ADDISON-WESLEY
SECONDARY MATH

Focus on
Advanced Algebra

AN INTEGRATED APPROACH

JOHN A. DOSSEY

CHARLES B. VONDER EMBSE

James R. Choike • David S. Daniels • Pamela Patton Giles

Howard C. Johnson • Sheryl M. Yamada

PROGRAM CONCEPTUALIZERS

Barbara Alcala

Randall I. Charles

John A. Dossey

Betty M. Foxx

Alan R. Hoffer

Roberta Koss

Sid Rachlin

Freddie L. Renfro

Cathy L. Seeley

Charles B. Vonder Embse

Scott Foresman
Addison Wesley

Editorial Offices: Menlo Park, California • Glenview, Illinois
Sales Offices: Reading, Massachusetts • Atlanta, Georgia •
Glenview, Illinois • Carrollton, Texas • Menlo Park, California

http://www.sf.aw.com

Cover images

Front:

Left: Italian ceramic tile by Cheryl Fenton*. *Right:* Fractal from the Mandelbrot Set by Antonio M. Rosario/The Image Bank.

Back:

Top left: Photo of financial district, Toronto, Ontario by Thomas Kitchin/Tom Stack & Associates. *Top center left: Castle and Sun,* 1928, by Paul Klee. Private Collection, London, Great Britain. Photo by Giraudon/Art Resource, NY. *Top center right: Kachina Song Poetry,* 1985, by Michael Kabotie (Hopi). Acrylic on canvas. Photo by Jerry Jacka Photography. *Top right:* Circuit board by Jon Feingersh/Tom Stack & Associates. *Bottom left:* Armillary (predecessor to the astrolabe) from the Vatican. Photo by Art Resource, NY. *Bottom center left: Wedding Basket,* 1989, by Mary Black (Navajo/Paiute). Courtesy of the Museum of Northern Arizona, Flagstaff. Photo by Jerry Jacka Photography. *Bottom center right:* Italian ceramic tile by Cheryl Fenton*. *Bottom right:* Fractal from the Mandelbrot Set by Antonio M. Rosario/The Image Bank.

ISBN 0-201-86980-2

2 3 4 5 6 7 8 9 10-VH-02 01 00 99 98

PROGRAM CONCEPTUALIZERS

Barbara Alcala
Whittier High School
Whittier, California

Randall I. Charles
San Jose State University
San Jose, California

John A. Dossey
Illinois State University
Normal, Illinois

Betty M. Foxx
Chicago Public Schools
Chicago, Illinois

Alan R. Hoffer
University of California
Irvine, California

Roberta Koss
Redwood High School
Larkspur, California

Sid Rachlin
East Carolina University
Greenville, North Carolina

Freddie L. Renfro
Fort Bend Independent
School District
Houston, Texas

Cathy L. Seeley
Texas Statewide
Systemic Initiative
Austin, Texas

Charles B. Vonder Embse
Central Michigan University
Mt. Pleasant, Michigan

FOCUS ON ADVANCED ALGEBRA AUTHORS

John A. Dossey
Lead author
Illinois State University
Normal, Illinois

Charles B. Vonder Embse
Associate lead author
Central Michigan University
Mt. Pleasant, Michigan

James R. Choike
Oklahoma State University
Stillwater, Oklahoma

David S. Daniels
Longmeadow High School
Longmeadow, Massachusetts

Pamela Patton Giles
Jordan School District
Sandy, Utah

Howard C. Johnson
Syracuse University
Syracuse, New York

Sheryl M. Yamada
Beverly Hills High School
Beverly Hills, California

OTHER SERIES AUTHORS

Barbara Alcala
Whittier High School
Whittier, California

Jerry D. Beckmann
East High School
Lincoln, Nebraska

Penelope P. Booth
Baltimore County Public Schools
Towson, Maryland

Randall I. Charles
San Jose State University
San Jose, California

Phillip E. Duren
California State University
Hayward, California

Trudi Hammel Garland
The Head-Royce School
Oakland, California

Virginia Gray
Columbia College
Sonora, California
(Formerly) South Medford
High School

Julia L. Hernandez
Rosemead High School
Rosemead, California

Alan R. Hoffer
University of California
Irvine, California

Roberta Koss
Redwood High School
Larkspur, California

Stephen E. Moresh
Seward Park
High School and
City College of New York
New York, New York

J. Irene Murphy
Ilisagvik College
(Formerly) North Slope Borough
School District
Barrow, Alaska

Andy Reeves
(Formerly) Florida Department
of Education
Tallahassee, Florida

Kathy A. Ross
(Formerly) Jefferson Parish
Public School System
Harvey, Louisiana

Beth M. Schlesinger
San Diego High School
San Diego, California

Cathy L. Seeley
Texas Statewide
Systemic Initiative
Austin, Texas

Alba González Thompson
(In Memoriam)

Catherine Wiehe
San Jose High Academy
San Jose, California

CONSULTANTS AND REVIEWERS

CONTENT REVIEWERS

William Babington
Glenbrook North High School
Northbrook, Illinois

Ruth F. Bolt
T. L. Hanna High School
Anderson, South Carolina

Sharon Cichocki
Hamburg Senior High School
Hamburg, New York

Margie Hill
Blue Valley School District #229
Overland Park, Kansas

Larry Kaber
Flathead High School
Kalispell, Montana

Gary S. Luck
Greendale High School
Greendale, Wisconsin

Patrick S. Mara
South High School
Pueblo, Colorado

Tom Oliver
Columbus Public Schools
Columbus, Ohio

Martha Ochoa
Edinburg High School
Edinburg, Texas

Beverly W. Nichols
Shawnee Mission Public Schools
Overland Park, Kansas

Linda Partridge
Norview High School
Norfolk, Virginia

Ernestina Rodríguez
Harlingen High School
Harlingen, Texas

MULTICULTURAL REVIEWERS

LaVerne Bitsie
Oklahoma State University
Stillwater, Oklahoma

Genevieve Lau
Skyline College
San Bruno, California

William Tate
University of Wisconsin
Madison, Wisconsin

INDUSTRY CONSULTANTS

Joseph M. Cahalen
Xerox Corporation
Stamford, Connecticut

Clare DeYonker
AMATECH
Bingham Farms, Michigan

Harry Garland
Canon Research Center
America, Inc.
Palo Alto, California

Timothy M. Schwalm, Sr.
Eastman Kodak Company
Rochester, New York

Diane Sotos
Maxim Integrated Products
Sunnyvale, California

Earl R. Westerlund
Eastman Kodak Company
Rochester, New York

Charles Young
General Electric Research and
Development Center
Schenectady, New York

John Zils
Skidmore, Owings & Merrill
Chicago, Illinois

Table of Contents

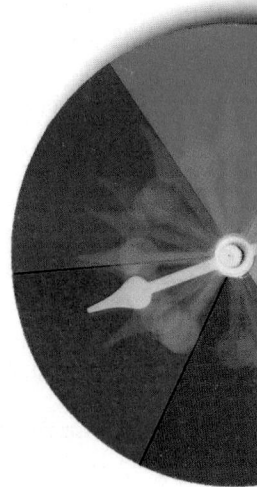

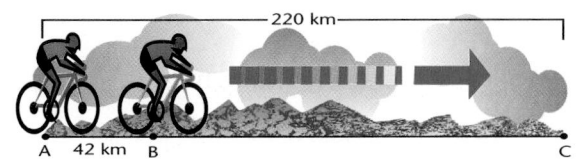

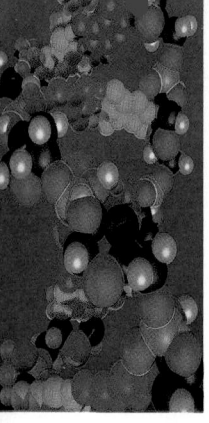

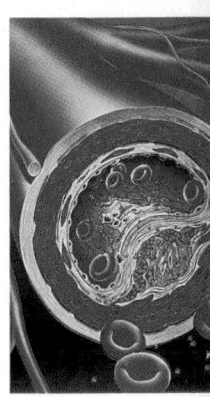

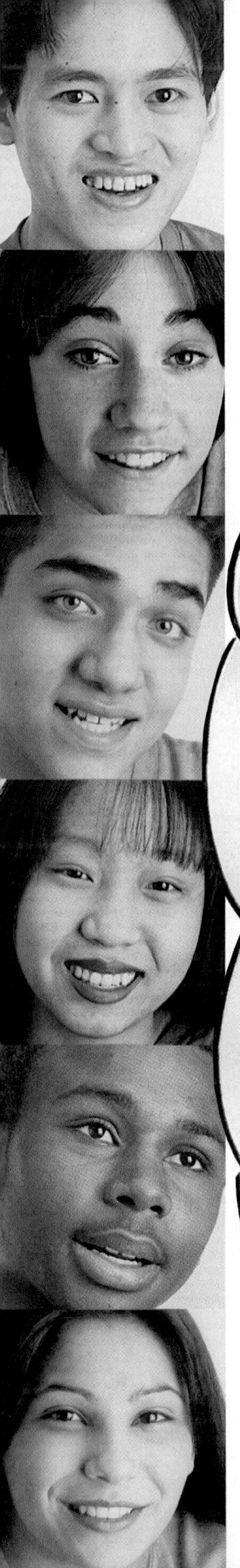

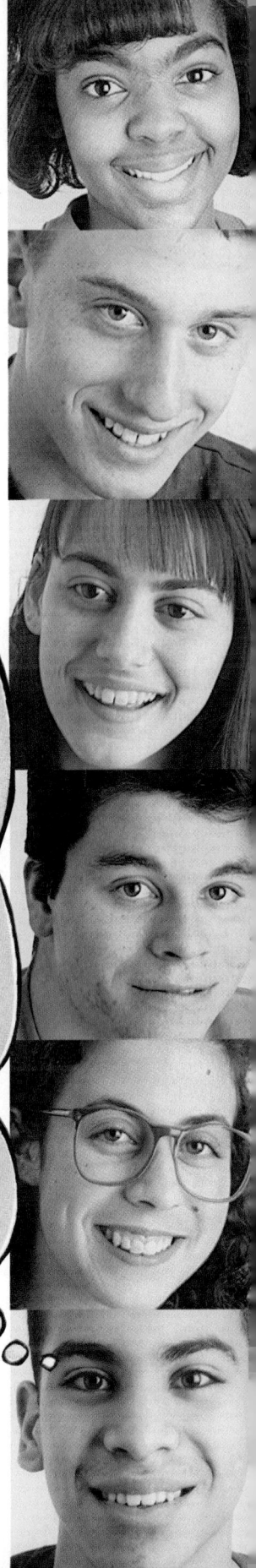

Getting Started

What Do YOU Think

In the twenty-first century, computers will do a lot of the work that people used to do. Even in today's workplace, there is little need for someone to add up daily invoices or compute sales tax. Engineers and scientists already use computer programs to do calculations and solve equations. By the twenty-first century, a whole new set of skills will be needed by almost everyone in the workforce.

Some important skills for the twenty-first century will be the ability to think creatively about mathematics, to reason logically, to work as a team member, and to be able to explain your thinking. Although people will still need to be able to do computations, they will also be required to analyze problems and determine the most appropriate ways to solve them. After all, what good is it to solve an equation if it is the wrong equation?

This course will help you to develop many of the skills you will need for the future. On the way, you will see the value of creative thinking. The students shown here will be sharing their ideas throughout this book. But the key question will always be "What do YOU think?"

1. In your last math class, what was the most interesting or useful thing you learned?
2. Why do you think teamwork is becoming more and more important in the workplace today? What are some advantages to working as a team?
3. Why is it important to be able to analyze and solve problems, even if a computer is available to help you do calculations?

← C O N N E C T → *There are times when working together can be more productive and motivating than working alone. If you've had experience working in groups, you are aware that it takes skill and planning to work together effectively. We will look at some ways to make working together effective.*

Working effectively as a team is an important skill in today's workplace, just as important as teamwork is in sports. Many industries assign teams of employees to work on projects. Each employee brings a different skill to the team.

Working in a group can also make learning more productive and enjoyable. In order to work together effectively, you must be able to communicate clearly with others. Communicating your ideas in a convincing way can also help you clarify your own thoughts.

CONSIDER

1. It is sometimes said that the sum of the parts can be greater than the whole. How do you think effective teamwork reflects this idea?

Here are some suggestions to consider when you are working in a group.

• Let everyone have a chance to participate.

• Everyone has a responsibility to participate. Don't be a *hitchhiker*.

• Each group member should be willing to help any other member of the group.

• Ask your teacher for help *only* after every member of your group has had a chance to resolve the issue.

• Talk only to members of your own group.

• Always be open-minded and show respect for one another. Work to problem solve rather than criticize.

EXPLORE: IN THE WINK OF AN EYE

MATERIALS

Stopwatch

1. While a classmate times you, count how many times you can wink your right eye in one minute. Make a table or organized list of the results for the members of your group.
2. Find the mean, median, and mode of the data for your group. If another person joined your group, how many times would this person have to wink in a minute to raise the group mean by five winks?
3. Repeat Steps 1 and 2 for winks of each group member's left eye. Was there a significant difference between the results for right eyes and left eyes? Explain how you decided.
4. Describe how you organized tasks within your group such as timing, calculation, answer checking, and so on.

Working cooperatively in groups can be an exciting and effective way to learn mathematics. You will have many opportunities for teamwork in this course.

REFLECT

1. What happens to a team when members don't communicate clearly or work together cooperatively?
2. Describe a situation, other than learning mathematics, in which teamwork plays an important role.
3. Are there situations where working individually is preferable to working in a group? Explain.

Exercises

1. Which two sets of numbers have the same mean (average)?
   (a) {−4, 6, 1, 2, 10, 3}   (b) {−14, 19, −33, −45, 68}   (c) {−13, 5, −3, 12, 10, 7}

2. Give an example of a team in the animal world. Write a brief explanation of how you think teamwork benefits the group of animals you described.

3. Describe a situation in which you worked in a group. How did teamwork help your group accomplish more than it might have if the members had worked individually?

4. Copy these three circles. For each pair of circles, draw the two lines that are externally tangent to both circles and mark the point where the lines intersect. What do you notice about the three points you've located in this way?

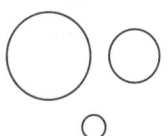

← **CONNECT** → *You have solved many problems before taking this class and have probably used various problem-solving guidelines and strategies. Many of these strategies and techniques can be used in this class.*

Problem solving means more than just finding the answer to a math problem. It means solving all types of problems, including those you encounter everyday. You may have trouble working a particular problem, or you may have a problem finding the time to do your homework. In either case, there is a problem to solve.

CONSIDER

1. What are some strategies you have used to solve problems?

Whenever the solution to a problem is not immediately apparent, it may be helpful to ask yourself some of the questions listed below.

PROBLEM-SOLVING GUIDELINES	
Understand the Problem What is the situation all about? What are you trying to find out? What are the key data/conditions? What are the assumptions?	**Develop a Plan** Have you ever worked a similar problem before? Will you estimate or calculate? What strategies can you use?
Implement the Plan What is the solution? Did you interpret correctly? Did you calculate correctly? Did you answer the question?	**Look Back** Could you work the problem another way? Is there another solution? Is the answer reasonable?

CONSIDER

2. Why is it useful to look back on a problem after you've solved it?

This problem appears in Leonardo Fibonacci's book *Liber Abaci,* published in 1202.

A man left to his oldest son one bezant and a seventh of what was left; then, from the remainder, to his next son he left two bezants and a seventh of what was left; then, from the remainder, to his third son he left three bezants and a seventh of what was left. He continued in this way, giving each son one bezant more than the previous son and a seventh of what remained. By this division it developed that the last son received all that was left and all the sons shared equally. How many sons were there and how large was the man's estate?

1. Solve Fibonacci's problem. As you work, think about the Problem-Solving Guidelines and strategies you are using to solve the problem.
2. Describe any Problem-Solving Guidelines or strategies you used and tell how they helped you solve the problem.

REFLECT

1. Would you apply the Problem-Solving Guidelines in a particular order, or can they be applied in any order? Explain.
2. Describe a helpful question or strategy you would add to the list of Problem-Solving Guidelines.

Exercises

1. What is the maximum number of pieces that a cubical block of wood can be cut into by making three plane cuts? Explain your reasoning.

2. For each formula, decide whether the value of E must be positive if all other variables have positive values.
   a. $E = 1 - x^4$ **b.** $E = mc^2$ **c.** $E = \frac{4}{3}\pi r^3$

3. Match each area formula with the geometric figure to which it applies. (A represents area, h represents height, and b, b_1, and b_2 represent top or bottom base lengths.)

   a. triangle   **i.** $A = \frac{1}{2}(b_1 + b_2)h$

   b. rectangle   **ii.** $A = \frac{1}{2}hb$

   c. trapezoid   **iii.** $A = hb$

4. Describe a problem you learned to solve in a previous mathematics course and solve the problem.

"*Now that desk looks better. Everything's squared away, yessir, squaaaaaared away.*"

← CONNECT → *You have worked in groups and used problem-solving guidelines and strategies to help you solve problems. There is often more than one approach to solving a problem. The features in this book can help you to develop your mathematical skills and choose problem-solving methods wisely.*

Throughout this book you will have many opportunities to work in groups (in Explore activities) and to practice what you have learned (in Try It activities). You will also see a feature called What Do YOU Think, in which you can share and compare the thinking of other students as they solve problems.

WHAT DO YOU THINK?

Find the solid that has 8 times the volume of a sphere with radius 1 ft.

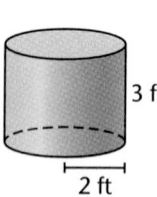 3 ft 2 ft

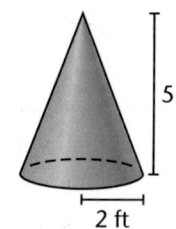 5 ft 2 ft

 2 ft

Kyle thinks...

The volume of a sphere with radius 1 ft is $V = \frac{4}{3}\pi r^3 = \frac{4}{3}\pi(1 \text{ ft})^3 = \frac{4}{3}\pi \text{ ft}^3$. So I'm looking for a solid with a volume of $8\left(\frac{4}{3}\pi \text{ ft}^3\right)$ or $\frac{32}{3}\pi \text{ ft}^3$.

The volume of the cylinder is $V = \pi r^2 h = \pi(2 \text{ ft})^2(3 \text{ ft}) = 12\pi \text{ ft}^3$.

The volume of the cone is $V = \frac{1}{3}\pi r^2 h = \frac{1}{3}\pi(2 \text{ ft})^2(5 \text{ ft}) = \frac{20}{3}\pi \text{ ft}^3$.

The volume of the sphere with radius 2 ft is $V = \frac{4}{3}\pi r^3 = \frac{4}{3}\pi(2 \text{ ft})^3 = \frac{32}{3}\pi \text{ ft}^3$.

So the sphere with radius 2 ft has 8 times the volume of the sphere with radius 1 ft.

Rita thinks...

The larger sphere is similar to the smaller sphere with twice the radius. I know that the ratio of the volumes of similar solids is the cube of their similarity ratio, so the sphere of radius 2 ft must have 2^3 or 8 times the volume of the smaller sphere.

1. Do you think problem-solving strategies are useful only for mathematics problems? Explain.

2. Why do you think it is important to understand the connections between mathematics and other disciplines?

Exercises

1. The diameter of Mars is only 53.2% of the diameter of Earth. How does the volume of Mars compare to that of Earth?

2. Find the solid that has 27 times the volume of a cylinder with height 5 cm and radius 2 cm.

(a)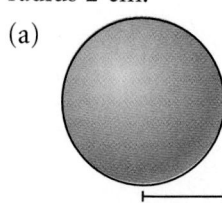

8 cm

(b)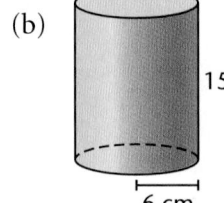

15 cm

6 cm

(c)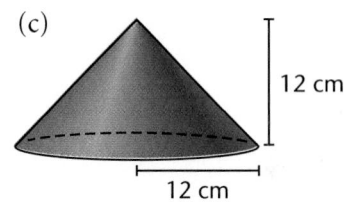

12 cm

12 cm

3. If a sphere has a surface area of 800 mm^2, what is the surface area of a sphere with twice the diameter?

4. During a storm, Matt put a 32-ounce pot under a drip in his living room. At 2 p.m. the pot was 10 ounces full. Now, at 3:30 p.m., the pot is 16 ounces full. If the storm continues as before, how long will it be before the pot overflows?

5. Which has the greater volume, a sphere or a cylinder with the same height and width as the sphere (that is, the height and base diameter of the cylinder are both equal to the diameter of the sphere)?

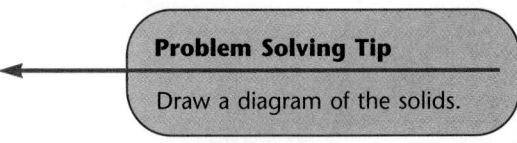

Problem Solving Tip

Draw a diagram of the solids.

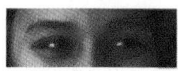 ***LOOK AHEAD***

Find the next two numbers in each pattern.

6. 4, 7, 11, 16, 22, 29, …

7. 2, 6, 18, 54, …

8. A meteorologist tells you that rain is twice as likely where you live as where she lives. She also tells you that it rained 37 days in her town last year. How many days do you expect it will rain this year where you live? Explain.

9. Suppose a friend's puppy has grown from 2 lb to 2.2 lb in the past two weeks. When would you predict the puppy will reach a weight of 3 lb? Explain.

Chapter 1 Mathematical Models

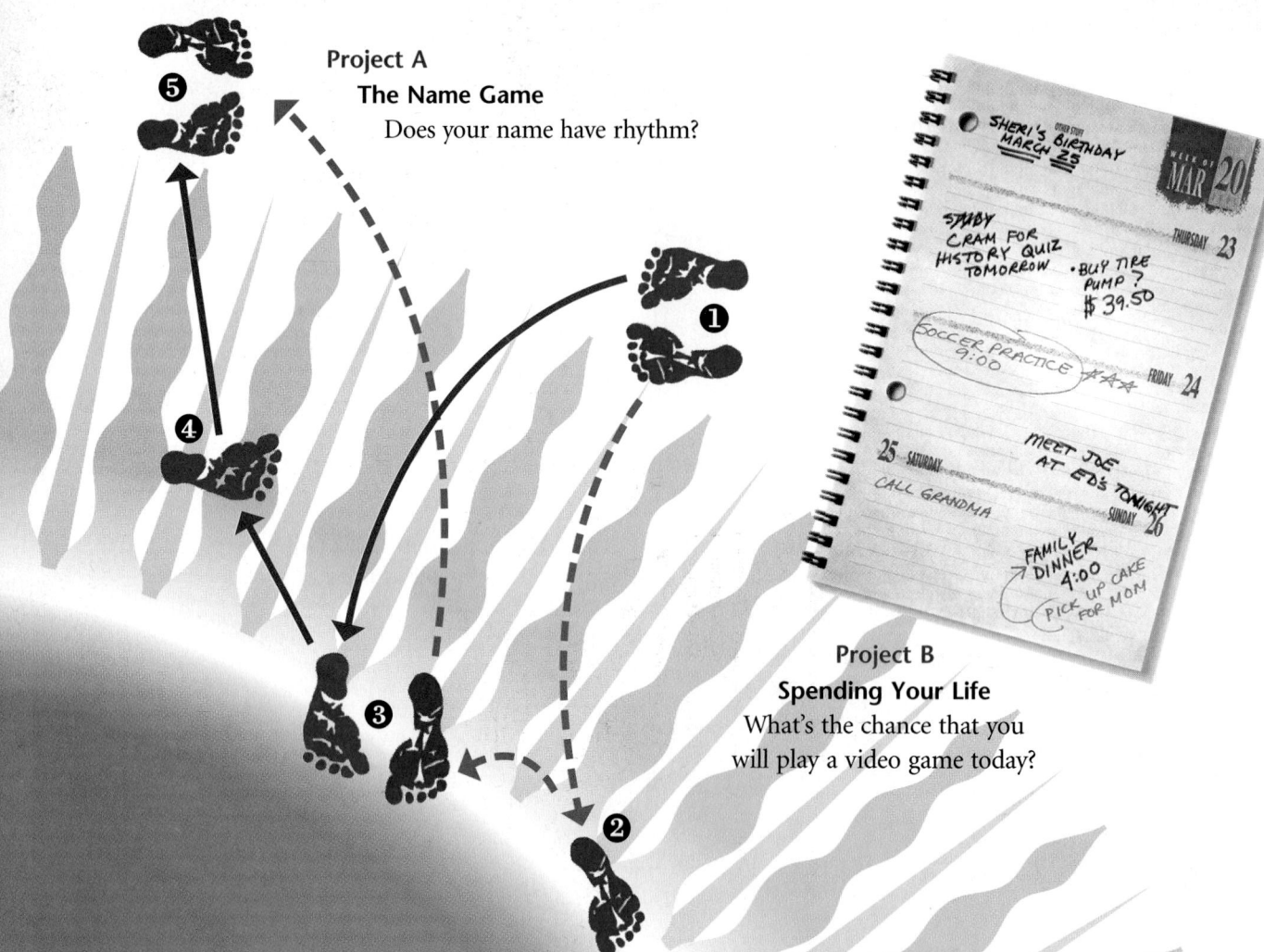

Project A
The Name Game
Does your name have rhythm?

Project B
Spending Your Life
What's the chance that you
will play a video game today?

Project C
We've Got Sol
How can we heat
our water for free?

I liked math in high school because I had a good teacher.

Math gives meaning to uncertainty. It helps reduce complexity to a simpler system. I use data, for instance, to learn what temperatures in the manufacturing process cause changes in the product. Each data gathering experiment can cost the company tens of thousands of dollars, so I have to know how to establish and apply the equations.

How Tsao
Statistician
Eastman Kodak Company
Rochester, New York

1-1
Graphical Models

In 1-1 you will find patterns in real-world data and learn to model the data mathematically. You will use the following skills from previous courses.

For each table, find a pattern relating x and y. [Previous course]

1.

x	2	7	12	23
y	11	16	21	32

2.

x	−3	0	5	12
y	6	0	−10	−24

3. Find the circumference and area of a circle with radius 3 in. [Previous course]

4. Graph $y = x^2$ by completing the table, plotting the points, and connecting them with a smooth curve. [Previous course]

x	−2	−1	0	1	2
y					

1-2
Experimental Probability and Simulation

In 1-2 you will be calculating probabilities from theory, experiments, and simulations. You will need the following skills from previous courses.

Write each of the following as percents and fractions. [Previous course]

5. 0.125   **6.** 0.06   **7.** 1 − 0.02   **8.** 100.001

Write each of the following as decimals and fractions. [Previous course]

9. 95%   **10.** 5%   **11.** 8.25%   **12.** 105%

1-3
Matrices

In 1-3 you will learn what matrices are and how to do operations with them. You will need to know the following properties from previous courses.

For each of the following, state its multiplicative inverse. [Previous course]

13. 8   **14.** $\dfrac{2}{3}$ **15.** −1   **16.** −0.1

Simplify. [Previous course]

17. $1 \cdot -1 + 2 \cdot \dfrac{1}{3} + 3 \cdot 1 + 4 \cdot 8$

18. $4 \cdot \dfrac{1}{2} + 3 \cdot \dfrac{-5}{6} + 6 \cdot 1 + 0 \cdot 8$

19. $7 \cdot -1 + 8 \cdot \dfrac{1}{3} + 9 \cdot 0 + (-10) \cdot 10$

20. $0.5 \cdot 1.1 + 0.5 \cdot 2.0 + 0.5 \cdot 8.9 + 0.5 \cdot -2.0$

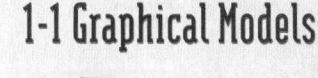

The Science of Patterns

What is mathematics? Is it working with numbers? counting? the study of shapes? a language? Over the years mathematics has been defined as all of these things. A definition of mathematics, however, that most mathematicians agree upon today is: *mathematics is the science of patterns.*

As a study of patterns, mathematics is a way of looking at the world. Some of the patterns in our world are easy to see, like those in a snowflake. Other patterns are not so obvious. Many real-world patterns in seemingly random events were not recognized until the 1970s. For instance, although it appears random, the dispersal of smoke into the air actually forms a "mathematical pattern."

Before computers, the beauty of mathematics was appreciated mostly by advanced mathematicians, who could read mathematical symbols like a musician reads notes. Today the mathematician can use a computer to arrange a "performance" of mathematics in much the same way that a musician performs a composition. A graph of an equation can be considered a "performance" of that equation. The fractal featured on the cover of this book is an example of a much more complex mathematical performance.

We are beginning to see that art and mathematics have much in common. Like artists, mathematicians think visually and use intuition. They often speak of their work in artistic terms—subtle, elegant, beautiful. Artists incorporate geometry and logic into their compositions. Both mathematicians and artists use their works to describe the world around them. In the words of G. H. Hardy, "A mathematician, like a painter or a poet, is a maker of patterns."

Fractal model resembling sand dunes

1. Give examples of patterns that you have observed in mathematics and in art.
2. In what ways is mathematics different from art? In what ways is it similar?
3. How could you use mathematics to analyze a work of art?

← C O N N E C T →
You live in an information age. Information is useless, however, unless you can see relationships between items of information. By graphing data, you will identify relationships and patterns in data.

The world changes from moment to moment, and we are swamped with data describing those changes. For instance:
- The number of crimes in one city increased by 3.2% in 1994.
- The population of the same city increased 4% in 1994.

Sometimes a change in one quantity produces a change in another. Did the population increase in this city cause the crime increase? It might have, since there were more potential criminals and victims. But we cannot be sure that the population increase alone *caused* the increase in crime.

A college recruiter noticed that there was a relationship between the number of students enrolled at the local campus and the unemployment rate for the region. She collected data and plotted them on the graph shown.

A line, called a **trend line,** can be drawn so that about half of the data points are above the line and half are below the line. The trend line helps us see the relationship between these two sets of data.

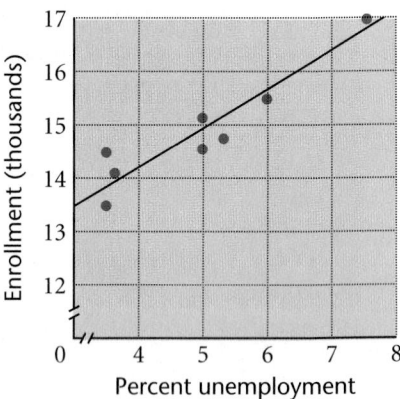

CONSIDER

1. How would you describe the relationship between the number of students enrolled at the local campus and the regional unemployment rate?

2. Could one of these changes have caused the other change? Explain.

A graph of real-world data rarely shows an exact relationship, but it can reveal a pattern or trend. By looking at this pattern, we may be able to develop a mathematical model to make predictions.

A **scatter plot** is a graph that shows a set of points, each based on paired data. In the following Explore, you will make a scatter plot of some real-world data and look for a pattern.

During the 1980s, a new type of music recording, the compact disc (CD), made vinyl records obsolete. The table below shows the change in U.S. production of CDs from 1984 to 1992.

MATERIALS

Graph paper
Graphing utility (optional)

CDs Shipped from U.S. Manufacturers	
Year	Number of CDs (in thousands)
1984	5,800
1985	22,600
1986	53,000
1987	102,100
1988	149,700
1989	207,200
1990	286,500
1991	333,300
1992	407,500

1. Draw a scatter plot of this data. Show the year on one axis of the graph and the number of CDs shipped on the other axis. Use an appropriate scale or viewing window if you are using a graphing utility.
2. Describe any patterns or trends you see in the data.
3. Draw a trend line for this scatter plot.
4. How many CDs do you think were shipped by U.S. manufacturers in 1994? Explain how you made your prediction.

Quality control is important in the CD manufacturing process.

CONSIDER
?

3. Why do you think the number of CDs shipped from U.S. manufacturers increased at such a rapid rate from 1984 to 1992, as shown in the table above?
4. Do you think this rate of increase will continue? Why or why not?

Although a scatter plot may not reveal a precise relationship between quantities, it may show a trend or **association.**

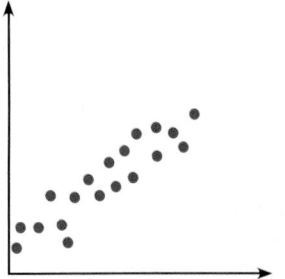

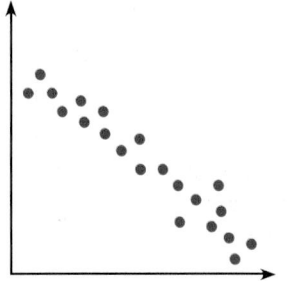

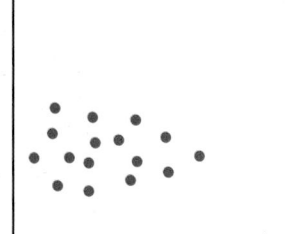

When two quantities increase or decrease together, the data show a *positive association.*

When one quantity decreases as the other increases, the data show a *negative association.*

When two quantities are unrelated, *no association* exists in the data, and the quantities are *independent.*

EXAMPLE

The scatter plot at the right shows the number of U.S. work stoppages (strikes, lockouts, etc.) involving 1000 workers or more from the years 1950 to 1991.

Draw a trend line for the scatter plot. What type of association do you observe?

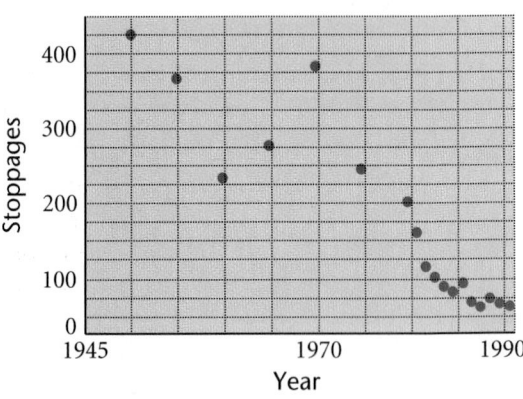

A trend line is shown. It passes through the "center" of the scattered data. The line shows a negative association between the data sets, since the number of work stoppages tends to decrease as the year increases.

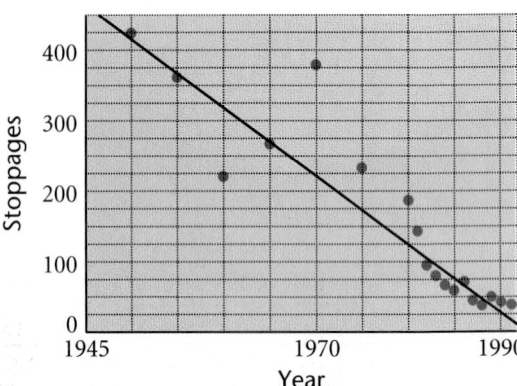

CONSIDER

5. Should the number of letters in a person's name and their shoe size have a positive association, negative association, or no association?

A fast-food chain test-marketed frozen yogurt desserts at a variety of different prices. This scatter plot shows the relationship between price and sales.

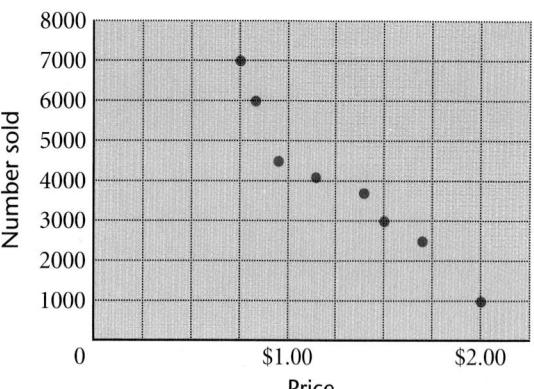

a. Draw a trend line for the scatter plot. What type of association do you observe?

You have seen how scatter plots are used to display data and you have looked for associations in that data. Finding associations in statistical data is very important to social scientists conducting experiments in psychology, sociology, and education.

REFLECT

1. How is a scatter plot useful in identifying a relationship between two types of data?

2. Suppose that a scatter plot shows a positive association between two quantities. Can you conclude that one quantity *causes* the other? Explain.

3. Name other ways of displaying data besides scatter plots. Identify some advantages and disadvantages of using each of these methods instead of a scatter plot.

Exercises

CORE

1. Getting Started

Expenditures on Books and Maps in the United States, 1986–1992							
Year	1 (= 1986)	2	3	4	5	6	7
Billions of dollars spent	8.6	9.5	14.6	15.8	17.5	18.3	20.2

a. Draw a graph showing the year on the horizontal axis and billions of dollars spent on the vertical axis.

b. Plot an ordered pair representing each pair of data in the table.

c. Draw a trend line for the scatter plot. What type of association do you observe?

d. Describe the trend shown in the scatter plot.

For each scatter plot, state whether there is a positive association, a negative association, or no association.

2.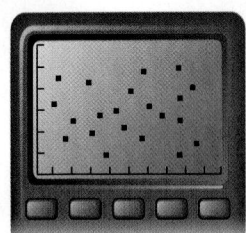

3.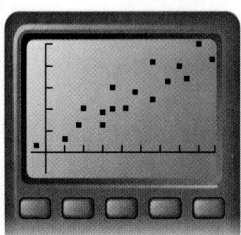

4.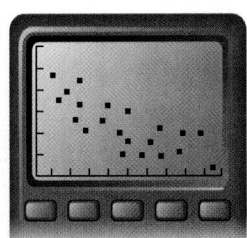

Determine whether each statement is true or false. If the statement is false, change the underlined word or phrase to make it true.

5. A scatter plot <u>always</u> reveals a relationship between the quantities that are graphed.

6. If one quantity increases while another quantity decreases, a scatter plot will show a <u>negative</u> association between the quantities.

State whether you believe there is a positive association, a negative association, or no association between each pair of quantities. Explain your reasoning.

7. the radius of a circle and the area of the circle

8. the age of a car and the value of that car

9. the height of a person in inches and the number in this person's street address

10. Where Have All the Farmers Gone? The table lists the farm population in the United States from 1910 to 1990.

Year	Population	Year	Population	Year	Population
1910	32,077,000	1940	30,547,000	1970	9,712,000
1920	31,974,000	1950	23,048,000	1980	6,051,000
1930	30,529,000	1960	15,635,000	1990	4,801,000

a. Make a scatter plot of the data.
b. Draw a trend line for the scatter plot. What type of association do you observe?
c. According to the trend line, will the farm population ever be zero?
d. Do you think the farm population will ever really be zero? Explain.

Give a real-world example of a pair of quantities showing each type of association.

11. a positive association   **12.** a negative association   **13.** no association

14. Swimming for the Gold The table lists the winning times in the Olympic Women's 200-Meter Breaststroke.

History

Year	Time (sec)	Year	Time (sec)	Year	Time (sec)	Year	Time (sec)
1928	193	1952	172	1968	164	1984	150
1932	186	1956	173	1972	162	1988	147
1936	184	1960	170	1976	153	1992	147
1948	177	1964	166	1980	150	1996	146

a. Make a scatter plot of the data.

b. Draw a trend line for the scatter plot. What type of association do you observe?

c. Predict the winning time for the event in the 2000 Olympics.

d. The Olympics were not held in 1940 and 1944 because of World War II. Estimate a winning time in this event for 1940 and 1944 as if the Olympics had been held.

LOOK AHEAD

Decide whether each quantity varies or stays the same.

15. the number of seconds in a minute   **16.** the cost of a pair of jeans

17. the number of breaths you take per minute   **18.** the measure of a right angle

For each table, find a pattern relating *x* and *y*. Then complete the table.

19.

x	−1	0	1	2	3
y	4	5	6		

20.

x	3	4	5	6	10
y	12	16	20		

MORE PRACTICE

For each scatter plot, state whether there is a positive association, a negative association, or no association.

21.

22.

23.

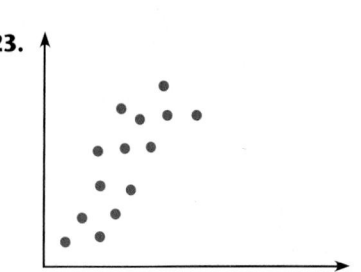

State whether you think there is a positive association, a negative association, or no association between each pair of quantities. Explain your reasoning.

24. the probability you will bowl a strike on your first ball and the number of years you have been bowling

25. the price of a dog and the weight of the dog

26. the average speed that a person travels in a car and the amount of time needed to travel a certain distance

27. Use a Graphing Utility

Latitude and Mean Temperatures in August, 1951–1980					
City	Lat. (°N)	Temp.	City	Lat. (°N)	Temp.
Mobile, AL	30	82	New Orleans, LA	29	82
Juneau, AK	58	55	Omaha, NE	41	75
Los Angeles, CA	34	70	New York, NY	40	75
Denver, CO	39	71	Raleigh, NC	35	77
Washington, DC	38	78	Seattle, WA	47	74
Jacksonville, FL	28	81	Sioux Falls, SD	44	72
Honolulu, HI	21	81	Nashville, TN	36	78

a. Make a scatter plot of the data in the table.
b. Copy the scatter plot onto graph paper and draw a trend line for the scatter plot.
c. Predict the mean August temperature of a city at latitude 45° N.

28. Use a Graphing Utility

U.S. Airline Departures, 1982–1992											
Year	1982	1983	1984	1985	1986	1987	1988	1989	1990	1991	1992
Departures (in millions)	5.0	5.0	5.4	5.8	6.4	6.6	6.7	6.6	6.9	6.8	6.9

a. Make a scatter plot of the data.
b. Copy the scatter plot onto graph paper and draw a trend line for the scatter plot.
c. What type of association do you observe?
d. Predict the number of airline departures for 1993.

MORE MATH REASONING

29. Use a Graphing Utility The table lists the life expectancies, in years, of girls born from 1920 to 1990.

Year of Birth	1920	1930	1940	1950	1960	1970	1980	1990
Life Expectancy	54.6	61.6	65.2	71.1	73.1	74.4	77.4	78.8

a. Make a scatter plot of the data.

b. Copy the scatter plot onto graph paper and draw a trend line for the scatter plot.

c. Use your trend line to predict the life expectancy of a girl born in 1955 and the life expectancy of a girl born in the year 2000.

d. In which of the predictions in **c** are you more confident? Explain.

30. Does it matter what units are used to graph data when determining whether or not there is an association in that data? Explain.

31. When you make predictions based on a trend line drawn through data points, how is your confidence in that prediction affected by the number of data points you have?

Patterns and Relationships

← CONNECT → *You have seen how a scatter plot can show relationships between two quantities. Now you will investigate other ways to discover and express specific patterns in data.*

Quantities in some relationships change from one moment to the next. Business profits change continually. Relationships between other quantities, however, may not change. The owner of a business can be confident that there will always be 100 cents in a dollar.

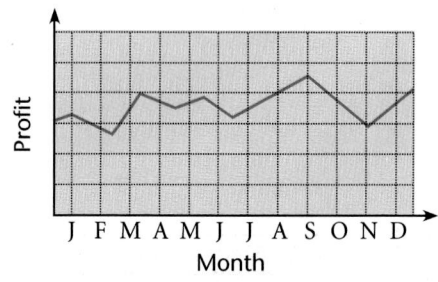

> **Variables** are quantities whose values can change or vary. We use letters like *x*, *y*, *t*, and *d* in algebraic expressions to represent possible values of such quantities. Quantities whose values do not change are **constants.**

Change lies at the heart of mathematics. How does a change in one variable affect another variable? How can that relationship be expressed? In the following Explore, you will begin to investigate these questions.

MATERIALS

Graph paper
Graphing utility (optional)

The art found in ancient Egyptian tombs has a flat, two-dimensional appearance. When the rules of perspective were discovered during the Renaissance, artists began to give a feeling of depth to their works. They altered the relative size of objects, reducing the size of those objects farther in the distance.

The figure below shows how perspective can be used to give the illusion of distance. The 1×1 square looks farther away than the 3×3 square does. Note that the smaller squares that make up the larger ones are actually the same size as the 1×1 square.

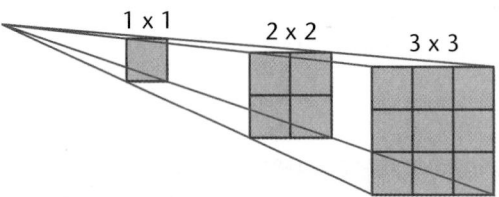

1 x 1   2 x 2   3 x 3

1. Copy and complete the table below.

Problem-Solving Tip

Look for patterns.

Type of square	1×1	2×2	3×3	4×4	5×5	6×6	7×7	8×8
Perimeter of square	4	8						
Number of 1×1 squares needed to construct the square	1	4						

2. a. Describe the relationship between the type of square and the perimeter.
  b. What is the perimeter of a 20×20 square? an $n \times n$ square?
  c. Describe the relationship between the side length of a square and its perimeter.
  d. Write an equation using variables to represent the relationship between the side length of a square and its perimeter.
3. a. Describe the relationship between the type of square and the number of 1×1 squares needed to construct it.
  b. How many squares are needed to construct a 12×12 square? an $n \times n$ square?
  c. Describe the relationship between the side length of a square and the number of squares needed to construct it.
  d. Write an equation using variables that expresses this relationship.

You may be able to discover a pattern in the data contained in a table. If so, you can write an equation relating the variables involved and then graph the equation.

1. Write and graph an equation relating x and y.

x	0	1	2	3	4	5
y	-5	-2	1	4	7	10

As the value of x increases by 1, the value of y increases by 3. This suggests that the change in y is related to 3 times the value of x.

To investigate this possibility, compare the value of y with the value of $3x$.

x	0	1	2	3	4	5
$3x$	0	3	6	9	12	15
y	-5	-2	1	4	7	10

Now the pattern is clear—the value of y is 5 less than the value of $3x$. Therefore, $y = 3x - 5$.

To graph the equation, plot ordered pairs (x, y) from the original table. Then, draw a line through the points.

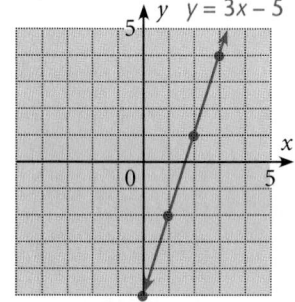

1. Why do we draw a line through the points plotted in Example 1?

For each table, write and graph an equation relating x and y. Check your work.

a.

x	-2	-1	0	1	2
y	-10	-5	0	5	10

b.

x	0	1	2	3	4
y	3	5	7	9	11

2. Suppose that it costs a printing company $500 to set up its equipment for a new job and $5 to print each book once the equipment has been set up. Write an equation for the total cost in terms of the number of books printed.

Let b be the number of books printed. The total cost (c) is equal to 5 times the number of books printed (b) plus 500. The equation is $c = 5b + 500$.

In Example 2, the total cost of printing the books depends on the number of books that are printed. Therefore, for this situation, the total cost is considered the *dependent variable* and the number of books printed is the *independent variable.*

> When the value of y depends on the value of x, y is called the **dependent variable** and x is called the **independent variable**.

In an ordered pair, the value of the independent variable is usually listed first. So when an equation is graphed, the **independent** variable is usually on the horizontal axis and the **dependent** variable on the vertical axis. The graph of the equation in Example 2 is shown. Note that b, the independent variable, is graphed on the horizontal axis.

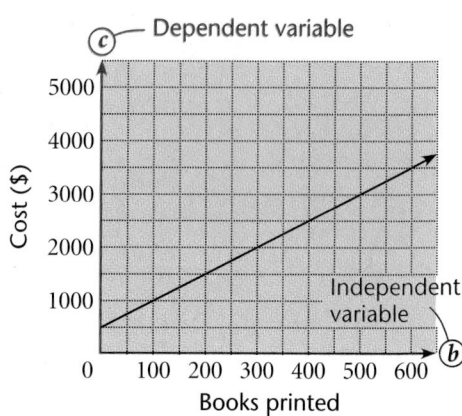

TRY IT

In 1993, the sales tax rate in Massachusetts was 5% (except for clothing and food items).

c. Write an equation for the amount of sales tax (t) paid on taxable purchases of d dollars.

d. Identify your equation's dependent variable and independent variable.

You've seen that an equation can be used to describe a relationship and that a graph can be drawn to represent the equation. Equations describing relationships are important to executives making business decisions, engineers designing new technology, and many other people in their everyday lives.

REFLECT

1. You have investigated three ways to express a relationship between two variables—a table of values, an equation, and a graph. Give an example of a situation where you would use each of these methods to show such a relationship. What are the advantages and disadvantages of each method?

2. The equation $m = 5k$ expresses a relationship between k and m. If you are given a value for either variable, you can find a value for the other. How would you choose which variable to call the independent variable and which to call the dependent variable?

Exercises

CORE

1. Getting Started

x	−2	−1	0	1	2	3	4	5
y	−6	−3	0	3				

a. Describe the relationship between x and y in the table above.
b. Complete the table for the values of y not given.
c. Write an equation to describe the relationship between x and y.
d. Find the value of y when $x = 25$.
e. Use the table to list eight ordered pairs you could use to graph the relationship.
f. Graph the relationship.

Write the word or phrase that best completes each statement.

2. In an hourly job, the number of hours that you work determines the amount you are paid. In this relationship, your pay is the ____ variable.

3. When you substitute Fahrenheit (F) temperatures in the equation $C = \frac{5}{9}(F - 32)$ to find the corresponding Celsius (C) temperatures, F is the ____ variable.

4. On a coordinate grid, the independent variable is graphed on the ____ axis.

Copy and complete each table. Then write and graph an equation relating x and y.

5.

x	0	1	2	3	4	5
y	6	7	8	9		

6.

x	0	1	2	3	4	5
y	0	−1	−2	−3		

7.

x	0	1	2	3	4	5
y	1	4	7	10		

8.

x	0	1	2	3	4	5
y	−2	−6	−10	−14		

9.

x	1	2	3	4	5	6
y	3	6	11	18		

10.

x	1	2	3	4	5	6
y	0	3	8	15		

(Hint: Compare y to x^2.)

11. The T's Have It A "1 T," a "2 T," a "3 T," and a "4 T" are shown.

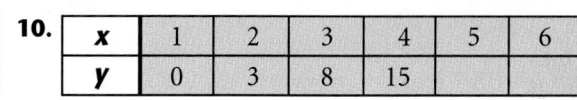

a. Write an equation relating n, the number in the name of the figure, and s, the number of squares needed to draw the figure.
b. Use your equation to find the number of squares needed to draw a "45 T."
c. Which T-figure uses 79 squares?

12. Spare Me The warehouse for a taxi company keeps two tires in stock for every taxicab the company owns plus fifteen spare tires.

   a. If 34 cabs are in the company's fleet, how many tires are in the warehouse?

   b. Write an equation relating c, the number of cabs in the fleet, and t, the number of tires in the warehouse.

   c. Identify which of your variables is the independent variable and which is the dependent variable. Justify your choices.

   d. If 53 tires are in the warehouse, how many cabs does the company own?

Make a table of values for each equation. Include at least six entries.

13. $y = 6x - 2$

14. $y = \frac{3}{4}x + 5$

15. $y = x^2 + x + 2$

Science

16. The Pressure's On The pressure that divers experience as they descend comes from the weight of the water resting on them. Ocean water exerts a pressure of 0.44 lb/in.^{2} for each foot that a diver descends.

   a. Write an equation relating P, the water pressure, and d, the depth descended. Identify which of the variables is independent and which is dependent.

   b. Find the water pressure at the ocean's deepest point, the bottom of the 35,840-foot deep Mariana Trench in the Pacific Ocean.

   c. An average bull elephant weighs 6.5 tons. Suppose that all of this weight is exerted on a one-square-foot surface. At what depth will the water pressure on a one-square-foot surface be equivalent to the pressure of the bull elephant?

Social Science

17. In the U.S. House of Representatives, the 435 seats are given out, or *apportioned*, to states based on their population. However, each state has two senators, regardless of its population. The number of electoral votes a state has in a presidential election is the total number of its senators and representatives.

   a. Based on the results of the 1990 Census, the number of representatives for each state is about $\frac{1}{572,000}$ of its population. Write an equation relating V, the number of *electoral votes* (not just representatives!) a state has, and p, its 1990 population.

   b. Identify which of the variables is independent and which is dependent.

   c. Use your equation to predict the number of electoral votes for each state.

   i. Wyoming, population 453,588   **ii.** Connecticut, population 3,294,394

   iii. Georgia, population 6,478,216   **iv.** California, population 29,760,021

LOOK BACK

Find the area of each figure. Round answers to the nearest tenth of a unit, if necessary. [Previous course]

18.
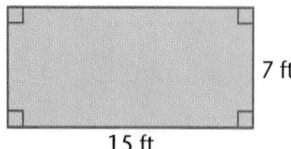
7 ft

15 ft

19.
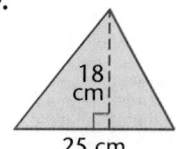
18 cm

25 cm

20.
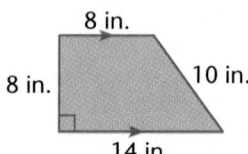
8 in.

8 in.   10 in.

14 in.

21.

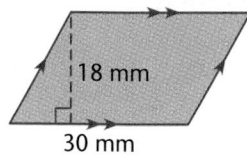

18 mm

30 mm

22.

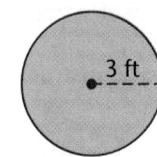

3 ft

23.

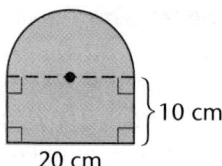

10 cm

20 cm

MORE PRACTICE

Copy and complete each table. Then write and graph an equation relating x and y.

24.

x	0	1	2	3	4	5
y	4	5	6	7		

25.

x	0	1	2	3	4	5
y	0	6	12	18		

26.

x	0	1	2	3	4	5
y	0	0.5	1	1.5		

27.

x	0	1	2	3	4	5
y	−1	1	3	5		

28.

x	0	1	2	3	4	5
y	0	1	4	9		

29.

x	0	1	2	3	4	5
y	−2	−1	2	7		

30. Lost in Space The Space Shuttle orbits the earth at a velocity of 26,500 km/hr.
  a. Write an equation relating t, the number of hours in orbit, to d, the distance traveled.
  b. Use your equation to find the distance an orbiting shuttle travels in one week.

31. Under normal conditions, Patty's heart beats 70 times per minute.

  a. Write an equation relating h, the number of heart beats, to t, the amount of time that Patty keeps count.
  b. About how many times will Patty's heart beat in 5 minutes?
  c. When Patty exercises, her heart rate is 95 beats per minute. Write an equation relating heart beats to time.
  d. How many more times will Patty's heart beat in 5 minutes while she exercises than when she is at rest and her heart is beating normally?
  e. Use a Graphing Utility Graph the two equations and compare the graphs.

Health

Make a table of values for each equation. Include at least six entries.

32. $y = x - 5$ **33.** $y = 0.5x + 5$ **34.** $y = x^2 - 4$

35. $y = \frac{2}{3}x + 3$ **36.** $y = 2x^2 - 1$ **37.** $y = x^3$

38. a. Write an equation relating s, the length of a side of a square, to A, the area of the square.
  b. Find the area of a square that measures 7 inches on each side.
  c. Find the length of the side of a square if its area is 121 square centimeters.

39. Let's Swim To change a temperature from degrees Celsius to degrees Fahrenheit, use the equation $F = \frac{9}{5}C + 32$.

 a. The weather report predicts the high for the day to be 15°C. What is the predicted high in degrees Fahrenheit?

 b. Would you plan to go swimming on a day with a high of 15°C? Why or why not?

MORE MATH REASONING

40. Postage Due In 1994, postage costs for a letter weighing up to 12 ounces were $0.29 for the first ounce plus $0.23 for each additional ounce. So it cost $0.52 to mail a letter weighing more than 1 ounce but less than or equal to 2 ounces.

 a. Write an equation using *n*, a letter's weight in whole ounces, and *p*, the postage required to mail the letter.

 b. How is the graph of this equation different from linear graphs?

 c. Now, make a graph showing the relationship between *n* and *p*, where *n* is not restricted to whole-number values. Describe your graph and explain your method for drawing it.

41. On the Road Again The line graph below shows speed and elapsed time for a road trip from Seattle to Spokane, Washington.

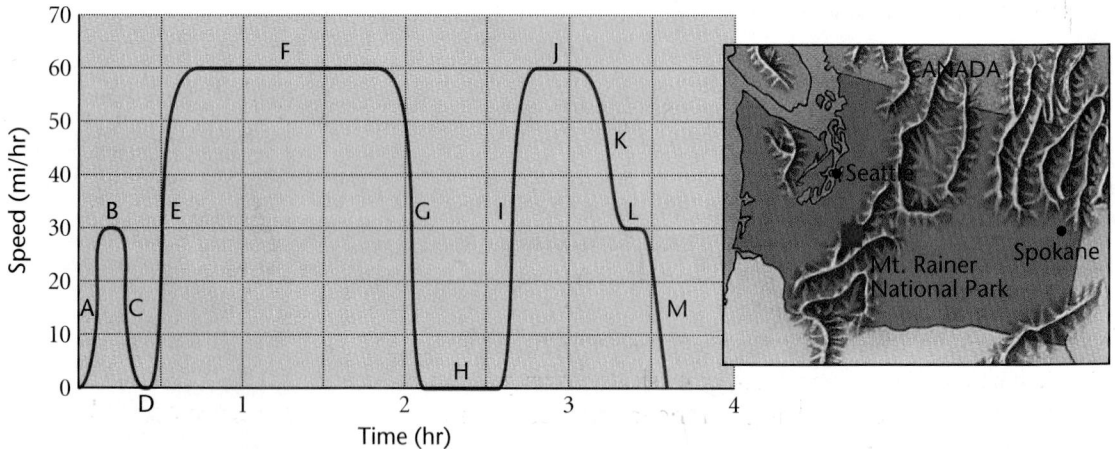

 a. What was the speed of the car 15 minutes after leaving Seattle? 2.5 hours after leaving?

 b. Which lettered intervals of the trip represent times when the car is not moving?

 c. What is the letter of the first interval when the car increases its speed? the first interval when it decreases its speed?

 d. What does a flat section of the graph represent?

 e. When did the car reach the freeway?

 f. Which interval represents a brief stop for gas before getting onto the freeway?

 g. For each time on the horizontal axis, only one point is plotted. Would it be possible for there to be *two* points plotted above a given time? Why or why not?

← **C O N N E C T** → *You've seen a relationship between two quantities expressed by a table of values, an equation, and a graph. Now you will investigate a special type of relationship that provides the foundation for much of the mathematics you will study this year.*

Computers have opened the way for the study of fractals. Fractals produce amazing images like the one shown at the right.

One important characteristic of fractals is *self-similarity*. A figure is self-similar if one part of the figure cannot be distinguished from the whole. The Sierpinski Gasket is a good example of self-similarity. This famous fractal is named after its discoverer, mathematician Waclaw Sierpinski.

EXPLORE: IT'S A GAS-KET!

MATERIALS

Graph paper
Graphing utility (optional)

Study the first four stages of the Sierpinski Gasket.

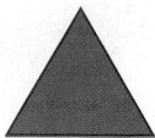    

Initial triangle (Stage 0) Stage 1 Stage 2 Stage 3 Stage 4

1. Make a table of the number of shaded triangles at each stage.
2. Write an equation based on the information in the table. Explain how you found your equation.
3. Graph the equation.
4. Are there any restrictions on the stage number and the number of triangles? Explain.
5. If the stage number is given, could you use your equation to predict the number of shaded triangles? Are there ever two possible answers for a given stage?

If you ordered two medium drinks at a concession stand, you would think it was very strange if the cashier said, "That'll be $1.98 *or* $2.10." There is only *one* correct price to charge for two medium drinks. In many situations, one quantity (here, the number of drinks) determines a unique value of the other quantity (the total cost).

This special type of relationship is called a *function*.

> A **function** is a relationship between two quantities in which the value of one quantity, the dependent variable, is uniquely determined by the value of the other quantity, the independent variable.
>
> The **domain** of a function is the set of all possible values of the independent variable. The **range** of a function is the set of all possible values of the dependent variable.

EXAMPLES

Determine whether each situation represents a function. If it does, identify the domain and range of the function.

1. The ordered pairs (1, 5), (2, 9), and (3, 12)

Recall that the first value in an ordered pair is a value of the independent variable. Since each of the three values of the first variable is matched with only one value, these ordered pairs do represent a function.

The domain of the function is the set {1, 2, 3}, and the range is {5, 9, 12}.

2. The data shown on the graph

There are two values of y, 2 and 4, for the value $x = 1$. Since x is the independent variable, this data does not represent a function.

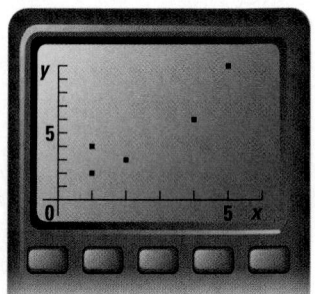

If the value of y depends on x, we can use **function notation** to make this relationship clear. In function notation, we use f (or g, h, etc.) to denote the association between the variables. We write $f(x)$ (or $g(x)$, $h(x)$, etc.), instead of y, to represent a value of the dependent variable. The parentheses in $f(x)$ are not multiplication parentheses—$f(x)$ does not mean f times x.

The x in $f(x)$ reminds us that the value of $f(x)$ depends on x. For instance, $f(x) = 3x + 2$ shows that the value of function f is three times the value of x plus two.

To find $f(x)$ for a particular value of x, substitute that value into the expression for $f(x)$. Here is the specific *order of operations* that is used to evaluate expressions:

1) operations inside parentheses
2) powers
3) multiplication and division (from left to right)
4) addition and subtraction (from left to right)

3. Your pay (P) for working part-time at the Aquarium is a *function* of the number of hours you work (h). If you make $5.25 an hour, then $P(h) = 5.25h$. Find your pay for 5 hours of work.

Since you worked 5 hours, $h = 5$. To find your pay, find $P(5)$.
$P(5) = 5.25(5) = 26.25$

Your pay for 5 hours of work is $26.25.

4. Let $f(x) = 3x^2 - 2x$. Find $f(4)$.

$f(4) = 3(4)^2 - 2(4)$	Substitute 4 for x.
$= 3(16) - 2(4)$	Evaluate powers first.
$= 48 - 8$	Multiply next.
$= 40$	Subtract last.

Give the domain and range of each function.

5. $f(x) = x^2$

Since the independent variable x can take on any value, the domain of the function is all real numbers. $x^2 \geq 0$ for all values in the domain, so the range is all real numbers greater than or equal to 0.

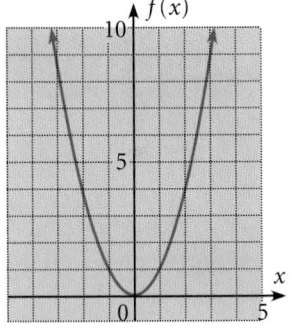

6. $g(x) = \dfrac{1}{\sqrt{x}}$

We cannot find a real-number square root for a negative number, so x cannot be negative. Since we cannot divide by zero, x cannot equal zero. Therefore, the domain is all positive real numbers. From the graph, the range is also all positive real numbers.

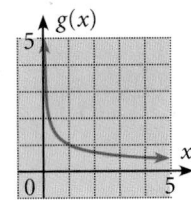

a. Let $f(x) = 8x - 5$. Find $f(-2)$.
b. Give the domain and range of the function $f(x) = |x| + 3$.
c. For the data shown in the graph at the right, is weight a function of height?

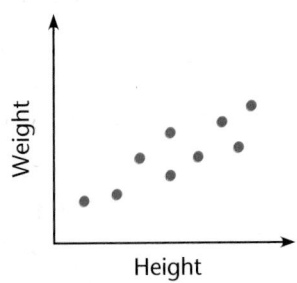

You've seen many types of relationships between quantities. A function is a special relationship where a value of the independent variable is associated with exactly one value of the dependent variable.

1. Is the area of a square a function of the length of a side of the square? Explain your answer.
2. Give an example of a relationship between two quantities that is *not* a function.
3. If a relationship between two quantities is a function, must there be exactly one value of the independent variable for each value of the dependent variable?
4. "The engine doesn't function." "Success is a function of hard work." Describe any connections you can find between the mathematical meaning and everyday meanings of the word *function*.

Exercises

CORE

1. **Getting Started** A car travels at a steady rate of 55 miles per hour.
   a. Write a function in the form $f(x) = \underline{\ ?\ } x$ that expresses $f(x)$, the number of miles the car travels, as a function of x, the number of hours it travels.
   b. Find $f(4)$.
   c. Explain why $f(x)$ is a function.
   d. Give the domain and range of $f(x)$.
   e. Draw a graph of the function. Use the horizontal axis for values of x and the vertical axis for values of $f(x)$.

Choose the best word or words to correctly complete each statement.

2. The number of rotations that an automobile tire makes is a ____ of the distance the car travels.

3. The ____ of the function (4, 5), (6, 7), and (8, 9) is the set of values {4, 6, 8}.

4. For each value of the ____ variable of a function, there is exactly one value of the ____ variable.

A. dependent
B. domain
C. function
D. independent
E. range
F. relationship

5. **Dollar Sense** Myesha's computer business has found that the profit (P) from selling one type of computer depends on the price (c). From sales data, her model is:

   $P(c) = -0.1(c - 1000)^2 + 7500$

   a. Find the company's profit on this type of computer for each price.
      i. $500   **ii.** $800   **iii.** $1000   **iv.** $1100   **v.** $1300
   b. Explain what a negative value of the profit function represents.
   c. What price do you think Myesha's company should charge? Why?

Tell whether each relationship is a function. If it is, state its domain and range.

6. {(23, 0.5), (14, 2.5), (25, 3.0), (18, 2.5), (14, 1.5), (22, 2.0)}

7. names of people in Florida (independent variable) and their telephone numbers (dependent variable)

8. names of cities in Pennsylvania (independent variable) and their 1990 census populations (dependent variable)

9. $f(x) = \sqrt{x - 1}$

10.

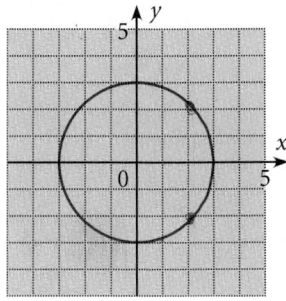

11.

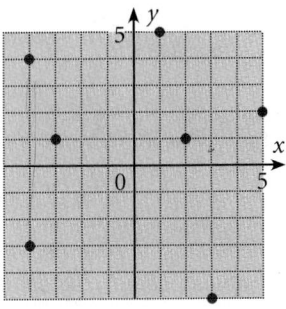

12.

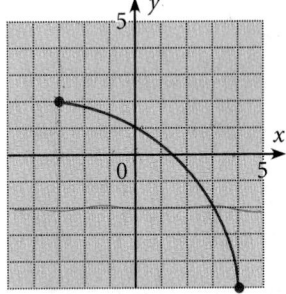

13. Let $f(x) = x^2 - x + 1$. Find each of the following.

   a. $f(1)$ **b.** $f(-3)$ **c.** $f(1.5)$ **d.** $f\left(\frac{1}{2}\right)$ **e.** $f(n)$ **f.** $f(2x)$

14. Let $h(x) = \frac{x - 4}{x}$. Find each of the following.

   a. $h(8)$ **b.** $h(0)$ **c.** $h(-2)$ **d.** $h(3.2)$ **e.** $h\left(\frac{1}{2}\right)$ **f.** $h(t)$

15. a. Find a relationship between x and $f(x)$.
    b. Complete the table.
    c. Graph the relationship.

x	0	1	2	3	4	5
$f(x)$	-2	0	2	4	6	

16. I Hear You! At sea level and at a temperature of 32°F, sound travels 1088 ft/sec.
    a. Write a function that gives the distance sound travels as a function of time.
    b. Make a table of values and use it to graph the function.
    c. Under the given conditions, how long would it take sound to travel 1 mile?

17. Just Weight The density of quartz is 165 lb/ft³.
    a. Write a function that gives the weight of a block of quartz as a function of its volume.
    b. Make a table of values and use it to graph the function.
    c. Find the volume of a 500-lb block of quartz.

18. The Vertical Line Test You can check whether a graph represents a function or not by passing a vertical line over the graph from left to right. If the vertical line ever touches the graph at two or more places at the same time, the graph does *not* represent a function. This is commonly known as the "vertical line test." Explain why the vertical line test works. Use the definition of a function in your explanation.

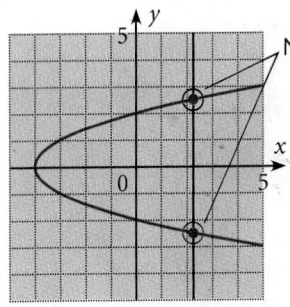

NOT a function

19. If you toss a penny, what is the probability that the penny will come up heads?

20. If you throw a die, what is the probability that you will get a 5?

21. If you throw a die, what is the probability that you will get a 1 or a 2?

22. If the weather report says there is a 30% chance of rain today, what is the probability it will not rain?

MORE PRACTICE

Tell whether each relationship is a function. If it is, state its domain and range.

23. $\{(-4, -3), (1, 0), (0, 0)\}$

24. $\{(-10, -5), (-3, -2), (-10, -6)\}$

25. meals on a menu (independent variable) and their prices (dependent variable)

26.

City name (independent variable)	Des Moines	Kansas City	New Orleans	Albany	Kansas City
State (dependent variable)	Iowa	Kansas	Louisiana	California	Missouri

27.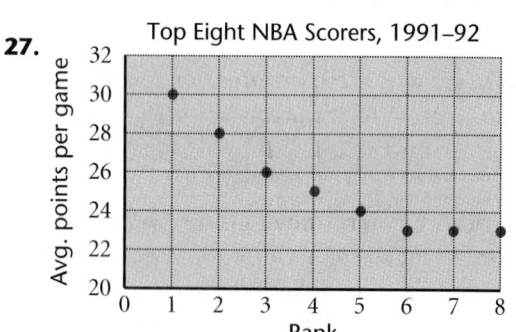

28.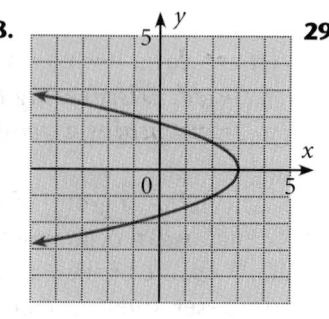

29.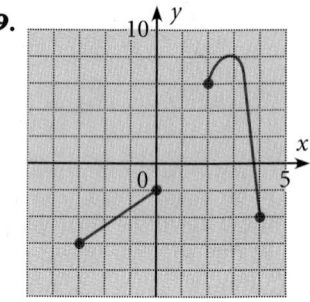

30. Let $f(x) = 2x + 4$. Find each of the following.
   a. $f(0)$ **b.** $f(1)$ **c.** $f(-1)$ **d.** $f(3x)$ **e.** $f\left(\frac{1}{2}\right)$ **f.** $f(e)$

31. Let $g(x) = |x| - 5$. Find each of the following.
   a. $g(-5)$ **b.** $g(0)$ **c.** $g(5)$ **d.** $g(-2)$ **e.** $g(-9)$ **f.** $g(n)$

32. a. Find a relationship between x and $f(x)$.
   b. Complete the table.
   c. Graph the relationship.

x	0	1	2	3	4	5
$f(x)$	5	4	3	2		

33. The surface area of a sphere is a function of its radius. The surface area is 4π times the square of the radius.
   a. Write an expression that gives the surface area of a sphere as a function of its radius.
   b. Make a table of values and use it to graph the function.
   c. Find the surface area of each spherical object.
      i. a soccer ball (radius 11 cm)   **ii.** the planet Venus (avg. radius 6050 km)

MORE MATH REASONING

34. Let $f(x) = 2x + 1$.
  a. Find $f(2)$, $f(3)$, and $f(5)$.   **b.** Is $f(2) + f(3) = f(5)$?
  c. Is $f(a) + f(b) = f(a + b)$? Explain.
  d. Does $nf(x) = f(nx)$? Test the conjecture using several examples of $f(x)$ and n.
      Then state whether you believe the conjecture is true, giving your reasons.

35. a. Sketch a graph where y is a function of x and x is a function of y.
  b. Sketch a graph where y is a function of x and x is not a function of y.
  c. Explain how you drew your graphs in **a** and **b**.

36. The **Cartesian product** of sets M and N is the set of all ordered pairs of elements from M
  and N where the first member is an element of M and the second is an element of N.
  a. Find the Cartesian product of {circle, square, triangle} and {red, blue, yellow, orange}.
  b. How can you tell how many ordered pairs the Cartesian product of two sets will have?
  c. Is taking the Cartesian product of two sets commutative? Why or why not?

1-1 PART D · Making Connections

← **C O N N E C T** → *Sets of data, even those with no apparent connection, may be closely related. Discovering those connections may not be easy. Now you will find relationships among a large amount of data.*

In the early 1800s, a group of American painters known as the Hudson River School began depicting the beauty of the American wilderness. Today, paintings by some of these artists sell for hundreds of thousands of dollars. Works by lesser known members of the group sell for less than $10,000.

Thomas Cole, *View Near the Village of Catskill,* 1827, oil on wood panel, 24.5" × 35"/ The Fine Arts Museums of San Francisco/ Gift of Mr. and Mrs. John D. Rockefeller III

You have $10,000 to spend on a painting by a member of the Hudson River School. To get the best value for your money, you collect data on past sales of such paintings to see which factors had the greatest influence on price. Since the price of a painting always depends on its artistic quality, you choose 20 works that are nearly equal in quality.

Artist (painting #)	Selling Price ($)	Area (nearest ft²)	Condition	Age (years)
James Brevoort (1)	8,800	7	7	110
James Brevoort (2)	5,500	17	4	96
Alfred Bricher (1)	4,000	20	5	118
Alfred Bricher (2)	10,000	9	9	122
Alfred Bricher (3)	8,100	6	9	94
John Casilear (1)	8,750	14	10	90
John Casilear (2)	6,800	5	8	100
Samuel Colman (1)	3,000	2	5	113
Samuel Colman (2)	9,600	8	8	110
Regis Gignoux (1)	8,500	13	8	123
Regis Gignoux (2)	6,000	16	6	112
Regis Gignoux (3)	7,250	16	6	97
David Johnson (1)	10,000	10	10	93
David Johnson (2)	5,000	2	3	125
Jervis McEntee (1)	7,500	7	7	110
Jervis McEntee (2)	9,200	10	10	103
James Smillie (1)	3,500	18	3	107
James Smillie (2)	4,000	3	4	92
John Williamson (1)	6,400	4	5	98
John Williamson (2)	9,000	9	9	114

You decide to investigate the relationship between price and each of the following:
1) the area of the painting in square feet
2) the condition of the painting (10 = excellent, 1 = poor)
3) the age of the painting

1. Make scatter plots plotting price against each of the other factors.
2. Describe any associations you find. Do they make sense? Explain.
3. Which factor(s) appear to be the best predictors of price? the worst predictors?
4. Describe the strategy you would use to make your purchase. Which painting would you buy?

1. Sketch scatter plots of data that exhibit positive association, negative association, and no association. Describe how you can identify each type of association.

2. How is the concept of a function similar to the idea of association between two types of data? How are they different?

3. Define independent variable and dependent variable in your own words.

Self-Assessment

State whether you believe there is a positive association, a negative association, or no association between each pair of quantities. Explain your reasoning.

1. phone number and monthly phone bill

2. number of students setting up for a meeting and time needed to complete the job

3. cost of motor oil and number of quarts purchased

4. Complete the table at the right. Then write and graph an equation relating x and y.

x	0	1	2	3	4	5
y	2	5	8	11		

5. Box Office Cash The table lists the average admission charge to see a movie in a theater from 1981 to 1992.

Year	Charge	Year	Charge	Year	Charge
1981	$2.78	1985	$3.55	1989	$4.45
1982	$2.94	1986	$3.71	1990	$4.75
1983	$3.15	1987	$3.91	1991	$4.89
1984	$3.36	1988	$4.11	1992	$5.05

a. Make a scatter plot of the data.
b. Draw a trend line for the scatter plot. What type of association do you observe?
c. Estimate the admission charge for 1980.

6. It's All Mine! The scatter plot shows the production of silver in the United States from 1930 to 1992.
a. Describe any associations you notice.
b. Copy the scatter plot and draw a trend line.
c. Estimate what you think the production of silver was in the United States in 1983. Explain.

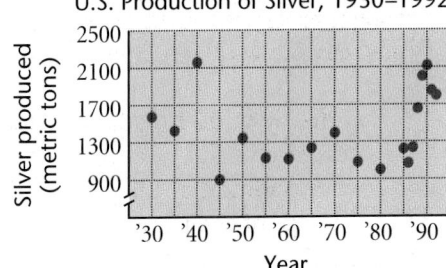

U.S. Production of Silver, 1930–1992

Copy and complete each table. Then write and graph an equation relating x and y.

7.

x	0	1	2	3	4	5
y	0	6	12	18		

8.

x	0	1	2	3	4	5
y	3	2	−1	−6		

Find the area of each figure. Round answers to the nearest tenth of a unit, if necessary. [Previous course]

9.

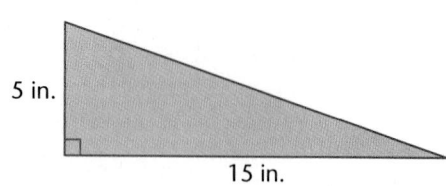

5 in.

15 in.

10.

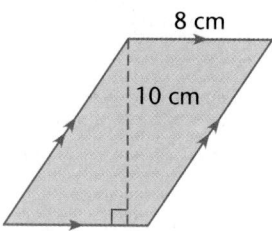

8 cm

10 cm

Health

11. Running burns about 13 calories per minute.
   a. If you run for 20 minutes, about how many calories will you burn?
   b. Write an equation relating r, the number of minutes that you run, and c, the number of calories that you burn.
   c. Identify which of your variables is the independent variable and which is the dependent variable. Justify your choices.
   d. How long would you have to run in order to burn 403 calories?

Tell whether each relationship is a function. If it is, state its domain and range.

12. the graph shown at the right

13. $\{(-2, -5), (-1, 0), (0, -1), (1, -2), (2, -1), (3, -3)\}$

14. $y = \dfrac{1}{x}$

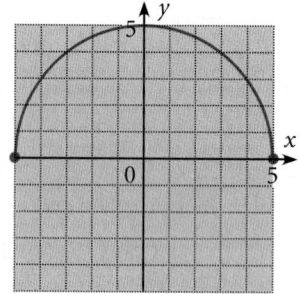

Choose the letter that correctly answers each question.

15. $f(x) = 4x - 3$. What is $f(0)$?
   (a) 0   (b) 1   (c) $\dfrac{3}{4}$ (d) -3

16. What is the domain of the function $f(x) = \sqrt{x + 2}$?
   (a) all real values of x (b) all real values of $x \geq 0$
   (c) all real values of $x \geq -2$ (d) all real values of $x \leq 0$

17. Let $f(x) = x^2 - 5x$. Find each of the following.
   a. $f(2)$ **b.** $f(0)$ **c.** $f(-3)$ **d.** $f(5)$ **e.** $f\left(-\dfrac{1}{5}\right)$ **f.** $f(n)$

18. Fare Enough! Suppose that a taxi cab fare is $4 plus $1.20 per mile for any part of a mile.
   a. Write a function expressing cab fare as a function of distance traveled.
   b. Use your function to complete the table below.

Distance (miles)	1	2	5	10
Cab Fare	$5.20			

   c. Give the domain and range of the function. Then graph the function.
   d. Find the fare for a trip of 9 miles. Locate the point on the graph.
   e. If the fare was $29, how far was the trip? Locate the point on the graph.

1-2 Experimental Probability and Simulation

"Nothing is certain except death and taxes." If this adage is true, all of the other events in our lives are uncertain. The study of uncertain events is called *probability*.

You take chances every day, from deciding what to eat to choosing a career. But how aware are you of the probabilities associated with making choices? For instance, you may keep a wary eye out for sharks when swimming in the ocean, but walk calmly through a thunderstorm. Yet the odds of being attacked by a shark are one in several million, while the chance that an American will be struck by lightning in her lifetime is many times higher, one in 9100.

Our personal probability estimates are not always accurate. They can be affected by what we see on television and in the movies, and by our individual hopes and fears. Which of the following events do you think is more likely:

- earning a degree in medicine, earning a degree in law, or beginning a career in the National Football League?

- that an airline loses your baggage (at least temporarily) or that a fiction novel becomes a best seller?

- seeing a UFO or winning the state lottery?

1. Give some reasons why people's fears about certain dangers are out of proportion to the actual likelihood of such events occurring.

2. The average chance of an American being struck by lightning is one in 9100. Do you think that every American has the same odds of being hit by lightning? If not, what might affect these odds?

3. Suppose that a high school student wants to become a veterinarian, but learns that the odds of being accepted to a veterinary school are not very good. What do you think this student should do?

← **C O N N E C T** → *You've looked at some ways to explore patterns in data. Now you will see how data can be used to estimate the probability that an event will occur.*

A probability is a number that measures the likelihood that an event will— or will not—happen. Recall that the probability of an event A, $P(A)$, is the fraction of time it is expected to occur. The probability of an event ranges from 0 (impossible) to 1 (certain).

Probability that a roll of a die comes up –13.4	Probability that a roll of a die comes up 1, 2, or 3	Probability that the word *probability* is on this page

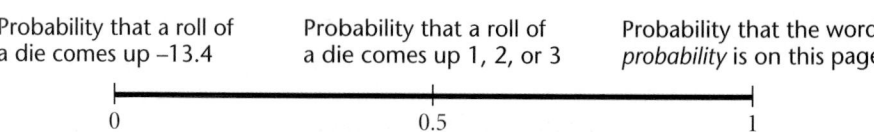

When we use probability to analyze a situation, we call any possible result an **outcome.** The **sample space** is the set of all possible outcomes. An **event** is any specified set of outcomes.

EXAMPLES

List the sample space for each situation.

1. taking a coin out of a pocket filled with pennies, dimes, and quarters

The three outcomes are a penny, a dime, or a quarter. The sample space is {penny, dime, quarter}.

2. the answers to a two-question true-or-false test

The outcomes are the possible arrangements of the two answers. The sample space is {(true, true), (true, false), (false, true), (false, false)}.

If you toss a quarter, there are two equally likely outcomes, heads and tails. The *theoretical probability* of tossing heads is therefore $\frac{1}{2}$, or 0.5. If you toss a quarter 10,000 times, you might expect to obtain 5,000 heads.

While a prisoner during World War II, mathematician John Kerrich tossed a coin 10,000 times. In his first 10 tosses he got 4 heads, a 40% ratio. As he made more tosses, his ratio of heads to tosses came closer and closer to 50%. His final total was 5,067 heads and 4,933 tails. The theoretical probability of tossing a head is still 0.5. But Kerrich's *experimental probability* was $\frac{5,067}{10,000}$, or 0.5067.

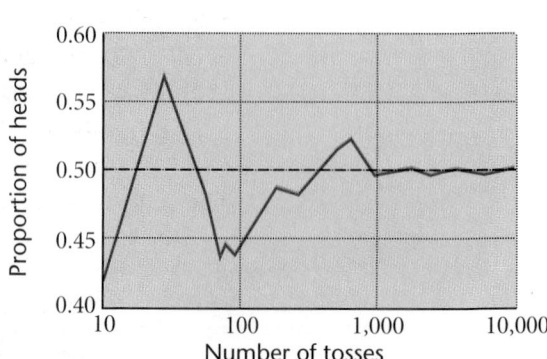

> If an event E consists of m outcomes out of a sample space of n possible equally likely outcomes, the **theoretical probability** of that event is $P(E) = \frac{m}{n}$. An **experimental probability** is found by collecting data or performing an experiment.

EXAMPLE

3. A box contains 52 blue pens, 25 black pens, 19 red pens, 15 green pens, and 6 purple pens. If one pen is chosen at random, what is the probability that it is green?

number of outcomes in sample space $= 52 + 25 + 19 + 15 + 6 = 117$

number of outcomes in event $= 15$

$$P(\text{green pen}) = \frac{15}{117} = \frac{5}{39}$$

The probability that a green pen is chosen is $\frac{5}{39} \approx 0.128$.

CONSIDER

1. How can you apply the definition of theoretical probability to show that a probability can never be less than 0 or greater than 1?

We are often interested in probabilities that involve geometric measurements. In **geometric probability,** the probability of an event is determined by comparing the areas (or perimeters, angle measures, etc.) of the "successful" regions to the total area of the sample space.

If point C is chosen at random from region B, then $P(C$ is in interior of region $A) = \frac{\text{area of region } A}{\text{area of region } B}$.

EXAMPLE

4. All of the skydivers in a competition landed randomly within the main 20-foot target square. What is the probability that a competitor landed in the 6-foot square marked "X"?

$$P(\text{"X"}) = \frac{\text{area of 6-ft square}}{\text{area of 20-ft square}} = \frac{36}{400} = 0.09$$

The probability that a diver landed in the "X" square is 0.09.

20 ft

EXPLORE: AROUND AND AROUND IT GOES

MATERIALS

Paper, Compass
Pin, Straw

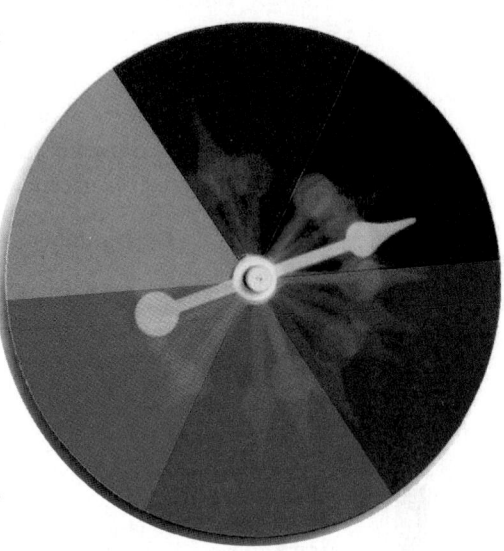

1. Design a spinner that has a 50% chance of landing on red, 30% on blue, and 20% on white. Explain how you designed your spinner.

2. Spin your spinner 25 times and record the results. How close were your experimental results to the theoretical probabilities?

3. Now suppose that an outcome consists of *two* spins of the spinner. List all of the possible outcomes in the sample space.

4. Use your spinner to generate 25 two-spin outcomes. From your results, find the approximate probabilities of all of the possible outcomes.

5. Combine your results in Step 4 with the results of your classmates. From the combined outcomes, find the approximate probabilities of all the possible outcomes.

6. Describe any connections you see between the one-spin theoretical probabilities and your two-spin results.

TRY IT

a. A die has sides numbered 1 to 6. Find the theoretical probability that one roll of the die gives a 2 or a 5.

b. The central angle of a spinner's only green sector measures 135 degrees. Find the theoretical probability that the spinner will land on green.

c. In an archery competition, 28 of Alicia's 40 arrows hit the bull's-eye. What is the experimental probability that one of her arrows hits the bull's-eye?

You've seen that the probability that an event will occur is the ratio of the number of outcomes in the event to the number of equally likely outcomes in the sample space. The probability that an impossible event will occur is 0 and the probability that a certain event will occur is 1. All other probabilities are between 0 and 1.

REFLECT

1. Give an example of an event with a probability of 0 and an example of an event with a probability of 1.

2. What does it mean to say that an event occurs "randomly"?

3. What is a "fair" coin?

4. Suppose you know the theoretical probability of an event occurring. How can you find the theoretical probability that the event will *not* occur?

Exercises

CORE

In the Exercises, assume that probability means "theoretical probability." Unless asked to do otherwise, express probabilities as decimals rounded to the nearest hundredth.

1. **Getting Started** A spinner with 8 congruent sectors is spun. The person spinning hopes to land on an even number.
   a. What is the sample space?
   b. What is the event?
   c. List the outcomes in the event.
   d. What is the probability that the spinner will land on an even number?

List the sample space for each situation.

2. the roll of a die

3. drawing a marble from a bag of green, yellow, and blue marbles

4. the answers to a three-question true-or-false test

5. the segments formed by joining points *A*, *B*, *C*, and *D*

Give the number of outcomes in each sample space.

6. the set of states in the United States

7. the set of letters in the alphabet

8. the set of sides in a rhombus

9. the set of vertices in an octagon

Give the number of outcomes in each event.

10. a digit from 0 to 9 is odd

11. a month of the year begins with J

12. a number less than 5 comes up when a die is rolled

13. In your own words, explain how to find the theoretical probability of an event.

14. Find the theoretical probability that one roll of a die results in each event. Express each answer as a fraction.
   a. you roll a 4   **b.** you roll an odd number   **c.** you roll a number less than 5
   d. you do not roll a 2 or a 3   **e.** you roll an 8

15. The central angles of a spinner's two red sectors measure 34 degrees and 48 degrees. Find the probability that the spinner lands on a red sector.

16. Eight sophomores, ten juniors, and six seniors are in one English class. One student is randomly chosen to be the first to give a report. What is the probability of each of the following events?
   a. a junior is chosen   **b.** a sophomore or a senior is chosen
   c. a sophomore is not chosen   **d.** a sophomore, a junior, or a senior is chosen
   e. a freshman is chosen

17. A doctor states that an operation has an 85% probability of success. Is this a statement of theoretical or experimental probability? Explain.

18. A penny is tossed 200 times and comes up heads 92 times and tails 108 times. Find the experimental probability of each outcome.
  a. tails   **b.** heads   **c.** heads or tails   **d.** neither heads nor tails

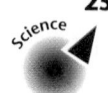

19. The vote totals in the 1992 presidential election for the state of Washington are shown below.

Clinton (Dem): 993,037   Bush (Rep): 731,234   Perot: 541,780   Others: 20,144

Find the probability that a randomly selected Washington voter chose:
  a. Clinton   **b.** Bush   **c.** Perot
  d. neither the Democratic nor the Republican candidate

20. But the Light's Better Over Here Melissa has lost her contact lens tonight somewhere inside the 10-m square shown. The streetlight lights up a circular region inscribed in this square. Assuming the contact has fallen randomly inside the square, what is the probability that her contact is in the lighted region?

10 m

Write the word or phrase that correctly completes each statement.

21. If a die is rolled, the ____ is the numbers 1, 2, 3, 4, 5, and 6.

22. A die is rolled. The ____ probability that a die will show a 1 is $\frac{1}{6}$.

23. The ____ probability that a die will show a 1 must be found by rolling the die many times and recording the results.

24. Watch Out for That Tree! Assume that a parachutist lands randomly within a rectangular field that measures 50 yards by 30 yards. At each corner of the field is a tree that covers a quarter-circle area with a radius of 5 yards. What is the probability that the parachutist does not land in a tree?

> **Problem-Solving Tip**
>
> Draw a picture to represent the situation.

25. Probabilities that parents will pass certain genes to their offspring were first studied by the Austrian monk Gregor Mendel. Mendel showed that if pea plants with yellow, round seeds were crossed with plants having green, wrinkled seeds, their offspring should occur in these proportions:

yellow, round: 0.5625   yellow, wrinkled: 0.1875

green, round: 0.1875   green, wrinkled: 0.0625

Suppose that pea plants with yellow, round seeds are crossed with those with green, wrinkled seeds, and they produce 1184 seeds. How many of each variety of seed would you expect to find?

 **LOOK BACK**

State whether you believe there is a positive association, a negative association, or no association between each pair of quantities. Explain your reasoning. [1-1]

26. the annual number of sunny days in a city and the percentage of its citizens who are retired

27. the number of miles on a car and the value of the car

28. Let $f(x) = x^2 - 2x + 4$. Find each of the following. [1-1]
   a. $f(2)$ **b.** $f(-3)$ **c.** $f(5)$ **d.** $f(10)$ **e.** $f(n)$

MORE PRACTICE

Give the number of outcomes in each sample space.

29. the set of months in a year

30. the set of hours in a day

31. the set of sides in a hexagon

32. the set of diagonals in a pentagon

Give the number of outcomes in each event.

33. a side of a trapezoid is a base

34. a digit is between 3 and 8

35. an odd number comes up when a die is tossed

36. Candidates' Forum The five female and four male candidates for mayor will draw names to determine who will speak first. Find the probability that the first speaker will be male. Express your answer as a fraction.

37. A spinner is divided into 10 congruent sectors. The sectors are numbered consecutively from 1 to 10. Two sectors are yellow, three are red, and five are blue. Find the probability that the spinner will land on each of the following.
   a. an even number   **b.** red   **c.** a prime number
   d. red or yellow   **e.** a number from 1 to 10   **f.** 1, 3, 8, or 9

38. A die is tossed 300 times. The 1 shows 55 times, the 2 shows 48 times, the 3 shows 52 times, the 4 shows 45 times, and the 5 shows 57 times. Give the experimental probability of each roll.
   a. 1   **b.** 4   **c.** an odd number   **d.** 2 or 3   **e.** 6   **f.** a number less than 7

39. A square flower garden has two triangles planted in roses, as shown in the figure. If a drop of rain falls randomly on the garden, what is the probability that it falls in a section with roses?

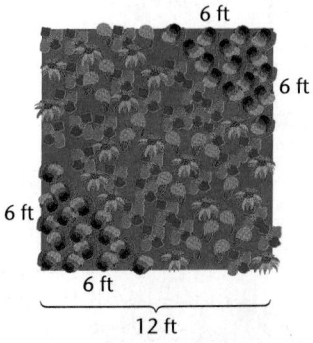
6 ft
6 ft
6 ft
6 ft
12 ft

40. The central angle of a spinner's sector labeled "Try Again" measures 75 degrees. Find the probability that the spinner will land on "Try Again."

41. Space Pollution The average radius of the earth is approximately 3,960 mi. Suppose that debris from a satellite lands randomly on the earth's surface. What is the probability that it lands:
   a. in the United States (area 3,615,100 mi^2)?   **b.** in the water?
   c. in South America (area 6,883,000 mi^2)?   **d.** on land (total area 58,433,000 mi^2)?

MORE MATH REASONING

42. The table at right shows the dollar amounts of currency in circulation reported by the U.S. Department of the Treasury on March 31, 1993.

Suppose you find a bill on the street. Assuming that it is "chosen" at random, what is the probability that it is:

a. a $1 bill? **b.** a $20 bill? **c.** a $100 bill?

d. worth at least $5 but no more than $50?

e. worth $1,000 or more(!!)?

f. Explain what you had to do before you could find these probabilities.

g. What are the four most common denominations? Why do you think these particular denominations are so plentiful?

Denomination ($)	Federal Reserve Notes ($)
1	5,154,336,328
2	784,359,718
5	6,186,740,170
10	12,109,938,660
20	70,182,595,780
50	37,649,949,450
100	179,868,854,100
500	146,431,000
1,000	169,645,000
5,000	1,725,000
10,000	3,450,000

h. There are about 260 million U.S. citizens. If the total value of all of these bills were divided equally among all citizens, how much would each person have in cash?

43. Suppose you believe that a die you have been using in a game is not fair. Describe an experiment you could conduct to test your conjecture.

1-2
PART B
Simulation

←CONNECT→ *You have seen how to find theoretical and experimental probabilities. Now you will investigate how to estimate probabilities by simulating experiments that are difficult to perform.*

Calculating the theoretical or experimental probability of a complex real-world event can be challenging. When a probability of a complex event is difficult or impossible to find theoretically, we can create a model of the situation by estimating the probability of a single event and using it to run an experiment. This model is called a **simulation.**

To estimate the probability that there are more than four shoppers in a supermarket line on a Saturday afternoon, a grocery chain might create a computer program that models the number of shoppers, number of open checkstands, the time it takes to serve a customer, etc.

If the simulation program is well-designed, it can provide a good estimate of the actual probability. Once the program is written, the store manager can easily see how making changes (for instance, adding more clerks) might affect the probabilities.

1. What is the probability that a family with four children will have two girls and two boys?

Step 1: State your assumptions.
Assume the probability that a baby is a girl is $\frac{1}{2}$.

Step 2: Select a model to generate the outcomes.
Since each birth can result in either a girl or a boy, we need a model for two equally likely outcomes. You could toss a coin or put two slips of paper in a bag. For this example, we will use a coin, letting H = girl and T = boy.

Step 3: Define a trial.
Tossing a coin four times will represent a four-child family.

Step 4: Collect data by repeating the trial.
The more times the simulation is repeated, the more accurate the results tend to be. The results of 50 trials are shown.

HHHH	**THHT**	**THHT**	**HTHT**	HTTT	HHTH	**HTHT**	**HTHT**	HHTH	**THTH**
HTTT	**HHTT**	HHHH	**THTH**	HTTH	**THHT**	HHTH	THHH	HHHH	THTT
TTHT	HTHH	TTTH	HTHH	HHHT	THTT	TTTT	TTHT	**HHTT**	HHHH
HTTT	**HHTT**	TTTH	TTTH	HHHT	**HHTT**	**THTH**	**HTTH**	TTTH	HHTH
HHTT	**THTH**	**HHTT**	**HTHT**	**HTTH**	HHHH	TTTH	**HTHT**	TTTT	**THHT**

Of the 50 simulations, 22 resulted in two girls and two boys. So we estimate the probability to be $\frac{22}{50} = 0.44$.

It is important to remember that experimental probabilities are *estimates*. In general, the more trials that are performed, the more closely the experimental probability approximates the true probability of the event.

The key to using simulation to estimate probability is finding a good model for the individual events that make up the simulation.

a. Describe a good method for modeling the selection of one out of six people several times.

b. Describe a good method for modeling a series of games between two evenly matched teams.

A table of random numbers is often used to simulate an event. This table consists of the digits from 0 to 9, listed in no predetermined order. The following is an example of a series of random numbers from a random number table.

60633   49280   77180   78540...

Some calculators have a *random number generator* that will provide random numbers between 0 and 1. The individual digits in these numbers are also random, and can be used like digits in a random number table.

We could have used random numbers to model the birth of a child in Example 1 by letting even numbers represent a girl and odd numbers represent a boy. Let each group of four digits represent a four-child "family."

6	0	6	3	3	4	9	2	8	0	7	7	1	8	0	7	8	5	4	0
G	G	G	B	**B**	**G**	**B**	**G**	**G**	**G**	**B**	**B**	**B**	**G**	**G**	**B**	G	B	G	G
2	3	7	3	5	4	9	5	0	9	4	9	8	4	4	5	4	5	4	6
G	B	B	B	B	G	B	B	**G**	**B**	**G**	**B**	G	G	G	B	G	B	G	G

From this simulation of 10 trials, the probability that a four-child family has two girls is estimated as $\frac{4}{10} = 0.4$.

CONSIDER

?

1. The simulation above using random numbers gave a different probability for a two-girl, two-boy result than did Example 1. Does this indicate that one of the simulations was done incorrectly? Explain.
2. How could you use a random number table to model probabilities involving a basketball player who makes 60% of his free throws?

EXAMPLE

2. A small grocery store throws away milk that has passed the expiration date. At this store, 70% of the milk cartons are sold before the expiration date. The store receives 8 new cartons every week. What is the probability that they throw out three or more of these cartons?

Step 1: State your assumptions. 70% of the cartons are sold. So 30%, or 3 out of 10, must be thrown out.

Step 2: Select a model to generate the outcomes. We will use random numbers. Let three digits, say 0, 1, and 2, represent the cartons that are thrown out. The other seven digits represent the cartons that are sold.

Step 3: Define a trial. We will look at eight numbers at a time to simulate the eight cartons.

Step 4: Collect data by repeating the trial. Thirteen random numbers (representing 13 weeks of milk shipments) are generated on a graphing calculator. We use the first eight digits of each to represent one week's shipment of milk cartons.

These numbers give the following results.

62173948	**88110630**	**12430305**	**45003086**	46658004
28603253	62789696	61740363	**80684182**	77343267
46384001	92517826	**62437622**		

Since at least three cartons of milk were thrown out in 8 of the 13 weeks, the simulation gives an estimated probability of $\frac{8}{13} \approx 0.62$ that three or more cartons are thrown out.

EXPLORE: COLLECT THE WHOLE SET!

MATERIALS

Random number generator or random number table

Solver's Cereal has randomly inserted collectible cards of five different mathematicians in boxes of cereal. You want to collect the entire set. Suppose that there is an infinite supply of each of the five cards, and that there is a probability of $\frac{1}{5}$ of getting any particular one in a given box.

1. Simulate buying two boxes of cereal 20 different times. What is the probability that you received two different cards?
2. Simulate buying three boxes of cereal 20 different times. What is the probability that all three of the cards were different?
3. Predict the number of boxes of cereal you would have to buy to get all five cards.
4. Using random numbers, "buy" boxes of cereal until you have all five cards. Record the number of boxes you had to buy to get all five cards. Repeat this step 10 times.
5. Make a table of your results. If this were a real situation, how many boxes of cereal would you expect to buy to collect the entire set? Explain your reasoning.

CONSIDER

3. Do you think it is easier to collect a complete set of collectible cards if the probability of getting each card is the same, or if some cards are found more frequently than others? Why or why not?

Simulation is an important way to estimate probabilities when it is too difficult, costly, or time-consuming to perform an actual probability experiment. Scientists and businesspeople often use computers to create detailed simulations of real-world events.

1. Name two events that could be illustrated or tested by simulation.
2. Give an example of a simulation where you would rather use a die instead of a random number generator and an example of a simulation where you would prefer to use a random number generator.
3. To generate a set of random numbers, one student rapidly wrote digits on a piece of paper. Were they random numbers? Explain.

Exercises

CORE

Unless asked to do otherwise, express probabilities as decimals rounded to the nearest hundredth.

1. **Getting Started** To simulate the number of girls and boys in a three-child family, three coins are flipped. The results of twenty trials are shown below.

| HHT | HTH | HTH | TTH | TTH | TTH | THH | HHH | THH | HHH |
| HHH | TTH | HTT | HHH | THT | HHT | THT | TTH | TTH | TTT |

   a. Let heads represent girls and tails represent boys. How many families had three girls? two girls? two boys? three boys?
   b. What is the estimated probability that there are exactly two boys in a three-child family?
   c. What is the estimated probability that there are three girls in a three-child family?

Describe an appropriate way to model each situation. (The probabilities given are from *What the Odds Are,* by Les Krantz.)

2. $\frac{1}{6}$ of all Americans will have some kind of cosmetic surgery.

3. $\frac{1}{3}$ of Americans eat in a restaurant once a week.

4. $\frac{1}{5}$ of all American men suffer some significant hair loss by the time they reach age 29.

State whether each statement is true or false. If the statement is false, correct it so that the revised statement is true.

5. A simulation can be used to find the exact value of a probability that is difficult to measure directly.

6. There may be more than one way to accurately simulate a situation.

7. Suppose that you have a coin, a die, and a calculator that generates random numbers. Describe one simulation that you could do using each of these tools. Then state which of the three is most useful in general and explain why.

8. Suppose that there is a 50% chance of rain tomorrow. Which of the following methods would *not* be a valid way to simulate tomorrow's weather?
   (a) flip a coin; let heads represent rain
   (b) roll a die; let odd numbers represent rain
   (c) use a random digit; let 0–5 represent rain
   (d) use a random digit; let 0–4 represent rain

9. In 1992, about 40% of the days in Jackson, Mississippi, were cloudy.
   a. Assume that cloudy days occur randomly. Use the series of random digits at the right to simulate 12 weeks of weather in Jackson. Estimate the probability that there are 3 or fewer cloudy days in a week. (Hint: Let any of the numbers 6–9 represent cloudy weather.)

1543639	4612310	3734077
2777330	6549652	3316937
8537709	3867611	0209183
8209377	0977130	2389191

   b. Do you think that cloudy days and clear days actually occur "randomly"? Explain your answer.

10. During the regular basketball season, Jovonne made 70% of her free throws, worth one point each. In the state championship game, her team is behind by one point with one second left. Jovonne has two free throws.
    a. Use the random numbers below to simulate Jovonne shooting two free throws 30 times. Explain your method.

0.8235090391	0.1278735876
0.3480635773	0.0195646032
0.3700634566	0.8864070497

    b. Use your results to estimate the following probabilities.
       i. Jovonne makes both free throws and her team wins the game.
       ii. Jovonne makes one of the free throws and the game goes into overtime.
       iii. Jovonne misses both free throws and her team loses.
    c. Do you think Jovonne's free throw percentage will actually be 70% in this situation? Explain.

JoeSam, *Boy in Wheelchair*, 1994, mixed media, 5'4" × 4'8"/ An original work commissioned by the State of Florida Arts Council for the University of Central Florida, Orlando, Florida

11. **That'll Never Happen To Me!** According to the *1992 Statistical Abstract of the United States,* there were about 143 million registered automobiles in the United States in 1990. The same year, there were 14.3 million cars involved in accidents.
    a. Based on these statistics, what is the estimated probability that a car was *not* involved in an accident in 1990? Guess the probability that a particular car will avoid an accident for five *consecutive* years.
    b. Use the random digits at the right to simulate 20 five-year sequences. Estimate the probability that a car avoids an accident for five consecutive years.

51275	75658	61962	11966	49046
06965	48613	58890	59220	07371
09569	28121	93532	97064	03536
49673	35029	59577	63577	08083

    c. How do your results in **b** compare to your guess in **a**?

12. Suppose your health clinic has six doctors who are assigned randomly to patients. You go to the clinic four times this year. Use a simulation to estimate the probability that you will see the same doctor at least twice. Explain how you did your simulation and tell how many trials you chose to do.

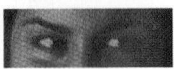 **LOOK AHEAD**

13. Use the graph at the right to make a table of the number of U.S. licensed male drivers in 1991 who were 19 years of age or younger using the given age categories.

14. Make a table of the number of licensed female drivers in 1991 who were 19 years of age or younger using the given age categories.

15. Make a table of the total number of licensed drivers in 1991 who were 19 years of age or younger using the given age categories. Describe how you could use the tables in **13** and **14** to do this.

U.S. Licensed Drivers by Age, 1991

Age	Female	Male
19	1,330,000	1,490,000
18	1,156,000	1,311,000
17	970,000	1,098,000
16	655,000	739,000
under 16	30,000	35,000

MORE PRACTICE

Describe an appropriate way to model each situation.

16. 10% of American men between the ages of 40 and 44 have never married.

17. About 40% of all residents of the state of Alaska live in the city of Anchorage.

18. About 60% of the television viewing audience watched the final episode of *M*A*S*H* in 1983.

19. Nearly $\frac{1}{3}$ of all U.S. cars sold in 1992 were small cars.

 Careers

20. Probably Sold Myrna is a real estate agent. Thirty percent of the homes listed are sold each week. Your family is moving out of state, so you have decided to have Myrna sell your home. What is the estimated probability that she will sell your home in less than 4 weeks? Use the random digits at the right to simulate twenty 4-week periods. (Hint: Let any of the numbers 0–2 represent your house being sold.)

0688	5735	6590	7371	5272
1097	8618	7578	2389	9160
2777	2299	1439	9380	9906
8934	9860	0406	2442	2962

21. Use a Graphing Calculator People often believe that there is a natural tendency for random events to "even out;" for example, that a run of four heads in a row is less likely than the result, "heads, tails, heads, tails."
   a. Guess the probability that a ten-digit random number has at least two consecutive equal digits, for instance, 0155234291.
   b. Use the random number generator on your graphing calculator to generate 25 numbers. Keep track of the ones that have two or more consecutive equal digits. From the results estimate the probability that a random number from your calculator has two or more consecutive equal digits. How did your results compare with your guess in **a**?

22. Quiz Kid! Phil was running out of time on his true-false test, so he had to guess the answers to the last three questions. The probability that Phil had a correct answer to any one of these questions is 50%.

Use a coin to simulate this situation. Complete 20 trials of 3 "questions" each, and record your results. Use your results to estimate:
a. the probability that Phil answered all 3 questions correctly
b. the probability that he answered exactly 2 of the questions correctly
c. the probability that he answered none of the questions correctly

MORE MATH REASONING

23. Use a Graphing Utility These two pictures were shown to 100 people, 59 of whom preferred the computer-generated art.

a. If you choose a person randomly out of a crowd, what is the probability that this person will prefer the Mondrian painting?

b. Suppose that a group of 3 people views these pictures. Use a random number generator to simulate this situation 9 times. Estimate the probability that exactly 2 of the people in the group will prefer the computer-generated picture to the Mondrian painting.

Piet Mondrian, *Composition with Lines*, 1917, Courtesy of Mondrian Estate/ Holtzman Trust. Rijksmuseum Kröller-Müller

A. Michael Noll, *Computer Composition with Lines*, 1964

24. Explain how you could use a six-sided die to simulate an event with eight equally likely outcomes.

25. Use a Graphing Utility Your favorite restaurant is giving out free plastic cups to promote a new movie. There are four different cups available, given out randomly.

You plan to keep going to the restaurant until you have the complete set of cups. Using a simulation technique, estimate how many trips you will need to make before you have the four different cups. Show the results of each of your trials, explain how you did your simulation, and tell how many trials you chose to do.

26. Use a Graphing Utility The Perkins Company produces computer memory chips and sells them in boxes of 5. Perkins knows that there is a 2% chance of any one chip being defective.

Krash Computers agrees to buy 100 boxes of Perkins's chips. If they find that over 95% of the boxes contain no defective chips, they will make Perkins their exclusive chip supplier. Use random numbers generated by a graphing utility to simulate this situation. Do you think that the Perkins Company will become Krash's exclusive supplier? Explain how you did your simulation and show your results.

Making Connections

← C O N N E C T → *You have calculated theoretical and experimental probabilities and used simulations to estimate probabilities that are difficult to find directly. All of these ways of finding probabilities are important in solving real-world problems.*

When studying the spread of communicable diseases, epidemiologists and other health professionals use probabilities and statistics. In the following Explore, you will use probability to investigate how a disease might spread to your family.

EXPLORE: CAN YOU TAKE THE STRAIN?

MATERIALS

Random number generator or random number table

A strain of influenza (the flu), similar to that shown in the photograph, has hit your town. Suppose that your family consists of you and two other people. You want to predict the chances of your family members catching the flu from someone outside the family.

1. You call your doctor to ask how likely it is that anyone will catch the flu from someone who already has it. She tells you about a recent study where 82 out of 410 people exposed to the virus became ill. What is the probability that someone who is exposed to this virus catches the flu? Is this a theoretical or an experimental probability?

2. Assume that each member of your family has come in contact with someone who has the flu. Using your result from Step 1, devise a way to model whether or not a member of your family catches the flu. Explain how you are going to model the events in your simulation and how you decided how many trials to run.

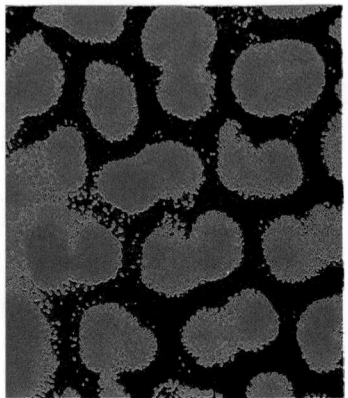

Influenza virus as seen through a scanning electron micrograph

3. Run your simulation several times, counting the number of times that 0, 1, 2, or 3 of your family members comes down with the flu. Calculate the following probabilities.
   a. 0 family members catch the flu   **b.** 1 family member catches the flu
   c. 2 family members catch the flu   **d.** 3 family members catch the flu
   e. at least 1 family member catches the flu
   f. at least 2 family members catch the flu

4. How would you change this experiment if the probability of contracting the flu from another person was 15%?

1. In your own words, explain how *theoretical probability, experimental probability,* and *simulation* are different.
2. Suppose you flipped a coin 10 times and found that the experimental probability of tails was 70%. Would you be surprised? What would you think if, after 1000 trials, your experimental probability of tails was still 70%? Explain.
3. Can you be sure that the results of a simulation give the actual probability of an event? Why or why not?

Self-Assessment

Give the number of possible outcomes in each event.

1. a month of the year begins with M

2. a random digit is greater than 6

3. a day of the week begins with the letter S

4. A coin was tossed and heads turned up 20 times out of 50. What is the experimental probability that the coin will land tails?
(a) $\frac{1}{2}$ (b) $\frac{2}{5}$ (c) $\frac{3}{5}$ (d) 2500   (e) 600

5. A set of cards consists of ten red cards numbered 1 to 10 and ten blue cards numbered 1 to 10. Give the probability of choosing:
a. a red card   **b.** a 1   **c.** a number evenly divisible by 4
d. a number greater than 7   **e.** a blue 3   **f.** a yellow card

6. A Matter of Age The numbers below give population projections (in thousands) for the United States in the year 2000.

Under age 25: 90,944   Between ages 25 and 64: 142,441   Over age 65: 39,604

What is the probability that a person chosen at random in the year 2000:
a. will be under the age of 25?   **b.** will be less than age 65?
c. will not be between ages 25 and 64?

7. Describe a situation where simulation would be the easiest way to estimate a probability. Explain why finding the theoretical probability would be more difficult.

8. State whether you believe there is a positive association, a negative association, or no association between the polar bear population of a region and the amount of territory available to each bear. [1-1]

9. If $f(x) = 6(x - 3) + 2$, find each of the following. [1-1].
a. $f(3)$ **b.** $f(-1)$ **c.** $f\left(\frac{1}{2}\right)$ **d.** $f(10)$ **e.** $f(n)$

10. A drug company reports that 95% of patients using a certain medication have no side effects. Is this a theoretical probability or an experimental probability? Do you think it is the result of a simulation? Explain.

11. **Defective Batteries** The quality control department of the Better Battery Company selects 300 of the company's batteries at random and tests them for endurance. Four of the batteries tested do not meet the company's standards for endurance. Based on this test, what is the probability that a customer who buys one battery will get a battery that does not meet the company's standards?

12. Alexia has spread her collection of 20 rectangular stamps on a circular table. The table is 4 ft in diameter, and each of the stamps is 2 in. × $1\frac{1}{2}$ in. Unfortunately, a drop of ink from Alexia's pen flies off and lands randomly somewhere on the table. What is the probability that the ink will land on one of her stamps?

13. The flag of Guyana is shown at the right. Suppose that a raindrop lands on the flag at random.

   a. What is the probability that the raindrop lands in the red or the yellow region? Justify your answer.

   b. Suppose that the length of the flag is 3.2 m and its width is 2.0 m. If the red triangle's altitude from its rightmost point is 1.5 m, find the probability that the raindrop lands in the red region.

14. **An "Eggzact" Science** When a bird breeder mates two of his gray cockatiels, he finds that 75% of the offspring are gray, but 25% are lutino (yellow). Suppose these parents have five chicks. Use the string of random digits from 1 to 4 shown to find the approximate probability that exactly two of the chicks are lutino. Simulate twenty sets of five chicks. Explain how you found your results.

32224	13411	24111	24244	21222
33331	14222	33332	23334	33412
43433	14142	12112	44232	42234
12433	11144	22242	12241	11332

15. According to *What the Odds Are*, U.S. airlines estimate that 9 out of 10 lost bags will eventually be returned to their owners. Suppose that an airline misplaces 5 bags on a given day. Use the string of random digits at the right to estimate the probability that all 5 will be returned. Explain how you found this probability.

20301	52310	28855	98311	75943
61868	66021	26565	37821	95791
70882	53420	46615	24653	91161
95603	89257	58094	44898	39646
71622	29832	57867	76963	52298

16. **Soccer or Rugby?** Each Saturday afternoon, a soccer game is played at North Park and a rugby match is played at South Park. A fan who lives halfway between the parks can never decide which game to attend. Therefore, he walks to the nearest bus stop at a random time on Saturday afternoon and takes the first bus. A bus for North Park arrives every ten minutes, and a bus for South Park also arrives every ten minutes. The fan thinks he will see about the same number of soccer games as rugby matches. But for some reason he ends up going to the rugby match about 90% of the time. Give a reasonable explanation for what has occurred.

Language by the Numbers

81,31,61,71,21,31,72,72,62,

61,21,42,12,
62,63,33

12,22,+83,53,62,

"Secret codes" are fun for children, but encoding and decoding messages, called cryptography, can be vitally important. For example, code breakers had a major impact on the outcome of both World Wars.

One of the few unbroken codes in military history belongs to the Navajo Code Talkers. During World War II, this elite group of 420 Navajos served in U.S. Marine Corps divisions in the Asian-Pacific theater. By using everyday Navajo words (with meanings that changed as vowel pitches rose and fell) and some 400 code words of their own, this elite group created a code that remained unbroken throughout the war. The Marine commanders were skeptical about using the Navajo Code Talkers at first, but when they realized the Navajos could code and decode secret messages more quickly than any machine, the Code Talkers became indispensable.

The code was top secret, as was the existence of the Code Talkers. Even though the code was never used again, it wasn't declassified until 1968. Nearly twenty-five years after World War II, the Navajo Code Talkers could finally be given the recognition they deserved.

Two members of the leatherneck unit, made up of Navajo Indians from Arizona and New Mexico, are seen during the battle for Bougainville in 1943.

?

1. Besides safeguarding military secrets, list three other ways codes are used.
2. What features does a good secret code have?
3. What effect do you think computers have had on breaking codes?

← C O N N E C T → *You've seen how data is displayed on a scatter plot. Now you will investigate another way to organize and store data.*

A matrix (plural: matrices) is a rectangular array of numbers arranged between brackets. The rows and columns are useful for classifying information. Matrices have applications in mathematics, business, and cryptography, where computers now create codes so complex they are practically unbreakable.

The following table shows the enrollment at Kennedy High School.

Kennedy High School Enrollment				
	9th Grade	**10th Grade**	**11th Grade**	**12th Grade**
Male	155	202	184	193
Female	186	175	179	182

The numbers in this table can be used to form a matrix.

$$A = \begin{bmatrix} 155 & 202 & 184 & 193 \\ 186 & 175 & 179 & 182 \end{bmatrix}$$

A matrix has a **dimension,** given by the number of horizontal rows and the number of vertical columns. In this case, there are 2 rows and 4 columns, so the dimension of matrix A is 2×4, read "2 by 4."

Each number in a matrix is an **entry.** The entry in row i and column j of matrix A is denoted a_{ij}. In the matrix above, the number in the second row and third column is $a_{23} = 179$. This entry gives us information about females (row 2) in 11th grade (column 3). Matrices are **equal** only if they have the same dimension and all of their corresponding entries are the same.

$$\text{Row} \begin{matrix} & & \text{Column} \\ & \begin{matrix} 1 & 2 & 3 & 4 \end{matrix} \\ \begin{matrix} 1 \\ 2 \end{matrix} & \begin{bmatrix} 155 & 202 & 184 & 193 \\ 186 & 175 & 179 & 182 \end{bmatrix} \end{matrix}$$
a_{23}

In business and other applications, tables of data are often stored as matrices. To update this data, these matrices must sometimes be added to each other, subtracted from each other, or multiplied by a number.

Matrix A represents the enrollment at Kennedy High School. Matrix B represents the numbers of students absent today.

$$A = \begin{matrix} & \text{Grade} \\ \begin{matrix} 9 & 10 & 11 & 12 \end{matrix} \\ \begin{bmatrix} 155 & 202 & 184 & 193 \\ 186 & 175 & 179 & 182 \end{bmatrix} \end{matrix} \qquad B = \begin{matrix} & \text{Grade} \\ \begin{matrix} 9 & 10 & 11 & 12 \end{matrix} \\ \begin{bmatrix} 8 & 16 & 12 & 10 \\ 14 & 12 & 18 & 22 \end{bmatrix} \begin{matrix} \text{Boys} \\ \text{Girls} \end{matrix} \end{matrix}$$

1. Identify b_{21}. What is the real-world meaning of this entry?

The entry in the second row and the first column of B is 14. $b_{21} = 14$. This represents the number of 9th grade girls absent today.

2. Find the matrix that represents the students present at Kennedy High School today.

$$A - B = \begin{bmatrix} 155 & 202 & 184 & 193 \\ 186 & 175 & 179 & 182 \end{bmatrix} - \begin{bmatrix} 8 & 16 & 12 & 10 \\ 14 & 12 & 18 & 22 \end{bmatrix}$$

$$= \begin{bmatrix} 155-8 & 202-16 & 184-12 & 193-10 \\ 186-14 & 175-12 & 179-18 & 182-22 \end{bmatrix} = \begin{bmatrix} 147 & 186 & 172 & 183 \\ 172 & 163 & 161 & 160 \end{bmatrix}$$

3. Tomorrow is picture day. If only half of each group of students who are absent today are absent tomorrow, find the matrix that represents the students who will be absent tomorrow.

$$\tfrac{1}{2}B = \tfrac{1}{2} \times \begin{bmatrix} 8 & 16 & 12 & 10 \\ 14 & 12 & 18 & 22 \end{bmatrix} = \begin{bmatrix} 4 & 8 & 6 & 5 \\ 7 & 6 & 9 & 11 \end{bmatrix} \qquad \begin{matrix} \text{Each entry in } B \text{ is} \\ \text{multiplied by } \tfrac{1}{2}. \end{matrix}$$

The process of multiplying a matrix by a number, as seen in Example 3, is called **scalar multiplication.** The product of a number r and a matrix A is the matrix rA.

4. What is the real-world meaning of the entry "9" in the $\tfrac{1}{2}B$ matrix?
Since 9 is in row 2, column 3, it represents the number of 11th grade girls absent on picture day.

$$A = \begin{bmatrix} 3 & 6 \\ 2 & -1 \end{bmatrix}, B = [5 \quad 7], C = \begin{bmatrix} -3 & 4 \\ 8 & 11 \end{bmatrix}$$

Find each entry or matrix, if possible.

a. c_{12} **b.** $A + C$ **c.** $B + C$ **d.** $3A$ **e.** $A - 2C$

CONSIDER

?

1. Do you think it is possible to add or subtract two matrices that do not have the same dimension? Explain.

In the following Explore, you will see a connection between matrices and geometric transformations.

EXPLORE: TRANSFORMATION MATRICES

MATERIALS

Graph paper
Geometry software (optional)

1. a. Plot and connect the points $A(1, -3)$, $B(2, 1)$, and $C(-3, -2)$ to form a triangle.

Let the matrix $V = \begin{bmatrix} 1 & 2 & -3 \\ -3 & 1 & -2 \end{bmatrix}$ represent the triangle.

b. Let $T = \begin{bmatrix} 4 & 4 & 4 \\ -2 & -2 & -2 \end{bmatrix}$.

Find $V + T$ and draw the resulting triangle on the same coordinate plane. Describe how adding T transformed the original triangle.

2. Choose a transformation matrix different from T. (It must have equal numbers across the top row and across the bottom row.) Add your matrix to V, plot the new coordinates, and sketch the resulting triangle. How does adding this matrix transform the triangle?

3. Choose three points on a coordinate plane that form the vertices of a triangle. Write a matrix that represents these points. Transform the triangle by multiplying the matrix by 2. Then transform the triangle by multiplying by other numbers of your choice. Describe your results.

4. Summarize the effects of changing the vertices of a polygon through matrix addition and scalar multiplication as explained above. Use the language of transformations in your summary.

5. Suppose that the vertices of a geometric figure represent a "message" you want to send. Explain how to use a transformation matrix to put your message into "code." How can the person who receives the message decipher it?

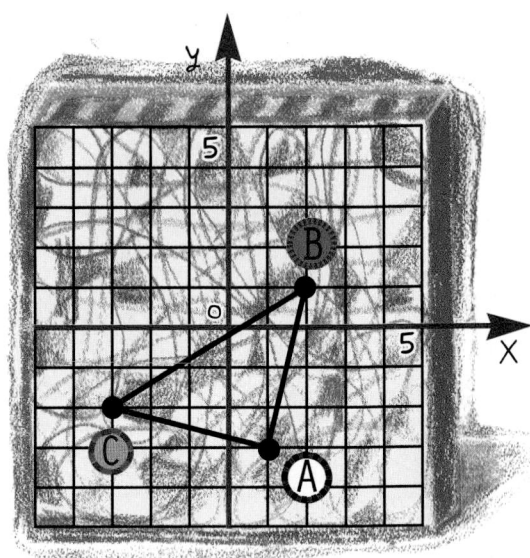

TRY IT

The vertices of a rectangle are represented by the columns of the matrix $V = \begin{bmatrix} -1 & 4 & 4 & -1 \\ -1 & -1 & 2 & 2 \end{bmatrix}$. Graph these vertices and sketch the rectangle.

Perform each transformation to V and sketch the transformed rectangle. Then use the language of transformations to describe the results.

f. Add $T = \begin{bmatrix} 3 & 3 & 3 & 3 \\ -1 & -1 & -1 & -1 \end{bmatrix}$.

g. Multiply V by 3.

You are familiar with some properties of addition for real numbers. Recall that, for real numbers a, b, and c, the Associative Property of Addition states that $(a + b) + c = a + (b + c)$, and the Commutative Property states that $a + b = b + a$.

CONSIDER

?

2. Is matrix addition associative? Is matrix addition commutative? Justify your answers.

You have seen how matrices can be added, subtracted, or multiplied by a number. The sum or difference of two matrices is the sum or difference of their corresponding entries. To multiply a matrix by a number, multiply each entry in the matrix by that number.

REFLECT

1. When can you add two matrices? Describe how you add matrices.
2. If you know that matrices G and H are equal, what conclusions can you make?
3. Describe a real-world situation where you could use a matrix to organize data.

Exercises

CORE

1. Getting Started
   a. What is the dimension of matrix A?
   b. Identify entry a_{13}.
   c. For what values of i and j does $a_{ij} = 8$?
   d. Find $2A$.

$$A = \begin{bmatrix} 0 & 3 & -5 & 3 \\ 5 & -7 & 2 & -1 \\ 4 & 8 & 2 & 6 \end{bmatrix}$$

Use the matrices below to find each of the following, if possible. If not possible, explain why.

$$W = \begin{bmatrix} 3 & -7 \\ 4 & 2 \end{bmatrix} \qquad X = \begin{bmatrix} -2 & -6 & 11 \\ 2 & -2 & -5 \\ 13 & 6 & 7 \end{bmatrix} \qquad Y = \begin{bmatrix} 9 & 7 \\ 3 & -2 \end{bmatrix} \qquad Z = \begin{bmatrix} 2 & 1 & 0 \\ -1 & 7 & 3 \\ 3 & -6 & 12 \end{bmatrix}$$

2. $W + X$

3. $W + Y$

4. $3Z$

5. $X - X$

6. $X + Z$

7. $\frac{1}{2}W$

8. $Z - X$

9. $-W$

10. $3X - 2Z$

11. Give an example of a 5×2 matrix.

12. Give an example of two matrices that cannot be added together.

13. Matrix Workout The Heartland Recreational Spa has two types of membership, basic and extended. Matrix A gives Heartland's membership at the beginning of the year based on gender and type of membership. Matrix B shows new memberships for the year, while matrix C shows membership losses.

$$
\begin{array}{ccc}
\begin{array}{c}
\text{Memberships at End} \\
\text{of 1995} \\
\begin{array}{cc} \text{Male} & \text{Female} \end{array} \\
A = \begin{bmatrix} 47 & 53 \\ 39 & 21 \end{bmatrix}
\end{array}
&
\begin{array}{c}
\text{New 1996} \\
\text{Memberships} \\
\begin{array}{cc} \text{Male} & \text{Female} \end{array} \\
B = \begin{bmatrix} 15 & 13 \\ 14 & 9 \end{bmatrix}
\end{array}
&
\begin{array}{c}
\text{Memberships Canceled} \\
\text{in 1996} \\
\begin{array}{cc} \text{Male} & \text{Female} \end{array} \\
C = \begin{bmatrix} 21 & 18 \\ 19 & 11 \end{bmatrix}
\begin{array}{l} \text{Basic} \\ \text{Extended} \end{array}
\end{array}
\end{array}
$$

    a. Find a matrix giving spa memberships at the end of the year.

    b. Which gender showed the most change? which membership type?

    c. The spa management projects a 5% growth in all categories of membership next year. Find a matrix showing the projected status of all membership categories.

14. The vertices of a triangle are represented by the columns of the matrix. Graph these vertices and sketch the triangle. Perform each transformation to V and sketch the transformed triangle. Then use the language of transformations to describe the results.

$$V = \begin{bmatrix} 3 & 5 & -2 \\ 0 & -1 & 6 \end{bmatrix}$$

    a. Add $T = \begin{bmatrix} -2 & -2 & -2 \\ 4 & 4 & 4 \end{bmatrix}$.

    b. Multiply V by $\frac{1}{2}$.

15. Who's Reading What? A book store orders mysteries (M), romance novels (R), and biographies (B) from three suppliers, Pager Books (P), Coverall Notes (C), and Literally Literature (L). The matrices give number of books sold for last year.

	First quarter (Jan.–Mar.)			Second quarter (Apr.–Jun.)			Third quarter (Jul.–Sep.)			Fourth quarter (Oct.–Dec.)		
	P	C	L	P	C	L	P	C	L	P	C	L
M	850	806	818	671	124	211	589	461	580	422	372	450
R	235	656	384	57	535	356	209	618	700	814	323	15
B	539	271	999	203	64	986	965	968	420	818	751	676

    a. Find and label matrices to represent sales by each distributor for the first half of last year, for the second half of last year, and for the entire year.

    b. Which distributor was the best seller over the entire year? Which type of book sold the most copies?

    c. Contrast book sales during the two half-years.

    d. If you had to discontinue one type of book, which would it be? Why? If you had to drop one distributor, which would it be? Why?

16. An international study of 13-year-old math students yielded the following data. Use this information to answer each question.

Country	School days per year	Minutes of math instruction per week	% with at least 2 hr of homework per day	% watching at least 5 hr of TV per day
Canada	188	225	27	14
France	174	230	55	5
Hungary	177	186	58	13
Ireland	173	189	63	9
Slovenia	190	188	28	4
South Korea	222	179	41	11
Taiwan	222	204	41	10
United States	178	228	29	20

a. Write a matrix M to represent the data in the table. What is the dimension of M?

b. Identify entry m_{42}. What does this entry represent?

c. For what values of i and j does the entry m_{ij} represent the percentage of 13-year-old math students in Taiwan who watch five or more hours of television per day?

d. Describe any associations that appear to link the data. What reasons can you give that might explain the associations? How could you confirm your conjectures?

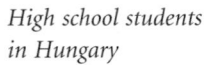

High school students in Hungary

High school students in Korea

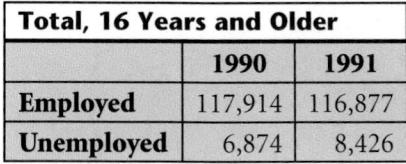

17. Help Wanted The following tables give U.S. employment figures for 1990 and 1991. Numbers given are in thousands.

Total, 16 Years and Older	1990	1991
Employed	117,914	116,877
Unemployed	6,874	8,426

Men, 20 Years and Older	1990	1991
Employed	61,198	60,174
Unemployed	3,170	4,109

Women, 20 Years and Older	1990	1991
Employed	50,455	50,535
Unemployed	2,555	3,028

a. Write and label a matrix to represent each table.

b. Find a matrix that represents the total number of employed and unemployed people 20 years old and above for 1990 and 1991. Explain how you found this matrix.

c. Find a matrix that represents the total number of employed and unemployed 16- to 19-year-olds in 1990 and 1991. Explain how you found this matrix.

d. Can you find a matrix that represents the number of employed and unemployed 16- to 19-year-old females in 1990 and 1991? If so, find the matrix; if not, explain why not.

e. Use the data in these tables to make a conjecture about the U.S. economy during this time period.

18. In 1992, the world population was about 5420 million. The populations of the five most populous countries in that year, given in millions, are shown below. [1-2]

China: 1186   India: 883   United States: 256   Indonesia: 185   Brazil: 151

Find the probability, expressed as a decimal rounded to the nearest hundredth, that a randomly chosen person:

a. lived in China   **b.** lived in India

c. lived in the United States, Indonesia, or Brazil

d. did not live in one of the five most populous countries

19. A restaurant finds that 47 customers out of 130 order a salad with dinner. What is the experimental probability that a customer orders a salad? Express your answer as a decimal rounded to the nearest hundredth. [1-2]

20. A box of canned food is packed as shown at the right. If a speck of dust lands randomly in the box, what is the probability that it lands in a space between the cans? [1-2]

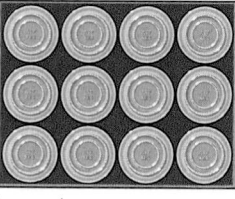

7 cm

MORE PRACTICE

$$A = \begin{bmatrix} 6 & 2 & -8 & 1 \\ 0 & 3 & 4 & 9 \\ 3 & -11 & 6 & 9 \end{bmatrix} \quad B = \begin{bmatrix} 5 & -1 \\ 7 & 6 \\ -2 & 0 \end{bmatrix}$$

21. Find the dimensions of A and B.

22. Identify entries a_{23} and b_{31}.

23. For which i and j does $a_{ij} = -8$?

24. Find $-3B$.

25. Pepperoni or Anchovies Sonny's Pizza Shop sells small, medium, and large pizzas. They sell pizzas with one, two, or three toppings as well as deluxe pizzas with everything except the anchovies on the pizzas. The first matrix lists the sales for Friday, the second matrix lists the sales for Saturday, and the third matrix lists the sales for Sunday.

	Friday Sales			Saturday Sales			Sunday Sales		
	S	M	L	S	M	L	S	M	L
One topping	34	52	44	45	57	38	30	40	23
Two toppings	45	48	27	34	66	37	56	38	36
Three toppings	25	28	38	22	34	29	19	35	28
Deluxe	12	24	26	18	23	14	24	15	25

a. Find a matrix showing the change in sales from Friday to Saturday.

b. Find a matrix showing the change in sales from Saturday to Sunday.

c. Find a matrix giving the total sales for Saturday and Sunday.

d. What was the most popular pizza sold on Saturday and Sunday?

e. Sonny hopes that the sales for the whole month will be 8 times the weekend (Saturday and Sunday) sales. Make a matrix showing what Sonny hopes to sell over the entire month.

Use the matrices below to find each of the following, if possible. If not possible, explain why.

$$A = \begin{bmatrix} 7 & 0 \\ 3 & -1 \\ -3 & 4 \end{bmatrix} \qquad B = \begin{bmatrix} 5 & -1 \\ 7 & 6 \\ -2 & 0 \end{bmatrix} \qquad C = \begin{bmatrix} 4 & -2 \\ 3 & 1 \end{bmatrix} \qquad D = \begin{bmatrix} -1 & 4 \\ 6 & 2 \end{bmatrix}$$

26. $A + B$

27. $-5C$

28. $A - C$

29. $3B$

30. $3B - 2A$

31. $A + B + C$

32. $C - D$

33. $D - C$

34. $B - A$

35. $0.5B$

36. $5D + 2C$

37. $2(A + B)$

38. Highs and Lows The matrices show the high and low temperatures in degrees Fahrenheit for selected cities for the months of January, April, and July.

	January High	January Low		April High	April Low		July High	July Low
Nairobi, Kenya	77	54		75	58		69	51
Rome, Italy	54	39		68	46		88	64
Sydney, Australia	78	65		71	58		60	46
Tokyo, Japan	47	29		63	46		83	70

a. Find a matrix that indicates the change in high and low temperatures for the four cities from January to April.

b. Find a matrix that indicates the change in high and low temperatures for the four cities from April to July.

c. Find a matrix that indicates the change in high and low temperatures for the four cities from January to July.

d. Which of the four cities has the least amount of temperature change?

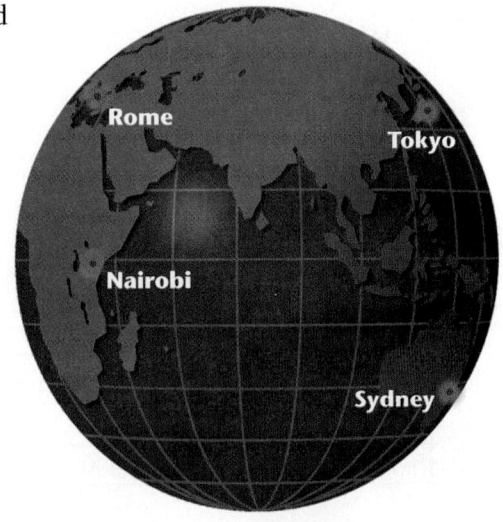

Rome · Tokyo · Nairobi · Sydney

MORE MATH REASONING

39. Crude Oil Production The bar graph shows the crude oil production in millions of barrels per day. The data covers three different years for several OPEC nations. Organize the data in a matrix and describe what is represented in each row and column. Which country seems to have the least fluctuation in production? Explain your answer.

40. What are the possible dimensions of a matrix with 18 entries? with 230 entries?

World Crude Oil Production
(millions of barrels)

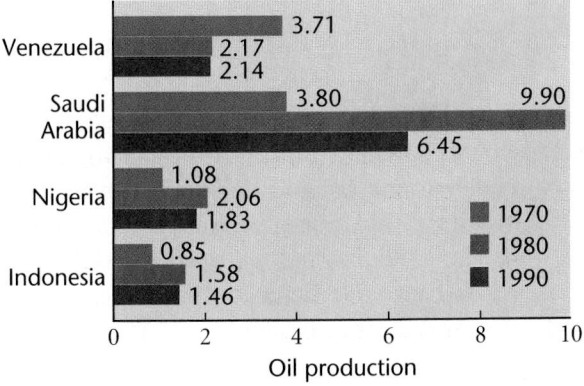

	1970	1980	1990
Venezuela	3.71	2.17	2.14
Saudi Arabia	3.80	9.90	6.45
Nigeria	1.08	2.06	1.83
Indonesia	0.85	1.58	1.46

Oil production

41. Suppose that the coordinates of the vertices of rectangle *ABCD* are transformed by scalar multiplication by *a*. What is the ratio of the area of the new rectangle to the area of the original rectangle? Explain your reasoning.

Multiplying Matrices

← **CONNECT** →   *You've seen how to add and subtract matrices and how to perform scalar multiplication. Now you will learn how to multiply matrices and use matrix multiplication to solve problems.*

By writing data in matrices, businesses can use computers to store, retrieve, and operate on such data with great efficiency. In the following Explore, you will use matrices to analyze data on sales of three grades of gasoline.

EXPLORE: SPLITTING THE PROFITS

Part of the price that you pay for a gallon of gasoline goes to the government as taxes. The rest of the money goes to the owners of the gas station. The tables below give data collected at the Highway Petrol gas station over two weeks. The table on the left gives numbers of gallons of gas sold. The table on the right breaks down the total cost of each gallon into the owners' revenues and taxes paid.

Gallons of Gas Sold			
	Regular	**Midgrade**	**Premium**
Week 1	18,100	4,500	10,200
Week 2	19,400	5,300	12,700

Dollar Amount Per Gallon		
	Revenues ($)	**Taxes ($)**
Regular	0.85	0.29
Midgrade	0.92	0.32
Premium	1.05	0.35

1. Write the information in the tables in two matrices. What is the dimension of each matrix?

2. Calculate the *total* owner revenues and the *total* taxes for all grades of gas for Weeks 1 and 2. Explain how you found these totals. (Hint: How can you find the Week 1 revenues for any one grade of gasoline?)

3. Create a matrix to record the totals. What is the dimension of this matrix? Compare the number of rows in the *totals* matrix with the number of rows in the gallons matrix, and compare the number of columns in the *totals* matrix with the number of columns in the dollar amount matrix. Describe your results.

4. The *totals* matrix is a **product matrix.** Explain how each entry in the product matrix was determined from the entries in the matrices in Step 1.

When you use the two matrices in the Explore to find the matrix of total revenues and total taxes, you are doing **matrix multiplication.** You may have seen that using matrix multiplication to find a product matrix involves adding individual products of entries.

1. Find product matrix CD, where $C = [3 \quad 1]$ and $D = \begin{bmatrix} -5 & 3 & -2 \\ 2 & 4 & 0 \end{bmatrix}$. Find the dimensions of C, D, and CD.

$$[3 \quad 1] \times \begin{bmatrix} -5 & 3 & -2 \\ 2 & 4 & 0 \end{bmatrix} = \begin{bmatrix} \mathbf{3 \cdot (-5)} & \mathbf{3 \cdot 3} & \mathbf{3 \cdot (-2)} \\ + & + & + \\ \mathbf{1 \cdot 2} & \mathbf{1 \cdot 4} & \mathbf{1 \cdot 0} \end{bmatrix} = [\mathbf{-13 \ 13 \ -6}]$$

The dimension of C is 1×2, the dimension of D is 2×3, and the dimension of CD is 1×3.

2. Find product matrix EF, where

$$E = \begin{bmatrix} 3 & -2 & 1 & 4 \\ -4 & 5 & 2 & 28 \end{bmatrix} \text{ and } F = \begin{bmatrix} -2 & -1 & 4 \\ 6 & 3 & 2 \end{bmatrix}.$$

When we try to multiply the first row of E by the first column of F, we find that they do not have the same number of entries—the 1 and the 4 in matrix E have no multipliers. Therefore, these two matrices cannot be multiplied.

It was possible to multiply the matrices in the Explore and in Example 1 because the number of *columns* in the first of the matrices multiplied was equal to the number of *rows* in the second. The product matrix has the same number of rows as the first matrix and the same number of columns as the second.

These must be equal.

$1 \times 2 \cdot 2 \times 3$ gives a 1×3

a. M has dimension 3×4. N has dimension 4×5. Find the dimension of MN.

$$A = \begin{bmatrix} 3 & -2 \\ -1 & 4 \end{bmatrix} \qquad B = \begin{bmatrix} 4 \\ 6 \end{bmatrix} \qquad C = [3 \quad 4] \qquad D = \begin{bmatrix} 1 \\ -3 \\ 5 \end{bmatrix}$$

Find each product, if possible. Remember that the number of columns in the first matrix must equal the number of rows in the second matrix.

b. AB **c.** AC **d.** CD **e.** DC

The Caiman Automobile company has fixed prices for four models, the Skink, the Iguana, the Python, and the Komodo. The tables give the number of each type sold during the first quarter, together with the dealer cost and price for each type. Find the total costs and total income from sales for each month.

Cost/Price	Dealer Cost	Selling Price
Skink	6,894	7,925
Iguana	8,668	9,850
Python	10,124	11,440
Komodo	11,871	13,339

Sales	Skink	Iguana	Python	Komodo
January	44	29	32	23
February	52	41	41	37
March	49	37	43	45

Arturo thinks...

To find the total cost for each month, I'll multiply the number of each type of car sold in that month by its cost and add the results. The total cost for January is $44 \times 6,894 + 29 \times 8,668 + 32 \times 10,124 + 23 \times 11,871 = \$1,151,709$. I can do the same for the car prices to find the total income for each month.

My results for the monthly costs are: January = $1,151,709, February = $1,568,187, and March = $1,628,049. My results for the monthly incomes are January = $1,307,227, February = $1,778,533, and March = $1,844,950.

Vanessa thinks...

I'll use my graphing calculator to find the matrix product. First, I enter the matrix that represents the sales table for matrix *A*, then I enter the matrix that represents the cost/price table for matrix *B*.

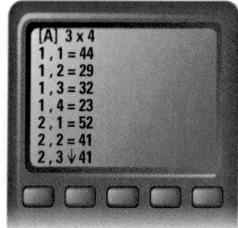

```
[A] 3 x 4
1 , 1 = 44
1 , 2 = 29
1 , 3 = 32
1 , 4 = 23
2 , 1 = 52
2 , 2 = 41
2 , 3 ↓ 41
```

```
[B] 4 x 2
1 , 1 = 6894
1 , 2 = 7925
2 , 1 = 8668
2 , 2 = 9850
3 , 1 = 10124
3 , 2 = 11440
4 , 1 ↓ 11871
```

Next, I multiply the two matrices, and store the result as matrix *C*.

```
[A] [B]
[ 1151709 13072...
[ 1568187 17785...
[ 1628049 18449...
```

```
[ 1151709 13072...
[ 1568187 17785...
[ 1628049 18449...
Ans → [C]
[ 1151709 13072...
[ 1568187 17785...
[ 1628049 18449...
```

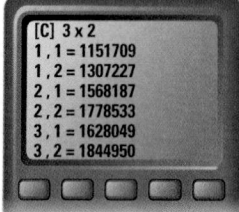

```
[C] 3 x 2
1 , 1 = 1151709
1 , 2 = 1307227
2 , 1 = 1568187
2 , 2 = 1778533
3 , 1 = 1628049
3 , 2 = 1844950
```

Although Arturo and Vanessa used different solution methods, their results are the same. Their results are shown as a table.

	Total Cost	Total Income
January	$1,151,709	$1,307,227
February	$1,568,187	$1,778,533
March	$1,628,049	$1,844,950

CONSIDER
?

1. Why did Vanessa multiply $A \times B$ and not $B \times A$ to find the totals for each month?
2. Describe the advantages and disadvantages of each student's method. If you had both methods available, how would you decide which one to use?

A matrix with the same number of columns and rows is a **square matrix.** A square matrix with a diagonal of 1's running from upper left to lower right and 0's for all other entries is a **multiplicative identity matrix,** sometimes denoted by I.

The matrix $\begin{bmatrix} 1 & 0 & 0 \\ 0 & 1 & 0 \\ 0 & 0 & 1 \end{bmatrix}$ is the 3×3 identity matrix. If you multiply any 3×3 matrix by the 3×3 identity matrix, the product is the original matrix, as shown below.

$$\begin{bmatrix} 5 & 1 & 3 \\ -2 & 0 & -4 \\ 2 & 2 & 1 \end{bmatrix} \times \begin{bmatrix} 1 & 0 & 0 \\ 0 & 1 & 0 \\ 0 & 0 & 1 \end{bmatrix} = \begin{bmatrix} 5 & 1 & 3 \\ -2 & 0 & -4 \\ 2 & 2 & 1 \end{bmatrix}$$

If the product of two matrices (in either order) is an identity matrix, the matrices are called **multiplicative inverse matrices,** or simply **inverse matrices.** If the inverse of A exists, we denote it A^{-1}.

EXAMPLE

3. $A = \begin{bmatrix} 2 & 4 \\ 6 & 8 \end{bmatrix}$ and $B = \begin{bmatrix} -1 & \frac{1}{2} \\ \frac{3}{4} & -\frac{1}{4} \end{bmatrix}$. Are A and B inverse matrices?

To see whether A and B are inverse matrices, find their product. If AB is the 2×2 identity matrix, A and B are inverses.

$$AB = \begin{bmatrix} 2 \cdot (-1) + 4 \cdot \left(\frac{3}{4}\right) & 2 \cdot \left(\frac{1}{2}\right) + 4 \cdot \left(\frac{-1}{4}\right) \\ 6 \cdot (-1) + 8 \cdot \left(\frac{3}{4}\right) & 6 \cdot \left(\frac{1}{2}\right) + 8 \cdot \left(\frac{-1}{4}\right) \end{bmatrix} = \begin{bmatrix} -2 + 3 & 1 - 1 \\ -6 + 6 & 3 - 2 \end{bmatrix} = \begin{bmatrix} 1 & 0 \\ 0 & 1 \end{bmatrix}$$

Therefore, A and B are inverse matrices.

When real-world data is stored in matrices, products of those matrices may also be meaningful. For instance, if the prices of items are stored in one matrix and the number of items sold are stored in another, the product of these matrices can show the total revenue. Important facts about matrix multiplication are summarized on page 62.

- To multiply two matrices, multiply elements in the rows of the first matrix by the corresponding elements in the columns of the second and add.
- Two matrices can be multiplied only if the number of columns in the first matrix is equal to the number of rows in the second matrix. The product matrix has the same number of rows as the first matrix and the same number of columns as the second.
- The multiplicative identity matrix is a square matrix with a diagonal of 1's running from the upper left to lower right. All other entries are 0's.
- If the product of two matrices is an identity matrix, the matrices are inverse matrices.

REFLECT

1. In order to be able to multiply matrix A by matrix B, what must be true of the dimensions of the two matrices?
2. In your own words, explain how to find the product of two matrices.
3. The number 1 is called the *multiplicative identity*. How is an identity matrix in matrix multiplication like the multiplicative identity?

Exercises

CORE

1. Getting Started $A = \begin{bmatrix} 1 & 2 \\ 3 & 4 \end{bmatrix}$ $\qquad B = \begin{bmatrix} 3 & -2 & 5 \\ 1 & 4 & -3 \end{bmatrix}$

a. What is the dimension of A? of B?
b. Find $1 \cdot 3 + 2 \cdot 1$. Place your answer in the first row, first column of AB.
c. Find $1 \cdot (-2) + 2 \cdot 4$. Place your answer in the first row, second column of AB.
d. Explain how to find the last number in the top row of the product matrix for AB. Then find this entry and use it to complete the top row of AB.
e. Complete the product matrix AB. What is the dimension of AB?

Copy and complete each matrix multiplication.

2. $\begin{bmatrix} 1 & 2 \\ 4 & 5 \end{bmatrix} \times \begin{bmatrix} 6 & 7 \\ -1 & -2 \end{bmatrix} = \begin{bmatrix} 1 \cdot 6 + 2 \cdot \square & \square \cdot 7 + 2 \cdot -2 \\ 4 \cdot \square + 5 \cdot \square & 4 \cdot 7 + \square \cdot -2 \end{bmatrix} = ?$

3. $\begin{bmatrix} 4 & -2 & 5 \\ 3 & 11 & 1 \end{bmatrix} \times \begin{bmatrix} -7 & 6 \\ 10 & 1 \\ 6 & -3 \end{bmatrix} = \begin{bmatrix} 4 \cdot -7 + \square \cdot 10 + 5 \cdot 6 & \square \cdot 6 + \square \cdot 1 + 5 \cdot -3 \\ 3 \cdot \square + 11 \cdot 10 + \square \cdot \square & \square \cdot 6 + 11 \cdot \square + 1 \cdot \square \end{bmatrix} = ?$

Decide if AB exists. If it does, find the dimension of AB.

4. A is a 3×7 matrix and B is a 7×3 matrix.

5. A is a 2×5 matrix and B is a 2×3 matrix.

6. A is a 1×4 matrix and B is a 4×4 matrix.

7. Suppose that you are given the matrices below with the entries filled in.

	Number of Customers				Average Number of Videos Rented

$$\begin{array}{cc} & \begin{array}{ccc} 1992 & 1993 & 1994 \end{array} \\ \begin{array}{c} \text{Store A} \\ \text{Store B} \end{array} & \left[\begin{array}{ccc} XX & XX & XX \\ XX & XX & XX \end{array}\right] \end{array} \qquad \begin{array}{cc} \begin{array}{c} 1992 \\ 1993 \\ 1994 \end{array} & \left[\begin{array}{c} XX \\ XX \\ XX \end{array}\right] \end{array}$$

a. Could you multiply these matrices? Why or why not?
b. Does the order in which you multiply the matrices matter? Explain.
c. What would the entries in the product matrix represent?

Use the matrices below to find each product matrix, if possible. If not possible, explain why.

$$A = \left[\begin{array}{ccc} -3 & 1 & 0 \\ 17 & 2 & -5 \end{array}\right] \qquad B = \left[\begin{array}{ccc} -7 & 22 & 0 \\ 4 & 0 & 17 \\ 4 & 13 & -5 \end{array}\right] \qquad C = [3 \ -2 \ 7]$$

8. AB **9.** AC **10.** BC **11.** BA **12.** CA **13.** CB

14. Making the Grade Ms. Lee teaches algebra. She is calculating semester grades. The grades for the first two grading periods are each worth three times the grade on the semester exam. The grades of four of her students are given below.

Student	First Period	Second Period	Semester Exam
Tomo	85%	82%	94%
Maria	89%	91%	85%
John	82%	79%	83%
Carol	75%	82%	79%

a. Write a matrix for the table.

b. Multiply this matrix by $\left[\begin{array}{c} 3 \\ 3 \\ 1 \end{array}\right]$ to help Ms. Lee determine the students' semester grades.

c. Who has the highest grade for the semester?

15. Write a 3×3 matrix of your choosing and the 3×3 identity matrix. Then find the product of the two matrices.

16. a. Find the product matrix AB, where $A = \left[\begin{array}{cc} 5 & 2.5 \\ -2 & 1 \end{array}\right]$ and $B = \left[\begin{array}{cc} 0.1 & -0.25 \\ 0.2 & 0.5 \end{array}\right]$
    b. How are A and B related?

Check whether each pair of matrices is a pair of inverse matrices.

$$C = \left[\begin{array}{cc} -5 & 7 \\ 2 & -3 \end{array}\right] \qquad D = \left[\begin{array}{cc} 5 & -7 \\ -2 & 3 \end{array}\right] \qquad E = \left[\begin{array}{cc} 3 & 7 \\ 2 & 5 \end{array}\right]$$

17. C and D **18.** D and E **19.** C and E

20. Don't Give Away the Store! The manager of Zooland Toy Store is promoting the store by giving away $300 worth of merchandise, at random, to customers this week. She would like to know if the promotion helped the week's sales and if it was worth $300. The tables show sales and prices of some of Zooland's big-selling items before and during the promotion.

Sales	Toys	Games	Stuffed Animals
Last Week	152	87	182
This Week	166	96	193

Average Prices	
Toys	$4
Games	$10
Stuffed Animals	$6

a. Write a matrix for each table.
b. Find the total sales for toys, games, and stuffed animals last week and this week by multiplying the matrices.
c. Can you tell whether the promotion was worth the $300 giveaway? If so, how? If not, what other information would you need to know to be able to decide?

LOOK AHEAD

Simplify each expression.

21. $9x - 13x$

22. $5y - (4 - 7y)$

23. $3(2c - 5) - 2(6c - 2)$

24. $\frac{7}{5}k + 12 - \left(6 - \frac{3}{10}k\right)$

25. a. What is true about the consecutive x-values in the table below? What is true about their corresponding y-values?

x	−2	−1	0	1	2	3
y	10	7	4	1	−2	−5

b. Graph the points representing the coordinates in the table. What do you notice about the graph?
c. Write and graph an equation relating x and y for the table. Check your work.

MORE PRACTICE

26. Copy and complete the matrix multiplication.

$$\begin{bmatrix} 11 & 7 \\ -3 & 0 \\ 1 & 2 \end{bmatrix} \times \begin{bmatrix} 4 & 14 \\ -1 & 0 \end{bmatrix} = \begin{bmatrix} 11 \cdot 4 + 7 \cdot \square & \square \cdot 14 + \square \cdot \square \\ \square \cdot 4 + 0 \cdot \square & -3 \cdot \square + 0 \cdot 0 \\ \square \cdot \square + 2 \cdot \square & 1 \cdot 14 + 2 \cdot \square \end{bmatrix} = ?$$

27. Decide if AB exists. If it does, find the dimension of AB.
   a. A is a 2×6 matrix and B is a 3×6 matrix.
   b. A is a 4×5 matrix and B is a 5×1 matrix.
   c. A is a 2×2 matrix and B is a 7×2 matrix.

Use the matrices below to find each product matrix, if possible. If not possible, explain why.

$$A = \begin{bmatrix} 5 & -8 \\ 4 & -1 \end{bmatrix} \qquad B = \begin{bmatrix} 2 & -5 \\ 0 & 11 \\ -2 & 3 \end{bmatrix} \qquad C = \begin{bmatrix} 2 \\ 4 \end{bmatrix}$$

28. AB **29.** AC **30.** BC **31.** BA **32.** CA **33.** CB

Use a Graphing Utility Use the matrices below to find each product matrix, if possible. If not possible, explain why.

$$J = \begin{bmatrix} 1 & -2 & 3 \\ 5 & 0 & 2 \\ -2 & 3 & 10 \end{bmatrix} \qquad K = \begin{bmatrix} 12 & 0 & -5 \\ 3 & -1 & 6 \\ 2 & 2 & -7 \\ 4 & 0 & 1 \end{bmatrix} \qquad L = \begin{bmatrix} 3 & 2 & -5 & 1 \\ 0 & 8 & 4 & 9 \\ -1 & -11 & 6 & 5 \end{bmatrix}$$

34. JK **35.** KJ **36.** KL **37.** LK

Check whether each pair of matrices is a pair of inverse matrices.

$$M = \begin{bmatrix} -2 & 0 \\ 12 & \frac{1}{2} \end{bmatrix} \qquad N = \begin{bmatrix} 5 & -7 \\ -2 & 3 \end{bmatrix} \qquad P = \begin{bmatrix} -\frac{1}{2} & 0 \\ 12 & 2 \end{bmatrix}$$

38. M and N **39.** M and P **40.** N and P

41. Apples and Bananas and Melons—Oh My! The tables show the sales and prices for the four best-selling fruits at a roadside fruit stand.

Sales				
	Apples	Bananas	Melons	Oranges
Last Month	530 lb	810 lb	1060 lb	620 lb
This Month	710 lb	910 lb	1290 lb	850 lb

Prices Per Pound	
Apples	$0.80
Bananas	$0.40
Melons	$0.30
Oranges	$0.70

a. Write a matrix for each table.
b. Find the matrix product.
c. Explain the significance of the entries in the matrix product.

42. Use a Graphing Utility The number of hours worked in a week and the hourly wages of a company's part-time employees are stored in a computer. Part of the company's data is shown below.

Hours Worked			
	Claudia	Dave	Elizabeth
Week 1	30	17	25
Week 2	22	25	32
Week 3	20	28	23

Hourly Wage	
	Wage
Claudia	$6.45
Dave	$5.80
Elizabeth	$7.00

Use matrix multiplication to find a matrix that shows the total amount paid to these employees for weeks 1, 2, and 3.

MORE MATH REASONING

43. Making a Splash The scores of the top three finishers in the 1992 Olympic women's 10-meter platform diving competition are organized by the degree of difficulty of the dives.

	Degree of Difficulty									
	1.6	1.9	2.0	2.1	2.4	2.7	2.8	3.0	3.2	3.3

Competitor	Scores									
Mary Clark (USA)	39.5	41	36	38.5	0	75	38.5	0	20.5	0
Fu Mingxia (China)	39	42	40.5	36	0	0	0	37	70.5	40.5
Yelena Miroshina (Unified Team)	39	30.5	40	38	38.5	0	0	32.5	67.5	0

Final scores are calculated by multiplying each score by the degree of difficulty, adding these, and multiplying the result by 0.6.

a. Find a scalar, d, and matrices A and B so that dAB is a 3×1 matrix listing the final scores of the three competitors.

b. Determine the divers' final scores and the order in which they finished.

44. Is matrix multiplication commutative? Explain your answer, giving examples to support your conclusions.

45. Use a Graphing Utility For any real numbers a, b, and c, if $ab = ac$ and $a \neq 0$, then $b = c$. Use the matrices below and your graphing utility to show that this property is *not* true for matrices.

$$A = \begin{bmatrix} -1 & 2 & 2 \\ 4 & 7 & -8 \\ 2 & 8 & -4 \end{bmatrix} \qquad B = \begin{bmatrix} 5 & -4 & 6 \\ 3 & -1 & 5 \\ 4 & 3 & 0 \end{bmatrix} \qquad C = \begin{bmatrix} 7 & 0 & 8 \\ 3 & -1 & 5 \\ 5 & 5 & 1 \end{bmatrix}$$

1-3 PART C Making Connections

← CONNECT → *You have added, subtracted, and multiplied matrices. Now you will use matrices to encode and decode a message.*

Cryptography is the study of the making and breaking of codes. At its simplest, a code simply replaces each letter in a message with another letter. Such codes are called substitution codes, or *ciphers,* and they have been in use since the time of Julius Caesar (100–44 B.C.). "MEET AT NOON" becomes "PHHW DW QRRQ" if we replace each letter in this message with the letter that follows three letters later in the alphabet. To de*cipher* "PHHW DW QRRQ," reverse the encoding steps, replacing each letter in the coded message with the letter that precedes it by three letters in the alphabet.

From such simple beginnings, codes of enormous complexity have evolved. Long in use for military and diplomatic purposes, cryptographers today also work in industry designing elaborate computerized coding systems for protecting data, like the symbols at the bottom of checks. In the following Explore, you will use matrices to encode and decode data.

EXPLORE: A PHRASE IN VERSE

Follow these steps to encode the message "PLANE ARRIVES TODAY."

1. Separate the message into pairs of letters. Replace each letter with the number that represents the letter's position in the alphabet.

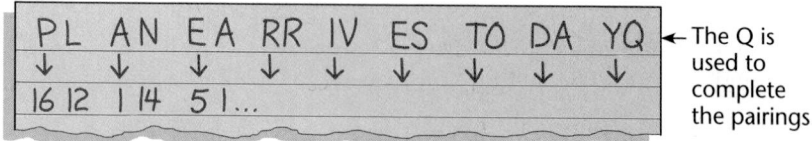

PL AN EA RR IV ES TO DA YQ ← The Q is
↓   ↓   ↓   ↓   ↓   ↓   ↓   ↓   ↓   used to
16 12 1 14 5 1...   complete
                                        the pairings

2. Three encoding matrices are shown below.

$$A = \begin{bmatrix} 7 & 5 \\ 4 & 3 \end{bmatrix} \qquad B = \begin{bmatrix} 3 & 4 \\ 2 & 3 \end{bmatrix} \qquad C = \begin{bmatrix} 4 & 3 \\ 5 & 4 \end{bmatrix}$$

Write each number pair as a 2 × 1 matrix: $\begin{bmatrix} 16 \\ 12 \end{bmatrix}, \begin{bmatrix} 1 \\ 14 \end{bmatrix}, \begin{bmatrix} 5 \\ 1 \end{bmatrix} \ldots$ Then multiply the encoding matrix A by each 2 × 1 message matrix. For example,

$\begin{bmatrix} 7 & 5 \\ 4 & 3 \end{bmatrix} \times \begin{bmatrix} 16 \\ 12 \end{bmatrix} = \begin{bmatrix} 172 \\ 100 \end{bmatrix}$. The message is sent as a sequence of numbers: 172, 100,.... List the numbers in the coded message.

3. The decoding matrices for the given encoding matrices are listed below.

$$A^{-1} = \begin{bmatrix} 3 & -5 \\ -4 & 7 \end{bmatrix} \qquad B^{-1} = \begin{bmatrix} 3 & -4 \\ -2 & 3 \end{bmatrix} \qquad C^{-1} = \begin{bmatrix} 4 & -3 \\ -5 & 4 \end{bmatrix}$$

Since matrix A was used to encode the message, use A^{-1} to decode the message. Explain your decoding method.

4. Use one of the other encoding matrices, either B or C, to write and encode a message. Identify the decoding matrix you used and exchange your encoded message with a partner. Translate the message you have received.

REFLECT

1. Describe how matrices can be used to store real-world data.
2. If two matrices are to be added, what must be true about their dimensions?
3. Explain the differences between scalar multiplication and matrix multiplication.

1. Find the value of entry a_{21} in matrix $A = \begin{bmatrix} 1 & -2 & 4 \\ 7 & -6 & 8 \end{bmatrix}$.

(a) 7   (b) -2 (c) 1   (d) -6

Determine whether each statement is true or false. If the statement is false, change the underlined expression or phrase to make it true.

2. A matrix with 4 columns and 5 rows has dimension <u>4×5</u>.

3. The matrix $\begin{bmatrix} 1 & 0 \\ 0 & 1 \end{bmatrix}$ is <u>an inverse</u> matrix.

4. Decide if AB exists. If it does, find the dimension of AB.
  a. A is a 4×4 matrix and B is a 4×1 matrix.
  b. A is a 3×1 matrix and B is a 3×1 matrix.
  c. A is a 2×8 matrix and B is a 8×5 matrix.

Use the matrices below to find each of the following, if possible. If not possible, explain why.

$$W = \begin{bmatrix} 2 & -3 & 3 \\ 0 & 1 & -1 \\ 5 & 4 & 2 \end{bmatrix} \quad X = \begin{bmatrix} 5 & 0 & 1 \\ -3 & 10 & 2 \\ 2 & 4 & -2 \end{bmatrix} \quad Y = \begin{bmatrix} -11 & 5 & 6 \\ 2 & 0 & 9 \end{bmatrix} \quad Z = \begin{bmatrix} -7 & 2 \\ 0 & 0 \\ 3 & -1 \end{bmatrix}$$

5. $W + X$

6. $4Y$

7. $Z - X$

8. $3X - 4W$

9. XW

10. YZ

11. XY

12. $YX + Y$

Use $A = \begin{bmatrix} 15 & -7 \\ 5 & -2 \end{bmatrix}$ to answer each of the following.

13. Multiply A by the 2×2 identity matrix. Show your work.

14. Determine whether $\begin{bmatrix} -0.4 & 1.4 \\ -1 & 3 \end{bmatrix}$ is the inverse of A.

15. A spinner is divided into 8 congruent sectors numbered 1 through 8. What is the theoretical probability of spinning an odd number? [1-2]

16. A spinner for a game comes up "go back 3 spaces" 42 times in 140 spins. What is the experimental probability of spinning "go back 3 spaces"? [1-2]

17. The target at right shows a square inscribed in a circle with a smaller circle inscribed in the square. A randomly thrown dart lands inside the outer circle. [1-2]
  a. What is the probability that it lands inside the square but outside the inner circle?
  b. Suppose you do not know the length of a side of the square. Can you still find the probability asked for in **a**? Why or why not?

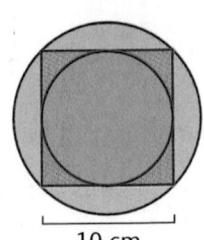

10 cm

18. It's Magic! A *magic square* is a square array of numbers with rows, columns, and diagonals that all add up to the same number. Archaeologists found records of the first known magic square in China around 2200 B.C. This type of matrix, called *lo-shu*, uses knots to represent numbers in the array.

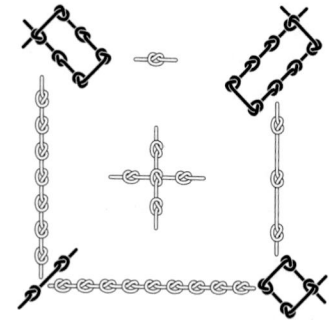

a. The order of a magic square, n, is the number of rows or columns of the square. The sum of each row, column, or diagonal is given by $f(n) = \frac{1}{2}(n(n^2 + 1))$. What is the sum of each row of this magic square?

b. The center of this ancient Tibetan seal represents a magic square. Write the matrix represented in the seal if $f(n) = 15$, $a_{11} = 4$, $a_{22} = 5$, and $a_{32} = 1$.

19. Alarming News Central Protection Alarm Company manufactures three models of alarm systems in two plants. The company's production for March is summarized in the following table.

	Model A	Model B	Model C
Uptown Plant	320	290	340
Downtown Plant	530	310	130

a. Let matrix M represent the data in the table. What is the dimension of M?
b. Management has decided to increase production in April by 10% over its March output in each plant. Write a scalar product representing the targeted output for April. Then evaluate the product.

20. The Great American Novel Suppose the table below left represents the number of books submitted to U.S. publishers, and the table below right represents the probability of publication for the books in 1991–1993.

Books Submitted			
	1991	**1992**	**1993**
Fiction	376,000	372,000	360,000
Juvenile	438,000	470,000	474,000
Medicine	156,000	148,000	151,000
Philosophy/Psychology	94,000	104,000	110,000

Probability of Publication, 1991–1993	
	Probability
Fiction	0.015
Juvenile	0.011
Medicine	0.025
Philosophy/Psychology	0.021

a. Write a matrix for each table.
b. Find the matrix product.
c. Explain the significance of the entries in the matrix product.

Chapter 1 Review

One of the principal purposes of mathematics is to model the world. You have looked at three types of mathematical models. Graphs allow you to see relationships in real-world data. Probability helps you investigate the uncertainties of the world. Matrices are an efficient way to handle data. All three of these tools help you organize and look for patterns in data.

KEY TERMS

association [1-1]	function notation [1-1]	range [1-1]
constant [1-1]	geometric probability [1-2]	sample space [1-2]
dependent variable [1-1]	independent variable [1-1]	scalar multiplication [1-3]
dimension [1-3]	matrix [1-3]	scatter plot [1-1]
domain [1-1]	matrix multiplication [1-3]	simulation [1-2]
entry [1-3]	multiplicative identity matrix [1-3]	square matrix [1-3]
equal matrices [1-3]	(multiplicative) inverse matrix [1-3]	theoretical probability [1-2]
event [1-2]	outcome [1-2]	trend line [1-1]
experimental probability [1-2]	probability [1-2]	variable [1-1]
function [1-1]	product matrix [1-3]	

Choose the word that best completes each sentence.

1. The set of all possible values of the independent variable of a function is the ____.
   (a) dependent variable   (b) sample space
   (c) range   (d) domain

2. Any possible result of an experiment is a(n) ____.
   (a) simulation   (b) outcome
   (c) event   (d) sample space

CONCEPTS AND APPLICATIONS

Tell whether each relationship is a function. If it is, state its domain and range. [1-1]

3. {(0, 1), (1, 2), (2, 3), (3, 4)}

4. the ages of Californians to the nearest year (independent variable) and their weights to the nearest pound (dependent variable)

5. Write and graph an equation relating x and y. [1-1]

x	0	1	2	3	4	5
y	−1	1	3	5	7	9

The scatter plot below shows the results of a survey of gas station owners that was conducted to investigate the association between the price of gas and the average number of gallons purchased by each driver. [1-1]

6. Identify the independent variable and the dependent variable.

7. Describe any association that you see.

8. At a price of $1.20 per gallon, how much gas would you expect drivers to purchase, on average? Explain how you found your answer.

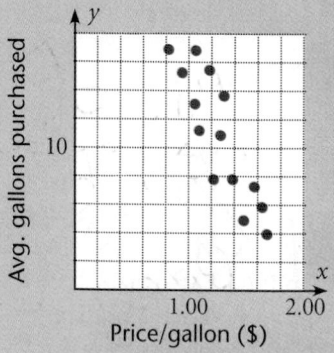

9. Let $f(x) = x^2 + 1$. Find each of the following. [1-1]
   a. $f(0)$ **b.** $f(3)$ **c.** $f(-2)$
   d. $f\left(\frac{1}{2}\right)$ **e.** $f(n)$

The table below shows the blood types of a group of donors at a blood bank. Find the probability that a randomly chosen person in the group: [1-2]

Blood Type	O+	A+	B+	AB+	O−	A−	B−	AB−
Number	182	75	72	42	35	34	31	29

10. has type B+ blood

11. has type O−, A−, B−, or AB− blood

12. Briefly explain the difference between experimental and theoretical probability.

13. Use the coin flip results at the right to simulate 18 families with four children. Use your results to approximate the probability that a four-child family has two girls and two boys. [1-2]

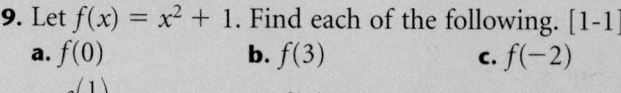

THTT   TTHH   TTHT   TTHT   THTH   THHT
TTHT   TTHH   TTTT   THHH   TTHH   TTTT
TTHT   THHT   HTTT   THTH   TTHH   HHHT

Use the matrices below to find each of the following, if possible. If not possible, explain why. [1-3]

$$A = [6 \;\; -4 \;\; 2] \qquad B = \begin{bmatrix} 1 & 4 \\ 2 & -3 \\ 5 & 3 \end{bmatrix} \qquad C = \begin{bmatrix} -5 & 4 \\ 6 & 3 \\ -3 & -6 \end{bmatrix}$$

14. $B + C$ 15. $-2C$ 16. AB

17. Scientific Supply sells three types of graphing calculators. The tables below give the calculator inventory at the company's stores and the calculator prices.

	Model Ex	Model K	Model S
Midtown	63	19	42
Suburban	58	37	61

	Price ($)
Model Ex	65
Model K	79
Model S	102

Write an inventory matrix and a price matrix. Then multiply the matrices to find the inventory values at the two stores. [1-3]

CONCEPTS AND CONNECTIONS

18. Astronomy The figure shows a star map measuring 10 degrees by 10 degrees. Each night an astronomer surveys a 1×1 square in search of comets. Let the matrix $V = \begin{bmatrix} a & c & e & g \\ b & d & f & h \end{bmatrix}$ represent the vertices of a square that the astronomer is watching (see the shaded square).

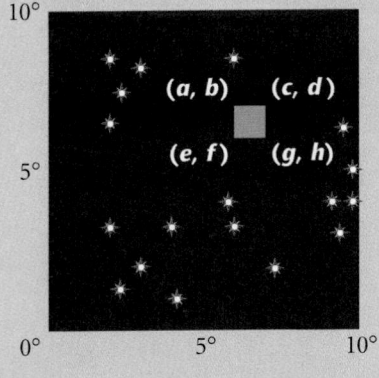

The observation begins with the first square in the lower left and moves right one square each night. At the end of a row, the astronomer moves to the left square of the row above.

a. Write a matrix which, when added to V, gives the coordinates of the vertices of the square for the following night:

  i. when the next square is in the same row   **ii.** when the next square is in the row above

b. An undiscovered comet is at a random point on the map. What is the probability that the astronomer will discover it on any given night?

c. What type of association do you believe there would be between the number of nights of study and the number of comets discovered? Justify your answer.

SELF-EVALUATION

Choose a subject that interests you that you can illustrate or describe using graphs, probability, and matrices. Show how each of these three tools can be used to model the subject you have chosen. Point out ways that graphs, matrices, and probability help a person understand your chosen subject, and areas where other methods are needed to illustrate or describe the subject.

Chapter 1 Assessment

TEST

Tell whether each relationship is a function. If it is, state its domain and range.

1. $\{(-2, 3), (-2, 4), (3, 5)\}$

2. the number of coins in a person's pocket (independent variable) and the amount of money the coins are worth (dependent variable)

3. the graph shown at the right

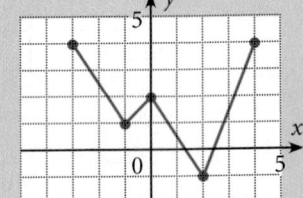

4. Let $f(x) = \sqrt{x - 1}$. Find each of the following.
  a. $f(10)$ **b.** $f(5)$ **c.** $f(3y)$

5. Write and graph an equation relating x and y.

x	0	1	2	3	4	5
y	−2	1	4	7	10	13

6. The table gives the results of bird counts for the male dusky seaside sparrow. The tallies were conducted at St. Johns Wildlife Refuge in Florida during the 1970s.

Science

Year	1970	1972	1973	1974	1975	1976	1977	1978
Number	143	110	54	37	47	11	12	9

a. Make a scatter plot of the data and draw a trend line. Describe any association seen.
b. Estimate the number of males in 1971. Explain how you made your estimate.

A survey of highest educational level reached had the results shown below.

Grade	0–6	7–12	2 Years of College	4 Years of College	Master's Degree	Doctoral Degree	Post-doctorate Work
Number	43	241	108	295	123	34	16

7. Find the probability that the highest level reached by a randomly chosen member of the group was 4 years of college.

8. Find the probability that the highest level reached was a Master's or a Doctoral degree.

9. Forty-two cars are parked on a car dealer's 80-ft square lot. The frame of each car is approximately rectangular, 12.8 ft long and 6.5 ft wide. What is the probability that, in a storm, the first drop of rain to land in the parking lot hits a car?

Use the matrices below to find each of the following, if possible. If not possible, explain why.

$$A = \begin{bmatrix} 2 & -4 & 5 \\ 1 & 6 & -3 \end{bmatrix} \qquad B = \begin{bmatrix} -7 \\ 6 \\ 2 \end{bmatrix} \qquad C = \begin{bmatrix} -2 & -3 & 8 \\ -4 & -3 & 5 \end{bmatrix}$$

10. $A + C$ **11.** $5C$ **12.** AB

13. The tables show data from Jefferson School. Write a student enrollment matrix and a cost matrix. Then find the total number of dollars spent on physics and chemistry texts by the school. Explain how you found your answer.

	Physics	Chemistry
Sophomores	0	18
Juniors	9	31
Seniors	42	22

	Book Cost ($)
Physics	42
Chemistry	35

PERFORMANCE TASK

You manage a clothing store. Over the past 12 weeks, you sold one style of jeans at 3 different prices. For 4 weeks, the jeans sold for $24; for the next 4 weeks, $20; and for the final 4 weeks, $17. Your supplier sells the jeans to you for $12 a pair.

Your boss asks you to report on the effect that the price has on (1) the number of pairs you sell, and (2) the profit you make. Explain how you can use the concepts of this chapter, including scatter plots and matrices, to prepare your report. Then make up data for jeans sales over the 12 weeks and create data displays for your report.

Chapter 2

Linear Functions, Equations, and Inequalities

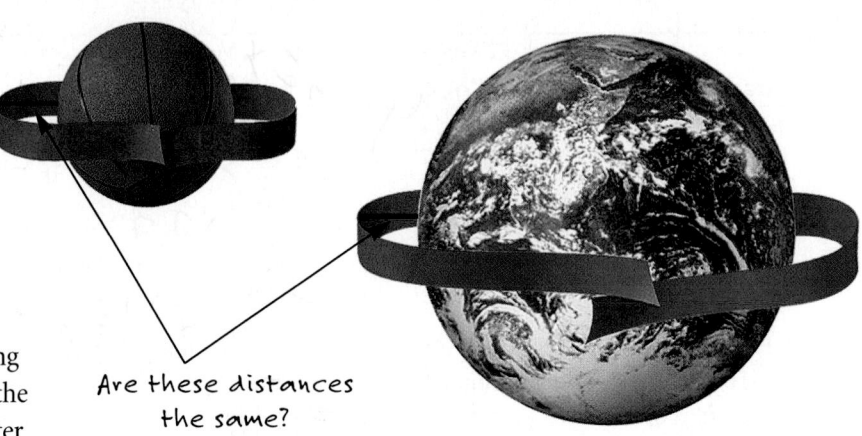

Project A
How's Your Intuition?
A ribbon around the earth is lengthened by a meter. A ribbon around a basketball is lengthened by a meter.

How much greater is the radius of the ribbon encircling the earth than the radius of the earth itself? How much greater is the radius of the ribbon encircling the basketball than the radius of the basketball itself? How do the increases in radii compare?

Are these distances the same?

Project B
The Pace of Life
How fast is the pace where you live?

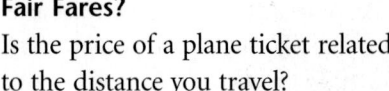

Project C
Fair Fares?
Is the price of a plane ticket related to the distance you travel?

As a high school student, I knew that I wanted to study mechanical engineering in college and that math would be an important part of my studies.

Working for an environmental engineering company, I use math daily. Our expertise is vehicles that run on alcohol, natural gas, electricity, or other environmentally friendly and domestically available fuels. For example, I use my math skills to compare emissions of pollutants from different engines and fuels, and to predict future pollution levels.

I feel very fortunate to be trained in a field which has given me an interesting, challenging job.

Charlotte Pera
Mechanical Engineer
Acurex Environmental
Mountain View, California

Worksheet

ng Thermodynamics (W.C. Reynol

4.696	psi =	0.101325
19.53	gal-kg/lbf-m^3 (at 3.2808	
1	Btu =	1.055 k
1	kg =	2.21 l

thane

P (psig)	P (MPa abs)	m^3/kg
0	0.101325	0.00238
4.54	0.1326	0.0023
13.14	0.1919	0.002
20.00	0.2392	0.00
24.38	0.2694	0.0
38.69	0.3681	0.
56.56	0.4913	0
60.00	0.5150	
78.46	0.6423	
85.00	0.6874	
100.00	0.7908	
104.89	0.8245	
136.29	1.041	
140.00	1.066	
173.42	1.29	

Emissions (g/bhp-hr)

0.16
0.14
0.12
0.10
0.08
0.06
0.04
0.02
0.00

California '91
92TA 350hp*
92TA 300hp*
92TA 300hp
300hp, M85
DT-466
Ald

METHANOL FUELED

699

3.10

weight(lbf/

2-1
Linear Functions and Equations

In 2-1 you will interpret linear models and graphs to make predictions. You will use the following algebra skills from previous courses.

Calculate the slope of the line containing the given points. [Previous course]

1. $(4, -3)$ and $(-2, 1)$ **2.** $(5, 7)$ and $(-10, 7)$

3. $(0, -1)$ and $(2, 2)$ **4.** $(3, 0)$ and $(3, 1)$

Solve each equation. Check your solution. [Previous course]

5. $2y - 5 = 17$ **6.** $2(y - 3) = 15$ **7.** $y + 4 = 17y$

8. $18 - 2(y - 5) = 0$ **9.** $y + (y + 1) = 3$ **10.** $y + 10 = 2y$

11. $9 - (12 - 7y) = 0$ **12.** $0.5y = 1 - 0.75y$

2-2
Fitting Linear Functions to Data

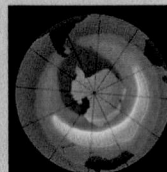

In 2-2 you will find the equation of a trend line using algebra and geometry. You will need the following skills from previous courses.

Match each equation with a line on the graph. [Previous course]

13. $y = 2x - 4$

14. $y = -3x + 6$

15. $y = 2x + 3$

16. $y = 7$

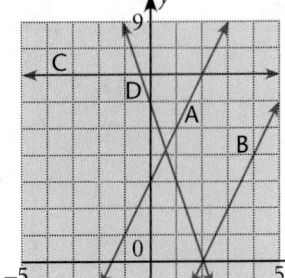

2-3
Linear Inequalities

In 2-3 you will graph inequalites and absolute value functions. You will need to use properties of inequalities from previous courses.

Graph on a number line. [Previous course]

17. $x < 5$ **18.** $x \leq 5$ **19.** $x > -1$ **20.** $x \geq -1$

Complete the table and graph on a coordinate plane. [Previous course]

21. $y = |x|$

x	−2	−1	0	1	2
y					

22. $y = |x - 3|$

x	−2	0	1	3	5
y					

★★LABOR DAY★★

Boy working in factory in the early 1900s.

Many students today have part-time jobs during the school year and in the summer. Balancing the responsibilities of a job and school requires discipline and organization. A job shouldn't interfere with your success in school.

Children didn't always have the *right* to go to school in this country. In 1910, nearly 2,000,000 youths 9 to 15 years old were working instead of attending school, like the boy in the photo.

In the coal mining industry, boys as young as 9 years old were hired as *coal-breakers*. A coal-breaker sat for ten or eleven hours a day on wooden boards placed over chutes through which coal passed. Their task was to pick out slate, stone, and other wastes from the passing coal. Coal-breakers had to endure cuts from sharp material, air filled with coal dust, and long hours in a stooped position, which often caused deformities such as rounded shoulders and narrow chests.

Public outrage over employment of youths in jobs like coal-breaking resulted in the formation of the National Child Labor Committee in 1904. Although labor problems for youths still exist, the deplorable conditions of the past have been dramatically reduced. ★

1. Why do you think a 9-year-old child would work at a job such as coal-breaking?
2. In 1909, workers in coal mines made 31 cents per hour and worked 37.5 hours per week, on average. About how much did these workers make per week? per year?
3. In 1991, the minimum wage was increased to $4.25 per hour. At this rate, how long would it take to earn the yearly wage of someone earning 31 cents per hour working 37.5 hours per week?

← **C O N N E C T** → *You've begun to work with patterns in data and functional relationships. Now you will learn to recognize linear functions, including those that represent direct variation. You will also learn to find the slope and rate of change of a linear function.*

Functions are useful tools for modeling a wide variety of relationships between real quantities. In the following Explore, you will use a function to model earnings.

EXPLORE: THE ROARING TWENTIES

In 1926, women working in manufacturing earned an average of about 40 cents per hour. However, the booming economy of the "roaring twenties" soon came to an end when the great depression hit. It would be another eight years before the average earning rate of women in manufacturing would surpass 40 cents per hour.

MATERIALS

Graphing utility or graph paper

1. Make a table of values that shows the number of hours worked per week (*h*) and the total weekly earnings (*E*) for a woman that earns 40 cents per hour.
2. How are total weekly earnings related to the number of hours worked? Write and graph an equation relating *E* and *h*. Describe the shape of your graph.

> **Problem-Solving Tip**
>
> Look for a pattern.

3. In 1926, women working in manufacturing worked an average of 43.5 hours per week. Use your equation or graph to find the average weekly salary of women working in manufacturing in 1926.
4. What features of your equation and graph do you think are similar for anyone earning an hourly wage? Explain.

The relationship that you worked with in the Explore is an example of **direct variation.** The earnings *vary directly* with the amount of time worked. That is, the earnings are *proportional* to the amount of time worked.

If *y* varies directly with *x*, you can express the relationship as an equation of the form $y = kx$, where *k* is a constant. The constant of variation (*k*) represents the **rate of change** of *y* with respect to *x*.

EXAMPLE

1. Jack tends the plants at Shrub Nursery after school. A week ago, he measured a plant at 0.8 cm tall. Today, the same plant is 2.3 cm tall. Find the constant growth rate of the plant and write an equation for the height (*y*) of the plant as a function of the time (*x*) since it sprouted.

Since $2.3 - 0.8 = 1.5$, the plant is growing at a rate of 1.5 cm/week. The plant's height (*y*) in centimeters *x* weeks after sprouting is given by the function $y = 1.5x$. The constant of variation, 1.5, is the growth rate or the rate of change of the height.

Direct variation is a kind of **linear function,** a function whose graph is a straight line. The rate of change of a linear function is constant, but not all linear functions represent direct variation.

A **linear function** is a function whose graph is a straight line. A linear function of *x* can be written in the form $f(x) = mx + b$ or as a linear equation $y = mx + b$, where *m* and *b* are constants.

If Jack's friend Maria buys the plant in Example 1 when it is 4 cm high and still growing 1.5 cm/week, then the plant's height *x* weeks after she buys it will be given by the linear function $f(x) = 1.5x + 4$. The growth rate is still 1.5 cm/week, but the height *does not* vary directly with the number of weeks.

We can represent a linear function in an equation, graph, or table of values.

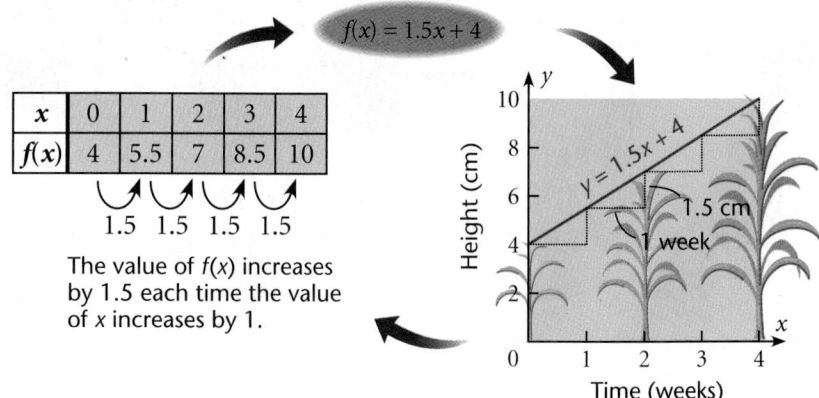

$$f(x) = 1.5x + 4$$

x	0	1	2	3	4
f(x)	4	5.5	7	8.5	10

1.5 1.5 1.5 1.5

The value of f(x) increases by 1.5 each time the value of x increases by 1.

1. **How can you recognize the rate of change of a linear function in an equation, table, or graph of the function?**

TRY IT

Decide whether each function is linear. If it is, state whether it represents direct variation.

a. $y = 2x + 4$ **b.** $y = 3x^2$

c. $f(x) = -3x$ **d.** $y = \frac{2x}{3}$

The steepness and direction of a line in a coordinate plane is determined by its **slope.** The slope of a line is the ratio of the *change in y* (Δy) to the *change in x* (Δx) as you move from one point on the line to another. This ratio is often referred to as the ratio of **rise** to **run.**

$$\text{Slope} = \frac{\text{change in } y}{\text{change in } x} = \frac{\Delta y}{\Delta x}$$

$$= \frac{\text{rise}}{\text{run}}$$

EXAMPLES

Graph each linear function and find its slope.

2. $f(x) = 2x + 1$ **3.** $y = -0.6x + 2.4$

The line contains the points $(-1, -1)$ and $(1, 3)$.

The line contains the points $(-3, 4.2)$ and $(0, 2.4)$.

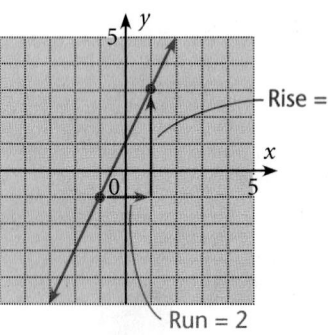

Xmin = –4.5
Xmax = 5
Xscl = 1
Ymin = –2
Ymax = 5
Yscl = 1

X = –3   Y = 4.2

$$\text{slope} = \frac{\text{rise}}{\text{run}} = \frac{4}{2} = 2$$

$$\text{slope} = \frac{\Delta y}{\Delta x}$$

$$= \frac{2.4 - 4.2}{0 - (-3)}$$

$$= \frac{-1.8}{3}$$

$$= -0.6$$

A line with a *positive slope* slants *upward* from left to right. The greater the positive slope, the steeper the line. A line with a *negative slope* slants *downward* from left to right. The more strongly negative the slope, the steeper the line.

CONSIDER

?

2. What is the slope of a horizontal line? Explain.

Examples 2 and 3 show that you can often recognize the slope of the graph of a linear function from its equation. The slope of a linear function is exactly the rate of change of *y* with respect to *x*.

> The slope of the graph of a linear equation $y = mx + b$ is m. The slope is equal to the rate of change of *y* with respect to *x*.

TRY IT

Find the slope of each line.

e. the line through the points (7, 2) and (1, 1)
f. the graph of the linear function $f(x) = -4x + 3$
g. the graph of the linear equation $y = 1.8x - 4.4$

The simplest linear function, $y = x$, is the *parent function* for all linear functions $y = mx + b$. The slope *m* rotates the line, and the constant *b* moves the line away from the origin.

REFLECT

1. How can you tell whether *y* varies directly with *x* from an equation?
2. Explain why the graph of a function that represents direct variation is a line that passes through the origin.
3. Explain how you can recognize a linear function in each representation.
  a. a table of values
  b. an equation
  c. a graph
4. Describe two ways to find a slope.
5. How is the slope of a line related to the rate of change of the variables that are graphed?
6. What happens to a line as *m* increases greatly in value? as *b* increases greatly in value?

Exercises

CORE

1. Getting Started Ahmed earns $10 for each lawn he mows.
  a. How much will Ahmed get paid for mowing 2 lawns? 3 lawns?
  b. Write an equation in the form $y = kx$ that shows that Ahmed's pay (y)
   varies *directly* with the number of lawns (x) he mows.
  c. What is the *rate of change* of y with respect to x?

Find the slope of each line.

2. line k

3. line ℓ

4. the line containing the points $(-2, 8)$ and $(13, 5)$

5. the line through the origin and $(3, -4)$

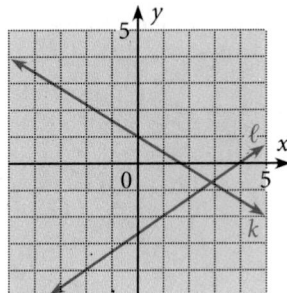

**Write the word or phrase that correctly completes
each statement.**

6. A ____ function is one whose graph is a straight line.

7. The ____ of a line is the ratio of the change in y to the change in x.

8. If the temperature outside was 54.1°F a half hour ago and is 55.6°F now, what is
the rate of change of the temperature in degrees per hour?

9. The Great Pyramid The Great Egyptian Pyramid of Khufu
(or Cheops) was built in 2680 B.C. at Giza near Cairo. It is one
of the Seven Wonders of the World and the largest pyramid
ever built. The pyramid is 756 feet along each side of its
square base. The peak of the pyramid, located above the
center of the square base, is 482 feet high. Find the positive
slope of the sides of the Great Pyramid.

10. The letter m, which is used to represent slope, comes from the
French word *monter,* meaning "to climb." Explain why this is
an appropriate choice to represent slope.

**Decide whether each equation or table represents a linear function. If it does,
give its slope and state whether it represents direct variation.**

11. $y = 6x + 12$

12. $y^2 = 6x + 12$

13. $f(x) = 2x^2 + 3$

14. $2y = 8x - 14$

15.

x	2	3	4	5	6
f(x)	13	11	9	7	5

16.

x	0	1	2	3	4
g(x)	0	-3	-6	-9	-12

17. The circumference of a circle is π times its diameter. Is circumference a linear function of diameter? Does the circumference vary directly with the diameter? Explain.

18. Horizontal and Vertical Lines Draw a graph of a horizontal and a vertical line. Find two points on each line and use them to justify the following facts.

> A horizontal line has slope 0.
> A vertical line does not have a slope.

19. Describe the basic differences in appearance between lines with positive, negative, and zero slopes. Sketch graphs to illustrate.

20. Computing for Cash Lianna is paid an hourly wage of $7.75 for part-time work doing computer data entry. Let $P(x)$ be her gross pay for x hours of work in a week. Write an expression for $P(x)$ and graph $y = P(x)$. Is $P(x)$ a linear function? Does y vary directly with x?

21. Up Stairs A stairway is made up of a set of steps. Each step consists of a *step riser* and a *step tread*.

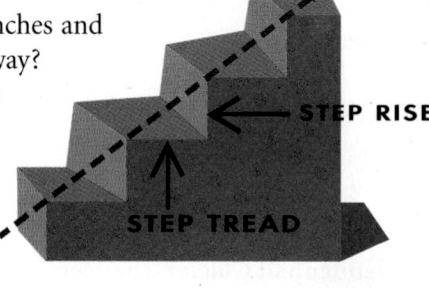

STEP RISER
STEP TREAD
STAIRWAY SLOPE

   a. A set of stairs is constructed with a step tread of 12 inches and a step riser of 6 inches. What is the slope of the stairway?

   b. Measure the step tread and step riser for a stairway at home or in your neighborhood. Then compute the slope of the stairway.

   c. For a step tread of 12 inches, estimate what the maximum step riser would be in order for most people to walk down stairs comfortably.

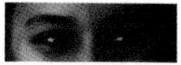 **LOOK AHEAD**

22. Sketch the graph of $y = 4x + 3$. Where does the line cross the y-axis?

23. A line contains the point $(1, 2)$. Let (x, y) represent any other point on the line. Write an expression for the slope of the line.

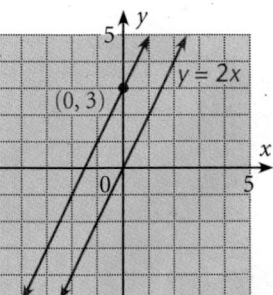

$y = 2x$

$(0, 3)$

24. The line $y = 2x$ is graphed at the right. A line parallel to $y = 2x$ is also graphed.

   a. Guess the slope of the line parallel to the graph of $y = 2x$.

   b. Using your answer to **a**, write the equation of the line parallel to $y = 2x$.

   c. Describe how the equations for the two lines are similar and how they are different.

MORE PRACTICE

Decide whether each equation or table represents a linear function. If it does, give its slope and state whether it represents direct variation.

25. $y = 9x - 13$

26. $f(x) = x + 2x$

27. $2x + y = 25$

28. $4y = 10x - 6$

29. $f(x) = 2x^2 - 3$

30. $x + \frac{1}{2}y = -24$

31. $6x + 5y = 15$

32. $f(x) = 7x + 0.6$

33. $y = -2x^3 + 3x^2$

34.

x	0	1	2	3	4
f(x)	0	3	5	7	9

35.

x	2	3	4	5	6
f(x)	−1	−1.5	−2	−2.5	−3

36.

x	1	2	3	4	5
g(x)	0	3	8	15	24

37.

x	0	2	4	6	8
g(x)	8	6	4	2	0

38. Joe is considering borrowing money from his sister, who will charge him 10% interest when he pays back the loan in a year. If he borrows x dollars, what is the *total* amount Joe will owe his sister in a year? What kind of function is this? Explain.

39. Mendenhall Glacier The Mendenhall Glacier in Alaska runs from the Juneau ice field to Mendenhall Lake. The glacier moves at a rate of 2 feet per day. Write an equation for the distance the glacier moves in x days. What kind of relationship is this? How is the rate of change shown in the equation?

40. If a kitten grows from 2 pounds to 4.4 pounds in 12 weeks, what is its average growth rate in pounds per week?

Find the slope of each line.

41. the line containing $(6, 12)$ and $(4, -4)$

42. the line containing $(0, -1)$ and $(-5, 8)$

43. the line containing $(-2, 4)$ and $(-4, -1)$

44. the line through $(-1, -4)$ and the origin

45. line m

46. line n

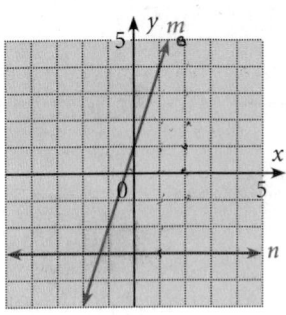

MORE MATH REASONING

47. Civil War The following graph represents the estimated strength of Union and Confederate troops at post-Gettysburg Civil War battles. The linear model contains $(0, 0)$ and the data point for the battle at Spotsylvania Court House, where an estimated 63,000 Confederates met 111,000 Union troops.

History

Civil War Areas Controlled, Mar./Apr., 1865

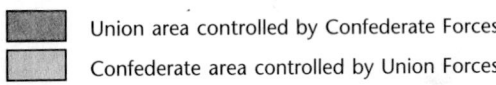 Union area controlled by Confederate Forces

Confederate area controlled by Union Forces

 Union route

Confederate route

Battle Site

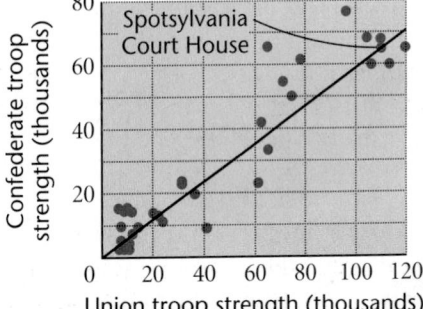

a. Write a linear equation that models Confederate troop strength as a function of Union troop strength.

b. What is the slope and what does it represent?

c. Why do you think the point $(0, 0)$ and the point for the battle at Spotsylvania were chosen? Describe some insights this graph may offer about the nature of Civil War battles following Gettysburg.

48. Cruise Control A cruising airplane is instructed to climb to 38,000 feet. After climbing at a rate of 35 feet for every 1000 feet it moves forward, the plane reaches its new cruising altitude after traveling a horizontal distance of 20 miles. What was its original cruising altitude?

2-1
PART B
Solving Equations

← CONNECT → *You have explored linear functions and their connections to slope and rate of change. The graph of a linear function can also be used to solve equations. After exploring this graphical method, you will see how properties of equality can help you solve equations symbolically.*

The **TRACE** feature on many graphing utilities allows you to move along the graph of a function while watching the changing values of x and y. You will use this feature in the Explore to help make a prediction.

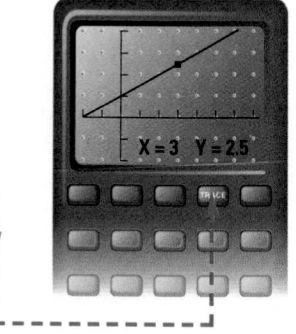

X = 3   Y = 2.5

EXPLORE: MINIMUM WAGE

MATERIALS

Graphing utility

Between 1974 and 1991 the minimum wage in the United States rose from $2 per hour to $4.25 per hour. Assuming the minimum wage grows at a constant rate, when will it reach $6 per hour? (A graphing utility can help you find out.)

1. What was the rate of change of the minimum wage (in dollars per year) during this period? At this rate, what will the minimum wage be x years after 1991? Explain.
2. Write a linear function of the form $y = mx + b$ that gives the minimum wage x years after 1991.
3. Graph the linear function on your graphing utility. *Trace* along the graph to find the point where the y-value is 6. What is the approximate value of x at this point?
4. Use your result to predict when the minimum wage will be $6 per hour. How accurate do you think this prediction is? Explain.

From APPLE HILL

Recall that a **solution** of an equation with one variable is a value of the variable that makes the equation true. For example, the value $x = 3$ is the solution of the equation $4x + 5 = 17$ since $4(3) + 5 = 17$ is true. *Solving* an equation means finding all of its solutions.

In 2-1A, we used the linear function $f(x) = 1.5x + 4$ to model the height (in centimeters) of a plant after x weeks. In how many weeks will the plant be 16 cm high? Answering this question means solving the equation $16 = 1.5x + 4$.

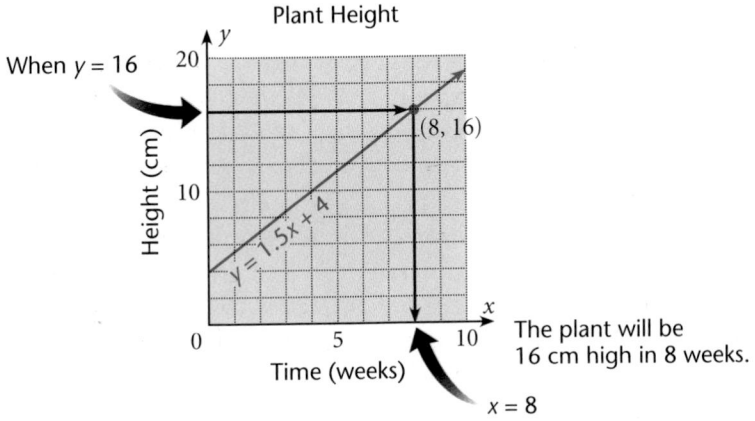

The plant will be 16 cm high in 8 weeks.

$x = 8$

By finding the x-value of the point on the graph where $y = 16$, we have solved the equation $16 = 1.5x + 4$. The solution is $x = 8$.

TRY IT

Use the graph of $y = 1.5x + 4$ to solve each equation.

a. $10 = 1.5x + 4$ **b.** $13 = 1.5x + 4$

You can also solve equations symbolically by using properties of algebra. Recall the following two properties of equality.

ADDITION PROPERTY OF EQUALITY

For any real numbers a, b, and c, if $a = b$, then $a + c = b + c$.

MULTIPLICATION PROPERTY OF EQUALITY

For any real numbers a, b, and c, if $a = b$, then $ac = bc$.

These properties of equality, along with the commutative, associative, and distributive properties of real numbers, give you the tools to solve many equations.

CONSIDER

?

1. If $a = b$, is it also true that $a - c = b - c$? If $a = b$ and $c \neq 0$, is it true that $\frac{a}{c} = \frac{b}{c}$? Explain.

Using the properties of equality, you can solve an equation by transforming it into simpler **equivalent equations**—equations with the same solutions.

EXAMPLES

Solve each equation.

1. $12x + 175 = 487$

$$12x + 175 = 487$$
$$12x + 175 - 175 = 487 - 175 \qquad \text{Subtract 175 from both sides.}$$
$$12x = 312$$
$$\frac{12x}{12} = \frac{312}{12} \qquad \text{Divide both sides by 12.}$$
$$x = 26 \qquad \text{This is a simpler equivalent equation.}$$

Check:

$$12x + 175 \stackrel{?}{=} 487$$
$$12(26) + 175 \stackrel{?}{=} 487$$
$$312 + 175 \stackrel{?}{=} 487$$
$$487 = 487 \checkmark$$

2. $5p - 9 = 3(p - 7)$

$$5p - 9 = 3(p - 7)$$
$$5p - 9 = 3p - 21 \qquad \text{Use the } \textit{distributive property.}$$
$$5p - 9 - 3p = 3p - 21 - 3p \qquad \text{Subtract } 3p \text{ from both sides.}$$
$$2p - 9 = -21 \qquad \text{Combine } \textit{like terms.}$$
$$2p = -12 \qquad \text{Add 9 to both sides and simplify.}$$
$$p = -6 \qquad \text{Divide both sides by 2.}$$

Literal equations are formulas involving several variables. To solve some problems, it is useful to use the properties of equality to *solve* a literal equation for one variable in terms of the other variables.

EXAMPLE

3. The equation $I = Prt$ relates the simple interest (I), initial investment or *principal* (P), interest rate (r), and time (t) for an investment.

a. Solve $I = Prt$ for r.

$$I = Prt$$
$$\frac{I}{Pt} = \frac{Prt}{Pt} \qquad \text{Divide both sides by } Pt.$$
$$\frac{I}{Pt} = r$$

b. Katya has $8000 to invest in a mutual fund. The funds that historically have higher rates of return also have greater risk, so she needs to choose wisely. Katya wants a return of at least $600 per year. What is the lowest rate of return that will meet her goal?

Let $P = \$8000$, $I = \$600$, and $t = 1$ year. Then $r = \frac{600}{8000} = 0.075$. Katya must choose a mutual fund with a rate of return of at least 7.5%.

Solve each equation.

c. $11 = 7z - 24$ **d.** $3x - 4 = 8x + 16$

e. The equation $d = rt$ relates the distance traveled (d) to the travel time (t) and rate (r). Solve the equation for t. In light traffic, a commuter can average 30 mi/hr on the 15-mile drive to work. In heavy traffic, she can only average 20 mi/hr. How long is her commute in each kind of traffic?

A graphing utility can make solving using graphs especially convenient, but may only yield approximate solutions. When you need an exact solution, it is often preferable to solve an equation by using the properties of equality.

REFLECT

1. Describe how you would use the graph of $y = -2x + 5$ to solve the equation $11 = -2x + 5$.
2. What is meant by an *equivalent equation*? Give an example of equivalent equations.
3. Which operation, when applied to both sides of the equation $5x + 9 = -x - 6$, is *not* a helpful first step in solving the equation? Explain.
   (a) subtract 9   (b) divide by 5   (c) add x

Exercises

CORE

1. **Getting Started** Tell how each equation was transformed from the previous equation.
   a. $8 + 6x = 11 + 4x$ **b.** $6x = 3 + 4x$ **c.** $2x = 3$ **d.** $x = 1.5$

2. Which equations are equivalent to $2x + 10 = 4$?
   (a) $2x + 4 = 10$ (b) $2x = -6$ (c) $x = -3$ (d) $10 = 4 - 2x$

3. Graph the function $y = 1.8x + 3.6$. Use your graph to solve each equation.
   a. $10.8 = 1.8x + 3.6$ **b.** $-5.4 = 1.8x + 3.6$ **c.** $0 = 1.8x + 3.6$

4. Use the graph of $y = 1.8x - 2.5$ to solve each equation to the nearest integer. Check your solution and tell if it is exact.
   a. $-0.7 = 1.8x - 2.5$ **b.** $3 = 1.8x - 2.5$

5. **Bok Choy Ahoy** In the vegetable section of the local grocery store, bok choy is selling for 79 cents a pound. Let x represent the number of pounds of bok choy. Write the amount you pay for bok choy as a function of x.

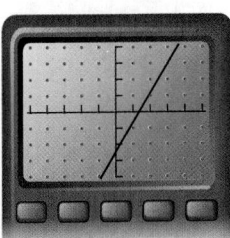

Xmin = –5
Xmax = 5
Xscl = 1
Ymin = –4
Ymax = 4
Yscl = 1

$y = 1.8x - 2.5$

Solve each equation. Check your solution.

6. $w + 31 = 17$

7. $25 = 4 - 7x$

8. $-3p + 9 = -15$

9. $1.4x + 3.7 = 13.5$

10. $\frac{1}{2}x + 13 = -28$

11. $72 = 5(12 - x)$

12. The literal equation $F = \frac{9}{5}C + 32$ relates Fahrenheit temperature (F) and Celsius temperature (C).
  a. Solve the equation for C in terms of F.
  b. Find the Celsius temperature if the Fahrenheit temperature is 84°.

Solve each equation. Check your solution.

13. $5x - 17 = 32 - 2x$

14. $6 + \frac{7}{4}z = 24 + z$

15. $1.7(x - 4) = x + 0.7(x + 1)$

16. $-4.5x - 7 = 14 - x$

17. $2(E - 3) = 5 + 2E$

18. $3(1 - 4a) - 2(7a + 1) = 27$

19. $1001x - 923 = 999x + 5$

20. $37(3x + 2) = 0$

21. $4(3 - x) = \frac{1}{2}(4x - 3)$

22. Gwen gets paid $5.50 an hour for wrapping gifts at the local department store. She wants to know how many hours she must work to earn $99.
  a. Write a function that relates the money Gwen earns (m) and the number of hours she works (h).
  b. Use the function to write an equation for finding the number of hours she must work to earn $99. Then solve the equation.

23. Own the Phone? The monthly rental fee for a telephone from the local telephone company is $4.89. An electronics store is selling telephones for $53.79. Maria wants to know how many months it will take the total fee to equal the cost of buying the phone.
  a. Write a function that relates the number of months (m) to the total amount she pays the telephone company (t).
  b. Write and solve an equation to determine when the rental fee equals the purchase price of the phone.

 **LOOK BACK**

24. If it rained in Seattle 73 days in the past year, give the experimental probability of rain in that city on any given day of the year. [1-2]

Find each product matrix. [1-3]

25. $\begin{bmatrix} -1 & 2 \\ 2 & 1 \end{bmatrix}\begin{bmatrix} 3 & 0 \\ 4 & -5 \end{bmatrix}$

26. $\begin{bmatrix} 11 & -7 \\ -4 & 17 \end{bmatrix}\begin{bmatrix} 3 \\ 5 \end{bmatrix}$

MORE PRACTICE

27. Which equation(s) are equivalent to $4x - 5 = 13$?
  (a) $4x = 18$ (b) $x = 9$ (c) $x = \frac{9}{2}$

28. Which equation(s) are equivalent to $-6x + 15 = -3$?
(a) $2x - 5 = -1$ (b) $-6x = 18$ (c) $x = 3$

29. Use a Graphing Utility Graph the function $y = 1.9x - 8.3$. Use the graph to solve each equation to the nearest tenth.
a. $-5.6 = 1.9x - 8.3$ **b.** $3.1 = 1.9x - 8.3$ **c.** $-14.2 = 1.9x - 8.3$

Solve each equation. Check your solution.

30. $4x - 13 = 35$ **31.** $96 = -12c + 36$ **32.** $5q + 9 = -12$

33. $8.7 = 2.3 - 2t$ **34.** $\frac{1}{5}x - 24 = 8$ **35.** $4(b - 3) = -8$

36. $1.7(h - 3) = -34$ **37.** $\frac{x}{7} + 3 = 13$ **38.** $13 + (8 + y)11 = 35$

39. Indian Cuisine Rajan is making his famous curry recipe for a party. He always uses $1\frac{1}{2}$ tablespoons of curry powder per serving plus 1 tablespoon extra "for good measure." However, he only has 10 tablespoons of curry powder left and no time to get more.
a. How much curry powder is needed for x servings?
b. Write and solve an equation to determine the number of servings Rajan can make with 10 tablespoons of curry powder.
c. Rajan invited seven people, but two said there was only a 50/50 chance that they could make it. Counting himself, do you think Rajan will have enough curry to go around? Explain.

Solve each equation. Check your solution.

40. $7x - 2 = 8x + 2$ **41.** $11p + 72 = 5p$ **42.** $5(3 - x) = 2 - 5x$

43. $\frac{x + 3}{6} = x - 17$ **44.** $(1 + R)3 = 13 - R$ **45.** $6x + 2 = 3(3 + 2x)$

46. $9x = -6(1.5 - 2x)$ **47.** $1.3z - 5 = 3z + 3.5$ **48.** $13j - 23 = 11j$

49. $7y - 4 + 2y = 6y + 11$ **50.** $4g - (2 + g) = 10 + 2g$ **51.** $1.45T + 5 = 2(T - 3)$

MORE MATH REASONING

52. Use a Graphing Utility Describe how you could solve the equation $-6x - 5 = 3x + 2$ using a graphing utility. Then solve the equation.

53. To find where the graph of the function $f(x) = 1200 - 1.5x$ crosses the x-axis, what single equation could you solve? What is the solution of that equation, and where does the graph cross the x-axis?

← CONNECT → *You've learned to recognize linear functions and to use them to solve problems. Now you will explore ways to find equations of lines. The ability to move freely between graphs and equations of linear functions is a vital part of linear modeling.*

William Pinkney sailed around the world on his 47-foot cutter, "Commitment." Through a satellite hookup, he maintained contact with students at his Chicago alma mater and kept them informed of his progress. Before sailing, he went over his route with the class.

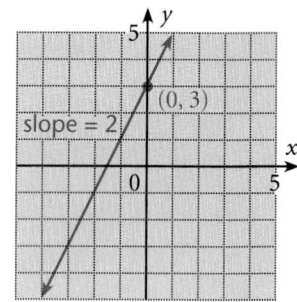

When navigating a boat, you can tell the boat's direction by using a compass. However, without landmarks, the navigator may only be able to estimate the boat's position. Similarly, the slope of a line describes its direction and steepness but not its location. A convenient way to locate a line is by giving its **y-intercept,** the value of y where the line crosses the y-axis.

The graph of $y = 2x + 3$ is a line with slope 2. The line crosses the y-axis at (0, 3), so the y-intercept is 3.

$$y = 2x + 3$$
$$\text{slope} \quad y\text{-intercept}$$

The **slope-intercept form** of an equation of a line with slope m and y-intercept b is $y = mx + b$.

EXAMPLE

1. Write the linear equation $3x + 2y = 8$ in slope-intercept form. Find the slope and y-intercept.

$$3x + 2y = 8 \qquad \text{Solve for } y.$$
$$2y = -3x + 8 \qquad \text{Subtract } 3x \text{ from both sides.}$$
$$y = -\frac{3}{2}x + 4 \qquad \text{Divide both sides by 2.}$$

The slope is $-\frac{3}{2}$ and the y-intercept is 4.

TRY IT

a. Write the linear equation $9x - 3y = 4$ in slope-intercept form. Find the slope and y-intercept.

b. Write an equation of the line shown on the graphing utility screen.

Xmin = –5
Xmax = 5
Xscl = 1
Ymin = –4
Ymax = 4
Yscl = 1

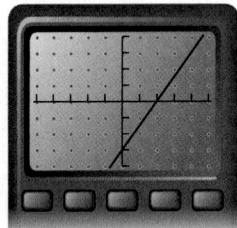

By using a proportion, you can also find an equation of a line if you know the slope and a point on the line other than the y-intercept.

EXAMPLE

2. Find an equation of the line through $(3, 5)$ with slope $\frac{1}{2}$.

Using the triangle, the slope from $(3, 5)$ to (x, y) is $\frac{y - 5}{x - 3}$. Since this slope must equal $\frac{1}{2}$ we can write a proportion.

$$\frac{y - 5}{x - 3} = \frac{1}{2}$$

Multiplying both sides by $(x - 3)$ gives an equation of the line.

$$y - 5 = \frac{1}{2}(x - 3)$$

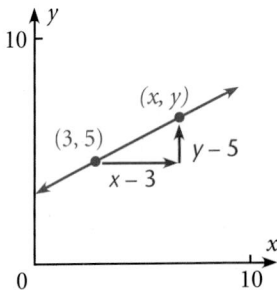

The **point-slope form** of an equation of a line through point (x_1, y_1) with slope m is $y - y_1 = m(x - x_1)$.

Using the point-slope form, you can also find the equation of a line through two points.

3. The water pressure in the ocean is a linear function of depth. Judy is diving in the ocean to collect data for her research project in marine biology. She measures a pressure of 27.8 lb/in.² (psi) at a depth of 30 feet, and a pressure of 32.1 psi at a depth of 40 feet.

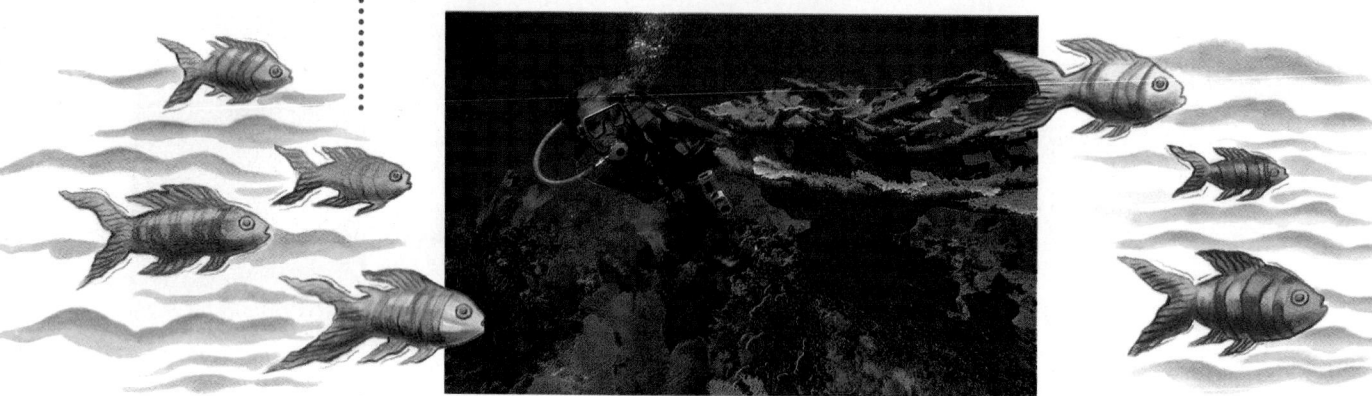

a. What is the pressure on the ocean floor at a depth of 60 feet?

Find the equation of the line through (30, 27.8) and (40, 32.1), where y is the pressure in psi and x is the depth in feet. First find the slope.

$$\text{slope} = \frac{\text{change in } y}{\text{change in } x} = \frac{(32.1 - 27.8)\text{ psi}}{(40 - 30)\text{ ft}} = \frac{4.3}{10} \text{ psi/ft} = 0.43 \text{ psi/ft}$$

This means that the rate of change of pressure is 0.43 psi per foot.

Choose either of the points and write an equation in point-slope form.

$$y - 27.8 = 0.43(x - 30)$$
$$y - 27.8 = 0.43x - 12.9$$
$$y = 0.43x + 14.9$$

When $x = 60$, $y = 0.43(60) + 14.9 = 25.8 + 14.9 = 40.7$. The pressure at 60 feet is 40.7 psi.

b. What is the pressure at the surface of the ocean?

When $x = 0$, $y = 14.9$. The pressure at the ocean surface, equal to the atmospheric pressure that day, is 14.9 psi.

c. Write an equation of the line through $(-3, 5)$ with slope -2.
d. Write an equation of the line through the points $(1, 2)$ and $(-4, 7)$.

EXPLORE: JUST THE RIGHT ANGLE

MATERIALS

Graph paper
Protractor

1. Choose four equations of linear functions, two with different positive slopes and two with different negative slopes. Graph each function on a separate coordinate grid.
2. Choose a point on each line. Then use your protractor to measure a 90° angle and draw the line **perpendicular** to the original line through that point.
3. Find the slope of each new line and compare the slopes of the perpendicular lines. Make a conjecture about the relationship between the slopes of perpendicular lines.
4. Test your conjecture by choosing two new slopes that you think will form perpendicular lines. Graph lines with these slopes and use your protractor to check that they are perpendicular.

Paul Klee, *Castle and Sun,* 1928/Private Collection/London, Great Britain

Comparing slopes of lines allows you to identify both **parallel lines** and **perpendicular lines.** If two lines have the same slope, then they are parallel. If the product of the slopes of two lines is −1, then the lines are perpendicular.

Parallel Lines

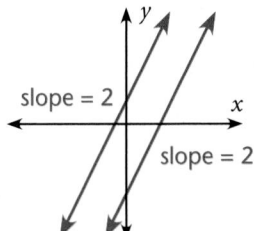

Perpendicular Lines

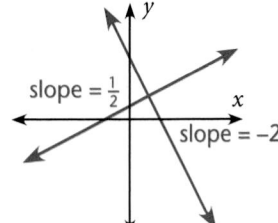

TRY IT

e. Find a pair of equations representing parallel lines and a pair representing perpendicular lines.
(i) $y = 3x − 2$ (ii) $y = \frac{1}{3}x + 2$ (iii) $y = \frac{1}{4}x + 1$
(iv) $y = 3x + 5$ (v) $y = −4x$

REFLECT

1. Summarize the different pieces of information that can be used to determine a line and write the equation of the line.
2. Describe the steps you would take to find an equation of the line through two points.
3. Can two parallel lines have the same y-intercept? Can two perpendicular lines have the same y-intercept? Explain.

Exercises

CORE

1. Getting Started Graph the linear equation $y = 2.5x + 6$.
  a. What is the slope of this line? How can you recognize the slope in the equation?
  b. What is the y-intercept of the line? How can you recognize the y-intercept in the equation?

Write the word or phrase that correctly completes each statement.

2. The equation $y = 9x - 11$ is in ____ form.

3. The equation $y + 3 = -2(x - 1)$ is in ____ form.

4. Give the slope and coordinates of a point on the graph of $y - 5 = -4\left(x - \frac{1}{6}\right)$.

5. Write an equation for a horizontal line 2 units above the x-axis.

6. Net Pay Nguyen has two pay receipts showing that he earned $58.00 for 12 hours work one week and $92.50 for 18 hours work another week.
  a. Express Nguyen's pay as a linear equation in the slope-intercept form.
  b. What is Nguyen's hourly rate of pay?
  c. What interpretation can you give for the y-intercept?

7. Write the slope-intercept form of the equation representing the line shown. Each grid mark is one unit.

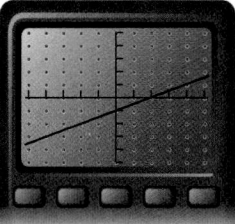

8. What is the slope of a line parallel to the graph of $y = 5x + 4$? What is the slope of a line perpendicular to this line?

9. What is the slope of a line parallel to the graph of the linear function $f(x) = -\frac{1}{2}x - 3$? What is the slope of a line perpendicular to this graph?

Give an equation for each line or function.

10. slope $= 2.5$ and contains $(8, 12)$

11. contains $(0, 2)$ and has slope -1

12. $f(2) = 5$ and has y-intercept 0

13. contains $(3, 0.12)$ and $(8, 0.045)$

14. contains $(6, -13)$ and is perpendicular to the graph of $y = 0.5x - 1$

15. contains $(100, 40)$ and is parallel to the graph of $2x + 6y = -5$

16. has y-intercept 4 and slope -3

17. $f(4.5) = 10$ and slope $= -4.5$

18. Explain why a vertical line is *not* the graph of a function. Which of the following equations represents a vertical line?
  (a) $y = 4$ (b) $x = 3$ (c) $y = x$

19. a. Write an equation of a horizontal line containing the point $(2, 4)$.
  b. Write an equation of a vertical line containing the point $(2, 4)$.

20. In each case, determine if enough information is given to determine a unique line. If so, write an equation of the line.

   a. slope = 3 and contains (2, 5)
   b. y-intercept = -2
   c. contains $(-\pi, -3.23)$ and $(\pi, 0)$
   d. the line is horizontal and contains $(-12, -10)$
   e. slope = -1.6 and y-intercept = $\sqrt{3}$
   f. slope = 0.01

Give the equation of each line.

21.

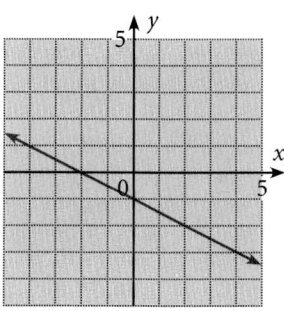

22.

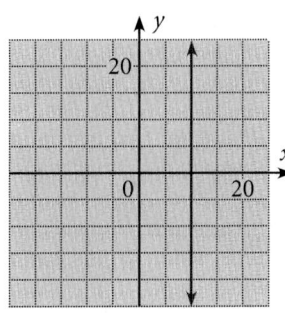

23.

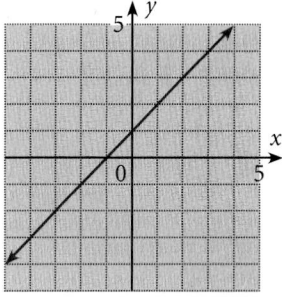

24. The equation of the line k is $y = 3x - 6$. Which equation describes a line parallel to k? Which equation describes a line perpendicular to line k?

   (a) $y = 6x - 3$ (b) $y = -\frac{1}{3}x + 3$ (c) $y = \frac{1}{6}x - \frac{1}{3}$ (d) $y = 3x + 5$

25. The line j has equation $y = -\frac{2}{3}x + 5$ and contains the point (6, 1).

   a. Write an equation of the line parallel to j containing (2, 3).
   b. Write an equation of the line perpendicular to j containing (6, 1).

26. Write an equation for the line containing $(5, -2)$ that is perpendicular to the line $9x - 3y = 14$.

27. Hardly Harley A new motorcycle is priced at $5380. After 9 years, its value has depreciated to $376.

   a. Express the value of the motorcycle as a linear function of the number of years since it was new. Graph the function.
   b. Interpret the slope and the y-intercept of the linear function given in **a.**
   c. What was the value of the motorcycle 3 years after it was new?
   d. According to your model, how many years will it take for the motorcycle to have no value? a negative value?
   e. Sketch a graph that you think might more accurately depict the market value of the motorcycle. Explain why it varies from the linear model.

28. 'Roo Tracks The faster a kangaroo hops, the longer the distance of the hop. Moving at less than 7 kilometers per hour, a kangaroo uses all four feet and its tail. At greater speeds, it hops on its two hind legs. When hopping, the length of stride can be modeled as a function of speed. At 7 kilometers per hour, the stride length is about 1 meter. The length increases approximately 0.1 meter for each increase of 1 kilometer per hour in speed.

a. What is the stride length for a speed of 10 kilometers per hour?

b. From the description, explain how you know this is a linear function.

c. Write the equation of this line.

d. While hiking in the bush, you spot fresh kangaroo tracks. The distance between prints is 2.1 meters. About how fast was the kangaroo going?

e. If the tracks are 10 minutes old and it has continued hopping at this speed, how far away is the kangaroo now?

 ## LOOK AHEAD

29. A trend line has been drawn on each scatter plot of data. Which line appears to fit the data best? Justify your choice.

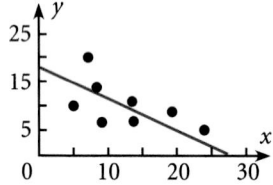 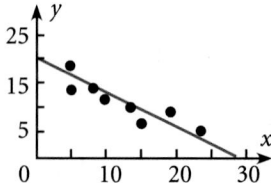

30. The mean of a set of numbers may be thought of as their balance point. What would be a geometrical description of the balance point of a line segment? Calculate the balance point of the segment with endpoints $(-3, 7)$ and $(4, 21)$.

MORE PRACTICE

Give the slope and coordinates of a point on the graph of each equation.

31. $y - 6 = -3(x - 10)$

32. $y + \frac{1}{2} = 7\left(x - \frac{2}{3}\right)$

Does each pair of equations represent parallel lines, perpendicular lines, or neither?

33. $y = -x + 3$ and $x - y = 2$

34. $8x - 4y = 10$ and $y = 2x$

35. $y + 3 = -2(x - 3)$ and $2x + y = -1$

36. $6x + 8y = -4$ and $8x - 6y = -12$

37. $x = 9$ and $y = 13.7$

38. $y = 2x$ and $2y + 1 = x$

Give an equation for each line.

39. with slope $= 4$ through $(1, 3)$

40. containing $(0, 0)$ and $(4, 6)$

41. containing $(-3, 5)$ and $(7, -1)$

42. containing $\left(2, \frac{3}{4}\right)$ and $\left(\frac{3}{2}, \frac{5}{4}\right)$

43. containing $(-25, 45)$ and having a y-intercept of 10

44. containing $(1, 3)$ and having a y-intercept of 5

45. Not-So-Free Delivery A furniture store charges a fee on all items delivered from the store to the customer. The delivery fee y is computed by a linear equation $y = mx + b$, where x denotes the amount of the purchase. Find the equation the furniture store might use to compute the fee if the store charges \$37.50 to deliver a purchase of \$525 and charges \$54.60 to deliver an \$810 purchase.

46. Write an equation for a line that has a slope of -7 and a y-intercept of 14. Sketch the graph of this line.

47. Find the equation $y = mx + b$ for the line that contains $(0, 3)$ and $(3, 9)$. Sketch the graph of this line.

Give an equation for each line.

48. containing $(6, -13)$ and parallel to the line $y = 0.5x - 1$

49. containing the point $(4, -5)$ and perpendicular to the line $y = -2x$

50. containing $(16, 9)$ and parallel to the line $1.5x - 3y = 12$

51. the vertical line containing $\left(\frac{3}{7}, -1\frac{1}{3}\right)$

52. the horizontal line through $(1, \pi)$

MORE MATH REASONING

53. The costs to a business to put an employee to work are more than just the employee's wages. A timber-cutting contractor pays each lumberjack \$26.50 an hour in wages, \$2.12 an hour in taxes, and fixed weekly benefits of \$23.80. Because accidents happen frequently in this industry, the employer also pays \$4 an hour in additional insurance.
   a. What is the total hourly cost of the employee? What is the fixed cost per week?
   b. Let x be the number of hours a lumberjack works in a week. Write an equation for the employer's total costs as a function of x.
   c. What are the employer's costs for the employee who works 28 hours in a week?
   d. If the employer's resources limit her to costs of no more than \$900 a week per employee, how many hours can the employee work? What will be the employee's wages?

54. Intercept Form Write the slope-intercept form of an equation for the line that contains the points $(a, 0)$ and $(0, b)$. Transform the equation so that its left side consists of an x-term and a y-term and its right side is 1. Explain why this form is called the **intercept form** of a linear equation.

55. Write a convincing argument that the triangle with vertices $(0, 5)$, $(1, 2.5)$ and $(-10, 1)$ is a right triangle.

Making Connections

← C O N N E C T → *You've explored and used relationships among slope, rate of change, and linear functions. You have also solved equations. Linear functions and equations are valuable tools to help you quantify trends and make predictions in a wide variety of real situations.*

In the United States, average weekly earnings have been increasing for decades. However, the economic outlook doesn't seem as promising when inflation is figured in. A dollar just doesn't stretch as far as it did in the past. How far do you think your money will go in a few years?

EXPLORE: WORKING IN A COAL MINE

MATERIALS

Graphing utility

The chart shows the average weekly earnings for workers in several industries during 1980 and 1990. Earnings are given in current dollars and in constant 1982 dollars, allowing you to compare the real buying power of earnings in 1980 and 1990. (Constant dollars have a set buying power unlike current dollars, which buy less and less each year due to inflation.)

Average Weekly Earnings

Industry	Current Dollars		Constant 1982 Dollars	
	1980	1990	1980	1990
Mining	397	603	464	453
Construction	368	526	430	395
Retail	147	194	172	146
Manufacturing	289	442	337	332

1. Choose one of these industries. Give the equation of the linear function that models earnings in current dollars and the equation of the linear function that models earnings in constant (1982) dollars.
2. If these trends continue, what do you predict the earnings in current dollars and in constant dollars will be in this industry when you are 20 years old?
3. The earnings in constant dollars take into account the decreased value due to inflation, as well as the increased value of salaries. What is the net effect of inflation and salary growth in the industry you chose? How could this affect future workers in that industry? Explain.

1. Describe how rate of change relates to slope.
2. How can you recognize that a function is linear from its equation?
3. If you know one point on a line, what other information can you use to graph a line and write its equation?

Self-Assessment

Decide whether each equation represents a linear function and whether it represents direct variation. If it is linear, give the slope.

1. $3x + 5 = 2y$

2. $y = x^2 - x$

3. $y = -4.2$

4. $y = x - \frac{2}{3}$

5. $x^2 + y^2 = 9$

6. $y = -7x$

7. Say It Ain't Joe Joe had 86 hits in 324 times at bat through July of this baseball season. By September he had a total of 163 hits in 563 at bats. What is the slope between these "points" if you think of hits as a function of at bats? Interpret the slope.

Find the slope of the line containing each pair of points.

8. $(3, 6)$ and $(5, 9)$

9. $(2, 8)$ and $(6, -3)$

10. $(-3, 1)$ and $(-1, 8)$

Indicate the slope and y-intercept for each linear equation. Then sketch its graph.

11. $y = -2x - 1$

12. $y = 4x + 3$

13. $3x + y = 12$

14. Jamal is weighing the merits of two part-time job opportunities. As an apprentice auto mechanic, Jamal would earn an hourly wage of $7. As a management trainee in a movie theater, he would earn $5 an hour plus $20 each week to update the movie titles on the marquee.

a. On the graph, which line, A or B, represents each job?

b. Write a function for each job expressing weekly earnings in terms of hours worked.

c. For which of the two jobs does the function represent direct variation?

d. If Jamal's goal is to earn at least $100 a week, what is the minimum number of hours he must work at each job?

e. Write a short paragraph on other factors that you would consider before choosing between job opportunities.

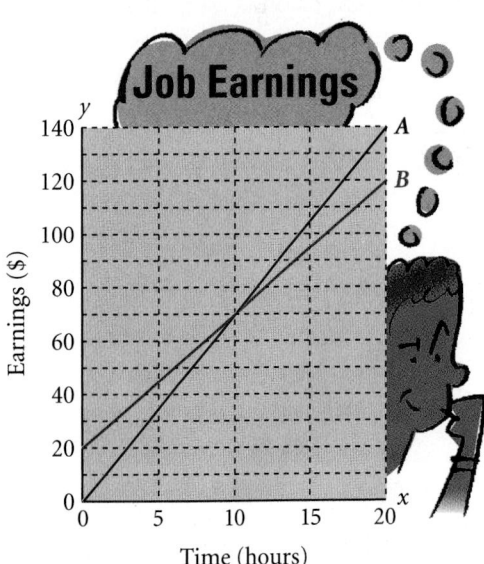

Job Earnings

Solve each equation.

15. $3x + 6 = -15$

16. $10 - 2y = -11$

17. $\frac{x}{9} = -18$

18. $5w - 2 = 4w + 11$

19. $3(2x - 1) + x = 5x - 11$

20. $3p - 1 = 3(2 + p)$

21. In 1975, 13.1% of economists were women. In 1992, that percentage had risen to 43.3%. At this rate, when would you predict half of all economists to be women?

22. Classy Shirts The senior class ordered T-shirts with the class logo from Bucky's Sporting Goods Store. Bucky's charges $245 for 25 T-shirts and $365 for 40 T-shirts. Find a linear function that relates the charge to the number of shirts. Interpret the function to find the fixed set-up cost and the charge per shirt.

Find an equation for each line.

23. with slope $= -1$ through $(-3, 5)$

24. through points $(2, 5)$ and $(5, 8)$

25. parallel to $y = -3x + 2$ through $(2, 4)$

26. perpendicular to $y = 4x$ through $(8, -6)$

27. Which equation describes a line parallel to $y = x - 7$?
    (a) $x + y = 9$ (b) $y - x = 2$ (c) $3x + y = -7$ (d) not here

28. Which equation describes a line with y-intercept -2?
    (a) $x + y = 2$ (b) $3x - y = -2$ (c) $x = -2$ (d) not here

29. Mr. Henderson is a repair person who charges a fee for coming to your home, plus an hourly rate. He charged Mrs. Wilson $95 for a repair that took 6 hours and Mrs. Rosario $65 for a repair that took 4 hours. How much will Mr. Henderson charge for a repair that takes 7 hours?

30. Larry earns $6.50 per hour as a helper on a delivery truck. He also earns $10 a week for working at the recycling center on Saturday mornings. How many hours must Larry work next week if he wants to earn $140?

31. If I Had a Hammer In 1860, carpenters earned an average of $1.65 per day. Assume a carpenter could save $0.85 of his daily pay and worked five days per week. If he had $16 saved, how many more weeks would he have to save to be able to buy a $50 horse?

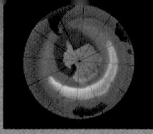

Exosphere
+300 km

2-2 Fitting Linear Functions to Data

Thermosphere
90–300 km

Blanket *for all* Seasons

Mesosphere 50–90 km

One of the atmosphere's most important functions is to keep the earth warm. Naturally occurring gases in the atmosphere allow sunlight to pass through to the earth's surface, but trap some of the radiation that would otherwise escape back into space. Over the past 1000 years this blanketing effect, called the *greenhouse effect*, has kept our planet about 33°C warmer than it would otherwise be.

This situation may be changing. Since the beginning of the Industrial Revolution, the burning of coal, oil, and other fossil fuels and the destruction of forests have released massive amounts of natural and unnatural greenhouse gases into the atmosphere, trapping large amounts of radiation. As a result, the National Academy of Sciences predicts that the average temperature of the planet will be 1.5°C to 4.5°C warmer in the next 75 years, compared with a 2°C rise in average temperature over the past 1000 years. These predictions are controversial, but the future could be a lot warmer for our descendants.

Stratosphere
20–50 km

Natural Greenhouse Gases	Gas Concentration (parts per million)	
	1800	1986
Carbon dioxide	275	346
Methane	0.75	1.65
Nitrous oxide	0.28	0.31

Troposphere
0–20 km

1. In percentages, which gas concentration has increased the most over the last 186 years?
2. Why might the temperature inside a parked car with closed windows be higher than the temperature outside?
3. What could be some effects of a marked increase in the earth's average temperature?

← CONNECT →   *In Chapter 1, you displayed data in scatter plots. If you could see an association in the data, you drew a trend line and used the line to make predictions. Now you will use the equation of a trend line to make predictions.*

In 1787, the French scientist Jacques Charles conducted experiments on gases by keeping the pressure of a sample of gas constant and measuring the volume at various temperatures. In the Explore, you will analyze the data and mathematics that Charles used to discover *absolute zero,* the lower limit of the temperature scale.

EXPLORE: DISCOVERING ABSOLUTE ZERO

1. Make a scatter plot of the data using temperature as the independent variable. Then draw a trend line. (You may want to use a straightedge or a piece of spaghetti or string as a guide to help you locate a good trend line.)
2. What happens to the volume of gas when the temperature increases? decreases? What rate of change does the slope of the line represent?
3. Write an equation for your trend line in the form $V = mT + b$, where T represents temperature and V represents volume.
4. Predict the volume of the gas when its temperature is $-300°C$. Is this prediction reasonable? Explain.
5. Charles was keenly interested in predicting the value of T when $V = 0$. This value is called *absolute zero,* the theoretical temperature when all heat is gone. Set $V = 0$ in your equation and solve for T either symbolically or using the trace feature on your graphing utility. What do you predict as the temperature of absolute zero?

MATERIALS

Graph paper or graphing utility
Straightedge
Piece of uncooked spaghetti or string (optional)

Temperature (°C)	Volume (ml)
−40	10.26
−30	10.68
−20	11.14
−10	11.59
0	12.00
10	12.43
20	12.87
30	13.34
40	13.79

With a linear model of data, you can make predictions using either a trend line or its equation. However, it is always important to interpret your prediction to make sure it is reasonable.

EXAMPLE

Seals can live comfortably in freezing water and in air temperatures of −20°C. Data was collected for 18 seals and compiled as a set of ordered pairs using the coordinates (air temperature, skin temperature). Draw a scatter plot and a trend line and find the equation of the trend line. Then use the equation or the graph to predict the skin temperature of a seal when the air temperature is −5°C.

Lucky: $(-22, 6)$	X: $(11, 31)$
Harper: $(-1, 19)$	Coogan: $(-19, 7)$
Royal: $(23, 31)$	Perma: $(19, 32)$
Mischa: $(-14, 11)$	Spot: $(18, 29)$
Calypso: $(22, 33)$	Prince: $(-9, 21)$
Homer: $(-2, 15)$	Lobelia: $(-1, 23)$
Astro: $(19, 31)$	Swak: $(21, 28)$
Smoke: $(2, 22)$	Approval: $(-7, 17)$
Ur: $(12, 28)$	Bono: $(10, 30)$

You can find the equation of a trend line for the data using the slope and y-intercept. The equation of the trend line shown is

$$y = \tfrac{3}{5}x + 20.$$

Now substitute −5 for x and solve.

$$y = \tfrac{3}{5}(-5) + 20$$

$$y = -3 + 20$$

$$y = 17$$

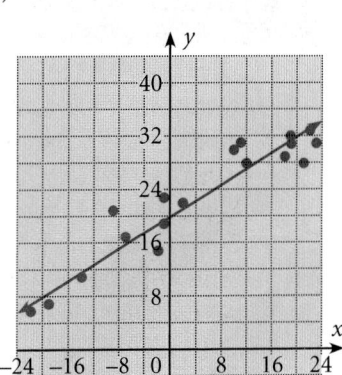

The predicted skin temperature of a seal is about 17°C when the air temperature is −5°C.

CONSIDER

?

1. Do you think the linear model in the Example is valid for all air temperatures? Explain.

TRY IT

Peter has been recording the temperature of the soil in his garden each week since early March. This scatter plot shows his data so far.

a. Find the equation of a trend line.
b. Use your equation to predict the temperature of the soil in the tenth week and in the thirtieth week. Do both of these predictions seem reasonable? Explain.

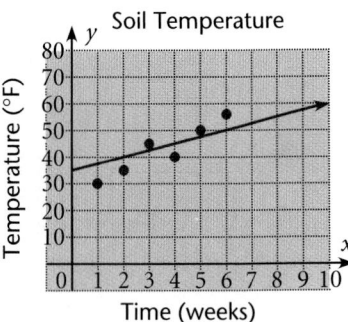

Soil Temperature

In 2-2B, you will explore a way to fit lines to data using both geometric and algebraic ideas.

REFLECT

1. Describe a situation in which making a prediction might be easiest and most accurate using the equation of a trend line.
2. Could two stock market analysts find different trends and make different predictions based on the same earnings data for a corporation? If so, would one of them necessarily have made a mistake? Explain your reasoning.
3. Give some quantities in which a weather forecaster might be interested in finding data and trends.

Exercises

CORE

1. Getting Started
  a. What is the slope of the trend line drawn for this scatter plot?
  b. What is its y-intercept?
  c. Write the equation of the trend line.
  d. If $x = 4.5$, predict the value of y.

2. Write the definition of a *trend line* for a scatter plot.

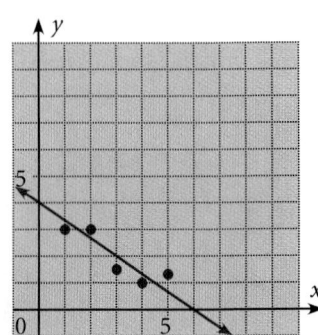

3. Choose the letter of the word or phrase that is related to *rate of change*.
(a) *y*-intercept (b) slope (c) the origin (d) a scatter plot (e) not here

4. How Tall? This graph compares children's heights at age 8 and at age 16.

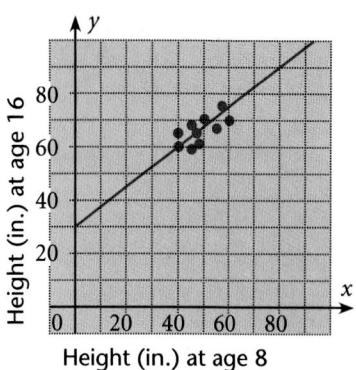

Height (in.) at age 8

a. How would you describe the association of data in this graph?
b. What is the equation of the trend line shown?
c. Use the equation to predict the height at age 16 of an 8-year-old child who is 52 inches tall.
d. How accurate do you think your prediction is? Explain.

Write an equation of the trend line for each scatter plot. Use your equation to predict the value of *y* for the given value of *x*.

5. $x = 30$
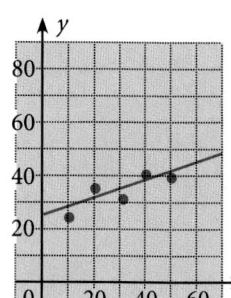

6. $x = 4$
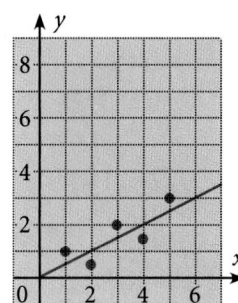

7. $x = 2.5$
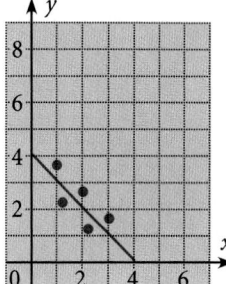

For each set of data, make a scatter plot, draw a trend line, and write its equation.

8. $(1, 2.8), (2, 3.2), (3, 3.2), (4, 2.8), (5, 3.1)$

9. $(1, 1.9), (1.5, 3), (2, 2.5), (2.5, 3.9), (3, 3.5), (3.5, 4.5), (4, 4.3)$

10. Spring Has Sprung A weight on a metal spring will cause the spring to stretch. This table shows data for a particular spring.

Weight (lb)	1	2	3	4	5	6	7	8
Stretch (in.)	0.5	1.1	1.7	2.3	2.6	3.1	3.6	4.2

a. Draw a scatter plot and trend line for the data.
b. Find the equation of your trend line.
c. Use your trend line to predict the amount the spring will stretch with a 12-pound weight.
d. Do you think your equation will work for any weight? Explain.

Give the median of each set of numbers.

11. 3, 9, 18, 7, 12, 27, 5   **12.** 22, 20, 33, 16, 30, 10, 27, 26

Find the midpoint of line segments with the given endpoints.

13. $(3, 5), (9, 11)$ **14.** $(-2, 7), (4, 3)$ **15.** $(5, 6), (8, -1)$

MORE PRACTICE

For each set of data, make a scatter plot, draw a trend line, and write its equation.

16. $(5, 10), (8, 14), (14, 6), (13, 10), (19, 8), (24, 4), (9, 6)$

17. $(4, 7), (3, 5), (5, 5), (2, 6), (1, 4), (3, 6), (1, 4), (4, 6), (7, 3)$

18. $(0, 15), (1.6, 2), (0.2, 5), (1.8, 3), (0.6, 12), (0.3, 10), (0.8, 8), (1.4, 7), (1, 4.5)$

Write an equation of the trend line for each scatter plot. Use your equation to predict the value of y for the given value of x.

19. $x = 3$ **20.** $x = 3$ **21.** $x = 2.7589$

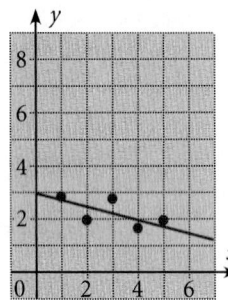   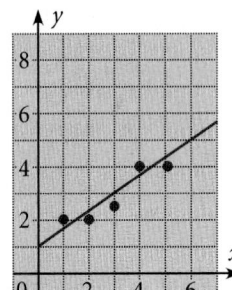   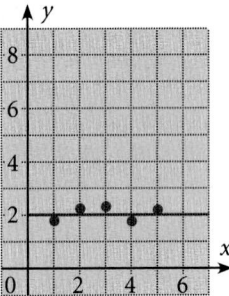

22. Speed Stocking In the early part of this century, a small stocking manufacturer recorded production figures for the number of hours (h) each employee worked per day and the number of stockings (s) that worker produced. The (h, s) data for several employees over several days were: $(10, 20), (8, 18), (9, 22), (6, 12), (12, 30), (8, 26), (5, 14), (7, 20), (9, 30), (11, 26)$.

a. Draw a scatter plot and trend line for the data.
b. Find the equation of your trend line.
c. Use your equation to predict the number of stockings that a worker could produce in 7 hours.
d. Do you think your equation could be used to predict the number of stockings a worker could have produced in a 15-hour day? Explain.

Industry

MORE MATH REASONING

23. To help analyze the expenses of his T-shirt manufacturing business, Alonzo plotted the number of T-shirts produced against his business expenses for each of the last 9 months. Then he fit a line to the data. After looking at the line, he was disturbed and told his foreman that the data must be wrong because the line should show no expenses when no shirts were produced. Do you agree with Alonzo or not? Explain.

24. Keeping On Track Track season, which lasts 15 weeks, starts the first week of February and ends with the state meet in mid-May. The coach thinks Paula can break the school record of 4 minutes 20 seconds in the 1500-meter run. Each week Paula has a time trial in practice or in competition with another school. Her actual running times for the first 8 weeks are plotted by the coach.

a. Paula drew a trend line for the data. Use it to predict whether or not she will be able to break the record by the time of the meet.

Week	Time (sec)
0	307.4
1	304.5
2	303.0
3	296.5
4	289.8
5	292.4
6	282.3
7	286.8
8	284.5

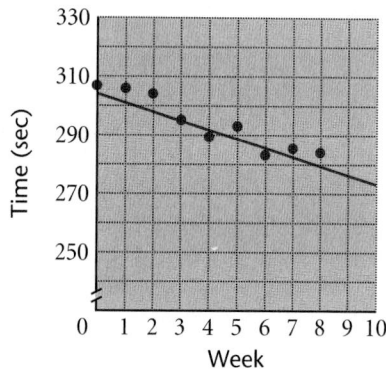

b. What does the line predict about Paula's time after 25 weeks of training?

c. Do you think a line is the best model for this data? Explain.

2-2 PART B · The Median-Median Line of Fit

← CONNECT → *You've fit trend lines to data and used their equations to make predictions. Now you will investigate a method for finding a line of best fit that utilizes ideas from both geometry and algebra.*

Two people who fit trend lines to a scatter plot will often find slightly different lines. However, there are mathematical methods you can use to fit a *unique* trend line to each set of data. A trend line that is found mathematically is called a **line of best fit.**

One algebraic and geometric method of fitting a line to data involves finding three vertices of a triangle and its balance point. In the following Explore, you will discover how to find a triangle's balance point.

EXPLORE: WHERE'S THE CENTROID?

MATERIALS

Cardboard, Scissors, Compass
Graph paper, Straightedge

The *center of gravity* of an object is the point where the object can be balanced.

1. Draw two congruent triangles, one on a piece of cardboard and one on a coordinate plane. Label the vertices of the graphed triangle *A*, *B*, and *C*, and find their coordinates.

2. Cut out the cardboard triangle. By trial and error, find and mark the point where you can balance the triangle on the end of a sharp pencil.

3. Find the mean of the *x*-coordinates of *A*, *B*, and *C*. Then find the mean of the *y*-coordinates of *A*, *B*, and *C*. Mark and label the point *D* with the mean *x*-coordinate and mean *y*-coordinate in your graphed triangle.

4. Cut out your graphed triangle and place the two triangles together so they match. What do you observe about the balance point on the cardboard triangle and point *D* of the graphed triangle?

The coordinates of the **centroid** (or balance point) of a triangle in a coordinate plane are the mean of the *x*-coordinates and the mean of the *y*-coordinates of the vertices of the triangle.

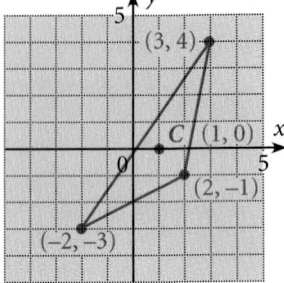

TRY IT

a. Give the coordinates of the centroid of the triangle with vertices (4, 21), (20, 150), and (13, 171).

Recall that the *median* is the middle value (or the mean of the middle two values) in a list of data arranged in numerical order. Finding medians and a centroid are the key steps in fitting the **median-median line** of best fit to data.

Find the equation of the median-median line for the set of data:
(1, 9), (5, 7), (2, 9), (10, 2), (2, 6), (7, 6), (8, 1), (4, 9), (6, 7).

Step 1: *Find three median points, A, B, and C.*

Sort the data into three groups in the order of their *x*-coordinates. Since there are nine data points, there are three points in each group.

Find the median *x*-coordinates of each group:

(2,)   (5,)   (8,)

Find the median *y*-coordinates of each group:

(, 9)   (, 7)   (, 2)

Combine the coordinates in each group to find the three *median points*.

$A(2, 9)$, $B(5, 7)$, and $C(8, 2)$.

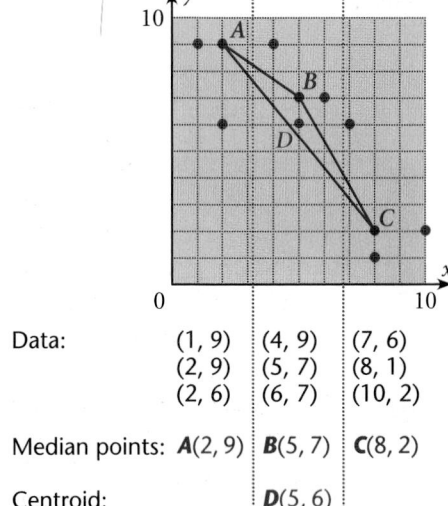

Data:	(1, 9)	(4, 9)	(7, 6)
	(2, 9)	(5, 7)	(8, 1)
	(2, 6)	(6, 7)	(10, 2)

Median points: **A**(2, 9) **B**(5, 7) **C**(8, 2)

Centroid: **D**(5, 6)

Step 2: *Find the centroid (D) of △ABC.*

The coordinates of the centroid are the mean of the *x*-coordinates and the mean of the *y*-coordinates.

$$\left(\frac{2 + 5 + 8}{3}, \frac{9 + 7 + 2}{3}\right) = D(5, 6)$$

Step 3: *Find the equation of the line parallel to $\overleftrightarrow{AC}$ through the centroid.*

$$\text{slope of } \overleftrightarrow{AC} = \frac{2 - 9}{8 - 2} = -\frac{7}{6}$$

Write the point-slope form of the equation of the line parallel to $\overleftrightarrow{AC}$ through $D(5, 6)$.

$$y - 6 = -\frac{7}{6}(x - 5)$$

$$y = -\frac{7}{6}x + \frac{71}{6}$$

The equation of the median-median line is $y = -\frac{7}{6}x + \frac{71}{6}$.

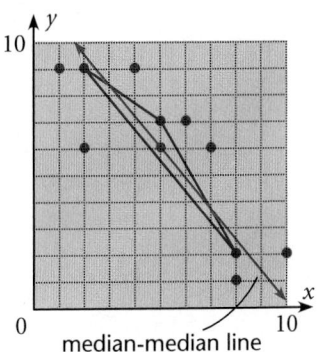

median-median line

If the number of data points *does not* divide evenly into three groups, use these guidelines:

If there is one point left over, place the point in the second group. So for 16 data points, divide the data into groups of 5, 6, and 5 points.

If there are two points left over, place one more point in the first and third groups. So for 17 data points, divide the data into groups of 6, 5, and 6 points.

CONSIDER

1. Could you have predicted that the slope of the median-median line in the Example would be negative? Explain.

TRY IT

b. Find the median point of points (2, 5), (4, 1), (7, 7), (6, 9).

c. To find three medians of 100 points of data, how many points would you include in each of the three groups of data?

A meteorologist found the three median points $A(2, 14.8)$, $B(4, 14.6)$, and $C(9, 14.4)$ for a set of data measuring time in hours and barometric pressures in psi.

d. Find the equation of the median-median line.

e. Predict when the barometric pressure will hit 14 psi.

The median-median line is a unique line of best fit found using geometric and algebraic ideas. In 2-2C, you will learn another method to fit a unique line to data using technology.

Barometers measure atmospheric pressure and help forecasters predict changes in the weather.

REFLECT

1. Name some of the geometric and algebraic ideas that are used to find a median-median line.
2. Suppose a scatter plot yields three noncollinear median points. In your own words, explain how to find the median-median line.
3. How does the association of the data affect the shape of the triangle formed by the median points? Explain.

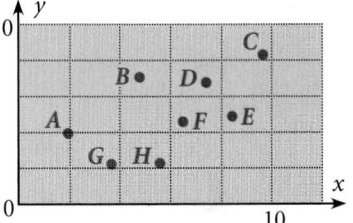

Exercises

CORE

1. Getting Started Find the centroid of the triangle with the vertices: $(10, 9)$, $(4, 6)$, $(1, 7)$.

2. Copy and complete the table to show how many points would be in each group when finding three median points of the data.

Number of Data Points	First Group (A)	Second Group (B)	Third Group (C)
32			
48			
13			

3. Choose the correct grouping of points to find the three median points of the data graphed in the scatter plot.

	First Group	Second Group	Third Group
(a)	A, B, G	F, H	C, D, E
(b)	B, D, C	A, F, E	G, H
(c)	A, G	B, H, F, D	C, E

4. Plot the points $A(1, 11)$, $B(4, 16)$, and $C(7, 3)$ on graph paper.
   a. What are the coordinates of the centroid of $\triangle ABC$? Plot the centroid on your graph.
   b. What is the slope of the line containing A and C?
   c. Write the equation of the line that contains the centroid and is parallel to $\overleftrightarrow{AC}$. Plot this line on your graph.

5. Getting Mobilized Classified ads to sell privately owned cars frequently list the miles the car has been driven. For example, 20K would mean 20,000 miles. The following table is from the classified section of a daily urban newspaper.
   a. Write three groups of data points (age, miles) to use in determining the median-median line for the data.
   b. Give the coordinates of the three median points and the centroid of the resulting triangle.
   c. Find the slope between the first and third median points. Then write the equation of the median-median line in slope-intercept form.
   d. What feature of the median-median line of best fit represents the distance an average car is driven per year? How far is the average car driven annually?
   e. Suppose you are considering buying a 6-year-old car that has been driven 57,000 miles. How does this car's use compare with the average usage predicted using the median-median line? How might this information affect your decision?

Age (yr)	Miles
4	42K
2	7K
4	20K
5	48K
7	65K
8	63K
10	101K
11	67K
1	1K
2	18K
2	23K
3	35K

Determine whether each statement is true or false. If the statement is false, change the underlined word or phrase to make it true.

6. The median-median line for a set of data contains the <u>median point</u>.

7. The median-median line is found using <u>all the data points in the set</u>.

8. The points shown in the graph are the median points of a set of data. Is the line shown the median-median line for the data? Explain.

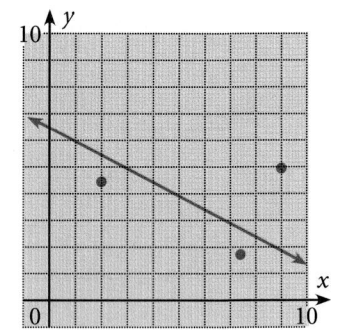

9. Graph the triangle with vertices $A(1, 1)$, $B(3, 6)$, and $C(10, 0)$. Draw a line segment from each vertex to the midpoint of its opposite side. These segments are the **medians of a triangle.**
   a. Give the coordinates of the point where the three medians intersect.
   b. Calculate the coordinates of the centroid of the triangle.
   c. Explain the relationship between the points in **a** and **b**.

10. Tall Stories This is a list of the skyscrapers in the United States that are more than 72 stories tall.
   a. Find the equation of the median-median line of best fit for the data.
   b. Use the median-median line to predict the height of an 88-story building.

Building	Stories	Height (ft)
Sears Tower	110	1454
World Trade Center	110	1377
Empire State	102	1250
Amoco	80	1136
John Hancock	100	1127
Chrysler	77	1048
First Interstate	73	1017
Texas	75	1002
Columbia Seafirst	76	943
Water Tower Place	74	859
Westin Peachtree	73	754
Detroit Westin	73	712

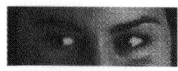 **LOOK BACK**

For each scatter plot, state whether the data show a positive association, negative association, or no association. [1-1]

11.

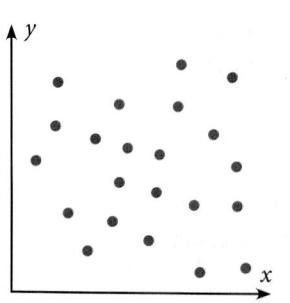

12.

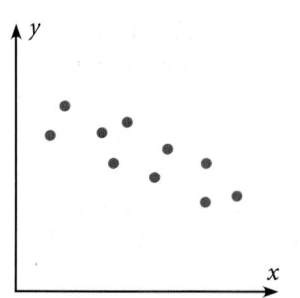

13.

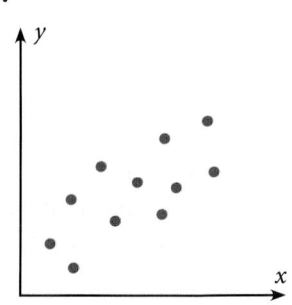

Find the slope of each line. [2-1]

14.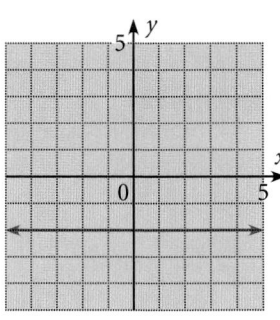

15.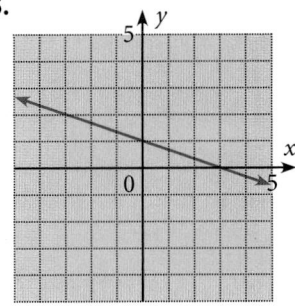

16.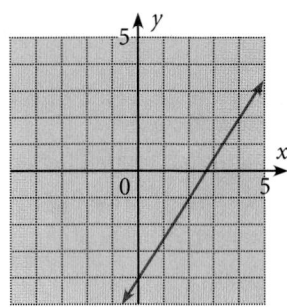

MORE PRACTICE

17. Copy and complete the table to show how many points would be in each group when finding three median points of the data.

Number of Data Points	First Group (A)	Second Group (B)	Third Group (C)
12			
20			
34			
42			
17			
23			

Find the coordinates of the centroid of each triangle.

18.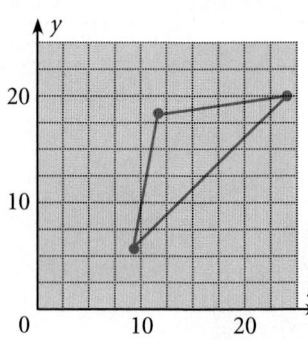

19.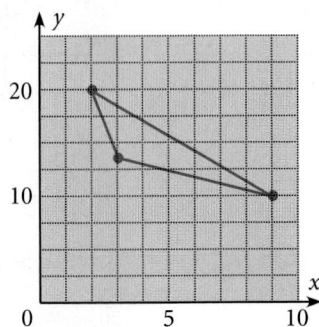

20. Plot the points (1, 16), (2, 11), (3, 10), (3, 14), (4, 5), and (8, 12) on graph paper.
  a. List the first, second, and third group of points for determining the median-median line.
  b. What are the coordinates of the three median points and the centroid of the resulting triangle?
  c. Find the slope of the line containing the first and third median points. Then write the equation of the median-median line. Plot this line on your graph.

21. Plot the points (1, 20), (2, 12), (2, 15), (3, 10), (6, 7), (9, 8), (11, 3), (15, 6), and (13, 8) on graph paper.

   a. List the first, second, and third group of points for determining the median-median line.

   b. What are the coordinates of the three median points and the centroid of the resulting triangle?

   c. Find the slope of the line containing the first and third median points. Then write the equation of the median-median line. Plot this line on your graph.

22. For the scatter plot, which letter represents the correct grouping of the points to find three median points of the data?

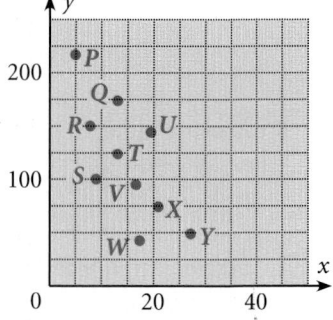

	First Group	*Second Group*	*Third Group*
(a)	P, Q, T	R, S, V, W	U, X, Y
(b)	P, Q, R	S, T, U	V, W, X, Y
(c)	P, R, S	Q, T, V, W	U, X, Y

23. To Rent or Not to Rent Attendance at crafts fairs and the rental fee for display space affect an artist's profits. Data from eight crafts fairs are given.

   a. Give the coordinates of the three median points and centroid for the data.

   b. Write the equation of the median-median line.

   c. What booth rental fee does the median-median line predict for a fair that is expected to draw 3000 people?

   d. Which of the shows listed are more expensive than average?

   e. Describe other factors that could influence whether you, as an artist, would rent space at a show that is more expensive than average.

Attendance	Rental Fee ($)
1200	120
1500	200
4000	300
6200	340
2900	250
800	100
3500	300
5500	370

24. a. Find the three median points of the data.

Group 1	Group 2	Group 3
(1, 3)	(4, 5)	(8, 8)
(1, 6)	(4, 8)	(9, 12)
(2, 5)	(5, 9)	(8, 13)

b. What special quality do the median points have?

c. Explain how this quality allows you to find the equation of the median-median line *without* first finding the centroid.

MORE MATH REASONING

25. Make a table and scatter plot of data about coin tosses: show the number of flips as the independent variable and number of heads as the dependent variable. First, flip the coin twice and record the data point. Repeat the process for 3, 4, 5, 6, 7, 8, 9, and 10 flips. Find the equation of the median-median line for the nine data points. Theoretically, what should be the equation for a line of best fit for this experiment? Explain why your line may differ from the theoretical line.

26. Draw a triangle, its three medians, and its centroid. Measure and record the length of each median. Then for each median, measure the distance of the centroid from each end of that median. Describe what you notice about the distances.

2-2
PART C Fitting Lines Using Technology

← CONNECT → *You have explored an algebraic and geometric method of finding a line of best fit. Now you will use a graphing utility to find a line of best fit called the regression line.*

The most common method used in science for finding a line of best fit is called **linear regression.** This method involves more calculations than the median-median method and generally yields a different line of best fit, called the **regression line.** Because of the calculations involved, computers and calculators are especially well suited to use this method.

Most graphing utilities allow you to enter data, draw a scatter plot, and find the regression line from the statistics menu (STAT). Some are programmed to find both the regression line and the median-median line.

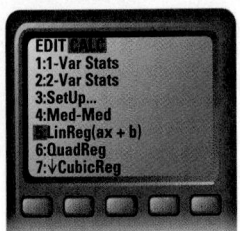

The data show the likely remaining years for people of different ages in 1990. Use a graphing utility to find the equations of the regression line and the median-median line. Graph each equation along with a scatter plot of the data and compare the two linear models. Then, using each model, give the likely remaining years of a 17-year-old.

Enter the data in the statistics menu. Then choose an appropriate window size to draw a scatter plot.

Age (1990)	Remaining Years
1	75.1
5	71.2
10	66.3
15	61.3
20	56.6
25	51.9
30	47.2
35	42.6
40	38.0
45	33.4
50	29.0
55	24.8
60	20.8
65	17.2
70	13.9
75	10.9
80	8.3

Xmin = 0
Xmax = 94
Xscl = 10
Ymin = 0
Ymax = 100
Yscl = 10

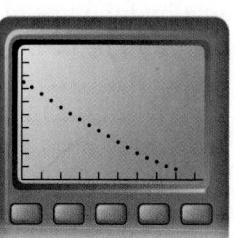

Enter the equation of the regression line and graph it along with the scatter plot. Then trace to find the y-value when $x = 17$.

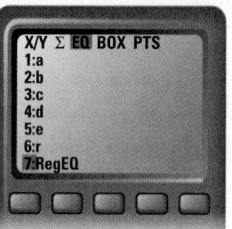

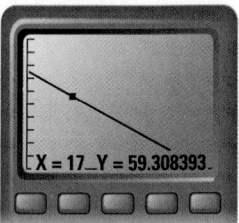

Regression line: $y = -0.86669049611754x + 74.04213105$

Then do the same for the equation of the median-median line.

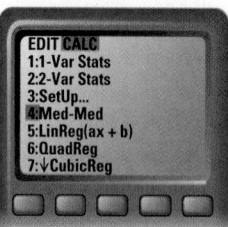

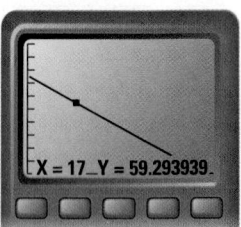

Median-median line: $y = -0.87727272727273x + 74.20757575$

The equations of the regression line and median-median line are different, but both lines fit the data very well. Both models indicate that a 17-year-old is likely to live about 59.3 more years.

1. Do you think the models in the Example are valid for ages above 90 years? Explain.

Have you ever done *the wave* at a sporting event? How long do you think it takes for a row of 10 people to do the wave? 20 people? *x* number of people? Here's your chance to find out!

EXPLORE: DO THE WAVE!

MATERIALS

Graphing utility
Stopwatch

1. Guess how long it would take 40 people in a row to do the wave.

2. Arrange chairs in a row and decide at which end the wave will begin. Agree on someone to be the timer and three or more students to sit together in the chairs.

3. When everyone is ready, the timer will say "GO," and the first seated student will quickly stand, raise her hands, drop her hands, and then sit down. When she finishes, the next student begins, continuing until the wave is completed and the last student is again seated. Record the number of students seated and the total time it took to complete the wave.

4. Repeat Steps 2 and 3 for at least five different numbers of students.

> **Problem-Solving Tip**
>
> Make an organized list of your data.

5. Find the equation of the regression line or median-median line that models wave time as a function of number of people.

6. Use your model to predict how long the wave would take for 40 people seated at a real sporting event. How does this compare with your initial guess?

TRY IT

a. Use a graphing utility to find the equation of the regression line for these data: (1, 2), (3, 5), (6, 13), (7, 15), (10, 19), (12, 24).

Linear regression is well suited to many technologies and the median-median method is straightforward to calculate by hand. Both methods are excellent for fitting lines to data with a positive or negative association.

1. Describe some data from your life that a line could help to model.
2. Do you think data is always best fit with a line? Explain.
3. Why is it useful to have more than one method of fitting lines to data?

Exercises

CORE

1. **Getting Started** Which linear equation fits these data best:
   $(2, 6), (4, 5), (5, 3), (6, 1), (8, 0)$?
   (a) $y = -3x + 2$ (b) $y = -x + 8$ (c) $y = x + 2$

2. A line that is *visually* fit to a scatter plot of data is called a ____.

3. **a.** Make a scatter plot of the data.
   b. Draw a trend line and find its equation.
   c. Find the equation of the regression line and graph it on the scatter plot.
   d. Find the equation of the median-median line and graph it on the scatter plot.
   e. Compare the equations and lines. Do they each fit the data well? Use each equation to predict the value of y when $x = 20$.

x	y
2	5
5	8
8	12
10	15
13	20
15	23

4. An equation written in the form $y = mx + b$ is in ____ form.

5. **It's a Growing World** The data show the increase in the world population over a 300-year period.
   a. Use your graphing utility to draw a scatter plot of the data.
   b. Find the equation of the regression line for the data. Graph the regression line along with the scatter plot. Does the regression line fit the data well?
   c. Find the equation of the median-median line for the data. Graph the median-median line.
   d. Compare the median-median line of best fit and the regression line of best fit for these data.
   e. Use each equation to predict the population of the world in the year 2020.

Year	Population (in millions)
1650	510
1700	625
1750	710
1800	910
1850	1130
1900	1600
1950	2510

Describe data that each person could model with a line of best fit. Tell what predictions could be made using the line.

6. the coach of the track team

7. the head of the purchasing department for a school district

8. a NASA engineer

9. a store owner

Solve each equation.

10. $9x = -81$

11. $15y + 13 = -32$

12. $\frac{c}{3} - 5 = 33$

Copy and complete each statement using $>$, $<$, or $=$.

13. -8 ____ -10

14. $\frac{8}{3}$ ____ $2\frac{1}{3}$

15. 6.8 ____ 6.69

MORE PRACTICE

16. a. Find the equations of the regression line and the median-median line for these data: (4, 5), (7, 5), (8, 1.5), (8, 4), (8.5, 4), (10, 2), (11, 5.5), (13, 3).
   b. Use a graphing utility to make a scatter plot of the data and graph both equations.
   c. Use each equation to predict the value of y when $x = 5$.

17. a. Find the equations of the regression line and the median-median line for these data: (2, 30), (6, 10), (4, 50), (4, 20), (2, 50), (3, 30), (6, 30), (2, 40), (8, 20).
   b. Use a Graphing Utility Make a scatter plot of the data and graph both equations.
   c. Use each equation to predict the value of y when $x = 10$.

18. Study Time Mr. Osipow's gymnastics team recorded the number of hours each athlete practiced the floor exercise the week before a meet and the score each received at the meet.
   a. Find the equation of the regression line for the data.
   b. Use the regression equation to predict the score a gymnast might expect to earn when practicing 16 hours per week. Do you think all gymnasts who practice 16 hours will earn this score? Explain.
   c. A new member of the class practiced 14.5 hours and earned a score of 4.25. Does this data fit the regression line? Does it have to? Explain.
   d. How would the line of best fit for these data be helpful to the coach? Explain.

Practice Hours	Score
4	4.25
12	5.50
8	4.75
6	4.75
10	5.25
8	4.50
16	5.50
6	4.75
20	5.75
14	5.50

MORE MATH REASONING

19. Head and Foot

a. Make a scatter plot of the data on a graphing utility.

b. Find the equation of the regression line and graph it with the scatter plot.

c. Suppose the data point (70, 9) is added to the set. Do you think this data point will change the line of best fit? Why or why not?

d. Add the data point (70, 9) to the original set of data. Find the equation of the regression line again. Compare this equation to the equation in **b** and tell whether the regression line changed.

Height (in.)	Shoe Size
60	6
64	7
63	$7\frac{1}{2}$
68	9
65	7
64	8
67	$8\frac{1}{2}$
66	8
58	5
61	$6\frac{1}{2}$

20. Regression Formula

The formula for the equation of the regression line of any set of data involves several means. Let $\bar{x}$ and $\bar{y}$ equal the means of the x- and y-values. Let $\overline{x^2}$ and $\overline{y^2}$ equal the means of the squares of the x- and y-values. And let $\overline{xy}$ equal the mean of the values of xy.

Choose data you've worked with before. Find each of the means given above. Then use the following formula to find the equation of the regression line.

Regression formula: $\quad y = mx + b$

where $m = \dfrac{\overline{xy} - (\bar{x})(\bar{y})}{\overline{x^2} - (\bar{x})^2}$ and $b = \dfrac{\bar{y}(\overline{x^2}) - \bar{x}(\overline{xy})}{\overline{x^2} - (\bar{x})^2}$

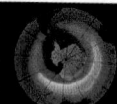

2-2
PART D Making Connections

· ·

← CONNECT → *You have learned three methods of fitting lines to data and have used the equations of the lines to make predictions.*

Lines of best fit allow us to *see* beyond a current set of data and predict future trends. One such trend is the increasing concentration of the greenhouse gas carbon dioxide (CO_2) in our atmosphere. Now you will analyze some real data on average carbon dioxide levels.

EXPLORE: THE RISE OF CO₂

These data give the average annual atmospheric concentrations of carbon dioxide in parts per million, by volume, as measured at the Mauna Loa Observatory in Hawaii.

MATERIALS

Graph paper or graphing utility (optional)
Spreadsheet program (optional)

Year	CO_2 Concentration (parts per million)	Year	CO_2 Concentration (parts per million)
1971	326.16	1981	339.75
1972	327.29	1982	340.96
1973	329.51	1983	342.61
1974	330.08	1984	344.25
1975	330.99	1985	345.73
1976	331.98	1986	346.99
1977	333.73	1987	348.79
1978	335.34	1988	351.35
1979	336.68	1989	352.75
1980	338.52	1990	353.95

1. Make a scatter plot of the data. Find a linear model for the carbon dioxide concentrations and graph the line on your scatter plot.
2. Predict the level of CO_2 concentration in 2010. What are some events that could occur before 2010 that might alter the trend and affect the accuracy of your prediction? Explain.

REFLECT

1. Why is it useful to fit a line to a scatter plot of data?
2. What does the slope of a line of best fit tell you about the association of the data?

3. If you were the owner of an ice cream cone factory, what kind of data might you collect and make predictions about using a linear model?

The scatter plot shows the data points (3, 24), (4, 20), (10, 35), (16, 47), (7, 40), (2, 18), (9, 27), and (14, 38) along with the graph of $f(x) = 2x + 15$.

1. Do the data show positive association, negative association, or no association?

2. Explain how the association of the data and the slope of a fitted line are related.

3. Based on the equation of the trend line, what value of y do you expect to get for an x-value of 11?

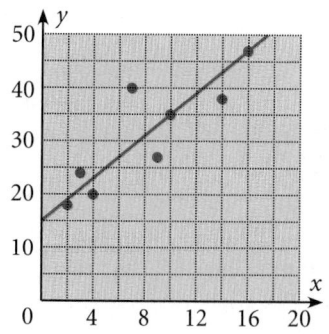

4. What Was It Like? Take a look at this amazing data on the average life expectancy of Americans.
  a. Draw a scatter plot of this data. Draw a trend line.
  b. What is the equation of your trend line?
  c. Use your equation to predict the average life expectancy of a person born in the year 2030.
  d. Describe some reasons that you think may have contributed to the increased life expectancy for Americans.

Social Science

Year of Birth	Life Expectancy
1900	47.3
1910	50.0
1920	54.1
1930	59.7
1940	62.9
1950	68.2
1960	69.7
1970	70.8
1980	73.7
1990	75.4

5. Describe how to find the coordinates of the centroid of a triangle. Give an example to illustrate.

6. Describe how to find the median-median line of best fit for a set of data.

7. Car Time The linear equation $y = 55t + 23$ models the location of an automobile traveling along a state highway, where t denotes time elapsed in hours since the beginning of the trip and y denotes distance from home in miles.
  a. What is the slope of the linear equation? What is the interpretation of slope in this situation?
  b. What is the y-intercept of the linear equation?
  c. Did this trip start from home? Explain how you can tell without transforming the equation.
  d. How would a graph of the real situation differ from the graph of the mathematical model?

8. Find the median-median line for these data: (1, 2), (2, 5), (3, 5), (4, 9), (5, 11), (6, 11), (7, 13), (8, 15), (9, 17).

9. The equation of a line of best fit is given on many graphing utilities as
$y = a + bx$.
a. What does b represent?
b. If $a = 15.67928$ and $b = -0.32761$, where will the line intersect the y-axis?

10. Use a Graphing Utility The table shows data for six months that relate the number of degree days in a month with the number of gallons of heating fuel used. (A degree day is a unit that indicates a change of one degree below the daily average of 65°F. So an average daily temperature of 50 would be 15 degree days.)
a. Find the equation of the regression line.
b. Use the equation to find the expected number of gallons of heating fuel that will be needed for a month of 800 degree days.

Month	Number of Degree Days	Gallons of Fuel
Oct.	217	92
Nov.	572	132
Dec.	1205	203
Jan.	724	169
Feb.	702	125
Mar.	612	80

11. A *curb cut* or ramp built into the sidewalk for wheelchair access must have a maximum rise-to-run ratio of 1:12 by federal law.
a. What positive slopes satisfy federal regulations?
b. If a curb height is 10 inches, what run is needed for the ramp to conform to federal regulations?
c. What do you think is the reason for specifying maximum slope for a curb cut?

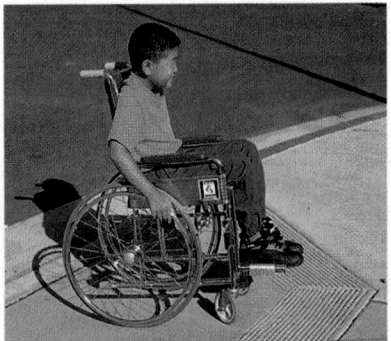

12. Dr. Eisenberg has started prescribing a new medicine with recommended dosages of 2.8 cc for children 4 to 6 years old, 4 cc for 7- to 9-year-olds, and 5.5 cc for 10- to 12-year-olds. Develop a linear model that the doctor could use, instead of these ranges, to find recommended dosages for children between 4 and 12 years of age.

13. Stop Making Sense A research lab is conducting a study on the distance it takes automobiles traveling at various speeds to come to a complete stop. The table shows a driver's reaction distance and braking distance. Reaction distance is the distance the automobile travels from the moment the driver decides to apply the brake to the moment the brake is applied. Braking distance is the distance traveled from the moment the driver applies the brake to the moment the auto comes to a complete stop.

a. Make a scatter plot of speed (x) in mi/hr and reaction distance (y) in feet. Plot speed and braking distance on another coordinate plane.

b. Model both relationships with lines and find their equations. What technique did you use to fit the lines?

c. What are two predictions you could make using your equations?

Speed (mi/hr)	Reaction Distance (ft)	Braking Distance (ft)
10	16.87	6.90
20	32.27	26.40
30	43.12	52.92
40	61.60	100.80
50	80.67	165.00
60	86.24	211.68
70	101.64	291.06
80	123.20	403.20
90	128.70	473.85

Social Science

14. Anthropologists can often use the length of a single human bone to estimate the height of a person when they were living. If an anthropologist knows the length (x) in centimeters of a humerus bone, she can estimate a male's height by using the linear function $y = 2.89x + 70.64$, and she can estimate a female's height by using $y = 2.75x + 71.48$.

a. At an anthropological dig, Professor Gallo discovered two partial skeletons. The male had a humerus 33 cm long and the female had a humerus 31 cm long. Estimate the height of each person when they were living.

b. Explain the significance of the slope of each linear function.

humerus

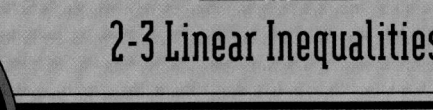

Florence Nightingale

Florence Nightingale had a profound influence on medical care and nursing in the nineteenth century. To this day, her name is associated with caring for others.

When Florence was a young adult, she begged her parents to let her study mathematics. Although they disapproved, she was finally allowed to study mathematics seriously. Soon she was tutoring students in arithmetic, geometry, and algebra, while making a particular effort to encourage girls in their studies.

Nightingale trained as a nurse in Germany and, when the Crimean War broke out in 1854, volunteered her nursing services. As head nurse, she found more men dying from fever and infection than from battle wounds. Enforcing sanitary regulations and special diets, Florence reduced the death rate in hospitals from 45% to 2%.

At the close of the war, Florence was given £50,000 (British pounds sterling) to found the Nightingale School for Nurses in England. The founding of this school marked the beginning of professional education in nursing. The school encouraged high standards of learning and raised the stature of the nursing profession.

Florence Nightingale's mathematical and medical excellence and devotion to public service have stood as a positive role model for those in the medical profession.

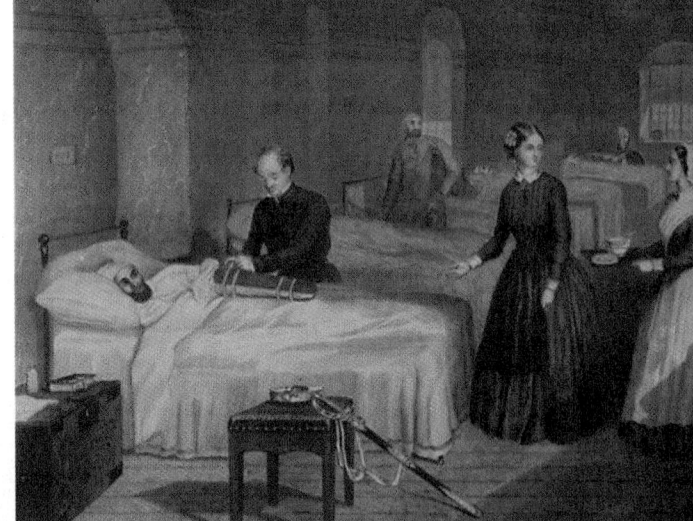

1. Describe how doctors and nurses might use mathematics to improve health care.
2. How are birth rates and death rates calculated?
3. Give an example of a probability that could be used in the health care profession.

One-Variable Inequalities

← C O N N E C T → *You've solved equations with one variable. Now you will solve and graph inequalities with one variable using properties similar to those that are used to solve equations.*

Many real-life situations involve minimum requirements or other limitations that can be modeled with **inequalities.** Inequalities allow us to compare quantities that typically have unequal values. The credit card and banking industries deal with inequalities on a daily basis.

Recall that an **inequality** consists of two expressions separated by an inequality symbol. The symbol $<$ means *is less than;* $>$ means *is greater than;* $\leq$ means *is less than or equal to;* and $\geq$ means *is greater than or equal to.* The **solutions of an inequality** are the variable values that make the inequality true and can be graphed much like solutions of equations. The solutions of a one-variable inequality are graphed on a number line.

The graph shows the solutions of $x > 30$. The open dot at the **boundary point** $x = 30$ indicates that 30 is *not* a solution. A solid dot is used with the symbols $\geq$ and $\leq$.

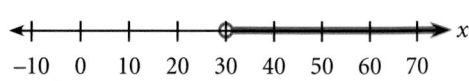

Just as you use properties of equality to help you solve equations, you can use properties of *inequalities* to help you solve inequalities. These properties are similar to the properties of equality, but something unexpected occurs when you multiply an inequality by a negative number: the inequality *reverses*! For example, $2 < 3$, but when you multiply both sides by -1, the inequality switches to $-2 > -3$.

ADDITION PROPERTY OF INEQUALITIES

For any real numbers a, b, and c, if $a > b$, then $a + c > b + c$.

MULTIPLICATION PROPERTY OF INEQUALITIES

For any real numbers a, b, and c, if $a > b$, then

$ac > bc$ if $c > 0$ and

$ac < bc$ if $c < 0$.

Combining these properties with the property of equality shows that the properties of inequalities are also true if $<$ is replaced with $\leq$ and $>$ is replaced with $\geq$.

1. Frank is at the store to pick up supplies for the athletic department. He must pick up 50 bandages and 3 ice packs, while spending at most $12. Prices vary for the different ice packs, but every brand of bandage costs $4.50 for 50. How much can Frank spend for each ice pack and keep within the budget?

Let x be the price of an ice pack.

$3x + 4.50 \le 12$	The total cost is at most $12.
$3x \le 7.50$	Subtract 4.50 from both sides.
$x \le 2.50$	Divide both sides by 3.

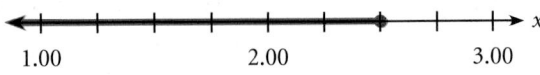

Frank can spend up to $2.50 per ice pack.

WHAT DO **YOU** THINK?

Solve $4 - 3p > 2p + 26$.

Andrea thinks...

I'll subtract 4 from both sides and then collect the variable terms on the left.

$$4 - 3p > 2p + 26$$
$$-3p > 2p + 22$$
$$-5p > 22$$

Now I'll divide by -5 and flip the inequality symbol.

$$p < -\frac{22}{5}$$

Jacy thinks...

I'll add $3p$ to both sides and collect the variable terms on the right.

$$4 - 3p > 2p + 26$$
$$4 > 5p + 26$$
$$-22 > 5p$$

Now I'll divide by 5. Since 5 is positive, the inequality symbol doesn't change.

$$-\frac{22}{5} > p$$

TRY IT

Solve and graph each inequality.

a. $2x - 5 \ge 11$ **b.** $-3s + 1.4 > 5$ **c.** $10w + 7 < 4(w - 2)$

In many situations, quantities are limited by more than one inequality. Now you will investigate how combining inequalities affects the graph of their solutions.

On some highways, there is a maximum speed limit of 65 miles per hour and a minimum speed limit of 45 miles per hour. Driving too slowly can be as hazardous as speeding.

1. Write two inequalities, one for each speed restriction. Graph each inequality.
2. Make a new graph of the speeds that satisfy *both* inequalities. How does this graph compare with the others?
3. Write two new inequalities, one for speeds that are faster than allowed and one for speeds that are slower than allowed. Graph each inequality.
4. Make a new graph of speeds that are either too fast *or* too slow. How does this graph compare with the others?
5. Describe how combining two inequalities so that *both* are true affects the graph of their solutions. Then describe how combining two inequalities so that *either* is true affects the graph of their solutions.

A **compound inequality** is the result of combining two inequalities with *and* or with *or*. For one inequality *and* another to be true, *both* inequalities must be true. So, the solutions of the compound inequality are the solutions that are common to both inequalities.

$-3 \leq x$ and $x < 2$

This compound inequality can also be written as $-3 \leq x < 2$.

For one inequality *or* another to be true, *either* inequality can be true. So, the solutions of the compound inequality are the combined solutions of the two inequalities.

$x < -2$ or $x \geq 1$

CONSIDER

1. Is it possible to write a compound inequality with no solutions? If so, give an example. If not, explain why it is impossible.
2. Is it possible to write a compound inequality for which every real number is a solution? If so, give an example. If not, explain why it is impossible.

A compound inequality written compactly, like $-3 \leq x < 2$, can always be written using *and*. There is no shorthand for compound inequalities with *or*.

EXAMPLE

2. Solve and graph the compound inequality $-3 < 1 - 2x \leq 9$.

$$-3 < 1 - 2x \leq 9$$
$$-4 < -2x \leq 8 \qquad \text{Subtract 1 from each expression.}$$
$$2 > x \geq -4 \qquad \text{Divide each expression by } -2 \text{ and}$$
$$\qquad \qquad \qquad \text{reverse the inequality signs.}$$

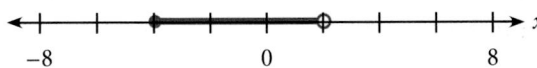

TRY IT

Solve and graph each compound inequality.

d. $-2 \leq 3x + 1 < 16$ **e.** $2x < -4$ or $3x > 27$

Inequalities are so common in life that you may not recognize them. When a menu says you must tip *at least 15%* for all groups of *eight or more,* you can clearly see the two inequalities.

REFLECT

1. Translate each phrase into an inequality symbol.
    a. at least   **b.** at most   **c.** no more than
2. How are the properties of inequalities similar to the properties of equality? How are they different?
3. When is it necessary to reverse the symbol in an inequality?

Exercises

CORE

1. Getting Started Match each inequality with its graph.

a. $x < -2$ **i.**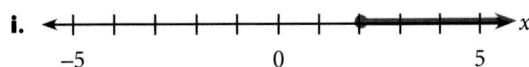

b. $x \geq 2$ **ii.**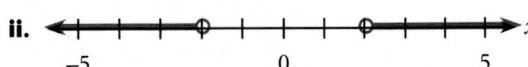

c. $-2 \leq x \leq 2$ **iii.**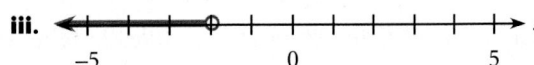

d. $x < -2$ or $x > 2$ **iv.**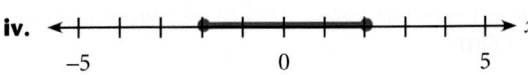

2. Which inequality below is not *equivalent* to $-3x + 12 \geq 6x$? That is, which inequality does not have all the same solutions as the given inequality?
(a) $-9x \geq -12$ (b) $4 - x \geq 2x$ (c) $x - 4 \leq -2x$ (d) $12 \leq 9x$ (e) not here

Solve and graph each inequality.

3. $3x < 9$

4. $3t + 5 < 14$

5. $10 - 1.8x > 3.4 + 9.2x$

6. $\frac{3}{4}x + 2 \leq \frac{5}{6}x + \frac{1}{2}$

7. $3(v - 6) - 12(v + 1) \geq 5$

8. $5p - 1 \geq 3(p - 2)$

9. Making Faces A cosmetologist makes a base salary of $225 per week plus 42.5% of the revenues from facials. What amounts of revenue would give the cosmetologist a weekly income of $500 or more?

10. Yoshi's method of solving inequalities is to solve the related *equality* to find the boundary point. Then he tests a point on one side of the boundary point to see which side the graph is on. Use his method to solve the inequality $2 - 3x > x + 22$.

   a. What is the boundary point of $2 - 3x > x + 22$? Should the boundary point be graphed as a solid dot or an open dot?

   b. Choose another point and test it in the inequality. Is the inequality true? Should you shade the graph on that side of the boundary point or on the opposite side?

   c. Solve the inequality using the properties of inequalities and verify that Yoshi's method gives the correct solution.

Solve and graph each compound inequality.

11. $x > -7$ and $x \leq 4$

12. $r \leq -7$ or $r > 4$

13. $1 \leq 3 - 8y \leq 7$

14. $-5 \leq 3z + 5 < 2$

15. $3.5x < -4.2$ or $14 - 5x < 0$

16. $2t - 1 \geq 9$ and $3t < 24$

17. Faster Than a Speeding Bullet The speed of supersonic aircraft is given in terms of the ratio of the speed of the aircraft (v) to the speed of sound (s), which is about 740 mi/hr. This ratio is called the *Mach number,* named after Austrian physicist Ernst Mach.

   a. Write a compound inequality for v, the aircraft speed in mi/hr, for a supersonic jet with an optimal speed range that is from Mach 1.5 to Mach 2.5.

   b. Write another inequality for the non-optimal speeds for this jet.

18. Solve the compound inequality $2x + 1 < 7$ and $4 - x \leq -1$. What is unusual about the solution set of this compound inequality?

19. Solve the compound inequality $3x - 5 \geq 4$ or $6(x - 2) + 1 < 13$. What is unusual about the solution set of this compound inequality?

20. How Cool The radiator of an automobile contains 16 liters of coolant and water. The mixture is 30% coolant and 70% water. What amounts of the mixture could be drained and replaced with pure coolant so that the mixture would be at least 50% coolant?

21. The following are the Kelvin temperature ranges on the surfaces of three planets:

   i. $103 \le K \le 623$ **ii.** $185 \le K \le 321$ **iii.** $187 \le K \le 244$

   a. The formula that expresses Kelvin temperature (K) as a function of Fahrenheit temperature (F) is $K = \frac{5}{9}(F - 32) + 273$. Give the corresponding ranges on the Fahrenheit scale for each of these planets.

   b. Do the temperature ranges for any of these planets offer the prospect of supporting human life? Explain.

   c. What planets do you think are represented here? Why?

 ## LOOK AHEAD

22. What is different about the routes to Transylvania and Frankenburg? What is the same about the routes?

23. What is different about the relationships of -5 and 5 to zero? What is the same about their relationships to zero?

24. You are on Highway 49 somewhere between Christieville and Asimovgrad. Describe your location without giving specific distances from either city.

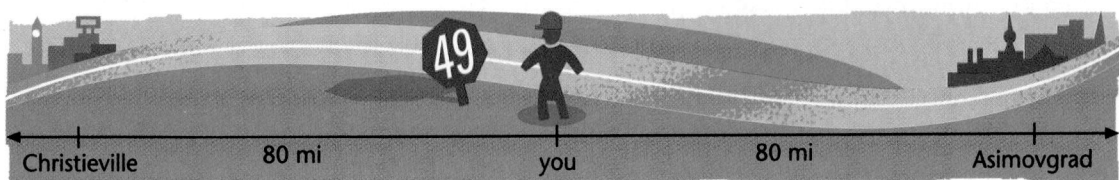

MORE PRACTICE

Solve and graph each inequality.

25. $x - 8 \ge 23$ **26.** $-y < -8$ **27.** $\frac{3}{4}x \le -9$

28. $0.9x > -45$ **29.** $-\frac{1}{3}x - 2 < 1$ **30.** $6(2 - x) + 4x < 48$

Write an inequality to match each graph.

31. 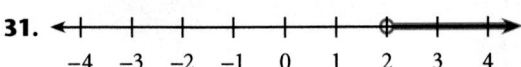   **32.**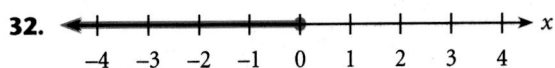

Health

33. Controlling Fat A nutritionist determines that one of her patients should have a daily intake of 2200 calories; no more than 20% of these calories should come from fat. There are 9 calories in each gram of fat. Describe the acceptable number of grams of fat this patient can consume in one day.

Solve and graph each compound inequality.

34. $x + 6 > 20$ or $x - 5 \le 1$ **35.** $5x - 3 \le 12$ and $4x + 7 > 8$

36. $2x - 7 < x < 5 + 2x$ **37.** $\frac{1}{5}x > -3$ or $\frac{5}{2}(x - 4) < 10$

Write a compound inequality to match each graph.

38.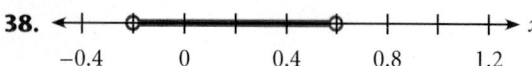

39.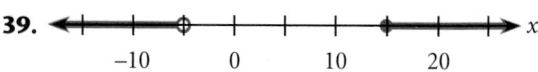

40. Refraction Action An incident ray of light enters a piece of crown glass at an angle (i) between 0° and 40°. It is refracted at an angle (r) between 0° and 25°. Write two compound inequalities describing the possible angle measures of the incident and refracted rays.

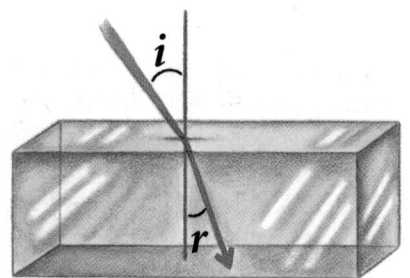

MORE MATH REASONING

41. Write a convincing argument using the properties of inequalities to show that the following statement is true.

For any real numbers a, b, and c, if $a < b$, then

$\frac{a}{c} < \frac{b}{c}$ if $c > 0$ and $\frac{a}{c} > \frac{b}{c}$ if $c < 0$.

42. Use a Graphing Utility Some graphing utilities and spreadsheets allow you to test inequalities using *Boolean algebra*. A Boolean value of 1 is assigned to a true statement, and a value of 0 is assigned to a false statement.

Give the Boolean value of the inequality $1.3x - 8 \leq 7 + x$ for each value of x.

a. $x = 33$ **b.** $x = 61$ **c.** $x = 50$

43. Graph the compound inequality $-2 < x \leq 5$ for each domain of x. Then describe how the choice of domain can affect the solutions and graph of an inequality.
a. {the real numbers}
b. {the integers}
c. {the positive real numbers}
d. {the positive integers}

44. At 12 midnight, the center of hurricane Jaime is 360 miles off the Florida coast. The hurricane has a radius of 125 miles. Its eye, or calm center, has a diameter of 20 miles. The hurricane is approaching Miami at a rate of 30 miles per hour. During what times will hurricane-force winds be hitting the Miami coast?

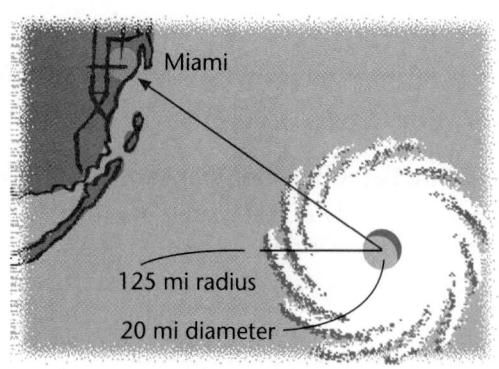

Miami

125 mi radius

20 mi diameter

Inequalities and Absolute Value

← **CONNECT** → *You have graphed inequalities and compound inequalities. Now you will solve and graph absolute value equations and inequalities. You will see how absolute value inequalities can describe distances and tolerances.*

Many comparisons in life can be described either in terms of an equation or an inequality. This is certainly true when comparing distances.

EXPLORE: CONVENIENCE WITHIN THE LAW

The figure below illustrates a stretch of Highway 51 showing the location of Rogers Elementary School and West High School. The point 0 is the intersection of Main Street with Highway 51. Each unit represents 1000 feet east or west of Main Street.

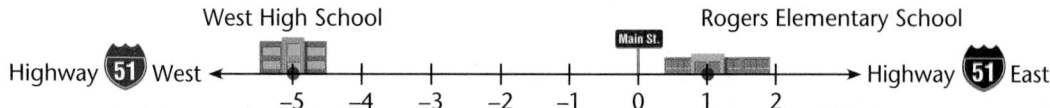

A convenience store chain would like to place a store along Highway 51. However, there is a city ordinance that states:

> "Whereas, by Ordinance 1407, Section 532 of the Public Welfare Code, no establishment selling alcohol or tobacco products shall be located within 2000 feet of any public/private school, playground, or other leisure areas planned for youths less than 18 years old."

1. Does the relative direction of the school and the liquor/tobacco-selling establishment matter in the above ordinance?
2. How would you describe the places along Highway 51 that are acceptable locations for a convenience store selling alcohol or tobacco?
3. How do you know that the locations you named are within the law?
4. Suppose a playground is placed at the intersection of Main Street and Highway 51. How would this change the acceptable locations of the convenience store?

The **absolute value** of a number can be thought of as its *distance* from 0 on a number line. Any positive number and any negative number are each a positive distance from 0. *The absolute value is concerned with distance rather than direction.*

> The **absolute value** of any real number (a), written as $|a|$, is defined as:
>
> $$|a| = a, \text{ if } a \geq 0$$
>
> $$|a| = -a, \text{ if } a < 0$$

1. If $a < 0$, does $-a$ represent a positive number or a negative number? Explain.

There are two values that have a distance of 3 from 0. They are 3 and -3. So, if $|x| = 3$, then $x = 3$ or $x = -3$.

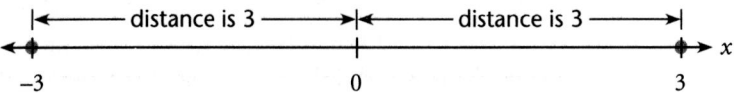

In order to solve an absolute value equation like $|x - 5| = 3$, solve the *compound equation* $x - 5 = 3$ or $x - 5 = -3$.

EXAMPLE

1. Solve and graph $|x - 5| = 3$.

$$|x - 5| = 3$$
$$x - 5 = -3 \text{ or } x - 5 = 3$$
$$x = 2 \quad \text{or} \qquad x = 8 \qquad \text{Add 5 to both sides of each equation.}$$

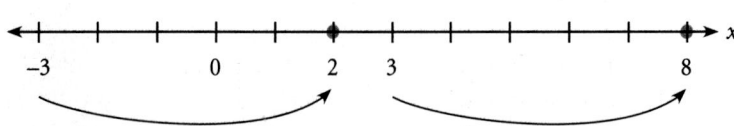

Each solution is translated 5 units to the right.

The solutions of $|x - 5| = 3$ are the **translations** of the solutions of $|x| = 3$, five units to the right.

The graph of all numbers with distance *less than 5* from 0 is shown.

This is the graph of $|x| < 5$. This graph can also be described as the compound inequality $x > -5$ and $x < 5$, which can be written as $-5 < x < 5$.

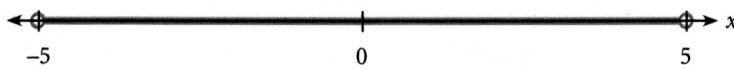

TRY IT

The graph of all numbers whose distance from 0 is greater than or equal to 5 is shown. We can write this as $|x| \geq 5$.

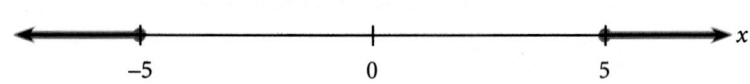

a. Write a compound inequality that describes this graph.

We can solve more complex absolute value inequalities by first rewriting them as compound inequalities.

EXAMPLE

2. Solve and graph the inequality $|x + 8| \geq 5$.

$$|x + 8| \geq 5$$

$x + 8 \leq -5$	or	$x + 8 \geq 5$
$x \leq -13$	or	$x \geq -3$

Subtract 8 from both sides of each inequality.

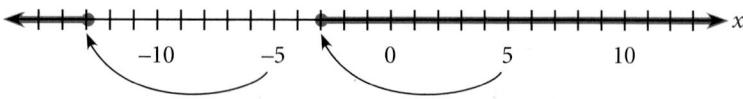

Each solution is translated 8 units to the left.

The solutions of $|x + 8| \geq 5$ are a translation of the solutions of $|x| \geq 5$ eight units to the left.

Maximum and minimum values play an important part in manufacturing and medicine. Manufacturers often have limits, called *tolerances,* that define acceptable margins for error in their products. Precision work in machine shops can require tolerances of 0.001 inch or even less. Doctors write prescriptions for medicines based on a range of recommended dosages.

EXAMPLE

3. Dr. Phillips usually writes prescriptions for a non-steroidal, anti-inflammatory medicine based on an 875-mg dosage per day. But she may vary this dosage for individual patients by up to 375 mg. What is the range of dosages she writes for this medicine?

$|x - 875|$ represents the difference between 875 mg and the actual amount prescribed.

So, $|x - 875| \leq 375$ states that the dosage is within 375 mg of 875 mg.

Solve as a compound inequality.

$x - 875 \geq -375$ and $x - 875 \leq 375$
    $x \geq 500$ and $x \leq 1250$ Add 875 to both sides of each inequality.

$500 \leq x \leq 1250$

The doctor prescribes daily dosages from 500 mg to 1250 mg.

Solve and graph each absolute value inequality.

b. $|x| > 5$ **c.** $|x - 3| > 5$ **d.** $|-x + 3| \le 4$

e. $|2x| < 2$ **f.** $|3x + 7| \ge 4$ **g.** $|x + 4| - 4 \ge 3$

REFLECT

1. What is the relationship between $|x| < 9$, $|x - 3| < 9$, and $|x + 5| < 9$?

2. What is the relationship between $|x| \ge 5$ and $|2x| \ge 5$?

3. The distance of x from -4 must be greater than or equal to 7. Write this requirement as an absolute value inequality.

4. The equation $|x - h| = c$ can be interpreted as either "x is at a distance c units from h" or as "x is c or $-c$ translated h units to the right." Show that both interpretations are accurate for the solutions of $|x - 10| = 3$.

Exercises

CORE

1. Getting Started Write an absolute value equation or inequality for each statement.

a. x is 3 units from zero on the number line.

b. x is less than or equal to 5 units from 0 on the number line.

c. x is more than 8 units from 0 on the number line.

2. Evaluate each absolute value.

a. $|4|$ **b.** $|-7|$ **c.** $|0|$ **d.** $|-0.4|$

Solve and graph each equation. (Hint: First isolate the absolute value on one side.)

3. $|x| = 8$ **4.** $|x - 1| = 8$ **5.** $|x + 3| = 8$

6. $|4x| = 8$ **7.** $|-2x| = 8$ **8.** $|3x + 1| = 8$

9. $3|2x - 3| = 15$ **10.** $|4 - 3x| + 1 = 6$ **11.** $|5 - (x - 3)| = 1$

12. a. Solve and graph the three equations: $|x| = 6$, $|x + 2| = 6$, and $|x - 2| = 6$.

     b. Look for patterns and describe how their solutions are related.

Decide if each statement is always, sometimes, or never true.

13. The absolute value of a number is its opposite.

14. The absolute value of a number is negative.

Solve and graph each inequality.

15. $|x - 2| < 4$ **16.** $|x + 2| \geq 3$ **17.** $-3|x| - 4 < 9$

18. $|-3x| > 6$ **19.** $|5x + 16| \leq 11$ **20.** $|4 - 3x| > 13$

21. Which of the following represents the restrictions on the highway speed of a vehicle if the minimum speed limit is 45 miles per hour and the maximum speed limit is 65 miles per hour?
(a) $|x - 55| \geq 10$ (b) $|x - 10| \leq 55$ (c) $|x - 45| \leq 20$
(d) $|x - 55| \leq 10$ (e) not here

Solve and graph each inequality.

22. $|3(x - 2)| \leq 4$ **23.** $3|x - 2| \leq 4$ **24.** $|3x| - 2 \leq 4$

25. $|-4x - 1| - 7 > 4$ **26.** $|x - 2(x + 3)| \geq 5$ **27.** $-5|x - 0.4| < 8$

28. Refer to the graph shown.

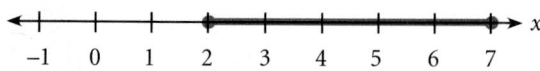

a. What is the midpoint of the segment?
b. What is the distance from the midpoint to either endpoint?
c. Write an absolute value inequality that represents the points on the graph.

Solve and graph each equation or inequality.

29. $12 \leq |-5x - 1|$ **30.** $12 > -|x| + 15$ **31.** $10 = 2|5x|$

32. $|-4x| \geq 16$ **33.** $|-8x + 7| = 16$ **34.** $|4x| - 8 < 16$

35. Is the solution of the absolute value inequality $|3x| < 4$ the same as the solution of the absolute value inequality $|-3x| < 4$? Explain.

36. Is the solution of the absolute value inequality $|2x| + 3 > 6$ the same as the solution of the absolute value inequality $|2x + 3| > 6$? Explain.

37. Manufacturing Limits The specifications for a piston cylinder call for a diameter of 6 ± 0.01 inches. ($\pm$ is read "plus or minus.")

a. What would be the largest diameter allowed for the cylinder? the smallest?
b. Write an absolute value inequality expressing when the diameter (d) of a cylinder, as described above, is within the tolerance.
c. A lathe is set to produce a cylindrical dowel with diameter d such that $|d - \frac{5}{8}| \leq \frac{1}{64}$ in. Write the specifications of the dowel diameter using $\pm$ notation.

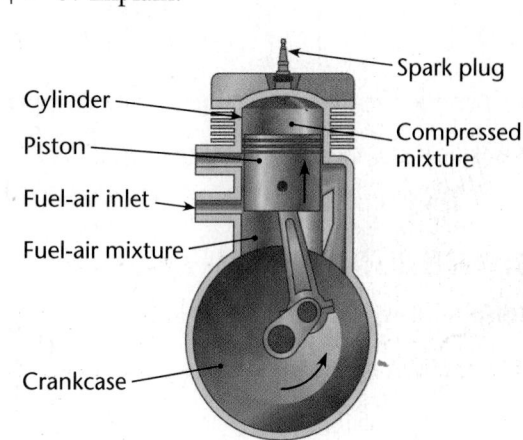

Spark plug
Cylinder
Compressed mixture
Piston
Fuel-air inlet
Fuel-air mixture
Crankcase

Write an absolute value equation or inequality for each graph.

38.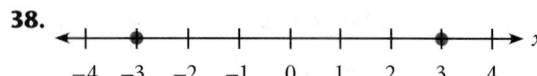

39.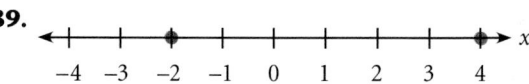

40.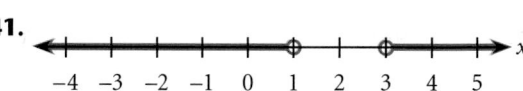

41.

42. Triangle Inequality The Triangle Inequality states that the sum of the lengths of any two sides of a triangle must be greater than the length of the third side.

   a. Draw a diagram and label sides *a*, *b*, and *c*. Write three different inequalities that illustrate this theorem.

   b. Can a triangle have side lengths of 4 ft, 5 ft, and 6 ft? Explain.

   c. Can a triangle have side lengths of 2 cm, 3 cm, and 5 cm? Explain.

43. Calibration Station To protect consumers, state agencies periodically inspect gasoline pumps for accuracy. A state inspection seal indicates that a gasoline pump is accurate to within a tenth of a gallon. Gasoline costs $1.19 per gallon. You fill up your auto's gas tank and the amount comes to $12.36.

   a. Write and solve an absolute value inequality to find the possible number of gallons you actually receive.

   b. How much might you be undercharged or overcharged due to the error in the pump?

 **LOOK BACK**

44. Add the matrices. [1-3]

$$\begin{bmatrix} 5 & -2 & 6 \\ 6 & 0 & 1 \\ 9 & 1 & -7 \end{bmatrix} + \begin{bmatrix} 7 & -1 & -1 \\ -1 & 5 & 11 \\ 8 & 0 & -4 \end{bmatrix}$$

45. Decide if each real number is rational or irrational. [Previous course]

   a. 5.4   **b.** π **c.** $\frac{2}{7}$ **d.** 0.22222…

MORE PRACTICE

Solve and graph each equation.

46. $|x + 3| = 7$ **47.** $|x - 5| = 1$ **48.** $|2 - x| = 3$

49. $|-2x| = 5$ **50.** $|4x| = 12$ **51.** $|-x| = 5$

52. $|3x - 1| = 2$ **53.** $|2x + 5| = 11$ **54.** $|1.2x - 4.3| = 0.8$

Write an equivalent absolute value sentence for each compound sentence.

55. $x = -1.5$ or $x = 1.5$

56. $r + 5 \le -12$ or $r + 5 \ge 12$

57. $-1 < x < 5$

58. $t - 4 < -6$ or $t - 4 > 6$

Solve and graph each absolute value inequality.

59. $|x - 1| > 4$

60. $|7x| \le 42$

61. $|x + 8| > 3$

62. $|2x - 1.2| < 9$

63. $|-3x| > 15$

64. $|4 - x| < 14$

65. $|3(4p - 1)| < 0$

66. $|8 - 3x| \le 0.6$

67. $|0.1t - 1.5| > 2.1$

68. $|2x - 4| \ge 13$

69. Hole Diameters A hole made by a machine is specified to have a diameter of 2.5 cm ± 0.02 cm. Write an absolute value inequality expressing the acceptable diameters for the hole.

70. Lab Conditions The temperature in a laboratory must not deviate from 23°C by more than 5°. Write this restriction on the temperature (t) as an absolute value inequality.

Solve and graph each equation or inequality.

71. $5 = |x + 9|$

72. $18 \le 9|x - 10|$

73. $10 = |2 - x| + 1$

74. $-32 = -8|-4x + 1|$

75. $|6x - 3| < 12$

76. $|6x| - 3 < 12$

77. $-7 < -4|x|$

78. $-7 = -4|x| + 3$

79. $-7 \ge -|4x + 3|$

80. $2|3y - 1| + 4 > 10$

MORE MATH REASONING

81. Survey Says... Public opinion polls often state that the polls are accurate within plus or minus 3%. What does this mean if a pollster finds that people are against a certain proposal, 44% to 42%?

82. Graph the solution of $|x + 5| < |3x|$.

83. Describe a real-life situation for which the solution of the associated absolute value inequality is the set $\{0, 1, 2, 3, \ldots, 12, 20, 21\}$. Write the absolute value inequality and its domain.

If money is saved by cutting government programs, should the savings be used to cut middle-class taxes, to reduce the deficit, or to increase spending on other government programs?

CUT TAXES	REDUCE DEFICIT	GOVERNMENT PROGRAMS
29%	34%	29%

From a telephone poll of 800 adult Americans by Yankelovich Partners Inc. Sampling error is ±3.5%.

← CONNECT → *You have studied linear functions and one-variable inequalities. Now you will study linear inequalities with two variables. Linear inequalities can help you describe restrictions in real relationships.*

Just as inequalities with one variable can help you describe restrictions on a single quantity, inequalities with *two variables* can help you describe restrictions in relationships between two quantities.

EXPLORE: QUININE QUALITY CONTROL

MATERIALS

Graph paper

Quinine is an important medicine that was first isolated from cinchona bark in 1820. It is especially useful for the control of malarial fever, but it is also found in everyday tonic water.

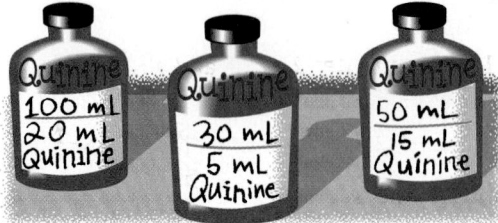

Total Volume (mL)	Quinine Volume (mL)
40	2
30	5
60	6
35	2
40	4
50	20
100	15
40	3
30	3
40	8
50	15
80	8
40	15
100	10

In a lab that makes quinine solution, batches are labeled with the total volume of the solution and the volume of quinine contained in the solution.

1. Graph these points using total volume as the independent variable.

2. A technician must identify all batches with less than 10% quinine. Find and circle the points on your graph that represent batches with less than 10% quinine. Place a star on any points that represent batches with exactly 10% quinine. Describe any patterns you notice in the arrangement of these points.

3. Based on your results, do you think that you can tell, just from its position, whether any point in the plane represents a solution with less than 10% quinine? Explain.

A region on one side of a line in a coordinate plane can be described by a **linear inequality** with two variables. The line is the **boundary line** of the linear inequality. The points in the region, possibly including the line, represent the **solutions of the linear inequality.**

1. Graph $y \geq 2x - 1$.

Graph the boundary line. A solid line shows that the line is part of the graph of the inequality. Test points and shade the region that represents the solutions of the inequality.

$(-4, 4)$ is a solution since $4 \geq 2(-4) - 1$, but $(5, 2)$ is *not* a solution since $2 < 2(5) - 1$.

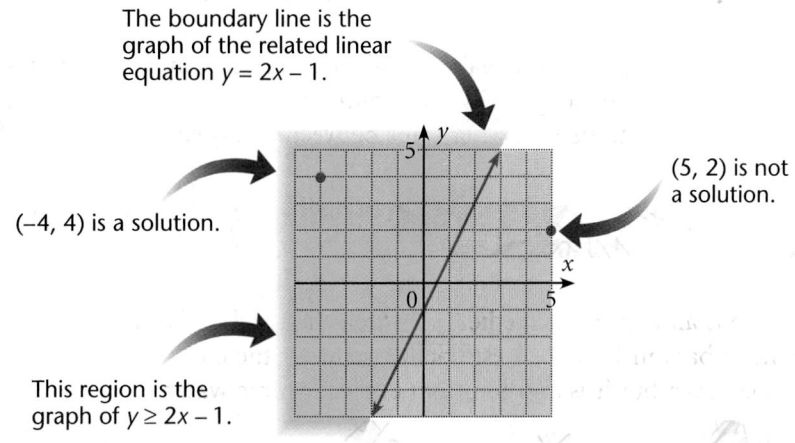

The boundary line is the graph of the related linear equation $y = 2x - 1$.

$(-4, 4)$ is a solution.

$(5, 2)$ is not a solution.

This region is the graph of $y \geq 2x - 1$.

The graph of $y \geq 2x - 1$ is the line $y = 2x - 1$ and all the points in the region above the line.

2. Graph $2x + y < 6$.

The equation of the boundary line is $2x + y = 6$. In y-intercept form, the equation is $y = -2x + 6$.

The strict inequality does not include the equation, so we draw a *dashed* boundary line to show that it is not part of the graph.

$(0, 0)$ is a solution since $2(0) + 0 < 6$. So shade the region below the line.

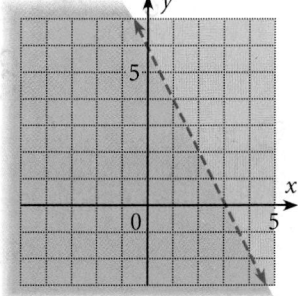

CONSIDER

1. How many test points do you think are necessary to determine which region to shade when you graph a linear inequality? Explain.

TRY IT

Graph each linear inequality.

a. $y < x + 2$　　　　　　**b.** $y \geq -2x - 5$　　　　　　**c.** $2x - 3y \leq 15$

This is the graph of the two-variable inequality $y \geq 3x - 4$.

If we assign y the constant value of 2, we get the one-variable inequality
$2 \geq 3x - 4$.

Solving the one-variable inequality gives:

$2 \geq 3x - 4$
$6 \geq 3x$
$2 \geq x$

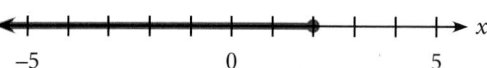

You can see the solution to this one-variable inequality in the graph of the two-variable inequality.

CONSIDER

2. Explain how you could use the graph of the inequality $y \geq 3x - 4$ to solve the one-variable inequality $-1 \geq 3x - 4$.

You can graph absolute value inequalities using almost the same technique you use to graph linear inequalities.

EXAMPLE

3. Graph $y \geq |x - 2|$.

The related equation is $y = |x - 2|$, which represents an **absolute value function.** Recall that an absolute value function has a V-shaped graph.

Plotting points or using a graphing utility yields the graph shown.

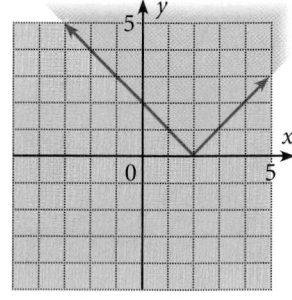

x	-2	-1	0	1	2	3	4
y	4	3	2	1	0	1	2

Testing points just as you do for linear inequalities, you find that the graph of the inequality is the region inside the V.

CONSIDER

3. How are the graphs of $y = x - 2$ and $y = |x - 2|$ similar and how are they different?

This is the graph of the two-variable absolute value inequality $y \leq 4|x + 1| - 3$.

If we assign y the constant value of 1, we get the one-variable inequality $1 \leq 4|x + 1| - 3$.

You can see the solution to this one-variable inequality in the graph of the two-variable inequality.

$x \leq -2$ or $x \geq 0$

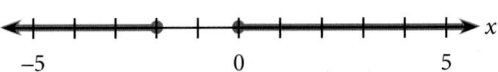

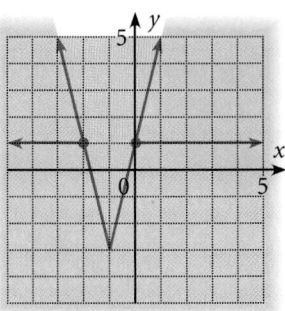

TRY IT

Graph each absolute value inequality.

d. $y < |x - 3|$ **e.** $y \geq 2|x + 1| + 3$

Equations and inequalities with two variables are graphed on a coordinate plane, while equations and inequalities with one variable are graphed on a number line. However, you can often see one-variable solutions hidden within graphs in the plane.

REFLECT

1. Describe how you can determine which region to shade when you graph an inequality.
2. A line in the coordinate plane can be said to divide the plane into three distinct sets of points. What are the three sets?
3. How are the graphs of linear inequalities and two-variable absolute value inequalities similar? How are they different?

Exercises

CORE

1. Getting Started Write an inequality for each graph.

a.

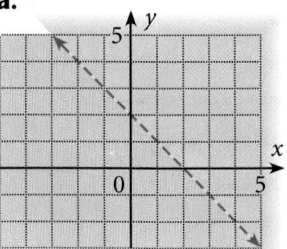

b.

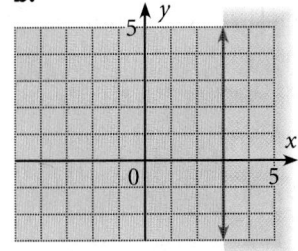

c.

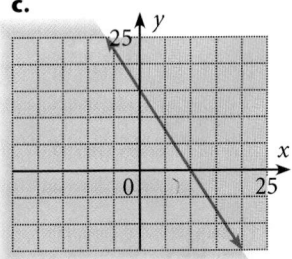

Graph each linear inequality.

2. $y < -2x$ **3.** $y > 3x + 2$ **4.** $y \geq 4$

5. $y \leq -5x$ **6.** $y < x + 2$ **7.** $y \geq 5 - x$

8. $x + y < 1$ **9.** $4x + 2y > 5$ **10.** $y - 3 \leq 2x$

11. Temperature Alert! The inequality $y \geq x + 10.8$ represents the relationship between lethal body temperature (y) for birds and mammals, based upon normal body temperature (x).

   a. The normal temperature of a bird is 104°F. Is a body temperature of 110° lethal for the bird?

   b. The normal temperature of an echidna (a spiny anteater) is 87°F. Is a body temperature of 101°F lethal for this animal?

12. Full Tank Will's car has a mileage rating of 18 mpg (miles per gallon) in the city and 26 mpg on the highway. The maximum capacity of the gasoline tank is 16 gallons. Let x denote the number of city miles and y the number of highway miles.

   a. How many gallons of gasoline are used driving x city miles? y highway miles?

   b. Write an inequality in x and y for the number of gallons of gasoline Will can use without refilling his tank.

13. Use the graph of the linear inequality $y < 3x - 4$ to solve the one-variable inequality $-1 < 3x - 4$. Explain how you used the graph.

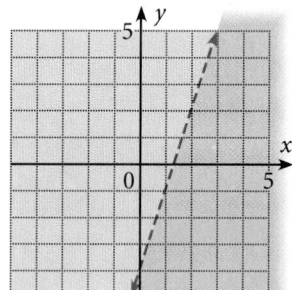

Graph each inequality.

14. $y < |x - 4|$ **15.** $y \geq 3|x|$

16. $y - 3 \geq |x|$ **17.** $y \leq -|5x|$

18. $y < |2x + 2| + 1$ **19.** $y + 1 \geq |5 - x|$

20. Graph and compare the inequalities $y \leq |x|$, $y \leq |x - 4|$, $y \leq |x + 3|$, $y \leq 5|x|$, and $y \leq -0.5|x|$. Explain how the constants a and h in an inequality of the form $y \leq a|x - h|$ affect its graph.

21. Rescue at Sea A volunteer rescue mission is being organized. There are two sizes of boats available: one requires a crew of 2, and the other a crew of 5. Let x represent the number of boats that require 2 crew members each and y represent the number of boats that require 5 crew members each. Write an inequality for the number of boats of each type that can be used if the total number of volunteer crew members is 65.

22. Graph $y \leq 2x + 1$. On the same coordinate plane, graph $y \geq -x + 1$. The region where both graphs overlap should be shaded more heavily than the single-shaded regions. What is true about the points that lie in this overlap region? Explain.

23. How could you describe the first quadrant using linear inequalities? How many linear inequalities are needed?

MORE PRACTICE

Write the inequality for each graph.

24.

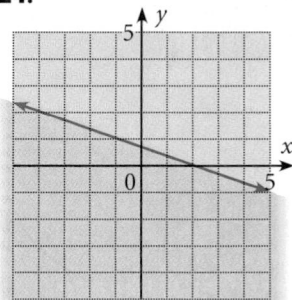

25.

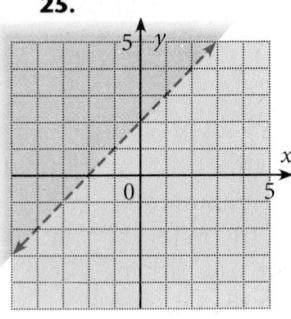

26.

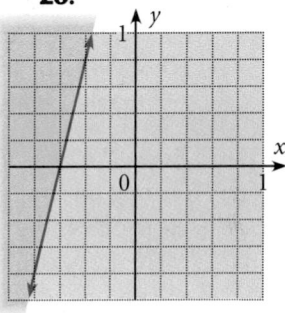

Graph each linear inequality.

27. $y < -2$

28. $y > x + 1$

29. $y \leq 6x$

30. $y > 4 - x$

31. $y \geq -x$

32. $x < 1$

33. $y \geq 2x - 3$

34. $y \leq x + 5$

35. $y > -1$

36. $2x - y < 4$

37. $x + y > -2$

38. $3x + 4y \leq -6$

39. High C Sandy's goal is to take a minimum of 450 units of vitamin C per day. *High CEE* vitamins provide 100 units of vitamin C, while *Happy Balance* vitamins provide 75 units of vitamin C. Write a linear inequality that shows the combinations of *High CEE* and *Happy Balance* tablets that would allow Sandy to meet her goal.

Graph each inequality.

40. $y < |x + 1|$

41. $y + 10 \geq |x + 10|$

42. $y \geq |2x|$

43. $y \leq 5.5 - |x - 3.5|$

44. $y < |x - 2| - 12$

45. $y + 7 \geq |5|$

46. $y \leq 3 - |13x + 13|$

47. $y < |4(x + 3)| + 1$

48. $y \geq |100 - x|$

49. The Play's the Thing! A community performing arts theater has 1200 general admission seats and 200 reserved seats. Let g denote the general admission seats sold and r denote the reserved seats sold. For each scenario given, write an inequality that relates g and r.

a. Attendance for a play is estimated to be at most 900 people.

b. Attendance for a concert is estimated to be at least 500 people.

c. The price of a general admission ticket is $15. The price of a reserved seat ticket is $25. The management must sell at least $500 worth of tickets for a performance to meet expenses.

MORE MATH REASONING

50. Use the graph of the inequality $y < 2|x - 1| - 2$ to solve the one-variable inequality $2 < 2|x - 1| - 2$. Explain how you used the graph.

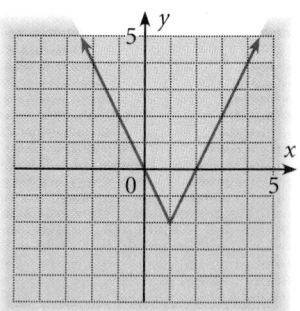

51. The *complement* of region S in a plane is the set of all points in the plane that are not in S. Isaac says he graphs a linear inequality by shading the complement of the region that represents the solutions of each inequality. Any region left unshaded is the solution.

a. Use Isaac's method to sketch the solution set of $y \leq -3x$.

b. Does Isaac's method work in all cases? If yes, explain why it would work for all inequalities. If no, give a counterexample.

52. Nick is planning to start a CD club. He will sell CDs for $11.98 each but will pay $6.25 for each CD returned in trade. He wants to average a profit of at least $7 per CD sold. Should he put a limit on the number of trades he takes? Explain.

53. A random number function on a computer generates a pair of numbers, each between 0 and 10. What is the probability that the numbers are the coordinates of a point in the first quadrant of the graph of the inequality shown at the right?

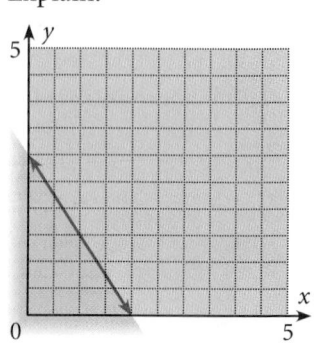

← C O N N E C T → *You have solved and graphed inequalities with one and two variables. You have also solved and graphed absolute value equations and inequalities. Inequalities and absolute values often arise as limitations and tolerances.*

Determining appropriate medical dosages for patients can speed recovery, reduce suffering, and save lives. Inequalities and absolute values are useful models for the restrictions and tolerances inherent in medicine.

EXPLORE: MEDICAL DOSAGES

MATERIALS

Graph paper

Cowling's Rule is a linear model for determining medical dosages for children. If *A* is the recommended dosage of a medicine for an adult, then $C(x) = \frac{A}{24}(x + 1)$ is the recommended dosage for a child *x* years old.

1. According to Cowling's Rule, at what age is it recommended that a child take half of an adult dosage? At what age is it recommended that a child take a full adult dosage? Do you think the model is valid past that age? Explain.
2. It is recommended that adults take at most 650 mg of aspirin in a 4-hour period. Using Cowling's Rule, write a linear inequality with two variables, giving acceptable aspirin dosages within a 4-hour period for children of any age. Graph your inequality.
3. How could you amend your graph to give acceptable aspirin dosages for both children and adults? Explain.

REFLECT

1. How are the symbolic methods for solving one-variable equations and inequalities similar? How are they different?
2. Describe how absolute value inequalities are related to compound inequalities.
3. Explain how the photo suggests the solutions of a linear inequality with two variables.

Self-Assessment

Solve and graph each inequality.

1. $x + 7 > -4$

2. $t + 10 < 8$

3. $5t \leq -15$

4. $2x + 3 \geq -7$

5. $9 - 2x \leq -3$

6. $4x - 2 > 5x + 2$

7. $x < 1$ or $x > 4$

8. $x + 5 > -2$ and $3x + 1 \leq 4$

9. $-2 < x < 3$

10. $x > 2$ or $x > 5$

11. $5x - 2 > 3x + 9$

12. $3 - 2(x - 3) < 4x + 15$

13. Overdose A certain drug comes in 2.5-mg tablets. The maximum dosage recommended for this drug is 40 mg per day. Write an inequality that expresses the restriction on the number of pills that can be taken safely per day. Then solve and graph the inequality. What is the interpretation of the boundary point in this situation?

14. High Wires An electric power line is suspended between two poles 1000 feet apart. What is the probability that a break in the line at a random point is less than 25 feet from a pole?

Solve and graph each absolute value equation or inequality.

15. $|x - 2| = 5$

16. $|3x| = 4$

17. $|x + 1| = 8$

18. $|2x + 8| = 7$

19. $|4 - x| = 2$

20. $|3x - 1| \geq 5$

21. $|x - 3| < 2$

22. $|x + 1| \geq 0$

23. $|2x| \leq -6$

24. $|7 - x| > 3$

25. Pipe Dream A pipe must be made with a diameter of 5.2 cm within a tolerance of 0.3 cm. Write an absolute value inequality that expresses the acceptable diameters. Graph the solutions of the inequality.

26. "Pentacular" Tiles in the shape of regular pentagons, with interior angles measuring 108°, do not *tessellate* (completely cover) a floor without gaps. Write an inequality that explains why three pentagons won't fit together without gaps at a point in a plane.

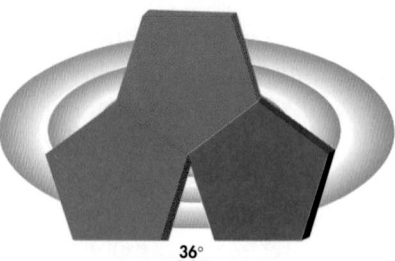

36°
GAP

Write an equation for each line. [2-1]

27. the line through $(-2, 1)$ with slope 3

28. the line through $(-1, 4)$ and $(2, 7)$

Perform the given matrix operations. [1-3]

$$A = \begin{bmatrix} 4 & -6 \\ 5 & 0 \\ -2 & 3 \end{bmatrix} \qquad B = \begin{bmatrix} 4 & -6 \\ 5 & 0 \\ -2 & 3 \end{bmatrix} \qquad C = \begin{bmatrix} 2 & -1 & 3 \\ 2 & -3 & 1 \end{bmatrix}$$

29. $A + B$

30. $-2C$

31. $B - A$

32. Which inequality matches this graph?
   (a) $y > 2x - 3$
   (b) $y < 2x - 3$
   (c) $y \le 3 - 2x$
   (d) $y \ge 3 - 2x$
   (e) not here

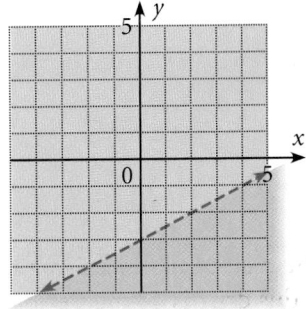

Graph each linear inequality.

33. $y > x - 7$

34. $y \ge 4 - x$

35. $y \le 3x - 1$

36. $x + y \le -4$

37. $2x - 3y > -9$

38. $\frac{x}{4} + \frac{3y}{2} \le 1$

39. The Best Investment Mrs. Kiley decides to invest some of her money in a bond that yields 5% annual interest, and some of her money in a little riskier bond that yields 6% annual interest. Mrs. Kiley wants to earn at least $500 interest per year, but she is worried about the riskier bond.
   a. Write a linear inequality that relates the amounts of money Mrs. Kiley can invest in each bond to earn at least $500 per year.
   b. Graph the inequality.
   c. Can Mrs. Kiley invest $9000 and make her goal without putting most of her investment in the riskier bond? Explain.

40. Wild Horses Adults' tickets at the rodeo sell for $15 and children's tickets sell for $7. The rodeo must take in more than $2100 to make a profit.
   a. Write and graph a linear inequality showing the numbers of each price ticket the rodeo must sell to make a profit.
   b. What do the intercepts on each axis represent for the rodeo?

Chapter 2 Review

Linear functions are useful models for a variety of patterns, trends, and relationships. You've investigated the features of linear functions, equations, and graphs and used them to fit data and model relationships. You've also discovered how restrictions and limitations in the real world can be described by linear inequalities and absolute value equations and inequalities.

KEY TERMS

absolute value [2-3]
absolute value function [2-3]
boundary line [2-3]
boundary point [2-3]
centroid [2-2]
compound inequality [2-3]
direct variation [2-1]
equivalent equations [2-1]
inequality [2-3]

line of best fit [2-2]
linear function [2-1]
linear inequality [2-3]
linear regression [2-2]
literal equation [2-1]
median-median line [2-2]
parallel lines [2-1]
perpendicular lines [2-1]
point-slope form [2-1]

rate of change [2-1]
regression line [2-2]
rise [2-1]
run [2-1]
slope [2-1]
slope-intercept form [2-1]
solution [2-1, 2-3]
translation [2-3]
y-intercept [2-1]

Decide whether each statement is true or false. If the statement is false, change the underlined word or phrase to make it true.

1. The equation $(y - y_1) = m(x - x_1)$ is the y-intercept form of a linear equation.

2. The function $y = kx$, where k is a constant, represents direct variation.

3. The weight per week that a cow grows is an example of a rate of change.

4. The centroid of a triangle is used to find the regression line.

5. The boundary line of a linear inequality may or may not be included in a graph.

CONCEPTS AND APPLICATIONS

6. Roberto's 6-year-old brother Carlos was 4 feet 4 inches tall 6 months ago and is 4 feet 5 inches tall now. Carlos wants to ride the Ferris wheel at the county fair in 3 months, but the minimum height requirement to enter the ride is 4 feet 6 inches. [2-1]
   a. Assuming Carlos is growing at a constant rate, what is his growth rate?
   b. Is Carlos's height directly related to his age? Explain.
   c. At his present growth rate, will Carlos be tall enough to go on the ride in 3 months?

7. Give the slope of each line shown. [2-1]

8. Write a linear equation for each line shown in slope-intercept form. [2-1]

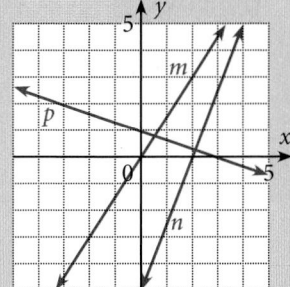

Write an equation for each line. [2-1]

9. with slope $\frac{2}{3}$ and y-intercept -2

10. parallel to $y = 4 - x$ and through $(3, 5)$

11. through points $(1, 2)$ and $(-6, 3)$

12. perpendicular to $y = 2x + 1$ and through $(2, 8)$

13. Describe the difference between a line with a negative slope and a line with a positive slope. [2-1]

Solve each equation. [2-1]

14. $4 - 2(x - 1) = 5$ **15.** $\frac{3x}{5} = -15$ **16.** $3x + 7 = 2(x - 29)$

17. For the linear function $f(x)$, $f(3) = 11$ and $f(7) = 27$. Find $f(-2)$. [2-1]

18. A storage tank that was full of fuel is being emptied. After 7 minutes, there are 1975 gallons left in the tank. After 11 minutes there are 1475 gallons left. [2-1]
 a. What is the rate of change of the amount of fuel remaining in the tank in gallons per minute?
 b. Write a linear equation that relates the number of gallons left in the tank to the number of minutes since it began draining.
 c. How many gallons were in the tank when it was full?
 d. How many minutes will it take to empty the tank completely?

19. This scatter plot shows the relationship between the number of people who visit a booth at the crafts fair and the amount of sales at that booth. [2-2]
 a. Write an equation of a trend line for this scatter plot.
 b. Predict the sales at a booth if they expect 50 visitors this morning.

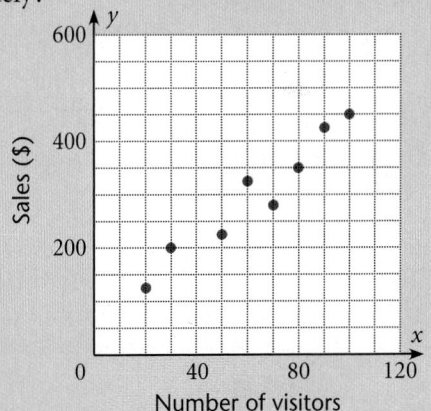

20. Graph the following data and find the equation of the median-median line. [2-2]

$(1, 5), (2, 5), (3, 8), (4, 9), (5, 10), (6, 11), (7, 11), (8, 13), (9, 12)$

Use your equation to predict the value of y when x is 20.

21. Use a Graphing Utility Find the equation of the regression line that fits these data on the height of a redwood tree at the beginning of each year. Then predict in which year the tree will reach a height of 50 feet.

Year	1973	1976	1981	1984	1989	1994
Height (ft)	31.9	34.0	37.7	40.0	43.5	47.2

Solve and graph each equation or inequality. [2-3]

22. $x + 11 \leq 14$

23. $5x - 2 \geq 8x + 25$

24. $-3 < x + 7 < 4$

25. $x + 5 < -4$ or $3x > 6$

26. $|2x + 23| = 17$

27. $|2x + 1| < 7$

Solve and graph each inequality on a coordinate plane. [2-3]

28. $3x + y < -1$

29. $y + 1 \geq |2x + 14|$

30. $2x - y < 3$

Write an inequality for each restriction. [2-3]

31. The cost of buying 4 tickets can be no more than $82.

32. The temperature in the room can vary from 70°F by no more than 3°F.

33. A printer produces 600 pages/hr on a high quality setting and 1000 pages/hr on a draft quality setting. Let x be the number of high quality pages printed in a day and let y be the number of draft quality pages printed in a day. The printer can be run for up to 8 hours a day. Write and graph a linear inequality that relates the number of pages of each quality that can be printed in a day.

CONCEPTS AND CONNECTIONS

34. Managing the Store A store hires full-time and part-time workers. Full-time employees work 40 hours per week and part-time employees work 25 hours per week. Each week, the store needs at least 450 hours of work from all employees.
a. Write and graph a linear inequality that relates the number of each type of employee needed to keep the store running.
b. Write a paragraph that describes how the store manager could use the equation or graph to make staffing decisions.

SELF-EVALUATION

Describe a trend in data or a relationship between quantities that you could model with a linear function. What predictions could you make using the model? How could you use a linear inequality or absolute value inequality to describe a restriction on the relationship? Indicate any concepts and skills about which you still do not feel confident.

Chapter 2 Assessment

TEST

1. Danny is growing carrots in his backyard. The carrots sprouted 2 weeks ago and the tops are now 1.6 inches long.
a. Assume the carrot tops grow at a constant rate. What is their growth rate?
b. Is the length of the carrot tops directly related to the number of weeks since they sprouted? Explain.
c. Danny wants to pick the carrots when their tops are 4 inches long. In how many weeks should Danny expect the carrots to be ready to pick?

2. Give the slope and an equation for each line.

   a. line p **b.** line q **c.** line r

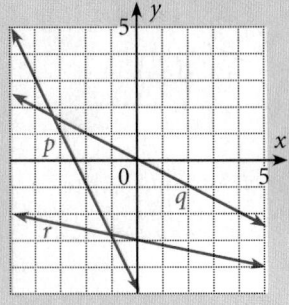

Write an equation of each line.

  3. through points $(-2, 4)$ and $(6, 20)$

  4. parallel to $y = 3x + 1$ and through $(3, 5)$

  5. perpendicular to $y = -\frac{1}{3}x + 2$ and through $(4, 1)$

Solve each equation.

  6. $\frac{x}{6} + 2 = -9$ **7.** $4x + 1 = x - 8$ **8.** $2(x - 1) = 5x$

9. This scatter plot shows the relationship between the number of hours of sunlight per day and the average daytime temperature inside a greenhouse.

   a. Write an equation of a trend line for the scatter plot.

   b. Predict the average daytime temperature on a day with 10 hours of sunlight.

   c. How many hours of sunlight per day would keep the greenhouse at an average daytime temperature of 75°F?

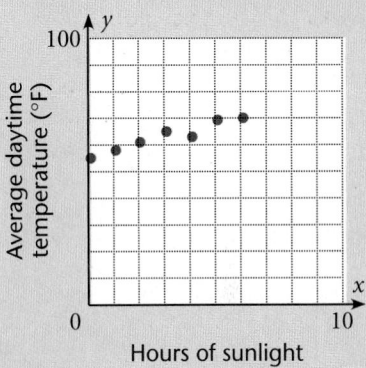

Solve and graph each equation or inequality.

  10. $x + 7 \leq -1$ **11.** $|1 - 2x| > 6$ **12.** $|2x - 7| = 13$

  13. $y \leq 3x - 1$ **14.** $y - 3 \geq 2|x + 2|$ **15.** $y + 2 \geq 3(x - 8)$

16. Frieda gets 3% commission on television sales and 4% commission on computer sales. Her goal is to earn at least $500 per week in commissions.

   a. Write and graph a linear inequality that shows the combinations of television and computer sales Frieda needs to make her goal.

   b. If she can sell only $6000 worth of computers this week, what is the minimum amount of television sales Frieda will need to meet her goal?

PERFORMANCE TASK

A small company makes small and large gift bags. The small gift bags cost $0.35 each to produce; they sell for $1.50 each. The large gift bags cost $0.75 each to produce and sell for $2.50 each. The company has standing orders for 2000 small gift bags and 5000 large gift bags each month. In addition to the standing orders, the sales staff has been bringing in orders of between 1000 and 3000 small bags and 2000 and 3000 large bags. Each month, these additional sales increase by about 4%. To help make production decisions for the next few months, write as many equations or inequalities as you can, based on these facts. Include at least two graphs. Describe any other information that might help the company to decide how many of each bag to produce for each of the next four months.

Chapter 3

Project A
Tune Me Up, Scotty!
How do tuning forks work?

Project B
Show Some Constraints
How does linear programming lead to important business decisions?

Project C
Simply Simplex
George Dantzig was late for class one day. How did that lead him to being recognized as a brilliant mathematician?

TOM WARREN

Math was challenging. There was a lot of competition among my friends to see who could do the best.

I am proud that I, with the help of my partner and a small group of dedicated employees, took a corporation that was in debt and made it into a successful business worth over a million dollars. I had to know when to borrow money to expand and when to hold back. Math was critical to all of these decisions. If a person is going to compete in the business world, mathematics is necessary.

Tom Warren
CEO, General Manager
Fluid Systems, Inc.
New Orleans, Louisiana

3-1
**Systems of
Linear Equations**

In 3-1 you will solve systems of linear equations by graphing, substitution, *and linear combination. You will use the following algebra skills from previous courses.*

Solve for y. [Previous course]

1. $5y = 3x + 10$ 2. $4x - y = 7$ 3. $x + 2y = 6$ 4. $3y + 9 = 0$

Graph. [Previous course]

5. $y = \frac{2}{3}x + 1$ 6. $x - y = 5$ 7. $2y = 6$

8. $x = 4$ 9. $2x + 2y = 5$

Simplify. [Previous course]

10. $3y + 2(y + 4)$ 11. $2x - 3(x - 7)$

12. $5(x + 3y) + 3(x - 5y)$ 13. $-6\left(\frac{1}{2}x + \frac{1}{3}y\right)$

14. $2(3x - y + 2z) + (-3)(2x + 3y - z)$

15. $12\left(\frac{5}{6}x - \frac{1}{2}y\right)$

Solve. [Previous course]

16. $5x = 25$ 17. $\frac{1}{7}x = 4$ 18. $\frac{2}{3}x = 24$

3-2
**Systems of
Linear Inequalities**

In 3-2 you will solve problems that involve systems of linear inequalities. You will *use the following graphing skills from previous courses.*

Name the point of intersection of each pair of equations. [Previous course]

19. $x = 3$ and $y = -2$ 20. $y = 2$ and $x + y = 3$ 21. $x = 0$ and $y = 2x + 7$

Graph each inequality on a coordinate plane. [Previous course]

22. $y \geq 0$ 23. $x \geq 0$ 24. $y \leq -2$

25. $y \leq -5$ 26. $y < x + 8$

Complete the table. [Previous course]

27. $8000 = 20x + 40y$

x	0		200
y		0	

28. $360,000 = 5000x + 12,000y$

x	0		50
y		0	

GOING
WIRELESS

Although you may not realize it, wireless phones have not always been a part of everyday life. Unheard of in the 1970s, cordless and cellular phones are found in cars, homes, and workplaces in ever-increasing numbers. The potential profits in the wireless telephone industry are enormous. An array of new services and a drop in prices may make portable phones as commonplace as VCRs. In fact, the wireless phone industry is adding 17,000 customers per day across the country.

In what is most certainly the largest auction ever held, the Federal Communications Commission sold licenses for the use of wavelengths not previously available for telephone communications. The winning bids in this 1994 auction were in the millions of dollars. The availability of the new wavelengths opened the market to new companies and new services in communications.

New services offered by competing companies will help make your life easier. For instance, one service will assign each customer one telephone number for a portable telephone. This telephone can be used as a cordless phone at home or as a cellular phone in your car, so people can call you wherever you (and your phone) happen to be. New companies have an advantage because they can build their networks from scratch, unencumbered by outdated technologies. The risk is that after paying millions of dollars at the auction and millions more to build a network, these companies may go broke if they cannot offer their services at a price that is competitive with older, well-established companies.

1. Why do you think companies were willing to bid so high for licenses for the new wavelengths?
2. The wireless industry is adding 17,000 customers per day. What type of function is suggested by this growth? Can this growth rate continue forever? Explain.
3. How might having a phone available at all times make your life easier? In what ways might your life be more difficult?

← CONNECT →

You have used linear equations to represent relationships in real-world data. Now you will investigate **systems of linear equations,** *where two or more of these relationships interact. The graphical methods you used to investigate functions and equations can also be used to solve systems of linear equations.*

A restaurant owner is glad to see more and more customers come through her door. As the number of customers increases, so does her revenue. But more customers also means increased costs: for instance, the owner must purchase more food from her suppliers and hire more chefs. She would like to know her *break-even* point, the point where costs and revenues are exactly equal. The answer to this question can be found by solving a *system of equations.*

THE FAR SIDE   By GARY LARSON

Down at the Eat and Slither.

Gary Larson, THE FAR SIDE © 1985 FARWORKS, INC./ Dist. by UNIVERSAL PRESS SYNDICATE. Reprinted with permission. All rights reserved.

A **system of linear equations** is a set of two or more linear equations *with the same variables.* The solution of the system is the set of all ordered pairs that make all of the equations true.

One way to find the solution to a system of equations is to look for the points where all of the equations intersect. The coordinates of the intersection point(s) solve the system. This method, called *solving by graphing,* is shown for the system of equations:

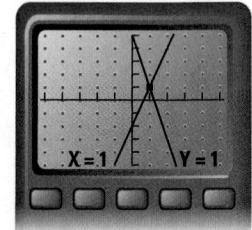

$$y = 3x - 2$$
$$y = -4x + 5$$

The point of intersection shows that the solution to this system is (1, 1), or $x = 1, y = 1$.

EXAMPLE

1. Cellular X Wireless charges its customers a base fee of $10.00 each month and $0.10 each minute for wireless phone service. A competitor, Call-Rite, charges $0.35 each minute with no base fee for the same service. Find the number of minutes of phone service for which the two companies charge the same amount.

First, write a system of linear equations to represent this situation. Let t = the number of minutes and c = the cost of the service.

$$c = 0.1t + 10 \qquad \text{Cellular X}$$

$$c = 0.35t \qquad \text{Call-Rite}$$

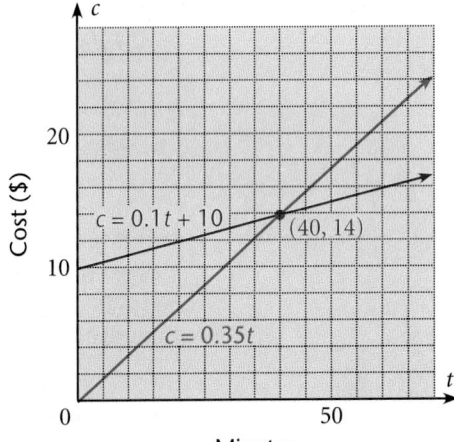

Graph the linear system on the same coordinate axes as shown. The graphs of the equations intersect at (40, 14), or $t = 40$, $c = 14$. This means that both Cellular X and Call-Rite charge $14 for 40 minutes of wireless phone service.

Graphing linear systems is often easiest if the equations are written in slope-intercept form, $y = mx + b$. In the following Explore, you will review slope-intercept form and investigate systems of linear equations.

EXPLORE: GRAPHIC INTERCEPTORS

MATERIALS

Graphing utility

Try the following game with a partner.

1. Using a graphing utility, input and graph a linear equation of your choice. Use the cursor to highlight a point on the graph. Record the equation of the line and the coordinates of the "target" point.

2. Have your partner choose a linear equation that he or she thinks will intersect the graph of the original equation at the highlighted point. Input and graph the equation. Record the equation and the actual point of intersection. (Hint: You may need to zoom in on your graphs to get a good estimate of the point of intersection.) Compare the actual point of intersection with the target point.

3. Switch roles, repeat Steps 1 and 2, and see whose second equation comes closer to intersecting the graph of the first equation at the target point. How did you decide whose equation came closest to solving the system at the target point?

Graphs of two linear equations in a coordinate plane may be related to each other in one of three ways. There are special terms used to describe these different situations.

$$x + 2y = 4$$
$$2x - y = 8$$

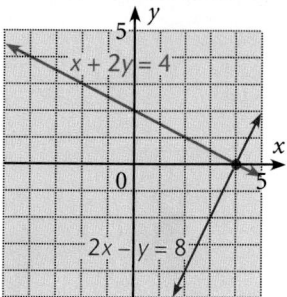

The graphs intersect in *exactly one* point, so there is one solution to the system. This is a **consistent system** since it has at least one solution.

$$y = 2x + 3$$
$$2y = 4x + 6$$

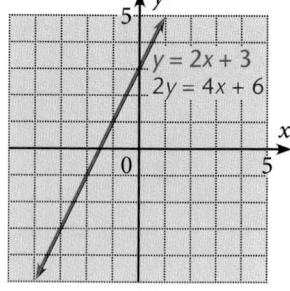

The graphs *coincide;* that is, there are an *infinite number* of solutions. The system is a **consistent system** since it has at least one solution, and the equations are **dependent equations.**

$$3x + y = 1$$
$$3x + y = 5$$

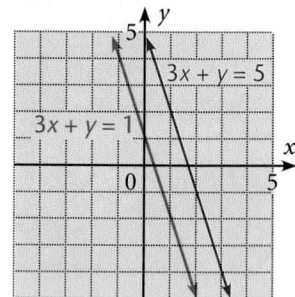

The graphs are *parallel.* They have no points in common. This system has *no solution.* Since the system has no solution, it is an **inconsistent system.**

CONSIDER

1. Write the equations of each line in the figures above in slope-intercept form. How can the slopes of the lines in a system of linear equations tell you whether the equations have a unique solution?
2. Suppose two equations represent perpendicular lines. Is the system consistent or inconsistent? How do you know?

EXAMPLE

Determine the number of solutions of the linear system. Tell whether the system is consistent or inconsistent.

2. $y - 5x = 3$
$\quad 2y = 6 + 10x$

First, put each equation into slope-intercept form by solving for y.

$$y - 5x = 3 \qquad\qquad 2y = 6 + 10x$$

$$y = 5x + 3 \qquad\qquad \frac{2y}{2} = \frac{6 + 10x}{2}$$

$$\qquad\qquad\qquad\qquad y = 5x + 3$$

The two equations represent the same line, so there are an infinite number of solutions. The equations are *dependent,* and the system is *consistent.*

Determine the number of solutions of the linear system. Tell whether the system is consistent or inconsistent.

3. $2x - y = 7$
$3x + y = -2$

Put each equation into slope-intercept form.

$2x - y = 7$ $\qquad\qquad$ $3x + y = -2$
$y = 2x - 7$ $\qquad\qquad$ $y = -3x - 2$

The lines have slopes of 2 and -3. Since the lines have different slopes, the graphs intersect in one point, and the system has one solution. The system is *consistent*.

TRY IT

Solve each system of linear equations by graphing. State the number of solutions and tell whether the system is consistent or inconsistent.

a. $4x - y = 5$ $\qquad\qquad$ **b.** $y = 2x + 5$
$\quad -3x + 3y = 3$ $\qquad\qquad\quad$ $y = 2x - 3$

You've seen that a system of linear equations can be solved by graphing. This visual technique is very useful, and graphing utilities can help find more precise solutions than can be estimated by hand. However, as you will soon see, there are several other methods for solving systems of linear equations.

REFLECT

1. Describe how you can use a graphing utility to solve a system of two linear equations with two variables.
2. Is it possible for a system of two linear equations to have exactly two solutions? Justify your answer.
3. What are some drawbacks to solving systems by graphing? Explain why you might need other methods to solve systems of linear equations.

Exercises

CORE

1. Getting Started Follow the given steps to solve the system below by graphing.

$3x + y = 11$
$6x - 3y = 9 \cdot 6x$

a. Rewrite each equation in slope-intercept form.
b. Graph each equation.
c. Find the point(s) of intersection of the two lines. If the system has only one solution, state its x- and y-values.

Write the word or phrase that correctly completes each statement.

2. An inconsistent system of linear equations has ____ solution(s).

3. If a system of equations has at least one solution, it is said to be ____.

4. If the two linear equations in a system represent the same line, the system is consistent and the equations are ____.

Determine the number of solutions of the linear system represented in each graph. Tell whether the system is consistent or inconsistent.

5.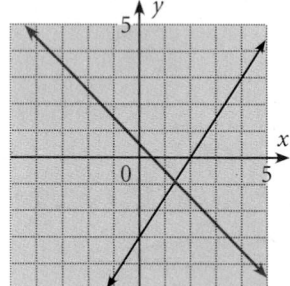

6.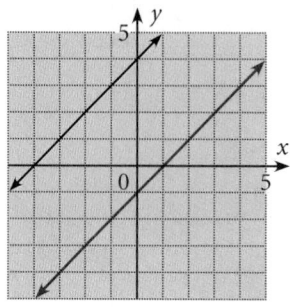

7.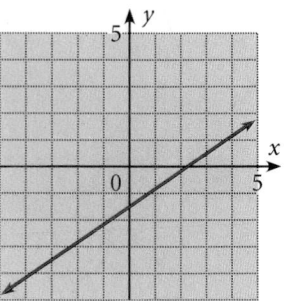

Solve each system of linear equations by graphing if possible.

8. $y = 2x + 10$
$y = 2x - 6$

9. $y = -3x$
$y = 4x - 5$

10. $y = 8x$
$x = \frac{1}{8}y$

11. $2x + 4y = -8$
$5x - y = -9$

12. $-4x + y = -2$
$2x - 3y = -9$

13. $4x - 7y = 28$
$-8x + 14y = 56$

14. Slice of Life Alyssa is running a marathon. Before starting the marathon, she ate a 400-calorie meal. During the marathon, she eats an 8-calorie orange slice every 30 minutes. Running burns 13 calories per minute. How long after the start of the race will she have used up all the calories from her meal and from the orange slices she has eaten up to that point?

For each system of equations, state the number of solutions and tell whether the system is consistent or inconsistent.

15. $y = 2.7x - 3$
$y = 2.7x - 13$

16. $y = -4x + 5$
$y = -9x + 5$

17. $y = -\frac{3}{4}x + 10$
$y = 10 - \frac{3}{4}x$

18. Fit in the Budget Nashota is thinking of joining a health club. Iron City charges a one-time membership fee of $400 and a monthly fee of $5. Universal Aerobics does not have a membership fee but charges a monthly fee of $30.
a. After how many months will the charges for the two clubs be equal?
b. Nashota is planning to move to another city in two years. Which club would be less expensive for her to join? Explain your answer.

19. Cruise CATastrophe Mr. and Mrs. Carlotta live 129 miles from Seattle. They leave for Seattle to catch a cruise ship for a two-month vacation across the Pacific. They drive to Seattle at a leisurely average speed of 42 miles per hour. Forty-five minutes later their friends, who are to feed the Carlottas' pet cats while the owners are away, realize that the Carlottas have forgotten to leave them the house keys. The friends try to catch the Carlottas before they reach the cruise ship. They drive at an average speed of 54 miles per hour.

a. How far from their house are the Carlottas when their friends start after them?

b. Let t denote the time (in hours) from the moment the Carlottas leave their house. Write two linear equations to model this situation, where the distance from the house (y) is expressed as a function of time (t). One equation should represent the Carlottas and the other should represent their friends.

c. Graph your system of linear equations. What is the point of intersection?

d. Describe what the solution of the system represents.

e. Will the friends catch the Carlottas in time?

 **LOOK AHEAD**

Simplify each expression.

20. $2(3x - 7) + 9$

21. $-4(5x - 3y)$

22. $-\frac{2}{3}(6x + 9y)$

Solve each equation.

23. $4x + 5 = 23$

24. $-2(7 - 2c) + 9c = -13$

25. $-\frac{1}{2}y + 3(y + 2) = 12$

MORE PRACTICE

Determine the number of solutions of the linear system represented in each graph. State whether the system is consistent or inconsistent.

26.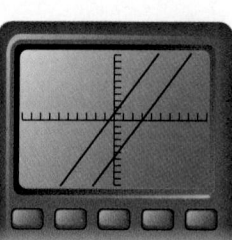

27.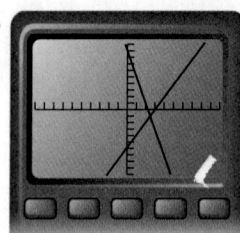

28.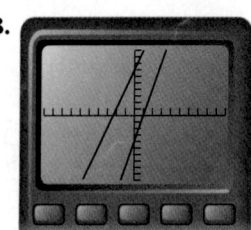

Solve each system of linear equations by graphing if possible.

29. $y = x + 3$
$y = -x + 7$

30. $y = -2x - 7$
$y = -3x + 10$

31. $y = 4x - 9$
$y = -2x + 6$

32. $3x + y = 6$
$x - 2y = 2$

33. $2x - y = 10$
$x + 2y = -5$

34. $y = 7 - 3x$
$2y + 6x = 14$

Use a graphing utility to solve each system of linear equations if possible.

35. $y = 3x - 2$
$2y = 5x + 4$

36. $9y - 6x = 12$
$3y - 2x = 4$

37. $0.5x - y + 2 = 0$
$2y = x$

38. $2930x - 4225y = 3992$
$-1457x + 2225y = -1945$

For each system of equations, state the number of solutions and tell whether the system is consistent or inconsistent.

39. $y = 5x - 5$
$y = 4x - 3$

40. $y = 0.3x - 0.3$
$y = -0.3x - 0.3$

41. $y = 7x + 2$
$y = 2x + 7$

42. $3x = 9$
$x = 3$

43. Popular Items As a fund-raiser last year, the school band purchased bags of popcorn from School Fund-Raising Ideas, Inc. The band paid the company $0.83 for each bag and sold the popcorn for $1.25 per bag. The band is considering making its own popcorn this year. A popcorn machine can be purchased for $240. Ingredients cost $0.48 per bag and the selling price will not be increased.
  a. On what basis would the band decide to make its own popcorn?
  b. Let y denote the profit (income minus expenses) earned for selling x bags of popcorn. Express y in terms of x if the band sells the company's popcorn. Express y in terms of x if the band sells its own popcorn.
  c. How many bags of popcorn must be sold to pay for the machine?
  d. How many bags must be sold to match the profit it can make from dealing with School Fund-Raising Ideas, Inc.?
  e. The band estimates between 550 and 650 bags of popcorn will be sold. Which plan should the band use? Explain the factors you considered.

44. Cycle Chase A cyclist starts cycling from Town A to Town C, which is 220 kilometers away, at 40 kilometers per hour. At the same time, a second cyclist starts toward C at 30 kilometers per hour from Town B, which is 42 kilometers down the road from A. A linear system can help determine when the first cyclist will overtake the second.

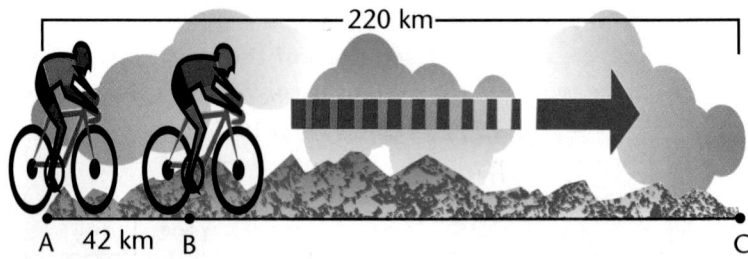

  a. Let y be each cyclist's distance from Town A x hours after starting. How far from A is the second cyclist at time 0? at 1 hour? at 2 hours?
  b. For each cyclist, write an equation expressing y as a function of x.
  c. **Use a graphing utility** to graph the two equations. What is their point of intersection? What do the x- and y-coordinates represent?
  d. Use the y-coordinate to determine whether the first cyclist will overtake the second before reaching Town C.

MORE MATH REASONING

45. Peak Performance A surveyor made sightings to the peak of a mountain from two points at the base. The two points were 8.1 miles apart on opposite sides of the mountain. He measured average slopes of 0.4 and -0.5 up the sides of the mountain. Write and solve a system of equations to find the mountain height from base to peak.

46. I Demand More! In economics, the *demand curve* for an item shows the sensitivity of the demand for a particular item in relation to its price. Customers usually purchase more of an item when its price is low than when it is high. The *supply curve* shows the sensitivity of the amount of the items produced in relation to its price. The point where these two curves intersect is called the *equilibrium point*. At the equilibrium point, the demand for an item is equal to the supply.

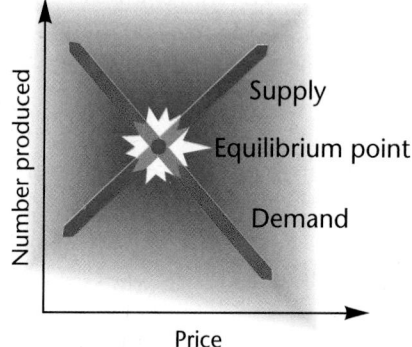

Suppose that the demand and supply curves for a new hand-held computer are linear. The manufacturer is willing to manufacture 60,000 computers if the asking price is $2,000 but only 27,000 if the asking price is $1,000. From a survey, the company estimates that if the computer is priced at $2,000, customers will buy 35,000 of them. But if the computer is priced at $1,000, then 59,000 people will be willing to buy one.

a. Write an equation for the demand curve and an equation for the supply curve. Explain how you found these equations.

b. Find the equilibrium point. What is the price of the hand-held computer at the equilibrium point? How many of the items are sold?

c. Do you think a demand curve would actually be linear? If not, explain why not and sketch a more typical demand curve.

47. Use a Graphing Utility The table shows the amount of money spent (in billions of dollars) in the United States from 1989 to 1992 to purchase new and used automobiles and to purchase tobacco products.

	1989	1990	1991	1992
Tobacco products	40.5	43.4	45.4	50.9
New/used autos	132.4	129.7	116.2	126.8

Assuming both trends are linear and that they continue, find the first year that Americans will spend more money on tobacco products than they will spend on new and used automobiles. Explain how you found your answer.

← CONNECT → *You've solved systems of linear equations graphically. Now you will investigate two ways to solve linear systems symbolically.*

It is difficult to find a precise intersection point for hand-drawn graphs. Even with a graphing utility, the solution is often only approximate. Therefore, it is important for you to work with other ways to solve systems of equations. These methods find the exact solution to a system of linear equations.

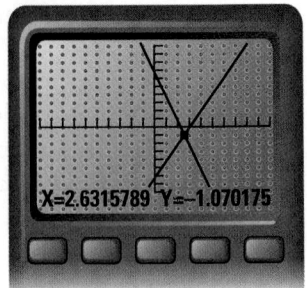

X=2.6315789 Y=-1.070175

You know how to solve any linear equation with only one variable, like $2x + 5 = 3x - 7$. Each of the solution methods you are about to investigate relies on reducing a system of equations to an equation with just one variable, which can then be solved using techniques from Chapter 2.

When using the **substitution** method, you reduce the number of variables in one equation by substituting for the other variable(s). Example 1 demonstrates the substitution method.

EXAMPLE

1. Solve the system by substitution.

$$4x + 2y = 8 \qquad ❶$$
$$3x - 7y = -11 \qquad ❷$$

Solve one of the equations for either of the variables. Since every constant in equation ❶ is divisible by 2, it is easiest to solve equation ❶ for y.

$$4x + 2y = 8$$
$$2y = -4x + 8$$
$$y = -2x + 4 \qquad ❸$$

By substituting $-2x + 4$ for y in equation ❷, we get a linear equation with only one variable, x. We can then solve for x. Note: It is not helpful to substitute into equation ❶, since the expression for y came from equation ❶.

$$3x - 7(\mathbf{-2x + 4}) = -11 \qquad \text{Substitute } -2x + 4 \text{ for } y.$$
$$3x + 14x - 28 = -11$$
$$x = 1 \qquad \text{Solve for } x.$$

To solve a system, we must find values for all of the variables.

To solve for y, we can substitute $x = 1$ into any of the equations above. However, equation ❸ is already solved for y, so it is the easiest one to use.

$y = -2x + 4$
$y = -2(\mathbf{1}) + 4$ Substitute 1 for x.
$y = 2$ Solve for y.

The solution to this system is $x = 1$, $y = 2$, or $(1, 2)$. To check our solution, we make sure that it makes *both* of the original equations true.

$$4x + 2y \overset{?}{=} 8 \qquad\qquad 3x - 7y \overset{?}{=} -11$$
$$4(\mathbf{1}) + 2(\mathbf{2}) \overset{?}{=} 8 \qquad 3(\mathbf{1}) - 7(\mathbf{2}) \overset{?}{=} -11$$
$$8 = 8 \checkmark \qquad\qquad -11 = -11 \checkmark$$

In the **linear combination** method, the equations in the system (or multiples of the equations) are added to each other to eliminate all but one of the variables. Once there is an equation with only one variable, the system can be solved.

EXAMPLE

2. Solve the system by linear combination.

$4y = 10x + 6$ ❶
$5x + 6y = -51$ ❷

So that the equations "line up" nicely, we begin by putting equation ❶ into the form $Ax + By = C$.

$4y = 10x + 6$
$-10x + 4y = 6$ ❸

Now, we look at the system:

$-10x + 4y = 6$ ❸
$5x + 6y = -51$ ❷

If these two equations are added as is, neither of the variables is eliminated. However, if we multiply equation ❷ by 2, the x-coefficients become additive inverses. Then the equations can be added to eliminate x, and the resulting equation can be solved for y.

$$-10x + 4y = 6 \rightarrow -10x + 4y = 6$$
$$\qquad\qquad 2 \cdot ❷$$
$$2(5x + 6y = -51) \rightarrow \underline{10x + 12y = -102}$$
$$16y = -96 \quad \text{Add.}$$
$$y = -6 \quad \text{Solve for } y.$$

Again, we need to substitute into one of the earlier equations to solve for x. We choose equation ❶, where the numbers appear small.

$4y = 10x + 6$
$4(\mathbf{-6}) = 10x + 6$ Substitute -6 for y.
$-24 - 6 = 10x$
$x = -3$ Solve for x.

The solution to this system is $x = -3$, $y = -6$. This solution checks.

CONSIDER

?

1. In Example 1, what would have happened if we had substituted $y = -2x + 4$ back into equation ❶? Why is it important that we substitute into the equation that we *did not use* to solve for y?
2. In Example 1, it was easiest to find the value of y by substituting $x = 1$ into an equation that was already solved for y. Will this always be possible when using the substitution method? Explain.

In the Explore, you will choose one of these methods to solve a system of linear equations.

EXPLORE: A FAST PROBLEM

MATERIALS

Graphing utility or graph paper

The table shows the winning Olympic times for men and women in the 100-meter dash. Times are rounded to the nearest tenth of a second.

1. Make a scatter plot of each set of data. Find an equation for the line of best fit for each.

2. Assume that these patterns continue to hold true. Use either substitution or linear combination to find the first year that the women's winning time will be faster than the men's. Project the winning time in that year. Explain how you found your answers and tell why you chose the method you used.

3. Do you think a linear model for this data is a good one? Why or why not?

Year	Men's Time (sec)	Women's Time (sec)	Year	Men's Time (sec)	Women's Time (sec)
1928	10.8	12.2	1968	9.9	11.0
1932	10.3	11.9	1972	10.1	11.1
1936	10.3	11.5	1976	10.1	11.1
1948	10.3	11.9	1980	10.3	11.1
1952	10.4	11.5	1984	10.0	11.0
1956	10.5	11.5	1988	9.9	10.5
1960	10.2	11.0	1992	10.0	10.8
1964	10.0	11.4			

The equations in the Examples and the Explore all had a unique solution. As you know, this is not always the case.

EXAMPLES

3. Solve the system:

$$x = 3y - 9 \qquad \text{❶}$$
$$2x - 6y = 3 \qquad \text{❷}$$

Since equation ❶ is already solved for x, it is most convenient to use substitution. We substitute the right side of equation ❶ into equation ❷.

$$2(\mathbf{3y - 9}) - 6y = 3 \qquad \text{Substitute } 3y - 9 \text{ for } x.$$
$$6y - 18 - 6y = 3$$
$$-18 = 3 \qquad \text{Simplify.}$$

Notice that solving this system gave us an equation that is *never* true, illustrating that there is no "true" solution to the system. Therefore, the system is inconsistent, and the lines are parallel.

4. Solve the system:

$$9x + 6y = 48 \qquad \text{❶}$$
$$\tfrac{3}{4}x + \tfrac{1}{2}y = 4 \qquad \text{❷}$$

First, clear the fractions from equation ❷ by multiplying through by 4.

$$4 \cdot \text{❷}$$
$$4\!\left(\tfrac{3}{4}x + \tfrac{1}{2}y = 4\right) \text{R } 3x + 2y = 16 \qquad \text{❸}$$

We can eliminate x if we multiply equation ❸ by -3 and add the result to equation ❶.

> **Problem-Solving Tip**
>
> Eliminate the variables with the smallest coefficients.

$$9x + 6y = 48 \qquad \text{❶}$$
$$-3 \cdot \text{❸}$$
$$-3(3x + 2y = 16) \text{ R } \underline{-9x - 6y = -48}$$
$$0 = 0 \qquad \text{Add.}$$

$0 = 0$ is an equation that is *always* true. This shows that any (x, y) pair that solves the first equation also makes the second equation true: the equations represent the same line. There are an infinite number of solutions to the system.

When solving by linear combination, you may need to multiply each of the equations by a different number before you can eliminate one of the variables.

5. Michelle and Julie are 17-year-old twins. They have decided to save all of the money they earn so that they can buy a car to share. One week Michelle worked 8 hours and Julie worked 14 hours, and they saved $128. The next week Michelle worked 12 hours, Julie worked 16 hours, and they earned $162. How much will they have saved after each works 100 hours?

First, we must find the respective hourly wages for Michelle and for Julie. Let M = Michelle's hourly wage and J = Julie's hourly wage. Then the problem can be represented by the system:

$8M + 14J = 128$ ❶
$12M + 16J = 162$ ❷

Since neither variable can be isolated or eliminated easily, we will solve this system by linear combination.

To eliminate M, multiply equation ❶ by 12 and equation ❷ by -8.

$$12 \cdot ❶$$
$$12(8M + 14J = 128) \rightarrow 96M + 168J = 1536$$
$$-8 \cdot ❷$$
$$-8(12M + 16J = 162) \rightarrow \underline{-96M - 128J = -1296}$$

$$40J = 240 \qquad \text{Add.}$$
$$J = 6 \qquad \text{Solve for } J.$$

We can now solve for M.

$8M + 14(\mathbf{6}) = 128$ Substitute 6 for J in equation ❶.
$\quad 8M + 84 = 128$
$\qquad\quad M = 5.5$ Solve for M.

Julie makes $6.00 an hour and Michelle makes $5.50 an hour.

In 100 hours, Julie makes $6 \times 100 = \$600$, and Michelle makes $5.50 \times 100 = \$550$. Their total earnings after each works 100 hours is $\$600 + \$550 = \$1150$.

TRY IT

Solve each system of linear equations if possible. State the number of solutions, and tell whether the system is consistent or inconsistent.

a. $3x + 2y = 5$
$\quad 4x + 4y = 10$

b. $4x - 2y = 3$
$\quad\quad y = x - 7$

c. $3x + y = 1$
$\quad 6x + 2y = 5$

You have seen that there is more than one way to solve a system of linear equations. The method you choose will depend on the equations of the system. Usually one method will make the process of eliminating a variable more convenient than another.

1. Describe how and why a variable is eliminated when you use the substitution method.
2. Describe how and why a variable is eliminated when you use the linear combination method.
3. Explain how you would decide whether to use linear combination or substitution to solve a system of linear equations. How do the coefficients of the variables help you make this decision?

Exercises

CORE

1. **Getting Started** Follow the steps to solve the system of equations by substitution.

$x - 3y = 3$ ❶
$2x + 4y = -14$ ❷

  a. Solve equation ❶ for x.
  b. Substitute the resulting expression into equation ❷. What variable has been eliminated in the new equation you obtained?
  c. Simplify the resulting equation. Solve this equation for the remaining variable.
  d. Use your answers in **a** and **c** to solve for the other variable.
  e. Write the solution of the system.

2. Follow the steps to solve the system of equations by linear combination.

$3x + 2y = 9$ ❶
$-2x + 4y = 10$ ❷

  a. Multiply equation ❶ by -2.
  b. Add the resulting equation to equation ❷. Which variable is eliminated?
  c. Solve for the remaining variable.
  d. Substitute your result from **c** into either equation ❶ or equation ❷ and solve for the other variable.
  e. Write the solution of the system.

Determine whether each statement is true or false. If the statement is false, change the underlined word to make it true.

3. If you solve a system by linear combination or substitution, you find an <u>approximate</u> solution to the system.

4. If, while solving a system of linear equations, you are left with an equation that can *never* be true, you know that the equations are <u>inconsistent.</u>

5. If, while solving a system of linear equations, you are left with an equation that can never be false, you know that the system has <u>no solution.</u>

Solve each system of linear equations by substitution. Then solve the same system by linear combination. State which method was more efficient for that problem and explain why it was better.

6. $y = 2x + 1$
$3x + 2y = 27$

7. $3x + 4y = 10$
$5x - 2y = 8$

Solve each system of linear equations if possible.

8. $x + y = 4$
$y = 2x + 1$

9. $2x - y = 5$
$3y - x = 5$

10. $x + 2y = 10$
$2x + 4y = 8$

11. The perimeter of a rectangle is 16 feet. Its length is four feet more than its width. Find the length and width of the rectangle.

12. What's the Point? In the 1986–87 National Basketball Association regular season, Michael Jordan became the first player in 24 years to score over 3000 points. He scored 3005 points on 2-point baskets and 1-point free throws. If he made a total of 1919 2-point baskets and free throws, how many free throws did he make?

Solve each system of linear equations if possible.

13. $x - y = 7$
$x + y = 3$

14. $\frac{2}{3}x + \frac{4}{3}y = -7$
$3x + y = -9$

15. $7x + 5y = 2$
$8x - 9y = 17$

16. Very Calculating Electronics City had a sale on two models of graphing calculators. One model sold for $85.75 and another model for $60.25. Thirty-two calculators were sold. The total amount of sales, excluding tax, was $2208.50. How many of each model were sold?

Solve each linear system if possible. State the number of solutions, and tell whether the system is consistent or inconsistent.

17. $6x + 2y = 4$
$10x + 7y = -8$

18. $x + 2y = 6$
$2x - 3y = 26$

19. $y = \frac{1}{3}x - 59$
$x - 3y - 15 = 0$

20. $3x + 2y = 16$
$7x + y = 19$

21. $2x - y + 2 = 0$
$6x + 12y - 1 = 0$

22. $5x - 3y = -1$
$-5x + 3y = -7$

23. Mixing It Up A chemist has a 10% solution (by volume) of alcohol and a 25% solution of alcohol. He needs to know how much of each to mix together to obtain 100 liters of a 20% alcohol solution. Let x be the number of liters of 10% solution and y be the number of liters of 25% solution in the mixture.

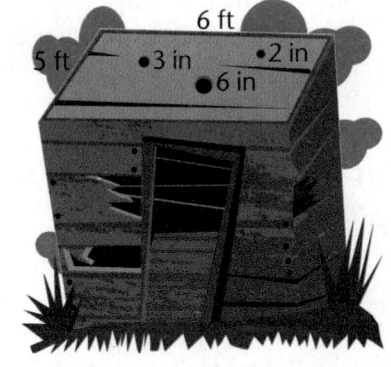

	Amount of Solution	Percent Alcohol	Amount of Alcohol
10% Solution	x		$0.1x$
25% Solution			
Mixture	100		$0.20(100)$

a. Copy and complete the table showing volumes before and after mixing.

b. Explain why the amount of alcohol in the mixture is given by $0.20(100)$, as shown in the table.

c. Write one equation to represent the "Amount of Solution" column. This equates the total amount of each type of solution used to the final volume of the mixture.

d. Write a second equation to represent the "Amount of Alcohol" column.

e. Solve the system of equations and describe how the chemist should proceed.

f. Show that your solution satisfies the two requirements stated in the problem.

LOOK BACK

24. Raindrops Keep Fallin' on My Shed An old shed with a flat, rectangular roof has three holes in it. The smallest hole has a diameter of 2 in., the next larger hole has a diameter of 3 in., and the largest hole has a diameter of 6 in. Find the probability that a raindrop that falls on the roof will go through one of the holes. Round your answer to the nearest hundredth. [1-2]

25. Write the equation of the line that contains the origin and is parallel to the graph of $2x + 3y = 7$. [2-1]

Find each product matrix if possible. If not possible, explain why. [1-3]

26. $\begin{bmatrix} 3 & 2 \\ -1 & 4 \end{bmatrix} \times \begin{bmatrix} 2 \\ 5 \end{bmatrix}$

27. $\begin{bmatrix} 7 & 8 \\ 5 & -4 \end{bmatrix} \times \begin{bmatrix} 10 \\ -6 \end{bmatrix}$

28. $\begin{bmatrix} 2 \\ 5 \end{bmatrix} \times \begin{bmatrix} 3 & 2 \\ -1 & 4 \end{bmatrix}$

29. Free T-Shirts! A company plans to spend at most $50,000 in an advertising campaign. The plan calls for $38,000 to be spent on TV commercials and the remainder on T-shirts that will be given away. The shirts will cost the company $3.00 each. What is the greatest number of T-shirts that can be given away? [2-3]

MORE PRACTICE

Solve each linear system if possible. State the number of solutions, and tell whether the system is consistent or inconsistent.

30. $y = x + 2$
$x + y = 8$

31. $x + 3y = -65$
$2x - y = -25$

32. $7x - 4y = 8$
$3x + 6y = 15$

33. $2x + 3y = 13$
$3x - 5y = 10$

34. $4x + 3y = 7$
$4x + y = 5$

35. $\frac{3}{5}y + \frac{2}{5}x = 4$
$-2x - 3y = -4$

36. $4.2x - 2.8y = 1.4$
$8.4x - 5.6y = 7$

37. $3x - y = 4$
$-1.5x + 0.5y = -2$

38. $\frac{3}{4}x - \frac{1}{2}y = -1$
$6x - 2y = -2$

39. Hi, Ethyl! The *octane* of gasoline measures the percentage of the hydrocarbon octane in the gasoline. At some gasoline stations, regular unleaded gasoline is 87 octane (87% octane), mid-grade unleaded is 89 octane, and premium unleaded is 92 octane.

A gasoline supplier has run out of mid-grade gasoline. One of his customers needs 1000 gallons of mid-grade gas. How many gallons of regular and premium need to be mixed to produce 1000 gallons of mid-grade?

40. The Leased Cost Holiday Rent-a-Car rents a compact car for $24.95 per day plus $0.23 per mile. Cargo Rent-a-Car rents a compact car for $22.95 per day plus $0.31 per mile.

a. For each car, write a function expressing daily cost as a function of miles driven.

b. What daily mileage gives the same rental charge for both cars? From which company would you choose to rent a car? Explain.

MORE MATH REASONING

41. The lines $2x + 3y = 12$, $x - 7y = -11$, and $-5x + 6y = 15$ contain the sides of a triangle. Find the coordinates of its vertices. Explain your solution method.

The *determinant* of a 2×2 matrix is found by subtracting the products of the diagonals. First, find the product of the number in the upper left times the number in the bottom right. Then, subtract the product of the upper right number times the lower left number. An example is shown.

The determinant of $\begin{bmatrix} 5 & 4 \\ 2 & 3 \end{bmatrix}$ is $(5 \cdot 3) - (4 \cdot 2) = 7$.

Find the determinant of each matrix.

42. $\begin{bmatrix} 9 & 4 \\ 3 & 2 \end{bmatrix}$

43. $\begin{bmatrix} -2 & -1 \\ 7 & -6 \end{bmatrix}$

44. $\begin{bmatrix} -6 & -3 \\ -10 & 5 \end{bmatrix}$

45. A general system of two equations with two variables is shown.

$$ax + by = c$$
$$dx + ey = f$$

a. Use linear combination to solve this system of equations for x. Your answer will be a fraction in terms of a, b, c, d, e, and f. (Hint: Multiply the first equation by $-e$.) Then use linear combination differently to solve for y. Compare your solution for x to the solution for y. What do you notice?

b. Cramer's Rule is another method of solving systems of linear equations by using determinants. According to this rule, the solution to the general system of two equations with two variables is given by the determinants of the matrices as shown. To solve any specific system of equations, you can substitute values for a–f, find the determinants, and simplify. Compare these expressions to the solutions for x and y that you found in **a.** Are they equivalent?

$$x = \frac{\begin{vmatrix} c & b \\ f & e \end{vmatrix}}{\begin{vmatrix} a & b \\ d & e \end{vmatrix}}, y = \frac{\begin{vmatrix} a & c \\ d & f \end{vmatrix}}{\begin{vmatrix} a & b \\ d & e \end{vmatrix}}$$

c. Use Cramer's Rule to solve the following system. Check your answer.

$$7x + 6y = 8$$
$$2x + 3y = 1$$

3-1
PART C Solving Systems Using Matrices

← **CONNECT** → *You've investigated matrix multiplication and worked with inverse matrices. Now you will see how inverse matrices can be used to solve systems of linear equations.*

When solving an equation like $3x = 12$, you need to cancel the multiplication of x by 3. To do this, you divide both sides of the equation by 3. Division by 3 cancels multiplication by 3 because division and multiplication are *inverse operations*.

Wouldn't it be nice to be able to solve a *system* of equations as easily as we can solve $ax = b$? We can—by using inverse matrices.

Suppose we have the matrix equation $AX = B$.

To "solve" this equation for X, we must cancel the multiplication by matrix A. To do this, multiply matrix A by its inverse matrix, called A^{-1}.

$A^{-1}AX = A^{-1}B$	Multiply both sides by A^{-1}.
$IX = A^{-1}B$	The product of A and A^{-1} is an identity matrix, denoted I.
$X = A^{-1}B$	Multiplication of X by an identity matrix gives X.

We have "solved" this matrix equation for matrix X. But how does this method apply to systems of equations? In the following Example, you will see how matrices can be used to solve a system of linear equations.

1. Solve the system using matrices.

$$3x - 6y = 21$$
$$-2x + 5y = 9$$

First, we represent this system as a matrix equation.

$$\begin{matrix} A & \times & X & = & B \end{matrix}$$
$$\begin{bmatrix} 3 & -6 \\ -2 & 5 \end{bmatrix} \times \begin{bmatrix} x \\ y \end{bmatrix} = \begin{bmatrix} 21 \\ 9 \end{bmatrix}$$

The 2×2 matrix on the left lists the coefficients of the variables. The 2×1 matrix on the left lists the variables. The 2×1 matrix on the right lists the constants.

The inverse matrix for $\begin{bmatrix} 3 & -6 \\ -2 & 5 \end{bmatrix}$ is $\begin{bmatrix} \frac{5}{3} & 2 \\ \frac{2}{3} & 1 \end{bmatrix}$. The product of these two

matrices is I, the 2×2 identity matrix $\begin{bmatrix} 1 & 0 \\ 0 & 1 \end{bmatrix}$. (You will see how you can find the inverse of a matrix later.) We now multiply both sides of the matrix equation by the inverse matrix. Note: On each side of the new equation, the inverse matrix should appear on the left.

$$\begin{matrix} A^{-1} & \times & A & \times & X & = & A^{-1} & \times & B \end{matrix}$$
$$\begin{bmatrix} \frac{5}{3} & 2 \\ \frac{2}{3} & 1 \end{bmatrix} \times \begin{bmatrix} 3 & -6 \\ -2 & 5 \end{bmatrix} \times \begin{bmatrix} x \\ y \end{bmatrix} = \begin{bmatrix} \frac{5}{3} & 2 \\ \frac{2}{3} & 1 \end{bmatrix} \times \begin{bmatrix} 21 \\ 9 \end{bmatrix}$$

$$\begin{matrix} I & \times & X & = & A^{-1} \times B \end{matrix}$$
$$\begin{bmatrix} 1 & 0 \\ 0 & 1 \end{bmatrix} \times \begin{bmatrix} x \\ y \end{bmatrix} = \begin{bmatrix} 53 \\ 23 \end{bmatrix} \qquad \text{Multiplying.}$$

$$X = A^{-1} \times B$$
$$\begin{bmatrix} x \\ y \end{bmatrix} = \begin{bmatrix} 53 \\ 23 \end{bmatrix}$$

The solution of this system of linear equations is $x = 53$, $y = 23$.

Write each equation in $AX = B$ form, where A is the coefficient matrix, X is the variable matrix, and B is the constant matrix.

a. $2x + 3y = 8$
$\quad -3x + 5y = 7$

b. $2.25x - 3.72y = 10.98$
$\quad x + 11.37y = 32.14$

CONSIDER ?

1. In Example 1, you were told that when multiplying each side of the matrix equation by the inverse matrix, the inverse matrix should appear on the left. Explain why this is important.

In Example 1, the inverse matrix just "appeared." Now you will see how to use technology to find an inverse matrix.

EXAMPLE

2. Using a graphing calculator, solve using matrices.

$$-4x - 8y = 16$$
$$2x + 5y = 12$$

Converting this system to a matrix equation of the form $AX = B$ gives:

$$\begin{bmatrix} -4 & -8 \\ 2 & 5 \end{bmatrix} \times \begin{bmatrix} x \\ y \end{bmatrix} = \begin{bmatrix} 16 \\ 12 \end{bmatrix}$$

Enter the variable and constant matrices into the calculator.

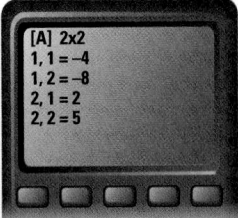
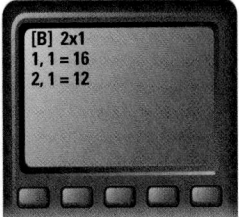

If you wish, you can look at the contents of the inverse matrix A^{-1}. (The calculator does not need to display the inverse before using it to solve the equation.)

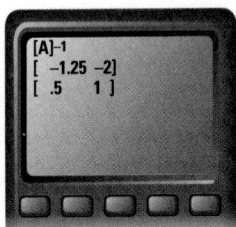

We now need to multiply both sides of our matrix equation $AX = B$ by A^{-1}. We know that $A^{-1}AX$ simplifies to X, the variable matrix. We can use the calculator to find $A^{-1}B$.

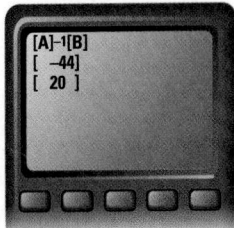

Therefore, $\begin{bmatrix} x \\ y \end{bmatrix} = \begin{bmatrix} -44 \\ 20 \end{bmatrix}$, or $x = -44$ and $y = 20$.

Checking the solution:

$$-4x - 8y \overset{?}{=} 16 \qquad\qquad 2x + 5y \overset{?}{=} 12$$
$$-4(\mathbf{-44}) - 8(\mathbf{20}) \overset{?}{=} 16 \qquad 2(\mathbf{-44}) + 5(\mathbf{20}) \overset{?}{=} 12$$
$$16 = 16 ✓ \qquad\qquad\qquad 12 = 12 ✓$$

2. Before using linear combination to solve a system of linear equations, it is convenient to put the equations into $Ax + By = C$ form. Is there a convenient form the equations should be in before solving by matrices? If so, what is that form and why is it convenient?

In the Explore, you will use matrices to analyze a business decision.

EXPLORE: OFF BROADWAY

MATERIALS

Graphing calculator

In 1994, renowned playwright Neil Simon chose to open his play "London Suite" Off Broadway. This choice was somewhat unusual, since important plays usually open in the larger, more well-known Broadway theaters. Mr. Simon's producer, Emanuel Azenberg, provided the information in the following table to the *New York Times*.

(In the table, the "money needed to open" is a one-time cost and is spent before the play is seen by the public.)

	Broadway	Off Broadway
Money Needed to Open ($)	1,295,000	440,000
Weekly Expenses ($)	206,500	82,000
Weekly Revenues ($)	250,000	109,000

1. Write an equation for the profit (revenues − expenses) of a Broadway play in terms of the number of weeks it has run. Then write a similar equation for an Off-Broadway play. Using matrices, solve this system of equations to find the point where the profit from an Off-Broadway play is equal to the profit from a Broadway play.

> **Problem-Solving Tip**
>
> Check to be sure that your answer makes sense.

2. Before the break-even point, would an Off-Broadway play or a Broadway play be more profitable? Which is more profitable after that point? Explain.

3. Why might Mr. Simon and Mr. Azenberg have decided to open "London Suite" Off Broadway?

Use a graphing calculator to solve each system of linear equations using matrices.

c. $2x - 9y = 4$
  $7x + 3y = -17$

d. $22.4y = -7.2x + 15.3$
  $2.13x + 11.11y = 3.75$

e. A precious metals dealer sold 4 oz of gold and 500 oz of silver to one customer for $3992. He sold a second customer 8 oz of gold and 200 oz of silver for $4088. Find the prices of an ounce of gold and an ounce of silver.

If A has an inverse, it is said to be an **invertible matrix.** Not all square matrices are invertible. If the coefficient matrix for a system of equations is invertible, then there is exactly one solution to the system. If not, either the system is inconsistent or the equations represent the same line.

EXAMPLE

3. Does the system below have a unique solution?
  $-x + 3y = 1$
  $2x - 6y = 3$

Write the coefficient matrix $\begin{bmatrix} -1 & 3 \\ 2 & -6 \end{bmatrix}$ and find its inverse.

When you try to find the inverse matrix on the calculator, you get an error message. This means that this matrix does not have an inverse.

Since the coefficient matrix does not have an inverse, the system does not have a unique solution. You must investigate the equations further to determine whether they represent parallel lines or the same line. (One way to do this is to put both equations in slope-intercept form.)

TRY IT

Determine whether each system of equations has a unique solution. If it does not, determine whether the system is inconsistent or the equations represent the same line.

f. $x + 3y = 9$
  $x + 3y = 4$

g. $6x - 4y = 18$
  $-9x + 6y = -27$

h. $2x = 4y - 9$
  $x + 2y = 9$

You are now familiar with four ways to solve a system of linear equations: graphing, substitution, linear combination, and matrices. You can use any of these methods to solve a system, but knowing all of them will help you choose an efficient way to solve a particular system.

REFLECT

1. Describe some advantages and disadvantages of using matrices to solve a system of linear equations. What characteristics of these equations might lead you to choose this method?
2. Suppose the coefficient matrix of a system is not invertible. Can you use this information to decide whether the equations have no solution or they represent the same line? If not, what would you do to determine this?
3. Explain how solving a matrix equation $AX = B$ is similar to solving a linear equation $ax = b$.

Exercises

CORE

1. **Getting Started** Follow the steps to solve the system of equations using matrices.

$4x + 2y = 8$
$7x + 4y = 14$

   a. Write the 2×2 coefficient matrix A, the 2×1 variable matrix X, and the 2×1 matrix B for the right-hand constants.
   b. Write the matrix equation $AX = B$ using your matrices from **a.**
   c. The inverse matrix for A is $A^{-1} = \begin{bmatrix} 2 & -1 \\ -\frac{7}{2} & 2 \end{bmatrix}$. Rewrite your equation from **b,** multiplying each side by A^{-1} on the *left* of the existing matrices.
   d. The left-hand side of your matrix equation simplifies to X, the variable matrix. Simplify the right-hand side using matrix multiplication.
   e. Write the solution of the system.

Write each system in $AX = B$ form, where A is the coefficient matrix, X is the variable matrix, and B is the constant matrix.

2. $x + y = 9$
   $x - y = 5$

3. $3x - y = 6$
   $5x - 2y = 2$

4. $-5x - 3y = 0$
   $3x + 2y = 7$

5. $x = 2y + 3$
   $y = -2x + 1$

The matrices in Exercises 6–9 are the inverses of the coefficient matrices for Exercises 2–5, respectively. With these inverses, solve the systems of equations in Exercises 2–5 using matrices.

6. $\begin{bmatrix} \frac{1}{2} & \frac{1}{2} \\ \frac{1}{2} & -\frac{1}{2} \end{bmatrix}$

7. $\begin{bmatrix} 2 & -1 \\ 5 & -3 \end{bmatrix}$

8. $\begin{bmatrix} -2 & -3 \\ 3 & 5 \end{bmatrix}$

9. $\begin{bmatrix} \frac{1}{5} & \frac{2}{5} \\ -\frac{2}{5} & \frac{1}{5} \end{bmatrix}$

10. Show that $\begin{bmatrix} 3 & -6 \\ -2 & 5 \end{bmatrix} \times \begin{bmatrix} x \\ y \end{bmatrix} = \begin{bmatrix} 21 \\ 9 \end{bmatrix}$ is equivalent to the system of equations $3x - 6y = 21$ and $-2x + 5y = 9$.

11. Confirm that $IX = X$ by showing that multiplying the 2×2 identity matrix $\begin{bmatrix} 1 & 0 \\ 0 & 1 \end{bmatrix}$ by the variable matrix $\begin{bmatrix} x \\ y \end{bmatrix}$ gives the variable matrix.

Write a matrix equation to represent each of the following situations. Do not solve.

12. Green Acres Mr. Douglas has 200 acres of farmland for tomatoes and peas. It costs $95 per acre to produce tomatoes and $150 per acre to produce peas. Mr. Douglas has $23,400 budgeted for producing these crops. If he uses all of his land and all the budgeted money, how many acres of each crop should be planted?

13. Welcome Home An apartment building contains 50 units. The one-bedroom units rent for $425 per month and the two-bedroom units rent for $550 per month. When the building is entirely rented, the total monthly income is $25,000. How many apartments of each type are there?

14. A "ReVolting" Development When two batteries are connected as shown, they are equivalent to one battery whose voltage is the sum of the individual voltages. Scientist Epson T. Mynded has large batteries and small batteries in his laboratory. When he connects 3 of the large batteries to 7 of the small ones, the total voltage is 99 volts. When he connects 7 of the large batteries to 4 of the small ones, the voltage is 120 volts. Find the voltages of the two types of batteries.

LOOK AHEAD

15. Is there a way to graph an equation with three variables on a coordinate plane? If so, explain how; if not, explain why not.

16. Sketch three planes whose common intersection is:
a. a point　　　　**b.** a line

17. You've explored solving systems of two equations with two variables using substitution and linear combination. To solve a 2×2 system (a system with two variables and two equations) by these methods, you first reduced the system to a "system" of one equation with one variable, which you already knew how to solve. If you were asked to solve a system of three equations with three variables, what would your general strategy be?

MORE PRACTICE

Use a graphing calculator to find the inverse of each matrix. If the inverse does not exist, say so.

18. $\begin{bmatrix} 5 & 2 \\ -2 & 1 \end{bmatrix}$

19. $\begin{bmatrix} 1 & 7 \\ 1 & -9 \end{bmatrix}$

20. $\begin{bmatrix} 1 & 3 \\ 7 & 5 \end{bmatrix}$

21. $\begin{bmatrix} 1 & 2 \\ 1 & 2 \end{bmatrix}$

22. $\begin{bmatrix} 4 & 7 \\ 2 & -1 \end{bmatrix}$

23. $\begin{bmatrix} -8 & 4 \\ -2 & 1 \end{bmatrix}$

24. $\begin{bmatrix} 0 & 1 \\ 1 & 0 \end{bmatrix}$

25. $\begin{bmatrix} 1 & 0 \\ 0 & 1 \end{bmatrix}$

26. $\begin{bmatrix} 0.4 & 0.25 \\ 0.4 & 0.75 \end{bmatrix}$

Write each system of linear equations as a matrix equation in the form $AX = B$. Use a graphing calculator to solve each system of linear equations using matrices if possible. If the system does not have a unique solution, determine whether the system is inconsistent or the equations represent the same line.

27. $3x + 4y = 10$
$-x + 2y = 0$

28. $3x + 6y = 5$
$-x - 2y = -4$

29. $22.3x + 14.3y = 15.4$
$7.5x - 15.2y = 3.3$

30. $2x = 3y - 6$
$5y = -7x + 10$

31. $y = 13x - 3$
$y = -x + 4$

32. $14 = 3x - 4y$
$y = 1$

33. Use a Graphing Calculator Solve Exercise **12** using matrices.

34. Use a Graphing Calculator Solve Exercise **13** using matrices.

35. Use a Graphing Calculator Solve Exercise **14** using matrices.

MORE MATH REASONING

36. Use A Graphing Calculator A botanist is testing the qualities of a particular type of soil. In one field with this soil, she planted 150 begonias and 220 nasturtiums. Of these plants, 297 survived. In another field, she planted 175 begonias and 196 nasturtiums, 301 of which survived.
  a. Use matrices to find the probability that each type of plant will survive in this soil.
  b. What difficulties might you have had in solving this problem using another method?

Science

37. Find It Yourself! It is possible to find the inverse of a 2×2 matrix by hand. We will demonstrate the method by finding the inverse of

$$\begin{bmatrix} 1 & -2 \\ -3 & 9 \end{bmatrix}.$$

Step 1: Interchange the element in the upper left with the element on the lower right. Change the signs of the other two elements. The resulting matrix is the *adjoint* of the original matrix.

$$\begin{bmatrix} 9 & 2 \\ 3 & 1 \end{bmatrix}$$

Step 2: Find the *determinant* of the original matrix. The determinant of a 2×2 matrix is found by multiplying the number in the upper left by the number in the lower right, then subtracting the product of the upper-right element times the lower-left element, as shown.

The determinant of $\begin{bmatrix} 1 & -2 \\ -3 & 9 \end{bmatrix}$ is $(1 \cdot 9) - ((-2) \cdot (-3)) = 3$.

Step 3: The inverse of the original matrix is the scalar product of the reciprocal of its determinant and the adjoint matrix.

$$\frac{1}{3}\begin{bmatrix} 9 & 2 \\ 3 & 1 \end{bmatrix} = \begin{bmatrix} 3 & \frac{2}{3} \\ 1 & \frac{1}{3} \end{bmatrix}$$

a. Confirm that $\begin{bmatrix} 3 & \frac{2}{3} \\ 1 & \frac{1}{3} \end{bmatrix}$ is the inverse of $\begin{bmatrix} 1 & -2 \\ -3 & 9 \end{bmatrix}$.

b. Find the inverse of $\begin{bmatrix} 2 & -2 \\ 5 & \end{bmatrix}$.

c. Use your answer from **b** to solve the system of equations:

$$2x - 2y = 12$$
$$5x - 4y = 16$$

38. Leg Count There are 27 centipedes and millipedes in a field. Each centipede has 175 pairs of legs and each millipede has 336 pairs. There are 14,924 legs in the field. Use matrices to find how many centipedes are in the field.

 **39. Doctor Data** In 1992, there were 548,303 physicians in the United States under 65 years old. 25.53415% of those under 45 were female and 11.67209% of those between 45 and 64 were female. There were 110,017 female physicians under 65. How many of them were under 45?

Systems with Three Variables

← CONNECT → *You have looked at methods for solving systems of two linear equations with two variables. Now you will use some of the same methods to solve linear systems with three variables.*

Although each of the systems of equations that we have looked at so far has had only two equations and two variables (known as a 2 × 2 system), many important real-world problems feature multiple variables and equations. Now you will see how the methods that you're familiar with can be used to solve a system of three equations and three variables.

You know that the graph of $Ax + By = C$ on a coordinate plane is a line. In much the same way, the graph of $Ax + By + Cz = D$ is a plane in coordinate space. Coordinate space has three axes, all perpendicular to each other.

Let's look at a system of three equations with three variables. Since we cannot represent three-dimensional space on two-dimensional paper, we show the *x*-axis in perspective. Only a portion of each plane can be shown.

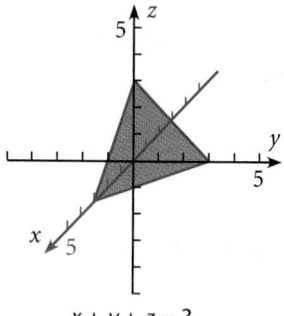

$x + y + z = 3$

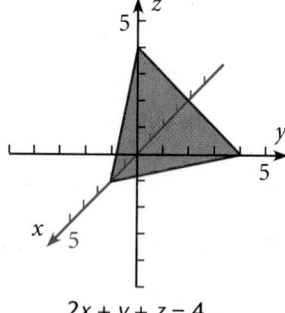

$2x + y + z = 4$

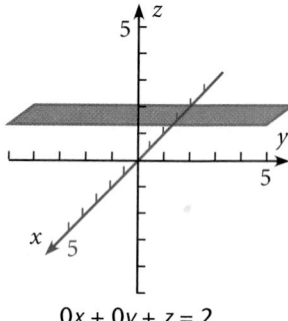

$0x + 0y + z = 2$

The solution of the system is the intersection of the three planes. As you can see, it is impractical to use graphing to solve a system of three equations in three variables!

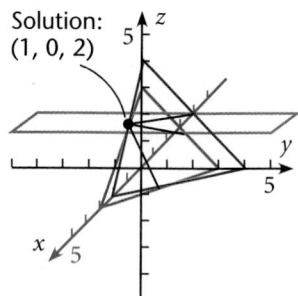

Solution: (1, 0, 2)

You can use linear combination or substitution to solve a linear system of three equations with three variables. In each case, your first goal is to reduce the system to two equations with two variables. Then you can solve this reduced system with our familiar techniques for 2 × 2 systems. When solving 3 × 3 systems, be sure that you find values for all three variables.

WHAT DO YOU THINK?

Mei Mei and Brian were asked to solve the following system of equations.

$x + 3y + 2z = 9$ ❶
$x - y + 3z = 16$ ❷
$3x - 4y + 2z = 28$ ❸

Mei Mei thinks...

I can easily eliminate x from equations ❶ and ❷ and from equations ❷ and ❸.

$$\begin{array}{rl} x + 3y + 2z = 9 & ❶ \\ -x + y - 3z = -16 & -1 \bullet ❷ \\ \hline 4y - z = -7 & ❹ \end{array} \qquad \begin{array}{rl} 3x - 4y + 2z = 28 & ❸ \\ -3x + 3y - 9z = -48 & -3 \bullet ❷ \\ \hline -y - 7z = -20 & ❺ \end{array}$$

Now I'll eliminate y from the new system and solve for z.

$$\begin{array}{rl} 4y - z = -7 & ❹ \\ -4y - 28z = -80 & 4 \bullet ❺ \\ \hline -29z = -87 & \\ z = 3 & \end{array}$$

Next, I need to find values for x and y. First, I'll use an equation with z and just one other variable, like equation ❹.

$$\begin{array}{rl} 4y - z = -7 & ❹ \\ 4y - \mathbf{3} = -7 & \text{Substituting 3 for } z. \\ y = -1 & \end{array}$$

Finally, I need to solve for x. I'll use equation ❶.

$$\begin{array}{rl} x + 3y + 2z = 9 & ❶ \\ x + 3(\mathbf{-1}) + 2(\mathbf{3}) = 9 & \text{Substituting } -1 \text{ for } y \text{ and 3 for } z. \\ x = 6 & \end{array}$$

The solution of the system is $x = 6$, $y = -1$, and $z = 3$.

Brian thinks...

I can use substitution to solve this system of equations. First, I'll solve equation ❶ for x, then substitute the result into equations ❷ and ❸. This will give me two equations with only two variables.

$$\begin{array}{rl} x + 3y + 2z = 9 & ❶ \\ x - y + 3z = 16 & ❷ \\ 3x - 4y + 2z = 28 & ❸ \\ x = -3y - 2z + 9 & ❹ \quad \text{Solving equation ❶ for } x. \end{array}$$

I've run out of space on this page, so I'll continue on the next page.

Substituting equation ❹ into ❷ and ❸ and simplifying:

$x - y + 3z = 16 \rightarrow \qquad -3y - 2z + 9 - y + 3z = 16 \rightarrow \qquad -4y + z = 7$ ❺
$3x - 4y + 2z = 28 \rightarrow 3(-3y - 2z + 9) - 4y + 2z = 28 \rightarrow -13y - 4z = 1$ ❻

I've gotten down to a 2 × 2 system, equations ❺ and ❻.

Now, I can solve equation ❺ for z and substitute the result into equation ❻.

$z = 4y + 7$ ❼   Solving equation ❺ for z.

Substituting ❼ into ❻ allows me to solve for y.

$-13y - 4z = 1$ ❻
$-13y - 4(4y + 7) = 1$ Substituting $4y + 7$ for z.
$-13y - 16y - 28 = 1$
$y = -1$

Now, I have to substitute to find the values of x and z. Equation ❼ is solved for z in terms of y only, so I'll use that to find z.

$z = 4y + 7$ ❼
$z = 4(-1) + 7$ Substituting -1 for y.
$z = 3$

Equation ❹ is already solved for x, so I'll use it to solve for x.

$x = -3y - 2z + 9$ ❹
$x = -3(-1) - 2(3) + 9$ Substituting -1 for y and 3 for z.
$x = 6$

The solution of the system is $x = 6$, $y = -1$, and $z = 3$.

CONSIDER

1. In What Do You Think? which approach did you prefer? Why?
2. Is it possible to use both substitution and linear combination to solve a 3 × 3 system? Explain.

Believe it or not, the system of equations in What Do You Think? were set up so they could be solved "easily" by linear combination and substitution. While these methods may be used to solve a 3 × 3 system, they can be quite time-consuming. Care must be taken to avoid computational errors, since one mistake can lead to several minutes of invalid work; you may not realize that an error has been made until you check your answer.

Fortunately, one of our methods works quite nicely for a 3 × 3 system, especially if you have suitable technology. In the Explore, you will use *matrices* to solve a 3 × 3 system.

EXPLORE: TECHNOLOGY TO THE RESCUE!

MATERIALS

Graphing calculator

You are operating a glass factory. You can assign apprentice glass blowers to a job at $20.25 an hour, journeyman glass blowers at $25.60 an hour, and master glass blowers at $31.50 an hour. From past experience, you know that an apprentice can make 3 glass pieces in an hour, a journeyman 4, and a master glass blower 5.

You have an order for 150 of these pieces . You have determined that total labor costs for the glassware should be $978, and there are 41 hours of time available on the oven needed to make these pieces .

1. Write three equations to represent the labor costs, the hours worked, and the glassware produced.
2. Write the system in the form $AX = B$, where A is the coefficient matrix, X is the variable matrix, and B is the constant matrix.
3. Use your calculator to find A^{-1}. Show that A^{-1} is the inverse matrix.
4. Use matrices to solve the system of equations. What does your solution mean?
5. In real life, some or all of the three equations in this system would probably be inequalities. Identify the equations that would likely be inequalities and rewrite them as inequalities. Explain your reasoning.

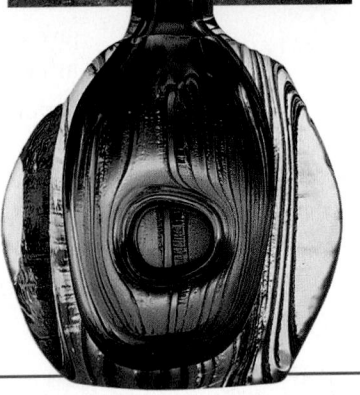

TRY IT

a. Solve the system of linear equations if possible.

$x + y + z = 5$
$x - 2y + z = -7$
$2x + y + 3z = 5$

b. A computer store offered special prices on a mouse, a track ball, and a joy stick. The chart below shows the sales for each of three days. Total sales revenues for the three days were $730, $595, and $770, respectively. What was the sale price of each item?

Day	Number of Items Sold		
	Mouse	Track Ball	Joy Stick
1	4	3	5
2	6	2	3
3	1	2	8

You've explored solution techniques for 3 × 3 systems. As you can probably imagine, solving larger systems of linear equations is best done with the help of technology.

REFLECT

1. The graph of $Ax + By = C$ on a coordinate plane is a line. What does the graph of $Ax + By + Cz = D$ in coordinate space look like? What does the graph of $Ax = B$ on a number line look like?

2. You have solved 2 × 2 systems of linear equations by graphing, linear combination, substitution, and matrices. Which of these methods seems least practical for solving a 3 × 3 system? Which seems most useful? Justify your choices.

3. Suppose you use either substitution or linear combination to reduce a 3 × 3 system to a 2 × 2 system. Do you have to continue using that method to solve the problem, or can you switch to another method at this point if it seems more convenient?

4. Does a 3 × 3 system always have a single solution? If so, explain why. If not, give examples or sketches of 3 × 3 systems with no solution or with an infinite number of solutions.

Exercises

CORE

1. Getting Started Copy and complete each statement to solve the 3 × 3 system.

$$x + y + z = 8 \quad \textbf{①}$$
$$x - y = 0 \quad \textbf{②}$$
$$z = 4 \quad \textbf{③}$$

a. Add equations ____ and ____ to obtain a new equation without the variable ____. Call the new equation, $2x + z = 8$, equation **④**.

b. To solve equation ____ for x, substitute ____ for variable ____. Solving the resulting equation gives $x = 2$.

c. To solve for ____, we can substitute $x = 2$ and $z = 4$ into equation ____ or ____. Solving gives ____ = ____.

d. The solution of the system is ____.

Solve each system of linear equations if possible.

2.
$$x = 2$$
$$2x + 3z = 13$$
$$x - 3y + z = -10$$

3.
$$x + z = 5$$
$$-2x + y + z = -5$$
$$3x - 2y - z = 9$$

4. $x - 2y + 3z = -3$
$$2x - 3y - z = 7$$
$$3x + y - 2z = 6$$

5. $x - 2y + 4z = -8$
$$2x + 2y - z = 11$$
$$x + y - 2z = 10$$

6. a. Write the system of linear equations as a matrix equation.

$$3x - 2y + 2z = -13$$
$$2x - y + z = -5$$
$$-6x + 4y - 3z = 19$$

b. The inverse matrix for the coefficient matrix you should have found in **a** is

$$\begin{bmatrix} -1 & 2 & 0 \\ 0 & 3 & 1 \\ 2 & 0 & 1 \end{bmatrix}.$$ Use this matrix to solve the system of equations.

7. The sum of three numbers is 24. The largest number is three times the smallest, and the middle number is four less than the largest. What are the three numbers?

8. Eulalia has 10 coins in her pocket—quarters, dimes, and nickels. She has 2 more dimes than nickels, and the coins are worth $1.50 in all. How many of each type of coin does she have?

9. Find the measures of the three angles of a triangle if the sum of the measure of the first angle and twice the measure of the second angle equals the measure of the third angle, and if four times the measure of the second angle is 15 degrees more than the measure of the third angle.

10. To predict fuel usage for new delivery routes, a distribution company conducted a study of the fuel usage of one typical truck. Use this information to find the rates of fuel usage in rush hour traffic, city traffic, and on the highway.

	Rush Hour Hours	City Traffic Hours	Highway Hours	Total Fuel Used (gal)
Week 1	4	18	6	30
Week 2	7	8	3	24
Week 3	3	9	3	17

11 Compare the difficulty of solving a 3×3 system to the difficulty of solving a 2×2 system.

 **LOOK BACK**

Solve each literal equation for the indicated variable. [2-1]

12. $s = \frac{1}{2}gt^2$, for g

13. $S = \dfrac{a}{(1 - r)}$, for a

14. $S = \frac{n}{2}(a + \ell)$, for ℓ

Solve and graph each inequality. [2-3]

15. $3x + 1 < 5$

16. $9 - 7.3k \le 9.1k - 7.5$

17. $\frac{2}{3}y - \frac{7}{3} > \frac{5}{6} + \frac{1}{3}y$

18. The U.S. center of population is the "balance point" of the population of the United States (assuming that every person weighs the same). The latitude of the center of population (about 38–39° N) has stayed fairly constant since the nation was formed. According to data from the Bureau of the Census, the longitude of the center of population has moved as shown in the table. Longitudes are rounded to the nearest degree.

1790	1810	1830	1850	1870	1890	1910	1930	1950	1970	1990
76° W	78° W	79° W	81° W	84° W	86° W	87° W	87° W	88° W	90° W	91° W

a. Give the equation of a line of best fit for the data in the table. State the method you used to find your equation. Then predict the longitude of the U.S. center of population in 2050. [1-1, 2-2]

b. For the figures from 1790 through the mid-1800s, the population data used to find these points was fully representative of U.S. citizens only. How might the centers of population be different if all people living within the current borders of the United States had been counted equally?

MORE PRACTICE

Solve each system of linear equations if possible.

19. $x + y = 3$
$2x - y = 9$
$3x + y + 2z = 1$

20. $2x + 3y = -2$
$4y + 2z = -10$
$3x + 5z = 1$

21. $2x - 3y - 4z = -21$
$4x + 2y - 3z = -14$
$-3x - 4y + 2z = -10$

22. $6x - y - 3z = 2$
$-3x + y - 3z = 1$
$-2x + 3y + z = -6$

23. $2x + y + z = 4$
$4x + 3y - 2z = 21$
$2x - 2y - z = -7$

24. $3x + 2y = z - 7$
$5x + 3y = -12 + 2z$
$2x + 3y = -5 + z$

Write each system of linear equations as a matrix equation in the form $AX = B$. Then use a graphing calculator to solve each system of linear equations using matrices if possible.

25. $2x + 5y - 3z = 6$
$3x + 3y + 7z = 23$
$5x - 4y + 6z = 9$

26. $3x + y = 7$
$-2x - z = 1$
$3y + 4z = 0$

27. $3x + 2y + z = 7.7$
$2x - y - z = 3.3$
$5x - 4y - 2z = 5.5$

28. $3.85x + 1.44y - 3.10z = -7.34$
$1.88x + 3.03y + 0.34z = 15.11$
$2.71x + 7.04y + 9.37z = -5.55$

29. $x + y + z = 180$
$\frac{x}{4} + \frac{y}{2} + \frac{z}{3} = 60$
$2y + 3z = 330$

30. $4.01k - 7.34m + 6.25n = 13.25$
$-7.92k + 10.25m + 1.03n = -7.61$
$12.11k - 9.21m + 11.04n = 1.71$

31. Use a Graphing Calculator Whenever Jessica goes to the grocery store, she buys bulk foods. She always buys granola, dried fruit, and trail mix. The table shows her purchases for three weeks. Assuming none of the prices has changed over this period, find the price per pound of each item.

	Granola	Dried Fruit	Trail Mix	Total
Week 1	0.88 lb	0.75 lb	0.50 lb	$4.68
Week 2	1.04 lb	0.95 lb	0.30 lb	$4.86
Week 3	0.92 lb	0.80 lb	0.40 lb	$4.59

MORE MATH REASONING

32. Use a Graphing Calculator A store began selling its line of fall sweaters. On the first day, 6 cotton, 4 orlon, and 5 wool sweaters were sold. On the second day, 3 cotton, 5 orlon, and 8 wool sweaters were sold. On the third day, 4 cotton, 1 orlon, and 4 wool sweaters were sold. Total sales for the three days were $395, $505, and $260, respectively. What was the sale price for each sweater?

33. Use a Graphing Calculator Suppose that a TV talent show ranks contestants on three traits: personality, talent, and star quality. Each of these three traits is a different percentage of the final score. For instance, personality might count for 50%, talent for 40%, and star quality for 10%. These *are not* the actual percentages.

The table shows the marks of five contestants and their total scores.

	Personality	Talent	Star Quality	Total
Dan Surr	6	10	7	8.05
Mac Gyshun	7	7	10	7.75
Voe Callist	7	10	6	7.95
Jo Kerr	9	7	8	7.85
Sam Antics	6	8	9	7.65

Dan Surr was declared the winner and was about to receive the grand prize. But as he stepped forward, one of the other contestants said, "Wait! You totaled my score incorrectly! *I* should be the winner!" After checking the scores, the judges found that this claim was correct, and they awarded the grand prize to the real winner. Who was it? Explain how you found the real winner.

193

← C O N N E C T → *Systems of linear equations have many applications in the real world. You have seen that several methods are available for solving systems of linear equations.*

EXPLORE: "PHONE-Y" PROFITS

You are the owner of a telecommunications company who won one of the bids at the FCC auction. After paying $120 million at the auction and $150 million more to build a network, you are ready to start looking for customers.

You are deciding between two ways to bill your customers. The first plan you consider charges a $40.00 monthly fee and $0.15 per minute for phone calls. The second plan charges no monthly fee but $0.40 per minute for calls.

MATERIALS

Graphing calculator or graph paper

1. Find the break-even point for these two plans. Explain how you solved the problem and how you decided which technique to use. What should you investigate before deciding which billing plan to offer your customers?

> **Problem-Solving Tip**
>
> Write equations to represent the two plans.

2. Market research indicates that your customers will use your service an average of 300 minutes a month. Which billing plan would you choose to offer? Explain how you made your decision.

3. Suppose each minute of phone service to your customers costs your company $0.05 and you have an average of 72,000 customers every month. (Hint: What is your monthly revenue for an average customer using the billing plan you chose in Step 2?) Find the length of time it would take for your company to become profitable. Explain how you found your answer.

1. Briefly describe each of the methods you have used to solve systems of linear equations. Give some of the strengths and weaknesses of each method.
2. Describe what happens when you try to solve an inconsistent 2 × 2 system by:
   a. graphing   **b.** linear combination
   c. matrices   **d.** using a graphing calculator
3. Maria's teacher had the class solve a system of equations. Then he asked, "Why did we say that $x = 1$ and $y = 2$ is the solution of this system? Shouldn't we say that these values are the *solutions* of the system?" Maria gave the correct answer to her teacher's question. What did she say?

Self-Assessment

1. Which system of linear equations has a unique solution?
   (a) $2x + 3y = -8$ (b) $4x - y = 9$ (c) $6x + 5y = 7$ (d) $y = 1$
        $6x + 9y = -24$ $y = 4x - 5$ $3x - 7y = 13$ $y = 3$

2. Identify the system that has an infinite number of solutions.
   (a) $x + y = 3$ (b) $x + y = 8$ (c) $3x - y = 10$ (d) $x - 6y = 12$
        $5x + 5y = 15$ $2x + 2y = 14$ $y = 4x + 5$ $2x + y = 14$

3. Identify the inconsistent system.
   (a) $x + 4y = -3$ (b) $y = 3x + 6$ (c) $x = 1$ (d) $x - y = 7$
        $x - 5y = 7$ $-6x + 2y = 12$ $y = 1$ $4x - 4y = 24$

Solve each linear system if possible. State the number of solutions, and tell whether the system is consistent or inconsistent.

4. $3x - 2y = 4$ 5. $2x + y = 5$ 6. $y = 9 - 4x$
     $x + 3y = 8$ $x - y = -2$ $4y - 9x = 11$

7. $y = x - 1$ 8. $y = 4x - 3$ 9. $y = 5x$
     $y = -3x + 2$ $y = 4x - 7$ $x = \frac{1}{5}y$

10. $3x + y = 10$ 11. $7x - 5y = -2$ 12. $8x + 6y = 10$
      $2x - y = 5$ $-8x - y = 9$ $-4x + 3y = -1$

13. **Painter's Brush** A paint store stocks one type of paint that is 25% linseed oil and another more expensive paint that is 35% linseed oil. Gnam figures he can cut costs and still do a quality job on his house with paint that is 31% linseed oil. He needs 20 gallons of paint for the job. How many gallons of each paint are needed to make the mixture?

Solve each literal equation for the indicated variable. [2-1]

14. $V = \ell wh$, for w 15. $A = \pi r^2$, for r 16. $A = \frac{1}{2}(b_1 + b_2)h$, for b_1

17. Whose Zoo? The table shows the 1993 attendance (in millions of people) and the 1993 budget (in millions of dollars) for some of the major zoos in the United States.

Name	Attendance	Budget
Bronx	2.1	24.6
Cincinnati	1.3	12.0
Cleveland	0.9	2.9
Houston	1.5	5.7
National (Washington, D.C.)	3.0	13.0
Philadelphia	1.2	16.0
St. Louis	2.7	14.7
San Antonio	1.0	7.3
San Diego	3.5	40.0

Give the equation of a line of best fit for the data in the table. State the method you used to find your equation. Then predict the 1993 budget at a zoo with an attendance of 2.5 million visitors. [1-1, 2-2]

18. Time Well Spent An advertiser plans to spend $220,000 on 30 one-minute TV commercials. A one-minute spot during prime time costs $10,000; after 10 p.m., the same spot costs $6,000. How many one-minute commercial spots can be bought during and after prime time?

Write each system of linear equations as a matrix equation in the form $AX = B$.

19. $3x + 7y = -4$
$2x + 5y = 3$

20. $3x + 4y = 26$
$x - 3y = 0$

21. $0.9x - 3.5y + 2.4z = -9.75$
$1.4x + 2.5y + 3z = 2.5$
$-3.4x - 1.8y - 5.6z = 10.14$

22. But I'm a Vegetarian! In 1989, Americans consumed an average of 115.9 pounds of red meat and 53.6 pounds of poultry. By 1991, the totals were 112.4 pounds and 58.2 pounds, respectively. If these trends continue, when will Americans, on average, eat equal amounts of red meat and poultry? Explain how you found your answer.

Solve each linear system if possible.

23. $2x + y - z = 2$
$x + y + z = 7$
$x + 2y + z = 4$

24. $x + 2y - z = 5$
$2x + z = -1$
$3x - 4y - 2z = 7$

25. In the Market? Computers Galore Store had personal computers (PCs) on sale. On the first day, three PC-160s, five PC-250s, and two PC-540s were sold. On the second day, five PC-160s, two PC-250s, and three PC-540s were sold. On the third day, four PC-160s, seven PC-250s, and five PC-540s were sold. Total sales for the three days were $18,700, $18,900, and $31,600, respectively. What was the sale price of each type of computer?

What's the Point?

Narenda Karmarkar

Linear programming, an organized method of making decisions mathematically, is a relatively new field. Linear programming was developed during and immediately after World War II in an attempt to allocate and move scarce military resources efficiently. In 1979, a Russian mathematician, L. G. Khachian, announced a new linear programming discovery. His work paved the way in 1984 for an American mathematician, Narenda Karmarkar, to discover a new *algorithm* (solution technique) that made solving complex linear programs faster and more efficient.

Today, many industries rely heavily on linear programming to help them improve profits, lower costs, and make efficient use of resources. Petroleum refineries were among the first industries to use linear programming, using it to help determine how gasolines should be blended. Airline and telephone companies use linear programming to determine the most efficient routing of planes and telephone calls.

Linear programming has saved companies large sums of money. A major oil refinery saved about 100 million dollars by using linear programming to select 200 energy-saving projects from over 600 proposed ideas. A company that produces artificial heart valves reduced their costs by over a million dollars per year when it applied linear programming to balance shipments from different suppliers.

1. Give an example of a resource that a business might want to use efficiently. Explain why it is important to use that resource wisely.

2. As mentioned, an oil refinery used linear programming to choose 200 energy-saving projects from a list of over 600 proposals. Why do you think the refinery did not adopt all 600 proposals? What characteristics of a particular project might have made it more likely to be adopted?

3. Suppose that you have two available methods for solving a problem. Method A gives the best possible solution to the problem; method B gives a very good solution that is not necessarily the best. Why might you choose method B to solve the problem?

Systems of Inequalities

← CONNECT → *You have seen several ways to solve systems of linear equations. Now you will investigate systems of linear inequalities.*

Much of the mathematics that we use in our daily lives does not come in the form of an equation. Statements like "I've got to have at least $15 for lunches this week," "You can miss no more than three practices before you're cut from the team," and "I want to find a job that pays more than the minimum wage" are statements of inequality.

We often find that more than one inequality applies to the same situation. For instance, you may need to buy enough gasoline to drive at least 40 miles to get home, but you can spend no more than the $5.00 you have in your pocket. Two or more linear inequalities that apply at the same time make up a **system of linear inequalities.** The solution set of a system of inequalities is the region of points whose coordinates satisfy every inequality in the system.

You have seen graphs of single inequalities on a coordinate plane. The following Examples will use the same technique as a basis for graphing systems of linear inequalities.

EXAMPLE

1. Graph the system of linear inequalities:

$$2x + y < 5$$

$$y \geq \frac{5}{4}x - 3$$

First, we graph $y < -2x + 5$. The boundary line is dashed since the inequality is strict.

We then repeat the process with $y \geq \frac{5}{4}x - 3$ on the same grid. Note that the boundary line of $y \geq \frac{5}{4}x - 3$ is solid since the inequality is not strict.

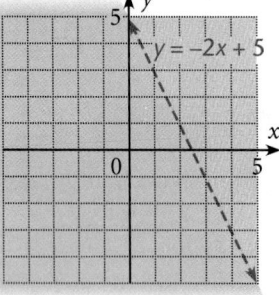

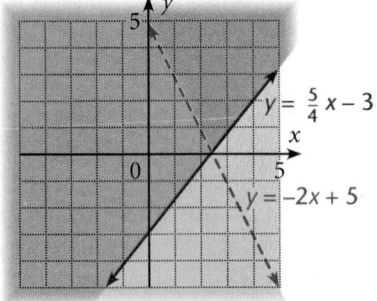

The region with the overlapped shading, plus the points on the solid portion of the line $y = \frac{5}{4}x - 3$ adjoining that region, represent the solution set to the system of inequalities.

2. Suppose that a doctor orders her patient to stay on a diet with at least 55 g (55,000 mg) of protein and at least 125 mg of vitamin C per meal. One of the dinners will be steak and broccoli. Graph the region that shows all possible combinations of steak and broccoli that satisfy these requirements.

Steak, 1 g	235 mg of protein, 0 mg of vitamin C
Broccoli, 1 g	33 mg of protein, $\frac{2}{3}$ mg of vitamin C

Let S = grams of steak and B = grams of broccoli. Begin by writing an inequality to represent each limitation.

Protein	$235S + 33B \geq 55{,}000$
Vitamin C	$\frac{2}{3}B \geq 125$

We can choose to plot either B or S on the vertical axis. We will arbitrarily choose to plot B on the vertical axis. Solving each inequality for B gives:

Protein	$B \geq -7.1S + 1{,}667$
Vitamin C	$B \geq 187.5$

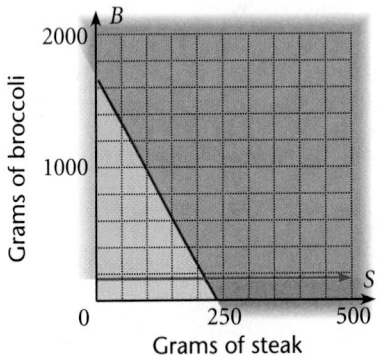

Graphing the related equations, testing points, and shading the appropriate regions gives the solution set shown.

Notice that any meal that satisfies both inequalities has at least 187.5 grams of broccoli. Moreover, if a meal has less than 1667 grams of broccoli, some amount of steak must be included.

CONSIDER

?

1. Why is the system of inequalities in Example 2 graphed in the first quadrant only?
2. In Example 2, why must any satisfactory meal contain some broccoli?

TRY IT

Solve and graph each system of inequalities.

a. $15x + 5y \leq 20$
   $2x - 3y > 6$

b. $y \geq -2$
   $y \leq 3x - 6$
   $2x + 4y < 14$

When you graph a system with more than two inequalities, the solution set may be a closed region. In the following Explore, you will design inequalities so that they "trap" a particular figure.

EXPLORE: TRIANGLE TRAP

MATERIALS

Graph paper

Write and graph a system of inequalities whose solution set is the interior of each of the following geometric figures.

- a right triangle
- a rectangle
- an isosceles triangle
- an equilateral triangle

Explain how you found each system of inequalities and why it gives the required figure.

You've seen that solving a system of inequalities involves graphing each individual inequality, then looking for the region where all of the individual regions overlap. When a real-world problem can be modeled by a system of linear inequalities, we may be able to solve it using a solution technique called *linear programming.* You will soon investigate this method.

REFLECT

1. Is it possible for a system of linear inequalities to have no solution? If so, describe or sketch such a system of inequalities; if not, explain why not.
2. Do you think that it is more unusual for a 2 × 2 system of linear inequalities to have exactly one solution or an infinite number of solutions? Justify your answer.
3. Suppose that the graph of the solution set for a system of inequalities is an enclosed region. Are there an infinite number of solutions? Explain.
4. Give an example of a real-world situation that can be modeled by a system of inequalities. Write an algebraic inequality to model each real-world inequality.

Exercises

CORE

1. Getting Started Follow the steps to graph the system of inequalities.

$y \leq x - 5$
$4x + 2y > 8$

a. Graph the line $y = x - 5$. Use a solid line, since the inequality features the "equal to" possibility.

b. Choose a point on either side of the line. (The origin is often a convenient point.) Substitute its x- and y-coordinates into the inequality $y \leq x - 5$. If these coordinates make the inequality true, shade the side of the line containing the point you chose; if they make the inequality false, shade the other side.

c. Graph $4x + 2y = 8$. Use a dashed line, since the inequality does not have the "equal to" possibility.

d. Using a different shading pattern than the one you used in **b,** shade the appropriate side of the line. The points in the region with the overlapped shading, plus the points on any solid portion of a line adjoining that region, represent the solution set to the system of inequalities.

Graph each inequality on a coordinate plane.

2. $x > 3$ **3.** $2y > x$ **4.** $y \leq \frac{1}{2}x + 1$ **5.** $3x - 9y \leq 18$

Write an inequality to describe each situation.

6. The water bottle can hold no more than two gallons.

7. The total number of reserved and general admission tickets sold cannot exceed 12,000.

8. The minimum balance for a savings account is $500.

9. A simple income tax schedule is shown.

Social Science

Income	Tax
Up to $20,000	15% of income
More than $20,000	$3,000 + 28% of income in excess of $20,000

a. For what incomes is the tax at least 20% of total income?

b. For what incomes is the tax at most 25% of total income?

c. Tony's employer wants him to work overtime hours in December. If Tony does this, his income for the year will barely exceed $20,000. Tony is worried that, since the additional income will change his tax bracket, he will actually *lose* money—that is, his additional taxes will exceed his added income—by working more hours. Are his fears justified?

Graph each system of linear inequalities.

10. $y \leq 6$
     $y \geq x - 7$

11. $y > 3x - 7$
      $y \leq 5x + 2$

12. $y \geq 3x$
      $-x + 3y \leq 8$

13. **Tanks a Lot** Gia's pickup truck has an EPA mileage rating of 18 miles per gallon (mpg) in the city, and 26 mpg on the highway. The maximum capacity of the gasoline tank is 16 gallons. Let x represent the number of city miles and y the number of highway miles.

a. How many gallons of gasoline are used when driving x city miles? y highway miles?

b. Write an inequality for the number of gallons of gasoline she can use without refilling.

c. Graph the region of all points whose coordinates satisfy this inequality.

d. Describe how the graph for the mathematical model differs from the graph for the real-world situation. What other inequalities should be included to represent the real situation?

Graph each system of linear inequalities.

14. $y \le x$
$x + 2y \ge -4$
$-2 \le x < 6$

15. $y \ge -3$
$3x - 6y \ge -12$
$4x - 5y \ge -5$

16. $2x + 3y < 6$
$3x - 2y \le 12$
$x - y \ge 0$
$x \ge 0$

17. Alice said, "I can tell which side of an inequality to shade without testing a point. First, I solve the inequality for y and graph the boundary line. Then, if the inequality says $y >$ (or $\ge$), I shade above the line. If the inequality says $y <$ (or $\le$), I shade below the line."

Is Alice correct? If so, explain why her method works; if not, explain why not.

18. **Growing Up Big and Strong** Kendrick wants to take a minimum of 450 units of vitamin C and 300 units of vitamin E per day. *C-Plus* vitamins provide 100 units of C and 50 units of E per tablet. *Vita-Balance* vitamins provide 75 units of C and 75 units of E.

Transmitted light micrograph of vitamin C

a. Write a system of inequalities that indicates how the daily minimum requirements for vitamins C and E can be met with combinations of the two brands.

Problem-Solving Tip

Write an inequality to represent each restriction.

b. Graph the solution set for the system.

c. Recommend to Kendrick two different vitamin plans that fit the restrictions.

d. What other factors would you consider before deciding on an acceptable plan using the products in this situation?

 **LOOK BACK**

Solve each linear system if possible. State the number of solutions, and tell whether the system is consistent or inconsistent. [3-1]

19. $2x + 5y = 24$
$\qquad x = 2$

20. $\quad C + G = 14$
$\qquad 2C + 3G = 56$

21. $7s + 3t = 74$
$\quad 2s + 5t = 46$

22. $6c + 3d = 108$
$\quad 5c + 4d = 114$

Solve and graph each inequality. [2-3]

23. $-12 \le 2x$ and $3x - 4 \ge 11$ **24.** $4x + 1 > 13$ or $x + 3 \le 9 - 3x$ **25.** $|3x - 12| < 15$

MORE PRACTICE

Graph each inequality on a coordinate plane.

26. $y \le 5$ **27.** $y < 2x - 3$ **28.** $3x + \frac{3}{5}y \ge 6$ **29.** $6x + 4y > 48$

Write an inequality to describe each situation.

30. The total number of Democratic and Republican members of the U.S. House of Representatives cannot exceed 435.

31. The minimum fine for a carpool lane violation is $271.

32. A city proposes to reduce the amount of soot in its air to an average of 30 micrograms or less per cubic meter of air.

Graph each system of linear inequalities.

33. $y > 3x$
$\quad y < -3$

34. $y \le 2x + 2$
$\quad y > x - 4$

35. $3x + y < 9$
$\quad 2x - y \le 4$

36. $y > x$
$\quad 3x - 6y > 15$
$\quad y \le 2$

37. $y \ge 0$
$\quad x \ge 0$
$\quad x + y \le 14$

38. $4x + 3y < 12$
$\quad -2 \le y \le 7$
$\quad 2y \ge 4x - 6$
$\quad x \ge -1$

39. If You Fail to Plan... Toshiko is starting to plan a monthly budget by classifying expenditures as rent (r) and other expenses and savings (x). Her total net income is $1400 per month. She can spend no more than 28% of her budget on rent.
   a. Write an inequality to express the fact that Toshiko can spend no more than $1400 per month.
   b. Write an inequality to express the 28% rent limitation. (Hint: What is 28% of $1400?)
   c. Do any other inequalities apply to this situation? Explain.
   d. Sketch a graph of the region that satisfies all of your inequalities in **a–c.**

MORE MATH REASONING

Use a graphing utility to graph each system of inequalities. Use an appropriate window size. Sketch each graph.

40. $y \geq x^2$
$y < 4$

41. $y \geq x$
$y \geq x^2$

42. $y \geq x^2$
$y \geq x^3$

43. A random number function on a computer generates a pair of numbers, each between 0 and 1. Let the first number generated represent the x-coordinate of a point and the second represent the y-coordinate. What is the probability that the numbers are the coordinates of a point inside the shaded quarter-circle shown on the graph? Explain your reasoning.

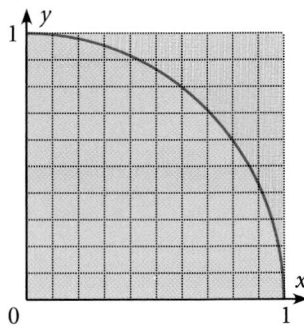

Linear Programming Constraints

← **CONNECT** → *You've solved systems of linear inequalities. Limitations, or constraints, on real-world situations can be modeled by systems of inequalities. Linear programming is used to solve problems defined by a system of linear constraints.*

People and businesses face problems every day where they must find a best solution given certain limitations. For instance, a business may have a limited amount of money to spend on raw materials or a limited amount of factory time to produce an item. **Linear programming** is a method of modeling and solving problems where these limitations, or **constraints,** can be modeled by linear inequalities.

The solution to the system of constraints is the **feasible region** for the linear programming problem. The feasible region includes all points whose coordinates satisfy every constraint. Today, you will be graphing feasible regions for linear programming problems.

1. Two astronomers, Ms. Brown and Mr. Chang, need to use a telescope next week for their research. Ms. Brown's work will require at least twice as much time as Mr. Chang's work. There are 45 hours of telescope time available, and the astronomers are unable to use the telescope at the same time. Write the constraints and graph the feasible region for this situation.

Let B = Brown's hours and C = Chang's hours. Then:

$B \geq 2C$ Ms. Brown's work will require at least twice as much time.

$B + C \leq 45$ There are 45 hours of time available.

$B \geq 0$ and $C \geq 0$ The astronomers cannot work for a negative amount of time.

To graph the first constraint, $B \geq 2C$, we start by graphing $B = 2C$. We can choose either axis to be the B-axis. Because there are usually several constraints for a linear programming problem, it is impractical to use shading for each inequality. Instead, we use arrows to indicate which side of the line solves the inequality.

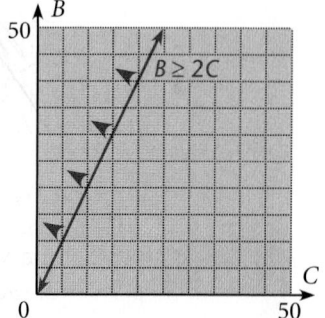

Graphing the other inequalities gives the graph shown at the right. The feasible region is the triangular region at the left of the graph. Notice that all sides of the feasible region have arrows pointing to its interior.

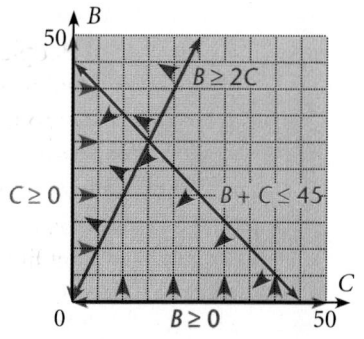

The shaded region is the feasible region—the region that satisfies all of the inequalities. To make the feasible region more obvious, we also remove any parts of the linear graphs that do not help delineate the feasible region.

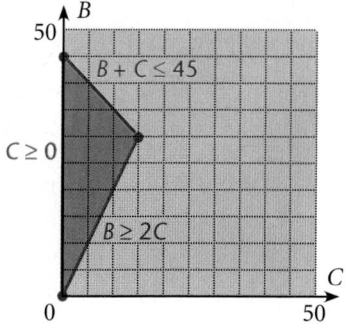

In the Explore, you will graph the feasible region for a problem involving a pizza parlor. Save your work from this Explore because you will use these results in the Explore in Part C.

EXPLORE: HOW MANY PIZZAS?

MATERIALS

Graph paper

You have just been hired as manager of Todaro's, a small business that makes frozen pizzas for sale to local markets. Todaro's makes 12-inch pizzas for a profit of $2 a box, and 16-inch pizzas for a profit of $4 a box. Preparation and packaging take 0.2 hours for each box of 12-inch pizzas and 0.25 hours for each box of 16-inch pizzas. The staff at Todaro's can put at most 240 hours into preparation and packaging per week, and they must meet the company quota of producing at least 1000 boxes of pizzas per week.

1. There are several constraints on the numbers of each type of box Todaro's can produce in a week. Write a linear inequality to represent each constraint. The last two constraints weren't explicitly stated in the problem. They represent the obvious fact that Todaro's can't produce a negative number of boxes.

2. Graph the feasible region described by the constraints in Step 1. Does the feasible region for this problem include the boundaries?

3. Now, find the coordinates of each corner point, or *vertex,* of your feasible region. If the coordinates of a vertex are not obvious, identify the two linear equations that intersect at the vertex. Then set up those equations as a system and solve. (You will see why it is important to be able to find the coordinates of the vertices in Part C.)

4. Guess the best production strategy for Todaro's. In other words, what number of 12- and 16-inch pizzas will give this business the maximum profit? Find the profit Todaro's could expect to make using this strategy. Explain how you made your guess.

In Example 1 and in Step 1 of the Explore, two of the constraints showed that the quantities in the problem could not be negative. When writing constraints for a real-world problem, think about whether or not negative values make sense for the variables. If they do not, include non-negativity constraints.

2. **Coffee Beans** Edwina Jackson is a coffee supplier with 4000 pounds of premium beans and 2000 pounds of bargain beans in stock this month. Edwina supplies coffee houses with *Edwina's Excellent Coffee,* a grind of 100% premium beans, and *Jackson's Regular Coffee,* a grind of one-third premium plus two-thirds bargain beans. Her company can grind, package, and ship at most 5000 pounds of coffee this month. Write the constraints for this situation. Then graph the feasible region and find the coordinates of the vertices of the feasible region.

Let E = number of pounds of Edwina's Excellent Coffee produced and shipped this month.

Let R = number of pounds of Jackson's Regular Coffee produced and shipped this month.

Constraints:

$E + R \leq 5000$	At most a total of 5000 lb of coffee can be shipped.
$E + \frac{1}{3}R \leq 4000$	At most 4000 lb of premium beans can be used.
$\frac{2}{3}R \leq 2000$	At most 2000 lb of bargain beans can be used.
$E \geq 0 \quad R \geq 0$	Amounts of coffee cannot be negative.

Feasible Region:

The graph of the system of constraints is the pentagon *STUVW* and its interior.

Vertices:

From the graph, the vertices are:
$S(0, 0)$, $T(0, 3000)$, $U(2000, 3000)$ $V(3500, 1500)$, and $W(4000, 0)$.

Although these coordinates seem clear from the graph, vertex points are not always so conveniently located, so we will illustrate an algebraic solution for the coordinates of *V.*

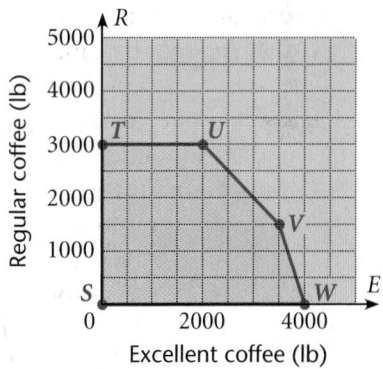

V is at the intersection of $E + R = 5000$ and $E + \frac{1}{3}R = 4000$. We can solve this system by linear combination, or by substitution, as shown below.

Solving $E + R = 5000$ for E gives $E = -R + 5000$.

$$-R + 5000 + \frac{1}{3}R = 4000 \quad \text{Substitute into } E + \frac{1}{3}R = 4000.$$
$$-\frac{2}{3}R = -1000$$
$$R = 1500$$

Substituting $R = 1500$ into $E = -R + 5000$ gives $E = 3500$. *V* has coordinates $(3500, 1500)$.

CONSIDER
?

1. In Example 2, what is the real-world meaning of point *U*?
2. In the Explore and the Examples, what type of geometric figure did the feasible region turn out to be? Do you think this is generally true? Explain why or why not.

TRY IT

a. Graph the feasible region for the following constraints. Then find the coordinates of the vertices.

$$x \geq 0 \qquad y \geq 0 \qquad x + y \leq 10 \qquad x + 3y \leq 24 \qquad 2x + y \leq 18$$

Write the constraints for each of the following situations. Be sure to include constraints that show that the quantities cannot be negative.

b. A bookstore can stock a total of 40,000 books. The store manager feels that there should be no more than 25,000 nonfiction books and 30,000 fiction books.

c. A cereal manufacturer is combining Blueberry Flakies and Corn Crunchies to make a new cereal. A serving of the new cereal cannot weigh more than 50 grams and cannot have more than 270 mg of sodium. Blueberry Flakies have 3 mg of sodium per gram and Corn Crunchies have 6 mg of sodium per gram.

A linear programming problem features restrictions, or constraints, that can be modeled by linear inequalities. You've seen how to write constraints and graph the feasible region for a linear programming problem. In 3-2C, you will discover how to find the best solution to the problem.

REFLECT

1. Look up the word *constraint* in the dictionary. How is the meaning of this word related to the inequalities in a linear programming problem?
2. What is a *feasible region* and what does it represent in real-world problems?
3. Explain how you can find the coordinates of a vertex of the feasible region.
4. The linear programming problems you've seen all have *nonnegativity* constraints of the type $B \geq 0$. Explain why they have these constraints.
5. Do you think all real-world linear programming problems must have nonnegativity constraints? If so, explain why. If not, describe a situation where they are not appropriate.

Exercises

CORE

1. **Getting Started** The feasible region is shown for the four inequalities below. Follow the steps to find the coordinates of each vertex.

    $x + y \leq 8$
    $2x + 4y \leq 20$
    $x \geq 0$
    $y \geq 0$

    a. Find the coordinates of A by substituting $x = 0$ into the equation $2x + 4y = 20$.
    b. Find the coordinates of B by solving the system of equations.
    $2x + 4y = 20$
    $x + y = 8$
    c. Find the coordinates of C by substituting $y = 0$ into $x + y = 8$.
    d. What are the coordinates of point D?

Write the word or phrase that correctly completes each statement.

2. In a linear programming problem, the ____ are a set of inequalities that model limitations.

3. The points that are possible solutions to a linear programming problem are in the ____.

Graph the feasible region for each of the following sets of constraints (inequalities). Then find the coordinates of the vertices.

4. $x \geq 0$
   $y \geq 0$
   $x + y \leq 8$

5. $x \geq 0$
   $y \geq 0$
   $x + y \leq 5$
   $3x + y \leq 9$

6. $x \geq 0$
   $y \geq 0$
   $50x + 40y \leq 5000$
   $x \leq 80$

Write a set of linear inequalities to model the constraints in each situation. Then graph the feasible region and find the coordinates of its vertices.

7. There are 1500 tickets available for sale for a show. Some of the seats are reserved, the rest are general admission. At most 500 of the tickets can be sold as reserved tickets.

8. **A Taste of the Tropics** A juice manufacturer imports 1200 quarts of guava juice and 500 quarts of mango juice each month. They sell 1-quart bottles of pure guava juice and also a 50/50 guava-mango punch. (Hint: Your variables should represent the amounts of bottled pure guava juice and of bottled guava-mango punch.) Note: The solution of this Exercise will help you find the answer to Exercise 6 on page 217.

9. **Happy "Hollow-Bead"** Bead-Counter stores sell necklaces that you make yourself. Customers create jewelry by selecting beads from various bins. Grace wants to design her own Halloween necklace from orange and black beads. She wants to make a necklace that is at least 12 inches long but no more than 24 inches long. Grace also wants her necklace to contain black beads that are at least twice the length of the orange beads. Finally, she wants her necklace to have at least 5 inches of black beads.

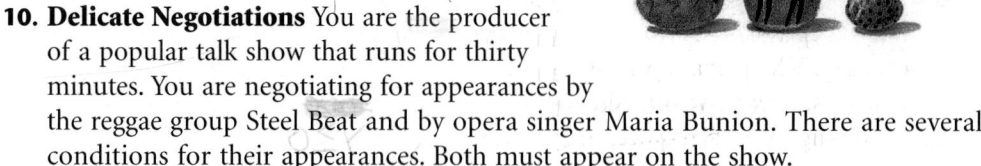

10. **Delicate Negotiations** You are the producer of a popular talk show that runs for thirty minutes. You are negotiating for appearances by the reggae group Steel Beat and by opera singer Maria Bunion. There are several conditions for their appearances. Both must appear on the show.
   - As producer, you have a maximum of $9000 to spend on entertainment for Monday's show. Steel Beat charges $600 for each minute they play. Bunion's performance fee is $300 for each minute that she sings.
   - Eight minutes is reserved for the show's opening, closing, and commercial segments. The remainder of the time is available for featured guests.
   - Steel Beat will not appear on the show unless they are allowed to perform at least one number lasting at least 3 minutes.
   - Maria Bunion will not appear unless she is allowed to perform at least as long as Steel Beat.

   Note: The solution of this Exercise will help you find the answer to Exercise 7 on page 217.

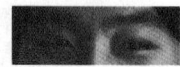

LOOK AHEAD

11. Graph the family of lines $2x + 3y = k$ for $k = 0, 6,$ and 12. Describe any patterns that you observe.

12. Name some quantities that each of the following types of people might want to maximize or minimize.
   a. a business owner   **b.** a park ranger   **c.** a principal
   d. the supervisor of a relief organization for refugee children

MORE PRACTICE

Graph the feasible region for each of the following sets of constraints (inequalities). Then find the coordinates of the vertices.

13. $x \geq 0$
   $y \geq 0$
   $3x + 5y \leq 15$

14. $x \geq 0$
   $y \geq 2$
   $x + y \leq 9$
   $y \geq 2x$

15. $x \geq 0$
   $y \geq 0$
   $12x + 10y \leq 2400$
   $y \leq 120$

Write a set of linear inequalities to model the constraints in each situation. Then graph the feasible region and find the coordinates of its vertices.

16. **Field Trip** An elementary school wants to send some children to a museum for a field trip. The museum staff has informed the school that tours can be scheduled for no more than 50 people and the school must provide at least one adult supervisor for every 9 students.

17. **Have a Heart** A group of artists has decided to produce hand-drawn cards for Valentine's Day and donate the money generated to charity. The artists will produce ink drawings and watercolors. They have volunteered to spend 120 hours for preparation of the valentines and 60 hours for packaging. The preparation of an ink drawing takes 0.3 hours, while a watercolor takes 0.5 hours. The packaging of each requires 0.2 hours. Graph the feasible region for these constraints. Then find the coordinates of the vertices.

18. **A Taxing Exercise?** The tax firm of D. Duction needs to determine the clientele it will seek for the upcoming tax season. The firm provides two services, a basic tax return and an in-depth return. The basic return requires 0.5 hours of preparation time and 0.6 hours of review time. The in-depth return requires 2 hours of preparation time and 1.2 hours of review time. The office has 700 hours of preparation time and 510 hours of review time available per week. Let x be the number of basic returns done per week and y be the number of in-depth returns. Graph the feasible region for these constraints. Then find the coordinates of the vertices.

Note: The solution to this Exercise will help you find the answer to Exercise 23 on page 219.

MORE MATH REASONING

19. **Park Place** Yamada Development Company will build a major shopping mall with 3 magnet (large) stores and 80 smaller shops. It must be decided how many public parking spaces and how many employee parking spaces the parking lot will have.
   - There is room available to build no more than 2500 parking spaces.
   - The city requires a minimum of 2000 total parking spaces, and also requires that there be at least 4 times as many public spaces as employee spaces.
   - Prospective businesses have been promised a minimum of 20 employee spaces for each magnet store and 2 employee spaces for each smaller shop.
   a. Graph the feasible region for these constraints. Then find the coordinates of the vertices.
   b. What are some objectives that the development company might consider when deciding on how many of each type of parking space to construct?

Note: The solution to this Exercise will help you find the answer to Exercise 25 on page 219.

20. Choose a product or service of a business that interests you. Describe at least 5 factors that could constrain the amount of product or service provided by the business. (You do not need to assign specific numbers to these constraints.) Try to be imaginative; that is, visualize each stage in providing the product or service.

← **C O N N E C T** → *You've seen how to write and graph constraints for a linear programming problem. You will now solve linear programming problems.*

Finding and graphing constraints for a linear programming problem gives a picture of *all* the points that satisfy every constraint. But which of these points is the "best" one—the **optimal solution** to the problem?

Before you can answer this question for a linear programming problem, you must know what your goal is. Is it to minimize waste? maximize profit? The equation that gives the value of the quantity you want to optimize in terms of the variables in the problem is called the **objective function.**

EXAMPLES

Write the objective function for each situation.

1. A wildlife photographer sells framed 12-in. × 20-in. prints for $240 and 18-in. × 30-in. prints for $365. His goal is to maximize total revenue.

Let S = the number of small prints sold and L = the number of large prints sold. The quantity to be maximized is R, total revenue.

The objective function is $R = 240S + 365L$.

2. A salesperson can travel from her office to City A, a 120-mile round-trip, and City B, an 85-mile round-trip. She wants to minimize the total distance she travels.

Let A = the number of trips to City A and B = the number of trips to City B. The quantity to be minimized is D, total distance.

The objective function is $D = 120A + 85B$.

An objective function needs to be linked to constraints for a problem to exist—otherwise, the photographer in Example 1 would sell an infinite number of each print and the salesperson in Example 2 would only make sales from her home! In the Explore, you will combine constraints with an objective function to solve a linear programming problem.

EXPLORE: HOW MANY PIZZAS?

Recall from the Explore in Part B that you have just been hired as manager of Todaro's, a small business that makes frozen pizzas that sell to local markets. Todaro's makes 12-inch pizzas for a profit of $2 a box, and 16-inch pizzas for a profit of $4 a box. Preparation and packaging take 0.2 hours for each box of 12-inch pizzas and 0.25 hours for each box of 16-inch pizzas. The staff at Todaro's can put at most 240 hours into preparation and packaging per week and must meet the company's weekly quota of producing at least 1000 boxes of pizzas. How many boxes of each type of pizza should you instruct the staff to make to maximize total profit?

1. Write the objective function for this situation using your variables from the Explore in Part B. Is your goal to minimize or maximize the value of this function?

2. From your work in the previous Explore, you should have a graph of the feasible region and a list of the coordinates of the vertices for this problem. Identify the coordinates of a point inside the feasible region. Then find the value of the objective function at that point by substituting each coordinate for the appropriate variable.

3. Search for the optimal solution to this problem by repeating Step 2 for other feasible points. Try points inside the region, points on the boundaries, and vertex points. Once you have found what you think is the best solution to the problem, state how many boxes of each type of pizza your staff should make and the amount of profit this will generate.

4. Explain any strategy that you used to look for the optimal point in Step 3.

5. Was the optimal point inside the feasible region, on one of its sides, or at one of its vertices? Do you think this will always be true? Why or why not?

3. Recall the coffee beans in Example 2, Part B. The variables were:

E = number of pounds of Edwina's Excellent Coffee produced and shipped this month;

R = number of pounds of Jackson's Regular Coffee produced and shipped this month.

The feasible region is shown.

The coordinates of the vertex points are:
$S(0, 0)$, $T(0, 3000)$, $U(2000, 3000)$, $V(3500, 1500)$ and $W(4000, 0)$.

Suppose Edwina Jackson makes a profit of $3 for each pound of Excellent coffee and $2 for each pound of Regular coffee she supplies. Find the point in the feasible region that maximizes her profit.

Let P = profit. Then the objective function is:
$P = 3E + 2R$

To find the optimal solution, substitute the coordinates of each vertex point into the objective function. Note: When doing this, we must remember that the first coordinate is an E-value!

Point	Profit
$S(0, 0)$	$P = 3(0) + 2(0) = \$0$
$T(0, 3000)$	$P = 3(0) + 2(3000) = \$6,000$
$U(2000, 3000)$	$P = 3(2000) + 2(3000) = \$12,000$
$V(3500, 1500)$	$P = 3(3500) + 2(1500) = \$13,500$
$W(4000, 0)$	$P = 3(4000) + 2(0) = \$12,000$

The optimal solution is for Edwina to supply 3500 pounds of Excellent coffee and 1500 pounds of Regular coffee. This gives the maximum possible profit for the month, $13,500.

CONSIDER

1. It was not absolutely necessary to check all five of the vertex points to find the optimal solution of Example 3. Which vertex points cannot possibly give the optimal solution? How do you know?

2. In Example 3, suppose that the profit on a pound of Excellent coffee increases to $7. Predict how such a steep increase will change the optimal solution. Then check your prediction by rewriting the objective function and checking the vertex points again.

The optimal solution of a linear programming problem can be found visually. This method helps illustrate why the optimal point is on the boundary of the feasible region.

Consider the feasible region for Example 3. We have graphed the objective function $P = 3E + 2R$ for a $9,000 profit. Notice that it cuts through the feasible region, showing that there are an infinite number of points that will give a $9,000 profit.

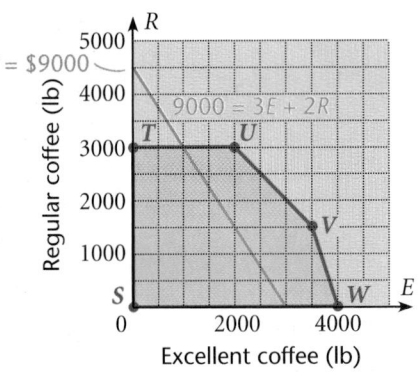

Now, we "slide" the objective function to higher and higher profit levels. Eventually, it touches the feasible region in just one point—(3500, 1500), the optimal solution—at a profit level of $13,500.

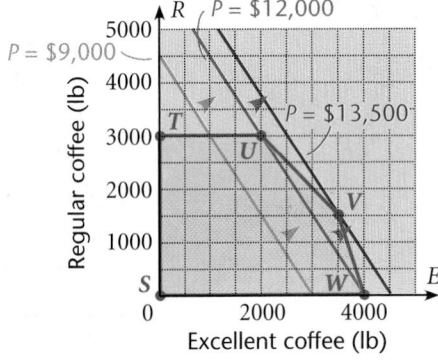

TRY IT

a. What is the maximum value of the objective function $F = 9x + 10y$ on the feasible region? At what point does it occur?

b. A pet food store sells birdseed for a profit of 40¢ per pound and mineral supplements for a profit of 60¢ per pound. The store must stock at least twice as much birdseed as mineral supplements, and can order no more than 90 pounds total of these two items in a month. Assuming the store can sell all that it buys, how many pounds of each item should be purchased each month in order to maximize profit?

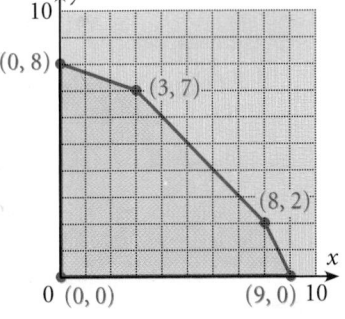

You have seen that the optimal solution to a linear programming problem is found at an extreme point of the feasible region.

> **VERTEX THEOREM**
>
> If a linear programming problem has an optimal solution, then one of the vertices of the feasible region represents an optimal solution.

Linear programming is a powerful tool for solving real-world problems. Scenarios involving hundreds of thousands of variables have been solved using linear programming techniques on computers.

REFLECT

1. Does it make sense that the optimal solution of a linear programming problem cannot occur at a point inside the feasible region? Why or why not?
2. Write a definition of an *objective function* in your own words.
3. Describe some quantities besides revenue, profit, and cost that a business might want to minimize or maximize.

Exercises

CORE

1. **Getting Started** What is the maximum value of the objective function $F = x + 3y$ on the feasible region? At what point does it occur?

2. What is the minimum value of the objective function $F = 5x - 2y$ on the feasible region? At what point does it occur?

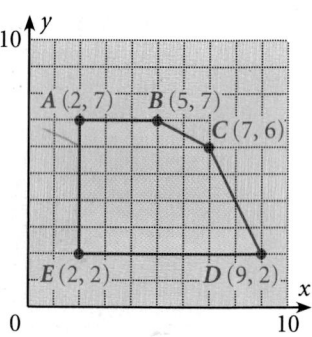

Write the objective function for each situation.

3. An ice show charges $15 for general admission tickets and $25 for reserved seats. The management wants to maximize its revenue.

4. A rental car agency finds that it costs $500 per year to maintain a midsize car and $300 per year to maintain a compact. The agency wants to minimize its costs.

5. A TV show finds that music acts attract m viewers and comedy acts attract n viewers. The show wants to attract the maximum possible number of viewers.

6. A Taste of the Tropics In Exercise 8 on page 209, you graphed constraints for a linear programming problem involving a juice manufacturer who produces two types of juice.

Suppose the manufacturer makes a profit of $0.80 per quart bottle of guava juice and $1.00 per quart bottle of guava-mango punch. They wish to maximize their profit. Write the objective function. Then find the optimal solution. How many bottles of each type should they produce, and how much profit will they make?

7. Delicate Negotiations In Exercise 10 on page 210 you graphed constraints for a linear programming problem involving musical guests on a television show.

As producer of the show, you want to minimize costs. Write the objective function. Then find the optimal solution. How long should each guest perform, and how much will this cost?

8. Little Shop O' Cheap Fertilizer A garden shop wishes to prepare a supply of special fertilizer at a minimal cost by mixing two fertilizers, A and B. The mixture is to contain at least 45 units of phosphate, at least 36 units of nitrate, and at least 40 units of ammonium. (The specifications for fertilizers A and B are listed in the table.) Fertilizer A costs the shop $0.97/lb and fertilizer B costs $1.89/lb.

Product	Phosphate (units per pound)	Nitrate (units per pound)	Ammonium (units per pound)
A	5	2	2
B	3	3	5

a. Write the cost (objective) function that is to be minimized. Use x to represent the amount of fertilizer A and y to represent the amount of fertilizer B.

b. Copy the following constraints and supply the missing coefficients:

Units of phosphate _____ x + _____ $y \geq 45$
Units of nitrate _____ x + _____ $y \geq 36$
Units of ammonium _____ x + _____ $y \geq 40$
$$x \geq 0, y \geq 0$$

c. Graph the feasible region. Calculate and label the coordinates of the vertices.

d. How many pounds of each fertilizer should be mixed to make the special fertilizer? What is the cost of this mixture?

Industry

9. Wise Acres A farmer has asked you for advice on the best strategy for planting wheat and corn on her 500-acre farm. To make it through harvest time, each acre of wheat she plants will require one person-day of labor and other expenses of $20, and each acre of corn she plants will require five person-days of labor and other expenses of $30. The farmer has $11,400 and 1480 person-days of labor available, and she expects to make a profit of $90 per acre of wheat and $120 per acre of corn.

a. What is the most profitable planting strategy for the farmer? How much total profit can she expect to make on her crops using this strategy?

b. The farmer discovers that wheat profits are expected to be $10 per acre *less* than she first estimated. What has changed in the linear programming problem? Solve the new problem and decide what planting strategy is best now. Did the farmer's best strategy change? How much total profit can she expect to make on her crops now?

c. The farmer also finds that corn profits will be $10 per acre *more* than she first estimated. Does this change the farmer's best strategy for planting her crops? What total profits can she expect to make now?

10. In 3 to 5 steps, describe the process of solving a linear programming problem.

 **LOOK BACK**

Solve each equation. [2-1]

11. $2x - 7 = 5x + 14$ **12.** $\frac{3}{4}x + \frac{7}{2} = \frac{1}{2}x - \frac{9}{4}$ **13.** $4(6x - 10) = -2(4 - 3x)$

Use the matrices below to find each of the following if possible. If not possible, explain why. [1-3]

$$A = \begin{bmatrix} 3 & -7 \\ -2 & 5 \end{bmatrix} \qquad B = \begin{bmatrix} 5 & -11 & 2 \\ -1 & 0 & 9 \\ 3 & -6 & 2 \end{bmatrix} \qquad C = \begin{bmatrix} -4 & 2 \\ -5 & 7 \end{bmatrix}$$

14. $A + C$ **15.** $2B$ **16.** $3A$

17. $A - B$ **18.** $2A + 4C$ **19.** $\frac{1}{2}C$

MORE PRACTICE

Write the objective function for each situation.

20. A software company sells word-processing software for a profit of $150 a copy and spreadsheet software for a profit of $60 a copy. The company wants to maximize its profits.

21. You need to buy Swiss cheese for $2.59 a pound and gouda cheese at $3.57 a pound. You want to minimize the amount you pay.

22. A grocery store finds that television ads attract x customers per dollar spent and coupon books attract y customers per dollar spent. Management wants to maximize the number of customers.

23. A Taxing Exercise? In Exercise 18 on page 211, you graphed constraints for a situation involving the tax firm of D. Duction, which needs to decide how many basic returns and in-depth returns it should provide.

The firm charges $50 for a basic tax return and $150 for an in-depth return. Write the objective function to maximize revenue. Then find the optimal solution. How many of each type of return should D. Duction provide, and how much revenue should this generate?

24. The Truck Shop's Here An automobile manufacturer makes cars and trucks in a factory that is divided into two shops. The first shop, which does the basic assembly, needs 5 worker-days per truck and 2 worker-days per car. The second shop, which does the finishing touches, needs 3 worker-days for both cars and trucks. The first shop has 180 worker-days available per week and the second shop has 135 worker-days available. The profit is $500 per car and $700 per truck. How many of each type of vehicle should the manufacturer produce each week to maximize profit? What is the maximum profit?

MORE MATH REASONING

25. Park Place In Exercise 19 on page 211, you graphed constraints for a situation involving public and employee parking at a new shopping mall.

a. Suppose that construction costs are $190 per public parking space and $215 per employee space. Write the objective function for the cost of constructing the parking lot. How many of each type of parking space should be constructed to minimize cost? What is the cost?

b. Instead of minimizing cost, assume the objective is to maximize the number of employee parking spaces in order to attract businesses. Write the objective function for this goal. How many of each type of parking space should be constructed?

c. Assume the objective is to maximize the number of public parking spaces in order to attract shoppers. Write the objective function. How many of each type of parking space should be constructed?

26. All of the constraints for the linear programming problems you have seen are either $\leq$ or $\geq$ inequalities. Would constraints with $<$ or $>$ signs present any problems in regard to our technique for solving linear programming problems? Why or why not?

27. All of the objective functions you have worked with so far are linear. Suppose your objective function for a system of linear constraints is *not* linear. Will an optimal solution necessarily be found at a corner point? Explain.

Industry

28. You are the manager of a mining company that owns two mines, each of which produces a particular kind of ore. The mines have different production capacities and different expenses. Mined ore is crushed and graded into three classes: high-grade, medium-grade, and low-grade. The mining company has contracted to provide a smelting plant with 12 tons of high-grade, 8 tons of medium-grade, and 24 tons of low-grade ore each week. The first mine costs $600 per day to run and produces 6 tons of high-grade, 2 tons of medium-grade, and 4 tons of low-grade ore each week. The second mine costs $450 per day to run and produces 2 tons of high-grade, 2 tons of medium-grade, and 12 tons of low-grade ore.

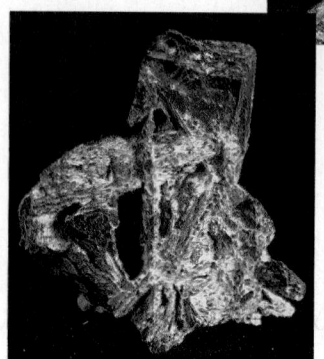
Native silver

Copper sulfite (indigo copper)

a. How many days per week should you operate each mine to minimize the company's weekly costs?

b. Use your answer from **a** to determine how much of each type of ore should be produced and what the minimum cost will be.

c. Due to an administrative error, the information you received about the costs of operating the mines was mistakenly reversed. How does this information affect your decision?

29. Integer Programming You may have noticed that corner points in the linear programming exercises you've solved have had integer coordinates. In cases where the variables represent integers (such as the number of people assigned to a certain task) and the best-corner point solution does *not* have integer coordinates, finding an optimal solution becomes more complex. Solutions of such problems are found using *integer programming*.

Your math teacher has designed a 25-minute quiz that includes a combination of 10-point and 5-point problems. You may choose to answer no more than six problems. On average, the 10-point questions take 7 minutes to answer and 5-point problems take 3 minutes. There is no partial credit, and you are not allowed to turn in an incomplete solution.

a. List and accurately graph the constraints for this situation. Find the coordinates for the vertices. Which of these points represent impossible answers?

b. Using your graph to help you, list *all* possible solutions for this situation. Explain how you found these solutions.

c. From past experience, you know that your probability of answering a 10-point problem correctly is 80% and your probability of answering a 5-point problem correctly is 90%. On average, how many points would you expect to get on each type of problem? You, of course, want to maximize your score.

d. Using your objective function and the list of possible solutions from **b,** find the number of each type of question you would answer to maximize your score. What score would you expect to receive? If you did not test all of the points from **b,** explain how you chose which points to examine.

e. Find the vertex point solution that maximizes your objective function. How does this compare to your optimal solution in **d**?

← CONNECT → *Linear programming finds optimal solutions of complex problems involving linear inequalities. By using graphs you can model and solve problems similar to those that people in business face every day.*

Important business decisions require careful consideration. Linear programming can be an invaluable tool that helps businesses decide how to make the best use of the resources they have.

EXPLORE: SOFTWARE PRODUCTION DECISIONS

MATERIALS

Graph paper

The MouseTrax software company produces both a word-processing program and a game for personal computers. Some of the work that goes into producing these products includes testing and debugging, maintenance and upgrading, and packaging and shipping.

The work requirements for one unit of each product are shown in the following table, along with the maximum weekly capacity for each type of work.

Work Requirement (hours per unit)			
	Testing and Debugging	Maintenance and Upgrading	Packaging and Shipping
Word-Processing Program	1.0	0.8	0.5
Game	0.1	0.2	0.5
Work Capacity (per week)	176.0	160.0	250.0

MouseTrax makes $85 profit on each word-processing program and $35 profit on each game.

1. How many programs and how many games should MouseTrax produce per week to maximize total profit on these two products? What is that profit?
2. Suppose that one of MouseTrax's competitors, Virtual Fun, introduces a new game. To compete with Virtual Fun, MouseTrax has decided to lower the price of its game by $20. Should MouseTrax alter its production strategy to maximize its weekly profits? What will the company's profits be now? Explain how you answered these questions.
3. Virtual Fun's new game has become a fad and is threatening to take over the market. In response, MouseTrax reduces the price of its game so that it now makes only $8 profit on each game. What production strategy should the company adopt in order to maximize its weekly profits now? Do you think the company's strategy would change if the price was cut further? Explain.

Linear programming is a cornerstone in the field of operations research. Graduates with degrees in operations research are employed in a wide variety of industries, such as communications, electronics, health care, and transportation, to help businesses improve the efficiency of their operations.

REFLECT

1. Write a brief paragraph describing what is meant by *linear programming*.
2. Write three phrases that could be translated into mathematical constraints.
3. Can an objective function in a linear programming problem reach its optimal value at an interior point of the feasible region? Justify your answer.
4. Explain how you can find the vertices of the feasible region of a linear programming problem. Why do you want to find these vertices?

Self-Assessment

Graph each system of linear inequalities.

1. $x > -3$
$y \le 2x - 6$

2. $y \ge 2x - 8$
$y > x + 2$

3. $y \ge \frac{3}{2}x$
$4x - 2y < 10$

Graph the feasible region for each of the following sets of constraints. Then find the coordinates of the vertices.

4. $y \ge 0$
$x \ge 0$
$x + y \le 6$

5. $y \ge 0$
$x \ge 0$
$2x + 4y \le 12$

6. $x + y \ge 4$
$x \ge 1$
$y \ge 0$

7. What is the maximum value of the objective function $F = 30x + 50y$ on the feasible region? At what point does it occur?

8. What is the minimum value of the objective function $F = 80x + 20y$ on the feasible region? At what point does it occur?

9. Write an objective function for which $(9, 3)$ is the optimal solution.

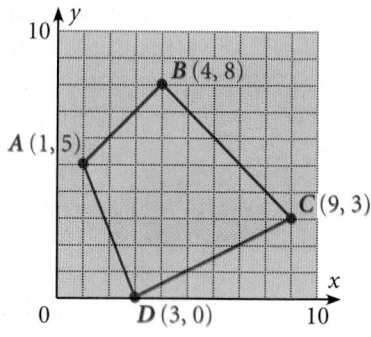

Write the objective function for each situation.

10. Your color television uses 0.2 kilowatt-hours of energy per hour and your radio uses 0.1 kilowatt-hours per hour. You want to minimize your energy consumption.

11. Your company produces paper from recycled paper costing x dollars a ton and wood pulp costing y dollars a ton. You want to minimize your costs.

Use the matrices below to find each of the following if possible. If not possible, explain why. [1-3]

$$A = \begin{bmatrix} 8 & -1 & -2 \\ -3 & 2 & 0 \\ 1 & -6 & 7 \end{bmatrix} \qquad B = \begin{bmatrix} 8 & 1 \\ -4 & -7 \end{bmatrix} \qquad C = \begin{bmatrix} -5 & 4 & 15 \\ 0 & 10 & 9 \\ 5 & -2 & 2 \end{bmatrix}$$

12. $A + C$ 　　　　　**13.** $2B$ 　　　　　**14.** $3A - 2C$ 　　　　　**15.** $6A + 4B - C$

Solve each linear system if possible. State the number of solutions, and tell whether the system is consistent or inconsistent. [3-1]

16. $x + y = 10$
$\quad\;\; 2x - 6y = 4$

17. $y = 2x - 6$
$\quad\;\; 3x - 2y = 22$

18. $7m - 5n = 31$
$\quad\;\; -6m + 2n = -22$

19. Years of Happy Ears A company produces two portable tape players, the ShuffleMan and the WalkOn. The profits per unit are $20 for the ShuffleMan and $15 for the WalkOn. The production time (in hours) for one unit of each product is given in the chart.

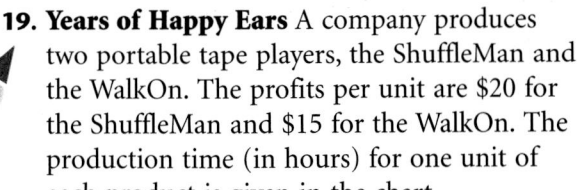

Product	Manufacturing Time (hr)	Shipping Time (hr)
ShuffleMan	0.4	0.1
WalkOn	0.6	0.2

The company has at most 750 worker-hours of manufacturing time available and 200 worker-hours of shipping time available each day. At least 300 ShuffleMan players and 500 WalkOn players must be produced each day.

a. Write the profit function to be maximized. How many of each product should be produced each day? What will the profit be?

b. If the profit for each ShuffleMan drops to $16 per unit, how many of each product should be produced? What will the new total profit be?

20. A Novel Idea A bookstore is placing an order from the publisher for a new best seller. The publisher requires at least 400 books per order. Wholesale prices to the store are $19.50 for each hardcover edition and $6.95 for paperbacks. At least 20% of each order must be hardcover books.

a. Write a set of linear inequalities to model these constraints. Then graph the feasible region and find the coordinates of its vertices.

b. The bookstore wants to minimize its expenses. Write the objective function.

c. How many of each type of book should the store order to minimize expenses?

d. What is the minimum cost to the bookstore for buying these books?

21. Don't Get Stamped Out! Cooper Stamp Company needs to determine how many stamps to bring to a stamp show. They sell basic stamps and rare stamps. Basic stamps provide an average profit of $2 each, and rare stamps average $18 profit each.

- The total available stock is 2700 stamps.
- The company wants to bring at least 3 times as many basic stamps as rare stamps.
- They have 2200 basic stamps available.

a. Write an inequality for each constraint and graph the feasible region.

b. Write the objective function for profit.

c. How many of each type of stamp should be brought to the show? How much profit will Cooper Stamp Company make?

Chapter 3 Review

In Chapter 3, you used graphing, substitution, linear combination, and matrices to solve systems of linear equations with two or more variables. You then found solutions of systems of linear inequalities by graphing. When using linear programming, an important problem-solving technique, you used all of these skills. When finding the feasible region, you graphed systems of linear constraints (inequalities). Finding coordinates of the vertex points where optimal solutions are found involved solving systems of linear equations.

KEY TERMS

consistent system [3-1]

constraints [3-2]

dependent equations [3-1]

feasible region [3-2]

inconsistent system [3-1]

invertible matrix [3-1]

linear combination method [3-1]

linear programming

objective function

optimal solution [3-2]

substitution method [3-1]

system of linear equations [3-1]

system of linear inequalities [3-2]

Vertex Theorem [3-2]

Write the word or phrase that correctly completes each statement.

1. A set of parallel lines illustrates a(n) ____ system of linear equations. [3-1]

2. The system of equations $y = 5x$ and $2y = 10x$ has ____ solutions. [3-1]

3. When a system is solved by ____, multiples of equations are added together to eliminate variables. [3-1]

4. When a square matrix is multiplied by its ____, the result is an identity matrix. [3-1]

5. Money, time, and labor are examples of ____ under which businesses must operate. [3-2]

6. ____ is a method of solving problems with a quantity to be maximized or minimized and limitations on resources. [3-2]

CONCEPTS AND APPLICATIONS

Solve each linear system if possible. Use each solution method available to you at least once. State the number of solutions, and tell whether the system is consistent or inconsistent. [3-1]

7. $y = 2x + 5$
   $y = -7 + 2x$

8. $-x + 6y = -1$
   $2x - 2y = 5$

9. $5x - 9y = 1$
   $5x - 3y = 7$

10. $3x - y = 8$
    $2x + y = 7$

11. $4x + 5y = 5$
    $6x + 2y = 2$

12. $y = \frac{1}{2}x - 8$
    $5x + 4y = 16$

Write each system of linear equations as a matrix equation in the form $AX = B$. [3-1]

13. $3x - 7y = 5$
$2x + y = 9$

14. $-x + y = 2$
$-2x + 3y = 0$

15. $3x + 6y = 5$
$-x - 2y = -4$

16. Solve the linear system.

$x - y + 2z = 4$
$3x + y - z = 16$
$-2x + 4y + 3z = -6$

Graph each system of linear inequalities. [3-2]

17. $y \geq 3x - 8$
$y < \frac{2}{3}x + 1$

18. $-2x + y \leq 8$
$x + 3y > 12$
$y \geq 2$

Graph the feasible region for each of the following sets of constraints (inequalities). Then find the coordinates of the vertices. [3-2]

19. $x \geq 0$
$y \geq 2$
$x + 2y \leq 10$

20. $x \geq 0$
$y \geq 0$
$x + y \leq 5$
$3x + y \leq 9$

21. $x \geq 0$
$y \geq 0$
$100x + 150y \leq 45,000$

22. Suppose that the objective function for Exercise 21 is $F = 3x + 5y$. Find the solution that maximizes the objective function. What is the value of the objective function at this point? [3-2]

CONCEPTS AND CONNECTIONS

23. The purity of a gold alloy is measured in *karats*. For example, 10-karat gold is $\frac{10}{24}$ gold; 24-karat gold is pure $\left(\frac{24}{24}\right)$ gold.

A jeweler finds 10-karat and 24-karat gold chains at an antique sale. She plans to melt them down and mix them together to make 120 grams of 18-karat gold. How much of each type of gold should she purchase?

24. The jeweler in Exercise 23 sells her 18-karat gold necklaces for a profit of $80 each and turquoise necklaces for a profit of $50 each. She can make no more than fifty necklaces a month and can afford enough gold to make only twenty 18-karat necklaces a month.
   a. Write the constraints to model this situation.
   b. Graph the feasible region and find the coordinates of its vertices.
   c. The jeweler wants to maximize her profit. Write the objective function. Then find the optimal solution of this problem. How many of each type of necklace should she make, and what profit will she earn?

SELF-EVALUATION

Write a paragraph comparing and contrasting the different methods of solving systems of equations. Then explain how solving systems of equations is similar to solving systems of inequalities and how the two processes are different. Identify the parts of the chapter that you found difficult and which sections you need to study further in order to better understand these topics.

Chapter 3 Assessment

TEST

Solve each linear system if possible. State the number of solutions, and tell whether the system is consistent or inconsistent.

1. $x + y = 9$
$5x - y = 3$

2. $4x - 3y = 7$
$12x - 9y = 7$

3. $3x + y = 5$
$2y = 10 - 6x$

4. Is $(-5, 3)$ a solution of the system $3x + 2y = 9$ and $-x + 4y = 17$? Justify your answer.

5. Consider the linear system:
$3x + y = 5$
$6x + 7y = 8$

  a. Solve this system graphically. Write the two functions you graphed.
  b. Solve this system by the substitution method. Show your work.
  c. Solve this system by the linear combination method. Show your work.
  d. Which of the three methods was easiest for you to use? Which was the most difficult? Why do you think this was the case?

6. Cassette Club A offers a membership fee of $50.00 and sells each music cassette for $5.00. Cassette Club B has a membership fee of only $10.00 but charges $7.00 for each cassette. How many cassettes would you have to buy for the costs of the two plans to be equal?

7. Graph the system of linear inequalities.
$x + y < 4$
$2x - y > 6$
$x \geq -3$

8. Graph the feasible region for the set of constraints (inequalities). Then find the coordinates of the vertices.
$x \geq 0$
$y \geq 0$
$x + y \leq 9$
$y \geq 1.5x$

9. A bicycle manufacturer makes two models of bikes, a professional racing bike and a mountain bike. Profits average $150 per mountain bike and $120 per racing bike. The company has the following constraints.
- The maximum total production possible is 1440 bikes per month.
- Consumer demand for the racing bike is no more than half the demand for the mountain bike.
- At least 400 mountain bikes per month must be made to satisfy a long-term contract.

  a. Write the profit (objective) function to be maximized in this problem. Use x to represent the number of mountain bikes and y to represent the number of racing bikes produced.

  b. Write inequalities for the constraints.

  c. Graph the feasible region for the constraints of this problem and find the coordinates of its vertices.

  d. What production strategy should be followed to maximize the profit? What is the maximum profit?

PERFORMANCE TASK

You've always been interested in running your own business. While in an ice cream store run by a national chain, you see a brochure entitled "Own Your Own Business!" Curious, you take one home and begin to read.

This chain sells two types of ice cream cones, gourmet (with sprinkles!) and regular. In order to make their gourmet ice cream seem truly special, they limit each store to 150 servings per day. Other information about a typical franchise is given.

- Average number of worker hours in a day: 16.
- Average number of minutes to complete a regular cone order: 2.
- Average number of minutes to complete a gourmet cone order: 3. (The sprinkles take time.)
- Average profit per gourmet cone: $0.70.
- Average profit per regular cone: $0.40.
- You can purchase a franchise from this chain for $8000.

Although you don't have the money just yet, you'd like to know whether this seems like a good business opportunity. Analyze this situation using any mathematical tools that seem appropriate. Include an analysis of how long it will take the average franchise owner to make back the purchase fee and what you might want to do differently than the average franchise store.

Chapter 4

Patterns and Structure in Algebra

Project A
In the Wild
How do birds know how many eggs are in their nests? Can birds count?

Project B
A Perfect Number
How can a number be perfect or abundant?

$$6 = 1 + 2 + 3$$

Project C
Multiply Like an Egyptian
How did people of ancient civilizations perform multiplication?

Math was a lot of fun in high school because we had a teacher who really challenged us.

In my research in preventive medicine, I have the opportunity to study how people's behaviors can protect them from disease or put them at greater risk. We assign numerical values to different types of behaviors, and do statistical analyses to test hypotheses about how and why people do the things they do. For example, I have studied how knowing about AIDS affects people's behavior.

Monica Ruiz, Ph.D.
Behavioral Researcher
USC School of Medicine
Los Angeles, California

**4-1
Analyzing
Arithmetic
Growth**

In 4-1 you will explore arithmetic sequences and their sums. You will use the following skills.

Describe the pattern and write the next number in the sequence. [Previous course]

1. 1, 3, 5, 7, 9, 11, ...

2. $\dfrac{1}{8}, \dfrac{1}{4}, \dfrac{3}{8}, \dfrac{1}{2}, \dfrac{5}{8}, \dfrac{3}{4}, \ldots$

Describe the pattern and find the sum of the numbers. [Previous course]

3. 100, 93, 86, 79, 72

4. 45.3, 45.8, 46.3, 46.8, 47.3, 47.8

5. 1, 2, 3, 4, ..., 10   **6.** 11, 12, 13, ..., 20   **7.** 2, 4, 6, 8, ..., 20

**4-2
Analyzing
Geometric
Growth**

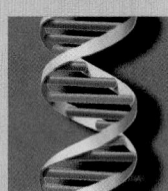

In 4-2 you will investigate geometric sequences and their sums. You will need the following skills.

Describe the pattern and write the next number in the sequence. [Previous course]

8. 2, 4, 8, 16, 32, ...

9. 50, 25, 12.5, 6.25, ...

10. 10, −30, 90, −270, 810, ...

11. 1, 0.5, 0.25, 0.125, ...

12. 1, −0.5, 0.25, −0.125, ...

13. 1, −1, 1, −1, ...

Describe the pattern and find the sum of the numbers. [Previous course]

14. 81, 27, 9, 3, 1

15. −1, −10, −100, −1000, −10000

**4-3
Algebraic
Structure and
Fractal Geometry**

In 4-3 you will investigate the structure of the real number system and the complex number system. You will use the following algebra skills from previous courses.

Name the variable that is an identity element. [Previous course]

16. $a + b = b + a = a$

17. $m \cdot n = n \cdot m = m$

Evaluate.

18. $\sqrt{\dfrac{25}{49}}$ **19.** $-\sqrt{169}$ **20.** $\sqrt{2.25}$ **21.** $\sqrt{12}\sqrt{3}$

Simplify. [Previous course]

22. $(5 + x) + (5 - x)$ **23.** $3(4 - x) - 3(5 - 4x)$ **24.** $(x + 3)(x - 3)$

25. $(2x + 1)(2x - 1)$ **26.** $(6 + x)(6 - x)$ **27.** $(4x + 3)(x - 5)$

PATTERNS IN NATURE

The sun rises and sets, the tides ebb and flow, temperatures rise and fall with the changing of the seasons. People around the globe have observed and pondered the patterns of nature for thousands of years. Their drive to measure, record, and understand these patterns and the forces behind them led to the development of mathematics.

The ancient Greeks are perhaps most famous for observing and measuring patterns in nature. They gave us the word *geometry*—measurement of the earth—and a logical system of mathematical thought that we use to this day.

Many American Indian cultures displayed an equal passion for observing patterns in nature. The Hohokam of Arizona aligned the windows of their massive adobe ceremonial buildings to admit the sun at the solstices and equinoxes. People of the Mississippi culture in Illinois made precise observations of the sun and may have developed the ability to predict solar and lunar eclipses. The Anasazi constructed magnificent observational sites in Chaco Canyon, New Mexico, including one that marked the zenith passage of the sun on the day of the summer solstice.

Archaeologist Kendrick Frazier paid tribute to the Anasazi with a statement that applies to many American Indian cultures: "The monumental quality of this solar construct reflects the profound beauty of ancient Pueblo culture. It is characterized by the Indians' sensitive integration of their structures with nature, light, and patterns of the solar cycle."

1. How might the development of mathematics enable people to gain an understanding of the forces behind patterns in nature?
2. Why would knowledge and an understanding of the movements of the sun and moon have been important to ancient cultures throughout the world?
3. What are some ways mathematics is used today to describe patterns in nature?

←**CONNECT**→ *Numbers create patterns in a multitude of ways. Now you will investigate the patterns that form arithmetic sequences and learn how to recognize, represent, and generate these patterns.*

Around 550 B.C., the Greek mathematician Pythagoras brought together a group of scholars that came to be known as the Pythagorean Society. The Pythagoreans were interested in patterns of numbers and the *theory* behind them, which they believed reflected the harmony of the universe. They devoted much of their study to number patterns found in geometrical figures.

EXPLORE: THE HARMONY OF NUMBERS

Triangular numbers, square numbers, pentagonal numbers, and hexagonal numbers are some of the *figurate numbers* that interested the Pythagoreans. Starting with 1, the triangular numbers are formed by successively adding 2, 3, 4, and so on.

Triangular Numbers

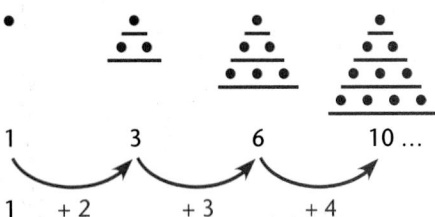

1   3   6   10 ...

1 + 2   + 3   + 4

Square Numbers

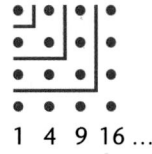

1 4 9 16 ...

Pentagonal Numbers

Hexagonal Numbers

1. Study these figures to see how each successive figurate number is formed from the previous one. Give the first six square numbers, the first six pentagonal numbers, and the first six hexagonal numbers.

> **Problem-Solving Tip**
>
> Look for patterns.

2. For each pattern of figurate numbers, give a rule telling how each successive figurate number can be found from the previous number. What is the connection between your rule and the number of sides of the polygon? Explain.

3. Using the connection you found in Step 2, give the first six figurate numbers for a 100-sided polygon.

A sequence is an ordered list of numbers. We denote these numbers, called **terms,** by a variable with a subscript that gives the term's place in the list.

For the sequence of positive odd integers, 1, 3, 5, 7, …, we can denote the first term, 1, by a_1, the second term, 3, by a_2, and so on. The **general term** or **nth term** in this sequence is denoted by a_n. A sequence that continues indefinitely, like the positive odd integers, is an **infinite sequence.**

Notice that any odd integer can be found from the previous odd integer by adding 2. A sequence which shows a constant change between terms represents *arithmetic growth*.

> A sequence in which a constant, *d,* is added to the previous term to get the next term is called an **arithmetic sequence.** The constant is called the **common difference.**

EXAMPLE

1. Is the sequence 5, 8, 11, 14, … an arithmetic sequence? If so, give the common difference and the next term in the sequence.

Each term is 3 more than the previous term, so the sequence is arithmetic with the common difference 3. The next term in the sequence is 17.

$$5, \quad 8, \quad 11, \quad 14, \quad 17, \ldots$$
$$\quad 3 \quad 3 \quad 3 \quad 3$$

TRY IT

Decide whether each sequence is an arithmetic sequence. If so, give the common difference and the next term in the sequence.

a. 13, 19, 25, 31, …   **b.** 1, 3, 9, 27, …   **c.** 35, 33, 31, 29, …

CONSIDER

1. If you know the first two terms of an arithmetic sequence, how can you find the third term?

The initial term and common difference of an arithmetic sequence give a rule for finding each subsequent term. A rule that tells how to find a term using previous terms is called a **recursive definition** of a sequence. The following recursive definition defines the arithmetic sequence 5, 8, 11, 14, 17, ….

$$a_1 = 5 \text{ and } a_n = a_{n-1} + 3 \text{ for each integer } n \geq 2$$

The recursive pattern that emerges in an arithmetic sequence with common difference d allows us to write an *explicit* formula for the nth term. With this formula we can find the value of any term without evaluating all of the previous terms.

n	Term
1	a_1
2	$a_1 + d$
3	$a_1 + 2d$
4	$a_1 + 3d$
⋮	⋮
n	$a_1 + (n-1)d$

> The nth term of an arithmetic sequence with first term a_1 and common difference d is given by $a_n = a_1 + (n-1)d$.

EXAMPLE

2. The period between full moons has been observed to be 29.53 days. If the first full moon of the year occurs 13.41 days into the year (the *fourteenth* day of the year), when will the ninth full moon of the year occur?

$$a_1 = 13.41 \text{ and } d = 29.53$$
$$a_n = 13.41 + (n-1)29.53$$
$$a_9 = 13.41 + (8)29.53 = 249.65$$

The ninth full moon will occur on the 250th day of the year. (It will occur at 3:36 p.m. since 0.65 days equals 15 hours 36 minutes.)

We can graph a sequence with general term a_n by graphing all of the points (n, a_n) for positive integers n.

This is the graph of the arithmetic sequence in Example 2.

Xmin = 0
Xmax = 10
Xscl = 1
Ymin = 0
Ymax = 300
Yscl = 100

 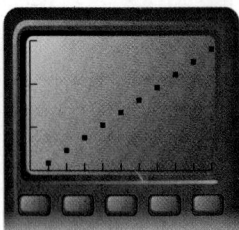

Writing x for n and $f(x)$ for a_n, we see that this is actually the graph of the *linear function* $f(x) = 13.41 + (x-1)29.53$ where the domain is the positive integers and the common difference is the slope or rate of change of successive term values.

The study of functions on countable domains, such as the integers, is called *discrete mathematics*.

CONSIDER

2. Explain why the common difference of an arithmetic sequence is the rate of change of successive term values.

TRY IT

d. Give the 37th term of the arithmetic sequence 164, 152, 140, 128, ….

e. What is the first term of the arithmetic sequence with common difference 6 and seventeenth term 111? Give the formula for the nth term of this sequence. Then graph the sequence.

Arithmetic sequences can be used to model many situations where quantities change in a constant, step-by-step manner. A savings account that grows in value by $5 per month and the level of a lake that falls 1.5 ft per month during a drought are examples of arithmetic sequences.

REFLECT

1. In your own words, describe what makes a sequence *arithmetic*.

2. How are arithmetic sequences like and unlike the linear functions you've studied and graphed?

3. Suppose you know the first term and the common difference of an arithmetic sequence. Describe how you can find the fifth term.

Exercises

CORE

1. Getting Started Examine the arithmetic sequence 17, 20, 23, 26, ….
   a. Give the common difference of the sequence.
   b. Give the next four terms of the sequence.
   c. To begin graphing this sequence, graph these ordered pairs: (1, 17), (2, 20), (3, 23), (4, 26).

Determine whether each statement is true or false. If the statement is false, change the underlined word or phrase to make it true.

2. A sequence is an ordered list of <u>numbers</u>.

3. The <u>common difference</u> of the arithmetic sequence 2, 6, 10, 14, … is 2.

4. Give the 25th term of the arithmetic sequence 3.2, 9.1, 15.0, 20.9, ….

5. Top That! A pizza parlor charges $4.99 for a medium cheese pizza plus $0.75 for each additional topping. Give the prices for medium pizzas with one, two, three, and four toppings. Do these prices form an arithmetic sequence? Explain.

Graph each sequence on a coordinate plane. Decide whether it is an arithmetic sequence. If so, give the common difference and the next term in the sequence.

6. 4, 14, 24, 34, …   **7.** 2, 4, 8, 16, 32, …   **8.** −6.7, −7.1, −7.5, −7.9, …

Decide whether the sequence graphed is an arithmetic sequence. If so, give the first term and the common difference.

9.

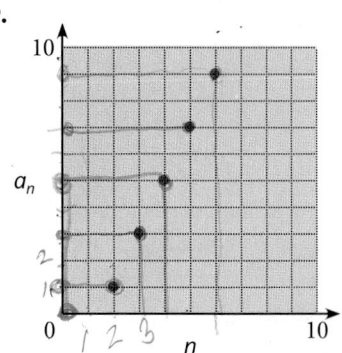

10.

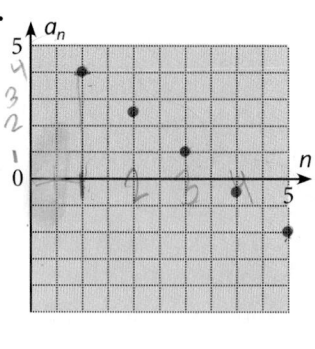

11.

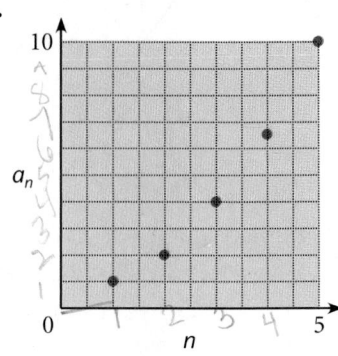

Give a formula for the *n*th term of each arithmetic sequence.

12. 2, 11, 20, 29, 38, …   **13.** 13, 10, 7, 4, 1, −2, …   **14.** $\frac{1}{3}$, 1, $\frac{5}{3}$, $\frac{7}{3}$, 3, …

15. Going First Class In 1995 the U.S. Postal Service charged the following rates for first class mail.

Weight	1 oz	2 oz	3 oz	4 oz	5 oz	•••
Postage	$0.32	$0.55	$0.78	$1.01	$1.24	•••

   a. Show that the postage prices form an arithmetic sequence.
   b. How much is the postage on a piece of first class mail weighing 9 ounces?
   c. How much is the postage on a piece of first class mail weighing *n* ounces?

16. A race car driver accelerates at a steady rate from 120 miles per hour to 190.4 miles per hour in 8 seconds.
   a. How much does the car's speed change each second?
   b. How fast is the car moving 3 seconds after it begins to accelerate?

17. What is the first term of the arithmetic sequence with common difference 6 and 21st term 971?
   a. Give the formula for the *n*th term of this sequence.
   b. Write the recursive definition of the sequence.
   c. Which formula would you find most useful for computing the 40th term? Why?

18. Julian is saving money to buy a CD player. He received $50 for his birthday and plans to save an additional $5 per week from his allowance and odd jobs.
   a. Write a formula for a_n, the amount Julian has saved up after *n* weeks.
   b. Draw a graph showing Julian's savings for the first ten weeks.
   c. How much will Julian have saved after 12 weeks?
   d. The CD player Julian wants costs $185. How long will it take him to save that amount?

19. a. Complete the arithmetic sequence 19, ___, ___, ___, 47. These three terms are called *arithmetic means* between 19 and 47.

b. Find four arithmetic means between 13 and 61.

 **LOOK BACK**

Solve each system. [3-1]

20. $3x + 2y = 4$
$-4x - 3y = -7$

21. $-x + 5y = 18$
$9x - 2y = 10$

22. Find the equation of the line with slope of 3 containing the point $(-1, 2)$. [2-1]

Find each matrix product. [1-3]

23. $\begin{bmatrix} -3 & 2 & 4 \\ 7 & -2 & -6 \end{bmatrix} \begin{bmatrix} -5 \\ 7 \\ 2 \end{bmatrix}$

24. $\begin{bmatrix} 2 & 5 \\ 3 & 8 \end{bmatrix} \begin{bmatrix} 8 & -5 \\ -3 & 2 \end{bmatrix}$

MORE PRACTICE

Graph each sequence on a coordinate plane. Decide whether the sequence is an arithmetic sequence. If so, give the common difference and the next term in the sequence.

25. 2, 8, 14, 20, …

26. $2\frac{1}{4}, 3, 3\frac{3}{4}, 4\frac{1}{2}, \ldots$

27. $-3, -7, -11, -15, \ldots$

28. $-5, -6, -7, -8, \ldots$

29. $64, $32, $16, $8, \ldots$

30. $5.7, 2.8, -0.1, -3, \ldots$

31. Long Play, Low Pay At Roy's Record Bin, the price of long-playing records was lowered by $1.49 five times, to $4.55 per record. Give each of the prices that has been charged for long-playing records at Roy's.

32. Use a Graphing Utility Enter the arithmetic sequence given by $a_n = 3 + 4(n - 1)$ in a table or list in your graphing utility. Then graph it and sketch the graph.

33. Hourly parking charges in a local garage form an arithmetic sequence. It costs $3.75 to park for 4 hours and $5.25 to park for 6 hours. How much does it cost to park for 1 hour?

34. Give the 47th term of the sequence 101, 98, 95, 92, ….

35. Give two arithmetic means between 51.6 and -32.4.

Decide whether the sequence graphed is an arithmetic sequence. If so, give the first term and the common difference.

36.

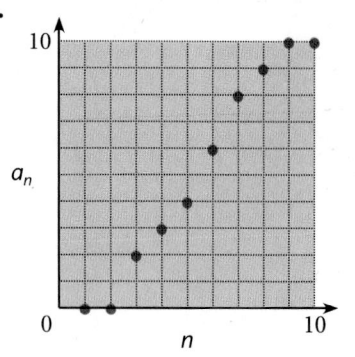

37.

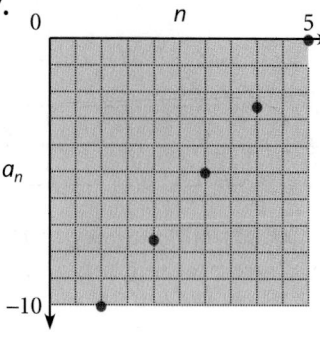

38.

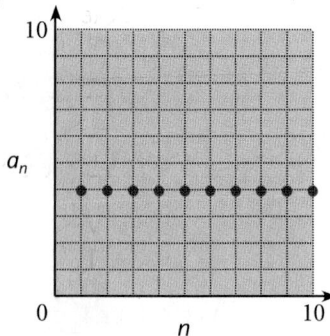

39.

Xmin = 0
Xmax = 5
Xscl = 1
Ymin = 0
Ymax = 10
Yscl = 1

40.

Xmin = 0
Xmax = 10
Xscl = 1
Ymin = 0
Ymax = 10
Yscl = 1

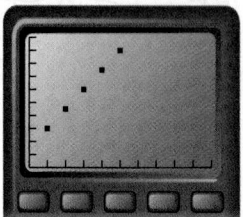

Give a formula for the nth term of each arithmetic sequence.

41. 7, 13, 19, 25, 31, …

42. −5, −1, 3, 7, 11, 15, …

43. 0.9, 0.75, 0.6, 0.45, …

44. Write the first five terms of the arithmetic sequence that has −13 as its first term and a common difference of 4.

45. What is the first term of the arithmetic sequence with common difference −1.5 and twentieth term 11? Give the formula for the nth term of this sequence.

46. An arithmetic sequence with a common difference of −2.4 has 45 as its first term and −29.4 as its last. How many terms are there in the sequence?

MORE MATH REASONING

47. This spreadsheet shows formulas for generating an arithmetic sequence.
   a. What is the common difference? Give the first six terms in the sequence.
   b. How would you change the formulas to generate the arithmetic sequence 100, 125, 150, 175, …?

	A	B
1	n	a_n
2	1	20
3	2	= B2 + 10
4	3	= B3 + 10
5	4	= B4 + 10

48. Show that if one arithmetic mean is inserted between two numbers, it is the average of the two numbers.

49. Raoul is an accountant for a software company. He decides to use *straight-line depreciation* to calculate the declining value of a new $26,000 copy machine over the next eight years. He projects that the machine will have a trade-in value of $2,100 at the end of eight years.

a. Complete Raoul's depreciation schedule for each of the next eight years.

Year	0	1	2	3	4	5	6	7	8
Value ($)	26,000								2,100

b. Why do you think this is called straight-line depreciation?
c. When will the copy machine have no value under this model?

4-1
PART B Arithmetic Series

← CONNECT →   *You have seen that arithmetic sequences produce recognizable patterns and graphs. Now you will investigate patterns in the sums of arithmetic sequences.*

You can often see patterns and formulate general rules in situations by investigating special cases. This strategy, known as **inductive reasoning,** is a simple yet powerful tool for discovering mathematical patterns and rules.

EXPLORE: A SERIES OF STEPS

MATERIALS

Graph paper
Scissors

1. This step-shaped array of squares represents the first four terms of the arithmetic sequence 2, 5, 8, 11, …. Cut two copies of this shape from a piece of graph paper and fit them together to form a rectangle.

2. What are the dimensions of the rectangle? What is the area of the rectangle? How is the area of each step shape related to the area of the rectangle? Explain.

3. Verify that the area of each step shape is equal to 2 + 5 + 8 + 11.

4. The height of the rectangle you formed is equal to the number of terms of the sequence represented. How is the length of the rectangle related to the first and last of these terms?

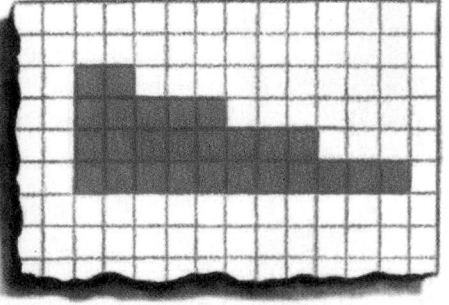

5. Repeat the investigation using the first several terms of another arithmetic sequence. Explain why the following statement makes sense:

The area of each step-shape equals the number of terms in the arithmetic sequence represented, multiplied by half the sum of the first and last of these terms.

The sum of the terms of an arithmetic sequence forms an **arithmetic series.** By adding all of the terms prior to any term, we can find any **partial sum** of the series, even when the arithmetic sequence is infinite.

Arithmetic Sequence	Arithmetic Series	Partial Sums
$5, 8, 11, 14, 17, \ldots$	$5 + 8 + 11 + \cdots$	$S_1 = 5$
		$S_2 = 5 + 8 = 13$
		$S_3 = 5 + 8 + 11 = 24$

The general pattern you discovered in the Explore gives a convenient way to find partial sums of any arithmetic series.

> The partial sums of an arithmetic series, $a_1 + a_2 + a_3 + \cdots$, are given by $S_n = \frac{n}{2}(a_1 + a_n)$.

WHAT DO YOU THINK?

The partial sums of the arithmetic series $1 + 4 + 7 + 10 + \cdots$ generate the *pentagonal numbers.* Find the fifteenth pentagonal number.

Kyle thinks...

The fifteenth pentagonal number is the partial sum S_{15}. To use the formula for S_{15}, I first need to find the fifteenth term in the arithmetic sequence.

The first term of the sequence is 1 and the common difference is 3, so $a_n = 1 + (n - 1)3$ and $a_{15} = 1 + (14)3 = 43$.

$$S_{15} = \frac{15}{2}(a_1 + a_{15}) = \frac{15}{2}(1 + 43) = \frac{15}{2}(44) = 330$$

The fifteenth pentagonal number is 330.

Darcy thinks...

Using $a_1 = 1$ and $d = 3$, the nth term of the sequence is $a_n = 1 + (n - 1)3$. I'll enter the first 15 terms of this sequence as a *list* L_1 in my graphing calculator and then find the *sum* of the list.

The fifteenth pentagonal number is 330.

```
seq(1 + (N – 1) *3, N, 1
, 15, 1) → L₁
{1  4  7  10  13  16 ...
sum L₁
                    330
```

CONSIDER

1. Explain why the following statement is true: "The sum of a finite arithmetic sequence equals the number of terms times the average of the first and last terms."

We can use the Greek letter Σ (sigma) to write a series in **sigma notation.**
The series in What Do You Think? has nth term $a_n = 1 + (n - 1)3 = 3n - 2$.
In sigma notation, the fifteenth partial sum of this series is written as

$$\sum_{n=1}^{15} (3n - 2).$$

This is read aloud as, "The sum from $n = 1$ to 15 of the terms $3n - 2$."

EXAMPLES

1. Give the sum $\sum_{n=1}^{8} (2n + 3)$.

$$\sum_{n=1}^{8} (2n + 3) = (2 \cdot 1 + 3) + (2 \cdot 2 + 3) + (2 \cdot 3 + 3) + \cdots + (2 \cdot 8 + 3)$$
$$= \quad 5 \quad + \quad 7 \quad + \quad 9 \quad + \cdots + \quad 19$$

Use the first and last terms in the formula for the sum.

$$\sum_{n=1}^{8} (2n + 3) = \tfrac{8}{2}(5 + 19) = 4(24) = 96$$

2. Write the arithmetic series $4 + 7 + 10 + \cdots + 58$ in sigma notation and find its sum.

The first term of the arithmetic sequence is 4 and the common difference is 3, so the nth term is $a_n = 4 + (n - 1)3 = 3n + 1$.

To write the series in sigma notation, we must determine the number of terms in the series, that is, the value of n when $a_n = 58$.

$$3n + 1 = 58$$
$$3n = 57$$
$$n = 19$$

There are 19 terms in the series. The series and its sum are:

$$\sum_{n=1}^{19} (3n + 1) = \tfrac{19}{2}(4 + 58) = 589$$

TRY IT

a. The partial sums of the arithmetic series $1 + 5 + 9 + 13 + \cdots$ generate the *hexagonal numbers.* Find the 31st hexagonal number.

b. Give the sum $\sum_{n=1}^{6} (5n - 3)$.

c. Write the arithmetic series $1 + 3 + 5 + \cdots + 41$ in sigma notation and find its sum.

Arithmetic series are useful for describing geometric patterns. Sigma notation is especially convenient for writing series of many terms. This notation and techniques for summing series are used extensively in many branches of engineering, science, and mathematics.

Pyramids in the Americas, such as this one in Chichén Itzá, Mexico, were frequently built with a series of steps.

1. Explain the difference between an arithmetic sequence and an arithmetic series.
2. What is an advantage of using sigma notation to write series?
3. How are the number of terms in a series shown in sigma notation?

Exercises

CORE

1. Getting Started Examine the arithmetic series $2 + 6 + 10 + 14 + \cdots$.
   a. Give the partial sums S_1, S_2, S_3, and S_4.
   b. Give the fifteenth term in the series.
   c. What is the average of the first and fifteenth terms?
   d. Compute S_{15} by multiplying the number of terms, 15, by your result in **c.**

Write the word or phrase that correctly completes each statement.

2. An arithmetic _____ is a sum of the terms of an arithmetic sequence.

3. S_n represents the _____ of a series.

Give the sum of each arithmetic series.

4. $-27 + (-17) + (-7) + \cdots + 43$ **5.** $1 + 4 + 7 + \cdots + 142$

6. $400 + 394 + 388 + \cdots + (-32)$ **7.** the first 20 terms of the series $13 + 20 + 27 + \cdots$

8. Give the partial sum S_{25} of the arithmetic series $50 + 58 + 66 + \cdots$.

9. Carl Friedrich Gauss, considered to be one of the greatest mathematicians of all time, found another way to sum an arithmetic sequence when he was only ten years old! When asked to compute the sum of the series $1 + 2 + \cdots + 49 + 50$, Gauss noticed a convenient way to pair the numbers.
   a. Rewrite the series by pairing the 1 and 50, 2 and 49, 3 and 48, and so on.
   b. What is the sum of each pair? How many pairs are there? What is the sum of the entire series?
   c. Use the formula for the sum of an arithmetic series to check your result.

Give each sum.

10. $\displaystyle\sum_{n=1}^{12} (4n - 1)$ **11.** $\displaystyle\sum_{n=1}^{25} (-n + 6)$ **12.** $\displaystyle\sum_{n=1}^{100} 10n$

13. **Birthday Present and Future** On each of Arlene's birthdays beginning with her first, Arlene's grandmother has deposited money in Arlene's college fund. The amount she has deposited is $10 times Arlene's age in years. Disregarding interest, how large will the fund be when Arlene reaches the age of 18?

14. Find the 30th pentagonal number, which is equal to S_{30} for the arithmetic series $1 + 4 + 7 + 10 + \cdots$.

15. There are 48 terms in an arithmetic series with a sum of 4560. If the first term is 1, give the last term.

16. The sum of an arithmetic series is 598.
    a. If the first term is 8 and the last term is 38, how many terms are there in the series?
    b. Give the common difference of the sequence forming the series.

Write each arithmetic series in sigma notation and find its sum.

17. $1 + 8 + 15 + \cdots + 43$

18. $25 + 32 + 39 + \cdots + 102$

19. $1.8 + 1.1 + 0.4 - 0.3 - \cdots - 8$

20. **Row, Row, Row** A display of toothpaste cartons in a pharmacy window has 12 rows, each containing 2 fewer cartons than the row below. The bottom row contains 30 cartons. How many cartons are there in the display?

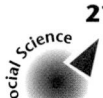

21. **Depreciation** is the loss in value of an item over time. One way to calculate annual depreciation is the *sum-of-the-years* method. The chart shows how the method is used to calculate annual depreciation over 7 years.

> Sum of the years: $1 + 2 + 3 + 4 + 5 + 6 + 7 = 28$
>
> First year: Depreciate $\frac{7}{28}$ of original value.
>
> Second year: Depreciate $\frac{6}{28}$ of original value.
>
> ...
>
> Seventh year: Depreciate $\frac{1}{28}$ of original value.

A transportation firm depreciated a $110,000 truck over 10 years.
   a. Write the amounts of depreciation for each year as a sequence.
   b. Show that this sequence is arithmetic.
   c. Find the total depreciation over 10 years.

22. Find the sum of the first ten terms of the sequence graphed at the right.

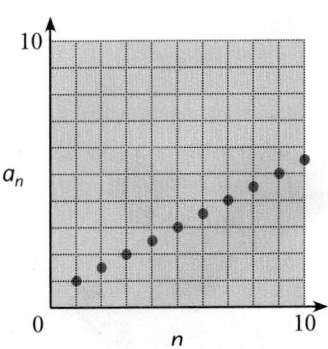

LOOK AHEAD

23. Find the next three terms in the sequence 1, 3, 9, 27, ...

Problem-Solving Tip

Look for a pattern.

24. Due to excessive hunting, a population of deer was reduced by one-fourth every 4 years. If the 1979 population was 1280, what was the 1995 population?

MORE PRACTICE

Give the sum of each arithmetic series.

25. $2 + 4 + 6 + \cdots + 100$

26. $1 + 5 + 9 + \cdots + 401$

27. $1 + 2 + 3 + \cdots + 1000$

28. $(-50) + (-35) + (-20) + \cdots + 400$

29. $600 + 595 + 590 + \cdots + 5$

30. $2 + 13 + 24 + \cdots + 79$

31. $1.2 + 0.2 - 0.8 - \cdots - 8.8$

32. the first 30 terms of the sequence 80, 82, 84, ...

33. $\displaystyle\sum_{n=1}^{20} n$

34. $\displaystyle\sum_{n=1}^{30} (2n - 4)$

35. $\displaystyle\sum_{n=1}^{50} (6n + 3)$

36. Give the partial sum S_{12} of the arithmetic series $7 + 11 + 15 + 19 + \cdots$.

37. Give the partial sum S_{100} of the arithmetic series $1 + 1.25 + 1.5 + 1.75 + \cdots$.

Write each arithmetic series in sigma notation and find its sum.

38. $3 + 6 + 9 + \cdots + 30$

39. $2 + 9 + 16 + \cdots + 65$

40. $10 + 12 + 14 + \cdots + 40$

41. $80 + 76 + 72 + \cdots + 4$

42. Find the seventeenth hexagonal number, which is equal to S_{17} for the arithmetic series $1 + 5 + 9 + 13 + \cdots$.

43. Inflation Nation In a country experiencing runaway inflation, the cost of a tomato increased $1 per day. On January 1 of a non-leap year, a tomato cost $1.
  a. Give the cost of a tomato on December 31 of the same year.
  b. Suppose that you bought a tomato every day. How much would you have spent on tomatoes during the year?

44. Find the sum of the first five terms of the sequence graphed at the right.

45. A city sets a fine of $10 for the first parking offense. The fine increases by $8 for each subsequent offense.
  a. Give the fine for the tenth offense.
  b. Give the total amount a driver would pay for ten offenses.

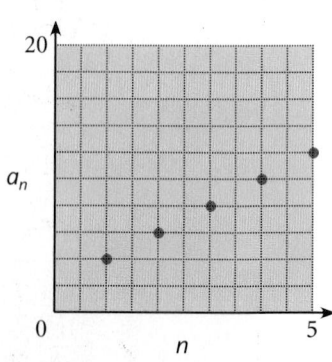

MORE MATH REASONING

46. Partridge in a Pear Tree In the song "The Twelve Days of Christmas," someone gets a partridge in a pear tree on the first day. She gets two turtle doves and a partridge in a pear tree on the second day. On the third day, she gets three French hens, two turtle doves, and a partridge in a pear tree. Each successive day, she gets a duplicate of what she got on the previous day plus as many new items as the number of the day. How many presents were given on the twelfth day?

47. Eight players are entered in a round-robin tennis tournament. The players will play each other one time.
   a. Give the number of matches the first player will play.
   b. Give the number of matches the second player will play (excluding the match she will play with the first player, which was already counted).
   c. Give the number of matches the third through eighth players will play (excluding those already counted).
   d. Find the total number of matches that will be played in the tournament.
   e. Forty players are entered in a two-day round-robin tournament. Fifteen courts are available each day from 10 a.m. to 5 p.m. The tournament director is trying to decide whether to have four round-robins of ten players each or five round-robins of eight players each. Matches take an average of one hour to play. Which choice should the director make? Explain.

48. a. Use the formulas $S_n = \frac{n}{2}(a_1 + a_n)$ and $a_n = a_1 + (n - 1)d$ to write a new formula that expresses S_n in terms of n, a_1, and d.
   b. Use your result to write a general formula for the nth pentagonal number.

4-1
PART C — Making Connections

← **CONNECT** → *You have investigated and characterized arithmetic growth in sequences and discovered patterns in arithmetic series. Sequences and series are valuable tools for modeling patterns in geometry and in nature.*

Patterns can be found in nature almost everywhere you look. Even the atoms that make up the matter in our bodies and around us can reveal predictable patterns.

EXPLORE: THE ELEMENT OF SURPRISE

MATERIALS

Graphing utility or graph paper
Chemistry textbook

The *atomic number* of an element is the number of protons in its nucleus. The *atomic mass* of an element is the average mass of an atom of the element in nature, usually measured in atomic mass units (amu). The table shows the atomic numbers and masses of the first twelve elements.

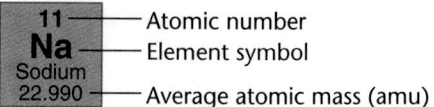

11 —— Atomic number
Na —— Element symbol
Sodium
22.990 —— Average atomic mass (amu)

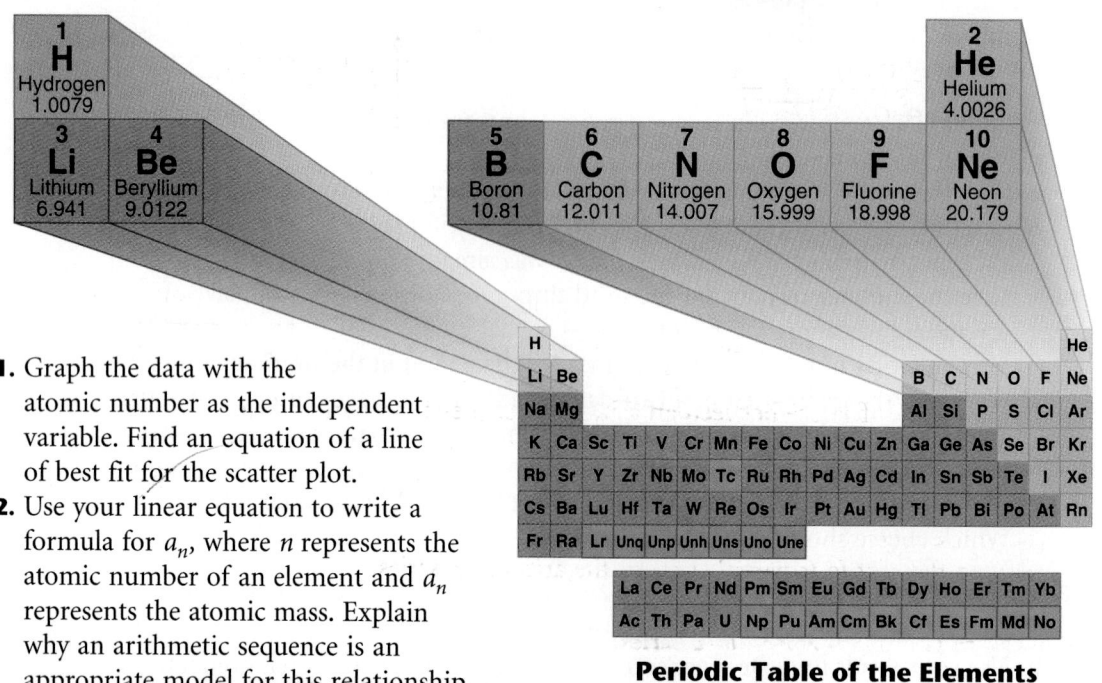

| 1
H
Hydrogen
1.0079 | | | | | | | 2
He
Helium
4.0026 |
| 3
Li
Lithium
6.941 | 4
Be
Beryllium
9.0122 | 5
B
Boron
10.81 | 6
C
Carbon
12.011 | 7
N
Nitrogen
14.007 | 8
O
Oxygen
15.999 | 9
F
Fluorine
18.998 | 10
Ne
Neon
20.179 |

Periodic Table of the Elements

1. Graph the data with the atomic number as the independent variable. Find an equation of a line of best fit for the scatter plot.

2. Use your linear equation to write a formula for a_n, where n represents the atomic number of an element and a_n represents the atomic mass. Explain why an arithmetic sequence is an appropriate model for this relationship.

3. Use your sequence to predict the atomic mass of each element.
   a. silicon (atomic number 14)   **b.** calcium (atomic number 20)
   c. silver (atomic number 47)   **d.** mercury (atomic number 80)

4. Compare your predictions with the actual atomic masses of silicon, calcium, silver, and mercury in a periodic table of a chemistry textbook. Discuss the accuracy of your model.

When data show a steady, step-by-step increase or decrease, an arithmetic sequence can provide a useful model for representing the data and making predictions.

REFLECT

1. Describe how you can recognize arithmetic growth in patterns and data.
2. Interpret the common difference in an arithmetic sequence as a rate of change.
3. If you know the average of the first and last terms in an arithmetic series, what else could you use to find the sum of the series? Explain.

Self-Assessment

Decide whether each sequence is an arithmetic sequence. If so, give the common difference.

1. 1, 4, 16, 64, …

2. 100, 90, 80, 70, …

3. −8, −4.3, −0.6, 3.1, …

4. 13, 13, 13, 13, …

5.

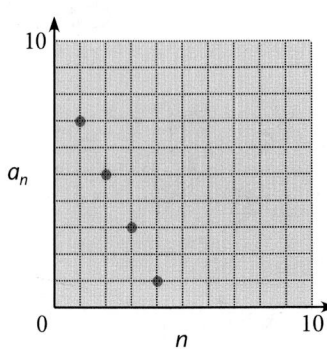

6.

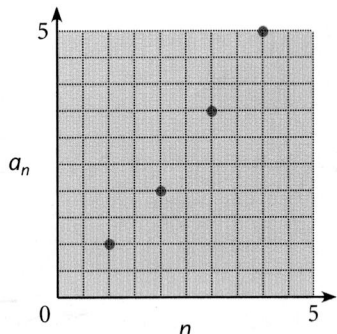

7. Explain the difference between an arithmetic sequence and an arithmetic series. Give an example of each.

8. The first two terms of an arithmetic sequence are 7 and 11.
   a. Find the next three terms in the sequence.
   b. Find the first four partial sums of the arithmetic series.

Give the sum of each arithmetic series.

9. $6 + 8 + 10 + 12 + \cdots + 46$

10. $80 + 75 + 70 + \cdots + (-35)$

11. the 25th partial sum of the series $-12.5 + (-9) + (-5.5) + (-2) + \cdots$

12. the series with 40 terms that ends $\cdots + 400 + 412 + 424$

13. $\displaystyle\sum_{n=1}^{15}(2n + 5)$

14. $\displaystyle\sum_{n=1}^{20}(-n + 1)$

15. Write the series $6 + 11 + 16 + 21 + \cdots + 91$ using sigma notation and find its sum.

16. Insert three arithmetic means between −23 and 35.

17. Find the product: $\begin{bmatrix} -4 & 2 \\ 5 & -6 \end{bmatrix}\begin{bmatrix} 9 \\ -3 \end{bmatrix}$. [1-3]

18. Solve the system: $5x + 4y = 5$ [3-1]
                    $-2x + 3y = 21$

19. Find the equation of the line parallel to the graph of $2x - 4y = 5$ that contains the point $(6, -1)$. [2-1]

20. Wire for Hire To work on a phone line in your residence, a local phone company charges $45 for the first 15 minutes and $16 for each additional 15 minutes of labor.

    a. Write a sequence giving the costs for labor times of 15 minutes, 30 minutes, 45 minutes, and so on, up to 2 hours.

    b. Is the sequence arithmetic? Justify your response.

    c. A private contractor charges $95 for the first hour or any part thereof, plus $14.50 for each additional 15 minutes. What is the minimum charge for which the private contractor is cheaper than the local phone company?

    d. Could a system of linear equations be used to solve **c**? Justify your response.

21. Choose the word or phrase that best completes the sentence. In the sequence 12, 18, 24, the middle term is the ____ of 12 and 24.

    (a) index   (b) arithmetic mean   (c) common difference   (d) general term

22. What Goes Around The days of an astronomical calendar are numbered consecutively beginning with day 1. The planet Mercury was observed to complete an orbit of the sun on days 49, 137, 225, and 313. Assuming that the sequence of days is arithmetic, when will Mercury complete its tenth orbit of the sun?

23. On-The-Aisle ticket agency charges a single-ticket price plus a flat service fee for tickets to the Barcelona Circus, regardless of the number of tickets purchased. The total charge for one ticket is $18.50 and the total charge for four tickets is $62.

    a. Give the single-ticket price.

    b. Give the service fee.

24. In Calcutta before the seventeenth century, cannonballs were stacked in pyramids. Knowledge of the *pyramidal numbers* made it easy to calculate the number of cannonballs there were in a pyramid of a given height and shape.

    a. Use the illustrations to list the first eight pyramidal numbers.

    b. What sequence has a related series with the pyramidal numbers as partial sums?

    c. Write a formula in sigma notation for the number of cannonballs in a pyramid ten rows high, and give the total number of cannonballs in the pyramid.

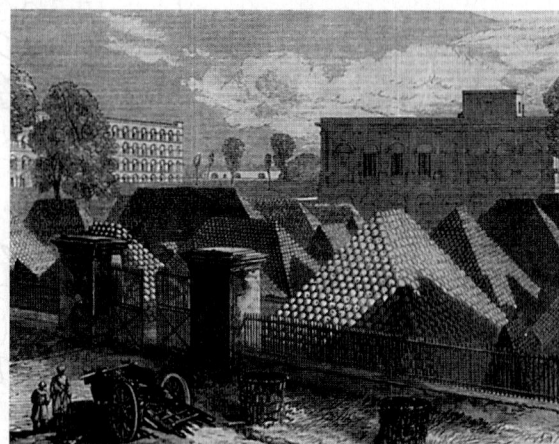

Pyramidal Numbers

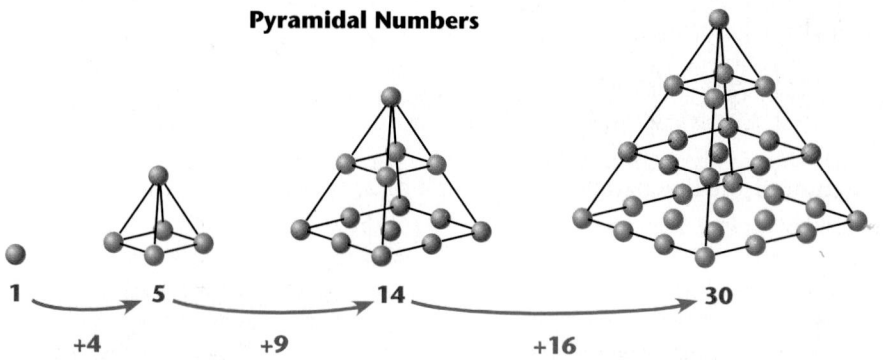

1   5   14   30

+4   +9   +16

Growing Up

Many living organisms begin with the union of two cells. If the growth that follows were to proceed arithmetically, organisms could never achieve the size or complexity of many forms of life we find on the earth. Cells do not reproduce arithmetically, however. They reproduce *geometrically*, dividing to produce twice as many cells in each succeeding generation.

Geometric growth can quickly surpass arithmetic growth, allowing an embryo of microscopic cells to develop within months into a living organism that is made up of trillions of cells.

As an animal embryo develops, groups of neighboring cells begin to develop different characteristics: for example, some form skin cells, stomach cells, or brain cells. The number of cells in the human body is truly amazing: about 100 trillion in a typical adult! Within humans and every other organism on the earth, genetic codes orchestrate the incredibly complex feat of timing and organization that has helped to develop all life on the planet.

?

1. Why would doubling the number of cells in an embryo at each new generation produce faster growth rates than arithmetic growth?
2. As you grow up, some types of cells no longer divide, while others continually reproduce and die. Why is it important for skin cells to continually reproduce?
3. If the cells of the human body grew arithmetically by 1000 cells per day, about how long would it take to reach the number of cells in a typical adult?

Screen shot from After Dark® artwork. ©1993 Berkeley® Systems, Inc.

← C O N N E C T →   *You've seen how to find new terms in an arithmetic sequence by adding a constant to preceding terms. Now you will explore geometric sequences in which new terms are found by multiplying preceding terms by a constant.*

Our bodies must replace a considerable number of cells every day. For example, red blood cells live about 120 days. Every second, your body replaces about two million red blood cells.

In the following Explore, you will investigate how cell division helps to produce the large numbers of cells within each of our bodies.

EXPLORE: THE NEXT GENERATION

MATERIALS

Graph paper
Graphing utility (optional)

A substantial number of cells can be generated from a single parent cell (generation 0) within a few generations. Each cell divides to produce two cells belonging to the next generation.

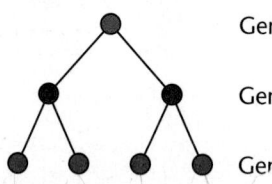

1. Copy and complete the table showing the number of cells in each new generation.

Generation	1	2	3	4	5	...	n
Number of Cells	2					...	

2. Write the numbers in the bottom row of your table as a sequence. What is the formula for the nth term of this sequence? Graph the sequence. Is this sequence arithmetic? Explain.

3. In which generation will the number of cells first exceed 100? 1000? Explain how you decided.

4. Suppose each cell divides once per day, resulting in two cells at the end of the first day, four cells at the end of the second day, and so on. In how many days will the number of cells reach 100 trillion (the number of cells in a typical adult human)? Do you think the cells that form a developing embryo can keep growing in this manner for many days? Explain.

In the Explore, you saw that cell division produces *double* the number of cells in each new generation. When the numbers in a sequence grow by a constant factor each successive term, we say the numbers grow *geometrically*.

> A sequence in which a constant (r) is multiplied by the previous term to get the next term is called a **geometric sequence.** The constant is called the **common ratio.**

Unlike the constant rate of change of an arithmetic sequence, the rate of change usually varies for a geometric sequence. The graph of the geometric sequence 1, 3, 9, 27, 81, … shows an increasing rate of change.

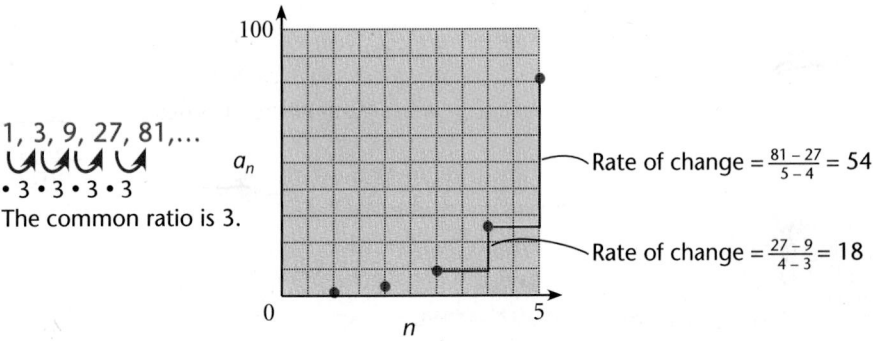

1, 3, 9, 27, 81,…
• 3 • 3 • 3 • 3
The common ratio is 3.

Rate of change $= \frac{81 - 27}{5 - 4} = 54$

Rate of change $= \frac{27 - 9}{4 - 3} = 18$

EXAMPLE

1. Is the sequence 400, 100, 25, 6.25, … a geometric sequence? If so, give the common ratio and the next term in the sequence.

$$\frac{100}{400} = 0.25 \qquad\qquad \frac{25}{100} = 0.25 \qquad\qquad \frac{6.25}{25} = 0.25$$

Each term is 0.25 times the previous term, so the sequence is geometric with common ratio 0.25. The next term is 0.25(6.25) = 1.5625.

TRY IT

Tell whether each sequence is a geometric sequence. If so, give the common ratio and the next term in the sequence.

a. 16, 24, 36, 54, … **b.** 10, 20, 30, 40, … **c.** 64, 48, 36, 27, …

CONSIDER

1. Can you use the common ratio to write a recursive definition for a geometric sequence? Explain.

We can rewrite the sequence in Example 1 as 400, $400(0.25)$, $400(0.25)^2$, $400(0.25)^3$, ...

A similar pattern of powers emerges for any geometric sequence, allowing us to write a general formula for the nth term in terms of the initial term and the constant ratio.

n	Term
1	a_1
2	$a_1 r$
3	$a_1 r^2$
4	$a_1 r^3$
⋮	⋮
n	$a_1 r^{n-1}$

> The nth term of a geometric sequence with first term a_1 and common ratio r is given by $a_n = a_1 r^{n-1}$.

EXAMPLES

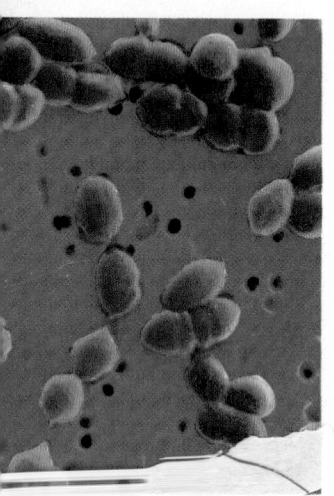

Streptococcus pneumoniae bacteria

2. Public health records show that the number of infections can grow geometrically during the initial phase of an outbreak of strep throat. If there were 5, 15, and 45 people infected on the first three days of an outbreak of strep throat and the geometric growth in the number of infections continues, how many people will be infected on the seventh day?

$a_1 = 5$ and $r = \dfrac{a_2}{a_1} = \dfrac{15}{5} = \dfrac{45}{15} = 3$

$a_n = a_1 r^{n-1}$

$\quad = 5(3^{n-1})$

$a_7 = 5(3^6) = 3645$

There will be 3645 people infected with strep throat on the seventh day.

3. The eleventh term of a geometric sequence with common ratio 2 is 7168. ...ve a formula for the nth term of the sequence.

$a_{11} = 7168$ and $r = 2$

$7168 = a_1(2^{11-1}) = a_1(2^{10}) = a_1(1024)$

$a_1 = \dfrac{7168}{1024} = 7$

$a_n = 7(2^{n-1})$

TRY IT

d. Give a formula for the nth term of the geometric sequence 1280, 640, 320, ...

e. The value of a "Herbert Hoover For President!" button increases 10% annually. The button sold for $100 in 1991. Use a geometric sequence to find its value this year.

Geometric sequences are useful models in a wide variety of situations where quantities increase or decrease geometrically. They can be used to model population growth, radioactive decay, or the value of an investment that earns compound interest.

REFLECT

1. Describe how the graphs and rates of change of arithmetic sequences and geometric sequences compare.
2. If you know the first and second terms of a geometric sequence, how can you find the common ratio? How can you find the sixth term?
3. Explain how the common ratio of a positive geometric sequence determines whether the terms increase or decrease.

Exercises

CORE

1. **Getting Started** Examine the geometric sequence 3, 6, 12, 24, ….
   a. Give the common ratio.
   b. Give the next four terms in the sequence.
   c. Graph the sequence.

2. Which formula gives the nth term of the geometric sequence 6.4, 8, 10, 12.5, …?
   (a) $a_n = 6.4^n$ (b) $a_n = 6.4(1.25^{n-1})$ (c) $a_n = 1.25(6.4^{n-1})$ (d) $a_n = 1.25^{n-1}$

Tell whether each sequence is geometric. If so, give the common ratio and the next term in the sequence.

3. 1, 4, 16, 64, …

4. 567, 189, 63, 21, …

5. $\frac{1}{2}, \frac{1}{3}, \frac{1}{4}, \frac{1}{5}, \ldots$

6. 1, −1, 1, −1, …

7. 36, 18, 6, 3, …

8. 12, 16, 20, 24, …

9.
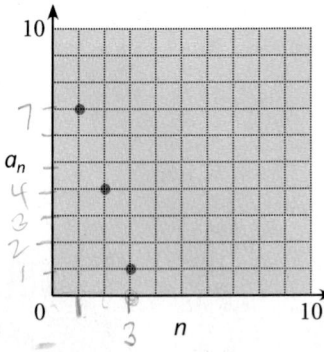

10.
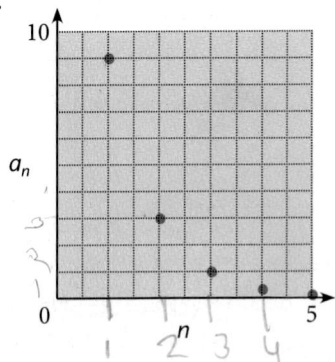

11. Records at City Hospital show 2, 10, and 50 new cases of chicken pox were reported for three consecutive days. Assuming that the number of new cases continues to increase geometrically, how many new cases will be reported on the fifth day?

Determine whether each statement is true or false. If the statement is false, change the underlined word or phrase to make it true.

12. To find each term of a geometric sequence, multiply the previous term by the <u>common difference</u>.

13. The fractions $\frac{1}{2}, \frac{1}{4}, \frac{1}{8}, \frac{1}{16}, \ldots$ form a <u>geometric</u> sequence.

14. $a_n = 5^{n-1}$ is the <u>fifth term</u> of the geometric sequence 1, 5, 25, 125, ….

15. The table gives the velocities of the Space Shuttle four times during its steady deceleration through the earth's atmosphere.
   a. Predict the Shuttle's velocity at 8:40 a.m. and 8:50 a.m.

Time	8:00 a.m.	8:10 a.m.	8:20 a.m.	8:30 a.m.
Velocity (mi/hr)	18,400	15,750	13,100	10,450

   b. If the Shuttle continues to decelerate at the same rate, when will its velocity reach 0? Do you think this velocity model is valid up to that point? Explain.

Give a formula for the nth term of each geometric sequence.

16. 40, 60, 90, 135, …

17. $-1, -2, -4, -8, \ldots$

18. 96, -48, 24, -12, …

19. The Earnings Are Mutual The value of Joe's investment in a mutual fund increased by 8% each year. After 4 years, Joe withdrew $12,597.12, the total value of his investment. Find the amount of Joe's initial investment.

20. a. Insert a positive term between 9 and 576 to form a geometric sequence. This value is called the positive *geometric mean* of 9 and 576. Its opposite is the negative geometric mean.
   b. Find the positive geometric mean of 3 and 147.

21. The eighth term of a geometric sequence with common ratio 3 is 10,935.
   a. Give the first term of the sequence.   **b.** Give the formula for the nth term.

22. Electronics industry analysts predict that the price of the Cine-Max video camera, which now retails for $1200, will fall 20% per year. The rival Videocam, which sells for $1000, should drop 15% per year. Assuming that the forecasts are accurate, when will the price of the Cine-Max first fall below that of the Videocam? Explain.

23. The first two terms of a sequence are 10 and 5.
   a. Write the first five terms of the sequence if it is arithmetic. Graph the sequence.
   b. Write the first five terms of the sequence if it is geometric. Graph the sequence.
   c. Compare and contrast the graphs and growths of these sequences.

24. In the decimal system (base 10), as you move left from the decimal point, the place values are 1, 10, 100, 1000, and so on.
   a. Show that these values form a geometric sequence.
   b. The Mayans of ancient Mexico and Guatemala used a vigesimal number system—base 20. Give the first five place values of the Mayan number system.

25. Give the 25th term of the arithmetic sequence $-36, -29, -22, -15, \ldots$ [4-1]

26. Give the 50th partial sum of the arithmetic series $1.3 + 2.6 + 3.9 + 5.2 + \cdots$. [4-1]

Solve each system of equations. [3-1]

27. $2.4x + 1.3y = 15.1$
$2x - y = 23$

28. $x + y + z = 0$
$2x - y + 3z = 11$
$-x + y + 2z = 0$

MORE PRACTICE

Tell whether each sequence is geometric. If so, give the common ratio and the next term in the sequence.

29. $5, 10, 15, 20, \ldots$

30. $7, 49, 343, 2401, \ldots$

31. $1, \dfrac{1}{4}, \dfrac{1}{16}, \dfrac{1}{64}, \cdots$

32. $1, -3, 9, -27, \ldots$

33. $1, 4, 9, 16, 25, \ldots$

34. $60, 90, 135, 202.5, \ldots$

35. $4, -6, 9, -13.5, \ldots$

36. $\dfrac{1}{2}, \dfrac{2}{3}, \dfrac{3}{4}, \dfrac{4}{5}, \cdots$

37. $-0.001, 0.01, -0.1, 1, \ldots$

38. Flu Epidemic On Monday, the first day of a flu epidemic, three employees of a company were absent. Throughout the week, absences mounted geometrically, peaking at 48 on Friday. Estimate how many employees were absent on Tuesday, Wednesday, and Thursday.

39. Use a Graphing Utility The first two terms of a sequence are 3 and 6.
a. Write the first five terms of the sequence if it is arithmetic. Graph the sequence.
b. Write the first five terms of the sequence if it is geometric. Graph the sequence.
c. How can the graph of a sequence help you to decide whether the sequence is arithmetic or geometric?

Give a formula for the nth term of each geometric sequence.

40. $1, 1.1, 1.21, 1.331, \ldots$

41. $256, 448, 784, 1372, \ldots$

42. $343, -98, 28, -8, \ldots$

43. $120, -60, 30, -15, \ldots$

44. $-1, -2, -4, -8, \ldots$

45. $2, 3.8, 7.22, 13.718, \ldots$

46. Give the sixth term of the geometric sequence $81, 108, 144, \ldots$.

47. Use a Graphing Utility Radioactive elements decay into other elements. The *half-life* of an element is the amount of time it takes for half of the substance to decay. The half-life of one type (*isotope*) of plutonium is 2.8 years.
a. Write a sequence showing the amount of plutonium that remains from a 100-gram sample after each of the first six half-lives.
b. Graph the sequence. Use time as the independent variable and amount of plutonium remaining as the dependent variable.

48. Find the positive geometric mean of 12 and 972.

49. The sixth term of a geometric sequence with a common ratio of 4.5 is 118,098. Give the first term and a formula for the nth term of the sequence.

MORE MATH REASONING

50. Give an example of a sequence that is both arithmetic and geometric.

51. a. Show that the positive geometric mean between 2 and 18 is the square root of their product.
b. Use the sequence $a, \sqrt{ab}, b, \ldots$ to explain why the positive geometric mean between any two positive numbers is the square root of their product.
c. The following theorem is proven in most geometry courses.

> The length of the altitude to the hypotenuse of a right triangle is the positive geometric mean between the lengths of the two segments of the hypotenuse that are determined by the altitude.

Use this theorem to find the lengths of the two segments that are formed when, in a right triangle, a 4-inch altitude divides a 10-inch hypotenuse.

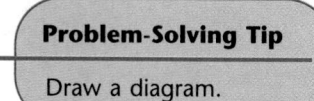

Problem-Solving Tip

Draw a diagram.

52. a. Give the first five terms of the sequence with nth term given by the formula
$a_n = \dfrac{n^4}{24} - \dfrac{n^3}{4} + \dfrac{23n^2}{24} - \dfrac{3n}{4} + 1$. What pattern do these terms *seem* to have?
b. Find the sixth term. Use your results to explain why a simple listing of the terms of a sequence is not sufficient to establish that the sequence is geometric.

4-2
PART B   Geometric Series

← **CONNECT** → *Like the terms of an arithmetic sequence, the terms of a geometric sequence can be added to produce a series. Now you will explore ways to sum and apply geometric series.*

Suppose one evening you call two people within 5 minutes to pass along some news. They each then pass along the news to two new people within 5 minutes, and so on. The number of people contacted in each 5-minute period forms a geometric sequence.

Time	8:00	8:05	8:10	8:15	8:20	8:25	8:30
People contacted	1	2	4	8	16	32	64

However, the total number of people with the news at each time is a *sum* of terms of this geometric sequence. The sum of the terms of a geometric sequence forms a **geometric series.** The partial sums of the geometric series $1 + 2 + 4 + 8 + \cdots$ give the total number of people who know the news.

$S_1 = 1$ 1 person knows the news at 8:00 p.m.

$S_2 = 1 + 2 = 3$ 3 people know the news at 8:05 p.m.

$S_3 = 1 + 2 + 4 = 7$ 7 people know the news at 8:10 p.m.

EXPLORE: A SERIES OF UPS AND DOWNS

1. Conduct several trials where you drop a ball from a known initial height and measure its rebound height after one bounce. Use a different initial height for each trial. Record the initial height and rebound height for each trial.

> **Problem-Solving Tip**
>
> Make a plan for measuring rebound height.

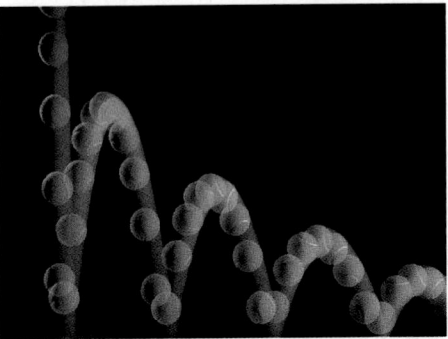

2. For each trial, calculate the *rebound ratio,* the ratio of the rebound height to the initial height. How do the rebound ratios compare for your trials? Find the average rebound ratio (r) from these trials.

3. Choose an initial ball height. Then write the first 12 terms of a sequence representing the initial height and each successive rebound height, assuming the rebound ratio is constant (r) for each bounce. What type of sequence is this? Do you think this is a good model for rebound heights of a bouncing ball? Explain.

4. Using your sequence, predict the total distance the ball will have traveled after 10 bounces and after 12 bounces. Do you think the ball will travel much farther after more bounces? Explain.

Writing a geometric series in terms of the first term and the common ratio allows us to give a convenient formula for evaluating partial sums.

The geometric series with first term a_1 and common ratio $r \neq 1$ is $a_1 + a_1 r + a_1 r^2 + a_1 r^3 + \cdots$. The partial sum of the first n terms is

$$S_n = a_1 + a_1 r + a_1 r^2 + a_1 r^3 + \cdots + a_1 r^{n-1}$$

If we multiply both sides of this equation by r, we get

$$r S_n = a_1 r + a_1 r^2 + a_1 r^3 + \cdots + a_1 r^{n-1} + a_1 r^n$$

Now if we subtract these two equations, only two terms remain.

$$S_n - r S_n = a_1 - a_1 r^n$$
$$S_n(1 - r) = a_1 - a_1 r^n$$
$$S_n = \frac{a_1(1 - r^n)}{1 - r}$$

> The partial sum of the first n terms of a geometric series with first term a_1 and common ratio $r \neq 1$ is given by $S_n = \frac{a_1(1 - r^n)}{1 - r}$.

CONSIDER

?

1. Why do only two terms remain when you subtract rS_n from S_n?

EXAMPLES

1. A tennis ball hit in the air 27 feet rebounds to two-thirds of its previous height after each bounce. Find the total vertical distance the ball has traveled when it hits the ground the tenth time.

Between bounces, the tennis ball travels twice its rebound height. The geometric series for the total distance traveled is $54 + 36 + 24 + \cdots$.

$$S_n = \frac{a_1(1 - r^n)}{1 - r} = \frac{54\left(1 - \left(\frac{2}{3}\right)^n\right)}{1 - \frac{2}{3}}$$ Use $a_1 = 54$ and $r = \frac{2}{3}$.

$$S_{10} = \frac{54\left(1 - \left(\frac{2}{3}\right)^{10}\right)}{1 - \frac{2}{3}} \approx 159.2$$

The ball has traveled about 159.2 feet by the tenth bounce.

2. Give the sum $\sum_{n=1}^{12} 2(3^n)$.

$$\sum_{n=1}^{12} 2(3^n) = 2(3) + 2(3^2) + \cdots + 2(3^{12})$$ Add the first 12 terms of the series.

$$= \frac{6(1 - 3^{12})}{1 - 3} = 1{,}594{,}320$$ Use $a_1 = 6$ and $r = 3$ to find S_{12}.

TRY IT

a. Jack calls 4 people within 10 minutes of his son's birth to pass along the news. They each pass along the news to 4 new people within 10 minutes, and so on. How many people have heard the news in 1 hour?

b. Give the sum $\sum_{n=1}^{8} 4(1.5^n)$.

c. Write the geometric series $3 + 6 + 12 + \cdots + 96$ in sigma notation and find its sum.

Geometric series can help you find long sums quickly. These series are also at the core of the theory of *power series*, an important subject in calculus.

REFLECT

1. How can you check whether a series is arithmetic or geometric?

2. Do you think a ball bounces an infinite distance by the time it stops? Explain.

3. If you know the common ratio and the first and last terms of a geometric series, how can you tell how many terms are in the series?

Exercises

CORE

1. Getting Started Examine the geometric sequence 2, 6, 18, ...
   a. Give the common ratio.
   b. Give the fourth term and the fifth term.
   c. Give the partial sums S_1, S_2, S_3, and S_4 for the geometric series $2 + 6 + 18 + \cdots$.

Write the word or phrase that correctly completes each statement.

2. A geometric ____ is the sum of the terms of a geometric ____.

3. Add the first five terms of a geometric series to find the fifth partial ____.

Give each sum.

4. the first 15 terms of $9 + 9 + 9 + \cdots$

5. the first 10 terms of $100 + 20 + 4 + \cdots$

6. $3 + 6 + 12 + \cdots + 6144$

7. $-32 + (-16) + (-8) + \cdots + (-0.0625)$

8. S_6 for the series $\frac{1}{2} + \frac{1}{3} + \frac{2}{9} + \cdots$

9. S_{39} for the series $-1 + 1 - 1 + 1 - 1 + \cdots$

10. $\sum_{n=1}^{8} 4^n$

11. $\sum_{n=1}^{6} 0.4(5)^n$

12. $\sum_{n=1}^{7} 4^n$

13. $\sum_{n=1}^{8} 625(0.8)^{n-1}$

14. $\sum_{n=1}^{8} (0.1)^n$

15. $\sum_{n=1}^{6} \left(\frac{1}{3}\right)^{n-1}$

16. That's the Way the Ball Bounces A golf ball that is thrown in the air to a height of 6 feet always rebounds to 40% of its previous peak height. Give the distance the ball has traveled when it strikes the ground for the sixth time.

> **Problem-Solving Tip**
>
> Draw a diagram.

Write each geometric series in sigma notation and find its sum.

17. $1 + 4 + 16 + \cdots + 4096$

18. $200 + 100 + 50 + \cdots + 1.5625$

19. the first 10 terms of the series $343 - 49 + 7 - 1 + \cdots$

20. What's My Line? Jackie belongs to the ninth generation of her family to be born in Arizona. She figures that she has two parents in the eighth generation, four grandparents in the seventh, eight great-grandparents in the sixth, and so on.
   a. How many ancestors does she have in the first generation of this direct parent-grandparent line?
   b. How many total members are there in the family line, including Jackie?

21. Give the first term of the five-term geometric series that has a common ratio of -3 and a sum of 244.

22. Extra Credit Nickels Department Store charges 1.5% interest per month on unpaid balances. In addition, the company charges a $10 late fee for payments received after the fifth of the month. Arthur made a $1000 purchase and made no payments for 6 months. How much does Arthur owe the department store?

Problem-Solving Tip

Make a table using a calculator or a spreadsheet.

23. You Haven't Seen the Half of It The radioactive substance strontium-90 has a half-life of 25 years, meaning that half of a given amount of the substance decays into other elements every 25 years. Begin with 400 grams of strontium-90.
  a. Write a sequence giving the amounts that decay every 25 years for 200 years.
  b. Calculate the sum of the sequence and use the sum to help you find the portion of the original amount that remains after 200 years.

24. The common ratio of a geometric series is $-\frac{2}{3}$. If the sum of the series is -55 and there are 5 terms, give the first term.

25. The sum of a geometric series is 635. The common ratio is 2 and the last term is 320. Give the first term.

26. Going Up, Slowing Down Because oxygen pressure decreases as altitude increases, humans perform less efficiently at higher altitudes. Suppose that a mountain climber who begins at 10,000 feet is able to climb 4,000 feet higher the first day, and each succeeding day is able to climb 75% of the previous day's climb.
  a. Write a sequence that gives the amount climbed each day for 1 week.
  b. What altitude has the climber reached after 1 week?

LOOK AHEAD

27. a. Use a scientific calculator, graphing calculator, or spreadsheet to generate partial sums of the geometric series $1 + 2 + 4 + 8 + \cdots$. Do the sums appear to be growing larger and larger without bound, or do they appear to be approaching a specific number?
  b. Answer the same question for the series $1 + \frac{1}{2} + \frac{1}{4} + \frac{1}{8} + \cdots$.

28. Account for the contrasting results that you obtained with the two series in **27.**

MORE PRACTICE

Give each sum.

29. the first 10 terms of $5 + 10 + 20 + \cdots$

30. the first 7 terms of $32 - 16 + 8 - 4 + \cdots$

31. the first 8 terms of $30 + 3 + 0.3 + \cdots$

32. the first 6 terms of $\frac{1}{27} - \frac{1}{9} + \frac{1}{3} - \cdots$

Give each sum.

33. $1 + 5 + 25 + \cdots + 15{,}625$

34. $800 + 200 + 50 + \cdots + 0.78125$

35. S_6 for the series $\frac{1}{2} + \frac{3}{8} + \frac{9}{32} + \cdots$

36. S_8 for the series $16 - 8 + 4 - \cdots$

37. $\displaystyle\sum_{n=1}^{6} 2^n$

38. $\displaystyle\sum_{n=1}^{4} 12(9^n)$

39. $\displaystyle\sum_{n=1}^{7} 3^n$

40. $\displaystyle\sum_{n=1}^{10} 1024(0.5)^{n-1}$

41. $\displaystyle\sum_{n=1}^{6} 125(-0.2)^{n-1}$

42. $\displaystyle\sum_{n=1}^{5} \left(\frac{1}{2}\right)^n$

43. A ball tossed to a height of 16 feet rebounds to one-half of its previous high point after each bounce. Find the total distance traveled when the ball hits the ground for the sixth time.

Write each geometric series in sigma notation and find its sum.

44. $1 + 3 + 9 + \cdots + 2187$

45. $256 + 192 + 144 + \cdots + 45.5625$

46. the first 20 terms of the series $-2 + 2 - 2 + \cdots$

47. the first 12 terms of the series $3240 + 540 + 90 + \cdots$

48. Cultural Growth For each bacterium in a culture, the culture grows by 6 bacteria in the first hour, 36 in the second hour, 216 in the third hour, and so on.
  a. How many bacteria are added during the tenth hour for each original bacterium?
  b. Give the total number of bacteria in the culture after 10 hours for each original bacterium.

49. The common ratio of a geometric series is $\frac{1}{2}$. If the sum of the first 5 terms of the series is 1.55, what is the first term?

50. A geometric series with 6 terms has a common ratio of 2 and a sum of 32. Find the first term of the series.

MORE MATH REASONING

51. Have You Heard the One About...? Suppose that one evening a person made up a joke. By 9 a.m. the following morning, the person had told the joke to 5 people. By 10 a.m., each of the 5 had told 5 more. Every hour, each person who had heard the joke the previous hour told 5 people who had never heard the joke, and then told no one else. There are about 5.5 billion people on the earth. How much time elapsed before everyone heard the joke?

52. Three consecutive terms of a geometric sequence have a sum of 15 and a product of -1000. Find the common ratio.

← CONNECT →   *Until now, you have investigated finite numbers of terms in sequences and series. Now you will investigate infinite sequences and series to see whether their terms and partial sums approach a definite value as you consider more and more terms.*

Twenty-five hundred years ago, the Greek philosopher Zeno of Elea devised a number of paradoxes based on infinite sequences and series. Here is one paradox:

If I want to go from Athens to Sparta, first I must travel half the distance. Then I must travel half the remaining distance. Then I must again travel half the remaining distance. The *halves* gets smaller and smaller, but there will always be another half ahead of me. Obviously, I will never reach Sparta.

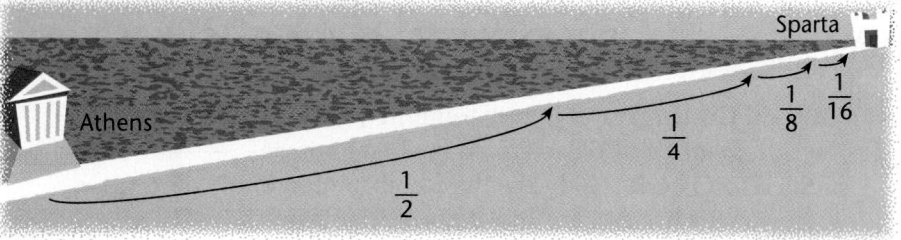

We can represent the progress of this trip with an infinite geometric series.

$$\frac{1}{2} + \frac{1}{4} + \frac{1}{8} + \frac{1}{16} + \cdots + \left(\frac{1}{2}\right)^n + \cdots$$

The partial sums give the portion of the journey completed after each stage.

Stage 1: $\frac{1}{2}$　　　Stage 2: $\frac{3}{4}$　　　Stage 3: $\frac{7}{8}$　　　Stage 4: $\frac{15}{16}$　　　$\cdots$

Notice the pattern: each numerator is 1 less than the denominator, so the partial sums get closer and closer to 1. Although they never reach 1, they get as close as we like. We say that the partial sums and the series **converge** to a **limit** of 1, and we *define* the sum of the infinite series to be this limit.

$$\frac{1}{2} + \frac{1}{4} + \frac{1}{8} + \frac{1}{16} + \cdots + \left(\frac{1}{2}\right)^n + \cdots = 1$$

In general, the common ratio determines whether an infinite geometric series converges or not.

> An infinite geometric series converges and thus has a sum if and only if $|r| < 1$, where r is the common ratio.

EXAMPLES

Determine whether each geometric series converges.

1. $3 + 6 + 12 + 24 + \cdots$

The common ratio is 2. Since $|2| > 1$, the series does not converge.

2. $4 - \frac{4}{3} + \frac{4}{9} - \frac{4}{27} + \cdots$

The common ratio is $-\frac{1}{3}$. Since $\left|-\frac{1}{3}\right| = \frac{1}{3}$ and $\frac{1}{3} < 1$, the series converges.

TRY IT

Determine whether each geometric series converges.

a. $64 + 16 + 4 + 1 + \cdots$ **b.** $1 - 5 + 25 - 125 - \cdots$

If an infinite geometric series converges, then we can use the formula $S_n = \frac{a_1(1 - r^n)}{1 - r}$ for the partial sums to find the sum (S) of the series. Since $|r| < 1$, r^n approaches 0 as n increases. Therefore, the numerator $a_1(1 - r^n)$ converges to a_1 as n increases and S_n converges to $\frac{a_1}{1 - r}$.

> The sum of an infinite geometric series with first term a_1 and common ratio r, where $|r| < 1$, is given by $S = \frac{a_1}{1 - r}$.

CONSIDER

1. Why does r^n approach 0 as n increases if $|r| < 1$?

EXAMPLE

3. The geometric series $32 + 24 + 18 + 13.5 + \cdots$ represents the lengths, in centimeters, of successive swings of a pendulum as it comes to rest. Find the total distance traveled by the pendulum before stopping.

The series converges, since $r = \frac{24}{32} = 0.75$ and $|r| < 1$.

$$S = \frac{a_1}{1 - r} = \frac{32}{1 - 0.75} = 128$$

The pendulum travels 128 cm.

c. A ball is tossed vertically and begins a series of bounces. The geometric series $90 + 60 + 40 + 26\frac{2}{3} + \cdots$ represents the total distance traveled, in inches, by the ball. How far does the ball travel before stopping?

Zeno's paradoxes have intrigued people for more than two thousand years. Among modern paradoxes, few have proven more puzzling than the Koch Snowflake, devised by the Swedish mathematician Helge von Koch in 1904.

EXPLORE: A FLAKE WITH A FLUKE!

1. Find the perimeter and the area of an equilateral triangle with side lengths of 27 units.

2. Enlarge the triangle by dividing each side in thirds and erecting an equilateral triangle on the middle third. How much did you increase the perimeter? How much did you increase the area?

3. Enlarge the figure again by dividing each edge in thirds and erecting an equilateral triangle on the middle third edge. How much did you increase the perimeter? How much did you increase the area?

4. Enlarge the figure as many times as needed to see geometric patterns in the perimeters and areas. Write a geometric series that represents the perimeter after enlarging the figure again and again. Write another geometric series that represents the area after enlarging the figure again and again.

5. Find the common ratio for each series. Does the perimeter converge or increase without bound? Does the area converge or increase without bound? Explain.

6. Do you find anything paradoxical about your results? Explain.

The concept of limit was first studied in depth by Isaac Newton and Gottfried von Leibniz, whose discoveries led them independently to the invention of calculus, an important branch of mathematics used by physicists, engineers, and economists.

REFLECT

1. Do you think Zeno will ever reach Sparta from Athens? Why or why not?
2. Why would an infinite geometric series not converge when the common ratio is greater than 1? Explain with an example.
3. Can an infinite arithmetic series have a limit? Explain.

Exercises

CORE

1. **Getting Started** Examine the infinite geometric series $1 + \frac{1}{4} + \frac{1}{16} + \cdots$.
   a. Give the common ratio (r).
   b. Give $|r|$. Explain how you know the series converges.
   c. Use $S = \frac{a_1}{1 - r}$ to find the sum of the infinite series.

Write the word or phrase that correctly completes each statement.

2. If the absolute value of the common ratio of an infinite geometric series is less than 1, then the series ____.

3. If each succeeding partial sum of an infinite geometric series gets closer and closer to 4, then the series has a ____ of 4.

Determine whether each geometric series converges.

4. $10 + 20 + 40 + 80 + \cdots$

5. $200 + 40 + 8 + 1.6 + \cdots$

6. $-27 - 9 - 3 - 1 - \cdots$

7. $1 - \frac{1}{5} + \frac{1}{25} - \frac{1}{125} + \cdots$

Give the sum of each infinite geometric series.

8. $9 + 6 + 4 + \cdots$

9. $25 - 5 + 1 - \cdots$

10. $4 + 3 + \frac{9}{4} + \cdots$

11. $\frac{9}{8} + \frac{3}{4} + \frac{1}{2} + \cdots$

12. Yolanda Ruiz is the marketing director for a company in a city of 4,000,000 people. Her advertising plan projects that 35% of the market will initially buy their new product. She then estimates that 35% of these people will like the product and convince another person to buy the product, and so on.
    a. In all, how many people does Ms. Ruiz project will buy the product?
    b. What percentage is this of the city's population?
    c. Suppose her 35% estimate is off by 2%. How many fewer people would buy the product?

13. Bouncing Back A ball tossed vertically 20 inches begins a series of bounces. If the ball travels a total of 160 inches before stopping, at what height does it rebound after its first bounce?

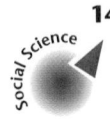

14. Multiplier Effect If the Federal Reserve was to set the reserve requirement for all federally insured banks at 15%, this would mean that Town Bank could only loan out 85% of a deposit. Suppose a local business deposits $10,000 in Town Bank, which in turn loans out 85% of that deposit, and this loan is redeposited and subsequently loaned to another at the maximum rate, and so on. Show how a geometric series can model the total effective influx to the economy in loans.

Using the symbol ∞ for infinity, $80 + 60 + 45 + \cdots$ can be written as $\sum\limits_{n=1}^{\infty} 80\left(\frac{3}{4}\right)^{n-1}$. Write each infinite geometric series using sigma notation and give its sum.

15. $16 + 8 + 4 + \cdots$

16. $625 + 500 + 400 + \cdots$

17. $1 + \frac{1}{2} + \frac{1}{4} + \cdots$

18. $9 - 3 + 1 - \cdots$

19. Squares in Squares in Squares Each side of a square measures 64 cm. A second square is drawn by joining the midpoints of the sides of the first. A third square is then drawn by joining the midpoints of the sides of the second. If this process is continued without end, what will be the sum of the areas of all the squares?

20. Shoot the Moon Following the shutdown of its engines, a rocket begins to decelerate. The following figures give hourly distances, in miles, traveled by a rocket sent to the moon during the first three hours: 25,000, 22,500, 20,250. If deceleration continues geometrically, will the rocket reach the moon, 240,000 miles from the earth? Explain.

21. Recall that we use bar notation for writing a repeating decimal:
$0.\overline{3} = 0.333\ldots$.
   a. Write $0.\overline{3}$ as an infinite geometric series with common ratio 0.1.
   b. Show that $0.\overline{3} = \frac{1}{3}$ by finding the sum of the above infinite series.

   Use this method to find a fractional equivalent of each repeating decimal.

   c. $0.\overline{7}$

   d. $0.\overline{15}$

   e. $0.\overline{61}$

 **LOOK BACK**

22. Give three arithmetic means between -32 and 28. [4-1]

23. Solve the system of inequalities:
$2x + 7 > 1$
$x - 3 \leq -5$ [3-2]

24. Find and graph an equation relating x and y. [1-1]

x	0	1	2	3	4	5
y	-3	1	5	9	13	17

MORE PRACTICE

Determine whether each geometric series converges.

25. $1 + 0.1 + 0.01 + 0.001 + \cdots$

26. $1 - 2 + 4 - 8 + \cdots$

27. $-10 + (-5) + (-2.5) + \cdots$

28. $30 + 10 + 3\frac{1}{3} + \cdots$

29. $12 + 18 + 27 + \cdots$

30. $6 + 6 + 6 + \cdots$

Give the sum of each infinite geometric series.

31. $30 - 3 + 0.3 - \cdots$

32. $1000 + 500 + 250 + \cdots$

33. $1 + \frac{2}{5} + \frac{4}{25} + \cdots$

34. $10 - 2.5 + 0.625 - \cdots$

35. $60 + 40 + 26\frac{2}{3} + \cdots$

36. $2 + 0.25 + 0.03125 + \cdots$

37. Let's Take a Cruise During the first minute of flight, a blimp ascended 600 feet. In each succeeding minute, the blimp rose 85% as much as in the previous minute, until it reached its cruising altitude.
a. Write the blimp's elevation gains during each of the first 4 minutes of flight.
b. Give the blimp's cruising altitude, which was reached after 4 minutes.

Write each infinite geometric series using sigma notation and give its sum.

38. $1 + 6 + 36 + \cdots$

39. $1 + 0.1 + 0.01 + \cdots$

40. $800 + 200 + 50 + \cdots$

41. $16 - 12 + 9 - \cdots$

MORE MATH REASONING

Social Science

42. College Bound On the day of her birth, Mr. and Mrs. Hwang bought $500 in bonds to help pay for their daughter's college education. The bonds paid 6% interest compounded annually. Each year on her birthday, the Hwangs bought another $500 in bonds paying the same interest rate. If they continue this tradition, how much will their daughter have in her college fund on her eighteenth birthday?

43. An Ant... A rubber strip is 5 inches long. An ant standing at one end of the strip starts walking toward the other end at a rate of 1 inch per second. After 1 second the strip is stretched to 125% of its original length. The ant keeps walking and after each additional second the strip is again stretched to 125% of its previous length. Will the ant ever reach the end of the strip? If so, how long will it take?

44. ...And a Bee... Two trains 150 miles apart are speeding toward each other on the same track. One train is going 80 mi/hr, the other 70 mi/hr. A bee on the engine of the faster train takes off toward the slower, flying at a speed of 120 mi/hr. On reaching the slower engine, the bee immediately reverses course and flies back to the first, then reverses again. The bee continues at the same rate, flying an infinite number of zigs and zags until the engines collide. How far does the bee fly altogether? Explain your answer.

← CONNECT → *You have examined geometric growth in sequences and series. You've also analyzed infinite geometric series to decide whether they converge and, if so, to find their sum.*

One of the principal tasks of demographers—people who study the dynamics of human populations—is to construct accurate models of populations so that governments and agencies can respond appropriately. In the following Explore, you will have an opportunity to construct such a model.

EXPLORE: MODELING THE WORLD

The table gives estimates of the world population for 14 years out of the past 2000 years.

MATERIALS

Graphing utility or graph paper

Year	Population (billions)	Year	Population (billions)
1	0.255	1930	2.070
1500	0.460	1940	2.295
1600	0.579	1950	2.515
1700	0.679	1960	3.019
1800	0.954	1970	3.698
1900	1.633	1980	4.450
1920	1.862	1990	5.292

1. Graph the population data. What can you learn from the shape of the graph?
2. If population grows at the rate of p percent per year, explain why the yearly populations form a geometric sequence. What is its common ratio in terms of p?
3. From years 1 to 1500, world population grew at an average rate of about 0.039 percent per year. Verify that your population formula gives a reasonable prediction of the population in 1500, given the population in year 1 and the average rate of growth.
4. Annual population growth since 1500 has ranged from a low of about 0.2% to a high of about 2%. Construct a population model for the period from 1500 to the present that reasonably generates values in the table. Either find a single annual growth percentage for the entire period or find the annual growth percentage for several shorter periods. Explain how you constructed your model.
5. Use your model to forecast the world population for the years 2000, 2050, and 2100. What could you do to make even better predictions? Explain.
6. Do you think the human population is converging or is it increasing without limit? Explain your decision.

1. Give a general description of the graphs of positive geometric sequences.
2. If one bacteria culture is growing by 10,000 bacteria per hour and a second culture is growing by 10% an hour, which culture would you model using a geometric sequence? Why?
3. How does the common ratio affect the growth of the terms of a geometric sequence? How does it affect the convergence of an infinite geometric series?

Self-Assessment

Tell whether each sequence is geometric. If so, give the common ratio and the formula for a_n.

1. 1, 4, 16, 64, ... **2.** 50, 40, 30, 20, ... **3.** −1, 2, −4, 8, ... **4.** 18, 6, 3, 1, ...

5. The first two terms of a geometric sequence are 27 and 18.
  a. Find the next three terms in the sequence.
  b. Find the first four partial sums of the geometric series.

Give each sum.

6. the first 6 terms of the series $120 + 90 + 67.5 + \cdots$

7. $1 + 2 + 4 + \cdots + 512$

8. $20 + 4 + 0.8 + \cdots + 0.0064$

9. S_6 for the series $\frac{1}{2} + \frac{1}{4} + \frac{1}{8} + \cdots$

10. S_7 for the series $-1 + 3 - 9 + 27 - \cdots$

11. $\sum_{n=1}^{5} 3(5)^n$

12. $\sum_{n=1}^{6} 1440\left(\frac{2}{3}\right)^{n-1}$

13. $32 + 16 + 8 + \cdots$

14. $-81 + 27 - 9 + \cdots$

15. $6 + 4 + 2\frac{2}{3} + \cdots$

16. $0.9 + 0.09 + 0.009 + \cdots$

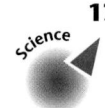

17. Many people are worried about the amount of radon in their homes. Radon is a radioactive gas that comes from soil containing uranium. The gas seeps into basements and, because homes today are less drafty than they once were, the radon tends to stay indoors for a prolonged period of time. The half-life of radon is 3.8 days. If you had a container of radon, about what percentage of radon would be left after one 30-day month?

Use sigma notation to write each series.

18. $1 + 7 + 49 + 343 + 2401$

19. $40 + 4 + 0.4 + \cdots$

20. Express the repeating decimal $0.\overline{45}$ as an infinite geometric series and as a fraction.

21. Snail's Pace A snail crawled 36 inches in one hour, 24 inches the next hour, 16 the third hour, and so on. Find the total distance the snail traveled.

22. The first two terms of a sequence are 3 and 9.
  a. Write the first five terms of the sequence if it is arithmetic.
  b. Write the first five terms of the sequence if it is geometric.

23. Insert three arithmetic means between 14 and 36. [4-1]

24. The results of several U.S. censuses for the population of Tennessee are given below. [4-1]

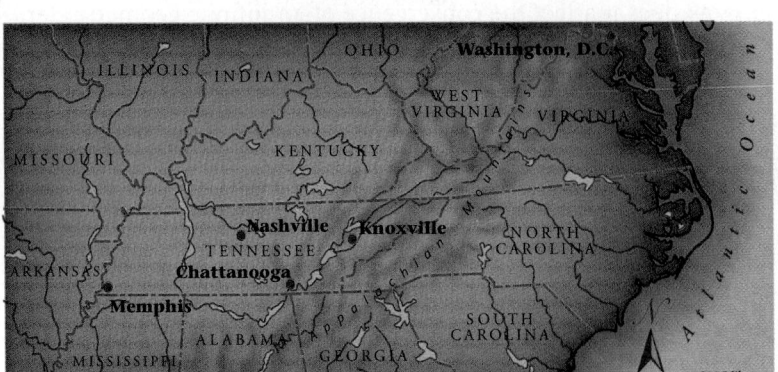

Year	Population
1900	2,020,616
1910	2,184,789
1920	2,337,885
1930	2,616,556
1940	2,915,841
1950	3,291,718
1960	3,567,089
1970	3,926,018
1980	4,591,023
1990	4,877,185

  a. Give the population increase for each decade and the mean increase per decade.
  b. Use the mean as the common difference and write an arithmetic sequence to model the census for Tennessee in the twenty-first century.
  c. What would you predict for the population of Tennessee in the year 2020?

25. In the geometric sequence with the first two terms 20 and 15, the third term is:
  (a) 5   (b) $1\frac{1}{3}$ (c) 11.25   (d) 10

26. Without finding the sum, we know that the infinite geometric series
  $8 + 4 + 2 + \cdots$ converges because:
  (a) $a_1 > 0$ (b) the series has an infinite number of terms.
  (c) $|r| < 1$ (d) each term is less than the last.

27. A Matter of Age Radiocarbon dating uses carbon-14 to determine the age of artifacts. Living things absorb carbon until they die, at which point the carbon-14 begins to decay with a half-life of 5,700 years. What percentage of carbon-14 will remain after 28,500 years?

28. Consider the infinite geometric series $1 + 2 + 4 + 8 + \cdots$.
  a. Compare S_n and 2^n for several values of n. How do they appear to be related?
  b. Use $S_n = \dfrac{a_1 - a_1 r^n}{1 - r}$ with $a_1 = 1$ and $r = 2$ to show how S_n is related to 2^n.

29. Pile It On A sheet of paper 0.002 in. thick is repeatedly folded in half.
  a. Write a sequence giving the total thickness after each of the first 8 foldings.
  b. Suppose that you could fold the paper in half 30 times. Give the total thickness in inches and in miles.

30. The Swing of Things You start a pendulum swinging at an angle of 30° from vertical. The maximum angle of each swing is 90% of the maximum angle of the previous swing. Find the maximum angle after 5 swings. How many swings will the pendulum make before the maximum angle is less than 1°?

The Fractal Nature of the World

The geometry of many objects in nature appears disorganized or extraordinarily complex. Three decades ago, the mathematician Benoit Mandelbrot began studying such geometry. He discovered that beneath the seemingly random, irregular shapes there is often a simple organizing principle of *self-similarity*. That is, these shapes look similar at a variety of scales. View a section of twisting coastline or the side of a craggy mountain from an airplane, at eye level, and at microscopic levels, and the shapes often look remarkably similar. Mandelbrot called these shapes *fractals* because they often seemed to have fractional dimension. A complex fractal curve with infinite length but no area may seem to be greater than one-dimensional but not quite two-dimensional.

Mandelbrot set out to model self-similarity mathematically. By continually recycling the outputs of certain *complex* functions back into these functions, a process known as *iteration*, the results, when graphed, often exhibit self-similarity. Computers can calculate and graph millions of iterations per second, producing fractal images of extraordinary beauty. Natural phenomena such as water turbulence, rock fractures, language patterns, and heart rhythms, once thought to be too complex or random for analysis, are now being modeled with fractals. Mandelbrot's discovery has opened up rich and seemingly endless possibilities for research and is justly regarded as one of the great developments in the history of mathematics.

1. In your own words, describe self-similarity.
2. Benoit Mandelbrot has stated that "Clouds are not spheres. Mountains are not cones. Lightning does not travel in a straight line." What point do you think he was making?
3. Choose one of the fractals and describe how it seems to have a fractional dimension. What integral dimensions does the fractal seem to be between?

← CONNECT → *You have used several general properties of real numbers to analyze patterns in sequences and series. Now you will investigate the general properties and structure of the real number system.*

You are already familiar with several properties of real numbers. Some of these properties we take for granted. Recall that you can add real numbers in any order or group them in any way and you always get the same result.

$3 + 4 = 4 + 3$ Addition is *commutative.*

$(3 + 4) + 1 = 3 + (4 + 1)$ Addition is *associative.*

Also recall that the number 0 is called the *additive identity* since 0 added to any real number yields the identical number.

$0 + 17 = 17$ The *additive identity* is 0.

A set of numbers is said to be **closed** under addition if the sum of any two numbers in the set is also a number in the set.

Consider the set of numbers {1, 2, 3} and the operation of addition.

Since addition can yield numbers not in the set {1, 2, 3}, this set is *not closed* under addition. It only takes one *counterexample* (for example, $3 + 3 = 6$, which is not in the set) to show that a set is not closed under an operation.

In the following Explore, you will investigate different sets, properties, and operations to discover the structure of various number systems.

EXPLORE: VALUABLE PROPERTIES

1. Answer these questions for each set of numbers, property, and operation in the chart. Then copy and complete the chart.
   a. Is the set closed under the given operation?
   b. Does the operation satisfy the commutative property?
   c. Does the operation satisfy the associative property?
   d. Is there an identity number in the set for the given operation? If so, what is it?

Note that © means *clock addition,* where 12 is equal to 0, 13 is equal to 1, −2 is equal to 10, and so on. For example, 5 © 8 = 1, just as 5 hours after 8 o'clock is 1 o'clock.

Set of numbers	Operation	Closed	Commutative	Associative	Identity
$\{-1, 0, 1\}$	+				
	×				
$\{0, 1\}$	+				
	−				
$\{-2, 0, 2\}$	+				
	×				
{whole numbers}	+				
	−				
{integers}	+				
	×				
$\{0, 1, 2, 3, \ldots, 11\}$	©				

2. Define a different set of numbers and an operation so that the set is closed under the operation and the commutative and associative properties are satisfied. Add the set to your table and complete the table.

The set with two operations that satisfies each of the following properties is called a **field.** The real number system is perhaps the best known example of a field, but it is not the only one as you will see.

A **field** is a set with two operations, + and •, that satisfies the following **field axioms.**

For any elements *a, b,* and *c* in the set,

	The operation +	**The operation •**
Closure Properties:	$a + b$ is also in the set.	$a \cdot b$ is also in the set.
Commutative Properties:	$a + b = b + a$	$a \cdot b = b \cdot a$
Associative Properties:	$(a + b) + c = a + (b + c)$	$(a \cdot b) \cdot c = a \cdot (b \cdot c)$
Identities:	There is a unique identity element, 0, so that for any *a*, $a + 0 = 0 + a = a$.	There is an unique identity element, 1, so that for any *a*, $a \cdot 1 = 1 \cdot a = a$.
Inverses:	For any *a*, there is an inverse, $-a$, so that $a + (-a) = -a + a = 0$.	For any $a \neq 0$, there is an inverse, $\frac{1}{a}$, so that $a \cdot \frac{1}{a} = \frac{1}{a} \cdot a = 1$.

Distributive Property of • over +: $a \cdot (b + c) = (a \cdot b) + (a \cdot c)$

1. In the field of real numbers, why is the inverse property for multiplication defined only for nonzero numbers?

EXAMPLES

1. Do the integers 2 and -8 have additive inverses within the set of integers? If so, give their additive inverses. Do all integers have additive inverses within the set of integers?

The additive inverse of 2 is the integer -2 since $2 + (-2) = 0$, the additive identity. Likewise, the additive inverse of -8 is 8 since $-8 + 8 = 0$. Every integer n has an additive inverse, its opposite $-n$, which is also an integer.

2. Is the set $\{-1, 0, 1\}$, with the real-number operations $+$ and $\cdot$, a field?

In order to be a field, all eleven field axioms must be satisfied. If any axiom fails (has a counterexample), the set is not a field.

Since $1 + 1 = 2$ and 2 is *not* in the set $\{-1, 0, 1\}$, the set is not closed under addition. So the set is not a field.

3. Does the set of even integers satisfy the distributive property of multiplication over addition?

Since the distributive property is true for all real numbers, it is true for any *subset* of the real numbers such as the even integers. For example:

$2(4 + 2) \overset{?}{=} 2(4) + 2(2)$

$2(6) \overset{?}{=} 8 + 4$

$12 = 12 \checkmark$

TRY IT

Determine whether all of the numbers in each set have multiplicative inverses. Justify your conclusions.

a. $\{-1, 0, 1\}$ **b.** {integers}   **c.** {positive real numbers}

d. Does the set of integer multiples of 3 satisfy the distributive property of multiplication over addition? Explain.

e. Does the set of integers with the operations $+$ and $\cdot$ form a field? Justify your conclusion.

The real number system was sufficient for problem solving until the mid-sixteenth century. Since then, many new algebraic structures have proven to be useful in areas such as physics and engineering. These structures include matrix groups, function fields, and the complex numbers, which you will study in 4-3C.

1. Give an operation and a set that is not closed under that operation.

2. Which field axioms refer strictly to addition? to multiplication? to both addition and multiplication?

3. Explain how subtraction and division can be defined from the existing field axioms and operations, and so need not have their own axioms.

Exercises

CORE

1. Getting Started Using real numbers, write an expression, equation, or sentence illustrating each field axiom.

    a. the associative property of multiplication

    b. the inverse property of addition

    c. the identity property of addition

    d. the distributive property of multiplication over addition

    e. the closure property of multiplication

    f. the commutative property of addition

Give each real number.

2. the multiplicative identity element

3. the additive inverse of 14.6

4. the additive identity element

5. the multiplicative inverse of $-\frac{1}{2}$

Write the word or phrase that correctly completes each statement.

6. The number 7 is the ____ of the number -7.

7. The equation $(8 + 7) + 6 = (7 + 8) + 6$ illustrates the ____ property of addition.

8. Because the product of two integers is always an integer, the set of integers is ____ under multiplication.

9. As part of a service project, Darlene and Alan are responsible for serving sandwiches at a soup kitchen. Alan counted 4 groups of 3 sandwiches on a tray, for a total of 12 sandwiches. Darlene counted 3 groups of 4 sandwiches, for a total of 12.

    a. What axiom(s) assure(s) that Darlene and Alan both counted 12 sandwiches?

    b. If the sandwiches were made with two different types of bread and three different kinds of cheese, how many different kinds of meat would be needed to insure that there would be 12 different sandwiches of cheese and meat? Explain your answer.

10. Kirk added a column of figures up, while Holly added the column down. What axiom(s) assure(s) that they both obtained the same sum?

Determine whether each statement is true or false. If the statement is false, provide a counterexample.

11. The set of odd integers is closed under multiplication.

12. The set of odd integers is closed under addition.

Give an example to illustrate each statement.

13. The set of positive real numbers is not closed under subtraction.

14. The set $\{-2, -1, 0, 1, 2\}$ is not closed under addition.

15. Subtraction of real numbers is not commutative.

16. Division of real numbers is not associative.

17. Clock Arithmetic Clock arithmetic, also known as *modular arithmetic*, can be illustrated on a diagram similar to a clock. In clock arithmetic with the set $\{0, 1, 2, 3, 4\}$, we add (◎) and multiply (⊗) numbers and give the remainder after dividing by 5.

    a. Decide whether the set $\{0, 1, 2, 3, 4\}$ is closed under each operation.

    b. Is there an identity element for each operation? If so, give the identity.

    c. Are there inverses for elements using each operation? If not, give counterexamples.

    d. Is the set $\{0, 1, 2, 3, 4\}$ with these operations a field? Explain.

Examples of clock arithmetic:

$2 \odot 2 = 4 \qquad 2 \otimes 2 = 4$
$2 \odot 3 = 0 \qquad 2 \otimes 3 = 1$
$3 \odot 3 = 1 \qquad 3 \otimes 3 = 4$

Decide whether each set is a field. If not, explain why.

18. the set of even integers

19. the set of positive numbers

20. the set of whole numbers

21. the set of odd integers

22. Suppose a new operation (∇) is defined as $a \nabla b = a + 3b$ for the set of integers. For example, $2 \nabla 6 = 2 + 3(6) = 20$.

    a. Is ∇ commutative for the set of integers? Explain.

    b. Is ∇ associative for the set of integers? Explain.

    c. Does ∇ distribute over regular addition? Explain.

 *LOOK AHEAD*

Write a definition for each set of numbers. Then give an example of a number in each set.

23. {rational numbers}

24. {irrational numbers}

25. Is the sum of two irrational numbers always irrational? Justify your answer.

MORE PRACTICE

26. Using real numbers, write an expression, equation, or sentence illustrating each field axiom.
  a. the commutative property of multiplication
  b. the closure property of addition
  c. the inverse property of multiplication
  d. the identity property of multiplication
  e. the associative property of addition

Give each real number.

27. the additive inverse of -13.72

28. the multiplicative inverse of 24

29. the multiplicative inverse of $\frac{4}{5}$

30. the additive inverse of $\sqrt{5}$

Give an example to illustrate each statement.

31. The set $\{1, 2, 3, ..., 9, 10\}$ is not closed under multiplication.

32. The set of multiples of 5 is not closed under division.

33. Subtraction of real numbers is not associative.

34. Division of real numbers is not commutative.

35. The operation of raising a number to a power is not associative.

Identify each field axiom illustrated.

36. $6 + 13 = 13 + 6$

37. $9 \cdot (-4)$ is a real number.

38. $7 \cdot (6 + 5) = 7 \cdot 6 + 7 \cdot 5$

39. $2 + 12 = 2 + 12 + 0$

40. $15 \cdot \frac{1}{15} = 1$

41. $3.4 \cdot 7.52 \cdot 1 = 3.4 \cdot 7.52$

42. $\sqrt{2} + \sqrt{3}$ is a real number.

43. $5(9 + 8) = (9 + 8)5$

MORE MATH REASONING

44. Let $\frac{a}{b}$ and $\frac{c}{d}$ represent two rational numbers, where a, b, c, and d are integers.
  a. Show that the product of two rational numbers is a rational number.
  b. Show that the sum of two rational numbers is a rational number.

45. Study these two attempts to simplify the expression $6(x + 4)(x + 3)$.

  (a) $6(x + 4)(x + 3) = (6x + 24)(x + 3)$
  (b) $6(x + 4)(x + 3) = (6x + 24)(6x + 18)$

  Which method is correct? Identify the mistake made using the other method.

46. Do you think that $\oplus$ and $\otimes$ can be used with the real numbers to form a field? Justify your response.
$$a \oplus b = 2ab \qquad a \otimes b = \tfrac{1}{2}(a + b)$$

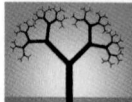

Rational and Irrational Numbers

← CONNECT → *You've examined the structure of fields. Now you will work with the rational and irrational numbers that make up the real number field.*

The real numbers are represented by all decimal numbers and by all numbers on a number line. Here are some of the subsets of the real numbers.

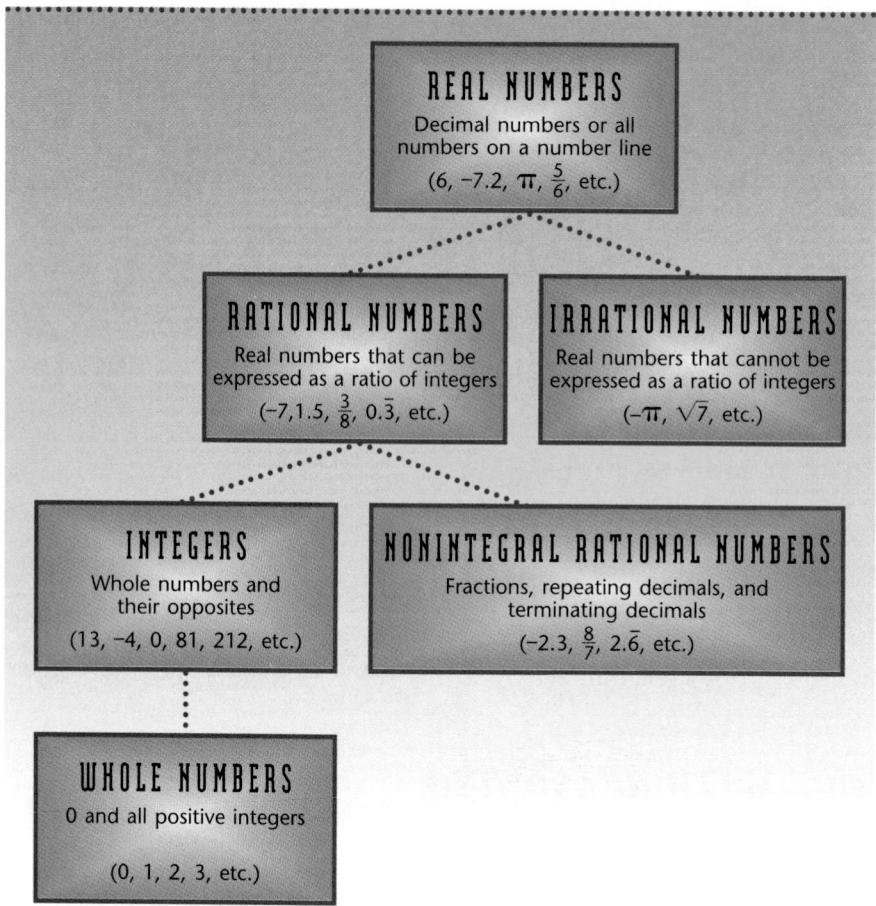

REAL NUMBERS
Decimal numbers or all numbers on a number line
$(6, -7.2, \pi, \frac{5}{6}, \text{etc.})$

RATIONAL NUMBERS
Real numbers that can be expressed as a ratio of integers
$(-7, 1.5, \frac{3}{8}, 0.\overline{3}, \text{etc.})$

IRRATIONAL NUMBERS
Real numbers that cannot be expressed as a ratio of integers
$(-\pi, \sqrt{7}, \text{etc.})$

INTEGERS
Whole numbers and their opposites
$(13, -4, 0, 81, 212, \text{etc.})$

NONINTEGRAL RATIONAL NUMBERS
Fractions, repeating decimals, and terminating decimals
$(-2.3, \frac{8}{7}, 2.\overline{6}, \text{etc.})$

WHOLE NUMBERS
0 and all positive integers
$(0, 1, 2, 3, \text{etc.})$

CONSIDER

1. How can you write a terminating decimal, such as 4.91, as a ratio of integers?

You will often encounter irrational numbers as **square roots.** Recall that a square root of a real number a is a real number c such that $c^2 = a$. If a is positive, then it has two square roots. The positive square root of a is called the **principal square root** and is written using the **radical symbol** as $\sqrt{a}$. The negative square root of a is $-\sqrt{a}$.

For example, $\sqrt{81} = 9$, $\sqrt{\frac{4}{9}} = \frac{2}{3}$, and $-\sqrt{0.0064} = -0.08$, since $9^2 = 81$, $\left(\frac{2}{3}\right)^2 = \frac{4}{9}$, and $(0.08)^2 = 0.0064$.

> If a is a positive integer, then $\sqrt{a}$ is rational only if a is the square of an integer. Similarly, if a and b are positive integers with no common factors, then $\sqrt{\frac{a}{b}}$ is rational only if a and b are both squares of integers.

EXAMPLES

Decide whether each square root is rational or irrational. If it is rational, give its value.

1. $-\sqrt{121}$

$-\sqrt{121}$ is rational since 121 is 11 squared.

$-\sqrt{121} = -11$

2. $\sqrt{\frac{3}{16}}$

$\sqrt{\frac{3}{16}}$ is irrational since 3 and 16 have no common factors and 3 is not the square of an integer.

3. $\sqrt{6.25}$

6.25 can be written as $\frac{25}{4}$; 25 and 4 are both squares of integers, so $\sqrt{6.25}$ is rational.

$\sqrt{6.25} = \sqrt{\frac{25}{4}} = \frac{5}{2}$ or 2.5.

TRY IT

Decide whether each square root is rational or irrational. If it is rational, give its value.

a. $\sqrt{225}$ **b.** $\sqrt{3.5}$ **c.** $-\sqrt{\frac{16}{49}}$

An important application of square roots in geometry is the Pythagorean Theorem, which states that a right triangle with legs of lengths a and b and hypotenuse of length c satisfies $a^2 + b^2 = c^2$. Therefore, $c = \sqrt{a^2 + b^2}$.

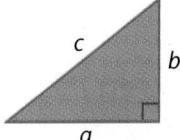

In the following Explore, you will use the Pythagorean Theorem to construct and analyze a sequence of lengths.

EXPLORE: GOING TO IRRATIONAL LENGTHS

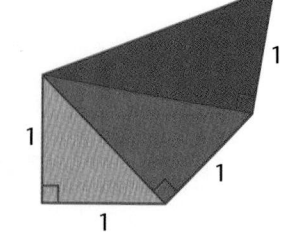

MATERIALS

Graph paper, Protractor
Straightedge

1. Construct a right triangle with each leg 1 unit in length. What is the exact length of the hypotenuse?

2. Using the first triangle, construct a new triangle with the hypotenuse of the first triangle as one leg and the second leg 1 unit in length. How long is the hypotenuse of the new right triangle?

3. Construct a third triangle with the hypotenuse of the second triangle as one leg and the second leg 1 unit in length. How long is the hypotenuse of the third right triangle?

4. Continue constructing triangles in this manner. What do you notice about the lengths of the hypotenuses?

> **Problem-Solving Tip**
>
> Look for a pattern.

5. Write a sequence representing the lengths of the hypotenuses of the triangles and give a formula for the *n*th term of the sequence. Which terms in the sequence are rational numbers and which are irrational numbers? Explain.

Notice that $\sqrt{7^2}$ and $\sqrt{(-7)^2}$ both equal $\sqrt{49}$, which equals 7. In both cases the principal square root is the *absolute value* of the number squared inside the radical symbol. This property is true for the square root of any square.

For any real number a, $\sqrt{a^2} = |a|$.

Using the following property, you can also simplify square roots of products and quotients.

For any positive real numbers a and b, $\sqrt{ab} = \sqrt{a}\sqrt{b}$ and $\sqrt{\dfrac{a}{b}} = \dfrac{\sqrt{a}}{\sqrt{b}}$.

By simplifying square roots using these properties and combining like terms involving square roots, you can simplify a variety of square root expressions.

Simplify each expression.

4. $\sqrt{\dfrac{45}{4}}$

$= \dfrac{\sqrt{45}}{\sqrt{4}}$

$= \dfrac{\sqrt{9} \cdot \sqrt{5}}{2}$

$= \dfrac{3\sqrt{5}}{2}$ or $\dfrac{3}{2}\sqrt{5}$

5. $\sqrt{12} - 5\sqrt{7} + 6\sqrt{3}$

$= \sqrt{4 \cdot 3} - 5\sqrt{7} + 6\sqrt{3}$

$= 2\sqrt{3} + 6\sqrt{3} - 5\sqrt{7}$

$= (2 + 6)\sqrt{3} - 5\sqrt{7}$

$= 8\sqrt{3} - 5\sqrt{7}$

6. $-2\sqrt{75n^2}$

$= -2\sqrt{25 \cdot 3 \cdot n^2}$

$= -2(5|n|\sqrt{3})$

$= -10|n|\sqrt{3}$

7. $2\sqrt{3x} \cdot \sqrt{6x}$

$= 2\sqrt{18x^2}$

$= 2 \cdot \sqrt{9} \cdot \sqrt{2} \cdot \sqrt{x^2}$

$= 2 \cdot 3 \cdot |x| \cdot \sqrt{2}$

$= 6|x|\sqrt{2}$

Simplify each expression.

d. $\sqrt{\dfrac{18}{100}}$

e. $-2\sqrt{3w^2}$

f. $8\sqrt{11} + 7\sqrt{5} - 2\sqrt{44}$

g. $3\sqrt{5k} \cdot 4\sqrt{15k}$

Rational and irrational numbers are important structures within the field of real numbers. Studying these numbers leads us to useful properties of square roots, square root expressions, and, later, rational expressions.

1. Why is there no real square root of a negative real number?

2. Describe other sets of numbers you could add to the chart on page 278.

3. A calculator gave the square root of 3 as 1.732050808. Was the square root exact or approximate? Since this value is a terminating decimal, is $\sqrt{3}$ rational? Explain.

Exercises

CORE

1. **Getting Started** Classify each number as real, rational, irrational, an integer, a nonintegral rational number, or a whole number. Most numbers have more than one classification.

   a. 34

   b. $-\frac{7}{8}$

   c. $-\sqrt{64}$

   d. 5.777

   e. π

   f. $-13\frac{2}{3}$

   g. $\sqrt{-100}$

   h. $\sqrt{3}$

   i. $\sqrt{5.29}$

Write the word or phrase that correctly completes each statement.

2. A rational number is a number that can be expressed as ____.

3. The whole numbers and their opposites comprise the set of ____.

4. The principal square root of a positive real number is ____.

5. The numbers on the number line comprise the set of ____.

Decide whether each square root is rational or irrational. If it is rational, give its value.

6. $-\sqrt{16}$

7. $\sqrt{0.909}$

8. $\sqrt{\frac{25}{36}}$

9. Use the Pythagorean Theorem to find the length of the hypotenuse of the right triangle. Is this length rational or irrational?

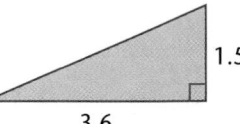

1.5

3.6

Simplify each expression. Check your work by comparing the decimal equivalent of the initial expression to your answer.

10. $\sqrt{12.1}$

11. $-\sqrt{416}$

12. $-\sqrt{\frac{1}{24}}$

Solve each equation.

13. $3x^2 = 12$

14. $\sqrt{x} = 13$

15. $\sqrt{2x} = 18$

16. **Double Dunk** The diameter of a basketball hoop is 46 cm. The surface area (S) of a basketball is 1810 cm^2.

   a. Find the radius (r) of a basketball using the formula $r = 0.5\sqrt{\frac{S}{\pi}}$. Use 3.14 for π.

   b. Can two basketballs be dunked through the hoop side by side? Explain.

Simplify each expression.

17. $\sqrt{4p^2}$

18. $5\sqrt{2} + 9\sqrt{2}$

19. $\sqrt{72} - \sqrt{50}$

20. $\sqrt{18}\,\sqrt{8}$

21. $(7\sqrt{3})^2$

22. $12\sqrt{75} \cdot 0.5\sqrt{12y^2}$

23. $\sqrt{8} + \sqrt{6} - \sqrt{12}$

24. $\dfrac{12\sqrt{60}}{3\sqrt{5}}$

25. $\dfrac{\sqrt{32x}\,\sqrt{18x}}{\sqrt{2}}$

26. $\sqrt{(x-3)^2}$

27. $-\sqrt{45h} + \sqrt{5h}$

28. $\sqrt{\dfrac{125}{k^2}}$

29. A Long Time This photo shows the world's longest pendulum, which measures 73 ft $9\frac{3}{4}$ in. It is part of the water-mill clock in the Shinjuku NS Building in Tokyo. Calculate the length of time (t) in seconds that it takes a standard pendulum of this length to make one complete swing.

Use $t = 2\pi\sqrt{\dfrac{L}{384}}$, where L is the length of the pendulum in inches.

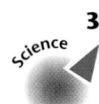

30. Special Delivery The formula $t = 0.25\sqrt{d}$ can be used to find the time (t) in seconds that it takes an object to fall a distance of d feet. Suppose that a mail bag accidentally fell from the cargo bay of a jet liner that was flying at an altitude of 6 miles. How long would it take the bag to reach the ground?

31. Let $i_1 = 2$ and let $i_{n+1} = \sqrt{i_n}$.
   a. Use a calculator to generate the first few terms in the sequence $i_1, i_2, i_3, \ldots$ Does the sequence appear to have a limit? If so, what is it?
   b. Choose different values for i_1 and repeat the calculations. Describe your results.

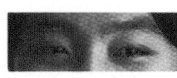 *LOOK BACK*

32. Rolling Down the Highway Rachel bought a new car for \$14,000. If the car depreciates $\frac{1}{5}$ of its value each year, find the value of the car in 6 years. [4-2]

33. Solve the system of equations graphically: [3-1]
$$y = 2x - 7$$
$$y = -4x + 5$$

34. The table shows the boiling point of water at various altitudes. [2-2]

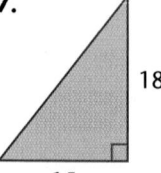

	Altitude (ft)	Boiling Point of Water (°F)
London, England	0 (sea level)	212.0
Dead Sea	−1,296	213.8
Denver, Colorado	5,280	203.0
Quito, Ecuador	9,350	194.0
Lhasa, Tibet	12,087	188.6
Mt. Everest (top)	29,002	159.8

a. Graph the data and sketch a line of best fit.

b. Write an equation for your line of best fit and use it to predict the boiling point of water at 20,000 ft.

c. Write a generalization about the relationship between altitude and the boiling point of water.

MORE PRACTICE

Define each set of numbers. Give an example of a number in each set.

35. {rational numbers}

36. {negative integers}

37. {real numbers}

38. {positive irrational numbers}

39. A square mile measures 5280 feet on a side. There are 640 acres in a square mile. Find the dimensions of a square-shaped acre.

40. Classify each number as real, rational, irrational, an integer, a nonintegral rational number, or a whole number. Most numbers have more than one classification.

a. -4.56119 **b.** $\sqrt{35}$ **c.** $20\frac{1}{4}$ **d.** $-\sqrt{225}$

e. $\sqrt{81}$ **f.** 1 **g.** -1000 **h.** $\sqrt{54.76}$

Decide whether each square root is rational or irrational; if rational, give its value.

41. $\sqrt{\dfrac{25}{16}}$ **42.** $\sqrt{108}$ **43.** $\sqrt{0.01}$

44. $\sqrt{45}$ **45.** $\sqrt{24}$ **46.** $\sqrt{\dfrac{27}{3}}$

Use the Pythagorean Theorem to find the length of the hypotenuse of each right triangle. Decide whether the length is rational or irrational.

47.

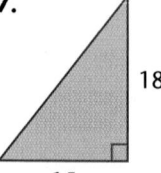

18

15

48.

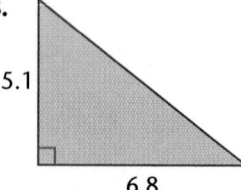

5.1

6.8

Simplify each expression. Check your work by comparing the decimal equivalent of the initial expression to your answer.

49. $\sqrt{360}$ **50.** $-\sqrt{605}$ **51.** $-2\sqrt{\dfrac{507}{50}}$

52. Time for a Brake Traffic accident investigators use the formula $s = \sqrt{30d}$ to estimate the speed (s) in miles per hour of a car with locked brakes that skids a distance of d feet. Estimate the speed of the car that left skid marks of each length.

a. 50 feet
b. 100 feet
c. 200 feet

Solve each equation.

53. $5x^2 = 125$

54. $\sqrt{x} = 7$

55. $\sqrt{3x} = 27$

56. $4x^2 = 64$

57. $\sqrt{x} = 19$

58. $\sqrt{5x} = 20$

Simplify each expression.

59. $\sqrt{18m^2}$

60. $-\sqrt{128d}$

61. $3\sqrt{5} - 8\sqrt{7} + 2\sqrt{5} - \sqrt{3}$

62. $\sqrt{48} - \sqrt{27}$

63. $\sqrt{200} + \sqrt{162}$

64. $\sqrt{(y+5)^2}$

65. $\dfrac{\sqrt{45}}{\sqrt{5}}$

66. $\dfrac{28\sqrt{96}}{7\sqrt{6}}$

67. $\sqrt{21}\sqrt{3} - \dfrac{\sqrt{84}}{\sqrt{3}}$

68. $\sqrt{18} - \sqrt{50} + 8\sqrt{2}$

69. $\sqrt{(-8m)^2}$

70. $\sqrt{3}\,(\sqrt{27} - \sqrt{12})$

MORE MATH REASONING

71. Shooting Stars Scientist F. L. Whipple of Harvard determined that the velocity of a shooting star or meteor can be found by using the formula $V = \dfrac{0.3(\sqrt{\lambda R})}{T}$ if λ is the wavelength of a transmitted radar signal in miles, R is the distance to the meteor in miles, and T is the time interval in seconds between the maximum and the first minimum of the received echo signal. Determine the value of T for a meteor traveling 25 miles per second at a height of 60 miles if the wavelength in use is 30 feet long.

72. Show that $\sqrt{9 - 4\sqrt{5}} = \sqrt{5} - 2$.

73. Some 2300 years ago, Euclid devised the following proof that $\sqrt{2}$ is irrational. Give a reason for each step of the proof. The proof is indirect, meaning that we begin by assuming that $\sqrt{2}$ is rational and then see if that assumption leads to a contradiction.

Assume that $\sqrt{2}$ is a rational number.

a. $\sqrt{2}$ equals $\frac{a}{b}$ for some integers a and b with no common factors greater than 1.

b. $2 = \dfrac{a^2}{b^2}$

c. $2b^2 = a^2$

d. a^2 must be an even number.

e. a must be an even number.

f. There must be an integer k such that $a = 2k$.

g. $2b^2 = (2k)^2 = 4k^2$

h. $b^2 = 2k^2$

i. b must be an even number.

j. This contradicts **a.**

Therefore, $\sqrt{2}$ is irrational.

74. Does taking the square root distribute over multiplication? Justify your answer.

75. Does taking the square root distribute over addition? Justify your answer.

← **CONNECT** → *Square roots of positive real numbers lead us to the study of rational and irrational numbers. By including the imaginary square roots of negative numbers, we can build a new field of complex numbers.*

In the sixteenth century, the Italian mathematician and physician Girolamo Cardano offered the "fictitious" solutions $5 + \sqrt{-15}$ and $5 - \sqrt{-15}$ to the problem of finding two numbers with a sum of 10 and a product of 40.

Sum:
$$(5 + \sqrt{-15}) + (5 - \sqrt{-15}) = 5 + 5 + \sqrt{-15} - \sqrt{-15} = 10$$

Product:
$$(5 + \sqrt{-15})(5 - \sqrt{-15}) = 5 \cdot 5 - 5\sqrt{-15} + 5\sqrt{-15} - (-15) = 25 + 15 = 40$$

By using square roots of negative real numbers, such as $\sqrt{-15}$, Cardano had *invented* a new type of number not in the real number system. These numbers came to be known as **imaginary numbers.**

The **imaginary unit** i is defined by $i = \sqrt{-1}$ and satisfies the equation $i^2 = -1$. An **imaginary number** is a number of the form bi, where b is a real number.

If c is a positive real number, $\sqrt{-c}$ is defined to be $i\sqrt{c}$. For example, Cardano's imaginary number $\sqrt{-15}$ is equal to $i\sqrt{15}$.

EXAMPLES

Simplify each expression.

1. $\sqrt{-18}$
$= \sqrt{18 \cdot -1}$
$= \sqrt{9 \cdot 2 \cdot -1}$
$= \sqrt{9} \cdot \sqrt{2} \cdot \sqrt{-1}$
$= 3i\sqrt{2}$

2. $-2i(\sqrt{-7})$
$= -2i \cdot i\sqrt{7}$
$= -i^2 \cdot 2\sqrt{7}$
$= -(-1) \cdot 2\sqrt{7}$
$= 2\sqrt{7}$

3. $\sqrt{-3}\sqrt{-5}$
$= i\sqrt{3} \cdot i\sqrt{5}$
$= i^2\sqrt{15}$
$= (-1) \cdot \sqrt{15}$
$= -\sqrt{15}$

TRY IT

Simplify each expression.

a. $\sqrt{-50}$

b. $\sqrt{-6}\sqrt{-8}$

c. $9i \cdot 6i \cdot \sqrt{-\dfrac{1}{4}}$

1. Is it true that $\sqrt{ab} = \sqrt{a}\sqrt{b}$ for any negative real numbers a and b? Explain.

2. Is the set of imaginary numbers closed under addition? under multiplication? Explain.

The imaginary unit i has some interesting properties, such as the pattern that emerges in the geometric sequence of powers of i.

EXPLORE: THE *i*'s HAVE IT

1. Copy and complete the table of powers of i.

Power	i^1	i^2	i^3	i^4	i^5	i^6	i^7	i^8
Value	i	-1						

2. Describe the pattern in the values of the powers of i.

3. Predict the values of i^{12} and i^{13}. Extend your table to these values to check.

4. Describe a method you can use to simplify i^n for any whole number n. Use your method to simplify i^{39}, i^{62}, and i^{101}.

By adding real numbers and imaginary numbers, we create **complex numbers,** which can be added by combining like terms and multiplied by extending the distributive property to all complex numbers.

The **complex numbers** consist of all sums $a + bi$, where a and b are real numbers. The **real part** of $a + bi$ is a, and the **imaginary part** is bi.

EXAMPLES

Simplify each expression.

4. $(3 + 7i) - 2(5 - 2i)$
$= 3 + 7i - 2(5) - 2(-2i)$ Use the distributive property.
$= 3 - 10 + 7i + 4i$ Combine real parts and combine
$= -7 + 11i$ imaginary parts.

5. $(3 + 4i)(5 + 2i)$
$= 3 \cdot 5 + 3 \cdot 2i + 4i \cdot 5 + 4i \cdot 2i$ Use the distributive property.
$= 15 + 6i + 20i + 8i^2$
$= 15 + 8(-1) + 6i + 20i$ Recall that $i^2 = -1$.
$= 7 + 26i$ Combine real parts and combine
    imaginary parts.

6. The formula $V = IZ$ relates the voltage (V), the current (I), and the resistance or *impedance* (Z) through an electrical component or circuit. Give the voltage across a stereo speaker system with an impedance of $(15 + 10i)$ ohms and a current flow of $(3 - 6i)$ amps.

$$V = IZ = (3 - 6i)(15 + 10i)$$
$$= 3 \cdot 15 + 3 \cdot 10i - 6i \cdot 15 - 6i \cdot 10i$$
$$= 45 + 30i - 90i - 60i^2$$
$$= 45 - 60(-1) + 30i - 90i$$
$$= 105 - 60i$$

The voltage across the speaker system is $105 - 60i$ volts.

TRY IT

Simplify each expression.

d. $3(4 - 9i) + (-13 + 3i)$ **e.** $(8 + 5i)(-3 - 7i)$

The complex numbers include every real number as numbers of the form $a + 0i$. The complex numbers also satisfy each of the field axioms, and so form a field that contains the real number field.

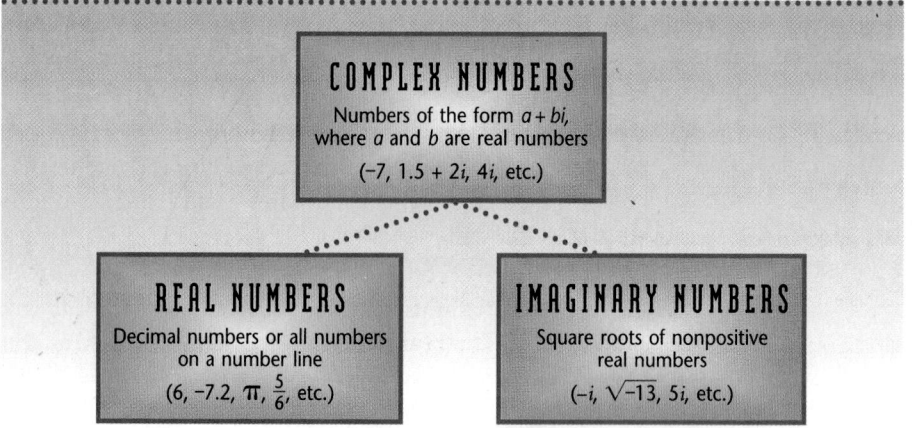

Imaginary and complex numbers have proven to be useful in many fields, most notably in electrical engineering, physics, medical imaging, and fractal geometry.

REFLECT

1. Write a description of complex numbers that would explain them to someone who has never heard of complex numbers.

2. Explain how you multiply two complex numbers.

3. Is there any number that is both real and imaginary? Explain.

Exercises

CORE

1. Getting Started Complete each step to express $\sqrt{-49}$ in terms of i.

   a. $\sqrt{-49} = \sqrt{\underline{\ ?\ } \cdot 49}$

   b. $= \sqrt{\underline{\ ?\ }} \ \sqrt{49}$

   c. $= \underline{\quad ?\quad}$

Express each imaginary number in terms of i.

2. $\sqrt{-11}$ **3.** $\sqrt{-100}$ **4.** $\sqrt{-75}$

5. Write the letter of the second pair that best matches the first pair.

Imaginary numbers: complex numbers as

(a) arithmetic series: arithmetic sequence
(b) integers: rational numbers
(c) real numbers: negative numbers
(d) field: axiom

Write the word or phrase that correctly completes each statement.

6. The number 3 is the ____ part of the complex number $3 - 6i$.

7. A(n) ____ is a number of the form bi, where b is a real number.

Simplify each expression.

8. $6 \cdot 9i$ **9.** $5i \cdot 12i$ **10.** $\sqrt{-8} \ \sqrt{-2}$

11. $13i + 15i$ **12.** $3i\sqrt{-6}$ **13.** $-\sqrt{-72}$

14. $-14i(-4)$ **15.** $\sqrt{20} \ \sqrt{-24}$ **16.** $\sqrt{-\dfrac{25}{36}}$

17. i^3 **18.** i^2 **19.** $-i^4$

20. $(5 + 6i) + (-2 + 4i)$ **21.** $(12 - 10i) + (7 - 16i)$ **22.** $(-3 + 2i) - (4 - 6i)$

23. $9 - (2 + 7i)$ **24.** $6 + (16 + 3i) - 13i$ **25.** $2i + (3i)^2$

26. $4i(6 - 2i)$ **27.** $9(-11 + 5i)$ **28.** $(3 - i)(6 + 2i)$

29. A Current Affair The current in an electronic circuit is $(6 - 9i)$ amps and the impedance is $(14 + 9i)$ ohms. Give the voltage, which is equal to the product of the current and the impedance.

Science

Give the additive inverse of each complex number.

30. $6 - 7i$ **31.** $22i$ **32.** $a + bi$

Give the missing length on each geometric figure. Decide whether the length is rational or irrational.

33.

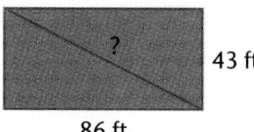

?

43 ft

86 ft

34.

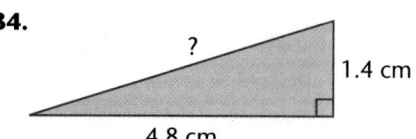

?

1.4 cm

4.8 cm

35. The *reactance* (r) of an electrical circuit is given by $r = r_I - r_C$, where r_I is the inductive reactance of the circuit and r_C is the capacitive reactance of the circuit. Suppose that a circuit with a reactance of $18i$ ohms has an inductive reactance of $22i$ ohms. Give the capacitive reactance of the circuit.

36. The function $f(z) = 2z - (4 + i)$ is to be *iterated*, that is, evaluated repeatedly using each output value (*iterate*) as the next input value.
   a. Find $f(z)$ for the initial value $z = 3 - i$.
   b. Find $f(z)$ for z equal to the value you obtained for $f(z)$ in **a.**
   c. Find the next two iterates of $f(z)$.

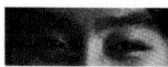 **LOOK AHEAD**

Evaluate $\dfrac{-b + \sqrt{b^2 - 4ac}}{2a}$ and $\dfrac{-b - \sqrt{b^2 - 4ac}}{2a}$ **for the given values of a, b, and c.**

37. $a = 3, b = 7, c = 2$ **38.** $a = 5, b = 6, c = 2$

39. Draw a line segment in a coordinate plane with one endpoint at the origin and the other at $(-12, 5)$. Draw a right triangle and use the Pythagorean Theorem to find the distance from $(-12, 5)$ to the origin.

MORE PRACTICE

Express each imaginary number in terms of i.

40. $\sqrt{-81}$ **41.** $\sqrt{-23}$ **42.** $\sqrt{-18}$

Simplify each expression.

43. $3i \cdot 3i$ **44.** $\sqrt{-5}\,\sqrt{-10}$ **45.** $6i + 11i$

46. $3(7i)$ **47.** $i\sqrt{-16}$ **48.** $6i + \sqrt{-49}$

49. $\sqrt{-4}\,\sqrt{8}$ **50.** $\sqrt{-\dfrac{64}{121}}$ **51.** $i(5i)$

52. $(12 - i) + (5 + 2i)$ **53.** $(-15 - 8i) + (6 - 7i)$ **54.** $(4 - i) - (4 + i)$

55. $(-13 + 10i) - (12 - 3i)$ **56.** $(3 + 2i)(5 + 4i)$ **57.** $(6 + i)(-2 - 3i)$

58. $(2 + 3i) + (4i)^2$ **59.** $\sqrt{-20} + \sqrt{-45}$ **60.** $\sqrt{-108} - \sqrt{-27}$

61. Give the voltage in a wall heater if the current is $(8 - 4i)$ amps and the impedance is $(12 + 5i)$ ohms.

MORE MATH REASONING

62. Lavonna and Roger simplified $\sqrt{-3}\ \sqrt{-5}$ as shown.

Lavonna's Method

$$\sqrt{-3}\ \sqrt{-5} = \sqrt{-1 \cdot 3}\ \sqrt{-1 \cdot 5}$$
$$= \sqrt{-1}\ \sqrt{3} \cdot \sqrt{-1}\ \sqrt{5}$$
$$= i\sqrt{3} \cdot i\sqrt{5}$$
$$= i^2\sqrt{3 \cdot 5}$$
$$= -\sqrt{15}$$

Roger's Method

$$\sqrt{-3}\ \sqrt{-5} = \sqrt{-3 \cdot -5}$$
$$= \sqrt{15}$$

Who was right? Why was the other method incorrect?

63. a. Choose two complex numbers.
   b. Find the product of the numbers.
   c. For each of the complex numbers $a + bi$ that you chose, write a matrix $\begin{bmatrix} a & b \\ -b & a \end{bmatrix}$. Find the product of the matrices.
   d. Compare the product of the complex numbers with the product of the matrices.
   e. Repeat the above steps using a different pair of complex numbers.
   f. Make a conjecture based on what you found.

4-3 PART D — Graphing Complex Numbers

← **CONNECT** → *Now that you've worked with and applied imaginary and complex numbers, you will see how these numbers can be graphed in a plane.*

The beautiful images of fractal geometry are graphs of sets of complex numbers graphed in the **complex plane,** sometimes called the Argand plane.

The method of graphing complex numbers was developed independently about two centuries ago by Carl Friedrich Gauss (1777–1855), Caspar Wessel (1745–1818), and Jean Robert Argand (1768–1822).

The complex plane has a horizontal **real axis** and a vertical **imaginary axis.** A complex number $a + bi$ is graphed in the complex plane as the point with coordinates (a, b).

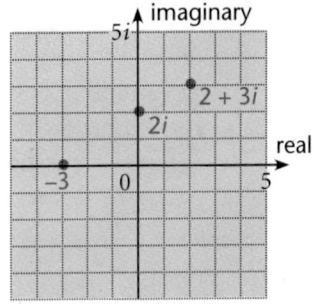

Graph each complex number in the complex plane.

a. $4 + 2i$ **b.** $-7i$

c. 2.5 **d.** $-2 - 5i$

CONSIDER

?

1. What complex number is represented by the origin of the complex plane?

The complex plane is not only useful for representing complex numbers, it is also useful for investigating complex operations. In the following Explore, you will investigate how some operations on complex numbers produce geometrical transformations in the complex plane.

EXPLORE: COMPLEX TRANSFORMATIONS

MATERIALS

Graph paper

1. Create a geometric figure by choosing three or more complex numbers, graphing them in the complex plane, and connecting the points consecutively.

2. Create a new figure by adding $2 + 4i$ to each of your original numbers, graphing the resulting numbers, and connecting the points consecutively. How did adding $2 + 4i$ transform your original figure?

3. Create a third figure by multiplying each of your original numbers by i, graphing the resulting numbers, and connecting the points consecutively. Describe how multiplying by i transformed your original figure.

4. Create a fourth figure in the same manner by changing the sign of the imaginary part of each of your original numbers. That is, replace $a + bi$ with $a - bi$. The complex number $a - bi$ is called the **complex conjugate** of $a + bi$. How did this operation transform your original figure?

5. Sketch a new transformation of your original figure and find a complex operation that performs this transformation.

You can visualize complex addition graphically by drawing a *parallelogram* in the complex plane. The complex numbers being added form two opposite vertices of the parallelogram, and their sum along with the origin form the other two vertices.

EXAMPLE

1. Add $(1 + 2i) + (-4 + 3i)$ graphically.

Draw the parallelogram with the origin as one vertex and the graphs of $1 + 2i$ and $-4 + 3i$ as opposite vertices.

The fourth vertex of the parallelogram represents $-3 + 5i$. This is the sum.
$(1 + 2i) + (-4 + 3i) = -3 + 5i$

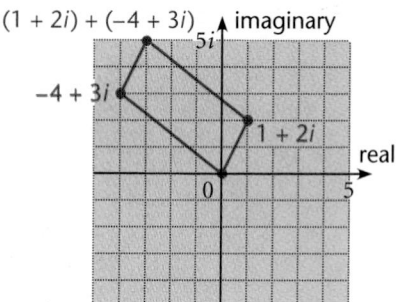

TRY IT

Add each pair of complex numbers graphically.

e. $(4 - i) + (-3 + 3i)$ **f.** $(9 + 6i) + (1 - 4i)$

We can also extend the idea of *absolute value* to the complex numbers. Recall that the absolute value of a real number is its distance from the origin on a number line. Likewise, the **absolute value of a complex number** is its distance from the origin in the complex plane.

EXAMPLE

2. Give $|4 - 3i|$.

Using the Pythagorean Theorem, the distance from $4 - 3i$ to the origin is 5.
$$\sqrt{4^2 + (-3)^2} = 5$$
$$|4 - 3i| = 5$$

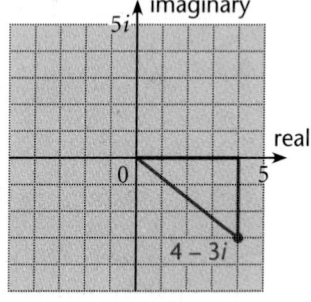

The Pythagorean Theorem shows that, in general, $|a + bi| = \sqrt{a^2 + b^2}$ for any real numbers a and b.

TRY IT

Give each absolute value.

g. $|5 + 12i|$ **h.** $|6i|$ **i.** $|3 - 7i|$

The complex plane allows you to visualize complex numbers and their operations. Note that, because points in the plane cannot be ordered linearly, the complex numbers cannot be compared and ordered using inequalities. Nevertheless, the field of complex numbers and the complex plane have developed into important tools for many engineers, artists, and scientists.

REFLECT

1. Compare and contrast graphing in the real number plane and graphing in the complex plane.
2. Jack claims that the graphs of a complex number $a + bi$ and its complex conjugate $a - bi$ are *reflections* of each other across the real axis. Do you agree with Jack? Explain.
3. How could you subtract two complex numbers graphically?

Exercises

CORE

1. **Getting Started** Give the complex number represented by each point.
   a. A
   b. B
   c. C
   d. D
   e. E

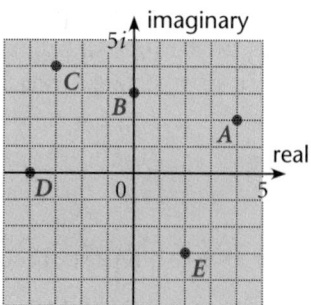

Graph each complex number.

2. $-4i$　　　　3. $1\frac{1}{2}$　　　　4. $-2 - i$　　　　5. $5 - 4i$

Write the word or phrase that correctly completes each statement.

6. The complex plane is defined by a horizontal ____ axis and a vertical ____ axis.

7. The ____ of a complex number is its distance from the origin in the complex plane.

The complex conjugate of a complex number $a + bi$ is $a - bi$. Give the complex conjugate of each number.

8. $2 + 8i$　　　　9. $14 - 7i$　　　　10. $3i$　　　　11. π

Give each absolute value.

12. $|8 - 6i|$　　　　13. $|-1|$　　　　14. $|-12 + 22.5i|$　　　　15. $|19i|$

16. One rich family of fractal images is called *Julia sets,* named for Gaston Julia, a twentieth-century French mathematician. The key to finding these sets is *iteration.*

Iteration is the process of repeatedly substituting the previous output value of a function, the iterate, back into the function to obtain a new *iterate.* This feedback process begins with an *initial value.*

The fractal shown was generated by iterating the complex function $f(z) = z^2 - 0.76906 + 0.10436i$ for thousands of complex initial values.

a. To see how iteration works, use the initial value $z = 0.1 - 0.02i$ and give $f(z)$. Then give the next two iterates.

b. Choose a different initial value and find the next two iterates using this value.

Add each pair of complex numbers graphically.

17. $(2 + i) + (-3 + 2i)$ **18.** $(-5 + 4i) + 3$ **19.** $(6 - 3i) + (-4 - 2i)$

20. Show that the product of any complex number, $a + bi$, and its complex conjugate, $a - bi$, is equal to the square of the absolute value of the complex number, $|a + bi|^2$.

21. a. Graph $3 - 4i$ and its opposite.
b. Choose three other complex numbers. Graph each number and its opposite.
c. Describe the geometric relationship between a complex number and its opposite.

LOOK BACK

22. The College Board reported these figures in 1994. [4-1]

Average Costs of Tuition and Fees at Four-Year Public Colleges, 1980–1993					
School Year	**Costs ($)**	**School Year**	**Costs ($)**	**School Year**	**Costs ($)**
1980–81	804	1985–86	1318	1990–91	1908
1981–82	909	1986–87	1414	1991–92	2137
1982–83	1031	1987–88	1537	1992–93	2315
1983–84	1148	1988–89	1646		
1984–85	1228	1989–90	1781		

a. Find the cost increase at public colleges from each year to the next.
b. Find the mean of the cost increases for the public colleges.
c. Use the mean increase as the common difference. Write the first four terms of an arithmetic sequence that could be used to estimate the costs of tuition and fees for public colleges in the mid-1990s.
d. Predict the costs for a public college in the 2004–05 school year.

23. Write an inequality to describe the fact that the elevator in Marshall High School may not safely hold more than eleven hundred pounds. [3-2]

24. Give the scalar product of -1 and the matrix $\begin{bmatrix} 2 & 8 & -4 \\ -6 & 13 & 1 \end{bmatrix}$. [1-3]

MORE PRACTICE

Graph each complex number.

25. $-i$ **26.** $4 - i$ **27.** $-5 - 3i$ **28.** 6

29. $2 + \frac{1}{2}i$ **30.** 0 **31.** $3 + 2.5i$ **32.** $-0.75 + 2i$

Give each absolute value.

33. $|15 + 7i|$ **34.** $|-2 - 6i|$ **35.** $|\sqrt{8} - i\sqrt{4}|$ **36.** $|0.2 + 0.8i|$

37. $|-14|$ **38.** $|-3.6i|$ **39.** $|20 + 21i|$ **40.** $|-30 - 5.5i|$

41. Give three complex numbers that would be graphed as points on the real axis of the complex plane. Then give three complex numbers that would be graphed as points on the imaginary axis of the complex plane.

The complex conjugate of a complex number $a + bi$ is $a - bi$. Give the complex conjugate of each number.

42. $2.3 - i$ **43.** $113 + 290i$ **44.** $0.004i$ **45.** $\sqrt{3}$

46. $\sqrt{-5}$ **47.** $17 - 17i$ **48.** $-1 + 2i$ **49.** 49

Add each pair of complex numbers graphically.

50. $(3i) + (8)$ **51.** $(-4 - 3i) + (2 - 2i)$

52. $(3 + 3i) + (3 - 3i)$ **53.** $(2) + (3i)$

54. $(2 + 3i) + (3 + 2i)$ **55.** $(4 - i) + (2 + 5i)$

56. This Julia set fractal (see **16**) is generated by iterating the complex function $f(z) = z^2 - 0.5122 + 0.5204i$.

    a. Give the value of $f(z)$ for the initial value $z = -1 - 1.2i$. Then give the next two iterates.

    b. Choose a different initial value and find the next two iterates using your value.

MORE MATH REASONING

57. Graph the set of all $a + bi$ such that $a \leq 3$ and $b \leq 2$. Describe the graph.

58. Graph the set of all $a + bi$ such that $|a + bi| \leq 4$. Describe the graph.

59. Show that each complex number has the same absolute value as its complex conjugate and its opposite.

4-3 PART E Making Connections

← **CONNECT** → *Complex numbers form a field that contains the real number field. These once "fictitious" numbers and their graphs are now a vital mathematical tool with many rich applications.*

One intriguing feature of fractals is the simple functions that are often used to generate them. Benoit Mandelbrot did much of his research on fractals generated by iterating functions of the form $f(z) = z^n + c$, where z is a complex variable and c is a complex constant. Strikingly intricate fractals are generated for most values of c, while more orderly graphs result for some special values of c. Now you will explore the simplest case, when $c = 0$.

EXPLORE: PRISONERS AND ESCAPEES

When you iterate a complex function $f(z)$ starting with an initial complex value, the outputs, or iterates, can behave in several ways. For some initial values, called *prisoner values*, the iterates approach a limit value. For other initial values, called *escape values*, the absolute value of the iterates increases without bound and the points drift away. The remaining initial values form the *Julia set*, the boundary between escape values and prisoner values.

The figure shows a unit circle in the complex plane with three points identified—one inside, one outside, and one on the circle.

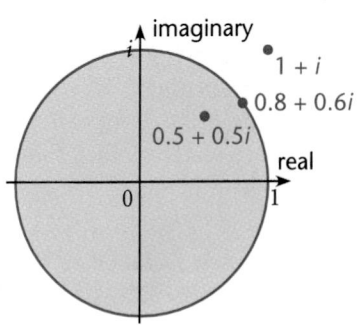

1. Using the function $f(z) = z^2$, find four or more iterates of each of the three points. Decide whether each initial point seems to represent a prisoner value, an escape value, or neither.
2. Choose three more points, one outside the unit circle, one inside, and one on the circle. Repeat Step 1.
3. For the function $f(z) = z^2$, what points do you think correspond to prisoner values? escape values? the Julia set?

1. How is a complex number different from an imaginary number?
2. In what sense are complex numbers two-dimensional?
3. What distance is measured by the absolute value of a complex number?
4. Why do you think computers have proven to be of immense value in generating fractals?

Self-Assessment

Identify each field axiom illustrated.

1. $5 \cdot 9 = 9 \cdot 5$

2. $6 + (-3)$ is a real number.

3. $4 \cdot \frac{1}{4} = 1$

4. $(10 + 3) + (-4) = 10 + (3 + (-4))$

5. $-7 + 0 = -7$

6. $8(-3 + 12) = 8 \cdot (-3) + 8 \cdot 12$

Decide whether each set is a field. If not, tell why.

7. {real numbers}

8. $\{-3, -2, -1, 0, 1, 2, 3\}$

9. {imaginary numbers}

10. {negative integers}

Decide whether the statement is true. If not, give a counterexample.

11. The set of integers is closed under the operation of division.

12. The set of counting numbers contains additive inverses.

13. Beyond the Horizon Have you ever been at the top of a tall building or cliff and wondered how far away you were from the horizon? There is a simple formula, $D \approx \sqrt{2rh}$, to approximate this distance, where D represents the distance to the horizon, r represents the radius of the earth (3960 miles), and h represents the height of the observer above the surface of the earth. If a person is about 300 feet above sea level, find the distance to the horizon in miles.

Classify each number as real, imaginary, or complex. A number may fall under several classifications.

14. $-2 + i$

15. $2i$

16. -1

17. $\sqrt{-7}$

18. A Square Diamond A baseball diamond is a square measuring 90 feet on a side. Find the distance from home plate to second base.

19. The Venn diagram shows that set A is a subset of set B and that sets C and D have no common elements. Draw a Venn diagram to represent the relationship between the following sets.

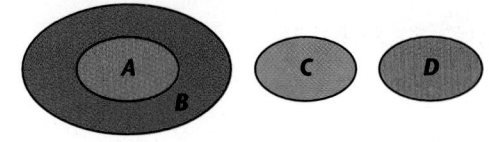

    a. real numbers and complex numbers   **b.** rational numbers and irrational numbers
    c. real numbers and imaginary numbers   **d.** counting numbers and positive numbers

Simplify each expression.

20. $-\sqrt{36}$

21. $\sqrt{-36}$

22. $\sqrt{32}$

23. $\sqrt{-8}$

24. $\sqrt{9n^2}$

25. $-\sqrt{\frac{36}{81}}$

26. $\sqrt{50} - \sqrt{18}$

27. $6i \cdot 7i$

28. $2i\sqrt{-4}$

29. i^2

30. $9i - 5\sqrt{-1}$

31. $(4 + 3i) + (-5 + 2i)$

32. $(-9 + 10i) - (8 - 4i)$

33. $3(-2 + i)$

34. $(5 + 2i)(4 - 3i)$

35. $(5 - 3i)^2$

Graph each complex number and its complex conjugate.

36. $-5 - 2i$

37. -3.5

38. $4i$

39. $3 + \frac{5}{2}i$

Add each pair of complex numbers graphically.

40. $i + (4 + 2i)$

41. $(1 - 3i) + (-2 - 2i)$

Give the missing length on each geometric figure. Decide whether the length is rational or irrational.

42.

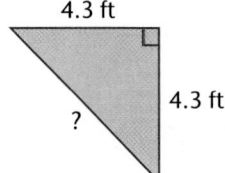

4.3 ft

4.3 ft

?

43.

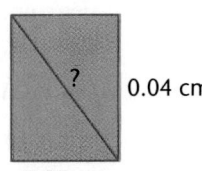

?

0.04 cm

0.03 cm

Choose the letter of the correct answer.

44. Give the absolute value of $8 - 6i$.
    (a) 14   (b) $2i$ (c) 10   (d) $8 + 6i$

45. Give the product $(4 + 2i)(4 - 2i)$.
    (a) 20   (b) 12   (c) $16 - 16i$ (d) $16 + 8i$

46. Give the sum: $\begin{bmatrix} -3 & 5 \\ 4 & 9 \\ -6 & -7 \end{bmatrix} + \begin{bmatrix} -5 & 6 \\ -1 & -9 \\ 2 & 0 \end{bmatrix}$. [1-3]

    $3x + y = -1$

47. Solve graphically: [3-1]
    $-5x - 2y = 3$

48. Find the sum of the infinite geometric series $12 + 6 + 3 + 1.5 + \cdots$.

49. Show that the set of 2×2 matrices does *not* form a field under the operations of matrix addition and multiplication.

Chapter 4 Review

You began this chapter by looking at sequential patterns and series of real numbers. Arithmetic sequences have terms with a common difference, while geometric sequences have terms with a common ratio. The sums of these sequences form arithmetic and geometric series. You continued looking at patterns by investigating the structures and patterns within the real and complex number systems. You also learned to use complex arithmetic and to graph complex numbers. The patterns and structures you've studied have a wide variety of applications, from the study of the atmosphere to the beautiful graphs of fractal geometry.

KEY TERMS

absolute value of a complex number [4-3]	field axioms [4-3]	nth term [4-1]
arithmetic sequence [4-1]	fractal [4-3]	partial sum [4-1]
arithmetic series [4-1]	general term [4-1]	principal square root [4-3]
closure [4-3]	geometric sequence [4-2]	radical symbol [4-3]
common difference [4-1]	geometric series [4-2]	real axis [4-3]
common ratio [4-2]	imaginary axis [4-3]	real part [4-3]
complex conjugate [4-3]	imaginary number [4-3]	recursive definition [4-1]
complex number [4-3]	imaginary part [4-3]	sequence [4-1]
complex plane [4-3]	imaginary unit [4-3]	sigma notation [4-1]
converge [4-2]	inductive reasoning [4-1]	square root [4-3]
field [4-3]	infinite sequence [4-1]	term [4-1]
	limit [4-2]	

Choose the letter of the word or phrase that best completes each sentence.

1. An ordered set of numbers in which a constant is added to the previous term to get the next term is a(n) ____.
(a) arithmetic sequence   (b) geometric sequence
(c) arithmetic series   (d) geometric series

2. The distance from the origin to a complex number is the ____ of the number.
(a) square root   (b) real part
(c) absolute value   (d) limit

3. For any element a in a field, there is a(n) ____, $-a$, so that $a + (-a) = 0$.
(a) common difference   (b) identity element
(c) field   (d) inverse

CONCEPTS AND APPLICATIONS

4. Give an example of an arithmetic sequence and of a geometric sequence. Describe the difference between the two types of sequences. [4-1, 4-2]

State whether each sequence is arithmetic or geometric. If it is arithmetic, give the common difference and the nth term. If it is geometric, give the common ratio and the *n*th term. [4-1, 4-2]

5. $-12, 24, -48, 96, \ldots$

6. $5, 25, 45, 65, \ldots$

7. The first two terms of a sequence are 2 and 6.
  a. If the sequence is arithmetic, what are the next three terms? Give the first four partial sums of the arithmetic series. [4-1]
  b. If the sequence is geometric, what are the next three terms? Give the first four partial sums of the geometric series. [4-2]

Give the sum of each series. [4-1, 4-2]

8. $1 + 5 + 9 + 13 + \cdots + 45$

9. the first 20 terms of the sequence $-8, -2, 4, 10, \ldots$

10. $3 + 6 + 12 + 24 + \cdots + 768$

11. the seventh partial sum of the series $\frac{1}{2} + \frac{1}{4} + \frac{1}{8} + \cdots$ $\frac{1}{16} \ \frac{1}{32} \ \frac{1}{64} \ \frac{1}{128}$

12. $\displaystyle\sum_{n=1}^{12} (2n - 3)$

13. $\displaystyle\sum_{n=1}^{6} 0.5(6)^n$

Write each series in sigma notation and give its sum. [4-1, 4-2]

14. $4 + 7 + 10 + 13 + \cdots + 64$

15. $1 + 8 + 64 + 512 + 4096$

16. Each of the 15 rows in a stack of bricks contains 3 fewer bricks than the row below. The bottom row has 43 bricks. How many bricks are in the stack? [4-1]

17. Radioactive Isotopes Cobalt-60 is a radioactive isotope used in medicine to help doctors diagnose certain diseases. Its half-life is 5 years, meaning that half of the cobalt-60 in a sample decays into other elements every 5 years. Suppose a hospital has 50 milligrams of cobalt-60. How much of this cobalt-60 will remain after 20 years? 50 years? [4-2]

Identify each field axiom illustrated. [4-3]

18. $6 \cdot (3 \cdot 8) = (6 \cdot 3) \cdot 8$

19. $5 \cdot (-2)$ is a real number.

20. $-3 + 3 = 0$

21. $19 \cdot 1 = 19$

Give an example to illustrate each statement. [4-3]

22. Multiplication of even integers is commutative.

23. The set $\{0, 1\}$ is not closed under addition.

24. Subtraction of real numbers is not associative.

Write an expression, equation, or sentence illustrating each field axiom. [4-3]

25. the associative property of multiplication

26. the inverse property of multiplication

27. the distributive property of multiplication over addition

Give each real number. [4-3]

28. the multiplicative inverse of -6 **29.** the additive inverse of 0.46

Find the absolute value and complex conjugate of each complex number. [4-3]

30. $-4.2i$ **31.** $24 - 10i$ **32.** 15

Simplify each expression if possible, and identify it as rational, irrational, or complex. [4-3]

33. $-\sqrt{100}$ **34.** $\sqrt{-49}$ **35.** $\sqrt{72}$

36. $\sqrt{-\dfrac{4}{25}}$ **37.** $3i \cdot 2i$ **38.** $\sqrt{12} + \sqrt{75}$

39. $(5 + 3i) + (-4 - 5i)$ **40.** $-7i + \sqrt{-64}$ **41.** $(3 + 2i)(5 - 3i)$

Graph each complex number. [4-3]

42. $-4 + i$ **43.** $6i$ **44.** -4.5

45. Give the sum of $(-3 - 2i) + (-2 + 4i)$ graphically. [4-3]

46. Give the voltage (the product of current and impedance) in an integrated circuit with an impedance of $(16 + 8i)$ ohms and a current flow of $(4 - 5i)$ amps. [4-3]

47. A tennis ball has a surface area (S) of 132.7 cm². Find the radius (r) of the ball using $r = 0.5\sqrt{\dfrac{S}{\pi}}$. Use 3.14 for π. [4-3]

CONCEPTS AND CONNECTIONS

48. Seismology Earthquake ground motion is commonly measured on the Richter scale. Each increase of 1 in the magnitude of an earthquake represents an increase by a factor of 10 in the intensity of the quake.

Compare the given magnitudes of the quakes with each other and with minor quakes of magnitudes less than 5. Use equations, inequalities, sequences, graphs, or any other means that might make the comparisons clearer to someone unfamiliar with the Richter scale.

Year	Location	Richter Magnitude
1993	Japan	7.8
1992	Egypt	5.9
1991	Pakistan	6.8
1989	San Francisco	7.1
1985	Mexico City	8.1
1983	Colombia	5.5
1933	Japan	8.9

SELF-EVALUATION

Each of the topics you have studied in this chapter involves patterns or algebraic structures. Taking each topic in turn, write a brief summary explaining what you think patterns or structures have to do with the topic. Be as specific as possible. Mention areas where you think the roles of patterns and structures are minor or where you had trouble finding evidence of them.

Chapter 4 Assessment

TEST

1. Examine the sequence 50, 46, 42, 38, ….
  a. Is the sequence arithmetic or geometric?
  b. Give the common difference or the common ratio.
  c. Find the 40th term of the sequence.
  d. Find the sum of the first 30 terms of the series.

2. The first term of a geometric sequence with common ratio $-\frac{1}{2}$ is 24.
  a. Write the first five terms of the sequence.
  b. Does the infinite geometric series summing this sequence converge? If so, find its limit. If not, explain why.

3. Write the terms of the series $\sum_{n=1}^{6} (n + 2)$ and give its sum.

4. Population Explosion Imagine that 2 sea stars could reproduce a full complement of offspring and that there were no predators or diseases to limit their existence. Assuming one of these is female and produces one million eggs, in the next year there would be 1,000,000 sea stars. If half of all sea stars are female and this pattern continues, how many generations will it take for the sea star population to exceed the 1991 human population of 5,423,000,000?

Give each real number.

5. the multiplicative inverse of 9

6. the additive inverse of -3.4

Give an example to illustrate the statement.

7. The set of negative numbers is not closed under multiplication.

8. The set of integers is not a field.

Simplify each number if possible, and identify it as rational, irrational, or complex.

9. $\sqrt{18}$ **10.** $(3 + i)(2 + 4i)$ **11.** $\sqrt{-64}$

12. Graph $9 + 12i$. Then give its complex conjugate and absolute value.

13. It takes a sky diver $t = 0.25\sqrt{d}$ seconds to free-fall d feet. Give the duration of an 800-ft free-fall in simplified radical form.

PERFORMANCE TASK

Growth characterizes many of the changes we see around us—the growth of plants, income, populations, and countless other quantities. Choose a type of growth that interests you. Explain how the concepts of this chapter can be used to analyze the type of growth you chose. Use equations, graphs, or any other concepts from the chapter to illustrate your point.

Chapter 5

Project A
Trajectory Tracking
What is the trajectory of an object launched from a catapult?

Project B
Which Falls Faster—
a Pickle or a Rock?
How does gravity affect falling objects?

Project C
Where Are We?
Find out how a navigation system works.

DAMIAN ROUSON

I had instructors who made math fun to learn. I loved it!

I am proud of a design I made for a lifting device that is now in use at the 3M Company. It was needed after a previous device failed and caused a fatal accident. Today I use math for computer simulations of how tiny particles interact with turbulent fluids, as in pollution control and rocket propulsion technologies.

Math helps you think critically and logically about the world around you. When newspapers cite polling data and meteorologists give forecasts, a good understanding of math helps you interpret the information.

Damian Rouson
Doctoral Candidate in
    Mechanical Engineering
Stanford University
Palo Alto, California

5-1
Quadratic Functions

In 5-1 you will learn about the characteristics of a quadratic function. You will use the following skills from previous chapters and courses.

Complete the table and graph the function. [Previous course]

1. $y = x^2 + 2x + 6$

x	−3	−2	−1	0	1
y					

2. $y = -x^2 + 3x + 6$

x	−1	0	1	2	3	4
y						

Replace the ? to make the trinomial a perfect square. [Previous course]

3. $x^2 + 4x + ?$ **4.** $x^2 - ? + 36$ **5.** $? + 8x + 16$ **6.** $4x^2 + 4x + ?$

5-2
Solving Quadratic Equations

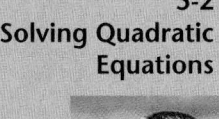

In 5-2 you will solve quadratic equations by graphing, factoring, and applying the quadratic formula. You will use the following skills from previous courses.

Factor out the common monomial factor. [Previous course]

7. $x^2 + 5x$ **8.** $75y^2 - 25$ **9.** $9w^2 + 18w$ **10.** $3ab + ab^2c$

Replace the ? to make a true sentence. [Previous course]

11. $x^2 + 5x + 6 = (x + ?)(x + ?)$ **12.** $x^2 - 2x - 8 = (x + ?)(x - ?)$

13. $3x^2 + 20x - 7 = (3x - ?)(x + ?)$ **14.** $2x^2 + 18x + 40 = 2(?)(?)$

5-3
Conic Sections

In 5-3 you will explore the circle, ellipse, and hyperbola. You will need the following skills from previous courses and chapters.

Simplify. [Previous course]

15. $\sqrt{(7 - 2)^2 + (4 - (-6))^2}$ **16.** $\sqrt{(-5 - 2)^2 + (9 - 0)^2}$

17. $\dfrac{16x^2}{144}$ **18.** $\dfrac{9y^2}{144}$

5-4
Quadratic Systems

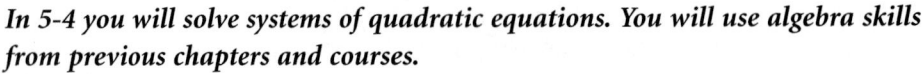

In 5-4 you will solve systems of quadratic equations. You will use algebra skills from previous chapters and courses.

Solve for y. [5-1]

19. $y^2 = 25$ **20.** $\dfrac{y^2}{4} = 9$ **21.** $y^2 + x = 49$ **22.** $y^2 - x^2 = 0$

OUT THERE
IS ANYBODY
OUT THERE?

IS ANYBODY
OUT THERE?

IS ANYBODY
OUT THERE?

When we think of astronomers, we may picture them peering into the eyepiece of a huge telescope, scanning the skies for new discoveries. However, only a small part of the information in the heavens can be seen through an optical telescope. Investigations of wavelengths outside the visible spectrum, such as infrared and X-ray, have provided some of the most important astronomical discoveries in recent history.

Radio telescopes use a curved "dish" made from metal or wire mesh to gather faint radio waves from distant sources. The *parabolic* shape of the dish gathers and focuses the weak signals efficiently.

The largest single-dish radio telescope in the world lies in the hills near Arecibo, Puerto Rico. The fixed telescope is 1000 feet in diameter.

Astronomers use the dish to collect signals from *pulsars*, rapidly spinning neutron stars that give off regular bursts of radio waves.

The Very Large Array Interferometer, or VLA, is located near Socorro, New Mexico. The VLA's computers combine the input from 27 radio telescope reflectors, each 82 feet in diameter, so that they act as one. The individual parabolic reflectors work as if they were one gigantic reflector.

The great power of these telescopes enables scientists to study celestial bodies billions of light-years away. Some scientists (and quite a few other curious individuals), however, have other hopes for the telescopes. They hope someday to pick up a faint signal from far away that they can interpret as, "Hello, is anybody out there?"

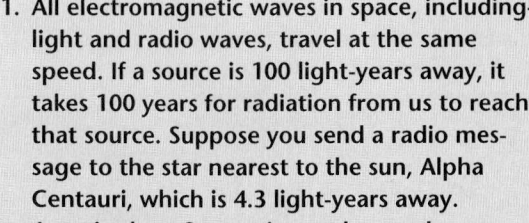

1. All electromagnetic waves in space, including light and radio waves, travel at the same speed. If a source is 100 light-years away, it takes 100 years for radiation from us to reach that source. Suppose you send a radio message to the star nearest to the sun, Alpha Centauri, which is 4.3 light-years away. Amazingly, a Centaurian understands your message and sends one back. How old will you be when you get the reply?

2. Why might we be interested in gathering information from sources billions of light-years away?

3. If one radio dish is twice the diameter of another, about how many times the signal-gathering capacity do you think the larger dish has? Explain your reasoning.

← CONNECT → *You have investigated linear functions. Now you will begin to explore another family of functions, quadratic functions, by examining their graphs and looking at a real-world quadratic model.*

A radio telescope takes signals that come in parallel to its line of symmetry and focuses them at a single point. The reflector of a narrow-beam flashlight directs the light from the bulb in one direction. The symmetrical U-shaped curve that gives the radio telescope and the reflector these abilities is called a **parabola.**

You have seen that the graphs of functions of the form $f(x) = ax + b$ are lines. Parabolas are the graphs of a family of functions known as quadratic functions. A quadratic function has a squared term.

> A **quadratic function** is a function of the form $f(x) = ax^2 + bx + c$, where a, b, and c are real-number constants and $a \neq 0$.

On a line, equal changes in the x-value give equal changes in the y-value. The rate of change of y with respect to x is constant.

On the graph of a quadratic function like $y = x^2$, the rate of change is not constant—it depends on the x-value.

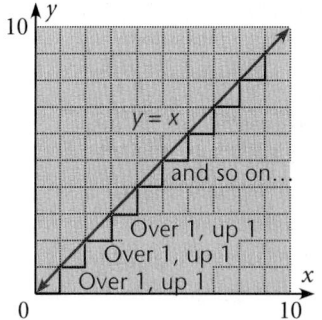

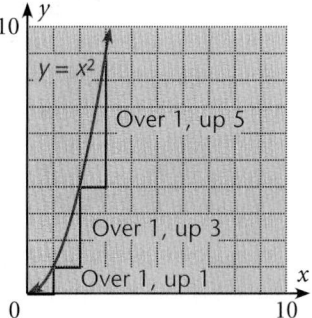

CONSIDER

1. A linear function can be described by its slope. Can a quadratic function be described by its slope? Explain why or why not.

The turning point of a parabola is its **vertex.** If a parabola opens upward, its *minimum y*-value is at its vertex; if it opens downward, its *maximum y*-value is at its vertex. For the most basic quadratic function $f(x) = x^2$, the vertex is $(0, 0)$.

A line of symmetry through the vertex divides the parabola into two mirror-image halves. For $f(x) = x^2$, the line of symmetry is $x = 0$, the *y*-axis. Every point on the parabola except its vertex has a reflection image with respect to the line of symmetry that is also on the parabola.

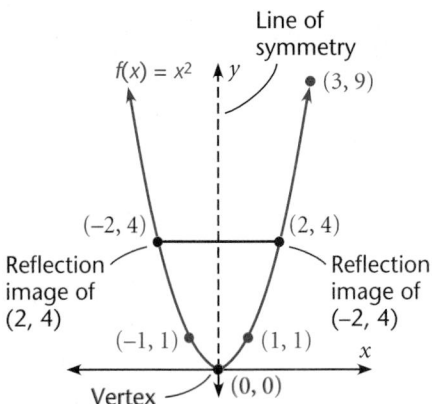

EXAMPLES

1. Graph the quadratic function $f(x) = 2x^2 - 8x + 3$.

Find the coordinates of the vertex, the line of symmetry, and the minimum or maximum value of the function.

You can plot points to sketch a graph or use a graphing calculator.

The vertex is the point $(2, -5)$.

The line of symmetry intersects the parabola at its vertex. Since it is a vertical line passing through $(2, -5)$, the line of symmetry is $x = 2$.

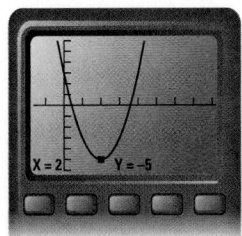

The upward-opening parabola has its minimum at the vertex, so the minimum value of $f(x)$ is -5, when $x = 2$.

2. The point $(4, 3)$ is on the graph of $f(x) = 2x^2 - 8x + 3$. Use symmetry to find the coordinates of another point on the parabola.

We are looking for the reflection image of $(4, 3)$ over the line of symmetry $x = 2$. You can see that the *y*-coordinate of the image point must also be 3, and that its *x*-coordinate is 2 units from $x = 2$, that is, at $x = 0$. The reflection image of $(4, 3)$ over $x = 2$ is $(0, 3)$, which is also on the parabola.

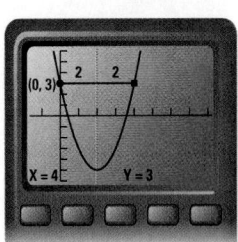

TRY IT

Graph the quadratic function $g(x) = x^2 + x - 2$.

a. Find the coordinates of the vertex.

b. Find the line of symmetry.

c. Find the minimum or maximum value of the function.

One of the more important roles of quadratic functions is modeling the path of a falling object.

Without gravity, if you threw a ball upward at 5 meters per second from 2 meters above the ground, the ball would keep moving upward at that velocity. After t seconds, it would be $5t + 2$ meters above the ground.

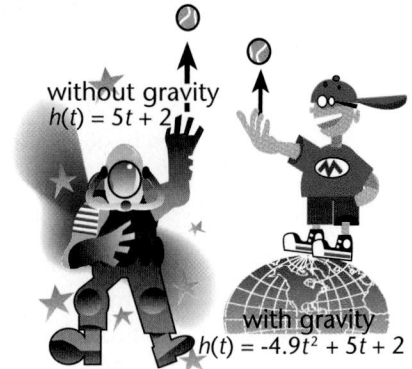
without gravity
$h(t) = 5t + 2$

with gravity
$h(t) = -4.9t^2 + 5t + 2$

But gravity pulls the ball downward, in the negative direction. The force of gravity is modeled by an additional term in the height equation, $-4.9t^2$.

We can write a quadratic function that models the height of an object influenced only by gravity near the earth's surface.

After t seconds, the height of an object with an initial upward velocity of v_0 meters per second and an initial height of h_0 meters is:

$$h(t) = -4.9t^2 + v_0 t + h_0 \text{ meters}$$

If h_0 is measured in feet and v_0 in feet per second, then the height is:

$$h(t) = -16t^2 + v_0 t + h_0 \text{ feet}$$

In each equation, the force of gravity is represented by a squared term in the negative direction. As the time increases, the t^2 term overpowers the t term, and the ball falls.

EXAMPLE

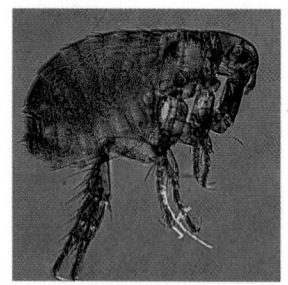

3. A flea jumps straight up from the ground with an initial upward velocity of 6 ft/sec. What will the height of the flea be after 0.2 sec?

The flea jumps from ground level, so $h_0 = 0$. Its initial upward velocity (v_0) is 6 ft/sec. So:

$h(t) = -16t^2 + 6t$ Use the equation for height in feet.
$h(0.2) = -16(0.2)^2 + 6(0.2)$ Substitute 0.2 for t.
$h(0.2) = 0.56 \text{ ft}$

After 0.2 seconds, the flea is 0.56 feet (about 6.75 inches) above the ground.

In Example 3, the height of the flea over time can be shown graphically. This graph is *not* the path of the flea, however, since the flea jumped straight up.

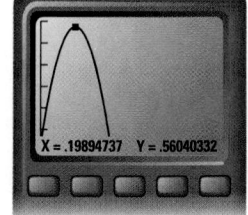
X = .19894737   Y = .56040332

Of course, not all jumps are straight up. If a platform diver did not jump horizontally as well as vertically, he would hit the board on his way down. In the Explore, you will see how to show the actual trajectory of a jump that has both an upward and an outward direction.

An Olympic diver in the 10-meter platform competition jumps with an initial vertical velocity of 3 m/sec and an initial horizontal velocity of 1.2 m/sec.

1. Write an equation for the height (h) of the diver as a function of time (t).

2. The gravity of the earth pulls us in one direction— down. So gravity has no effect on horizontal distance. To find an equation for the horizontal distance, you can use the familiar formula $d = rt$. Find an equation for the horizontal distance (p) in terms of t. (Hint: What is the horizontal velocity of the diver?)

   You now have two equations for the position of the diver, one for vertical distance and one for horizontal distance. Both h and p are expressed in terms of the same variable, t. When the position of a point in an x-y plane is described in terms of a third variable, the third variable is a **parameter.**

3. Put your graphing utility in parametric mode. Then enter your equation for the horizontal distance of the diver as the equation for x and your equation for the height (vertical distance) of the diver as the equation for y. Explain why these choices make sense.

4. Now, set the range for the graph. An appropriate range for this situation has t from 0 to 2 at steps of 0.05, x from 0 to 3, and y from 0 to 12. Graph the function. What is the shape of the graph?

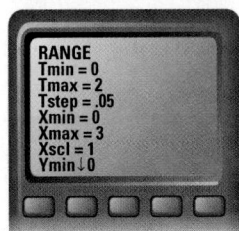

5. Graph the path of the diver. Investigate how TRACE works for a parametric graph. Then find the following.
   a. the maximum height of the diver and the time when he reached this height
   b. the height of the diver 1 sec after the jump and his horizontal distance from the board at this point
   c. the time when the diver hit the water and his horizontal distance from the board at that time
   d. how far the diver was from the board when he passed it on the way down

6. Investigate how changes in the initial horizontal and vertical velocities affect the diver's path. Briefly describe the effect of increasing each initial velocity.

The height of a falling object, in meters, is modeled by a quadratic function $h(t) = -4.9t^2 + v_0 t + h_0$. The horizontal distance from the starting point is a linear function of time, $d = v_h t$, where v_h is the initial horizontal velocity.

1. Why is the restriction $a \neq 0$ included in the definition of a quadratic function?

2. What feature of a parabola corresponds to a maximum or minimum point? How is this feature related to the line of symmetry of the parabola?

3. How can you tell from the coordinates that two points are reflections of each other over the line $x = a$?

Exercises

CORE

1. Getting Started Use the graph of $f(x) = x^2 - 2x - 1$ to find:

a. the coordinates of the vertex and the line of symmetry

b. the minimum value for $f(x)$ and the corresponding x-value

c. the reflection image with respect to the line of symmetry for the point $(0, -1)$ on the parabola

d. the reflection image with respect to the line of symmetry for the point $(3, 2)$ on the parabola

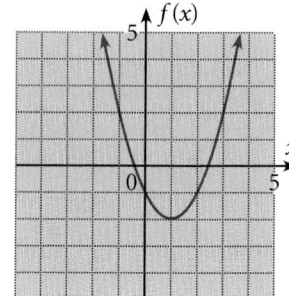

Plot points to graph each quadratic function. For each, find the coordinates of the vertex, the line of symmetry, and the maximum or minimum value of the function.

2. $y = -x^2 + 4x - 3$ **3.** $y = -2x^2 + 5x + 3$ **4.** $y = 4x^2 - 6$

Write the word or phrase that correctly completes each statement.

5. $y = mx + b$ is to *line* as $y = ax^2 + bx + c$ is to ____.

6. The maximum or minimum value of a quadratic function occurs at its ____.

Given each pair of reflection image points on a parabola, find the equation of the line of symmetry.

7. $(0, 2)$; $(4, 2)$ **8.** $(3, -2)$; $(-8, -2)$ **9.** $(-4.6, 5)$; $(0, 5)$ **10.** $(18.8, -6)$; $(-29.6, -6)$

Given the vertex (*V*) of a parabola and a second point (*P*) on the parabola, find the coordinates of a third point on the parabola.

11. $V(0, 0)$; $P(3, 4)$ **12.** $V(2, 3)$; $P(-1, 6)$ **13.** $V(-2, 4)$; $P(1.5, -8)$

14. Write an equation for a quadratic function that models the height of a ball t seconds after it was thrown downward at a speed of 10.8 m/sec from a height of 43.5 m off the ground. Then find the height of the ball after 2 seconds.

Identify each set of points as a linear function or quadratic function. Explain your reasoning. Write an equation for each set of points.

15.

x	1	2	3	4	5	6
y	1	4	9	16	25	36

16.

x	2	4	6	8	10	12
y	8	9	10	11	12	13

Give the coordinates of the vertex, the equation of the line of symmetry, and the image point of the labeled point for each parabola. What is the maximum or minimum value of the function that each represents?

17.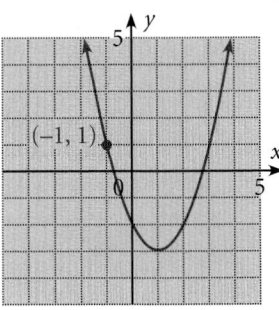

18.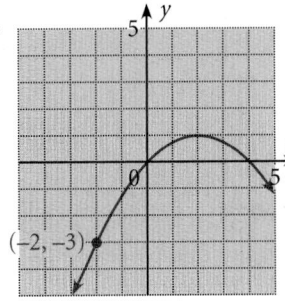

19. Graph the points $(-2, 9)$, $(1, 0)$, and $(-6, -7)$.
    a. If these three points lie on the graph of a quadratic function, and one of the three points is the vertex, find the line of symmetry.
    b. Use the symmetry of the parabola to find two other points on the parabola.
    c. Draw a smooth parabola through your five points. Do you think more than one parabola can be drawn through the points? Explain.

Determine whether each function is quadratic. If it is, write its equation in the form $y = ax^2 + bx + c$.

20. $f(x) = 3x(x + 1) - x$ 21. $y = -(x + 3) + x^2 + (x - 3)$

22. $D(x) = (x + 4)(x - 4)$

23. **Sew, Sew** A designer wants to use a 36-inch piece of heirloom lace around the edge of a pillow. What is the maximum area of a pillow that can made before sewing on the lace? What are its dimensions?

24. A tennis ball at an initial height of 1.5 meters is hit upward with an initial vertical velocity of 25 meters per second.
    a. Write the quadratic function $g(t)$ for the height (in meters) of the tennis ball after t seconds.
    b. Copy the table and find the height of the ball after 0, 1, 2, 5, and 6 seconds.

t	0	1	2	5	6
$g(t)$					

    c. Interpret your mathematical answer for $g(6)$. Does that answer make sense in the real world?
    d. The vertex of the parabola for this function is approximately $(2.6, 33.4)$. What is the maximum height reached by the ball?

25. Ayanna kicks a ball into the air. After 0.1 seconds, the ball is 10 feet above the ground. After 1.3 seconds, it reaches its maximum height of 33 feet. At what time will the ball be at a height of 10 feet on its descent?

LOOK BACK

Solve each inequality. Then graph its solution. [2-3]

26. $2.50(x - 0.4) < 3.75$ **27.** $\frac{3}{4} \le \frac{1}{2}t + \frac{1}{8} \le 1$ **28.** $3 > -2s + 1 \ge 2$

Find the sum of each series. [4-1 and 4-2]

29. $\displaystyle\sum_{n=1}^{4} (n + 2)$ **30.** $\displaystyle\sum_{n=1}^{4} 2^n$ **31.** $\displaystyle\sum_{n=1}^{6} (2n - 1)$ **32.** $\displaystyle\sum_{n=1}^{3} 3^n$

MORE PRACTICE

Determine whether each function is quadratic. If it is, write its equation in the form $y = ax^2 + bx + c$.

33. $f(x) = 4x^2 + 5x$ **34.** $16x^2 + 4y = \frac{3}{2}$

35. $y = 10x^4 - 5x^2$ **36.** $g(x) = (x - 1)(x + 2)$

Given each pair of reflection image points on a parabola, find the equation of the line of symmetry.

37. $(3, 2); (-1, 2)$ **38.** $(-3, 5); (25, 5)$ **39.** $(13.1, -7.1); (-29.2, -7.1)$

40. $(-0.1, 17); (0.1, 17)$ **41.** $(-7, -7); (6.2, -7)$ **42.** $(\pi, 3); (-2\pi, 3)$

Use a graphing calculator to find the coordinates of the vertex, the equation of the line of symmetry, and the maximum or minimum value of each function.

43. $y = x^2 + 6x$ **44.** $f(x) = -x^2 - 4x + 3$

45. $y = -5x^2 + 3.5x - 0.5$ **46.** $h(x) = -4.9x^2 + 10x + 3$

47. Use a Graphing Utility A bale of hay for cows trapped by a blizzard is dropped from an airplane so that the height in meters above ground level is given by the formula $h(t) = -4.9t^2 - 2t + 500$. The bale's horizontal velocity is 75 m/sec, so its horizontal distance from the drop point is given by $p(t) = 75t$.

a. Using parametric mode, enter both of these equations and graph the path of the hay bale. Find an appropriate window of t-, x-, and y-values for viewing the entire path. What is your viewing window?

b. Find the height and horizontal distance from the launch point when t is 0, 4, 6, and 8 seconds.

c. Find the time and horizontal distance when the hay bale is 100 feet above the ground.

d. At what time does the hay bale strike the ground? What is its horizontal distance from the launch point at that time?

Identify each set of points as a linear function or quadratic function. Explain your reasoning. Write an equation for each set of points.

48.

x	−2	−1	0	1	2	3
y	14	7	0	−7	−14	−21

49.

x	−1.5	−1	−0.5	0	0.5	1
y	10	5	2	1	2	5

Given the vertex (V) of a parabola and a second point (P) on the parabola, find the coordinates of a third point on the parabola.

50. $V(0, 2)$; $P(1, 4)$ **51.** $V(-3, -4)$; $P(5, 6)$ **52.** $V(3, -16)$; $P(9.2, -42)$

53. Foundation Calculation The foundation of a rectangular house is to be 10 ft longer than it is wide.
  a. Write an equation for the area of the foundation.
  b. Use a graphing utility to graph your equation.
  c. The area of the house being built on the foundation is to be 1575 square feet. What should the length and width of the foundation be? Explain.

MORE MATH REASONING

54. Which Falls Faster? Rumor has it that Galileo Galilei (1564–1642) simultaneously dropped a 10-kg cannonball and a 1-kg stone from the 55-meter Leaning Tower of Pisa to contradict the long-held notion from Aristotle that heavier objects fall faster than lighter ones. The objects hit the ground at virtually the same time.
  a. Write a function $h(t)$ for the height of the objects after falling for t seconds.
  b. What does the vertex correspond to in the real situation?
  c. Use a graphing utility to graph the height function. How long did the objects fall before they hit the ground?
  d. For what domain is $h(t)$ valid for the experiment? Explain.

55. Use a Graphing Utility You have used linear regression models to fit a line to data points. Some graphing utilities will find a quadratic model for a set of data points. Suppose a store manager has been varying the price of a software package to see how the price affects the net profit made on sales of the package. She has tabulated her results.

Price ($)	79	85	89	95	99	105	114
Profit (× $100)	−2.5	2.4	10.9	16.1	17.9	11.8	8.2

  a. Enter the data in your calculator and select quadratic regression. What is the equation of the quadratic function that best fits the data?
  b. Make a scatter plot of the data and overlay it with a graph of the regression equation. What is the vertex of the graph? What does it represent?
  c. On the scatter plot, the point representing a price of $105 shows a sharply lower profit than the point representing a price of $99. Give some possible explanations for this.
  d. On the regression curve, trace to find the prices (to the nearest dollar) that correspond to a zero profit. Explain the significance of these points.

Sketching Parabolas: $f(x) = ax^2$

← CONNECT → *You've identified characteristics of the graphs of quadratic functions. But to predict their behavior, you have to study their equations. To do this, you will first examine how the coefficient "a" affects the graph of $f(x) = ax^2$.*

You know that $h(t) = -4.9t^2 + v_0t + h_0$ meters gives the height of an object having initial velocity v_0. If you just need to know the *distance* an object falls from rest in t seconds, affected only by gravity, then $v_0 = 0$ and $h_0 = 0$. Distance is positive, so you're left with $d(t) = 4.9t^2$ meters.

The coefficient 4.9 was found experimentally and reflects the acceleration caused by Earth's gravity. On other planets, this value is different—the smaller the mass, the less the gravitational attraction. On Earth, you can model the effect of less gravity by rolling a ball down a ramp instead of free-falling.

EXPLORE: ROLLIN', ROLLIN', ROLLIN'...

MATERIALS

*Cardboard (at least 4 ft long)
Ruler, Ball, Stopwatch
Graphing utility or
graph paper*

1. Slightly fold the cardboard lengthwise to direct the ball. Prop up one end of the cardboard to make a ramp with a slight incline. Mark distances at regular intervals along the ramp.
2. Record at least four data points of the form (t, d), where t is the time it takes the ball to roll varying distances d down the ramp.
3. Average the ratio $\dfrac{d}{t^2}$ for all your data points. Then use this average, $a = \dfrac{d}{t^2}$, to write the quadratic function $d(t) = at^2$, which models the motion of the ball.
4. Repeat your experiment at two other inclinations to find two more models of the form $d(t) = at^2$. For each inclination, graph the data points and your model. Graph all three of your models together, along with the model for free fall.
5. Compare the shape, orientation, vertices, and lines of symmetry of the four graphs. Write down your results. How does the steepness of the ramp correspond to the values for a? How do the values for a correspond to the shape of the graphs?

If your ramp in the Explore just happened to be placed at the proper angle, you might have observed objects "falling" as they would on the moon. The falling distance formula, in meters, for the moon is $d(t) = 0.8t^2$.

1. A ball is dropped from a high cliff. After 2 seconds, how far will it have fallen on Earth? on the moon?

The coefficient for t^2 on Earth is 4.9; for the moon, the coefficient is 0.8.

On Earth

$d(t) = 4.9t^2$

$d(2) = 4.9(2)^2$

$d(2) = 19.6$ m

On the moon

$d(t) = 0.8t^2$

$d(2) = 0.8(2)^2$

$d(2) = 3.2$ m

The greater force of gravity on Earth makes a ball fall faster than it would on the moon.

When the distance functions for Earth and the moon are graphed on the x-y plane, some patterns become evident.

- The graphs open upward.
- The graphs share the line of symmetry $x = 0$.
- The graphs share the vertex $(0, 0)$ and have a *minimum* y-value of 0.
- The greater the coefficient, the narrower the corresponding parabola.

The graph for Earth (coefficient 4.9) is narrower than the graph for the moon (coefficient 0.8).

You can think of changing the width of these graphs as stretching the graph of $f(x) = x^2$, the **parent function** for quadratic functions. On the graph of the parent function, $y = 1$ when $x = 1$. On the graph for Earth, the y-value for $x = 1$ is stretched to 4.9, and the graph appears narrower. For the moon, the y-value for $x = 1$ is pulled down to 0.8, and the graph appears wider.

CONSIDER

?

1. A function $f(x) = ax^2$ always opens upward and always has a minimum value of 0 when a is positive. Explain why this is true.

Compare the graph of $y = x^2$ to the graphs of $y = -x^2$, $y = -3x^2$, and $y = -\frac{1}{3}x^2$. Notice the following characteristics of graphs of quadratic functions with negative a values.

- The graphs open downward.
- The graphs share the line of symmetry $x = 0$.
- The graphs share the vertex $(0, 0)$.
- The graphs all have a maximum y-value of 0.
- The graphs have the same shapes as those for positive values of a, but now they open downward.

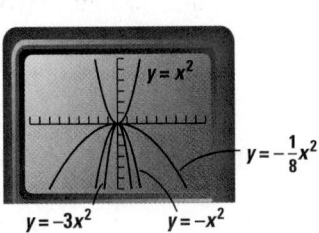

Notice that the graph of $y = -x^2$ is a reflection of the graph of $y = x^2$ over the x-axis. This is true for all coefficients a in $y = ax^2$ and $y = -ax^2$.

EXAMPLES

2. Write the equation of the quadratic function that has the graph shown.

The graph opens downward from its vertex at $(0, 0)$, so the quadratic function must have the form $y = ax^2$ with $a < 0$.

Since $-3 = a(-1)^2$, $a = -3$. The quadratic function is $y = -3x^2$.

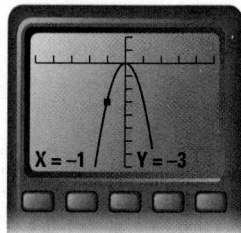

3. Write the equation of the reflection of the graph of $y = -3x^2$ over the x-axis.

Reflecting the graph of $y = ax^2$ over the x-axis gives $y = -ax^2$. So the reflection of $y = -3x^2$ over the x-axis is $y = 3x^2$.

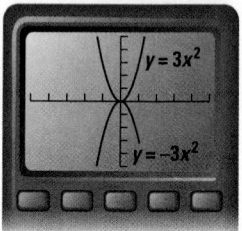

4. Write an equation that contains $(-2, 8)$ in the form $y = ax^2$.

$y = ax^2$
$8 = a(-2)^2$ Substitute $x = -2$, $y = 8$.
$8 = a(4)$
$2 = a$

The equation is $y = 2x^2$.

TRY IT

a. Write the equation of the parabola that has its vertex at the origin and contains the point $(2, 10)$.
b. Write the equation of the reflection over the x-axis of this parabola. Give the image point on the reflection of the point $(2, 10)$.
c. Sketch graphs of $y = 2x^2$ and $y = -\frac{1}{3}x^2$ on the same set of axes.

To visualize the graph of $f(x) = ax^2$, you only need to understand how the coefficient a modifies the graph of $f(x) = x^2$. Different values of a stretch the graph, and different signs reflect the graph over the x-axis, but they cannot move the vertex from the origin.

REFLECT

1. For what values of a is the graph of $f(x) = ax^2$ narrower than the graph of $f(x) = x^2$, and for what values of a is it wider?
2. Identify features of the graph of $f(x) = ax^2$ that are unaffected by the value of a. Explain why changes in the a coefficient do not affect these features.
3. Using symmetry, explain why, if $f(x) = ax^2$ has a minimum of 0, then $g(x) = -ax^2$ has a maximum of 0.

Exercises

CORE

1. **Getting Started** Consider the functions $f(x) = x^2$, $g(x) = -3x^2$, $h(x) = -5x^2$, and $j(x) = 12x^2$.
   a. List the functions whose graphs open upward and those whose graphs open downward.
   b. List the functions from widest to narrowest as their graphs would appear on a coordinate plane.
   c. List the functions that reach a maximum at their vertex and those that reach a minimum at their vertex. What do these points have in common?

2. Match the letter corresponding to each function with the number corresponding to its graph.
   a. $y = -2.3x^2$ b. $y = 2.3x^2$
   c. $y = -0.9x^2$ d. $y = -0.2x^2$

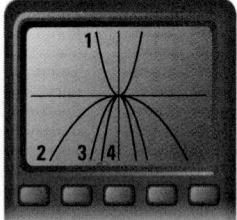

3. On the same axes, graph each quadratic function: $y = 0.5x^2$, $y = 2x^2$, $y = -3x^2$ for the values $x = -4, -2, 0, 2,$ and 4.
   a. What point do all three graphs have in common?
   b. Name the line of symmetry for each graph.
   c. Write a short paragraph that compares the widths and orientation of the graphs.

4. a. Sketch the parabola $y = -2.5x^2$ and its reflection across the x-axis.
   b. Write the equation of its reflection.
   c. What is the vertex of each parabola?
   d. What is the equation of the line of symmetry between the parabola and its reflection?
   e. If the point $(4, -40)$ lies on $y = -2.5x^2$, name a point that lies on its reflection.

Graph each set of functions on the same set of axes.

5. $f(x) = x^2$ and $g(x) = -x^2$

6. $f(x) = \frac{1}{2}x^2$, $g(x) = -\frac{1}{2}x^2$, and $h(x) = 2x^2$

7. $f(x) = 4x^2$ and $g(x) = -4x^2$

8. $f(x) = 0.1x^2$, $g(x) = -0.1x^2$, and $h(x) = -0.2x^2$

Tell whether each statement is true or false for the graphs of quadratic functions of the form $f(x) = ax^2$. If the statement is false, rewrite it so that it is true.

9. The point $(0, 0)$ is the vertex of the graph.

10. The line $x = 0$ is the line of symmetry of the graph.

11. If $|a| > 1$, the graph is wider than the graph of $g(x) = x^2$.

12. The parabola opens upward if $a < 0$.

13. The height of wind-blown waves is a function of wind speed. For wave height H in feet and wind speed v in knots, the approximate wave height is $H = 0.025v^2$. If the wind speed triples, from 6 knots to 18 knots, by how many times will the wave height increase? What will the new height be?

14. Support Your Local Bridge Engineers often use parabolic bridge supports to distribute the weight of the road over the bridge. Suppose the support for a bridge is approximately at a height of $h(x) = -0.016x^2$ meters, where the point $(0, 0)$ is counted as the center of the span of the road. If the support extends 45 meters to the right and left of the center of the bridge, how far above or below the bridge are the ends of the support? Explain how you solved this problem.

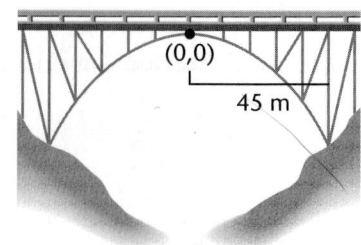

15. What are the possible values for a if you want the graph of $y = ax^2$
   a. to be wider than the graph of $y = 6x^2$?
   b. to be narrower than the graph of $y = -4x^2$?
   c. to be wider than the graph of $y = 2x^2$, narrower than the graph of $y = 0.8x^2$, and to have a maximum at its vertex?

Write an equation in the form $y = ax^2$ that contains each point.

16. $(1, 1)$ **17.** $(1, -4)$ **18.** $(2, -4)$ **19.** $(-3, -45)$

20. Copy and complete the table. Describe how the values $3x^2$ and $0.5x^2$ relate to the value of x^2 for a given value of x. Explain how the coefficient a in $y = ax^2$ makes the graph of $y = x^2$ appear wider or narrower.

x	$y = x^2$	$y = 3x^2$	$y = 0.5x^2$
-2	4	12	___
-1	___	___	___
2	___	___	___
5	___	___	___

Write the equation of each graph. Then write the equation of its reflection with respect to the x-axis.

21.
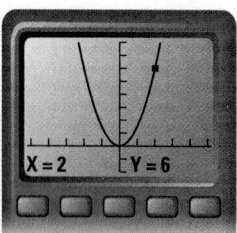
X = 2   Y = 6

22.
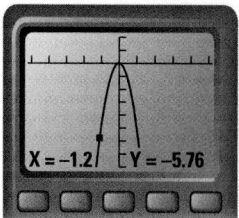
X = -1.2   Y = -5.76

23.
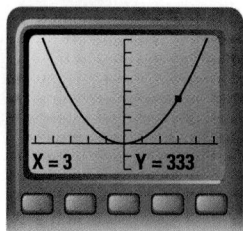
X = 3   Y = 333

24. Full Swing Ahead The *period* of a pendulum (the time it takes to complete a full swinging cycle—from one side to the other and back again) depends on its length (ℓ). If ℓ is in meters and the period (p) is in seconds, $\ell = 9.8\left(\dfrac{p}{2\pi}\right)^2$.
   a. Write the equation in the form $\ell(p) = ap^2$, with a rounded to the nearest hundredth.
   b. Without graphing, compare the graph of $\ell(p)$ to the graph of $f(x) = x^2$.
   c. What pendulum lengths correspond to periods of 1, 2, 4, and 8 seconds?
   d. If you want the pendulum to swing from side to side (one-half of a period) in one second, how long should the pendulum be?

25. Plant specialists in the U.S. Forest Service have kept records that show how the growth (g) of redwood trees in their first year depends on rainfall (r).

r (in.)	0	3	5	12	17	22	34	35	50
g (in.)	1	4	6	9.5	10.8	10.9	6	5.3	1

a. Does this data suggest a quadratic or linear model? Explain. If it suggests a linear model, what is the approximate slope of the line? If it suggests a quadratic model, what is the vertex of the parabola?

b. Given what you know about trees and other plants, does this model make sense? Why or why not?

c. Graph the data. Can you write an equation that models it? If so, give the equation and explain how you found it; if not, explain why not.

LOOK AHEAD

26. Sketch the graphs of $y = x$, $y = x + 3$, and $y = x - 2$ on the same set of axes. Describe the differences between the graphs.

Expand each squared binomial.

27. $(x + 2)^2$

28. $(x - 6)^2$

29. $(2x - 1)^2$

30. $\left(4 - \frac{1}{2}x\right)^2$

Factor each expression.

31. $x^2 + 6x + 9$

32. $x^2 - 14x + 49$

33. $x^2 + 5x + 6.25$

MORE PRACTICE

34. Match the letter corresponding to each function with the number corresponding to its graph.

a. $y = -2x^2$

b. $y = 1.6x^2$

c. $y = -2\pi x^2$

d. $y = \sqrt{6}x^2$

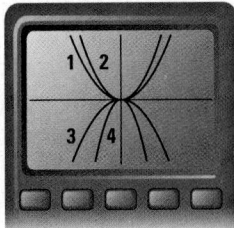

Graph each set of functions on the same set of axes.

35. $f(x) = 3x^2$ and $g(x) = -3x^2$

36. $f(x) = 5x^2$ and $g(x) = -5x^2$

37. $f(x) = \frac{1}{4}x^2$, $g(x) = -\frac{1}{4}x^2$, and $h(x) = 3x^2$

38. $f(x) = 9x^2$, $g(x) = -9x^2$, and $h(x) = 6x^2$

Write the equation of each graph. Then write the equation of its reflection with respect to the x-axis.

39.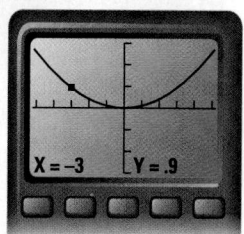

X = -3   Y = .9

40.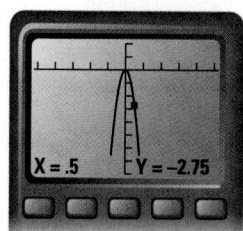

X = .5   Y = -2.75

41.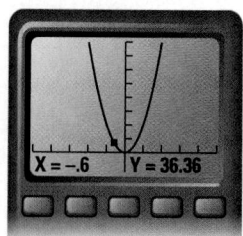

X = -.6   Y = 36.36

42. Use a Graphing Utility The falling-distance formula for the moon, in meters, is $d(t) = 0.8t^2$, and the corresponding formula for Earth is $d(t) = 4.9t^2$.

a. Sketch a graph of these functions on the same set of axes.

b. How far will a ball that is dropped from a cliff fall in 5 seconds on the moon? on Earth?

c. How much longer will it take a ball to fall 40 meters on the moon than it will on Earth?

d. Suppose a feather is dropped from a height of 100 meters on Earth and on the moon. Will the feather take longer to fall on Earth or on the moon? Explain.

MORE MATH REASONING

43. Great Reception Suppose that a radio telescope whose cross sections are parabolas has a diameter of 250 feet and a depth of 100 feet. Using the center of the dish as (0, 0), write an equation that models the cross section of the dish.

44. Show that the triangle formed by the vertex and any two reflection image points on the graph of $y = x^2$ is isosceles.

45. A Speedy Question If you take one hour to make a 50-mile trip, your *average speed* for the trip is 50 mi/hr. However, your speed on the speedometer at any instant (*instantaneous speed*) may be far different than 50 mi/hr. You will now investigate the instantaneous speed of a falling object.

a. Using the function $d(t) = 16t^2$ for the number of feet a dropped object falls in t seconds, find the distance the object drops between $t = 2.0$ and $t = 2.5$.

b. Find the average speed during the interval from $t = 2.0$ to $t = 2.5$.

c. Find the average speed during the interval from $t = 2.0$ to $t = 2.1$.

d. Find the average speed during the intervals from $t = 2.0$ to $t = 2.01$, from $t = 2.0$ to $t = 2.001$, and from $t = 2.0$ to $t = 2.0001$.

e. What do you think the instantaneous speed of the object is at $t = 2$ seconds? Explain your reasoning.

> **Problem-Solving Tip**
>
> Look for a pattern.

← **CONNECT** → *You've studied parabolas that are reflections and stretches of the graph of $f(x) = x^2$. Now you will learn how to use translations to identify and sketch graphs of more complicated quadratic functions.*

When using a quadratic function to model a real-world situation, its maximum or minimum point often provides important information. The quadratic function $y = x^2$ has its vertex at $(0, 0)$. Since it opens upward, its vertex also represents its minimum.

Other quadratic functions are more complicated, but if you know how they are related to the parent quadratic function $f(x) = x^2$, you can quickly find maximum or minimum values.

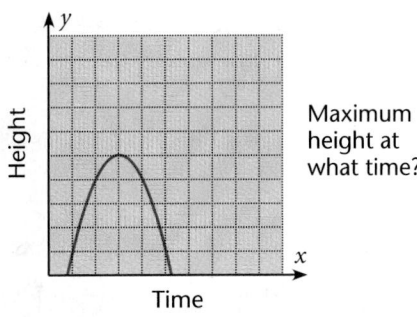

Maximum height at what time?

Time

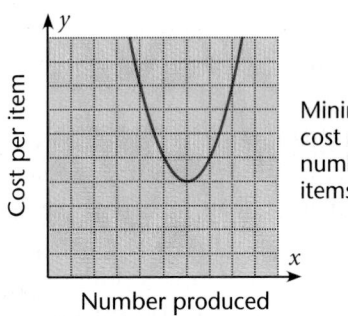

Minimum cost at what number of items made?

Number produced

Any quadratic function can be written in the form $f(x) = a(x - h)^2 + k$, where $a \neq 0$. How can we identify the maximum or minimum value of a quadratic function in this form? We begin by investigating the case where h is 0 and $f(x) = ax^2 + k$.

Compare the graph of $f(x) = \frac{1}{2}x^2$ with those of $f(x) = \frac{1}{2}x^2 + 4$ and $f(x) = \frac{1}{2}x^2 - 4$. Adding a constant (k) *translates* (slides) the graph of $f(x) = \frac{1}{2}x^2$ upward or downward. However, k doesn't change the shape, orientation, or line of symmetry of the graph.

For $k = 4$ (as an example of $k > 0$), the graph is translated *upward* 4 units. For $k = -4$ ($k < 0$), the graph is translated *downward* 4 units.

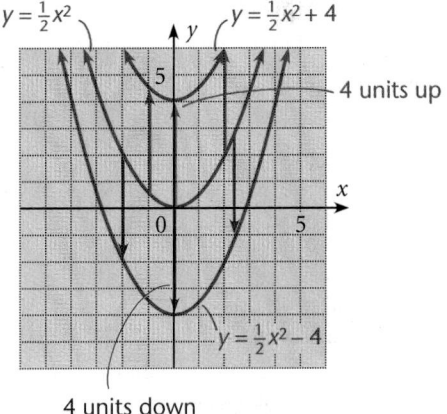

4 units up

4 units down

1. What are the coordinates of the vertex of $f(x) = ax^2 + k$? Justify your answer. Is the y-value of the vertex the minimum or maximum value for the function?

For each set of quadratic equations, sketch the graphs on the same set of axes. Then give the coordinates of the vertex and any two points on each parabola that are reflections of each other.

a. $y = x^2$, $y = x^2 + 4$, and $y = x^2 - 5$
b. $y = -2x^2$, $y = -2x^2 + 3$, and $y = -2x^2 - 2$

In the following Explore, you will investigate graphs of quadratic equations in the form $f(x) = a(x - h)^2 + k$.

EXPLORE: THE LATEST TRANSLATION

MATERIALS

Graphing utility
Graph paper

1. Use your graphing utility to graph $y = x^2$. Then graph $y = (x + 3)^2$, $y = (x - 2)^2$, and $y = (x + 5)^2$. Make a conjecture about the effect of subtracting a constant (h) from x *before* squaring.

2. Graph equations $y = -2x^2$, $y = -2(x - 2)^2 - 3$, and $y = -2(x + 4)^2 + 1$. Record the values of h and k for each function, and give the coordinates of the vertex and equation of the line of symmetry for each graph. Do the graphs have the same shape and orientation? How are their vertices related to the h and k values?

3. Compare graphs of other quadratic functions with the same a values, but different h and k values, until you are confident that you see a pattern. Then give a brief written summary of the effect of each of the following on the graph of the equation $f(x) = a(x - h)^2 + k$.

a. the size of the a value   **b.** the sign of the a value
c. the h value   **d.** the k value

4. Write equations for three quadratic functions with different a, h, and k values. Sketch the graph of each function on graph paper. Then confirm your sketches by graphing the functions with a graphing utility or by plotting points.

5. Suppose you model a real-world situation with a quadratic function in the form $f(x) = a(x - h)^2 + k$. Explain how you can quickly find the maximum or minimum value of the function and how you can tell whether it is a maximum or minimum.

The graph of any quadratic function $f(x) = a(x - h)^2 + k$ can be sketched quickly by analyzing the effects of the a, h, and k values. The y-coordinate of the vertex gives the maximum or minimum value of the function.

Find the coordinates of the vertex of each quadratic function, and state whether the vertex represents a maximum or a minimum. Then give the equation of the function's line of symmetry.

c. $y = x^2 + 6$ **d.** $y = 2(x - 3)^2 - 12$ **e.** $y = -\frac{1}{32}(x + \pi)^2 + 1066$

EXAMPLE

1. A ticket sales manager for the Algebra on Ice Show believes that revenue (R) will be a function of ticket prices (P) according to:

$$R = -500(P - 8.5)^2 + 36{,}125$$

Which ticket prices result in maximum revenue? Which ticket prices give the minimum revenue? (Assume revenue cannot be negative.)

Because a is negative, the function has a maximum value at the vertex; $h = 8.5$ and k is 36,125, so the vertex is (8.5, 36,125). A ticket price of $8.50 gives Algebra on Ice its maximum revenue of $36,125.

Graphing, you can *trace* to see that a ticket price of $0 results in a revenue of $0, the minimum possible.

Since $P = 8.5$ is the line of symmetry, the reflection image of (0, 0) is (17, 0). So, a ticket price of $17 also results in $0 revenue.

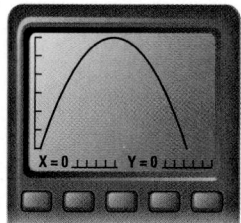

WHAT DO **YOU** THINK?

Drew and Rita were asked to sketch the graph of $g(x) = -(x - 4)^2 + 2$.

Drew thinks...

I'll begin by sketching a graph of $y = x^2$. For $g(x) = -(x - 4)^2 + 2$, $a = -1$. So I'll first sketch the reflection of the graph of x^2 over the x-axis.

Now, $h = 4$ and $k = 2$, so I'll translate my reflected graph 4 units to the right and 2 units upward and sketch $g(x)$.

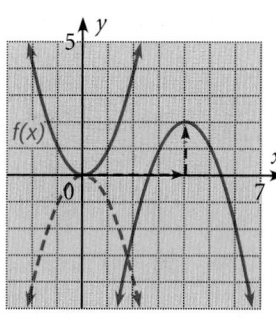

Rita thinks...

I'll begin by sketching a graph of the parent function $y = x^2$. For $g(x) = -(x - 4)^2 + 2$, $h = 4$ and $k = 2$, so I'll translate the graph 4 units to the right and 2 units upward.

$a = -1$ for $g(x)$, so $g(x)$ opens downward. I'll reflect my translated graph to point downward and sketch $g(x)$.

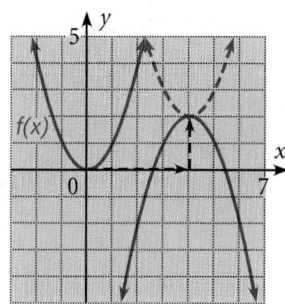

CONSIDER

2. Why did Rita reflect her sketch over the line $y = 2$ ($y = k$) instead of over the x-axis?

Quadratic functions are important mathematical models in many real-world contexts. The y-value of the vertex of a parabola gives the maximum or minimum value of the function. So it is helpful to have a quadratic function in a form where its vertex can be identified immediately.

You've seen that the values of h and k in $f(x) = y = a(x - h)^2 + k$ represent translations of the graph of the parent function. By knowing the effects of a, h, and k, you can quickly identify the maximum or minimum value of a quadratic function and sketch its graph.

When quadratic functions in the form $f(x) = a(x - h)^2 + k$ are graphed, the vertex is (h, k), and the line of symmetry is $x = h$.

If $a > 0$, the parabola opens upward, the vertex is the lowest point on the graph, and k is the minimum value of the function.

If $a < 0$, the parabola opens downward, the vertex is the highest point on the graph, and k is the maximum value of the function.

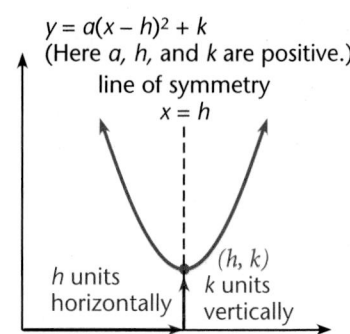

$y = a(x - h)^2 + k$
(Here a, h, and k are positive.)
line of symmetry
$x = h$

(h, k)
h units
horizontally
k units
vertically

REFLECT

1. Give a function whose graph would be positioned like a translation and reflection of the graph of $f(x) = x^2$ but would be narrower than the parent graph.
2. Describe all of the transformations you would use to change the graph of $y = x^2$ into the graph of $y = -(x - 3)^2 - 1$.
3. Explain why $f(x) = a(x - h)^2 + k$, where $a > 0$, has a minimum value at k. (Hint: What is the smallest possible value of $(x - h)^2$?)
4. Explain how you can find the line of symmetry for $f(x) = a(x - h)^2 + k$.

Exercises

CORE

1. **Getting Started** For $f(x) = a(x - h)^2 + k$, which constant, a, h, or k:
   a. affects the shape of the graph?   **b.** translates the graph vertically?
   c. translates the graph horizontally?
   d. determines whether the function has a maximum or a minimum value?
   e. represents the maximum or minimum value of the function?
   f. determines the line of symmetry?

2. Match each function to its graph at the right.

a. $f(x) = 1.5(x - 5.4)^2 + 1.7$
b. $f(x) = -1.7 + 1.5(x + 5.4)^2$
c. $f(x) = -(-1.5(x - 5.4)^2 + 1.7)$
d. $f(x) = (x + 5.4)^2(1.5) + 1.7$

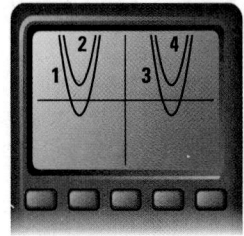

Graph each set of functions on the same set of axes.

3. $f(x) = x^2$ and $h(x) = (x + 1)^2 - 4$

4. $f(x) = x^2 + 4$, $g(x) = (x - 2)^2$, and $h(x) = (x - 2)^2 + 1$

5. $f(x) = -2x^2$, $g(x) = -2x^2 + 4$, and $h(x) = -2(x + 3)^2 + 4$

6. $f(x) = \frac{1}{2}(x - 3)^2$, $g(x) = -\frac{1}{2}(x - 3)^2$, and $h(x) = \frac{1}{2}(x - 3)^2 + 2$

For each quadratic function, find the vertex of its graph and state whether the y-coordinate of the vertex is the maximum or minimum value for that function.

7. $f(x) = 3(x - 5)^2 + 7$ **8.** $g(x) = -(x + 7)^2 + 2$

9. $h(t) = -\frac{1}{2}(t - 3)^2 - 3$ **10.** $k(t) = \frac{9}{2}t^2 - 2$

11. It's a Toss-Up A carpenter is tossing a bag of washers up to his partner who is on a scaffold above him. The height of the bag (in feet) is given by $h(t) = -16(t - 1.2)^2 + 24$. His partner catches the bag just as it reaches its highest point.

a. How long does the bag take to reach the carpenter, and at what height above the ground does he catch it? Explain how you found these values.

b. If the bag was not caught, how long would it take to reach the ground?

Write a quadratic function of the form $f(x) = a(x - h)^2 + k$ for each parabola.

12. vertex $(1, 3)$, $a = 5$ **13.** vertex $(-5, 0)$, $a = -3$

14. vertex $(0, 0)$, $a = 1$ **15.** vertex (p, q), $a = r$

Write a sequence of transformations that will produce the graph of each function from the graph of $y = x^2$.

16. $y = -x^2 + 2$ **17.** $y = -(x - 7)^2 - 3$ **18.** $y = (x - 2.1)^2$

19. The point (m, n) lies on the graph of $f(x) = x^2$. If $f(x)$ is transformed by reflection, vertically "stretched," and translated to become $g(x) = -4\left(x - \frac{1}{2}\right)^2 - 3$, what point on $g(x)$ corresponds to (m, n)?

20. When he projects profits from previous years, the financial manager of an observatory star show concludes that the profit (P) from the show should be related to the ticket price in dollars (T) by the function $P = -500(T - 7.5)^2 + 56,000$. What should the ticket price be to make the maximum profit?

21. A Quick Aside All of the parabolas you have looked at so far are generated by equations with squared terms in x. Now you will investigate equations with a squared y-term.

   a. By plotting points, sketch a graph of the equation $y^2 = x$. (Hint: It may be easier to substitute for y than for x.)

   b. Describe your graph. How does it compare to the graph of $y = x^2$? Can it be seen as a transformation of the graph of $y = x^2$? If so, how?

   c. Graph $x = 2y^2 - 4$ and $x = -(y - 2)^2 + 4$. Describe your results.

   d. Give as much information as you can about the graph of $x = a(y - k)^2 + h$. Include information about its vertex, line of symmetry, width, and direction.

   e. Is $x = a(y - k)^2 + h$ ($a \neq 0$) a function? Explain why or why not.

22. Parabolic Tourist Site The Gateway Arch of the Jefferson National Expansion Memorial in St. Louis, Missouri, has a shape approximated by a parabola with equation $f(x) = -\frac{2}{315}(x - 315)^2 + 630$, where x and $f(x)$ are in feet. If the x-axis is at ground level, what is the height of the arch? How wide is it? Explain your reasoning.

Graph each inequality.

23. $y \geq 2(x - 3)^2 - 2$ **24.** $y \leq (x + 1)^2 - 4$

25. $y > x^2$

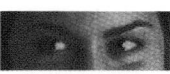 **LOOK BACK**

Find the equation of each line, given a point on the line and the slope, or given two points on the line. [2-1]

26. $(1, 3)$, $m = -2$ **27.** $(-5, -3.5)$, $m = 0.5$ **28.** $(4, 7)$, $(-3, 2)$

29. Graph the region defined by the inequalities $x \geq 0$, $y \leq 5$, $1.6x + 6y \leq 24$, $3y \geq x$, and $3y \leq x + 6$. Label the coordinates of the vertices. [3-2]

Give the formula for the nth term in each sequence. [4-1]

30. 3, 9, 15, 21, 27, ...   **31.** 15, 10, 5, 0, -5, ...   **32.** $\frac{1}{2}$, 2, $3\frac{1}{2}$, 5, $6\frac{1}{2}$, ...

MORE PRACTICE

Graph each set of functions on the same set of axes.

33. $f(x) = x^2$ and $h(x) = (x - 1)^2$ **34.** $f(x) = x^2 + 3$ and $g(x) = (x - 1)^2 + 3$

35. $f(x) = 3x^2$, $g(x) = 3x^2 + 1$, and $h(x) = 3(x + 2)^2 + 1$

36. $f(x) = \left(x - \frac{1}{2}\right)^2$, $g(x) = -\frac{1}{3}\left(x - \frac{1}{2}\right)^2$, and $h(x) = -\frac{1}{3}\left(x - \frac{1}{2}\right)^2 + 4$

For each quadratic function, find the vertex of its graph and state whether the y-coordinate of the vertex is the maximum or minimum value for that function.

37. $f(x) = -7(x - 11)^2$ **38.** $f(x) = 1.5(x + 4)^2 + 9$ **39.** $f(x) = -2(x + 4)^2 + 3$

Write a quadratic function of the form $f(x) = a(x - h)^2 + k$ for each parabola.

40. vertex $(2, -3)$, $a = 2$ **41.** vertex $(0, 0)$, $a = -3$ **42.** vertex $(3.2, -1.1)$, $a = 3.7$

43. vertex $(m, 2m)$, $a = 1$ **44.** vertex $(0, -4)$, $a = -2$ **45.** vertex $(1.87, 56.2)$, $a = -16$

Write a sequence of transformations that will produce the graph of each function from the graph of $y = x^2$.

46. $y = -(x - 2)^2$ **47.** $y = (x - 5)^2 + 3$ **48.** $y = -2.5(x + 11)^2 - 4$ **49.** $y = -(x - 2)^2 + 4$

50. Use a Graphing Utility A factory manager finds that the average cost per unit of producing an automobile part on an assembly line depends on the amount produced over the year (n). The equation that models the cost (c) is $c = \dfrac{1}{100{,}000}(n - 5000)^2 + 5$.

    a. What production level gives the minimum cost per item? What is that minimum cost?

    b. Find the annual cost per part for the following production levels.

      i. 1 part   **ii.** 2,000 parts   **iii.** 6,000 parts   **iv.** 10,000 parts

    c. In the real world, why might costs be high for low levels of production? for high levels of production?

MORE MATH REASONING

Use a graphing utility to help you write each quadratic function in the form $f(x) = a(x - h)^2 + k$. (Hint: Find the vertex.)

51. $f(x) = x^2 + x - 6$ **52.** $f(x) = 2x^2 + 10x + 8$

53. $f(x) = -x^2 + x + 3$ **54.** $f(x) = -4x^2 - 8x + 21$

55. Foul Up Sometimes a basketball player intentionally fouls an opponent who is taking an easy shot. The fouler is gambling that the opponent will miss one or both one-point free throws, instead of making two sure points. A player with a probability r of making each free throw has a probability $1 - r^2$ of missing at least one foul shot.

    a. What is the probability that a 90% ($r = 0.9$) shooter will miss at least one of two free throws? that a 60% shooter will miss at least one?

    b. The probability that a player will miss *both* free throws is $(1 - r)^2$. Find the probabilities that the 90% and 60% shooter will miss both shots.

    c. Write the probabilities $1 - r^2$ and $(1 - r)^2$ in the form $p(r) = a(r - h)^2 + k$. Give the vertex of the graph of each function, tell whether it represents a minimum or a maximum, and describe what it represents.

    d. Use a graphing utility to graph each probability function. *Trace* to find the highest value of r for which it is at least as likely that the shooter will miss at least one shot as make both shots. Then find the lowest value of r for which the probability that the shooter will miss both shots is no more than 10%.

← CONNECT →   *You've discovered that it's easy to graph and find the maximum or minimum value of a quadratic function when it is written in the form $f(x) = a(x - h)^2 + k$. Now you'll discover how you can write any general quadratic function $f(x) = ax^2 + bx + c$ in this form.*

Mohammed ibn Musa al-Khowarizmi, an Islamic professor at the Arab University in Baghdad, was a well-known ninth-century mathematician. His use of the Hindu-Arabic numerals that we take for granted (1, 2, 3, …) helped to spur the change from the system of Roman numerals. Al-Khowarizmi wrote his book *Al-jabr w'al muqabalah* to help settle legal disputes and to measure land, using geometric models to solve quadratic equations. The title of Al-Khowarizmi's book may remind you of the name of the subject matter you're studying right now!

His geometric models resemble the use of algebra tiles to **complete the square,** the process by which you can write any general quadratic function $f(x) = ax^2 + bx + c$ in the form $f(x) = a(x - h)^2 + k$, where the vertex of its graph can be immediately identified.

EXPLORE: SMILE WHILE YOU TILE

MATERIALS

Algebra tiles

With an x^2-tile, 8 x-tiles, and some unit tiles, how can you create a square?

1. Begin by dividing your x-tiles evenly. Arrange them on two consecutive sides of the x^2-tile as shown.

2. Complete the square by adding unit tiles. How many did you need to add to $x^2 + 8x$ to complete the square?

3. Write an expression for the length of an edge of this square. Use this side length to write an expression for the area of the square. Do not expand your expression.

4. Write an equation setting your area result from Step 3 equal to the sum of the areas of the algebra tiles, $x^2 + 8x +$ ____.

5. Repeat Steps 1–4 at least twice. Each time, use one x^2-tile, and choose a different *even* number of x-tiles.

6. Look for a pattern in your results. If you start with one x^2-tile and a certain number of x-tiles, how can you tell, without actually arranging the tiles, how many unit tiles it will take to complete the square?

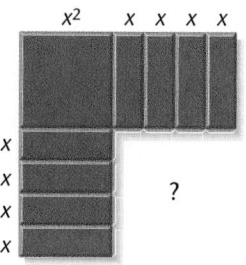

When completing the square in the Explore, you had to choose an even number of x-tiles, but only because it's hard to cut an algebra tile in half! Your pattern will work for any quadratic function $f(x) = ax^2 + bx + c$, no matter what the value of b is.

In previous courses, you factored *trinomial squares*, like $x^2 + 16x + 64$ and $x^2 - 14x + 49$.

$$x^2 + 16x + 64 = (x + 8)^2 \qquad\qquad x^2 - 14x + 49 = (x - 7)^2$$

To identify these trinomials, you checked whether the constant term was a perfect square and the coefficient of the x-term was either positive or negative 2 times its square root. If both of these were true, you could factor the trinomial as a binomial squared. Notice that the constant in the squared binomial is half the coefficient of the x-term.

Unfortunately, quadratic functions are seldom perfect squares, so you have to "complete" them before you can put them into the form $f(x) = a(x - h)^2 + k$.

EXAMPLE

1. Write $y = x^2 + 3x + 40$ in completed-square form. Find the vertex and line of symmetry of its graph.

$$y = x^2 + 3x + 40$$
$$y - 40 = x^2 + 3x \qquad\qquad \text{Isolate the } x\text{-terms.}$$

The number needed to complete the square is the square of half the coefficient of the x-term.

$$y - 40 + 2.25 = x^2 + 3x + 2.25 \qquad \left(\tfrac{3}{2}\right)^2 = \tfrac{9}{4} = 2.25$$
$$y - 37.75 = x^2 + 3x + 2.25 \qquad\qquad \text{Simplify.}$$

Factor the trinomial square as a binomial squared. The constant term in the squared binomial is half the coefficient of the x-term.

$$y - 37.75 = (x + 1.5)^2 \qquad\qquad \tfrac{3}{2} = 1.5$$
$$y = (x + 1.5)^2 + 37.75 \qquad\qquad \text{Solve for } y.$$

So, the vertex is $(-1.5, 37.75)$ and the line of symmetry is $x = -1.5$.

TRY IT

Complete the square to find the vertex and the line of symmetry of the graph of each function.

a. $y = x^2 + 6x$ **b.** $f(x) = x^2 - 10x - 90$

c. $g(x) = x^2 - 5x + 5$ **d.** $y = x^2 + 7x - 3$

In all of the cases you have looked at so far, the coefficient of the squared term was 1. When this is not the case, you will need to do some factoring before completing the square.

2. A science class launches a model rocket. When its fuel runs out, it is 170 meters above the ground, and traveling upward at 39.2 meters per second. What is the maximum height the rocket reaches, and how long after the fuel runs out does it reach that height?

By completing the square of the free-fall formula with the given information, we can find the vertex of the graph of the function.

$h(t) = -4.9t^2 + 39.2t + 170$ Use the free-fall equation in meters, $v_0 = 39.2$, $h_0 = 170$.

$h(t) - 170 = -4.9t^2 + 39.2t$ Isolate the t-terms.

Before completing the square, factor out the coefficient of t^2.

$h(t) - 170 = -4.9\left(t^2 - \frac{39.2}{4.9}t\right)$ Factor out -4.9.

$h(t) - 170 = -4.9(t^2 - 8t)$ Simplify.

Now complete the square of $t^2 - 8t$. Adding a number inside the parentheses means you're really adding -4.9 times that number to the right side, so you must add -4.9 times the number to the left side of the equation.

$h(t) - 170 - 4.9(16) = -4.9(t^2 - 8t + 16)$ $\left(-\frac{8}{2}\right)^2 = 16$

$h(t) - 248.4 = -4.9(t - 4)^2$ Factor the trinomial.

$h(t) = -4.9(t - 4)^2 + 248.4$ Solve for $h(t)$.

The vertex, (h, k), is $(4, 248.4)$. The rocket reaches its maximum height of 248.4 meters 4 seconds after its fuel runs out.

CONSIDER

1. In Example 2, how can you tell, without solving for $h(t)$ in the height function or graphing and tracing, that once the fuel runs out, the rocket is at the same height after 3 seconds as after 5 seconds?

TRY IT

Complete the square to find the vertex and the line of symmetry of the graph of each function.

e. $y = -3x^2 - 6x + 1$ f. $f(x) = 2x^2 - 4x - 7$

REFLECT

1. Explain how to complete the square of $x^2 + bx$.
2. What information can you "read" from a quadratic function in $f(x) = a(x - h)^2 + k$ form that you cannot read from $f(x) = ax^2 + bx + c$ form?
3. What modern word is descended from *Al-jabr w'al muqabalah*?

Exercises

CORE

1. Getting Started Complete the square for $y = x^2 + 6x + 1$ by supplying the value for each question mark.

a. $y + \underline{\ ?\ } = x^2 + 6x$

b. $y - 1 + \underline{\ ?\ } = x^2 + 6x + \underline{\ ?\ }$

c. $y + \underline{\ ?\ } = (x + \underline{\ ?\ })^2$

d. $y = (x + \underline{\ ?\ })^2 - \underline{\ ?\ }$

Copy and complete each equation.

2. $x^2 + 10x + \underline{\ \ \ } = (x + 5)^2$ **3.** $y^2 + \underline{\ \ \ } + 49 = (y - 7)^2$ **4.** $z^2 - 20z + \underline{\ \ \ } = (z - 10)^2$

5. $m^2 + \underline{\ \ \ } + 1 = (m - 1)^2$ **6.** $p^2 + \underline{\ \ \ } + \frac{1}{9} = \left(p + \frac{1}{3}\right)^2$ **7.** $n^2 + 0.5n + \underline{\ \ \ } = (n + 0.25)^2$

8. Complete the square for $y = 3x^2 + 15x + 1$ by supplying the value for each question mark.

a. $y + \underline{\ ?\ } = 3x^2 + 15x$

b. $y - 1 = 3(x^2 + \underline{\ ?\ } x)$

c. $y - 1 + \underline{\ ?\ } = 3(x^2 + 5x + \underline{\ ?\ })$

d. $y + 17.75 = 3(x + \underline{\ ?\ })^2$

e. $y = 3(x + \underline{\ ?\ })^2 - \underline{\ ?\ }$

9. Name That Model Julio has discovered a way to model completing the square of $x^2 + 3x$ using algebra tiles. Instead of using 3 x-tiles, he arranges 6 x-tiles next to the x^2-tile as shown, and renames the x-tiles as one-half x-tiles. Then, when he adds the unit tiles to complete the square, he must rename them, too.

a. What should Julio call the unit tiles? Explain.

b. Sketch the completed square. What number completes the square?

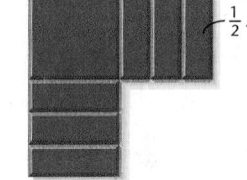

Complete the square to find the vertex and the line of symmetry of the graph of each function. Find the maximum or minimum value of the function.

10. $y = x^2 + 16x$

11. $y = x^2 - 8x - 5$

12. $y = x^2 - 7x + 5$

13. $y + 2 = x^2 + \frac{3}{4}x + 6$

14. $g(x) = 0.4x^2 + 2x + 3$

15. $f(x) = -5x(x - 2)$

16. $y = 2x^2 + 4x - 6$

17. $m = -3k^2 + 9k - 10$

18. $h = 4t^2 - 12t$

19. Out to Launch When a satellite is launched, it is powered into space by a rocket with several parts, or *stages*. When the fuel in each stage is exhausted, the stage falls back to earth. Suppose that the second stage of a satellite is released at an altitude of 85 miles. Its vertical velocity at this point is 7500 feet per second.

a. Write the height function for the second stage. Then convert the function into completed-square form.

b. What will the maximum height of the second stage be? When will it reach this height? Explain how you found your answer.

20. a. A student wrote $(x + 3)^2 = x^2 + 9$. Show that this equation is generally *incorrect* by comparing the graphs of $y = (x + 3)^2$ and $y = x^2 + 9$.

    b. Are there *any* values of x that make $(x + 3)^2 = x^2 + 9$ true? If so, find them and explain your method.

21. Suppose a quadratic function in $f(x) = ax^2 + bx + c$ form is converted to $f(x) = a(x - h)^2 + k$ form by completing the square. Are the two a-values equal in both equations? Do they both give the same information about the width and direction of the parabola? Explain.

22. "Jean-eology" A store owner sells an average of 36 pairs of jeans weekly at a price of \$30 per pair. From past sales, she estimates that each \$1 decrease in the price will increase weekly sales by 12 pairs, as long as prices aren't below half price.

    a. If $r =$ revenue and $d =$ the number of \$1 decreases, explain why this situation is modeled by $r = (36 + 12d)(30 - d)$ or $r = -12d^2 + 324d + 1080$.

    b. Write your model equation in $f(x) = a(x - h)^2 + k$ form by completing the square. If the owner wants to maximize revenue, at what price should she sell the jeans?

    c. Does maximizing revenue necessarily mean maximizing profit? Explain.

LOOK AHEAD

Find the vertex of each function and determine if the y-value is a maximum or minimum value. Tell how many times you think the function intersects the x-axis.

23. $y = x^2 + 4x - 2$ **24.** $f(x) = x^2 - 2x + 1$ **25.** $y = x^2 + 6x + 5$

Factor each trinomial.

26. $x^2 + 3x + 2$ **27.** $x^2 - 10x - 39$ **28.** $t^2 - 12t + 32$ **29.** $x^2 + 8x - 9$

MORE PRACTICE

Copy and complete each equation.

30. $x^2 + 6x + \underline{\hspace{1em}} = (x + 3)^2$ **31.** $y^2 + \underline{\hspace{1em}} + 36 = (y - 6)^2$

32. $c^2 - 1600c + \underline{\hspace{1em}} = (c - 800)^2$ **33.** $d^2 + 7d + \underline{\hspace{1em}} = \left(d + \frac{7}{2}\right)^2$

34. $k^2 - 10k + \underline{\hspace{1em}} = (k - 5)^2$ **35.** $r^2 + \underline{\hspace{1em}} + 1 = (r + 1)^2$

36. $n^2 + 1.2n + \underline{\hspace{1em}} = (n + 0.6)^2$ **37.** $p^2 + \underline{\hspace{1em}} + \frac{9}{16} = \left(p + \frac{3}{4}\right)^2$

Complete the square to find the vertex and the line of symmetry of the graph of each function. Find the maximum or minimum value of the function.

38. $y = x^2 - 10x$ **39.** $y = x^2 + 4x$ **40.** $y = x^2 - 9x$

41. $v = d^2 + 8d - 7$ **42.** $y = x^2 - 12x + 15$ **43.** $y = x^2 + 5x + 4$

44. $g(x) = x^2 + \frac{1}{2}x - \frac{3}{4}$ **45.** $g(x) = x^2 + 0.6x - 11$ **46.** $f(x) = 4x^2 + 16x + 1$

47. $f(x) = -x^2 - 3x - 0.25$ **48.** $h = 3g(g + 2) + 7$ **49.** $y = -2x^2 + 20x - 3$

50. Fireworks Burnout A chrysanthemum, one of the most spec-
tacular fireworks, is intended to burst at its highest point
between 1000 and 1200 feet above the ground.

  a. If the charge is traveling upward at 128 feet per second
  when the propelled "burn" ends at a height of 900 feet,
  write the general form of the height function, with time in
  seconds. Then complete the square to write the function in
  $f(x) = a(x - h)^2 + k$ form.

  b. When is the best time after the burn ends for the chrysanthemum to burst? At what height would this burst occur?

  c. In reality, fireworks operators usually use "rules of thumb"
  to time the bursts. If the burn lasts 3.5 seconds, and the
  operator sets the burst for 8 seconds after launch, at what
  height will the chrysanthemum burst?

MORE MATH REASONING

51. Ticket Prices A theater complex charging $7.00 per ticket is averaging
640 customers per evening. They estimate that each $0.50 price cut will
bring in 80 more customers.

  a. Let $m =$ each $0.50 price cut. Write an expression for the cost of each
  discounted ticket and an expression for the expected number of ticket sales.

  b. The total revenue equals the number of tickets sold times the cost of each
  ticket. Write a quadratic model for the revenue.

  c. If the theater wants to maximize revenue, at what price should they sell tickets?
  Explain how you solved this problem.

52. For a rectangle of width w, length ℓ, and given perimeter p, $p = 2w + 2\ell$.

  a. Write an area function $A(w)$ in terms of w, where p is constant.

  b. Complete the square for the area function. Write it in $f(x) = a(x - h)^2 + k$ form.

  c. For what width and length is the area maximum? What is the maximum area in
  terms of the perimeter?

  d. What do your results say about the shape of a rectangle with the maximum
  area for a given perimeter?

53. Use a Graphing Utility If you have three noncollinear points, no two of which
have the same k-value, you can find a quadratic function that fits the three data
points. There are 136 connections required between 16 electrical posts, 210
between 20 posts, and 325 between 25 posts.

  a. Write the data as three ordered pairs of the form (number of posts, number of
  connections).

  b. You are looking for a function of the form $ax^2 + bx + c = y$. Write three equations by substituting each ordered pair for x and y and simplifying. For example,
  the first ordered pair gives $a(16)^2 + b(16) + c = 136$ before simplification.

  c. You now have three equations with the three unknowns a, b, and c. Write a
  3×3 coefficient matrix, A, and a 3×1 constant matrix, B. Enter the matrices
  on your graphing calculator.

  d. Find A^{-1}. Then find the product $A^{-1}B$ to find the variable matrix.

  e. What is the equation of the quadratic function that fits the data? Use the
  function to find the number of connections needed between 70 posts.

Making Connections

← **CONNECT** → *You've explored quadratic functions and seen how writing quadratic functions in the form $f(x) = a(x - h)^2 + k$ can help you picture their graphs and find the maximum and minimum values of the functions.*

A parabolic shape has important properties. A parabolic reflector focuses parallel incoming signals—for example, sound, light, or radio waves—to a single point. In the Explore, you will discover what makes a parabola a parabola.

EXPLORE: BACK IN THE FOLD

MATERIALS

*Copy or typing paper
Straightedge*

1. Mark a point about two inches from the center of the bottom edge of the paper. Fold from the lower right corner as shown, so that the bottom edge of the paper touches the point. Mark the crease by inserting a pencil into it or by using a straightedge.

2. Moving from left to right, make several more folds through the point. Each time, mark the crease.
3. Repeat the process, this time folding up the lower left corner and moving from right to left. Draw the curve suggested by the folds. What shape does this curve remind you of?
4. Measure the distance from each point on the curve to the bottom edge of the page and to the original point that you drew. What do you notice? (Hint: How do you measure the distance from a point to a line?) Make a conjecture about the points on a parabola.
5. Assuming that your conjecture is true, write a geometric definition of a parabola as a set of points that follows certain guidelines based on distance.
6. How might the original point that you drew relate to the focusing point for a radio collector dish?

REFLECT

1. Describe the roles of *a*, *h*, and *k* in $f(x) = a(x - h)^2 + k$ in transforming the graph of $f(x) = x^2$.
2. When you use a quadratic function to model a real-world situation, why might finding its vertex be important?
3. Outline as many similarities and differences as you can between linear functions and quadratic functions. Be sure to discuss the rates of change of the two types of functions.

1. Consider the functions $f(x) = 4x^2$, $g(x) = -5x^2$, $h(x) = 6x^2 + 2$, and $j(x) = -3(x + 1)^2$.
   a. List the functions whose graphs open upward and those whose graphs open downward.
   b. List the functions from widest to narrowest as their graphs would appear on a coordinate plane.
   c. List the functions that reach a maximum at their vertex and those that reach a minimum at their vertex.

Given the vertex (V) of a parabola and a second point (P) on the parabola, find the coordinates of a third point on the parabola.

2. $V(1, 1)$; $P(3, 4)$ **3.** $V(4, -6)$; $P(-3.2, 11)$ **4.** $V(-5, 6)$; $P(0, -5)$

5. Write the equation of each graph. Then write the equation of its reflection over the x-axis.

   a. 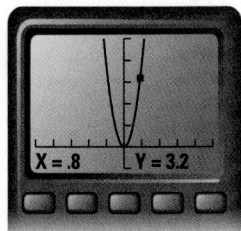   **b.** 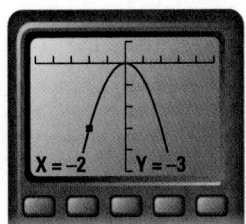   **c.**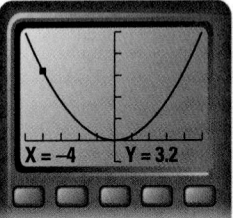

6. Which function has a graph with its vertex at the origin?
   (a) $f(x) = x^2 + 3$ (b) $y = (x - 2)^2 - 2$ (c) $f(x) = (x - 1)^2$ (d) $y = -399x^2$

7. Suppose a golf ball is hit with an initial vertical velocity of 30 m/sec. The height function for the ball on the moon is $h(t) = -0.8t^2 + 30t$. For Earth, the function is $h(t) = -4.9t^2 + 30t$.
   a. Complete the square to write each function in $f(x) = a(x - h)^2 + k$ form.
   b. What is the maximum height of the ball on Earth? on the moon?

8. The screen shows the height of a golf ball hit with an initial vertical velocity of 30 m/sec on the moon and on each of the given planets. Match each graph with its heavenly body and corresponding coefficient of t^2.
   a. Earth: -4.9 **b.** Moon: -0.8 **c.** Mars: -1.9

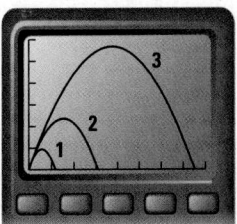

For each quadratic function, find the vertex of its graph and the line of symmetry. Then state whether the y-coordinate of the vertex is the maximum or minimum value for that function.

   9. $D(x) = -9(x - 4)^2 + 16$ **10.** $f(x) = 0.2(x + 1)^2$ **11.** $y = 4x^2$

12. Graph the region defined by the inequalities $y \le x$, $y \le -x + 4$, $y \ge -x$, and $y \ge x - 4$. Label the coordinates of the vertices. [3-2]

Find the sum of each series. [4-1 and 4-2]

13. $\displaystyle\sum_{n=1}^{5} (n - 1)$

14. $\displaystyle\sum_{n=1}^{3} 4^n$

15. $\displaystyle\sum_{n=1}^{4} (4n + 3)$

16. $\displaystyle\sum_{n=1}^{5} (-2)^n$

17. The graph of $y = 2x^2$ is labeled A. Graph A is transformed into graph B, graph B is transformed into C, and graph C is transformed into D. Describe each transformation and write the equation of each new graph.

    a. A into B   **b.** B into C   **c.** C into D

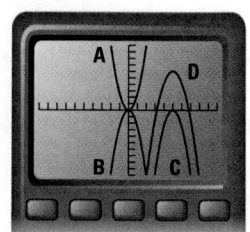

18. Oh, Buoy! As the lifeguard at a lake, you must rope off a safe area for recreation. The shoreline is virtually straight, and you have a 600-ft rope and two buoys to form three sides of a rectangle. You want to maximize the recreation area.

    a. Express the length of the rectangle in terms of its width. Then express its area as a function of its width.

    b. How do you know, without graphing, that the graph of the area function is a parabola?

    c. Use a graphing utility to graph the area function. What is the maximum area that can be enclosed, and what are the rectangle's dimensions?

Graph each set of functions on the same set of axes.

19. $f(x) = x^2 - 5$, $g(x) = (x - 5)^2$, and $h(x) = (x - 5)^2 + 2$

20. $f(x) = \frac{1}{2}x^2$, $g(x) = -\frac{1}{2}x^2 + 3$, and $h(x) = -\frac{1}{2}(x + 1)^2 + 3$

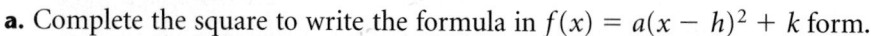

Complete the square to find the vertex and the line of symmetry of the graph of each function. Find the maximum or minimum value of the function.

21. $f(x) = x^2 + 10x$

22. $y = x^2 - 6x + 3$

23. $g(x) = 2x^2 + 8x + 10$

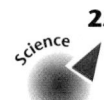

24. An insurance company is using the formula $y = 0.009x^2 - 0.90x + 27$ to predict the number of accidents per million driving miles (y) for drivers of different ages (x) between 16 and 70.

    a. Complete the square to write the formula in $f(x) = a(x - h)^2 + k$ form.

    b. For what age does the model predict the fewest accidents? What accident rate does it predict for this age group?

25. Getting Our Signals Crossed The diagram shows the cross section of a parabolic reflector. It also shows four signals, each parallel to the axis of symmetry of the parabolic reflector.

    a. Carefully trace the diagram. Two signals are shown bouncing off the surface of the reflector. Where do the other two signal reflections intersect?

    b. Where should the device that collects the signals be located?

    c. Why are reflectors with parabolic cross sections used in radio and optical telescopes?

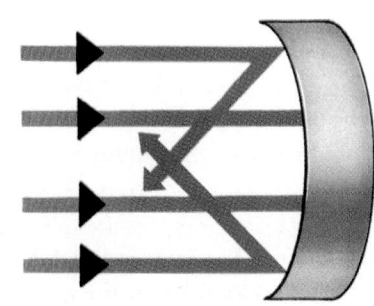

WORLD SPEED RECORD

Soaring high above a rugged canyon or a city street, a peregrine falcon spots its prey. The falcon accelerates, then transforms its body into the shape of a speeding bullet by pointing its head down and tucking in its wings and feet. Within seconds of beginning its dive, called a *stoop*, the peregrine falcon can reach speeds of up to 217 miles per hour!

The peregrine falcon is as much "at home" in the high-rise buildings of the city as it is in the cliffs and mountains. A special program designed to save this bird from extinction has helped it adapt to city life.

About the same size as a crow, peregrine falcons are predators with streamlined bodies and long, pointed wings. The falcon's wings are strong enough to give it the power to carry its prey back to a nest in the cliffs or atop a high-rise city building. But the specialized wings of this falcon provide more than just strength. They also enable the peregrine falcon to claim the title of the fastest-moving animal on the earth.

?

1. Write an inequality to describe the range of a peregrine falcon's speed.
2. Why does the falcon tuck in its wings and feet during its dive?

3. Why do you think the fastest moving animal is found in the air, rather than on land or in the sea?

← CONNECT →
You have solved linear equations graphically. Now you will use a similar method to solve quadratic equations.

A quadratic function, like $f(x) = x^2 + 6x - 4$, represents an infinite set of points, including $(-2, -12)$, $(0, -4)$, $(1.5, 7.25)$, and $(\sqrt{3}, 6\sqrt{3} - 1)$.

When a quadratic function takes on a particular value, you have a **quadratic equation**, such as $-12 = x^2 + 6x - 4$. You can use the graph of the related function $f(x) = x^2 + 6x - 4$ to see that the solutions of $-12 = x^2 + 6x - 4$ are $x = -2$ or $x = -4$.

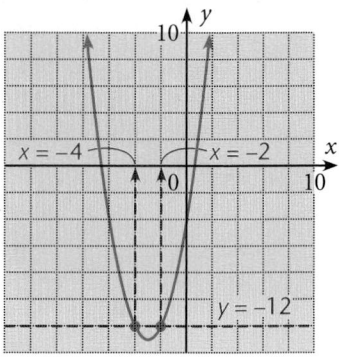

There are many ways to find the solutions of a quadratic equation. In the Explore, you will use graphing to approximate the solutions of a quadratic equation.

EXPLORE: STOOPING TO CONQUER

MATERIALS

Graphing utility

Suppose that the height, in feet, of a peregrine falcon t seconds after it starts diving toward its prey is modeled by the quadratic function $h(t) = -16t^2 - 53t + 1000$.

1. Graph the function that shows the height of the falcon over time. (Do not use parametric mode.) Experiment to find appropriate values for t on the x-axis and $h(t)$ on the y-axis. Give your values and explain why they produce an appropriate graph.

2. Write a quadratic equation that shows that the height of the falcon is 500 feet. Use the ZOOM and TRACE features to find an approximate solution to this equation. What does your solution represent?

3. Change your viewing window so that x ranges from -10 to 10 and y ranges from 0 to 1100. What does the graph of the function look like now?

4. Use your graph to find *all* of the x-values that solve your equation in Step 2. How do your results differ from your answer in Step 2? Explain how you should interpret these results.

5. Using an appropriate viewing window, find the times when the height of the falcon is:

a. 800 feet   **b.** 600 ft

c. 400 ft   **d.** 200 ft

What do you notice about these times?

6. Using your results from Step 5, estimate the time when the falcon will reach the ground. Then use your graph to confirm your estimate.

7. Do you think that this quadratic free-fall model of the falcon's dive is a good approximation for the entire dive? If not, explain how and when the actual dive might be different than the free-fall model.

As you saw in the Explore, a quadratic equation can have two real solutions. When using a quadratic model for a real-world situation, check to make sure each solution makes sense.

EXAMPLE

1. Use the graph of the related function to solve each equation.

a. $-1 = (x - 2)^2 - 3$

Graph $y = (x - 2)^2 - 3$ and find the x-values of the points where $y = -1$. The vertex of the parabola is at $(2, -3)$. Approximate solutions are $x \approx \frac{1}{2}$ or $x \approx 3\frac{1}{2}$.

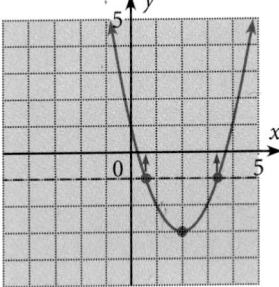

b. $5 = x^2 - 6x + 10$

Graph $y = x^2 - 6x + 10$. If you use a graphing utility, you can use TRACE to find the x-values of the points where $y = 5$. The solutions are $x = 1$ or $x = 5$.

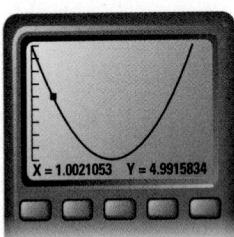

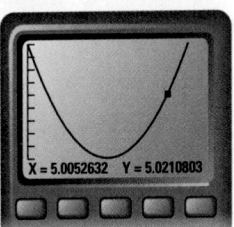

1. How many real solutions does $n = (x - h)^2 + k$ have if $n > k$? if $n = k$? if $n < k$? Explain.

EXAMPLE

2. A projectile is shot upward from the surface of the earth at an initial velocity of 234 ft/sec. When will the projectile reach a height of 650 feet?

Use the equation $h(t) = -16t^2 + v_0t + h_0$.

Since the initial velocity is 234 ft/sec and the initial height is 0, graph the function $h(t) = -16t^2 + 234t$. Then, check for places where $-16t^2 + 234t = 650$.

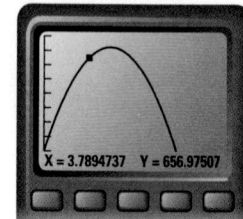

On the graph, these occur at $t \approx 3.7$ and $t \approx 10.9$. Both of these solutions are meaningful: the projectile will be at this height on its way up, at 3.7 sec, and on its way down, at 10.9 sec.

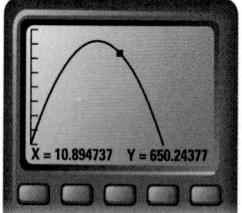

> **Problem-Solving Tip**
>
> Check to be sure your answer makes sense.

TRY IT

Use the graph of the related function to solve each equation.

a. $(x + 1)^2 + 4 = 5$
b. $11 = -x^2 + 2x + 10$
c. $-2x^2 + 2x - 1 = -6$
d. $x^2 + 6x + 1 = -7$

As you will soon see, it is often most convenient to solve a quadratic equation when one side is set equal to zero.

$0 = ax^2 + bx + c$ is the **standard form** for a quadratic equation. The solutions to an equation in standard form are called its **roots.** The roots of a quadratic equation are the **zeros** of its corresponding function $f(x) = ax^2 + bx + c$.

3. During the opening ceremony of a baseball game, a colorful display is to be dropped by a blimp, hitting the pitcher's mound during the last note of the Star Spangled Banner. The blimp will be at an altitude of 1000 ft. A student will signal the blimp with a light when it is time to drop the display. How much earlier than the last note should the signal be sent?

Graph $y = -16t^2 + 0t + 1000$.

On the graphing utility, we can use the TRACE and ZOOM functions to find the times when the height $= 0$, that is, the zeros of the function.

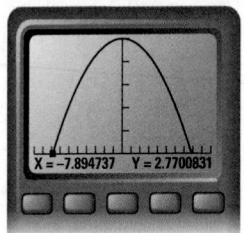

The zeros are $t \approx 7.91$ and $t \approx -7.91$. Only the positive number makes sense in this problem, so the signal should be sent about 8 sec before the last note is played.

You've seen that a quadratic equation can have two real roots. (If it is in standard form, this means that its related function has two real zeros.) It is also possible for a quadratic equation to have one real root or no real roots, as shown.

$y = x^2 - 2x - 3$

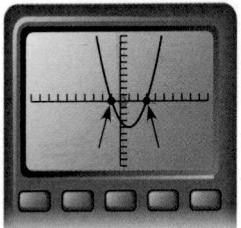

$0 = x^2 - 2x - 3$ has two real roots.

$y = x^2 - 2x + 1$

$0 = x^2 - 2x + 1$ has one real root.

$y = x^2 - 2x + 3$

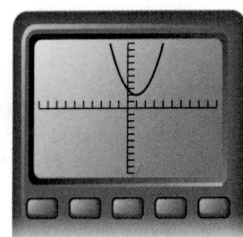

$0 = x^2 - 2x + 3$ has no real roots.

REFLECT

1. Briefly explain the differences between a quadratic function and a quadratic equation. How can you use a quadratic function to solve a quadratic equation?

2. Compare the number of possible real solutions for a linear and a quadratic equation.

3. The y-intercept of the graph of a linear function in slope-intercept form $f(x) = mx + b$ is $(0, b)$. What is the y-intercept of a quadratic function in standard form? Explain.

Exercises

CORE

1. Getting Started The graph of $f(x) = x^2$ is shown.

  a. Graph $y = (x + 3)^2 - 12$.

  b. Find the x-values of the points where $y = 4$.

  c. Find the x-values of the points where $y = 0$.

  d. Which values are called the zeros of the function $f(x) = (x + 3)^2 - 12$?

  e. Which values are called the solutions to the equation where $(x + 3)^2 - 12 = 4$?

  f. Which values are called the roots of the equation $(x + 3)^2 - 12 = 0$?

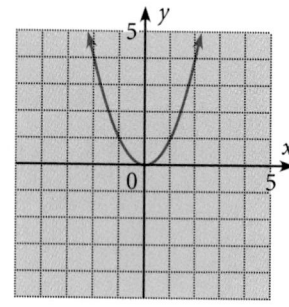

How many zeros does each quadratic function have?

2.
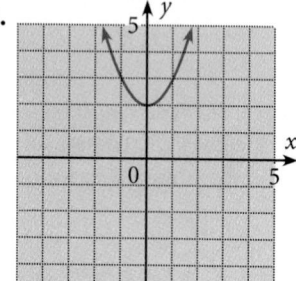

3.
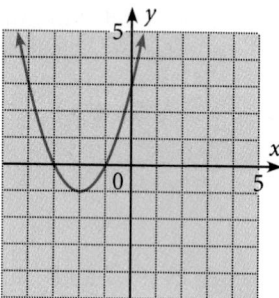

4.
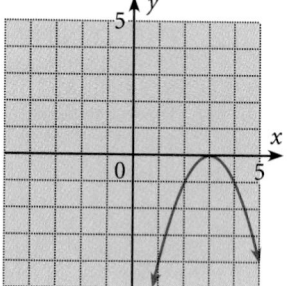

Write the word or phrase that correctly completes each statement.

5. The equation $4x^2 - 2x + 7 = 3$ is an example of a _____ equation.

6. The _____ of a quadratic equation in standard form can be found by determining the values of x where the function crosses the x-axis.

7. Graph the quadratic function $y = -x^2$. Use the graph to solve each quadratic equation.

  a. $-9 = -x^2$ **b.** $0 = -x^2$ **c.** $9 = -x^2$

Use the graph of the related function to solve each equation. Estimate answers where necessary. If an equation appears to have no real solutions, say so.

8. $x^2 = 4$ **9.** $-6 = -2x^2 + 10$ **10.** $5 = (x + 3)^2 - 4$

11. $-2(x - 1)^2 + 5 = 8$ **12.** $(x + 2)^2 = 4$ **13.** $3x^2 + 2x = 1$

Rewrite each quadratic equation in standard form.

14. $3x(x + 2) = 8$ **15.** $0 = (x + 4)^2$ **16.** $5x^2 - 7 + 3x = 7$

17. **Kinetic Energy in King Arthur's Court** The *kinetic energy* of an object measures its energy due to motion. In the metric system, the basic unit of kinetic energy is a *Joule*.

When the velocity of an object (v) is measured in m/sec and its mass (m) is measured in kilograms, its kinetic energy (KE), in Joules, is:

$$KE = \tfrac{1}{2}mv^2$$

Sir Lancelot and Sir Galahad are going to a tournament. In the joust, Sir Lancelot will ride Camelot Slough and Sir Galahad will ride Water Biscuit. Their masses are shown.

	Sir Lancelot	Camelot Slough	Sir Galahad	Water Biscuit
Weight (in armor)	130 kg	870 kg	110 kg	830 kg

For each combination of horse and rider, find the velocity necessary to generate a kinetic energy of 10,000 Joules.

18. Explain how the location of the vertex of the graph of a quadratic function and whether it is a maximum or minimum point can tell you how many x-intercepts the graph of the function has.

Use the graph of the related function to find the roots of each equation. Estimate answers where necessary. If an equation appears to have no real solutions, say so.

19. $x^2 - 2x + 1 = 0$

20. $-3x^2 + 12 = 0$

21. $\frac{1}{2}(x + 4)^2 - 6 = 0$

Graph each quadratic function and estimate its zeros.

22. $y = (x - 2)^2 - 4$

23. $h(x) = 4x^2 - 1$

24. $y = -2(x + 3)^2 - 5$

25. $f(x) = x^2 - 5x + 6$

26. **Deck Me** Your company is building a wooden deck of uniform width around a 20-ft by 40-ft swimming pool. The cost of decking is $4.20 per square foot, and you need to know the maximum width deck that can be built within the budget of $2400.
   a. Sketch a diagram of the pool and surrounding deck.
   b. Write a quadratic equation representing the situation. Graph the related function.
   c. Use your graph to solve the quadratic equation you wrote in **b.**
   d. What would a deck with a width of 6 ft cost?
   e. If boards are only available in widths that are multiples of two inches, what width deck should you build? Assume there is no gap between adjacent boards.

For each quadratic function, find the vertex of its graph and the line of symmetry. Then state whether the *y*-coordinate of the vertex is the maximum or minimum value for that function. [5-1]

27. $D(x) = 4(x - 4)^2 + 16$ **28.** $f(x) = -4(x + 1)^2$ **29.** $y = 2x^2$

Simplify each expression. [4-3]

30. $(4 + 2i) + (8 - 7i)$ **31.** $(9 - 4i) - (-7 + 2i)$ **32.** $(2 + 6i)(5 - 9i)$ **33.** i^{23}

MORE PRACTICE

34. Graph the quadratic function $y = 2x^2$. Use the graph to solve each equation.
    a. $0 = 2x^2$ **b.** $-7 = 2x^2$ **c.** $8 = 2x^2$

Use a graphing utility to graph the related function for each equation. Then solve the equation. Where necessary, round answers to the nearest tenth. If an equation has no real solutions, say so.

35. $2x^2 = 9$ **36.** $6 = -x^2 - 2x + 1$ **37.** $5x^2 - 6 = 75$

38. $-x^2 - 2x + 1 = -6$ **39.** $2x^2 + 6x = -4.5$ **40.** $5 = -2x^2 + 6$

41. $2.23x^2 + 17.4x = 78.1$ **42.** $-16x^2 + 53x + 1000 = 700$

Rewrite each quadratic equation in standard form.

43. $0 = (2x + 3)(x - 2)$ **44.** $(x + 4)(x + 4) = 0$ **45.** $(x + 2)x = 5$

Using a graphing utility, graph the related function to find the roots of each equation. Where necessary, round answers to the nearest tenth. If an equation has no real roots, say so.

46. $0 = x^2 + 7x + 12$ **47.** $0 = -3x^2 + 22x - 2$ **48.** $0 = 7.7x^2 + 13.8x - 18.2$

Use a graphing utility to graph each quadratic function and estimate its zeros.

49. $2x^2 - x = y$ **50.** $f(x) = x^2 + 2x - 3$ **51.** $-4.9t^2 + 32t + 400 = h(t)$

52. $x^2 + 5x = y + 4$ **53.** $x^2 - 4x - 3 = g(x)$ **54.** $y = 10.4x^2 - 27.5x + 7.7$

55. Use a Graphing Utility If a savings account earns interest compounded annually, the money in the account earns interest once a year. If you invest *P* dollars in an account with an interest rate of *r*, the amount of money (*A*) you will have after *n* years (assuming you make no other deposits or withdrawals) is $A = P(1 + r)^n$.
    a. Suppose you invest $500 in a savings account. Write the function for the amount of money in the account after two years. Graph your equation.
    b. At the end of two years, the account has $550 in it. What is the interest rate for this account?

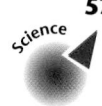

56. Use a Graphing Utility Suppose that a falcon starts its stoop at 800 feet. Its initial vertical velocity is -40 ft/sec.

a. Write and graph a function that models the height of the falcon.

b. Find the times when the falcon is at a height of 200 feet.

c. What is the real-world meaning of the zeros of the function you wrote in **a**? Find the zeros of the function.

MORE MATH REASONING

57. Pipe Down As fluid flows through a thin cylindrical pipe, the velocity of one of the fluid's molecules varies with its distance from the center of the cylinder. When a fluid is somewhat *viscous* (thick and slow flowing), the molecules near the inner surface of the pipe are slowed down more than those near the center. A quadratic equation can be used to approximate this effect.

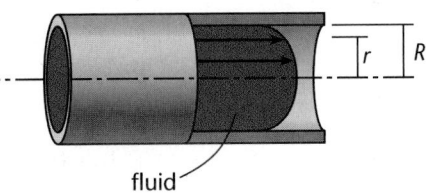

fluid

The equation that approximates the velocity of the molecule is:

$$v = v_{max}\left(1 - \frac{r^2}{R^2}\right)$$

where v is the velocity of a molecule at a distance r from the center of the pipe, R is the inside radius of the pipe, and v_{max} is the fluid's maximum velocity.

a. Oil with a maximum velocity of 10 cm/sec flows through a pipe with a 0.5-cm inside radius. Write an equation for the velocity of a molecule. What does $r = 0$ represent in the real situation?

b. Use a graphing utility to graph the velocity function. At what distances from the center is the fluid's velocity half of its maximum velocity?

c. According to this model, at what distances from the center is the fluid's velocity *zero*? Do you think that molecules at this distance from the center of the pipe are really stationary? Explain.

58. Ancient Textbooks Thousands of clay tablets record Babylonian mathematics prior to 1600 B.C. Many of the tablets are problem *texts,* similar in purpose to modern math texts. According to *Treasury of Mathematics,* line 5 of one tablet presents a problem on rectangular area:

"1 bur'u is the area; the length exceeded the width by 2,25. What are the length and the width?"

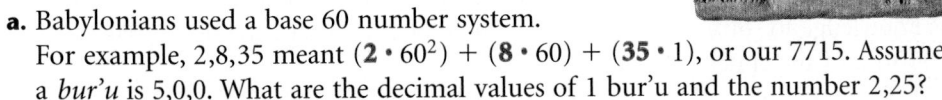

a. Babylonians used a base 60 number system. For example, 2,8,35 meant $(2 \cdot 60^2) + (8 \cdot 60) + (35 \cdot 1)$, or our 7715. Assume a *bur'u* is 5,0,0. What are the decimal values of 1 bur'u and the number 2,25?

b. Write an equation using w to represent the width in the problem and solve. What are the width and length?

c. Convert your dimensions to base 60 to show how an ancient Babylonian might express the answer to this problem.

← C O N N E C T →   *You've found approximate solutions to quadratic functions by graphing. However, it is possible to find exact solutions to some quadratic equations by factoring. You will see how to use this method to solve quadratic equations.*

Because quadratic equations are important mathematical models for many real-world situations, inexact solutions may not be adequate. In the following Explore, you will discover a different method for solving quadratic equations.

EXPLORE: FOLLOW THE BOUNCING BALL

You have landed your spaceship on the moon of a distant planet. Through quick experimentation, you find that the force of gravity there is $\frac{1}{16}$ that of Earth. Therefore, the equation for free fall, in feet, on this moon is $h(t) = -t^2 + v_0 t + h_0$.

1. For a publicity photo, you toss a tennis ball off the rim of a crater 300 feet above its floor. The initial vertical velocity of your toss is 20 feet per second. Write a function to model the height of the tennis ball.

2. When will the tennis ball hit the bottom of the crater? Write an equation to show that the height of the ball is zero to help you answer this question.

In the strange atmosphere of this moon, your graphing calculator will not work! You must find a new solution method.

3. Begin by multiplying both sides of your equation by -1 so that the coefficient of t^2 is positive. Then factor the trinomial expression.

4. When the product of two factors is equal to zero, what do you know about the individual factors? (In other words, if $a \times b = 0$, what must be true about a or b?) Use this knowledge to solve your equation. How long does it take the tennis ball to hit the bottom of the crater?

5. Write a short paragraph explaining how you solved this problem.

You can find the roots of some quadratic equations by factoring. This solution method is based on the following principle.

Exercises

CORE

1. Getting Started

a. What polynomial is represented by the algebra tiles?

b. Sketch a rectangle that could be formed from the algebra tiles.

c. What are the dimensions of the rectangle?

d. What is the factorization of the polynomial in **a**?

Match each trinomial with its factors.

2. $x^2 + 5x + 6$ **A.** $(x + 2)(x - 3)$

3. $x^2 + x - 6$ **B.** $(x + 2)(x + 3)$

4. $3x^2 + 9x + 6$ **C.** $(x - 2)(x + 3)$

5. $x^2 - x - 6$ **D.** $(x - 2)(x - 3)$

6. $3x^2 + 5x + 2$ **E.** $(3x + 2)(x + 1)$

7. $x^2 - 5x + 6$ **F.** $(3x + 3)(x + 2)$

Solve each equation using the Principle of Zero Products. If the equation cannot be solved by factoring, say so.

8. $x^2 + 5x + 4 = 0$ **9.** $x^2 - 2x - 8 = 0$ **10.** $x^2 + 4x = 0$

11. $x^2 - 11x + 22 = 0$ **12.** $4x^2 - x - 42 = 0$ **13.** $x^2 = -2x$

14. $2y^2 - 4y - 48 = 0$ **15.** $4x^2 + 16x - 48 = 0$ **16.** $9x^2 - 25 = 0$

17. $3x^2 - 4x - 7 = 0$ **18.** $2x^2 + 11x + 15 = 0$ **19.** $b^2 = 48 - 13b$

20. Print It!

A print of a square photograph has a 2-inch white mat on the left and right sides, and a 3-inch white mat on the top and the bottom. The area of the print, including the mats, is 143 in^2.

a. Write an equation that summarizes the known information about the area of the print. Rewrite the equation as a quadratic equation in standard form.

b. Factor the trinomial expression. Then solve the equation by factoring.

c. What are the dimensions of the print with the mats? What are the dimensions of the photograph? Explain how you found your answers.

William Wegman, *Wedding. With Battina and Chundo*, 1991, Polaroid print

21. It's Easy The equation for the distance fallen for an object on the earth, given in feet, is $d = 16t^2$, where t is the number of seconds of free fall.

   a. Suppose an object has fallen 400 feet. Write an equation and solve by factoring. How long ago was the object dropped?

   b. Suppose an object has fallen 600 feet. Write an equation for this situation. Can this equation be solved by factoring? Explain.

   c. Can you find another way (besides graphing) to solve the equation in **b**? If so, solve it and explain your technique.

   d. Explain how any quadratic equation of the form $ax^2 + c = 0$ can be solved without factoring or graphing.

Solve each equation. Where necessary, round your answer to the nearest tenth.

22. $2x^2 = 72$ **23.** $3x^2 - 18 = 0$ **24.** $-4.9x^2 + 1000 = 0$

25. If r is a root of $ax^2 + bx + c = 0$, write one of the factors of $ax^2 + bx + c$. Explain why this must be a factor.

26. Choose the function or functions represented by the graph.

   (a) $y = (x + 2)(x + 4)$
   (b) $y = 2(x - 2)(x - 4)$
   (c) $y = x^2 - 6x + 8$
   (d) $y = -x^2 + 6x - 8$

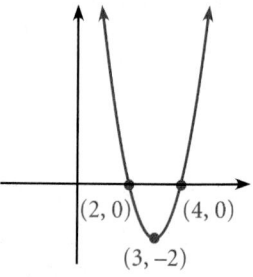

27. a. What are the zeros of the function $y = (x - 5)(x - 11)$? What is the vertex of its graph?

   b. What is the quadratic function with the same zeros as in part **a**, but whose vertex has a y-coordinate of -18?

28. Facts for Everyone The length and width of the pages of the large-print version of an almanac are 3 in. larger than the length and width of the regular-print book. The area of a page of the large-print version is 77 in². What are the dimensions of the larger book if the length of the smaller book is twice its width?

LOOK AHEAD

Complete the square to find the vertex and the line of symmetry of the graph of each function. Find the maximum or minimum value of the function.

29. $y = x^2 + 10x$ **30.** $y = 3x^2 + 9x - 4$ **31.** $y = 2x^2 + 5x + 6$

32. In your own words, explain what a formula is and why formulas are useful.

MORE PRACTICE

Solve each equation using the Principle of Zero Products. If the equation cannot be solved by factoring, say so.

33. $x^2 - 2x + 1 = 0$

34. $x^2 + 5x + 6 = 0$

35. $x^2 - 11x + 24 = 0$

36. $a^2 - 3a = 0$

37. $x^2 + 12x - 28 = 0$

38. $x^2 = 6x$

39. $10 - x^2 = 3x$

40. $c^2 + 7c - 14 = 0$

41. $x^2 - 16 = 0$

42. $2y^2 - 8y - 20 = 0$

43. $3x^2 + 12x + 9 = 0$

44. $16x^2 - 64 = 0$

45. $2x^2 - 7x + 5 = 0$

46. $3x^2 + 16x + 10 = 0$

47. $25x^2 - 20x + 4 = 0$

Solve each equation. Where necessary, round your answer to the nearest tenth.

48. $3x^2 = 27$

49. $4x^2 - 44 = 0$

50. $-16x^2 + 1400 = 0$

51. More for Your Money A pizzeria sells a rectangular pizza 16 in. wide and 12 in. long. As a sales promotion, they increase the length and width of the pizza by the same amount. The area of the enlarged pizza is 357 in^2. By how many inches did the pizzeria increase the dimensions of the pizza?

MORE MATH REASONING

52. Use a Graphing Calculator The number of angles formed by n rays drawn from a common endpoint follow a quadratic pattern. When one ray is drawn, no angles are formed. When two rays are drawn, one angle is formed. When three rays are drawn, three angles are formed, as shown.

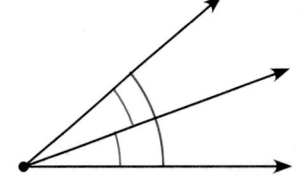

  a. Write the data as three ordered pairs of the form (number of rays, number of angles).
  b. You are looking for a function of the form $ax^2 + bx + c = y$. Write three equations by substituting each ordered pair for x and y and simplifying. The first ordered pair gives $a(1)^2 + b(1) + c = 0$ before simplification.
  c. You now have three equations with the three unknowns a, b, and c. Write a 3×3 coefficient matrix, A, and a 3×1 constant matrix, B.
  d. Find A^{-1}. Then find the product $A^{-1}B$ to obtain the variable matrix. What is the equation of the quadratic function that fits the data?
  e. Check your function by using it to predict the number of angles formed by four rays, then use your function to check your results with a sketch.
  f. Use your function to find the number of rays needed to form 21 angles.

53. New Way A concrete walkway x feet wide is being built around a 40 ft × 30 ft garden. The area of the walkway is 984 ft^2. What is the width of the walkway? Explain how you solved this problem.

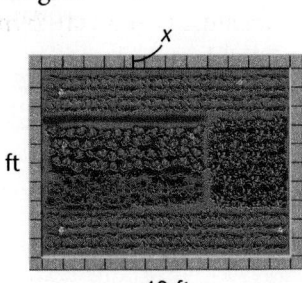

30 ft

40 ft

Using the Quadratic Formula

← C O N N E C T → *You can find exact solutions to some quadratic equations by factoring. The quadratic formula will enable you to solve any quadratic equation. You will derive the quadratic formula and use it to solve equations.*

A general formula known as the **quadratic formula** can be used to find the roots of any quadratic equation. In the Explore, you will derive this formula by completing the square.

EXPLORE: FIND THE FAMOUS FORMULA

By finding the solution to the general quadratic equation $ax^2 + bx + c = 0$, you will discover a formula that can be used to solve *any* quadratic equation.

1. Begin with $ax^2 + bx + c = 0$. Subtract c from both sides.
2. Factor a out of the left side of the equation.
3. Complete the square on the left side. Add a times the new constant term to the right side. Why do you need to multiply the new term by a?
4. Write the right side of the equation as a single fraction by finding a common denominator. Then divide each side of the equation by a.
5. Write the left side of the equation as a binomial square.
6. Find the square root of both sides of the equation. (Hint: $\sqrt{n^2}$ can equal n or $-n$, written $\pm n$.) The denominator of the fraction on the right side should be a perfect square, which can be simplified.
7. Solve for x by subtracting a term from each side. Use the common denominator to write the right side as a single fraction.

The formula you developed in the Explore can be used to solve any quadratic equation. Notice that this formula gives *two* solutions to the equation.

QUADRATIC FORMULA

For any quadratic equation in standard form $ax^2 + bx + c = 0$, the exact solutions (roots) are given by:

$$x = \frac{-b \pm \sqrt{b^2 - 4ac}}{2a}$$

1. Solve $3x^2 - 4x - 7 = 0$ by using the quadratic formula.
   This equation is already in standard form. $a = 3$, $b = -4$, and $c = -7$.

   $x = \dfrac{-(-4) \pm \sqrt{(-4)^2 - 4(3)(-7)}}{2(3)}$ Substitute for a, b, and c.

   $x = \dfrac{4 \pm \sqrt{16 - (-84)}}{(6)}$ Simplify.

   $x = \dfrac{4 \pm \sqrt{100}}{6}$

   $x = \dfrac{4 + 10}{6}$ or $x = \dfrac{4 - 10}{6}$

   $x = \dfrac{7}{3}$ or $x = -1$

2. You have a can of varnish that will cover 3800 in². You want to build a small box with a square base and a height of 10 in. and use the varnish to finish it. What is the side length of the base of the largest box you can build?

   Let s = the measure of the square side. The box has two square bases, each with area s^2, and four rectangular sides, each with area $10s$. The total area of the box is $2s^2 + 4(10s)$. So we must solve the equation $2s^2 + 40s = 3800$.

   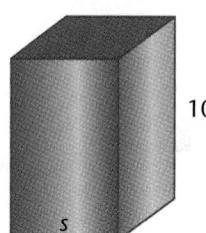

   $2s^2 + 40s - 3800 = 0$ Put the equation into standard form.

   $s = \dfrac{-40 \pm \sqrt{40^2 - 4(2)(-3800)}}{2(2)}$ Apply the quadratic formula with $a = 2$, $b = 40$, and $c = -3800$.

   $s \approx 34.72$ in. or $s \approx -54.72$ in.   Solve for s.

   Since length cannot be negative, the side length of the base should be about 34.72 in.

TRY IT

Use the quadratic formula to solve each equation.

a. $2x^2 - 13x - 15 = 0$ **b.** $3x^2 + 6x + 2 = 0$

c. A falcon enters its dive 800 feet above the ground. Its initial vertical velocity is -50 feet per second. When will it be 300 feet above the ground?

CONSIDER

1. Do all quadratic equations have two different roots? Explain your reasoning.

When you investigated solving quadratic equations by graphing, you saw that not all quadratic equations have real roots. But does this mean that some quadratic equations have no roots at all? Consider the following Example.

3. Find the roots of the equation $2x^2 - 4x + 3 = 0$.

$$x = \frac{-(-4) \pm \sqrt{(-4)^2 - 4(2)(3)}}{2(2)}$$ Apply the Quadratic Formula with $a = 2$, $b = -4$, and $c = 3$.

$$x = \frac{4 \pm \sqrt{16 - 24}}{4}$$ Simplify.

$$x = \frac{4 \pm \sqrt{-8}}{4}$$

$$x = \frac{4}{4} \pm \frac{2i\sqrt{2}}{4}$$ $\sqrt{-8} = 2i\sqrt{2}$

$$x = 1 \pm \frac{1}{2}i\sqrt{2}$$ Simplify.

The roots of the equation are $x = 1 + \frac{1}{2}i\sqrt{2}$ and $x = 1 - \frac{1}{2}i\sqrt{2}$.

These solutions are *complex* numbers. They cannot be "seen" on a graph that shows only real numbers, but they *are* solutions to the equation.

When solving an equation using the quadratic formula, it is important to remember that $-b \pm \sqrt{b^2 - 4ac}$ is *all* divided by $2a$. However, if we think of the quadratic formula as two fractions instead of one, we find an easy way to find the vertex of a quadratic function in $y = ax^2 + bx + c$ form.

$$x = \frac{-b}{2a} + \frac{\sqrt{b^2 - 4ac}}{2a} \text{ or}$$

$$x = \frac{-b}{2a} - \frac{\sqrt{b^2 - 4ac}}{2a}$$

As you can see, $x = -\frac{b}{2a}$ is the line of symmetry of the parabola, and $-\frac{b}{2a}$ is the x-value of its vertex.

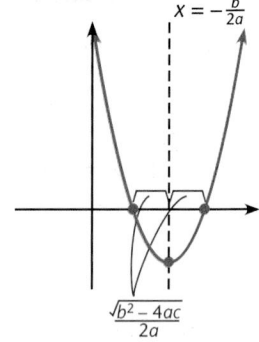

$x = -\frac{b}{2a}$

$\frac{\sqrt{b^2 - 4ac}}{2a}$

Use $x = -\frac{b}{2a}$ to find the vertex of each parabola. Use a graphing utility to check your answer.

d. $y = x^2 - 4x + 6$ **e.** $y = 2x^2 + 7x - 1$

All quadratic equations can be solved using the quadratic formula. The roots of some quadratic equations may involve complex numbers.

1. Discuss the advantages and disadvantages of solving a quadratic equation by using the quadratic formula.

2. If a quadratic equation can be solved by graphing, can the same equation be solved by factoring? by using the quadratic formula? Explain your reasoning.

3. In deriving the quadratic formula in the Explore, we used general coefficients a, b, and c instead of specific numbers. Why was this necessary?

Exercises

CORE

1. Getting Started Follow the steps to solve $2x^2 + 7x + 3 = 0$ using the quadratic formula.

  a. For this equation, $a = \underline{\ \ ?\ \ }$, $b = \underline{\ \ ?\ \ }$, and $c = \underline{\ \ ?\ \ }$.

  b. Substituting these values into the quadratic formula gives:

$$x = \frac{-\underline{\ ?\ } \pm \sqrt{(\underline{\ ?\ })^2 - 4(\underline{\ ?\ })(\underline{\ ?\ })}}{2(\underline{\ ?\ })}$$

  c. Simplify each product and square in this expression.

  d. Simplify the expression under the radical. If possible, simplify the radical itself.

  e. Write the resulting expression as two individual expressions, one using the $+$ from the $\pm$, the other using the $-$. Simplify each as far as possible. These are the solutions of the equation.

Determine whether each statement is true or false. If the statement is false, change the underlined word or phrase to make it true.

2. If a quadratic equation can be solved by factoring, it <u>can</u> be solved by applying the quadratic formula.

3. If an equation can be solved by applying the quadratic formula, you <u>will</u> be able to solve it by factoring.

4. If one of two roots of a quadratic equation is a complex number, the other solution is a <u>real</u> number.

Solve each equation. Leave answers in exact form.

5. $x^2 + 7x + 12 = 0$ **6.** $x^2 + 6x - 1 = 0$ **7.** $x^2 + 8x + 4 = 0$

8. $5m^2 - 8m + 4 = 0$ **9.** $2x^2 - 5x = 4$ **10.** $3b^2 + 3b - 1 = 0$

11. The surface area of a right circular cylinder is given by $SA = 2\pi rh + 2\pi r^2$. What is the radius, rounded to the nearest hundredth, of a right circular cylinder of height 5.5 m and surface area 120 m²?

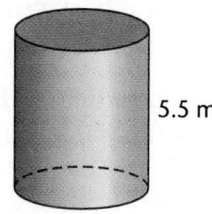

5.5 m

Solve each equation. Where necessary, round answers to the nearest hundredth.

12. $x^2 - 4x - 7 = 0$ **13.** $x^2 + 10x + 25 = 0$

14. $-4.9x^2 + 23.5x + 104 = 0$ **15.** $6k + 11 = k^2$

16. $3x^2 + 5x = 10$ **17.** $0.01x^2 - 0.05x - 0.04 = 0$

18. $x^4 + 2x^2 - 10 = 0$ (Hint: Let $x^2 = z$.)   **19.** $2t^4 - 6t^2 = 7$

20. Brake Time Suppose a car is traveling at a rate of

66 ft/sec (45 mi/hr) when the brakes are applied. The function for the car's position (p) after t seconds is $p(t) = -8.25t^2 + 66t$.
   a. How long will it take the car to travel 120 feet? Round your answer to the nearest tenth.
   b. How long will it take the car to stop? How far will the car have traveled?

21. It's Not the Cold, It's the Chill The *windchill* measures

how cold the temperature feels at different wind speeds. The faster the wind carries away the warm air around your body, the colder you feel.

The windchill (c) at a given temperature is approximately a quadratic function of the wind speed (s). The function $c = 0.028s^2 - 2.52s + 2.7$ models the windchill at 0°F. This is a reasonably good model for wind speeds from 0 to 45 mi/hr.
   a. Graph the windchill function. Explain why the model would not seem reasonable for wind speeds above 45 mi/hr.
   b. Find the wind speeds for windchills of $-10°$, $-20°$, and $-30°$. Round your answers to the nearest tenth.

22. Which equation(s) have the solutions -2 and 3?

   I. $(x + 3)(x - 2) = 0$ II. $(x - 3)(x + 2) = 0$ III. $x^2 - x - 6 = 0$

   (a) only I   (b) only II   (c) only III   (d) I and III   (e) II and III

23. Which equation(s) can be solved by using the quadratic formula?

   I. $3x^2 + 5x + 8 = 0$ II. $3x + 5 = 0$ III. $x^4 - 3x^2 - 5 = 0$

   (a) only I   (b) only II   (c) only III   (d) I and III   (e) I and II

24. The quadratic formula can be used to solve any equation of the form $0 = ax^2 + bx + c$. Is there a *linear* formula that solves all equations in $0 = mx + b$ form? If so, give the formula; if not, explain why not.

25. The length of a side of a triangle exceeds the altitude to that side by 5.1 cm. If the area of the triangle is 14.8 cm², what are its base and altitude?

26. Falconry Suppose that the height, in feet, of a falcon t seconds after it starts

its dive (stoop) toward its prey is modeled by the quadratic function $h(t) = -16t^2 - 53t + 1000$.
   a. To the nearest tenth of a second, how long will it take the falcon to reach a height of 400 feet?
   b. If the falcon has no initial vertical velocity, how much longer will it take to reach a height of 400 feet?

Find the *y*-intercepts for the graph of each equation and explain how you found them.

27. $x = y^2 + 4y - 12$ **28.** $x = y^2 - 5y + 8$

Use $x = \dfrac{-b}{2a}$ to find the vertex of each parabola.

29. $y = x^2 + 12x - 4$ **30.** $y = 3x^2 - 36x + 22$ **31.** $f(x) = -16x^2 - 53x + 1000$

 ## LOOK BACK

32. A die is rolled 18 times, and the results are recorded as shown. [1-2]

  1 5 6 1 2 3 4 2 3 5 1 6 4 3 1 2 6 5

   a. What is the experimental probability of rolling a 1?
   b. What is the theoretical probability of rolling a 1?
   c. How many times would a 1 have been rolled if the experimental probability
      had matched the theoretical probability?

Graph each set of functions on the same set of axes. [5-1]

33. $f(x) = 3x^2$ and $g(x) = -3x^2$ **34.** $f(x) = 4x^2$ and $g(x) = -4x^2 + 10$

35. $f(x) = x^2$, $g(x) = (x - 2)^2$, and $h(x) = (x - 2)^2 - 3$

MORE PRACTICE

Solve each equation. Leave answers in exact form.

36. $x^2 + 12x - 28 = 0$ **37.** $x^2 + 9x + 10 = 0$ **38.** $x^2 - 8x - 4 = 0$

39. $4x^2 + 4x + 1 = 0$ **40.** $5c^2 - 3c + 9 = 0$ **41.** $4x - 2x^2 = 8$

Solve each equation. Where necessary, round answers to the nearest hundredth.

42. $x^2 + 2x - 4 = 0$ **43.** $x^2 = 4x + 5$ **44.** $2x^2 - 3x - 5 = 0$

45. $6x^2 + 13x + 5 = 0$ **46.** $c^4 + 9c^2 + 4 = 0$ **47.** $0.28x^2 - 1.45x + 0.17 = 0$

48. $x^4 - 3x^2 - 6 = 0$ (Hint: Let $x^2 = z$.)

49. $-4.9t^2 + 44.2t + 503 = 0$

50. The area of a trapezoid is given by $A = \dfrac{b_1 + b_2}{2}h$,
where b_1 and b_2 are the lengths of the bases and h is
the height. The area of this trapezoid is 255.8 m².
Find its height and the length of the unknown base.

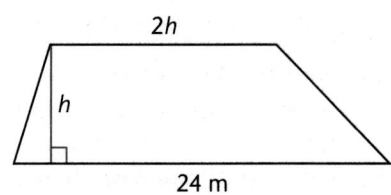

51. The Sound of Money A music store finds that its annual revenue from cassette
tapes (R) is approximately equal to the function:

$R = -6{,}800p^2 + 130{,}000p$

where p is the price of the tapes. Find the prices for which the store's annual
revenue from cassette tapes would be $600,000.

MORE MATH REASONING

52. A Hooded Stove You are designing the ventilation hood for a restaurant's stove. The hood is to be made by cutting squares from the corners of a piece of sheet metal, then folding the corners and welding them together. The piece of sheet metal is 5 ft wide. The length of the finished hood should be 9 ft, and its volume must be 22 ft³. The height of the hood should not exceed 1 ft.

a. Let h = the length of the square cut. Write and solve a quadratic equation representing the volume inside the hood.

b. What are the length and width of the original piece of sheet metal and the side length of the square cut, accurate to 0.1 inch?

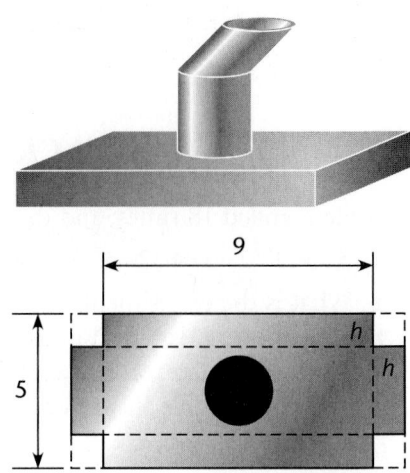

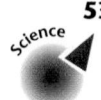

53. (your name here) Saves the Day! A mild-mannered student by day, you assume your secret superhero identity by night. Your sidekick has spotted a gang of jewel thieves on the roof of a building 100 feet away. The building is 240 feet tall and 100 feet wide. You plan to fire a hook with a rope attached to it onto the roof of the building, climb to the top, and capture the thieves.

a. The vertical velocity setting of your hook-firing bazooka is jammed at 128 feet per second! Will the hook go high enough to reach the top of the building?

b. Fortunately, your horizontal velocity control is still operating. Since gravity does not affect horizontal motion, the horizontal velocity of the hook does not change much during its flight. Write a function for the distance covered by the hook in terms of time and horizontal velocity.

c. You must set the horizontal velocity so that the hook lands on the roof. For what range of horizontal velocities will your hook land on the roof of the building? Explain how you found your answer.

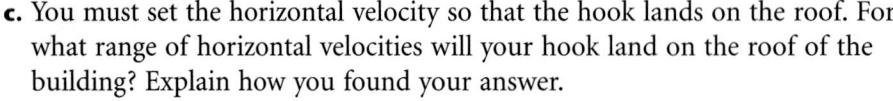

54. The Right Price The MathFun Corporation sells 40,000 software packages at a price of $60 each. Research shows that every $5 increase in the price decreases the demand for this software by 8000 units.

a. Write an equation modeling the demand for this software in terms of its price.

b. Write an equation modeling the revenue from this software.

c. MathFun plans to earn $2.5 million in revenue from this software. Find the minimum and maximum selling price.

Classifying Solutions

← **C O N N E C T** → *You have found the roots of a quadratic equation by applying the quadratic formula, and have seen that they may be complex numbers. Now you will see a way to quickly determine the nature of these roots without solving the equation.*

In solving real-world problems, we are usually looking for real solutions. All quadratic equations have solutions; however, these solutions are not always real numbers. In the Explore, you will discover a quick way to determine the nature of the roots of a quadratic equation.

EXPLORE: IDENTIFICATION, PLEASE

MATERIALS

Graphing utility

1. Use the quadratic formula to solve each equation in the table. Record the value of $b^2 - 4ac$ and the value or values of the roots. Then describe the nature of the solutions as shown below.

Equation	$b^2 - 4ac$	Roots	Description
$2x^2 + 9x + 7 = 0$	25	$x = -3.5$ or -1	two real numbers
$2x^2 + 9x + 11 = 0$			
$x^2 - 6x + 9 = 0$			
$-2x^2 + 8x + 24 = 0$			
$-x^2 + 6x - 10 = 0$			
$3x^2 + 12x + 12 = 0$			
$x^2 + 4x + 8 = 0$			
$5x^2 + 2x - 10 = 0$			

2. When the solutions to a quadratic equation are not real numbers, do they show any special relationship to each other?

3. Describe any patterns that you find in your table. How can you use the value of $b^2 - 4ac$ to predict the nature of the roots of a quadratic equation?

4. Graph the function $f(x) = ax^2 + bx + c$ for each equation $0 = ax^2 + bx + c$ in the table. How do the graphs of the functions relate to the roots of the equations?

The **discriminant** of a quadratic equation is the quantity $b^2 - 4ac$ (the number under the square root sign). The value of the discriminant of a quadratic equation can tell us a great deal about its solutions.

CONSIDER

1. Explain why there is one real root to a quadratic equation whose discriminant is 0.

EXAMPLES

1. Without solving, determine the nature of the roots of $3x^2 - 7x + 10 = 0$. For this quadratic equation, $a = 3$, $b = -7$, and $c = 10$. The value of the discriminant is:

$$(-7)^2 - 4(3)(10) = 49 - 120 = -71$$

Since the value of the discriminant is negative, the equation has two complex conjugate roots.

2. Write a quadratic equation that has two different real solutions.

A quadratic equation in standard form has two real number solutions when $b^2 - 4ac > 0$. Choose any values of a and c, then find a value of b that satisfies this inequality.

For instance, use $a = 2$ and $c = 10$.

$b^2 - 4ac > 0$
$b^2 - 4(2)(10) > 0$ Substitute $a = 2$ and $c = 10$.
$b^2 - 80 > 0$
$b^2 > 80$

A value of b whose square is greater than 80 is $b = 9$. Use these a, b, and c values to write an equation.

$2x^2 + 9x + 10 = 0$ has two real solutions.

TRY IT

Without solving, determine the nature of the roots of each equation.

a. $-4x^2 - 3x + 5 = 0$
b. $x^2 + 16 = 8x$

c. Write a quadratic equation that has two complex conjugate roots.

We can use the discriminant to check whether a real-world problem has meaningful solutions before solving the problem.

EXAMPLE

3. One cost of operating a car is a function of its speed. When speeds are low, the engine operates inefficiently; when they are high, it must work to overcome wind resistance. So a quadratic model is a reasonable one to relate speed to cost per mile.

Suppose *Road Rider* magazine collects data on a new car, the Constellation, and fits a mathematical model to the results. The Constellation's cost of operation, in cents per mile, is related to its operating speed by the quadratic model:

$$M = \frac{1}{64}S^2 - \frac{3}{2}S + 72$$

Dave wants to buy a car with operating costs of not more than 32¢ a mile. Are there speeds where the Constellation has an operating cost of 32¢ per mile? First, write an equation.

$\frac{1}{64}S^2 - \frac{3}{2}S + 72 = 32$ 　　　　Cost desired is 32¢ per mile.

$\frac{1}{64}S^2 - \frac{3}{2}S + 40 = 0$ 　　　　Rewrite the equation in standard form.

Then, investigate the discriminant.

$b^2 - 4ac = \left(-\frac{3}{2}\right)^2 - 4\left(\frac{1}{64}\right)(40)$ 　　　$a = \frac{1}{64},\ b = -\frac{3}{2},\ c = 40$

$= \frac{9}{4} - \frac{160}{64} = \frac{9}{4} - \frac{10}{4} = -\frac{1}{4}$ 　　　Evaluate the discriminant.

Since the discriminant is negative, there is no real solution, and there is no way to operate the Constellation for 32¢ a mile. Dave needs to look at other cars.

As the $\pm$ sign in the quadratic formula implies, quadratic equations generally have two solutions. When the discriminant is zero, however, the "+ version" and the "− version" of the roots are equal, and there is only one solution to the quadratic equation.

So that we can say that a quadratic equation *always* has two solutions, we call the single solution a **double root.**

Discriminant is:	Solution	Graph
Positive	Two real roots	
Negative	Two complex conjugate roots	
Zero	One real root (a double root)	

2. A quadratic function whose graph does not intersect the *x*-axis still has zeros. Explain how this is possible, given that its graph shows no points where *y* = 0.

By evaluating the discriminant of a quadratic equation, you can determine whether it has real roots and, if so, how many. This information can be very helpful in analyzing real-world problems.

REFLECT

1. What information can the discriminant of a quadratic equation $0 = ax^2 + bx + c$ give you about the graph of its related function $f(x) = ax^2 + bx + c$?

2. Explain why complex-number solutions of a quadratic equation are always conjugates of each other.

3. Suppose you model a real-world problem with a quadratic equation. Using the discriminant, you find that the equation has two real-number roots. Does this necessarily mean that the problem has two meaningful answers? Explain why or why not.

Exercises

CORE

1. Getting Started Copy and complete the table.

Quadratic Function	Number of Real Zeros	Is the Discriminant $b^2 - 4ac = 0, < 0, \text{ or } > 0$?
a.		
b.		
c.		

2. Sketch the graph of a quadratic function with no real zeros.

3. Sketch the graph of a quadratic function whose discriminant is positive and whose vertex is in the second quadrant.

Without solving, determine the nature of the roots of each quadratic equation.

4. $x^2 + 2x + 3 = 0$ **5.** $3x^2 + 4x + 2 = 0$ **6.** $0.12x^2 + x + 2.7 = 0$

7. $x^2 - 6x + 5 = 0$ **8.** $x^2 - 6x + 9 = 0$ **9.** $w^2 - 2w + 13 = 0$

Write a quadratic equation that has each of the following types of solutions.

10. two real solutions

11. two complex conjugate solutions

12. one real solution

13. Consider $f(x) = -6x^2 + 7x - 2$. For what values of x is $y = 0$? For what values of x is $y < 0$? $y > 0$?

Find the number of zeros of each function.

14. $y = x^2 + 5x - 6$ **15.** $y = 2x^2 - 12x + 7$ **16.** $f(x) = 3x^2 + 5x + 1$

17. $y = 5x^2 - 3x + 9$ **18.** $h(t) = -4.9t^2 + 40t + 500$ **19.** $y = \frac{1}{2}x^2 - \frac{3}{4}x + \frac{2}{5}$

20. Which function could represent the graph? Explain how you found your answer.
  (a) $y = x^2 - 3x + 4$
  (b) $y = -x^2 - 3x + 4$
  (c) $y = x^2 - 3x - 4$
  (d) $y = -x^2 - 3x - 4$

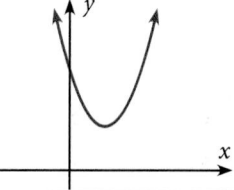

21. Sketch the graph of a quadratic function that opens upward and whose discriminant is positive.

22. Sketch the graph of a quadratic function that opens downward and whose discriminant is negative.

23. Explain why a quadratic equation whose discriminant is negative has two complex conjugate roots.

Use the discriminant to determine whether each of the following has at least one real-number answer. If it does not, say so and explain how you can tell. If it does, find the solution.

24. A football is kicked upward with an initial vertical velocity of 63 ft/sec. If the football stadium is 70 feet tall, at what times will the football be the same height as the top of the stadium?

25. A company's profit (P) depends on the number of items it produces (n) according to $P = -0.02n^2 + 250n$. What number of items should it produce to make a profit of $500,000?

26. It's Not Worth the Wait Suppose that a restaurant finds that the probability (p) that a customer who puts her name on the waiting list will be present when her name is called can be modeled by a quadratic function. The function is $p = \frac{1}{1600}t^2 - \frac{1}{20}t + 1$, where $t =$ the number of minutes until the name is called.

a. What waiting time will result in a 50% chance of the customer leaving the restaurant before her name is called?

b. What domain makes sense for this mathematical model? Why?

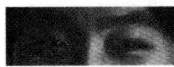 **LOOK AHEAD**

27. In your own words, give definitions for a *circle* and an *ellipse*.

28. Consider the equation $x^2 + y^2 = 4$. Give *all* real y-values that satisfy the equation when:

a. $x = 0$ **b.** $x = 1$ **c.** $x = 2$ **d.** $x = \sqrt{2}$

29. Solve $x^2 + y^2 = 4$ for y.

MORE PRACTICE

Without solving, determine the nature of the roots of each quadratic equation.

30. $9x^2 + 6x + 1 = 0$ **31.** $1.5x - x^2 = 0.7$ **32.** $2b^2 + 5b = 1$

33. $4y^2 = 15 - 7y$ **34.** $3x^2 - 27 = 0$ **35.** $m^2 - \frac{2}{3}m + 13 = 0$

Find the number of zeros of each function.

36. $y = x^2 + 7x - 6$ **37.** $y = 4x^2 - 29x + 83$ **38.** $f(x) = 9x^2 - 12x + 4$

39. $f(x) = 3x^2 - 5x + 7$ **40.** $h(t) = -4.9t^2 + 17.9t + 309$ **41.** $y = 0.03x^2 - 0.8x - 9.1$

42. Sketch the graph of a quadratic function that opens downward and whose discriminant is zero.

43. Sketch the graph of a quadratic function that opens upward and whose discriminant is positive.

Use the discriminant to determine whether each of the following has at least one real-number answer. If it does not, say so and explain how you can tell. If it does, find the solution.

44. A swimming pool is 20 ft wide and 30 ft long. It is surrounded by a concrete walkway that is x feet wide. The area of the walkway is 216 ft². What is the width of the walkway?

45. A flea jumps up with an initial vertical velocity of 2 m/sec. When will the flea be 1 m off the ground?

Science

MORE MATH REASONING

46. In *History of Mathematics, Vol. II*, David E. Smith mentions that several solutions of quadratic equations exist from Indian sources. Bhāskara (ca. 1150) quotes another Hindu mathematician, Srīdhara (ca. 1025), as having presented the following method. Assume that the initial equation is in the form $ax^2 + bx = c$.

"Multiply both sides of the equation by a number equal to four times the [coefficient of the] square, and add to them a number equal to the square of the original [coefficient of the] unknown quantity. [Then extract the root.]"

a. Begin with the original equation. Show the two steps prescribed by Srīdhara. Take the square root of both sides, then solve for x.

b. How and why does your solution differ from the quadratic formula? Is it accurate?

c. How do Srīdhara's first two steps in the solution process help solve the equation?

d. Hindu mathematics in Srīdhara's time produced only one root of a quadratic equation. Where in the solution process would the omission of the second root most likely occur?

47. For the general quadratic function $f(x) = ax^2 + bx + c$:

a. Use the quadratic formula to derive the sum of its zeros. What is the product of the zeros?

b. Without solving, what are the sum and product of the zeros of $y = 6x^2 + 9x + 1$?

c. Write a quadratic function whose zeros have a sum of 9 and a product of 20.

48. Just Imagine! Using two sheets of graph paper, you can create a visual model of the quadratic function $y = x^2 + 4$ and its imaginary zeros.

a. Find the zeros of $y = x^2 + 4$.

b. On one sheet of graph paper, sketch the graph of $y = x^2 + 4$ using real values, $x = a$, for instance, $x = 2$. Then set up an *imaginary plane* on the other grid and sketch the graph of $y = x^2 + 4$ using imaginary values, $x = bi$, for instance, $x = -1i$.

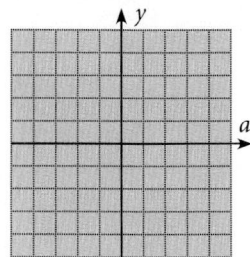

Real plane

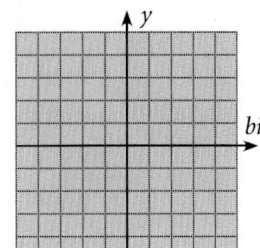

Imaginary plane

c. Cut one grid along the positive half of the y-axis and the other along the negative half. Then join the planes at right angles. Describe the 3-dimensional graph of $y = x^2 + 4$ you have created. Where are the zeros of this function located? Do you think you could graph the function for complex values of x that *aren't* real or imaginary? Explain.

← CONNECT → *You have investigated quadratic equations and have found their solutions by graphing, factoring, and applying the quadratic formula.*

Quadratic equations can help solve real-world problems. Physicists need to solve quadratic equations as they study projectile motion.

You have been told that the equations for free fall on Earth are:

$h(t) = -4.9t^2 + v_0t + h_0$ (height in meters)

$h(t) = -16t^2 + v_0t + h_0$ (height in feet)

Both of these come from the theoretical equation $h(t) = -\frac{1}{2}gt^2 + v_0t + h_0$. The values -4.9 and -16 represent $\frac{1}{2}$ of the acceleration due to gravity on Earth's surface, about 9.8 m/sec² (32 ft/sec²). But where did these numbers come from? In the Explore, you will approximate one of these values through an experiment.

EXPLORE: HAVE A NICE FALL

MATERIALS

Stopwatch
Coin or other small object
Meterstick

To find the value of g in the free-fall equation $h(t) = -\frac{1}{2}gt^2 + v_0t + h_0$, you can perform a simple experiment.

1. Drop an object with very little wind resistance, such as a coin, from several different heights. Use your stopwatch to measure the time it takes to fall. Record your results in a table.

2. Take the values for time and height from your first experiment. By substituting these values for t and h_0 into $0 = -\frac{1}{2}gt^2 + v_0t + h_0$, you can write an equation whose only unknown is g. Solve this equation for g.

3. Repeat Step 2 using your time and height data for each experiment. Then average your values for g. How close is your experimental value to the theoretical value?

4. Describe some possible sources of error in your experiment. Given these, would you expect your experimental value for g to be larger or smaller than the theoretical value? Explain.

1. Write a short paragraph discussing the strengths and weaknesses of solving a quadratic equation by graphing, factoring, or using the quadratic formula.
2. How many solutions does a quadratic equation have? What can the discriminant of the equation tell you about its solutions?
3. Give a brief definition of each term.
   a. quadratic *function*   **b.** quadratic *equation*   **c.** quadratic *formula*

Self-Assessment

1. Which of the functions does the graph represent?
   (a) $y = \frac{1}{2}(x + 1)(x - 2)$ (b) $y = \frac{1}{2}(x - 7)(x + 3)$
   (c) $y = -\frac{1}{12}(x + 7)(x - 3)$ (d) $y = -x^2 + 4x - 4$

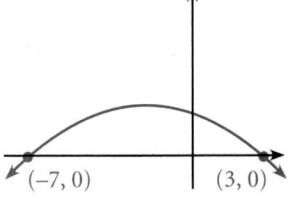

2. Which of the following methods can be used to find the exact values of the zeros of any quadratic function: graphing, factoring, or using the quadratic formula?

Use the graph of the related function to solve each equation. Estimate answers where necessary. If an equation appears to have no real solutions, say so.

3. $(x - 1)^2 - 4 = 0$ 4. $-3x^2 = -20$ 5. $2x^2 - 7x = 10$

6. Graph the function $f(x) = (x - 4)(x + 2)$. Determine the equation of another quadratic function with the same zeros and a maximum value of 20.

Simplify each expression. [4-3]

7. $(9 - 3i) + (2 - 12i)$ 8. $(6 - 4i) - (7 - 5i)$

9. i^{62} 10. $(1 + 2i)(8 - 11i)$

Graph each set of functions on the same set of axes. [5-1]

11. $f(x) = 2x^2$ and $g(x) = -2x^2$ 12. $f(x) = 5x^2$ and $g(x) = -5(x - 3)^2$

13. $f(x) = x^2$, $g(x) = -(x + 3)^2$, and $h(x) = -(x + 3)^2 - 6$

14. You are interested in the function $y = -0.32x^2 + 1.908x + 3.666$. For each application below, which solution method would you choose: graphing, factoring, using the quadratic formula, or checking the discriminant? Write a sentence to explain your choice.
    a. You need to know whether a positive solution exists when $y = 7.2$.
    b. You need to find the values of the zeros of the function.
    c. A friend working on a physics experiment has derived this function. She needs a quick confirmation that it actually does have real zeros.

Solve each equation. Where necessary, round your answers to the nearest tenth. Explain your choice of solution technique.

15. $x^2 + 6x + 8 = 0$

16. $4x^2 - 8 = 0$

17. $2b^2 + 5b = 3$

18. $-4.9t^2 + 88t + 15 = 212$

19. $2.8x(x - \pi) = 0$

20. $\frac{1}{3}x^2 + \frac{2}{3}x + \frac{1}{3} = 0$

21. The product of two consecutive even integers is 728. What are the integers?

22. Find the y-intercepts of $x = 2y^2 + 3y - 5$. Explain your method.

Solve each equation. Leave answers in exact form.

23. $x^2 + 4x - 11 = 0$

24. $2x^2 - 9x = 15$

25. $-16t^2 + 80t = 64$

26. What values may k assume for $f(x) = 4x^2 + kx + 5$ to have real zeros? Explain how you found these values.

27. Drop That Ball A ball is dropped from a height of 1000 feet. One second later a second ball is dropped from a height of 75 feet. Which ball hits the ground first? Is it easier to solve this problem using a graphing utility or by using the quadratic formula? Explain your choice.

Without solving, determine the nature of the roots of each quadratic equation.

28. $3x^2 - 4x - 2 = 0$

29. $x^2 + 2x = -3$

30. $6(x^2 - 1) = x + 20$

31. $2.4x^2 + 9.12x - 7.8 = 0$

32. Recall the formula $h(t) = -16t^2 - 53t + 1000$ for the height of a falcon during a stoop.
  a. Find the times when the height of the falcon is:
    i. 500 feet
    ii. 250 feet
    iii. 75 feet.
  b. An object is dropped from a plane so its initial velocity is 0 and its initial height is h_0. Find h_0 so that the height of the object matches the height of the falcon throughout its dive. Explain how you found this height.

33. In about 825 A.D., Mohammed ibn Musa al-Khowarizmi used this figure to solve the quadratic equation $x^2 + px = q$.
  a. How long is a side of the largest square? What is its area?
  b. Explain why the total unshaded area is q.
  c. Write an equation stating that the area of the large square is the same as q plus the total area of the shaded squares. Take the positive square root of both sides, and then solve for x. Why do you think al-Khowarizmi would only find the positive root of the equation?
  d. Using the equation you derived with al-Khowarizmi's method, find the positive root of $x^2 + 8x = 11$.

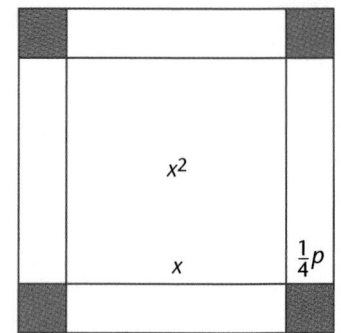

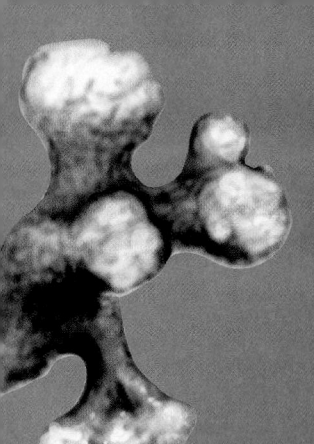

Shocking News

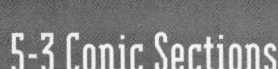

A kidney stone is a mass of mineral salts that accumulates in the kidneys. Until recently, anyone who had a kidney stone that would not pass and needed removal had to undergo a major operation. Now, thousands of kidney stone operations are avoided because of a new technique, called kidney stone lithotripsy. Lithotripsy was developed in Germany and accepted for use in the United States in 1984. The lithotripter produces electronic shock waves that pulverize the stones into small fragments.

In lithotripsy, the reflective property of the ellipse is used to direct the shock waves. Because your body has the same acoustical properties as water, your body is not hurt by the shock waves. Moreover, lithotripsy involves no radiation. Complications such as bleeding, infection, or reactions to drugs, which may occur with other methods, are avoided.

During the procedure, the patient lies in a tub of water, with an elliptical ring positioned so that the kidney stone is located at one focus point inside the ellipse and the transmitter at the other focus point. The shock waves are reflected off the sides of the ring at different places. But they are all reflected back to a single point—the other focus. The concentrated energy of the shock waves blasts the kidney stone. It may take as many as 2000 shocks over 30 minutes to break a stone into sand-sized particles.

1. What are some of the advantages of undergoing lithotripsy rather than a surgical procedure?
2. Draw a diagram of the lithotripsy procedure and the possible path of the shock waves.
3. Why do you think a circular tub is not used in lithotripsy?

← CONNECT →   *You have investigated parabolas, which are graphs of a particular type of quadratic relation. Now you will investigate the graph and equation for a different type of quadratic relation—the circle.*

The four curves known as **conic sections** can be generated by shining a flashlight on a wall.

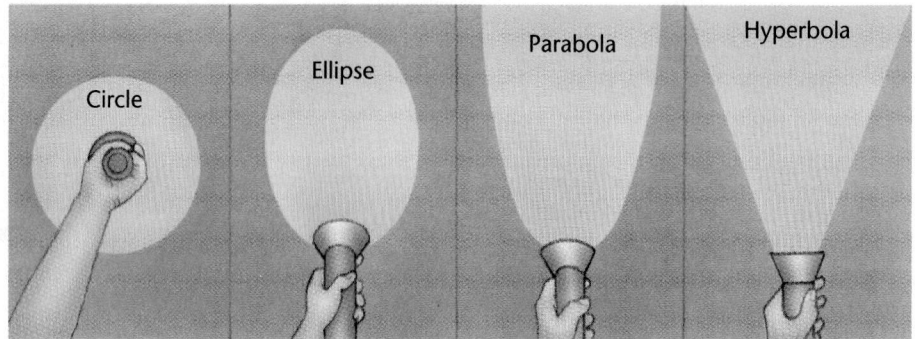

As you will see, each conic section is the graph of a quadratic relation. (Recall that a relation is any set of ordered pairs.) However, each conic section also has a geometric definition that involves distances.

You've already seen your first conic section. A parabola can be generated by graphing $y = ax^2 + bx + c$. In 5-1E, you found that a parabola can also be made by finding the set of points in a plane equidistant from a point and a line.

Since distances are important in the study of conic sections, we review the formula for the distance between two points on a coordinate plane.

The distance between two points on a coordinate plane whose coordinates are (x_1, y_1) and (x_2, y_2) is:

$$D = \sqrt{(x_1 - x_2)^2 + (y_1 - y_2)^2}$$

TRY IT

Find the distance between each pair of points.

a. $(1, 3)$ and $(4, 7)$ **b.** $(-1, -4)$ and $(-3, 2)$ **c.** $(0, 0)$ and $(6, -9)$

CONSIDER

1. What geometric theorem is related to the distance formula? Explain the relationship.

MATERIALS

Graph paper
Compass
Ruler

The diatom is a microscopic sea plant. Some diatoms are approximately circular.

1. Place graph paper over the enlargement of the diatom. Draw the axes so that the origin (0, 0) is in the middle of the circle.

2. Find the distance from the origin to several points on the circle. What do you notice? What is this distance called?

3. Using the distance formula, write an equation that shows that the distance from (0, 0) to a general point (x, y) is the distance you found in Step 2. Simplify your expression.

4. Square both sides of your equation. Describe your result. How is the constant term related to the radius of the circle?

5. Will the coordinates of any point on the circle satisfy your equation from Step 4? Explain.

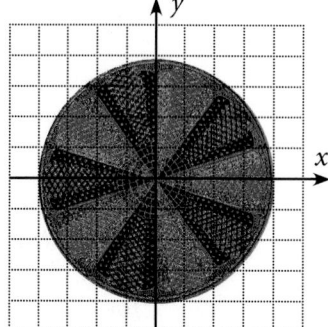

A **circle** is the set (*locus*) of points in a plane equidistant from a given point. The point is the **center** of the circle and the distance is the **radius.**

Suppose the center of a circle is located at (0, 0) and *r* is the radius. Let *P*(x, y) be any point on the circle. The distance from (x, y) to (0, 0) is equal to the radius *r*, so:

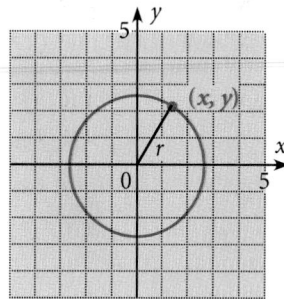

$$\sqrt{(x - 0)^2 + (y - 0)^2} = r$$ Use the distance formula.

$$\sqrt{x^2 + y^2} = r$$ Simplify.

$$x^2 + y^2 = r^2$$ Square both sides.

The **standard form** of the equation of a circle with radius *r* and center (0, 0) is $x^2 + y^2 = r^2$.

---

1. Sketch the circle whose equation is
$x^2 + y^2 = 36$.
The center of the circle is $(0, 0)$. Since $r^2 = 36$, the radius of the circle is 6. Some of the points that are 6 units away from the center are $(0, 6)$, $(6, 0)$, $(0, -6)$, and $(-6, 0)$. Plot these points and draw a smooth curve that connects them.

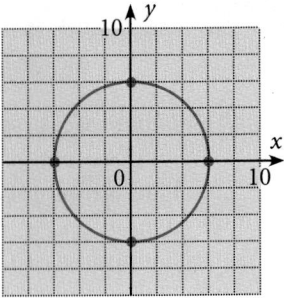

Suppose that the center of a circle is not at the origin. Is it possible to write an equation for the circle?

The center of the circle is $(2, 1)$ and its radius is 3. So the distance from any point (x, y) on the circle to its center $(2, 1)$ is 3. Using the distance formula:

$\sqrt{(x - 2)^2 + (y - 1)^2} = 3$

$(x - 2)^2 + (y - 1)^2 = 9$ Square both sides.

The equation of the circle is
$(x - 2)^2 + (y - 1)^2 = 9$.

Notice that the center of the circle $(2, 1)$ appears in the equation!

> The **standard form** of the equation of a circle with radius r and center (h, k) is $(x - h)^2 + (y - k)^2 = r^2$.

TRY IT

Write an equation for each circle in standard form.

d. center $(0, 0)$ and radius 2   **e.** center $(0, 0)$ and radius $\sqrt{5}$
f. center $(3, 4)$ and radius 7   **g.** center $(-2, -1)$ and radius $\sqrt{3}$

EXAMPLE

2. The equation $x^2 + 4x + y^2 - 8y = 5$ is an equation for a circle. Write it in standard form.

To convert this form of the equation to standard form, we must complete the square in x and y.

$(x^2 + 4x) + (y^2 - 8y) = 5$

$(x^2 + 4x + 4) + (y^2 - 8y + 16) = 5 + 4 + 16$ Complete the square in x by adding $\left(\frac{4}{2}\right)^2$; in y by adding $\left(\frac{-8}{2}\right)^2$.

$(x + 2)^2 + (y - 4)^2 = 25$ Factor and simplify.

Graph each equation.

h. $x^2 + y^2 = 121$

i. $16x^2 + 16y^2 = 32$

j. $(x - 2)^2 + (y + 1)^2 = 50$

k. $x^2 - 2x + y^2 + 6y = 39$

You can use a graphing utility to graph conic sections. However, you may have to rewrite the equations before you can enter them into the graphing utility. This is because the equations of most conic sections are relations, not functions.

CONSIDER

2. Explain why the equation for a circle is a quadratic relation. Tell why the equation is *quadratic,* and why it is not a function.

EXAMPLE

3. On a graphing utility, graph the circle whose equation is $x^2 + y^2 = 25$.

A circle is not a function, but it is made up of two semicircles, each of which can be described as a function. To do this, you must first solve the equation for y.

$$x^2 + y^2 = 25$$
$$y^2 = 25 - x^2 \qquad \text{Subtract } x^2 \text{ from both sides.}$$
$$y = \pm\sqrt{25 - x^2} \qquad \text{Take the square root of both sides.}$$

Enter $y = -\sqrt{25 - x^2}$ and $y = \sqrt{25 - x^2}$ into the calculator.

The graph on your screen may appear to be an oval, even though it is actually a circle. This is because the spacing between units on the axes is not consistent. Some calculators have a SQUARE option that will adjust the axes for you.

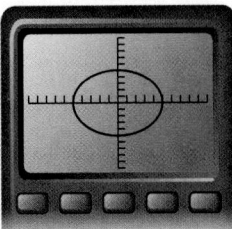
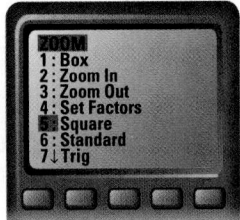
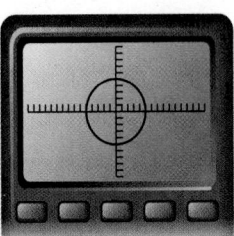

The standard-form equation for a circle comes directly from the distance formula. If you forget the standard form, you can apply the distance formula or Pythagorean Theorem to derive it.

1. How is the standard form of the equation of a circle similar to the $y = (x - h)^2 + k$ form of the equation for a parabola?

2. Monica said, "The standard form for the equation of a circle is just its definition translated into algebra." Is she correct? Explain.

3. Suppose that you are given the equation of a circle. If you know the coordinates of a point, how can you determine whether it lies on the circle, inside the circle, or outside the circle?

4. Are the two standard forms of the equations of a circle actually different? Explain your answer.

Exercises

CORE

1. **Getting Started** Determine the center and radius of each circle whose equation is given.

   a. $x^2 + y^2 = 169$ **b.** $(x - 9)^2 + (y - 3)^2 = 49$

   c. $4x^2 + 4y^2 = 1$ **d.** $(x - 1)^2 + (y + 5)^2 = 25$

Write an equation for each circle in standard form.

2.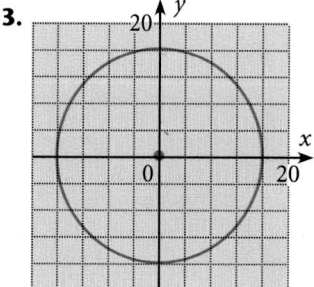

3.

4.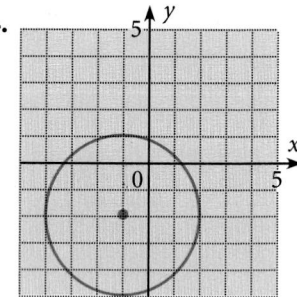

Graph each equation.

5. $x^2 + y^2 = 25$ 6. $x^2 + y^2 = 1$ 7. $(x - 2)^2 + (y - 5)^2 = 4$

8. $2x^2 + 2y^2 = 98$ 9. $x^2 + y^2 = 60$ 10. $4x^2 + 4y^2 - 32 = 0$

Write an equation for a circle with center (0, 0) and the given radius. Then sketch a graph of the circle.

11. $r = 2$ 12. $r = 5$ 13. $r = 9$

14. **A Revolutionary Equation** Earth's orbit around the sun is nearly circular. The radius of the orbit is approximately 9.3×10^7 mi. If the center of the sun is located at (0, 0), write an equation for the orbit of Earth around the sun.

Find the distance between each pair of points. Where necessary, round answers to the nearest hundredth.

15. $(3.2, 7.1)$ and $(-4.5, 6.8)$ **16.** $(3, -8)$ and $(11, -12)$ **17.** $(-1, 6)$ and $(4, -2)$

Write an equation for a circle with center (0, 0) that contains the given point. Then sketch a graph of the circle.

18. $(2, 4)$ **19.** $(-3, 5)$ **20.** $(-4, -3)$

21. The design for an archery target is drawn with circles of radius 4.8 in., 9.6 in., 14.4 in., 19.2 in., and 24 in.
  a. Write a set of equations to model these circles.
  b. What is the probability that an arrow that hits the target randomly lands:
    i. in the bull's-eye (center circle)?
    ii. in the outermost ring?

Write an equation for each circle in standard form.

22. center $(7, 3)$ and radius $\sqrt{2}$ **23.** center at $(-3, 3)$ and radius 4

24. center $(0, 0)$ and containing $(-6, 1)$ **25.** center $(2, 5)$ and containing $(5, 1)$

26. Supernova When a dying star collapses, the pressure and heat generated cause a massive explosion, called a *supernova*. The light produced by this explosion travels from the supernova in all directions at the speed of light, about 300,000 km/sec. Consider a coordinate plane with the supernova located at the origin.
  a. Write an equation for the outer edge of the light from the supernova 10 sec after the explosion.
  b. Write an equation for the outer edge of the light 50 sec after the explosion.
  c. Write an equation for the outer edge of the light n sec after the explosion.
  d. Suppose we do not simply look at one plane. What is the "shape" of the outer edge of the light from the supernova? Explain your answer.

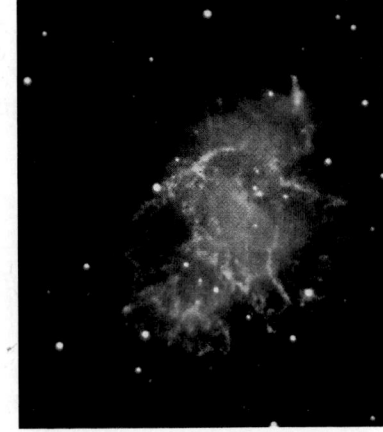

The Crab Nebula is believed to be the remains of a supernova.

Write an equation for each circle in standard form. Then state the center and radius of the circle.

27. $x^2 - 6x + y^2 = 0$ **28.** $x^2 + y^2 + 4y = 5$

29. $2x^2 + 16x + 2y^2 + 4y = 8$ **30.** $x^2 + 5x + y^2 - 9y = 6$

Graph each inequality.

31. $x^2 + y^2 \leq 10$ **32.** $(x - 3)^2 + (y + 1)^2 > 4$

33. Go Fish! The artist M. C. Escher based the art piece *Six Fish Pattern* on a circular pattern. Write equations for the circle that borders the art and the four circles that intersect the four central fish. Assume the center of the pattern is (0, 0) and its radius = 1.

34. A Circular City The Roman poet Virgil wrote a story about Queen Dido. After Queen Dido's brother killed her husband, she fled to Africa, where she begged King Iarbus for land. The king did not want to give her much land, so the queen requested only the land she could enclose with the hide of an ox. King Iarbus granted her request. The queen cut the ox hide into very thin strips, then used the strips to form a circle. According to this story, her circular city became the great city of Carthage, near what is now Tunis.

a. Suppose that the total length of the oxhide strips was 7 miles. Find the area of Queen Dido's city. Then write an equation that models its boundary.

b. Explain why Queen Dido arranged the strips in a circle instead of using some other figure.

LOOK BACK

Write a formula for the *n*th term of each sequence. [4-1 and 4-2]

35. 1, 4, 7, 10, …   **36.** $-2, 4, -8, 16, …$ **37.** 81, 27, 9, 3, …

Solve each equation. Where necessary, round your answers to the nearest tenth. [5-2]

38. $x^2 - 2x - 5 = 0$ **39.** $k^2 - 10k + 30 = 0$ **40.** $d^2 - d - 1 = 0$ **41.** $2n^2 - 8n - 3 = 0$

MORE PRACTICE

Write an equation for each circle in standard form.

42.
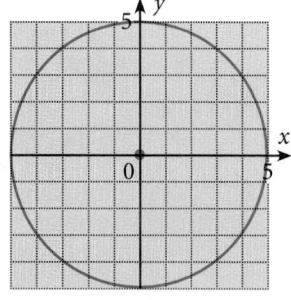

43.
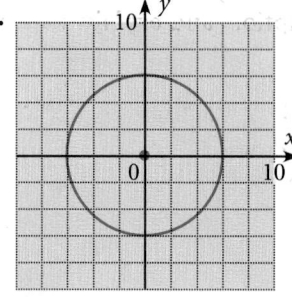

44.
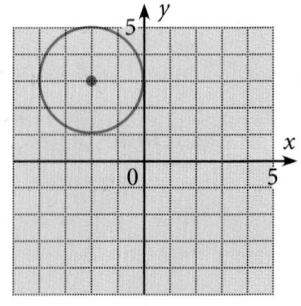

Find the distance between each pair of points. Where necessary, round answers to the nearest hundredth.

45. $(4, 2)$ and $(-7, 2)$

46. $(-12, -20)$ and $(-5, 4)$

47. $(2.3, -3.4)$ and $(8.7, 2.6)$

48. $(-1.9, 8)$ and $(9.1, -6)$

Solve each equation for y. (Hint: Your equation should have a ± sign.) Then graph each circle on a graphing utility. Sketch your result, and state your window for x and y.

49. $x^2 + y^2 = 16$

50. $x^2 + y^2 = 121$

51. $x^2 + y^2 = 225$

52. $3x^2 + 3y^2 = 75$

53. $5x^2 + 5y^2 - 85 = 0$

54. $x^2 + y^2 = 20$

Write an equation for each circle in standard form. Then state the center and radius of the circle.

55. $x^2 + y^2 + 10y = 0$

56. $3x^2 + 9x + 3y^2 - 12y = 0$

57. $x^2 + 6x + y^2 - 2y = 14$

58. $x^2 - 8x + y^2 = 9$

59. $x^2 - 7x + y^2 + 11y = 20$

60. $x^2 + x + y^2 - 5y = \frac{1}{2}$

61. Circular Crops You may have seen circular fields while flying in an airplane. These fields are watered by *central pivot irrigation,* where sprinklers rotate around a pivot in a circular pattern.

a. Suppose that the line of sprinklers turning around the central pivot is 0.25 mi long. Write an equation to model the circular boundary of the field. Assume that the central pivot is at $(0, 0)$.

b. Use a graphing utility to graph this circle. If you are on the edge of the field and your y-coordinate is 0.2, what is your x-coordinate? Explain how you found your answer.

MORE MATH REASONING

62. Plot each set of points and draw a triangle. By guess-and-check, find an equation for a circle that contains the three vertices. Then find an equation for a circle that is tangent to the three sides of the triangle.
  a. $(-3, 0)$, $(12, 0)$, $(9, 9)$ **b.** $(3, 2)$, $(3, -10)$, $(0, 0)$ **c.** $(-3, 5)$, $(7, 8)$, $(4, -2)$

63. What does the graph of $(x - 10)^2 + (y + 3)^2 + (z - 8)^2 = 25$ look like? Be as specific as you can in your description, and explain your reasoning.

64. a. Solve $x^2 + y^2 = r^2$ for y.
  b. Use your result from **a** to write an equation for a semicircle that is the top half of a circle whose center is $(0, 0)$ and radius is r.
  c. Write an equation for a semicircle that is the top half of a circle whose center is at $(0, 0)$ and radius is 9.

← C O N N E C T →   *You've worked with equations of circles. Now you will investigate a conic section that is closely related to the circle—the ellipse.*

Early astronomers believed that planets traveled in circular orbits. Thanks to the mathematician Johannes Kepler (1571–1630), modern astronomers know that planetary orbits are actually flattened circles—*ellipses.*

In the following Explore, you will sketch an ellipse.

EXPLORE: DON'T LOSE YOUR FOCUS!

MATERIALS

Cardboard
Thumbtacks
String

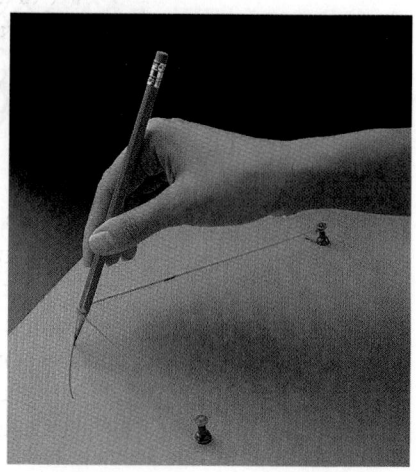

1. Push two thumbtacks into a piece of cardboard. Label the thumbtacks F_1 and F_2. Make a loop of string that fits loosely around the thumbtacks. Put your pencil point inside the loop. Keeping the string taut to form a triangle, move your pencil so that a closed curve is drawn. Describe the shape of the curve.

2. Choose a point on the curve. Measure the distances from that point to F_1 and F_2. Choose other points and repeat your measurements until you find a pattern. What do you notice? Why does this make sense, given the method you used to draw the ellipse?

3. With the thumbtacks different distances apart, draw several ellipses. How does the distance between the thumbtacks affect the shape of the curve?

4. Using a string with a different length, draw more ellipses. How does the length of the string affect the ellipse?

The construction of the ellipses in the Explore depended on the placement of points F_1 and F_2. These points have a special name.

An **ellipse** is the set of all points P in a plane where the sum of the distance from P to two fixed points is a constant. Each of the fixed points is a **focus** (plural: foci) of the ellipse.

The **center** of an ellipse is the midpoint of the line segment joining its foci.

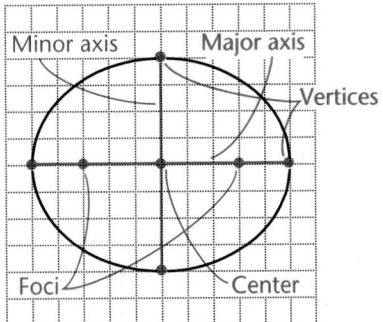

The two points on the ellipse that are farthest from its center are the endpoints of the **major axis.** The **minor axis** joins the two points on the ellipse nearest its center. Notice that both line segments are axes of symmetry for the ellipse.

The endpoints of the major and minor axes are the **vertices** of the ellipse.

The standard equation for an ellipse enables you to find the lengths and orientations of its major and minor axes quickly.

The **standard form** of the equation of an ellipse with center $(0, 0)$ *and major axis on the x-axis* is:

$$\frac{x^2}{a^2} + \frac{y^2}{b^2} = 1, \text{ where } a^2 > b^2 \text{ and } a > b > 0$$

The standard form of the equation of an ellipse with center $(0, 0)$ *and major axis on the y-axis* is:

$$\frac{x^2}{b^2} + \frac{y^2}{a^2} = 1, \text{ where } a^2 > b^2 \text{ and } a > b > 0$$

The vertices on the major axis are a units from the center and the vertices on the minor axis are b units from the center. The foci are on the major axis, c units from the center, where $c^2 = a^2 - b^2$. The sum of the distances from the foci to any point on the ellipse is $2a$.

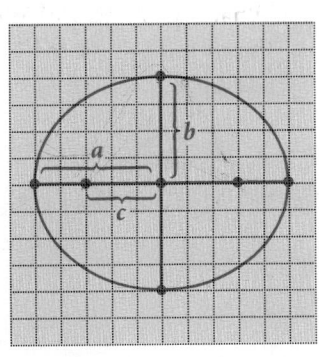

1. Graph the ellipse $\frac{x^2}{25} + \frac{y^2}{9} = 1$ and give the coordinates of its foci.

The center of the ellipse is $(0, 0)$. Since the denominator of the x-fraction is larger than the denominator of the y-fraction, the major axis of the ellipse is along the x-axis.

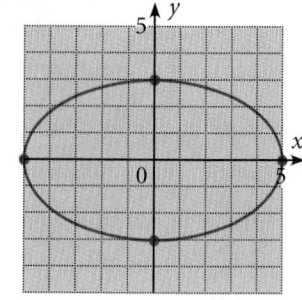

$25 = a^2$, so $a = 5$. The vertices on the major axis are 5 units from $(0, 0)$ on the major axis, at $(-5, 0)$ and $(5, 0)$.

$9 = b^2$, so $b = 3$. The vertices on the minor axis are at $(0, -3)$ and $(0, 3)$. Draw a smooth curve to connect the vertices.

To find the coordinates of the foci, first find c.

$c^2 = a^2 - b^2$
$c^2 = 25 - 9$
$c^2 = 16$, so $c = 4$. The foci are on the major axis, 4 units from $(0, 0)$, at $(-4, 0)$ and $(4, 0)$.

2. Write an equation in standard form for the ellipse shown.

The center of the ellipse is $(0, 0)$, and its major axis is on the y-axis. The vertices on the major axis are 4 units from the center, so $a = 4$. The vertices on the minor axis are 2 units from the center, so $b = 2$. The equation is:

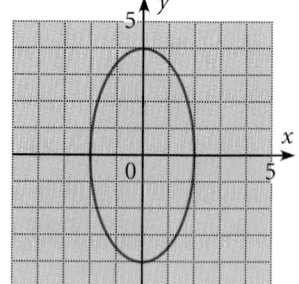

$$\frac{x^2}{2^2} + \frac{y^2}{4^2} = 1$$
$$\frac{x^2}{4} + \frac{y^2}{16} = 1$$

a. Graph the ellipse $\frac{x^2}{36} + \frac{y^2}{9} = 1$. Give the coordinates of its foci.

b. Write an equation in standard form for the ellipse shown.

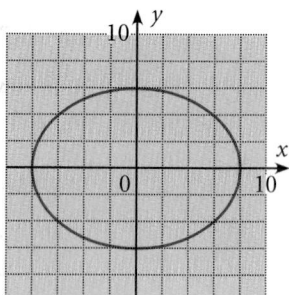

Ellipses are used to create art in the *Iliad Sculpture* in Seattle, Washington.

One important quality of an ellipse is its reflection property. Any signal emitted at one focus is reflected by the ellipse to the other focus. In an elliptical room, like the Statuary Hall in the United States Capitol, a whisper at one focus is clearly heard at the other focus. This property has been used by acoustical engineers in designing concert halls.

EXAMPLE

3. As discussed on page 371, a lithotripter is a medical device used to break up kidney stones. Shock waves produced at one focus of an elliptical ring are reflected to the person's kidney stone at the other focus. Suppose that the major axis of the elliptical ring is 10 units long and the minor axis is 4 units long. Use a graphing utility to draw a graph that models the lithotripter.

For convenience, center the ring at $(0, 0)$ and place its major axis on the x-axis. $a = \frac{10}{2} = 5$ and $b = \frac{4}{2} = 2$. An equation for the ellipse is $\frac{x^2}{5^2} + \frac{y^2}{2^2} = 1$ or $\frac{x^2}{25} + \frac{y^2}{4} = 1$.

The equation must be solved for y before it can be graphed in function mode.

$100\left(\frac{x^2}{25} + \frac{y^2}{4}\right) = 100 \times 1$ Multiply by 100 to clear fractions.

$4x^2 + 25y^2 = 100$

$25y^2 = 100 - 4x^2$ Isolate terms in y.

$y^2 = \frac{100 - 4x^2}{25}$

$y = \pm\frac{\sqrt{100 - 4x^2}}{5}$ Take the square root of both sides.

As was the case for a circle, we graph this relation as two functions, $y = \frac{\sqrt{100 - 4x^2}}{5}$ and $y = -\frac{\sqrt{100 - 4x^2}}{5}$. To see the ellipse without distortion, be sure that the spacing is consistent on both axes.

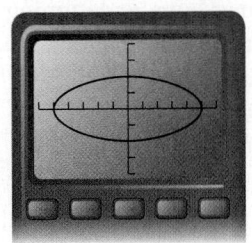

1. Suppose the distance between the foci of an ellipse is very small. What will the ellipse look like and why?
2. Compare the reflective properties of an ellipse with those of a parabola. In a radio telescope, why is a parabolic reflector used instead of an elliptical one?
3. On an ellipse, the closest points to its center are the vertices on the minor axis. Where is the closest point(s) to a focus of the ellipse? Explain.
4. Explain how you could use a string and thumbtacks to draw a circle. Why does your method work?

Exercises

CORE

1. **Getting Started** Follow the steps to sketch a graph of $\frac{x^2}{16} + \frac{y^2}{4} = 1$.
   a. The denominator of the fraction involving x^2 is the larger of the two denominators, so it is equal to a^2. Find a.
   b. The center of the ellipse is at $(0, 0)$. The vertices of the ellipse on the x-axis (the major axis) are a units away from $(0, 0)$. Find their coordinates and graph these points.
   c. The denominator of the fraction involving y^2 is equal to b^2. Find b.
   d. The vertices of the ellipse on the y-axis (the minor axis) are b units away from $(0, 0)$. Find their coordinates and graph these points.
   e. Draw a smooth curve connecting the vertices.

Graph each ellipse and give the coordinates of its foci.

2. $\frac{x^2}{9} + \frac{y^2}{25} = 1$

3. $\frac{x^2}{49} + \frac{y^2}{16} = 1$

4. $\frac{x^2}{36} + \frac{y^2}{100} = 1$

5. $25x^2 + 9y^2 = 225$

Write the word that correctly completes each statement.

6. The sum of the distances from any point on an ellipse to its ____ is a constant.

7. The foci of an ellipse are on its ____ axis.

8. **Garden in the Park** Qin-Zhong is designing an elliptical garden for an office park. The ratio between the lengths of the major and minor axes will be $\frac{3}{2}$. If the land available for the garden is 60 ft long and 30 ft wide, what are the maximum lengths of the axes?

Write an equation for each ellipse in standard form.

9.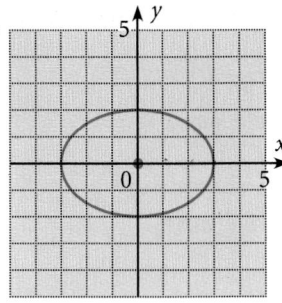

10.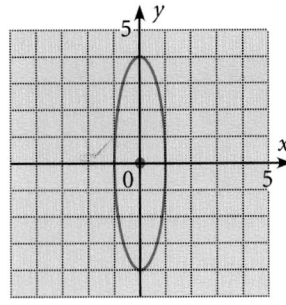

11.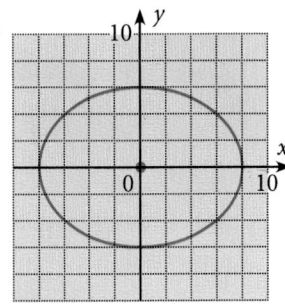

12. Earth's orbit around the sun is actually elliptical, with the center of the sun at one focus. The length of the major axis is 186 million miles, and the two foci are 3.2 million miles apart.

   a. What is the length of the minor axis of the ellipse? Explain your reasoning.

   b. Sketch a graph of Earth's orbit, showing the location of the sun.

   c. What is the greatest distance between Earth and the sun? At what point on the ellipse does this occur?

   d. What is the smallest distance between Earth and the sun? At what point does this occur?

13. Kepler's second law states that, for a given time period, the areas swept out by the elliptical orbit of a planet is constant. In the figure, the planet takes the same amount of time to move from *A* to *B* as from *C* to *D*, given that the two gray areas are equal. In its orbit, is a planet moving faster when it is nearer the sun or farther away? Explain your reasoning.

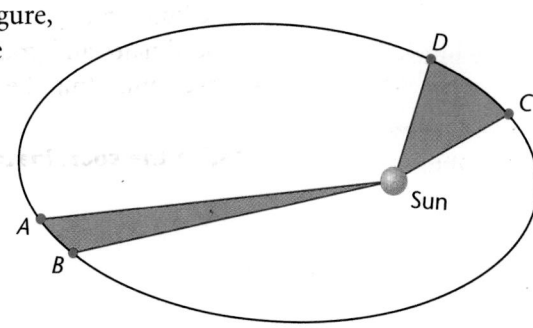

Find the sum of the distances from the foci to any point on each ellipse.

14. $\frac{x^2}{81} + \frac{y^2}{25} = 1$

15. $\frac{x^2}{4} + y^2 = 1$

16. $\frac{x^2}{27} + \frac{y^2}{21} = 1$

17. **I Hear You!** As noted on page 383, Statuary Hall, in the United States Capitol building, is an elliptical room. A whisper spoken at one focus can clearly be heard at the other focus. Elaine stands at one focus of the room and whispers quietly. Manuel moves around the room until he can hear Elaine whispering. At this point, the two are about 84 feet apart. If the minor axis of Statuary Hall is 46 feet long, what is the sum of the distances from Elaine and Manuel to one of the paintings on the wall? Explain how you found your answer.

As you have probably noticed, some ellipses are "flatter" than others. A ratio called the *eccentricity* measures the flatness of an ellipse.

> The *eccentricity* of an ellipse is $\frac{c}{a}$.

Graph each ellipse and find its eccentricity rounded to the nearest hundredth.

18. $\frac{x^2}{9} + \frac{y^2}{36} = 1$ **19.** $\frac{x^2}{9} + \frac{y^2}{16} = 1$ **20.** $\frac{x^2}{81} + \frac{y^2}{9} = 1$

21. a. What is the largest value that the eccentricity of an ellipse can have? the smallest? Explain your reasoning.
 b. What does an ellipse with the largest possible eccentricity look like? the smallest? Explain.

22. Is a circle an ellipse? Why or why not?

23. Using the data given in Exercise 12, find the eccentricity of Earth's orbit. Then comment on the statement, "Earth's orbit around the sun is nearly circular."

24. Using the data in Exercise 17, find the eccentricity of Statuary Hall.

As was the case with circles, the centers of ellipses are not necessarily located at $(0, 0)$. The standard forms of the equations of an ellipse with center (h, k) and $a^2 > b^2$ are:

major axis parallel to the x-axis   *major axis parallel to the y-axis*

$$\frac{(x-h)^2}{a^2} + \frac{(y-k)^2}{b^2} = 1$$ $$\frac{(x-h)^2}{b^2} + \frac{(y-k)^2}{a^2} = 1$$

The lines of symmetry are $x = h$ and $y = k$.

Sketch the graph of each ellipse. Give the coordinates of its center, foci, and lines of symmetry.

25. $\frac{(x-2)^2}{64} + \frac{(y+1)^2}{16} = 1$ **26.** $\frac{(x-3)^2}{4} + \frac{(y-4)^2}{9} = 1$

Graph each inequality.

27. $\frac{x^2}{4} + y^2 \le 1$ **28.** $\frac{(x-1)^2}{16} + \frac{(y+2)^2}{25} > 1$

By completing the square in x and y, write an equation for each ellipse in standard form. Then give the center of the ellipse.

29. $2x^2 + 4x + y^2 = 8$ **30.** $4x^2 + 24x + 3y^2 - 12y = 78$

31. Bridging the Gap The underside of a bridge is shaped like a semi-ellipse. The bridge spans 140 ft and the height of the bridge at its center is 30 ft.
 a. Suppose you draw a model of the bridge on a coordinate plane with the origin located on the bridge halfway between the ends of the bridge. Write an equation of the ellipse representing this model.
 b. Write an equation of the ellipse if the origin is at one end of the bridge.

Solve each system of equations if possible.

32. $2x - y = 5$
  $x + 3y = 6$

33. $5x + 4y = -2$
  $x - y = 4$

34. $y = 2x + 5$
  $3y - 2x = 6$

35. $y = -x - 5$
  $y = -x + 2$

36. $4x - 3y = 5$
  $7x + 3y = 1$

37. $y = 3x$
  $y = x^2 - x + 5$

MORE PRACTICE

Graph each ellipse and give the coordinates of its foci.

38. $\dfrac{x^2}{4} + \dfrac{y^2}{49} = 1$

39. $\dfrac{x^2}{25} + \dfrac{y^2}{16} = 1$

40. $\dfrac{x^2}{64} + \dfrac{y^2}{25} = 1$

41. $16x^2 + 9y^2 = 144$

Graph each ellipse and find its eccentricity. Express the eccentricity as a decimal rounded to the nearest hundredth.

42. $\dfrac{x^2}{16} + \dfrac{y^2}{9} = 1$

43. $\dfrac{x^2}{36} + \dfrac{y^2}{16} = 1$

44. $\dfrac{(x-1)^2}{49} + \dfrac{(y+2)^2}{9} = 1$

45. $\dfrac{(x+3)^2}{39} + \dfrac{(y+2)^2}{50} = 1$

46. Arch Rival An arch is to be built in the shape of a semi-ellipse. The opening is to have a height of 50 ft at the center and a span of 200 ft. Write an equation of an ellipse that represents this arch.

Solve each equation for y. (Hint: Your equation should have a ± sign.) Then graph each ellipse on a graphing utility. Sketch your result, and state your window for x and y.

47. $\dfrac{x^2}{9} + y^2 = 1$

48. $\dfrac{x^2}{4} + \dfrac{y^2}{36} = 1$

49. $4x^2 + 25y^2 = 100$

By completing the square in x and y, write an equation for each ellipse in standard form. Then give the center of the ellipse.

50. $x^2 + 4x + 2y^2 = 12$

51. $2x^2 + 16x + y^2 = 4$

52. $3x^2 + 18x + 2y^2 - 8y = 32$

53. $2x^2 - 12x + y^2 - 10y = 21$

54. Not So Eccentric At its closest approach to Earth, the moon is about 221,500 miles away. At its farthest, it is 253,700 miles away. The eccentricity of the moon's orbit is about 0.07. Write an equation to model this orbit.

MORE MATH REASONING

55. Satellite Orbit A satellite follows an elliptical orbit around the earth with the center of the earth as one of the foci. At its farthest, the satellite is 2500 miles from the earth's surface, and at its closest it is 1000 miles from the earth's surface. Using 4000 miles as the radius of the earth, write an equation to model the satellite's orbit.

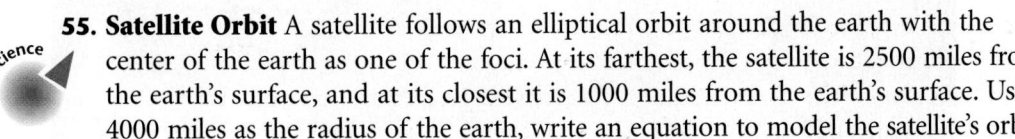

56. Low Bridge The opening of a stone bridge across a river is the top half of an ellipse described by $\frac{x^2}{625} + \frac{y^2}{256} = 1$. Units are given in feet.

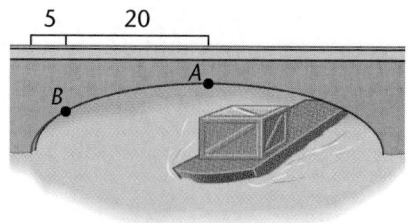

a. Find the height of the opening at point *A*.

b. Find the distance between points *A* and *B*.

c. The deck of a barge is 1 foot above water level. Find the size of the largest cube that the barge could transport under the bridge.

d. On weekends, all barge traffic must stay on one side of point *A*. Find the size of the largest cube the barge can transport on weekends.

57. As you've seen in Exercises 29, 30, and 50−53, an equation in the form $Ax^2 + Bx + Cy^2 + Dy = E$ can be rewritten as an equation in standard form by completing the square. But can you tell whether the equation represents a circle or not *without* completing the square?

a. By completing the square in *x* and *y*, write each equation in standard form for an ellipse. Which of these equations represent circles? How can you tell?

   i. $x^2 + 2x + y^2 + 4y = 4$ **ii.** $2x^2 + 12x + y^2 + 4y = 3$

   iii. $2x^2 + 4x + 3y^2 - 12y = 4$ **iv.** $x^2 + 6x + y^2 - 10y = 2$

b. Explain how you can tell whether or not an equation for an ellipse in the form $Ax^2 + Bx + Cy^2 + Dy = E$ represents a circle.

5-3
PART C   Hyperbolas

← CONNECT →   *You've investigated the ellipse, where the sum of the distances from its points to its foci is a constant. Now you will work with the hyperbola, where the **difference** in these distances is a constant.*

Comets are mixtures of rock and ice, "dirty snowballs" that orbit the sun. When a comet gets close enough to the sun, the sun's heat vaporizes part of the comet, creating a bright tail pointing away from the sun. Parts of the orbits of some comets are nearly parabolic. Others follow the curve of a different conic section, the *hyperbola.*

The heat generated by nuclear power plants is dissipated in huge cooling towers. The curved sides of the towers shown in the photograph are hyperbolic.

In the Explore, you will investigate a real-world situation that leads to a hyperbolic curve.

EXPLORE: WHOSE FAULT IS IT, ANYWAY?

MATERIALS

Graph paper
Compass

While a geologist is working at a geological station (S_1), its seismograph detects a moderate earthquake. Seven seconds later, her colleague at a second station (S_2) detects the same earthquake. The stations are located 120 kilometers apart. Suppose that the earthquake moves at 8 km/sec. Where might the epicenter of the earthquake be located?

1. How much farther away from the epicenter is the second station? Call this difference in distances d. Explain how you found d.
2. You need to find all of the points that are d kilometers farther from S_2 than they are from S_1. To begin searching for the epicenter of the quake, sketch locations of your two stations on graph paper. (Let each unit on your graph paper represent 8 km.)
3. Around each station, draw concentric circles whose radii are multiples of 8. Use these circles to find all points whose distance from S_2 is d kilometers greater than its distance from S_1.
4. Connect these points with a smooth curve. Describe the curve that results. Does it have symmetry? Does the curvature of this figure change as you move away from the stations? If so, how?

5. What other information might you need before you could pinpoint the epicenter of the earthquake? Explain how this additional information would help you locate the epicenter.

In the Explore, you found the locations where the difference in the distances to two points was the same. The curve you graphed was one branch of a hyperbola.

A **hyperbola** is the set of all points P in a plane where the absolute value of the difference between the distances from P to two fixed points is a constant. The two fixed points are the **foci** of the hyperbola.

A hyperbola has two **branches.** The **center** of the hyperbola is the midpoint of the line segment joining its foci, and the **vertices** are the two points on the hyperbola nearest its center. As the branches of a hyperbola move away from its center, they approach, but never reach, the dashed lines shown. These lines are the **asymptotes** of the hyperbola.

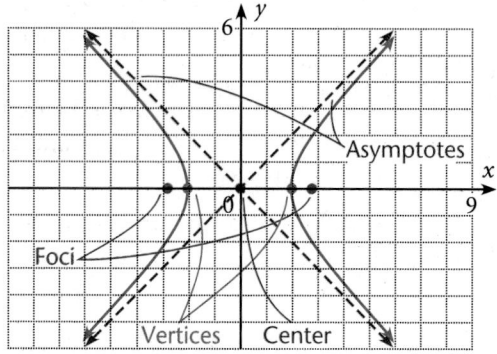

The **standard form** of an equation of a hyperbola with center $(0, 0)$ and *vertices on the x-axis* is:

$$\frac{x^2}{a^2} - \frac{y^2}{b^2} = 1$$

The standard form of an equation of a hyperbola with center $(0, 0)$ and *vertices on the y-axis* is:

$$\frac{y^2}{a^2} - \frac{x^2}{b^2} = 1$$

The foci are on the line joining the vertices of the hyperbola. They are c units from the origin, where $c^2 = a^2 + b^2$. The absolute value of the difference of the distances from the foci to any point on the hyperbola is $2a$. The equations of the asymptotes are $y = \frac{b}{a}x$ and $y = -\frac{b}{a}x$, for hyperbolas whose equations are in the first standard form. The asymptotes for equations in the second form are $y = \frac{a}{b}x$ and $y = -\frac{a}{b}x$.

CONSIDER

1. Briefly describe the differences between the standard equation for a hyperbola and the standard equation for an ellipse.

1. Graph the hyperbola $\frac{y^2}{16} - \frac{x^2}{9} = 1$ and give the coordinates of its foci.

The center of the hyperbola is $(0, 0)$. Since the y-term is positive, the vertices of the hyperbola lie on the y-axis. $a^2 = 16$, so $a = 4$. The vertices are at $(0, -4)$, and $(0, 4)$. $b^2 = 9$, so $b = 3$.

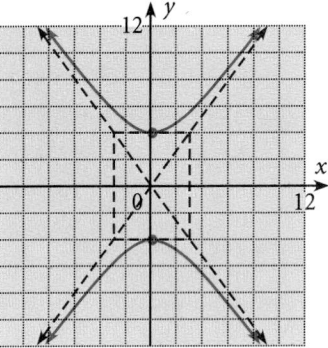

To guide the graph, draw a rectangle that extends 4 units from the center in the y-direction and 3 units in the x-direction. The asymptotes of the hyperbola contain the diagonals of the rectangle.

Using your vertices and the asymptotes, sketch the hyperbola. Remember that the graph comes closer and closer to the asymptotes but never intersects them.

To find the coordinates of the foci, first find c.

$c^2 = a^2 + b^2$

$c^2 = 16 + 9$

$c^2 = 25$, so $c = 5$. The foci are 5 units from $(0, 0)$ on the y-axis, at $(0, -5)$ and $(0, 5)$.

2. Write an equation in standard form for the hyperbola shown.

The center of the hyperbola is $(0, 0)$ and its vertices are on the x-axis. The vertices are 3 units from the center, so $a = 3$. The slopes of the asymptotes are $\pm\frac{2}{3} = \pm\frac{b}{a}$, and $a = 3$, so $b = 2$. The equation is:

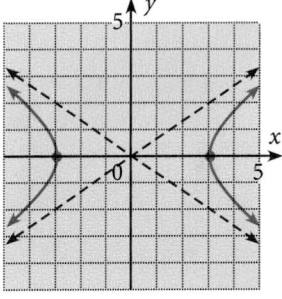

$\frac{x^2}{3^2} - \frac{y^2}{2^2} = 1$

$\frac{x^2}{9} - \frac{y^2}{4} = 1$

Graph each hyperbola and give the coordinates of its foci.

a. $\frac{y^2}{25} - \frac{x^2}{144} = 1$

b. $\frac{x^2}{36} - \frac{y^2}{12} = 1$

c. Write an equation in standard form for the hyperbola shown.

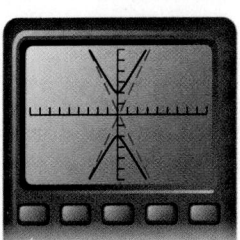

1. Describe similarities and differences between a hyperbola and an ellipse.
2. What happens to the curvature of a hyperbola as the asymptotes get farther apart?

Exercises

CORE

1. **Getting Started** Follow the steps to sketch a graph of $\frac{x^2}{16} - \frac{y^2}{4} = 1$.

    a. The fraction involving x^2 is positive, so its denominator is equal to a^2. Find a.

    b. The center of the hyperbola is at $(0, 0)$. The vertices of the hyperbola are on the x-axis (since the x^2 fraction is positive) and are a units away from $(0, 0)$. Find their coordinates and graph these points.

    c. The denominator of the y^2 fraction is equal to b^2. Find b.

    d. The equations of the asymptotes are $y = \frac{b}{a}$ and $y = -\frac{b}{a}$. Use dashed lines to sketch the asymptotes.

    e. Starting from each vertex, draw symmetric smooth curves which approach the asymptotes on either side. The curves should approach the asymptotes more and more closely the farther they get from the vertex.

Graph each hyperbola. Give the coordinates of its foci and the equations for its asymptotes.

2. $\dfrac{x^2}{9} - \dfrac{y^2}{16} = 1$ 3. $\dfrac{y^2}{36} - \dfrac{x^2}{25} = 1$ 4. $\dfrac{y^2}{9} - \dfrac{x^2}{40} = 1$ 5. $16x^2 - 9y^2 = 144$

Write an equation for each hyperbola in standard form.

6.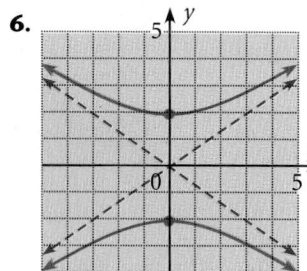

7.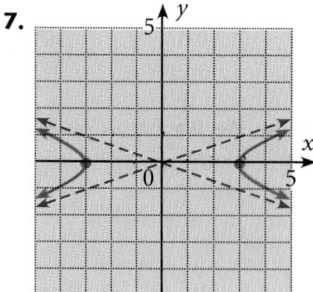

8.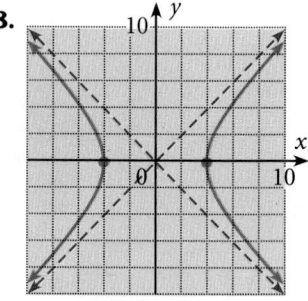

9. **One Step Beyond!** In literature, an exaggeration, especially an unreasonable one, is referred to as *hyperbole*. "This backpack is as heavy as an elephant!" is an example of hyperbole. The words *hyperbole* and *hyperbola* both come from the Greek *hyper,* beyond. Explain how hyperbole and hyperbolas both "go beyond." (Hint: Compare a hyperbola to a circle and an ellipse.)

10. How can you determine which axis the graph of a hyperbola with center $(0, 0)$ crosses by looking at its standard-form equation?

Find the difference in the distances from the foci to any point on each hyperbola.

11. $\dfrac{x^2}{25} - \dfrac{y^2}{9} = 1$

12. $\dfrac{y^2}{16} - x^2 = 1$

13. $\dfrac{x^2}{8} - \dfrac{y^2}{12} = 1$

14. So Repulsive! When two particles have the same electrical charge, they repel each other. Suppose that two negatively charged electrons move toward each other along the line $y = x$. As they approach each other, the repulsion forces the particles away from each other in a hyperbolic path. Suppose that the vertex of one of the branches of the hyperbola is at $(3, 0)$ and its center is at $(0, 0)$. Write an equation to model the paths of the electrons.

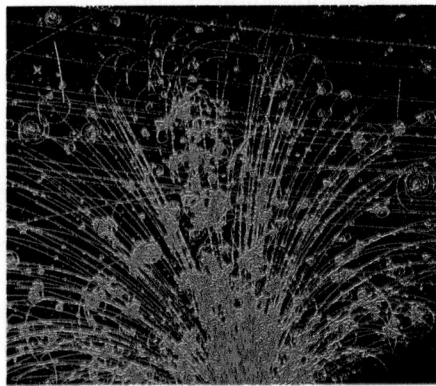

Tracks left by subatomic particles in a bubble chamber

The centers of hyperbolas are not necessarily located at $(0, 0)$. The standard forms of the equations of a hyperbola with center (h, k) are:

vertices on an axis parallel to the *x*-axis

$\dfrac{(x - h)^2}{a^2} - \dfrac{(y - k)^2}{b^2} = 1$

vertices on an axis parallel to the *y*-axis

$\dfrac{(y - k)^2}{a^2} - \dfrac{(x - h)^2}{b^2} = 1$

The lines of symmetry are $x = h$ and $y = k$.

Graph each hyperbola. Give the coordinates of its center, foci, and lines of symmetry.

15. $\dfrac{(x - 5)^2}{16} - \dfrac{(y + 3)^2}{9} = 1$

16. $\dfrac{(y + 2)^2}{4} - \dfrac{(x - 3)^2}{9} = 1$

17. $\dfrac{(x + 1)^2}{4} - y^2 = 1$

18. $\dfrac{(y + 2)^2}{25} - \dfrac{(x - 5)^2}{64} = 1$

By completing the square in *x* and *y*, write an equation for each hyperbola in standard form. Then give the center of the hyperbola.

19. $x^2 + 2x - y^2 = 15$

20. $y^2 - 4y - x^2 = 5$

21. $2y^2 + 16y - 3x^2 - 12x = 29$ (Hint: Factor out a -3 from the *x*-terms.)

22. SOS Two Coast Guard stations are located 600 mi apart at points $A(0, 0)$ and $B(600, 0)$. A distress signal from a ship is received at slightly different times by the two stations. It is determined that the ship is 200 mi farther from station A than it is from station B. Find the equation of a hyperbola that passes through the location of the ship.

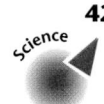
23. Seven freshmen, ten juniors, and eight seniors are in the school chorus. One student is randomly chosen to perform a solo. What is the probability of each of the following events? [1-2]

    a. a senior is chosen   **b.** a freshman is chosen

    c. a sophomore is chosen   **d.** a freshman or a junior is chosen

Simplify each radical expression. [4-3]

24. $\sqrt{28}$ **25.** $\sqrt{18}$ **26.** $\sqrt{147}$ **27.** $\sqrt{720}$

Without solving, determine the nature of the solutions of each equation. [5-2]

28. $2x^2 + 3x + 7 = 0$ **29.** $5 - 7x - 2x^2 = 0$

30. $x^2 = -2x - 1$ **31.** $x^2 + 7x = 9$

MORE PRACTICE

Graph each hyperbola. Give the coordinates of its foci and the equations for its asymptotes.

32. $\dfrac{x^2}{4} - \dfrac{y^2}{9} = 1$ **33.** $\dfrac{y^2}{25} - \dfrac{x^2}{100} = 1$ **34.** $\dfrac{x^2}{20} - \dfrac{y^2}{18} = 1$

35. $y^2 - 4x^2 = 16$ **36.** $\dfrac{x^2}{36} - \dfrac{y^2}{25} = 1$ **37.** $\dfrac{y^2}{32} - x^2 = 1$

Graph each hyperbola. Give the coordinates of its center and foci.

38. $\dfrac{(x + 3)^2}{64} - \dfrac{(y - 1)^2}{16} = 1$ **39.** $\dfrac{(y - 1)^2}{28} - \dfrac{(x + 6)^2}{48} = 1$ **40.** $\dfrac{(y + 2)^2}{9} - \dfrac{x^2}{16} = 1$

41. Booming Business During a season of high fire danger, a forest ranger hears the thunderclap from a lightning strike. Six seconds later, the thunderclap is heard at a ranger station 8 km away. Make a diagram to show all possible locations of the lightning strike. Use $\frac{1}{3}$ km/sec as an approximation for the speed of sound.

42. Suppose that part of a comet's path approximates a branch of a hyperbola with the sun at the focus. At its closest approach to the sun, the comet is 25 million miles away. Assume that the center of its path is at $(0, 0)$ and its vertex is 9 million miles from the center. Write an equation for a hyperbola with one branch that models the path of this comet.

By completing the square in x and y, write an equation for each hyperbola in standard form. Then give the center of the hyperbola.

43. $x^2 - 6x - y^2 = 0$

44. $y^2 + 10y - x^2 = 24$

45. $4x^2 + 16x - 2y^2 + 4y = 7$ (Hint: Factor out a -2 from the y-terms.)

Solve each equation for y. (Hint: Your equation should have a ± sign.) Then graph each hyperbola on a graphing utility. Sketch your result, and state your ranges for x and y.

46. $\frac{x^2}{16} - y^2 = 1$ **47.** $\frac{y^2}{4} - \frac{x^2}{36} = 1$

48. $4x^2 - 16y^2 = 64$ **49.** $y^2 - \frac{x^2}{4} = 1$

50. $9x^2 - 81y^2 = 81$ **51.** $\frac{x^2}{9} - \frac{y^2}{36} = 1$

MORE MATH REASONING

52. Use a Graphing Utility A *rectangular hyperbola* has an equation of the form $xy = k$, where $k \neq 0$. Graph each rectangular hyperbola. Make a conjecture about the asymptotes of rectangular hyperbolas.

    a. $xy = 4$ **b.** $xy = 1$ **c.** $xy = -3$ **d.** $xy = -8$

53. Mirror Speculation A *hyperbolic* mirror is shaped like one branch of a hyperbola. It reflects any light directed toward one focus of the hyperbola through the other focus. Suppose that the center of a hyperbolic mirror is at $(0, 0)$, the vertex of the mirror's branch is at $(3, 0)$, and the focus of the mirror's branch is at $(5, 0)$, as shown. The equations of its asymptotes are $y = \pm\frac{4}{3}x$.

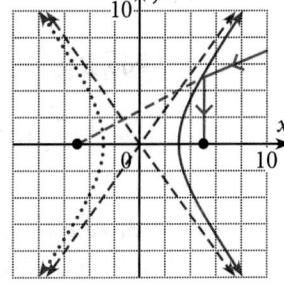

    a. Write an equation that models the surface of the mirror. Where is the focus of the other branch of the hyperbola located?

    b. Suppose light from $(20, 7)$ is directed toward the focus of the imaginary branch. Where will it intersect the mirror?

54. An equation for any of the conic sections you have worked with can be written in the form $Ax^2 + Bx + Cy^2 + Dy = E$. You can tell whether the equation represents a parabola, a circle, an ellipse, or a hyperbola by looking at the coefficients A and C. For instance, if A and C have different signs, the equation represents a hyperbola. What is true about A and C if:

    a. the equation represents a parabola? Why?

    b. the equation represents an ellipse?

    c. the equation represents a circle?

    d. Identify the conic section for each of the following equations.

        i. $2x^2 + 6x + 3y^2 + 7y = 10$ **ii.** $6x - 4y^2 - 9y = 4$

        iii. $x^2 - 6x + y^2 = 39$ **iv.** $x^2 - 6x - y^2 + 2y = 14$

← **C O N N E C T** → *You've investigated circles, ellipses, and hyperbolas. These conic sections can each be described by a geometric definition involving distance and an algebraic equation.*

The *conic sections* (the parabola, the circle, the ellipse, and the hyperbola) have applications in astronomy, engineering, and navigation. In the Explore, you will see why these figures are known as conic sections.

EXPLORE: CONE CUTTER

1. Use a compass to draw a circle. Cut out the circle and cut a slit from its outside to its center. Roll up the circle to make a right cone as shown and fasten it with tape.

MATERIALS

*Cardboard, Marking pen
Construction paper, Compass
Scissors, Tape*

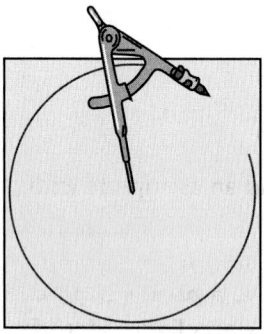  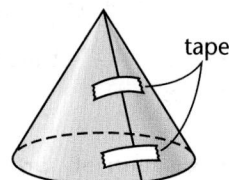

tape

2. Using a sheet of cardboard to represent a plane, find a way to cut the cone with a plane so that the cross section is a circle. With your marking pen, sketch the circle on your cone. Describe the relationship between the plane and the cone.

3. Repeat Steps 1 and 2 for an ellipse, a parabola, and a hyperbola.

4. Look for other shapes that you can generate by cutting a cone with a plane. Describe or illustrate these figures and explain how they can be formed.

5. Explain why the ellipse, circle, parabola, and hyperbola are known as conic sections.

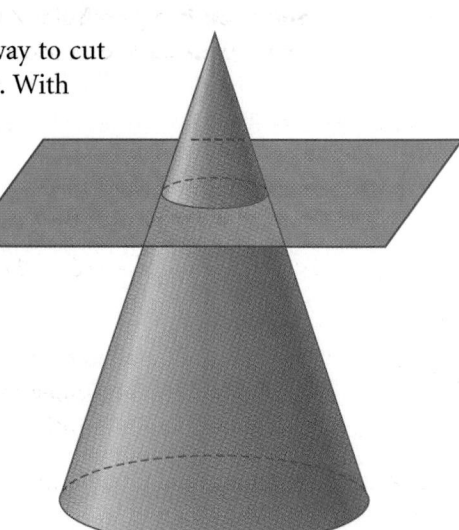

By slicing a single cone, you can get only one branch of a hyperbola. Conic sections are actually considered slices of a *double-napped cone.*

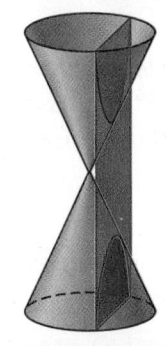

REFLECT

1. Using distance, define a circle, an ellipse, and a hyperbola.
2. How are a parabola and a hyperbola different?
3. The architectural design shown involves the equation $\frac{y^2}{b^2} - \frac{x^2}{a^2} = \frac{z}{c}$. What two conic sections do you think are involved?

Self-Assessment

Write an equation in standard form for each conic section.

1. A circle with center $(2, -4)$ and radius 9

2. An ellipse with vertices $(-6, 0)$, $(6, 0)$ and foci $(-5, 0)$, $(5, 0)$

3. A hyperbola with center at the origin, a vertex at $(0, -2)$, and an asymptote with equation $y = -x$

State whether the graph of each equation is a circle, an ellipse, a parabola, or a hyperbola. If it is a circle, identify its center and radius; if it is an ellipse, identify its center and foci; if a parabola, its vertex; and if a hyperbola, its center and vertices. Then graph each equation.

4. $x^2 + y^2 = 25$

5. $\frac{x^2}{25} - \frac{y^2}{16} = 1$

6. $\frac{x^2}{9} + \frac{y^2}{16} = 1$

7. $y = (x + 4)^2 - 2$

8. $(x - 1)^2 + (y + 3)^2 = 4$

9. $\frac{(y - 1)^2}{36} - \frac{(x + 4)^2}{9} = 1$

10. $(x + 3)^2 + 4(y - 2)^2 = 16$

11. $\frac{(x + 8)^2}{5} - \frac{(y - 10)^2}{12} = 1$

12. $(x + 2)^2 + \frac{y^2}{9} = 1$

Science
13. In a lithotripter, described on page 371, shock waves at one focus of an elliptical ring are reflected to the kidney stone of a patient located at the other focus. Explain why the ring is elliptical and not circular or hyperbolic.

Science
14. Although parts of the paths of comets can be nearly parabolic or hyperbolic, they cannot have parabolic or hyperbolic *orbits*. Explain why it is impossible for comets to have such orbits.

By completing the square in *x* and *y*, write an equation for each conic section in standard form. State whether the conic is a circle, an ellipse, a parabola, or a hyperbola. Then give the center of the conic.

15. $x^2 + 4x + y^2 - 8y = 2$ 16. $x^2 + 4x + 2y^2 - 8y = 2$ 17. $x^2 + 4x - 2y^2 - 8y = 2$

18. Write a short paragraph that explains how to graph the equation for a conic section using a graphing utility.

19. The orbit of Mercury is an ellipse with the center of the sun at one focus. It has an eccentricity of about 0.205. The sun is 7.4 million miles from the center of Mercury's orbit. What is Mercury's greatest distance from the sun? Explain how you found your answer.

20. In 1964, an elliptical billiard (pool) table was introduced. The table had a pocket at one focus and a mark at the other focus. What would happen if you placed a ball at the mark and hit it off one of the sides? Why would this happen?

Write a formula for the *n*th term of each sequence. [4-1 and 4-2]

21. 4, 8, 16, 32, ...   22. $-2, -5, -8, -11, ...$ 23. $-16, 4, -1, \frac{1}{4}, ...$

Without solving, determine the nature of the solutions of each equation. [5-2]

24. $3x^2 - 3x + 9 = 0$ 25. $x^2 = 6x - 9$

26. $8 + 7x^2 = 2x$ 27. $6x^2 + 6x = -4$

28. You know that the sum of the angle measures of a triangle on a flat plane is 180°. But this is only true for surfaces with zero curvature. Using the figures, make a conjecture about the sum of the angle measures of a triangle in hyperbolic geometry (left) and spherical geometry (right).

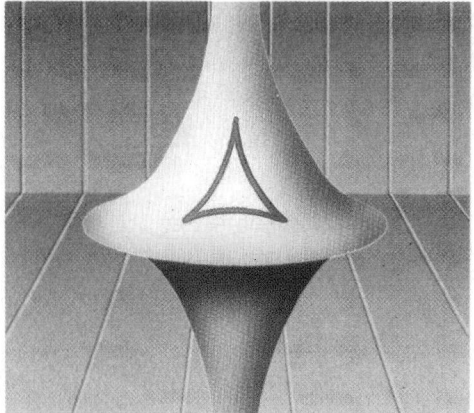
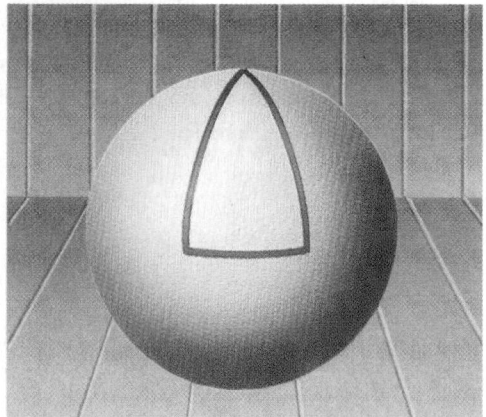

29. As seen in the Explore on page 336, a parabola is a set of points equidistant from a given point (*focus*) and a given line (*directrix*). A parabola with vertex (0, 0), focus (0, *p*), and directrix $y = -p$ satisfies the equation $x^2 = 4py$. Sketch a graph of $x^2 = 16y$ and identify its focus and directrix.

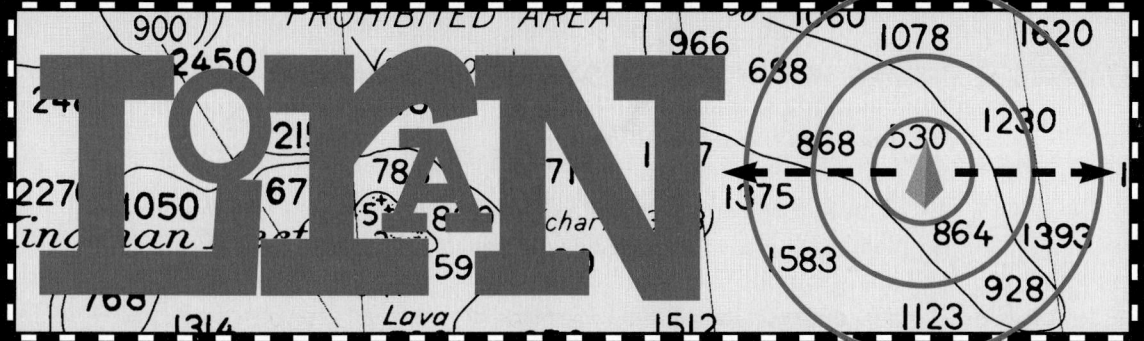

For centuries, ships have been using the stars as an aid in navigating the oceans. Airline pilots have also used celestial maps to determine their plane's location during long flights. Since World War II, ships and planes have used another navigational aid, the LORAN. The name LORAN comes from the phrase LOng RAnge Navigation. The LORAN system makes use of radio pulses that are broadcast at the same time from widely separated positions.

The radio signals allow a ship to locate itself at the intersection of hyperbolic curves.

Pairs of shore-based transmitters send out high-powered pulses of low-frequency radio waves that are received by the ship's LORAN receiver. These signals are used to locate the ship.

Suppose one pair of transmitters, located at F_1 and F_2, sends the same signal, which is received by the ship at two different times. The navigator can then determine the difference in distances from the two transmitters. This locates the ship on a hyperbola with F_1 and F_2 as foci. Using signals from points F_2 and F_3, the ship can be located on another hyperbola. The ship must be located at a point where the hyperbolas intersect.

Modern ships have onboard computers that are programmed to receive the radio signals from the three stations. Using the locations of the three transmitting stations, the program determines the two hyperbolas and finds the intersection point, thereby locating the ship.

Master Station

Base Line

Base Line

Slave Station

Slave Station

Location of Ship

?

1. What would it mean if two signal pulses were received at the same time?

2. Draw a diagram to show how the LORAN navigation system works.

3. Do you think a conic section other than the hyperbola could be used to locate ships? Why or why not?

Quadratic-Linear Systems

← C O N N E C T → *You've seen that a system of linear equations can be solved graphically. You can also use graphs to find the intersection of a linear function and a quadratic relation.*

You've used conic sections to model many real-world phenomena, from falling objects to medical devices. Linear equations are also powerful mathematical models. At times, both of these models apply to the same situation. For instance, the demand for a resource may be growing quadratically while the production is growing linearly. When will the demand exceed the supply?

A **quadratic-linear system** of equations includes an equation of one of the conic sections and a linear equation.

EXPLORE: SKETCHY ARRANGEMENTS

MATERIALS

Graph paper

1. Draw several different sketches showing intersections of a line and a parabola that result in different numbers of intersection points. How many points of intersection are possible for a line and a parabola?

2. Repeat Step 1 for a line and a circle, a line and an ellipse, and a line and a hyperbola.

3. What conclusions can you draw about the intersection of a line and the different conic sections?

You can find the real-number solutions of a quadratic-linear system by graphing the equations and finding the points of intersection.

EXAMPLE

1. Solve the system of equations by graphing.

$$y = -2x + 2$$
$$x^2 + y^2 = 25$$

The first equation represents a line with a slope of -2 and a y-intercept of 2. The graph of the second equation is a circle with center $(0, 0)$ and radius 5. The intersection points appear to be near $\left(-1\frac{1}{2}, 5\right)$ and $(3, -4)$.

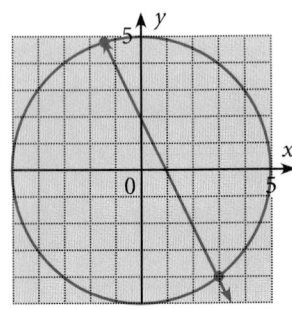

2. A stunt skydiver has opened his parachute and is falling to earth at a constant speed of 10 ft per second. When he is at a height of 150 ft, a softball is fired upward from the ground at a speed of 100 ft/sec. He hopes to catch the softball. At what times is the catch possible?

Use the free-fall equation $h(t) = -16t^2 + v_0 t + h_0$.

The height of the skydiver is given by $h(t) = 150 - 10t$.

The height of the softball is $h(t) = -16t^2 + 100t$.

By graphing both of these equations on a graphing utility, we can see that this system has two points of intersection, one at $t \approx 2$ sec, $h \approx 130$ ft and another at $t = 5$ sec, $h = 100$ ft.

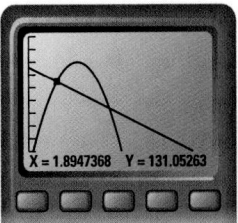
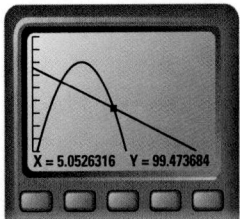

The skydiver can try to catch the ball about 2 seconds after it is fired, and if he misses, 5 seconds after it is fired.

If you are using a graphing utility to solve a system of equations that involves a circle, ellipse, or hyperbola, remember that you will need to solve for y and input *two* equations for the conic section.

TRY IT

Graph and estimate the solutions of each system of equations.

a. $y = 3x - 5$

$y = x^2 + 4x - 8$

b. $y = -\frac{3}{4}x + 6$

$\dfrac{x^2}{64} + \dfrac{y^2}{36} = 1$

CONSIDER

1. When graphing, how can you tell that a quadratic-linear system has no real-number solution?

You can also solve a system of equations symbolically.

3. Solve the system by substitution. Round answers to the nearest hundredth.

$y = x + 1$ **❶**

$x^2 + y^2 = 20$ **❷**

$x^2 + (x + 1)^2 = 20$ Use equation **❶** to substitute for y in equation **❷**.

$x^2 + x^2 + 2x + 1 = 20$ Simplify.

$2x^2 + 2x - 19 = 0$ Put the quadratic equation into standard form.

$x = \dfrac{-2 \pm \sqrt{4 + 152}}{4} = \dfrac{-2 \pm \sqrt{156}}{4}$ Use the quadratic formula.

$x \approx 2.62, -3.62$ Use an approximation for $\sqrt{156}$ and simplify.

The corresponding y-values are found by substituting the x-values back into one of the original equations (preferably **❶**!).

The points of intersection are approximately $(2.62, 3.62)$ and $(-3.62, -2.62)$. These answers check. When solving these systems symbolically, it is important to check for extraneous solutions.

TRY IT

Solve each system of equations symbolically.

c. $x^2 - y^2 = 1$
$2x - y = 4$

d. $y = x^2 - 5$
$y - x = 1$

A quadratic-linear system may have 0, 1, or 2 real-number solutions. As is the case with systems of linear equations, you can find approximate solutions by graphing, or exact solutions by symbolic methods.

REFLECT

1. It is possible to have a system of linear equations with an infinite number of solutions. Is this possible for a quadratic-linear system? Explain.

2. In general, will using substitution be a more complicated solution method for a system of linear equations or for a quadratic-linear system? Explain.

3. What are some of the strengths and weaknesses of using a graphing utility to solve a quadratic-linear system?

Exercises

CORE

1. Getting Started Use the graph to estimate the coordinates of the points of intersection of the line and ellipse.

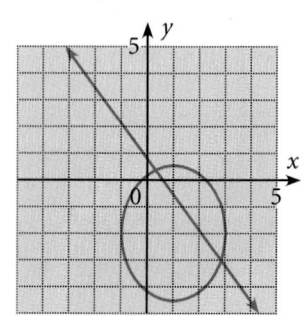

Graph and estimate the solutions of each system of equations.

2. $25x^2 - 9y^2 = 400$
$y = x$

3. $3x - 4y = 0$
$x^2 + y^2 = 25$

4. $y = x^2 + 1$
$y = -2$

Solve each system of equations symbolically.

5. $y = x^2 - 3x$
$y = x$

6. $2x + 3y = 6$
$4x^2 + 4y^2 = 36$

7. $2x - y = 1$
$y^2 - x^2 = 1$

8. $64 = x^2 + 4y^2$
$y = 4$

9. Find the dimensions of a rectangle if its area is 12 cm^2 and its length is 2 cm less than twice its width.

Graph each system of inequalities.

10. $x^2 + y^2 \le 25$

$y > x - 2$

11. $\frac{x^2}{16} + \frac{y^2}{25} > 1$

$y \le \frac{1}{2}x - 2$

12. Exploring the Planets Suppose that a space probe from Earth is sent to photograph the planet Neptune. If the sun is at $(0, 0)$, the equation of the path of the probe can be modeled by the linear equation $y = 3x$ in the plane of Neptune's orbit. Neptune's orbit is nearly circular. Neptune's average distance from the sun is about 2.8×10^9 mi. Find the coordinates of the points of intersection of the satellite and Neptune's orbit. Are both intersection points actually possible? Why or why not?

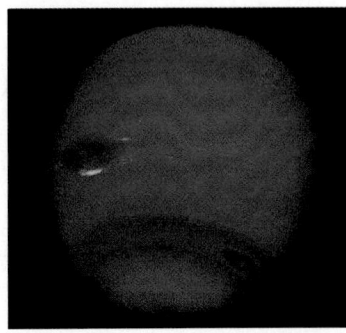

LOOK BACK

13. Find $C + D$, if $C = \begin{bmatrix} 2 & -1 \\ 3 & 5 \end{bmatrix}$ and $D = \begin{bmatrix} 4 & 3 \\ -1 & 2 \end{bmatrix}$. [1-3]

14. Find AB, where $A = \begin{bmatrix} 1 & 1 \\ 1 & 1 \end{bmatrix}$ and $B = \begin{bmatrix} 2 & 5 \\ -2 & -5 \end{bmatrix}$. [1-3]

Tell whether the following sets of numbers are closed under multiplication. [4-3]

15. the set of positive even integers

16. the set of odd integers greater than -1 and less than 6

Name the coordinates of the foci of each ellipse described below. The major axis is horizontal. [5-3]

17. Center $(0, 0)$, $a = 6$, $b = 4$

18. Center $(5, -1)$, $a = 8$, $b = 5$

MORE PRACTICE

Use a graphing utility to graph and estimate the solutions of each system of equations. (Hint: In some cases, you will need to solve the quadratic equations for *y* before graphing.)

19. $y = x^2 + 1$
$y = 10$

20. $x - y = 1$
$x^2 = 2y + 3$

21. $x^2 - y^2 = 14$
$x + y = 7$

22. $36x^2 + 9y^2 = 144$
$3x + y = -6$

23. Find the dimensions of a rectangle having a perimeter of 20 m and an area of 21 m².

24. Contract Bridge Suppose that you are building a bridge, whose base is a semi-ellipse as shown, over a canyon. You have strung a cable to haul building supplies from the base of the canyon. At what points will the cable meet the underside of the bridge?

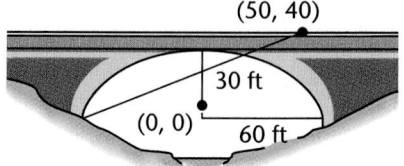

(50, 40)

30 ft

(0, 0)

60 ft

Solve each system of equations symbolically.

25. $25 = x^2 + y^2$
$x + y = 7$

26. $x + 3 = y^2$
$2y = x + 4$

27. $2y^2 + xy = 5$
$4y + x = 7$

28. $x^2 + y^2 = 5$
$y = 2x + 5$

29. $y^2 - x^2 = 9$
$y = 2x - 3$

30. $x^2 + 4y^2 = 25$
$x + 2y = 7$

MORE MATH REASONING

31. By the Numbers The sum of the squares of two numbers is 25. The difference of twice the first and three times the second is −1. Find the numbers.

32. Use a Graphing Utility The original height of the Great Pyramid of Khufu was about 482 feet, and the length of one of the sides of its square base was 756 feet. Suppose that when it was completed, an architect standing at its peak tossed a pebble into the air in triumph. The pebble had a vertical velocity of 55 ft/sec, an initial horizontal velocity of 60 ft/sec, and its path was in a vertical plane that bisected a face of the pyramid. Will the pebble strike the pyramid? If so, at what height and at what vertical distance from the peak? Explain how you solved this problem.

← **C O N N E C T** → *You've used graphing and substitution to solve quadratic-linear systems. Now you will investigate quadratic-quadratic systems.*

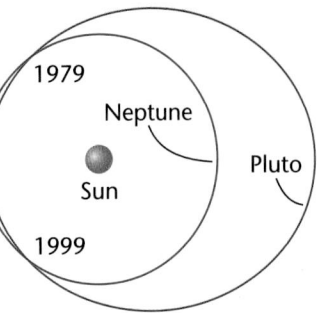

A system of two or more quadratic relations or conic sections is a **quadratic-quadratic system.** An example of a quadratic-quadratic system is seen in the elliptical paths of Neptune and Pluto. If their orbits are viewed in the same plane, you can see that they intersect. Pluto is typically considered the "farthest" planet from the sun. However, Neptune is sometimes farther from the sun than Pluto. Pluto has been nearer the sun than Neptune since 1979, and will remain the eighth planet until 1999.

CONSIDER

?

1. **Does the fact that the orbits of Pluto and Neptune intersect mean that the planets will collide? Why or why not?**

In the following Explore, you will investigate the points of intersection of a circle and an ellipse.

EXPLORE: CATCH A FALLING TELSTAR

A satellite is circling the earth in an elliptical orbit in the plane of the earth's equator. The satellite's orbit has been decaying, and the satellite is nearing the earth's atmosphere, where it will begin to burn up. At what locations in its orbit will the satellite enter the atmosphere?

MATERIALS

Graphing utility

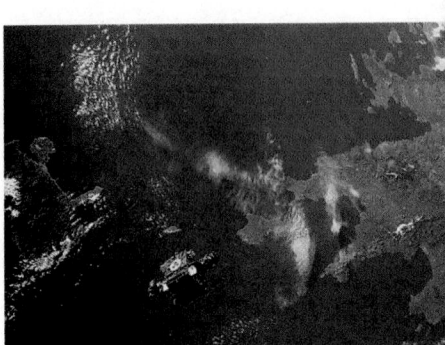

1. The average diameter of the earth is about 7920 miles. The upper reaches of its atmosphere reach approximately 600 miles above the earth's surface. Write an equation that models the earth and its atmosphere as a circle, as viewed from above the North Pole. Explain how you found your equation.

2. Suppose the satellite's orbit is modeled by the equation:

$$\frac{x^2}{4200^2} + \frac{y^2}{5500^2} = 1$$

At what (x, y) locations will the satellite enter or leave the atmosphere? How many intersection points are there? Explain how you found these points.

3. If the satellite follows this path, will it strike the earth? Explain how you can tell.

A quadratic-quadratic system can have more than one real solution. The graphs of an ellipse and a hyperbola illustrate that a quadratic-quadratic system may have 0, 1, 2, 3, or 4 real-number solutions.

0 points   1 point   2 points

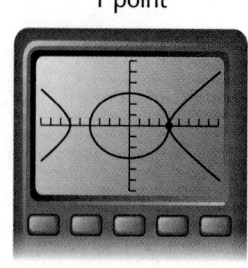 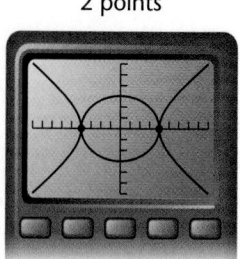

3 points   4 points

 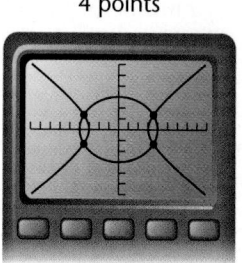

EXAMPLE

1. Graph the quadratic-quadratic system. Determine the number of real-number solutions visually. Then solve the system.

$x^2 + y^2 = 36$
$y = (x - 2)^2 - 3$

The graph of $x^2 + y^2 = 36$ is a circle with center at the origin and radius 6.

The graph of $y = (x - 2)^2 - 3$ is a parabola that opens upward with a vertex of $(2, -3)$.

The parabola intersects the circle in two points. This system has two real solutions near $(-1, 6)$ and $\left(4\frac{1}{2}, 4\right)$.

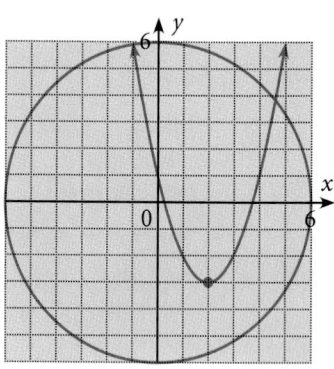

TRY IT

a. Graph the quadratic-quadratic system. Determine the number of real-number solutions visually. Then solve the system.

$(x - 1)^2 + (y + 3)^2 = 16$
$\dfrac{x^2}{9} + \dfrac{y^2}{4} = 1$

It is possible to solve a quadratic-quadratic system symbolically. Both substitution and linear combination approaches can be used.

EXAMPLE

2. Solve the system symbolically. Round answers to the nearest hundredth.

$x^2 + y^2 = 16$ ❶

$\frac{x^2}{25} + \frac{y^2}{4} = 1$ ❷

From the equations, we know we are looking for intersection points for a circle and an ellipse.

First, we clear the fractions in equation ❷.

$$\frac{x^2}{25} + \frac{y^2}{4} = 1 \quad \xrightarrow{100 \cdot ❷} \quad 4x^2 + 25y^2 = 100 \quad ❸$$

Solve for y by adding equations to eliminate one variable.

$$\begin{aligned} 4x^2 + 25y^2 = 100 \quad &\rightarrow \quad 4x^2 + 25y^2 = 100 \\ x^2 + y^2 = 16 \quad &\xrightarrow{-4 \cdot ❶} \quad -4x^2 - 4y^2 = -64 \end{aligned}$$

$$\begin{aligned} 21y^2 &= 36 \\ y^2 &= \frac{36}{21} \approx 1.71 \\ y &\approx \pm 1.31 \end{aligned}$$

Solve for x by substitution. Notice that we can substitute for y^2 directly.

$x^2 + y^2 = 16$ ❶

$x^2 + 1.71 = 16$ Substitute for y^2.

$x^2 = 14.29$

$x \approx \pm 3.78$

There are four possible answers, representing the possible positive and negative combinations. The four solutions are: $(-3.78, -1.31)$, $(-3.78, 1.31)$, $(3.78, -1.31)$, $(3.78, 1.31)$. These answers check.

TRY IT

b. Solve the system symbolically.

$y = 2x^2$

$x^2 + y^2 = 20$

When solving a quadratic-quadratic system, it is helpful to know which conic sections you are working with. As seen in 5-3B (Exercise 57 on page 388) and in 5-3C (Exercise 54 on page 395), you can identify the conic when its equation is in the form $Ax^2 + Bx + Cy^2 + Dy = E$ by using the following rules.

$A = C$	Circle	$2x^2 + 3x + 2y^2 - 4y = 7$
$A \neq C$, A and C have the same sign	Ellipse	$2x^2 + 3x + 3y^2 - 4y = 7$
A and C have different signs	Hyperbola	$2x^2 + 3x - 2y^2 - 4y = 7$
$A = 0$ or $C = 0$ (but not both)	Parabola	$3x - 2y^2 - 4y = 7$

REFLECT

1. Is it possible to have a quadratic-quadratic system with an infinite number of solutions? If so, give an example of such a system. If not, why not?
2. Describe some differences and similarities between quadratic-linear systems and quadratic-quadratic systems.
3. Give an example of a real-world situation that can be modeled by a quadratic-quadratic system.

Exercises

CORE

1. **Getting Started** Use the graph to estimate the coordinates of the points of intersection of the circle and parabola.

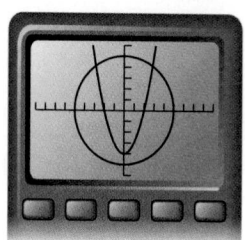

2. Draw a sketch of a hyperbola and an ellipse that intersect in two points.

Graph and estimate the solutions of each system of equations.

3. $(x - 2)^2 + (y - 2)^2 = 16$
   $2y = (x - 2)^2 - 1$

4. $16x^2 - 9y^2 = 144$
   $x^2 + y^2 = 16$

5. **Time for a Station Shake** Suppose that the epicenter of an earthquake is located 10 miles from a geological station situated at $(0, 0)$, 13 miles from a station at $(6, 3)$, and 20 miles from a station at $(-6, 12)$. What are the coordinates of the epicenter of the earthquake? Explain how you solved this problem.

Solve each system of equations symbolically.

6. $x^2 + y^2 = 74$
   $y^2 - x^2 = 24$

7. $4x + 2y^2 = 4$
   $x = 2y^2$

8. $5x^2 = y^2$
   $3x^2 - 4y^2 = 0$

9. $y = 2x^2$
   $x^2 + 3y = 16$

Graph each system of inequalities.

10. $x^2 + y^2 \leq 36$
    $y > x^2 - 2$

11. $\frac{x^2}{16} + \frac{y^2}{25} < 1$
    $x^2 + y^2 \geq 9$

12. Look, It's Halley's Comet! Halley's Comet appears about every 75 years. (Its next appearance is due in 2062.) It follows an elliptical path whose major axis is approximately 36 astronomical units (A.U.) and minor axis is about 9 A.U. The sun is at one focus of its orbit. Earth's orbit is approximately circular with a radius of 1 A.U.

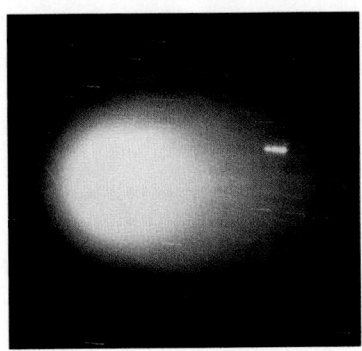

  a. Assuming the orbits are coplanar, does the path of Halley's Comet intersect the orbit of Earth? Explain how you found your answer.

  b. Is it possible that Halley's Comet will collide with Earth? If so, do you think such a collision is likely? Why or why not?

Graph each system of inequalities.

13. $x^2 + y^2 > 36$

$\dfrac{x^2}{9} + \dfrac{y^2}{16} > 1$

14. $y \geq (x - 3)^2 + 2$

$(x - 3)^2 + (y - 2)^2 < 25$

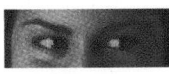 ## LOOK AHEAD

Simplify.

15. $6 \cdot 5 \cdot 4 \cdot 3 \cdot 2 \cdot 1$

16. $5 \cdot 4 \cdot 3 \cdot 2 \cdot 1 + 3 \cdot 2 \cdot 1$

17. $4 \cdot 3 \cdot 2 \cdot 1 - 2 \cdot 1$

18. $\dfrac{6 \cdot 5 \cdot 4 \cdot 3 \cdot 2 \cdot 1}{3 \cdot 2 \cdot 1}$

MORE PRACTICE

Use a graphing utility to graph and estimate the solutions of each system of equations. (Hint: You will need to solve the quadratic equations for y before graphing.)

19. $x^2 + y^2 = 7$

$3x^2 + 3y^2 = 12$

20. $\dfrac{x^2}{9} - \dfrac{y^2}{4} = 1$

$\dfrac{x^2}{25} + \dfrac{y^2}{9} = 1$

21. $9x^2 + 25y^2 = 225$

$y^2 = 2x + 4$

22. The area of a rectangle is 240 cm^2 and the length of one of its diagonals is 26 cm. Find the dimensions of the rectangle.

Solve each system of equations symbolically.

23. $x^2 - y^2 = 1$

$y = 2x^2 + 3$

24. $x^2 + y^2 = 10$

$x^2 - y^2 = 17$

25. $2x^2 + 3y^2 = 12$

$3x^2 + 4.5y^2 = 18$

26. $y = 2x^2 - 3$

$x^2 + y^2 = 16$

27. $x^2 + y^2 = 25$

$x^2 - y^2 = 9$

28. $y = x^2 - 7$

$2x^2 - 4y^2 = 2$

29. Increasing Revenue In 1994, Lila opened a business selling interactive computer software. Her revenue from one item was $26,554. In 1995, she cut the price of this software $5 and sold 195 more units of this item. The revenue increased to $28,304. How many units did she sell each year? What were the prices? Explain how you solved this problem.

MORE MATH REASONING

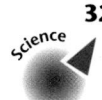

30. Find all possible lengths for the legs of a right triangle whose hypotenuse is $\sqrt{10}m$ long and area is $2m^2$.

31. Identical Roots Find the square roots of $12 + 16i$. (Hint: Let one of the square roots be $x + yi$, where x and y are real.)

32. Hurricane Alert! Hurricanes usually follow a path that is approximately parabolic. Suppose a hurricane tracking station, located at position $(0, 0)$ on the island shown, finds that the eye (center) of Hurricane Kim passes through points $(8, -25)$, $(7, -16)$, and $(6, -9)$.

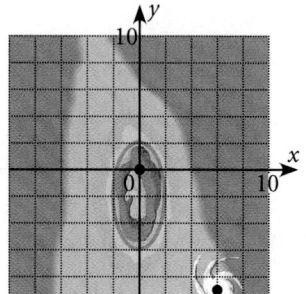

  a. By substituting values for x and y into $ax^2 + bx + c = y$, use the three locations of the hurricane to write a system of three equations.

  b. Use a graphing calculator to solve your system for a, b, and c by using matrices. Then write an equation to model the path of Hurricane Kim. (For specific information on how to do this, see 5-2B, Exercise 52 on page 353.)

  c. Does the eye of Hurricane Kim pass over the island where the tracking station is situated? If not, about how close does it come? Explain how you solved this problem.

5-4
PART C Making Connections

· ·

← CONNECT → *You've solved quadratic-linear and quadratic-quadratic systems by graphing and by analytical methods.*

Quadratic-linear and quadratic-quadratic systems can be used to find the intersection of a line and a conic section and of two conic sections. The LORAN navigation system uses intersecting hyperbolas to pinpoint the location of a ship.

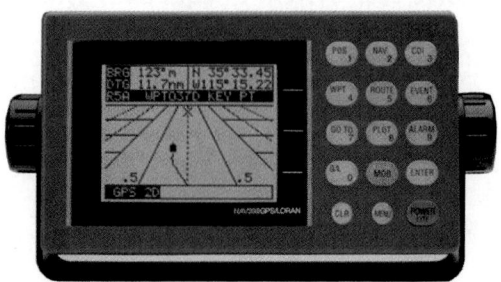

Your ship has been buffeted by a storm and has gone off course. Fortunately, your LORAN system is still working.

1. Your (x, y) position on a map is at an intersection point of the hyperbolas:

$$\frac{x^2}{9} - \frac{y^2}{16} = 1$$

$$\frac{y^2}{4} - \frac{x^2}{9} = 1$$

Where could you be? Explain your solution method.

2. Suppose that each unit on the map represents ten nautical miles. You know that you were at $(-8, 12)$ four hours ago. Your ship's top speed is 25 knots (nautical miles per hour). Where are you? How do you know?

George Philip Reinagle, *A First Rate Man of War Driving on a Reef of Rocks Foundering in a Gale,* Royal Albert Memorial Museum, Exeter, Great Britain

REFLECT

1. How is a system of linear equations similar to a quadratic-quadratic system? How are the systems different?

2. Suppose that the vertex of a comet's parabolic path is nearer the sun than any point on Earth's elliptical orbit. If the orbits are coplanar, in how many places will the comet's path intersect Earth's orbit? How do you know? Will the comet collide with Earth?

Self-Assessment

1. On the same axes, accurately draw the graphs of $x^2 - 4y^2 = 16$, $4y^2 - x^2 = 16$, and $x^2 + 4y^2 = 16$. Identify the conic sections, and describe and estimate any points of intersection.

Graph and estimate the solutions of each system of equations.

2. $2x^2 + 2y^2 = 72$
$4x^2 + y^2 = 100$

3. $y + 5 = x^2$
$2y = -x^2 + 6$

4. $y = 3x^2 - 5$
$y + 3x = 1$

5. The perimeter of a rectangle is 44 cm and its area is 57 cm². Find the dimensions of the rectangle.

6. Write equations for a parabola and an ellipse that intersect only at the point (0, −3).

> **Problem-Solving Tip**
>
> Make a sketch of the two figures.

Solve each system of equations symbolically.

7. $x^2 + y^2 = 100$
   $x^2 - 2y = 0$

8. $x^2 + y^2 = 25$
   $x + y = 7$

9. $x^2 + y^2 = 16$
   $x^2 - y^2 = 4$

10. **Cheers Across the Charles** Carla's dorm room is in Cambridge, just across the Charles River from Fenway Park, the baseball stadium in Boston. Alex's apartment is in Boston. The coordinates of their rooms are (0, 0) and (4, −2), respectively. Each unit represents 1 km.

During a baseball game, one of the Red Sox players hits a home run. Alex hears the cheers 9 seconds after they actually happen, and Carla hears the cheers 6 seconds after they happen. If the speed of sound is $\frac{1}{3}$ km/sec, what are the possible locations of Fenway Park?

Tell whether the following sets of numbers are closed under multiplication. [4-3]

11. The set of negative integers

12. {−1, 0, 1}

Name the coordinates of the foci of each ellipse described below. The major axis is horizontal. [5-3]

13. Center (0, 0), $a = 5$, $b = 3$

14. Center (−2, 3), $a = 10$, $b = 1$

Graph each system of inequalities.

15. $(x + 1)^2 + (y - 3)^2 \le 9$
    $y \le 2x - 1$

16. $\frac{x^2}{4} + \frac{y^2}{9} < 1$
    $y > x^2 - 4$

17. **Quadratic programming** is used to solve problems with linear constraints but with a quadratic objective function.

The Hedlund-Price Glork company produces regular glorks and Ultra glorks. They can produce a total of 20 glorks in a day, but no more than 4 of these can be Ultra glorks. Because Ultra glorks are in such high demand, they want to maximize the sum of the square of the number of Ultra glorks they produce plus the number of regular glorks; that is, the objective function is $U^2 + r$.

Find the number of Ultra glorks and regular glorks that the company should produce each day to maximize its objective function. Explain how you found your answer.

Chapter 5 Review

In Chapter 5, you worked with quadratic functions, equations, and relations. You investigated quadratic functions and their graphs, then used several different methods to solve quadratic equations. You also explored the different conic sections (parabolas, circles, ellipses, and hyperbolas) and saw real-world situations that could be modeled by these figures. Finally, you solved quadratic-linear and quadratic-quadratic systems of equations both symbolically and by graphing.

KEY TERMS

asymptote [5-3]

branches of a hyperbola [5-3]

center (of a circle, ellipse, hyperbola) [5-3]

circle [5-3]

complete the square [5-1]

conic section [5-3]

discriminant [5-2]

double root [5-2]

ellipse [5-3]

foci (of an ellipse, hyperbola) [5-3]

hyperbola [5-3]

major axis [5-3]

minor axis [5-3]

parabola [5-1]

parameter [5-1]

parent function [5-1]

quadratic equation [5-2]

quadratic formula [5-2]

quadratic function [5-1]

quadratic-linear system [5-4]

quadratic-quadratic system [5-4]

radius [5-3]

roots of an equation [5-2]

standard form (for a circle, ellipse, hyperbola) [5-3]

standard form (for a quadratic equation) [5-2]

vertex (of a parabola) [5-1]

vertices (of an ellipse, hyperbola) [5-3]

zeros of a function [5-2]

Determine whether each statement is true or false. If the statement is false, change the underlined word or phrase to make it true.

1. An <u>ellipse</u> is easier to sketch if you draw its asymptotes.

2. The <u>quadratic function</u> can be used to solve any quadratic equation.

3. The standard form of a <u>quadratic equation</u> is $ax^2 + bx + c = 0$.

4. Conic sections include <u>parabolas</u>, <u>circles</u>, <u>functions</u>, and <u>ellipses</u>.

5. The <u>roots</u> of a quadratic function are its x-intercepts.

6. The <u>minor axis</u> of an ellipse passes through its foci.

7. The minimum or maximum value of a quadratic function $y = ax^2 + \underline{bx} + c$ is at its <u>focus</u>.

CONCEPTS AND APPLICATIONS

Copy and complete the chart. [5-1]

$f(x) = a(x - h)^2 + k$	Vertex	Value of a	Transformations to the Graph of $y = x^2$		
			Reflect Across x-axis?	**Horizontal Translation**	**Vertical Translation**
$f(x) = -4(x + 1)^2 + 3$	$(-1, 3)$	-4	yes	left 1	up 3
8. $f(x) = 0.75x^2 - 2$					
9.		0.4	no	right 1.6	down 7
10. $f(x) = -8(x + 5)^2$					
11.	$(2, 5)$	-3			

Graph each set of functions on the same set of axes. [5-1]

12. $f(x) = x^2 + 3$, $g(x) = (x - 1)^2$, and $h(x) = (x - 1)^2 + 3$

13. $f(x) = 3x^2$, $g(x) = -3x^2 - 1$, and $h(x) = -3(x + 2)^2 - 1$

Complete the square to find the vertex and the line of symmetry of the graph of each function. Find the maximum or minimum value of the function. [5-1]

14. $f(x) = x^2 + 6x$ **15.** $y = x^2 - 8x + 5$ **16.** $g(x) = 3x^2 + 9x - 1$

17. A report by a telemarketing company indicates that there is a close connection between the number of different products the company sells and the number of successful sales contacts per month. The report states that the number of products the company sells (x) is related to the number of successful contacts (y) by the equation $y = -x^2 + 30x + 4$.

How many products should the company market to have the maximum number of successful sales contacts per month? What will be the maximum number of sales contacts per month? Explain how you solved this problem. [5-1]

Solve each equation. Where necessary, round your answer to the nearest tenth. Explain your choice of solution technique. [5-2]

18. $14x - x^2 = 49$ **19.** $5x^2 + 8x - 4 = 0$ **20.** $0 = x^2 + 2x - 63$ **21.** $3x^2 - 12x = 10$

22. Win Valuable Prizes! In a carnival test of strength, contestants strike a pad with a hammer. The force of the blow propels a ringer upward toward a bell. If the bell rings, the contestant wins. Marcel swings the hammer and knocks the ringer upward from ground level at 10 m/sec. [5-2]

a. Write a function $h(t)$ for the height of the ringer after t seconds.

b. Will Marcel ring the bell 6 m above the ground? Explain.

Without solving, determine the nature of the roots of each quadratic equation. [5-2]

23. $x^2 - 20x + 7 = 0$ **24.** $4x^2 - 10x + 5 = 0$

State whether the graph of each equation is a circle, an ellipse, a parabola, or a hyperbola. If it is a circle, identify its center and radius; if it is an ellipse, identify its center and foci; if a parabola, its vertex; and if a hyperbola, its center and vertices. Then graph each equation. [5-3]

25. $x^2 + y^2 = 81$

26. $\frac{x^2}{36} - \frac{y^2}{16} = 1$

27. $\frac{(x-1)^2}{9} + \frac{(y+2)^2}{4} = 1$

28. The major axis of Mercury's orbit is about 72,000,000 miles long. If the eccentricity of its orbit is about 0.205, what is the closest Mercury comes to the sun? [5-3]

Graph and estimate the solutions of each system of equations. [5-4]

29. $(x + 1)^2 + (y - 2)^2 = 36$
$y = 2x + 1$

30. $y = x^2 - 4$
$\frac{x^2}{16} + \frac{y^2}{4} = 1$

Solve each system of equations symbolically. [5-4]

31. $x^2 + y^2 = 125$
$y = 2x$

32. $4x^2 + y^2 = 16$
$y = x^2 - 1$

33. Suppose that the total daily cost of manufacturing n items is approximated by $C = n^2 - 50n + 225$. Items sell for $10 each, so the revenue for n items is $10n$. How many items should the company produce in order to break even? Explain your solution method. [5-4]

CONCEPTS AND CONNECTIONS

34. Astronomy The Cassegrain telescope shown uses parabolic and hyperbolic mirrors. Copy the sketch and show how the light rays are reflected. Then explain how the telescope works. Note: The focus of the branch of the hyperbola is the same as the focal point of the parabola.

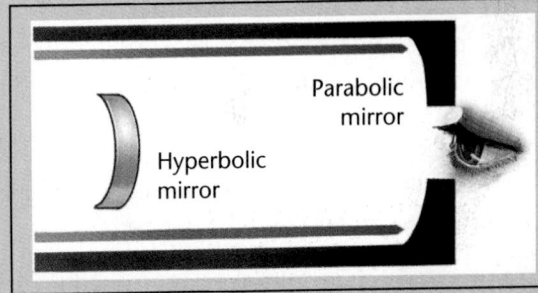

SELF-EVALUATION

Describe what you have learned about quadratic functions and quadratic equations. Identify the similarities and differences between the different conic sections. Determine how quadratic-linear systems and quadratic-quadratic systems can be solved. Mention any parts of the chapter that were difficult for you.

TEST

1. Graph the points $(2, 8)$, $(3, 9)$, $(0, 12)$, and $(5, 17)$.
  a. If these points lie on a parabola and one of the points is the vertex, find the line of symmetry.
  b. Use the symmetry of the parabola to find three other points on the parabola.
  c. Draw a smooth parabola through your points. Do you think more than one parabola can be drawn through the points? Explain.

Write a sequence of transformations that will produce the graph of each function from the graph of $y = x^2$.

2. $y = (x - 3)^2$ **3.** $y = -(x - 0.3)^2 + 18$ **4.** $y = (x + 2)^2 - 3$

Graph each set of functions on the same set of axes.

5. $f(x) = x^2$, $g(x) = (x + 2)^2$, and $h(x) = (x + 2)^2 - 3$

6. $f(x) = 2x^2$, $g(x) = -2(x + 1)^2$, and $h(x) = -2(x + 1)^2 + 2$

7. Parabolic Path Galileo used the equation $y = x - 8x^2$ to describe the path of a cannonball. Graph this equation and identify its line of symmetry.

Complete the square to find the vertex and the line of symmetry of the graph of each function. Find the maximum or minimum value of the function.

8. $y = x^2 - 4x$ **9.** $y = 4x^2 - 16x + 7$

10. The free-fall equation for the moon, with distance in meters, is $h(t) = -0.8t^2 + v_0 t + h_0$. Find the maximum height reached by a ball thrown with an initial upward velocity of 24 m/sec on Earth and on the moon. Explain how you found your answers.

Solve each equation. Where necessary, round your answer to the nearest tenth. Explain your choice of solution technique.

11. $x^2 - 100 = 0$ **12.** $x^2 - 5x + 10 = 0$ **13.** $6x^2 - 4x - 2 = 0$ **14.** $2x^2 + 3x = 1$

15. The Golden Rectangle The golden rectangle is found in nature, and in the art and architecture of many cultures. The ratio of the length of a golden rectangle to its width is the *golden ratio*.

If you cut a golden rectangle into a square and a smaller rectangle, the smaller rectangle is a golden rectangle. Using this fact, use the quadratic formula to find $\frac{\ell}{w}$, the golden ratio. (Hint: Let $w = 1$ for convenience.)

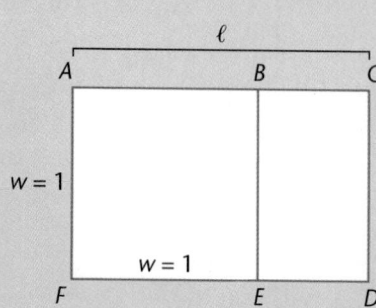

Without solving, determine the nature of the roots of each quadratic equation.

16. $3x^2 - 4x + 2 = 0$

17. $-16t^2 + 20t = 100$

State whether the graph of each equation is a circle, an ellipse, a parabola, or a hyperbola. If it is a circle, identify its center and radius; if it is an ellipse, identify its center and foci; if a parabola, its vertex; and if a hyperbola, its center and vertices. Then graph each equation.

18. $x^2 + y^2 = 9$

19. $\dfrac{y^2}{64} - \dfrac{x^2}{9} = 1$

20. $\dfrac{(x+3)^2}{16} + \dfrac{(y-4)^2}{25} = 1$

21. Martian Orbit At its nearest approach, Mars is 128.5 million miles from the sun. At its greatest distance, it is 155 million miles away. Find the eccentricity of Mars' orbit. (Hint: First find the distance from the center of its orbit to the sun, one focus of its orbit.)

Graph and estimate the solutions of each system of equations.

22. $y = (x - 2)^2 + 5$

$y = -\dfrac{1}{2}x + 6$

23. $(x + 5)^2 + (y + 3)^2 = 49$

$\dfrac{x^2}{25} + \dfrac{y^2}{16} = 1$

Solve each system of equations symbolically.

24. $x^2 + y^2 = 40$

$y = 3x^2$

25. $x^2 + 2y^2 = 24$

$y = x + 2$

26. While talking on the phone, Reggie and Alicia both notice a flash of lightning. By counting the seconds from lightning flash to thunderclap, Reggie determines that the lightning is 5 km away. Alicia finds that the lightning is 8 km away. If Reggie's house is at $(0, 0)$ and Alicia's is at $(2, 11)$, find the possible locations for the lightning strike. Explain how you solved this problem.

PERFORMANCE TASK

You are hired to design a logo for a company that sells books and toys that teach children about astronomy. The company wants its logo to include at least two conic sections. Since the logo will be produced by computer, the company also wants you to provide equations for the conic sections.

Design a logo for this company. Explain why you chose the conic sections that you used. Include the equations for your conic sections and explain how you determined them.

Chapter 6

Counting and Arranging Discrete Objects

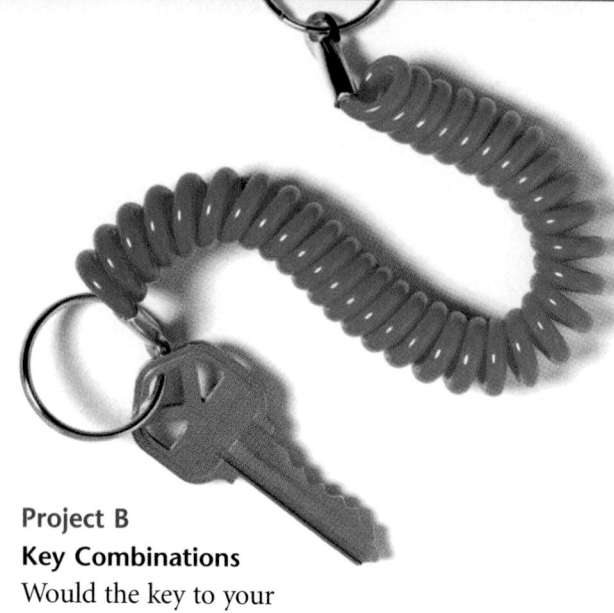

Shall I compare thee to a summer's day?

And make the earth devour her own sweet brood;

Rough winds do shake the darling buds of May

And burn the long-liv'd phoenix in her blood;

Sometime too hot the eye of heaven shines,

And do whate'er thou wilt, swift footed Time,

And every fair from far sometime declines,

But I forbid thee one most heinous crime:

But thy eternal summer shall not fade

Nor draw no lines there with thine antique pen!

So long as men can breathe or eyes can see,

For beauty's pattern to succeeding men.

So long lives this, and this gives life to thee.

My love shall in my verse ever live young,

Project B
Key Combinations
Would the key to your
front door open anyone
else's front door?

Project A
A Hundred Thousand
Billion Sonnets
How does poetry relate
to mathematics?

Project C
Celebrating Change
Is there a specific pattern
to bell ringing?

ELIZABETH FLINT

In high school it was never quite clear to me how I would be able to use the math I was learning.

As a biologist, I use math almost every day in activities such as making and reading maps, or using statistics to help me answer scientific questions and make decisions that may affect the welfare of endangered species.

All students should study math because it teaches you quantitative thinking, which gives you an advantage when problem-solving.

Elizabeth Flint
Wildlife Biologist
U.S. Fish and Wildlife
    Service
Department of the Interior
Honolulu, Hawaii

6-1
Counting Objects and Permutations

In 6-1 you will explore principles that help you count objects and events. You will use the following skills.

Evaluate. [Previous course]

1. $4 \cdot 26^2 \cdot 10^3$ **2.** $6 \cdot 5 \cdot 4 \cdot 3 \cdot 2 \cdot 1$ **3.** $\dfrac{7 \cdot 6 \cdot 5 \cdot 4 \cdot 3 \cdot 2 \cdot 1}{4 \cdot 3 \cdot 2 \cdot 1 \cdot 3 \cdot 2 \cdot 1}$

How many outcomes are possible for each of the following events? [Previous course]

4. flipping a coin

5. rolling a die

6. selecting a letter of the alphabet

7. selecting one card from a 52-card deck

8. selecting a heart from a standard deck of playing cards

9. selecting a one-digit positive odd number

10. spinning a spinner with 4 equal sections.

6-2
Combinations and the Binomial Theorem

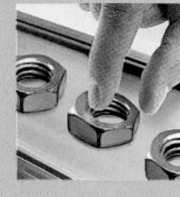

In 6-2 you will count combinations of objects and events where the order of the objects does not matter. You will need the following algebra skills.

Simplify. [Previous course]

11. $(-3)^2$ **12.** $(5 - 4)^2$ **13.** $(a + 5)^2$ **14.** $(b - 3)^2$

15. $(2c + 7)^2$ **16.** $(3d - 8)^2$ **17.** $(-2y)^2$ **18.** $(-2x)^3$

19. $-(3y)^5$ **20.** $\dfrac{4 \cdot 3 \cdot 2 \cdot 1}{(2 \cdot 1)(2 \cdot 1)} x^2 5^2$

21. $\dfrac{5 \cdot 4 \cdot 3 \cdot 2 \cdot 1}{(3 \cdot 2 \cdot 1)(2 \cdot 1)} x^3 (-3)^2$ **22.** $\dfrac{5 \cdot 4 \cdot 3 \cdot 2 \cdot 1}{(2 \cdot 1)(3 \cdot 2 \cdot 1)} (2x)^2 (-5)^3$

Solve. [Previous course]

23. The fifth row of Pascal's Triangle is 1 4 6 4 1. Write the next two rows.

6-1 Counting Objects and Permutations

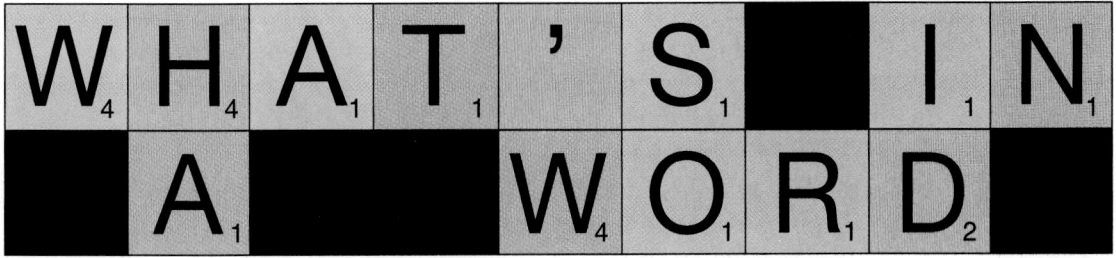

People of all ages enjoy playing with words. Children often delight in rhyming, creating amusing poems, and even making up their own words. Many of us enjoy puns, riddles, and phrases with double meanings. We may rearrange the letters of a word to form an anagram or create a palindrome, a phrase that reads the same forward and backward.

It's probably not surprising that people of many cultures indulge in a wide variety of word puzzles and word games such as crossword puzzles, acrostics, hangman, and the popular board game Scrabble®.

Scrabble was invented in 1931 and has become a favorite pastime in homes and organized clubs. In 1987, 326 contestants competed in an international Scrabble competition, which was won by computer science graduate Rita Norr of New York. In 1988, Clive Spate scored a record 979 points in a competitive Scrabble match. His score included an amazing 320 points in a single turn for the word *waltzing.* In the process, he also set a new record for the greatest winning margin when he outscored his opponent by 705 points!

The pleasure derived from playing with words has also influenced many poets, lyricists, and writers. The writer and mathematician Lewis Carroll is perhaps best known for the ingenious word play and word puzzles found throughout his book, *Alice's Adventures in Wonderland.*

Word games continue to be a source of pleasure, entertainment, and creativity for millions of people.

1. Describe some mathematics that could be related to word games or word puzzles.
2. Give three examples of word pairs that rhyme.
3. Examine this phrase, which could have been uttered by Napoleon while exiled on the island of Elba: Able was I ere I saw Elba. What do you notice about this phrase?

Methods of Counting

Counting methods can help you count the members of a set and the outcomes in an event. Counting events is an important part of finding theoretical probabilities.

Counting has been a basic skill of mathematics since people first invented the counting numbers. A more modern tool available to help you count in complex situations is the **tree diagram.** In the following Explore, you will complete a tree diagram to help you investigate possible schedules.

EXPLORE: TOURNAMENT TIME

A committee is planning a Scrabble tournament and has chosen sites in Albuquerque, Chicago, Dallas, and San Diego for the four rounds. However, the committee has not yet chosen which site will host each round.

1. This tree diagram shows some of the possibilities for assigning sites for the tournament rounds. What site assignments do you think are represented by this tree diagram?

2. Suppose Dallas is chosen to host the first round of the tournament. How many cities can be chosen to host the second round? After the second site is chosen, how many cities can be chosen to host the third round? the fourth round? How many possible ways can the tournament sites be scheduled with Dallas as the site of the first round?

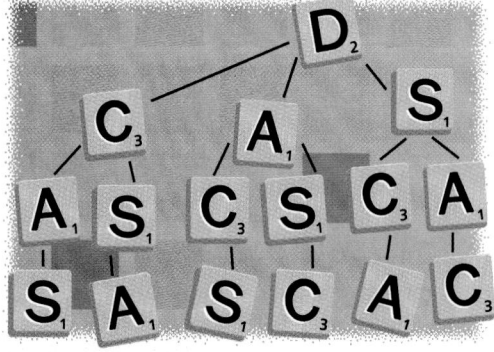

3. Copy and complete the tree diagram to show all possibilities for scheduling the sites for the tournament. How many ways can the sites for the four-round tournament be scheduled?

4. How many ways could the five sites for a five-round tournament be scheduled? six sites? Generalize to find the number of ways to schedule a tournament with any number of rounds at an equal number of sites.

When you count the number of ways a series of events can occur, such as the rounds of the tournament above, it is often useful to look at each event separately. The notation $n(A)$ means the number of ways an event A can occur. For example, if A represents the event that a state's name has *New* in it, then $n(A) = 4$ (New Hampshire, New Jersey, New Mexico, and New York). Using this notation, we can give a simple principle for counting series of events.

The number of ways a series of events, A_1 through A_k, can occur is
$n(A_1) \cdot n(A_2) \cdot \cdots \cdot n(A_k)$.

EXAMPLES

1. A concession stand has a special price for complete meals. A meal consists of a main item, a side order, and a drink. The main items are hot dogs and hamburgers. The side orders are french fries, onion rings, and salad. The drinks are colas, lemonade, and iced tea. How many different complete meals does the vendor offer?

The vendor offers 2 main items, 3 side orders, and 3 drinks. Therefore, there are $2 \cdot 3 \cdot 3 = 18$ possible complete meals. The tree diagram shows the 18 possible meals.

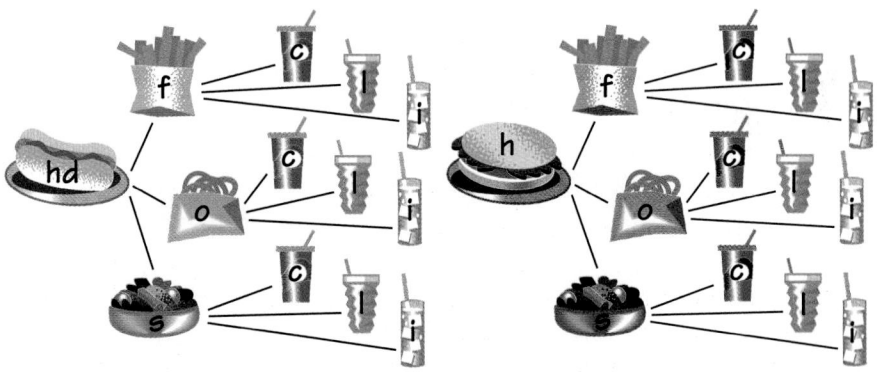

2. A locksmith manufactures combination locks with numbers from 0 to 39. Each lock uses a unique combination of three of these whole numbers, not necessarily all different. How many lock combinations can the locksmith use without repeating a combination?

There are 40 possible numbers to use for each of the three numbers on a lock. Therefore, there are 40^3 or 64,000 different combinations possible.

CONSIDER

1. How would your method and result differ in Example 2 if numbers could not be repeated in any lock combination? Explain.

TRY IT

a. Shauna invented a game in which each move is determined by choosing one card marked A, B, C, D, or E, and a second card numbered 0, 1, 2, 3, 4, 5, or 6. How many choices of the two cards are possible?

In the Explore, there were 4 choices for the first site, 3 choices for the second site, 2 choices for the third site, and 1 choice for the last site. Multiplying gives 4 • 3 • 2 • 1 or 24 possible ways to choose the four sites. This product is denoted by **4!** and is read "four **factorial.**"

$0! = 1$, $1! = 1$, and $n! = n \cdot (n - 1) \cdot (n - 2) \cdot \cdots \cdot 3 \cdot 2 \cdot 1$ gives the value of n **factorial** for any integer $n > 1$.

TRY IT

b. How many ways can the top three finishers at a Scrabble tournament line up in a row for the awards photograph?

c. Evaluate 6!.

To count the possible ways an event can occur, it is sometimes helpful to think of the event as two or more **mutually exclusive events,** events that have no common outcomes. For such events, you can add the number of ways each event can occur to find the total number of ways any of the events can occur.

ADDITION COUNTING PRINCIPLE

If A and B are mutually exclusive events, then $n(A \text{ or } B) = n(A) + n(B)$.

EXAMPLE

3. Suppose you play a game in which you win your turn by rolling a 7 or 11 with two dice. How many ways can you win a turn?

There are 6 ways to roll a total of 7, and 2 ways to roll a total of 11.

Rolling a total of 7 and rolling a total of 11 are mutually exclusive events, since it is impossible to do both. Therefore, there are 6 + 2 or 8 ways to roll a total of 7 or 11 and win the turn.

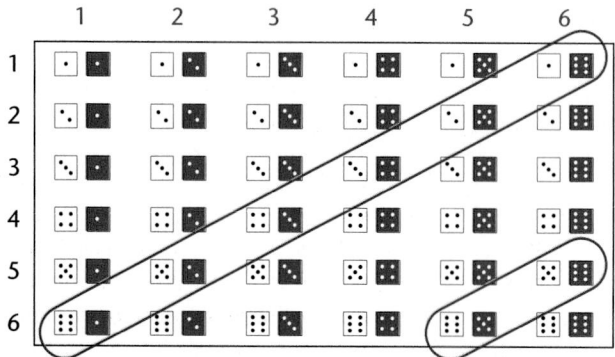

d. Suppose you roll two 8-sided dice, each numbered 1 through 8. How many ways can you roll a total of 3 or 13?

These two counting methods provide an important foundation for later work with permutations, combinations, and probability.

REFLECT

1. Explain what is shown in a tree diagram and explain how it can help you count the number of ways a series of events can occur.

2. Describe a situation in which an event has 5! ways of occurring.

3. How does your counting strategy differ when outcomes in a series of events can or cannot be repeated? Explain.

4. Explain how you can tell if two or more events are mutually exclusive.

Exercises

CORE

1. Getting Started A game company makes two versions of a game, one version for two or more players and the other for solitaire play (one player). The game is made for four levels of playing abilities: beginner, intermediate, advanced, and genius.

a. Copy and complete the tree diagram showing all possible games the company makes.

b. How many different games does the company make?

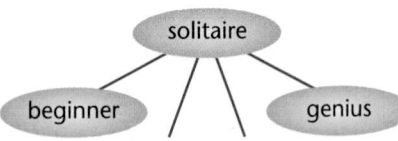 

2. At Romano's Pizzeria, you can order pizza with thin or thick crust and with any of five toppings.

a. How many types of crust are there?

b. How many choices of toppings are there?

c. How many different types of one-topping pizza can be ordered?

3. During your turn in a game, you toss two dice.

a. How many ways can you get a sum of 5?

b. How many ways can you get a sum of 10?

c. How many ways you can get a sum of 5 or 10?

4. You are given a test with four true-false questions and six multiple-choice questions, each with three possible answers.

a. How many possible answers are there for each true-false question? How many possible ways are there to complete the whole true-false section?

b. How many possible answers are there for each of the remaining questions?

c. Use the Multiplication Counting Principle to find out how many different answer sheets could be filled out.

5. **Family Tree** If you go back one generation, you have two genetic ancestors, your parents. How many genetic ancestors do you have four generations back?

6. Yaël is planning her day off. During the day, she can go shopping, visit the zoo, or play tennis. For her evening meal, she can buy Italian, Chinese, or Mexican food. After dinner, she can go to a movie or read a book. Draw a tree diagram to show and count Yaël's options for spending her day off.

Evaluate each expression.

7. 10!

8. 4! + 5!

9. 6! − 3!

10. $\frac{8!}{6!}$

11. **Voting Booth** In an upcoming primary election, a Republican, a Democrat, and an Independent candidate will be chosen to represent their parties. Two Republicans, four Democrats, and six Independent Party candidates are campaigning. How many ways can a representative from each party be chosen?

12. A club is holding an election for a president, a secretary, and a treasurer. One person can hold only one office in the club. If there are 25 members in the club, how many different ways can these offices be filled?

13. U.S. radio stations have three- or four-letter station codes, with one letter that cannot be selected. (Station codes east of the Mississippi River typically begin with W, and station codes west of the Mississippi River typically begin with K.)
   a. If the letters can be repeated, how many different three-letter station codes can be assigned? How many four-letter station codes can be assigned? How many station codes can be assigned all together?
   b. How would your answers to **a** differ if the letters could not be repeated?

14. Totolospi is a game of chance invented by the Hopi. The materials used to play the game include three cane dice, each with a round side and a flat side, a counting board, and a game piece for each player. The two players place their game pieces at opposite ends of the board. The object is to reach the other side of the board. Players toss three cane dice to determine their moves. If three round sides are tossed, the player moves up two spaces. If three flat sides are tossed, the player moves up one space. If any other combination is tossed, the turn is lost.

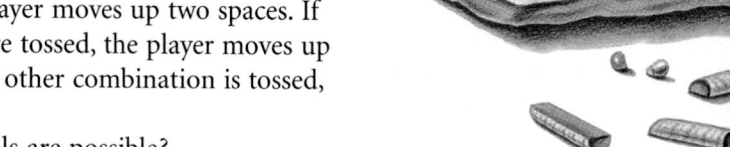

   a. How many rolls are possible?
   b. How many ways can you get three flat sides?
   c. How many ways can you get three round sides?
   d. How many ways can you get three flat sides or three round sides?

 **LOOK AHEAD**

Evaluate each expression.

15. $\frac{5!}{(5-3)!}$

16. $(6 \cdot 5 \cdot 4) \cdot 3!$

17. $\frac{6!}{(3! \cdot 2!)}$

MORE PRACTICE

18. **Dial-a-Code** In the United States, each region has its own area code made up of three digits. Prior to 1995, the first digit could be any number other than 0 or 1, and the second digit could only be 0 or 1. The third digit could be any of the digits 0 through 9, as long as there were not two consecutive zeros or ones.
    a. How many area codes with a first digit of 2 are possible?
    b. How many area codes with a middle digit of 0 are possible?
    c. How many area codes with a middle digit of 1 are possible?
    d. How many area codes are possible?

Evaluate each expression.

19. $9!$

20. $3! + 6!$

21. $8! - 5!$

22. $\dfrac{9!}{5!}$

23. $6 \cdot 5!$

24. $0! + 1!$

25. **Hit the Trail** A ranger at a national park posts the day's scheduled activities. In the morning, visitors can choose a 0.5-mile hike, a 1.2-mile hike, or a 2.5-mile hike. In the afternoon, visitors can choose to watch a nature film, canoe on a river, or take a horseback ride. In the evening, visitors can choose a sing-along, a lecture, or a crafts demonstration. Make a tree diagram to show how many different ways a visitor to the park can take advantage of the day's scheduled activities.

26. A customer ordering a dinner entree at Johnson's Restaurant must choose between soup or salad; potato, rice, or french fries; and a dinner roll or garlic bread. If chicken is the entree, make a tree diagram to show how many different meals can be ordered.

27. At 30 Flavors Yogurt Shoppe, a sundae can be made from one of 30 flavors of yogurt; one of 5 flavors of syrup; one of 10 toppings; with or without whipped cream; and with or without a cherry. How many different sundaes can be made?

28. The password on a home security system consists of a sequence of any six digits, not necessarily all different. How many different passwords are possible?

29. How many outfits can be made from 3 skirts, 5 blouses, and 3 pairs of shoes?

30. The Huskies and the Wombats are playing a best-of-five game series, which means that the series is over when one team has won three games. Make a tree diagram to find the number of ways the Huskies can win the series.

MORE MATH REASONING

31. How many different paths can be taken from A to B along the edges of the figure without crossing any edge or vertex more than once?

32. Find the nth term of the sequence with the following recursive definition: $a_1 = 1$ and $a_n = n \cdot a_{n-1}$ for $n > 1$?

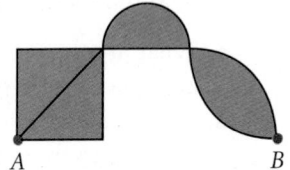

Decide whether each equation is true for every positive integer n. Explain.

33. $n! = n(n - 1)!$

34. $(n + 1)! = 2n!$

Arrangements and Permutations

← **CONNECT** → *The Multiplication Counting Principle allows you to count the number of possible ways to arrange a set of items in order. Now you will examine the number of possible ways to arrange items in a set, both when the items are all different and when some items are repeated.*

An *anagram* is a word or phrase formed by rearranging letters in an existing word or phrase. For example, the word *redo* is an anagram of the word *rode*. Arrangements can be applied to words and used in many other situations.

EXPLORE: COOL SKATES

Four speed skaters are scheduled to compete in a 1000-meter race. They skate in pairs and then their times are compared to determine the finishing order. The officials assign the numbers 1, 2, 3, and 4 to the skaters before they compete.

1. Assuming each skater finishes with a different time, what are all of the possible finish orders for the skaters? How many possible race results are there?

> **Problem-Solving Tip**
>
> Make an organized list or a tree diagram of the possible results.

2. Only the two fastest finishers go on to the regional finals. What are all of the possible results for first and second place? How many possible results are there for first and second place?
3. Three medals—gold, silver, and bronze—are awarded to the top three finishers. What are the possible medal results? How many possible medal results are there?

Skaters 1 and 2 are members of the East team, and skaters 3 and 4 are members of the West team. As far as team results are concerned, there is no difference between the finishing orders 1, 2, 3, 4 and 2, 1, 4, 3. Both represent the result E, E, W, W; that is, East coming in first and second, and West coming in third and fourth.

4. What are the possible finishing orders for all four skaters as far as the team results are concerned? How many possible team race results are there?
5. All else being equal, what is the probability that one team will have both skaters advance to the regional finals? Describe at least one other probability you can find using your results from Steps 1–4.

The order in which things are arranged is an important consideration in many situations, such as determining race results or deciding how you will arrange your daily tasks.

A **permutation** of a set of items is an ordered arrangement of the items.

EXAMPLE

1. In a Scrabble game, Mario drew the letters E, W, L, N, S, F, and O. How many permutations of four of these letters are possible?

There are 7 choices for the first letter, 6 choices for the second letter, 5 choices for the third letter, and 4 choices for the fourth letter. Using the Multiplication Counting Principle, there are $7 \cdot 6 \cdot 5 \cdot 4$ or 840 permutations of these 7 letters taken 4 at a time.

We denote the number of permutations of 7 distinct items taken 4 at a time by $_7P_4$, which can be evaluated on many calculators. We can also express this number as a product or by using factorials.

7 nPr 4
840

$$_7P_4 = 7 \cdot 6 \cdot 5 \cdot 4 = \frac{7 \cdot 6 \cdot 5 \cdot 4 \cdot 3 \cdot 2 \cdot 1}{3 \cdot 2 \cdot 1} = \frac{7!}{3!}$$

If n and r are positive integers with $r \leq n$, then $_nP_r$ denotes the number of permutations of n distinct items taken r at a time. $_nP_r$ is given by

$$_nP_r = \underbrace{n(n-1)(n-2)\cdots(n-r+1)}_{r \text{ factors}} = \frac{n!}{(n-r)!}.$$

TRY IT

a. Evaluate $_{11}P_5$.

b. How many permutations of 6 letters are there from A, E, B, L, N, O, S, T, and Y?

c. A chemist is making a solution of 5 chemicals in water. How many possible orders are there to add the chemicals one at a time?

CONSIDER

?

1. What does $_nP_n$ represent? Explain why $_nP_n = n!$.

When items in a set are repeated, some permutations yield the same arrangement. For example, there are 5! permutations of the digits in 11123, but for each permutation, there are 3! ways to permute the 1's that are *indistinguishable*. There are only $\frac{5!}{3!}$ or 20 *distinguishable* permutations.

> If n items include q copies of one item, r copies of another item, s copies of a third item, and so on, then the number of distinguishable permutations of all n items is $P = \frac{n!}{q!r!s!...}$.

EXAMPLE

2. How many distinguishable permutations are there of the letters in the phrase **THE EYES**? Can you find an anagram among these permutations?

There are 7 letters. The only repeated letter is E, which occurs 3 times.

$$P = \frac{7!}{3!} = 840$$

There are 840 distinguishable permutations of the letters in **THE EYES**.

One of these permutations is the anagram **THEY SEE**.

TRY IT

d. Give the number of distinguishable permutations of these letters.

MISSISSIPPI

CONSIDER **2.** Renata noticed that when she added an *s* to the end of a word that previously had no *s*, the number of distinguishable permutations tripled. What can you deduce about her original word?

The counting principles lead naturally to the study of arrangements and permutations. Situations that involve permutations have been studied for hundreds of years and can be found, for example, in the writings of the Hindu mathematician Bhāskara (ca. 1150).

REFLECT

1. What does the symbol $_8P_5$ represent in terms of permutations?

2. How can the items in a set be permuted in different ways, yet yield the same arrangement? Give an example to explain.

3. Would you use the product form or the factorial form to evaluate $_{26}P_{10}$? Explain your choice.

CORE

1. **Getting Started** Examine the letters in the word FAMILY.
   a. Consider all 4-letter permutations from these letters, such as FLAM. How many choices are there for the first letter? second letter? third letter? fourth letter?
   b. Calculate the product of the numbers in **a** to find the number of 4-letter permutations in the word FAMILY.
   c. How many 6-letter permutations are there in FAMILY?

Write the word or phrase that correctly completes the statement.

2. A ____ is an ordered arrangement of a group of items.

Determine whether each statement is true or false. If the statement is false, change the underlined word or phrase to make it true.

3. ABC and <u>BAC</u> are permutations of the letters in the word CAB.

4. There are 3 <u>distinguishable permutations</u> of the letters in the name ANN.

5. List all 3-letter permutations in the name STU.

6. **Say Cheese!** How many ways can a family of 6 line up for a photograph?

7. **The Hands of Siva** Answer the following ques-  tions adapted from the writings of the twelfth-century Hindu mathematician Bhāskara.
   a. How many permutations are there of these items held in the hands of the god Siva (Sambu): a rope, elephant's hook, serpent, tabor, skull, trident, bedstead, dagger, arrow, and bow?
   b. How many permutations are there of these items held by the god Hari: a mace, discus, lotus, and conch?

An eighteenth-century gilded-bronze statue of the Indian god, Siva

Evaluate each expression.

8. $_8P_6$

9. $_{10}P_{10}$

10. $_{15}P_5$

11. 8!

12. **Name That Tune** How many ways can the 8 notes of a C scale be arranged to form an 8-note melody if:
   a. no note can be repeated?
   b. notes can be repeated, but the melody must begin on low C and end on high C?

13. **Get the Vote Out** How many ways can a president, vice-president, secretary, and treasurer be elected from a club with 15 members?

14. a. How many permutations are there of 6 letters taken 6 at a time?
  b. If 4 of the letters are identical and the other 2 are different, how many ways can you permute the 4 letters among themselves to yield the same arrangement?
  c. Divide your result in **a** by your result in **b** to give the number of *distinguishable* permutations of the 6 letters taken 6 at a time.

15. List all distinguishable permutations of the letters VENN taken 4 at a time. How many distinguishable permutations are there?

Give the number of distinguishable permutations of all letters in each word.

16. BOOTH   **17. MATHEMATICS**   **18. SCIENCE**

19. How many different ways can these four states on the map be colored, if six colors are available and each state must be a different color?

20. Mix Up How many distinguishable permutations can be made using the letters in PLEASED? If you can, find a word or phrase that forms an anagram of this word.

Utah   Colorado

Arizona   New Mexico

LOOK BACK

Solve each system of linear equations by using substitution or linear combinations. [3-1]

21. $4x - y = 14$
  $5x + 3y = 9$

22. $4x + 3y = 17$
  $2x + 3y = 13$

23. Which term of the geometric sequence 5, −10, 20, … is equal to 320? [4-2]

Give the coordinates of the foci of the ellipse given by each equation. [5-3]

24. $x^2 + \dfrac{y^2}{4} = 1$ **25.** $\dfrac{x^2}{169} + \dfrac{y^2}{144} = 1$ **26.** $4x^2 + 16y^2 = 16$

MORE PRACTICE

27. How many permutations are there of all letters in the word PRICE? How many permutations of 3 letters are there?

Evaluate each expression.

28. $_5P_3$ **29.** $_6P_2$ **30.** $_8P_8$

31. $_{25}P_3$ **32.** 7!   **33.** $_9P_1$

34. How many 2-letter permutations can be formed from the letters A, W, S, and M?

35. How many permutations of the letters in LEARN begin with 2 vowels?

36. Eight parking spaces are to be assigned to the eight executives who form the executive committee of a large corporation. How many different ways can the parking spaces be assigned?

37. A computer lab has 10 computers. How many ways can the computers be assigned to a group of 15 students?

Give the number of distinguishable permutations of all letters in each word.

38. APPROACH

39. TOGETHER

40. INTRODUCTORY

41. CONNECTICUT

42. AVAILABLE

43. ESSENCE

44. How many 3-digit even integers can be formed using the digits 2, 3, 4, 5, and 6:
   a. if repetition is not allowed?   **b.** if repetition is allowed?

45. How many different 6-digit integers can be formed by arranging the digits in the number 384,883?

46. In the 1992–93 season, the Atlantic Coast Conference had nine teams in its basketball program. Before the season began, one of the school newspapers did a report on some of the possible outcomes of the season.
   a. Assuming no ties, in how many different orders was it possible for the nine teams to finish the season?
   b. How many different possibilities were there for the first- and second-place teams?

47. Send a Wire How many distinguishable permutations can be made using the letters in TELEGRAPH? If you can, find a word or phrase that forms an anagram of this word.

48. How many distinguishable ways can 3 red, 2 white, and 5 blue marbles be lined up in a row?

MORE MATH REASONING

49. *The Once and Future King* by T. H. White is one of many books that describe the legend of Camelot. How many ways can eight Knights of the Round Table be seated if one of them, Sir Lancelot, must sit to the right of King Arthur?

50. Anagram Anagram How many distinguishable permutations can be formed from the letters in NAMELESS? Give two anagrams of the word.

51. An arrangement of items in a circle is called a *circular permutation*. If one arrangement is a rotation of another arrangement, then the two arrangements are considered to be the same circular permutation.
   a. Explain why there are $(n - 1)!$ circular permutations of n distinct items.
   b. How many circular permutations are there of the numbers on the face of a clock?

52. How many ways can 6 different keys be arranged on a key ring? Note that there is no fixed starting place on a key ring. Also note that you get the same arrangement if you flip over a key ring, reversing the order of the keys.

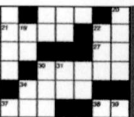

6-1 PART C Making Connections

← CONNECT → *Word games offer many opportunities to study permutations and apply counting methods. However, permutations and counting methods can also be applied to find probabilities in complex situations.*

Recall that cryptography is the study of writing and deciphering encoded messages, called ciphers. A substitution code is one of the easiest ways to encode and decipher messages. Substitution codes involve substituting letters and numbers for the letters and numbers in the original message. For example, if we replace each letter with the following letter in the alphabet, and replace Z with A, we can encode the word CIPHER to get DJQIFS. Permuting and substituting the letters of the Roman alphabet in such a way yields 26! or about 4×10^{26} possible codes!

EXPLORE: ELEMENTARY, MY DEAR WATSON!

You have intercepted the following secret message encoded using a substitution code. Your mission is to crack the code and decipher the message.

Use one or more of the following strategies to help you find the correct substitution code and decipher the secret message.

1. Find the letter frequency for each letter in the cipher. The five letters used most often in the English language are E, T, A, O, and I. Try substituting some of these letters for the most frequently used letters in the cipher.

QEFP PBZOBQ JBPPXDB TXP TOFQQBK FK QEB ZXBPXO ZFMEBO

Problem-Solving Tip

Make an organized chart or list.

2. Look for some common short English words that fit with any substitutions you have already made. Some of the most common short words are *the, a, in, of, and, is, was,* and *to.* Remember to complete each substitution throughout the cipher when you guess what a letter stands for. Change any previous guesses as needed if you think you are on the wrong track.

3. Look for common letter patterns such as *th, he, in, er, an, ing,* and *es.* Then try to piece together one or more of the longer words. Continue to look for words and complete your substitutions until you have deciphered the whole message.

The decoded message refers to one of the first persons to use this type of code. If the message makes sense, you have deciphered it!

1. Explain how a tree diagram can help you count the number of ways events can occur.
2. When does the Multiplication Counting Principle apply and how is it used?
3. When does the Addition Counting Principle apply and how is it used?
4. Explain how and why having repeated items affects the number of permutations of the items.

Self-Assessment

1. The Braille alphabet consists of raised dots that can be touched and read by hand. A character is formed by six dots arranged in a 2-by-3 rectangular array, and each dot can be raised or not raised. How many characters can be formed in Braille?

2. **Neat 'Keets** A pet store has both English and American parakeets. Each variety of parakeet is found in four different colors, and there are males and females of each variety.
   a. Draw a tree diagram showing all of the possible types of parakeets available at the store. How many types are there?
   b. How would your answer to **a** change if the store had only two different colors of English parakeets?

3. **Hit Parade** A radio disk jockey plans to play four songs between the next two commercial breaks. In how many different orders can the songs be played?

4. An Olympic event has 20 contestants. How many possible ways can the gold, silver, and bronze medals be awarded for this event?

5. **Up, Up, and Away** An airline flying out of Chicago's O'Hare International Airport has flights to London, Paris, Hawaii, Mexico City, Rome, and Tokyo. There are six capable pilots available: Adams, Beck, Cole, Doi, Ebrahimi, and Fernandez.
   a. How many ways can the pilots be scheduled for the flights if each pilot is scheduled for only one city?
   b. Adams requests to be scheduled to Mexico City, and Doi requests Tokyo. How many ways can the remaining pilots be scheduled?
   c. Because of bad weather, the flights to Paris and Rome are canceled. Now there are six pilots available to fly to four cities. How many ways can the schedule be made if requests are not considered?

6. **History in the Making** During World War II, the U.S. Navy succeeded in cracking the Japanese fleet code, and the English mathematician Alan Turing cracked the German military code called *Enigma*. How many ways can ENIGMA be encoded by substituting any six letters of the alphabet (even the original ones) for its letters?

7. The 12 chromatic tones in an octave are A, A#, B, C, C#, D, D#, E, F, F#, G, and G#. In one form of musical composition, a melodic sequence using each of the twelve tones exactly once is used as a theme. How many themes are possible?

8. Early Bird Special Kerry's Restaurant offers an *early bird* dinner special before 5 p.m. with a choice of one of 5 entrees, soup or salad, baked potato or rice, one of three drinks, and chocolate cake. How many dinner combinations are possible?

Solve each system of equations. [5-4]

9. $x^2 + y^2 = 36$
$(x + 2)^2 = y + 3$

10. $x = 3y - 4$
$y = x^2 - 2x + 2$

11. Evaluate $f(z) = z^2 - 2z + 3$ when $z = 4 + 7i$. [4-3]

12. One of the oldest books in the world, probably dating back to China in the eighth century B.C., is the *I Ching* (oracle of change). Characters in the book are formed from six stacked horizontal segments, each either a broken or solid line. How many characters are possible?

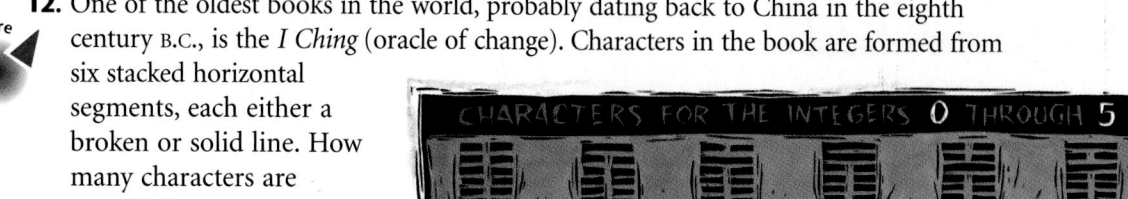
CHARACTERS FOR THE INTEGERS 0 THROUGH 5

13. In a state lottery, if you pick the correct sequence of five integers from 1 to 25, you win. How many ways can you pick a sequence of five different integers from 1 to 25? If you choose your five numbers, what is the probability that your numbers will win, if the winning numbers are chosen at random?

14. There are six national parks in northern California, four in central California, and three in southern California.
   a. Marsha plans to visit one national park from each region, starting in the north and heading south. How many ways can she plan her trip?
   b. How many ways can she plan her trip if she can visit the three regions in any order?
   c. If Marsha finds that she only has time to visit three national parks in northern California, how many ways can she plan her trip?

Evaluate each expression.

15. $_8P_3$

16. $_{10}P_5 \cdot {_5P_3}$

17. Kipling's Cipher A substitution code is described in Rudyard Kipling's story "The First Letter" from his book *Just So Stories*. Create your own substitution code for the 26 letters of the alphabet and write a coded and decoded message.

18. The possible ways to enter or exit a stage are upstage left, downstage left, upstage right, downstage right, or upstage center. Determine the number of ways a person can enter and exit the stage if a different entrance and exit are used.

19. The Super Sub Shop makes a variety of submarine sandwiches: Italian beef, tuna, vegetarian, ham, and meatball. Each sandwich is made on white or whole wheat buns and comes with or without cheddar cheese. How many sandwich varieties are offered at the shop? Draw a tree diagram to show the choices.

QUALITY CONTROL

During World War II, engineers began to study a field known as Statistical Process Control and developed a system to increase efficiency and production quality in factories and plants. The system requires manufactured items to fall within a certain acceptable range of quality. The quality might be a measure of length, weight, purity, accuracy, or any other critical parameter that can be measured. The upper limit of the acceptable range is the Upper Control Limit (UCL), and the lower limit of the acceptable range is the Lower Control Limit (LCL).

Data from samples are taken and graphed on quality control charts. If certain indications occur, the process is considered to be "out of control" and an adjustment is necessary. Here are possible indications that a process is out of control:

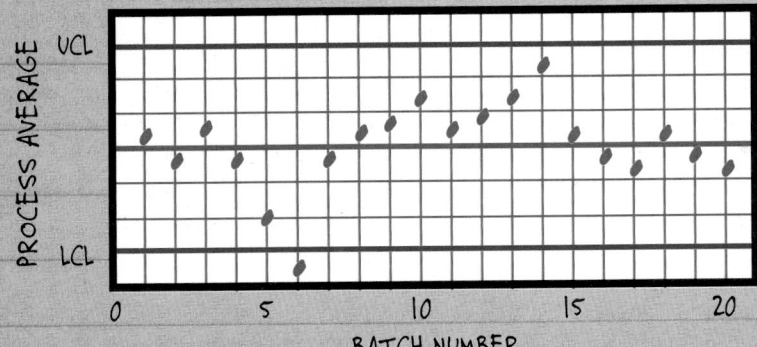

- A sample is outside the acceptable range.
- Seven or more consecutive samples are above or below the process average.
- Less than 40% of the samples lie within the middle third of the acceptable range.

To bring the process back under control, machinery might be adjusted, operators might be given a break or extra training, or higher quality materials might be used. This system helped to increase production and improve quality in a variety of manufacturing industries.

?

1. Which sample was outside the acceptable range in the graph? Does it appear that the process was adjusted afterwards? Explain.

2. Does it seem that at least 40% of the samples shown lie within the middle third of the acceptable range? Explain.

3. Why do you think seven consecutive samples above or below the process average would be considered out of control? Does the graph show any such samples? If so, which batch shows that the process was adjusted?

437

← **CONNECT** → *You have learned to count permutations where the order of objects is important. Now you will learn to count selections of objects in situations where their order doesn't matter.*

Permutations such as ABC and CBA can use the same items but in different arrangements. In some situations, such as choosing vertices of a triangle, the arrangement is not important. Only which vertices are chosen is important. Collections of items without regard to order are called **combinations.**

EXPLORE: COUNTING TRIANGLES

1. Draw a circle and label any three points on the circle *A*, *B*, and *C*. How many different permutations of the letters *A*, *B*, and *C* are possible? Draw all of the triangles you can with vertices from the points you labeled. How many different triangles can you form using these three points?

2. Draw another circle and label any four points on the circle *A*, *B*, *C*, and *D*. How many permutations are there of the four letters taken three at a time? Draw all of the triangles you can with vertices from the points you labeled. How many different triangles can you form using any three of the points?

3. Draw another circle and label any five points on the circle *A*, *B*, *C*, *D*, and *E*. How many permutations are there of the five letters taken three at a time? Draw all of the triangles you can with vertices from the points you labeled. How many different triangles can you form using any three of the points?

4. How does the number of permutations of *n* points taken three at a time seem to relate to the number of different triangles that can be formed from *n* points?

MATERIALS

Protractor
Straightedge

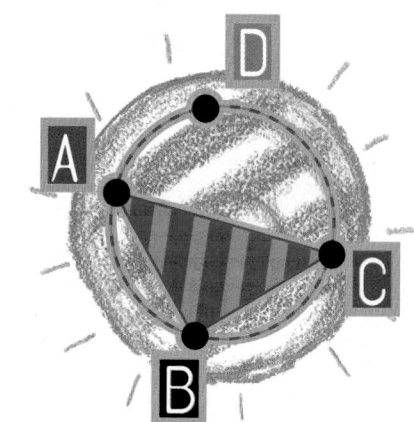

Problem-Solving Tip

Look for a pattern.

In the Explore, each triangle was determined by a combination of three vertices. We denote the number of combinations of *n* items taken *r* at a time by $_nC_r$. We can count combinations by relating them to permutations.

1. Susan is packing for a vacation and wants to choose three of her twelve novels to take along. How many possible combinations of three novels can she choose?

For any 3 of the 12 novels Susan chooses, there are 3! ways to arrange them. Therefore, there are 3! times as many permutations of 3 novels as there are combinations. We can use this fact to solve for the number of combinations.

$$3!(_{12}C_3) = {_{12}P_3}$$

$${_{12}C_3} = \frac{_{12}P_3}{3!} = \frac{1320}{6} = 220 \qquad \text{Solve for } _{12}C_3.$$

There are 220 combinations of 3 novels Susan can choose.

In general, there are $r!$ times as many permutations of r items as there are combinations of r items. Therefore, $_nC_r = \frac{_nP_r}{r!} = \frac{n!}{r!(n-r)!}$.

> If n and r are whole numbers with $r \le n$, then $_nC_r$ denotes the number of combinations of n items taken r at a time. $_nC_r$ is given by $_nC_r = \frac{n!}{r!(n-r)!}$.

WHAT DO YOU THINK?

Ms. Stanley plans to choose four students to construct the set for a play her drama class is putting on. How many ways can she choose this crew of four from the six volunteers?

Vinh thinks...

I will write a list of possibilities using the letters a, b, c, d, e, and f to represent the six volunteers. I can list the possibilities in alphabetical order to avoid duplicates.

abcd	abce	abcf	abde	abdf
abef	acde	acdf	acef	adef
bcde	bcdf	bcef	bdef	cdef

There are 15 ways for Ms. Stanley to choose the crew of four students.

LeRon thinks...

There are $_6C_4$ combinations of four students from the six volunteers.

$$_6C_4 = \frac{6!}{4!(6-4)!} = \frac{6!}{4!2!} = \frac{6 \cdot 5 \cdot 4 \cdot 3 \cdot 2 \cdot 1}{4 \cdot 3 \cdot 2 \cdot 1 \cdot 2 \cdot 1} = \frac{6 \cdot 5}{2} = \frac{30}{2} = 15$$

Ms. Stanley can choose four students from six volunteers in 15 ways.

a. Evaluate $_8C_3$.   **b.** Evaluate $_7C_5$.

c. How many ways can a music store choose four of their ten best-selling CDs for a display?

Counting combinations can also help you calculate probabilities.

EXAMPLE

2. Suppose you draw 2 cards at random from a deck of 52 playing cards. What is the probability that both cards will be hearts?

There are 13 hearts in a deck, so there are $_{13}C_2$ ways to draw 2 hearts from a deck. There are $_{52}C_2$ ways to draw any 2 cards from a deck.

Dividing the number of favorable outcomes, $_{13}C_2$, by the total number of outcomes, $_{52}C_2$, gives the probability of drawing 2 hearts.

$$P(\text{drawing 2 hearts}) = \frac{_{13}C_2}{_{52}C_2} = \frac{78}{1326} = \frac{1}{17} \approx 0.0588$$

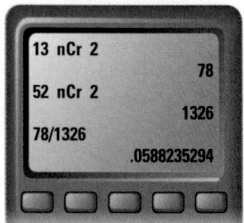

13 nCr 2	
	78
52 nCr 2	
	1326
78/1326	
	.0588235294

CONSIDER

1. How can you use the result in Example 2 to find the probability that two cards drawn from a deck will be the same suit?

TRY IT

d. Suppose you draw three cards from a deck of 52 playing cards. What is the probability that all three cards will be black (clubs or spades)?

e. There is only one winning ticket in a hat holding 100 tickets. What is the probability that you won't win if you draw two tickets from the hat?

One use of counting combinations is in analyzing surveys. Pollsters can often only survey a portion of a population. Counting combinations can help pollsters calculate probabilities and estimate the accuracy of their surveys.

REFLECT

1. Write a brief paragraph comparing permutations and combinations.

2. How is the formula for $_nP_r$ related to the formula for $_nC_r$?

3. Describe a situation in which you might want to know the number of combinations.

Exercises

CORE

1. **Getting Started** Without answering either question, decide which of these situations involves combinations.
   a. Twenty-five students are applying for three $1000 scholarships. How many different ways can the scholarships be awarded?
   b. Twenty-five students are applying for three scholarships—one for $500, one for $1000, and one for $1500. How many different ways can the scholarships be awarded?

Evaluate each expression.

2. $_{25}C_5$

3. $_{31}C_{10}$

4. $_{100}C_{95}$

5. $_{50}C_{50}$

6. $_{73}C_0$

Decide whether each statement is always true, sometimes true, or never true. If the statement is sometimes or never true, rewrite it so that it is always true.

7. The symbol $_nC_r$ is defined for whole numbers r and n when $r \leq n$.

8. When you choose objects and order is important, you are choosing combinations.

9. $_nC_n = {_nC_0}$ for all positive integers n.

10. How many ways can you choose two pizza toppings from a choice of eight?

11. **Hearty Handshakes** A conference group on open-heart surgery included 12 heart surgeons. If each surgeon shook hands with every other surgeon, how many handshakes were exchanged?

12. **Emergency Planning** A new communications hotline is to connect the fire station, police station, hospital, school, and city hall. If there is to be exactly one connection between any two of these places, how many connections are necessary?

13. **Genetic Codes** Genes are made up of a nucleic acid, deoxyribonucleic acid, more commonly known as DNA. The differences between DNA molecules lie in the arrangement of their organic bases: adenine (A), thymine (T), cytosine (C), and guanine (G). The sequence of A, C, T, and G molecules constitutes the genetic code. How many sequences of 8 organic bases are possible, assuming the bases can be repeated?

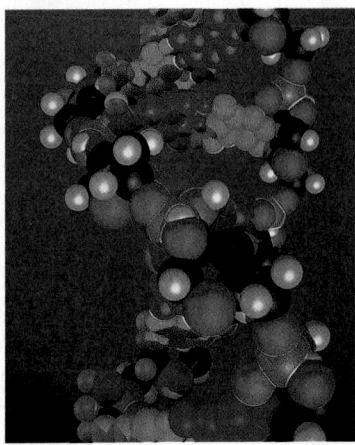

14. Twelve members of a 50-member club are randomly chosen for a publicity photo.
   a. How many ways can the 12 members be chosen?
   b. If the 2 senior members are automatically chosen, then how many ways can the rest be chosen?

15. There are six points on a circle.
   a. How many different chords can be drawn by connecting any two of the points?
   b. How many different triangles can be inscribed in the circle using any three of the points?

16. What is the probability that two cards drawn from a deck of 52 playing cards will be face cards?

17. Five women and three men each take turns to choose one ticket from the eight tickets in a hat. Three tickets will win prizes and the others are valueless.
   a. What is the probability that all three prizes will be won by women?
   b. What is the probability that two women and one man will win prizes?
   c. What is the probability that at least two women will win prizes?

18. Color Combinations Psychologists have determined that colors affect people in many ways. Depending on the person, different colors seem to evoke different emotions. Four prominent colors are red, orange, green, and blue. Red and green are complementary colors, as are orange and blue. What is the probability that two of these colors chosen at random will be complementary?

The Sadness of the King, by Henri Matisse, 1952

 **LOOK AHEAD**

Expand each expression.

19. $(x + 5)^2$
20. $(3x + 2)^3$
21. $(x - 2)^4$

MORE PRACTICE

Evaluate each expression.

22. $_{12}C_{11}$
23. $_{19}C_{15}$
24. $_{45}C_1$
25. $_{36}C_{36}$

26. $_{22}C_3$
27. $_{37}C_0$
28. $_{120}C_{96}$
29. $_{40}C_{40}$

30. A geometric design is to use three different colors. There are ten colors from which to choose. How many different ways can the three colors be chosen?

31. Jorge's Pizzeria offers 8 different pizza toppings. How many different choices of exactly three toppings can be made? at most three toppings?

32. Take-Out A Chinese restaurant has 60 items on its menu.
   a. How many different combinations of 6 items can be ordered?
   b. If there are an equal number of meat, seafood, vegetable, and noodle dishes, how many ways can 2 of each type of dish be ordered?

33. Fifteen percent of the students in a class of twenty are absent today. What is the probability that all of the first five students called on the roll sheet will be present?

34. Senate Committees The Senate of the 100th Congress consisted of 54 Democrats and 46 Republicans.

   a. How many different committees of 7 senators from either party could be formed?
   b. How many committees of 5 Democratic senators could be formed?
   c. How many committees of 8 Republican senators could be formed?
   d. What is the probability that three senators standing outside the Senate chambers are all Democrats?

35. Euchre A card game known as euchre is played with a deck of 32 cards. Half of the cards are red and half are black. Each player is dealt a hand of 5 cards at the start of the game.

   a. How many different playing hands are possible?
   b. How many different hands contain only red cards?
   c. What is the probability of being dealt an all-red hand?

36. Chess Champs There are 20 members of the Chess Club.

   a. How many ways can a team of 4 be selected to compete in an interscholastic competition?
   b. If there are 15 seniors and 5 juniors in the club, how many different teams can be formed with 2 seniors and 2 juniors?

MORE MATH REASONING

37. Show that $_nC_r = {_nC_{n-r}}$ for any positive integers r and n when $r \leq n$.

38. Calculate values of $\dfrac{16^n}{\pi n(_{2n}C_n)^2}$ for several large values of n. What do you notice?

39. Twelve jars of preserves are to be placed in a basement in three boxes, with four jars per box. Ignoring the arrangement of jars within each box, how many ways are there to place the jars in the boxes?

6-2 PART B The Binomial Theorem

← CONNECT →   *You will now explore a connection between counting combinations and expanding powers of binomials.*

Recall that a *binomial* is an expression consisting of a sum of two terms, such as $a + b$ or $2x + 5$. Using the distributive property, you can expand powers of binomials. For example, $(a + b)^2 = a^2 + 2ab + b^2$.

In the following Explore, you will discover a connection between numbers of combinations and expansions of powers of binomials. This connection will give you an effective method for expanding any power of a binomial.

EXPLORE: TOSSED POSSIBILITIES

1. If you toss two coins, how many ways can you get two heads? a head and a tail? two tails?
2. Consider the coefficients of this expanded square of a binomial: $(h + t)^2 = h^2 + 2ht + t^2$. What connection do you see between these coefficients and your results in Step 1?
3. If you toss three coins, how many ways can you get all heads? two heads and a tail? one head and two tails? all tails?
4. Copy and complete the expansion of $(h + t)^3$ by using the distributive property.
   $(h + t)^3 = (h + t)(h^2 + 2ht + t^2) = \underline{\quad}$
5. What connection do you see between your results in Steps 3 and 4?
6. Make a conjecture about the connection between the numbers of combinations when tossing n coins and the coefficients of expansion of $(h + t)^n$. Check your conjecture when $n = 4$.

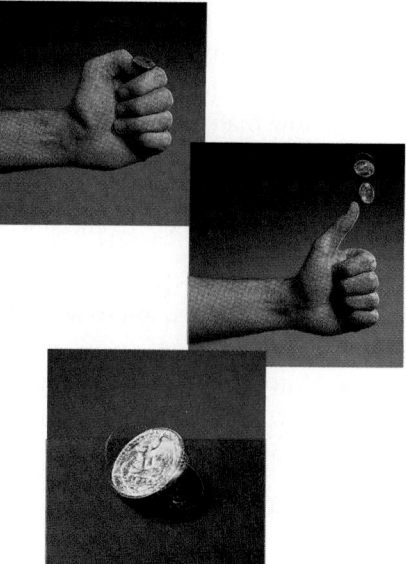

The connection between binomial powers and combinations that you investigated in the Explore can be stated in the following theorem.

BINOMIAL THEOREM

For any binomial $(a + b)$ and any positive integer n,
$$(a + b)^n = {_nC_0}a^n + {_nC_1}a^{n-1}b + {_nC_2}a^{n-2}b^2 + \cdots + {_nC_{n-1}}ab^{n-1} + {_nC_n}b^n.$$

EXAMPLE

1. Expand $(2x - 5)^4$.

$(2x - 5)^4$

$= {_4C_0}(2x)^4 + {_4C_1}(2x)^3(-5) + {_4C_2}(2x)^2(-5)^2 + {_4C_3}(2x)(-5)^3 + {_4C_4}(-5)^4$

$= 1(16x^4) + 4(8x^3)(-5) + 6(4x^2)(25) + 4(2x)(-125) + 1(625)$

$= 16x^4 - 160x^3 + 600x^2 - 1000x + 625$

TRY IT

a. Expand $(x + 2)^5$.

b. Expand $(3c - 4)^3$.

Pascal's Triangle is an intriguing arrangement of the binomial coefficients. The fourth row of the triangle, for example, shows the coefficients of $(a + b)^3 = a^3 + 3a^2b + 3ab^2 + b^3$.

The triangle is named for the seventeenth-century French mathematician Blaise Pascal who explored many of the triangle's patterns and properties. However, the triangle had been studied by Hindu, Arab, and Chinese mathematicians earlier.

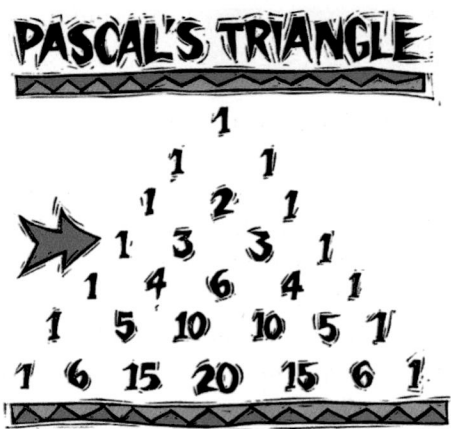

EXAMPLE

2. Expand $(x + 2)^5$.

The sixth row of Pascal's Triangle gives the binomial coefficients for a fifth power.

$$(x + 2)^5 = 1x^5 + 5x^4(2) + 10x^3(2^2) + 10x^2(2^3) + 5x(2^4) + 2^5$$
$$= x^5 + 10x^4 + 40x^3 + 80x^2 + 80x + 32$$

CONSIDER

1. For any pair of adjacent numbers in Pascal's Triangle, what do you notice about the value in the next row between the two numbers? How can this help you to write more rows of Pascal's Triangle?

TRY IT

c. Expand $(3x + 1)^6$.   **d.** Expand $(-2y + 10)^5$.

One of the many interesting properties within Pascal's Triangle can be seen by expanding 2^n in the form $(1 + 1)^n$ using the binomial theorem.

$$(1 + 1)^n = {}_nC_0 + {}_nC_1 + \cdots + {}_nC_n$$

This shows that the sum of the numbers in the $(n + 1)$ row of Pascal's Triangle is 2^n.

REFLECT

1. What is a binomial? Give an example.

2. How many terms are there in the expanded nth power of a binomial?

3. How does the expansion of $(x - y)^6$ compare to the expansion of $(x + y)^6$?

CORE

1. **Getting Started** Consider the binomial power $(x + 3)^5$.
   a. How many terms are in its expansion?
   b. Write the coefficients of each term using combination notation.
   c. Write the complete expansion in simplest form.

2. Which of the following are binomials?
   (a) $2x$ (b) $x + 3$ (c) $4x^2$ (d) $3y^2 + 2$ (e) $x^2 + 2x + 1$

3. Write an informal description of each word.
   a. term   **b.** power   **c.** coefficient   **d.** exponent

4. Write the fourth term of the expansion of $(2x + 1)^8$.

5. Write the third term of the expansion of $(4 - 3p)^7$.

6. Write the first three terms of $(x + y)^9$.

7. Write the last three terms of $(x - 6)^8$.

Expand.

8. $(x + 6)^5$

9. $(x - y)^7$

10. $(5 + y)^4$

11. $(2x + 0.5)^3$

12. $(3x - 4)^4$

13. $(2 + x)^5$

14. Draw a tree diagram showing all the possible outfits that can be created with a skirt, blouse, and hat from a choice of 4 skirts, 2 blouses, and 3 hats.

15. **Toss Five** Expand $(h + t)^5$ as a model for flipping a coin five times. The coefficient of $h^c t^{5-c}$ is the number of ways to flip c heads in five tosses.
   a. What is the total number of outcomes possible from five coin flips?
   b. How many of the outcomes have two heads and three tails?
   c. How many of the outcomes have at least two heads?
   d. What is the probability of flipping a coin five times and getting at least two heads?

16. **Hybrid Watermelons** Two watermelons each pass on a pair of biological traits, GS, Gs, gS, or gs. Of the four inherited traits, the offspring can be either green (GG, Gg, or gG) or striped (gg), and either short (SS, Ss, or sS) or long (ss). List the traits of all possible offspring of two short green watermelons, and describe some probabilities related to these traits.

17. Family Figures If G represents having a baby girl and B represents having a baby boy, the coefficient of $G^c B^{4-c}$ in the expansion of $(0.5G + 0.5B)^4$ gives the probability of a family having c girls out of 4 children.

a. What is the probability that a family of 4 children will have 3 girls and 1 boy?

b. What is the probability that a family of 4 children will have 2 girls and 2 boys?

18. Recall that the triangular numbers, 1, 3, 6, 10, 15, 21, …, are the partial sums of the counting numbers. Copy Pascal's Triangle and identify the triangular numbers in the triangle. Write a general formula for the nth triangular number in terms of combination symbols.

19. Chinese/Moslem Triangle Historical records indicate that what later became known as Pascal's Triangle was studied by the Moslems in the eleventh century and by the Chinese around 1300 A.D. Describe any patterns you see in this triangle, which is from a book written in 1303 by the Chinese mathematician Chu Shih-Chieh.

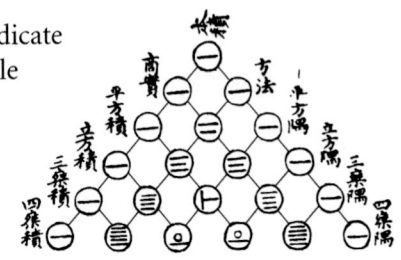

 **LOOK BACK**

20. Find the twentieth term of the sequence 3, 7, 11, 15, …. [4-1]

21. Solve $x^2 - 7x + 12 = 0$. [5-2]

22. A license plate will use 2 letters followed by 4 digits. Assuming letters and numbers can be repeated, how many different license plates are possible? How would your answer change if repetition was not allowed? [6-1]

MORE PRACTICE

23. How many terms are in the expansion of $(2w + 7y)^6$?

24. What is the exponent of w in the third term of $(4 - w)^8$?

25. One term of $(5m + 2q)^9$ contains m^6. What is the exponent of q in that term?

26. Write the fourth term of $(x^2 - 3)^5$.   **27.** Write the third term of $(2c + 3)^7$.

28. Mr. McIlroy is going to appoint a committee of 3 or 4 students to plan the refreshments for the band picnic. Roberto, Alison, Penny, Lee, Carl, Aram, and Nathan have volunteered to be on the committee. How many possible committees can Mr. McIlroy appoint? Which binomial coefficients did you use to decide?

Decide which choice is correct.

(A) The quantity in Column A is greater.   (B) The quantity in Column B is greater.
(C) The two quantities are equal.   (D) The relationship cannot be determined.

	Column A	Column B
29.	$(x + 1)^4$	$4x^3 + 4x$
30.	$(2y + 1)^3$	$6y^2 + 12y + 1$

Expand each binomial.

31. $(x - 2)^7$

32. $(x + y)^3$

33. $(2x - 3)^5$

34. $(4x + 1)^3$

35. $(x + 0.1)^4$

36. $(x - 3)^5$

37. $(x + 0.3)^3$

38. $(2x - 9)^4$

39. $(-0.4 + x)^5$

40. There is a 30% chance of rain for each of the next 7 days. The coefficient of $x^h y^{7-h}$ in the expansion of $(0.3x + 0.7y)^7$ gives the probability of exactly h days of rain this week. What is the probability of exactly 3 days of rain?

MORE MATH REASONING

Simplify each expansion.

41. $\left(x + \dfrac{1}{x}\right)^3$

42. $(1 + i)^8$

43. $(2 - i)^6$

44. Quiz-a-Phobia Steve did not study for his science quiz. There were 20 true-false exercises for which he guessed. Describe how you can use a binomial expansion to determine the probability that Steve got exactly 14 of the answers correct.

45. Identify the *tetrahedral numbers*, 1, 4, 10, 20, …, in Pascal's Triangle, and write a formula for the nth tetrahedral number.

46. Use a Graphing Calculator Expand $(0.5h + 0.5t)^{10}$. Use the coefficients to determine the probability of tossing 10 coins and getting 4, 5, or 6 tails.

47. Chances of Failing Three trials are conducted on an experiment with a 65% probability of producing successful results and a 35% probability of failure. Write and expand an expression to determine the probability of each possible event.

6-2
PART C
Making Connections

← CONNECT → *You have studied combinations and how they are applied to counting and finding probabilities. You have also discovered the connection between combinations and binomial coefficients.*

In the following Explore, you will see how binomial powers can help you to generate probabilities that are useful for studying quality control.

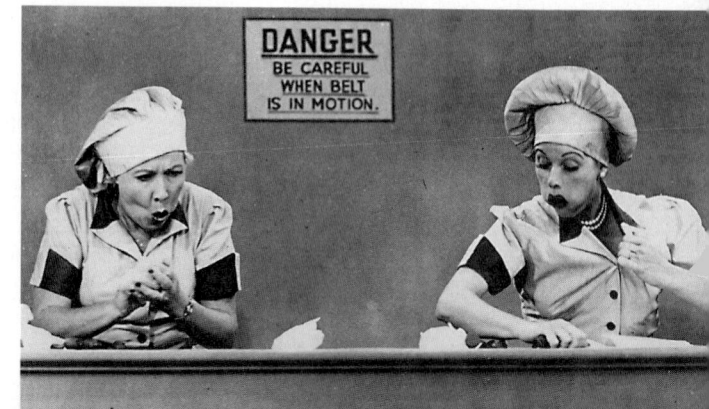

The Louisville Bat Company manufactures baseball bats. The following chart shows the acceptable weight range (0.94 lb to 1.06 lb) for one model of bat, along with data taken from samples.

Assume that 60% of the manufactured bats are in the middle third of the acceptable weight range (0.98 lb to 1.02 lb). Four bats are sampled and weighed each work shift. If at least 50% or two of these bats are in the middle third of the acceptable weight range, then the process is running fine and needs no adjustment.

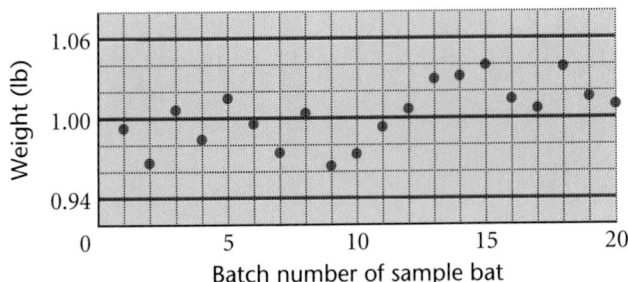

1. Expand $(0.6m + 0.4x)^4$. The coefficient of $m^c x^{4-c}$ gives the probability that exactly c of the four bats are in the middle third of the acceptable range.
2. What is the probability that all four bats sampled will be in the middle third of the acceptable range? What is the probability that three of the bats will be in the middle third? two of them?
3. What is the probability that at least 50% of the bats will be in the middle third of the acceptable weight range?
4. How often would you estimate that the process will need readjustment? Explain.

The serious study of permutations, combinations, and probabilities began in the sixteenth century. A commentary on Dante's *Divine Comedy* shows that people had considered the probabilities of dice rolls as early as 1477.

REFLECT

1. How do you know when a counting problem is a combination rather than a permutation?
2. Explain why $_nC_0 = 1$ for all values of n.
3. Write a set of directions for finding the expansion of $(x + 1)^4$.
4. Describe how Pascal's Triangle can be used to find $_nC_r$.
5. Describe how a binomial expansion can be used to model the experiment of tossing a coin six times.

Self-Assessment

Evaluate each expression.

1. $_6C_4$ **2.** $_7C_3$ **3.** $_7C_6$ **4.** $_8C_4$

5. Project Volcano There are ten books about volcanoes in the library. A patron may not check out more than four books on any one subject at a time. How many different ways can Darryl choose four of the books to check out?

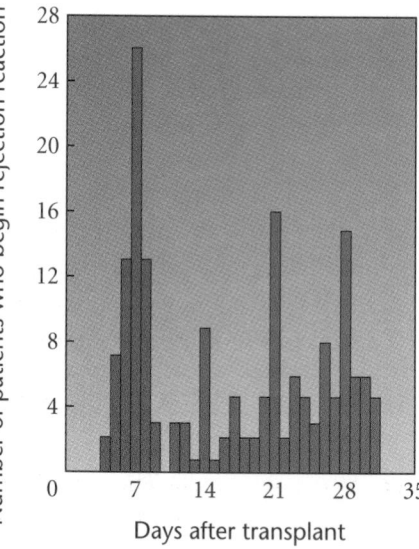

6. How many terms will be in the expansion of $(x + y)^{10}$?

7. Which of these is a term of $(x - y)^7$?

     (a) x^2y^5 (b) $21x^5y^2$ (c) $-21x^5y^2$ (d) $7x^2y^5$ (e) not here

Expand each expression.

8. $(x + 12)^4$ **9.** $(2a - b)^4$ **10.** $(-3 + 2y)^3$

Science

11. The graph illustrates the days when rejections of transplanted kidneys threatened to occur among 508 patients. Use this information to predict the days when a transplant will have a greater chance of being rejected, and explain how you made your prediction.

12. Explain how to obtain a number in row $(n + 1)$ of Pascal's Triangle if you know the numbers in row n.

13. You draw 4 cards from a deck of 52 playing cards. Give the probability that all four are red face cards.

History

14. Prior to the development of telephone and radio, Morse code enabled messages to be transmitted by wire over long distances. The code, devised in 1837 by Samuel F. Morse, uses a series of dots and dashes to represent messages. Each letter consists of up to four dots and dashes.

A	·–	G	––·	M	––	T	–	W	·––
B	–···	H	····	N	–·	U	··–	X	–··–
C	–·–·	I	··	O	–––	V	···–	Y	–·––
D	–··	J	·–––	Q	––·–	P	·––·	Z	––··
E	·	K	–·–	R	·–·				
F	··–·	L	·–··	S	···				

How many characters of one, two, three, or four dots and dashes are possible? Are there enough characters to represent all digits as well as all letters? Are these codes examples of combinations or permutations? Explain.

15. Use the expansion of $(0.5G + 0.5B)^8$ to determine the probability that a couple planning to have 8 children will have at most 1 girl.

16. Find the 21st term of the sequence 5, -1, -7, -13, ... [4-1]

Solve each equation. [5-1]

17. $x^2 - 8x = 20$

18. $x^2 + 3x = 70$

19. Joe is holding four cards in a game of Old Maid. How many ways can he arrange the cards in a row? [6-1]

20. Be Alert! Scientists believe that research known as *chronobiology* can determine the most effective time schedule for individual workers. A study of high school students and teachers classified the following students and teachers as morning alert, afternoon alert, or evening alert.

Morning alert:
Students: Cindy, Hua Mei, Amy, Isabel, and Ado
Teachers: Ms. Jackson, Mr. Sato, Mrs. McNamara

Afternoon alert:
Students: Guido, Elana, and Lee
Teachers: Ms. Green, Mr. Weismann, and Mrs. Minor-Forman

Evening alert:
Students: Guillaume, Carlotta, Maureen, and Ricardo
Teachers: Mr. Cuadra and Ms. Chouteau

Plan a school schedule that takes this information into account. Each teacher needs at least 5 students and 3 classes. How many classes of 5 students are possible? Justify the arrangements that you think will be most effective.

21. Show that, in general, $_nC_{r-1} + {}_nC_r = {}_{n+1}C_r$, for any positive integers r and n when $1 \le r \le n$.

22. At the Thai Oasis, there are 30 dinner entrees to choose from, and every meal comes with noodles or rice. How many different meals with 3 entrees and rice or noodles can be ordered from the restaurant?

23. Ten students volunteered to paint a mural for the community. The mayor and school principal are to choose six of the volunteers to plan and paint the mural. How many ways can they choose the six students?

24. At Maria's fifth birthday party, her mother fills a bag with 8 quarters, 10 nickels, and 5 dimes. She then blindfolds Maria and lets her choose 6 coins. What is the probability that Maria gets a dollar or more?

Chapter 6 Review

In Chapter 6, you have seen how to use the principles of counting to count arrangements of objects and calculate probabilities. You have also seen the connection between the algebraic expansion of a binomial expression and numbers of combinations.

KEY TERMS

Addition Counting Principle [6-1]

Binomial Theorem [6-2]

combinations [6-2]

factorial [6-1]

Multiplication Counting Principle [6-1]

mutually exclusive events [6-1]

Pascal's Triangle [6-2]

permutation [6-1]

tree diagram [6-1]

Write the word or phrase that correctly completes each statement.

1. The product of the first n counting numbers is ____.

2. To determine the number of ways a series of events can occur, use the ____ Counting Principle.

3. An ordered arrangement is called a(n) ____.

4. A choice of items without regard to their arrangement is called a(n) ____.

CONCEPTS AND APPLICATIONS

5. In a game of Scrabble, a player drew the letters D, E, N, T. Draw a tree diagram to show all the possible arrangements of three of these letters. [6-1]

6. Suppose there is a committee of five people: Ann, Benito, Chris, Ding, and Elise. How many possible ways can a recorder and a leader be chosen? [6-1]

7. The lock on a briefcase uses four digits from the numbers 0, 1, 2, 3, 4, and 5. How many different arrangements of four numbers are possible if a number can be used more than once? [6-1]

Evaluate each expression. [6-1]

8. $8!$

9. $5! - 4!$

10. $\frac{10!}{5!}$

11. It's your turn in a game using two dice. With the two dice, how many ways can you throw a sum of six to win the game? [6-1]

12. What is the probability of choosing a red ace or a black nine from a deck of 52 playing cards?

13. How many ways can you get a sum of 6 or 11 from tossing two dice? [6-1]

Evaluate each expression. [6-1]

14. $_6P_3$ **15.** $_8P_5$ **16.** $_2P_0$ **17.** $_{11}P_{11}$

18. A *Greek Square*, which substitutes a two-digit number for each letter, was used to make the following encoded message. [6-1]

    23 11 44 32   42 34   52 35 31 42 44 42 33 22

    a. How many unique letters were used?
    b. Since the first word has 4 letters, how many distinguishable letter arrangements are possible?
    c. If 11 represents *A*, how many distinguishable letter arrangements are possible for the first word?
    d. Decode the cipher if 11 represents *A* and 42 represents *I*.

How many distinguishable permutations can be made with the letters of each word? [6-1]

19. IMAGE   **20.** IMAGINATION

21. CHARACTER   **22.** ALGEBRA

23. A submarine sandwich shop offers the following toppings: mayonnaise, mustard, lettuce, onions, green peppers, pickles, and olives. How many possible combinations of three sandwich toppings are available? [6-2]

24. Ten women are on a volleyball team and six players are on the court at a time. [6-2]
    a. How many different groups of six players can be formed from a team of ten?
    b. Only one of the two setters is on the court at a time. How many groups of six can be formed now?

Evaluate each expression. [6-2]

25. $_7C_4$ **26.** $_9C_6$ **27.** $_{10}C_8$ **28.** $_{20}C_{20}$

29. Of 35 students in a history class, 8 students are randomly chosen to change classes in order to reduce the size of the class. [6-2]
    a. How many possible ways can the 8 students be chosen?
    b. If 5 students have chemistry first period and cannot change their schedules, how many possible ways are there now to choose the 8 students?

30. In a lottery drawing, six numbers are drawn from the numbers 1 through 54. [6-2]
    a. How many possible combinations are there?
    b. What is the probability of randomly choosing the one winning combination?

31. If you draw three cards from a deck of 52 playing cards, what is the probability that you will choose three spades that are not face cards? [6-2]

Expand each binomial using the binomial theorem. [6-2]

32. $(3x + 2)^5$ **33.** $(2x - 2)^4$ **34.** $(6 + 4y)^3$

35. On a quiz, there were 10 true-false questions. Use $(T + F)^{10}$ to find the possibility of getting 70% if a student answers true to all the questions. [6-2]

CONCEPTS AND CONNECTIONS

36. A cell is made of chemical compounds, each of which has specific functions. Proteins make up the essential structure of the cell and are made of amino acids, which are molecules of carbon, hydrogen, nitrogen, and oxygen. Scientists have found that there are 20 different amino acids used to build proteins. Proteins differ because of the arrangements of these amino acids. If a typical protein is made up of a sequence of about 100 amino acids, how many possible proteins are there?

37. A Different Word Game The game of Boggle® uses 16 six-sided dice with different letters on each face that are arranged in a 4-by-4 square. Once the dice are rolled, how many ways are there to arrange the dice in a 4-by-4 square? (Hint: It is the same number of ways you can arrange them in a row.)

SELF-EVALUATION

Write a summary of what you learned in this chapter. Explain how counting techniques can help you analyze word puzzles or count in other situations. Which techniques discussed in this chapter were confusing to you? Explain how you can relate these techniques to everyday activities, so that they will be easier to remember.

Chapter 6 Assessment

TEST

1. In a game of Scrabble, a player drew the letters H, O, P, E, S. Draw a tree diagram to show all the possible arrangements of three of these letters.

2. Suppose there is a board of directors of five people: Allie, Bob, Carmen, Dana, and Emanuel. How many possible ways can they choose a treasurer and a president?

3. A bike lock uses three numbers from 0, 1, 2, 3, 4, 5, or 6. How many different arrangements of three numbers are possible if repetition is allowed? not allowed?

Evaluate each expression.

4. $4!$ **5.** $2(7! - 6!)$ **6.** $\frac{12!}{5!}$

7. How many ways can you get a sum of 7 or more from a roll of two dice?

8. How many ways can you toss two dice and get an even sum? What is the probability of tossing an even sum with two dice?

Evaluate each expression.

9. $_8P_4$ **10.** $_6P_5$ **11.** $_{12}P_3$

How many distinguishable permutations can be made with the letters of each word?

12. COMPUTER   **13.** COMMITTEE   **14.** EXERCISE

15. A club has 20 members.
   a. A president, vice-president, secretary, and treasurer are to be elected. How many possible ways can these four offices be filled by different people?
   b. Assume the four elected officers will serve as a general executive board, none with any title or influence greater than any other. How many possible executive boards can be elected?

16. A restaurant specializes in offering customers the chance to create their own hamburgers. Customers may choose from the following selections: lettuce, tomatoes, mushrooms, onions, bacon, olives, guacamole, and 4 kinds of cheese. How many possible combinations of 2 toppings are available?

Evaluate each expression.

17. $_6C_3$ **18.** $_8C_5$ **19.** $_{12}C_4$

20. Thirty-five orchestra positions are open, and 9 musicians are to try out at a time.
   a. How many different groups of 9 musicians can be made from the 35?
   b. Only 1 of 5 percussionists can play at a time. How many groups of 9 can be formed now?

21. Ten jurors are to be selected at random from 38 potential jurors.
   a. How many choices of a jury are possible?
   b. If six potential jurors know the defendant and are dismissed for the day, how many possible juries remain?

22. In a drawing for door prizes, five winners are identified from the tickets 1 through 42. Assuming no one bought more than one ticket, how many possible combinations of winners are there?

23. Write the third term of the expansion of $(5x - 3y)^7$.

Expand each binomial using the binomial theorem.

24. $(2x - 1)^3$ **25.** $(13 + 13y)^4$ **26.** $(x - 2.5)^5$

27. On a quiz, there were 5 true-false questions. Expand $(0.5T + 0.5F)^5$ and use it to find the probability that a student guessing the answers will get at least 3 correct.

PERFORMANCE TASK

Create a substitution code for encoding messages. Write a message and use your code to create a cipher—the encoded message. Analyze the possible number of substitution codes someone could try if they wanted to break your code. Write some clues to your code or cipher, enough so that the number of possible solutions is less than 100. Show how each clue decreases the number of possible solutions.

Chapter 7

Investigating Roots and Powers

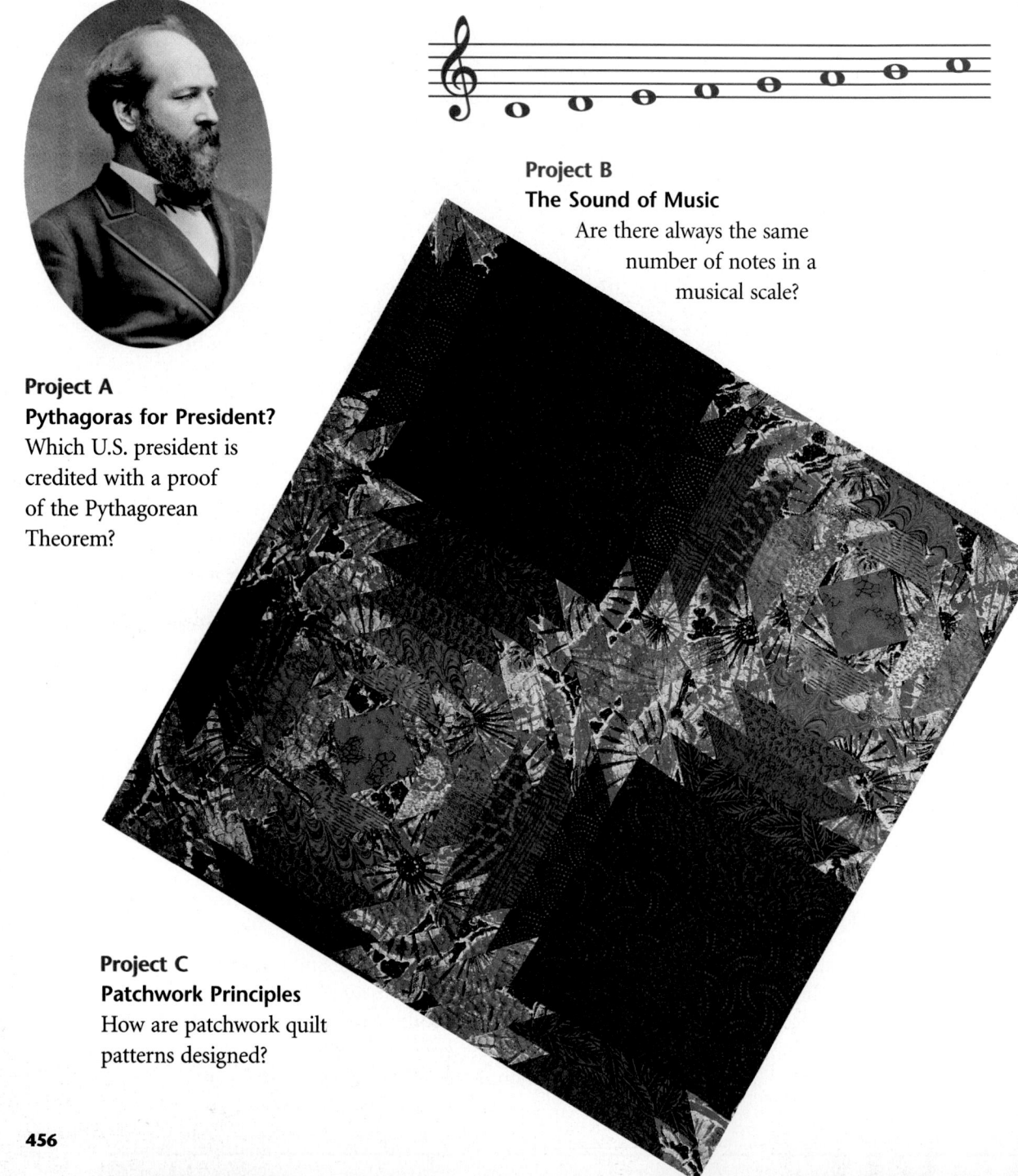

Project A
Pythagoras for President?
Which U.S. president is
credited with a proof
of the Pythagorean
Theorem?

Project B
The Sound of Music
Are there always the same
number of notes in a
musical scale?

Project C
Patchwork Principles
How are patchwork quilt
patterns designed?

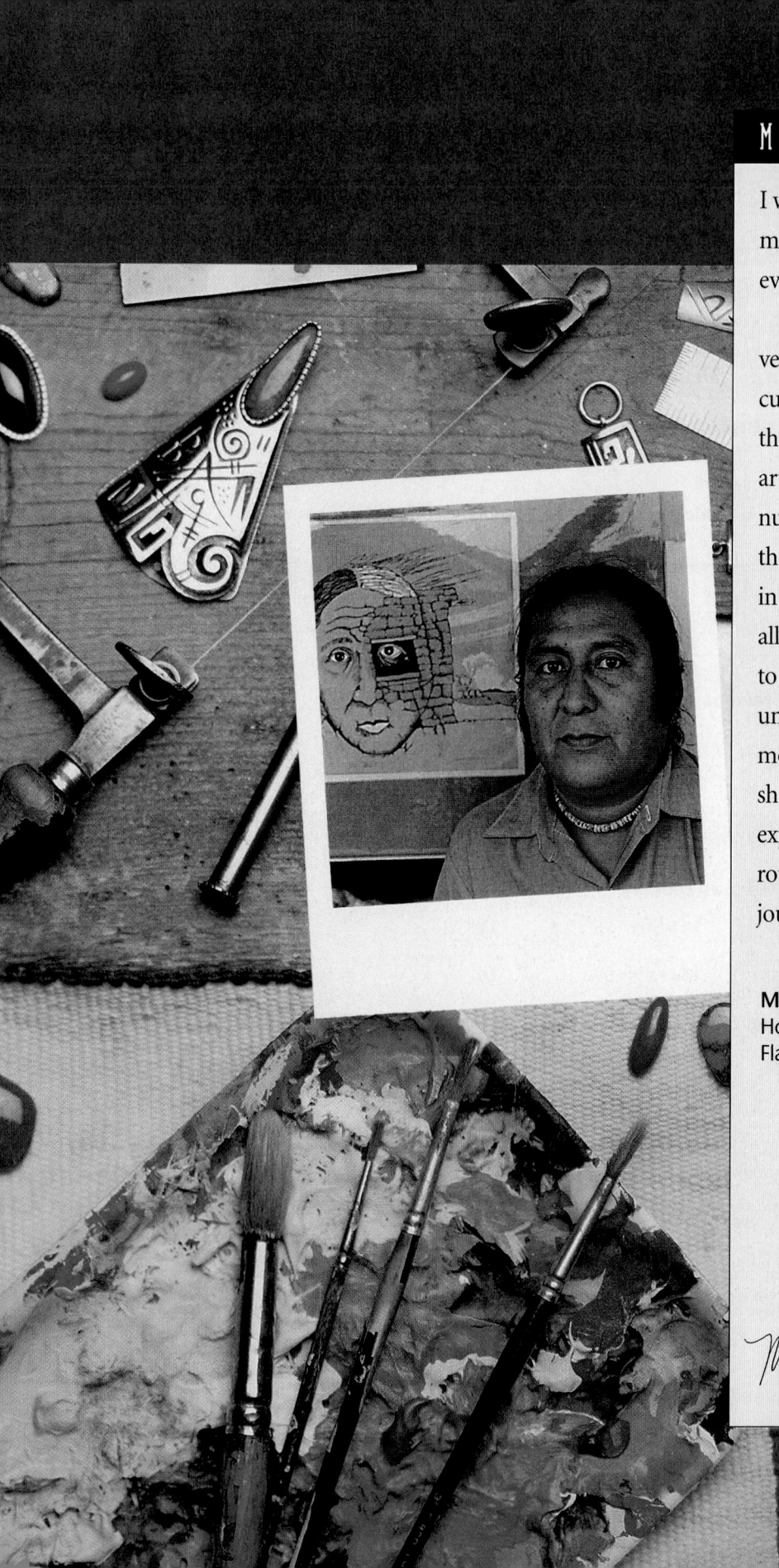

MICHAEL KABOTIE

I wasn't very good at math in high school, but even so, I enjoyed it.

I think there is a universal language of lines, curves, angles, or patterns that we all feel. I'm an artist, not a precision number person, but I think there's a basic truth in numbers that we can all experience. My urge to create comes from understanding more and more about life. Everyone should have some math experience. It helps to round out our life's journey.

Michael Kabotie
Hopi Artist
Flagstaff, Arizona

Michael Kabotie

7-1
**Variation
and Integral
Exponent Powers**

In 7-1 you will see how change can be expressed mathematically with powers. You will use the following algebra skills relating to powers.

Solve for k. [Previous course]

1. $24 = k(72)$ **2.** $\dfrac{1}{5} = \dfrac{k}{125}$ **3.** $8 = \dfrac{k \cdot 100}{20^2}$

Complete each table and graph the equation. [Previous course]

4. $y = x^2$

x	$\frac{1}{5}$	$\frac{2}{5}$	$\frac{3}{5}$	$\frac{4}{5}$	1
y					

5. $y = x^3$

x	-2	-1	0	1	2	3
y						

Simplify. [Previous course]

6. $d^4 \cdot d^5$ **7.** $(k^3)^5$ **8.** $\dfrac{m^5}{m^2}$ **9.** $(ab)^4 \cdot a$

7-2
**Roots, Radicals,
and Rational
Exponents**

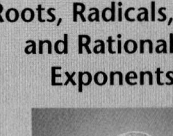

In 7-2 you will investigate operations on roots and powers. You will use the following skills involving radicals.

Simplify. [Previous course]

10. $\sqrt{48}$ **11.** $\sqrt{x^2}$ **12.** $\sqrt{72}$ **13.** $\sqrt[3]{27}$

14. $\sqrt[3]{x^3}$ **15.** $(x + 5)^2$ **16.** $\left(\sqrt{x}\right)^2$ **17.** $\left(\sqrt{x - 3}\right)^2$

Solve. [Previous course]

18. $\sqrt{x} = 5$ **19.** $\sqrt{x} + 4 = 7$ **20.** $x^2 + 4x - 21 = 0$

7-3
**Combining
Functions**

In 7-3 you will combine functions to create a new function. You will use the following algebra skills.

If $f(x) = x^2 - 3x + 5$, find each of the following. [Previous course]

21. $f(2)$ **22.** $f(-5)$ **23.** $f\!\left(\dfrac{5}{8}\right)$ **24.** $f(0)$

State whether or not the relation is a function. If it is a function, give its domain and range. [Previous course]

25. $(5, 7), (4, -3), (12, 7), (-2, -1)$ **26.** $y = 3x - 5$

27. $y = x^2$ **28.** $x^2 + y^2 = 49$

Capturing LIGHT AND LIFE

During the Great Depression of the 1930s, documentary photographer Dorothea Lange (1895–1965) roamed the roads of America's back country recording the terrible economic conditions that afflicted the nation. Her powerful images of migrant farmworkers showed Americans the oppressive conditions under which these people lived and helped create support for government relief programs. Lange's portrait, Migrant Mother, which hangs in the Library of Congress, was chosen as one of the 50 best photographs of the first half of this century.

In theory the photographer's job is easy: capture light on a photographic plate. In practice it is extremely difficult. Dorothea Lange confronted many different lighting conditions, from the scorching sunlight of the Great Plains to the dim interiors of unlighted shacks. Each potential photo brought a new set of conditions and the need to balance a new set of variables.

Suppose Dorothea Lange wanted to take a photograph in bright sunlight. She could deal with the problem of excessive brightness in several ways. She might choose a less light-sensitive film, close down the aperture (opening) of the camera, increase the shutter speed, or move farther from the subject. Each answer solves one problem but creates others. The ability to produce memorable images while juggling so many variables distinguishes the work of great photographers like Dorothea Lange, and helps us understand why photography is not merely a skill, but an art.

Dorothea Lange, *Migrant Mother*, 1936, Library of Congress

1. Choose one of the solutions given for the problem of excessive brightness. How might that solution create other problems for a photographer?
2. Dorothea Lange's photographs helped generate public support for government relief programs. Explain how a photograph can affect public opinion.
3. Suppose you doubled your distance from a source of light. How would this affect how bright the light seemed to you? Explain.

459

← CONNECT → *You've used equations to show how change in one variable affects change in another. Now you will more closely investigate certain types of relationships between variables.*

The *intensity* (light energy) of a light source is measured in *candela* (cd) or *candlepower*. *Illuminance* is the light energy per unit area. Naturally, illuminance decreases as we move farther from the source. But if we do not change our distance, illuminance is directly related to light intensity.

Recall that when y varies *directly* with x, we can express the relationship between the two variables with the equation $y = kx$, where k is the *constant of variation*. If we know a pair of (x, y) values for the relationship, we can solve for the constant of variation.

EXAMPLE

1. At a distance of 12 feet from a 60-cd light source, a photographer's light meter registers an illuminance of 18 units. Find the constant of variation. Then use the constant to find the illuminance of a 45-cd light source at the same distance.

Let I represent intensity and E represent illuminance. Since illuminance is proportional to intensity at a given distance, we can write $E = kI$.

$E = kI$

$18 = k(60)$ Substitute values for the known situation.

$k = 0.3$ Solve for the constant of variation.

We can now find the illuminance of the 45-cd source at this distance.

$E = 0.3I$ Write the equation of variation.

$E = 0.3(45)$ Substitute values for the unknown situation.

$E = 13.5$ Solve for E.

The illuminance is 13.5 units.

TRY IT

a. A light meter is the same distance from two light sources. When the first source (a 90-cd lamp) is turned on, the light meter reads 7.2 units of illuminance. When the 90-cd lamp is turned off and the second light source is turned on, the light meter reads 6 units. Find the intensity of the second light source.

CONSIDER

?

1. Suppose that *y* varies directly with *x*. Describe the graph of the ordered pairs (*x*, *y*). What does *k* represent?

When two variables are in direct variation, they increase or decrease together. In the Explore, you will investigate variation where one variable increases as the other decreases.

EXPLORE: FOCUS ON VARIATION

MATERIALS

Graph paper
Graphing utility (optional)

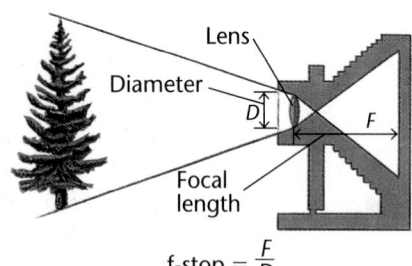

f-stop = $\frac{F}{D}$

The focal length of a camera lens is the distance from the lens to the point where the image is focused. The f-stop (*f*) of an exposure is the quotient of the focal length and the diameter (*D*) of the lens. With a focal length of 100 mm and a lens diameter of 50 mm, the f-stop is $\frac{100}{50} = 2$.

1. The table gives standard photographic f-stops. Complete the table for a focal length of 100 mm. Round your values for the lens diameter to the nearest tenth.

Focal length: 100 mm										
f-stop	1.4	2	2.8	4	5.6	8	11	16	22	32
Diameter		50								

2. Graph the values in the table. Describe your results. Have you ever seen a graph similar to this one before? If so, state what the graph was called and describe similarities and differences between this graph and the kind you saw before.

3. As the f-stop increases, what happens to the lens diameter? What happens when the f-stop decreases?

When two positive quantities are related in such a way that one increases as the other decreases, we say that the quantities are *inversely related*. If *y* varies inversely with *x*, the equation of **inverse variation** can be written $y = \frac{k}{x}$.

4. Write an inverse variation equation for the relationship between the f-stop and the lens diameter. What is the constant of variation?

5. Predict the equation for the relationship between the f-stop and the lens diameter for a focal length of 200 mm. Explain how you made your prediction.

CONSIDER

?

2. An inverse variation can also be expressed by the equation *xy* = *k*. Explain why this equation shows inverse variation.

The graph of an inverse relationship is a **rectangular hyperbola.** This is a pair of curves in opposite quadrants that approach the coordinate axes as asymptotes. In real-world contexts where variables have only positive values, only the branch of the hyperbola in the first quadrant applies.

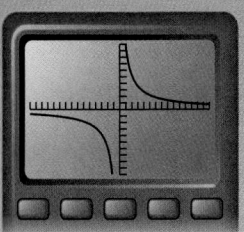

EXAMPLE

The current (I) in an electrical conductor varies inversely with the resistance (R) of the conductor. The current is $\frac{1}{3}$ amp (amperes) when the resistance is 360 ohms.

2. a. Graph the relationship between current and resistance.

First, find the constant of variation.

$I = \frac{k}{R}$ Write the equation of inverse variation.

$\frac{1}{3} = \frac{k}{360}$ Substitute values for the known situation.

$120 = k$ Solve for k.

The equation for the relationship is $I = \frac{120}{R}$.

The graph is shown at the right. Since the values of I and R must be positive, the graph is in the first quadrant.

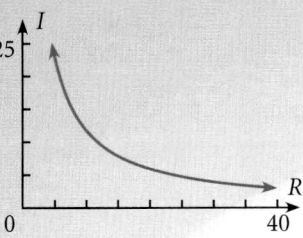

b. Find the current when the resistance is 15 ohms.

The solution can be found algebraically, as shown below, or approximated graphically, as shown at the right.

$I = \frac{120}{15}$ Substitute 15 for R.

$I = 8$ Solve for I.

The current is 8 amps.

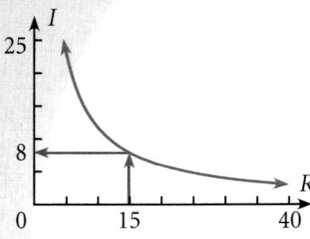

TRY IT

b. Suppose that the time needed to do a job varies inversely with the number of people working on the job. If it takes 8 hours for 3 people to load a moving van, how long would it take 4 people?

You've seen that the illuminance from a light source varies directly with the intensity of the light. However, your distance from the source also affects the illuminance—the farther you are from a reading lamp, the dimmer your book page gets.

3. The illuminance (E) of a light varies directly with the intensity (I) of the light and inversely with the square of the distance (D) from the light. At a distance of 20 feet, a light meter reads 6 units for a 100-cd lamp. Find the illuminance reading of a 54-cd lamp at a distance of 18 feet.

$$E = k\frac{I}{D^2}$$ Write the equation of variation.

$$6 = \frac{k \cdot 100}{20^2}$$ Substitute values for the known situation.

$$k = 24$$ Solve for k.

$$E = \frac{24 \cdot 54}{18^2}$$ Substitute in the new situation to find the unknown value.

$$E = 4$$ Solve.

The lamp gives an illuminance reading of 4 units.

As shown in Example 3, more than one variation may apply in a given situation. When a relationship shows both inverse and direct variation (as in Example 3), you have **combined variation.** If one variable varies directly with two or more other variables, but does not vary inversely with any other variable, the variation is called **joint variation.**

c. Suppose z varies jointly with x and the square of y. When $x = 4$ and $y = 5$, $z = 300$. Find z when $x = 6$ and $y = 2$.

d. The current (I) in an electrical circuit varies directly with the voltage (E) and inversely with the resistance (R). When the voltage is 8 volts and the resistance is 4 ohms, the current is 2 amps. Give the current when the voltage is 10 volts and the resistance is 20 ohms.

e. The illuminance (E) of a light varies directly with the intensity (I) of the light and inversely with the square of the distance (D) from the light. At a distance of 12 feet, a light meter reads 8 units for a 72-cd lamp. Find the illuminance reading of a 108-cd lamp at a distance of 20 feet.

Real-world situations often involve complex interrelationships among several variables. In such a situation, you may be able to write an equation for direct, inverse, joint, or combined variation relating the variables.

1. How can you decide whether two quantities vary directly or inversely?

2. Give an example of two real-world quantities that vary inversely. Explain why they have an inverse relationship.

3. The volume of a cone varies jointly with its height and the square of its radius. What type of variation does the height of the cone have with its volume and radius? Explain.

4. Explain why the illuminance of a light varies directly with the intensity of the source but inversely with the *square* of the distance from the source.

Exercises

CORE

1. **Getting Started** y varies directly with x. When $x = 12$, $y = 36$.
   a. Write the variation equation using k as a constant of variation.
   b. Substitute values for the known situation and solve for k. Rewrite your variation equation using this value.
   c. Suppose $x = 32$. Substitute 32 for x and solve the equation for y.
   d. Suppose $y = 49.5$. Solve the equation for x.
   e. Find three ordered pairs and graph the relationship.
   f. What happens to the value of x as y increases? to the value of y as x increases?

Write the word or phrase that correctly completes each statement.

2. When one quantity increases as another decreases, the quantities vary ____.

3. A rectangular hyperbola is the graph of a(n) ____ relationship.

Find each constant of variation.

4. y varies inversely with x. $y = 30$ when $x = 5$.

5. y varies directly with the square of x. $y = 24$ when $x = 2$.

6. Suppose h varies directly with g. When $g = 3$, $h = 12$. Find h when $g = 15$.

7. Suppose t varies inversely with s. When $s = 15$, $t = 20$. Find t when $s = 18$.

8. Suppose y varies jointly with the square of w and the cube of x. When $w = 4$ and $x = 2$, $y = 72$. Find y when $w = 1$ and $x = 5$.

9. **Dial Trial** Suppose that the cost of a 15-minute phone call varies directly with the distance to the person being called. On your phone bill, you find that a 15-minute, 2000-mile call costs $22.
   a. Graph the relationship between the cost of a phone call and the distance called.
   b. Find the cost of a 15-minute, 90-mile call algebraically.
   c. Explain how you could check your solution using your graph.

10. **Keeping Current** The current (I) in an electrical conductor, such as a wire, varies inversely with the resistance (R) of the conductor. The current is $\frac{1}{3}$ ampere when the resistance is 360 ohms.
    Science
    a. Write the variation equation.
    b. Find the constant of variation. Then sketch a graph of the variation equation. Describe your graph.
    c. Suppose the resistance of the conductor drops to 50 ohms. What is the current in the wire?

11. **A Place in Space** The force (F) that holds the moon in orbit around Earth varies jointly with the mass (m) of the moon and the mass (M) of Earth, and inversely with the square of the radius (r) of the orbit. Write the equation of variation.
    Science

For each of the following, determine the effect on y when x is doubled.

12. y varies directly with x

13. y varies inversely with x

14. y varies directly with the square of x

15. y varies inversely with the square of x

For each equation tell how the dependent variable varies in its relationship with the independent variable(s).

16. distance and time in $D = 65t$

17. base, area, and height in $b = \frac{2A}{h}$

18. Flat Tire The pressure (P) in a tire in lb/in.^{2} varies directly with the weight (W) of the car and inversely with the area (A) of contact of each tire with the ground.
   a. Write the variation equation.
   b. Find the constant of variation if a car that weighs 4000 lb has a tire pressure of 32 lb/in.^{2} and the area of contact of each tire with the ground is 31.25 in^2. Explain why this constant makes sense.
   c. Suppose the tire pressure drops to 24 lb/in^2. Find the area of contact of each tire with the ground.

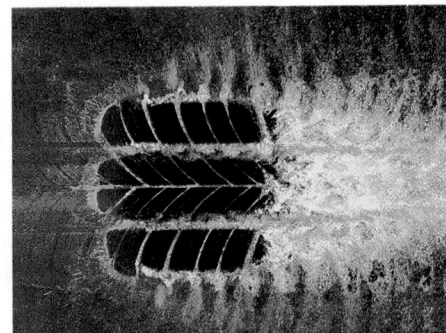

19. Putting the Right Spin on It If you spin a weight on the end of a string, the force (F) on the string varies directly with the square of the velocity (v) of the weight and inversely with the radius (r) of the circle. What happens to the force if:
   a. the length of the string is doubled?
   b. the velocity is tripled?
   c. the length of the string is halved and the velocity is increased by 50%?

LOOK BACK

20. Find the product of the complex numbers $(3 + 4i)$ and $(-2 + i)$. [4-3]

Solve each equation. Where necessary, round answers to the nearest tenth. [5-2]

21. $x^2 - 5x - 7 = 0$

22. $x^2 - 4x - 32 = 0$

23. $2x^2 + 3x = -5$

24. Da Da Da Dummm Beethoven had 12 notes to choose from for the first 4 notes in his Fifth Symphony. How many different arrangements of these notes are there? [6-1]

MORE PRACTICE

Find each constant of variation.

25. y varies directly with x. $y = 4$ when $x = 16$.

26. y varies inversely with x. $y = 9$ when $x = 6$.

27. Suppose y varies directly with x. When $x = 10$, $y = 25$. Find y when $x = 6$.

28. Suppose b varies inversely with a. When $a = 8$, $b = 60$. Find b when $a = 3$.

29. Suppose p varies jointly with m and the cube of n. When $m = 5$ and $n = 3$, $p = 270$. Find p when $m = 4$ and $n = 2$.

30. Use a Graphing Utility According to Boyle's Law, the volume of a gas varies
inversely with the pressure on the gas, when temperature is held constant.
   a. Find the constant of variation if the gas occupies 180 in.³ when the pressure
   is 15 lb/in².
   b. Graph the equation of variation on a graphing utility. Then use your graph to
   estimate, to the nearest tenth, each of the following.
      i. the pressure when the volume of the gas is 120 in.³
      ii. the volume when the pressure is 22 lb/in.²
      iii. the pressure when the volume of the gas is 3000 in.³

31. Political Timing According to a local comedian, the amount of time spent
discussing an issue at a town meeting varies inversely with the amount of money
involved. If the statement were true and an elementary school bond issue for
$1.5 million required 2.4 hours of discussion, how long would it take to discuss a
$6000 park for dogs?

**For each equation, state how the dependent variable varies in its relationship
with the independent variable(s).**

32. width and area in $w = \frac{A}{7}$

33. width, volume, and height in $w = \frac{V}{5h}$

34. time and rate in $t = \frac{50}{r}$

35. area and radius in $A = \pi r^2$

36. The volume of a cylindrical soda can varies directly with its height and the square
of its radius. Suppose that the radius is 3.2 cm, the height is 11.1 cm, and the
volume is 357.1 cm³.
   a. Write a variation equation. Solve for the variation constant.
   b. What would the height of a can with the same radius need to be to hold 524 cm³?

MORE MATH REASONING

37. Wind Power The power (P) in watts generated by a windmill varies
jointly with its efficiency (E), the square of the diameter (D) of its
blades in feet, and the cube of the wind velocity (V) in feet per
second. A windmill whose blades have a 10-ft diameter and whose
efficiency is 0.40 generates 10,000 watts of power at a wind velocity of
9.3 ft/sec. How much power does the windmill generate when the
wind velocity is 25 ft/sec? Explain how you solved this problem.

38. An "Eggcellent" Problem Suppose that two hens lay two eggs in two days.
   a. How long will it take four hens to lay four eggs?
   b. Explain what this problem has to do with variation.

39. More Than You Think A 3-inch-tall bottle of perfume costs $27. How much
should a geometrically similar 5-inch-tall bottle of perfume cost?

40. The graph of $xy = 4$ is a rectangular hyperbola appearing in the first and third
quadrants.
   a. Explain why neither branch of the hyperbola intersects the axes.
   b. Give the equation whose graph is a 90° rotation, in either direction, of the
   graph of $xy = 4$.

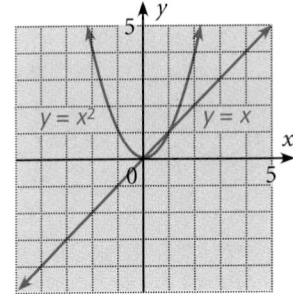

7-1
PART B

Positive Integer Exponents

← C O N N E C T → *You are very familiar with the graphs of y = x and y = x². You will now investigate the behavior of the graphs of y = xⁿ for values of n greater than 2.*

You know that the graph of the linear equation $y = x^1$ is a line and that the graph of the quadratic equation $y = x^2$ is a parabola.

In the Explore, you will investigate graphs of equations of the form $y = ax^n$ for higher values of n.

EXPLORE: INCREASING YOUR POWERS

MATERIALS

Graphing utility

1. Graph $y = x^3$ in a suitable viewing window. Describe your graph. What happens to the graph as the x-values take on larger and larger positive values? What happens as the x-values become more and more negative?

2. On the same set of axes, graph $y = x^4$. Compare its characteristics to those of $y = x^3$. Do the graphs have any points in common? If so, what are their coordinates?

3. Graph several other equations of the form $y = x^n$, where n is a positive integer. Describe any patterns you observe.

4. Change your viewing window so that the x-values are between 0 and 2 and the y-values are also between 0 and 2. On the same set of axes, graph $y = x^3$ and $y = x^4$. Which function has greater y-values? Continue graphing equations with higher powers of x until you are confident that you see a pattern. Make a conjecture about the graphs.

5. By making a sketch of each, predict the graphs of $y = -x^3$ and $y = -x^4$. Describe how you made your predictions. Then check your graphs on the graphing utility.

6. Summarize your results from Steps 1–5. Be sure to describe: any common points for the graphs; how the exponent affects their shape; and their behavior for positive and negative x-values, as those values get farther and farther from $x = 0$.

EXAMPLE

1. Sketch a graph of $f(x) = x^5$.

Substituting $x = 0$ and $x = 1$ into this equation, we see that the graph contains $(0, 0)$ and $(1, 1)$. As the x-values take on larger and larger positive values, the graph increases more and more quickly; as the x-values become more and more negative, the graph decreases more and more quickly.

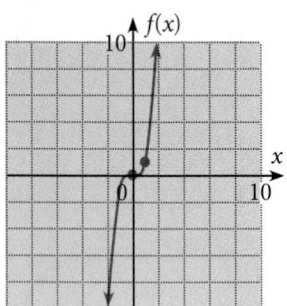

TRY IT

Graph each pair of equations on the same set of coordinate axes. Use different coordinate axes for each pair.

a. $y = x^4$ and $y = x^8$ **b.** $y = x^3$ and $y = -x^5$

In 5-2B, you saw how the value of a in $y = ax^2$ affects the graph. This effect is the same for all graphs of $y = ax^2$.

Some real-world relationships can be modeled by equations in this form.

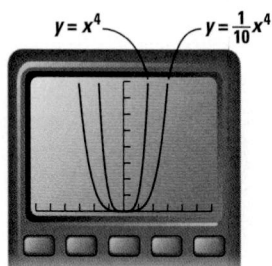

CONSIDER

1. Make a sketch of the graphs of $y = x^2$ and $y = |x^3|$ on the same set of axes. Explain how you graphed $y = |x^3|$.

2. Sketch a graph of $y = 2x^4 + 1$. Describe how its graph compares to that of $y = x^4$.

EXAMPLE

2. The total amount of life insurance in force (I) in the United States from 1945 to 1990, in billions of dollars, can be approximated by $I = 1.8 \times 10^{-13}x^7$, where x is the year ($1945 = 45$). Graph this function and estimate the amount of life insurance in force in 1975.

We can graph the function on a graphing utility and *trace* to estimate the I-value, where $x = 75$. From the graph, we estimate that the total amount of life insurance in 1975 was 2.4 billion dollars.

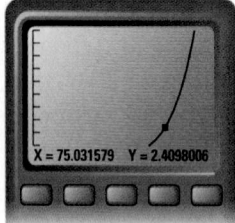

If a figure coincides with itself after a 180°
rotation around a point, it has **point symmetry**
with respect to the point. The figure shown has
point symmetry.

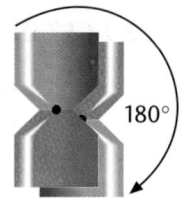

As you may have noticed, the graphs of
$f(x) = x^n$ have point symmetry with
respect to the origin when n is odd.

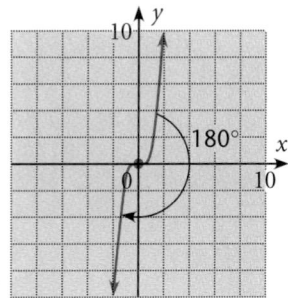

CONSIDER

**3. Do the graphs of functions of the form $f(x) = x^n$, where n is even,
show symmetry? If so, describe their symmetry or symmetries as
completely as you can.**

The properties of the graphs of functions of the form $y = x^n$ are summarized
below.

For all graphs:
- the graph contains the points $(0, 0)$ and $(1, 1)$;
- in the interval $-1 < x < 1$, the greater the value of n, the flatter the graph;
- for $x < -1$ and $x > 1$, the greater the value of n, the steeper the graph
  appears.

If n is even:
- the graph is "U-shaped," that is, the
  y-values become more and more positive as the x-values take on larger and
  larger positive values or more and more
  negative values;
- the graph has line symmetry with respect
  to the y-axis.

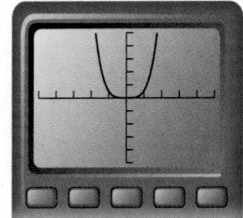

If n is odd:
- the graph resembles the graph of $y = x^3$, that
  is, the y-values become more positive as the
  x-values take on larger and larger positive
  values and more negative as the x-values take
  on more and more negative values;
- the graph has point symmetry with respect
  to the origin.

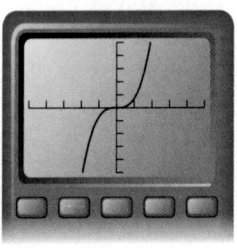

1. Describe the graph of the equation $y = x^7$.

2. By looking at a graph of $y = x^n$ or $-x^n$ for a particular value of n, how can you tell whether n is odd or even? How can you tell whether the sign in front of x^n is positive or negative?

3. If $n > m$, why does the graph of $y = x^n$ appear to climb less steeply than the graph of $y = x^m$ for values of x between 0 and 1, but more steeply for values of x greater than 1?

Exercises

CORE

1. Getting Started Answer each question to analyze the graph of $y = x^8$.

   a. Does the graph resemble a quadratic or a cubic curve? Explain.

   b. Give the coordinates of three points on the graph.

   c. Does the graph have line symmetry or point symmetry? Explain.

   d. Describe the behavior for positive and negative x-values of the graph as those values get farther from 0.

   e. For values of x greater than 1, does the graph rise more steeply or less steeply than the graph of $y = x^2$?

   f. For values of x between 0 and 1, does the graph appear to rise more steeply or less steeply than the graph of $y = x^2$?

Choose the letter of the graph that most resembles the graph of the given equation.

2. $y = -x^5$ **3.** $y = x^{18}$ **4.** $y = x^{13}$ **5.** $y = -x^6$

A. 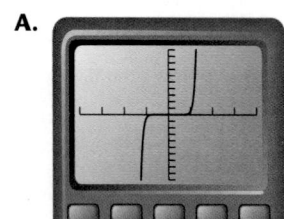   **B.** 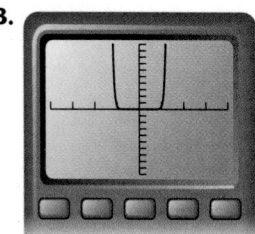   **C.** 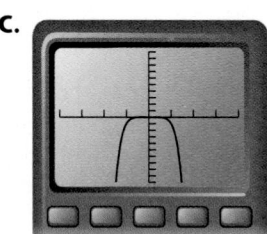   **D.**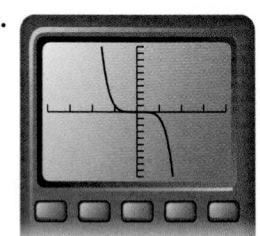

6. The figure below shows sections of the graphs of $y = x^{11}$ and $y = x^{12}$. Which graph is which? Explain.

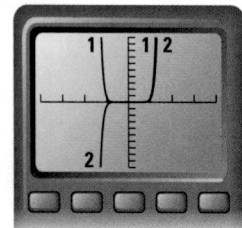

7. The figure below shows sections of the graphs of $y = x^9$ and $y = x^{13}$. Which graph is which? Explain.

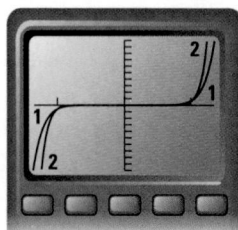

Graph each pair of equations on the same set of coordinate axes. Use different coordinate axes for each exercise.

8. $y = x^2$ and $y = x^{10}$

9. $y = x^3$ and $y = x^7$

10. $y = x^2$ and $y = -x^6$

11. $y = -x^3$ and $y = x^{11}$

12. The volume of a cube with side length x is given by $V = x^3$.
   a. Graph this equation.
   b. Use your graph to estimate, to the nearest half-unit:
      i. the volume of a cube whose side length is 1.5 units
      ii. the side length of a cube whose volume is 10 units

13. Engine Power According to a National Automobile Chamber of Commerce formula, the horsepower (h) of a 6-cylinder engine with a *bore* (cylinder diameter) of D inches, is given by

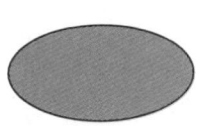

$$h = 2.4D^2$$

(This assumes a piston speed of 1000 ft/min and a mean pressure of 90 lb/in^2.)

   a. Graph this equation.
   b. Use your graph to estimate, to the nearest half-unit:
      i. the horsepower of a 6-cylinder engine with a 3-in. bore
      ii. the horsepower of a 6-cylinder engine with a 4-in. bore
      iii. the bore of a 29.4-horsepower, 6-cylinder engine

14. Sketch each figure. If the figure has line symmetry, draw the lines of symmetry; if it has point symmetry, sketch the point around which the figure is symmetric.

a.

b.

c.

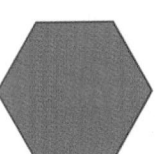

15. An *even* function is one whose graph has line symmetry with respect to the y-axis. An *odd* function is one whose graph has point symmetry with respect to the origin. Classify $y = x^2$, $y = x^3$, $y = x^4$, and $y = x^5$ as even or odd functions. Then explain why functions with these types of symmetry are called "odd" or "even."

LOOK AHEAD

Write in expanded notation. (Example: $m^3 \cdot m^2 = m \cdot m \cdot m \cdot m \cdot m$)

16. $k^4 \cdot k^3$

17. $\dfrac{x^4}{x^2}$

18. $-(3k)^3$

19. $(-3k)^3$

20. $\dfrac{n^3 n^1}{n^2}$

21. $(v^4)^2$

Replace each question mark with a missing numeral to make a true equation.

22. $8.2567 \times 100 = \underline{\ ?\ }$

23. $\dfrac{7.36}{10^3} = \underline{\ ?\ }$

24. $325{,}000 = 10^5 \times \underline{\ ?\ }$

MORE PRACTICE

25. Answer each question to analyze the graph of $y = x^{19}$.
  a. Does the graph resemble a quadratic or a cubic curve? Explain.
  b. Give the coordinates of three points on the graph.
  c. Does the graph have line symmetry or point symmetry? Explain.
  d. Describe the behavior for positive and negative x-values of the graph, as those values get farther from 0.
  e. For values of x greater than 1, does the graph appear to rise more steeply or less steeply than the graph of $y = x^2$?
  f. For values of x between 0 and 1, does the graph appear to rise more steeply or less steeply than the graph of $y = x^2$?

Choose the letter of the graph that most resembles the graph of the given equation.

26. $y = x^6$

27. $y = x^3$

28. $y = -x^{13}$

29. $y = -x^8$

A. **B.** **C.** **D.**

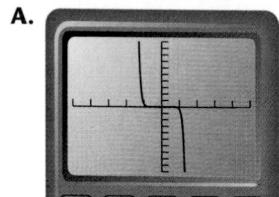

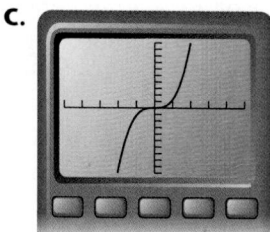

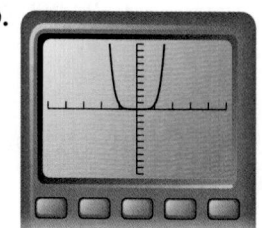

30. The figure below shows parts of the graphs of $y = -x^{17}$ and $y = -x^{20}$. Which graph is which? Explain.

31. The figure below shows parts of the graphs of $y = x^{11}$ and $y = x^{15}$. Which graph is which? Explain.

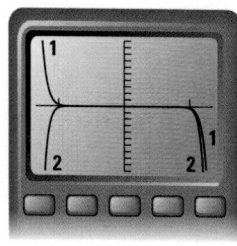

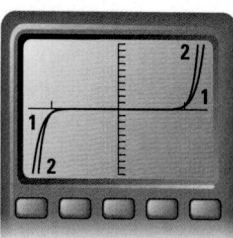

Graph each pair of equations on the same set of coordinate axes. Use different coordinate axes for each exercise.

32. $y = x^4$ and $y = x^6$

33. $y = x^3$ and $y = x^{11}$

34. $y = -x^2$ and $y = -x^4$

35. $y = -x^5$ and $y = -x^7$

36. $y = x^3$ and $y = x^4$

37. $y = -x^5$ and $y = -x^4$

38. Sketch a figure with:
  a. line symmetry over exactly one line
  b. line symmetry over three lines
  c. point symmetry

39. Tournament Time If the probability that your team wins a game is p, the probability that it will win n games in a row is p^n. Suppose that your team plays a four-game tournament. If it wins all four games, your team wins the tournament.
  a. What is the function that represents the probability that your team will win the tournament? What is the domain of this function? Explain.
  b. Use a graphing utility to graph the function. Then find the probability, to the nearest hundredth, that your team will win the tournament if your probability p of winning one game is:
  i. 30%   **ii.** 50%   **iii.** 70%   **iv.** 90%

40. According to projections cited in *The World Almanac and Book of Facts, 1995,* the percentage (p) of U.S. households with computers that have installed CD-ROM drives is approximated for the years 1994−1997 by:

$p = 0.65y^2$

where y is the year from 1994–1997 (1994 = 4).
  a. Use a graphing utility to graph this function.
  b. Use your graph to estimate, to the nearest percent, the percentage of U.S. households that will have such computers in:
  i. 1994   **ii.** 1995   **iii.** 1996   **iv.** 1997

MORE MATH REASONING

41. The Power of Medicine One characteristic of the life-threatening disease of atherosclerosis is a shrinking of the radii of the arteries due to a buildup of plaque on the inner walls. Poiseuille's Law states that the blood flow in an artery varies directly with the fourth power of the radius. Suppose that, due to treatment, the radius of an artery is increased by one-fifth. By what percent is blood flow through the artery increased?

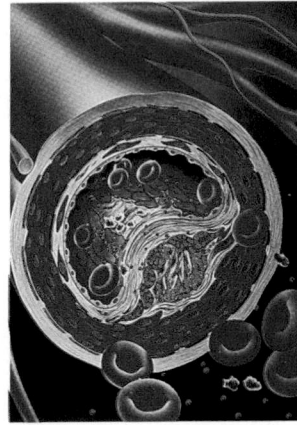

42. Use a graphing utility to graph the functions for the surface area of a sphere and its volume, $SA = 4\pi r^2$ and $V = \frac{4}{3}\pi r^3$. What do the points of intersection of these two functions represent? Explain.

43. Use a Graphing Utility
  a. On the same set of axes, graph $y = x^3$, $y = 2x^3$, and $y = 3x^3$. Describe the effect of a on the graph of $y = ax^n$.
  b. On the same set of axes, graph $y = x^3$, $y = x^3 + 1$, and $y = x^3 + 2$. Describe the effect of b on the graph of $y = ax^n + b$.
  c. On the same set of axes, graph $y = x^4$, $y = (x + 1)^4$, and $y = (x - 2)^4$. Describe the effect of c on the graph of $y = (x - c)^n$.
  d. Are these effects consistent with ones you have seen earlier? Explain.

← CONNECT →   *You have worked with exponents throughout this course. Now you will formalize the properties of exponents so that you can use them more efficiently and work easily with very large and very small numbers.*

We use **exponential notation** to write a product of equal factors in a compact form.

$$3 \cdot 3 \cdot 3 \cdot 3 \cdot 3 = 3^5$$

Here, 3 is the **base** and 5 is the **exponent.** We read 3^5 as "3 to the fifth **power**," "the fifth power of 3," or simply "3 to the fifth."

EXAMPLES

1. There are 10^2 centimeters in a meter and 10^3 meters in a kilometer. How many centimeters are there in a kilometer?

$10^2 \cdot 10^3 = (10 \cdot 10) \cdot (10 \cdot 10 \cdot 10)$ Using the definition of exponent.

$\qquad\quad = 100,000$ Multiply.

$\qquad\quad = 10^5$ Rewrite in exponential form.

There are 10^5 centimeters in a kilometer.

Simplify each expression.

2. $(d^3)^2$

$(d^3)^2 = (d \cdot d \cdot d)(d \cdot d \cdot d) = d^6$

3. $\dfrac{m^5}{m^2}$

$\dfrac{m^5}{m^2} = \dfrac{m \cdot m \cdot m \cdot m \cdot m}{m \cdot m}$

$\qquad = m \cdot m \cdot m$

$\qquad = m^3$

The Examples above suggest some easier ways to simplify expressions involving exponents.

CONSIDER

?

1. Describe an easy method to simplify each of the following:

$6^{13} \cdot 6^9 \qquad \dfrac{6^{13}}{6^9} \qquad (6^{13})^9$

Explain why each of your methods makes sense.

EXAMPLE

Simplify.

4. $6x^2(2x)^3$

$$6x^2(2x)^3 = 6x^2(2^3x^3) \qquad\qquad (2^1x^1)^3 = 2^3x^3$$
$$= 6x^2(8x^3) = (6)(8)(x^2)(x^3) \qquad 2^3 = 8$$
$$= 48x^5 \qquad\qquad (x^2)(x^3) = x^5$$

TRY IT

Simplify.

a. $(3k)^4$ **b.** $-(2a)^4$ **c.** $(-2a)^4$ **d.** $(n^3)^4$ **e.** $\dfrac{10^{11}}{10^7}$

You've seen negative exponents in earlier courses. The following pattern helps illustrate the meaning of zero as an exponent and the meaning of negative exponents.

$$10^2 = 100$$
$$10^1 = 10$$
$$10^0 = ?$$
$$10^{-1} = ?$$
$$10^{-2} = ?$$

By continuing the pattern, we see that $10^0 = 1$, that $10^{-1} = \frac{1}{10}$, and that $10^{-2} = \frac{1}{100}$. These results are summarized below.

ZERO AND INTEGER EXPONENTS

Any real number (besides zero) raised to the zero power equals 1: $x^0 = 1$.

For any nonzero real number b and integer n, $b^{-n} = \frac{1}{b^n}$ and $\frac{1}{b^{-n}} = b^n$.

When simplifying an expression with exponents, leave your answer so that it has only positive exponents.

EXAMPLES

Write using only positive exponents.

5. k^{-3}

$$k^{-3} = \frac{1}{k^3}$$

6. $(x^6)(x^{-13})$

$$(x^6)(x^{-13}) = x^{-7} = \frac{1}{x^7}$$

Simplify $\dfrac{14x^8y^{-5}}{8x^{-4}y^3}$. Write your answer using only positive exponents.

Vanessa thinks...

I'll simplify the fraction first. To divide powers, I subtract their exponents.

$$\frac{14x^{8-(-4)}y^{-5-3}}{8} = \frac{7x^{12}y^{-8}}{4}$$

I need to have all the exponents positive. Since y^{-8} means $\dfrac{1}{y^8}$, I can rewrite the fraction with a positive power of y in the denominator.

$$\frac{7x^{12}y^{-8}}{4} = \frac{7x^{12}}{4y^8}$$

Jacy thinks...

First, I'll rewrite the fraction so that it has only positive exponents. I know that $\dfrac{1}{x^{-4}} = x^4$ and $y^{-5} = \dfrac{1}{y^5}$.

$$\frac{14x^8y^{-5}}{8x^{-4}y^3} = \frac{14x^8x^4}{8y^3y^5}$$

Now, I can multiply by adding the exponents.

$$\frac{14x^8x^4}{8y^3y^5} = \frac{7x^{12}}{4y^8}$$

We can use integer exponents to express very large and very small numbers in **scientific notation.** A number in scientific notation is in the form $a \times 10^n$, where $1 \le |a| < 10$ and n is an integer. Since a is a number between 1 and 10, there is always one digit to the left of the decimal point for a number in scientific notation.

Standard notation	Scientific notation
56,000,000	5.6×10^7

7 places to the left

0.0003099	3.009×10^{-4}

4 places to the right

In the Explore, using scientific notation will help you do calculations involving large numbers.

If Earth were made of sand, would it contain more or less than a googol (10^{100}) grains of sand?

1. Draw a 1-inch segment. Mark pencil points along the segment to get an estimate of the number of tightly packed grains of sand in one linear inch.
2. Calculate the number of grains of sand in one cubic foot.
3. Earth's radius is about 4000 miles. Use the formula for the volume of a sphere, $V = \frac{4}{3}\pi r^3$, and the fact that there are 5280 feet in a mile to calculate the number of grains in a sandy Earth. Is it more or less than a googol?
4. Explain why scientific notation is useful for doing calculations involving very large or very small numbers.

TRY IT

Write using only positive exponents.

f. $(c^{-3})(c^{-6})$

g. $\left(\dfrac{m^3}{m^{-5}}\right)^{10}$

h. $\dfrac{4x^{12}y^{-4}}{10x^{-4}y^{-13}}$

i. Einstein's formula, $E = mc^2$, shows a connection between matter and energy. E is the energy produced, in Joules, by converting m kg of matter to energy; c is the speed of light, approximately 3×10^8 m/sec. Find the amount of energy produced when a hydrogen atom, with a mass of 1.67×10^{-27} kg, is converted to energy. Express your answer in scientific notation.

The properties of exponents are summarized below.

For all real numbers a and b and integers m and n:

$$a^m \cdot a^n = a^{m+n} \qquad \text{(Product of Powers)}$$

$$(a^m)^n = a^{mn} \qquad \text{(Power of Powers)}$$

$$(ab)^m = a^m b^m \qquad \text{(Power of Products)}$$

$$\frac{a^m}{a^n} = a^{m-n},\, a \neq 0 \qquad \text{(Quotient of Powers)}$$

$$\left(\frac{a}{b}\right)^m = \frac{a^m}{b^m},\, b \neq 0 \qquad \text{(Power of Quotients)}$$

The properties of exponents simplify calculations by: reducing the multiplication of powers to the addition of their exponents; reducing the division of powers to the subtraction of their exponents; and reducing the raising of a power to a power to the multiplication of their exponents.

1. State each of the properties of exponents in your own words.
2. Explain the difference between $a^m \cdot a^n$ and $(a^m)^n$.
3. Suppose that ▢ represents 10^{50}. Sketch a rectangle representing 10^{51}.

Exercises

CORE

Getting Started Determine if each equation is true or false. If the equation is true, name the property of exponents that justifies it. If it is false, change the equation to make it true.

1. $9^4 \cdot 9^6 = 9^{24}$ **2.** $(2^7)^8 = 2^{56}$ **3.** $(3 \cdot 7)^4 = 3^4 \cdot 7^4$ **4.** $\dfrac{13^{10}}{13^2} = 13^{12}$

5. $\left(\dfrac{3}{4}\right)^5 = \dfrac{3^5}{4^5}$ **6.** $\dfrac{8^{12}}{8^4} = 8^8$ **7.** $11^3 \cdot 11^2 = 22^5$ **8.** $\dfrac{7^3}{7^3} = 0$

Write the word or phrase that correctly completes each statement.

9. The number 8.3×10^{-4} is written in ____ notation.

10. The number 7^3 is written in ____ notation.

11. In the expression 5^6, 5 is called the ____.

Simplify. Write answers without negative exponents.

12. $(4m)^3$ **13.** $4m^3$ **14.** $(-4m)^3$

15. $-4m^3$ **16.** $-(4m)^3$ **17.** $-4m^{-3}$

18. $(-8b^3)^0$ **19.** $-3(2m)^4$ **20.** $a^{-7} \cdot a^{-2} \cdot a^5$

21. $(-2x^{-4})(5x^5)$ **22.** $(7a^8b^{-3})(3a^{-9}b^3)$ **23.** $\dfrac{8^{-3}}{8^{-4}}$

24. $\dfrac{mn^4}{m^3n}$ **25.** $\dfrac{-24h^4k^{-6}}{8h^7k^9}$ **26.** $(2^3x^4)^{-3}$

27. $\dfrac{(3x^2)^3}{6x^5}$ **28.** $\dfrac{10(x^5y^7)^6}{5(x^3y^6)^6}$ **29.** $\dfrac{4(c^5d^{-3})^{-2}}{6(c^{-2}d^4)^5}$

Write each number in standard notation.

30. The interior temperature of the sun is about 3.5×10^7 °F.

31. The Gulf of Mexico covers about 5.96×10^5 mi².

Write each number in scientific notation.

32. The mean wavelength of sodium light is 0.000059 cm.

33. An amoeba is about 0.0003 m in length.

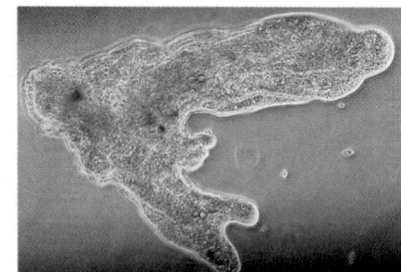

Amoeba

Simplify and write in scientific notation.

34. $(8 \times 10^{-10})(3 \times 10^{13})$

35. $\dfrac{5 \times 10^7}{8 \times 10^3}$

36. $(2.32 \times 10^3)(3.5 \times 10^2)$

37. Traveling Light A *light-year*, a unit of distance used in astronomy, is the distance that light travels in one year.
   a. If the velocity of light in a vacuum is 3.0×10^5 km/sec, find the length of one light-year in km.
   b. In 1994, the farthest-known object from Earth was the quasar PC 1247+3406, at a distance of 1.3×10^{10} light-years. Write this distance in km.

38. The volume of a sphere of radius r is $V = \frac{4}{3}\pi r^3$. The diameter of the sun is about 1.4×10^6 km. Find the volume of the sun.

39. The Beat Goes On Count the number of times your heart beats in one minute. Assuming your heart continues to beat at this rate, calculate how many times it will beat in the next 80 years. Write your result in scientific notation.

40. Deficit Reduction In 1993, the U.S. population was about 260,000,000 people and the total U.S. public debt was $\$4.3512 \times 10^{12}$. Find the average amount of money each person in the United States would have had to contribute to pay off the 1993 deficit.

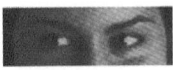

LOOK BACK

Graph each conic section. [5-3]

41. $(x - 1)^2 + (y + 3)^2 = 16$

42. $\dfrac{(x + 1)^2}{9} + \dfrac{y^2}{16} = 1$

43. $\dfrac{(y + 3)^2}{25} - \dfrac{(x + 2)^2}{4} = 1$

44. Jenny has 2 different choices for her first period class, 4 choices for her second period class, and 5 choices for her third period class. What is the probability that she has the same schedule as her friend Soraya, who has the same choices? [6-2]

MORE PRACTICE

Simplify. Write answers with positive exponents.

45. $(-2h)(-2h)(-2h)$

46. 18^0

47. $(2p)^2(3p)^3$

48. $(x^4)^{-3}$

49. $(x^{-3}y^4)(x^6y^{-4})$

50. 13^{-4}

51. $\dfrac{20^{15}}{20^9}$

52. $\dfrac{5k^7}{15k^2}$

53. $(-3)^{-5}$

54. $a^6 \cdot a^{10}$

55. $(14^3)^5$

56. $(4m^3n^{13})(-12m^{-1}n^7)$

57. $(-3m^9)(4m^{-5})$

58. $\dfrac{(3y^5)^2}{(3y^{-3})^3}$

59. $\dfrac{1}{a^0 + b^0}$

60. $(2 \times 10^{72})^{-1}$

61. $2c^7 \cdot c^9$

62. $\dfrac{3^7}{3^{-11}}$

63. $(2k^4)^7$

64. $\dfrac{(4x^2)^{-2}}{(2x^4)^2}$

65. $\dfrac{c^{-12}}{c^{-15}}$

66. $\dfrac{20m^4n^5}{5(mn^2)^3}$

67. $\dfrac{54(x^{-4}y^3)^2}{144(x^{-2}y^3)^{-4}}$

68. $\dfrac{(r^3s^{-5}t^{12})^2}{(r^{-3}s^{15}t^{-6})^{-1}}$

Write each number in standard notation.

69. The mass of an electron is 9.11×10^{-28} g.

70. The distance to the nearest galaxy is 9.6×10^{11} miles.

71. The area of Russia is 6.5928×10^6 mi².

Write each number in scientific notation.

72. The probability that a professional golfer will get a hole in one is approximately 0.00065.

73. There are 10,800,000,000,000,000,000,000,000 atoms of iron in a kilogram.

Simplify and write in scientific notation.

74. $(2 \times 10^6)(4.5 \times 10^8)$ **75.** $(1.2 \times 10^{-6})(8.4 \times 10^{10})$ **76.** $\dfrac{9.6 \times 10^{-3}}{2.4 \times 10^{-7}}$

77. The three-toed sloth is the slowest-moving mammal. Its average ground speed is about 0.083 mi/hr. Express this speed in mi/sec.

78. In 1983, the spacecraft *Pioneer 10* passed the orbit of the planet Pluto, a distance of 5×10^9 km from Earth. How long did it take a radio signal from *Pioneer 10*, traveling at the speed of light (3.0×10^5 km/sec), to reach Earth?

MORE MATH REASONING

Solve for x.

79. $4^{3x} = 8$ **80.** $4^{6x+2} = 16^x$ **81.** $81 = 27^{x-3}$ **82.** $4^{3x} = 32^{x+2}$

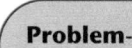

> **Problem-Solving Tip**
>
> Rewrite the equation using the same base on both sides.

83. a. Is $2^{(3^4)} = (2^3)^4$? Explain.
   b. Give an order-of-operations rule for the expression a^{b^c}. Explain your reasoning.

84. High Class Living Suppose that each person in the world (approximately 5.5×10^9 people) were allotted an area the size of your classroom in which to live. How much area would be needed to house the world's population? Express your answer as a comparison to one of the areas below.
   (a) Asia, 1.7×10^7 mi²
   (b) North America, 9.4×10^6 mi²
   (c) The Gulf of Mexico, 5.96×10^5 mi²

← CONNECT → *Unusually large and small numbers are common in astronomy, making the field ideally suited for the use of scientific notation. You will apply scientific notation and direct variation to calculate an extremely large number, the velocity of quasar 3C 273.*

Visible light has properties similar to those of ocean waves. A light wave can be characterized by its wavelength (ℓ), which is the distance between two successive crests, and by its frequency (f), the number of crests passing a given point in one second, measured in Hertz (Hz). Of the colors we can see, violet light has the shortest wavelength and red light the longest.

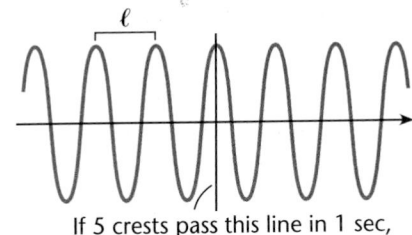

If 5 crests pass this line in 1 sec, the frequency is 5 Hz.

By photographing and analyzing light that arrives from faraway objects, such as the Andromeda Galaxy, astronomers can learn the chemical composition, age, and even the velocity of heavenly bodies.

Andromeda Galaxy

First, a spectrograph is used to split the light from a source into a spectrum (similar to the colors formed by a prism) and photograph it. The spectrum has *absorption lines,* five of which are shown. These indicate chemical elements in the object being photographed.

$\ell(\times 10^{-5}$ cm$)$ Spectrum of Stationary Object

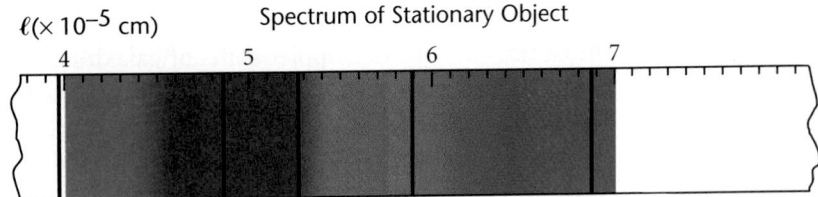

If an object is moving toward us, the lines shift toward the violet end of the spectrum because the wavelengths appear compressed. If an object is moving away from us, the lines shift toward the red. This *Doppler shift* is of great importance, for the velocity of the object varies directly with the shift in wavelength. By measuring the shift in the positions of absorption lines, we can determine how fast and in what direction an object is traveling.

EXPLORE: THE SPEED OF QUASARS

MATERIALS

Graph paper
Graphing utility (optional)

1. Estimate the wavelength of the light at the position of each of the five absorption lines in the spectrum on the previous page.

2. The wavelength and frequency of a ray of light are related to the speed of light (c) (approximately 3×10^{10} cm/sec) by the equation $\ell f = c$. Use $\ell f = c$ to find the frequency of the light at each position.

3. Graph the frequency of light against wavelength. Is the relationship between the two variables direct or inverse?

4. Quasars are the most remote and fastest moving objects in the universe. The quasar known as 3C 273 was discovered in 1963 by astronomer Maarten Schmidt. The absorption lines in the spectrum below have been drawn to reflect the Doppler shift observed by Schmidt.

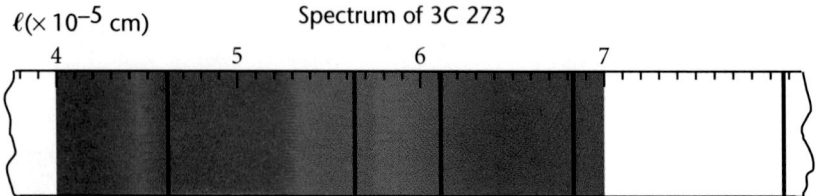

$\ell(\times 10^{-5}$ cm$)$ Spectrum of 3C 273

Estimate the position of each absorption line. For each line, calculate D, the *percentage* change in the wavelength compared to the standard wavelength seen in the spectrum on page 481. This change is caused by the Doppler shift. Use the mean of the five values as your value for D.

5. The velocity of a source of light (v) varies directly with the percent change in the wavelength of the light due to motion (D). The constant of variation (c) is the speed of light. Therefore, we have the equation:

$$v = cD$$

Calculate the velocity of 3C 273. Express the velocity in cm/sec and mi/sec. Is the quasar moving toward us or away from us? Explain how you can tell.

Measurements of the Doppler shifts of galaxies during the 1920s led to one of the most important discoveries of our century. Astronomers Edwin Hubble and Vesto Slipher found that all other galaxies are moving away from us. The farther the galaxy, the faster it is traveling. This discovery showed that we live in an expanding universe.

REFLECT

1. Briefly define direct, inverse, combined, and joint variation.

2. Why is scientific notation useful? Why do you think it is called *scientific* notation?

3. Describe how the value of n affects the steepness of the graph of a function $f(x) = x^n$. Consider all possible x-values in your description.

Self-Assessment

1. The graph shows the curves $y = x$, $y = x^2$, $y = x^3$, and $y = x^4$.
   a. Identify the range of x- and y-values shown. Explain how you can tell.
   b. Match each equation with one of the graphs.

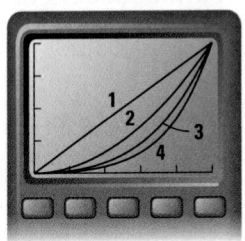

Write the word or phrase that correctly completes each statement.

2. In the expression 7^4, the number 4 is the ____.

3. Combined variation involves both ____ and ____ variation.

Give the constant of variation.

4. y varies directly with x. $y = 20$ when $x = 4$.

5. y varies inversely with x. $y = 4.5$ when $x = 6$.

6. y varies inversely with the square of x. $y = 2$ when $x = 5$.

7. Suppose y varies inversely with x. When $x = 25$, $y = 10$. Find y when $x = 12$.

8. Suppose h varies jointly with f and the square of g. When $f = 11$ and $g = 6$, $h = 88$. Find h when $f = 9$ and $g = 22$.

Solve each equation. Where necessary, round answers to the nearest hundredth. [5-2]

9. $x^2 - 3x - 2 = 0$

10. $x^2 + x - 20 = 0$

11. $7x^2 + 2x = -11$

12. **Opposites Attract** The force of attraction between two magnets varies inversely with the square of the distance between them. The force is 8 newtons when the magnets are 3 centimeters apart. Give the force when the magnets are 4 centimeters apart.

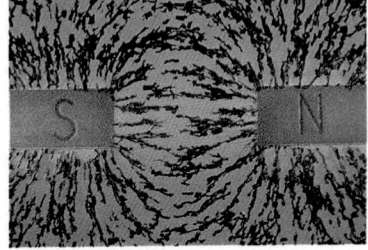

13. How many different committees of 3 can be chosen from 8 student council members? [6-2]

14. **News Copy** The time required to make copies of a newsletter varies jointly with the number of copies needed and the number of pages in the newsletter, and inversely with the number of photocopy machines used. It takes 5 machines 20 hours to make 10,000 copies of a four-page newsletter. How long would it take 1 machine to make 200 copies of a two-page newsletter?

15. **Fill It Up** Under steady driving conditions, the amount of gas a car uses varies directly with the distance driven. Mario drove 353.4 miles on 12.4 gallons of gas.
   a. Write the variation equation and find the constant of variation. What is the meaning of this constant?
   b. Use the equation to find the distance Mario can drive on 16 gallons of gas.

Graph each pair of equations on the same set of coordinate axes. Use different coordinate axes for each exercise.

16. $y = x^2$ and $y = x^6$ **17.** $y = x^3$ and $y = x^5$

18. Name the points of intersection of the graphs of $y = x^9$ and $y = x^{10}$.

19. For values of x greater than 1, does the graph of $y = x^7$ appear to rise more steeply or less steeply than the graph of $y = x^8$?

20. For values of x between 0 and 1, does the graph of $y = x^{10}$ appear to rise more steeply or less steeply than the graph of $y = x^{11}$?

Simplify. Choose the letter of the correct answer.

21. $(2 \times 10^3)(6 \times 10^8)$
    (a) 12×10^{24} (b) 1.2×10^{10} (c) 1.2×10^{11} (d) 1.2×10^{12}

Decide which choice is correct.

(A) The quantity in Column A is greater.   (B) The quantity in Column B is greater.
(C) The two quantities are equal.   (D) The relationship cannot be determined.

	Column A	Column B
22.	x^{12}	x^{11}
23.	$-x^{27}$	$(-x)^{27}$

Simplify. Write answers with positive exponents.

24. 4^{-7} **25.** $(6k^4)^0$ **26.** $\dfrac{15x^2y^6}{-3x^8y^{-3}}$

27. $(2p^3)^4(-p^2)^3$ **28.** $\left(\dfrac{2d}{3}\right)^3\left(\dfrac{d}{6}\right)^2$ **29.** $\dfrac{7.5 \times 10^6}{5 \times 10^{17}}$

Write each number in scientific notation.

30. 56,700,000,000,000   **31.** 0.0000000001043

Write each number in standard notation.

32. 8.035×10^{-9} **33.** 6×10^8

34. Night Light The illuminance (E) of a light varies directly with the intensity (I) of the light and inversely as the square of the distance (D) from the light. At a distance of 40 feet, a light meter gives a reading of 12 units for a 160-cd lamp. Find the reading of a 90-cd lamp at a distance of 60 feet.

35. Going Against the Grains The area of the Sahara Desert is about 3.5×10^6 square miles. Suppose that the average depth of sand in the Sahara is 12 feet and that the volume of a grain of sand is 1.5×10^{-9} cubic feet.
    a. Find the volume of sand in the Sahara in cubic feet.
    b. Find the number of grains of sand in the Sahara. Assume there is no space between grains of sand.

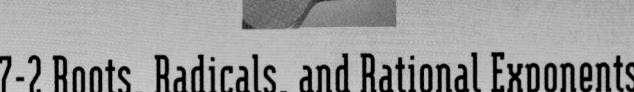

The Language of Sound

For more than a decade, Wynton Marsalis has been widely regarded as one of the world's premier jazz *and* classical trumpet players. Jazz, however, is his first love.

In a 1982 interview for *Down Beat* magazine, he said, "Listen to the music. High schools all over the country should have programs where the kids can listen to the music. Schools should have the records, and the students should be required to listen to them all.... They should listen to Parker and Coltrane and some of the more creative cats."

The language of the trumpet, like the language of all sound, begins with *vibration*. The sounds of speech are produced by the vibrations of the vocal cords. Similarly, music is produced by vibrations—a trumpet player's lips, an oboe player's reed, a violinist's strings. The faster the speed of vibration (the *frequency*), the higher the note produced. To change the frequency of a note, a musician has several options. A guitarist, for example, can produce a higher note by shortening a string (moving to a higher fret), by tightening the string, or by choosing a thinner string. Therefore, frequency is a function of three variables: length, tension force, and mass per unit length.

The language of mathematics may not seem as expressive as the trumpet of Wynton Marsalis, but it is central to the language of sound.

1. Does the frequency of a guitar note vary directly or inversely with the length of the string? Explain.
2. Do you think a large organ-pipe produces a lower note or higher note than a small, thin one? Justify your answer.
3. Suppose that a guitarist buys a guitar, smaller than her own, for her child to learn on. If both guitars' strings have the same mass per unit length, which guitar will need to be strung more loosely to produce the same notes? Explain.

Rational Exponents

← CONNECT → *You've investigated the properties of integral exponents and the graphs of functions that involve integral powers of x. Now you will extend your investigation to include exponents that are rational numbers.*

OH   YOU   SEE

    OH   CAN

       SAY

If you sing the first six notes of our national anthem, you will hear that the note for the word *see* is higher than the note for *say*, but that they sound similar. That is because the frequency of the higher note is exactly 2 times that of the lower.

The frequencies of the 12 notes in the musical interval from "say" to "see" form a geometric sequence. So, the common ratio is a number that gives a product of 2 when multiplied by itself 12 times. We write the positive real number with this property as $\sqrt[12]{2}$, called the *twelfth root* of 2. The number inside the radical sign, 2, is the **radicand.** The number 12 is the **index.**

Every positive number has two real-number square roots, one positive and one negative. The positive real root of the number is its principal root, and it is this number that we look for when simplifying a radical. This is also true for fourth roots, sixth roots, and in general, any even roots.

No confusion arises with odd roots. An odd root is positive if the radicand is positive and negative if the radicand is negative.

$$\sqrt{16} = 4 \qquad\qquad -\sqrt[4]{81} = -3 \qquad\qquad \sqrt[6]{x^{18}} = |x|^3$$

$$\sqrt[3]{125} = 5 \qquad\qquad \sqrt[3]{-125} = -5 \qquad\qquad \sqrt[9]{x^{27}} = x^3$$

CONSIDER

1. Suppose that $x^4 = 16$. How many real solutions are there to this equation? Which of these numbers is equal to $\sqrt[4]{16}$?

2. Explain why $\sqrt[6]{x^{18}} = |x|^3$.

In the Explore, you will investigate the relationship between roots and exponents.

EXPLORE: THE ROOT OF THE MATTER

MATERIALS

Scientific calculator

1. Evaluate $4^{\frac{1}{2}}$, $9^{\frac{1}{2}}$, $16^{\frac{1}{2}}$, and $25^{\frac{1}{2}}$. Explain what it means to raise a number to the $\frac{1}{2}$ power.

2. Evaluate $8^{\frac{1}{3}}$, $27^{\frac{1}{3}}$, $64^{\frac{1}{3}}$, and $125^{\frac{1}{3}}$. Explain what it means to raise a number to the $\frac{1}{3}$ power.

3. Predict the values of the $\frac{1}{4}$ power of 16 and the $\frac{1}{5}$ power of 32. Check your prediction on your calculator. Explain what it means to raise a number to the $\frac{1}{4}$ and to the $\frac{1}{5}$ power.

4. Compare the following. Then make a conjecture about the meaning of $x^{\frac{m}{n}}$.

   • 4 to the $\frac{3}{2}$ power and 4^3 to the $\frac{1}{2}$ power

   • 27 to the $\frac{4}{3}$ power and 27^4 to the $\frac{1}{3}$ power

   • 16 to the $\frac{7}{4}$ power and 16^7 to the $\frac{1}{4}$ power

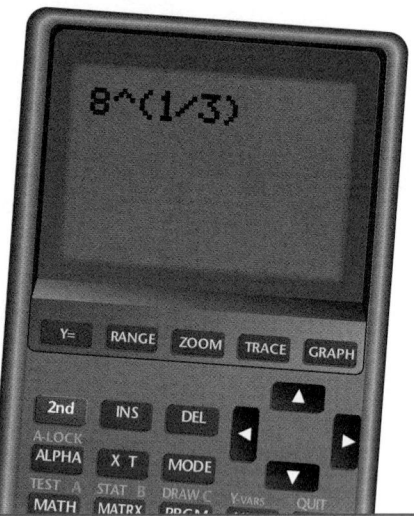

The following shows the relationship between rational exponents and roots.

For integers p and q, $q > 0$, and any nonzero real number a,

$$a^{\frac{p}{q}} = \sqrt[q]{a^p} = \left(\sqrt[q]{a}\right)^p$$

except when a is negative and q is even.

All of the properties of integral exponents also hold for rational exponents. Thus, you may add exponents when you are multiplying expressions that have the same base, subtract exponents when you are dividing such expressions, and so on.

EXAMPLES

Evaluate each expression.

1. $27^{\frac{2}{3}}$

$27^{\frac{2}{3}} = \left(\sqrt[3]{27}\right)^2 = 3^2 = 9$

2. $125^{-\left(\frac{4}{3}\right)}$

$125^{-\left(\frac{4}{3}\right)} = \dfrac{1}{125^{\frac{4}{3}}} = \dfrac{1}{\left(\sqrt[3]{125}\right)^4}$

$= \dfrac{1}{5^4} = \dfrac{1}{625}$

3. Simplify $x^{\frac{1}{5}} \cdot x^{\frac{3}{5}}$.

$$x^{\frac{1}{5}} \cdot x^{\frac{3}{5}} = x^{\frac{1}{5}+\frac{3}{5}} = x^{\frac{4}{5}} = \sqrt[5]{x^4}$$

4. Rewrite $(m^2n^3)^{\frac{1}{4}}$ using a radical.

$$(m^2n^3)^{\frac{1}{4}} = \sqrt[4]{m^2n^3}$$

5. Rewrite $\sqrt[5]{(xy^2)^3}$ using a rational exponent.

$$\sqrt[5]{(xy^2)^3} = (xy^2)^{\frac{3}{5}}$$

Evaluate each expression.

a. $32^{\frac{6}{5}}$

b. $25^{-\left(\frac{1}{2}\right)}$

Simplify each expression.

c. $\dfrac{9^{\frac{7}{12}}}{9^{\frac{1}{12}}}$

d. $\left(8^{\frac{3}{5}}\right)^{\frac{5}{3}}$

e. Rewrite $(c^3)^{\frac{4}{5}}$ using a radical.

f. The resting heart rate (h) for a mammal is related to its body mass (M) in kilograms by the equation $h \approx \dfrac{241}{\sqrt[4]{M}}$. Rewrite this equation using a rational exponent.

g. Rewrite $\left(\sqrt[6]{m^2n}\right)^5$ with a rational exponent.

By rewriting a radical expression using rational exponents, you may be able to simplify the expression. However, you should always express your final answer in radical form unless asked to do otherwise.

6. Simplify $\sqrt[12]{d^4}$.

$$\sqrt[12]{d^4} = d^{\frac{4}{12}} = \left|d^{\frac{1}{3}}\right| = \sqrt[3]{|d|}$$

Because the exponent is even, our answer must be nonnegative.

Simplify.

h. $\sqrt[10]{36^5}$

i. $\sqrt[8]{m^4n^2}$

You've explored the meaning of rational-number powers, such as $x^{\frac{3}{4}}$. You may wonder whether these exponents can also be written in decimal form, that is, whether $x^{\frac{3}{4}} = x^{0.75}$. You will investigate this possibility in 7-2B.

REFLECT

1. Why is it possible to take the cube root of a negative number but not its square root?
2. How could you estimate the three-halves power of a number without using a calculator?
3. Explain some of the advantages of using rational exponents instead of radicals when simplifying radical expressions.

Exercises

CORE

1. **Getting Started** Replace each question mark with the correct value.

   a. $a^{\frac{3}{4}} = \sqrt[?]{a^?} = \left(\sqrt[?]{a}\right)^?$

   b. $\sqrt[5]{a^2} = \left(\sqrt[?]{a}\right)^? = a^?$

2. Write the words that correctly complete the statement.
   In the expression $\sqrt[5]{8}$, 8 is the ____ and 5 is the ____.

If the expression has a fractional exponent, rewrite it using a radical. If the expression has a radical, rewrite it using exponents.

3. $7^{\frac{1}{3}}$ **4.** $n^{\frac{2}{5}}$ **5.** $\sqrt[4]{19}$ **6.** $\sqrt[4]{p^9}$

7. $(a + 3b)^{\frac{5}{7}}$ **8.** $\sqrt[10]{m^3 n^9}$ **9.** $(n^5)^{\frac{2}{3}}$ **10.** $(k + 1)^{-\frac{1}{2}}$

11. $\left(\sqrt[6]{(2x - y)}\right)^5$ **12.** $\dfrac{1}{\sqrt[3]{p^2}}$ **13.** $(a^3 b^4)^{\frac{2}{7}}$ **14.** $\sqrt[8]{(2mn^2)^3}$

If $x < 0$, tell whether the principal root for each expression is positive, negative, or does not exist.

15. $\sqrt[3]{x}$ **16.** $\sqrt[8]{x}$ **17.** $x^{\frac{3}{4}}$ **18.** $x^{\frac{3}{7}}$

19. **Going, Going, ...** Carbon-14 is a radioactive form of carbon. The amount of carbon-14 in an organism decreases with time, following the death of the organism. The amount (A) left after 5000 years is given by $A = A_L(2.7)^{-\frac{3}{5}}$, where A_L is the amount that was originally present in the living organism. Rewrite in radical form the formula for the amount of carbon-14 that is present after 5000 years.

Mammoth bones

Evaluate each expression.

20. $(-64)^{\frac{1}{3}}$

21. $100^{\frac{1}{2}}$

22. $25^{\frac{3}{2}}$

23. $49^{-\left(\frac{1}{2}\right)}$

24. $(-8)^{-\left(\frac{2}{3}\right)}$

25. $9^{\frac{5}{2}}$

26. How Long Is a Year? In 1618, German astronomer Johannes Kepler showed that the time (t) that it takes a planet to orbit the sun, in days, is related to the planet's mean distance from the sun (d), in kilometers, by the equation $t \approx (2 \times 10^{-10})d^{\frac{3}{2}}$. Approximate the orbital period for each planet to the nearest tenth of a day.

Planet	Distance from Sun (km)
Mercury	5.79×10^7
Venus	1.08×10^8
Earth	1.50×10^8
Mars	2.28×10^8
Jupiter	7.78×10^8
Saturn	1.43×10^9
Uranus	2.87×10^9
Neptune	4.50×10^9
Pluto	5.90×10^9

Simplify each expression.

27. $36^{\frac{1}{4}} \cdot 36^{\frac{1}{4}}$

28. $x^{\frac{1}{3}} \cdot x^{\frac{1}{2}}$

29. $\dfrac{5^{\frac{2}{3}}}{5^{\frac{1}{2}}}$

30. $\left(81^{\frac{1}{5}}\right)^{\frac{5}{2}}$

31. $\sqrt[6]{h^4}$

32. $\sqrt[9]{(-64)^3}$

33. $\sqrt[4]{\dfrac{2^2}{3^2}}$

34. $\sqrt[3]{\sqrt{27}}$

35. Get a Tune Up Members of symphony orchestras traditionally tune their instruments to the note "Concert A," which has a frequency of 440 vibrations per second (Hertz).

a. Notes an octave apart sound similar, but the higher note has twice the frequency of the lower. Give the frequencies of the notes one octave above and one octave below Concert A.

b. There are twelve intervals in an octave, so the frequency of each note is $\sqrt[12]{2}$ times the frequency of the next lower one. Find the frequency of each note in the scale.

Pitch	A	A#	B	C	C#	D	D#	E	F	F#	G	G#
Frequency	440											

36. Clock Work A pendulum's *period* is the time it takes to make one complete swing. The period (T), in seconds, is given by $T = 2\pi\sqrt{\dfrac{\ell}{g}}$, where ℓ is the length of the pendulum in meters and g is the acceleration due to gravity (about 9.8 m/sec²).

a. Rewrite the formula for the period of a pendulum using exponents.

b. Find the period of the 1.2-m-long pendulum of a grandfather clock.

Foucault pendulum at the United Nations

LOOK AHEAD

Rewrite each fraction as a decimal.

37. $\frac{3}{4}$
38. $\frac{7}{10}$
39. $\frac{9}{5}$
40. $\frac{5}{8}$

Rewrite each decimal as a fraction in lowest terms.

41. 0.6
42. 1.75
43. 2.875
44. 2.62

MORE PRACTICE

If the expression has a fractional exponent, rewrite it using a radical. If the expression has a radical, rewrite it using exponents.

45. $6^{\frac{1}{4}}$
46. $v^{\frac{1}{5}}$
47. $\sqrt[3]{15}$
48. $12^{\frac{5}{6}}$

49. $\sqrt{b^3}$
50. $\sqrt[7]{6^3}$
51. $(x-y)^{\frac{2}{5}}$
52. $\sqrt[8]{ab^3}$

53. $\sqrt[4]{(m+2n)^3}$
54. $\left(p^{\frac{1}{3}}\right)^3$
55. $(y+3z^2)^{-\left(\frac{1}{5}\right)}$
56. $\frac{1}{a^{\frac{3}{7}}}$

57. $\frac{1}{\sqrt[5]{x^2y}}$
58. $\left(mn^{\frac{4}{5}}\right)^{\frac{5}{2}}$
59. $\sqrt[9]{(5h^2k^3)^5}$
60. $\left(\sqrt[7]{8x^3yz^2}\right)^3$

61. Use a Graphing Utility The graphs of $y=\sqrt{x}$, $y=\sqrt[3]{x}$, $y=\sqrt[4]{x}$, and $y=\sqrt[5]{x}$ are shown. The x-values range from 0 to 2 and y-values range from 0 to 1.2.
a. Which graph is which?
b. Identify the points where the graphs intersect.
c. Graph the same equations for x-values from -2 to 2 and y-values from -2 to 2. Sketch your results on graph paper and label each graph. Describe what is happening.

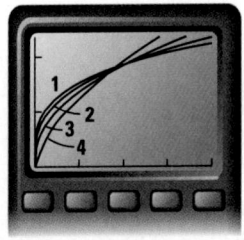

62. The formula $r \approx 0.62\sqrt[3]{V}$ can be used to approximate the radius (r) of a sphere from its volume (V). Rewrite the formula using a rational exponent.

Evaluate each expression.

63. $9^{\frac{1}{2}}$
64. $125^{\frac{1}{3}}$
65. $1000^{-\left(\frac{1}{3}\right)}$
66. $625^{\frac{1}{4}}$

67. $81^{\frac{3}{2}}$
68. $16^{\frac{5}{4}}$
69. $27^{-\left(\frac{2}{3}\right)}$
70. $0^{\frac{5}{4}}$

Simplify each expression.

71. $29^{\frac{1}{3}} \cdot 29^{\frac{2}{3}}$
72. $49^{\frac{1}{6}} \cdot 49^{\frac{1}{3}}$
73. $\frac{8^{\frac{7}{9}}}{8^{\frac{4}{9}}}$
74. $\left(32^{\frac{3}{4}}\right)^{\frac{4}{5}}$

75. $\sqrt[10]{x^5}$
76. $\sqrt[12]{n^9}$
77. $\sqrt[3]{125^2}$
78. $\sqrt[5]{-32x^{15}}$

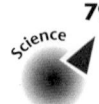

79. Take a Deep Breath According to *Animal Physiology: Adaptation and Environment,* by Knut Schmidt-Nielsen, the volume of oxygen (V), in liters per hour, that is consumed by a mammal can be approximated by the function $V = 0.676 m^{\frac{3}{4}}$, where m is the animal's mass in kilograms. Approximate the oxygen consumption rate for each animal.

a. a chipmunk, 0.12 kg

b. a goat, 33 kg

c. a Siberian tiger, 265 kg

MORE MATH REASONING

80. Stringy Roots A guitar string with a length (ℓ) of 64 cm and a mass per unit length (m) of 2×10^{-1} g/cm is strung at a tension force (F) of 2.048×10^8 g-cm/sec^2.

Find the frequency of vibration (f) of the string, where $f = \frac{1}{2\ell}\sqrt{\frac{F}{m}}$.

81. Heavy Metal O'Carroll's formula is used to compare weights lifted by different-sized weightlifters, so that lighter lifters can compete with heavier ones on an equal basis. For a weightlifter whose mass is b kg and who lifts w kg, the handicapped weight (W) is $W = \dfrac{w}{\sqrt[3]{b - 35}}$.

a. Rewrite this equation using fractional exponents.

b. Suppose Ted weighs 60 kg and lifts 70 kg, while Alex, who is 80 kg, lifts 90 kg. Who has lifted a greater handicapped weight?

7-2
PART B   Real-Number Exponents and Modeling

· ·

← CONNECT →   *You've explored the meanings of rational exponents. Now you will see how to use exponents in decimal form to model real-world situations.*

As you learned in Chapter 2, data graphed in a scatter plot can often be approximated by a *line of best fit*, also known as a *regression line*. You've seen how you can use a graphing utility to find the slope and y-intercept of a line of best fit. Once the equation for the line is written, you can use it to make predictions.

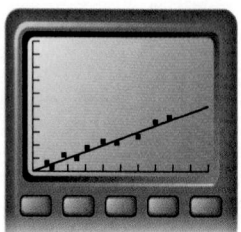

Some scatter plots show a relationship between variables that is obviously not linear. To approximate a scatter plot of the data, we use a curve instead of a line.

The equation of such a curve may take the form $y = Ax^B$. When we use this type of equation to model the data, we call the curve of best fit a **power regression** curve.

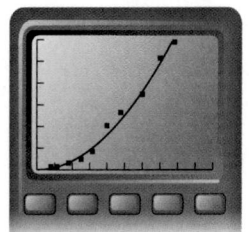

EXPLORE: THE CURVE OF SECURITY

MATERIALS

Graphing utility

The Social Security Act was passed by Congress and signed by President Franklin Roosevelt in 1935. It provides retirement, unemployment, and other benefits to Americans. Social Security expenses have risen steadily since passage of the act.

Year	Expenses (millions of $)	Year	Expenses (millions of $)
1940	28	1985	169,210
1950	784	1990	223,481
1960	11,073	1991	241,316
1970	27,321	1992	256,239
1980	103,228		

1. Enter the data into your graphing utility. Number years from 1 (1940) to 53 (1992). Make a scatter plot of this data. Does a straight line or a curve seem to model the data more closely? Explain.
2. Use your graphing utility to perform a power regression on the data. Write down the two numbers that the calculator gives you. One of these is a coefficient and the other is an exponent. Identify which is which and tell how you know.
3. Predict social security expenditures for the year 1975. Explain how you made your prediction.
4. Explain the meaning of the decimal exponent in the equation that you found.

CONSIDER

?

1. How would you decide whether linear regression or power regression is more appropriate to use in modeling a set of data?

It seems reasonable that we can write $x^{\frac{1}{2}}$ as $x^{0.5}$, $x^{\frac{3}{4}}$ as $x^{0.75}$, and so on. In fact, for a positive base, an exponent can be *any* real number. The rules for operations on exponents that applied for integer and rational exponents apply to all real-number exponents.

EXAMPLES

Evaluate each expression. Where necessary, round answers to the nearest hundredth.

1. $81^{1.25}$

$81^{1.25} = 81^{\frac{5}{4}}$

$= \left(\sqrt[4]{81}\right)^5 = 3^5 = 243$

2. $7^{2.06}$

$7^{2.06} \approx 55.07$ Use a calculator.

3. According to *Animal Physiology: Adaptation and Environment*, by Knut Schmidt-Nielsen, the lung volume in liters (V) and the mass of a mammal in kilograms (M) are related by the equation $V \approx 0.046M^{1.06}$. Find the approximate lung volume of a 5900-kg African elephant.

$V \approx 0.046(5900)^{1.06}$

$\approx 0.046(9933.5)$ Evaluate powers

≈ 456.9 before multiplying.

The volume of the elephant's lungs is approximately 457 liters.

4. Simplify $\left(c^{3.2}\right)^5$.

$\left(c^{3.2}\right)^5 = c^{3.2 \times 5} = c^{16}$

TRY IT

Evaluate. If necessary, round answers to the nearest hundredth.

a. $25^{2.5}$

b. $4^{1.83}$

c. Simplify $\left(\dfrac{x^{4.64}}{x^{3.17}}\right)^2$.

Real-world data can often be closely approximated by a power regression equation of the form $f(x) = Ax^B$. With A and B in decimal form, the function can easily be evaluated for specific values of x using a calculator.

REFLECT

1. Explain what $x^{3.8}$ means.

2. Give an example of a real-world relationship that a curve would model more closely than a straight line.

3. If $a > b$, is $x^a > x^b$? Explain.

Exercises

CORE

Getting Started For each scatter plot, state whether linear regression or power regression models the data more closely.

1.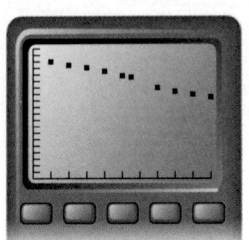

2.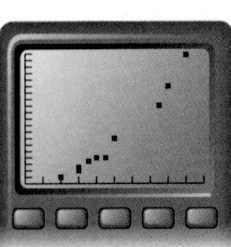

3.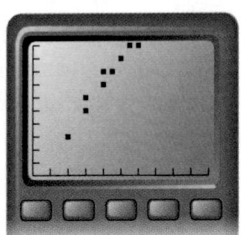

Evaluate each expression. Where necessary, round answers to the nearest hundredth.

4. $4^{2.5}$

5. $49^{1.5}$

6. $1^{6.772}$

7. $81^{0.5}$

8. $27^{1.\overline{3}}$

9. $9^{3.5}$

10. $11^{2.16}$

11. $39.764^{1.048}$

12. $0^{5.9912}$

13. $3.81^{\frac{5}{9}}$

14. $8.04^{\frac{11}{17}}$

15. $3.9^{\frac{4}{11}} \cdot 3.9^{\frac{7}{11}}$

16. Shifting Gears The velocity (v), in kilometers per hour, at which a running animal switches from an easy trot to a gallop can be approximated by the function $v = 5.5m^{0.24}$, where m is the animal's mass in kilograms. Approximate the transition speed for the animal.
a. horse, 700 kg   **b.** dog, 20 kg   **c.** mouse, 0.03 kg

Simplify each expression.

17. $a^{2.57} \cdot a^{3.49}$

18. $\left(x^{0.56}y^{-3.45}\right)^{2.4}$

19. $\dfrac{k^{7.17}}{k^{-3.53}}$

20. a. Graph the following data:
   (2, 2.5), (3, 7.4), (4, 15.8), (5, 28.5), (6, 46.1).
   b. Which function better fits the data, $y = 0.40x^{2.65}$ or $y = 9.0x - 14.7$? Explain.

21. A person's surface area (S) can be approximated by the function $S = (90.1)w^{0.425}h^{0.725}$, where w is weight in pounds and h is height in inches. Find the approximate surface area of each person.
   a. the world's tallest man, whose height was 8 ft 11 in. and whose weight was 491 lb
   b. the average 6-month-old girl, with height 2 ft 2 in. and weight 16 lb

22. Using data from *The World Almanac and Book of Facts,* *1995,* world automobile production can be modeled by the equation:

$$A = 300y^{2.68}$$

where A is total production and y is the year ($1900 = 0$). Use this function to predict automobile production in each year.

a. 1965   **b.** 1985   **c.** 2000

d. According to this model, what was the first year that automobiles were produced? How many were produced in that year? Is this prediction historically accurate? Explain.

 ## LOOK BACK

23. Find the equation of a circle of radius 6 with its center at $(3, -2)$. [5-3]

Evaluate each of the following. [6-1]

24. $_5P_3$

25. $_4P_3$

26. $_6P_2$

27. Alfredo has room for 5 of his 7 textbooks on the bottom shelf of his locker. How many different arrangements are there for the textbooks on the bottom shelf? [6-1]

28. y varies inversely as x, and $y = 9$ when $x = 6$. Find the constant of variation. Then evaluate y when $x = 4$. [7-1]

MORE PRACTICE

Evaluate each expression. Where necessary, round answers to the nearest hundredth.

29. $64^{0.5}$

30. $9^{1.5}$

31. $11^{2.0}$

32. $8^{1.\overline{3}}$

33. $27^{1.\overline{6}}$

34. $32^{1.6}$

35. $1^{5.5096}$

36. $4^{2.34}$

37. $6.71^{1.85}$

38. $2.08^{-3.7}$

39. $8.77^{-0.71}$

40. $1^{-9.65}$

41. $5^{\frac{2}{3}}$

42. $17.31^{\frac{7}{6}}$

43. $0.721^{-\frac{5}{8}}$

44. $10.11^{\frac{7}{9}}$

45. $38.508^{\frac{14}{11}}$

46. $177.6^{\frac{2}{3}}$

Simplify each expression.

47. $e^{0.89} \cdot e^{1.45}$

48. $n^{-5.28} \cdot n^{3.79}$

49. $\left(a^{3.98}b^{-6.15}\right)^{-1.7}$

50. $\dfrac{x^{0.04}}{x^{0.52}}$

51. $x^{2.04} \cdot x^{0.57}$

52. $\dfrac{d^{5.1} \cdot d^{3.8}}{d^{4.2}}$

53. Use a Graphing Utility The table shows life expectancy data for the United States.

Year	1920	1930	1940	1950	1960	1970	1980	1990
Average Life Expectancy (years)	54.1	59.7	62.9	68.2	69.7	70.8	73.7	75.4

a. Find the power regression function that best fits the data. (Hint: Let 1920 = year 20.)

b. Use your function to predict the U.S. life expectancy in the year 2000.

54. Use a Graphing Utility The table below shows average lifespans and gestation periods for several mammals.

Animal	Mouse	Moose	Tiger	Zebra	Goat	Horse
Lifespan (years)	3	12	16	15	8	20
Gestation Period (days)	21	240	105	365	151	330

a. Find the power regression function that best fits the data.

b. Use your function to predict the gestation period of a mammal whose average lifespan is 22 years.

c. Does your function do a good job of predicting the human gestation period? Explain.

MORE MATH REASONING

55. Use a Graphing Utility The table gives the lengths and midshaft diameters of the humerus bones (upper forelegs) of 12 African antelopes.

Diameter (mm)	Length (mm)	Diameter (mm)	Length (mm)
17.6	159.9	58.1	351.7
26.0	206.9	64.7	377.6
31.9	236.8	66.4	384.1
38.9	269.9	73.1	409.3
45.8	300.6	80.8	437.2
51.2	323.6	82.9	444.7

a. Make a scatter plot of this data. Then use power regression to find the function $y = Ax^B$ that best fits the data.

b. In your own words, describe the relationship between the length of an antelope's upper foreleg and the diameter of its humerus bone. If the two quantities are not directly proportional, explain why the relationship makes sense.

56. Can any positive real number be expressed as a power of 10? If so, explain why you believe this is true; if not, explain why not.

57. Taking It In Stride As an animal begins to gallop, its "stride frequency" (f)—the number of strides it takes per minute—is related to its mass (m), in kilograms, by the formula $f \approx 269m^{-0.14}$.

a. Do stride frequency and mass vary directly or inversely? Explain.

b. Approximate the stride frequency of an animal with a mass of 800 kg.

c. Find the mass of an animal that has a stride frequency of about 250 strides per minute when it begins to gallop.

7-2
PART C Solving Radical Equations

← **CONNECT** → *You have worked extensively with radical expressions and with rational exponents. Now you will solve equations involving radicals and rational exponents.*

A **radical equation** contains at least one radical expression. For example,

$$\sqrt{x} = 5 \qquad\qquad x - 3 = \sqrt{x + 2} \qquad\qquad \sqrt[3]{x^2 - x} = 6x + 3$$

The Explore will introduce you to a radical equation that models a real-world situation. By solving this equation, you will find out what might have happened at the scene of an accident.

EXPLORE: THE SKIDS WILL TELL

Police were called to the scene of an accident that occurred when a deer unexpectedly darted in front of a truck on the freeway. The driver slammed on the brakes, then the truck skidded and overturned. The driver claimed to have been traveling under the 55 mi/hr speed limit. Investigators measured skid marks 124.6 feet in length. The brakes and tires were new, and the road surface dry.

The formula $s = \sqrt{30d}$ can be used to estimate the initial speed (s), in miles per hour, of a vehicle that skids a distance of d feet after the driver applies the brakes. The formula assumes good tires and brakes and a dry road surface.

1. Use the equation to approximate the truck's speed.
2. Was the driver telling the truth? Explain.
3. The driver of a car traveling 45 mi/hr slammed on the brakes. Write a radical equation you could solve to find the approximate distance the car skidded.
4. Solve the equation. Describe the method you used.

EXAMPLE

Solve each equation.

1. Solve $\sqrt{x} = 7$.
$$\left(\sqrt{x}\right)^2 = 7^2$$

Square both sides of the equation to clear the square root.

$$x = 49$$
Check: $\sqrt{49} = 7 \checkmark$

2. Solve $x = \sqrt{x + 7} + 5$.

$x = \sqrt{x + 7} + 5$	
$x - 5 = \sqrt{x + 7}$	Isolate the radical.
$(x - 5)^2 = \left(\sqrt{x + 7}\right)^2$	Square both sides of the equation.
$x^2 - 10x + 25 = x + 7$	Simplify. The result is a quadratic equation.
$x^2 - 11x + 18 = 0$	Put the quadratic equation into standard form.
$(x - 9)(x - 2) = 0$	Factor.
$x = 9$ or $x = 2$	Solve for x.

Check:

$\underline{x = 9}$	$\underline{x = 2}$
$9 \stackrel{?}{=} \sqrt{9 + 7} + 5$	$2 \stackrel{?}{=} \sqrt{2 + 7} + 5$
$9 \stackrel{?}{=} 4 + 5$	$2 \stackrel{?}{=} 3 + 5$
$9 = 9 \checkmark$	$2 \neq 8$

Note that the solution $x = 2$ does not check. It is an example of an invalid **extraneous solution** (or *extra solution*) that is sometimes produced when both sides of an equation are raised to a power. Notice what happens when we square both sides of a very simple equation.

$x = 5$	The "solution" to this equation is $x = 5$.
$x^2 = 25$	Square both sides. Since $5^2 = 25$ and $(-5)^2 = 25$, the new equation has two solutions, $x = 5$ and $x = -5$. We have introduced the extraneous solution $x = -5$.

CONSIDER

1. Explain *why* squaring both sides of an equation may generate an extraneous solution.

Because of the possibility of extraneous solutions, you should check the solutions of any equation that you solve by raising both sides of the equation to a power.

TRY IT

Solve each equation and check your solutions.

a. $\sqrt{x} = 16$ **b.** $\sqrt{x + 2} = 8$

c. $x = \sqrt{x}$ **d.** $5 + \sqrt{18 - 2x} = x$

CONSIDER

2. Explain why $x = k$ and $x^2 = k^2$ do not have the same solutions.

3. What is the solution to the equation $\sqrt{x} = -2$? Explain.

Radical equations may involve roots other than square roots or rational exponents. To solve such equations, it is still useful to clear the radicals by raising both sides of the equation to an appropriate power.

EXAMPLES

3. Solve $2 + \sqrt[3]{x - 5} = 7$.

$$2 + \sqrt[3]{x - 5} = 7$$

$$\sqrt[3]{x - 5} = 5 \qquad \text{Isolate the radical.}$$

$$\left(\sqrt[3]{x - 5}\right)^3 = 5^3 \qquad \text{Cube both sides of the equation.}$$

$$x - 5 = 125 \qquad \text{Simplify.}$$

$$x = 130 \qquad \text{Solve for } x.$$

The solution checks.

4. Solve $4x^{\frac{3}{4}} = 108$.

$$4x^{\frac{3}{4}} = 108$$

$$x^{\frac{3}{4}} = 27 \qquad \text{Isolate the variable.}$$

$$\left(x^{\frac{3}{4}}\right)^{\frac{4}{3}} = 27^{\frac{4}{3}} \qquad \text{Raise both sides to the reciprocal of the exponent of the variable.}$$

$$x = \left(3^3\right)^{\frac{4}{3}} \qquad \text{Write the base in exponential form.}$$

$$x = 3^4 \qquad \text{Simplify.}$$

$$x = 81 \qquad \text{Solve for } x.$$

The solution checks.

CONSIDER

4. In solving Example 4, why did we raise both sides of the equation to the power that was the reciprocal of the exponent?

There is no danger of *losing* solutions when you raise both sides of an equation to an integral power. The solutions to the original equation will continue to be solutions to the new equation. As you have seen, however, you may have introduced extraneous solutions. Eliminate those by checking all of your solutions. The ones that check are the solutions to the original equation; the others can be ignored.

REFLECT

1. In your own words, describe a general strategy for solving an equation with one exponential expression. Explain why this strategy works.

2. If you solve an equation by raising both sides of the equation to a power, why is it necessary to check your solutions?

3. Give an example of a radical equation with no real-number solution.

CORE

1. **Getting Started** Follow these steps to solve $3 + \sqrt{x} = 8$.
   a. Isolate the radical by subtracting 3 from both sides of the equation.
   b. Square both sides of the equation.
   c. Check your solution by substituting it in the original equation.

Write the word or phrase that correctly completes each statement.

2. When solving radical equations by raising both sides to a power, you should check your answers to find any ____.

3. A radical equation contains at least one ____.

Solve each equation.

4. $\sqrt{x} = 1.5$

5. $\sqrt{2x - 3} = 1$

6. $\sqrt{3x + 4} = 5$

7. $1 = 7 + \sqrt{x - 1}$

8. $4 - \sqrt{x + 3} = 0$

9. $1 - x = \sqrt{x + 5}$

10. $\sqrt{2x - 1} = x - 2$

11. $x - 3 = \sqrt{3x + 1}$

12. $\sqrt[3]{x - 6} = -2$

13. $3 = \sqrt[4]{3x - 9}$

14. $x^{\frac{1}{2}} = 13$

15. $x^{\frac{2}{3}} = 16$

16. $x^{\frac{3}{2}} + 6 = 33$

17. $7x^{\frac{2}{5}} + 3 = 31$

18. $\sqrt[3]{x^4} = 9.1$

19. **A Fish Story** "Arrrr, matey!" says Captain Spindrift. "Ye should have seen the Pacific Halibut I caught back in '83! Full 2 meters long he were, and he weighed in at 30 kilograms." You know that the length of a Pacific Halibut is approximated by $L = 0.46\sqrt[3]{W}$. Do you believe Captain Spindrift? Explain.

Solve for the given variable.

20. $h = \dfrac{V^2}{g}$, for V

21. $F = \dfrac{kMm}{d^2}$, for d

22. $a = \sqrt{b^2 + c^2}$, for b

23. $f = \dfrac{1}{2\ell}\sqrt{\dfrac{F}{m}}$, for m

24. **Found Horizon** The formula $d = 1.23\sqrt{h}$ approximates the distance (d), in miles, that a person can see to the horizon from a height of h feet.
   a. About how far can you see if you are standing at sea level? (Assume your eyes are 5 in. below the top of your head.) What is the approximate area of the region that you can see?
   b. How much farther can you see if you climb to the top of a 2200-ft hill? What is the approximate area of the visible region now?
   c. The CN Tower in Toronto, the world's tallest self-supporting tower, can broadcast a straight-line TV signal a distance of 52.4 miles. About how tall is the tower?

25. a. Write an equation expressing the radius of a circle in terms of its area.

b. You have enough cake batter to make a rectangular cake 12 in. wide and 18 in. long. What is the radius of the largest round cake of the same height that you can make with this amount of batter?

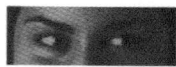 **LOOK AHEAD**

Find each product.

26. $(x - 7)(x + 7)$

27. $(4 + t)(4 - t)$

28. $\left(\sqrt{x} + 3\right)\left(\sqrt{x} - 3\right)$

Find each binomial square.

29. $(x - 7)^2$

30. $(4 + t)^2$

31. $\left(\sqrt{x} - 3\right)^2$

MORE PRACTICE

Solve each equation.

32. $\sqrt{x} = 8$

33. $\sqrt{x} + 5 = 17$

34. $\sqrt{x - 4} = 12$

35. $-9 = -\sqrt{3x + 5}$

36. $\sqrt{7x + 1} - 8 = -2$

37. $5 = 11 + \sqrt{x + 3}$

38. $5.6 + \sqrt{x + 1.56} = 9$

39. $x - 4 = \sqrt{4x + 5}$

40. $\sqrt[3]{x} = 7$

41. $\sqrt[3]{x + 3} = -5$

42. $\sqrt[3]{2x - 5} + 2 = 4$

43. $\sqrt[7]{x} = -1$

44. $\sqrt[5]{5x - 3} + 11 = 13$

45. $x^{\frac{1}{2}} = 3$

46. $x^{\frac{1}{3}} = 1.2$

47. $x^{\frac{2}{3}} = 25$

48. $2x^{\frac{3}{5}} - 9 = 45$

49. $x^{\frac{4}{5}} = 11.3$

Solve for the given variable.

50. $A = \pi r^2$, for r

51. $t = \sqrt{\dfrac{2s}{g}}$, for s

52. $r = \dfrac{1}{2}\sqrt{\dfrac{S}{\pi}}$, for S

53. $t = (2 \times 10^{-10})d^{\frac{3}{2}}$, for d

54. Very Interesting If you invest P dollars in an account whose annual yield is r, the amount (A) of money you will have after n years (assuming you make no other deposits or withdrawals) is:

$A = P(1 + r)^n$

Suppose that you have $1000 to invest, and that you will need that money to grow to $2500 in 15 years. At what interest rate will you need to invest the money?

55. The surface area (S) of a sphere with radius r is given by:

$S = 4\pi r^2$

a. Solve this equation for r.

b. The surface area of Io is about 4.16×10^7 km^2. What is its radius?

Io is a moon of Jupiter.

MORE MATH REASONING

56. It's All Relative According to scientific theory, it is impossible to travel faster than the speed of light. You may wonder what makes such speeds impossible to reach.

The *rest mass* (m_0) of an object is its mass in kilograms when at rest relative to an observer. However, its mass (m) when it is in motion is given by $m = \dfrac{m_0}{\sqrt{1 - \dfrac{v^2}{c^2}}}$

where v is its velocity and c is the speed of light (approximately 300,000 km/sec).
   a. According to this equation, does the mass of an object increase or decrease as it approaches the speed of light? Explain.
   b. According to the *Guinness Book of World Records,* the fastest speed reached by a human is about 40,000 km/hr, in the command module of *Apollo X.* What was the mass of a 70-kg astronaut in the module (relative to a stationary observer)? Is the difference from the rest mass noticeable?
   c. Suppose that *Apollo X* traveled at $\frac{9}{10}$ the speed of light. What would the mass of the 70-kg astronaut be? What would the astronaut's mass be at $\frac{99}{100}$ the speed of light?
   d. Assuming this equation is accurate, explain why faster-than-light speeds are theoretically impossible.

57. It'll Probably Happen The probability that an earthquake will occur in a particular region over the next 30 years (P_{30}) is related to the probability that it will occur in any one year (p) by the equation:

$$P_{30} = 1 - (1 - p)^{30}$$

   a. Solve this equation for p.
   b. Suppose geologists predict that there is a 70% chance of a severe quake in a particular region in the next 30 years. What is the probability that it will happen next year? Explain how you found your answer.
   c. What is the probability that the quake will occur sometime in the next 60 years?

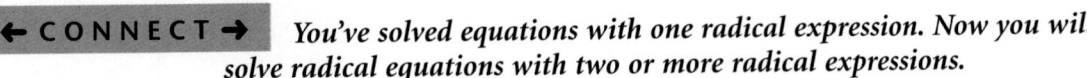

7-2 PART D Other Radical Equations

← CONNECT →   *You've solved equations with one radical expression. Now you will solve radical equations with two or more radical expressions.*

The figure illustrates a graphical method for solving the linear equation $\frac{1}{2}x = -x + 3$. To solve graphically, we can set each side of the equation equal to y and graph the resulting equations. Here, we graph $y = \frac{1}{2}x$ and $y = -x + 3$. The point of intersection is (2, 1). The x-value of the point of intersection gives us the solution to the original equation, $x = 2$.

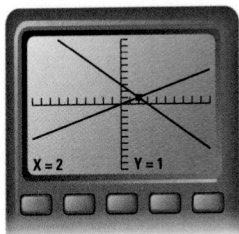

In the Explore, you will use this method to solve an equation involving two radicals.

EXPLORE: A RADICAL SOLUTION

MATERIALS

Graph paper
Graphing utility (optional)

Follow these steps to solve the equation $\sqrt{2x - 5} = 1 + \sqrt{x - 3}$ graphically.

1. Graph $y = \sqrt{2x - 5}$. Explain how you drew the graph. What is the domain of this function? Explain why the domain has restrictions.

2. On the same set of coordinate axes, graph $y = 1 + \sqrt{x - 3}$. What is its domain?

3. Give the point(s) of intersection of the graphs.

4. Give the solution(s) to the original equation.

5. What are the advantages and disadvantages of this method of solving an equation?

TRY IT

Solve by graphing.

a. $\sqrt{5x - 16} + 2 = \sqrt{3x + 4}$

When using the distance formula, you often deal with expressions that involve radicals. These expressions can be worked with symbolically as well as graphically.

EXAMPLE

1. You are lost in a forest. Your friends are located at $(0, 0)$ and $(4, 8)$. By listening to their shouts, you estimate that you are equidistant from their positions. Write an equation to describe your possible locations.

We are looking for all points (x, y) where the distance from $(0, 0)$ is equal to the distance from $(4, 8)$.

The distance from (x_1, y_1) to (x_2, y_2) is given by

Henri Rousseau, *Jungle with Horse Attacked by a Jaguar*, Pushkin Museum of Fine Arts, Moscow, Russia

$$D = \sqrt{(x_1 - x_2)^2 + (y_1 - y_2)^2}.$$

$\sqrt{(x - 0)^2 + (y - 0)^2} = \sqrt{(x - 4)^2 + (y - 8)^2}$	Use the distance formula.
$\sqrt{x^2 + y^2} = \sqrt{x^2 - 8x + 16 + y^2 - 16y + 64}$	Simplify.
$x^2 + y^2 = x^2 - 8x + 16 + y^2 - 16y + 64$	Square both sides.
$0 = -8x - 16y + 80$	Simplify.

This is a linear equation. We write it in slope-intercept form.

$$16y = -8x + 80$$
$$y = -\frac{1}{2}x + 5$$

You are on a straight line that is the perpendicular bisector of the segment joining your friends.

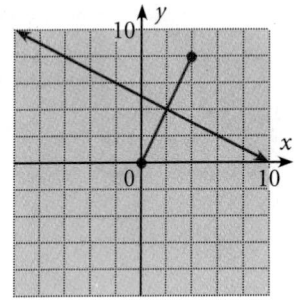

To solve an equation containing more than one radical, you may have to raise it to a power more than once. This will increase the likelihood that you find one or more extraneous solutions.

EXAMPLE

2. Solve $\sqrt{x + 2} + \sqrt{3x + 4} = 2$.

$\sqrt{x + 2} + \sqrt{3x + 4} = 2$	
$\sqrt{x + 2} = -\sqrt{3x + 4} + 2$	Subtract $\sqrt{3x + 4}$ from both sides of the equation.
$\left(\sqrt{x + 2}\right)^2 = \left(-\sqrt{3x + 4} + 2\right)^2$	Square both sides.
$x + 2 = \left(-\sqrt{3x + 4}\right)^2 + 2(2)\left(-\sqrt{3x + 4}\right) + 2^2$	Expand the squared binomial on the right side.
$x + 2 = (3x + 4) - 4\sqrt{3x + 4} + 4$	Simplify.
$-2x - 6 = -4\sqrt{3x + 4}$	Combine like terms and isolate the radical.
$x + 3 = 2\sqrt{3x + 4}$	Simplify by dividing by -2.
$(x + 3)^2 = \left(2\sqrt{3x + 4}\right)^2$	Square both sides again.
$x^2 + 6x + 9 = 4(3x + 4)$	
$x^2 + 6x + 9 = 12x + 16$	
$x^2 - 6x - 7 = 0$	Collect like terms.
$(x - 7)(x + 1) = 0$	Factor.
$x = 7$ or $x = -1$	Solve for x.

Check: $x = 7$

$\sqrt{7 + 2} + \sqrt{3 \cdot 7 + 4} \stackrel{?}{=} 2$

$\sqrt{9} + \sqrt{25} \stackrel{?}{=} 2$

$8 \neq 2$

$x = -1$

$\sqrt{-1 + 2} + \sqrt{3(-1) + 4} \stackrel{?}{=} 2$

$\sqrt{1} + \sqrt{1} \stackrel{?}{=} 2$

$2 = 2$ ✓

The solution is $x = -1$; $x = 7$ is an extraneous solution.

1. Why did we begin the above solution by subtracting $\sqrt{3x + 4}$ from both sides of the equation?

TRY IT

b. Solve: $\sqrt{x + 4} - \sqrt{x + 20} = -2$

Another method of solving radical equations applies to equations that are in quadratic form. An equation is in **quadratic form** if it is a trinomial with a variable raised to powers that are multiples of 2, 1, and 0. The following equations are in quadratic form.

$$
\begin{array}{ccc}
2 & 1 & 0 \\
\downarrow & \downarrow & \downarrow \\
5x^2 & - 3x & + 6 = 0
\end{array}
\qquad
\begin{array}{ccc}
2 \cdot 5 & 1 \cdot 5 & 0 \cdot 5 \\
\downarrow & \downarrow & \downarrow \\
-4x^{10} & + 3x^5 & - 1 = 0
\end{array}
\qquad
\begin{array}{ccc}
\frac{1}{4} \cdot 2 & \frac{1}{4} \cdot 1 & \frac{1}{4} \cdot 0 \\
\downarrow & \downarrow & \downarrow \\
c^{\frac{1}{2}} & + 4c^{\frac{1}{4}} & - 8 = 0
\end{array}
$$

If an equation containing a radical is in quadratic form, you can solve it by factoring or using the quadratic formula.

EXAMPLE

3. Solve $x - 3\sqrt{x} - 5 = 0$.

The equation is in quadratic form. This is more easily seen if we write it using exponents.

$$x^1 - 3x^{\frac{1}{2}} - 5 = 0$$

$$x^{\frac{1}{2}} = \frac{-(-3) \pm \sqrt{(-3)^2 - 4(1)(-5)}}{2} \qquad \text{Use the quadratic formula, } x = \frac{-b \pm \sqrt{b^2 - 4ac}}{2a}.$$

$$x^{\frac{1}{2}} = \frac{3 \pm \sqrt{29}}{2} \qquad \text{Simplify.}$$

$$x^{\frac{1}{2}} \approx 4.19, \; x^{\frac{1}{2}} \approx -1.19 \qquad \text{Find the two possible values for } x^{\frac{1}{2}}.$$

Now, solve for x.

If $x^{\frac{1}{2}} \approx 4.19$, $x \approx 17.6$. This solution checks.

Since $\sqrt{x}$ cannot be negative, the second solution, $x^{\frac{1}{2}} \approx -1.19$, is extraneous.

TRY IT

Solve each equation.

c. $x + 2\sqrt{x} - 3 = 0$ **d.** $x - 3\sqrt{x} + 5 = 0$

1. Explain how you can solve an equation by graphing.
2. How can you tell whether a trinomial is in quadratic form?
3. When solving an equation with two or more square roots, why might you need to square both sides more than once?

Exercises

CORE

1. Getting Started Complete each step to solve the equation $\sqrt{x+3} = \sqrt{x} + 1$.

a. $(\sqrt{x+3})^2 = (\underline{\hspace{0.5cm}})^2$

b. $x + 3 = \underline{\hspace{0.5cm}} + \underline{\hspace{0.5cm}} + \underline{\hspace{0.5cm}}$

c. $\underline{\hspace{0.5cm}} = 2\sqrt{x}$

d. $\underline{\hspace{0.5cm}} = \sqrt{x}$

e. $\underline{\hspace{0.5cm}} = x$

f. Check: $\sqrt{\underline{\hspace{0.8cm}} + 3} \stackrel{?}{=} \sqrt{\underline{\hspace{0.8cm}}} + 1$

g. The solution _____ (checks, does not check).

Solve each equation by graphing.

2. $\sqrt{x} + \sqrt{x+1} = 2$

3. $\sqrt{2x+3} + \sqrt{3x+3} = 11$

4. $\sqrt{2x+3} + 1 = \sqrt{6x+7}$

Solve each equation.

5. $\sqrt{x} + \sqrt{x-5} = 5$

6. $\sqrt{x-2} + 3 = \sqrt{4x+1}$

7. $\sqrt{x} + \sqrt{x+4} = 3$

8. $3 = \sqrt{x+9} - \sqrt{x-6}$

9. City A is located at $(-3, 2)$ and City B is located at $(4, 8)$. If City C is equidistant from both cities, find a linear equation that represents all possible locations of City C.

State whether each equation is in quadratic form.

10. $5x^2 - 2.6x - 7.4 = 0$

11. $x^6 + 2x^5 - 8x^4 = 0$

12. $-3x^8 + 2x^4 - 1 = 0$

13. $2x + 5\sqrt{x} + 3 = 0$

14. $x + \sqrt[3]{x} - 12 = 0$

15. $\sqrt[4]{x} - 9.22\sqrt[8]{x} + 16 = 0$

Solve each equation.

16. $x - 4\sqrt{x} + 3 = 0$

17. $x^{20} + x^{10} + 5 = 0$

18. $x - 5\sqrt{x} + 6 = 0$

19. $\sqrt[3]{x^4} - 6\sqrt[3]{x^2} + 10 = 0$

20. The amount of time (t) it takes for an object dropped from a height of h meters to reach the ground is given by $t = \sqrt{\dfrac{h}{4.9}}$.

a. Find the time it takes for a ball dropped from a height of 10 meters to reach the ground.

b. Explain the derivation of this formula.

Science

21. Seeing Farther The formula $d = 1.23\sqrt{h}$ approximates the distance (d), in miles, that a person can see to the horizon from a height of h feet. Tinisha is standing on top of a mountain, and Linda is climbing the mountain 1000 feet below Tinisha. Tinisha can see 8 miles farther than Linda. How tall is the mountain?

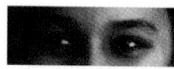 **LOOK BACK**

Evaluate each of the following. [6-2]

22. $_3C_2$

23. $_5C_3$

24. $_7C_2$

25. Mike wants to go through the express lane at the grocery store. He has 11 items in his basket, but he must have 9 items or less to go through the express lane. How many possible combinations of 9 of the 11 items can he keep? [6-2]

26. On the same coordinate axes, sketch graphs of $y = x^3$ and $y = x^6$. [7-1]

MORE PRACTICE

Solve each equation by graphing.

27. $\sqrt{x + 8} = 7 - \sqrt{x + 1}$

28. $\sqrt{x + 8} - \sqrt{3x + 1} = -1$

29. $\sqrt{2x - 3} + \sqrt{x + 3} = 6$

Solve each equation.

30. $\sqrt{x} = 3 - \sqrt{x - 3}$

31. $\sqrt{x} - \sqrt{x - 7} = 1$

32. $\sqrt{x} = 2 + \sqrt{x - 24}$

33. $\sqrt{3x + 7} + \sqrt{x + 3} = 2$

34. $\sqrt{4x + 5} - \sqrt{2x - 1} = 2$

35. $\sqrt{x + 12} + \sqrt{-4x + 4} = 7$

36. Two right triangles have hypotenuses of equal length. One leg of the first triangle measures 6 cm, while a leg of the other measures 9 cm. The other leg of the first triangle is twice as long as the other leg of the second. Find the lengths of the unknown legs.

State whether each equation is in quadratic form.

37. $x^4 + 2x^2 - 3x^3 = 0$

38. $x^4 - 2x^2 + 1 = 0$

39. $3x^2 + 16x - 11 = 0$

40. $5x + 2\sqrt{x} = 0$

41. $x^{18} + 4x^{12} - 5x^6 = 0$

42. $2x^{\frac{3}{5}} - x^{\frac{4}{5}} + 1 = 0$

43. $-3x + 4\sqrt{x} - 5 = 0$

44. $9x^{20} - 3x^{10} - 7 = 0$

Solve each equation.

45. $x + 2\sqrt{x} - 3 = 0$

46. $x - 6\sqrt{x} + 5 = 0$

47. $x - 4\sqrt{x} + 4 = 0$

48. $x - 3\sqrt{x} - 18 = 0$

49. $x - 12\sqrt{x} + 35 = 0$

50. $2x - 5\sqrt{x} = 3$

51. Swing Time For a pendulum, the period (T), in seconds, is given by $T = 2\pi\sqrt{\dfrac{\ell}{g}}$, where ℓ is its length in meters and g is the acceleration due to gravity, approximately 9.8 m/sec². Glenn is swinging back and forth on a swing. Suddenly, he sees the neighbor's dog leaping at him from the ground below. He quickly scrambles halfway up the rope to safety. Relaxing, he finds that the period of his swing is one second shorter now that his "pendulum" is half its original length. How long is the swing?

MORE MATH REASONING

Solve each equation.

52. $\dfrac{\sqrt{3x+1} + \sqrt{3x}}{\sqrt{3x+1} - \sqrt{3x}} = 2$

53. $\dfrac{1}{\sqrt{x-1}} - \dfrac{1}{\sqrt{x+1}} = \dfrac{1}{\sqrt{x^2-1}}$

54. Unequal Forces The gravitational attraction between two bodies of masses M and m that are a distance d apart is given by:

$$F = \frac{kMm}{d^2}$$

where k is a constant. Suppose that an asteroid is equidistant from Jupiter (mass $\approx 1.9 \times 10^{27}$ kg) and the sun (mass $\approx 2.0 \times 10^{30}$ kg). What is the ratio of the asteroid's gravitational attraction to Jupiter to its attraction to the sun?

7-2
PART E — Making Connections

· ·

← CONNECT → *You have learned to work with exponents and radicals. Now you will use what you have learned to search for a relationship between the velocity of a sound wave and the temperature of the air.*

Sound travels in waves. Like other waves, a sound wave can be characterized by its wavelength and its frequency. As you saw on page 481, the wavelength is the distance between successive crests of a wave, and the frequency is the number of crests that pass a given point each second.

The frequency of the note called "Concert A" is 440 vibrations per second (Hertz). A trumpeter playing Concert A sends out a sound wave that causes air molecules to vibrate 440 times per second. When the wave reaches your ear, your eardrum vibrates 440 times per second, allowing you to hear Concert A. The speed of sound is 332.2 m/sec at a temperature of 0°C. We must specify the temperature, because the velocity of sound varies with temperature. The Explore will give you an opportunity to investigate this relationship and to see how a change in temperature can affect the wavelength of a sound wave.

EXPLORE: DEGREES OF SOUND

MATERIALS

Graphing utility

1. The frequency (f), wavelength (ℓ), and velocity (v) of a sound wave—the speed of sound—are related by the equation:

$$v = f\ell$$

Describe the relationship between frequency and wavelength. Then graph frequency versus wavelength, assuming a temperature of 0°C.

2. Give the wavelength of each musical note at 0°C. Explain how you found these wavelengths.

   a. 16 Hz, the lowest note the average human ear can hear

   b. 261.63 Hz, "Middle C" on a piano

   c. 440 Hz, Concert A

   d. 3729.3 Hz, the highest note on a piccolo

   e. 20,000 Hz, the highest note the average human ear can hear

3. Suppose that you perform an experiment to measure the velocity of sound at various temperatures. Your thermometer measures temperature on the *Kelvin scale*. Data collected during the experiment are given in the table. Enter the data and make a scatter plot. Describe your scatter plot.

Temperature (K)	Velocity (m/sec)	Temperature (K)	Velocity (m/sec)
230	304.83	350	376.04
250	317.81	370	386.63
270	330.28	390	396.94
290	342.29	410	406.99
310	353.90	430	416.80
330	365.13	450	426.39

4. Kelvin temperature (K) and Celsius temperature (C) are related by the formula

$$K = C + 273.15$$

What would a graph of Kelvin temperature versus Celsius temperature look like? Explain.

5. Use a power regression to find the equation $v = At^B$ that best fits the data, where v = velocity of sound and t = temperature (in K).

6. Use your power regression equation to predict each of the following. Explain how you made each prediction.

   a. the velocity of sound at a temperature of 50°C

   b. the temperature at which sound travels 200 m/sec

   c. the wavelength of Concert A at 20°C

   d. the wavelength of Concert A at 40°C

The velocity of sound is a function not only of temperature, but also of humidity and of the medium through which it travels. Some musical instruments are fitted with tuning adjustments that allow the musician to compensate for the effects of temperature and humidity.

REFLECT

1. Give strengths and weaknesses of radical notation, rational exponents, and decimal exponents.
2. In your own words, explain why squaring both sides of an equation can lead to extraneous solutions.
3. When Carole graphed $y = (-2)^x$ on her graphing utility, she got several dots instead of a smooth curve. Why did this happen?

Self-Assessment

1. Solving the equation $x - 2 = \sqrt{2x - 1}$ yields the solutions $x = 5$ and $x = 1$. Which solution is extraneous?

Choose the letter that represents the correct answer.

2. Evaluate $8^{\frac{2}{3}}$.
   (a) 2   (b) 4   (c) $3\sqrt{8}$ (d) 64

3. Simplify $\sqrt[4]{k^2}$.
   (a) k (b) k^8 (c) $\sqrt[3]{k}$ (d) $|k|^{\frac{1}{2}}$

4. The graphs of $y = x^2$, $y = \sqrt{x}$, and $y = \sqrt[4]{x}$ are shown.
   a. Which graph is which?
   b. Identify the points where the graphs intersect.

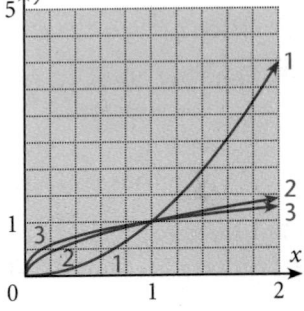

5. Su-Ching's CD changer can play 5 CDs. She has 12 CDs to choose from.
   a. How many different sets of 5 CDs can Su-Ching put into the changer? [6-2]
   b. How many different ways can Su-Ching put the 5 CDs into the changer? [6-1]

6. Give the equation of a circle of radius 2 with its center at $(-1, 4)$. [5-3]

Decide which choice is correct.

(A) The quantity in Column A is greater.
(C) The two quantities are equal.

(B) The quantity in Column B is greater.
(D) The relationship cannot be determined.

	Column A	Column B	
7.	$x^{0.6}$	$x^{\frac{3}{5}}$	when $x \geq 0$
8.	$\sqrt{x}$	x^2	

Simplify each expression.

9. $9^{\frac{1}{4}} \cdot 9^{\frac{1}{4}}$

10. $k^{\frac{1}{2}} \cdot k^{\frac{1}{3}}$

11. $\sqrt{\sqrt{\sqrt{x}}}$

12. $\dfrac{x^{3.5}y^{-0.7}}{x^{2.7}y^{7.5}}$

13. $\left(c^{\frac{2}{3}}\right)^{\frac{5}{4}}$

14. $\left(m^{0.7}n^{1.8}\right)^{2.6}$

Evaluate each expression. If necessary, round answers to the nearest hundredth.

15. $\sqrt[9]{-1}$

16. $32^{\frac{3}{5}}$

17. $25^{1.5}$

18. $1.32^{2.41}$

19. $36^{-\frac{1}{2}}$

20. $100^{0.5}$

21. Rewrite $\sqrt[5]{(x + y^2)^3}$ in exponential form.

22. Rewrite $(xy^3)^{\frac{1}{4}}$ using a radical.

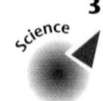

23. The depth (d), in feet, of the water in which an earthquake occurred is related to the velocity (v), in mi/hr, of a tidal wave unleashed by the earthquake according to the formula $v \approx 3.86d^{0.5}$.

a. Rewrite the formula in radical form.

b. Solve the formula for d.

c. Calculate the velocity of a tidal wave set off by an earthquake at a depth of 18,000 feet.

Solve each equation.

24. $\sqrt{x} = 6.2$

25. $\sqrt{x - 6} = 2$

26. $\sqrt{x + 8} = x - 4$

27. $5\sqrt[3]{x - 7} = -15$

28. $x^{\frac{3}{2}} - 6 = 2$

29. $\sqrt{2x + 3} = \sqrt{5x - 6}$

30. $x - 10\sqrt{x} + 21 = 0$

31. $x + \sqrt{x} = 10$

32. $x + 7\sqrt{x} = 12$

33. $\sqrt{x + 4} + \sqrt{x - 1} = 5$

34. $\sqrt{2x - 2} - \sqrt{3x - 2} = -1$

35. Solve $V = \frac{4}{3}\pi r^3$ for r.

36. Showing Some Interest The $2400 that Eduardo put in a savings account 3 years ago has grown to $2778.30. Find the interest rate he has been earning. Use the formula $A = P(1 + r)^n$, where A is the amount in an account after n years and P is the principal, the amount initially invested.

37. I Need My Space! An empirical study of territoriality in animals suggests that the area (A) an animal will defend varies directly with the 1.31 power of the animal's weight in pounds.

a. In the study, a 40-pound beaver defended a territory of 2700 square feet. Find the constant of variation.

b. Find the size of the territory that a 1200-pound Kodiak bear will defend.

c. An unknown animal left remains of its prey scattered over a 7000-square-foot area. Estimate the predator's weight.

The Functions of Weather and Climate

On June 27, 1915, the temperature reached 100°F in frigid Fort Yukon, Alaska. On January 30, 1966, the mercury dipped to –27°F in balmy New Market, Alabama. Although the *weather* on those days was unusual, the *climate* in each town stayed the same.

The difference between *weather* and *climate* is the difference between your mood and your personality. Weather changes from day to day, sometimes from hour to hour. A region's climate is the long-term atmospheric conditions that prevail in that area. Even though the weather is occasionally uncomfortably hot in Alaska, Alaska's climate is classified as cold. On the other hand, Alabama's climate is generally warm and humid, despite occasional snow flurries.

Climatologists study the changes in and the effects of the earth's climate. To help do this, they create mathematical models and use computer simulations, which must take a complex set of factors into account. Climate is a function of temperature, rainfall, elevation, ocean currents, air pressure, and wind. Each of these factors, in turn, is a function of others. The temperature of a region, for example, is a function of the region's latitude and the time of the year.

So we can describe climate as a function of temperature, and temperature as a function of latitude. To show the interrelationship between all three variables, we can use a *composite function* that combines both temperature and latitude. By combining functions in different ways, climatologists can make elaborate mathematical models.

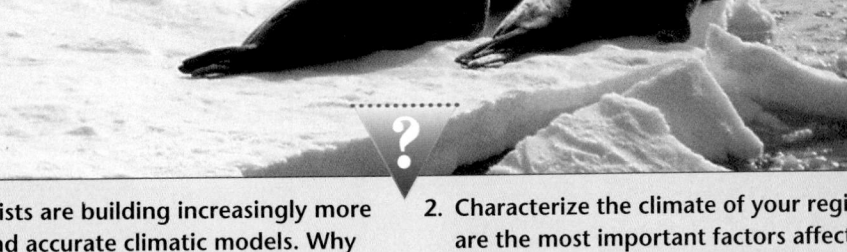

1. Climatologists are building increasingly more complex and accurate climatic models. Why might modern climatologists be able to build and use more elaborate models than their predecessors did?

2. Characterize the climate of your region. What are the most important factors affecting your climate?

3. Give an example of a composite function from your everyday life.

← CONNECT →
You've worked with functions before. Now you will use addition, subtraction, and multiplication to create new functions.

Heat is one of the principal components of climate. The source of Earth's heat is the sun. The amount of solar radiation that strikes Earth at a given point is a function of the latitude and the time of year.

Polar latitudes receive less radiation than temperate and tropical latitudes, and every latitude receives less radiation in winter than it does in summer. The net radiation received is the difference between the incoming energy from the sun and the energy lost back in space.

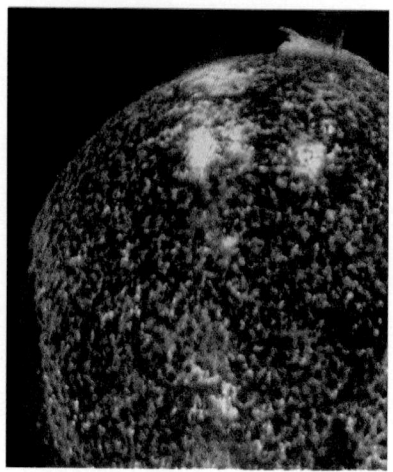

In the Explore, you will combine data from two graphs to produce a graph of net solar radiation as a function of latitude and time of year.

EXPLORE: JANUARY HOT AND COLD

MATERIALS

Graph paper

According to Reginald Newell in *Climate and the Ocean*, the first graph shows total radiant energy received from the sun as a function of latitude for the month of January. Energy is given in watts/m². Latitudes run from the South Pole (90° S) to the North Pole (90° N). The second graph shows radiant energy lost (reflected) back into space during the same period.

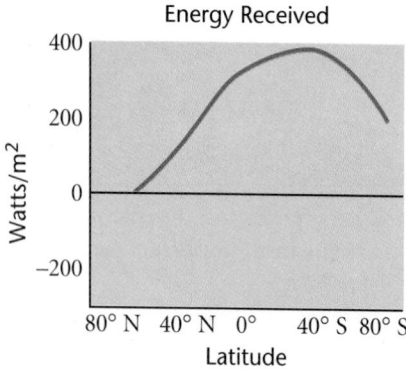

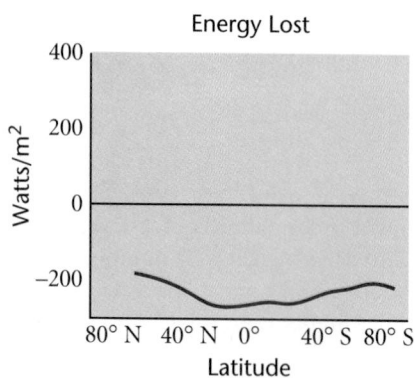

1. The graph of energy received (incoming radiation) shows that the maximum radiation received in the month of January is at about 30° S. Why is this the case? It also shows that extreme northern latitudes receive *no* solar radiation at this time. Can this be correct? If so, explain how this is possible.

2. Estimate and record the energy received and the energy lost at each latitude that is a multiple of 10. Then find the net radiation at each of these latitudes.

3. Make a graph of net solar radiation for January. Explain how your graph can be described as a sum or difference of two functions.

4. Where on Earth's surface is there a net loss of heat during January? Where is the net gain the greatest?

Problem-Solving Tip

Check to be sure that your answer makes sense.

Recall that a function is a relationship between two quantities where the value of one quantity, the dependent variable, is uniquely determined by the value of the other quantity, the independent variable. The set of all possible values of the independent variable is the domain. The set of all possible values of the dependent variable is the range.

A function is like a machine that takes members of the domain and turns them into members of the range. The "function machine" for $f(x) = x^2$ is shown.

We can add, subtract, or multiply two functions to create a new function.

Let $f(x)$ and $g(x)$ be two functions. Their *sum* $f + g$, their *difference* $f - g$, and their *product* $f \cdot g$ are defined as follows.

The *sum* of f and g, $(f + g)(x) = f(x) + g(x)$.

The *difference* of f and g, $(f - g)(x) = f(x) - g(x)$.

The *product* of f and g, $(f \cdot g)(x) = f(x) \cdot g(x)$.

EXAMPLE

1. Find $(f + g)(x)$, $(f - g)(x)$, and $(f \cdot g)(x)$ for $f(x) = 2x + 1$ and $g(x) = x - 1$.

$(f + g)(x) = (2x + 1) + (x - 1) = 3x$

$(f - g)(x) = (2x + 1) - (x - 1) = 2x + 1 - x + 1 = x + 2$

$(f \cdot g)(x) = (2x + 1)(x - 1) = 2x^2 - x - 1$

2. Find $(f + g)(x)$, $(f - g)(x)$, and $(f \cdot g)(x)$ for $f(x) = x^2 + 3x - 4$ and $g(x) = 3x^3 - 2x^2 + 7$.

$(f + g)(x) = (x^2 + 3x - 4) + (3x^3 - 2x^2 + 7) = 3x^3 - x^2 + 3x + 3$

$(f - g)(x) = (x^2 + 3x - 4) - (3x^3 - 2x^2 + 7)$

$\qquad\qquad = x^2 + 3x - 4 - 3x^3 + 2x^2 - 7 = -3x^3 + 3x^2 + 3x - 11$

To multiply polynomials, use the distributive property. Be sure that each term in f multiplies every term in g.

$(f \cdot g)(x) = (\mathbf{x^2 + 3x - 4})(3x^3 - 2x^2 + 7)$

$\qquad\qquad = \mathbf{x^2}(3x^3 - 2x^2 + 7) \mathbf{+ 3x}(3x^3 - 2x^2 + 7) \mathbf{- 4}(3x^3 - 2x^2 + 7)$

$\qquad\qquad = 3x^5 - 2x^4 + 7x^2 + 9x^4 - 6x^3 + 21x - 12x^3 + 8x^2 - 28$

$\qquad\qquad = 3x^5 + 7x^4 - 18x^3 + 15x^2 + 21x - 28 \qquad$ Combine like terms.

3. If $m(x) = 3x^2 + 8$ and $n(x) = 2x - 4$, find $(m + n)(-3)$.

$(m + n)(x) = (3x^2 + 8) + (2x - 4) = 3x^2 + 2x + 4$

$(m + n)(-3) = 3(-3)^2 + 2(-3) + 4 = 27 - 6 + 4 = 25$

Notice that we have arranged the terms in the answers to Examples 1 and 2 so that their exponents are in *descending order*.

CONSIDER

1. In Example 3, we found $(m + n)(-3)$ by finding $(m + n)(x)$, then substituting -3 for x. Describe another way to find $(m + n)(-3)$.

You can use the graphs of two functions to find the graph of their sum, difference, or product. For instance, we can use the graphs of $f(x) = x + 2$ and $g(x) = -2x - 4$ to find the graph of $(f + g)(x)$.

First, graph $f(x)$ and $g(x)$ on the same set of axes. Then choose a value of x. To find the y-value of $(f + g)(x)$ for that x-value, add the individual values of f and g. Repeat this process for more x-values until you have enough information to sketch the graph of $(f + g)(x)$.

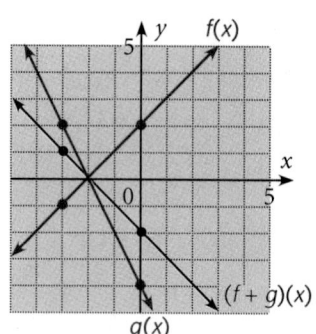

The blue line represents the sum. From the slope and y-intercept of the line, we can give its equation as $y = -x - 2$. Note that we obtain the same sum algebraically:

$(f + g)(x) = (x + 2) + (-2x - 4) = -x - 2$.

Let $f(x) = -3x - 2$ and $g(x) = 2x + 3$.

a. Find $(f + g)(x)$, $(f - g)(x)$, and $(f \cdot g)(x)$.

Let $f(x) = -2x^3 + 5x - 1$ and $g(x) = 3x^2 - 4$.

b. Find $(f + g)(x)$, $(f - g)(x)$, and $(f \cdot g)(x)$.

c. Find $(f \cdot g)(2)$.

REFLECT

1. Give an example of a real-world function that can be described as the sum, difference, or product of two individual functions.

2. What is $(f + g)(x) - (f - g)(x)$? Explain.

3. Suppose $f(x)$ is a linear function and $g(x)$ is a quadratic function. Classify $(f + g)(x)$, $(f - g)(x)$, and $(f \cdot g)(x)$ as linear, quadratic, or neither.

Exercises

CORE

1. Getting Started Let $f(x) = x + 1$ and $g(x) = 2x$. Find each value or expression.
    a. $f(2)$ **b.** $g(2)$ **c.** $(f + g)(2)$ **d.** $(f - g)(2)$
    e. $(f \cdot g)(2)$ **f.** $(f + g)(x)$ **g.** $(f - g)(x)$ **h.** $(f \cdot g)(x)$

Let $p(x) = 6x - 2$ and $q(x) = -3x^2 + 2x + 1$. Find each value or expression.

2. $(p + q)(-1)$ **3.** $(p - q)(2)$ **4.** $(q - p)(0)$

5. $(p \cdot q)(-2)$ **6.** $p(\pi)$ **7.** $q(k)$

For each pair of functions, find $(f + g)(x)$, $(f - g)(x)$, and $(f \cdot g)(x)$.

8. $f(x) = 5$, $g(x) = 2x - 3$ **9.** $f(x) = -x + 2$, $g(x) = 3x - 5$

10. $f(x) = x + 1$, $g(x) = 2x^2 - 3$ **11.** $f(x) = x^3 - 2$, $g(x) = 3x^2 + 2x$

12. $f(x) = x^2 + 6x - 2$, $g(x) = 2x^2 - 3x + 1$ **13.** $f(x) = 3x^4 - x^2 + 3$, $g(x) = x^3 + 5x + 4$

14. Budget Balance The net income, in billions of dollars, for the United States government for the years 1990–1993 can be modeled by the function $r(t) = 40.4t + 1021.9$, where t is the year $(1990 = 0)$. The net expenses can be modeled by the function $e(t) = 52.6t + 1262.6$.

    a. Write a function $d(t)$ that models the budget deficit for these years.

    b. If this function continues to model the deficit for years beyond 1993, will the budget deficit increase or decrease? Explain how you know.

    c. Use $d(t)$ to find each of the following. Explain the real-world meaning of each.
        i. $d(2)$ **ii.** $d(0)$ **iii.** $d(3)$

Social Science

15. The function f is the set of ordered pairs $(1, 5)$, $(2, 7)$, $(3, 9)$, $(4, 11)$. The function g is the set of ordered pairs $(1, -3)$, $(2, -6)$, $(3, -9)$. Find each value.

    a. $(f + g)(1)$ **b.** $(f - g)(3)$ **c.** $(f \cdot g)(2)$

16. Alice's job pays \$12 per hour for the first forty hours she works each week. For overtime hours she is paid \$18 per hour. She always works at least 40 hours.

    a. Write functions for Alice's regular pay and her overtime pay.

    b. Write a function for Alice's net pay. Explain how you found this function.

    c. Alice worked 48 hours this week. What will her net pay be?

17. Let $b(x) = x + 3$ and $c(x) = 4x$.

    a. Show that $b(-2) + c(-2) = (b + c)(-2)$.

    b. Show that $b(3) - c(3) = (b - c)(3)$.

    c. Suppose that f and g are functions and that a is a real number. Describe two ways to find $(f + g)(a)$.

For each pair of functions, graph f and g on the same set of axes. Then use your graphs to find the graph of $(f + g)(x)$.

18. $f(x) = -x + 3$, $g(x) = 2x - 4$ **19.** $f(x) = -5$, $g(x) = x^2$

20. Pet Project During her first year as a veterinary assistant, Angela earned \$6 per hour, plus an average of \$36 per week in overtime pay. At the beginning of her second year, she received a \$1.50 per hour raise and began earning an average of \$6 more in overtime pay weekly.

    a. Write a function f relating the number of hours (h) that she worked weekly during her first year and her total weekly wages $f(h)$.

    b. Write a function g representing her additional wages $g(h)$ during the second year.

    c. Find the sum of the functions $(f + g)(h)$. Explain what the sum represents.

    d. If Angela works 36 hours before being paid overtime, find her earnings for a typical week during the second year.

 **LOOK BACK**

Expand each expression. [6-2]

21. $(x + 1)^3$ **22.** $(x - 3)^4$ **23.** $(3c + 2)^3$

Solve each equation. [7-2]

24. $\sqrt{x + 6} = 3$ **25.** $\sqrt{x^2 - 5} = x + 2$ **26.** $x + 3\sqrt{x - 3} = 0$

MORE PRACTICE

Let $h(x) = 2x + 5$ and $k(x) = -2x^2 + x$. Find each value or expression.

27. $(h + k)(1)$ **28.** $(h - k)(-2)$ **29.** $(k - h)(-3)$

30. $(h \cdot k)(3)$ **31.** $h(n)$ **32.** $k(T)$

For each pair of functions, find $(f + g)(x)$, $(f - g)(x)$, and $(f \cdot g)(x)$.

33. $f(x) = x, g(x) = -3x$

34. $f(x) = -2x + 1, g(x) = -x + 3$

35. $f(x) = 4x + 1, g(x) = 3x - 2$

36. $f(x) = 0.5x - 6, g(x) = x - 2.5$

37. $f(x) = 2x - 2, g(x) = x^2 + 4$

38. $f(x) = x^2 + 1, g(x) = x^2 - 1$

39. $f(x) = x^2 - 2x + 3, g(x) = 2x^2 - x - 2$

40. $f(x) = 4x^3 - 2x^2 + 1, g(x) = 2x^5 - 5x^3 + 2$

For each pair of functions, graph f and g on the same set of axes. Then use your graphs to find the graph of $(f + g)(x)$.

41. $f(x) = x + 1, g(x) = x - 1$

42. $f(x) = 2x + 5, g(x) = x - 2$

43. $f(x) = -3x - 2, g(x) = x + 2$

44. Education Costs A teacher drove to a conference. She figured that it cost her $0.06/mi for gasoline and $0.22/mi for other car expenses.
  a. Write a function $f(m)$ for the total gasoline cost for the teacher in terms of the number of miles driven (m).
  b. Let $g(m) = 0.22m$. Find $(f + g)m$ and explain what the sum represents.
  c. Find the cost of driving the car for 250 miles.

45. Use a Graphing Utility The table shows the number of employed and unemployed people, age 16 and over, in the United States for the years 1988–1991.

Year	1988	1989	1990	1991
Employed (millions)	114.9	117.3	117.9	116.9
Unemployed (millions)	6.7	6.5	6.9	8.4

  a. Use linear regression to find an equation to model the number of people employed, and find a different equation to model the number of people unemployed.
  b. Find a function that models the *total* number of employed and unemployed U.S. citizens, ages 16 and over, for those years. Explain how you found this function.
  c. Use your function to approximate the total number of employed and unemployed U.S. citizens, 16 and over, for 1988 and 1991. Then check your answers by using the table. Are your approximations close to the actual values?

MORE MATH REASONING

46. Suppose that the functions f and $f + g$ were graphed on the same coordinate axes. Explain how you could graph the function g.

47. Use the definitions of $(f + g)(x)$ and $(f \cdot g)(x)$ to prove the following theorems.
  a. $(f + g)(x) = (g + f)(x)$
  b. $(f \cdot g)(x) = (g \cdot f)(x)$

48. If the domains of two functions that are being added, subtracted, or multiplied are different, the domain of their sum, difference, or product is the *intersection* of the domains of the two functions.
  a. Let $f(x) = \sqrt{x + 3}$ and $h(x) = \frac{2}{4x - 2}$. Find $(f + h)(x)$ and state its domain.
  b. Explain why this restriction makes sense.

← **CONNECT** →   *Through the use of arithmetic operations you have created new functions from old ones. Now you will do the same thing by finding "functions of functions."*

In some cities, TV weathercasters announce the "Comfort Index" for the day. This index, a measure of how comfortable the weather is supposed to feel, is a function of the day's temperature and humidity. The temperature, in turn, is a function of many factors such as altitude, latitude, and time of year, while the humidity is a function of the water content of the air. We can write a "chain" of functions showing that the Comfort Index is ultimately a function of many factors.

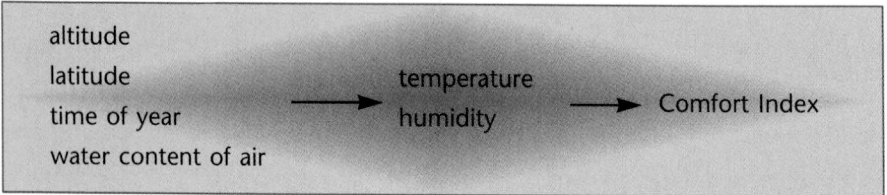

altitude		
latitude	temperature	
time of year	→ humidity	→ Comfort Index
water content of air		

The idea that a variable can be a function *of a function* underlies the concept of *composite functions*. You will investigate composite functions in the Explore.

EXPLORE: BALLOONING

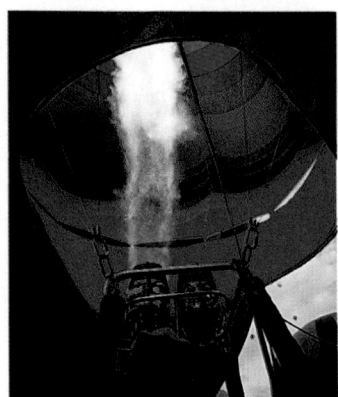

Suppose a spherical balloon is being inflated. The volume (V) of the balloon is a function of the radius (r) and is given by the formula $V = \frac{4}{3}\pi r^3$. The radius is increasing at a rate of 2 cm per second.

1. Let t represent time in seconds. If $r = 0$ at $t = 0$, give the radius at each whole number of seconds from $t = 1$ to $t = 5$.
2. Express r as a function of t.
3. Express V as a function of t. Explain how you did this.
4. Suppose instead that the *volume* increases at 20 cm³/sec. Express r as a function of t.
5. Which of the two types of increase is more realistic? Why?

We use the familiar algebraic process of substitution to compose functions.

> Let f and g be any two functions such that the range of g is in the domain of f. The **composite** (or **composition**) of f and g is the function $f(g(x))$.

We indicate the composite of f and g by $f(g(x))$ or by the notation $(f \circ g)(x)$. Both notations are read "f of g of x."

EXAMPLES

1. Let $f(x) = 3x - 1$ and $g(x) = x + 5$. Find $f(g(2))$ and $g(f(2))$.

$f(g(2)) = f(2 + 5) = f(7)$ Find $g(2)$.

$\quad\quad\quad = 3(7) - 1 = 20$ Substitute $g(2)$ into f and evaluate.

$g(f(2)) = g(3(2) - 1) = g(5)$ Find $f(2)$.

$\quad\quad\quad = 5 + 5 = 10$ Substitute $f(2)$ into g and evaluate.

2. Let $f(x) = x^2$ and $g(x) = x - 2$. Find $(f \circ g)(x)$ and $(g \circ f)(x)$.

$(f \circ g)(x) = f(g(x))$

$\quad\quad\quad = f(x - 2) = (x - 2)^2$ Substitute $g(x) = x - 2$ for x in $f(x)$.

$\quad\quad\quad = x^2 - 4x + 4$ Simplify.

So, $(f \circ g)(x) = x^2 - 4x + 4$

$(g \circ f)(x) = g(f(x))$

$\quad\quad\quad = g(x^2) = x^2 - 2$ Substitute $f(x) = x^2$ for x in $g(x)$.

So, $(g \circ f)(x) = x^2 - 2$

3. Fahrenheit temperature (F) is a function of Celsius temperature (C), with $F = 1.8C + 32$. Celsius temperature is a function of Kelvin temperature (K), with $C = K - 273.15$. Express Fahrenheit temperature as a function of Kelvin temperature.

$F = 1.8C + 32$

$\quad = 1.8(K - 273.15) + 32$ Substitute the expression for C.

$\quad = 1.8K - 491.67 + 32$ Simplify.

$F = 1.8K - 459.67$

CONSIDER

1. Is composition of functions commutative; that is, is $f(g(x)) = g(f(x))$? Justify your answer.

TRY IT

a. Let $f(x) = x + 2$ and $g(x) = -x - 3$. Find $(f \circ g)(-4)$ and $(g \circ f)(-4)$.

b. Let $f(x) = (x - 1)^2$ and $g(x) = x + 1$. Find $(f \circ g)(x)$ and $(g \circ f)(x)$.

c. The cost (c) of \$1.12/gal gasoline is a function of the number of gallons (n) purchased, with $c = 1.12n$. The number of gallons used in a car getting 28 mi/gal is a function of the number of miles driven (m), with $n = \frac{m}{28}$. Express the cost of gasoline as a function of the distance driven.

As you have seen, real-world variables are often dependent on variables that are in turn dependent on other variables. Composite functions allow you to express these chains of functions mathematically.

REFLECT

1. Explain how substitution is used to find the composite function $f(g(x))$.
2. Describe as many ways as you can to combine two functions to make a third function.
3. Suppose that the height of an animal is a function of its age, and the weight of the animal is a function of its height. Describe a third function that is a composition of these two functions.

Exercises

CORE

1. **Getting Started** Let $f(x) = 3x - 1$ and $g(x) = x + 4$. Follow the steps to find $f(g(x))$.
   a. Begin with the expression $f(g(x))$. Rewrite this expression by substituting $x + 4$ for $g(x)$.
   b. Substitute $x + 4$ for x in the expression $3x - 1$.
   c. Simplify the expression from **b** as far as possible. This is your result for $f(g(x))$.

2. Complete the statement using *domain, range, h,* and *k:* In order to form the composite function $h \circ k$, the ____ of ____ must be a subset of the ____ of ____.

Let $m(x) = 3x - 5$ and $n(x) = x^3$. Find each value or expression.

3. $m(4)$ 4. $n(-3)$ 5. $m(n(2))$

6. $n(m(-5))$ 7. $m(n(x))$ 8. $(n \circ m)(x)$

9. **Cheap, Cheaper** As an employee of Tires Are Us, Tim is entitled to a 20% discount off the advertised price of tires. During the store's anniversary sale, all tires were advertised at 25% off the regular price.
   a. Let x represent the regular price of a tire before the sale. Write a function $f(x)$ that represents the price that Tim pays.
   b. Write a function $g(x)$ that expresses the price of the tire during the anniversary sale.
   c. Write a composite function that expresses the twice-discounted price Tim pays for a tire that regularly sells for x dollars.
   d. Find the price that Tim pays during the sale for a tire whose regular price is $60.

For each pair of functions, find $f(g(2))$ and $g(f(2))$.

10. $f(x) = 2x + 5$, $g(x) = 3x - 1$ 11. $f(x) = x + 1$, $g(x) = x^2$

12. $f(x) = x^2$, $g(x) = -4x$ 13. $f(x) = x^2 + x$, $g(x) = x - 1$

For each pair of functions, find $(h \circ j)(x)$ and $(j \circ h)(x)$.

14. $h(x) = 3x + 7$, $j(x) = 2x - 4$

15. $h(x) = x^2$, $j(x) = 2x - 1$

16. $h(x) = 3x + 2$, $j(x) = 5x - 7$

17. $h(x) = 2x^2 - 3x$, $j(x) = x + 2$

18. $h(x) = 3x^2 + 2$, $j(x) = x - 1$

19. $h(x) = x^3 - x$, $j(x) = 3x$

20. The volume (V) of a cylinder equals the area of the base (B) multiplied by the height (h).
   a. Write an expression for the volume as a function of the area of the base and the height.
   b. Write an expression for the area of the base as a function of the radius (r).
   c. Write an expression for the volume as a function of the radius and the height.

Let $f(x) = 2x$, $g(x) = x + 1$, and $h(x) = x^2 - 1$. Find each composite function.

21. $(f \circ f)(x)$

22. $(g \circ g)(x)$

23. $(f \circ g \circ h)(x)$

24. Let $f(x) = x^2$ and $g(x) = x + 2$. For what value(s) of x is $(f \circ g)(x) = (g \circ f)(x)$?

25. Time, Temperature, and Culture The number of bacteria (n) in a culture is given by $n = -5T^2 + 600T - 16{,}000$, where T is the temperature in °C. The temperature is given by $T = h + 40$, where h is the number of hours since the experiment began.
   a. Write and simplify an expression giving the number of bacteria as a function of time.
   b. Find the number of bacteria after 8 hours.
   c. When will the culture contain 2000 bacteria? What will the temperature be at that time?

 **LOOK AHEAD**

For each pair of functions, find $f(g(x))$ and $g(f(x))$.

26. $f(x) = x + 1$, $g(x) = x - 1$ **27.** $f(x) = \sqrt[3]{x}$, $g(x) = x^3$ **28.** $f(x) = \frac{x + 2}{3}$, $g(x) = 3x - 2$

MORE PRACTICE

For each pair of functions, find $(h \circ k)(-3)$ and $(k \circ h)(-3)$.

29. $h(x) = x + 4$, $k(x) = 5x$

30. $h(x) = 4x - 2$, $k(x) = 3x + 2$

31. $h(x) = -x$, $k(x) = x^2 + 4$

32. $h(x) = -x + 8$, $k(x) = x - 2$

33. $h(x) = 2x + 1$, $k(x) = x^2$

34. $h(x) = (x - 5)^2$, $k(x) = x^3$

35. Video to Go You have a coupon for $5.00 off the price of a video. In addition, the video store is having a "20% off" sale.

a. Write a function $c(d)$ that describes the cost of a video whose regular price is d dollars if you use your coupon. (Do not include the 20% discount.)

b. Write a function $s(d)$ that describes the sale price of a video whose regular price is d dollars.

c. Find $s(c(d))$ and $c(s(d))$. What is the real-world meaning of each function?

d. If you use your coupon to buy a sale video, would you prefer to use it before or after 20% is taken off the original price? Explain.

For each pair of functions, find $f(g(x))$ and $g(f(x))$.

36. $f(x) = -3x$, $g(x) = 2x + 6$ **37.** $f(x) = 9$, $g(x) = x$

38. $f(x) = 2x$, $g(x) = 3x - 2$ **39.** $f(x) = x^2 - 2x + 1$, $g(x) = x + 1$

40. $f(x) = -10x$, $g(x) = -0.1x$ **41.** $f(x) = x + 2$, $g(x) = x^2$

42. $f(x) = 2x - 4$, $g(x) = 0.5(x + 4)$ **43.** $f(x) = x^2 + 4x$, $g(x) = x - 1$

44. Oil Spill Oil leaking from a disabled tanker is spreading in a circle around the tanker. The radius (r), in feet, of the circle is given by $r = \sqrt{1000t}$, where t is the time in minutes since the spill.

a. Write a function expressing the area of the spill (A) as a function of time.

b. Find the area of the spill after 15 minutes.

c. When will the area surpass 100,000 ft²?

MORE MATH REASONING

45. Find two different functions $f(x)$ and $g(x)$, such that $f(g(x)) = g(f(x))$.

46. The definition of a composite function $f(g(x))$ states that the range of g must be in the domain of f.

a. Suppose that $f = \{(1, 4), (2, 8), (3, 5)\}$ and $g = \{(7, 2), (-1, 3)\}$. Find $f(g(x))$ and $g(f(x))$. Use your results to explain the domain and range restrictions in the definition.

b. Let $p(x) = \dfrac{4}{x - 8}$ and $q(x) = x^3$. Find $p(q(x))$ and state whether it exists for all real numbers. If it does not, specify appropriate restrictions on the domain of $p(q(x))$.

47. Use a Graphing Utility The table below shows the average temperature and the *apparent* temperature (assuming a humidity of 20%) for Los Angeles for the months of February through August.

Social Science

Month	Feb.	Mar.	Apr.	May	June	July	Aug.
Average Temperature (°F)	60	61	63	66	70	74	75
Apparent Temperature (°F)	56	57	59	61	65	69	71

Use regression to write functions for average temperature in terms of the month and apparent temperature in terms of average temperature. Then use these functions to write a function for the apparent temperature in terms of the month.

← CONNECT →   *As you have seen, composition of functions is not generally commutative. You will investigate a special class of functions that is not only commutative, but whose members "undo" each other, producing an output after composition that is equal to the original input.*

A relation is a set of ordered pairs. By interchanging the domain and range of a relation, you create a new relation that is the **inverse** of the original one.

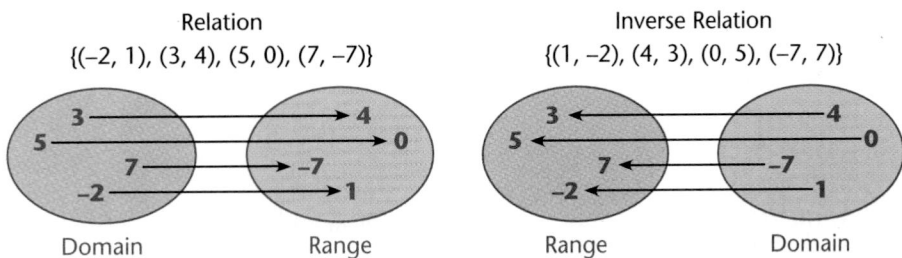

Relation	Inverse Relation
{(–2, 1), (3, 4), (5, 0), (7, –7)}	{(1, –2), (4, 3), (0, 5), (–7, 7)}

A function is a special type of relation in which each member of the domain is matched with exactly one member of the range. If the inverse relation of a function $f(x)$ is also a function, it is called the **inverse function** of $f(x)$ and is denoted by $f^{-1}(x)$, read "the inverse of f" or "f inverse of x."

Note that the -1 in the notation is not an exponent and that $f^{-1} \neq \dfrac{1}{f}$.

EXAMPLE

1. State whether the relation is a function and whether the inverse relation is a function: {(1, 6), (2, 7), (3, 7)}

Each member of the domain {1, 2, 3} is matched with exactly one member of the range {6, 7}, so the relation is a function.

The inverse relation is {(6, 1), (7, 2), (7, 3)}. The number 7 in the domain is matched with *two* members of the range, 2 and 3, so the inverse relation is not a function.

TRY IT

State whether the relation is a function and whether the inverse relation is a function.

a. {(−2, 5), (−7, −4), (0, 0)}   **b.** {(8, 5), (4, −1), (2, 1), (13, 5)}

In the Explore, you will use parametric equations to investigate the relationship between the graph of a function and the graph of its inverse.

EXPLORE: PARAMETRIC GRAPHING

MATERIALS

Graphing utility, Graph paper

For the relation $x = y^2$, there are two values of y for every positive value of x. Therefore, the relation is not a function. Nevertheless, you can graph the relation on a graphing utility by introducing a new variable **T**, called a *parameter*, then graphing the ordered pairs $(\mathbf{X_T}, \mathbf{Y_T})$ that satisfy the *parametric equations* $\mathbf{X_T} = \mathbf{T^2}$ and $\mathbf{Y_T} = \mathbf{T}$.

1. What is $(\mathbf{X_T}, \mathbf{Y_T})$ when $\mathbf{T} = 2$? when $\mathbf{T} = -1.5$? Verify that the ordered pairs satisfy the relation $x = y^2$.

2. Set your graphing utility on parametric mode. Enter the parametric equations, and set the range of **T**-values and screen window as shown. Graph the relation and sketch the graph.

Tmin $= -3$	Xmin $= -9$	Ymin $= -6$
Tmax $= 3$	Xmax $= 9$	Ymax $= 6$
Tstep $= 0.1$	Xscl $= 1$	Yscl $= 1$

3. Interchange the parametric equations for $\mathbf{X_T}$ and $\mathbf{Y_T}$ to represent the quadratic function $y = x^2$. Enter the parametric equations along with the previous ones and graph *both* the relations $x = y^2$ and $y = x^2$ on the same screen. Sketch the graphs.

4. *Trace* to one value of **T** and move from one graph to the other. Label the coordinates of the points on your sketch. *Trace* to two more values of **T** and label those points on your sketch. How are the coordinates of these pairs of points on the two graphs related? Explain why this pattern makes sense.

5. Draw the dashed line $y = x$ on your sketch. For a given value of **T**, how are the points on the two graphs related to the line?

The ordered pairs of an inverse relation are obtained by interchanging the x- and y-values of the ordered pairs of the original relation.

The figure shows the graph of the relation $\{(-2, 1), (-3, 4), (2, 5)\}$ and its inverse $\{(1, -2), (4, -3), (5, 2)\}$. As you can see, interchanging the x- and y-values *reflects* the relation across the line $y = x$, producing the inverse.

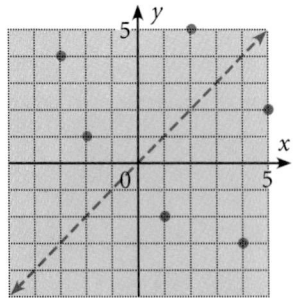

The same is true of the graphs of any relation and its inverse. Each is a reflection of the other over the line $y = x$.

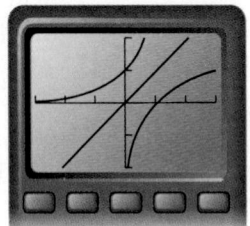

CONSIDER
?

1. If the point (a, b) is on the graph of a relation, what point must be on the graph of its inverse? Why?

One way to find the inverse of a function is to reverse the operations it specifies.

$$f(x) = 2x + 1 \rightarrow \boxed{1} \text{ Multiply } x \text{ by } 2. \rightarrow \boxed{2} \text{ Add } 1.$$

$$\downarrow \text{ Reverse steps.}$$

$$f^{-1}(x) = \frac{x - 1}{2} \leftarrow \boxed{4} \text{ Divide by } 2. \leftarrow \boxed{3} \text{ Subtract } 1 \text{ from } x.$$

This technique works for many, but not all, functions. Another way to find the inverse of a function involves interchanging two variables. As above, let $f(x) = 2x + 1$.

$$y = 2x + 1 \qquad \text{Replace } f(x) \text{ with } y.$$

$$x = 2y + 1 \qquad \text{Interchange the variables.}$$

$$x - 1 = 2y$$

$$\frac{x - 1}{2} = y \qquad \text{Solve for } y.$$

$$\frac{x - 1}{2} = f^{-1}(x) \qquad \text{Replace } y \text{ with } f^{-1}(x).$$

To confirm that f^{-1} is the inverse of f, we need to check that it "undoes" f. In other words, if $f(a) = b$, then $f^{-1}(b) = a$. We can check this for a particular value, for example, $x = 6$.

$$f(6) = 2(6) + 1 = 13 \qquad\qquad f^{-1}(13) = \frac{13 - 1}{2} = \frac{12}{2} = 6$$

But is this true for *all* values of x? If we substitute any value x into $f(x)$, then take the result and substitute it into $f^{-1}(x)$, will we always get x back?

We check this by taking the composition of f and f^{-1}.

$$f^{-1}(f(x)) = f^{-1}(2x + 1) = \frac{(2x + 1) - 1}{2} = \frac{2x}{2} = x$$

If two functions are inverses of each other, this property works both ways.

> $f(x)$ and $g(x)$ are inverses of each other if and only if
> $f(g(x)) = x$ for all x in the domain of g, and
> $g(f(x)) = x$ for all x in the domain of f.

2. Show that $f(x) = 5x$ and $g(x) = \frac{x}{5}$ are inverses of one another.

$f(g(x)) = 5\left(\frac{x}{5}\right) = x \checkmark \qquad g(f(x)) = \frac{5x}{5} = x \checkmark$

3. $f(x) = x^3 - 8$. Find $f^{-1}(x)$.

$y = x^3 - 8$	Replace $f(x)$ with y.
$x = y^3 - 8$	Interchange the variables.
$x + 8 = y^3$	
$\sqrt[3]{x + 8} = y$	Solve for y.
$\sqrt[3]{x + 8} = f^{-1}(x)$	Replace y with $f^{-1}(x)$.

c. Show that $f(x) = 4x + 2$ and $g(x) = \frac{x - 2}{4}$ are inverses of one another.

d. $f(x) = 4x - 1$. Find $f^{-1}(x)$.   **e.** $h(x) = \frac{x^5}{7}$. Find $h^{-1}(x)$.

Like the inverse operations of addition and subtraction, a function or relation and its inverse undo each other. Graphs of a relation and its inverse can be thought of as mirror images.

1. How can you decide whether a relation is a function?

2. How can you determine whether two functions are inverses of one another?

3. Describe how the "square" key and the "square root" key on a calculator act like inverse functions. How are they different from inverse functions?

Exercises

CORE

1. Getting Started Use the relation $f = \{(-4, -2), (-1, 1), (0, -2)\}$.

a. Is the relation a function? Explain.

b. Find the inverse relation f^{-1}. Is the inverse relation a function? Explain.

c. Graph both relations. How can you tell by looking at the graphs that the relations are inverses of one another?

Write the word or phrase that correctly completes each statement.

2. A(n) ____ is a relation in which each member of the domain is matched with exactly one member of the range.

3. The graphs of a relation and its inverse are ____ of each other over $y = x$.

4. $f(x) = 8.2x^{21} + 17.6x^3 + 4.3x$. Find $f(f^{-1}(178))$. Explain how you found your answer.

State whether each relation is a function and whether its inverse relation is a function.

5. $\{(-3, 4), (0, 0), (4, -3), (0, -3)\}$

6. $\{(-7, 8), (-7, 9), (-7, 10), (-7, 11)\}$

The graph of a relation is shown. Copy the graph. Then sketch the graph of the inverse relation.

7.

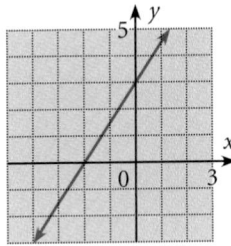

8.

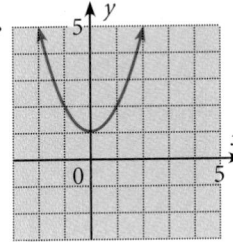

Graph each function and its inverse.

9. $f(x) = 2x$

10. $f(x) = -3x + 2$

11. $f(x) = \frac{3}{4}x$

For each pair of functions, show that the functions are inverses of one another.

12. $f(x) = x - 3, \; g(x) = x + 3$

13. $f(x) = 4x, \; g(x) = \frac{1}{4}x$

14. $f(x) = 3x - 1, \; g(x) = \frac{x + 1}{3}$

15. $f(x) = -2x + 4, \; g(x) = -\frac{1}{2}x + 2$

16. $f(x) = x^5 - 1, \; g(x) = \sqrt[5]{x + 1}$

17. Which Conversion Version? The formula for converting Celsius temperature to Fahrenheit temperature is $F = \frac{9}{5}C + 32$, and the formula for converting Fahrenheit to Celsius is $C = \frac{5}{9}(F - 32)$.

  a. Show that these formulas are inverses of each other. Explain why it makes sense that they are inverses.

  b. Graph the two formulas on the same set of axes. Show that they are reflections of each other over $y = x$.

Find the inverse of each function.

18. $f(x) = x + 8$

19. $f(x) = 3x + 8$

20. $f(x) = 2x - 1$

21. $f(x) = \frac{4x + 7}{3}$

22. $f(x) = \frac{1}{x}$

23. $f(x) = x^3 - 5$

24. Testing, Testing A function has an inverse function if it is *one-to-one*, that is, if each number in its domain corresponds to a unique number in its range, and vice versa.

  The vertical line test, described in Exercise 18 on page 25 in 1-1C, is a way to test the graph of a relation to see whether it is a function. Describe a test to see whether the function has an inverse function. Explain why your test works.

25. a. Let x represent the radius of a circle. Write a function $f(x)$ that represents the circumference.

  b. Find $f^{-1}(x)$. What does the inverse function represent?

  c. Show that $f(f^{-1}(x)) = x$.

26. Breathless The breathing rate (B), in breaths per minute, for a mammal weighing m kilograms, can be approximated by $B = 53.5m^{-0.26}$.
   a. Solve this equation for the mass of the animal.
   b. While camping one night, you hear an animal outside your tent. It is breathing every 6 seconds. Should you be scared? Explain.

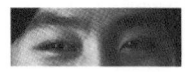

LOOK BACK

27. Use the expansion of $(0.5G + 0.5B)^3$ to determine the probability that a couple planning to have 3 children will have at most 1 boy. [6-2]

28. The frequency of the pitch produced by an organ pipe varies inversely with the length of the pipe. [7-1]
   a. If the pitch of an 8-ft pipe is 64 Hz, find the constant of variation.
   b. Find the length of a pipe that produces a pitch of 440 Hz.

MORE PRACTICE

For each pair of functions, show that the functions are inverses of one another.

29. $f(x) = x + 3$, $g(x) = x - 3$ **30.** $f(x) = 2x$, $g(x) = \frac{1}{2}x$ **31.** $f(x) = 0.1x$, $g(x) = 10x$

32. $f(x) = 4x + 5$, $g(x) = \frac{x-5}{4}$ **33.** $f(x) = 3x + 1$, $g(x) = \frac{x-1}{3}$

34. Use a Graphing Utility Let $f(x) = x^3 + 3x + 2$.
   a. Find $f^{-1}(x)$ algebraically if possible. If not possible, explain why.
   b. Use parametric mode on a graphing utility to graph this function. Let $X_{1T} = T$ and $Y_{1T} = T^3 + 3T + 2$. Let Tstep $= 0.05$ and set the ranges of **T**, **X**, and **Y** from -6 to 6. Make a sketch of the graph.
   c. To graph $f^{-1}(x)$, set $X_{2T} = T^3 + 3T + 2$ and $Y_{2T} = T$. Graph the function and make a sketch of the graph. Explain why these equations for X_{2T} and Y_{2T} give the graph of $f^{-1}(x)$.
   d. Use your graphs to find each of the following.
   i. $f^{-1}(6)$ **ii.** $f(-1.5)$ **iii.** $f^{-1}(-5.875)$

Use a graphing utility to graph each function and its inverse. Sketch copies of your graphs.

35. $f(x) = -x + 2$ **36.** $f(x) = 2x - 4$ **37.** $f(x) = 3x + 4$ **38.** $f(x) = x^3 + 5$

Find the inverse of each function.

39. $f(x) = x - 2$ **40.** $f(x) = -5x$ **41.** $f(x) = 3x + 7$

42. $f(x) = \frac{x-4}{6}$ **43.** $f(x) = \frac{2}{x}$ **44.** $f(x) = \sqrt[3]{x} + 2$

45. The density of gold is 19.3 g/cm³. Therefore, the mass (m) of a spherical piece of gold whose radius, in centimeters, is r is given by $m = 19.3\left(\frac{4}{3}\pi r^3\right)$.
   a. Solve this equation for r.
   b. Find the radius of a spherical piece of gold that weighs 20 g.

MORE MATH REASONING

46. Use a Graphing Utility A ball is thrown directly upward from an initial height of 20 m with an initial velocity of 15 m/sec.

    a. Write an equation modeling the height of the ball.

    b. Using parametric mode, graph the relation that gives time in terms of height. Sketch a copy of your graph. Is this relation a function? Explain.

    c. Using your graph, find the time(s), to the nearest tenth of a second, when:

        i. the height of the ball is 25 m   **ii.** the height of the ball is 15 m

        iii. the height of the ball is 5 m   **iv.** the ball hits the ground

47. Use a Graphing Utility Write a function of your choice. Use parametric mode to graph the function and its inverse. Then choose two points on your original function and find the slope between them. Do the same for the two corresponding points on the inverse. Repeat until you are confident of a pattern. What seems to be true about the slopes of these lines?

7-3 PART D Making Connections

← **CONNECT** → *You have learned to operate, compose, and find the inverses of functions.*

In 1901, German climatologist Wladimir Köppen proposed a system for classifying the world's climates. His system, which has become standard, establishes five types of climates.

A. Hot, humid climates

B. Dry climates

C. Humid climates with mild winters

D. Humid climates with cold winters

E. Cold climates

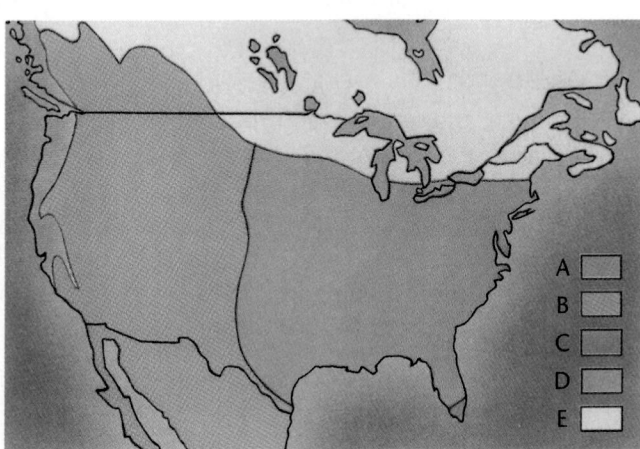

B (dry) climates are subdivided into *desert* (or *arid*) climates and *semiarid* climates. The *Köppen ratio*, $K = \dfrac{2tr - w}{4r}$, is used to distinguish between these two climates. It is a function of three variables: the mean annual temperature (t), the mean total annual rainfall (r), and the mean total rainfall for the months December–February (w).

In the Explore, you will use the Köppen ratio to classify the climate of Reno, Nevada.

EXPLORE: FROM NORDEN TO RENO

MATERIALS

Graph paper
Graphing utility (optional)

Reno, Nevada, is located at an elevation of 4500 feet and is 35 miles northeast of Norden, California, elevation 7200 feet. The table gives mean monthly precipitation and temperature figures for Norden. Reno's precipitation and temperature figures are closely related to those of Norden.

1. Temperature is a function of altitude. In general, temperature falls 3.3°F for each 1000 feet of elevation gain. Write a function that expresses the temperature at Reno as a function of the temperature in Norden.

2. Find the mean annual temperature for Norden. Explain how you found the figure. Then use the function you wrote above to estimate the average annual temperature for Reno.

Norden is located in California's Sierra Nevada mountains. Rain clouds moving eastward from the Pacific are cooled as they cross the mountains, causing them to drop most of their moisture. Norden, therefore, receives a great deal of rain.

Norden, California		
	Mean Precipitation (in.)	**Mean Temperature (°F)**
January	9.8	23
February	8.2	28
March	5.7	32
April	4.2	37
May	5.8	46
June	2.4	53
July	2.5	61
August	2.5	58
September	2.2	51
October	2.6	41
November	4.9	31
December	9.8	24

3. East of Norden lies the crest of the Sierras and *rain shadow* of the range. The farther east of the crest a region near the Sierras is, the more it lies in the rain shadow, and the less rain it receives. If P_N represents precipitation in Norden, the precipitation in a region in the Sierra rain shadow is approximately $(1.06^{-d})P_N$, where d is the distance from Norden in miles. Use this function to estimate the mean annual precipitation in Reno and the mean winter (December–February) precipitation for Reno. Explain how you found these figures.

4. Recall the Köppen ratio, $K = \frac{2tr - w}{4r}$. If $r < \frac{1}{2}K$, a dry climate is classified as a desert. If $\frac{1}{2}K \le r \le K$, a dry climate is classified as semiarid. (If $r > K$, a region does not have a dry climate.) Calculate K, the Köppen ratio for Reno. Use it to classify Reno's climate.

5. Did you use a composite function to find the Köppen classification for Reno? If so, explain how.

Climbing a tall mountain in the tropics may allow a traveler the opportunity to see climate types from all of the Köppen classifications. An ascent of Mount Kilimanjaro in Tanzania or a volcano in Ecuador begins in hot, humid jungle, ascends through a temperate region, and eventually reaches the polar climate of the summit.

REFLECT

1. Explain the difference between $(f \circ g)(x)$ and $(f \cdot g)(x)$.
2. The function $y = \sqrt[3]{x}$ is the inverse function for $y = x^3$. However, $y = \sqrt{x}$ is not the inverse function for $y = x^2$. Explain why this is the case.
3. What is the relationship between inverse functions and composition of functions?
4. Explain why the graphs of a function and its inverse are reflection images of each other over the line $y = x$.

Self-Assessment

Let $f(x) = 2x + 3$ and $g(x) = 5x - 3$. Find each value or expression.

1. $(f + g)(x)$ **2.** $(f + g)(-3)$ **3.** $(f - g)(x)$ **4.** $(f \cdot g)(x)$

5. $(f \cdot g)(-1)$ **6.** $(f \circ g)(x)$ **7.** $g(f(x))$ **8.** $(f \circ f)(-5)$

For each pair of functions, find $(m + n)(x)$, $(m - n)(x)$, and $(m \cdot n)(x)$.

9. $m(x) = 2x - 5$, $n(x) = x + 1$ **10.** $m(x) = 3x$, $n(x) = 2x^2 - 7$

11. $m(x) = x^2 - 7x + 1$, $n(x) = 2x^2 + 6$ **12.** $m(x) = x^3 + 2x + 6$, $n(x) = 2x^2 + 5x - 4$

13. For the years 1960−1990, U.S. energy consumption $C(t)$, in quadrillion Btu, and the domestic energy production $P(t)$, can be modeled by:

$$C(t) = 1.18t + 48.8 \qquad P(t) = 0.81t + 46.5,$$

where t is the year ($1960 = 0$).

a. According to this model, which is increasing more rapidly: production or consumption? Explain.

b. Using these functions, write a function that models the net energy imports for the United States during those years. Explain how you found this function.

c. Use your function to estimate net U.S. energy imports for each of the following years. Round answers to the nearest tenth.

i. 1960   **ii.** 1970   **iii.** 1980   **iv.** 1990

14. Use the expansion of $(0.5W + 0.5L)^3$ to determine the probability that a softball team playing a series of 3 games against an evenly matched opponent will win exactly two of the games. [6-2]

Solve each equation. [7-2]

15. $\sqrt{x-4}=7$

16. $\sqrt{4x-1}=x+2$

17. $x+5\sqrt{x}-14=0$

For each pair of functions, find $b(c(3))$ and $c(b(3))$.

18. $b(x)=2x-1$, $c(x)=x^2+4$

19. $b(x)=\frac{x}{3}+2$, $c(x)=4x$

20. $b(x)=x^2+1$, $c(x)=-x^2-1$

21. $b(x)=6x-2$, $c(x)=-3x^2+2x+1$

For each pair of functions, find $f(g(x))$ and $g(f(x))$.

22. $f(x)=3$, $g(x)=x+8$

23. $f(x)=6x-2$, $g(x)=\frac{x}{3}$

24. $f(x)=x-3$, $g(x)=x^2$

25. $f(x)=5x$, $g(x)=\frac{x+5}{10}$

26. The surface area (S) of a sphere equals 4π times the radius (r) squared.
   a. Write an expression for the surface area as a function of the radius.
   b. Write an expression for the radius as a function of the diameter (d).
   c. Write and simplify an expression for the surface area as a function of the diameter.

27. Is the relation $\{(3,-1),(2,-1),(1,3)\}$ a function? Is its inverse relation a function? Explain.

For each pair of functions, show algebraically and graphically that the functions are inverses of one another.

28. $f(x)=x-5$, $g(x)=x+5$

29. $f(x)=2x+4$, $g(x)=\frac{1}{2}x-2$

Find the inverse of each function.

30. $f(x)=0.25x$

31. $f(x)=-3x+12$

32. $f(x)=8x^3$

33. $f(x)=\frac{2x-3}{5}$

34. If $f(x)=2x$ and $g(x)=\frac{x}{4}$, then $\frac{x}{2}=$
   I. $f^{-1}(x)$

   II. $f(g(x))$

   III. $g(f(x))$

   (a) only I
   (b) only II
   (c) I and II
   (d) I and III
   (e) I, II, and III

35. Family admission to a benefit concert is $4 per family member plus a $5 charity donation for each family.
   a. Write a function that expresses $f(x)$, the total admission charge, in terms of x, the number of family members.
   b. Find $f^{-1}(x)$. What does the function represent?
   c. Write a problem you can solve using the inverse function. Solve the problem.

36. Suppose you have graphs of $f(x)$ and $g(x)$ as shown. Sketch graphs of each of the following. Explain how you made your sketches.
   a. the graph of $(f+g)(x)$
   b. the graph of $f^{-1}(x)$
   c. the graph of $g^{-1}(x)$

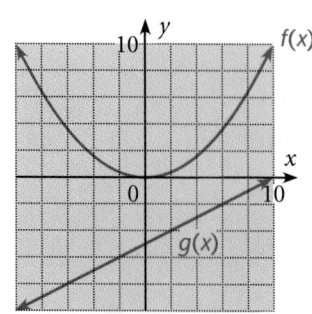

Chapter 7 Review

In Chapter 7, you worked with different types of variation that relate two or more variables; you explored roots and exponents, including negative, rational, and decimal exponents; and you investigated different ways to combine functions. With these concepts, you extended your ability to model complex real-world situations.

KEY TERMS

base [7-1]
combined variation [7-1]
composite function [7-3]
exponent [7-1]
exponential notation [7-1]
extraneous solution [7-2]
index [7-2]

inverse function/relation [7-3]
inverse variation [7-1]
joint variation [7-1]
point symmetry [7-1]
power [7-1]
power regression [7-2]

quadratic form [7-2]
radical equation [7-2]
radicand [7-2]
rectangular hyperbola [7-1]
relation [7-3]
scientific notation [7-1]

Write the word or phrase that correctly completes each statement.

1. When the quotient of two variables is a constant, the quantities vary ____.

2. A(n) ____ is sometimes produced when both sides of an equation are raised to a power.

CONCEPTS AND APPLICATIONS

3. Classify each equation as direct, inverse, or joint variation. [7-1]

    a. $y = kx$ **b.** $y = \dfrac{kx}{z}$ **c.** $y = \dfrac{3z}{kx}$ **d.** $xy = k + 4$

4. a. Graph $y = x^3$ and $y = x^7$ on the same set of coordinate axes. [7-1]
    b. Describe how the graphs differ. What points do they have in common?

Simplify. Write each answer with positive exponents. [7-1]

5. $x^5 \cdot x^{-8}$ **6.** $(w^{-4}y^3)(5w^{-6}y^{-3})$ **7.** $\sqrt[4]{64a^8b^{12}}$ **8.** $\dfrac{8a^5b^3}{-4a^8b^2}$

9. The sound of thunder travels about 1100 feet per second. [7-1]
    a. If it takes 10 seconds for the sound to reach you after you see the flash, how far away is the lightning? Write your answer in scientific notation.
    b. Light moves at a speed of about 186,000 miles per second. How much faster does light move than sound? Write your answer in scientific notation.

Evaluate each expression. Round answers to the nearest hundredth. [7-2]

10. $64^{\frac{2}{3}}$ **11.** $16^{-\frac{3}{2}}$ **12.** $32^{2.2}$ **13.** $14,641^{1.7}$

If the expression has a fractional exponent, rewrite it using a radical. If the expression has a radical, rewrite it using exponents. [7-2]

14. $x^{\frac{3}{2}} \cdot x^{\frac{5}{4}}$ **15.** $\sqrt[3]{4^4} \cdot \sqrt[6]{2^5}$ **16.** $\left(\sqrt[5]{6x^2y^3} \right)^8$ **17.** $\dfrac{\sqrt[3]{729}}{\sqrt[3]{64}}$

Solve each equation. [7-2]

18. $\sqrt{5x - 2} = 4$ **19.** $\sqrt{x + 3} = \sqrt{2x - 5}$

20. $x - 2\sqrt{x} + 1 = 0$ **21.** $\sqrt{6x + 12} - \sqrt{4x + 9} = 1$

Let $f(x) = 3x + 2$ and $g(x) = 6 - 5x$. Find each value or expression. [7-3]

22. $(f + g)(8)$ **23.** $(f \cdot g)(x)$ **24.** $g(f(-1))$ **25.** $f(g(x))$

26. $(g \circ f)(x)$ **27.** $f^{-1}(x)$ **28.** $g^{-1}(x)$ **29.** $g(g^{-1}(x))$

30. As a clothing store manager, it is your responsibility to price items that are received in your store. [7-3]

    a. If items are usually priced 50% higher than your cost, write a function that represents the price you normally charge for an item.

    b. A sale advertises 30% off the regular price. Write a function to represent the sale price of an item.

    c. Write a function that shows the sale price of an item if x represents the cost to your store.

CONCEPTS AND CONNECTIONS

31. Physics When electricity flows, the substance it passes through resists the electrical current to some extent and generates power. The power (W), in watts, varies directly with the square of the voltage (V), in volts, across the resistance and inversely with the resistance (R), in ohms.

    a. A light bulb with a 192-ohm resistance uses 100 watts of power when on a 120-volt line. Write the variation equation and solve for the constant of variation.

    b. Solve your equation from **a** for W.

    c. Suppose the bulb in **a** is replaced by one with a higher resistance. Is the power generated by the new bulb higher or lower if the voltage is the same? Explain.

    d. If the resistance of the bulb in **c** is 240 ohms, what is the power used by this bulb?

SELF-EVALUATION

Write a summary of what you learned in this chapter. Explain how the concepts explored in this chapter can help you understand relationships that exist in the real world. Which techniques discussed in this chapter were confusing for you? Explain how you can connect these techniques to concepts that you have already learned so that they will be easier to remember.

Chapter 7 Assessment

TEST

1. The volume of a right circular cone varies jointly with the square of the radius and the height. If the volume of a cone with height 4 and radius 3 is approximately 37.7, what is the approximate volume of a cone with height 8 and radius 6?

2. **a.** Graph $y = x^2$ and $y = x^5$ on the same set of coordinate axes.
   b. Describe how the graphs differ. What points do they have in common?

Simplify. Write each answer with positive exponents.

3. $\left(y^{\frac{3}{2}}\right)^{-4}$

4. $(8x^{-3}y^{-5})(x^4y^{-6})$

5. $\dfrac{-45r^3s^{10}}{9rs^{15}}$

6. The *covalent atomic radius* of oxygen is 6.6×10^{-9} m. Use the formula $V = \frac{4}{3}\pi r^3$ to find the volume of a sphere with this radius.

Evaluate each expression. Round answers to the nearest hundredth.

7. $4^{-\frac{5}{2}}$

8. $64^{\frac{3}{2}}$

9. $3^{1.25}$

10. $64^{-0.33}$

Simplify. If the expression has a fractional exponent, rewrite it using a radical. If it has a radical, rewrite it using exponents.

11. $x^{\frac{2}{3}} \cdot x^{\frac{2}{3}}$

12. $(y^3)^{\frac{4}{5}}$

13. $\sqrt[3]{5^2}$

14. $\left(\sqrt[5]{3x^2y^3}\right)^4$

Solve each equation.

15. $3 + \sqrt{7x} = 10$

16. $\sqrt{x-3} = 3\sqrt{x+12}$

17. $x + 2\sqrt{x} = 3$

18. $\sqrt{x+20} - \sqrt{x} = 2$

Let $f(x) = 2x$ and $g(x) = x^3 + 3$. Find each value or expression. [7-3]

19. $(f - g)(3)$

20. $(f \cdot g)(x)$

21. $g(f(x))$

22. $g^{-1}(x)$

23. **Feed the Dog** A dog food manufacturer has determined by data analysis that dog weight (w), in pounds, and ideal feeding amount (c), in cups, are related by the equation $w = 4.647c^{1.756}$.
    a. Solve this equation for c.
    b. Use your answer to estimate the ideal feeding amount for:
      i. a 4-lb Chihuahua   **ii.** a 40-lb Australian Shepherd   **iii.** a 130-lb Great Dane

PERFORMANCE TASK

Collect numerical data on two quantities of your choice that you think may be related. Choose a dependent and independent variable and make a scatter plot of your data.

Use linear regression and power regression to model the data. Decide which of these two models seems to fit the data more closely and explain why. Finally, solve the equation that you feel is the better model for the dependent variable. In which forms do you think the equation is most useful? Explain your choice.

Chapter 8

Polynomials and Polynomial Functions

Project A
Building Boxes
What things need to be considered when determining the size and material of a box?

Project B
"I Think, Therefore I Am."
Who was Descartes and why did he say this?

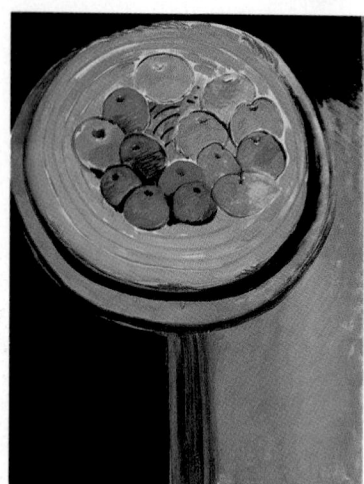

Project C
It's an Odd Thing to Be Even
How does an artist use the principles of even and odd functions?

In high school, math was straightforward and made perfect sense to me, but I had no idea how I would use the math I was learning.

Today, my math education enables me to use numbers to see patterns of human behavior. I am proud of my ability to do research in behavioral and social science areas. For example, we examine health care quality issues from the patient's perspective and track quality changes over time.

Julie Ballou Swaroff
Industrial Organizational
Psychologist
Gallup Organization
Lincoln, Nebraska

8-1
Polynomial Functions and Their Graphs

In 8-1 you will investigate polynomial functions other than linear and quadratic functions. You will use the following algebra skills.

Graph each of the following and state the maximum or minimum value of y. [Previous course]

1. $y = x^2$

2. $y = -x^2 - 1$

3. $y = (x - 3)^2$

4. $y = x^2 - 13x + 42$

Factor completely. [Previous course]

5. $x^2 - 5x - 84$ **6.** $2x^2 + 9x - 18$ **7.** $x^3 - 2x^2 - 15x$ **8.** $x^4 - 29x^2 + 100$

8-2
The Fundamental Theorem of Algebra

In 8-2 you will solve polynomial equations by factoring. You will use the following skills.

Graph each equation and estimate x when y = 5. [Previous course]

9. $y = x^2 - 4$ **10.** $y = x^2 - 4x + 3$ **11.** $y = x^2 + 5x + 6$

Solve over the complex numbers. If necessary, first factor completely. [Previous course]

12. $(x + 3)(x - 5)(x + 11) = 0$ **13.** $m(2m - 5)(m + 7) = 0$

14. $(x - i)(x + i) = 0$ **15.** $x^2 + 13x + 40 = 0$

16. $x^2 = 12x$ **17.** $x^2 + 9 = 0$

Evaluate each of the following if P(x) = x³ + 3x² - 2x - 4. [Previous course]
18. $P(0)$ **19.** $P(100)$ **20.** $P(1)$ **21.** $P(-1)$ **22.** $P(-100)$

8-3
Rational Expressions and Functions

In 8-3 you will investigate the characteristics of rational expressions and functions. You will use the same skills necessary to work with fractions.

Evaluate.

23. $\dfrac{5}{8} + \dfrac{5}{6}$ **24.** $\dfrac{7}{12} - \dfrac{4}{9}$ **25.** $\dfrac{24}{36} \cdot \dfrac{108}{48}$ **26.** $\dfrac{54}{60} \div \dfrac{27}{100}$

Find the products. [Previous course]
27. $(3i)(4i)$ **28.** $(2 + 3i)(2 - 3i)$ **29.** $4i(i - 2)$ **30.** $(5 + 3i)(6 - i)$

Factor completely over the complex numbers.
31. $36x^2 - 25$ **32.** $x^2 + 21x + 80$ **33.** $2x^2 - x - 3$

The Not-So-Lowly Aluminum Can

When you reach for a can of juice or soda, you probably don't give a second thought to the container. After all, many of us drink from aluminum cans every day. But the aluminum beverage can has gone high tech. The United States alone produces 100 *billion* beverage cans per year, so there's quite an incentive to keep improving the cans.

Designers enlist the best modeling techniques, as they continue to make cans lighter to conserve aluminum. At the same time, cans must support 250 pounds and withstand more than 90 pounds per square inch of internal pressure.

The designers of the models consider how the volume of a can relates to a given surface area, how cans are formed, and how the shape distributes stress. They also consider aesthetics and usability. They work to minimize the size of the lid, which by itself makes up nearly 25 percent of the can's weight.

These models exemplify many kinds of functions. Quadratic functions represent surface area. Cubic functions represent volume. Other parts of the models may contain terms such as $3x^4$ or $7x^5$. And yet these are some of the simplest models involved in the manufacture of aluminum cans.

The next time you reach for a cold soda, take a moment to consider the (not-so-lowly) aluminum can.

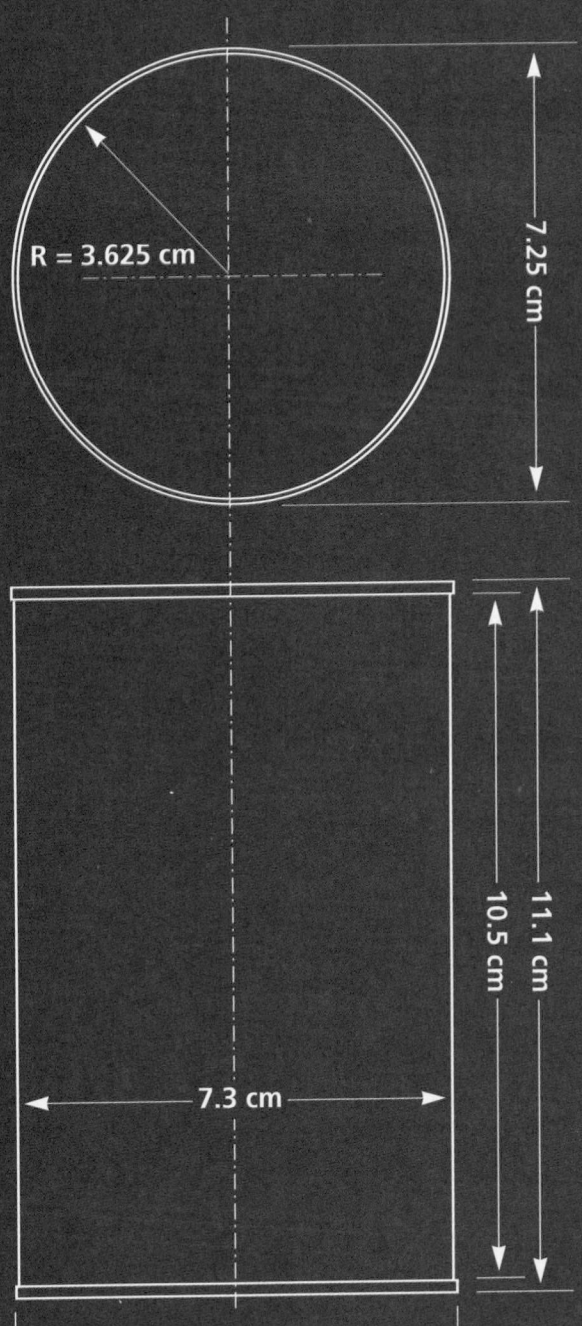

1. Describe some other factors that designers of models for aluminum cans might have to consider.
2. Why do you think the top of a soda can is designed to be narrower than the body of the can?
3. Why do you think the bottom of a soda can is bowed inward?
4. In any expression for volume, what exponent is used to describe the measurement units?

Graphing Polynomial Functions

← CONNECT →
You have already worked with polynomial expressions and you have graphed quadratic functions, which are one type of polynomial function. You will now explore other polynomial functions and their characteristics.

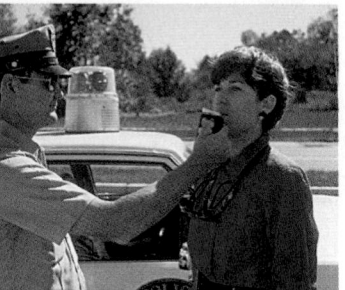

When you model the volume of an aluminum can or anything else, you find yourself working with expressions involving the exponent "3." Likewise in engineering, business, economics, science, or medicine, you encounter models involving the third, fourth, or higher powers of a variable.

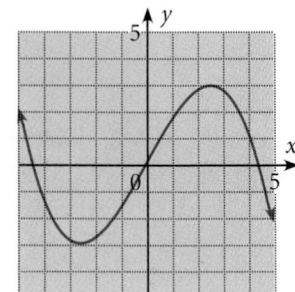

The function $a(x) = -0.0915x^3 + 1.771x$ models the approximate alcohol concentration, in hundredths of a percent, in an average person's bloodstream x hours after one drink.

By looking at the graph of this function, you have a visual sense of how quickly the alcohol enters the bloodstream and is metabolized.

You know that the expression $5x^2 + 4x + \sqrt{2}$ contains the *terms* $5x^2$, $4x$, and $\sqrt{2}$. You are experienced at dealing with *monomials*, which have one term; *binomials*, which have two terms; and *trinomials*, which have three terms. These are a few examples of *polynomials*.

A **polynomial** in x is any expression of the form

$$a_n x^n + a_{n-1}x^{n-1} + \cdots + a_1 x + a_0,$$

where n is a nonnegative integer and the coefficients $a_0, \dots, a_n$ are complex numbers.

The **degree of the polynomial** with one variable is the greatest exponent of the variable that appears in any term. The coefficient of the term with the greatest exponent is the **leading coefficient,** and the **constant term** is the term that is not multiplied by a variable.

The polynomial $-2x^4 + 7x^3 - x + 4$ has degree 4.

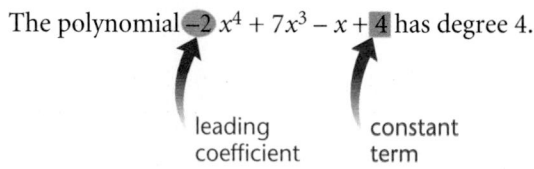

leading
coefficient

constant
term

For any polynomial expression, you can write the corresponding **polynomial function,** such as $f(x) = -2x^4 + 7x^3 - x + 4$ or $y = -2x^4 + 7x^3 - x + 4$.

You've looked at the graphs of first-degree and second-degree polynomial functions. Let's explore the graphs of polynomial functions with higher degrees.

EXPLORE: FUNCTIONAL GRAPHS

MATERIALS

Graphing utility
Graph paper

1. Graph the third-degree polynomial functions listed below. Make a sketch of each graph on graph paper and label your sketch with the equation. Use the graphing utility settings shown.

$y = x^3$ $y = x^3 - 4x - 1$

$y = x^3 - 2x^2 - x - 2$ $y = 4x - 2x^3$

$y = x^3 - 3x + 2$ $y = -x^3$

$y = 2x^3 - x + 2$ $y = -x^3 + 2x^2 + 3x + 1$

a. How are these graphs alike? How are they different? Make up and graph your own third-degree polynomial functions. Does the shape of the graph resemble any you have already seen?

b. How are the graphs with positive leading coefficients different from the graphs with negative leading coefficients? Explain how you can tell from the graph of a third-degree equation whether the leading coefficient is positive or negative.

2. Graph the fourth-degree polynomial functions listed. You may need to modify the graphing utility range settings of x and y to see the shape of each graph. Make a sketch of each graph, and label each with the equation. Describe the similarities and differences in these graphs.

$y = x^4$ $y = x^4 - 5x^2 + 4$

$y = -x^4$ $y = -x^4 + 3x^3 + x^2 - 3x - 3$

$y = x^4 - 3x^3 - x^2 + 3x + 3$ $y = -x^4 + 5x^2 - 4$

3. How can you determine from the graph whether the degree of the polynomial is 3 or 4?

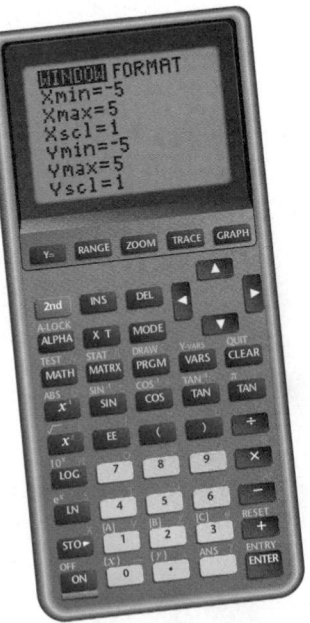

Several types of polynomial functions have names, some of which are familiar to you.

A polynomial function of degree zero is called a *constant* function.

A polynomial function of degree one is called a *linear* function.

A polynomial function of degree two is called a *quadratic* function.

A polynomial function of degree three is called a **cubic** function.

A polynomial function of degree four is called a **quartic** function.

Polynomial functions with higher degrees are named by their degree. For example, $y = x^7 + 5x^3 + 4x^2$ is a seventh-degree polynomial function.

Identify the degree of each function by name.

a. $f(x) = x^3 - 4x + 8$
b. $f(x) = 6 + 5x + 3x^2 - x^4$
c. $f(x) = x^5 + x^3 - 4x^2$

The terms of a polynomial are often listed in **descending order,** such as in Try It **a** and **c.** The term with the greatest exponent for x is listed first, the term with the next greatest exponent second, and so on, with the constant term last.

In many situations, the domain of any polynomial function is the set of real numbers, though you may have to restrict the domain to make sense for a given application.

EXAMPLE

When a person takes medication, the medicine becomes effective as it enters the bloodstream. It can be useful to know just how much medicine is in the bloodstream at different times.

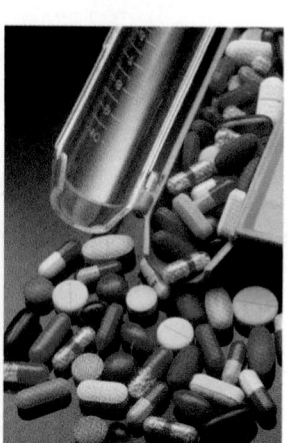

Karen is a volunteer in a drug-testing program at a pharmaceutical company. The function $A(x) = -0.015x^3 + 1.058x$ approximates the amount of a new medicine (in tenths of a percent) in Karen's bloodstream x hours after the medicine is taken. For what values of x does the graph make sense?

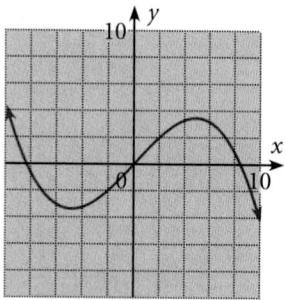

The graph of $A(x)$ is shown. Since time cannot be negative, negative values of x do not make sense. Medication concentration can't be negative either, so values of x greater than 8 do not make sense. Therefore, the situation only makes sense for values from $x = 0$ to about $x = 8$.

If you can work with polynomial expressions and quadratic functions, graphing polynomial functions of degree greater than two becomes fairly easy.

REFLECT

1. How can you determine the degree of a function from its equation?
2. How does the leading coefficient of a polynomial function affect the graph of the function?
3. Why is it sometimes necessary to restrict the domain of a polynomial function when using it to model a real-world situation? Give an example.
4. How are the graphs of linear and cubic functions similar? How are the graphs of quadratic and quartic functions similar?

Exercises

CORE

1. Getting Started Use the polynomial function $P(x) = 6 - 2x + 3x^2 - 4x^3 - 7x^5$.
  a. What is the leading coefficient?   **b.** What is the degree of this function?
  c. Identify the constant term.   **d.** How many terms does this polynomial have?

2. Match each term with its corresponding example.
  a. constant function   ~~|~~
  b. cubic function   3
  c. linear function   2
  d. quadratic function   3
  e. quartic function   4

  i. $f(x) = x^2 + 7$
  ii. $f(x) = 2x - 8$
  iii. $f(x) = 20$
  iv. $f(x) = 4x^3 + 8x^2 - 3x$
  v. $f(x) = x^4 + x - 9$

Match each function with its graph. Explain your choice.

3. $f(x) = -3x^2 + 8x - 4$

4. $f(x) = -x^4 + x^3 + 4x^2 + 2x - 1$

5. $f(x) = -2x^3 - 3x^2 + 7$

6. $f(x) = 4x - 5$

7. $f(x) = 2x^4 - 2x^3 - 5x^2 + 7x - 2$

8. $f(x) = x^3 - 4x^2 - 3x + 2$

A.

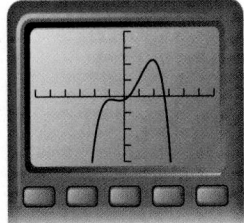

B.

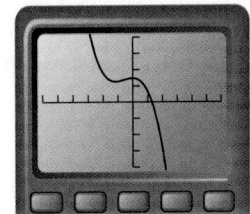

C.

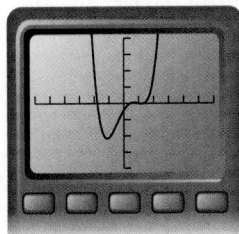

D.

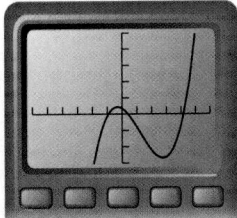

E.

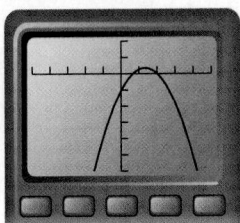

F.

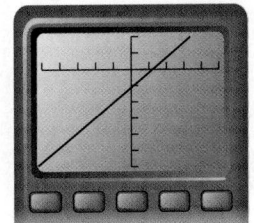

9. Martin must receive an injection to combat his illness. The function $A(x) = -0.0125x^3 + 1.052x$, shown on the graph, approximates the amount of medicine (in tenths of a percent) in his bloodstream x hours after the solution is initially given. For what values of x does the graph make sense? Explain.

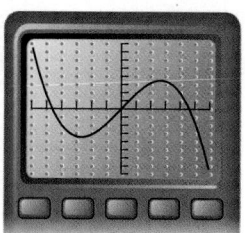

Xmin = –12
Xmax = 12
Xscl = 2
Ymin = –8
Ymax = 8
Yscl = 1

For each pair of polynomial functions, find $(P + A)(x)$ and $(P - A)(x)$.

10. $P(x) = -x^4 - 13x^3 + 2x^2 + 16x - 1$, $A(x) = x^6 - 17x^3 + 6x^2 - 10x + 8$

11. $P(x) = x^5 + x^4 - 5x^2 + x - 21$, $A(x) = x^5 - 9x^3 + 2x^2 + 4x - 5$

12. $P(x) = -3x^3 - 4$, $A(x) = x^5 - 2x^4 - x^3 + 4$

13. Kerry modeled the cost to operate her car at different speeds. The polynomial function $C(s) = 0.002s^2 - 0.21s + 15$ approximates her cost, in cents per mile, as a function of her speed (s), in miles per hour.

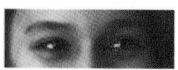

Problem-Solving Tip

Draw a graph if necessary.

  a. How much does it cost Kerry to operate her car at 30 miles per hour? 50 miles per hour? 65 miles per hour?
  b. Would Kerry save more if she takes a 100-mile trip averaging 30 miles per hour, or averaging 65 miles per hour? Are there other considerations besides cost that Kerry might need to consider? Explain.

Simplify each polynomial, and determine the leading coefficient and degree of the polynomial function.

14. $f(x) = (x - 3)^2 + 5$

15. $g(x) = (x - 3)(x + 3)(x - 4)$

16. $h(x) = x(2x - 1)(4x + 3)$

17. $m(x) = -4(x^2 + 5)(x^2 - 5)$

18. Recently the tax (T) for a married person filing jointly was $5,370 plus 28% of the difference between the taxable income (x) and $35,800.
  a. Write a polynomial function for $T(x)$.
  b. What is the degree of this polynomial function?
  c. Find the amount of tax paid if a married person had a taxable income of $48,000.

LOOK AHEAD

Determine the point(s) where each graph crosses (a) the x-axis, and (b) the y-axis.

19.

Xmin = –5
Xmax = 5
Xscl = 1
Ymin = –5
Ymax = 5
Yscl = 1

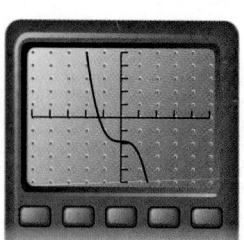

20.

Xmin = –5
Xmax = 5
Xscl = 1
Ymin = –16
Ymax = 6
Yscl = 2

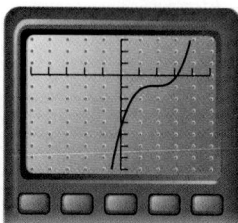

21.

Xmin = –5
Xmax = 5
Xscl = 1
Ymin = –5
Ymax = 5
Yscl = 1

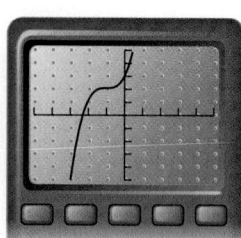

MORE PRACTICE

22. Use the polynomial function $P(x) = -7x + 3x^7 - 4x^3 + 6x^5 + 11$.
   a. What is the leading coefficient?
   b. What is the degree of this function?
   c. Identify the constant term.

Match each function with its graph. Explain your choice.

23. $f(x) = 9x^3 - 4 + x^2$

24. $f(x) = 0.4x^2 - x + 3$

25. $f(x) = x^4 - 4x^3 + x^2 - 6$

26. $f(x) = -3x^3 - 8x^2 - x + 1$

27. $f(x) = 8 - x$

28. $f(x) = -x^4 - 4x^3 + x^2 + 6x - 2$

A.

B.

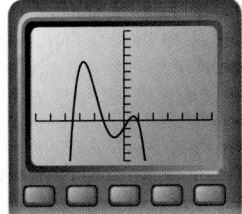

C.

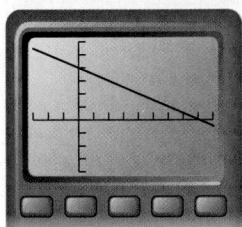

D.

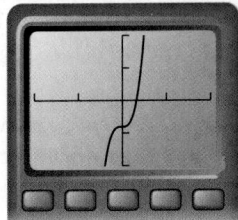

E.

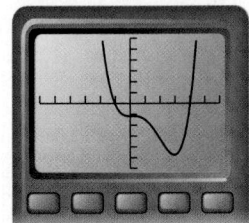

F.

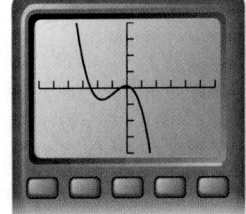

For each pair of polynomial functions, find $(P + A)(x)$ and $(P - A)(x)$.

29. $P(x) = x^4 - 22x^3 + 5x^2 + 16x - 7$, $A(x) = -x^6 - 15x^3 - 3x^2 - 4x + 12$

30. $P(x) = -x^5 + x^4 - 7x^3 + x + 24$, $A(x) = x^5 - 4x^3 + 6x^2 - 3x - 10$

31. $P(x) = x^6 + 3x^5 - 6x^2 + x - 4$, $A(x) = -x^6 + 4x^4 + 5x^3 - x^2 + x + 8$

Use a Graphing Utility Graph each function. Sketch the general shape of each function on graph paper and indicate the window setting that you used to see the shape of each graph.

32. $y = x^3 - 3x^2 - 4x$

33. $y = x^4 + 4x^3 - x^2 - 6x - 10$

34. $y = -2x^5 - 15x^4 + 8x^3 + x^2$

35. $y = -3x^3 - x^2 + 11x - 7$

MORE MATH REASONING

36. Use a Graphing Utility Graph each function. You may need to experiment with the window settings to see the shape of the graph. *Trace* each to determine what happens to the y-values at the ends of each graph, as x increases or decreases. Is there a relationship between this behavior and the sign of the leading coefficient of each function? Explain.

a. $y_1 = -x^3 + 4x^2 - 6x + 3$ **b.** $y_2 = -x^3 + x^2 - x + 1$

c. $y_3 = x^3 - 5x^2 - 10x + 6$ **d.** $y_4 = 6x^3 - 3x^2 + 1$

37. Use a Graphing Utility If the solid shown is built from four cubes, each with a side length of x, write a polynomial $V(x)$ that represents its volume and another polynomial $A(x)$ that represents its surface area.

Find the volume and surface area for a cube of side length 1.5 cm. Graph these two functions to check your result. What does your graph tell you about the volume of a solid compared to its surface area, as the sides of the solid become larger or smaller?

8-1
PART B   Maximums and Minimums

← **CONNECT** →   *You've analyzed the graphs of quadratic functions to easily find maximum and minimum values and other information. Now you will investigate maximums and minimums of graphs of polynomial functions with degrees greater than two.*

As with linear and quadratic functions, you can substitute values into polynomial functions, make a table, and plot a graph. For example, the function $f(x) = 2x^4 + 4x^3 - 4x^2 - 6x + 1$ takes on the values shown for the given values of x.

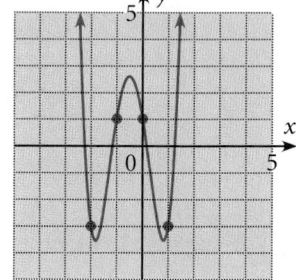

x	-3	-2	-1	0	1	2
$f(x)$	37	-3	1	1	-3	37

The graph is a smooth curve. Like the graphs of all polynomial functions, it is **continuous**—if you traced along the graph with a pencil, you would never have to lift the pencil.

Notice, however, that the points plotted have missed much of the information about the curve, such as where the peaks and valleys are located.

You will learn ways to predict the general shapes of graphs of polynomial functions of degree greater than two. But the complexities of such graphs will often force you to rely on graphing technology to picture the graphs.

EXPLORE: ALL BOXED IN

MATERIALS

Graph paper
Graphing utility

1. Following the instructions below, make a box out of an $8\frac{1}{2}$" × 11" sheet of graph paper. Before you begin, plan your strategy carefully so that your box has the largest possible volume.

  a. Cut a square out of each of the four corners of the sheet of paper.

  b. Fold up the edges to form the sides of the box.

2. Compare your box with those of your classmates and estimate which box has the largest volume.

3. Determine the volume of your box. Then compare this computed volume with those of other boxes. Did you estimate correctly?

4. Write a function $V(x)$ for the volume of the box, letting x be the length in inches of each side of the squares that are cut out.

5. Graph your volume function $V(x)$ on a graphing utility. What values of x make sense for this problem?

6. *Trace* along the graph to determine the value of x that gives you the largest value for y. Since y is the same as $V(x)$, this is the largest possible volume. What are the dimensions, to the nearest tenth of an inch, of the box with the largest possible volume?

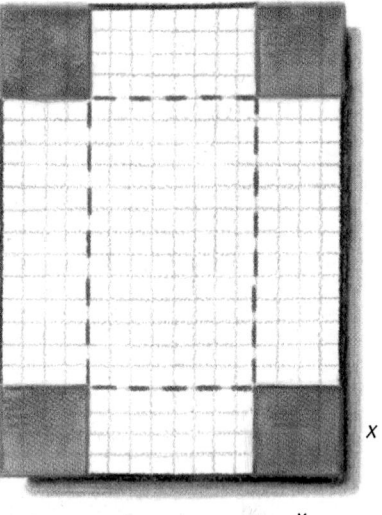

x

x

Quadratic functions have exactly one maximum or minimum value. With cubics, quartics, and higher-degree polynomial functions, it isn't as simple.

Cubic functions have neither a maximum nor a minimum, but they may have *relative maximum* or *relative minimum* values in certain intervals.

There is no maximum for the function $y = x^3 - 3x^2 - 6x + 2$ because *y increases without bound* as x increases.

Likewise, there is no minimum value since *y decreases without bound* as x decreases.

However, in the interval from $x = -2$ to $x = 1$, the maximum value for y is about 4.4. This is called a *relative maximum*.

There is also a *relative minimum* value of about -16.4 in the interval from $x = 1$ to $x = 5$.

Cubic Function

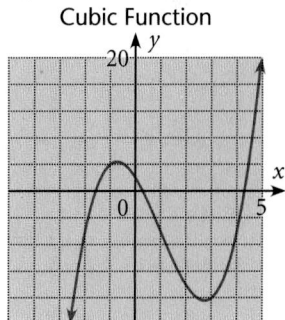

Quartic functions have *either* a maximum *or* a minimum value. They can also have other relative maximum and/or minimum values within intervals.

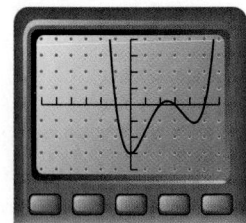

Quartic Function

The function $y = x^4 - 9x^3 + 21x^2 + x - 30$ has a minimum y-value at $x \approx 0$. The minimum y-value is about -30.

This function does not have a maximum value. However, in the interval from $x = 1$ to $x = 4$, there is a relative maximum of $y \approx 2$.

CONSIDER

?

1. Can you tell whether the graph of the function $-3x^4 + 2x^3 + 3x - 5$ has a maximum or a minimum without graphing the function? Explain your answer.

An **absolute maximum** is the largest y-value of the function.
A **relative maximum** is the largest y-value within a specified interval.

An **absolute minimum** is the smallest y-value of the function.
A **relative minimum** is the smallest y-value within a specified interval.

EXAMPLES

1. The graph of $y = x^5 + 3x^4 - 11x^3 - 27x^2 + 10x + 24$ is shown with lettered "points of interest."

a. Does this function have an absolute maximum? an absolute minimum?

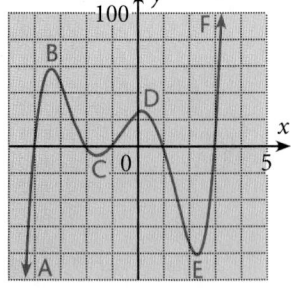

Since the y-value increases without bound as the x-value increases (F), there is no absolute maximum.

Likewise, the y-value decreases without bound as the x-value decreases (A). So there is no absolute minimum.

b. Identify relative maximums and relative minimums, and indicate an appropriate interval for each.

There is a relative maximum value of y at B between $x = -2$ and $x = -4$. If you have a graphing utility, you can use the TRACE key to approximate this relative maximum value for y, which is $y \approx 55.5$. The relative maximum, 55.5, occurs when $x \approx -3.2$.

Xmin = –6
Xmax = 6
Xscl = 1
Ymin = –100
Ymax = 100
Yscl = 25

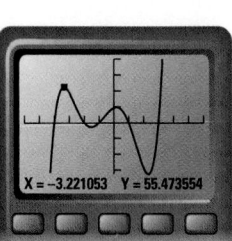

X = –3.221053   Y = 55.473554

There is also a relative maximum value of y at D between $x = -1$ and $x = 1$. There are relative minimum values of y at E between $x = 1$ and $x = 3$ and at C between $x = -2$ and $x = -1$.

2. Psychologists often study how long it takes a subject to learn a task. The data collected is then modeled by a *learning curve,* which indicates the percentage of a task mastered in a certain time.

For example, a manufacturer has determined that, for the first five days, trainees learn to assemble parts according to the learning curve $f(t) = -0.2t^3 + t^2 + 1.2t + 0.1$, where t is the time in days and f measures the percentage of the assembly task learned on day t. Graph the function and use the graph to determine on which day trainees learn the most.

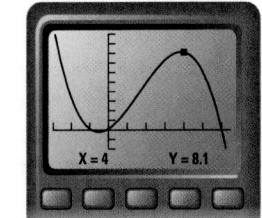

The maximum y-value, which is the same as $f(t)$, occurs just before $x = 4$, where $y = 8.1$. So trainees learn the most on the fourth day, when they learn 8.1% of the task.

TRY IT

The graph of $y = x^5 + x^4 - 13x^3 - 13x^2 + 36x + 36$ is shown.

a. Does this function have an absolute maximum? an absolute minimum?

b. Identify relative maximums and relative minimums, and indicate an interval for each.

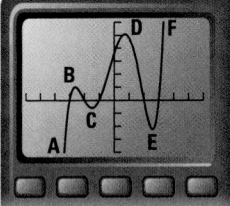

```
Xmin = -6
Xmax = 6
Xscl = 1
Ymin = -40
Ymax = 60
Yscl = 10
```

c. Use the TRACE key on a graphing utility to find the maximum value of the function in Example 1 between $x = -1$ and $x = 2$.

d. Use the TRACE key to find the minimum value of the function in Example 1 between $x = 2$ and $x = 3$.

Finding maximum and minimum values is the key to optimizing quantities in real situations, such as maximizing profits and minimizing production times.

REFLECT

1. Describe how you decide if a function has an absolute maximum or minimum.

2. How do you locate relative maximums on a graph? relative minimums?

3. Are the absolute maximums or minimums usually the most important values for a real-world situation? Explain.

Exercises

CORE

1. **Getting Started** Use the graph of the function $y = x^5 - 2x^4 - 10x^3 + 20x^2 + 9x - 18$.
   a. Does this function have an absolute maximum? If so, what is it?
   b. Does this function have an absolute minimum? If so, what is it?
   c. Which letter corresponds to the relative minimum in the interval from $x = 2$ to $x = 3$?
   d. Which letter corresponds to the relative maximum in the interval from $x = -3$ to $x = 1$?

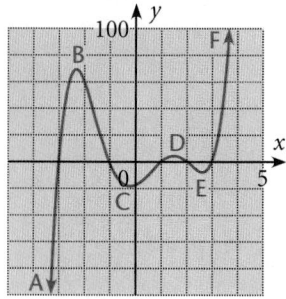

Write the word or phrase that best completes each statement.

2. A(n) _____ is the largest y-value of the function.

3. A(n) _____ is the smallest y-value of the function.

Match each function with its corresponding graph. Explain your choice.

4. $f(x) = x^3 + 8$ 5. $f(x) = x^4 + 8$ 6. $f(x) = x^3 + 4$ 7. $f(x) = x^4 + 4$

A. Xmin = –3
Xmax = 3
Xscl = 1
Ymin = –2
Ymax = 18
Yscl = 1

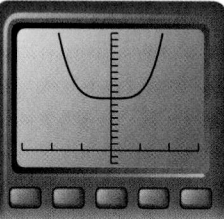

B. Xmin = –3
Xmax = 3
Xscl = 1
Ymin = –2
Ymax = 18
Yscl = 1

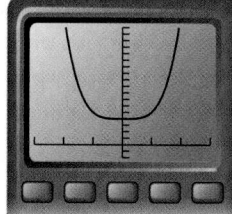

C. Xmin = –3
Xmax = 3
Xscl = 1
Ymin = –6
Ymax = 14
Yscl = 1

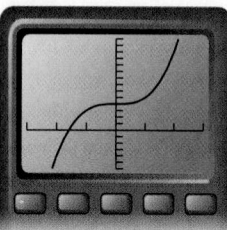

D. Xmin = –3
Xmax = 3
Xscl = 1
Ymin = –6
Ymax = 14
Yscl = 1

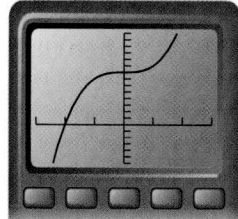

8. A pencil box is to be constructed out of a square sheet of cardboard by cutting out four squares of equal size at the corners and folding up the sides. The cardboard is 12 in. by 12 in.
   a. Write a polynomial function $f(x)$ for the volume of the pencil box.
   b. Graph the function.
   c. Determine what domain is reasonable for this situation.
   d. Use the graph to determine what size the square cutout should be in order to make a box that has the greatest volume. (Hint: Find the value of x for the largest volume.)

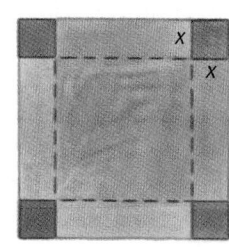

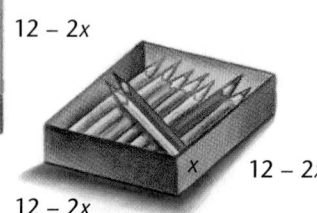

For each function, (a) identify an absolute maximum or minimum if one or both exist, and (b) approximate the y-values at A, B, and C. Identify each point as a relative maximum or a relative minimum, and indicate an interval for each.

9.

Xmin = –6
Xmax = 6
Xscl = 1
Ymin = –35
Ymax = 10
Yscl = 5

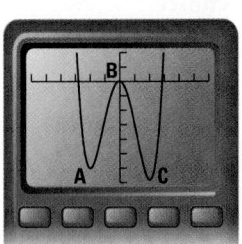

10.

Xmin = –4
Xmax = 4
Xscl = 1
Ymin = –4
Ymax = 4
Yscl = 1

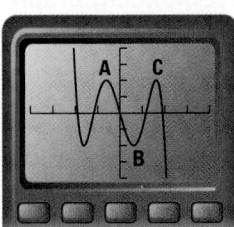

11.

Xmin = –6
Xmax = 6
Xscl = 1
Ymin = –5
Ymax = 50
Yscl = 5

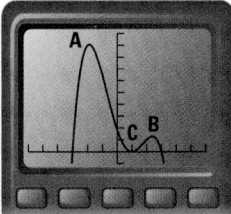

12. When the local movie theater charges $5 for admission, there is an average attendance of 100 people. For every $0.50 increase in admission, there seems to be an average loss of 5 people. Let *x* be the number of $0.50 increases.

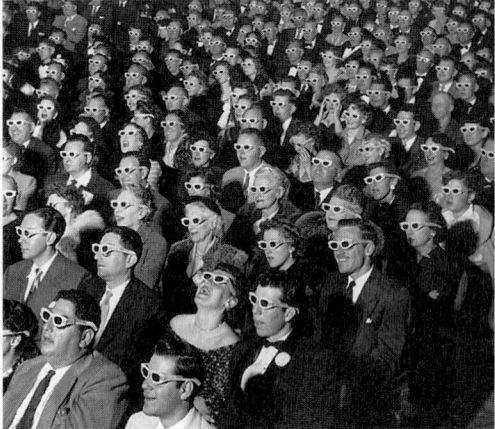

   a. Write an expression for the admission price increased by $0.50 *x* times.
   b. Write an expression for the number of people decreased by 5*x*.
   c. Determine a function for the revenue, which is the admission multiplied by the number of people.
   d. Graph the function that you found in **c** to find the admission price that will yield the maximum revenue.

LOOK BACK

13. Let $f = \{(-2, 6), (4, 0)\}$ and $g = \{(0, 7), (8, -3), (6, -5)\}$. Find $f \circ g$ and $g \circ f$ if they exist. [7-3]

14. In the novel *Little Women* by Louisa May Alcott, the daughters were named Meg, Jo, Beth, and Amy. List these four names in all possible ways. [6-1]

15. Tell whether the sequence 20, 8, 3.2, 1.28, … is a geometric sequence. If so, give the common ratio. [4-2]

MORE PRACTICE

16. Use the graph of the function $y = x^4 + x^3 - 7x^2 - x + 6$.

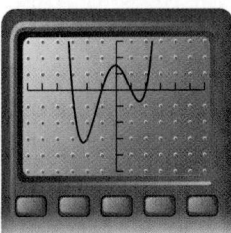

Xmin = –6
Xmax = 6
Xscl = 1
Ymin = –20
Ymax = 12
Yscl = 4

   a. Does this function have an absolute maximum? Explain.
   b. Does this function have an absolute minimum? Explain.
   c. Estimate the relative minimum in the interval from $x = 1$ to $x = 2$.
   d. Estimate the relative maximum in the interval from $x = -1$ to $x = 1$.

17. Use a Graphing Utility *Trace* to find the minimum value in the function $y = x^4 - 6x^3 + 4x^2 + 6x - 5$.

18. Use a Graphing Utility *Trace* to find the maximum value in the function $y = -x^5 - 3x^4 - 2x^3 + x^2 + 3x + 2$ between $x = -1$ and $x = 1$.

Match each function with its corresponding graph. Explain your choice.

19. $y = x^2 - 3x + 6$

20. $y = x^3 - 3x + 6$

21. $y = x^4 - 3x^2 + x$

22. $y = x^5 - 3x^3 + 2x$

A. Xmin = –5
Xmax = 5
Xscl = 1
Ymin = –4
Ymax = 5
Yscl = 1

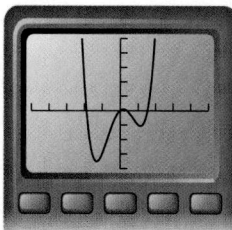

B. Xmin = –5
Xmax = 5
Xscl = 1
Ymin = –4
Ymax = 5
Yscl = 1

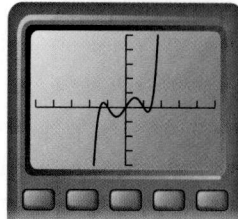

C. Xmin = –4
Xmax = 4
Xscl = 1
Ymin = –2
Ymax = 10
Yscl = 1

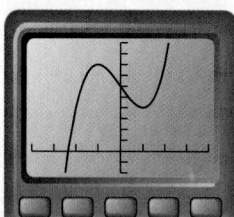

D. Xmin = –4
Xmax = 4
Xscl = 1
Ymin = –2
Ymax = 10
Yscl = 1

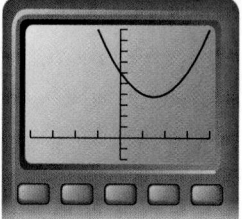

Use a Graphing Utility Graph each function. *Trace* **to find maximum and minimum values.**

23. $f(x) = x^4 + 5x + 4$

24. $f(x) = -x^3 + 4x$

25. $f(x) = x^5 + 10$

26. $f(x) = -x^5 + 6$

27. $f(x) = -x^4 + 4x$

28. $f(x) = x^3 - 4$

For each function, approximate the *y*-value at A and B. Identify each as a relative maximum or a relative minimum.

29.

Xmin = –4
Xmax = 4
Xscl = 1
Ymin = –18
Ymax = 8
Yscl = 2

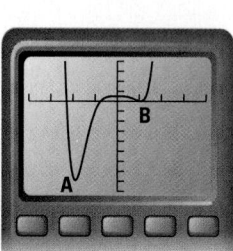

30.

Xmin = –6
Xmax = 6
Xscl = 1
Ymin = –10
Ymax = 8
Yscl = 2

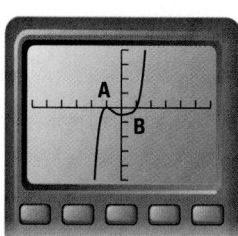

31.

Xmin = –6
Xmax = 6
Xscl = 1
Ymin = –4
Ymax = 4
Yscl = 1

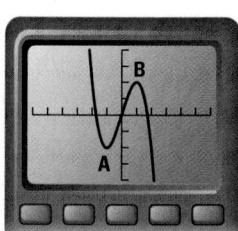

MORE MATH REASONING

32. Bursting with Boxes The monthly profit formula for a mailing company is $P = R - C$. *R* is the total revenue generated by the business and is determined by the function $R(x) = 0.0125x^2 + 412x$. *C*, the total cost of operating the business, is determined by the function $C(x) = 12{,}225 + 0.001435x^3$. The number of boxes sold is *x*.

a. Find the number of boxes that must be sold this month to make a profit.

b. How many boxes must the business sell to realize a monthly profit of $60,000?

Zeros of a Function

← CONNECT →   *In polynomial applications, you often need to know where the function equals zero. For quadratic functions, you used the quadratic formula to find zeros. For higher-degree polynomial functions, you will begin by using graphs to find zeros.*

You've seen that lines can have an x-intercept, and that parabolas can have two x-intercepts. You may have noticed that graphs of higher-degree polynomial functions sometimes have several x-intercepts. The graph of $y = 0.1x^5 - 2x^3 + 6.4x$ has five x-intercepts: -4, -2, 0, 2, and 4.

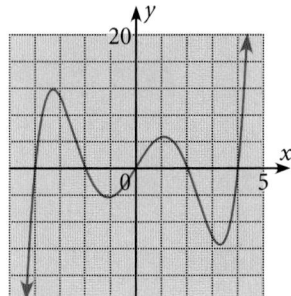

With a graphing utility, you can easily estimate x-intercepts of polynomial graphs and study what happens as $|x|$ gets larger.

EXPLORE: COUNTDOWN TO INTERCEPT

MATERIALS

Graphing utility

1. Graph $y_1 = x^3$, $y_2 = x^3 - 12x^2 + 44x - 48$, and $y_3 = -x^3 - 19x^2 - 116x - 220$. (You can use the same graphing screen.)
   a. *Trace* to estimate the x-intercepts of each graph to the nearest tenth.
   b. How can you modify the constant term of y_3 so that the new graph has three x-intercepts? Give a value for the constant term that meets this condition.
   c. What is the minimum number of x-intercepts that a cubic can have? What is the maximum number of x-intercepts that a cubic can have?
2. Graph $y_1 = x^4$, $y_2 = x^4 - 28x^3 + 289x^2 - 1302x + 2164$, and $y_3 = -x^4 - 18x^3 - 116x^2 - 312x - 288$.
   a. *Trace* to estimate the x-intercepts of each graph.
   b. Give a new value of the constant term for y_2 so that the new graph has two x-intercepts, and give a new value of the constant term for y_3 so that the new graph has four x-intercepts.
   c. What is the minimum number of x-intercepts that a quartic can have? What is the maximum number of x-intercepts that a quartic can have?
3. How many x-intercepts can the graph of a linear function have? What is the maximum number of x-intercepts that the graph of a quadratic function can have? Make a conjecture about the maximum number of x-intercepts that the graph of a fifth-degree function can have.

If a graph has an *x*-intercept, the value of the function at that point is zero.

> For a polynomial function $p(x)$, if r is an *x*-intercept of the graph of $p(x)$, then $p(r) = 0$, and r is called a **zero** of $p(x)$.

Recall that the *zeros* of a function are *roots* of an equation. So the zeros that occur at *x*-intercepts are the **real roots** of an equation.

Profit equals revenue minus cost, or $P(x) = R(x) - C(x)$. Every company has a person or department that is devoted to computing these figures. Once a profit function has been determined, a computer is usually programmed to do the profit and loss calculations quickly.

EXAMPLE

1. The AWSM company finds that for the past year, $R(x) = 0.01x^2 + 400x$ and $C(x) = 0.0015x^3 + 50{,}750$, where *x* is the number of items sold and function values are in dollars. Write the profit function for the company. Then find the first *break-even* point, the first point where $P(x) = 0$.

The profit function is $P(x) = R(x) - C(x)$.

$P(x) = (0.01x^2 + 400x) - (0.0015x^3 + 50{,}750)$
$\qquad = -0.0015x^3 + 0.01x^2 + 400x - 50{,}750$

The relevant portion of the graph of $P(x)$ is shown. The break-even point is a zero of the function. *Tracing* until the curve intersects the *x*-axis (and then *zooming* in) shows that the company must sell 136 items to reach the break-even point.

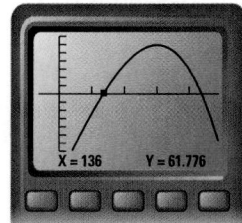

TRY IT

a. The concentration in the bloodstream (in parts per million) of a certain dose of medication after *x* hours is about $C(x) = -0.05x^3 + 2x - 0.5$. Using your graphing utility, find the meaningful zeros of the function to the nearest tenth, and describe what they represent.

CONSIDER

?

1. If a polynomial function has both positive and negative *y*-values, can we say that it must have at least one zero? Explain.

You have used the quadratic formula to find zeros of quadratic functions. There are complex formulas for the zeros of cubic and quartic functions, but they are of limited use compared to graphical and other methods of finding zeros. The French mathematician Evariste Galois proved in 1832 that no general algebraic formulas exist for finding the zeros of polynomial functions of degree greater than or equal to five.

You can occasionally use factoring and the Principle of Zero Products to find zeros of a function.

EXAMPLES

2. Find the zeros of the function $f(x) = x^3 - 2x^2 - 8x$.

Since zeros occur when the value of the function is zero, we will write the equation $0 = x^3 - 2x^2 - 8x$ and solve by factoring.

$$0 = x^3 - 2x^2 - 8x$$
$$0 = x(x^2 - 2x - 8) \qquad \text{Factor.}$$
$$0 = x(x - 4)(x + 2) \qquad \text{Factor completely.}$$
$$x = 0 \text{ or } (x - 4) = 0 \text{ or } (x + 2) = 0 \qquad \text{Use the Principle of Zero Products.}$$
$$x = 0 \text{ or } \qquad x = 4 \text{ or } \qquad x = -2$$

Check to see if each gives a zero value for $f(x)$.

$$f(0) \ = 0^3 - 2(0)^2 - 8(0) \qquad = 0 - 0 - 0 \ \ = 0 \ \checkmark$$
$$f(4) \ = 4^3 - 2(4)^2 - 8(4) \qquad = 64 - 32 - 32 = 0 \ \checkmark$$
$$f(-2) = (-2)^3 - 2(-2)^2 - 8(-2) = -8 - 8 + 16 = 0 \ \checkmark$$

They are all zeros of the function $f(x) = x^3 - 2x^2 - 8x$.

3. Find the zeros of the function $g(x) = x^4 - 13x^2 + 36$.

$$0 = x^4 - 13x^2 + 36 \qquad \text{Set the expression equal to zero.}$$
$$0 = (x^2 - 4)(x^2 - 9) \qquad \text{Factor.}$$
$$0 = (x - 2)(x + 2)(x - 3)(x + 3) \qquad \text{Factor completely.}$$

$$x - 2 = 0 \text{ or } x + 2 = 0 \ \text{ or } x - 3 = 0 \text{ or } x + 3 = 0$$
$$x = 2 \text{ or } \qquad x = -2 \text{ or } \qquad x = 3 \text{ or } \qquad x = -3$$

TRY IT

Find the zeros of the function.

b. $f(x) = x^3 - x^2 - 6x$

c. $g(x) = 2x^4 - 52x^2 + 50$

Few polynomials can be factored easily, if at all. In these cases, you can always look at the graph of the function and approximate any x-intercepts.

REFLECT

1. How can you use a graph to find the zeros of a function?

2. How can you use the factors of a polynomial to find the zeros of the related function?

3. Describe how you might check to see if $x = 4$ is a zero of the function $f(x) = x^4 - 3x^2 + 1$.

Exercises

CORE

1. Getting Started Use the graph of the function
$f(x) = x^4 - 2x^3 - 15x^2 + 32x - 16$.
  a. Give the values of the x-intercepts of this function.
  b. Give the zeros of this function.
  c. Find $f(-4)$.

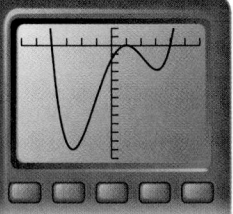

Xmin = −6
Xmax = 6
Xscl = 1
Ymin = −130
Ymax = 20
Yscl = 10

2. Describe how you could use these graphs from a graphing utility to estimate a zero of the given function.

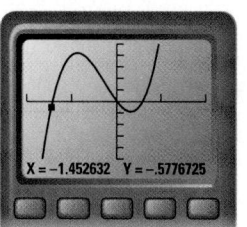

X = −1.452632   Y = −.5776725

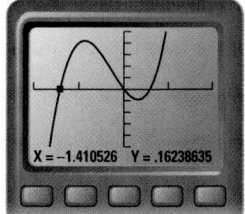

X = −1.410526   Y = .16238635

Find the zeros of each function.

3.

Xmin = −6
Xmax = 6
Xscl = 1
Ymin = −8
Ymax = 4
Yscl = 1

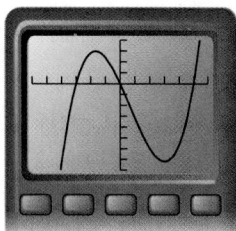

4.

Xmin = −6
Xmax = 6
Xscl = 1
Ymin = −40
Ymax = 20
Yscl = 5

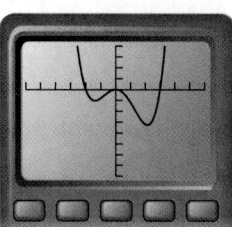

5.

Xmin = −6
Xmax = 6
Xscl = 1
Ymin = −40
Ymax = 20
Yscl = 5

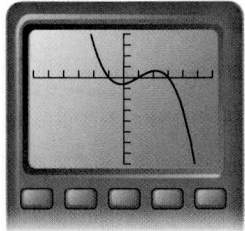

6. Wally evaluates the function $P(x)$ for $x = 5$ and finds that $P(5) = 0$. What conclusion can he make about the graph of $P(x)$?

Find the zeros of each function. Tell what method you used. Check your answers.

7. $f(x) = -16x^2 + 30x + 100$

8. $f(x) = 8x^5 + 12x^4 + 6x^3$

9. $f(x) = x^4 - 15x^2 + 16$

10. $f(x) = x^3 - 3x^2 + 2x$

11. The Hornets' all-state quarterback threw a pass on the run, straight toward the goal line 40 yards away. Unfortunately, no players were near the goal line. The ball was 2 yards above the ground when he released it, and it followed the parabolic path $f(x) = -0.03x^2 + 1.2x + 2$, with $f(x)$ representing the height of the ball in yards and x representing the number of yards traveled toward the goal line.

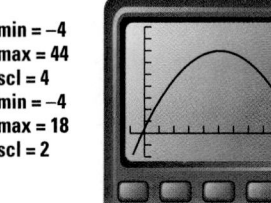

Xmin = –4
Xmax = 44
Xscl = 4
Ymin = –4
Ymax = 18
Yscl = 2

  a. What was the maximum height the ball reached? Where did this happen?
  b. What was the height of the ball when (and if) it reached the goal line?
  c. Where did it hit the ground?

Science

12. Why We're MADD The polynomial function $a(x) = -0.0915x^3 + 1.771x$ gives the approximate alcohol concentration (in hundredths of a percent) in an average person's bloodstream x hours after one drink.

  a. From the graph estimate the number of hours necessary for the alcohol concentration to return to 0.
  b. Check your answer to **a** by solving $a(x) = 0$. What is an appropriate domain for x?
  c. Using the graph, at what time is the concentration of alcohol the greatest? Estimate the maximum alcohol concentration.
  d. In California, a person is legally drunk if the blood alcohol concentration exceeds 0.08%. Use your graph to estimate the length of time it takes an average person to be legally drunk after consuming an alcoholic drink.

Xmin = –5
Xmax = 5
Xscl = 1
Ymin = –5
Ymax = 5
Yscl = 1

LOOK AHEAD

Make a table of values for each pattern.

13. 2^x for $x = 0, 1, 2, 3, 4, 5, 6$

14. 3^x for $x = 0, 1, 2, 3, 4, 5, 6$

15. 5^x for $x = 0, 1, 2, 3, 4, 5, 6$

16. 10^x for $x = 0, 1, 2, 3, 4, 5, 6$

17. 2^{-x} for $x = 0, 1, 2, 3, 4, 5, 6$

18. 3^{-x} for $x = 0, 1, 2, 3, 4, 5, 6$

19. 5^{-x} for $x = 0, 1, 2, 3, 4, 5, 6$

20. 10^{-x} for $x = 0, 1, 2, 3, 4, 5, 6$

MORE PRACTICE

21. Describe how you could use these graphs from a graphing utility to estimate a zero of the given function.

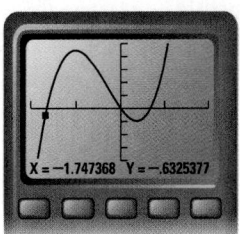
X = –1.747368   Y = –.6325377

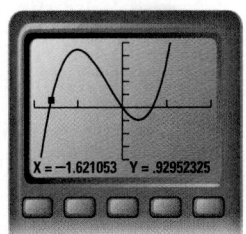
X = –1.621053   Y = .92952325

22. Use the graph of $f(x) = -0.2x^4 + 3x^2 - 8$.

    a. How many x-intercepts are there on the graph of $f(x) = -0.2x^4 + 3x^2 - 8$?

    b. Find the zeros of this function. Estimate if necessary.

Xmin = –6
Xmax = 6
Xscl = 1
Ymin = –10
Ymax = 10
Yscl = 2

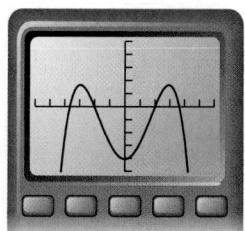

Estimate the zeros for each graph. Check your answers.

23. $f(x) = x^3 - x^2 - 6x$ **24.** $f(x) = -x^5 + 10x^3 - 9x$ **25.** $f(x) = -x^4 + 2x^3 + 3x^2 - 8x + 4$

Xmin = –3
Xmax = 4
Xscl = 1
Ymin = –10
Ymax = 6
Yscl = 2

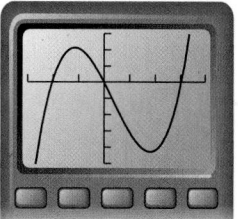

Xmin = –4
Xmax = 4
Xscl = 1
Ymin = –40
Ymax = 40
Yscl = 10

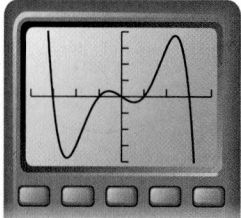

Xmin = –3
Xmax = 3
Xscl = 1
Ymin = –2
Ymax = 14
Yscl = 2

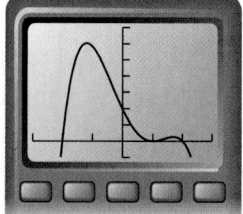

Factor or use a graphing utility to determine the number of zeros and their approximate values.

26. $f(x) = x^3 - x^2 + x - 1$ **27.** $f(x) = x^3 - 4x$

28. $f(x) = -x^5 + x^3$ **29.** $f(x) = x^4 + 2x^3 - x - 1$

MORE MATH REASONING

30. Bushel Bummer The number of bushels of barley an acre of land will yield depends on how many seeds the farmer plants per acre. 200,000 seeds per acre leads to a harvest of 22 bushels an acre, and 400,000 seeds per acre yields a harvest of 40 bushels an acre. It is known that the harvest yield is a quadratic function of the number of seeds planted per acre. As more seeds are planted the harvest increases to a maximum and then declines, as the plants compete for minerals and moisture in the soil.

    a. Using another obvious ordered pair to describe the harvest situation, write a function describing the harvest yield.

    b. How many bushels per acre would you expect if you planted 800,000 seeds per acre? 1.4 million seeds per acre?

    c. How many seeds should you plant per acre to maximize the harvest yield in bushels? What would this harvest yield be?

    d. Can you plant so many seeds that there would be no harvest? Explain the potential of this in terms of your model, and discuss its validity.

31. Look at the graph of $y = 33x^3 - 100x^2 + 101x + 5$ in a variety of graphing utility settings to make a conjecture about whether this function is increasing or decreasing as x increases.

← CONNECT → *You've seen that polynomial models give you the tools to examine zeros, maximums, and minimums, and interpret them in real-world situations.*

On page 541, you read about some factors that designers of aluminum beverage cans must consider while doing their work. Now you will look at a model for a cylindrical can. Do you think that the typical beverage can is designed to hold the maximum amount of beverage?

EXPLORE: YES, YOU CAN!

By approximating a beverage can as a cylinder, you can estimate its surface area and volume. Since the surface area affects the amount of aluminum in a can, manufacturers might want to maximize volume for a given surface area. You can test whether or not this is what they have actually done. A diameter of 2.56 inches and a height of 4.5 inches are typical dimensions of most beverage cans.

The surface area of a cylinder is twice the area of the base plus the area of the sides (the circumference times the height), or $A = 2\pi r^2 + 2\pi rh$.

MATERIALS

Graphing utility

$V = \pi r^2 h$
$A = 2\pi r^2 + 2\pi rh$

1. Estimate the surface area of a typical beverage can.

2. To maximize the volume for this surface area, find a volume function that includes the information about the surface area. To do this, use your estimated area and solve the surface area function for h. Then substitute this expression for h into the volume formula. What is the volume function written as a cubic polynomial?

3. Use your graphing utility to graph the volume function. What do the x-values represent? Describe the domain restrictions that make the model relevant.

4. What dimensions maximize the volume, and what is this volume? What is the volume of a typical beverage can? How do these volumes compare?

5. Are beverage cans today designed to hold the greatest volume of beverage? Can you think of some reasons why cans are made in this design?

6. Convert the volume of a typical beverage can into fluid ounces by multiplying by $0.554 \frac{\text{fl oz}}{\text{in.}^3}$. Is this the amount of beverage in a typical beverage can? Can you explain the difference?

Soon you will learn additional ways to find zeros of polynomial functions. If you study calculus, you will learn other ways to find maximums and minimums for some polynomial functions. But at any level that you study, a graphing utility will remain indispensable for modeling polynomial applications.

REFLECT

1. How do you determine the leading coefficient of a polynomial? How do you determine the degree of a polynomial?
2. How do you know that a third-degree polynomial function must have at least one zero?
3. Without graphing, how can you tell whether a fourth-degree polynomial has an absolute minimum or an absolute maximum?
4. A polynomial function has three relative maximums, but no absolute maximum. How many relative minimums might the function have?

Self-Assessment

Identify the leading coefficient and tell the degree of each function.

1. $y = -0.4x^4 - x^3 + 4x^2 + x$

2. $f(x) = 15 + 4x - 3x^2$

3. $P(x) = -x^3 - 6x^2 + 3$

4. $g(x) = 1 - 0.05x$

5. $h(x) = x^2 - 4 + x^7 + 23x^3$

6. $y = -x^5 + 1$

Use the graph of $y = x^4 - x^3 - 16x^2 + 2x + 15$ to decide if each item is true or false.

7. Point A gives a relative minimum value for the function.

8. Point B gives the absolute maximum of the function.

9. One of the zeros of this function is at point C.

10. The absolute minimum value of this function is at D.

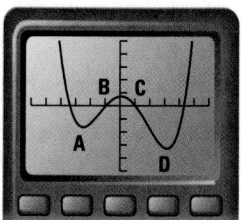

11. Robin has a collection of books by bestselling author Barbara Kingsolver: *Homeland, Animal Dreams, Pigs in Heaven,* and *The Bean Fields.* How many different ways can she arrange this collection on the shelf? [6-1]

Decide which choice is correct.

(A) The quantity in Column A is greater.
(B) The quantity in Column B is greater.
(C) The two quantities are equal.
(D) The relationship cannot be determined.

	Column A	Column B	
12.	$-x^3 + 4$	$x^3 + 4$	when $x < 0$
13.	$(x - 2)(x + 7)$	$(x - 2)$	when $x > 0$
14.	$(x + 2)(x + 3)$	$(x + 2)^2$	when $x > -2$
15.	x^4	$(x + 1)^3$	when $x < -1$

16. A company has pieces of cardboard, 36 inches by 18 inches. The cardboard is used for specimen boxes, which will be made by the biology class using the template shown.

    a. What values make sense for the side lengths of the square cutouts?

    b. Write an equation for the volume of the box.

    c. Describe how you could use your equation for volume to find the size cutout that results in the box with the greatest volume.

    d. **Use a graphing utility** to estimate the dimensions of the squares to cut out to get a box with the greatest volume. What is the greatest volume?

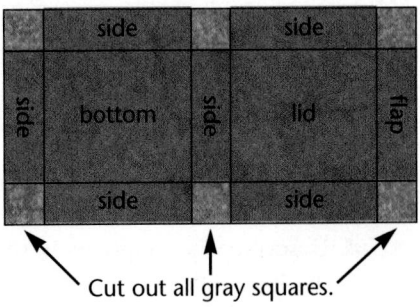

17. Tell whether the sequence 300, -100, 66.666, ... forms a geometric sequence. If so, give the common ratio. [4-2]

18. Suppose a farmer has 1000 yards of fencing, which is to be used to make a rectangular pigsty along the riverbank. Assuming that fencing is not needed along the riverbank side, what dimensions will give the farmer the maximum area for his pigs? [5-2]

Use the graph of each function to find its zeros. Approximate your answers when necessary.

19. $P(x) = -3x^3 + 9x^2 + 4$

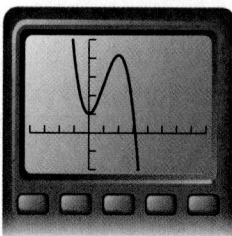

Xmin = –4
Xmax = 8
Xscl = 1
Ymin = –8
Ymax = 20
Yscl = 4

20. $y = x^4 - x^3 - 7x^2 + 4x + 12$

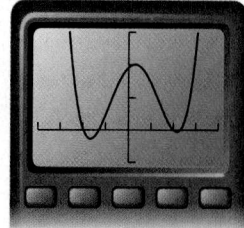

Xmin = –4
Xmax = 4
Xscl = 1
Ymin = –6
Ymax = 18
Yscl = 6

21. $f(x) = -x^5 + 4x^3 + x^2 - 4$

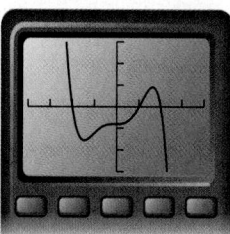

Xmin = –4
Xmax = 4
Xscl = 1
Ymin = –15
Ymax = 15
Yscl = 5

22. $y = 3x^5 - 3x^4 - 4x^3 + 1$

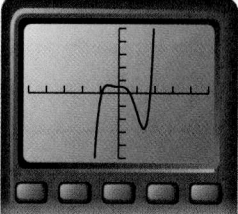

Xmin = –5
Xmax = 5
Xscl = 1
Ymin = –10
Ymax = 10
Yscl = 2
Xres = 1

23. Use the graph of $y = -x^4 + x^3 + 7x^2 - 4x - 12$.
   a. Find an absolute maximum or minimum of the function.
   b. Give a relative minimum within the interval from $x = -1$ to $x = 1$.
   c. Give two zeros of the function and verify your answers.
   d. Describe what happens to the value of the function as x increases beyond 2.

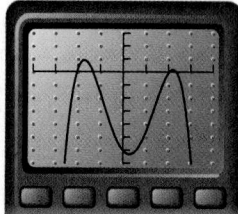

Xmin = –4
Xmax = 4
Xscl = 1
Ymin = –14
Ymax = 6
Yscl = 2

24. Find the zeros of the function $A(x) = x^3 - 7x^2 + 12x$. Describe your method of solution.

Using the following functions, fill in the chart numerically to compare the value of the leading term in a polynomial with the value of the entire polynomial, as the values for x move away from 0 in both positive and negative directions.

25. $2x^3 - 7x^2 - 8x + 16$

26. $-0.5x^4 + 5x^3 - 10x + 1$

27. $-2x^3 - x^2 + 3x + 5$

28. $3x^4 - 2x^3 + x^2 - x + 5$

x	Value of Leading Term	Value of Polynomial
20		
50		
100		
–20		
–50		
–100		

Seeing the Forest for the Trees

Today, lumber is an essential product in our economy and in the construction industry. Yet to obtain lumber at competitive prices, loggers have been depleting *old-growth* forests, which have stood for centuries.

Not surprisingly, political issues surrounding the lumber industry often cause people a variety of concerns and emotions. From one viewpoint, the livelihood of loggers is at stake. Furthermore, the more land that is restricted from logging, the higher the price of lumber and construction. On the other hand, environmentalists argue that 90 percent of old-growth forests in the United States have already been cut down and we must save the remaining 10 percent. The 8.3 million acres of remaining old-growth forest are home to many species that might perish if these ecosystems are destroyed.

Despite the controversy, the health of American forests is generally improving. Since 1945, the forested portion of the United States has steadily grown, not declined. About 35 percent of the area of Vermont was forest a century ago, yet today about 76 percent of Vermont is forest. Although issues surrounding forests and the lumber industry will undoubtedly be argued in the future, figures such as these give us hope that we can continue to sustain healthy forests.

The northern spotted owl is an endangered species found in old-growth forests.

The ecosystem of an old-growth forest cannot be easily replanted or replaced.

Traditional wood frame construction of a new home being built.

?

1. What are some advantages of maintaining healthy forests?
2. Describe a mathematical model that could help you to monitor and predict the health of a forest.
3. List some items that are made from wood products. How might issues regarding forests and logging affect the supply and prices of these items?

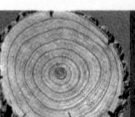

8-2 PART A Solving Polynomial Equations by Graphing

← CONNECT → *You have solved linear and quadratic equations graphically. Now you will use graphing to solve other polynomial equations.*

In Chapter 5, you used graphs of quadratic functions to find the real solutions of quadratic equations. This method can also be used to find the real solutions of any **polynomial equation,** $P(x) = c$, where $P(x)$ is a polynomial with real coefficients and c is a real constant.

EXAMPLE

Hans designs and builds handmade wood furniture. He is designing a new chest to have a volume of 48 cubic feet. All of the chests he builds are 2 feet wider than their height and 2 feet longer than their width. What dimensions should he choose for the new chest?

Let x represent the height, in feet, of the chest. The width is $x + 2$ and the length is $x + 4$. The volume (V) is the product of the height, width, and length.

$$V(x) = x(x + 2)(x + 4)$$
$$= x^3 + 6x^2 + 8x$$

The height that gives a volume of 48 ft³ is the solution of the equation $48 = x^3 + 6x^2 + 8x$. To solve this equation, graph $y = x^3 + 6x^2 + 8x$ on a graphing utility and *trace* to find (or estimate) the value of x where $y = 48$.

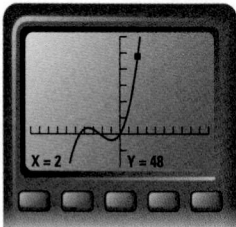

The real solution of $48 = x^3 + 6x^2 + 8x$ is $x = 2$. Hans should design the chest to be 2 feet high, 4 feet wide, and 6 feet long.

CONSIDER

1. In the Example, how many zeros does the polynomial function $y = V(x)$ have? These zeros are solutions of what equation?

TRY IT

Solve each equation graphically.

a. $x^3 - 21x + 15 = -5$ **b.** $x^4 - 5x^3 + 3x^2 + 9x = 0$

c. Graph $y = 2x^3 + 5x^2 - 2x$. How many real solutions does the equation $2x^3 + 5x^2 - 2x = 5$ have? Explain.

In the following Explore, you will write and solve a polynomial equation to help make a design decision.

EXPLORE: SILO DESIGN

You've been asked to design a grain silo in the shape of a cylinder with a hemispherical top. The silo must be 60 feet tall and have a total volume of 20,000 ft³. Recall that the volume of a cylinder with radius r and height h is $\pi r^2 h$, and the volume of a sphere with radius r is $\frac{4}{3}\pi r^3$.

1. Give the total volume of the silo as a polynomial function of the radius (r) of the base of the silo. What is the degree of this polynomial function?

2. Graph the volume function. In your design, what should be the radius of the base of the silo? Explain how you decided. Also give the height of the cylindrical part of the silo.

MATERIALS

Graphing utility or graph paper

Graphing polynomial functions can be a powerful tool to help you solve polynomial equations. For a polynomial equation of the form $P(x) = 0$, the solutions are the zeros of the corresponding function $y = P(x)$.

REFLECT

1. Explain how you can determine the number of real solutions of a polynomial equation of the form $P(x) = c$ from the graph of the related polynomial function $y = P(x)$.

2. A quadratic equation can have as many as two real solutions. Can other polynomial equations have more solutions? Explain.

3. Explain how the zeros of a polynomial function and the x-intercepts of the function's graph are related to the roots of a polynomial equation.

Exercises

CORE

1. Getting Started The graph of a polynomial function $y = P(x)$ is shown.

a. What are the x-intercepts?

b. What are the solutions of the polynomial equation $P(x) = 0$?

c. Give a solution of the polynomial equation $P(x) = -2$. Is there more than one solution?

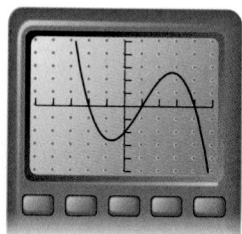

Xmin = –5
Xmax = 5
Xscl = 1
Ymin = –5
Ymax = 5
Yscl = 1

Sketch the graph of each function. Find the x-intercepts.

2. $y = 3x + 1$

3. $y = x^2 - 0.75x - 0.25$

Solve each equation graphically. Estimate the solutions if necessary.

$y = 0.5x^3 - x^2 - 1.5x$

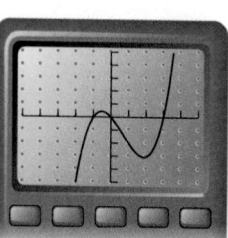

Xmin = –5
Xmax = 5
Xscl = 1
Ymin = –5
Ymax = 5
Yscl = 1

$y = 0.5x^4 + 2.5x^3 + 1.5x^2 - 4.5x$

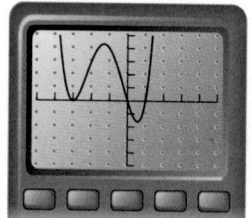

Xmin = –5
Xmax = 5
Xscl = 1
Ymin = –5
Ymax = 5
Yscl = 1

4. $0.5x^3 - x^2 - 1.5x = 0$

5. $0.5x^4 + 2.5x^3 + 1.5x^2 - 4.5x = -1$

6. $0.5x^3 - x^2 - 1.5x = -5$

7. $0.5x^4 + 2.5x^3 + 1.5x^2 - 4.5x = 0$

8. $0.5x^3 - x^2 - 1.5x = 4$

9. $0.5x^4 + 2.5x^3 + 1.5x^2 - 4.5x = 2$

10. Pill Fill Pill-Tech makes time-release capsules for several medications. The company needs to design a new capsule in the shape of a cylinder with a hemisphere on each end. The capsule is to be 14 mm long with a radius sufficient for the capsule to hold 300 mm³ of medication.

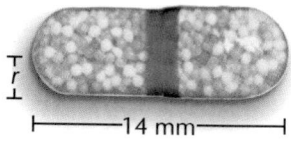

a. Explain why the volume of the capsule is modeled by the function $V(r) = -\frac{2}{3}\pi r^3 + 14\pi r^2$. What type of polynomial function is this?

b. Write a polynomial equation that can be solved to find the capsule radius Pill-Tech should use so that a capsule holds 300 mm³.

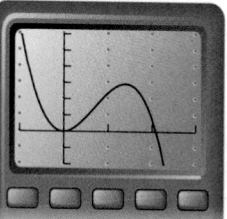

Xmin = –10
Xmax = 30
Xscl = 10
Ymin = –2000
Ymax = 6000
Yscl = 1000

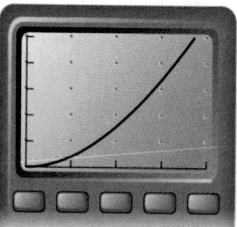

Xmin = 0
Xmax = 4
Xscl =1
Ymin = 0
Ymax = 500
Yscl = 100

c. Both graphs show the function $V(r)$ in different viewing windows of a graphing utility. Solve your polynomial equation graphically. What radius should Pill-Tech use for these capsules?

11. Find the number of distinguishable permutations of the letters in the word BOOKKEEPER. [6-1]

12. a. Evaluate $8^{4.6}$ to the nearest hundredth. [7-2]
   b. What power of 7 equals $7^3 \cdot (7^4)^5$?

MORE PRACTICE

13. Explain the difference between a polynomial function and a polynomial equation.

Sketch the graph of each function. Find the x-intercepts.

14. $y = -5x + 7$ **15.** $y = x^2 + 5x - 6$ **16.** $y = x^3 - 4x$

Solve each equation graphically. Estimate the solutions if necessary.

$$y = -x^3 + 4.5x^2 - 3.5x$$

17. $-x^3 + 4.5x^2 - 3.5x = 0$

18. $-x^3 + 4.5x^2 - 3.5x = 2$

19. $-x^3 + 4.5x^2 - 3.5x = -4$

20. $-x^3 + 4.5x^2 - 3.5x = -6$

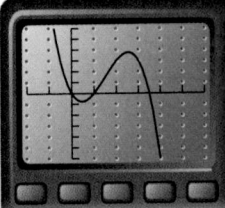

Xmin = -2
Xmax = 6
Xscl = 1
Ymin = -6
Ymax = 6
Yscl = 1

$$y = -x^4 + 4x^3 - 2.5x^2 - x$$

21. $-x^4 + 4x^3 - 2.5x^2 - x = -2$

22. $-x^4 + 4x^3 - 2.5x^2 - x = 0$

23. $-x^4 + 4x^3 - 2.5x^2 - x = 2$

24. $-x^4 + 4x^3 - 2.5x^2 - x = 4$

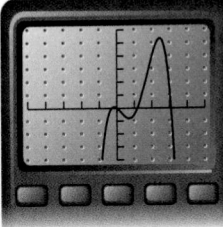

Xmin = -5
Xmax = 5
Xscl = 1
Ymin = -4
Ymax = 6
Yscl = 1

25. Sketch a graph to explain each answer. Can a third-degree polynomial equation have:
   a. no x-intercepts?   **b.** exactly one x-intercept?   **c.** exactly two x-intercepts?

Use a Graphing Utility Solve each equation graphically. Give each solution to the nearest tenth.

26. $x^3 + 7x^2 + 10x = 8$ **27.** $x^4 - 5x^3 + 9x = -28$

28. $2x^3 - 9x = -2$ **29.** $x^5 = 6 - 4x$

30. Which types of polynomial equations can have exactly two solutions?
   I. linear   II. quadratic   III. cubic
   (a) only I   (b) only II   (c) only III   (d) II and III   (e) I, II, and III

31. What's the Scoop? For their ice cream stores, Scoops wants to design a new cone that is 12 cm high and holds $\frac{1}{4}$ liter (250 cm³) of ice cream when completely filled and topped with a hemispherical scoop. Recall that the volume of a cone of height h and radius r is $\frac{1}{3}\pi r^2 h$.

    a. Give a polynomial function $V(r)$ for the volume of the cone and hemisphere. What type of polynomial is $V(r)$?

> **Problem-Solving Tip**
>
> Draw and label a diagram of the filled cone.

    b. Use a Graphing Utility Graph the volume function. Use your graph to decide what radius the cone should be in order to hold $\frac{1}{4}$ liter.

MORE MATH REASONING

32. Can you always use graphing to approximate solutions of a polynomial equation? Explain your reasoning.

33. If $P(x)$ is a cubic polynomial and the equations $P(x) = -4$ and $P(x) = 2$ each have three solutions, can there be a value c between -4 and 2 so that the equation $P(x) = c$ has fewer than three solutions? Explain.

34. Without graphing these functions, explain how you can locate the points where the graph of $f(x) = 2x^3 + 3x^2 - 7x - 4$ intersects the graph of $g(x) = 2x^3 + 2x^2 - 7x + 5$. Give the exact coordinates of each intersection point. Verify by graphing.

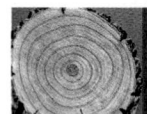

8-2
PART B Factors and Roots of Polynomials

← **C O N N E C T** → *You've solved polynomial equations graphically. Now you will investigate how dividing and factoring polynomials can help you to solve polynomial equations.*

Recall that factoring quadratic polynomials is one method you can use to solve quadratic equations. You've also factored to find zeros of polynomial functions. Factoring can also be a useful method for solving polynomial equations of degree greater than 2.

Solve each equation by factoring.

1. $x^3 - 6x^2 = 7x$

$x^3 - 6x^2 - 7x = 0$ Subtract $7x$ from both sides to get 0 on the right.

$x(x^2 - 6x - 7) = 0$ Factor out x.

$x(x + 1)(x - 7) = 0$ Factor the quadratic expression.

$x = 0, x = -1,$ or $x = 7$ Use the Principle of Zero Products.

2. $x^4 - x^2 = 72$

$x^4 - x^2 - 72 = 0$ Subtract 72 from both sides to get 0 on the right.

$(x^2 - 9)(x^2 + 8) = 0$ Factor the expression.

$x^2 = 9$ or $x^2 = -8$ Use the Principle of Zero Products.

$x = \pm 3$ or $x = \pm\sqrt{8}i$ Solve each equation to find the four roots.

$x = \pm 3$ or $x = \pm 2i\sqrt{2}$

TRY IT

Solve each equation by factoring.

a. $x^3 + 8x^2 = 20x$

b. $x^3 = 9x$

c. $2x^4 + x^2 = 6$

Most polynomials are difficult to factor. Even when you can find one factor, it may be difficult to factor it out and obtain other factors.

EXPLORE: FIND THE FACTORS

MATERIALS

Graphing utility

1. Graph the polynomial function $P(x) = x^3 + x^2 - 2x - 8$. Use your graph to find a real root r of the polynomial equation $x^3 + x^2 - 2x - 8 = 0$. Substitute the value r into $P(x)$ and verify that $P(r) = 0$.

2. Explain why r is also a root of any polynomial of the form $(x - r)(x^2 + ax + b)$, where a and b are real numbers.

3. Show that $P(x)$ can be factored in the form $(x - r)(x^2 + ax + b)$, where r is the real root of $P(x)$ you found in Step 1 and a and b are real numbers. Describe the method you used to factor $P(x)$.

4. Using the factored form you found in Step 3, find *all* of the roots of the polynomial equation $x^3 + x^2 - 2x - 8 = 0$.

In the Explore, you factored a cubic polynomial and used the factored form to solve a polynomial equation. There is a systematic way to divide polynomials that can help you to factor them.

3. Divide $2x^2 + 6x + 7$ by $x + 1$. Is $x + 1$ a factor of $2x^2 + 6x + 7$?

To find the first term of the *quotient*, divide the highest degree term of $2x^2 + 6x + 7$ by the highest degree term of the $x + 1$, giving $\frac{2x^2}{x}$, or $2x$.

The *divisor* is $x + 1$. →

Multiply $x + 1$ by $2x$. →

$$
\begin{array}{r}
2x \\
x + 1 \overline{)2x^2 + 6x + 7} \\
2x^2 + 2x \\
\hline
4x + 7
\end{array}
$$

← $\frac{2x^2}{x} = 2x$

← Subtract and bring down the next term.

To find the next term, divide the highest degree term of $4x + 7$ by the highest degree term of $x + 1$, giving $\frac{4x}{x}$, or 4.

Continue in this manner until you get an expression of degree less than the degree of the *divisor*, $x + 1$. This final expression is the *remainder*. Since $x + 1$ has degree 1, the remainder is a constant (degree 0).

Multiply $x + 1$ by 4. →

$$
\begin{array}{r}
2x + 4 \\
x + 1 \overline{)2x^2 + 6x + 7} \\
2x^2 + 2x \\
\hline
4x + 7 \\
4x + 4 \\
\hline
3
\end{array}
$$

← The quotient is $2x + 4$.

← The remainder is 3.

$2x^2 + 6x + 7$ divided by $x + 1$ equals $2x + 4$ with a remainder of 3.

Check: divisor · quotient   +   remainder $\stackrel{?}{=} 2x^2 + 6x + 7$

        $(x + 1)(2x + 4)$ +   3 $= 2x^2 + 6x + 7$ ✓

Since the remainder is not 0, $x + 1$ is not a factor of $2x^2 + 6x + 7$.

In Example 3, by writing the polynomial $P(x) = 2x^2 + 6x + 7$ in the form $P(x) = (x + 1)(2x + 4) + 3$, we see that $P(-1) = 3$. Notice that since the factor $(x + 1)$ equals 0 when $x = -1$, the value of $P(-1)$ is same as the remainder.

REMAINDER THEOREM

If a polynomial $P(x)$ is divided by $(x - a)$, where a is a constant, then the remainder is $P(a)$.

The Remainder Theorem gives a simple way to check whether a polynomial has a factor of the form $x - a$. If a is a zero of $P(x)$, then the remainder is zero when you divide $P(x)$ by $(x - a)$, and $(x - a)$ is a factor of $P(x)$. This result is called the Factor Theorem.

FACTOR THEOREM

For any polynomial $P(x)$, if $P(a) = 0$ for a constant a, then $(x - a)$ is a factor of $P(x)$.

EXAMPLE

4. Show that 3 is a zero of the polynomial $P(x) = x^3 - 7x^2 + 11x + 3$. Then verify that $(x - 3)$ is a factor of $P(x)$ by dividing.

$P(3) = 3^3 - 7 \cdot 3^2 + 11 \cdot 3 + 3$

$\qquad = 27 - 63 + 33 + 3$

$\qquad = 0\ ✓$

$$
\begin{array}{r}
x^2 - 4x - 1 \\
x - 3 \overline{)x^3 - 7x^2 + 11x + 3} \\
\underline{x^3 - 3x^2} \\
-4x^2 + 11x \\
\underline{-4x^2 + 12x} \\
-x + 3 \\
\underline{-x + 3} \\
0
\end{array}
$$

$x^3 - 7x^2 + 11x + 3$ divided by $x - 3$ equals $x^2 - 4x - 1$, so $x^3 - 7x^2 + 11x + 3 = (x - 3)(x^2 - 4x - 1)$.

CONSIDER

1. **How many factors of the form $(x - a)$ do you think a cubic polynomial can have? Explain.**

TRY IT

Divide each pair of polynomials. Verify the Remainder Theorem by finding each remainder in two ways.

d. $(x^3 + 2x^2 - 3x + 4) \div (x - 2)$

e. $(x^3 + 3x^2 - 2x + 11) \div (x + 4)$

f. Show that 5 is a zero of the polynomial $P(x) = x^4 - 4x^3 - 6x^2 + 3x + 10$. Then verify that $(x - 5)$ is a factor of $P(x)$ by dividing.

Factoring polynomials isn't always possible or convenient, but when it is, factoring can be a valuable method for finding and verifying zeros of polynomial functions and roots of polynomial equations.

REFLECT

1. If the constant term of a polynomial is 0, what can you say about factors of the polynomial?

2. When you are dividing a polynomial by a first-degree polynomial, how do you know when you are finished?

3. Describe the relationship between the factors of polynomials and roots of polynomial equations.

Exercises

CORE

1. Getting Started Complete each statement to solve $x^3 - 6x^2 = 16x$.

a. $x^3 - 6x^2 - \underline{\quad} = 0$

b. $x(\underline{\quad}) = 0$

c. $x(x - \underline{\quad})(x + \underline{\quad}) = 0$

d. $x = 0, x = \underline{\quad}$, or $x = \underline{\quad}$

2. Is 17 a factor of 359? How do you know?

Solve each equation by factoring.

3. $x^3 - 4x^2 - 5x = 0$

4. $x^4 + 6x^2 = 40$

5. $x^2 = 2x(x^2 - 3)$

6. $(x^2 + x)(x - 1) = 27 - x$

Copy and complete each division of polynomials.

7.
$$
\begin{array}{r}
x + ? \\
x + 3 \overline{\smash{)}x^2 + 6x + 14} \\
\underline{x^2 + ?x} \\
3x + 14 \\
\underline{3x + ?} \\
?
\end{array}
$$

$(x^2 + 6x + 14) \div (x + 3) =$

quotient _____

with remainder _____

8.
$$
\begin{array}{r}
2x^2 + ?x + ? \\
x - 4 \overline{\smash{)}2x^3 - 3x^2 - 15x + 3} \\
\underline{2x^3 - 8x^2} \\
?x^2 - 15x \\
\underline{?x^2 - 20x} \\
? + 3 \\
\underline{?} \\
?
\end{array}
$$

$(2x^3 - 3x^2 - 15x + 3) \div (x - 4) =$

quotient _____

with remainder _____

Use division to find each quotient and remainder.

9. $(3x^2 - 8x + 7) \div (x - 1)$

10. $(x^3 + 5x^2 - 3x - 4) \div (x + 6)$

11. $(x^2 + 3x - 8) \div (x - 5)$

12. $(4x^3 - 2x + 1) \div (2x + 1)$

13. a. What value of x makes $2x + 1$ equal to 0?
  b. Is $6x^2 - 11x - 7$ equal to zero for that value of x?
  c. Is $2x + 1$ a factor of $6x^2 - 11x - 7$? Explain how you know.

14. Show that 4 is a zero of the polynomial $P(x) = x^3 - 3x^2 + x - 20$. Then verify that $(x - 4)$ is a factor of $P(x)$.

Find each remainder when the first polynomial is divided by the second polynomial.

15. $3x^2 - 2x + 9; \; x - 4$

16. $4x^3 - 2x^2 + 11x; \; x + 10$

17. $4x^3 + 5x^2 - 6x + 7; \; x - 1$

18. $2x^4 + 5x^3 - 8x^2 + 12x - 9; \; x + 3$

Write the word or phrase that correctly completes each sentence.

19. When dividing one polynomial by another, the degree of the remainder must be ____ the degree of the divisor.

20. If $x - 8$ is a factor of the polynomial $P(x)$, then ____ is a root of the equation $P(x) = 0$.

21. If 6 is a root of the polynomial equation $P(x) = 0$, then ____ is a factor of $P(x)$.

22. Boxing Day Construct a box with an open top by cutting squares from the corners of a 12-inch by 16-inch piece of cardboard. Find the side length of the squares you can cut out to make a box with a volume of 180 in³. Show that there are two possible dimensions for the box and explain how you found them.

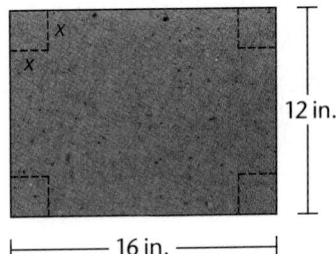

23. Find a polynomial $P(x)$ that has quotient $3x - 7$ and remainder 0 when divided by $2x + 3$.

24. When polynomial $P(x)$ is divided by $x - 5$, the quotient is $3x^2 - 2$ and the remainder is 3. What is the value of $P(5)$?

25. What can you say about factors of the polynomial $Q(x)$ if 5 is a root of the equation $Q(x) = 0$?

26. Explain how you know that $x - 1$ is a factor of $x^{19} - 1$ without actually dividing.

27. Give a polynomial function that has x-intercepts of $-2, -1,$ and 1.

28. a. Write a polynomial equation with roots $-2, 7,$ and 10.
  b. Write a polynomial function with zeros $1, 3i,$ and $-3i$.

29. An industrial psychologist, who works to help employees improve their memory while learning new languages, establishes that a person is able to memorize M words after t minutes, where $M(t) = -0.001t^3 + 0.1t^2$.

    a. Write $M(t)$ in its factored form. What does this tell you about the graph of $M(t)$? What domain do you think would yield the most helpful graph? Explain.

    b. How might knowledge of the graph of $M(t)$ be useful to the psychologist?

LOOK AHEAD

Evaluate each expression for $x = 0$, 1, and i.

30. $\dfrac{3x^2(x - 5)}{x^2 + 2}$

31. $\dfrac{12}{x^3 + x}$

MORE PRACTICE

Solve each equation by factoring.

32. $x^3 + 13x^2 = -40x$

33. $x^4 - 7x^2 = 18$

34. $x = 3x^3 - 2x$

35. $3x^2 - 5x^3 = 2x^4$

36. $x^4 = 121$

37. $(x^2 + 1)(x + 2) = 2$

38. $x^3 - 2x^2 = -x$

39. $x^4 - 4x^2 + 4 = 0$

40. $x^5 = 256x$

Use division to find each quotient and remainder.

41. $(8x^2 + 14x) \div (2x + 5)$

42. $(27x^3 - 1) \div (x - 1)$

43. $(x^4 + x^3 + x^2 + x) \div x$

44. $(x^2 - 16) \div (x - 4)$

45. $(2x^2 + x - 5) \div (2x + 3)$

46. $(18x^3 - 12x^2 + 10x) \div 2x$

47. $(2x^4 + 8x^3 + 3x) \div (x + 4)$

48. $(5x^5 - 30x^4 + x - 1) \div (x - 6)$

49. $(x^8 - 1) \div (x - 1)$

50. $(3x^5 + 5x^4 + 2x^3 - x^2 + 4x) \div (x + 1)$

51. Trash It A trash can manufacturer is designing a new can in the shape of a cylinder with a hemispherical top. The can must be 4 ft tall and hold a volume of $4\frac{1}{3}$ ft^3. What radius (r) should the designer plan to use for the trash can?

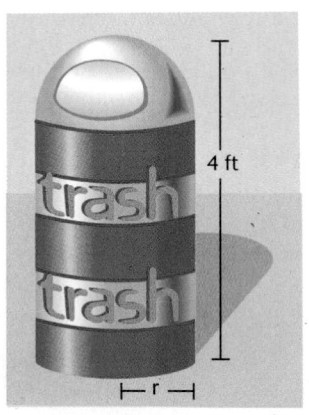

52. $2y - 3$ is a factor of $2y^3 - y^2 - y - 3$. Find another factor.

53. For a polynomial $P(x)$, suppose $P(4) = 0$. What conclusions can you draw about factors of $P(x)$?

54. Is $x - 8$ a factor of $P(x) = 2x^3 - 16x^2 - 4x - 32$? Explain.

55. When a polynomial $Q(z)$ is divided by $z + 1$, the remainder is 5. Find $Q(-1)$.

56. If $x - \sqrt{2}$ is a factor of $T(x)$, name a zero of $T(x)$.

Find each remainder when the first polynomial is divided by the second polynomial.

57. $x^3 - 2x^2 + 10x - 18$; $x + 1$

58. $x^3 - 14x^2 + 5x - 8$; $x - 1$

59. $3x^4 - x^3 + 5x^2 - x + 4$; $x - 2$

60. $5x^4 - 6x^3 + 4x^2 - x + 12$; $x + 2$

61. $x^4 - 2x^3 + 11x^2 - x$; $x - 4$

62. $7x^4 - 7x^3 + 7x^2 + 12$; $x + 5$

Write a polynomial with the given roots.

63. $x = 2, 5$, and -4

64. $x = -4, 0, 3i$, and $-3i$

65. $x = 3, 10, 1 + i$, and $1 - i$

66. $x = i, -i, 2i$, and $-2i$

MORE MATH REASONING

67. For which values of b is $x + 1$ a factor of $x^2 + bx + 1$?

68. Explain how the Factor Theorem follows from the Remainder Theorem.

69. Divide $x^3 - 3x + 2$ by $x^2 - x$. What is the quotient? What is the remainder?

70. Find the quotient of each polynomial when it is divided by $x - 1$.

    a. $x^2 - 1$ **b.** $x^3 - 1$ **c.** $x^4 - 1$

    d. Make a conjecture about the quotient of any polynomial of the form $x^n - 1$ when it is divided by $x - 1$. Verify your conjecture for $n = 5$.

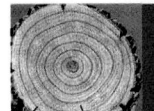

8-2 PART C   The Fundamental Theorem

← CONNECT →   *You will continue to explore methods of factoring polynomials and solving polynomial equations. In the process you will discover how many roots a polynomial can have.*

Once you find a zero of a polynomial, the Factor Theorem tells you one of the factors of the polynomial. You can then divide to factor the polynomial. But how can you find zeros in the first place? Graphing often doesn't give exact values, but the following theorem can help.

RATIONAL ROOTS THEOREM

Let $P(x) = a_nx^n + a_{n-1}x^{n-1} + \cdots + a_1x + a_0$ be any polynomial with integer coefficients. If b and c are integers with no common factors and $\frac{b}{c}$ is a rational root of the equation $P(x) = 0$, then b is a divisor of a_0 and c is a divisor of a_n.

---

1. Solve $x^3 + x^2 + 4x + 4 = 0$.

The possible divisors of 4, the constant term, are $b = -4, -2, -1, 1, 2,$ or 4. The possible divisors of 1, the coefficient of x^3, are $c = -1$ or 1. Therefore, the possible rational roots of the polynomial equation are $\frac{b}{c} = -4, -2, -1,$ 1, 2, or 4.

Check these values for a zero of $P(x) = x^3 + x^2 + 4x + 4$.

$P(-4) = -60; P(-2) = -8; P(-1) = 0$ ✓

Since -1 is a zero, $(x + 1)$ is a factor of the polynomial. Divide the polynomial by $(x + 1)$ and then continue to factor.

$$
\begin{array}{r}
x^2 + 0x + 4 \\
x + 1 \overline{)x^3 + x^2 + 4x + 4} \\
\underline{x^3 + x^2} \\
0 + 4x \\
\underline{0} \\
4x + 4 \\
\underline{4x + 4} \\
0
\end{array}
$$

$x^3 + x^2 + 4x + 4 = (x + 1)(x^2 + 4) = 0$

Using the Principle of Zero Products, the other roots of the polynomial equation are the roots of $x^2 + 4 = 0$. We can solve this directly or by using the quadratic formula.

$x^2 + 4 = 0$

$x^2 = -4$

$x = \pm\sqrt{-4} = \pm 2i$

The roots of $x^3 + x^2 + 4x + 4 = 0$ are $x = -1, 2i,$ and $-2i$.

Using these solutions, we can write the polynomial $x^3 + x^2 + 4x + 4$ completely factored as $(x + 1)(x - 2i)(x + 2i)$.

EXPLORE: HOW MANY ROOTS?

1. Solve each equation.
   a. $3x - 9 = 0$
   b. $x^2 - 5x + 6 = 0$
   c. $x^3 + 2x^2 - x - 2 = 0$
   d. $x^4 - 16 = 0$
2. How many roots does each equation have? How many roots do you think a fifth-degree polynomial equation would have?
3. Make a conjecture about the total number of roots of any polynomial equation. Explain why you think your conjecture is reasonable.

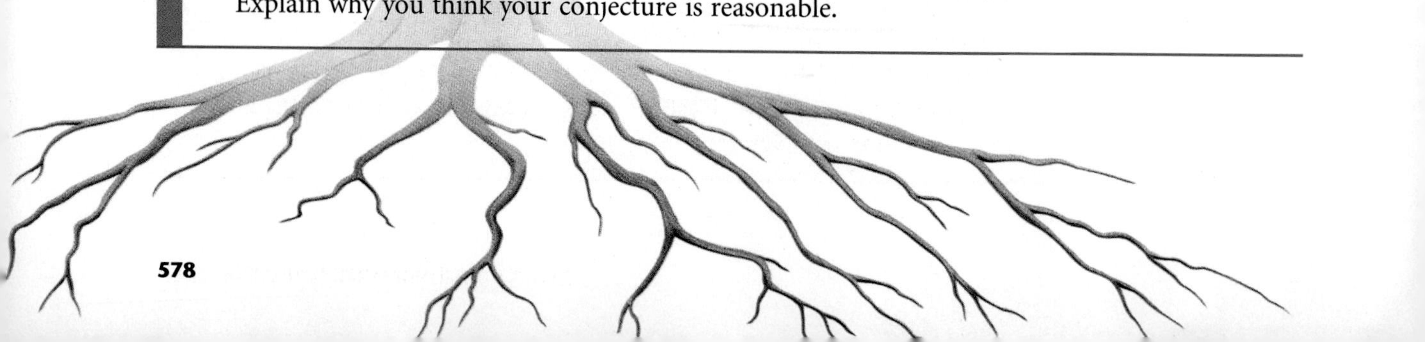

The factors of a polynomial don't have to be different. If a polynomial $P(x)$ has two or more equal factors of the form $(x - a)$, then a is called a **multiple root** of the polynomial equation $P(x) = 0$.

EXAMPLE

2. Solve $x^3 + x^2 - 5x + 3 = 0$.

Using the Rational Roots Theorem, the possible rational roots are -3, -1, 1, or 3. Checking the first value, -3, shows that it is indeed a root.

Divide the polynomial $x^3 + x^2 - 5x + 3$ by $(x + 3)$.

$$
\begin{array}{r}
x^2 - 2x + 1 \\
x + 3 \overline{) x^3 + x^2 - 5x + 3} \\
\underline{x^3 + 3x^2} \\
-2x^2 - 5x \\
\underline{-2x^2 - 6x} \\
x + 3 \\
\underline{x + 3} \\
0
\end{array}
$$

$x^3 + x^2 - 5x + 3 = (x + 3)(x^2 - 2x + 1)$. Recall that $x^2 - 2x + 1$ is the square of $(x - 1)$. So, the polynomial can be completely factored as $x^3 + x^2 - 5x + 3 = (x + 3)(x - 1)^2$.

The roots of the equation $x^3 + x^2 - 5x + 3 = 0$ are $x = -3$ and 1. The root $x = 1$ is a multiple root.

TRY IT

Solve each equation.

a. $x^3 + 2x^2 - 13x + 10 = 0$ **b.** $2x^3 - x^2 - 5x - 2 = 0$

CONSIDER

1. Can a fourth-degree polynomial equation have exactly 3 roots? Can a third-degree polynomial equation have exactly 4 roots? Explain.

You have solved some polynomial equations, but does every polynomial equation have a root? The answer is yes, even for equations with complex coefficients such as $2x^3 + 3ix + 1 = 0$.

FUNDAMENTAL THEOREM OF ALGEBRA

Every polynomial $P(x)$ of degree at least 1 and with complex coefficients has at least one complex zero.

The German mathematician Carl Friedrich Gauss proved the Fundamental Theorem of Algebra in 1799 when he was 22. An important consequence of this theorem is that every polynomial $P(x)$ of degree n can be *completely factored* into n linear factors. Since each factor corresponds to a root of the polynomial equation $P(x) = 0$, this equation has exactly n complex roots, counting multiplicity.

REFLECT

1. For what type of polynomial equation does the Rational Roots Theorem apply? What type of roots does it help you find?

2. Can methods of solving quadratic equations help you to solve higher degree polynomial equations? Explain.

3. How can you recognize a multiple root of a polynomial equation from the factored form of the related polynomial?

Exercises

CORE

1. Getting Started Consider the equation $2x^3 + 5x^2 - 11x + 4 = 0$.
   a. Is -1 a root? Is 1 a root?
   b. Write $2x^3 + 5x^2 - 11x + 4$ as a product of a linear factor and a quadratic factor.
   c. What are the roots of the quadratic factor?
   d. Give the three roots of the equation.
   e. Write $2x^3 + 5x^2 - 11x + 4$ as a product of linear factors.

2. a. Explain how grouping the terms of $P(x) = x^3 - 3x^2 + 2x - 6$ as $(x^3 - 3x^2) + (2x - 6)$ and factoring each group separately can help you factor $P(x)$.
   b. Can grouping the terms of $P(x)$ as $(x^3 + 2x) + (-3x^2 - 6)$ also help you factor $P(x)$? Explain.

Write the word or phrase that correctly completes each sentence.

3. A ____ root of an equation is a root of the form $\frac{b}{c}$, where b and c are integers with c not equal to 0.

4. A polynomial equation $P(x) = 0$ has a ____ root if $P(x)$ has two or more equal linear factors.

5. Consider $P(x) = 6x^4 - 4x^3 + 3x^2 + 13x - 10$.
   a. List the integer divisors of 6, the leading coefficient.
   b. List the integer divisors of -10, the constant term.
   c. Give all possible ratios of a divisor of -10 to a divisor of 6.
   d. The Rational Roots Theorem guarantees that if $P(x) = 0$ has a rational root, it will be one of the rational numbers in **c.**
   Find a root of $P(x) = 0$ from the rational numbers you found in **c.**

> **Problem-Solving Tip**
>
> Make an organized list.

Solve each polynomial equation.

6. $2x^3 + x^2 - 7x - 6 = 0$

7. $6x^3 - 19x^2 + 8x + 5 = 0$

8. $x^3 - 4x^2 - 4x + 16 = 0$

9. $2x^3 - 9x^2 + 4x + 15 = 0$

10. $3x^3 + 5x^2 - 26x + 8 = 0$

11. $6x^3 - x^2 - 27x - 20 = 0$

12. $x^4 - 2x^3 - 24x^2 + 50x - 25 = 0$

13. $x^4 - 3x^3 - 12x^2 + 52x - 48 = 0$

14. Assume that the leading coefficient of a polynomial with integer coefficients is 1. Explain why you only need to consider divisors of the constant term when looking for roots of the related polynomial equation.

15. Two roots of the polynomial equation $x^3 + 5x^2 + x + 5 = 0$ are i and $-i$. How many other roots can there be? Solve the equation completely.

Decide whether each polynomial equation has multiple roots. If so, state which root. Then give the total number of roots of the equation, counting multiplicity.

16. $(x - 2)^2(x + 1) = 0$

17. $(x^2 - 1)(x^4 - 1) = 0$

18. $x^3 - 2x^2 - x = -2$

19. Does $x^5 - 7x^4 + 12x^3 - 4x^2 + 10x - 18 = 0$ have six roots? Explain how you know.

 **LOOK BACK**

Find each product matrix. [1-3]

20. $\begin{bmatrix} 2 & -1 & 7 \\ 4 & 3 & 5 \end{bmatrix} \begin{bmatrix} 2 & -1 & 8 & 9 \\ 4 & 3 & -1 & 2 \\ 0 & 8 & 1 & -4 \end{bmatrix}$

21. $\begin{bmatrix} 2 & -3 & 0 \\ 1 & 0 & 6 \\ 5 & -8 & 4 \end{bmatrix} \begin{bmatrix} 1 \\ 2 \\ 3 \end{bmatrix}$

22. For $f(x) = x^2$ and $g(x) = 3x - 1$, give $(f \circ g)(x)$ and $(g \circ f)(x)$. [7-3]

MORE PRACTICE

Find all roots of each polynomial equation.

23. $x^3 - 3x^2 - 10x + 24 = 0$

24. $x^3 - 3x^2 + 2 = 0$

25. $x^3 - 2x^2 + 5x + 26 = 0$

26. $4x^3 + 16x^2 - 22x - 10 = 0$

27. $6x^4 - 5x^3 - 65x^2 + 85x - 21 = 0$

28. $x^4 - x^3 + 19x^2 + 79x + 58 = 0$

29. $2x^4 - 5x^3 - 17x^2 + 41x - 21 = 0$

30. $x^4 - 6x^3 - 24x^2 - 26x - 9 = 0$

31. $9x^4 + 3x^3 - 30x^2 + 6x + 12 = 0$

32. $x^4 - 8x^3 + 73x^2 - 228x + 212 = 0$

33. $x^5 - 4x^4 + 4x^3 + 2x^2 - 5x + 2 = 0$

34. $x^5 + x^4 - 8x^3 - 8x^2 + 16x + 16 = 0$

35. Show that the two polynomial equations $x^2 + 3x = 4$ and $x^3 + 2x^2 - 7x = -4$ have the same solutions. How can polynomial equations with different degrees have the same solutions?

Decide whether each polynomial equation has multiple roots. If so, state which root. Then give the total number of roots of the equation, counting multiplicity.

36. $(x + 5)^5(2x - 1) = 0$ **37.** $x^3 + 4x^2 - 3x = 12$ **38.** $(4x^2 + 4x + 1)(x - 5) = 0$

39. $7x^3 - 2x = 5$ **40.** $(x^3 - 1)(x - 1) = 0$ **41.** $6x^2 - x^4 = 9$

MORE MATH REASONING

42. Given that $\sqrt{2}$ is a root of $x^4 + 7x^2 - 18 = 0$, solve this equation completely.

43. A polynomial equation of degree n has n roots counting multiplicity. Explain how this is a consequence of the Fundamental Theorem of Algebra.

44. Descartes' Rule of Signs There are three sign changes in the coefficients of the polynomial function $P(x) = x^6 + 7x^4 - x^3 - 2x^2 + 6x - 5$. One sign change occurs at the term $-x^3$, another at the term $6x$, and a third at the term -5. *Descartes' Rule of Signs* states that the number of positive real zeros of a polynomial function with real coefficients is either equal to the number of sign changes of the polynomial or less than that number by a positive even integer. Verify Descartes' Rule of Signs for the function $P(x)$.

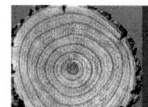

8-2

PART D **Making Connections**

←**CONNECT**→ *You've seen how to solve polynomials by graphing and by factoring. You've also learned some important strategies for dividing and factoring polynomials. The Fundamental Theorem of Algebra guarantees that every polynomial equation has a solution.*

Animal populations almost never remain constant. Increases in a population may lead to a scarcity of food, which in turn may cause the population to decrease. Polynomial functions can be useful models for describing the changes in some populations.

EXPLORE: DEER ME

MATERIALS

Graphing utility

During the early part of the twentieth century the mule deer of the Kaibab National Forest, near the Grand Canyon in Arizona, experienced a rapid increase in population. Hunting had reduced the number of coyotes, wolves, and mountain lions, which prey on the mule deer. This allowed the mule deer population to temporarily increase. However, the greater population caused diminished food supplies, eventually resulting in a decrease in the mule deer population.

The following polynomial function models the mule deer population from 1905 to 1930. The variable x represents the number of years since 1905.

$$D(x) = -0.125x^5 + 3.125x^4 + 4000$$

1. What is the degree of this polynomial function? What domain applies to the model? Explain why this function would not be a good model for every year after 1905.

2. Graph the function and give several values of the population during the period from 1905 to 1930.

3. According to the model, when was the population increasing? When was it decreasing? What was the maximum population and when did it occur?

4. Suppose you were a ranger in Kaibab National Forest during this period. You've decided that if the mule deer population reaches 20,000, you will control the mule deer population by issuing no new permits for hunting coyotes, wolves, or mountain lions. Write and solve an equation to determine when the deer population reached 20,000 and when the measures to control the population would have begun. Explain what method you used to solve the equation.

REFLECT

1. How are the factors of a polynomial $P(x)$ related to the roots of the related polynomial equation $P(x) = 0$?

2. Under what circumstances will the number of x-intercepts of the graph of $y = P(x)$ be different from the number of roots of $P(x) = 0$? Which number will be greater? Explain.

3. Choose one of the theorems you've learned about polynomials and describe how it applies to factoring polynomials and solving polynomial equations.

Self-Assessment

1. Show that $x^3 - 3x^2 + 3x - 1 = 0$ has only one solution. Does this contradict the Fundamental Theorem of Algebra? Explain.

2. How many x-intercepts is it possible for a cubic polynomial function with real coefficients to have? How many real roots can a cubic equation with real coefficients have? How many complex roots that are not real can a cubic equation with real coefficients have? Explain.

3. Give a cubic polynomial equation with roots 5, −6, and 7. Then give a quartic polynomial equation with the same roots and no others.

4. Describe the graph of each polynomial function. What does each graph tell you about the zeros of the function and the real roots of a related equation?
   a. $g(x) = x^4 + 5x^2 + 4$
   b. $h(x) = x^4 - 2x^3 - 4$

Solve each equation. Describe which method you used.

5. $(x - 5)^3(x + 2) = 0$

6. $x^3 - 4x^2 - 3x = -12$

7. $x^3 + 64 = 0$

8. City Trees City foresters give the following breakdown of environmental benefit values per year from a single tree: air conditioning = \$73; control of erosion and storm water runoff = \$75; wildlife shelter = \$75; control of air pollution = \$50. What is the total value of environmental benefits a tree provides each year?

If these amounts increase at 5% per year for a typical 50-year life of a tree, what is the total value of this single tree? [4-2]

9. Write the equation of an ellipse with center at the origin and vertices at $(-10, 0)$, $(10, 0)$, $(0, 6)$, and $(0, -6)$. [5-3]

10. Another type of substitution code uses a two-digit number substituted for each letter. The letters are written in a 5-by-5 grid called a *Greek square.* [6-2]

In the Greek square shown, the letter M would be substituted by 32. The first digit represents the row and the second digit represents the column. The letters I and J are given the same code, requiring the decoder to decide from the context which letter is appropriate. How many different codes based on Greek squares are possible?

Solve each radical equation. [7-2]

11. $\sqrt{2x + 5} = x + 1$

12. $\sqrt{2x + 4} = 2 + \sqrt{x}$

Use division to find each quotient and remainder.

13. $(x^4 + 3x^3 + 14x - 3) \div (x + 5)$

14. $(17 - 2x + 3x^3) \div (3 + x)$

15. The relationship between the height (h) in meters and the diameter (d) in centimeters of a giant sequoia (redwood) tree in a forest can be modeled by the function

$$d = 2.0121h + 0.1814h^2 - 0.00076045h^3.$$

   a. Graph this function and describe the shape of the graph.
   b. Use the model and solve an equation to predict the height of the largest known giant sequoia, the General Sherman, which has a diameter of 985 cm, the size of a small house!

8-3 Rational Expressions and Functions

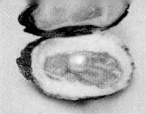

A Pearl of a Job

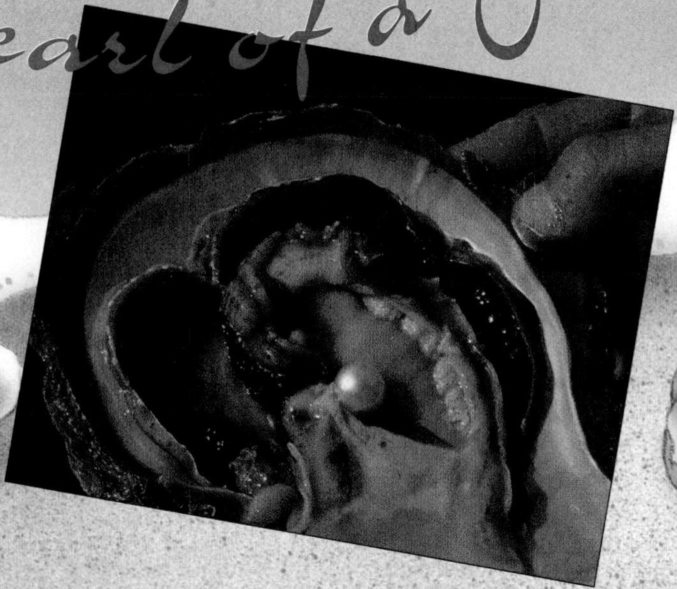

Until recently, Japanese divers, called the ama, *dived in the coastal waters off Japan collecting abalone, sea snails, oysters, and other bounty from the sea. Primarily women, the ama used very little diving equipment and followed traditions passed down over 2000 years.*

The ama typically dived for a minute or more on each breath of air, sometimes reaching depths as great as 75 feet. On deep dives, an ama diver usually wore a weighted belt, a face mask, and modeling clay in her ears to help protect them against the water pressure. When she was ready to surface, she would tug on a rope attached to her waist, signaling a helper waiting in a boat to pull her to the surface.

The ama tradition of diving has virtually disappeared in recent times. Today, most deep-sea diving is done with scuba gear *for purposes other than fishing. Scuba, or* Self-Contained Underwater Breathing Apparatus, *is one of the most important innovations in diving technology in the past century. Scuba equipment allows individual divers to dive deeper and stay underwater longer than ama ever could. However, scuba divers have their own dangers to contend with. They must carefully monitor their depth and time underwater to avoid getting* the bends, *a dangerous condition caused by the release of nitrogen in the bloodstream when a person returns too quickly to the surface.*

1. What factors could make it more difficult to hold your breath while diving?
2. What factors might have contributed to the decline of the ama tradition?
3. What variables do you think scuba divers must keep track of during dives?

Rational Expressions

← CONNECT → *Just as dividing integers yields rational numbers, dividing polynomials yields rational expressions. Now you will write, evaluate, and simplify rational expressions.*

The acceleration of gravity at the surface of the earth is 9.8 m/sec². However, this acceleration decreases the higher an object is above the earth. Now you will write and evaluate an expression that gives gravitational accelerations at different altitudes.

EXPLORE: DOWN TO EARTH

In the seventeenth century, Isaac Newton discovered that at any point above the earth, the gravitational acceleration towards the earth is inversely proportional to the square of the distance from the center of the earth.

1. The radius of the earth at the equator is 6378 km. A point x km above the earth's surface is what distance from the earth's center?

2. Write an expression for the earth's gravitational acceleration at a point x km above the earth. Use your knowledge of the acceleration of gravity at the earth's surface to find the constant of proportionality.

   Problem-Solving Tip

   Write a proportion.

3. Evaluate your expression to find the gravitational acceleration at each altitude above the earth's surface. How does each acceleration compare to the acceleration at the earth's surface?
   a. 1 km, the altitude of a low cloud
   b. 6 km, the cruising altitude of a commercial jet airliner
   c. 50 km, the edge of the stratosphere   **d.** 190,000 km, halfway to the moon

4. What happens to the value of your expression when $x < 0$? when $x = -6378$? Do you think the expression is valid for distances below the earth's surface? Explain.

Recall that rational numbers are ratios of integers. Similarly, **rational expressions** are ratios of polynomials, such as $\dfrac{3x^2 + 2x - 5}{4x - 7}$ and $\dfrac{2x - 1}{x(x + 3)}$.

In the Explore, you wrote and evaluated a rational expression with real variable values. You can also evaluate rational expressions for complex values. Doing so involves dividing complex numbers by using *complex conjugates*. Recall that the complex conjugate of $a + bi$ is $a - bi$.

EXAMPLE

1. An electrician connects an audio component *in parallel* with a 2-ohm resistor, as shown. The expression $\dfrac{2z}{z + 2}$ gives the total *impedance* (in ohms) of the parallel components if the audio component has an impedance of z ohms. Give the total impedance of the parallel components if the audio component has an impedance of $z = 1 - 4i$ ohms.

z ohms

2 ohms

$$\frac{2z}{z + 2} = \frac{2(1 - 4i)}{(1 - 4i) + 2} \qquad \text{Substitute } 1 - 4i \text{ for } z.$$

$$= \frac{2 - 8i}{3 - 4i} \qquad \begin{array}{l}\text{The complex conjugate of the denominator is} \\ 3 + 4i. \text{ Multiply by } \frac{3 + 4i}{3 + 4i}.\end{array}$$

$$= \frac{(2 - 8i)(3 + 4i)}{(3 - 4i)(3 + 4i)}$$

$$= \frac{6 + 8i - 24i + 32}{9 + 12i - 12i + 16}$$

$$= \frac{38 - 16i}{25} \qquad \text{The denominator is real.}$$

$$= 1.52 - 0.64i \qquad \text{Simplify.}$$

The total impedance is $1.52 - 0.64i$ ohms.

TRY IT

Let z be the impedance of an electrical component in ohms. The expression $\dfrac{3z}{z + 3}$ gives the total impedance (in ohms) of a 3-ohm resistor connected in parallel with the other electrical component. Give the total impedance of the parallel components for each value of z.

a. $z = 6$ ohms   **b.** $z = -2 + 3i$ ohms   **c.** $z = 1 + 2i$ ohms

CONSIDER

1. Assume a and b are real numbers. Explain why the product of $a + bi$ and its complex conjugate $a - bi$ is always real. How is this product related to $|a + bi|$?

You can often simplify rational expressions, making them easier to evaluate. To simplify a rational expression, first factor the polynomials in the numerator and in the denominator. Then find any factors common to both the numerator and denominator and simplify.

EXAMPLES

2. Simplify $\dfrac{x^3 - 8}{x^2 + x - 6}$.

Notice that 2 is a zero of the numerator. Use long division to factor $(x - 2)$ out of the numerator. Then factor the denominator and simplify using $\dfrac{x - 2}{x - 2} = 1$.

$$\frac{x^3 - 8}{x^2 + x - 6} = \frac{(x - 2)(x^2 + 2x + 4)}{(x - 2)(x + 3)}$$

$$= \frac{x^2 + 2x + 4}{x + 3}$$

$$\begin{array}{r} x^2 + 2x + 4 \\ x - 2 \overline{)x^3 + 0x^2 + 0x - 8} \\ \underline{x^3 - 2x^2} \\ 2x^2 + 0x \\ \underline{2x^2 - 4x} \\ 4x - 8 \\ \underline{4x - 8} \\ 0 \end{array}$$

3. Multiply and simplify $\dfrac{t^2 - 1}{t^2 - 2t - 3} \cdot \dfrac{3t - 9}{t^2 + 5t + 6}$.

$$\frac{t^2 - 1}{t^2 - 2t - 3} \cdot \frac{3t - 9}{t^2 + 5t + 6}$$

$$= \frac{(t + 1)(t - 1)}{(t - 3)(t + 1)} \cdot \frac{3(t - 3)}{(t + 3)(t + 2)} \qquad \text{Factor each polynomial.}$$

$$= \frac{(t - 1)}{1} \cdot \frac{3}{(t + 3)(t + 2)} \qquad \text{Simplify using } \frac{t + 1}{t + 1} = 1 \text{ and } \frac{t - 3}{t - 3} = 1.$$

$$= \frac{3(t - 1)}{(t + 3)(t + 2)} \qquad \text{Multiply the numerators and multiply the denominators.}$$

To divide by a rational expression, multiply by its reciprocal.

EXAMPLE

4. Divide and simplify $\dfrac{y^2 - 25}{y^2 - 4} \div \dfrac{y^2 + 2y - 15}{y^2 + 2y}$.

$$\frac{y^2 - 25}{y^2 - 4} \div \frac{y^2 + 2y - 15}{y^2 + 2y}$$

$$= \frac{y^2 - 25}{y^2 - 4} \cdot \frac{y^2 + 2y}{y^2 + 2y - 15} \qquad \text{Rewrite as a product.}$$

$$= \frac{(y - 5)(y + 5)}{(y + 2)(y - 2)} \cdot \frac{y(y + 2)}{(y - 3)(y + 5)} \qquad \text{Factor each polynomial.}$$

$$= \frac{(y - 5)}{(y - 2)} \cdot \frac{y}{(y - 3)} \qquad \text{Simplify.}$$

$$= \frac{y(y - 5)}{(y - 2)(y - 3)} \qquad \text{Multiply the numerators and multiply the denominators.}$$

Simplify each expression.

d. $\dfrac{x^4 - 16}{3x^2 - 8x + 4}$

e. $\dfrac{-3a^2}{4b} \cdot \dfrac{2b^3}{9a}$

f. $\dfrac{x^2 + x}{3x^2} \cdot \dfrac{18x^3}{2x^2 - x - 3}$

g. $\dfrac{z^2 + 10z + 25}{3z + 4} \div \dfrac{2z^2 - 50}{4z^2 - 26z + 30}$

Simplifying and evaluating rational expressions can help you use formulas in a variety of subjects, such as physics, chemistry, and electronics. Remember that many of the properties and tools you use to work with fractions also apply to rational expressions.

REFLECT

1. How are rational expressions similar to rational numbers? How are they different?

2. Explain how you divide two complex numbers.

3. How are multiplying and dividing rational expressions similar to multiplying and dividing rational numbers?

Exercises

CORE

1. Getting Started Determine whether each expression is a rational expression.

a. $\dfrac{2}{3x}$

b. $\sqrt{x + 5}$

c. $\dfrac{-3}{5}$

d. $\dfrac{x^2 - 1}{2x^2 + 7x - 10}$

2. Choose the correct letter to complete the statement.

A rational expression is a ratio of ____.

(a) integers   (b) rational numbers   (c) polynomials   (d) not here

Evaluate each rational expression for the given value of the variable.

3. $\dfrac{1}{x + 3}$ for $x = 6$

4. $\dfrac{2y + 5}{y^2}$ for $y = -3$

5. $\dfrac{3a + 2}{a - 7}$ for $a = -1$

Divide each pair of complex numbers.

6. $(8 + 4i) \div (1 + 2i)$

7. $26 \div (-2 + 3i)$

8. Let z be the impedance of an electrical component in ohms. The expression $\dfrac{5z}{z + 5}$ gives the total impedance (in ohms) of a 5-ohm resistor connected in parallel with the other electrical component. Give the total impedance of the parallel components for each value of z.

a. $z = 20$ ohms

b. $z = -1 - 3i$ ohms

c. $z = 1 + 8i$ ohms

9. Write a rational expression for the partial sum of the first ten terms of a geometric series with first term a and common ratio r. Evaluate your expression to find the tenth partial sum of the series $0.2 + 0.4 + 0.8 + 1.6 + \cdots$.

Simplify each expression.

10. $\dfrac{-40x^3y}{80xy^2}$

11. $\dfrac{a + 3}{a^2 + a - 6}$

12. $\dfrac{y^3 - 27}{2y^2 + 6y + 18}$

13. $\dfrac{2n^2 - 32}{n^2 + 11n + 28}$

14. $\dfrac{-a}{bc^2} \cdot \dfrac{c^3}{ab}$

15. $\dfrac{x^2}{y} \div \dfrac{x^3}{y}$

16. $\dfrac{3x}{x^2 - 4} \cdot \dfrac{x^2 + 5x + 6}{3x - 21}$

17. $\dfrac{2y - 5}{2y^2 - 3y + 1} \cdot \dfrac{y^2 - 1}{2y^2 - 3y - 5}$

18. $\dfrac{a^3}{a^2 - 9} \div \dfrac{2a^2 + a}{2a^2 + 7a + 3}$

19. $\dfrac{b^2 - 81}{2b^2 - 50} \div \dfrac{3b - 27}{b^2 + 10b + 25}$

History

20. In the book *The Spirit of St. Louis*, Charles Lindbergh recorded an anxious moment over the ocean on his historic flight from New York to Paris in 1927. "What I wouldn't give for a high cloud's shadow on the surface to tell me the wind drift aloft! What should I allow for the wind?"

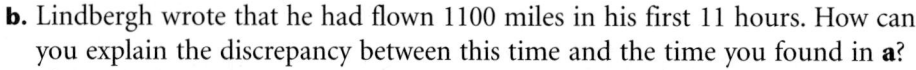

a. Lindbergh's log relates that in the eleventh hour he was over Newfoundland flying at an air speed of 92 mi/hr with a tailwind of 20 mi/hr. Explain why $\dfrac{1100}{92 + 20}$ hours is the time it would take to fly 1100 miles in these conditions. How would the time differ if he had a 20 mi/hr *headwind*?

b. Lindbergh wrote that he had flown 1100 miles in his first 11 hours. How can you explain the discrepancy between this time and the time you found in **a**?

c. If the wind speed and direction remained the same and Lindbergh had aborted the flight at 1100 miles and returned to New York at an average air speed of 95 mi/hr, what expression would give the time for his return trip?

Social Science

21. Fly Away The distance between Washington, D.C., and San Francisco is 2800 miles. An airplane flies at a speed of 400 miles per hour in still air. Suppose a wind of w miles per hour blows from west to east across the country.

a. Write a rational expression for the time for a flight from San Francisco to Washington, D.C. Then write a second rational expression for the time for a flight from Washington, D.C., to San Francisco.

b. What is the flight time in each direction if the wind speed is 10 miles per hour?

LOOK AHEAD

Evaluate each expression.

22. $\dfrac{3}{4} + \dfrac{7}{12}$

23. $\dfrac{3}{5} - \dfrac{1}{3}$

24. $\dfrac{7}{9} - \dfrac{1}{6}$

MORE PRACTICE

Evaluate each rational expression for the given value of the variable.

25. $\dfrac{13 + x}{2x}$ for $x = -21$

26. $\dfrac{3a - 5}{a + 4}$ for $a = 3$

27. $\dfrac{3y^2 - 7}{y - 5}$ for $y = -1$

28. $\dfrac{b^3}{b^2 + 2b - 3}$ for $b = -2$

29. $\dfrac{10}{-3x - 1}$ for $x = 3$

30. $\dfrac{6}{a + 2}$ for $a = -2$

Divide each pair of complex numbers.

31. $100i \div (3 - 4i)$

32. $(12 + 8i) \div (3 + i)$

33. $(9 + 5i) \div 10i$

34. Prepayment Formula The expression $\dfrac{M[1 - (1 + r)^{-q}]}{r}$ gives approximate prepayment amounts for making house payments in advance. M is the monthly payment, r is the monthly interest rate, and q is the number of remaining payment periods. Rewrite the formula without a negative exponent.

Simplify each rational expression.

35. $\dfrac{-15xy^2}{24x^3}$

36. $\dfrac{(x - 2)^3}{x^2 - 4}$

37. $\dfrac{y^2 - 1}{2y^2 + 3y + 1}$

38. $\dfrac{4n^2 + 8n}{n^3 + 8}$

39. $\dfrac{6y^2 - 5y - 6}{10y^2 - 11y - 6}$

40. $\dfrac{15ab^3}{8b} \cdot \dfrac{12a^3}{-10ab^2}$

41. $\dfrac{t^4 - 16}{6t + 12} \cdot \dfrac{3t^2 - 6t}{t^2 - 2t + 4}$

42. $\dfrac{3a^2}{4b^2} \div \dfrac{b}{2}$

43. $\dfrac{8}{xy} \div \dfrac{16x^2}{y}$

44. $\dfrac{2y^2 + 4y}{y^2 - 25} \cdot \dfrac{2y - 10}{3y^2 + 5y - 2}$

45. $\dfrac{y^2 + 3y}{9y^2} \div \dfrac{y^2 - 9}{12}$

46. $\dfrac{a^2 - 4a - 5}{a^2 + 4a + 4} \cdot \dfrac{a^2 + a - 2}{a^2 - 1}$

47. $\dfrac{2c^2 + 3c + 1}{2c^2 - c - 3} \cdot \dfrac{2c^2 - 3c}{c + 2}$

48. $\dfrac{4x^2}{x + 2} \div \dfrac{x^2 + 4x + 4}{2x^3 - 8x}$

49. $\dfrac{b^2 - 6b + 5}{b^2 + 3b + 2} \div \dfrac{b^2 - 25}{b^2 + 6b + 5}$

50. Big Pipes A pipe manufacturer has 690 cubic feet of iron to make into pipe that has an inside radius of two feet. Let x represent the thickness of the pipe.

   a. The volume of iron in a pipe is the length of the pipe multiplied by the cross-sectional area. Using this fact, write an expression for the length of the pipe that can be made from 690 ft^3 of iron.

   b. If the manufacturer needs to cast 2-inch-thick pipes in 8-foot lengths, how many lengths of pipe can be produced?

   c. Cast iron weighs 450 lb/ft^3. How much would each length of pipe weigh?

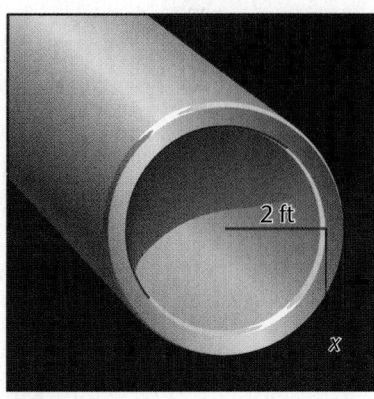

MORE MATH REASONING

51. For what values of x would the following product equal zero?

$$\frac{x^2 + x - 2}{x^2 - x + 5} \cdot \frac{x^2 + 2x - 3}{x - 5}$$

Simplify each expression.

52. $\dfrac{\frac{a}{b}}{\frac{a^2}{b^2}}$

53. $\dfrac{\frac{2xy^2}{y^3}}{\frac{x^2}{4y}}$

54. $\dfrac{\frac{5t^2}{t^2 - 9}}{\frac{15t^2 + 45t}{t^2 - 6t + 9}}$

Adding and Subtracting Rational Expressions

← CONNECT → *You've multiplied, divided, and simplified rational expressions. Now you will add and subtract rational expressions and simplify the results.*

Recall that to add fractions, you must first write them with the same denominator. Can the same idea work for adding rational expressions? You will investigate this question in the following Explore.

EXPLORE: THE SUM OF THE PARTS

MATERIALS

Graphing utility
Graph paper

1. Graph each equation on a graphing utility. Sketch each graph.

  a. $y = \dfrac{1}{x} + \dfrac{1}{2x}$

  b. $y = \dfrac{1}{x - 4} - \dfrac{1}{x + 4}$

  c. $y = \dfrac{3}{x(x + 3)} - \dfrac{1}{x}$

2. Graph each equation on a graphing utility. Identify any graph that seems to match a graph in Step 1.

  a. $y = \dfrac{1}{x(x + 3)}$ **b.** $y = \dfrac{3}{2x}$

  c. $y = -\dfrac{1}{x + 3}$ **d.** $y = \dfrac{8}{x^2 - 16}$

3. For each pair of matching graphs, compare the expressions of x in their equations. Use what you know about adding and subtracting rational numbers to determine how to simplify or begin to simplify the expression from Step 1 to match the expression from Step 2.

To add or subtract rational expressions, they must first be written with a common denominator. The **least common denominator** (LCD) is the least common multiple of the denominators and can be found by factoring each denominator.

1. a. Find the LCD of $\dfrac{4}{a^2 + 3a}$ and $\dfrac{5}{a^3 - 2a^2}$.

First factor each denominator: $a^2 + 3a = a(a + 3)$ and $a^3 - 2a^2 = a^2(a - 2)$.

The LCD is the product of the greatest power of each factor in the denominators. The greatest powers of a, $a + 3$, and $a - 2$ are a^2, $a + 3$, and $a - 2$, respectively.

The LCD of $\dfrac{4}{a(a + 3)}$ and $\dfrac{5}{a^2(a - 2)}$ is $a^2(a + 3)(a - 2)$.

b. Simplify $\dfrac{4}{a^2 + 3a} + \dfrac{5}{a^3 - 2a^2}$.

$= \dfrac{4}{a(a + 3)} + \dfrac{5}{a^2(a - 2)}$ Factor each denominator.

To write each expression with the least common denominator, multiply the first expression by $\dfrac{a(a - 2)}{a(a - 2)}$ and the second one by $\dfrac{a + 3}{a + 3}$.

$= \dfrac{4a(a - 2)}{a^2(a + 3)(a - 2)} + \dfrac{5(a + 3)}{a^2(a + 3)(a - 2)}$ Rewrite each expression with the LCD.

$= \dfrac{4a^2 - 8a}{a^2(a + 3)(a - 2)} + \dfrac{5a + 15}{a^2(a + 3)(a - 2)}$

$= \dfrac{4a^2 - 8a + 5a + 15}{a^2(a + 3)(a - 2)}$ Add the numerators.

$= \dfrac{4a^2 - 3a + 15}{a^2(a + 3)(a - 2)}$ Simplify.

2. Simplify $\dfrac{2x + 4}{x^2 - x} - \dfrac{x + 4}{x^3 - x}$.

$= \dfrac{2x + 4}{x(x - 1)} - \dfrac{x + 4}{x(x + 1)(x - 1)}$ Factor each denominator.

$= \dfrac{(2x + 4)(x + 1)}{x(x + 1)(x - 1)} - \dfrac{x + 4}{x(x + 1)(x - 1)}$ Rewrite each expression with the LCD.

$= \dfrac{(2x^2 + 6x + 4) - (x + 4)}{x(x + 1)(x - 1)}$ Subtract the numerators.

$= \dfrac{2x^2 + 5x}{x(x + 1)(x - 1)}$

$= \dfrac{x(2x + 5)}{x(x + 1)(x - 1)}$ Factor the numerator.

$= \dfrac{2x + 5}{(x + 1)(x - 1)}$ Simplify.

Simplify each expression.

a. $\dfrac{1}{x^2 + x} + \dfrac{1}{x^2 - x}$

b. $\dfrac{1}{s^2 - 2s} - \dfrac{1 - s}{s^2 - 4}$

Once you've simplified a sum or difference of rational expressions, you have a single convenient expression to evaluate.

EXAMPLE

3. Jacqueline races in triathlons and can swim 50 meters per minute in calm water. The swimming part of her next race is out to a buoy and back, covering a total of 1500 m.

a. Write an expression for Jacqueline's total swimming time if there is a current of x m/min from the buoy towards the start during the race.

The formula relating distance (d) to rate (r) and time (t) is $d = rt$, so $t = \dfrac{d}{r}$.

For the 750-m swim to the buoy, Jacqueline will be going *against* the current, so she can only swim at a speed of $(50 - x)$ m/min. Her time for this half will be $\dfrac{750}{50 - x}$ minutes.

For the 750-m swim back, she will be swimming *with* the current, so she can swim at $(50 + x)$ m/min. Her time for this half will be $\dfrac{750}{50 + x}$ minutes.

Jacqueline's total time for the swim will be $\dfrac{750}{50 - x} + \dfrac{750}{50 + x}$ minutes.

$$\dfrac{750}{50 - x} + \dfrac{750}{50 + x} = \dfrac{750(50 + x)}{(50 + x)(50 - x)} + \dfrac{750(50 - x)}{(50 + x)(50 - x)}$$

$$= \dfrac{750 \cdot 50 + 750x + 750 \cdot 50 - 750x}{2{,}500 - x^2}$$

$$= \dfrac{75{,}000}{2{,}500 - x^2}$$

b. At the race Jacqueline found out that the current is 10 m/min. What time should she expect for the swimming part of the triathlon?

$x = 10$, so $\dfrac{75{,}000}{2{,}500 - x^2} = \dfrac{75{,}000}{2{,}400} = 31.25$.

Jacqueline can expect to take 31.25 minutes for the swim.

CONSIDER

1. What is the fastest time Jacqueline can swim the 1500 meters? Under what conditions can she swim that time?

The way you combine rational expressions by adding and subtracting is similar to the way you combine fractions. Using the LCD of rational expressions allows you to write their sum or difference as a single rational expression.

REFLECT

1. How are adding and subtracting rational expressions like adding and subtracting fractions?
2. Describe how to find the least common denominator of two rational expressions.
3. Dave said, "Instead of finding the LCD, I find a common denominator by multiplying all of the denominators of the rational expressions together." Will this method work? What are its disadvantages?

Exercises

CORE

1. Getting Started Simplify each sum.

a. $\dfrac{a}{4a} + \dfrac{3}{4a}$

b. $\dfrac{4}{c+1} + \dfrac{2}{c+1}$

c. $\dfrac{3}{3+x} + \dfrac{x}{3+x}$

2. In your own words, explain the meaning of *least common denominator*.

Find the least common denominator of each pair of rational expressions.

3. $\dfrac{14}{b-3}; \dfrac{1}{2b+6}$

4. $\dfrac{5}{a^2+a}; \dfrac{7}{a}$

5. $\dfrac{2x}{x^2-9}; \dfrac{1}{x^2+6x+9}$

6. $\dfrac{5}{z^2-8z+15}; \dfrac{7}{z^2-2z-3}$

Simplify each expression.

7. $\dfrac{3}{4m} + \dfrac{1}{10m^2}$

8. $\dfrac{4}{q^2+2q+1} - \dfrac{q}{7(q+1)}$

9. $\dfrac{5p}{p+1} + \dfrac{7}{p^2+p}$

10. $\dfrac{3}{x^2} + \dfrac{x+1}{x+x^2}$

11. $\dfrac{1}{2x^2-5x-3} + \dfrac{7}{x-3}$

12. $\dfrac{y}{y^2-9} - \dfrac{2}{y^2-2y-3}$

13. Let There Be Light If two electrical components with resistances of r_1 ohms and r_2 ohms are connected in parallel, the total resistance is the reciprocal of $\dfrac{1}{r_1} + \dfrac{1}{r_2}$.
Assume two light bulbs are connected in parallel and that one (r ohms) has a resistance 4 ohms greater than the other. Give a rational expression for the total resistance of the connected light bulbs.

14. **On the Road** A research team for a county transportation department polled drivers who commute about 20 miles to work. They found that the people drive about 5 mi/hr slower going the 20 miles home than they do driving into work in the morning. Let r be a driver's average speed (in mi/hr) driving into work.

   a. What does the expression $\frac{20}{r-5} - \frac{20}{r}$ represent? Simplify this expression. If the typical driver averages 45 mi/hr on the morning drive, what does the expression tell the researchers?

   b. What does the expression $\frac{20}{r-5} + \frac{20}{r}$ represent? Simplify this expression. Using the typical speed given in **a,** what does this expression tell the researchers?

15. Two rectangles each have an area of 12 in.^{2}, but one rectangle is 1 inch more than twice as long as the other. Write a rational expression that gives the difference in the widths of the two rectangles. What is this difference if the longer rectangle is 9 inches long?

> **Problem-Solving Tip**
>
> Draw a diagram.

LOOK BACK

16. Mile-High Car Rental in Denver, Colorado, charges $25 per day plus $0.18 per mile to rent a compact car. [2-1]
   a. Write a linear function that expresses the cost (C) to rent a compact car for one day as a function of the distance (d), in miles, that the car is driven.
   b. Graph the function and tell what the y-intercept represents.

Simplify each expression. [4-3]

17. $\sqrt{45}$
18. $-5\sqrt{96}$
19. $\sqrt{144 + 25}$
20. $6\sqrt{-54}$

21. Sketch the graph of each equation. [5-3]
   a. $(x-3)^2 + (y-2)^2 = 25$
   b. $\frac{x^2}{9} + \frac{y^2}{4} = 1$

MORE PRACTICE

Find the least common denominator of each pair of rational expressions.

22. $\frac{2}{5v}; \frac{v+1}{10v^2}$

23. $\frac{3}{10a^2 + 5a}; \frac{7}{4a^2 - 1}$

24. $\frac{1}{3t+9}; \frac{1}{t^2 - 9}$

25. $\frac{3}{4a-8}; \frac{5}{6a-12}$

26. $\frac{5}{x^2 - 3x - 4}; \frac{x}{x^2 - 6x + 8}$

27. $\frac{2}{b^2 + 4b + 4}; \frac{1}{b^2 - b - 6}$

Simplify each expression.

28. $\dfrac{2}{7a} - \dfrac{1}{4a^2}$

29. $\dfrac{a}{2a^2 - 2} + \dfrac{2}{a^2 + a}$

30. $\dfrac{3a}{a - 4} - \dfrac{12}{a - 4} \;=\; \dfrac{3a - 12}{a - 4}$

31. $\dfrac{x + 1}{x + 5} + \dfrac{2}{x - 3}$

32. $\dfrac{2y}{y^2 + 3y + 2} + \dfrac{3y - 1}{y^2 - 1}$

33. $\dfrac{4}{a + 2} - \dfrac{3}{a - 2}$

34. $\dfrac{2}{x^3 - 2x^2} - \dfrac{1}{3x^2 + 3x}$

35. $\dfrac{n}{3n^2 - 10n + 8} - \dfrac{2}{9n^2 - 9n - 4}$

36. $\dfrac{p + 1}{p^2 - 1} + \dfrac{p - 1}{p^2 + 2p + 1}$

37. $\dfrac{m - 1}{m + 5} - \dfrac{m + 2}{m - 3}$

38. Joanna flies her airplane at an air speed of 300 mi/hr. If there is an x mi/hr wind from the north and Joanna is planning a round-trip to an airport 76 miles south, how long will her total travel time be as a rational expression of x? Evaluate the expression for several reasonable values of x.

39. On Ice The team accountant for the North Dakota Ice Cubes keeps track of finances using these variables and expressions:

S = the income from regular ticket sales; p = the price for each regular seat;

$p - x$ = the price for a bleacher seat; $p + 2x$ = price for reserved seats.

a. The accountant has found that the income from bleacher seats is usually 80% of the income from regular seats, and the income from reserved seats is usually 150% of the income from regular seats. What does the expression $\dfrac{S}{p} + \dfrac{0.8S}{p - x} + \dfrac{1.5S}{p + 2x}$ represent?

b. Simplify the expression in **a.** If $p = \$6$ and $x = \$2$, what does the expression tell you about a game where the income from regular tickets was \$9000?

MORE MATH REASONING

40. Demonstrate that you can also simplify rational expressions with *complex* coefficients by simplifying the expression $\dfrac{2x}{ix + 1} + \dfrac{2ix^2}{x^2 + 1}$.

41. Ringing Up Sales Frankie and Carla each make custom beaded jewelry and have decided to start a business together. It takes Frankie 10 minutes more on average to make a beaded bracelet than it takes Carla.

a. Write and simplify a rational expression for the number of bracelets Frankie and Carla can make in an hour working together, if x is the average number of minutes it takes Frankie to make a bracelet.

b. If it takes Frankie an average of 30 minutes to make a bracelet, how many bracelets can Frankie and Carla expect to produce per hour in their business?

← C O N N E C T →   *You have worked with rational expressions. Now you will investigate*
rational functions and their graphs. The graphs of rational functions have
some characteristics you don't see in the graphs of polynomial functions.

Ballooning has captured the imaginations of people ever since the French
scientist Jean Francois Pilatre de Rozier became the first person to ride in a
hot-air balloon in October of 1783. Since then, balloons, dirigibles, and
blimps filled with hot air, helium, or other gases have been used for sport,
meteorological research, and even as passenger ships.

EXPLORE: UP, UP, AND AWAY!

The volume of gas in a sealed balloon depends on
the outside air pressure. The lower the pressure, the
greater the volume, causing the balloon to expand.
If the temperature of the gas stays constant, the
volume varies inversely with the pressure.

1. While on the ground preparing for flight,
a weather balloon is filled with 1000 m³ of
helium at a pressure of 1 atm (1 atm =
average atmospheric pressure at sea level).
Give the volume (V) of helium in the balloon
as a function of the pressure (p). What type
of function is $V(p)$?
2. For altitudes up to several kilometers, the
atmospheric pressure decreases about 0.1 atm
for every kilometer the balloon rises. Give the pressure (p) as a function of the
balloon's altitude (a). What type of function is $p(a)$?
3. Give the volume of helium in the balloon as a function of its altitude. Explain how
you found this function. What type of function is $V(a)$?
4. What altitudes should the balloon be restricted to if the balloon can safely hold up
to 1250 m³ of helium?

Rational expressions lead naturally to **rational functions,** functions of the
form $r(x) = \dfrac{p(x)}{q(x)}$, where $p(x)$ and $q(x)$ are polynomials. The domain of a
rational function is all real numbers except the zeros of the denominator,
where the function is *undefined.* Near these values, the graph of a rational
function has features you don't see in the graphs of polynomial functions.

EXAMPLE

Sketch the graph $f(x) = \dfrac{x^2 + 5x}{x + 2}$.

The function is undefined when $x = -2$, so the domain of $f(x)$ is all real numbers except $x = -2$. The function has zeros when the numerator is 0, at $x = 0$ and $x = -5$. We can use a graphing utility or make a table of values to sketch the graph.

x	-7	-5	-3	-2.5	-1.5	-1	0	1	4
f(x)	-2.8	0	6	12.5	-10.5	-4	0	2	6

The graph is **discontinuous** at $x = -2$; that is, there is a break in the graph. We also say that the graph has a *discontinuity* at $x = -2$. The line $x = -2$ is a **vertical asymptote** of the graph.

The graph of a rational function can be discontinuous at a value of x without having an asymptote there. This can occur if there is a common factor in the numerator and denominator of the function.

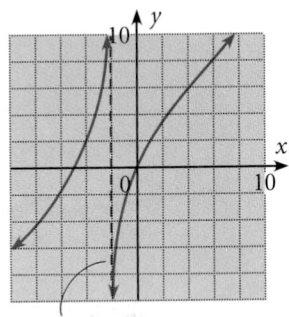

Vertical asymptote
at $x = -2$

WHAT DO **YOU** THINK?

Graph $y = \dfrac{x^2 - 1}{x^2 - x - 2}$ and describe any discontinuities in the graph.

Arturo thinks...

First, I'll factor the denominator. $x^2 - x - 2 = (x + 1)(x - 2)$, which equals zero when $x = -1$ or $x = 2$. So the graph is discontinuous at $x = -1$ and $x = 2$.

Plotting points and sketching the graph shows that there is a vertical asymptote at $x = 2$. At $x = -1$ there is just a "hole" in the graph where the function is undefined.

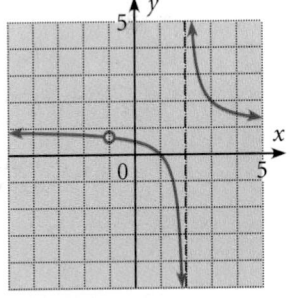

Darcy thinks...

The graph will have discontinuities at $x = -1$ and $x = 2$ since the value of the denominator is 0 for these x-values. I'll graph the function on a graphing utility and investigate these points.

There is a vertical asymptote at $x = 2$. *Tracing* to $x = -1$ shows that there is a break in the graph there, but no asymptote.

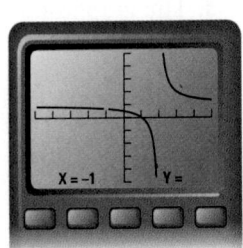

1. What factor is common to both the numerator and denominator of the function graphed by Arturo and Darcy? If you simplify the rational expression, how will the domain and graph of the new function differ from the original one? Explain.

TRY IT

Sketch the graph of each function. Describe any discontinuities in the graph.

a. $f(x) = \dfrac{x + 2}{x - 3}$

b. $y = \dfrac{x^2 + 3x + 2}{2(x + 1)}$

c. $\dfrac{x^2 + x - 6}{x^2 - 4}$

Rational functions can be difficult to graph by merely plotting points. Identifying discontinuities before you graph can help you find key features so you can make a reasonable sketch of the graph.

REFLECT

1. How do you find the domain of a rational function?

2. Do rational functions include polynomial functions? Explain.

3. Describe the types of discontinuities a rational function can have.

4. What other graphs have you worked with that have asymptotes?

Exercises

CORE

1. Getting Started Find the zeros of each function. Then find the values of x that make the denominator of each function 0, and explain why the function is undefined at these values.

a. $f(x) = \dfrac{2x}{x + 1}$

b. $g(x) = \dfrac{3x - 5}{x^2}$

c. $h(x) = \dfrac{x^2 - 3x}{2x + 5}$

Choose the word or phrase that best completes each statement.

2. If $f(x)$ is given by a ratio of polynomials, then it is a ____ function.

3. The graph of a function is ____ at a value of x if there is a break in the graph at that value.

4. If the graph of a rational function approaches a vertical line at a discontinuity, then the line is called a ____.

Determine where any discontinuities will occur in the graph of each rational function.

5. $f(x) = \dfrac{5}{x-1}$

6. $r(x) = \dfrac{3x-2}{3x^2 + 13x - 10}$

7. $g(x) = \dfrac{x^2 + 9x + 14}{x^2 - 7x + 10}$

8. $k(x) = \dfrac{x^2 - 4}{x+2}$

9. Match each function with its graph. Explain how you decided. Locate each discontinuity and tell whether there is a vertical asymptote or a "hole" there.

a. $f(x) = \dfrac{x^2 - 3x}{x^2 - x - 6}$

b. $g(x) = \dfrac{x^2 + 7x + 10}{2x + 4}$

c. $h(x) = \dfrac{x^2 + 1}{x^2 + 2x + 1}$

i.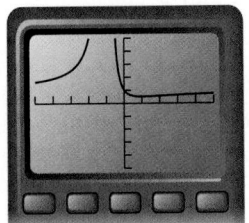

ii.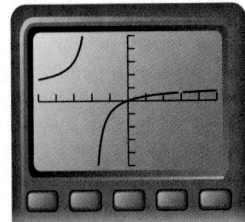

iii.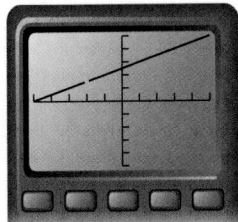

Make a table of values and sketch the graph of each rational function. Describe any discontinuities in the graphs.

10. $f(x) = \dfrac{1}{x+3}$

11. $g(x) = \dfrac{1}{x^2}$

12. $h(x) = \dfrac{12x + 24}{x^2 + 2x}$

13. $k(x) = \dfrac{x^2 - 1}{x^2 + 3x + 2}$

14. Boxing It Up The initial investment for the Burton Box Company was $225,000. Each box the company makes costs an additional $0.25 to produce.
   a. Write the unit cost per box as a function of the number of boxes produced. What is the domain of the function that makes sense in this situation?
   b. Will the unit cost of producing a box ever fall below $0.25? Explain.
   c. Sketch the graph of the function. Locate any asymptotes of the graph.

15. Sketch the graphs of the functions $f(x) = \dfrac{x^2 - 1}{x^2 - 2x - 3}$ and $g(x) = \dfrac{x-1}{x-3}$.
   a. How are the graphs similar? How are they different?
   b. Compare the expressions of x in both functions. What do you notice?

16. Jesse can paint a room in 1 hour less than Carl can.
   a. Let t be the time it takes Jesse to paint a room in a house. How fast does he paint in rooms per hour? How fast does Carl paint in rooms per hour?
   b. Add the rates in **a** to find how fast both can paint a room together. Simplify this expression.
   c. Using the expression in **b,** write a function $f(t)$ that gives the time it takes the two of them to paint a room together.
   d. If Jesse can paint each bedroom of a large 3-bedroom house in 3 hours, how long will it take both Jesse and Carl working together to paint all 3 bedrooms?

Solve each equation.

17. $12p^2 + 11p - 5 = 0$ **18.** $3x^3 = 75x$ **19.** $2y^2 + 10y = 28$

MORE PRACTICE

Determine where any discontinuities will occur in the graph of each rational function.

20. $f(x) = \dfrac{4}{x - 5}$

21. $g(x) = \dfrac{3x}{x^2 + 2}$

22. $y = \dfrac{x - 1}{x^2 + 5x + 6}$

23. $y = \dfrac{x^2 - 25}{2x^2 - 7x - 15}$

24. $h(x) = \dfrac{5}{8x^3 - 18x}$

25. $R(x) = \dfrac{2x - 4}{3x^2 + 5x + 1}$

26. Use a Graphing Utility Graph each function and sketch the graph. Locate and describe any discontinuities in the graphs.

a. $y = \dfrac{x + 7}{3x^2 - 11x - 20}$

b. $y = \dfrac{x^3 - 64}{x^2 - 16}$

27. A chemist has 500 milliliters of a solution that is 25% acid. If she mixes this solution with m milliliters of pure acid, the following function gives the concentration of the acid in the resulting solution:

$$C(m) = \frac{(0.25 \cdot 500 + m)}{(500 + m)}$$

a. What domain makes sense in this situation? Graph $C(m)$.

b. Does the graph have an asymptote in the relevant domain?

c. Can the value of C ever be greater than 1? Explain.

Make a table of values and sketch the graph of each rational function. Describe any discontinuities in the graphs.

28. $F(x) = \dfrac{x + 3}{1 - x}$

29. $F(x) = \dfrac{1}{x^2 + 6x + 5}$

30. $F(x) = \dfrac{12}{x^2 + 4}$

31. $F(x) = \dfrac{2x}{x^2 + 8x - 9}$

32. $F(x) = \dfrac{x^2 + x - 2}{x^2 + 4x + 3}$

33. $F(x) = \dfrac{2x^2 - 6x}{x^2 - 9}$

34. Use a Graphing Utility Graph $y = \dfrac{x^2 - 1}{x + 1}$ and $y = x - 1$. Compare the equations and the graphs and describe what you notice.

MORE MATH REASONING

Write a rational function that matches each description.

35. zeros: $x = 2$ and $x = 5$; "holes": none; asymptote: $x = -4$

36. zeros: none; "hole": $x = 2$; asymptotes: $x = 3$ and $x = -2$

37. Graph some functions of the form $f(x) = \dfrac{ax + b}{x + c}$. Every such function has a *horizontal asymptote* as well as a vertical asymptote. Give the location of both the horizontal and vertical asymptotes in terms of a, b, and c.

8-3 PART D · Solving Rational Equations

← **CONNECT** → *You've solved various types of equations, including radical and polynomial equations. You can solve rational equations by using many of the same techniques and properties you use to solve other equations.*

An equation involving rational expressions is called a **rational equation.** As with other types of equations, one way to solve a rational equation is to use the graph of the related rational function.

EXAMPLE

1. A spacecraft is heading from Earth directly toward the moon, 240,000 miles away. If x is the distance to Earth in thousands of miles, then $240 - x$ is the distance to the moon. At these distances gravity accelerates the craft at $\dfrac{154}{x^2}$ m/sec^2 toward Earth and at $\dfrac{1.9}{(240 - x)^2}$ m/sec^2 toward the moon. At what distance from Earth will the net gravitational acceleration acting upon the spacecraft from Earth and the moon be 0?

The net acceleration toward Earth, in m/sec^2, is given by the function

$$A(x) = \frac{154}{x^2} - \frac{1.9}{(240 - x)^2}, \text{ where } 0 \le x \le 240.$$

The solution of the rational equation

$$\frac{154}{x^2} - \frac{1.9}{(240 - x)^2} = 0$$

gives the distance from Earth at which the net acceleration is 0. Graph the function in this range and *trace* to find the x-intercept, where $A(x) = 0$.

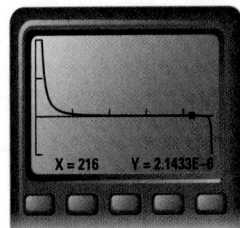

X = 216   Y = 2.1433E–6

The solution is $x \approx 216$. The net acceleration is 0 when the spacecraft is about 216,000 miles from Earth, 90% of the way to the moon.

You can also solve rational equations symbolically, using properties of algebra. The first step is to multiply by the least common denominator. You can then solve the resulting polynomial equation by one of the methods you used in 8-2.

EXAMPLES

2. Solve $\frac{3}{x} + \frac{6}{x+3} = 2$.

Keep in mind that x cannot equal 0 or -3 since one of the rational expressions is undefined for each of these values.

$$x(x+3)\left(\frac{3}{x} + \frac{6}{x+3}\right) = 2x(x+3)$$ Multiply both sides by the LCD.

$$3(x+3) + 6x = 2x(x+3)$$ Simplify.

$$3x + 9 + 6x = 2x^2 + 6x$$

$$2x^2 - 3x - 9 = 0$$ Solve the resulting polynomial equation.

$$(2x+3)(x-3) = 0$$

$$x = -\frac{3}{2} \text{ or } x = 3$$

3. Solve $\frac{x-2}{x^2+3x-10} - \frac{x}{x+5} = 4$.

$$\frac{x-2}{(x+5)(x-2)} - \frac{x}{(x+5)} = 4$$ Factor the denominators. Note that $x \neq -5$ or 2.

$$x - 2 - x(x-2) = 4(x+5)(x-2)$$ Multiply by the LCD, $(x+5)(x+2)$, and simplify.

$$-x^2 + 3x - 2 = 4x^2 + 12x - 40$$

$$5x^2 + 9x - 38 = 0$$ Solve.

$$x = \frac{-9 \pm \sqrt{9^2 - 4(5)(-38)}}{10}$$

$$= \frac{-9 \pm 29}{10}$$

$$x = -\frac{19}{5} \text{ or } x = 2$$

Since the first rational expression is undefined when $x = 2$, the only solution is $x = -\frac{19}{5}$.

TRY IT

Solve each equation.

a. $\frac{4x^2 - 9}{3x + 1} = 0$

b. $\frac{p}{4} = \frac{3}{p-3} + 1$

c. $\frac{2y-3}{5} - \frac{y}{2} = \frac{y-1}{3}$

CONSIDER

1. What must be true about the expressions in a rational equation so that there will be no real values of the variable for which the expressions are undefined?

In the following Explore, you will write and solve rational equations to decide how to keep a research project on schedule.

EXPLORE: "X" MARKS THE SPOT

A group of researchers is planning a one-week trip to dive, explore, and photograph the sunken wreckage of a ship. The site of the wreckage is 150 nautical miles from the port where their research vessel is moored. On the trip to the site, they must travel *against* a current of 2 knots (nautical miles per hour). On the return trip they will travel *with* the 2-knot current. They would like to limit their total travel time to at most 24 hours so they will have 6 days on site to do their research.

1. If s is the speed of the research vessel relative to the water, then the vessel will make an overall speed of $s - 2$ knots going to the site and $s + 2$ knots returning. Give the total travel time $T(s)$ as a function of the vessel's speed relative to the water.

2. Write and solve an equation to find the minimum water speed that will limit the total travel time to 24 hours.

3. The research vessel has a top speed of 15 knots. What is the maximum current for which the total travel time can still be limited to 24 hours? Explain how you arrived at your conclusion.

4. Describe at least two reasons why the researchers might not want to travel at full speed to reduce their travel time further when the current is 2 knots.

When solving rational equations, you must keep in mind the domain of the rational expressions involved. Only the values you find that are in the domain are actual solutions of the rational equation.

REFLECT

1. Compare the methods of solving rational equations with the methods for solving other types of equations. What are the similarities and differences in each method?

2. How does the LCD help you solve a rational equation?

3. Explain why some values that you find when solving rational equations are not actual solutions.

Exercises

CORE

1. **Getting Started**   Multiply by the LCD and solve each equation.

   a. $\dfrac{a+7}{4} = \dfrac{2a-1}{3}$

   b. $\dfrac{2x+1}{5} = \dfrac{10}{3}$

   c. $\dfrac{y^2}{60} = \dfrac{y-1}{15}$

Write the word or phrase that correctly completes each sentence.

2. A rational expression is equal to zero when its ____ is equal to zero.

3. A rational expression is undefined when its ____ is equal to zero.

Solve each equation.

4. $\dfrac{1}{3p} + \dfrac{1}{2p} = 10$

5. $\dfrac{y-7}{5} + 2 = \dfrac{3y}{4}$

6. $\dfrac{5a^2 + 19a - 1}{3a} = a + 6$

7. $\dfrac{5}{x} + \dfrac{1}{2} = \dfrac{7}{x}$

8. $\dfrac{x}{x+2} = \dfrac{3x+1}{x-1} + \dfrac{4}{x^2+x-2}$

9. $\dfrac{n}{n+3} - 2 = \dfrac{-3}{n+3}$

10. $\dfrac{x^2 - 4x - 5}{x+1} + 4x + 11 = x^2$

11. $\dfrac{6y^2 + 13y - 8}{2y - 1} = 2y^2 + 9$

12. A group of friends planned a trip and chartered a bus for $247.50. When they got four more friends to join the trip, the cost for the bus was $6 less per person. In all, how many people made the trip?

13. The basic lens equation is $\dfrac{1}{p} + \dfrac{1}{q} = \dfrac{1}{f}$, where p is the distance of an object from the lens, q is the distance of the image from the lens, and f is the focal length of the lens. Suppose the focal length of a lens is 10 centimeters and the distance of the image is one fourth the distance of the object from the lens. Find the distances of the object and the image from the lens.

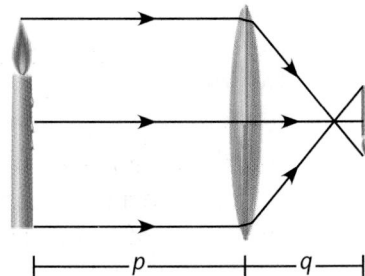

14. Assume there is a 10 mi/hr wind blowing from the north. Yolanda is planning to fly her plane on a round-trip to an airfield 120 miles north.
    a. Write the round-trip time as a function of Yolanda's air speed.
    b. At what air speed should she fly to make the round-trip in 1 hour and 25 minutes?

15. The volume of a sphere of radius r is $\frac{4}{3}\pi r^3$, and the volume of a cylinder with the same radius and height h is $\pi r^2 h$. Solve for h in terms of r if the sphere and the cylinder have the same volume.

 **LOOK BACK**

16. A jar contains 15 black balls and 3 white balls. If you choose a ball, replace it, and choose a ball again, what is the probability you will choose the same color ball each time? [1-2]

17. Solve $|3x + 1| \leq 7$. [2-3]

18. Solve $3x^2 + 5x + 1 = 0$. [5-2]

MORE PRACTICE

Solve each equation. Indicate any necessary restrictions.

19. $\dfrac{x}{3} - \dfrac{3}{x} = \dfrac{-3}{x}$

20. $\dfrac{4n + 2}{3} + 1 = \dfrac{2}{n}$

21. $\dfrac{4a^2 - 4a - 35}{4a + 10} = 0$

22. $\dfrac{9y^4 - 4y^2}{9y^2 + 12y + 4} = 0$

23. $\dfrac{5b^2 + 6b - 3}{3b^2 + 14b + 8} - \dfrac{1}{b + 4} = \dfrac{b}{3b + 2}$

24. $\dfrac{-x + 3}{x - 3} + \dfrac{1}{x} = -3$

25. $\dfrac{3p^2 + 14p + 11}{p^2 - 121} = 0$

26. $\dfrac{t}{3t - 3} + \dfrac{2}{t^2 - 1} = \dfrac{1}{3}$

27. $\dfrac{3}{b - 1} + 2 = \dfrac{5}{2b - 2}$

28. $\dfrac{8y^3 - 50y}{y^2} = 0$

29. $\dfrac{-3x^2 - 15x - 12}{x^2 + 5x + 4} = 0$

30. $\dfrac{x}{5x - 10} - \dfrac{1}{x^2 - 4} = \dfrac{2}{5}$

31. A jogger ran two miles per hour faster than a hiker walked. If the jogger ran 15 miles in the time it took the hiker to walk 10 miles, what was the speed of each?

 Science

32. a. An 8-ohm resistor is to be connected in parallel to a second resistor (r ohms) so that the connected resistors have a total resistance of 4.8 ohms. Solve the equation $\dfrac{1}{4.8} = \dfrac{1}{r} + \dfrac{1}{8}$ to find the necessary resistance of the second resistor.

b. An audio component with an impedance of $0.5 - i$ ohms is to be connected in parallel with another component so that the connected components have a total impedance of 1 ohm. Solve the equation $1 = \dfrac{1}{z} + \dfrac{1}{0.5 - i}$ to find the necessary impedance of the second component.

MORE MATH REASONING

Solve each equation. Then interpret your results.

33. $\dfrac{-x}{x^2 - 25} + \dfrac{3}{x + 5} = \dfrac{2}{x - 5}$

34. $\dfrac{5}{x + 3} - \dfrac{2x + 1}{x^2 + 5x + 6} = \dfrac{3}{x + 2}$

35. In an ice cream cone factory, machine A can produce a case of ice cream cones in 4 minutes, machine B in 3 minutes, and machine C in 6 minutes. If all three machines are running, how long will it take to produce a case?

Making Connections

← **CONNECT** → *You've learned to write rational expressions to describe quantities and you've simplified them when possible. You've also explored features of the graphs of rational functions and solved rational equations.*

Pressure underwater requires scuba divers to breathe compressed air, which forces extra nitrogen into the bloodstream. The deeper or longer a dive, the more nitrogen builds up. If enough nitrogen builds up, a diver coming directly to the surface can get *the bends*, a dangerous condition caused by the release of nitrogen in the bloodstream. To avoid the bends, scuba divers must make decompression stops during deep or long dives to allow nitrogen to be slowly and safely released.

In the following Explore, you will investigate a rational function that models data related to decompression stops from the Professional Association of Dive Instructors (PADI).

EXPLORE: STOPPING THE BENDS

MATERIALS

Graphing utility or graph paper

Let *d* be the maximum depth, in feet, to which a scuba diver intends to dive. If $d < 33$, then a diver can surface without decompression stops after any amount of time underwater.

For depths over 33 feet, the function $T(d) = \frac{1700}{d - 33}$ models the longest total dive time in minutes that a scuba diver can breathe compressed air and still surface at 60 ft/sec with no decompression stops.

1. Sketch the graph of the function $T(d)$.
   a. Are decompression stops needed for dives plotted above or below the graph?
   b. Where is the asymptote on the graph? What is the significance of the asymptote for the diving model?

2. Hector is planning to go scuba diving at the bottom of a lagoon with a depth of 60 feet. If he places no restriction on the depth he maintains, how long can he stay underwater and still avoid decompression stops upon surfacing?

3. If Hector ventures out into the open ocean, what depths should he limit himself to so that he can stay underwater at least 30 minutes? Explain how you decided.

1. What are some properties of algebra that you use when simplifying rational expressions and solving rational equations?
2. What information can be determined about the nature of the graph of a rational function from its equation alone? Explain.
3. How do you find the LCD of two rational expressions?

Self-Assessment

Evaluate each rational expression for the given value of the variable.

1. $\dfrac{3a^2 - 1}{a + 5}$ for $a = 2$

2. $\dfrac{7}{x^2 + 2x - 11}$ for $x = -3$

Simplify each expression.

3. $\dfrac{x + 1}{x + 5} + \dfrac{2}{x - 3}$

4. $\dfrac{-3p}{p^3 - 9p} - \dfrac{3}{p^2 + 5p + 6}$

5. $\dfrac{3a^2 + 6a}{a^2 - 25} \cdot \dfrac{2a^2 + 11a + 5}{3a^2 + 3a - 6}$

6. $\dfrac{-15y^2}{3y + 12} \div \dfrac{5y^3 - 5y}{3y^2 + 14y + 8}$

7. **a.** How can you find x-intercepts of the graph of a rational function from the equation of the function?
   b. How can you find the discontinuities of the graph of a rational function from the equation of the function?
   c. If the graph of a rational function has a "hole" discontinuity at $x = 3$, what can you say about the equation of the function?

Give the values of x where each function is undefined.

8. $f(x) = \dfrac{3x + 5}{x^2 + 6x + 8}$

9. $g(x) = \dfrac{x^2 - 16}{2x^2 + 11x + 12}$

Make a table of values and sketch the graph of each rational function. Describe any discontinuities of the graphs.

10. $f(x) = \dfrac{10x^2 - 7x - 12}{3x + 4}$

11. $g(x) = \dfrac{2x^2 + 8}{2x^2 + 3x + 14}$

12. $y = \dfrac{3}{x - 2}$

13. $y = \dfrac{x + 2}{x + 5}$

14. $h(x) = \dfrac{1}{x^2 + 2x - 3}$

15. $k(x) = \dfrac{x^3 + 1}{2x^2}$

16. A grocer wants to mix 30 lb of candy, which sells for \$0.49/lb, with x lb of a different kind of candy, which sells for \$0.79/lb. How many pounds does he end up with? What is the total price for which the two kinds of candy would have sold? Write the price per pound of the mix as a function of x. How much of the cheaper candy should he blend in if he wants to sell the mix for \$0.59/lb?

Solve each rational equation.

17. $\dfrac{a - 6}{2} + 3 = \dfrac{2a}{5}$

18. $\dfrac{n}{5n - 5} = \dfrac{1}{5} - \dfrac{2}{n^2 - 1}$

19. $\dfrac{6x^2 + 7x + 2}{9x^2 - 4} = 0$

20. $\dfrac{x^2 - 1}{3x^3 + 6x^2 + 3x} = 0$

21. Magic Cube To find a formula for partial sum $S_n = 1^2 + 2^2 + 3^2 \cdots + n^2$, some students constructed a rectangular solid with edge lengths of n, $n + 1$, and $2n + 1$ using six identical pyramids like the one shown. What formula did they find for S_n? [4-1]

22. After two years, Joel had earned a total of $25 interest from a savings account earning simple annual interest. If his original investment was $300, what annual interest rate was he earning? [5-2]

23. If you choose two cards from a deck of 52 playing cards, what is the probability that you will choose two red face cards? [6-2]

24. Hot Metal Many materials expand when heated and contract when cooled. Steel expands by 1.2×10^{-5} times its original length for every 1°C increase in its temperature. (1.2×10^{-5} is called the *coefficient of thermal expansion* for steel.) If a steel girder on a bridge is 12 feet long in the morning when the temperature is 5°C, how long will it be in the afternoon when the bridge has heated up to 40°C? [7-1]

Find the least common denominator of each pair of rational expressions.

25. $\dfrac{8}{x + 4}$; $\dfrac{3}{5x + 20}$

26. $\dfrac{2w}{w^2 - 36}$; $\dfrac{1}{w^2 + 12w + 36}$

27. $\dfrac{p + 1}{p^3}$; $\dfrac{5}{p^5 - p}$

28. $\dfrac{7}{t^2 - 5t + 6}$; $\dfrac{4}{t^2 + t - 12}$

29. When a bicyclist rode 3 miles an hour slower, it took her 3 hours longer to make a 70-mile trip. What was her slower speed?

30. Kaboom! If an explosion in a fireworks display radiates sound uniformly in all directions, the intensity at any distance r is $I = \dfrac{P}{4\pi r^2}$, where P is the sound power of the explosion. What is the intensity detected by a listener who is 160 meters away from the explosion if the sound reaches a second listener who is 640 meters away from the explosion at an intensity of 0.10 watts per meter^2?

31. Tennis Anyone? Three tennis balls are packed in a cylindrical tube. If r is the radius of each ball and of the tube, what is the total volume of the three balls? of the tube? What is the ratio of the volume of the balls to the volume of the tube?

Chapter 8 Review

In Chapter 8, you have extended your knowledge of functions by exploring the characteristics of polynomial functions and rational functions. You have seen how algebra can help you describe the graphic behaviors of these functions. There are many real-world phenomena that can be studied by using graphic representations of polynomial and rational functions and by solving related equations.

KEY TERMS

absolute maximum [8-1]

absolute minimum [8-1]

constant term [8-1]

continuous [8-1]

cubic function [8-1]

degree of a polynomial [8-1]

descending order [8-1]

discontinuous [8-3]

Factor Theorem [8-2]

Fundamental Theorem of Algebra [8-2]

leading coefficient [8-1]

least common denominator (LCD) [8-3]

multiple root [8-2]

polynomial [8-1]

polynomial equation [8-2]

polynomial function [8-1]

quartic function [8-1]

rational equation [8-3]

rational expression [8-3]

rational function [8-3]

Rational Roots Theorem [8-2]

real root [8-1]

relative maximum [8-1]

relative minimum [8-1]

Remainder Theorem [8-2]

vertical asymptote [8-3]

zeros of a function [8-1]

Write the word or phrase that correctly completes each statement.

1. In a polynomial expression, the greatest exponent that appears in any term with a nonzero coefficient is the _____.

2. If we know that r is a root of $P(x) = 0$, then _____ is a factor of $P(x)$.

3. If R is the remainder after dividing the polynomial $P(x)$ by $x - a$, then $P(a) =$ _____.

4. Discontinuities of a rational function occur when the _____ is equal to zero.

5. A vertical line that the graph of a rational function approaches is called a(n) _____.

CONCEPTS AND APPLICATIONS

Perform the indicated operations and write each result in descending order. Identify the leading coefficient and the degree of the polynomial function. [8-1]

6. $f(x) = 2(6x^2 + 1)(6x^2 - 1)$

7. $g(x) = (4x^2 - 5x^3) + (13x^3 + 4x^2 + 11x)$

8. $h(x) = (3.5x^8 + 7x^6) - (1.4x^6 - x^8 + 2.8x^{10})$

Match each function with its graph. Explain your choice. [8-1]

9. $f(x) = 4.7x + 20$

10. $f(x) = -x^2 + 3x + 5$

11. $f(x) = x^3 - 2x^2 + 10$

12. $f(x) = 2x^4 - x^3 - 10x^2 + 15$

a. **b.** **c.** **d.** not here

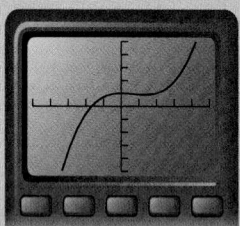 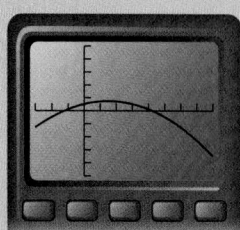 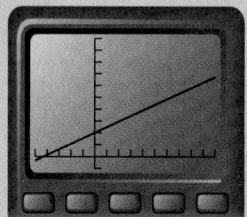

13. Examine the graph of $f(x) = x^4 - 3x^2 + 3$. [8-1]
   a. Is the function a quadratic, cubic, or quartic function?
   b. Does this function have an absolute maximum? Explain.
   c. Does this function have an absolute minimum? Explain.
   d. Estimate relative maximums and relative minimums, if any, and indicate an interval for each.

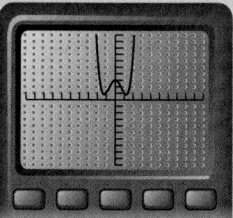

Xmin = –10
Xmax = 10
Xscl = 1
Ymin = –10
Ymax = 10
Yscl = 1

14. A company found that the profit per month (R) is related to the charge per item (p) by the function
   $R = 120p - 10p^2 - 150$.

   a. Estimate the lowest price for which the company makes a profit.
   b. Estimate the price it should charge for the product to receive maximum profit.
   c. What is the maximum price the company can charge and receive any profit? [8-1]

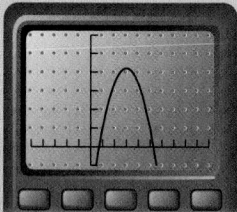

Xmin = –10
Xmax = 20
Xscl = 2
Ymin = –50
Ymax = 300
Yscl = 50

15. The graph of $f(x) = x^5 - 3x^3 + 2$ is shown. [8-1]
   a. How many real zeros does the function appear to have?
   b. Estimate the value of the real zeros.
   c. What is the value of the function at each of your estimated zeros?
   d. How can you be sure that you have found all the real roots of the equation?

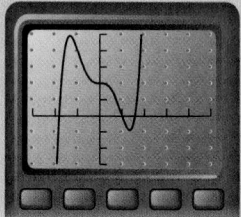

Xmin = –3
Xmax = 5
Xscl = 1
Ymin = –3
Ymax = 5
Yscl = 1

16. Find the zeros of the function $g(x) = x^3 - x^2 - 12x$ by factoring. [8-1]

17. Solve $3x^4 + 192 = -60x^2$ by factoring. [8-2]

Find $f(3)$ for each polynomial function. Then verify whether $(x - 3)$ is a factor of each function by dividing. [8-2]

18. $f(x) = 3x^3 - 6x^2 + 8x + 2$

19. $f(x) = x^3 - x^2 - 5x - 3$

Use the Factor Theorem to decide whether $(x + 1)$ is a factor of each function. If so, find the quotient by dividing. [8-2]

20. $f(x) = x^3 - x^2 + 8x - 8$

21. $f(x) = x^5 + 4x^3 - 5x$

22. When a polynomial $h(x)$ is divided by $x - 3$, the remainder is 2. Find $h(3)$. [8-2]

Solve each equation. [8-2]

23. $5x^2 - 241 = 4$

24. $4x^4 - 12x^3 - x^2 + 27x - 18 = 0$

25. Write a polynomial equation with the given roots $\frac{-2}{3}$ and $\frac{4}{5}$. [8-2]

26. Find the least common denominator of the expressions $\frac{5}{x^2 - x - 6}$ and $\frac{3}{x^2 - 9}$. [8-3]

Simplify each expression and evaluate it when $x = 2$. [8-3]

27. $\frac{4x - 5}{3x + 2} + \frac{2x^2}{4x - 5}$

28. $\frac{x^3 - 2x^2}{5x^4} \div \frac{x}{10x^6}$

29. $\frac{8x^3 - 2}{25x^3} - \frac{4x^2}{x^3 - x^2}$

30. Find the zeros of the rational function, $f(x) = \frac{x^2 - 6x + 9}{x^2 + 3x + 2}$, then determine where the discontinuity, if any, will occur in its graph. [8-3]

Sketch the graph of each rational function. Identify any asymptotes or any "holes" in the graph. [8-3]

31. $f(x) = \frac{x^2 - 6x + 8}{x + 3}$

32. $f(x) = \frac{x - 3}{x^2 - x - 6}$

Solve each rational equation. [8-3]

33. $\frac{8}{x^2 - 2} = 4$

34. $\frac{x}{x - 8} = 0$

CONCEPTS AND CONNECTIONS

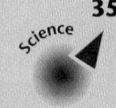

35. Lighting the Night The luminous intensity (I) of a light source is measured in candles. The illumination (E) from the light source is given by $E = \frac{I}{R^2}$, where R is the distance from the light source. The total illumination at a point is the sum of the illuminations from all light sources. One night Pauly stood between two street lights. Each light had a luminous intensity of 600 candles. If Pauly was 5 feet closer to one source than the other, write a rational expression that could describe the total illumination at the point where Pauly stood.

SELF-EVALUATION

Write a summary of what you learned in this chapter. Explain how these concepts can help you understand graphic representations that exist in the real world. Which techniques discussed in this chapter were confusing for you? Explain how the algebraic concepts in this chapter are related to arithmetic processes you learned in the past.

Chapter 8 Assessment

TEST

Perform the indicated operations. Write each result in descending order. Identify the leading coefficient and the degree of the polynomial function.

1. $(7x^3 + 2x - 3) - (10x^3 + 14x^2 - 5x)$

2. $(12x^5 + 28x^3 - 6x^2) \div 4x^2$

3. Which function is represented by the graph?
   (a) $f(x) = \dfrac{x+1}{x}$
   (b) $f(x) = 2x^4 - x^3 - 10x^2 + 15$
   (c) $f(x) = x^2 + 3x$
   (d) not here

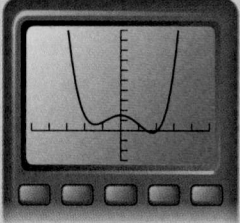

4. a. Is the function $f(x) = x^3 - 6x + 3$ a quadratic, cubic, or quartic function?
   b. Does this function have an absolute maximum? Explain.
   c. Does this function have an absolute minimum? Explain.
   d. Estimate relative maximums and relative minimums, if any, and indicate an interval for each.
   e. Estimate the real zeros of the function.
   f. What is the value of $f(x)$ when x is a zero?

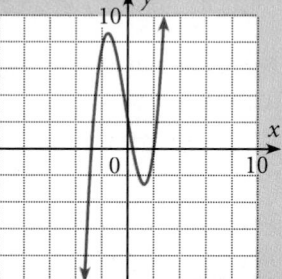

5. The surface area of a balloon increases as the volume of air inside the balloon increases. The volume of a sphere is $\frac{4}{3}\pi r^3$ and the surface area is $4\pi r^2$. Draw a graph to show the ratio of volume to surface area. What does the graph tell you about the maximum value of the ratio as the radius increases?

6. Write a polynomial equation whose roots are 9, −5, and 2.

7. Use the Factor Theorem to decide whether $f(x) = x^3 + 4x^2 - 6x - 24$ has a factor of $(x + 4)$. If it is a factor, find the quotient.

Solve each equation.

8. $x^3 - 2x^2 + 9x = 18$

9. $(x^2 - 5)(x - 3) = (x^2 - 5)(x + 2)$

Find the least common denominator of each pair of rational expressions.

10. $\dfrac{5}{4t + 4}$; $\dfrac{8}{t^2 + t}$

11. $\dfrac{x + 1}{x^3 + 2x^2}$; $\dfrac{3}{x^2 - 4}$

Use the Factor Theorem to decide whether $(x - 2)$ is a factor of each function. If so, find the quotient by dividing.

12. $f(x) = x^3 - 5x^2 + 7x - 2$

13. $g(x) = x^6 - 2x^5 + x$

Simplify each expression.

14. $\dfrac{2x + 2}{x - 2} - \dfrac{x + 1}{x}$

15. $\dfrac{8x^3 - 27}{-2x} \cdot \dfrac{6x^2 + 10x^4}{8x^2 + 12x + 18}$

16. Use long division to find the quotient and remainder if the first polynomial is divided by the second.
   a. $x^2 + 5x + 6$, $x + 3$
   b. $x^2 - 7x - 10$, $x + 8$
   c. $x^2 - 15$, $x - 3$
   d. $x^2 + 9x - 6$, $x - 2$

17. Find the discontinuities of the rational function $f(x) = \dfrac{x^2 - x - 6}{x^2 + 9}$.

18. Determine where the discontinuities, if any, will occur in the graph of the rational function $f(x) = \dfrac{x^2 + 3x - 10}{x^2 - 4}$.

19. Sketch the graph of the rational function $f(x) = \dfrac{2x + 4}{x^2 - 6x - 16}$. Identify any vertical asymptotes or any "holes" in the graph.

Solve each rational equation.

20. $\dfrac{10}{x + 2} = 2$

21. $\dfrac{x^2 + 9}{x - 1} - \dfrac{x^2 - 3}{x + 5} = 0$

22. When a motorcyclist rode 10 miles an hour slower, it took her 1 hour longer to make a 100-mile trip. What was her slower speed?

23. **When Will We Get There?** The Farzin family is traveling from their house in Yuma to a friend's house in Los Angeles. The distance between the two houses is 270 miles. If the average speed is increased by 9 miles per hour, the Farzin family will arrive at their destination an hour ahead of schedule. What is the Farzins' average speed for the trip?

PERFORMANCE TASK

Write a rational function of x with a vertical asymptote at $x = 3$ and a "hole" at $x = -1$. Sketch a graph of your function. Give the real zeros of your function and describe any relative or absolute maximums or minimums.

Chapter 9

Exponential and Logarithmic Functions

Project A
Whom Do You Know?
You're closer to the president than you think.

Project B
Unclear on Nuclear
What are the positive and negative effects of using nuclear power to generate electricity?

Project C
So Hot It's Cool
How fast will your ice cream melt?

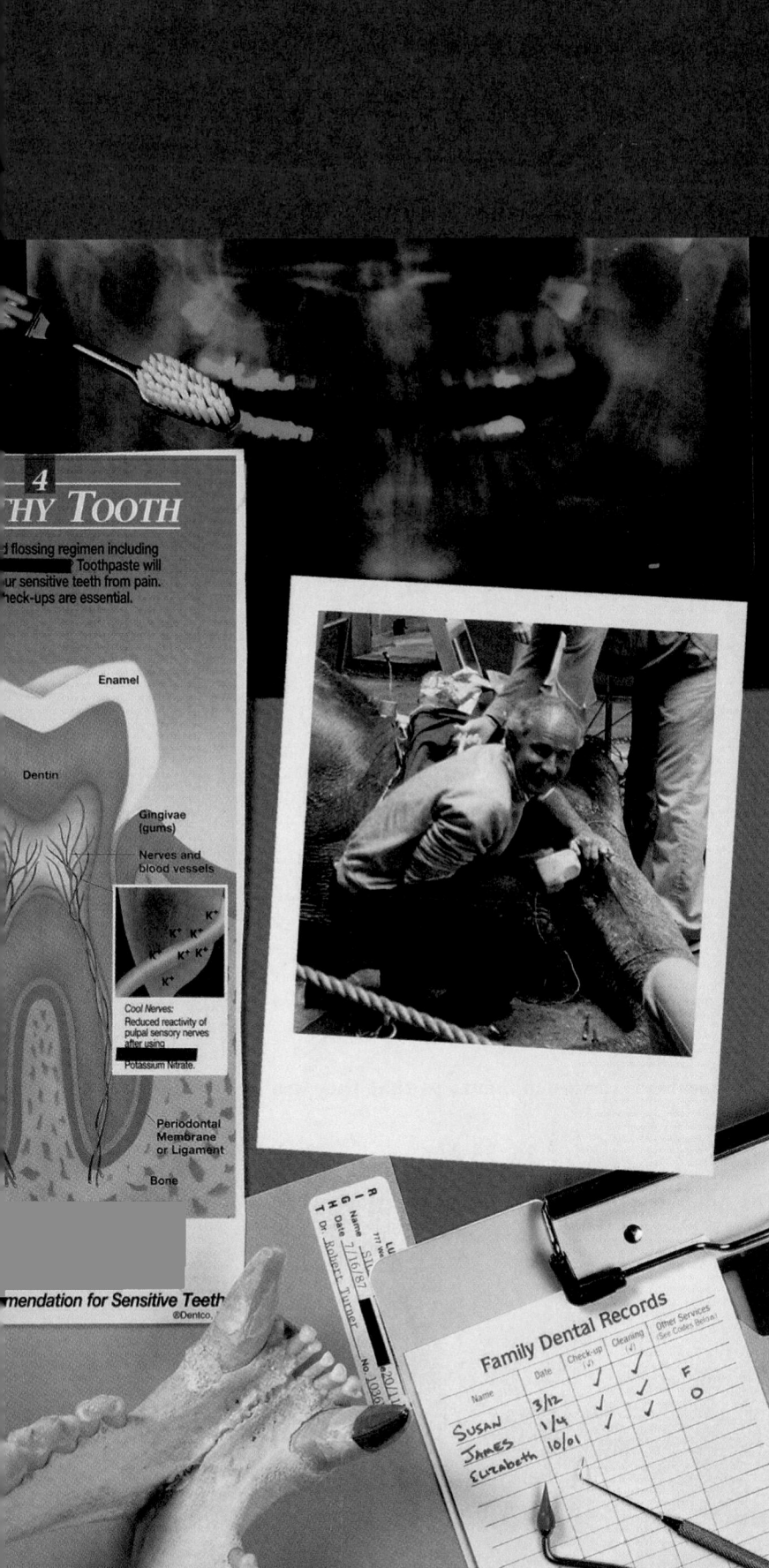

ROBERT W. TURNER

In high school, advanced math courses were difficult and very challenging for me.

In addition to my successful dental practice, I am the dental consultant for the San Francisco Zoo and for Marine World/Africa USA in Vallejo, California. I use oversize instruments that have been specially made to do dental work on lions, tigers, elephants, chimpanzees, gorillas, baboons, and other exotic animals. Math is important to the business side of my practice, but I also use it every day on the job. Math is everywhere, even at the zoo!

Robert W. Turner
Dentist
Robert W. Turner D.D.S. Inc.
Palo Alto, California

**9-1
Exponential
Patterns
and Graphs**

In 9-1 you will investigate exponential growth and decay functions. You will use the following skills with exponents.

Evaluate. [7-1]

1. 5^4

2. -5^4

3. $(-5)^4$

4. $-2^3 \cdot 7^4$

5. $63(0.5)^4$

6. $42,816(1.1)^3$

Write each of the following using exponents and a base of 2. [7-1]

7. 128

8. -8

9. $\dfrac{1}{64}$

10. 16^x

11. 32^{2x}

Complete the table and make a graph. [Previous course]

12. $y = 2^x$

x	−2	−1	0	1	2	3
y						

13. $y = \left(\dfrac{1}{2}\right)^x$

x	−3	−2	−1	0	1	2
y						

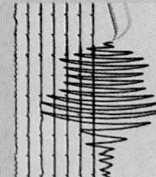

**9-2
Logarithmic
Functions**

In 9-2 you will learn how to solve problems using logarithms. You will use the following skills.

Rewrite each pair of numbers using exponents so that they are written with the same base. [7-1]

14. 32, 256

15. 216, 36

16. 3^x, 27

17. 25^x, 625

Rewrite each of the following with a single base. [7-1]

18. $5^x \cdot 5^y$

19. $(7^a)^b$

20. $\dfrac{9^m}{9^n}$

DID WHALES SWIM OR WALK TO MICHIGAN?

X-ing

Detroit

In the late 1920s and early 1930s, whale bones were found in Michigan in Lenawee County, at Oscoda in Iosco County, and near Therford Center, Genesee County. The question immediately arose, "How did whales get to Michigan when the nearest ocean is hundreds of miles away?"

To solve this mystery, scientists needed to know the age of the bones. If the whales lived a long time ago, when water levels were higher, they might have been able to swim to the Great Lakes from the Atlantic Ocean. However, if the whales lived relatively recently, they could not possibly have swum to Michigan, and another explanation would need to be found.

Carbon dating is used to estimate the age of organic remains. Carbon-14, a radioactive form of carbon, is produced by cosmic rays bombarding the earth. When an animal dies, it stops taking in carbon-14. Every 5,730 years, half of the carbon-14 changes to nitrogen through radioactive decay. If the animal has 8 grams of carbon-14 in its body when it dies, 4 grams will be left after 5,730 years, 2 grams after 11,460 years, and so on. By estimating the amount of carbon-14 that should have been present when the animal died and comparing it to the amount in its remains, the time since the animal's death can be estimated.

Paleontologist C. R. Harington used carbon dating to find the age of three different Michigan whale bones and solve the mystery. Later, you will estimate the ages of the whale bones and solve the mystery for yourself.

1. Suppose the whale bones are relatively recent. Form a hypothesis that explains how the bones got to Michigan.
2. Explain why the carbon dating process only gives an estimate and not the precise age of an object. What assumptions are made in the process?
3. Another radioactive substance, iron-55, decays to 50% of its original amount every 4 years. Assuming that iron-55 is also present in animal remains, do you think "iron dating" would be a useful process to estimate the age of a fossil? Why or why not?

← CONNECT → *You've investigated powers, which have a variable base and a constant exponent. Now you will explore what happens when the base of a power is a constant and the exponent is a variable.*

You've done a great deal of work with functions of the form $y = x^n$. In these functions, the base is a variable and the exponent is a constant. You know that these functions grow very quickly as x increases from 0 when $n > 1$.

Now you will begin your investigation of functions of the form $f(x) = b^x$, where the base is constant but the exponent is variable. These functions are called *exponential functions*.

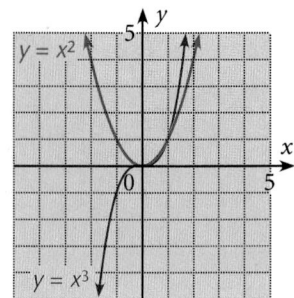

In the Explore, you will use a graphing utility to investigate the behavior of exponential functions.

EXPLORE: REVERSING THE SCHEME

MATERIALS

Graphing utility
Graph paper

1. Make a table of values and sketch the graph for the exponential function $y = 2^x$ on graph paper. Describe each of the following:
   a. the domain of the function
   b. the range of the function
   c. the behavior of the graph as x increases from 0
   d. the behavior of the graph as x decreases from 0
   e. any maximum or minimum points

2. Using your graphing utility, graph $y = 2^x$ and $y = 5^x$ on the same screen. How are the graphs similar? How are they different? Do they have any points in common? If so, why is this point on both graphs?

3. Predict the shape of the graph of $y = 10^x$. Now add the graph of $y = 10^x$ to your screen. How does it compare to the other graphs?

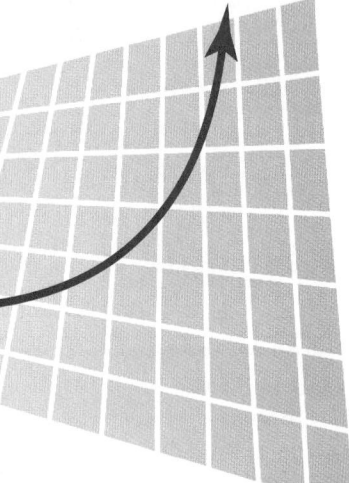

4. Clear the graphs of $y = 5^x$ and $y = 10^x$. From the graph of $y = 2^x$, predict the shape of the graph of $y = 2^{-x}$. Now graph $y = 2^{-x}$. Was your prediction accurate?

5. Add the graph of $y = \left(\frac{1}{2}\right)^x$ to your screen. What happens? Explain why this result makes sense.

6. Clear your screen of other graphs, then graph $y = (-2)^x$. Explain what you see.

7. Summarize your conclusions about the graphs of exponential functions. Include comparisons of the graphs for bases greater than 1 and between 0 and 1, and an explanation of the effect of a negative exponent.

An **exponential function with base b** is defined by an equation of the form $y = ab^x$, where a, b, and x are real numbers, $b > 0$, and $b \neq 1$:

An exponential function has a constant base and a variable exponent.

CONSIDER
?

1. Explain why the definition of an exponential function specifies that $b > 0$.

When a function is linear, you always *add* the same number to the *y*-value for a given change in *x*. For example, if your job pays $7 an hour, your pay increases by $7 for every hour you work.

With exponential functions, you always *multiply* the *y*-value by the same number for a given change in *x*. If you put your paycheck in a bank account earning 10% interest, your balance is *multiplied* by 1.10 every year.

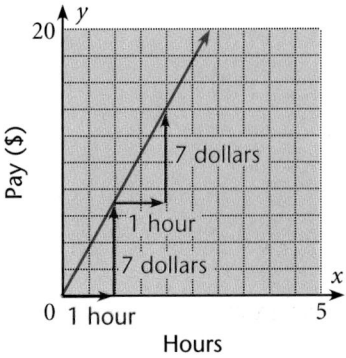

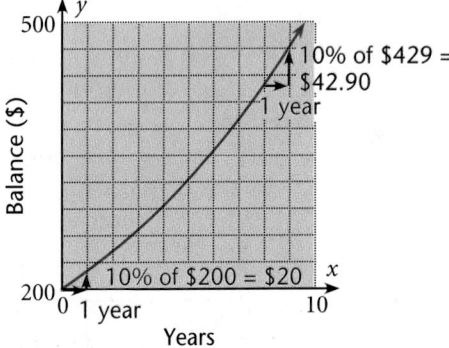

Many real-world situations can be modeled by exponential functions of the form:

$$A = Pb^t$$

where P is an initial amount, b is the factor you multiply the amount by every time period, and A is the amount present after t time periods. These situations include population growth, radioactive decay, and the growth of money in a bank account.

1. Bill has $500 in a savings account that pays 5% interest annually. Write an equation that models the amount of money he has in x years, assuming no deposits or withdrawals. Then use the equation to find how much money Bill will have in the account in 4 years.

The initial amount in the account is $500. Since the annual interest rate is 5%, the amount in the account is multiplied by 1.05 each year, so the equation is $A = 500(1.05)^t$.

To find the amount in the account after 4 years, let $t = 4$.

$A = 500(1.05)^4$

$A \approx 500(1.2155)$ Use a calculator to approximate 1.05^4.

$A \approx 607.75$

Bill will have about $607.75 in the account after 4 years.

In Example 1, we used algebra (and a calculator) to find the amount of money after a given time. However, we need to use other methods when the final amount is known and we want to solve for the amount of time.

WHAT DO **YOU** THINK?

In 1950, the population of Boston was 801,444. Over the next 40 years, Boston's population declined at a rate of about 0.83% per year. If this trend continues, when will Boston's population reach 500,000?

Kyle thinks...

Boston's population declined at the rate of 0.83% per year. So after one year, $100 - 0.83 = 99.17\%$ of the population is left. The equation for Boston's population is $A = 801,444(0.9917)^t$.

To find out when the population is 500,000, I can use a table of values to look for the time when the population = 500,000. I could do this by hand, but it's easier to use a spreadsheet or a table on a graphing utility. I'll start with 10-year intervals, using 1950 as year 0.

Year	0	10	20	30	40	50	60
Population	801,444	737,354	678,390	624,141	574,230	528,310	486,062

The year must be between and 50 and 60. I'll search one-year intervals between these values to find the nearest year.

Year	51	52	53	54	55	56	57
Population	523,925	519,576	515,264	510,987	506,746	502,540	498,369

Boston's population will be about 500,000 57 years after 1950, in 2007.

Mei Mei thinks...

The equation for Boston's population is:

$A \approx 801{,}444(1 - 0.0083)^t$

$A \approx 801{,}444(0.9917)^t$

I'll graph this function on my graphing utility and *trace* to the point where $y = 500{,}000$.

Boston's population will be 500,000 about 57 years after 1950, in the year 2007.

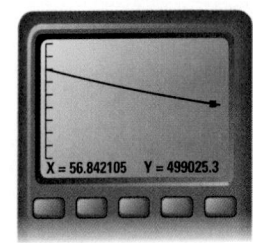

X = 56.842105   Y = 499025.3

An **exponential equation** has a variable as an exponent. One method of solving such equations is to express each term as a power with the same base. If two powers with the same base are equal, their exponents are equal.

EXAMPLE

2. Solve $64 = 8^{x-2}$.

Write each side of the equation as an exponential expression having the same base.

$64 = 8^{x-2}$

$2^6 = (2^3)^{x-2}$ $64 = 2^6;\ 8 = 2^3$

$2^6 = 2^{3x-6}$ Use properties of exponents.

Thus, $6 = 3x - 6$.   If $a^m = a^k$, then $m = k$.

       $12 = 3x$

          $4 = x$ Solve for x.

Check:

$64 \stackrel{?}{=} 8^{4-2}$

$64 \stackrel{?}{=} 8^2$

$64 = 64$ ✓

TRY IT

a. The population of Zaire is projected to increase at an average rate of 3.9% a year from 1994 to 2020. If Zaire's population in 1994 was about 42,684,000, what is its projected population for the year 2020?

b. Solve $2^x = 8$ for x.

c. Solve $9^{x-2} = 27$.

As you have seen, reversing the scheme of variables for bases and numbers for exponents produces exponential functions of the form $y = b^x$. The value of the base b affects the shape of the graph of the function.

As shown in the graph, exponential functions with a base greater than 1 contain (0, 1), approach the x-axis as x-values decrease, and increase very quickly for large, positive x-values. The graph of an exponential function with a base between 0 and 1 also contains (0, 1), but it approaches the x-axis as x-values increase.

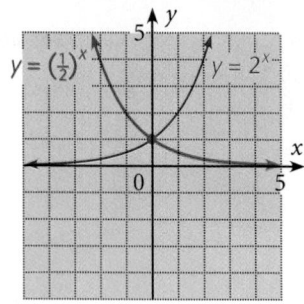

Whenever a real-world quantity has a consistent percentage increase or decrease over time, an exponential function can be used as a model. When using such a model, remember that real-world data may have restricted values—they may always be whole-number values, for example.

REFLECT

1. Why do you think that $y = 1^x$ is not typically considered to be an exponential function?

2. Compare the graphs of polynomial functions of the form $y = x^n$ to exponential functions of the form $y = b^x$. Explain any differences or similarities.

3. You have seen interest payments and population changes modeled by exponential functions. What other kinds of real-world situations might be modeled by exponential functions? Explain.

Exercises

CORE

1. Getting Started State whether or not each of the functions below is an exponential function.

a. $f(x) = 2^x$ **b.** $f(x) = (-2)^x$ **c.** $f(x) = x^2$ **d.** $f(x) = 1^2$ **e.** $f(x) = \left(\frac{1}{2}\right)^x$

Write the words or phrases that correctly complete each statement.

2. In an exponential function, the base is a ____ and the exponent is a ____.

3. The graph of an exponential function $y = b^x$ contains the point ____ and has ____ as an asymptote.

Let $f(x) = 3^{x+2}$. Evaluate $f(x)$ for each value of x.

4. $f(0)$ **5.** $f(-2)$ **6.** $f(-4)$ **7.** $f(3)$

8. $f(2)$ **9.** $f(-1)$ **10.** $f(-1.5)$ **11.** $f(h + 3)$

Graph each exponential function. Label the coordinates of at least two points on each curve.

12. $y = 2^x$

13. $y = 5^x$

14. $y = \left(\frac{1}{4}\right)^x$

15. Use your answer from Exercise 12 to graph each of the following. Explain how you made each graph.

a. $y = 2^{-x}$

b. $y = 2^{(x-3)}$

c. $y = 2^x + 2$

16. In 1991, Guatemala had a population of approximately 9,000,000 people. Its population has been growing at a rate of 2.7% per year.

a. Write a function that relates t, in years, to the population (P) of Guatemala t years after 1991.

b. Use the function from **a** to estimate the population of Guatemala in 2011.

17. A Penny Saved... Sharonda is investing $1000 in a certificate of deposit that pays 5.8% interest each year. If she keeps the money in the account, how much will she have after 6 years?

18. If you know that an exponential function of the form $f(x) = ab^x$ passed through the point $(0, 3)$, what else do you know about that function? Explain.

19. Sketch graphs of $y = x^2$ and $y = 2^x$ on the same set of axes. Compare the two graphs. Which function is greater for large x-values? Explain.

Solve each equation.

20. $2^x = 4$

21. $8^x = 32$

22. $27^x = 3$

23. $2^{x+2} = 16$

24. $2^{-x} = 8$

25. $\left(\frac{1}{4}\right)^x = 64$

26. A Small Reward In *History of Mathematics, Vol. II*, David E. Smith discusses a famous problem relating to a chessboard. This problem was described by the Arabian biographer Ibn Khallikan (1211–1282).

"When Sissah ibn Dahir invented the game of Chess, the king, Shirhram, was filled with joy... and commanded Sissah to ask for any reward he pleased. Thereupon Sissah asked for one grain of wheat for the first square [of the chessboard], two for the second, four for the third, and so on...."

a. Make a table of values for the number of grains of wheat for squares 1–16 and for the total number of grains up to a given square.

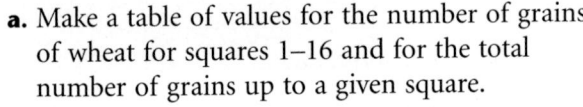

Square	1	2	3	4	...
Grains for square	1	2	4		...
Total grains	1	3			...

b. Write an equation to model the number of grains for each square. Explain how you found this equation. What domain makes sense for this situation?

c. Use your equation to find the number of wheat grains for the 24th, 36th, 48th, and 64th squares. Do you think Sissah ibn Dahir got his reward? Explain.

LOOK AHEAD

Sketch the graph of each function and its inverse on the same set of coordinate axes.

27. $y = 2x - 4$

28. $f(x) = \frac{3x}{5}$

29. $y = x^3$

Solve each equation.

30. $x^3 = 64$

31. $x^{\frac{3}{2}} = 8$

32. $10^{-4} = x$

33. $7^{-1} = x$

MORE PRACTICE

34. Use a Graphing Utility Graph each equation. Sketch copies of your graphs on the same set of axes.

a. $y = 3^x$

b. $y = 10^x$

c. $y = \left(\frac{1}{5}\right)^x$

d. $y = 0.6^x$

Solve for x.

35. $2^x = 32$

36. $3^x = 9^3$

37. $4^{x+1} = 16$

38. $5^{3x} = 25^{x-1}$

39. $3^x = \frac{1}{9}$

40. $2^{x+1} = 64$

41. $\left(\frac{1}{3}\right)^x = 27$

42. $3^{2x} = 81$

Let $f(x) = 2^{x+3}$. Evaluate $f(x)$ for each value of x.

43. $f(0)$

44. $f(-2)$

45. $f(-4)$

46. $f(3)$

47. $f\left(\frac{1}{2}\right)$

48. $f(1.3)$

49. $f(-7)$

50. $f(g - 2)$

51. Use a Graphing Utility Tokyo-Yokohama, Japan, is an example of a megacity, one of about 20 such urban population centers around the world. The 1995 population of Tokyo-Yokohama, the world's largest megacity, was estimated at 28.4 million, with an annual growth rate of 0.86%. This yearly growth is modeled by the equation $A = 28.4(1.0086)^t$, where t = the number of years since 1995.

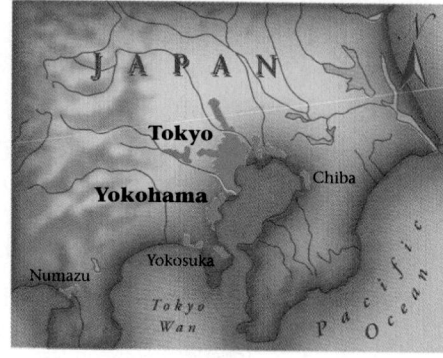

a. If Tokyo-Yokohama's growth rate remains constant, describe graphically, numerically (in a table), and in writing how its population will change over the next ten years.

b. Use a graph to estimate when Tokyo-Yokohama's population will reach:
  i. 30 million   **ii.** 40 million   **iii.** 50 million
c. In 1995, Mexico City was the second-largest megacity, with a population of 23.9 million. This population was growing at 2.69% per year. When will the population of Mexico City exceed the population of Tokyo-Yokohama?

52. Use a Graphing Utility Graph $y = 2^x$, $y = 3^x$, $y = 5^x$, and $y = 8^x$ on the same set of axes. Explore which graph is above or below the other graphs. Using inequality symbols, order 2^x, 3^x, 5^x, and 8^x for values of $x < 0$ from smallest to largest. Then order 2^x, 3^x, 5^x, and 8^x for values of $x > 0$. Describe any patterns you notice.

Solve each equation.

53. $2^x = \frac{1}{2}$

54. $3^x = 27$

55. $2^{-x} = 16$

56. $4^x = 0.25$

57. $25^{2x} = 125$

58. $3^{x-2} = 9$

MORE MATH REASONING

59. Use a Graphing Utility Combine the idea of a polynomial and an exponential function by exploring the graphs of the functions $y = x^x$, $y = x^{2x}$, and $y = x^{3x}$. First predict what the graphs might look like. Then graph each function on your graphing utility and sketch your results. Describe any patterns that you see, and discuss the domain, range, end behavior, and maximum or minimum points.

60. Recruiting Your friend has founded a new organization, the Society for the Promotion of Mathematics. As the founder, she is the only Level 1 member. You and four other people have been asked to join as Level 2 members. One rule of the society is that each member must recruit five new members.

a. How can you use an exponential function to model the growth of the society? Write an equation to model its growth.

b. The current population of the world is about 5.5 billion people. What number of levels can the society have? Explain your answer.

9-1
PART B
Exponential Growth and Decay

← **CONNECT** → *You've seen that the graphs of exponential functions whose bases are greater than 1 increase as x increases, while those with bases less than 1 decrease as x increases. Now you will use these properties to model exponential growth and decay.*

As you've seen, exponential functions model quantities that increase or decrease at a constant percentage rate over time. If the base of the function is greater than 1, the quantity shows **exponential growth;** if the base of the function is less than 1, it shows **exponential decay.** One application of exponential decay is in the study of radioactive substances.

A radioactive substance does not stay radioactive forever. As time passes, the atoms emit radiation and change into a new element. The amount of time that it takes for half of the radioactive material to decay is called the *half-life* of a substance.

1. The half-life of an *isotope* (type) of thorium, thorium-234, is 25 days. If you start with 70 g of thorium-234, how much do you have left after 100 days?

Since the amount of the substance decreases 50% every 25 days, the equation for the decay is $y = 70(0.50)^t$, where t is the number of half-lives that have elapsed.

There are $\frac{100}{25} = 4$ half-lives in 100 days.

$y = 70(0.50)^4$ Substitute 4 for t.

$y = 70(0.0625)$

$y = 4.375$

There are 4.375 grams of thorium-234 left after 100 days. The other 65.625 grams have emitted radiation and changed into another element.

Excessive radiation levels are toxic to humans, so safe storage of radioactive isotopes is important. In the Explore, you will investigate a radioactive substance whose half-life is much longer than 25 days.

EXPLORE: DECADES OF DECAY

Plutonium-239 is an extremely toxic radioactive isotope used in nuclear power reactors. The half-life of plutonium-239 is 24,400 years. Suppose a reactor uses 200 g of plutonium-239.

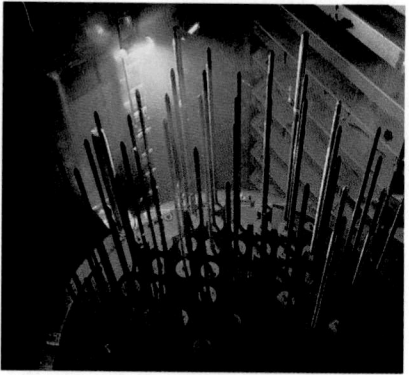

1. The average lifespan of an American is 75.5 years. What percentage of the plutonium-239 will be left after one lifespan?

2. How long will it take the 200 g of plutonium-239 to decay to 25 g?

3. The first known cities, located in Mesopotamia, arose about 3500 B.C. Therefore, all of human civilization spans about 5500 years. How much of the 200 g of plutonium-239 will be present 5500 years from now?

4. What are some issues that must be considered when constructing nuclear power plants that use isotopes like plutonium-239?

TRY IT

a. The half-life of nitrogen-13 is 10 minutes. If you start with 200 g of nitrogen-13, how much will you have left after an hour?

b. Suppose the half-life of a radioactive isotope is 10,000 years. How long will it take for this substance to decay to $\frac{1}{16}$ of its original amount?

You can use your knowledge of exponents to calculate the average annual growth or decay rate for a quantity that is growing or decaying exponentially.

EXAMPLE

2. The 1990 U.S. Census revealed that the population of Peoria, Illinois, declined from 124,813 inhabitants in 1980 to 113,504 in 1990. Calculate the average annual rate of decline for Peoria.

We know that the initial population of 124,813 declined to 113,504 in 10 years.

$$113{,}504 = 124{,}813(b)^{10}$$

$$\frac{113504}{124813} = b^{10}$$

$$0.9094 \approx b^{10}$$

$$0.9094^{\frac{1}{10}} \approx (b^{10})^{\frac{1}{10}} \qquad \text{Take both sides to the } \frac{1}{10} \text{ power.}$$

$$0.991 \approx b$$

Since the base is 0.991, the population decreases to 99.1% of its former value in one year. Therefore, the average annual rate of decrease is 0.9%.

In Example 2, notice that b can be thought of as $1 \pm r$, where r is the growth or decay rate. Therefore, if you find the value of b, you can find the growth or decay rate by subtracting 1. In Example 2, $0.991 - 1 = -0.009$, meaning that the population is *decreasing* at a rate of 0.9% per year.

As you've seen, populations grow exponentially. As human populations increase, so does their demand for resources. In Example 3, we look at the implications of exponential growth for resource production.

EXAMPLE

3. The production of copper increased at a rate of about 4.9% per year between 1988 and 1993. In 1993, copper production was 1.801×10^9 kg.

If this trend continues, when will world copper production exceed 10^{10} kg?

The equation for exponential growth is $A = Pb^t$.

The amount of copper produced in 1993 was 1.801×10^9 kg, and the annual growth rate is 4.9%. So the equation modeling copper production is $A = 1.801 \times 10^9(1.049)^t$.

We can graph this function on a graphing utility and *trace* to find the first year where production exceeds 10^{10} kg.

According to the graph, the copper production exceeds this level 36 years after 1993, in 2029.

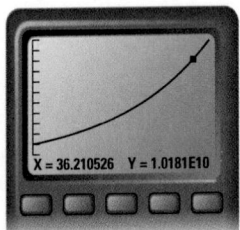

EXAMPLE

4. The number of Dalmatian dogs registered with the American Kennel Club grew from 38,927 in 1992 to 42,816 in 1993. If this trend continues, when will the number of registered Dalmatians exceed 70,000?

The population increased by 42,816 − 38,927 = 3,889 in one year, so the growth rate is $\frac{3,889}{38,917} \approx 0.10$.

Assuming this rate continues, we model the growth by:

$A = 42,816(1.1)^t$

We can graph this function on a graphing utility and *trace* to find the first year where the Dalmatian population exceeds 70,000.

According to the graph, the population exceeds 70,000 about five years after 1993, in 1998.

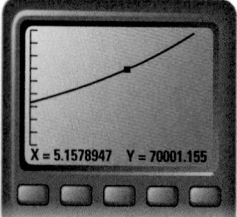

X = 5.1578947   Y = 70001.155

CONSIDER

1. Can the production of copper increase at 4.9% a year indefinitely? Explain why or why not.

TRY IT

c. In Example 3, we assume that world copper production increases at 4.9% a year. Suppose that this rate of increase was reduced to 2.5% per year starting in 1993. What would be the world copper production in 2029 using this growth rate?

Any real-world quantity that increases or decreases at a constant percentage rate can be modeled by an exponential function. These quantities include populations, radioactive materials, and resource production figures.

REFLECT

1. Suppose it takes 45 years for 4 of 8 grams of a radioactive isotope to decay. How long will it take the next 3 grams to decay? Explain.
2. Explain the difference between linear growth and exponential growth.
3. A biologist is observing a strain of bacteria growing in a Petri dish. Their population increases exponentially over time. If the first bacterium took 4 hours to divide into 2 bacteria, how long will it take for the 500,000 bacteria in the dish to increase to 1,000,000? Explain.

Exercises

CORE

1. **Getting Started** The average U.S. per capita income rose from $9,494 in 1980 to $18,696 in 1990. Follow the steps to find the average annual rate of growth in per capita income for those years. Express your answer in percentage form.
   a. Use the equation $A = Pb^t$. Substitute the known values for the final per capita income (A), the initial per capita income (P), and the number of years (t).
   b. Divide both sides of the equation by P to isolate b^t.
   c. To solve for b, take both sides of the equation to the exponent $\frac{1}{t}$. (This should leave b on the right side of the equation.)
   d. To solve for b, evaluate the left side of the equation.
   e. To find the average annual growth rate, subtract 1 from b. To convert to percentage form, multiply your result by 100.

2. Using your answer from **d** in Exercise 1, write an equation to model the growth in U.S. per capita income. Use your equation to predict the per capita income in the year 2000.

The equation $A = 15,383(1.019)^t$ models the growth in the world production of aluminum since 1980 (in thousands of metric tons). Use this equation to estimate the aluminum production in each year.

3. 1990   **4.** 1996   **5.** 2000   **6.** 2100

7. The half-life of radon-222 is 3.8 days. How much radon-222 will be left in a 16-mg sample after:
   a. 3.8 days?   **b.** 7.6 days?   **c.** 15.2 days?

8. Between 1980 and 1990, the population of Cleveland, Ohio, declined from 573,822 to 505,616.
   a. Find the average yearly rate of decline.
   b. Write an equation to model the decline in Cleveland's population. Then predict Cleveland's population in 2005.

9. **Blue Book Special** Qin bought a used car for $6500. This car is *depreciating* (declining in value) at the rate of 1.25% per month. Qin's auto loan is for 3 years. How much will this car be worth when Qin makes the final payment?

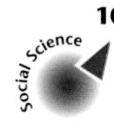

10. **Boomtown** The population of São Paulo, Brazil, increased from 18.7 million in 1991 to 21.5 million in 1995. Find the average annual rate of increase. Then use your result to predict the population of São Paulo in the year 2000.

Carnaval in Brazil

11. **A Growing Controversy** Maricela and Samuel found that their school's enrollment had increased from 1241 in 1994 to 1365 in 1996.

   a. Maricela and Samuel found the average annual growth rate for this period to be approximately 4.9%. Check their answer and explain how you checked it.

   b. To predict the 1998 enrollment, Samuel used the equation $A = 1241(1.049)^4$ and Maricela used $A = 1365(1.049)^2$. Do both equations give approximately the same result? If so, explain why both equations work; if not, tell which student used an incorrect equation and how you can tell.

12. **Where Did My Gold Go?** The radioactive isotope gold-201 has a half-life of 26 minutes. (Fortunately, this is not a naturally occurring isotope!)

   a. Write an equation to model the decay of this isotope. (Hint: Let $t =$ the number of 26-minute periods.)

   b. How much gold-201 is left in a 10-mg sample after:

   i. 10 minutes? **ii.** 45 minutes? **iii.** 3 hours?

13. **Half a Student is Better Than None!** The publication *Everybody Counts* states that the half-life of a mathematics student is approximately one year. Every year in the United States from ninth grade through the Ph.D. level, we lose half of our mathematics students. If this model is correct, how many mathematics students must we start with in ninth grade to produce one Ph.D. mathematician? Assume four years of high school, four years of undergraduate study, and eight years of graduate study. Explain how you solved this problem.

14. Explain how exponential growth and decay are related to geometric sequences.

15. **To Decay or Not to Decay** You can use probability to model radioactive decay.

   a. Take 10 coins and toss them. If a coin comes up tails, it has "decayed." Make a table to record how many coins remain after each toss.

Toss	0	1	2	...
Coins remaining	10			

   Remove the "decayed" coins. Then toss the remaining coins again and repeat the process until all of the coins have decayed.

   b. Make a graph of the data in your table. How is this graph similar to the graph of an exponential function with a base less than 1? How is it different?

   c. According to your experiment, what is the approximate "half-life" of your coins? Repeat the experiment to confirm this value.

   d. Explain how this experiment models radioactive decay.

 **LOOK BACK**

Solve each equation. [8-3]

16. $\frac{x}{5} + \frac{2x}{15} = 8$

17. $\frac{x}{2} + 4x = \frac{x}{4} - 64$

18. $\frac{2k}{5} - \frac{3k}{4} = 10$

Use division to find each quotient and remainder. [8-2]

19. $(x^3 + 7x^2 - 3x + 8) \div (x - 2)$ **20.** $(4x^2 - 6x + 1) \div (x + 5)$

21. $(2x^3 - 6x + 3) \div (x - 4)$ **22.** $(5x^3 - 3x^2 + 6x + 9) \div (x + 1)$

MORE PRACTICE

The equation $A = 61{,}671(1.029)^t$ models the growth in the number of cars and taxis registered in the United States, in thousands, since 1960. Use this equation to estimate the number of cars and taxis registered in each year.

23. 1970   **24.** 1980   **25.** 1996   **26.** 2005

27. Use a Graphing Utility Mayfield and Harborview are two small, rapidly growing cities. In 1990 Mayfield had 50,000 people and was growing at a rate of 7.9% per year. Harborview's 1990 population was 75,000 and increasing at a rate of 5% per year. Assuming these growth rates remain the same, investigate the change in population of these two cities over the next 20 years. Which city will reach 100,000 first? Which will reach 150,000 first?

28. Half a Life is Better Than None! The half-life of vanadium-53 is 2 minutes.
  a. Write an equation that models the decay of 1000 grams of vanadium-53 over time.
  b. Use a graphing utility to draw a graph showing this model for 0 to 24 minutes.
  c. *Trace* to find how many minutes must pass until there are less than 100 grams of vanadium-53 remaining. How long will it be before there is less than one gram of vanadium-53 remaining?
  d. Protactinium-236 has a half-life of about 12 minutes. Write an equation for the decay of protactinium-236, and find how long it will take for 1000 grams to decay to less than one gram.
  e. Compare the protactinium-236 graph to the vanadium-53 graph. How are they similar and how are they different?

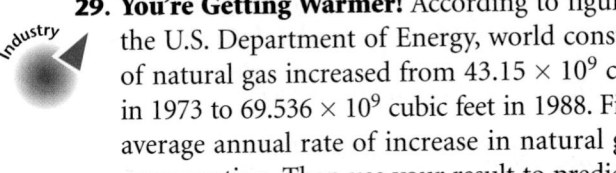

29. You're Getting Warmer! According to figures from the U.S. Department of Energy, world consumption of natural gas increased from 43.15×10^9 cubic feet in 1973 to 69.536×10^9 cubic feet in 1988. Find the average annual rate of increase in natural gas consumption. Then use your result to predict the quantity of natural gas that the world will consume in 2001.

American Gas Association

MORE MATH REASONING

30. Biohazard A laboratory technician is growing a bacteria culture. The experiment starts with 100 bacteria that double every 12 hours. After 3 days, the culture is subjected to a drug treatment and the bacteria stop reproducing and begin to die at the rate of 25% every 12 hours. How long does it take until the culture is smaller than it was at the beginning of the experiment?

31. The Big Blue Marble The U.S. Bureau of the Census published the following data on world populations. Numbers are given in millions.

Location	1900	1950	1980	1991
World	1600	2564	4478	5423
Africa	118	281	594	817
Asia	932	1368	2494	3046
Europe	400	392	484	502
North America	106	166	252	279

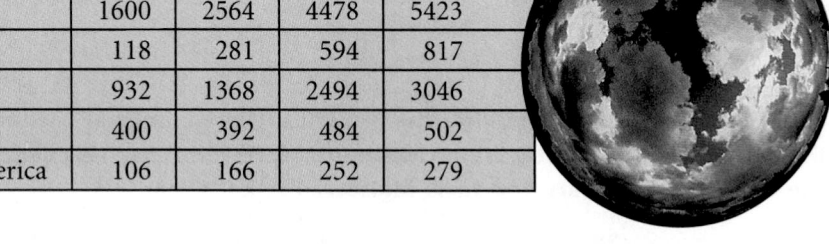

a. There is only one example of a population *decline* in the table above. Where and when did this decline occur? What do you think caused this decline?

b. Considering only the data for 1900 and 1991, calculate average annual growth rates for 1900–1991 for the world as a whole and then for each continent. Use your growth rates to predict the population of each continent and of the world in:
  i. 2050   **ii.** 2100   **iii.** 2200

c. Suppose that the world population growth rate is 1% more than your predicted rate. What is the estimated population in 2200 using this rate? What will the 2200 population be if the growth rate is 1% *less* than your predicted rate?

d. Calculate the world population growth rate for 1980-1991. Compare this rate to your answer from **b.** Does the growth rate seem to be increasing or decreasing?

e. What are some of the problems caused by world population growth?

9-1
PART C
Modeling Exponential Growth and Decay

← CONNECT →

You have already used exponential functions to model growth and decay. Now you will see how to write equations to model data that show exponential growth.

You've seen how you can use linear regression and power regression features on a graphing utility to find a line or curve that is a good model for data on a scatter plot. You've investigated many real-world examples of exponential growth and decay. Now you will use a graphing utility to determine the *best* exponential curve that fits a data set.

CONSIDER

?

1. Under what circumstances would an exponential function be a better model for data than a linear function?

EXPLORE: HEART DATA

The National Center for Health Statistics published the following data on the number of heart bypass surgeries performed between 1980 and 1990.

MATERIALS

Graph paper
Graphing utility

Year	Year Number	Number of Bypass Surgeries Performed
1980	0	137,000
1981	1	159,000
1982	2	170,000
1983	3	191,000
1984	4	202,000
1985	5	230,000
1986	6	284,000
1987	7	332,000
1988	8	353,000
1989	9	368,000
1990	10	392,000

1. Make a scatter plot of the year number versus the number of surgeries. Describe any trend that you see.

2. Find the percentage growth for each one-year period in the table. Use your results to estimate an "average" growth rate for bypass surgery in the United States from 1980 to 1990. Explain how you made your estimate.

3. Enter this data on your graphing utility. Then use *exponential regression* to find the best a and b values for the model $y = ab^t$. What are these values? Compare the growth rate given by this model to the estimate of the average growth rate you made in Step 2.

4. Graph the exponential regression equation that models this data set and draw the graph of the function through your scatter plot.

5. *Trace* the graph of the regression equation to compare the regression model to the actual data. Make a table to compare the number of surgeries the model predicts to the actual number of surgeries for the years 1980 through 1990.

6. Use your model to predict the number of bypass surgeries for each year. Explain how you made these predictions.

    a. 1998   **b.** 2005   **c.** 2050

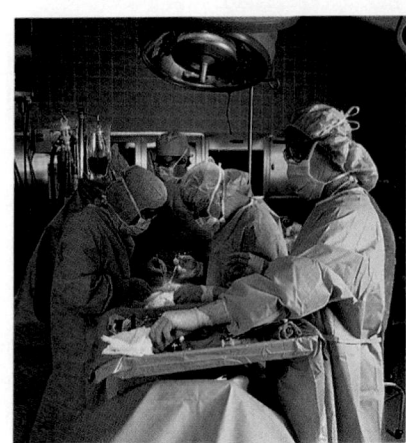

In the Explore, you used a mathematical model to predict the value of y when you were given different values for x. You can also use the same type of mathematical model to find the value of x when you know the value of y.

EXAMPLE

The city of New Milford has been experiencing rapid growth. Determine an exponential model for the following data. Then predict the year when New Milford's population will reach 75,000.

Years since 1980	0	1	2	3	4	5	6	7
Population	18,940	21,150	23,490	27,570	29,610	35,480	38,190	41,670

Use the exponential regression function on your graphing utility to find a and b for $y = ab^x$.

The graphing utility gives values

$a = 18,950.71$

$b = 1.12$

So $y \approx 18,951(1.12)^x$.

To find the year when the population will reach 75,000, graph $y = 18,950(1.12)^x$.

Then *trace* until $y \approx 75,000$.

$x \approx 12$

X = 12.157895 Y = 75161.727

The population of New Milford should have reached 75,000 twelve years after 1980, in 1992.

TRY IT

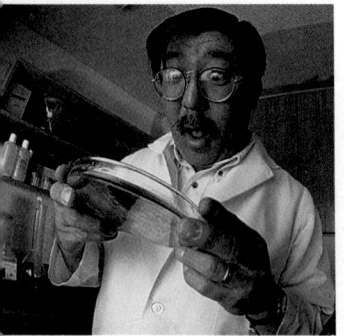

a. A microbiologist at Microbio-Tech Labs notices that a new strain of bacteria has begun to grow in the same culture as an older strain. The growth data on the new strain is given in the table below.

Days	5	8	10	12	15
Count	16,487	26,952	27,183	30,000	44,817

Graph the data and find the exponential regression equation. Then estimate the number of bacteria present after 18 days.

Many situations in real life can be modeled mathematically using an exponential equation. The exponential regression equation allows us to estimate the amount of something that is present at a particular time. We can use the graph of the equation to estimate the time when a given amount is present.

1. Explain why exponential functions are a good model for quantities that grow at a given percentage each year.
2. If the last point in a data set has an *x*-coordinate of 10 and you need to predict the *y*-coordinate for the *x*-coordinate 27, how accurate do you think the *y*-coordinate will be? Explain.
3. A town was founded in 1951. In attempting to model its population growth exponentially, John used 1950 as year 0, and entered $(0, 0)$ as a data point. When he tried to do an exponential regression on his graphing utility, he got an error message. Explain what the problem is.

Exercises

CORE

Getting Started State whether a linear or an exponential model is more appropriate for each of the following situations.

1. Your pay increases by $7.50 for each hour you work.

2. Your hourly wage increases 5% each year.

3. The length that a spring can stretch is directly proportional to the force on the spring.

4. Half of the carbon-14 in a sample decays every 5730 years.

Evaluate each expression. If necessary, round to the nearest hundredth.

5. $3(2)^3$ **6.** $4(1.05)^3$ **7.** $2.97(0.975)^{10}$ **8.** $1095(1.0083)^{2.5}$

9. For the years 1970–1991, the median price of a single-family home in the United States can be approximated by the exponential regression equation $A = 25690(1.072)^t$, where *t* is in years $(1970 = 0)$.
  a. According to this equation, what is the growth rate of housing prices for this period?
  b. Use this equation to estimate or predict the median price of a home in:
    i. 1970   **ii.** 1980   **iii.** 1990   **iv.** 2025

10. The graph shows a function that models the Gross Domestic Product (the total value of all goods and services produced) in the United States for the years 1960–1990. Use the graph to estimate the year when the Gross Domestic Product was:
  a. 1000 billion dollars   **b.** 2000 billion dollars
  c. 3500 billion dollars   **d.** 5000 billion dollars

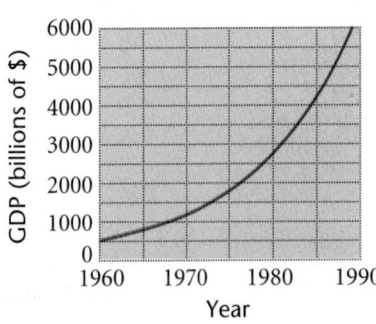

11. **The New System** Generally, prices of items tend to increase as time passes. This general increase in prices over time is called *inflation*. During the early 1990s, the former Soviet Union radically reorganized its political and economic structure. The fundamental change was the move from socialism to a free-market economy. At times during this upheaval, the inflation rate in Russia reached 200% per year. Assume this rate was constant from 1990–1996.
   a. Suppose that in 1990, a loaf of bread cost $1.50 and a pair of shoes cost $70. Make a table showing the increase in price of these items from 1990 to 1996.
   b. Discuss the implications of inflation. How does inflation affect people on a fixed income?

12. The value of a complete 1971 set of Topps baseball cards, from 1971−1995, can be modeled by the equation $A = 20(1.222)^t$, where t is in years (1971 = 0). The graph of this equation is shown.
   a. Estimate the value of the set in:
      i. 1975   **ii.** 1980   **iii.** 1986
   b. Estimate the year when the set was worth:
      i. $100   **ii.** $500   **iii.** $1000   **iv.** $1500

13. **Pricey Flour** In wartime, restricted supplies can cause prices to skyrocket. In 1861, right before the Civil War, flour cost about $7 per barrel in the United States. From 1861 to 1863, prices rose about 50 percent per year. In the Confederate states, the price of flour rose about 100 percent per year over the same time period. Write equations that model both price increases. Then use your equations to predict the price of flour in the Union and in the Confederacy in:
   a. 1863   **b.** 1864   **c.** 1865

 LOOK AHEAD

Find the inverse of each function.

14. $f(x) = 2x + 7$ 15. $g(x) = 8x^3$ 16. $h(x) = \dfrac{3x + 2}{8}$

17. What is the relationship between the graph of a function and the graph of its inverse?

MORE PRACTICE

Use a graphing utility to make a scatter plot for each set of data. Then find an exponential regression equation in the form $y = ab^x$ to model each data set.

18.

x	1	4	9	12	17	19
y	35	98	148	279	381	563

19.

x	3	9	12	18	24	37
y	0.1	0.9	2.3	5.7	16.4	29.7

20. The Consumer Price Index is used to measure inflation in the United States. An exponential regression equation that models the Consumer Price Index from 1960 to 1991 shows that prices rose about 5.4% per year during that period.

People often laugh at the low prices in old catalogs. Use an inflation rate of 5.4% per year to estimate prices of each of the following items in 1950 and 2030.

a. a spool of thread, 1996 price 79¢
b. a hamburger, 1996 price $1.99
c. a pair of jeans, 1996 price $30
d. a new car, 1996 price $13,000

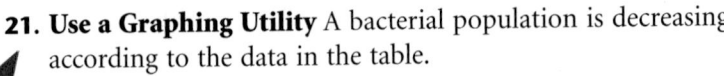

21. Use a Graphing Utility A bacterial population is decreasing according to the data in the table.

Days	1	2	3	4	5
Population	4094	3367	2735	2278	1895

a. Use the data to draw a scatter plot. Then find an exponential regression equation that models this data.
b. Predict the bacterial population:
   i. after 10 days   **ii.** after 15 days   **iii.** at the beginning of the experiment

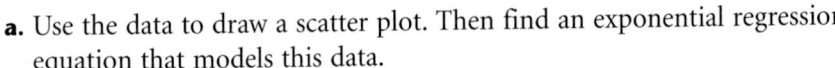

22. Use a Graphing Utility Consumer goods that use new technologies often come on the market at a relatively high price, but then the price drops over time. This pattern has been true for calculators, VCRs, CD players, and computers. Suppose that the following data represents the price drop for a new computer system.

Introductory Price, Jan. 1, 1994	$1599.00
Price, July 1, 1994	$1303.00
Price, Jan. 1, 1995	$1062.00
Price, July 1, 1995	$865.60

a. Find a regression equation to model the price of this computer. According to this equation, what is the rate of decline of the price?
b. If this rate stays the same, when will the price drop below $500? below $300?

MORE MATH REASONING

23. Steeliness According to *Van Nostrand's Scientific Encyclopedia*, Seventh Edition, the grain size for steel is expressed by a number from 1 to 8. A grain size from 1 to 3 is *coarse*, from 4 to 6 is *intermediate*, and from 7 to 8 is *fine*. If $n = 2^{N-1}$ where N is the grain size and n is the number of grains per square inch, make a table that relates n to the three categories of grain size.

24. Use a Graphing Utility You have studied the graphs of $y = x^2$ and $y = 2^x$. Use what you know about these two functions to predict the shape of the graph of $y = 2^{(x^2)}$. Check your prediction with your graphing utility. Extend your exploration of this type of function by using at least five other polynomial functions as the exponent for an exponential function. From what you know about exponential and polynomial functions, explain the shape and position of each graph.

← CONNECT → *You've worked with exponential functions with many different bases. Now you will investigate a new base that is very important in mathematics.*

Radioactive substances decay exponentially. Fortunately, money earning interest in a bank account *grows* exponentially. You may have seen advertisements that seem to show two different interest rates for an account.

Most banks *compound* interest by paying the interest every quarter or month instead of every year. If your money is in an account that pays 6% interest compounded monthly, you earn $\frac{6\%}{12} = 0.5\%$ interest every month. In the second month, you earn interest on your initial investment *and* on the interest from the first month. Because you earn interest on interest, your *effective annual yield* is more than the 6% *nominal* rate.

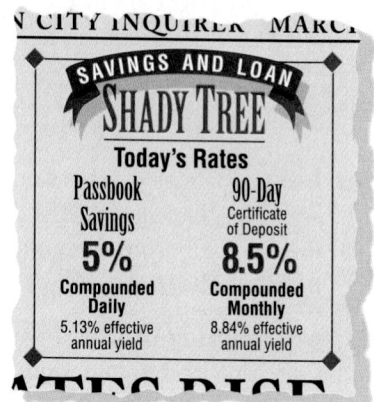

Suppose a bank pays *r* percent interest, expressed in decimal form. If interest is paid *n* times a year for *t* years, the exponential growth equation is:

$$A = P\left(1 + \frac{r}{n}\right)^{nt}$$

where *P* is the initial investment.

EXAMPLE

1. A bank advertises that it pays 4% interest on a savings account, compounded quarterly. If you put $100 in the account, how much will you have after 1 year?

Interest is paid 4 times a year, so $n = 4$. The balance in the account is:

$A = 100\left(1 + \frac{0.04}{4}\right)^{4t}$ Substitute $n = 4$, $r = 0.04$, and $P = 100$.

$A = 100\left(1 + \frac{0.04}{4}\right)^{4(1)}$ To see the amount after 1 year, let $t = 1$.

$ = 100(1.01)^4$

$ = 100(1.04060401)$

$ = 104.060401$

Round this answer to the nearest cent. You will have $104.06 after one year.

Notice that you actually made $4.06 on your $100 deposit. The effective yield on this account is 4.06%, higher than the 4% nominal rate.

Suppose you deposit $1200 in a savings account paying 8% interest for 10 years. Let's see how different compounding periods affect the growth of your investment.

Initial Deposit ($)	Compounding	Mathematical Model	Total $ After 10 Years
1200	1 (annually)	$y = 1200\left(1 + \frac{0.08}{1}\right)^{10}$	2590.71
1200	4 (quarterly)	$y = 1200\left(1 + \frac{0.08}{4}\right)^{4 \cdot 10}$	2649.65
1200	12 (monthly)	$y = 1200\left(1 + \frac{0.08}{12}\right)^{12 \cdot 10}$	2663.57
1200	365 (daily)	$y = 1200\left(1 + \frac{0.08}{365}\right)^{365 \cdot 10}$	2670.41
1200	365·24 (each hour)	$y = 1200\left(1 + \frac{0.08}{365 \cdot 24}\right)^{(365 \cdot 24) \cdot 10}$	2670.64
1200	365·24·60 (each minute)	$y = 1200\left(1 + \frac{0.08}{365 \cdot 24 \cdot 60}\right)^{(365 \cdot 24 \cdot 60) \cdot 10}$	2670.65

CONSIDER

1. What is happening to the total value of the investment as the compounding period gets shorter? How would you describe the pattern you see in the totals?

By taking the idea of compounding to the extreme, we can investigate *continuous* exponential growth.

To simplify matters, let the original amount (P) equal 1 and the yearly rate (r) equal 1 (or 100%) for 1 year of growth, compounded k times.

$$A = P\left(1 + \frac{r}{n}\right)^{nt} = \left(1 + \frac{1}{k}\right)^{k}$$

k	1	10	100	1,000	10,000	1,000,000
A	2	2.59374...	2.70481...	2.71692...	2.71814...	2.71828...

As k increases, A approaches a limiting value. This value is an irrational number (e), whose decimal expansion begins $e = 2.718281828...$. Although this value may not seem remarkable, it is the most important base value for exponential functions.

There is a formula involving e for continuous compounding.

The value of an original investment of P dollars with an interest rate r compounded continuously for t years is $A = Pe^{rt}$.

Notice that r is the nominal growth rate. The effective annual growth rate is somewhat higher than this.

2. Suppose $2000 is invested in a three-year certificate of deposit (CD) that earns 6% interest, compounded continuously. How much will the investment be worth after three years?

$A = Pe^{rt}$

$A = 2000e^{(0.06)(3)}$

$A = 2000e^{0.18}$

$A = (2000)(1.197217363)$ Use a calculator to evaluate $e^{0.18}$.

$A = 2394.434726$

The investment will be worth about $2394.43.

EXPLORE: SO YOU WANT TO BE AN INVESTOR

MATERIALS

Graphing utility

1. Suppose you have $1000 to invest. Your local bank is offering a savings account that pays 3.5% interest, compounded continuously. Write an equation to model the growth of your money in this account.

2. Graph this equation on your graphing utility. *Trace* to find out how many years it will take to double your money (the *doubling time*) if you put it in this account.

3. Each of the following investments are also available to you. Write an equation to model each, graph the equation, and *trace* to find the doubling time.

   a. *a certificate of deposit paying 7%, compounded continuously* You may not withdraw money before a specified time without paying a penalty.

   b. *stock in a computer software company* The value of this stock has risen 12% per year since the company started up two years ago.

   c. *a rare stamp valued at $1000* This stamp has increased in value at an average rate of 14% per year since 1972.

A mistake in printing makes this 1918 airmail stamp rare and valuable.

4. For each investment, compare the doubling time to the interest rate. Describe any pattern that you see.

5. It might seem that people should take their money out of the bank and buy stock or rare collectibles. But the investments in **3a, b,** and **c** each have a "hidden cost." Explain what the "hidden cost" of each investment is.

6. Which of these investments would you choose? Explain your choice. For each of the others, describe a person for whom that investment might be suitable.

CONSIDER

2. Using your results from the Explore, explain what the "Rule of 70" is.

a. If you invest $250 in an account that pays 5%, compounded continuously, how much will you have after 8 years?

b. How long will it take money invested at 5% to double in value?

c. Suppose one of your ancestors invested $1 in a bank account in 1700. The account paid 7%, compounded continuously. You have just inherited the account. How much is it worth?

You now have two equations available for modeling exponential growth or decay of an initial amount P over a t-year period.

$A = Pe^{rt}$, where r is the continuously compounded growth rate.

$A = Pb^t$, where b is the factor you multiply the amount by every time period.

Both are useful ways to model exponential growth. The first formula is exact only for continuous compounding situations. However, it gives good approximations in most other cases.

REFLECT

1. Three banks advertise the same nominal interest rate. One compounds interest quarterly, one monthly, and one continuously. Which bank gives the highest effective interest rate?

2. Explain what the number e is. What characteristics does it share with π?

3. Suppose you know that the population growth of a city can be modeled by $A = 500{,}000e^{0.02t}$. Is the city's population increasing 2% per year? Explain.

Exercises

CORE

Getting Started Use the Rule of 70 to estimate each of the following.

1. The doubling time for the balance in a bank account paying 5% interest.

2. The interest rate needed so that the value of an investment will double in 10 years.

3. The doubling time for the world's population if it increases at 1.4% per year.

For each function, find $f(x)$ for $x = 0$, 1, 2, 6, and 10.

4. $f(x) = 14{,}000e^{0.15x}$

5. $f(x) = 2{,}500e^{-0.055x}$

6. Use the formula $A = P\left(1 + \dfrac{r}{n}\right)^{nt}$ to find the value of a $1000 investment at 6% interest after 10 years, compounded:

   a. annually   b. semiannually   c. quarterly   d. monthly   e. daily

7. Use the formula $A = Pe^{rt}$ to find the value, after 10 years, of a $1000 investment at 6% interest, compounded continuously. Compare your answer to your results from Exercise 6.

Find the value of each investment. Assume interest is compounded continuously.

8. $100 invested at 5% for 6 years

9. $2500 invested at 10% for 4 years

10. 25¢ invested at 12% for 300 years

11. Use the graphs of $y = 2^x$ and $y = 3^x$ to help you sketch the graph of $y = e^x$. Do not use a calculator to find coordinates.

12. Waiting Time Suppose that the probability of waiting less than x minutes for a radio station operator to take your dedication is $P(x) = 1 - e^{\frac{-x}{t}}$, where t represents the average time, in minutes, for the operator to take a dedication.
   a. Operator A answers the phone in an average of 3 minutes. What is the probability that this operator will answer your call within 2 minutes? 4 minutes? 7 minutes?
   b. Suppose operator B takes an average of 5 minutes to answer the phone. What is the probability that your call is answered in 2 minutes when operator B is working? 4 minutes? 7 minutes?

13. Saving for College Maria's parents deposited $2500 in a savings account that pays 5.5% yearly interest, compounded continuously.
   a. Write and graph a function that shows the growth of this money over the next 15 years.
   b. Make a table to compare the amount in this account after 15 years when compounding is done yearly, quarterly, monthly, and continuously.
   c. What would happen to the total amount in the account if the interest rate changed? Compare the amount in the account after the first year for 5.5%, 7%, and 10%.

14. Power Trip Suppose that a nuclear-powered satellite has a power output of $P = 60e^{\frac{-t}{300}}$, where t is the time, in days, since the satellite was launched. The satellite requires 20 watts of power to operate. Will it still be operational after 2 years?

15. Find S_n for $\frac{1}{0!} + \frac{1}{1!} + \frac{1}{2!} + \cdots + \frac{1}{n!}$ as n increases. Do the partial sums appear to approach a limit? If so, what is it?

16. The Money Tree The Final National Bank offers several types of savings accounts with different interest rates and compounding periods. The Money-Market account pays 3.8% interest, compounded quarterly. Standard savings accounts earn 3.55% interest, compounded monthly. And the All-in-One account pays 3.2% interest, compounded continuously. You have $2000 to deposit. Make a table comparing the balance in each of these accounts after 25 years. Which plan is best? Why?

Solve each equation. [8-2]

17. $x^3 - 4x^2 + 3x = 0$ **18.** $x^3 - 2x^2 - 5x + 6 = 0$ **19.** $2x^3 - 3x^2 + 2x - 3 = 0$

20. An airplane travels 300 miles per hour in still air. The plane takes 4.8 hours to make a 1400-mile round-trip with a headwind on the outbound flight and a tailwind on the return flight. What is the wind speed? [8-3]

MORE PRACTICE

Use the Rule of 70 to estimate each of the following.

21. The doubling time for a bank account that pays 12% interest.

22. The interest rate needed so that the value of an investment will double in 7 years.

23. The time it will take U.S. oil consumption to quadruple if it increases 3.5% per year.

For each function, find $f(x)$ for $x = 0, 1, 3, 6,$ and 10.

24. $f(x) = 20e^{0.06x}$ **25.** $f(x) = 785e^{0.18x}$ **26.** $f(x) = 11{,}000e^{-0.085x}$

27. Use the formula $A = P\left(1 + \dfrac{r}{n}\right)^{nt}$ to find the value of a $200 investment at 8% after 15 years, compounded:
   a. annually   **b.** quarterly   **c.** monthly   **d.** continuously

28. The Second Savings Bank offers a passbook savings account paying 4.25% interest, compounded daily. Make a table showing the growth of this account for the next 10 years if the original deposit was $1300.

29. The Golden Years When Roland was born, his father deposited $2000 in a retirement account for him. The account has grown at a rate of 8% per year, compounded continuously. Roland is 65 years old and ready to retire. How much is the account now worth?

MORE MATH REASONING

30. A supervisor at MaxiCore has observed that the maximum number of control levers an employee can produce per day is 300 units. In approaching this production level, the learning curve is modeled by $P(x) = 300(1 - e^{-0.05x})$, where $P(x)$ is the number of units that will pass quality control after x days on the job.
   a. Use a graphing utility to graph this model and use it to predict when a new employee should be expected to produce 100, 200, and 300 units per day.
   b. The supervisor checks each employee's monthly output for the 90-day probation period. At each check, the employee must be within 5% of the predicted production output. According to the model, what is the least number of units that must pass quality control after 30, 60, and 90 days of training?

31. **Down with Inflation** You've decided that, to retire comfortably, you will need to be able to spend $30,000 each year. Assuming a 20-year retirement, you will need $600,000 in the bank when you reach retirement age. That way, you can spend $30,000 each year, in addition to Social Security, interest, and other income.

a. Suppose inflation averages 3.5% per year. Then $100 at the beginning of the year will buy $\frac{\$100}{1.035}$ worth at the end of the year. What is this amount?

b. Suppose you plan to retire in 50 years. How much will $600,000 be worth then, in today's dollars? Explain how you found this value.

c. How much will you need in the bank in 50 years to have a sum that is comparable to $600,000 today?

d. There is a second invalid assumption in the retirement plan outlined above. What is it?

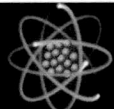

9-1 PART E Making Connections

← CONNECT → *You've seen how real-world quantities can be modeled by exponential functions. Now you will use an exponential function to help solve a paleontological mystery.*

A living animal or plant takes in carbon-14, a radioactive isotope of carbon. As the carbon-14 decays, it emits beta particles that can be measured with a *Geiger counter.* By finding the number of beta particles emitted from a bone sample, the age of the fossil can be calculated. This technique is known as *carbon dating.*

On page 619, you learned about a mystery involving whale bones found in Michigan, hundreds of miles from the ocean. You now have the mathematical tools needed to solve this mystery.

EXPLORE: SOLVING THE MICHIGAN WHALE MYSTERY

MATERIALS

Graphing utility

A living organism emits approximately 918 beta particles of radiation per gram each hour. When the organism dies, it stops absorbing carbon-14 and the decay process continues with a half-life of 5,730 years. After 5,730 years, a one-gram bone sample emits $918\left(\frac{1}{2}\right) = 459$ beta particles per hour. After 11,460 years, it emits $918\left(\frac{1}{2}\right)^2 = 229.5$ particles per hour.

How old are the whale bones found in Michigan? Paleontologist C. R. Harington used carbon dating to find the ages of three samples taken from different whales: a bowhead whale, a fin whale, and a sperm whale.

Archaeological evidence indicates that water levels during the last 20,000 years were not high enough for the Michigan whales to swim into the Eastern Great Lakes area. However, historic records tell of more recent trading routes that connected the Great Lakes area with the Atlantic coast, and fossil artifacts from the Atlantic coast dating from the same period have been found throughout Michigan.

1. Write an equation to describe the exponential decay of the number of beta particles emitted. Graph the equation on your graphing utility.
2. The sample from the bowhead whale fossil was found to emit 838 beta particles per gram each hour. *Trace* the graph of your equation to find the age of this fossil.
3. The fin whale fossil emitted 841 beta particles per gram each hour, and the sperm whale fossil emitted 896. Estimate the age of each fossil.
4. How do you think the whales got to Michigan? Explain.

REFLECT

1. In your own words, define *exponential growth* and *exponential decay*.
2. Describe the differences between a graph of an exponential function whose base is between 0 and 1, and that of an exponential function whose base is greater than 1.
3. Suppose carbon-14 decayed *linearly* so that half of it was left after 5730 years. Would it be useful for dating very old fossils? Why or why not?

Self-Assessment

For each function, find $f(t)$ for the values $t = 0, 1, 2, 6,$ and 10.

1. $f(t) = 3(2)^t$
2. $f(t) = 1200(1.10)^t$
3. $f(t) = 150e^{-0.6t}$

Graph each exponential function. Label the coordinates of at least two points on each curve.

4. $y = 3^x$
5. $y = 6^x$
6. $y = \left(\frac{1}{2}\right)^x$

Solve each equation.

7. $2^x = 16$
8. $9^x = 27$
9. $\left(\frac{1}{4}\right)^x = 32$

10. Uranium-238 has a half-life of 4.5×10^9 years. How long will it take the uranium-238 in a sample to decay to $\frac{1}{8}$ of its original amount?

11. If a radioactive isotope has a half-life of 5 days, how long will it be until a sample is less than 1% of its original amount? Will this be true for any size sample? Explain.

12. An algae population is growing at a rate equal to 10% of its population each day. Its initial size is 10,000 organisms. How many algae organisms are present after 10 days? after 30 days?

Solve each equation. [8-2, 8-3]

13. $x^3 - 5x^2 - 14x = 0$ **14.** $x^3 - 6x^2 + 3x + 10 = 0$ **15.** $\frac{x}{2} + \frac{3x}{4} = 15$

16. Suppose the population of a town has doubled in 5.6 years. What is the approximate average annual growth rate of its population?
    (a) 3.92%   (b) 5.6%   (c) 12.5%   (d) 15%

17. Suppose you deposit $100 in a bank account. How much will you have after 5 years if the account earns 4% interest:
    a. compounded semiannually (twice a year)?   **b.** compounded continuously?

Decide which choice is correct.

(A) The quantity in Column A is greater.   (B) The quantity in Column B is greater.
(C) The two quantities are equal.   (D) The relationship cannot be determined.

Column A	Column B
18. 2^x	3^x
19. 2^x	$\left(\frac{1}{2}\right)^{-x}$

20. According to World Health Organization (WHO) estimates, 10 to 12 million adults and 1 million children were infected with the AIDS virus worldwide as of mid-1992. The WHO estimates that up to 40 million people will be infected by the year 2000. The Global AIDS Policy Coalition, based at Harvard University, estimates that as many as 110 million people may be infected by the year 2000.

    a. Using the WHO estimates for 1992 and 2000, find the average annual growth rate of the number of people infected with the AIDS virus. Explain how you found this growth rate.
    b. Using the WHO estimate for 1992 and the Global AIDS Policy Coalition figures for 2000, find the average annual growth rate of the number of people infected with the AIDS virus. Compare this rate to the rate you found in **a.**

21. Guitar Strings The frequency of a note on the chromatic musical scale is approximately 1.05946 times the frequency of the previous note.
    a. Use this information to write the equation of the graph. The frequency of low E is 165 Hertz. (Hint: Let $x =$ the number of notes above low E.)
    b. Use your equation to find the frequency of each of the notes shown.

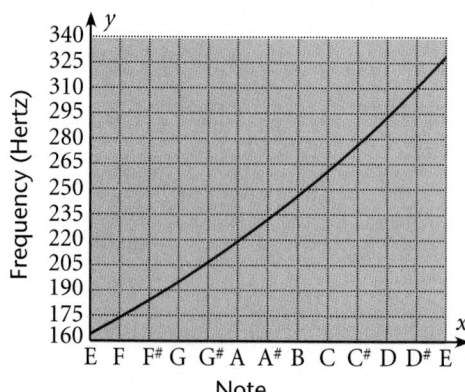

Problem-Solving Tip

Check your answers graphically.

DEVASTATING VIBRATIONS

On October 17, 1989, just minutes before the start of World Series Game 3 between the Oakland Athletics and the San Francisco Giants, the Loma Prieta earthquake struck the San Francisco Bay Area. Buildings collapsed and freeways buckled under the stress of this earthquake, which measured 7.1 on the Richter scale. You may have experienced, or seen on television, the effects of the Northridge earthquake, magnitude 6.8, that jolted Los Angeles on January 17, 1994. Other serious earthquakes around the world occurred on July 28, 1976, in Tangshan, China (magnitude 8.2); on September 19, 1985, in Mexico (magnitude 8.1); and on January 17, 1995, in Kobe, Japan (magnitude 7.2).

What do the numbers on the Richter scale mean? Named for American seismologist Charles F. Richter (1900–1985), this scale was developed to measure the intensity of an earthquake. An increase of one full point in magnitude on this scale represents a tenfold increase in the ground motion produced by the quake.

The quake with the greatest measured magnitude in North America occurred in Alaska on March 27, 1964. The ground motion of this magnitude 8.4 quake was about 20 times greater than that of the Loma Prieta quake and almost 40 times as great as that of the Northridge quake. In the Alaska quake, the earth shook for minutes, and houses broke from their foundations and shuffled down toward the seashore. The quake produced a 50-foot-high tidal wave that traveled nearly 8500 miles.

1. How much greater is the ground motion of a 6.0 earthquake than a 4.0? Explain.

2. Is the Richter scale linear? How do you know?

3. Do you think today's cities are likely to suffer more or less damage from an earthquake than cities 100 years ago? Explain.

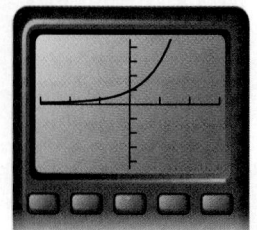

← C O N N E C T →

You've explored exponential functions and their graphs. Now you will take a look at inverses of exponential functions.

You're familiar with many of the characteristics of exponential graphs. For instance, you've seen that the graph of $y = 3^x$ approaches the x-axis as x decreases, and the graph grows rapidly as x increases from 0.

Now you will investigate inverses of exponential functions. In the Explore, you will begin this investigation by looking at the graphs of these inverses.

EXPLORE: SWITCH IT AROUND

MATERIALS

Graph paper
Graphing utility

1. Copy and complete the table. Then use your results to graph $y = 2^x$ on graph paper.

x	-4	-3	-2	-1	0	1	2	3	4
$y = 2^x$									

2. Using your results from Step 1, copy and complete the table for $x = 2^y$. Graph $x = 2^y$ on the same axes you used to graph $y = 2^x$. Describe the relationship between the two graphs and explain why this relationship makes sense.

$x = 2^y$									
y	-4	-3	-2	-1	0	1	2	3	4

3. Give a complete description of the graph of $x = 2^y$. Discuss any asymptotes and intercepts that you see. Is $x = 2^y$ a function? What is its domain? its range? How does the graph behave as x increases?

4. Put your graphing utility into parametric mode. Graph $x = 2^y$ by letting $x_{1T} = 2^t$ and $y_{1T} = t$. Check your answers from Step 3 by exploring this graph.

5. Now add the graph of $x = 10^y$ to your screen by letting $x_{2T} = 10^t$ and $y_{2T} = t$. Compare the graph of $x = 2^y$ to the graph of $x = 10^y$. Do the graphs have any points in common?

6. You've investigated the graphs of the inverses of some exponential functions whose bases are greater than 1. Give as complete a description as you can of the graphs of these inverse exponential functions. Compare their characteristics to those of the graphs of the exponential functions.

The inverse of the exponential function $y = 10^x$ is the function $x = 10^y$. This function is usually written as $y = \log_{10} x$ (read "log to the base 10 of x"). This is an example of a *logarithmic function*.

CONSIDER
?

1. The graphs of all logarithmic functions have one point in common. What is this point? Why is it on the graph of every logarithmic function?

It is important to remember that a *logarithm is an exponent*. Think of $y = \log_b x$ as the answer to the question: To what power must b be raised to obtain the number x?

This suggests the following definition.

This base   to this power

$$\log_b x = y$$

is equal to this.

> The **logarithmic function** $y = \log_b x$ is the inverse of the exponential function $y = b^x$, where $b \neq 1$ and $b > 0$. That is, $y = \log_b x$ if and only if $x = b^y$. A **logarithm** is a value of the logarithmic function.

Equations in exponential form can be rewritten in logarithmic form, and vice versa.

Exponential Form	**Logarithmic Form**
$2^3 = 8$	$\log_2 8 = 3$
$10^2 = 100$	$\log_{10} 100 = 2$
$4^{-2} = \frac{1}{16}$	$\log_4 \frac{1}{16} = -2$
$3^4 = 81$	$\log_3 81 = 4$

When evaluating a logarithmic expression or solving a logarithmic equation, it is often helpful to rewrite it in exponential form.

EXAMPLE

1. Evaluate $\log_{10} 10{,}000$.

Let $y = \log_{10} 10{,}000$.

$10^y = 10{,}000$ Rewrite in exponential form.

$10^y = 10^4$ Write as powers with the same base.

$y = 4$ Since powers with the same base are equal, their exponents are equal.

2. Evaluate $\log_{0.5} 32$.

Let $y = \log_{0.5} 32$.

$(0.5)^y = 32$ Rewrite in exponential form.

We need to rewrite the two expressions so that they have the same base.

$(0.5)^y = 2^5$ $32 = 2^5$

$2^{-y} = 2^5$ $0.5 = \frac{1}{2} = 2^{-1}$

$-y = 5$ Since powers with the same base are equal, their exponents are equal.

$y = -5$

TRY IT

a. Evaluate $\log_{10} \frac{1}{100}$.

b. Evaluate $\log_{\frac{1}{3}} 27$.

CONSIDER

?

2. What is $\log_b b^x$? What is $b^{\log_b x}$? Explain your answers.

You can use the definition of a logarithm to solve logarithmic equations.

EXAMPLES

3. Solve $\log_3 x = 4$.

$\log_3 x = 4$

$3^4 = x$ Rewrite in exponential form.

$81 = x$

4. Solve $\log_x \frac{8}{27} = 3$.

$x^3 = \frac{8}{27}$ Rewrite in exponential form.

$x^3 = \left(\frac{2}{3}\right)^3$ Rewrite as expressions with equal exponents.

$x = \frac{2}{3}$ Since equal powers have equal exponents, their bases are equal.

TRY IT

Solve each equation.

c. $\log_3 x = 4$

d. $\log_x \frac{1}{4} = \frac{1}{2}$

e. $\log_x \frac{1}{81} = -4$

f. $\log_2 x = 7$

Certain bases for logarithmic functions are especially common. In fact, logarithms whose base is 10 are called **common logarithms.** The base is not shown when writing a common logarithm, so "log k" is understood to mean $\log_{10} k$. The LOG key on your calculator gives base 10 logarithms.

5. The altitude of an aircraft is a function of the outside air pressure. The higher the aircraft, the thinner the air around it, and the lower the pressure. When the outside pressure is P, the altitude (h), in miles, is given by $h = \frac{-100}{9} \log \frac{P}{B}$, where B is the atmospheric pressure at sea level. P and B must be measured in the same units.

Find the altitude of an airplane if the pressure at sea level is 30 inches of mercury and the outside air pressure is 18.2 inches of mercury.

$h = \frac{-100}{9} \log \frac{P}{B}$

$h = \frac{-100}{9} \log \frac{18.2}{30}$ Substitute values for P and B.

$h \approx \frac{-100}{9} (-0.217)$ Use your calculator to approximate $\log \frac{18.2}{30}$.

$h \approx 2.41$

The plane is approximately 2.41 miles high.

The number e is also an important base for logarithms. Base e logarithms are known as **natural logarithms,** and are written ln. So "ln x" means $\log_e x$.

6. Evaluate 3.5 ln 9.1. Round your answer to the nearest tenth.

3.5 ln 9.1

$\approx 3.5(2.21)$ Use a calculator to approximate ln 9.1.

≈ 7.7

It is important to remember that logarithmic functions are inverses of exponential functions. This will help you remember that the graph of a logarithmic function has an asymptote on the y-axis and contains (1, 0). Also, graphs of logarithmic functions with bases greater than 1 grow very slowly as x-values take on larger and larger positive values.

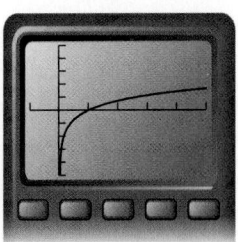

1. Explain why the domain of a logarithmic function does not include negative numbers.
2. The graph of $y = \log x$ contains the point (100, 2). How much will the x-value have to increase if y is to increase from 2 to 3?
3. What is $\log (10^x)$? Explain.

Exercises

CORE

1. **Getting Started** Follow the steps below to draw the graphs of $y = 3^x$ and its inverse, $y = \log_3 x$.
   a. Make a table of values for $y = 3^x$. Include both positive and negative x-values in your table. Graph these points and draw a smooth curve through them.
   b. To find values for points on the graph of $y = \log_3 x$, interchange the x- and y-values of the points on $y = 3^x$. Graph these points. Draw a curve that contains these points. This is a graph of $y = \log_3 x$.

2. Graph the function $y = 5^x$ by plotting points for $-4 \leq x \leq 5$ in steps of 0.5 units. Then graph the inverse function on the same set of axes. Draw the line $y = x$ and fold the graph paper along this line. Explain what happens and why.

Write the word or phrase that correctly completes each statement.

3. A base ten logarithm is also known as a(n) ____.

4. A logarithmic function is the inverse of a(n) ____ function.

Graph each logarithmic function. Label the coordinates of at least two points on each curve.

5. $f(x) = \log_4 x$ 6. $f(x) = \log_{\frac{1}{2}} x$ 7. $g(x) = \log (x + 3)$ 8. $g(x) = \log x + 3$

Rewrite each equation. If it is in exponential form, rewrite it in logarithmic form; if it is in logarithmic form, rewrite it in exponential form.

9. $\log_2 4 = 2$ 10. $(3)^3 = 27$ 11. $\left(\frac{1}{4}\right)^{-3} = 64$ 12. $\log 10 = 1$

13. $8^{\frac{2}{3}} = 4$ 14. $\log_5 \frac{1}{625} = -4$ 15. $2^{-6} = \frac{1}{64}$ 16. $\ln e^2 = 2$

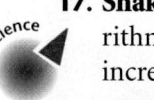

17. **Shake-up!** The Richter scale, used to measure the magnitude of earthquakes, is logarithmic. A difference of 1 in the magnitudes of two earthquakes indicates a tenfold increase in the ground motion of the earthquakes. What is the difference in ground motion between an earthquake that measures 6.5 and one that measures 4.5 on the Richter scale? Explain.

Evaluate each expression. If necessary, round answers to the nearest hundredth.

18. $\log_2 64$ 19. $\log_2 \frac{1}{4}$ 20. $\ln e$ 21. $\log 22.7$

22. $\log_3 \frac{1}{27}$ 23. $\log_3 1$ 24. $2.4 \ln 1.78$ 25. $\log_{\frac{1}{2}} 16$

26. **Acid Measure** The pH of a solution is a measure of its acidity. The lower the pH of a liquid, the more acidic it is. pH is defined as: $\text{pH} = -\log [H^+]$, where $[H^+]$ represents the concentration of H^+ (hydronium) ions in moles per liter.
   a. For pure water, $[H^+] = 10^{-7}$ moles per liter. Find the pH of pure water.
   b. Stomach acid has an $[H^+]$ of about 2.5×10^{-2} moles per liter. Find its pH.

27. Suppose $x = \log_b a$. If $b > a$, what do you know about the size of x? Explain.

Solve each equation.

28. $\log_2 x = 4$ **29.** $\log_{0.5} x = 3$ **30.** $\log_3 x = 5$ **31.** $\log_4 x^2 = 2$

32. $\log_x 4 = \frac{1}{2}$ **33.** $\log_x 0.25 = -2$ **34.** $\log_5 125 = x$ **35.** $\log_6 1296 = x^2$

36. Base 2 is also an important base for logarithms. Since computers work in base 2, this base has applications in computer science. Evaluate each base 2 logarithm.
      a. $\log_2 128$ **b.** $\log_2 512$ **c.** $\log_2 131{,}072$

37. Stormy Weather An altimeter measures the height of an airplane above sea level. It measures the difference between the air pressure outside the aircraft (P) and the current atmospheric pressure at sea level (B). The altitude of the aircraft (h), in miles, is modeled by $h = \left(\frac{-100}{9}\right)\log \frac{P}{B}$. P and B must be measured in the same units.

     a. Suppose the air pressure outside an airplane is 21 inches of mercury. If the air pressure at sea level is 31 inches of mercury, what is the airplane's altitude?

     b. Suppose that, due to a storm, the air pressure at sea level drops to 29 inches of mercury. If the pilot does not reset the altimeter to reflect this change, it will still show the altitude you found in **a** when the outside air pressure (P) is 21 inches of mercury. What is the plane's true altitude? Why is it dangerous to fly for long periods without resetting the sea level air pressure?

 ## *LOOK AHEAD*

Simplify each exponential expression.

38. $x^4 \cdot x^5$ **39.** $\dfrac{z^{11}}{z^{15}}$ **40.** $(v^3 \cdot v^5)^4$ **41.** $5 \times 10^8 \cdot 8 \times 10^{-4}$

42. Suppose you invest $300 in an account that pays 6% interest. What will be the balance in the account after 5 years, if the interest is compounded:
     a. annually?   **b.** continuously?

MORE PRACTICE

43. Use a Graphing Utility Using parametric mode, graph each of the following. Sketch copies of your graphs on the same set of axes.
     a. $y = \log_4 x$ **b.** $y = \log_{0.8} x$ **c.** $y = \log_9 x$

Rewrite each equation. If it is in exponential form, rewrite it in logarithmic form; if it is in logarithmic form, rewrite it in exponential form.

44. $\log_{10} 1000 = 3$ **45.** $3^6 = 729$ **46.** $\log_5 0.2 = -1$ **47.** $5^{-2} = \frac{1}{25}$

48. $16^{\frac{3}{2}} = 64$ **49.** $\log_7 49 = 2$ **50.** $20^{-3} = \frac{1}{8000}$ **51.** $\log_{\frac{1}{3}} \frac{1}{9} = 2$

Evaluate each expression. If necessary, round answers to the nearest hundredth.

52. $\log 10000$ **53.** $\log_2 8$ **54.** $\log_3 1$ **55.** $5.3 \ln 5.84 - 3$

56. $\log_6 36$ **57.** $\log_{\frac{1}{2}} 8$ **58.** $6.8 \log 9.11$ **59.** $\log_{\frac{1}{3}} 27$

60. Cooling-Off Period Newton's law of cooling states that the time (t), in minutes, it takes for a warm object to cool from an initial temperature (T_0) to a lower temperature (T) is given by $kt = \ln \dfrac{T - S}{T_0 - S}$, where k is a proportionality constant and S is the surrounding temperature.

  a. Suppose that you make a cup of hot cocoa on a cold winter day. The air temperature is 32°F, and you find that the cocoa cools 15°, from 125°F to 110°F, in 8 minutes. Find k, the constant of proportionality.

  b. Predict whether it will take more time or less time for the cocoa to cool another 15° to 95°F. Does Newton's law confirm your prediction?

Solve each equation.

61. $\log x = 100$ **62.** $\log_x 64 = 3$ **63.** $\log_{27} 81 = x$ **64.** $\log_x 2 = \dfrac{1}{2}$

65. $\log_{0.5} x = -6$ **66.** $\log_{\frac{1}{8}} \dfrac{1}{16} = x$ **67.** $\log_9 x = -1$ **68.** $\log 0.0001 = x^2$

MORE MATH REASONING

69. The graph of the exponential function $y = b^x$ passes through $(0, 1)$ and $(1, b)$. What are the corresponding points on the graph of the logarithmic function $y = \log_b x$?

70. Sound level is measured in decibels (dB). The equation for sound level (S) is: $S = 10 \log \left(\dfrac{I}{10^{-12}} \right)$, where I represents the intensity of the sound in watts per square meter. The table shows some sound intensities for various sources.

Sound	Intensity (W/m^2)	Sound Level (dB)
Threshold of hearing	10^{-12}	
Average whisper	10^{-10}	
Ordinary conversation	3.2×10^{-6}	
Busy street traffic		70
Riveter	3.2×10^{-2}	
Threshold of pain		120
Ear injury	10^4	

  a. Copy and complete the table. Explain how you found the missing values.

  b. How much louder (in decibels) is a sound that causes pain than one that can barely be heard? How many times greater is the louder sound's intensity?

  c. Use a graphing utility to graph the relationship between sound intensity (on the x-axis) and the sound level. Describe the graph. What happens to the sound level as intensity increases?

  d. The sound level was measured at 110 dB from the fifth row at a concert. Use your graph to estimate the intensity of this sound.

  e. How does sound level increase when the intensity increases by a factor of 100? Explain this in terms of the equation and the concept of logarithms.

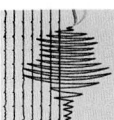

← C O N N E C T →   *You have seen that logarithmic functions are inverse exponential functions. Now you will use logarithms to help solve for unknown exponents.*

You've been introduced to logarithmic functions, which are inverse exponential functions. In the Explore, you will become more familiar with some of the properties of a logarithmic function.

EXPLORE: NEVER-ENDING LOGARITHMS

1. Make and complete a table of values. In the "Exponential form" column, write the powers of 10 from 10^0 through 10^9. In the "Logarithm (base 10)" column, write the logarithms, or exponents. Then evaluate the powers and record them in a third column labeled "Numerical value." The first row should read 10^0, 0, 1.

Exponential form	Logarithm (base 10)	Numerical value
10^0	0	1
10^1		
10^2		
10^3		

2. You know that $10^2 = 100$ and $10^3 = 1000$. Without using a calculator, estimate the value of $10^{2.5}$. Explain the strategy you used to make your estimate. Then find the actual value of $10^{2.5}$ and compare your estimate to the calculated value. Explain any differences.

3. Make and complete a table of values similar to the table you made in Step 1. Use powers of 10 from $10^{2.0}$ through $10^{3.0}$ in intervals of 0.1.

4. Pick any two successive rows from your table in Step 3 and create a new table of values using intervals of 0.01. For example, use $10^{2.3}$ and $10^{2.4}$ for the first and last rows, and fill in rows for $10^{2.31}$, $10^{2.32}$, $10^{2.33}$, and so on.

5. Are there any positive real numbers that cannot be the result of 10 raised to some power? Explain.

6. Choose ten numbers greater than 1 and make a table with columns labeled "Number," "Logarithm (base 10)," and "Power of 10." For example, your first row might read: 56.237, 1.750022145, $10^{1.750022145} = 56.237$.

7. Choose ten numbers between 0 and 1 and make a table similar to the one you made in Step 6. For example, your first row might read: 0.0356, -1.448550002, $10^{-1.448550002} = 0.0356$.

8. Summarize what you have discovered about numerical values, logarithms, and powers of 10.

Many real-world situations can be modeled by exponential functions of the form $A = Pe^{rt}$. Until now, we could only solve graphically for the exponents of the related exponential equation of such a function. Now, you can find their values algebraically as well. In the following Examples, you will see how you can use logarithms to solve exponential equations.

EXAMPLES

1. Solve $10^x = 758$. Round your answer to the nearest hundredth.

$$10^x = 758$$

$$\log (10^x) = \log 758 \qquad \text{Take base 10 logs of both sides.}$$

$$x = \log 758 \qquad \text{Use the meaning of inverse functions.}$$

$$x \approx 2.88 \qquad \text{Evaluate log 758 using a calculator.}$$

2. Ki Chong invests \$100 in a bank account that earns 7% interest, compounded continuously. How long will it take for the account to be worth \$180? Round your answer to the nearest tenth of a year.

Use $A = Pe^{rt}$.

$$180 = 100e^{0.07t} \qquad \text{Substitute } P = 100, A = 180, \text{ and } r = 0.07.$$

$$\frac{180}{100} = e^{0.07t} \qquad \text{Isolate the term with the variable exponent.}$$

$$\ln 1.8 = 0.07t \qquad \begin{array}{l}\text{Take natural logs of both sides. Note that}\\ \ln (e^{0.07t}) = 0.07t.\end{array}$$

$$0.5878 \approx 0.07t \qquad \text{Evaluate ln 1.8 using a calculator.}$$

$$\frac{0.5878}{0.07} \approx t$$

$$8.4 \approx t$$

The account will be worth \$180 in about 8.4 years.

CONSIDER

?

1. Why were common logs used to solve the equation in Example 1, while natural logs were used in Example 2?

TRY IT

Solve each equation. Where necessary, round answers to the nearest hundredth.

a. $10^x = 250$ **b.** $10^x = 0.025$

c. $265e^{2x} = 1400$ **d.** $150e^{0.05t} = 300$

You may recall from 9-1D that the value of r in $A = Pe^{rt}$ is *not* an annual growth rate—if you invest \$100 at 6%, compounded continuously, you have more than \$106 after 1 year. However, the r value is a reasonable approximation for annual growth rates that are less than 10%.

3. In 1992, the population of New Delhi, India, was 8.8 million people. Experts predict that New Delhi will grow to 11.7 million people by the year 2000. Use the equation $A = Pe^{rt}$ to find the approximate annual growth rate for the population of New Delhi. Round your answer to the nearest tenth of a percent.

$A = Pe^{rt}$

$11.7 = 8.8e^{8r}$ Use $t = 8$ for the number of years between 1992 and 2000.

$1.33 \approx e^{8r}$ Divide by 8.8.

$\ln 1.33 \approx 8r$ Take the natural log of both sides.

$0.285 \approx 8r$

$0.0356 \approx r$

Rounding to the nearest tenth of a percent, the annual growth rate is about 3.6%.

4. Use the equation $A = Pb^t$ to solve for the annual growth rate of New Delhi from 1992 to 2000.

$A = Pb^t$

$11.7 = 8.8b^8$ Use $t = 8$ for the number of years between 1992 and 2000.

$1.33 \approx b^8$ Divide by 8.8, rounding to two decimal places.

$1.33^{\frac{1}{8}} \approx b$ Take both sides to the $\frac{1}{8}$.

$1.0362 \approx b$

The annual growth rate is 3.625%, which also rounds to 3.6%.

From Examples 3 and 4, you can see that the continuous compounding formula $A = Pe^{rt}$ gives a good approximation for the annual growth rate when growth rates are low. However, this approximation decreases in accuracy as growth rates increase, and should not be used when growth rates exceed 10%.

Exponential equations can be solved by taking logarithms of both sides of an equation. Because natural logs and base 10 logs are available on calculators, this technique is most convenient when the base is e or 10.

REFLECT

1. Explain how to solve the continuous compounding formula $A = Pe^{rt}$ for time. What information must you have to be able to find a value for t?

2. Can you solve $y = 10^x$ for x *without* using logs? If so, explain how; if not, explain why logs are necessary.

3. Explain how you would estimate the value of $10^{2.4}$ *without* using a calculator.

Exercises

CORE

1. Getting Started Follow the steps to find an approximate solution to $10^x = 300$.
   a. To solve $10^x = 300$, make an initial guess of the value of x based on the fact that $10^2 = 100$ and $10^3 = 1000$. Test your guess with a calculator.
   b. Based on your initial guess, try another value for x and test with the calculator. Continue this process of approximation until you solve the equation.
   c. Now solve the equation for x by using logarithms and your calculator. Compare your answer to your answer from **b**. Explain any differences.

Solve each equation. Where necessary, round answers to the nearest hundredth.

2. $10^x = 2681$ **3.** $10^{3x} = 0.005$ **4.** $e^x = 12$

5. $e^m = \pi$ **6.** $e^{2x} = 25$ **7.** $10^{2n} = 40.2$

8. $1000 = 500e^{0.08t}$ **9.** $10^{x^2 + 4x - 6} = 100$ **10.** $2861 = \log (x + 4)$

11. $\log x = 2.096910013$ **12.** $\ln g = -2.39$ **13.** $\log 2x = 3.23$

14. You're Saving for Grace You are very fond of your baby cousin Grace, so you put $50 in a bank account in her name. You hope to use the money in this account to give her a $250 present when she graduates from high school.
   a. Suppose that the account pays 5.25% interest, compounded continuously. Write an equation to represent this situation.
   b. How long will it take before the account has a balance of $250? Will the account be worth $250 when your cousin graduates from high school?
   c. Find the interest rate that will give a balance of $250 in 17 years. Do you think you can find a bank account that pays this interest rate? Explain.

15. You have invested $100 in a bank account that earns 4% interest, compounded continuously. You make no deposits to or withdrawals from the account. In how many years will the balance in the account be:
   a. $200?   **b.** $350?   **c.** $1000?   **d.** $10,000,000?

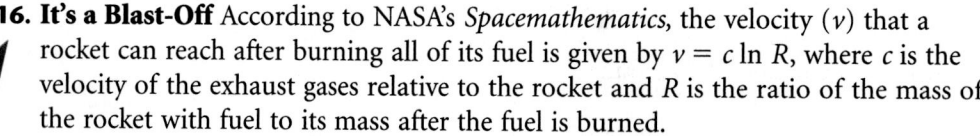

16. It's a Blast-Off According to NASA's *Spacemathematics,* the velocity (v) that a rocket can reach after burning all of its fuel is given by $v = c \ln R$, where c is the velocity of the exhaust gases relative to the rocket and R is the ratio of the mass of the rocket with fuel to its mass after the fuel is burned.
   a. Find the velocity of a rocket whose R-value is 2 and exhaust velocity is 2 km/sec.
   b. The velocity needed to escape the earth's gravitational field is 11.2 km/sec. If the exhaust gas velocity of a rocket is 2 km/sec, what R value would the rocket need to achieve escape velocity? What percentage of the rocket's total weight before launch would need to be fuel?

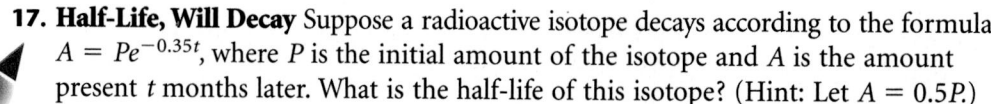

17. Half-Life, Will Decay Suppose a radioactive isotope decays according to the formula $A = Pe^{-0.35t}$, where P is the initial amount of the isotope and A is the amount present t months later. What is the half-life of this isotope? (Hint: Let $A = 0.5P$.)

18. Use Your Census According to U.S. census figures, the U.S. population grew from 131,669,275 in 1940 to 150,697,361 in 1950. Estimate, to the nearest hundredth, the annual percentage growth rate for that period:
   a. using $A = Pe^{rt}$ **b.** using $A = Pb^t$
   c. Does the continuous growth formula give a good approximation for the annual growth rate?

19. Fifteen Minutes of Fame After being featured in a prominent magazine, the paintings of Phil Palette increased in value. In 1990, one of his paintings sold for $200. By 1992, the same painting sold for $2500. Estimate, to the nearest hundredth, the annual percentage growth rate for that period:
   a. using $A = Pe^{rt}$ **b.** using $A = Pb^t$
   c. Does the continuous growth formula give a good approximation for the annual growth rate?

 ## LOOK BACK

Solve each equation. [9-1]

20. $3^x = 9$ **21.** $16^x = 8$ **22.** $\left(\dfrac{1}{2}\right)^x = 16$ **23.** $2^{3x} = 64$ **24.** $5^{x-3} = \dfrac{1}{125}$

Divide and simplify [8-2]

25. $\dfrac{1}{i}$ **26.** $\dfrac{8}{2+i}$ **27.** $\dfrac{2+4i}{6-3i}$ **28.** $\dfrac{3-5i}{3+5i}$

MORE PRACTICE

Solve each equation. Where necessary, round answers to the nearest hundredth.

29. $10^x = 15$ **30.** $10^{2p} = 0.125$ **31.** $e^x = 6.5$ **32.** $e^{3t} = 24$

33. $10^r = 0.0002$ **34.** $e^x = 100$ **35.** $10^{4x-3} = 1200$ **36.** $10^{x^2} = 600$

37. $1776 = 1812e^t$ **38.** $2500 = 1200e^{0.05t}$ **39.** $\log x = 1.4149$ **40.** $\ln 3x = -0.5003$

41. You have invested $100 in a bank account that earns 8% interest, compounded continuously. You make no deposits to or withdrawals from the account. In how many years will the balance in the account be:
   a. $200?   **b.** $350?   **c.** $1000?   **d.** $10,000,000?
   e. Compare your results for this problem to your results for Exercise 15.

42. Because of inflation, the cost of an oak bookcase is increasing at an average rate of 3.5% each year. If the bookcase costs $109.95 today, in how many years will it cost $200?
   a. Solve this problem numerically by making a table of values.
   b. Write an equation for the increase in the price of the bookcase.
   c. Use a graphing utility to graph this equation. Solve the problem graphically by *tracing* to find the time when the price will be $200.
   d. By using the equation you found in **b,** solve the equation algebraically.

43. Twinkle, Twinkle, Little Star The *apparent magnitude* of a star is a measure of its brightness as seen from Earth. The lower the magnitude, the brighter the star. Betelgeuse, a bright star in Orion, has a magnitude of about 0.41, while Polaris, the North Star, has a magnitude of 2.0. On a clear night away from city lights, you can see stars as faint as magnitude 6 without a telescope.

If you look through a telescope with an *aperture* (opening) of 1 inch, you can see stars as faint as magnitude 9. The apparent magnitude of the faintest visible star is the *limiting magnitude* of the telescope. The relationship between telescope aperture in inches (a) and limiting magnitude (m) is $m = 9 + 5 \log a$.

a. Use a graphing utility to graph this function. Compare its graph to that of the parent function $y = \log x$. How has the function been transformed?

b. Refracting telescopes with 2.4-inch and 3-inch apertures, and reflecting telescopes with 4.25-inch and 6-inch reflectors, are very popular among amateur astronomers. *Trace* to find the limiting magnitude of each of these telescopes.

c. The largest refracting telescope in the United States is the 40-inch one at Yerkes Observatory in Wisconsin. The 200-inch Hale reflecting telescope sits atop Mount Palomar in California. Calculate the limiting magnitudes that can be seen with these telescopes.

d. If you wanted to observe stars as faint as magnitude 16.8, what is the smallest aperture telescope you could use?

MORE MATH REASONING

44. Use a Graphing Utility Graph the function $y = \log (10^x)$ using a graphing utility. Explain what you see in terms of the definition of a logarithm. What is the domain of this function? Can you make a general rule for this function? (Hint: What is the base of the "log" function?)

45. It'll Grow on You Given data on growth in terms of age and height, you can use your graphing calculator to perform a *logarithmic regression* to find a logarithmic equation that models the data. The age and height data for girls in the table below is based on information from the National Center for Health Statistics of the U.S. Public Health Service.

Age (years)	13	15	16	18	20
Height (inches)	62.0	63.8	64.0	64.2	64.6

a. Use a graphing utility to graph the data on a scatter plot. Display ages on the *x*-axis and heights on the *y*-axis.

b. Perform a logarithmic regression on the data. Find values for the constant term *a* and the coefficient *b* to write an equation in the form $y = a + b \ln x$.

c. Graph the equation on your graphing calculator and explore the behavior of the function numerically.

d. Use the logarithmic regression equation to estimate the average height of a 14-year-old girl and a 17-year-old girl.

46. Use a Graphing Utility Draw the graph of the function $y = 10^{\log x}$ on a graphing utility and compare it to the graph of $y = \log (10^x)$. How are these two functions similar and different? Explain.

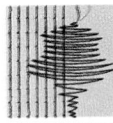

9-2 PART C Properties of Logarithms

← CONNECT →   *You have been exploring logarithmic functions graphically and numerically. Now the rules for manipulating logarithmic expressions will be formalized. You will use these properties to solve equations.*

The properties of exponents that you used in Chapter 7 helped you work with exponential expressions and solve exponential equations. Similar properties can help you work with logarithmic expressions and equations. Look for patterns as you complete the following Explore.

EXPLORE: LAW AND ORDER

Use the following information to explore the rules for manipulating logarithms.

$\log 2 = 0.30103$	$\log 8 = 0.90309$
$\log 3 = 0.47712$	$\log 9 = 0.95424$
$\log 4 = 0.60206$	$\log 12 = 1.07918$
$\log 6 = 0.77815$	$\log 16 = 1.20412$

1. Find each of the following sums.
   a. $\log 2 + \log 3$ **b.** $\log 3 + \log 4$ **c.** $\log 2 + \log 4$
   Compare these sums to the logarithms in the table. What do you notice?

2. Find each of the following differences.
   a. $\log 6 - \log 2$ **b.** $\log 4 - \log 2$ **c.** $\log 12 - \log 3$
   Compare these differences to the logarithms in the table. Describe any patterns that you see.

3. Find each of the following products.
   a. $2 \times \log 2$ **b.** $3 \times \log 2$ **c.** $2 \times \log 3$
   Compare these products to the logarithms in the table. Do you see any patterns?

4. Use the results from Steps 1–3 to make conjectures about sums of logarithms, differences of logarithms, and the product of a logarithm and a constant. Check your conjectures by using your calculator to test other values.

Remember that logarithms of numbers are really exponents. A review of the rules for operations on powers will help clarify the rules for operating with logarithms.

$10^2 \times 10^3 = 10^{2+3} = 10^5$ To multiply powers, add exponents.

$10^{12} \div 10^3 = 10^{12-3} = 10^9$ To divide powers, subtract exponents.

$(10^3)^2 = 10^{3 \times 2} = 10^6$ To take a power to a power, multiply exponents.

A summary of the properties for logarithms is listed below.

PROPERTIES OF LOGARITHMS

For $b > 0$ ($b \neq 1$), positive real numbers x and y, and any real number n:

Logarithm of a Product $\log_b (xy) = \log_b x + \log_b y$

Logarithm of a Quotient $\log_b \left(\dfrac{x}{y}\right) = \log_b x - \log_b y$

Logarithm of a Power $\log_b (x^n) = n \log_b x$

CONSIDER

1. How are the rules for operations on powers related to the properties of logarithms?

You can use the properties of logarithms to help simplify and solve logarithmic equations and expressions.

EXAMPLES

Simplify each expression by rewriting as a single logarithm.

1. $\log 2x + \log (3x - 7)$

Since the sum of two logs can be written as the log of the product:

$\log 2x + \log (3x - 7) = \log [2x(3x - 7)] = \log (6x^2 - 14x)$

2. $4 \log k - \log (k + 3)$

$4 \log k - \log (k + 3)$

$= \log k^4 - \log (k + 3)$ Use the property for the logarithm of a power.

$= \log \left(\dfrac{k^4}{k + 3}\right)$ The difference of two logs is the log of the quotient.

3. Write $\log \dfrac{ab}{c}$ without using multiplication or division.

$\log \dfrac{ab}{c} = \log ab - \log c = \log a + \log b - \log c$

4. Solve $3 \ln x = \ln 8$.

To "undo" a natural log, we can take e to that power. Before doing this, we need to deal with the 3 multiplying $\ln x$. We can use a property of logarithms to help us.

$3 \ln x = \ln 8$

$\ln x^3 = \ln 8$ Use the property for the logarithm of a power.

$e^{\ln x^3} = e^{\ln 8}$ Use inverse functions.

$x^3 = 8$

$x = 2$

If an exponential equation has a base that is neither 10 nor e, the equation can still be solved by taking base 10 logs or natural logs of both sides.

WHAT DO **YOU** THINK?

Solve $9^x = 250$. Round your answer to the nearest hundredth.

Drew thinks...

If I take logarithms of both sides, I can rewrite the exponent so that it multiplies the logarithm. I'll start by taking the common log of both sides of the equation.

$9^x = 250$

$\log 9^x = \log 250$

$x \log 9 = \log 250$

$x = \dfrac{\log 250}{\log 9} \approx 2.51$

Vinh thinks...

I can solve this equation by taking natural logs of both sides.

$\ln 9^x = \ln 250$

$x \ln 9 = \ln 250$

$x = \dfrac{\ln 250}{\ln 9} \approx 2.51$

TRY IT

Simplify each expression by rewriting as a single logarithm.

a. $\log x - 3 \log y$
b. $2 \log k + 3 \log m - \log (n + 10)$
c. Write $\log x^3 y^2$ without using multiplication or division.
d. Solve $4 \log x = \log 81$.

You can use properties of logarithms to help solve exponential equations when the base is neither 10 nor e.

EXAMPLE

5. The 1991 population of Cairo, Egypt, was 10,099,000. This population is expected to grow at a rate of approximately 2.2% per year. At this rate of increase, when will the population exceed 15 million?

The population of Cairo is modeled by:

$A = 10{,}099{,}000(1.022)^t$

$15{,}000{,}000 = 10{,}099{,}000(1.022)^t$

$\dfrac{15{,}000{,}000}{10{,}099{,}000} = 1.022^t$

$1.49 \approx 1.022^t$

At this point, we could take $\log_{1.022}$ of both sides. However, $\log_{1.022} 1.49$ is not convenient to calculate. Instead, we take the base 10 log of both sides.

$\log 1.49 \approx \log 1.022^t$

$\log 1.49 \approx t \log 1.022$ Use the property for the logarithm of a power.

$\dfrac{\log 1.49}{\log 1.022} \approx t$ Solve for t.

$\dfrac{0.1732}{0.0095} \approx t$ Use a calculator to approximate the logs.

$18.3 \approx t$

The population will reach 15 million about 18 years after 1991, in 2009.

Logarithms were originally developed to simplify computations. You've seen how properties of logarithms can help solve difficult equations.

REFLECT

1. Which is correct: $\log 5 - \log 3 = \log \frac{5}{3}$, or $\log 5 - \log 3 = \dfrac{\log 5}{\log 3}$? Explain.
2. Using the rule for multiplication of powers to help you, show why the property for the logarithm of a product is true.
3. Explain how the property for the logarithm of a power can help you solve exponential equations where the base is neither 10 nor e.

Exercises

CORE

1. Getting Started Match each equation or statement with its name.

a. $\log_b \left(\frac{x}{y}\right) = \log_b x - \log_b y$

b. If $y = \log_b x$, then $x = b^y$.

c. $\log_b x^y = y \log_b x$

d. $\log_b (xy) = \log_b x + \log_b y$

A. Logarithm of a Power

B. Logarithm of a Product

C. Definition of Logarithm

D. Logarithm of a Quotient

Classify each statement as true or false. If a statement is true, explain why it is true. If false, change the statement to make it true.

2. $\log 5 + \log 3 = \log 15$

3. $\log x^r = x \log r$

4. $\log 10^5 - \log 10^3 = \dfrac{\log 10^5}{\log 10^3}$

Simplify each expression by rewriting as a single logarithm.

5. $\log x + \log y$

6. $2 \log m$

7. $3 \log a - 5 \log b$

8. $4 \ln r + \ln s - 3 \ln t$

9. $4 \log xy - \log x$

10. $7 \log a - (2 \log b + 5 \log c)$

Rewrite each expression as a sum or difference of logarithms.

11. $\log tus$

12. $\ln x^4 z$

13. $\log (gh)^3$

14. $\log \left(\dfrac{xy}{z^2}\right)$

Solve each equation. Where necessary, round answers to the nearest hundredth.

15. $2 \log_3 x = \log_3 36$

16. $7^x = 22$

17. $15 = 12(1.05)^t$

18. $2 \log x = \log 9 + \log 8 - \log 18$

19. $\log_2 (x - 1) + \log_2 (x + 1) = 3$

20. The 1994 population of Indonesia was about 200.4 million. If the population is growing at a rate of 1.6% per year, when will Indonesia's population exceed:

a. 250 million? **b.** 300 million? **c.** 400 million?

21. Absolutely Bright The *absolute magnitude* of a star is its relative brightness when the distance to the star is taken into account. The distance to a star in parsecs (D) can be found if its apparent magnitude (m) and absolute magnitude (M) are known. (See Exercise 43, page 662 for an explanation of apparent magnitude.) These quantities are related by the formula
$m - M = -5 \log D - 5$.

a. Find the distance in parsecs to the star Antares if its apparent magnitude is 1.22 and its absolute magnitude is 24.0.

b. A parsec is approximately equal to 1.92×10^{13} miles. Find the distance to Antares in miles.

As you know, it is more convenient to find common logs and natural logs than other logs. The *change of base property* allows you to convert logarithms in one base to a quotient of two logarithms with another base.

The *change of base* rule for logarithms is:

$$\log_a x = \frac{(\log_b x)}{(\log_b a)},$$

where a, b, and x are positive real numbers and a and b are *not* equal to 1.

22. Using the Change of Base Rule To evaluate $\log_{2.4} 7$, let $a = 2.4$, $x = 7$, and $b = 10$ in the change of base rule shown above. Then $\log_{2.4} 7 = \dfrac{\log_{10} 7}{\log_{10} 2.4}$.

    a. Evaluate $\log_{2.4} 7$ by using your calculator to evaluate $\dfrac{\log_{10} 7}{\log_{10} 2.4}$.
    b. Use the change of base rule to evaluate:
        i. $\log_6 12$ **ii.** $\log_{3.14} 2.72$ **iii.** $\log_{0.58} 15.82$

23. Car Crash Ralph's car is depreciating in value at 13% per year. If he bought the car for \$3500 in 1995, when will its value be:
    a. \$1800?   **b.** \$1000?   **c.** \$400?   **d.** \$10?
    e. According to this model, when will Ralph's car be worthless? Does this result make sense in the real world? Explain why or why not.

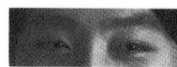 ## LOOK AHEAD

Find the measure of the complement of each angle.

24. $19°$ **25.** $35°$ **26.** $71°$ **27.** $x°$ **28.** $(90 - x)°$

Solve each equation.

29. $\dfrac{x}{14} = 0.9396$ **30.** $\dfrac{a}{335.8} = 0.4771$ **31.** $\dfrac{117}{h} = 1.732$ **32.** $\dfrac{45.7}{b} = \dfrac{22.9}{12.7}$

MORE PRACTICE

Simplify each expression by rewriting as a single logarithm.

33. $\log M - \log N$ **34.** $3 \log x$ **35.** $8 \log a + 2 \log b$

36. $\frac{1}{2} \log k - 3 \log m$ **37.** $4 \ln bc + 2 \ln c - 3 \ln b$ **38.** $6 \log x - (2 \log y + 9 \log z)$

Rewrite each expression as a sum or difference of logarithms.

39. $\log x^5 y$ **40.** $\log \left(\dfrac{x}{z}\right)$ **41.** $\log (cd)^4$

42. $\ln \dfrac{a}{3b}$ **43.** $\log (mn)^{\frac{1}{2}}$ **44.** $\log (x^{\frac{1}{3}} \cdot y^4)$

45. According to Census statistics, the 1990 population of the state of Colorado was 3,294,394. If the population is increasing at a rate of 1.3% per year, when will Colorado's population exceed:
    a. 4 million?   **b.** 5 million?   **c.** 248 million (the U.S. population in 1990)?

Social Science

Solve each equation. Where necessary, round answers to the nearest hundredth.

46. $3 \log_2 x = \log_2 64$

47. $3^x = 7$

48. $1500(0.5)^t = 100$

49. $1200(1.075)^x = 3600$

50. $\log x - \log 0.25 = 2$

51. $\log x + \log 15.5 = \log 50.375$

52. $\log (x + 3) + \log 2x^2 - \log x = 3 \log 2$

53. Wild Blue Yonder The altitude of an aircraft (h), in miles, is given by $h = \left(\frac{-100}{9}\right) \log \frac{P}{B}$, where P = the outside air pressure and B = the atmospheric pressure at sea level. Let $B = 30$.

a. Rewrite this function with $x = P$.

b. Use a **graphing utility** to draw the graph of this function for $0 \le x \le 30$. Set the vertical axis to an appropriate scale to show a complete graph. Describe the relationship between air pressure and altitude.

c. The earth's atmosphere is approximately 200 miles thick. Reset your viewing window for altitudes between 100 and 200 miles. If a space station is orbiting the earth at an altitude of 160 miles, what is the air pressure outside the station? What percentage of the sea level pressure does this represent?

MORE MATH REASONING

54. Use a Graphing Utility Compare graphs of $y = \log (x - 2)^2$ and $y = 2 \log (x - 2)$. According to the rule for logarithms of a power, these two expressions should be the same, since $\log (x - 2)^2 = 2 \log (x - 2)$. Explain why the graphs are different.

55. Antique Calculators Before electronic calculators (as late as the mid-1970s), students in math and science classes used *slide rules* to do mathematical calculations, including multiplication, division, logarithms, and trigonometry.

A simplified version of two scales on a slide rule is shown. Distances between numbers on the C and D scales are logarithmic. On a 10-inch scale, the 2 is 10 log 2 inches from the 1 on the left, the 3 is 10 log 3 inches, and so on.

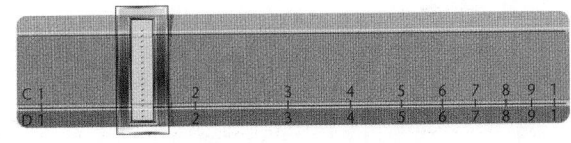

To multiply 2×3 on a slide rule, you slide the C scale until the 1 aligns with the 2 on the D scale as shown. The answer is on the D scale, directly beneath the 3 mark on the C scale.

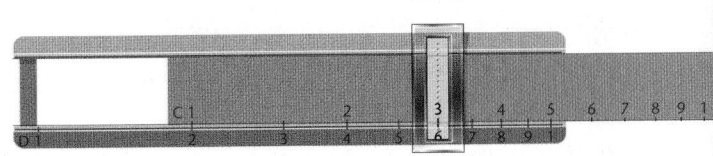

You can see that the slide rule also shows that $2 \times 4 = 8$ and $2 \times 5 = 10$.

a. Explain why this technique for multiplying works.

b. Make your own slide rule by marking lengths of log 2 through log 10 inches on the bottom of one strip of paper and the top of a second strip. Use your "slide rule" to multiply 3×3. Draw a sketch showing how you found this product.

c. How can you use your slide rule to multiply 5×4? Describe your method.

d. Explain how you can use a slide rule to *divide* two numbers? Why does this technique work?

56. Logistics Growth At times, a population appears to be growing exponentially, but the growth rate then slows dramatically. This is often the case with epidemics: as a virus spreads through a community, the infection rate is extremely rapid at first but then slows. Such growth can be modeled by a *logistics function* of the form $y = \dfrac{N}{1 + be^{-ct}}$. Suppose that the population (P) of an island is given by $P = \dfrac{8500}{1 + 25e^{-0.12t}}$, where t is the time, in years, since the first people arrived.

a. Find the population of the island after:
  i. 10 years   **ii.** 30 years   **iii.** 100 years   **iv.** 1000 years
b. What is happening to the population? Why might this make sense in this case?
c. When will the island's population be 7000? Explain how you found your answer.

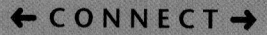

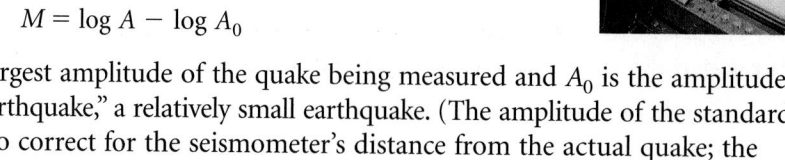

9-2 PART D Making Connections

← CONNECT → *The exponential functions $y = 10^x$ and $y = e^x$, and their inverses $y = \log x$ and $y = \ln x$, are useful in modeling real-world situations.*

As inverses for exponential functions, logarithmic functions help solve exponential equations that model many real-world situations. Logarithms are useful models themselves and are especially important in several common scales of measurement. In the Explore, you will see how the Richter scale works, and you will compare the sizes of several major earthquakes.

EXPLORE: SCALING UP

When Charles Richter developed his scale for earthquake measurement in the 1930s, he used an instrument called the *seismograph* to measure the size of an earthquake. The greater the *amplitude* of the curve recording the earthquake, the larger the earthquake.

The magnitude (M) of an earthquake on the Richter scale is:

$$M = \log A - \log A_0$$

where A is the largest amplitude of the quake being measured and A_0 is the amplitude of a "standard earthquake," a relatively small earthquake. (The amplitude of the standard quake is scaled to correct for the seismometer's distance from the actual quake; the standard quake amplitude is larger for a nearby quake than for a distant one.)

1. Suppose that an earthquake 100 km from a geological station has a maximum amplitude of 20, and that the amplitude of the standard quake for that distance is 0.001. Find the magnitude of the quake.

2. Suppose this geological station had been 100 km from the Northridge quake (magnitude 6.8). What would be the maximum amplitude reading for the Northridge quake? Explain how you found this value.

3. Find the maximum amplitudes for a seismograph 100 km from each of the following quakes:
   a. Japan, 1995 (magnitude 7.2)
   b. Mexico, 1985 (magnitude 8.1)
   c. Alaska, 1964 (magnitude 8.4)
   d. Japan, 1933 (estimated magnitude 8.9)

4. A magnitude 5 quake shakes very noticeably. How many times greater is the amplitude of an 8.9 quake than a 5.0 quake?

5. Why do you think a logarithmic scale is used instead of a linear scale to measure earthquakes?

Freeway damage from Kobe, Japan earthquake

REFLECT

1. In your own words, define *logarithm*.

2. Explain the product, quotient, and power properties of logarithms.

3. Why are logarithms important for solving exponential equations? Without logarithms, how would you solve an equation for the value of an exponent?

Self-Assessment

1. Describe the relationship between the graphs of $y = \log_2 x$ and $y = 2^x$. Sketch the graphs of these two equations.

2. If (6, 15,625) is on the graph of $y = 5^x$, what point must be on the graph of $y = \log_5 x$?

Graph each logarithmic function. Label the coordinates of at least two points on each curve.

3. $f(x) = \log_4 x$ **4.** $f(x) = \log_{\frac{1}{3}} x$ **5.** $g(x) = \log x + 2$

Rewrite each equation. If it is in exponential form, rewrite it in logarithmic form; if it is in logarithmic form, rewrite it in exponential form.

6. $\log 10,000 = 4$ **7.** $2^3 = 8$ **8.** $\log_4 \frac{1}{16} = -2$

9. $10^{-3} = 0.001$ **10.** $\log_6 1 = 0$ **11.** $81^{\frac{3}{4}} = 27$

Evaluate each expression. If necessary, round answers to the nearest hundredth.

12. $\log_6 36$ **13.** $\log_2 \frac{1}{8}$ **14.** $\log 8.87$ **15.** $3.5 \ln 4.58$

16. A patient was suffering from a bacterial infection. After an antibiotic was given to the patient, the bacteria began to die. The number of hours (H) it takes for an initial number of bacteria (P) to decrease to a smaller number (A) at a rate (r) is given by $H = \left(\frac{1}{r}\right)(\ln P - \ln A)$. How long will it take for an infection of 6000 bacteria to decline to 500, if the rate of decline (r) is 0.16?

Decide which choice is correct.

(A) The quantity in Column A is greater.   (B) The quantity in Column B is greater.

(C) The two quantities are equal.   (D) The relationship cannot be determined.

	Column A	Column B
17.	$\log_2 x$	$\log_4 x$
18.	$\log_{\frac{1}{3}} x$	$\log_3 x$

Divide and simplify. [8-2]

19. $\frac{2}{i}$ **20.** $\frac{5}{3-i}$ **21.** $\frac{3-2i}{4+3i}$ **22.** $\frac{1+i}{1-i}$

Simplify each expression by rewriting as a single logarithm.

23. $\log x + 2 \log y$ **24.** $3 \log a - 2 \log b$ **25.** $5 \ln mn + 3 \ln m - 8 \ln n$

Rewrite each expression as a sum or difference of logarithms.

26. $\log x^2 y^3$ **27.** $\log \left(\frac{c}{d}\right)$ **28.** $\log km^{\frac{1}{2}}$

29. Prehistoric Earthquakes According to the *McGraw-Hill Yearbook of Science and Technology*, the magnitude of an earthquake that happened long ago can be estimated from the maximum single-event fault displacement. This displacement is a measure of how far the earth slipped along a fault line during the quake. If the displacement (D) is given in meters, the magnitude (M_s) is given by the formula $M_s = 7.00 + 0.782 \log D$. If the evidence shows that an earthquake's displacement was 0.25 meters, what was its magnitude?

Solve each equation. Where necessary, round answers to the nearest hundredth.

30. $\log_2 x = 5$ **31.** $\log_x 27 = -3$ **32.** $\log 100,000 = x$ **33.** $\log_3 x = -4$

34. $10^x = 381$ **35.** $e^{3x} = 1.57$ **36.** $2500 = 500e^{0.15x}$ **37.** $\log x = 5.5$

38. $2 \log_3 x = \log_3 25$ **39.** $8^x = 397$ **40.** $\log (4x - 2) - \log (x - 2) = 1$

41. The 1991 population of London was about 9.1 million. If the population is declining at a rate of 0.48% per year, when will London's population fall below:
a. 8 million?   **b.** 5 million?   **c.** 3 million?

42. You are planning to invest $1000 in a savings account. If you want to have at least $1400 in the account in 6 years, at what minimum continuously compounded interest rate can you invest the money?

Chapter 9 Review

In this chapter, you have modeled real-world growth and decay using exponential and logarithmic functions. You have examined the inverse relationship of exponential functions and logarithmic functions, and used logarithms to solve exponential equations.

KEY TERMS

common logarithm [9-2]   exponential equation [9-1]   logarithm [9-2]

e (number) [9-1]   exponential function [9-1]   logarithmic function [9-2]

exponential decay [9-1]   exponential growth [9-1]   natural logarithm [9-2]

1. Which of the following is *not* an example of an exponential function?
   (a) $y = 2^x$ (b) $y = e^x$ (c) $y = x^2$ (d) $y = \left(\frac{1}{2}\right)^x$

2. Write the word or phrase that best completes the statement: A logarithmic function is the ___ of the exponential function with the same base.

CONCEPTS AND APPLICATIONS

3. On the same set of axes, sketch graphs of $y = 4^x$ and $y = \log_4 x$. Label the coordinates of at least two points on each curve. [9-1, 9-2]

Solve each equation. [9-1]

4. $8^x = 2$

5. $2^{x+2} = 16$

6. $16^x = \frac{1}{64}$

7. Find the value of $10,000 after 10 years at 8% interest, compounded:
   a. annually   **b.** quarterly   **c.** continuously [9-1]

 8. Krypton-91 has a half-life of 10 seconds. If you start with a sample of 80 mg of krypton-91, how long will it take before 20 mg are left? [9-1]

Rewrite each equation. If it is in exponential form, rewrite it in logarithmic form; if it is in logarithmic form, rewrite it in exponential form. [9-2]

9. $4^5 = 1024$

10. $\log_{10} 10,000 = 4$

11. $6^{-2} = \frac{1}{36}$

12. $\log_4 0.25 = -1$

13. $\log_{0.5} \frac{1}{4} = 2$

14. $36^{\frac{1}{2}} = 6$

15. The number of cattle in the United States decreased from 111 million in 1980 to 98 million in 1990.
    a. Find the annual rate of decline for the cattle population from 1980–1990. [9-1]
    b. Use your result to predict the cattle population in the year 2005. [9-1]
    c. If this trend continues, when will the cattle population reach 6 million? [9-2]

Evaluate each expression. [9-2]

16. $\log_{10} 100,000$

17. $\log_2 32$

18. $\log_{10} 0.0001$

19. $\log_{\frac{1}{3}} 27$

Solve each equation. Where necessary, round answers to the nearest hundredth. [9-2]

20. $\log_x 2 = \frac{1}{2}$　　　**21.** $\log_8 \frac{1}{32} = x$　　　**22.** $10^{2x} = 500$　　　**23.** $3 \log x = \log \frac{1}{8}$

24. Marta deposited $1000 in an account that compounds interest continuously. If the account grows to $1300 in 4 years, what is the interest rate?

Science

25. The sound level in decibels (S) of a sound whose intensity is I watts per square meter is given by $S = 10 \log \left(\frac{I}{10^{-12}} \right)$. Find the sound level of a loud stereo if the intensity is measured at 3.2×10^{-4} watts per square meter.

CONCEPTS AND CONNECTIONS

Social Science

26. The table shows census data for the population of Canada from 1901 to 1971.

Year	1901	1911	1921	1931	1941	1951	1961	1971
Population (millions)	5.4	7.2	8.8	10.4	11.5	14.0	18.2	21.6

a. Make a scatter plot of the data. Does it appear to be exponential? Explain.
b. Estimate the annual growth rate of the Canadian population. Explain how you made your estimate. Draw a graph of your model.
c. Find the difference between the actual population and what your model predicts for each year shown. These differences are called *residuals*. Display the year, the population, your predicted population, and the residuals in a table.
d. Predict the population of Canada in 1981 and 1991.
e. The Canadian census found the 1981 population to be 24,343,181 and the 1991 population to be 27,296,859. Compare your predicted values to the actual figures.

SELF-EVALUATION

Write a summary of the most important concepts from Chapter 9. Include descriptions of exponential and logarithmic functions, their graphs, and their relationship to each other. Identify real-world situations that can be modeled with these functions. In your summary, mention areas where you had difficulty and how you plan to review them.

Chapter 9 Assessment

TEST

1. Describe the relationship between the functions $y = 3^x$ and $y = \log_3 x$. Graph both functions on the same set of axes. Identify at least two points on each graph.

2. Rewrite $3^2 = 9$ in logarithmic form.

3. Rewrite $\log_5 125 = 3$ in exponential form.

Solve each equation. Where necessary, round answers to the nearest hundredth.

4. $3^{x+2} = 81$

5. $\log_x 7 = 1$

6. $2 \log x = \log 144$

7. $\left(\frac{1}{3}\right)^x = 27$

8. $\ln x = 7.94$

9. $\log_4 (x - 1) + \log_4 (x + 1) = 3$

10. The cost of a house is increasing at the rate of 4% each year.
    a. If the house costs \$125,000 today, predict its cost for each of the next 4 years.
    b. About how long will it take for the house to double in value?

11. Lead-210 has a half-life of 22 years. If an original sample contains 100 kilograms, when will 6.25 kilograms of the lead-210 remain?

12. The population of Taegu, South Korea, was about 2.65 million in 1991 and was projected to increase at a 3.77% annual rate from 1991 to 1995.
    a. Predict the population of Taegu in 1995.
    b. If this growth rate continues, when will the population reach 6 million?

13. Malika is comparing banks to decide where to deposit her \$3000 summer earnings. First Bank pays 6% interest, compounded quarterly, while Second Bank pays 5.5% interest, compounded continuously. Which bank offers the better deal?

Simplify each expression by rewriting as a single logarithm.

14. $8 \log x - 2 \log y$

15. $\frac{1}{2} \ln a + 2 \ln b$

16. $\log gh + 2 \log hk - 4 \log gk$

Rewrite each expression as a sum or difference of logarithms.

17. $\log \frac{xy}{z}$

18. $\ln \frac{a^2}{b}$

19. $\log (m^2 n^3)^4$

20. The altitude of an aircraft (h), in miles, is given by $h = \left(\frac{-100}{9}\right) \log \frac{P}{B}$, where P = the outside air pressure and B = the atmospheric pressure at sea level.
    a. Suppose the atmospheric pressure at sea level is 29.5 inches of mercury. If the pressure outside the airplane is 20.2 inches of mercury, what is its altitude?
    b. The plane moves to an altitude of 6.2 miles. What is the outside pressure?

PERFORMANCE TASK

A prescription contains 400 units of a drug per milliliter. The drug decomposes over time. There must be at least 300 units per millimeter for the drug to be effective.

Days	3	6	7	9	11	13	18
Units of prescription	380.1	361.2	355.1	343.3	331.8	320.7	294.6

The director of the company that manufactures the drug is trying to decide whether or not to invest in research to extend the shelf life of the drug. You are to prepare a report, including any necessary charts and graphs, to help the director make a good decision. The director needs to know:
• what the current shelf life of the drug is;
• whether the decay process can be modeled mathematically; and
• the effect of cutting the decay rate in half.

Chapter 10 Trigonometry

Project A
How High Is the Ceiling?
How do air traffic controllers determine
the height of the cloud ceiling?

Project B
Catch Some Rays
Does the amount of sunlight you get in
your town follow a pattern?

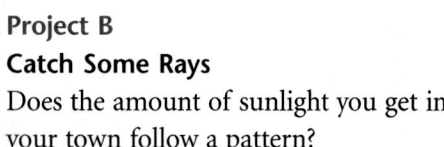

Project C
Sail Away
When sailing, how does
one account for wind when
setting the sail?

DEBORA COMPTON

I enjoyed math in high school. It was like learning all the grammar of a foreign language.

Uncertainty analysis is one way we use math. Say we want to measure the velocity in a wind tunnel, using a pressure probe. Physics tells us that the velocity is determined by the difference between total and static pressures. However, each of the instruments used has limits on its precision. When we report to a scientific journal, we must report on our confidence in the accuracy of velocity. We use mathematical models to determine the uncertainty.

Debora Compton
Assistant Professor,
    Aerospace &
        Mechanical Engineering
Boston University
Boston, Massachusetts

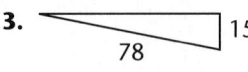

Chapter 10 GETTING READY

Trigonometry

10-1
Trigonometric Ratios

In 10-1 you will study angles and geometric ratios involving triangles. You will use the following skills from geometry.

Find the third side of each right triangle rounded to the nearest tenth. [Previous course]

1.
25
30

2.
120
80
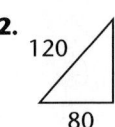

3.
78
15
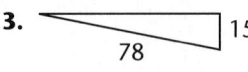

The circumference of a circle is 48 cm. Find the length of the arc intercepted by the given central angle. [Previous course]

4. 30°   **5.** 45°   **6.** 60°   **7.** 90°   **8.** 180°

10-2
Laws of Cosines and Sines

In 10-2 you will find lengths of sides and angles of triangles that are not right triangles. You will use the following skills.

Name the side opposite ∠A. [Previous course]

9.
B
A C
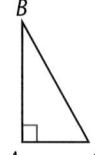

10.
D
E A
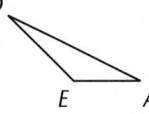

11.
A
F G
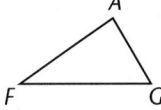

Evaluate, rounding answers to the nearest hundredth. [Previous course]

12. $14^2 + 21^2 - 2(14 \cdot 21 \cdot 0.632)$ **13.** $\dfrac{52^2 + 48^2 - 35^2}{2 \cdot 52 \cdot 48}$

10-3
Trigonometric Functions

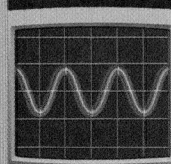

In 10-3 you will investigate the periodic nature of trigonometric functions. You will use the following skills.

Describe how the graph of $y = x^2$ is translated by each equation. [Previous course]

14. $y = x^2 + 3$ **15.** $y = -x^2$ **16.** $y = -x^2 - 5$

17. $y = (x - 3)^2$ **18.** $y = (x + 7)^2$ **19.** $y = 1 - x^2$

10-1 Trigonometric Ratios

Spherical
Geometry

Los Angeles

Tokyo

80° N

75° N

70° N

65° N

60° N

55° N

Is the shortest path between two points always a line segment? Not if you're a pilot flying from Los Angeles to Tokyo. The shortest path between Los Angeles and Tokyo, without passing through the earth, is an arc of a *great circle*. A great circle is the intersection of the surface of a sphere with a plane that passes through the center of the sphere.

Because the earth is a sphere, or practically so, *spherical geometry* is central to the study of geography and navigation. Many familiar concepts from plane geometry, such as the idea that a line segment is the shortest path between two points, must be discarded or modified when we work with spherical geometry.

One modification that is made in spherical geometry is to the coordinates used to locate points. Geographers often locate a point on the earth's surface by giving its *latitude* and *longitude*. Latitude is measured in degrees north or south of the equator (0° latitude). Longitude is measured in degrees east or west of the prime meridian, the great circle that passes through both poles and Greenwich, England (0° longitude).

The applications of this coordinate system and spherical geometry are not limited merely to the earth. Engineers and astronomers use similar systems to study the dynamics of rotating satellites, the solar system and other planetary systems, and even our own Milky Way galaxy.

50° N

45° N

40° N

?

1. The earth is not a perfect sphere. Its equatorial diameter is 7926.5 miles while its polar diameter is 7899.6 miles. What are some possible causes of this difference?

2. Are circles of longitude and circles of latitude great circles? Explain.
3. How could you find the shortest path between two cities?

35° N

30° N

679

← CONNECT → *You've worked with right triangles in previous courses. Now you will use similarity to develop trigonometric ratios for right triangles and use these ratios to find side lengths and angle measures in right triangles.*

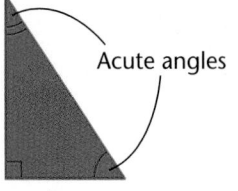

Acute angles

Right angle

The word **trigonometry** means *triangle measurement*. The relationships among the angle measures and side lengths of triangles are important building blocks used in surveying, engineering, and architecture.

Recall that a right triangle has one 90° angle and two acute angles. In the Explore, you will investigate right triangles that have the same pairs of acute angles.

EXPLORE: BIG TRIANGLES, LITTLE TRIANGLES

MATERIALS

Protractor
Ruler

1. Draw a right triangle $\triangle ABC$ with $m\angle A = 38°$. Then draw a larger right triangle $\triangle DEF$, where $m\angle D = 38°$, and a smaller right triangle $\triangle GHK$, where $m\angle G = 38°$. Describe any relationship you see among these three triangles.

2. Measure the second acute angle in each of your triangles. What do you notice? Explain why your observation makes sense.

3. Use a ruler to measure all of the side lengths of your triangles to the nearest millimeter. Then find each of the following ratios for all three triangles.

  a. the ratio of the length of the leg opposite the 38° angle to the length of the hypotenuse of the triangle (The hypotenuse is the side opposite the right angle.)

  b. the ratio of the length of the leg adjacent to the 38° angle to the length of the hypotenuse

  c. the ratio of the length of the leg opposite the 38° angle to the leg adjacent to it

4. What do you notice about all of these ratios? Make a conjecture about the values of these ratios for any right triangle where one of its acute angles measures 38°.

5. Using a different acute angle measure, draw two right triangles of different sizes. Repeat your measurements and ratios from Step 3. What do you notice?

6. Suppose two different right triangles each have an acute angle that measures $x°$. Make a conjecture about the ratios of their corresponding side lengths.

38°

38°

38°

38°

Recall that similar figures have congruent corresponding angles and the lengths of their corresponding sides are proportional. The symbol for similarity is ~.

In the figure, $\triangle ABC \sim \triangle FGH$. This means that $\angle A \cong \angle F$, $\angle B \cong \angle G$, and $\angle C \cong \angle H$, and that $\frac{AB}{FG} = \frac{BC}{GH} = \frac{CA}{HF}$. Notice that each of these side length ratios equals $\frac{1}{2}$.

You may recall the AA Similarity Postulate for triangles, which states that triangles with two pairs of corresponding congruent angles are similar.

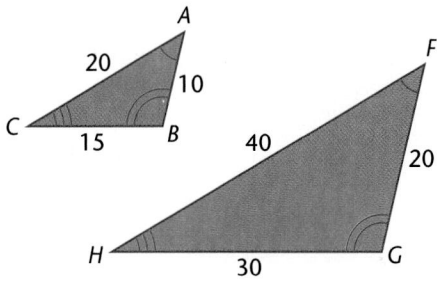

CONSIDER

?

1. Explain why any two right triangles that have a pair of corresponding congruent acute angles are similar.

As you discovered in the Explore, all right triangles with a given acute angle measure are similar. If you know the measure of an acute angle of a right triangle, you can determine the ratio of any two side lengths.

In $\triangle ABC$, notice that the side with length a is opposite $\angle A$, the side with length b is opposite $\angle B$, and the side with length c is opposite $\angle C$. We will use this naming convention throughout this chapter. Using $\triangle ABC$, the following three ratios are the *primary* trigonometric ratios.

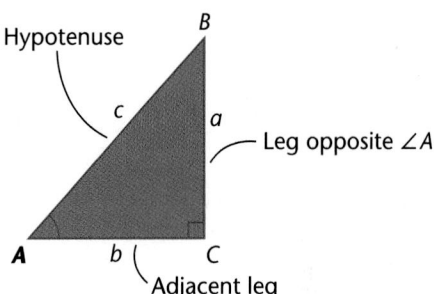

sine of $\angle A = \sin A = \dfrac{\text{length of opposite leg}}{\text{length of hypotenuse}} = \dfrac{a}{c}$

cosine of $\angle A = \cos A = \dfrac{\text{length of adjacent leg}}{\text{length of hypotenuse}} = \dfrac{b}{c}$

tangent of $\angle A = \tan A = \dfrac{\text{length of opposite leg}}{\text{length of adjacent leg}} = \dfrac{a}{b}$

The reciprocals of the primary ratios also have special names.

cosecant of $\angle A = \csc A = \dfrac{1}{\sin A} = \dfrac{c}{a}$

secant of $\angle A = \sec A = \dfrac{1}{\cos A} = \dfrac{c}{b}$

cotangent of $\angle A = \cot A = \dfrac{1}{\tan A} = \dfrac{b}{a}$

1. Find the sine, cosine, tangent, cosecant, secant, and cotangent of $\angle X$ in $\triangle XYZ$. If necessary, round these values to the nearest thousandth.

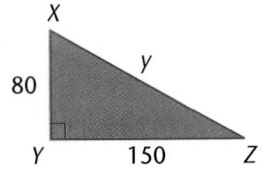

First, we will need to find y.

$x^2 + z^2 = y^2$ Use the Pythagorean Theorem.

$150^2 + 80^2 = y^2$

$28{,}900 = y^2$

$170 = y$ The length is the positive square root.

Now use the side lengths to compute the trigonometric ratios.

$\sin X = \frac{x}{y} = \frac{150}{170} \approx 0.882$ $\cos X = \frac{z}{y} = \frac{80}{170} \approx 0.471$ $\tan X = \frac{x}{z} = \frac{150}{80} = 1.875$

$\csc X = \frac{y}{x} = \frac{170}{150} \approx 1.133$ $\sec X = \frac{y}{z} = \frac{170}{80} = 2.125$ $\cot X = \frac{z}{x} = \frac{80}{150} \approx 0.533$

If you know the measure of an acute angle, you can use a calculator to find its sine, cosine, or tangent ratio. These ratios can help you solve problems involving side lengths in right triangles.

2. A 12-ft ladder is placed against a building so that the ladder makes an angle of 50° with the ground.

a. To the nearest tenth of a foot, at what height does the ladder touch the building?

We know the length of the hypotenuse is 12 feet. We are looking for the length of the leg opposite the given angle. So, we want to use a ratio that involves these sides, the sine ratio.

$\sin 50° = \frac{h}{12}$

$0.7660 \approx \frac{h}{12}$ Use your calculator in degree mode to find $\sin 50°$.

$9.2 \approx h$ Solve for h.

The ladder touches the building at a height of about 9.2 feet.

b. How far from the base of the building is the foot of the ladder?

$12^2 \approx d^2 + 9.2^2$ Use the Pythagorean Theorem.

$144 \approx d^2 + 84.64$

$59.36 \approx d^2$

$7.7 \approx d$

The foot of the ladder is about 7.7 feet from the base of the building.

An **angle of elevation** or **angle of depression** to an object is formed by the line of sight and a horizontal line. The vertex of the angle is the eye of the person looking at the object.

If two sides of a right triangle are known, then measures of the acute angles can be found using inverse keys on your calculator.

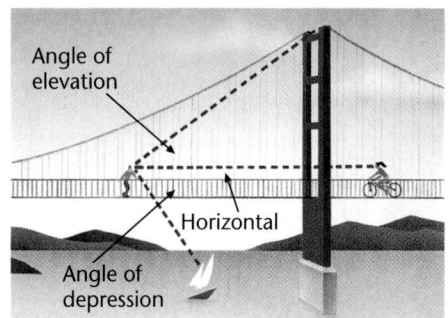

Angle of elevation

Horizontal

Angle of depression

3. An airplane is headed for Chicago's O'Hare airport, 12.5 miles away. If the airplane is at an altitude of 5000 ft, what is the angle of depression, to the nearest degree, from the airplane to the airport?

We know the lengths of the sides of the opposite and adjacent legs for the angle we want to find. Therefore, we will use the tangent ratio.

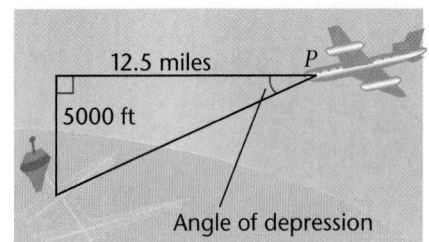

12.5 miles

5000 ft

Angle of depression

$$\tan P = 5000\left(\frac{1}{5280}\right)$$

$$= 0.07575\ldots \text{ or } 0.076$$

We know the value of the tangent of *P*; we need to find the angle that gives that value. This angle can be found by using the $\boxed{\text{TAN}^{-1}}$ key on some scientific calculators. (Other calculators use a two-key sequence, $\boxed{\text{INV}}$ $\boxed{\text{TAN}}$, $\boxed{\text{2ND}}$ $\boxed{\text{TAN}}$, or $\boxed{\text{ARC}}$ $\boxed{\text{TAN}}$.)

Entering 0.076 $\boxed{\text{TAN}^{-1}}$ gives an answer of 4.346124355....
The angle of depression is approximately 4.3°.

a. Find the sine, cosine, tangent, cosecant, secant, and cotangent of $\angle A$ in $\triangle ABC$. Express your answers as simplified fractions.

b. Find $m\angle A$ to the nearest tenth of a degree.

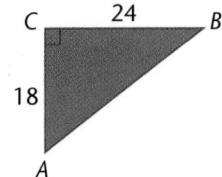

C   24   B

18

A

c. When the angle of elevation of the sun is 36°, a flagpole casts an 11.1-m long shadow. How tall is the flagpole?

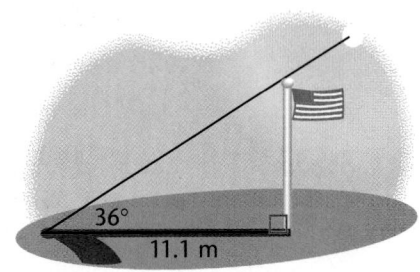

36°

11.1 m

Trigonometric ratios can be used to solve for a side length of a right triangle when a side length and the measure of an acute angle are known, or to solve for the measure of an angle when two side lengths are known.

REFLECT

1. Suppose one of the acute angles in a right triangle measures 42°. Explain why the sine of the 42° angle does not depend on the size of the triangle.

2. The hypotenuse of a right triangle is always its longest side. What does this tell you about the possible values of the sine and cosine of any acute angle?

3. If you know the lengths of two sides and the measure of one acute angle of a right triangle, how can you find the length of the other side and the measure of the other acute angle *without* using trigonometry?

Exercises

CORE

1. Getting Started Refer to right triangle △*KLM*.
   a. What is the length of the leg opposite ∠*L*? opposite ∠*K*?
   b. What is the length of the side adjacent to ∠*L*? adjacent to ∠*K*?
   c. Give sin *K*, sin *L*, cos *K*, tan *K*, and sec *L*.

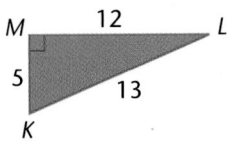

2. Which triangles are similar?

I. 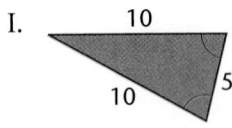   II. 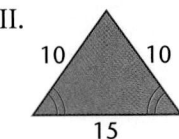   III. 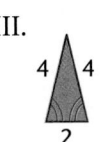   IV.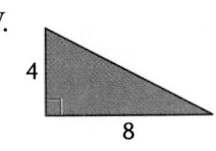

   (a) I and II only   (b) I and III only   (c) II and IV only   (d) none

3. Match the name of each trigonometric ratio with the correct ratio of side lengths of a right triangle.

   a. sine   **b.** cosine   **c.** tangent   **d.** cosecant   **e.** secant   **f.** cotangent

   i. $\dfrac{\text{opposite}}{\text{adjacent}}$ **ii.** $\dfrac{\text{hypotenuse}}{\text{opposite}}$ **iii.** $\dfrac{\text{adjacent}}{\text{hypotenuse}}$ **iv.** $\dfrac{\text{adjacent}}{\text{opposite}}$ **v.** $\dfrac{\text{opposite}}{\text{hypotenuse}}$ **vi.** $\dfrac{\text{hypotenuse}}{\text{adjacent}}$

Use △ABC to find each trigonometric ratio.

4. sin *A*   **5.** cos *A*   **6.** tan *A*

7. sin *B*   **8.** cos *B*   **9.** tan *B*

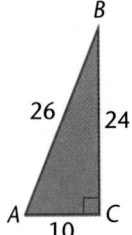

10. Shadows The shadow of a flagpole is 16 feet at the same time that a 6-foot person casts a 4-foot shadow. How tall is the flagpole?

Give the sine, cosine, tangent, cosecant, secant, and cotangent of each angle measure.

11. $37°$ **12.** $89°$ **13.** $10°$

14. Draw a right triangle $\triangle PQR$ with right angle at R. Label each side length of your triangle. Find $\sin P$ and $\cos Q$. What do you notice about these values?

15. Lean on Me A 20-ft ladder is placed against a building so that it makes an angle of 55° with the ground.
   a. At what height, to the nearest foot, does the ladder touch the building?
   b. How far from the base of the building is the foot of the ladder?

16. How Low Does It Go? Scientists use photographs and shadows to calculate heights and depths on the moon. Suppose that the shadow of the rim on the crater's floor is 275 meters long at a time when the rays of the sun make an angle of 20° above the horizon. Measuring from the rim, how deep is the crater?

17. Recall that the two acute angles of a right triangle are called *complementary angles*. Tracy says that the cosine, cosecant, and cotangent of an angle are the same as the sine, secant, and tangent of the complementary angle, respectively. Do you agree? Justify your answer.

Give the measure of the acute angle with each given value.

18. $\sin A = 0.5$ **19.** $\cos B = 0.9$ **20.** $\tan C = 1.2$

Use $\triangle XYZ$ to find each length or angle measure.

21. x **22.** y **23.** $m\angle Y$

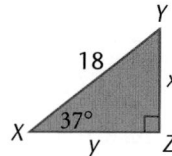

Use $\triangle DEF$ to find each length or angle measure.

24. f **25.** $m\angle D$ **26.** $m\angle E$

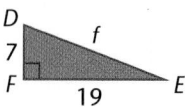

27. Grand Canyon At a certain point along the Grand Canyon, the North Rim is higher than the South Rim, as shown. How much higher?

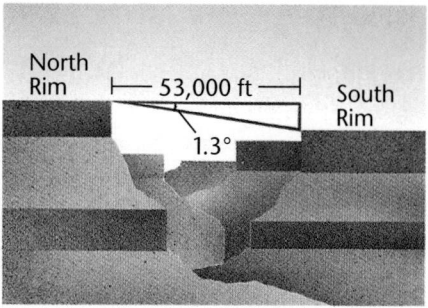

28. A medivac helicopter is headed for a hospital 4 miles away. If the helicopter is flying at an altitude of a half mile, what is the angle of depression to the hospital heliport, 300 feet above ground?

29. Fly Me to the Moon Hipparchus, an ancient mathematician and astronomer, calculated the distance to the moon during the second century B.C. He used the following information.

A person at point A observes the moon directly above at the same time that a person at point B observes the moon centered on the horizon. Using latitude and longitude, Hipparchus found that $m\angle BOA = 89.05°$. He also knew that the radius of Earth was about 3960 miles. Because $\overleftrightarrow{MB}$ is tangent to Earth, $\angle MBO$ is a right angle. Use this information to find the distance to the moon that Hipparchus calculated.

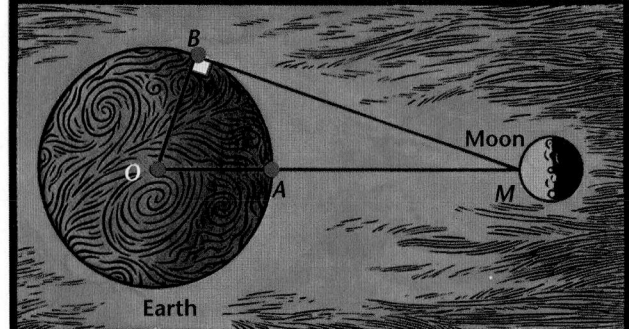

Earth

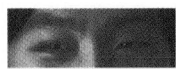

LOOK BACK

30. Add matrices A and B. [1-3]

$$A = \begin{bmatrix} 3 & 4 & -2 \\ 0 & 5 & 7 \end{bmatrix} \qquad B = \begin{bmatrix} -1 & 5 & 0 \\ 9 & -2 & 4 \end{bmatrix}$$

31. Expand the binomial power $(x + 3)^7$. [6-2]

32. Use the formula $A(t) = P\left(1 + \dfrac{r}{n}\right)^{nt}$ to find the balance if $5000 is invested at 6% annual interest, compounded quarterly for 8 years. [9-1]

MORE PRACTICE

33. Draw two similar triangles using a ruler and protractor, and label the side lengths and angle measures of each triangle.

34. Are all equilateral triangles similar? Explain.

Use △ABC to find each trigonometric ratio.

35. $\sin A$	**36.** $\cos A$	**37.** $\cot A$	
38. $\sin B$	**39.** $\csc B$	**40.** $\tan B$	
41. $\tan A$	**42.** $\sec A$	**43.** $\cos B$	

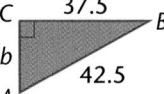

Give the sine, cosine, tangent, cosecant, secant, and cotangent of each angle measure.

44. $26°$	**45.** $1°$	**46.** $40°$	**47.** $77°$

48. An astronomer in an observatory sights a meteor when it is directly over a town 5 miles away. The angle of elevation from the observatory to the meteor is 38°. How high is the meteor, relative to the observatory, when the astronomer sights it?

Use △JKL to find each length or angle measure.

49. j

50. $m\angle J$

51. $m\angle K$

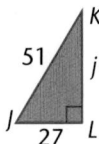

Use △RST to find each length or angle measure.

52. s

53. r

54. $m\angle R$

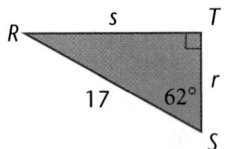

55. Timber! During a violent storm, a tree in front of a library is broken by the wind. The top part of the tree is bent over and touches the ground 14 feet from the base of the tree. If the top part of the tree makes a 35° angle with the ground, how tall was the tree before it was damaged by the storm?

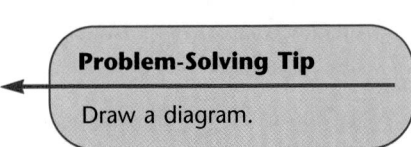

Problem-Solving Tip

Draw a diagram.

56. Traveling Through the Grapevine In southern California, a section of Interstate 5, commonly called the Grapevine, drops from 3000 feet above sea level to 500 feet above sea level in 6 miles. If the highway descends at a constant rate, what angle does the highway make with the horizontal?

MORE MATH REASONING

57. Can the cosine of an acute angle ever have a value greater than 1? If so, give the measure of such an angle. If not, explain why.

58. Assume a right triangle △ABC has right angle ∠C and hypotenuse of length 1. Let θ (the Greek letter *theta*) represent the measure of ∠A.
   a. Give the lengths of the legs in terms of θ.
   b. Use the Pythagorean Theorem to write an equation with the variable θ. Choose two values of θ and verify that the equation is true for these values.

59. Cubism Consider a cube with edges one unit long.
   a. Give the length of a diagonal of the cube. Explain your method.
   b. To the nearest degree, give the measure of the angle formed by a diagonal of the cube and the diagonal of one of its faces.

← CONNECT → *As you've worked with triangles and trigonometric ratios, you've used degrees to measure angles. Now you will learn another useful unit for measuring angles. You will also investigate some special angles for which you can find exact trigonometric ratios.*

The earth serves as a convenient setting for studying and applying angles.

EXPLORE: WHERE IS ALBORG?

This figure shows the locations and approximate coordinates of four cities with longitudes of 10° E. The cities are Oslo, Norway; Cremona, Italy; Ghadamis, Libya; and Libreville, Gabon.

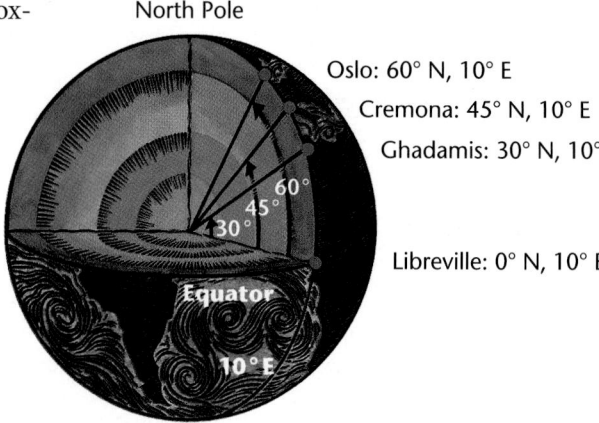

North Pole

Oslo: 60° N, 10° E
Cremona: 45° N, 10° E
Ghadamis: 30° N, 10° E
Libreville: 0° N, 10° E

The cutaway view shows the **central angles** formed by connecting these cities with the earth's center.

1. The radius of the earth is about 3960 miles. Explain why the straight-line distance *OL* (through the earth!), from Oslo (*O*) to Libreville (*L*), is 3960 miles.

2. The figure shows the relative positions of Libreville (*L*) and Alborg, Denmark (*A*), both at longitude 10° E. The distance between the cities along arc *AL* is about 3960 miles. Is the measure (θ) of the central angle ∠*ACL* greater than 60° or less than 60°? Is Alborg north or south of Oslo? Explain.

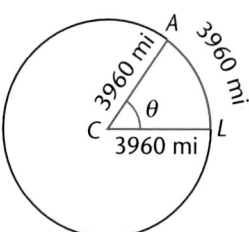

3. Give the circumference of the earth.

4. Write a proportion involving θ, 360°, and the earth's radius and circumference that you can solve to find θ. Solve the proportion and give θ to the nearest thousandth of a degree.

5. If two cities form a central angle with measure 0.5θ, how far apart are they along the surface of the earth? Explain how the value of θ could be a convenient unit of measurement when applying angles to measure distances on the earth.

A convenient way to measure some angles, such as central angles, is **radian measure,** the ratio of arc length to the radius of a circle.

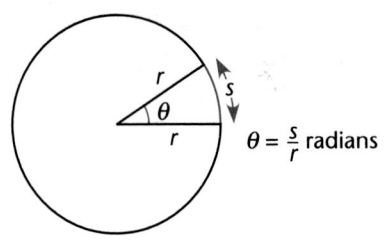

$$\theta = \frac{s}{r} \text{ radians}$$

On a circle of radius r, the radian measure of a central angle θ that intercepts an arc of length s is given by $\theta = \frac{s}{r}$.

The entire circle has circumference $s = 2\pi r$, giving a central angle of measure $\theta = \frac{s}{r} = \frac{2\pi r}{r} = 2\pi$ radians. In degrees, this angle measures 360°. Therefore, $360° = 2\pi$ radians and $180° = \pi$ radians. This gives us these two convenient *conversion factors:* $\frac{180°}{\pi \text{ radians}} = 1$ and $\frac{\pi \text{ radians}}{180°} = 1$.

CONSIDER
?

1. How is the radian measure of a central angle related to the length of an arc in a unit circle (a circle of radius 1)?

EXAMPLES

1. Convert 60° to radians.

$60° = 60° \cdot \frac{\pi \text{ radians}}{180°}$ Multiply by 1 in the form $\frac{\pi \text{ radians}}{180°}$.

$= \frac{60\pi}{180}$ radians

$= \frac{\pi}{3}$ radians

We usually omit the word *radians* with the understanding that when there is no degree symbol, the units are radians.

$60° = \frac{\pi}{3}$

2. Convert $\frac{5\pi}{4}$ to degrees.

$\frac{5\pi}{4} = \frac{5\pi}{4} \cdot \frac{180°}{\pi}$ Multiply by 1 in the form $\frac{180°}{\pi}$.

$= \frac{5(180°)}{4}$

$= 225°$

TRY IT

a. Convert 30° to radians.   **b.** Convert $\frac{7\pi}{6}$ to degrees.

Use a calculator to evaluate each trigonometric ratio of the radian measure.

c. $\sin \frac{\pi}{16}$ **d.** $\csc 0.17$

e. $\tan \frac{\pi}{10}$ **f.** $\sec \frac{\pi}{4}$

There are a few special angles for which you can find *exact* trigonometric ratios without using a calculator.

In a right triangle with two angles measuring 45° or $\frac{\pi}{4}$, both legs have the same length. We can use this fact to find the trigonometric ratios for 45°.

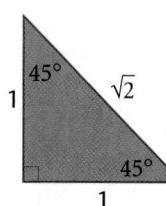

$$\sin 45° = \sin \frac{\pi}{4} = \frac{1}{\sqrt{2}} = \frac{\sqrt{2}}{2}$$

$$\cos 45° = \cos \frac{\pi}{4} = \frac{1}{\sqrt{2}} = \frac{\sqrt{2}}{2}$$

$$\tan 45° = \tan \frac{\pi}{4} = \frac{1}{1} = 1$$

A right triangle with acute angles measuring 30° and 60° $\left(\frac{\pi}{6} \text{ and } \frac{\pi}{3}\right)$ is half of an equilateral triangle.

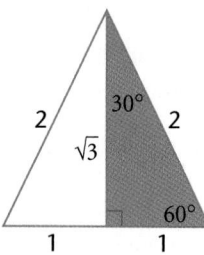

$$\sin 30° = \sin \frac{\pi}{6} = \frac{1}{2} \qquad\qquad \sin 60° = \sin \frac{\pi}{3} = \frac{\sqrt{3}}{2}$$

$$\cos 30° = \cos \frac{\pi}{6} = \frac{\sqrt{3}}{2} \qquad\qquad \cos 60° = \cos \frac{\pi}{3} = \frac{1}{2}$$

$$\tan 30° = \tan \frac{\pi}{6} = \frac{1}{\sqrt{3}} = \frac{\sqrt{3}}{3} \qquad \tan 60° = \tan \frac{\pi}{3} = \sqrt{3}$$

CONSIDER

2. How do you know that an equilateral triangle with side length 2 has height $\sqrt{3}$?

TRY IT

Give the exact value of each trigonometric ratio.

g. sec 60° 　　　　　**h.** csc $\frac{\pi}{4}$ 　　　　　**i.** cot 30°

Since π radians is 180°, 1 radian $= \frac{180°}{\pi} \approx 57.29578°$. Because of its definition, the radian is a convenient unit for measuring angles when you are working with arcs and *sectors* of circles, as you will see in 10-1C.

REFLECT

1. If you know the ratio of the lengths of an arc and radius of a circle, what else can you say about the circle or arc?
2. Why do many convenient measurements in degrees have π in them when you convert to radians?
3. What are the measures of the angles of an equilateral triangle?

Exercises

CORE

1. **Getting Started**
   a. Convert 30° to radians by answering these questions. What fraction of 180° is 30°? What is that same fraction of π, the number of radians in 180°?
   b. Which conversion factor can you multiply 30° by to get the same result as in **a**?
   (i) $\dfrac{180°}{\pi}$ (ii) $\dfrac{\pi}{180°}$
   c. Convert $\dfrac{\pi}{4}$ to degrees by answering these questions. What fraction of π is $\dfrac{\pi}{4}$? What is the same fraction of 180°, the number of degrees in π radians?
   d. Which conversion factor can you multiply $\dfrac{\pi}{4}$ by to get the same result as in **c**?
   (i) $\dfrac{180°}{\pi}$ (ii) $\dfrac{\pi}{180°}$

Write the word or phrase that correctly completes each statement.

2. In a circle, the radian measure of a central angle is the ratio of the arc length of the intercepted arc to ____.

3. The angle measure 2π radians is the same as the angle measure ____ degrees.

Convert each angle measure to radians.

4. 135°   5. 100°   6. 225°   7. 216°

Convert each angle measure to degrees.

8. $\dfrac{7\pi}{10}$ 9. $\dfrac{13\pi}{15}$ 10. $\dfrac{5\pi}{12}$ 11. $\dfrac{4\pi}{9}$

12. **Big Angles** The minute hand of a clock makes a complete 360° rotation every hour.
   a. Explain why the expression $360t$ gives the degree measure of the angle that the minute hand has rotated through t hours after noon.
   b. What is the value of the expression in **a** at 12:15 p.m.? 1:15 p.m.? How do you explain the difference in values when the minute hand is in the same position at both of these times?
   c. At what time has the minute hand rotated 1710°?

13. A 45-rpm record makes 45 revolutions every minute. Give the number of radians through which the record turns in one minute and in one second.

Use a calculator to evaluate each trigonometric ratio of the radian measure.

14. $\cos \dfrac{\pi}{4}$ 15. $\sin \dfrac{\pi}{6}$ 16. $\cos 1.362$ 17. $\tan 0.589$

Give the exact value of each trigonometric ratio.

18. $\sec \frac{\pi}{6}$

19. $\cot \frac{\pi}{4}$

20. $\csc 60°$

21. Around the World in 2π Radians The average radius of the earth is about 3960 miles.

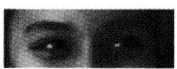

a. Two cities are separated by a 1.73-radian central angle (the angle between the radii from the center of the earth to each city). Give the arc distance between the cities.

b. The distance from New York City to Los Angeles is 2451 miles. Give the measure of the central angle formed by these cities in radians and degrees.

22. Each guy wire used to reinforce a 30-ft pole makes a 60° angle with the ground. Give the distance between the base of the pole and the point where the wire is attached to the ground. Also give the length of the wire.

LOOK AHEAD

23. a. What is the area of a pizza with a radius of 10 inches? If the pizza is sliced into 8 slices, what is the area of each slice?

b. What is the number of slices and the total area of these slices if they form a central angle of $\frac{\pi}{2}$ radians? $\frac{3\pi}{4}$ radians?

c. Do you see any connection between the radian measure of the central angle and the area in each case? Explain.

MORE PRACTICE

Convert each angle measure to radians.

24. 120°

25. 225°

26. 180°

27. 240°

28. 108°

29. 315°

30. 255°

31. 144°

Convert each angle measure to degrees.

32. $\frac{4\pi}{3}$

33. $\frac{5\pi}{4}$

34. $\frac{11\pi}{6}$

35. $\frac{5\pi}{9}$

36. $\frac{13\pi}{10}$

37. $\frac{23\pi}{15}$

38. $\frac{7\pi}{12}$

39. $\frac{19\pi}{20}$

40. Give the degree and radian measures of the angle that a discus thrower rotates through if she makes $2\frac{1}{2}$ revolutions before releasing the discus.

41. Getting in Gear A gear is turning at a rate of 1 revolution every 4.8 sec. Through how many radians does the gear turn in 1 second?

Use a calculator to evaluate each trigonometric ratio of the radian measure.

42. $\sin \frac{\pi}{2}$

43. $\cos \frac{\pi}{3}$

44. $\tan \frac{\pi}{6}$

45. $\cos \frac{\pi}{2}$

46. $\tan 1.5$

47. $\cos 0.14$

48. $\sin 0.919$

49. $\tan 0.588$

Give the exact value of each trigonometric ratio.

50. $\csc \dfrac{\pi}{6}$ **51.** $\sec \dfrac{\pi}{4}$ **52.** $\cot 60°$

53. The Hands of Time Give the measure, in both degrees and radians, of the central angle formed by the hands of a clock at 4 p.m.

54. Give the measures, in radians, of the angles of a 30°-60°-90° triangle.

MORE MATH REASONING

55. What's So Great About It? The figure shows two great circles inclined at an angle of θ radians. The crescent-shaped figure on the surface of the sphere is called a *lune*. The area A of a lune is given by $A = 2\theta r^2$, where r is the radius of the sphere.

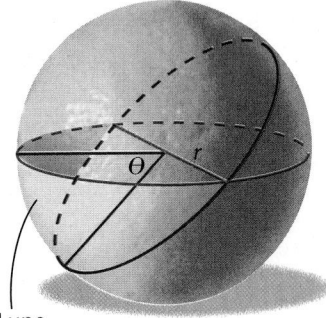

Lune

  a. An orange has a radius of 4 cm. Suppose that by slicing along halves of great circles inclined at 30°, you remove a section of the orange to eat. Give the area of the lune-shaped peel of the section that you remove.
  b. Show that the total surface area of a sphere of radius r is $4\pi r^2$.

56. If you express the measure of an angle in radians, you can use the following infinite series to calculate the sine and cosine of the angle.

$$\sin x = x - \frac{x^3}{3!} + \frac{x^5}{5!} - \frac{x^7}{7!} + \cdots$$

$$\cos x = 1 - \frac{x^2}{2!} + \frac{x^4}{4!} - \frac{x^6}{6!} + \cdots$$

Use the first three terms of each series to approximate the values of sin 30° and cos 30°. Compare your values with those given by your calculator.

10-1 PART C   Arc Length and Sector Area

← CONNECT → *You've seen how radian measure is related to lengths of arcs. Now you will investigate arc length more closely. You will also find areas of sectors and investigate rotating objects.*

Recall that the radian measure of a central angle θ that intercepts an arc of length s is given by $\theta = \dfrac{s}{r}$, where r is the radius of the circle. By multiplying both sides of this equation by r, we obtain an expression for **arc length,** $s = r\theta$.

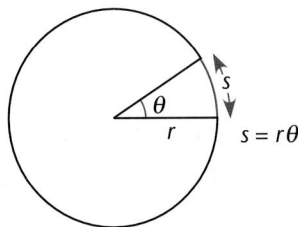

1. Give the length of an arc that is intercepted by a central angle of $\frac{\pi}{8}$ on a circle of radius 24 cm.

$s = r\theta = 24 \cdot \frac{\pi}{8} = 3\pi$

The length of the arc is 3π cm or about 9.4 cm.

2. New Orleans, latitude 29.95° N, is due south of St. Louis, latitude 38.63° N. Give the distance between the cities.

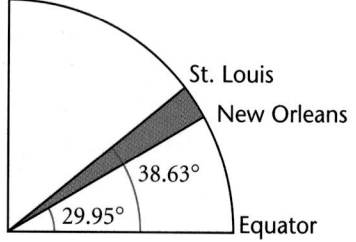

St. Louis

New Orleans

38.63°

29.95°

Equator

Problem-Solving Tip

Draw a diagram.

The difference in the latitudes of the two cities gives the measure of the central angle θ that they form.

$\theta = 38.63° - 29.95°$

$= 8.68°$

$= 8.68° \cdot \frac{\pi}{180°}$ Convert to radians.

≈ 0.1515

$s = r\theta \approx 3960(0.1515)$ The earth's radius is about 3960 miles.

≈ 600 miles

The distance from New Orleans to St. Louis is about 600 miles.

a. Find the length of an arc intercepted by a central angle of 48° on a circle of radius 30 cm.

b. Spokane, Washington, latitude 47.65° N, is due north of Los Angeles, latitude 34.05° N. Give the distance between the cities.

A portion of a circle bounded by an arc and the radii drawn to its endpoints is a **sector.** In the figure, the region *CMNP* is a sector of $\odot C$, a circle with center C and radius r.

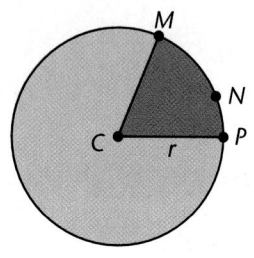

We can write a proportion to find an expression for A, the area of the sector.

$$\frac{\text{area of sector } CMNP}{\text{area of } \odot C} = \frac{\text{length of arc } MNP}{\text{circumference of } \odot C}$$

$$\frac{A}{\pi r^2} = \frac{r\theta}{2\pi r}$$

Solving for A gives $A = \pi r^2 \cdot \frac{r\theta}{2\pi r} = \frac{1}{2}r^2\theta.$

3. The signal from an FM radio station reaches 40 miles in all directions, except for a 20° angle where the signal is blocked completely by a nearby mountain. In order to attract advertisers, the marketing manager of the station needs to know the area served by the station. What is this area?

The measure of the central angle of the sector, where the station's signal reaches, is 360° − 20° = 340°, or about 5.934 radians. The radius of the signal area is 40 miles. So the area of the sector is $A \approx \frac{1}{2} \cdot 40^2(5.934) \text{ mi}^2 \approx 4747 \text{ mi}^2$.

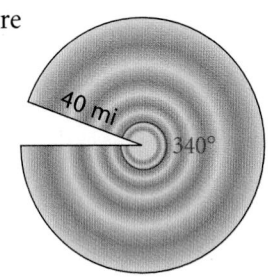

TRY IT

c. A directional microphone can pick up human voices in a 30° angle up to 200 m away. Give the area of the region where voices can be picked up by the microphone.

CONSIDER

1. If you know the area and angle of a sector, can you find the radius? Explain.

The study of rotating objects is one of the most useful applications of formulas relating to circles.

EXPLORE: SPINNING WHEEL

The three-wheel pulley in the figure rotates as a single unit. The radii of the three wheels are 2 in., 4 in., and 6 in., respectively. Points A, B, and C lie on the circumferences of the inner, middle, and outer wheels.

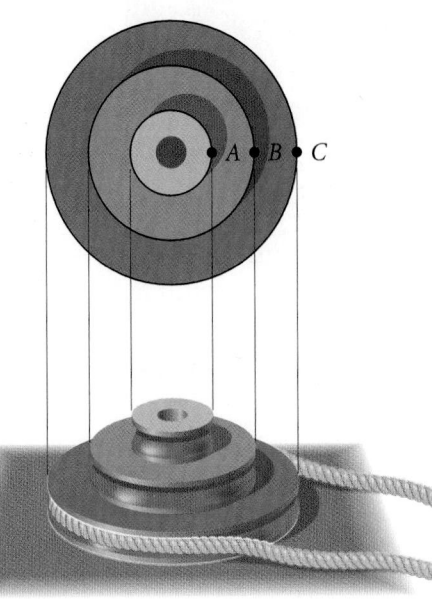

1. Suppose the pulley rotates at a rate of 1 revolution per second. How many revolutions per second do each of the points A, B, and C make?

2. Give the distance traveled in 1 second by each of the points A, B, and C. At what speed is each point moving?

3. Assume a rope runs over one of the wheels of the pulley to another pulley with a radius of 1 inch. How many revolutions per second will the other pulley make?

4. In general, explain the relationship between the rate of rotation of a circle and the speed of a point on its perimeter.

The rate of circular motion can be described in two ways.

The **angular speed** (ω, the Greek character *omega*) of a rotating point or object is its rate of revolution, usually given in revolutions or radians per unit time. For example, the angular velocity of the earth's rotation about its axis can be given as 2π radians per day or about 365 revolutions per year.

The **linear speed** (v) of a point is the distance it travels per unit time. We can relate the angular and linear speeds of a rotating point by using the formula for arc length.

If a point on a circle of radius r rotates θ radians in time t, then $\omega = \frac{\theta}{t}$ is its angular speed. In that same time, the point has moved through an arc of length $s = r\theta$, so its linear speed is $v = \frac{s}{t} = \frac{r\theta}{t}$, which is equal to $r\omega$.

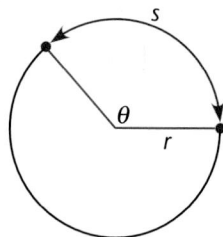

If a point rotates on a circle of radius r with linear speed v and angular speed ω in radians per unit time, then $v = r\omega$.

EXAMPLE

4. The 4-ft-diameter wheels of a steam locomotive can turn up to 600 revolutions per minute (rpm). What is the top speed of the locomotive?

To use the formula $v = r\omega$, first convert ω to radians per minute.

$\omega = 600\ \frac{\text{revs}}{\text{min}} \cdot \frac{2\pi}{1\ \text{rev}}$ Multiply by 1 in the form $\frac{2\pi}{1\ \text{rev}}$.

$\approx \frac{3770}{\text{min}}$

$r = \frac{1}{2}(4\ \text{ft}) = 2\ \text{ft}$ The radius is half the diameter.

$v = r\omega \approx (2\ \text{ft})\left(\frac{3770}{\text{min}}\right) = 7540\ \frac{\text{ft}}{\text{min}}$

$= 7540\ \frac{\text{ft}}{\text{min}} \cdot 60\ \frac{\text{min}}{\text{hr}} \cdot \frac{1\ \text{mile}}{5280\ \text{ft}}$ Convert to miles per hour.

$\approx 85.7\ \text{mi/hr}$

The maximum speed of the locomotive is about 86 mi/hr.

TRY IT

d. A $33\frac{1}{3}$-rpm record has a diameter of 30 cm. Give the linear speed of a point on the rim.

Angular and linear speeds clearly have applications to the study of motors and other machinery with rotating parts. Another important application is the rotation of satellites in order to stabilize their paths.

1. How do arc length and sector area vary with the central angle? How do they vary with the radius?
2. Why is it convenient to measure angles in radians when you are interested in finding arc length or sector area?
3. How are linear speed and angular speed similar and how are they different?

Exercises

CORE

1. **Getting Started** A central angle in a 12-cm-diameter circle measures 60°.
   a. Give the radius of the circle.
   b. Draw a diagram showing the arc intercepted by a 60° central angle, and give the measure of this angle in radians.
   c. Multiply the radius by the measure of the central angle to find the length of the arc that is intercepted by the angle.

Write the word or phrase that correctly completes each statement.

2. A sector of a circle is a region bounded by two radii and ____.

3. The number of revolutions of a point on a circle per unit time is its ____ speed.

4. The distance a point travels along a circle per unit time is its ____ speed.

5. The radius of the circle is 18 cm, $m\angle AOC = \frac{5}{12}\pi$, and $m\angle BOC = \frac{2}{9}\pi$. Give the length of $\overset{\frown}{APB}$.

6. Give the length of the arc intercepted by a central angle measuring $\frac{\pi}{4}$ in a 16-in.-radius circle.

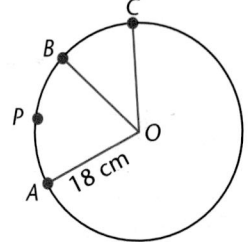

7. A central angle measuring 150° is drawn in a circle with radius 7.8 cm. Give the length of the arc that is intercepted by the angle.

8. **Tropic Topic** Antofagasta, Chile, is on the Tropic of Capricorn (the circle at latitude 23.45° S) and is due south of Boston. Boston's latitude is 42.35° N. Give the distance between the two cities.

9. Seattle, Washington, latitude 47.6° N, lies directly north of San Francisco, California, latitude 37.7° N. Give the distance between Seattle and San Francisco.

10. A sector of a circle has an arc length of 7 in. and a central angle of $\frac{\pi}{8}$ radians. Give the area of the sector.

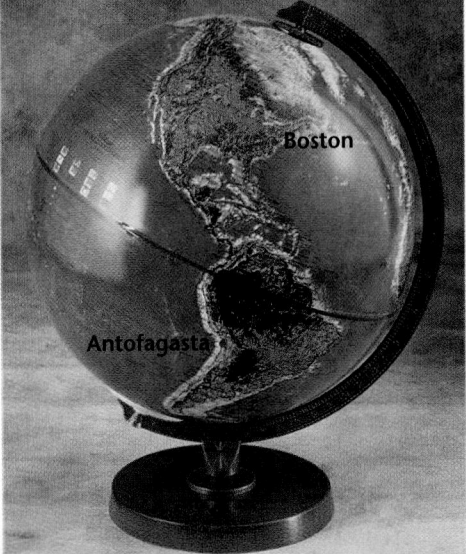

11. Windshield Vipers Each of two windshield wipers on a car is 20 inches long and wipes a 130° sector of the 4-ft. by 2-ft. windshield. If there is a 20-in.² area in the middle of the windshield wiped by both wipers, what percentage of the windshield is wiped by the windshield wipers?

12. A flywheel with a 6-in. radius revolves 200 times per minute. Give the linear speed of a point on the rim.

13. The foghorn on a ship can be heard for 1 mile in a 250° sector. In what area of the ocean can the ship's horn be heard?

14. As the World Turns The radius of the earth is 3960 miles.
  a. Give the angular speed of the earth in its daily rotation about its axis.
  b. Give the linear speed of a point on the equator, in mi/hr, due to the earth's rotation about its axis.

15. How Wide the Moon The moon appears 0.5° wide when seen from Earth, 240,000 miles away. Find the diameter of the moon.

16. What is the angular speed of a 2-ft-diameter automobile wheel on a car that is being driven along a freeway at 55 mi/hr?

17. A cylindrical tank that is lying on its side is partially filled with oil to a depth of 3 feet. The tank is 15 feet long and 6 feet in radius. Find the volume of oil in the tank to the nearest tenth of a foot.

LOOK BACK

18. Give the center and radius of the circle $x^2 + y^2 - 4x + 6y = -9$. [5-3]

19. $f(x) = 2x - 1$ and $g(x) = 3x + 5$. Give $(f \circ g)(x)$. [7-3]

20. Solve $\log_3 (5x + 1) = 4$. [9-2]

MORE PRACTICE

The radius of a circle and the measure of a central angle are given. Give the length of the arc that is intercepted by the angle.

21. 10 in., $\frac{2\pi}{5}$

22. 14.3 cm, 1.6 radians

23. 22 in., 75°

24. 9 in., π

25. 36 cm, 60°

26. 64 mm, $\frac{3\pi}{4}$

27. All Around the Island An island is approximately circular with a diameter of 4 miles. As seen from the air, there is an arc of 38° of the coastline with rocky cliffs. The rest of the coastline has sandy beaches. What is the length of coastline with sandy beaches?

Give the area of the sector of the circle with the given radius and central angle.

28. 4 cm, $\frac{\pi}{2}$

29. 10 in., π

30. 6 cm, $\frac{2\pi}{3}$

31. 9 in., $\frac{4\pi}{9}$

32. 28.6 cm, 4.6 radians

33. 45.7 cm, 135°

34. Give the linear speed of the teeth on a circular saw with a blade 9 inches in diameter that turns at 2000 revolutions per minute.

35. The signal from a radio beacon reaches 60 miles in all directions, except for a 15° angle where the signal is blocked completely by a nearby mountain. In what area can the radio beacon's signal be received?

36. A bicycle has 27-in.-diameter wheels. A cyclist turns the wheels at 4 revolutions per second as she rides.
  a. Give the angular speed of the wheel in radians per second.
  b. Give the linear speed of a point on the rim.
  c. How many revolutions per second must the wheels turn for the cyclist to be riding 25 mi/hr?

37. The radius of a pulley is 14 cm. The pulley turns at a rate of 6 revolutions per second. Give the linear speed of the drive belt that is turning the pulley.

MORE MATH REASONING

38. Measuring the Earth More than 2000 years ago, the Greek mathematician Eratosthenes of Cyrene (275−194 B.C.), director of the library in Alexandria, Egypt, calculated the earth's circumference with amazing accuracy. At a moment when the sun was directly overhead in Syene, Egypt, Eratosthenes placed a pole in the ground in Alexandria and measured the angle of the sun. The angle measured 7.2°. Eratosthenes assumed that the sun was far enough away so that $\overleftrightarrow{AM}$ and $\overleftrightarrow{ON}$ were parallel.

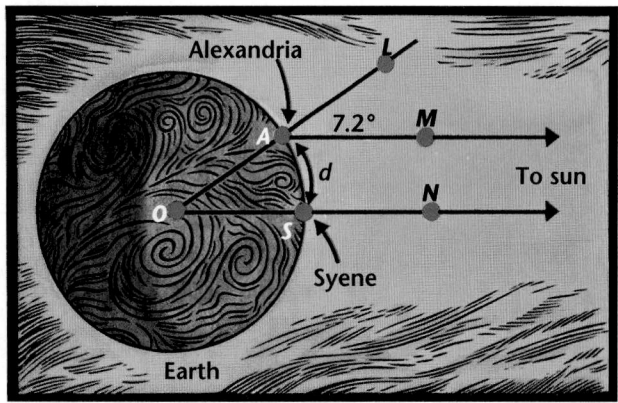

  a. Why is $m\angle AOS = 7.2°$?
  b. Let C represent the earth's circumference and d represent the arc distance from Alexandria to Syene. Write a proportion relating C, d, 7.2°, and 360°.
  c. The arc distance from Alexandria to Syene was 5000 Greek stades, where 1 stade ≈ 0.098 mile. Give the earth's circumference, in miles, according to Eratosthenes's measurements.
  d. The accepted equatorial circumference of the earth today is 24,901.55 mi. Find the percent error in Eratosthenes's calculation.

39. Fast Feet For maximum efficiency, it is recommended that bicyclists choose gears that allow them to cycle at 90 revolutions per minute (rpm). On flat ground, Carlos can race at this pace in gears with a 4-to-1 ratio, giving his 27-in.-diameter wheels an angular speed of 360 revolutions per minute. How fast does Carlos race his bicycle on flat ground?

40. Given a circle with a diameter of 12, find the length of the chord joining the endpoints of an arc with a central angle measuring $\frac{2\pi}{3}$.

41. Let θ be the radian measure of a central angle in a circle of radius 1. Consider the sector described by this angle and the isosceles triangle with the vertex angle at the origin and inscribed inside the sector. What happens to the ratio of the triangle's area and the sector's area as θ gets closer and closer to 0?

10-1 PART D Extended Trigonometric Values

← CONNECT → *So far, you've worked with acute angles when finding trigonometric values. Now you will discover how to find trigonometric values for any angle.*

When we work with angles other than acute angles, it is convenient to represent the angle on a coordinate plane. The vertex of the angle is placed at the origin with one ray, called the **initial side,** along the positive x-axis.

The other ray is called the **terminal side** and may be located by rotating in a positive direction (counterclockwise) or in a negative direction (clockwise). The angle shown is about 135° or −225°.

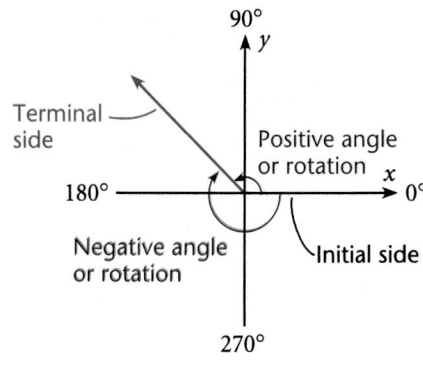

Several angles can have the same terminal side and are therefore equivalent in terms of position. This occurs when these angles differ by an integer multiple of 360° or 2π radians.

TRY IT

For each angle measure, give an equivalent angle measure between 0° and 360°, and tell in which quadrant the terminal side lies.

a. 502°   **b.** $\frac{10}{3}\pi$ **c.** −75°   **d.** 1111°

Now you will discover how angles can help you predict a celestial event.

EXPLORE: COMING FULL CIRCLE

Jupiter orbits the sun in the same direction as Earth, but takes 11.86 earth years to complete each orbit. The orbits of both planets are nearly circular. On June 1, 1995, Jupiter and the sun were in *opposition* with Earth, as shown. That is, the sun, Earth, and Jupiter lined up, with the sun and Jupiter on opposing sides of Earth.

1. In a year, Earth will have returned to the same position, but Jupiter will have moved to a new position. Estimate when Earth will catch up to Jupiter, resulting in the next opposition of the sun and Jupiter with Earth.

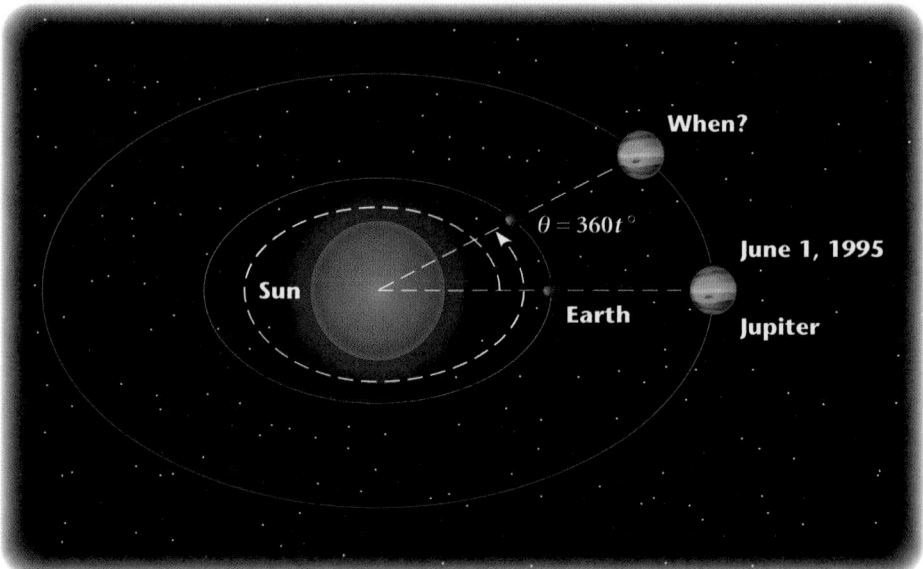

2. Explain why Earth's position will have changed by 360t degrees in t years. Give an equivalent angle measure for this position between 0° and 360° when 1 < t < 2.
3. How do the angular speeds of Jupiter and Earth compare? By how many degrees will Jupiter's position have changed in t years when 1 < t < 2?
4. Write and solve an equation to determine when the sun and Jupiter will next be in opposition with Earth. Compare your result to your estimate in Step 1.

If you know the coordinates of a point on the terminal side of an angle in quadrant I, you can find the trigonometric ratios of the angle.

For example, the point (3, 4) is on the terminal side of the angle shown. The primary trigonometric ratios of the angle are:

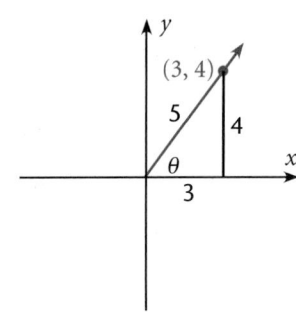

$$\sin \theta = \frac{4}{5} \qquad \cos \theta = \frac{3}{5} \qquad \tan \theta = \frac{4}{3}$$

In general, an angle θ in a right triangle in the first quadrant with leg lengths x and y and hypotenuse length r has the following trigonometric ratios:

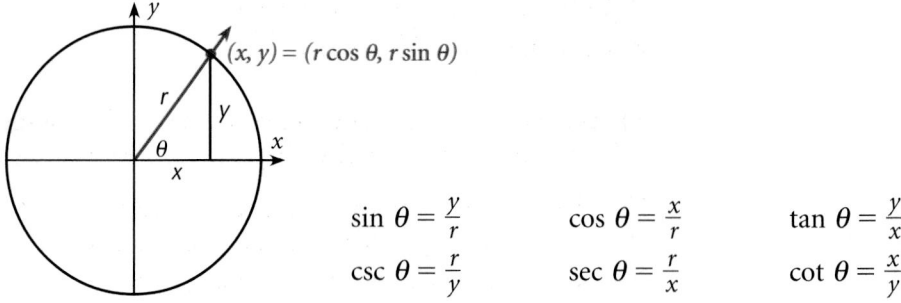

$$\sin \theta = \frac{y}{r} \qquad \cos \theta = \frac{x}{r} \qquad \tan \theta = \frac{y}{x}$$

$$\csc \theta = \frac{r}{y} \qquad \sec \theta = \frac{r}{x} \qquad \cot \theta = \frac{x}{y}$$

These same relationships are used to define the trigonometric ratios for angles in *any* quadrant. To find the ratios, choose a convenient right triangle with its hypotenuse on the terminal side of the angle and one leg on the x-axis. Use the quadrant and the **reference angle,** the acute angle formed by the terminal side and the x-axis, to find the values of x and y. Then use the above relationships to find the trigonometric ratios.

EXAMPLES

1. Give sin 300°, cos 300°, and tan 300°.

Notice that 300° is 360° − 60° and has its terminal side in quadrant IV. The reference angle is 60° and a convenient right triangle is one with hypotenuse of length 2 and leg lengths of 1 and $\sqrt{3}$.

The point $\left(1, -\sqrt{3}\right)$ is on the terminal side of the angle. Use these values of x and y, along with $r = 2$, to find the trigonometric ratios.

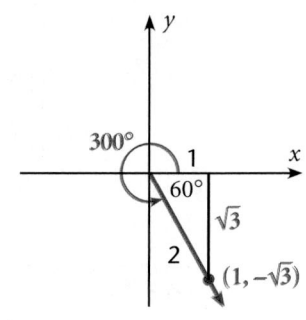

$x = 1;\; y = -\sqrt{3};\; r = 2$

$\sin 300° = \frac{y}{r} = -\frac{\sqrt{3}}{2};\; \cos 300° = \frac{x}{r} = \frac{1}{2};\; \tan 300° = \frac{y}{x} = -\sqrt{3}$

2. Give sin 180°, cos 180°, tan 180°, and cot 180°.

A right triangle can't be drawn for 180° (not for 0°, 90°, or 270° either), but you can easily choose a point on the terminal side, such as (−1, 0), and use that to find the trigonometric ratios.

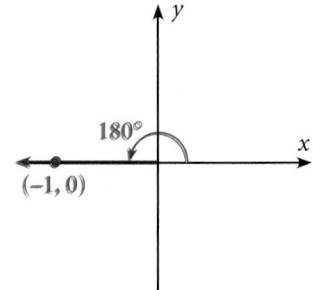

$x = -1;\; y = 0;\; r = 1$

$\sin 180° = \frac{y}{r} = 0;\; \cos 180° = \frac{x}{r} = -1;$

$\tan 180° = \frac{y}{x} = 0;\; \cot 180° = \frac{x}{y} = \frac{-1}{0}$ is undefined.

e. Give sin 330°, cot 330°, and sec 330°.

f. Give cos 90°, tan 90°, and csc 90°.

g. Give sin $\frac{4\pi}{3}$, cos $\frac{4\pi}{3}$, and tan $\frac{4\pi}{3}$.

In general, you can find a trigonometric ratio by finding that ratio using the reference angle and then deciding if it is positive or negative.

The signs of x and y in each quadrant determine the signs of the trigonometric ratios. For example, $y < \theta$ in quadrants III and IV, so sin $\theta = \frac{y}{r}$ is negative for angles with terminal sides in these quadrants. The chart summarizes the signs of the primary trigonometric ratios.

Note that r is positive in all of these quadrants since it is the distance from the point to the origin. The Pythagorean Theorem shows that

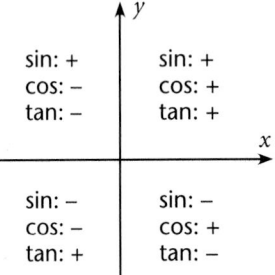

$x^2 + y^2 = r^2$, so also $\left(\frac{x}{r}\right)^2 + \left(\frac{y}{r}\right)^2 = 1$. Writing this in terms of trigonometric ratios gives the following important trigonometric *identity,* an equation that is true for all angles. Note that we generally write sin² θ for (sin θ)² and cos² θ for (cos θ)².

For any angle measure θ, sin² θ + cos² θ = 1.

CONSIDER

1. Explain how you can use the above trigonometric identity or the Pythagorean Theorem to write an identity for tan² θ + 1.

Reference angles help you to determine trigonometric ratios of any angle. These ratios can then help you to analyze situations involving any triangle, including those with obtuse angles.

REFLECT

1. Describe a situation in which an angle of rotation is greater than 360°.

2. How do you find the reference angle for any angle? What is a reference angle used for?

3. Are ratios like $\frac{\text{length of opposite leg}}{\text{length of hypotenuse}}$ for the sine still useful when working with angles that aren't acute? Explain.

CORE

1. **Getting Started**

   a. Name the initial side of the angle of rotation shown in the figure.

   b. Name the terminal side of the angle.

   c. Name the reference angle.

   d. Give the length of the hypotenuse and the side opposite and the side adjacent to the reference angle.

   e. Give each trigonometric ratio of the original angle of rotation.

i. sine	**ii.** cosine	**iii.** tangent
iv. cosecant	**v.** secant	**vi.** cotangent

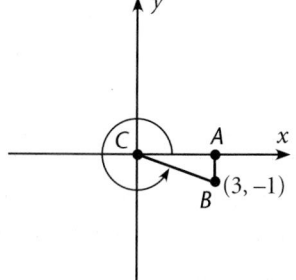

Write the word or phrase that correctly completes each statement.

2. The reference angle of an angle of rotation is the angle formed by the x-axis and the ____.

3. The initial side of an angle of rotation is placed along the ____.

For each angle measure, give an equivalent angle measure between 0° and 360°, and tell in which quadrant the terminal side lies.

4. 473°

5. −299°

6. $-\dfrac{10\pi}{6}$

7. **Spinning Wheels** A game is designed with a spinner that can spin up to 10 times for each spin. Describe a test that can be conducted to determine the average angle of rotation of each spin during a game. Give possible sample results.

A point on the terminal side of an angle of rotation is given. Give the sine, cosine, and tangent of each angle.

8. $(-3, -4)$

9. $(12, 5)$

10. $(-8, 15)$

Give the value of each trigonometric ratio.

11. $\cos 45°$

12. $\sin 150°$

13. $\tan 300°$

14. $\cos (-240°)$

15. $\sec \dfrac{\pi}{3}$

16. $\csc 675°$

17. $\cot 315°$

18. $\tan \dfrac{7\pi}{6}$

19. **Satellite Contact** As viewed from above our solar system, a satellite orbits the earth once every 5 hours in the same direction as the earth rotates. Assume that the satellite is above Greenwich, England, at $t = 0$. Write a function $\theta_e(t)$ giving the angle the earth has rotated in t hours. Then write a function $\theta_s(t)$ giving the angle the satellite has rotated in t hours. When will the satellite again be directly over Greenwich? Explain your conclusion.

20. Angles of rotation with the same terminal side are called *coterminal angles*. Give the measures of four angles with positive measures that are coterminal with a 40° angle.

21. a. Sketch the graph of $y = \sin x$, where x is radian measure, by making a table of values or a list of ordered pairs, graphing them, and then connecting them to form the graph. Be sure and graph some negative values of x as well as some values greater than 2π.

    b. Describe how this graph is different from the graphs of other functions you've studied so far in this course.

MORE PRACTICE

For each angle measure, give an equivalent angle measure between 0° and 360°, and tell in which quadrant the terminal side lies.

22. 495°   **23.** $-\dfrac{213\pi}{2}$ **24.** 204.5°   **25.** 7.2π

A point on the terminal side of an angle of rotation is given. Give the sine, cosine, and tangent of each angle.

26. $(3, 4)$ **27.** $(-8, -6)$ **28.** $(12, -5)$ **29.** $(8, 15)$

30. Nonvisual Instructions A visually impaired student loves to dance and wants to take ballet. Describe how the ballet teacher could use extended angles to help describe arm movements to teach the student.

Give the value of each trigonometric ratio.

31. $\sin 60°$ **32.** $\tan 30°$ **33.** $\cos 45°$

34. $\sin \dfrac{2\pi}{3}$ **35.** $\tan 210°$ **36.** $\sec 150°$

37. $\cot 330°$ **38.** $\cos \dfrac{5\pi}{4}$ **39.** $\csc 240°$

40. What Time Is It? Write expressions for the positions of the minute and hour hands on a clock, t hours after noon. Measure angles clockwise from 12 o'clock. When is the first time after noon when the minute hand and hour hand of the clock will be in the same position? Give the time to the nearest tenth of a second.

MORE MATH REASONING

Give two solutions of each equation between 0 and 2π.

41. $\cos x = \dfrac{1}{2}$ **42.** $\sin x = -\dfrac{1}{\sqrt{2}}$ **43.** $\cos x = -\dfrac{\sqrt{3}}{2}$

44. Angle Sums and Differences The following formulas relate the sine and cosine for two angle measures and their sum or difference.

$\sin (a + b) = \sin a \cos b + \cos a \sin b$ $\sin (a - b) = \sin a \cos b - \cos a \sin b$

$\cos (a + b) = \cos a \cos b - \sin a \sin b$ $\cos (a - b) = \cos a \cos b + \sin a \sin b$

    a. Give the exact value of the sine and cosine for angle measures of 75° and 105°.

    b. Let $a = b = 15°$. Use the formula for $\cos (a + b)$ along with the fact that $\sin^2 \theta + \cos^2 \theta = 1$ for any θ to find $\sin 15°$ and $\cos 15°$.

←CONNECT→ *You have studied radian measure and how it is used to find arc lengths and sector areas. You've also calculated and used trigonometric values for angles with terminal sides in any quadrant.*

Geometry means *earth measurement,* and for centuries plane geometry was adequate for measuring small regions on the earth. However, as people began to travel greater distances, they found that plane geometry was not always sufficient. The development of spherical geometry and trigonometry provided a basis for accurate measurement and navigation on the earth.

EXPLORE: SPHERICAL TRIANGLES

London, England, is located at latitude 51.5° N and longitude 0° (the prime meridian). New Orleans, Louisiana, is located at latitude 30° N and longitude 90° W. These cities, along with the North Pole, form a *spherical triangle* by connecting each pair of sites with the arc of a great circle.

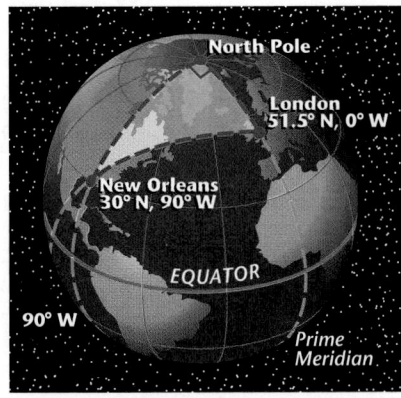

Because the longitudes of London and New Orleans differ by 90°, the angle of the spherical triangle formed at the North Pole is 90°. Can we use the Pythagorean Theorem on this *spherical right triangle* to find the distance from London to New Orleans?

1. The latitude of the North Pole is 90° N. Find the radian measure of the central angle of the arc from the North Pole to each city. Then find the length of the arc from the North Pole to each city. (Recall that the radius of the earth is about 3960 miles.)
   a. London   **b.** New Orleans
2. The arcs from the North Pole to London and to New Orleans are the *legs* of the spherical right triangle. If the Pythagorean Theorem applies to spherical right triangles, what is the distance from London to New Orleans?
3. The measure of the central angle (C) formed by radii from two points on the earth's surface to the center of the earth can be calculated using the following formula, where a and b are the latitudes of the two points and L is the difference of the longitudes of the points.

$$\cos C = (\sin a \sin b) + (\cos a \cos b \cos L)$$

   Use the formula to find the measure of the central angle of the arc between London and New Orleans. Then find the distance from London to New Orleans.
4. Compare the distances you found in Steps 2 and 3. Do you think the Pythagorean Theorem applies to spherical right triangles? Explain.

1. How can trigonometry help you measure the heights of tall objects that are inconvenient to measure directly?
2. Describe a situation where radian measure might be a more convenient choice than degree measure.
3. If you know the sine and cosine of an angle, how can you find the other trigonometric ratios?

Self-Assessment

Choose the letter of the correct answer.

1. Convert 90° to radians.
   (a) π (b) $\frac{\pi}{2}$ (c) 2π (d) $\frac{\pi}{4}$

2. Give the length of the arc of a 12-in. radius circle intersected by a central angle of $\frac{\pi}{6}$.
   (a) 2π in.   (b) 360 in.   (c) 24 in.   (d) 4π in.

3. An angle of $\frac{4\pi}{3}$ is equal to one of
   (a) 240°   (b) 135°   (c) 480°   (d) 120°   (e) not here

4. **Go Fly a Kite!** Jasper is flying a kite. After a while, he decides to put a second kite into the air, so he ties the first kite to a stake on the ground. If the first kite is on a 250-foot string and the string makes a 75° angle with the ground, how high is the first kite above the ground?

5. Rita stands 100 meters from a tree and finds that the angle of elevation to the top of the tree is 30°. Give the height of the tree.

6. How many radians does the hour hand of a clock rotate in one day?

7. A pie has a radius of 9 cm. Give the area of a slice of pie with a central angle of measure $\frac{\pi}{5}$.

8. **Circles of Latitude** The radius of the earth at the equator is 3960 miles, but other radii of circles of latitude are less, as shown.
   a. Explain why $m\angle CLA = \theta$.
   b. Let r represent the radius of circle of latitude θ. Write an equation relating $\cos\theta$ and r. Solve the equation for r.
   c. Indianapolis is located at 39.7° N, 86.2° W. Denver is located at 39.7° N, 105.0° W. Give the radius of the circle of latitude where both cities lie.
   d. Give the arc distance on this circle between Indianapolis and Denver.
   e. Use the method in the Explore on page 706 to find the actual distance (along a great circle) between Indianapolis and Denver. How does this distance compare to the distance along the circle of latitude?

Social Science

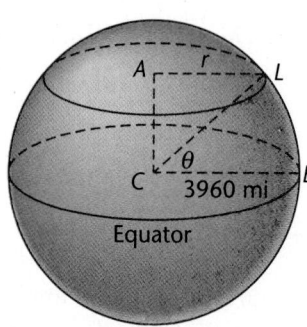

9. In a vacuum, a ray of light hits a piece of crown glass at
a 30° angle and is refracted (bent). The mathematics
of this phenomena is described in Snell's Law:
$n_1 \sin i = n_2 \sin r$, where $n_1 = 1$ (index of refraction
in a vacuum), i represents the angle of incidence,
$n_2 = 1.52$ (index of refraction of crown glass), and r
represents the angle of refraction in crown glass. Apply
Snell's Law to determine the angle of refraction.

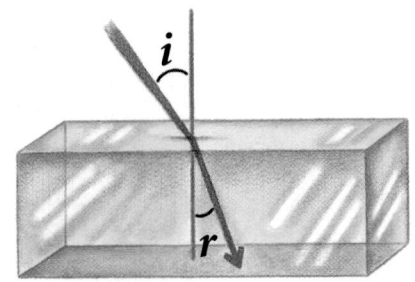

10. A car with 30-in.-diameter tires is traveling 60 mi/hr. Give the angular speed of
the tires, in revolutions per second.

11. A circular gear with a radius of 22 mm revolves 8 times per second.
  a. Give the angular speed of the gear.
  b. Give the linear speed of a point on the edge of the gear.

Give the value of each trigonometric ratio.

12. $\tan 45°$ **13.** $\sin \dfrac{5\pi}{6}$ **14.** $\cos (-390°)$ **15.** $\sin 270°$

16. $f(x) = 3x + 4$ and $g(x) = \dfrac{x - 4}{3}$. Give $(f \circ g)(x)$. [7-3]

17. Two resistors are connected in parallel. Their resistances are 8 ohms and 15 ohms.
Use the equation $\dfrac{1}{r} = \dfrac{1}{8} + \dfrac{1}{15}$ to find the resistance of the combination. [8-3]

18. Solve for x: $\log_2 (x^2 - 4) = 5$. [9-2]

19. A *triangle* created from three great circles drawn on the surface of a
sphere is a *spherical triangle*. The sum of the measures of its angles,
unlike that of a plane triangle, is greater than 180°.
  a. Give the sum of the measures of the angles of the spherical
    triangle in the earth's northern hemisphere formed by the
    equator, the prime meridian, and the 45° E line of longitude.
  b. The area of a spherical triangle with radian angle measures A,
    B, and C is given by $(A + B + C - \pi)r^2$, where r is the radius
    of the sphere. Give the area of the spherical triangle in **a.**

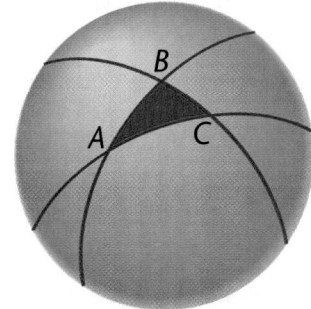

20. Drawing Circles Each side of a regular pentagon is 25 centimeters long.
  a. Find the radius of a circle circumscribed around the pentagon.
  b. Find the radius of a circle inscribed in the pentagon.

21. The Girth of the Earth The following describes an ancient way to
calculate the radius of the earth. Suppose a mountain is 3 miles high
and the angle between the horizon and the top of the mountain is
87.77°. Write an equation for the sine of the angle. Use this equation
to find the radius of the earth.

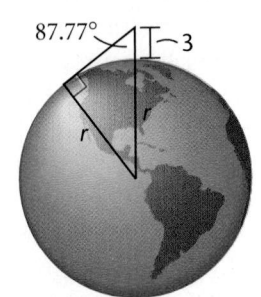

22. If an explorer at the North Pole walked 1 mile south, 1 mile east, and
1 mile north, the explorer would be back at the starting point. There
are an infinite number of points near the South Pole with the same
property—walk 1 mile south, 1 mile east, and 1 mile north, and you
will be back where you started. Where are they?

10-2 Laws of Cosines and Sines

SURVEYING THE SCENE

Ever since the concept of land ownership began, humans have needed to accurately measure the side lengths and areas of plots of land. From ancient Babylon and Egypt to the present day, surveyors have used mathematics to find measurements that are otherwise impractical or impossible to measure directly.

Before mathematics can be used to calculate indirect measurements, some measures must be made directly. The earliest surveyors used measuring ropes to find distances; steel measuring tapes are still used today. However, the *Electronic Distance Measurement* (EDM) system, which measures the time it takes for laser light to travel from a transmitter to a receiver and back, is now more commonly used to find distances. To measure angles, surveyors use a *theodolite* or a *transit*. Both of these instruments measure the angle of rotation of a telescope as it moves from one sight line to another. Modern surveying stations contain both an EDM system and a theodolite.

One mathematical technique frequently used by surveyors is called *triangulation*. In this method, a set of points on the perimeter of a plot of land is used to divide the plot into a series of triangles. Each triangle shares at least one side with the adjacent triangles. The length of one side, called the *baseline*, is measured,

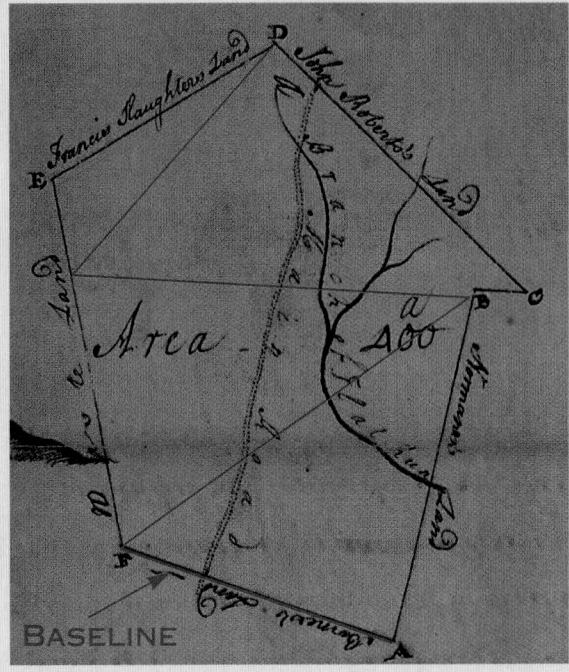

Compass traverse made by George Washington at age 17

and the measures of all of the angles in the triangles are found.

By applying a trigonometric rule called the Law of Sines, the lengths of all other sides of the triangles can be found. The area of each triangle can then be calculated mathematically. You will soon discover the formulas that solve these problems and then learn how to use them.

?

1. Give some examples of measurements that would be impractical or impossible to measure directly.
2. Why might it be helpful to divide a plot of land into triangular regions before finding its area?

3. What are some advantages of using an EDM system to measure a distance instead of a measuring tape? Are there situations where the measuring tape might be more convenient to use? Explain.

Law of Cosines

← CONNECT → *You have learned about right triangle trigonometry. Now you will extend trigonometry to cover acute and obtuse triangles. You will see how the Law of Cosines can be used to find side lengths and angle measures.*

You've used trigonometry to solve for side lengths and angle measures in right triangles. Of course, not all triangles are right triangles. By using the Law of Cosines and the Law of Sines (which you will see in 10-2B), you can apply trigonometry to investigate acute and obtuse triangles.

LAW OF COSINES

For any $\triangle ABC$, $c^2 = a^2 + b^2 - 2ab \cos C$.

The Law of Cosines involves three side lengths and the measure of one angle. Note that side c and angle C are opposite each other in the Law of Cosines, just as they are in a triangle.

If you know the lengths of two sides of a triangle and the measure of the included angle, you can use the Law of Cosines to find the length of the third side.

EXAMPLE

1. In $\triangle RST$, $r = 20.4$, $s = 16.4$, and $m\angle T = 128°$. Find t, rounding your answer to the nearest tenth.

Using the Law of Cosines for $\triangle RST$,

$t^2 = r^2 + s^2 - 2rs \cos T$

$t^2 = 20.4^2 + 16.4^2 - 2(20.4)(16.4) \cos 128°$

$t^2 \approx 20.4^2 + 16.4^2 - 2(20.4)(16.4)(-0.6157)$

$t^2 \approx 416.16 + 268.96 - (-411.95)$

$t^2 \approx 1097.07$

$t \approx 33.1$ Remember to take the square root.

CONSIDER

?

1. The Law of Cosines may look familiar. What happens to the Law of Cosines if the angle used is a right angle? Explain.

If the side lengths of all three sides of a triangle are known, you can use the Law of Cosines to find the measure of an angle.

EXAMPLE

2. In $\triangle ABC$, find $m\angle B$. Round your answer to the nearest tenth of a degree.

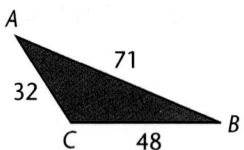

Since you are looking for $\angle B$, use the form of the Law of Cosines that involves $\cos B$.

$$b^2 = a^2 + c^2 - 2ac(\cos B)$$

Solve the formula for $\cos B$.

$$\cos B = \frac{a^2 + c^2 - b^2}{2ac}$$

$$\cos B = \frac{48^2 + 71^2 - 32^2}{2(48)(71)}$$

$$\cos B \approx 0.9274$$

$$m\angle B \approx 22.0°$$ Use your calculator to find the inverse cosine.

TRY IT

a. In $\triangle DEF$, $d = 15.8$, $e = 22.5$, and $m\angle F = 49°$. Find f. Round your answer to the nearest tenth.

b. In $\triangle DEF$, $d = 10$, $e = 12$, and $f = 20$. Find $m\angle F$. Round your answer to the nearest tenth of a degree.

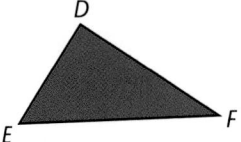

Trigonometry can be used to solve problems that involve forces, velocities, and other quantities that can be characterized both by a number or *magnitude* and a *direction*. For instance, to fully describe the flight of an airplane, you must state its speed and its direction. Such quantities are called **vectors.**

Vectors are often represented by arrows. The length of the arrow shows the magnitude of the vector. The vector $\overrightarrow{MN}$ points from its *origin* to its *endpoint*. A vector can be named using its endpoints or with a single letter. Absolute value bars are used to denote the magnitude of a vector.

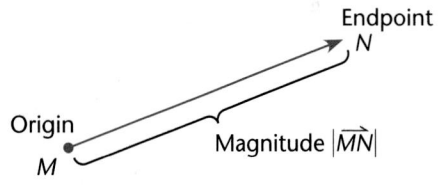

When two or more vectors act on the same object, we can add the vectors to find the **resultant vector.** To add two vectors, move one of them parallel to itself so that its origin is at the endpoint of the other. Notice that the vector that you move retains its length and direction.

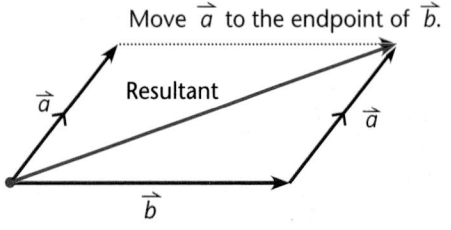

As you can see, the diagram showing the addition of two vectors involves a triangle. These triangles can be analyzed by using trigonometry. In the Explore, you will use the Law of Cosines to investigate a vector sum.

EXPLORE: WHICH WAY DID WE GO?

MATERIALS

Ruler
Protractor

You are the pilot of an airplane that is flying due east at a speed of 390 mi/hr. Suddenly, you enter the jet stream, an 80-mi/hr wind, whose direction is 70° to the north of due east, as shown.

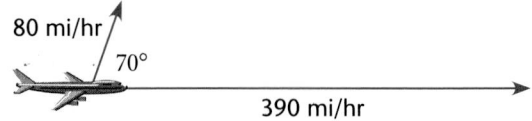

1. Use your protractor and ruler to sketch a diagram to represent the sum of the airplane velocity vector and the wind velocity vector. Use an appropriate scale to represent the lengths of the vectors. Be sure to draw the resultant vector in your sketch.

2. What is the measure of the angle opposite the resultant vector? How do you know? (Hint: If two lines are parallel, what is true about interior angles on the same side of a transversal?)

3. Use the Law of Cosines to find the magnitude of the vector sum. What is the real-world meaning of this number?

4. What is the measure of the angle that the actual path of the plane makes with respect to due east? Explain how you found this angle measure.

5. Briefly summarize how you can use the Law of Cosines to find the magnitude of the resultant vector for the sum of two vectors.

EXAMPLE

3. Elaine and Yumiko are pulling down an old fence post. Elaine pulls with a force of 73 lb, Yumiko pulls with a force of 80 lb, and the angle between their ropes is 40°. Find the resultant force on the rope and the angle that the resultant force makes with Yumiko's direction of pull. Round your answers to the nearest tenth of a pound and the nearest degree.

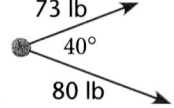

First, we sketch the vector sum. Since we will want to find the angle that the resultant vector makes with Yumiko's direction, we "move" Elaine's force vector. The 73-lb vector is moved parallel to itself, so the measure of the angle opposite the resultant vector is 180° − 40° = 140°.

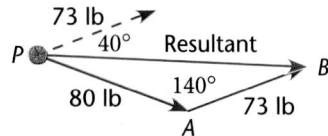

To find the magnitude of the resultant force, we use the Law of Cosines.

$|\overrightarrow{PB}|^2 = 80^2 + 73^2 - 2(80)(73)(\cos 140°)$

$|\overrightarrow{PB}|^2 \approx 6400 + 5329 - 11680(-0.7660)$

$|\overrightarrow{PB}|^2 \approx 20676.40$

$|\overrightarrow{PB}| \approx 143.8$

The resultant force (the net force on the rope) is about 143.8 lb.

We use the Law of Cosines again to find the angle measure.

$73^2 \approx 80^2 + 143.8^2 - 2(80)(143.8) \cos \angle BPA$

$0.9453 \approx \cos \angle BPA$

$19° \approx m\angle BPA$

The resultant force makes an angle of about 19° with Yumiko's pull.

CONSIDER

?

2. In Example 3, vectors with forces of 80 lb and 73 lb were added. The resultant force was about 143.8 lb. Explain why the resultant force was not 153 lb.

3. In Example 3, what angle between the force vectors would give the maximum resultant force? What would that force be? What angle would give the minimum force, and what would that force be? Explain your answers.

The Law of Cosines can be used in any triangle where all three side lengths or the lengths of two sides and the measure of the included angle are known. When two vectors are added, the Law of Cosines can be applied to find the resultant vector.

REFLECT

1. In $\triangle ABC$, how does length c compare to $\sqrt{a^2 + b^2}$ when:
a. $\angle C$ is acute?　　　**b.** $\angle C$ is obtuse?　　　**c.** $\angle C$ is a right angle?
2. When trying to find the magnitude of the resultant of two forces, why is the direction of the forces important?

Exercises

CORE

1. Getting Started Follow the steps and use the Law of Cosines to find side length a in $\triangle ABC$, if $m\angle A = 65°$, $b = 24$, and $c = 15$.
a. Write the Law of Cosines so that a^2 is isolated.
b. Substitute $b = 24$, $c = 15$, and $\cos A = \cos 65°$ into the Law of Cosines. Use your calculator to find an approximation for $\cos 65°$.
c. Simplify the resulting expression. Solve for a by taking the positive square root.

Determine whether each statement is true or false. If the statement is false, change the underlined word or phrase to make it true.

2. In any $\triangle ABC$, $\underline{a^2 + b^2 = c^2}$.

3. The Law of Cosines can be used to find an unknown <u>side length or angle measure</u>.

4. The <u>direction</u> of a vector is called its magnitude.

5. When two forces are exerted on the same object, the magnitude of the resultant force <u>is not necessarily</u> the sum of the magnitudes of the two individual forces.

Find each indicated side length for $\triangle ABC$. Where necessary, round answers to the nearest tenth.

6. $m\angle A = 18°$, $b = 20$, $c = 28$. Find a.

7. $a = 5.8$, $m\angle B = 53°$, $c = 3.5$. Find b.

8. $a = 85$, $b = 67$, $m\angle C = 117°$. Find c.

9. $m\angle A = 130°$, $b = 7.3$, $c = 6.1$. Find a.

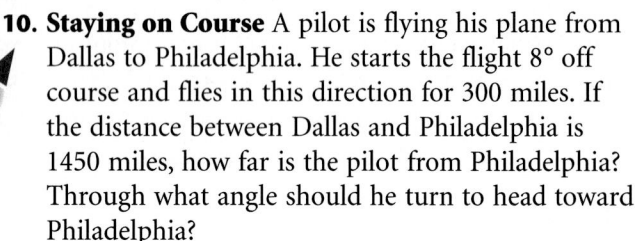

10. Staying on Course A pilot is flying his plane from Dallas to Philadelphia. He starts the flight 8° off course and flies in this direction for 300 miles. If the distance between Dallas and Philadelphia is 1450 miles, how far is the pilot from Philadelphia? Through what angle should he turn to head toward Philadelphia?

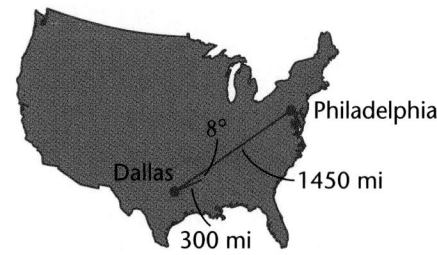

11. Betty is piloting her remote-controlled boat across an east-west stream. In still water, the boat travels 45 meters per minute. The stream has a current of 6 meters per minute heading directly to the east.
  a. Find the actual speed of the boat if Betty steers it directly north as shown. Explain how you found this speed.
  b. Find the actual speed of the boat if Betty steers it 33° east of due north. Compare your answer and the method you used to find it to those in **a.** Explain any differences.

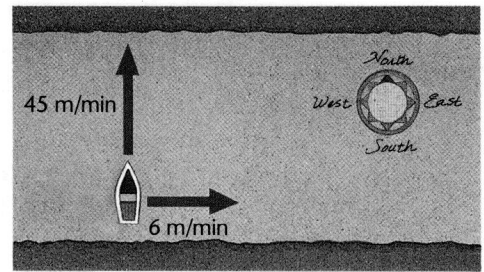

Find each indicated angle measure for $\triangle XYZ$. Where necessary, round answers to the nearest tenth of a degree.

12. $x = 57$, $y = 84$, $z = 71$. Find $m\angle X$.

13. $x = 8.7$, $y = 11.2$, $z = 14.3$. Find $m\angle X$.

14. $x = 70$, $y = 50$, $z = 90$. Find $m\angle Y$.

15. $x = 5$, $y = 12$, $z = 13$. Find $m\angle Z$.

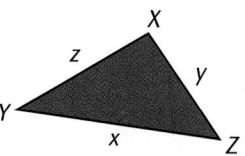

16. Halfback Option Pass A football quarterback laterals the ball to the halfback, 8 yards away. The halfback then passes the ball downfield 25 yards to a wide receiver, who is immediately tackled. The net gain on the play is 18 yards. What was the angle from the quarterback to the halfback to the wide receiver?

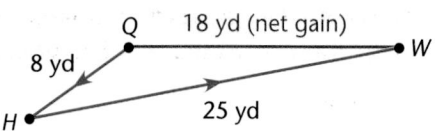

17. Three circles are externally tangent, as shown. If their respective radii are 5 cm, 7 cm, and 10 cm, find the measures of the three angles of the triangle that is formed by joining their centers.

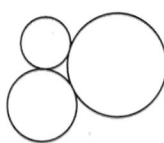

18. I Saw It First! Sal and Al are at a discount sale, fighting over a stylish necktie that is hanging on a rack. Sal pulls with a force of 102 lb and Al pulls with a force of 120 lb. If the angle between their forces is 48°, find the magnitude of the resultant force on the tie.

LOOK BACK

19. Solve the system of linear equations: [3-1]

$$3x - 6y = 6$$
$$-6x + 8y = 24$$

a. by graphing   **b.** algebraically

Solve each equation. Where necessary, round answers to the nearest hundredth. [9-2]

20. $\log_3 x = 2$ **21.** $\log_x 9 = \frac{1}{2}$ **22.** $\log 1000 = x$ **23.** $\log_2 x = -4$

24. Which of the radian measures gives the same terminal side as 75°? [10-1]

I. $\frac{12\pi}{5}$ II. $\frac{5\pi}{12}$ III. $-\frac{19\pi}{12}$

(a) only I   (b) only II   (c) only III   (d) II and III   (e) I, II, and III

MORE PRACTICE

Find each indicated side length for △WXY. Where necessary, round answers to the nearest tenth.

25. $m\angle W = 64°$, $x = 4.7$, $y = 8.1$. Find w.

26. $w = 45$, $m\angle X = 94°$, $y = 55$. Find x.

27. $m\angle W = 125°$, $x = 42$, $y = 42$. Find w.

28. $w = 2.7$, $x = 3.8$, $m\angle Y = 45°$. Find y.

29. $w = 10$, $m\angle X = 55°$, $y = 15$. Find x.

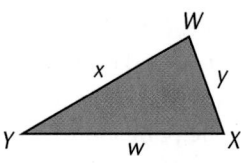

30. On the Diagonal The lengths of two sides of a parallelogram are 10 inches and 15 inches, and one angle of the parallelogram measures 35°. Find the lengths of the diagonals of the parallelogram.

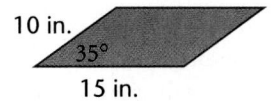

10 in.
35°
15 in.

31. Leticia's flight from El Paso to Washington, D.C., had a stopover in New Orleans. The distance from El Paso to New Orleans is 980 miles and the distance from New Orleans to Washington, D.C., is 970 miles. If the angle between the two flight paths is 125°, what is the length of a direct flight from El Paso to Washington, D.C.? Round your answer to the nearest ten miles.

New Orleans
El Paso   Washington, D.C.

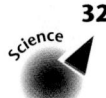

32. The speed of an airplane in still air is 520 km/hr. There is a 105-km/hr wind slowing the plane, blowing at an angle of 137° with respect to the path of the plane. What is the speed of the plane in the wind?

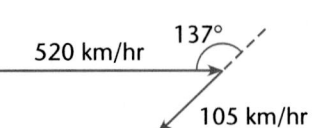

137°
520 km/hr
105 km/hr

Find each indicated angle measure for △ABC. Where necessary, round answers to the nearest tenth of a degree.

33. $a = 7$, $b = 8$, $c = 5$. Find $m\angle A$.

34. $a = 89$, $b = 62$, $c = 73$. Find $m\angle A$.

35. $a = 8$, $b = 15$, $c = 17$. Find $m\angle C$.

36. $a = 5.9$, $b = 8.3$, $c = 10.4$. Find $m\angle B$.

37. $a = 16.7$, $b = 29.5$, $c = 37.2$. Find $m\angle C$.

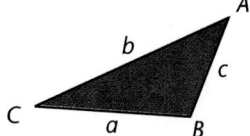

A
b
c
C
a   B

MORE MATH REASONING

38. △ABC is superimposed on a coordinate system, as shown. By the distance formula, $c^2 = (x - a)^2 + y^2$.

Find an expression for x in terms of $\cos C$ and for y in terms of $\sin C$. By substituting these expressions into the equation above, derive the Law of Cosines. (Hint: You will need to use the fact that $\sin^2 C + \cos^2 C = 1$.)

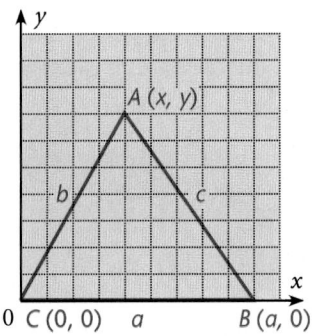

y
A (x, y)
b   c
x
0 C (0, 0)   a   B (a, 0)

39. Course Correction A pilot wants to fly due west at a speed of 400 mi/hr. There is a 70-mi/hr wind 40° south of due west. Find the airplane speed and direction that the pilot should maintain so that the plane travels at the desired speed and direction.

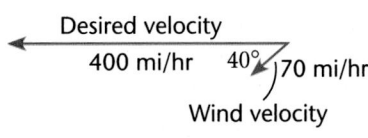

Desired velocity
400 mi/hr   40° 70 mi/hr
Wind velocity

← **CONNECT** → *You have used the Law of Cosines to find side lengths and angle measures in triangles. Now you will investigate the Law of Sines.*

You've seen that you can use the Law of Cosines to solve for the measure of an angle in a triangle if you know the lengths of all three sides. To solve for a side length, you need to know the lengths of two of the sides and the measure of the included angle.

If you know two angle measures and the length of only one side, you need another law to find measurements in triangles. In the Explore, you will discover the Law of Sines and see how it can be applied to solve a problem.

EXPLORE: SIGNS OF A METEOR

The Barringer Crater, near Winslow, Arizona, is approximately 30,000 years old. The meteorite that produced it is estimated to have weighed over 110,000 tons.

Suppose you are a surveyor interested in finding the diameter of the Barringer Crater. As shown in the figure, you have identified landmarks at points *A*, *B*, and *C*. You need to find *b*, the distance across the crater.

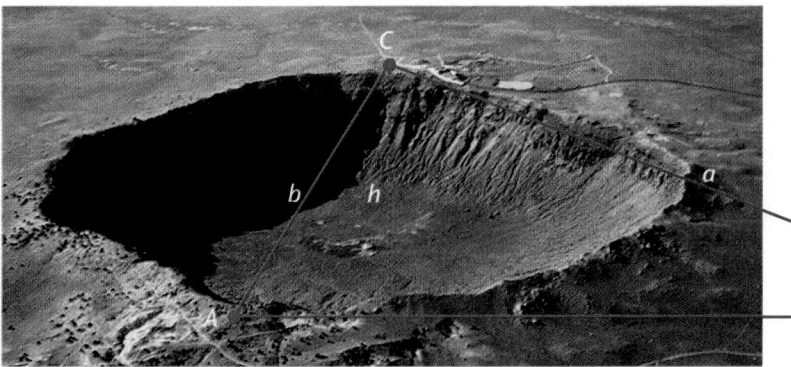

1. Use the sine ratio to write an expression for *h* using *m*∠*A* and a different expression for *h* using ∠*B*. Since both of these expressions are equal to *h*, they are equal to each other. Write one equation with the expressions involving ∠*A* and ∠*B*.
2. Rewrite the equation you found in Step 1 as a proportion by dividing both sides by (sin *A*)(sin *B*). Describe this proportion in words.
3. Using your surveying instruments, you determine that *m*∠*A* = 60° and *m*∠*B* = 51°. You also find that *a* = 2.4 km. Use your equation from Step 2 to find the diameter of the Barringer Crater, to the nearest tenth of a kilometer. Explain how you solved this problem.

In the Explore, you discovered a proportion involving the sines of two angles in a triangle. The Law of Sines generalizes that conclusion to include the third angle.

LAW OF SINES

In any $\triangle ABC$, $\dfrac{a}{\sin A} = \dfrac{b}{\sin B} = \dfrac{c}{\sin C}$.

When using the Law of Sines, you can write a proportion involving any two of the three equal ratios shown.

If one side length and two angle measures of a triangle are known, you can use the Law of Sines to find the length of a second side.

EXAMPLE

1. In $\triangle XYZ$, $z = 17$, $m\angle Y = 119°$, and $m\angle Z = 21°$. Find y. Round your answer to the nearest tenth.

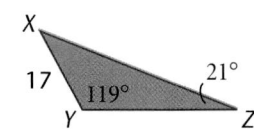

$$\dfrac{z}{\sin Z} = \dfrac{y}{\sin Y}$$ Use the appropriate proportion.

$$\dfrac{17}{\sin 21°} = \dfrac{y}{\sin 119°}$$

$$y = \dfrac{17(\sin 119°)}{\sin 21°}$$ Solve for y.

$$y \approx 41.5$$

CONSIDER

?

1. In Example 1, how could you have used the Law of Sines to find x? What would you need to determine first? How would you do this?

TRY IT

Find each indicated value in $\triangle ABC$ using the given information. Round your answers to the nearest tenth.

a. $m\angle A = 72°$, $m\angle B = 43°$, $a = 28$. Find b.
b. $m\angle B = 98°$, $m\angle C = 40°$, $b = 15$. Find c.

Recall that if two triangles have three pairs of congruent sides, the triangles are congruent by the Side-Side-Side Congruence Postulate (SSS). Triangles can be proved congruent by SSS, SAS, ASA, and AAS.

From the SSS postulate, we know that *all* triangles with three given side measures must have the same angle measures. In other words, given SSS information, we can find the measures of the three other parts of the triangle. This is also true for the SAS, ASA, and AAS patterns.

Given SSS, SAS, ASA, or AAS information for a triangle, you can use the Law of Cosines, the Law of Sines, and the fact that the sum of the angle measures in a triangle is 180° to find the measures of the other three parts of the triangle.

EXAMPLE

2. A triangular plot of land has side lengths of 31.8 m and 58.6 m. The measure of their included angle is 70.4°. Find the length of the third side and the measures of the two other angles. Round your answers to the nearest tenth.

Begin by sketching the situation and adding labels to the sketch.

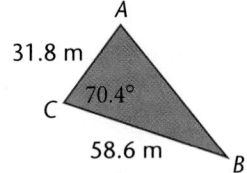

> **Problem-Solving Tip**
>
> Analyze the given information.

Since we know the lengths of two sides and their included angle, we can use the Law of Cosines to find the length of the third side.

$$c^2 = 31.8^2 + 58.6^2 - 2(31.8)(58.6)(\cos 70.4°)$$

$$c^2 \approx 1011.24 + 3433.96 - 2(31.8)(58.6)(0.3355)$$

$$c^2 \approx 3194.80$$

$$c \approx 56.5$$

We now know all of the side lengths and one angle measure. We will use the Law of Cosines to solve for $m\angle A$.

$$a^2 = b^2 + c^2 - 2bc(\cos A)$$

$$\cos A = \frac{b^2 + c^2 - a^2}{2bc} \qquad \text{Solve the formula for } \cos A.$$

$$\cos A = \frac{31.8^2 + 56.5^2 - 58.6^2}{2(31.8)(56.5)}$$

$\cos A \approx 0.2142$ Since the cosine of the angle is positive, the angle must be acute.

$m\angle A \approx 77.6°$ Use your calculator to find the inverse cosine.

Once we have the measures of two of the angles, the measure of the third angle can be found by subtracting from 180°.

$$m\angle B \approx 180° - 70.4° - 77.6 = 32.0°$$

To check our work, we make sure that the shortest side is opposite the smallest angle and the longest side is opposite the largest angle.

The smallest angle, $\angle B$, measuring 32°, is opposite the shortest side (31.8 m). The largest angle, $\angle A$, measuring 77.6°, is opposite the longest side (58.6 m). Our answers make sense.

TRY IT

c. In $\triangle DEF$, $m\angle D = 22°$, $m\angle E = 84°$, and $f = 15.2$. Find $m\angle F$, d, and e. Round your answers to the nearest tenth.

d. In $\triangle GHK$, $m\angle G = 38°$, $m\angle H = 103°$, and $h = 39.7$. Find $m\angle K$, g, and k. Round your answers to the nearest tenth.

You are familiar with the triangle area formula $A = \frac{1}{2}bh$, where b is the length of the base of a triangle and h is the length of the altitude to the base. However, there are other formulas for the area of a triangle. The following formula allows you to find the area of a triangle if you know the length of two sides and the measure of their included angle.

> For any $\triangle XYZ$, $A = \frac{1}{2}xy \sin Z$.

Heron's (or Hero's) Formula can be used to find the area of a triangle if you know the lengths of its sides.

> **HERON'S FORMULA**
>
> For any $\triangle XYZ$, $A = \sqrt{s(s - x)(s - y)(s - z)}$, where s equals half of the perimeter (the *semiperimeter*) of the triangle.

EXAMPLES

In $\triangle FGH$, $f = 7$, $g = 10$, $h = 15$, and $m\angle H = 123°$.

3. Use the trigonometric area formula to find the area of $\triangle FGH$ to the nearest tenth.

We know lengths f and g and the measure of the included angle, $\angle H$.

$$\begin{aligned} A &= \frac{1}{2}fg \sin H \\ &= \frac{1}{2}(7)(10) \sin 123° \\ &\approx 29.4 \end{aligned}$$

4. Use Heron's Formula to find the area of $\triangle FGH$ to the nearest tenth.

The semiperimeter $s = \frac{1}{2}(7 + 10 + 15) = 16$.

$$\begin{aligned} A &= \sqrt{s(s - f)(s - g)(s - h)} \\ &= \sqrt{16(16 - 7)(16 - 10)(16 - 15)} \\ &= \sqrt{864} \\ &\approx 29.4 \end{aligned}$$

Find each area. Round your answers to the nearest tenth.

e. $x = 5$, $y = 11$, and $z = 13$. Find the area of $\triangle XYZ$.
f. $m\angle D = 73°$, $e = 17.5$, and $f = 23.2$. Find the area of $\triangle DEF$.

When finding measures of unknown parts in a triangle, it is helpful to remember that the Law of Cosines can be used only when you know the lengths of three sides (SSS) or the lengths of two sides and the measure of the included angle (SAS). When you are given ASA or AAS information, you must use the Law of Sines to find the length of a second side.

REFLECT

1. When solving for a side length in a triangle, how do you decide whether to use the Law of Sines or the Law of Cosines?
2. Suppose you are given AAS information for a triangle. Explain how you would find the lengths of the two other sides and the measure of the third angle.
3. If you know that the cosine of one angle of a triangle is positive, can you tell whether the angle is acute or obtuse? Explain. If you know that the sine is positive, can you tell whether the angle is acute or obtuse? Why or why not?

Exercises

CORE

1. Getting Started Write the three ratios for $\triangle FGH$ that are equal by the Law of Sines.

Find each indicated side length for $\triangle RST$. Where necessary, round answers to the nearest tenth.

2. $m\angle R = 35°$, $m\angle S = 72°$, $r = 11$. Find s.

3. $m\angle S = 128°$, $m\angle T = 17°$, $r = 35$. Find t.

4. $m\angle R = 45°$, $m\angle T = 55°$, $r = 7.9$. Find t.

5. $m\angle S = 79°$, $m\angle T = 37°$, $r = 152$. Find s.

6. $m\angle R = 101°$, $m\angle S = 56°$, $t = 2.9$. Find r.

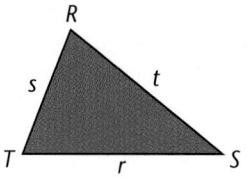

7. Getting a Better Altitude Two surveyors are measuring the height of a mountain. Thea finds that the angle of elevation to the top of the mountain is 37°. Ed, who is 900 m closer to the mountain, finds that the angle of elevation is 43°. Find the height of the mountain and describe your method.

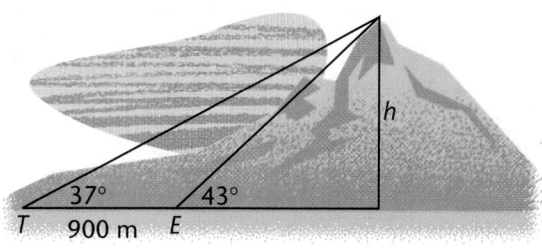

Find each area. Round answers to the nearest tenth.

8. $a = 4$, $b = 5$, and $c = 8$. Find the area of $\triangle ABC$.

9. $m\angle M = 73°$, $n = 12.4$, and $p = 8.7$. Find the area of $\triangle MNP$.

10. $d = 105$, $e = 228$, and $f = 331$. Find the area of $\triangle DEF$.

11. $m\angle A = 101°$, $b = 47.5$, and $c = 88.6$. Find the area of $\triangle ABC$.

12. Treading Water The distance from Shore Haven to Lake's Edge is 28 km, $m\angle L = 59°$, and $m\angle S = 36°$.
  a. To the nearest kilometer, what is the distance from Point Ilisum to Shore Haven?
  b. What is the area of $\triangle PLS$? Round your answer to the nearest tenth of a square kilometer.

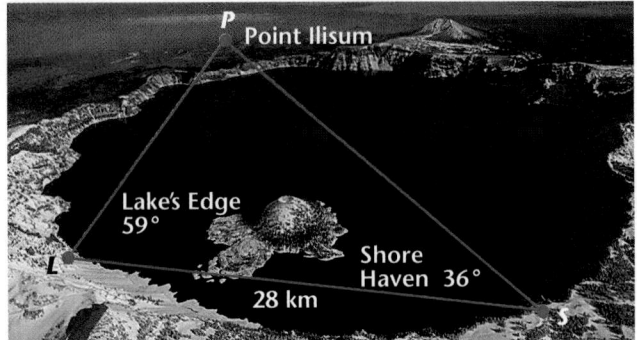

13. To the nearest hundredth, what is the area of a parallelogram whose sides are 20.8 cm and 10.9 cm long, if the measure of one of its angles is 53°? Explain how you solved this problem.

Find the missing measures for each $\triangle ABC$. Round answers to the nearest tenth.

	$m\angle A$	$m\angle B$	$m\angle C$	a	b	c	Area $\triangle ABC$
14.		70°	49°		9		
15.	82°		71°		5.7		
16.			115°	22	17		
17.				10.5	15.8	22.7	

18. Towering Tower A 40-foot tower is located on the top of a hill. A person observes that the angle of elevation to the top of the tower is 31° and the angle of elevation to the top of the hill is 26°. How far is the person from the bottom of the tower?

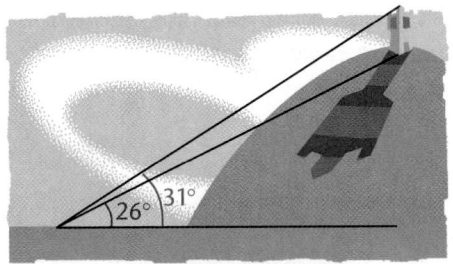

19. The painting *Across* by Kenneth Noland is on a 2.46-m by 3.2-m canvas. Estimate the areas of the subregions. Explain your method of determining each area.

©1996 Kenneth Noland/
Licensed by VAGA, New York, NY

20. Caution! Ambiguity Ahead! Although it is possible to use the Law of Sines to find an angle measure, you must be careful when doing so.

   a. If $0° < \theta < 180°$, find *all* possible measures for θ if $\sin \theta = 0.5$.

   b. In $\triangle ABC$, $a = 10$, $b = 12$, and $m\angle A = 24°$. Use the Law of Sines to find *both* possible values of $m\angle B$. Explain why you cannot eliminate either possibility.

   c. Assume that $\angle B$ is acute. Find $m\angle C$ and c.

   d. Assume that $\angle B$ is obtuse. Find $m\angle C$ and c.

   e. In **b**, you were given SSA information about a triangle: the lengths of two sides, and the measure of an angle opposite one of the known sides. Sketch the triangles for your answers to **c** and **d**, including side lengths and angle measures, to show that there are *two* triangles where $a = 10$, $b = 12$, and $m\angle A = 24°$.

   f. Explain why there is no SSA congruence postulate for triangles.

   g. Suppose that in $\triangle ABC$, $a = 12$, $b = 10$, and $m\angle A = 24°$. Use the Law of Sines to find the *only* possible value of $m\angle B$. Explain why this situation differs from **b**.

 ## *LOOK AHEAD*

Graph each set of functions on the same set of axes.

21. $f(x) = x^2$ and $h(x) = -x^2$

22. $f(x) = x^2$, $g(x) = (x + 1)^2$, and $h(x) = (x + 1)^2 - 2$

23. $f(x) = x^2$, $g(x) = 3x^2$, and $h(x) = -3x^2$

24. Write a sequence of transformations that will produce the graph of $y = 2(x - 4)^2 + 3$ from the graph of $y = x^2$.

MORE PRACTICE

Find each indicated side length for $\triangle FGH$. Where necessary, round answers to the nearest tenth.

25. $m\angle F = 12°$, $m\angle G = 67°$, $f = 9.5$. Find g.

26. $m\angle G = 149°$, $m\angle H = 11°$, $h = 82$. Find g.

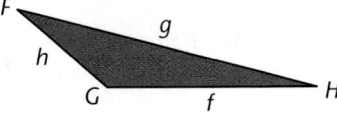

27. $m\angle F = 65°$, $m\angle H = 65°$, $g = 32$. Find f.

28. $m\angle G = 100°$, $m\angle H = 50°$, $g = 3.7$. Find h.

29. $m\angle G = 58°$, $m\angle H = 109°$, $f = 900$. Find h.

30. $m\angle F = 74°$, $m\angle G = 14°$, $f = 68$. Find g.

31. $m\angle F = 88°$, $m\angle H = 39°$, $g = 15$. Find f.

32. Going Around The length of one of the congruent sides of an isosceles triangle is 18 cm and the measure of the vertex angle is 40°. Find the perimeter.

33. Distances Apart A lighthouse is visible to two sailboats 310 m apart. Use the angle measures shown to find each sailboat's distance from the lighthouse.

34. A triangular target with sides 22 cm, 18 cm, and 12 cm is drawn on a square 40 cm on a side. If a dart strikes the square randomly, what is the probability that it lands inside the triangle?

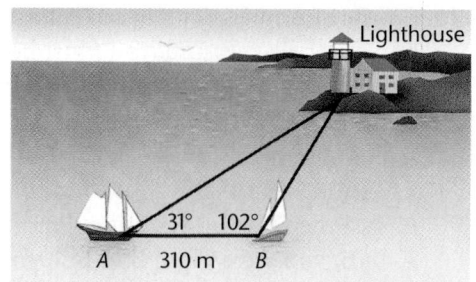
Lighthouse

31° 102°

A 310 m B

Find the missing measures for each △ABC. Round answers to the nearest tenth.

	$m\angle A$	$m\angle B$	$m\angle C$	a	b	c	Area △ABC
35.		17°	29°			8	
36.		60°	60°	1.9			
37.			133°	62.7	23.5		
38.	91°	62°			28		
39.				5.7	3.9	8.5	
40.		47°	51°	39			

History

41. The Taj Mahal in Delhi, India, was built by Shah Jahan in memory of his wife, Mumtaj-i-Mahal. There are four towers at the corners of the Taj Mahal. At a certain distance from one of the towers, the angle of elevation from the ground to the tower is 25°; 110 feet nearer the tower, the angle of elevation is 37.2°. Find the height of the tower to the nearest foot.

MORE MATH REASONING

42. In △ABC, if $m\angle A = x°$, $m\angle B = 2x°$, $m\angle C = 3x°$, and $b = 15$, find a.

43. Find the side lengths and angle measures for *all* possible triangles RST that satisfy each set of SSA information given.
   a. $m\angle S = 24°$, $r = 18$, and $s = 14$. Find $m\angle R$, $m\angle T$, and t.
   b. $m\angle S = 24°$, $r = 14$, and $s = 18$. Find $m\angle R$, $m\angle T$, and t.
   c. $m\angle S = 68°$, $r = 18$, and $s = 12$. Find $m\angle R$, $m\angle T$, and t.

44. a. Using the diagram shown, derive the trigonometric area formula for triangles. (Hint: Start with the geometric area formula.)
   b. Use the trigonometric area formula to write three different expressions for the area of the triangle. Using these expressions, derive the Law of Sines.

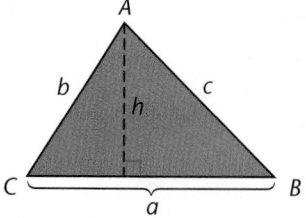
A
b
c
h
C
a
B

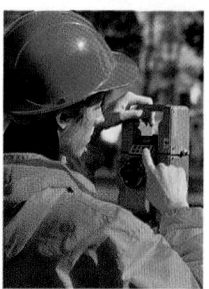

← C O N N E C T → *You have used the Laws of Cosines and Sines to find unknown measurements in acute and obtuse triangles. You have also seen how such measurement techniques are a vital part of practical problem solving.*

The Law of Cosines and the Law of Sines can be used to find triangle side lengths and angle measures indirectly. Surveyors can make use of these laws to measure the width of a river, the height of a mountain, or the dimensions of a plot of land.

Triangulation is a classic surveying technique. In the Explore, you will use triangulation to find the dimensions of a lot.

EXPLORE: LOTS OF LOTS

Mia Berger is a surveyor working on a subdivision of vacation home lots, some of which have lake frontage on Lake Lorentz. The lots are priced at $1.85 per square foot, with a premium of $20.00 for every linear foot of the property along the lake.

The Marlow family is considering buying the lakefront lot shown. They can afford to spend no more than $30,000.

Mia plans to use triangulation to find the measurements of the lot. She has established baseline $\overline{AB}$, found its length, and measured the angles as shown.

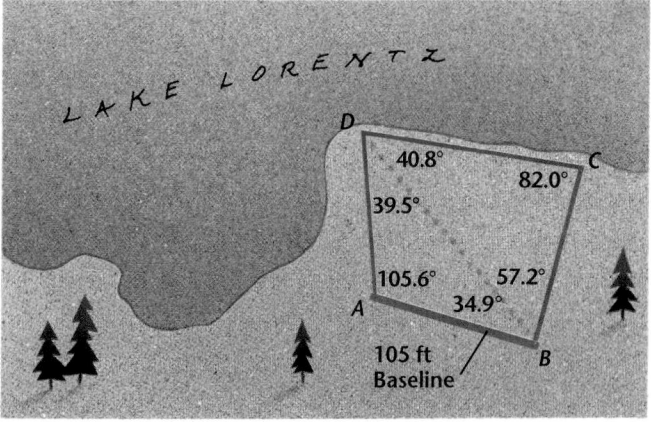

1. Using this information, find the lengths of all of the other sides shown in the figure, including lake frontage $\overline{CD}$. Explain how you found these dimensions.
2. Find the area of the lot. Describe how you found this area.
3. What is the price of the lot? Does it fit the Marlows' budget?
4. In using triangulation, what trigonometric law do you rely on to find the side lengths?
5. Another surveying technique is called *trilateration.* In trilateration, one initial direction is determined (like $m\angle A$), then all side lengths are measured. Explain how the measures of all other angles could be calculated from this information.

1. When you are given SSS, SAS, ASA, or AAS information about a triangle and you need to find the measures of the other parts, how do you decide which to use first: the Law of Cosines or the Law of Sines?
2. A plane whose speed in still air is 360 mi/hr flies in a 75-mi/hr wind. What is the range of possible speeds for the plane in this wind? Explain.
3. Give three different formulas for the area of a triangle. Describe the information you would need to be able to use each.

Self-Assessment

Find each indicated side length for △ABC. Where necessary, round answers to the nearest tenth.

1. $m\angle A = 37°$, $m\angle B = 59°$, $a = 15$. Find b.

2. $a = 124$, $m\angle B = 63°$, $c = 92$. Find b.

3. $m\angle A = 47°$, $m\angle B = 43°$, $c = 29$. Find a.

4. $a = 4.7$, $b = 6.9$, $m\angle C = 53°$. Find c.

5. $a = 142$, $m\angle B = 65°$, $m\angle C = 79°$. Find c.

6. $a = x$, $m\angle B = 60°$, $c = 2x$. Find b.

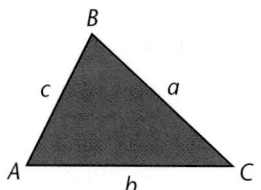

7. **Survey Says...** A surveyor needs to find the distance from point B to point C. The distance from A to B and the measures of $\angle A$ and $\angle B$ are shown. Find the distance from B to C.

8. Solve the system of linear equations: [3-1]

$$2x + 4y = 16$$
$$-5x + 5y = -60$$

   a. by graphing   **b.** algebraically

9. **Rescuing Rover** Rowena and Grover are rescuing their dog Rover, who has fallen into a hole. After Rover obediently crawls into a basket they've lowered into the hole, the dog's owners pull the basket up by using ropes.

   a. Rowena pulls with a force of 55 lb and Grover pulls with a force of 46 lb. When the angle between the forces is 37°, what is the magnitude of the resultant force on the basket?

   b. As the basket rises, what will happen to the angle between the forces? Will this make pulling Rover up easier or more difficult? Explain.

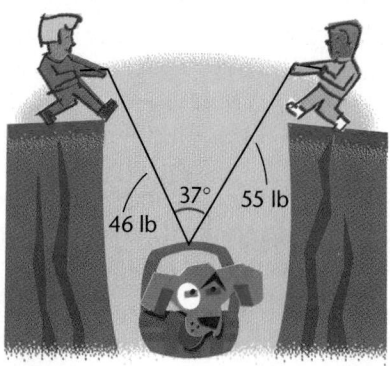

Solve each equation. Where necessary, round answers to the nearest hundredth. [9-3]

10. $\log_4 x = 3$ **11.** $\log_x \frac{8}{27} = -3$ **12.** $\log x = 5$ **13.** $\log_{125} x = \frac{1}{3}$

14. Which of the degree measures gives the same terminal side as $\frac{5\pi}{6}$ radians? [10-1]

   I. 150°   II. −210°   III. 3750°

   (a) only I   (b) only II   (c) only III   (d) I and III   (e) I, II, and III

15. The Chemistry Angle The bond angle for the F−O−F (Fluorine-Oxygen-Fluorine) bond in oxygen fluoride (OF_2) is 103.2°. If the average length of an O−F bond is 1.418×10^{-8} cm, find the distance between the centers of the fluorine (F) atoms.

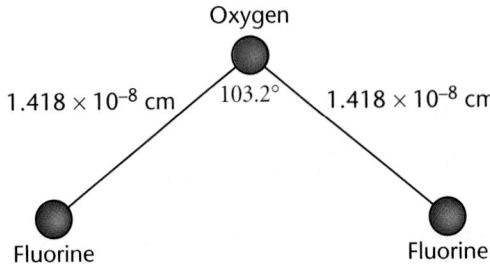

Find each indicated angle measure for △FGH. Where necessary, round answers to the nearest tenth of a degree.

16. $f = 8$, $g = 15$, $h = 10$. Find $m\angle H$.

17. $f = 132$, $g = 57$, $h = 83$. Find $m\angle F$.

18. $f = 2.7$, $g = 3.9$, $h = 4.1$. Find $m\angle F$.

19. $f = 7$, $g = 25$, $h = 24$. Find $m\angle G$.

20. $m\angle F = 121°$, $g = 58$, $h = 73$. Find $m\angle G$.

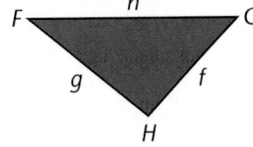

21. Can you find the lengths of the sides of △ABC if you know that $m\angle A = 27°$, $m\angle B = 105°$, and $m\angle C = 48°$? Explain your answer.

22. A surveyor finds that the sides of a triangular plot of land measure 155 m, 228 m, and 289 m.
   a. What is the measure of the largest angle of the triangle?
   b. Find the area of the plot of land. Explain your method, then describe another method you could have used to find the area.

23. In △ABC, $m\angle A = 76°$, $m\angle B = 25°$, and $c = 27$. Find the perimeter of △ABC.

24. Stopping the Steal A baseball diamond is a square 90 feet on a side. The pitcher's mound is located on a diagonal between second base and home plate and is exactly 60.5 feet from home plate.
   a. A pitcher needs to throw the baseball from the pitcher's mound to second base to prevent a steal. How long is the throw?
   b. If the pitcher throws the ball from the pitcher's mound to first base, how long is the throw?

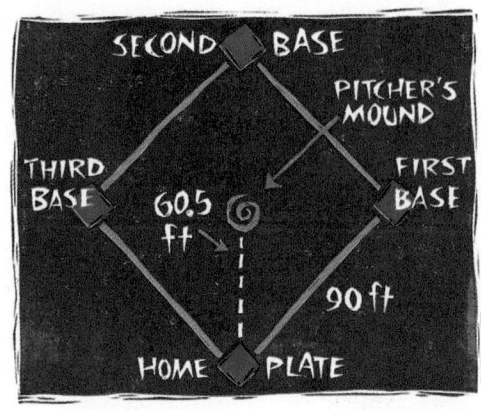

Decide which choice is correct. (Assume all angle measures are between 0° and 180°.)

(A) The quantity in Column A is greater.   (B) The quantity in Column B is greater.
(C) The two quantities are equal.   (D) The relationship cannot be determined.

	Column A	Column B
25.	$m\angle A$, if $\cos A > 0$	$m\angle A$, if $\cos A < 0$
26.	a, if $m\angle A > m\angle B$ in $\triangle ABC$	b, if $m\angle A > m\angle B$ in $\triangle ABC$

Find the missing measures for each △ABC. Round answers to the nearest tenth.

	$m\angle A$	$m\angle B$	$m\angle C$	a	b	c	Area $\triangle ABC$
27.	65°		71°		10		
28.			140°	11.4	15.6		
29.	15°				9	9	
30.	100°	60°			50.7		
31.		32°		1.7		2.4	
32.				12	16	8	

33. Crocodile Fears Kai and Alice row to the center of Lake Aothachos. A fierce crocodile springs suddenly from the lake, forcing the terrified twosome to row frantically for shore. Kai rows with a force of 36 newtons. Alice rows with a force of 42 newtons, and her intended direction makes a 54° angle with Kai's intended direction. Find the magnitude of the resultant force on the canoe.

34. Find the angle measures of $\triangle ABC$ if $a = 14$, $b = 12$, and $c = 31$. What did you discover? Why did this happen?

35. In *History of Mathematics, Vol. II*, David E. Smith states that the following formula was published in 1627 by W. Snell:

$$\frac{2ab}{[c^2 - (a - b)^2]} = \frac{1}{1 - \cos C}$$

a. Show that this formula is equivalent to the Law of Cosines for all triangles.
b. Snell also gave a version of the triangle area formula as 1: $\sin A = bc$: $2\triangle$.
   Show that this is equivalent to the area formula shown on page 720.
   (Hint: Each ":" represents a fraction bar.)

36. Suppose you are solving for the measure of an angle in a triangle. All of your calculations are correct. What do you know if you find:
a. that the cosine of the angle is negative?
b. that the sine of the angle is negative?

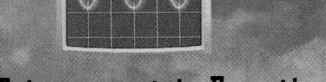

10-3 Trigonometric Functions

Mayan ASTRONOMICAL Beliefs

In early civilization, the Mayan Indians viewed time as a majestic succession of cycles without beginning or end. Their priests were astronomers who used the cycles of the Earth, moon, sun, and planets to guide many aspects of Mayan life. Important Mayan buildings were often constructed to conform to astronomical events. Orientations of some doorways and statues were based on the effects of sunlight and shadows at particular times of the year, such as the summer and winter solstices.

One of the best preserved Mayan sites in Mexico is at Palenque. The palace at Palenque is arranged so that on the winter solstice, as the sun disappears behind a ridge, the main center is covered with an advancing shadow. At the same time, a depression in the ridge allows the sun to shine fully on an altar, creating an effect like a spotlight.

Some experts still believe the Mayan calendrical system is superior to any system in use today. The Mayans had a 260-day sacred year and a solar year divided into 18 months of 20 days each. Dates were chronicled with respect to both types of time and enumerated by the number of cycles of the least common multiple of 260 and 365, which is 18,980 days or 52 years.

?

1. The rainy season usually begins 20 days after the vernal (spring) equinox. How could astronomy help the Mayan priests predict the beginning of the rainy season?
2. Why do you think the time of the winter solstice would be important in Mayan religious ceremonies?
3. What are some activities in your life that are based on the cyclical nature of our calendar?

← CONNECT → *You have learned to evaluate trigonometric functions for all angle measures. Now you will look at the sine and cosine ratios as functions. These functions are the basis for the study of all periodic functions.*

This graph shows the number of hours of daylight per day, at latitude 50° N, as a function of the time of year.

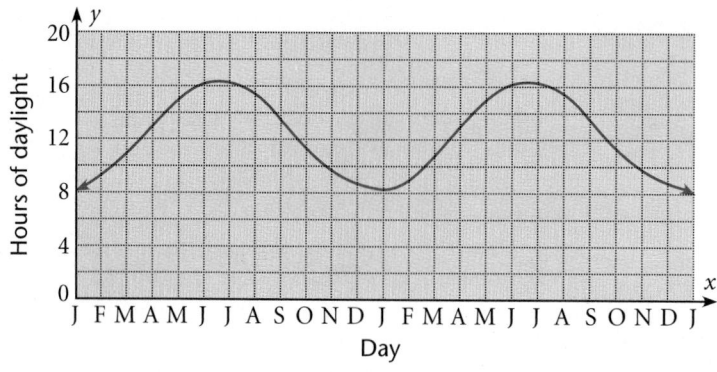

The basic pattern in the graph from January through December repeats every year. If $D(t)$ represents this function, where t is time in days, then the repeating pattern means that $D(t + 365) = D(t)$ for every value of t. Many functions in nature display similar repeating patterns and are called *periodic functions*.

> A function $f(x)$ is **periodic** if there is a constant $p > 0$ so that $f(x + p) = f(x)$ for all values of x. The smallest such value of p is the **period** of the function, the length of one repeating pattern in the graph. The **amplitude** of the function is half of the difference between the maximum and minimum function values.

The daylight function has a period of about 365 days. The amount of daylight per day at latitude 50° N varies between about 8 hours and 16 hours, with an average of 12 hours and an amplitude of 4 hours.

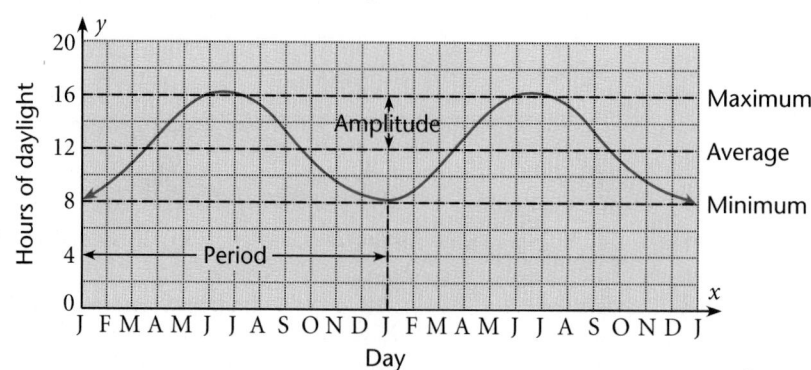

Sound is made up of pressure waves. For many sounds, such as musical notes, these waves can be modeled using periodic functions.

1. This graph, found using an oscilloscope, was produced by a note played on a trumpet and shows the change in air pressure from atmospheric pressure (1 atm) as a function of time. Give the amplitude and period of the function.

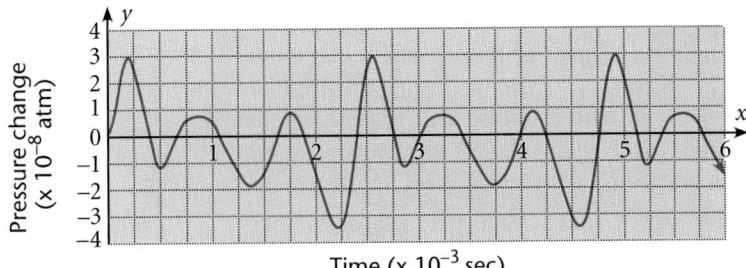

Time (x 10^{-3} sec)

The pressure change varies from about -3.5×10^{-8} atm to 3×10^{-8} atm, a difference of 6.5×10^{-8} atm. The amplitude (A) is half this difference.

$A = \frac{1}{2}(6.5 \times 10^{-8} \text{ atm}) = 3.25 \times 10^{-8}$ atm

At 0 milliseconds, the pressure change is zero followed by a maximum. At 2.4 milliseconds, there is another zero followed by a maximum. The same occurs at 4.8 milliseconds. The basic pattern repeats about every 2.4×10^{-3} seconds, so the period (p) is about 2.4×10^{-3} seconds.

$p \approx 2.4 \times 10^{-3}$ seconds

The reciprocal of the period is the frequency of the note in Hertz (cycles/sec). This note has a frequency of about 417 Hz, which corresponds to the note G#. (The other peaks and valleys mark a strong overtone that has one third the period and three times the frequency.)

a. Give the amplitude and period of the graph of the periodic function. This graph is called a *sawtooth wave*.

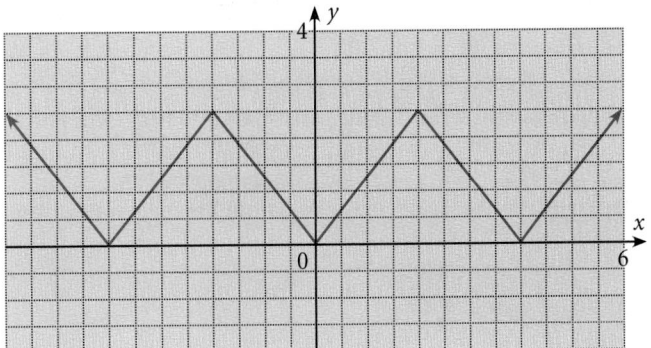

The trigonometric ratios you've studied can be used to create **trigonometric functions,** such as $y = \sin x$, $V = 2 \cos 3t$, and $f(\theta) = 1.5 + 0.7 \sin 0.2(\theta - \frac{\pi}{6})$. In the Explore, you will investigate the periodic nature of some basic trigonometric functions. These functions are typically written using radian measure, as we will do throughout 10-3.

EXPLORE: WHAT PERIOD IS THIS?

MATERIALS

Graph paper, Graphing utility

Problem-Solving Tip

Make an organized list or table.

1. Without using your graphing utility, plot points on the graph of $y = \sin x$ and sketch the graph of this trigonometric function. Include values of x from -2π to 4π.

2. Use your sketch to determine the amplitude and period of $y = \sin x$.

3. Using your graphing utility, graph $y = A \sin x$ for several values of A. Compare the amplitude and period of each function with those of $y = \sin x$. Describe any conclusions you reach.

4. Using your graphing utility, graph $y = \sin Bx$ for several values of B. Compare the amplitude and period of each function with those of $y = \sin x$. Describe any conclusions you reach.

5. Make a conjecture about the effects of A and B on the graph of $y = A \sin Bx$. Test your conjecture by graphing a few functions of this form. Modify your conjecture to match your observations if necessary.

Adding 2π to any angle gives an equivalent angle with the same trigonometric ratios. Therefore, $y = \sin x$ and $y = \cos x$ are periodic functions with period 2π. Their graphs also show that each function has amplitude 1 and average value 0.

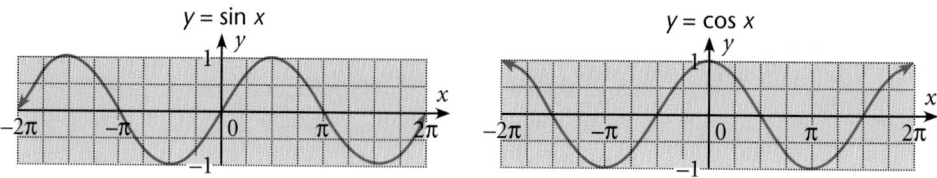

Notice that $y = \sin x$ has zeros at each integer multiple of π, while $y = \cos x$ has a maximum or minimum value at each integer multiple of π.

 **CONSIDER**

1. How can you obtain the graph of $y = \cos x$ by a translation of the graph of $y = \sin x$?

Using the graphs and properties of the basic trigonometric functions $y = \sin x$ and $y = \cos x$, you can sketch and analyze other periodic functions.

EXAMPLE

2. Sketch the graph of $y = 3 \sin 2x$, and give its amplitude and period.

The value of $\sin 2x$ varies from -1 to 1, so the value of $3 \sin 2x$ varies from -3 to 3. Therefore, the amplitude is 3.

The function goes through one basic pattern or cycle as the angle $2x$ varies from 0 to 2π. This occurs as x varies from 0 to π, so the period of the function is π.

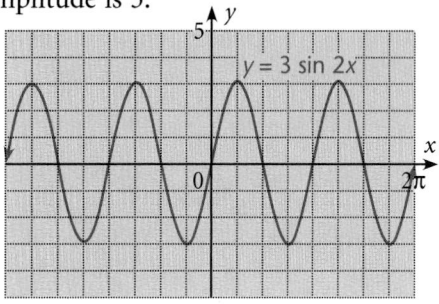

In general, functions of the form $f(x) = A \sin Bx$ and $g(x) = A \cos Bx$ vary in value from $-|A|$ to $|A|$, so each has amplitude $|A|$. The angle Bx repeats as $|Bx|$ varies from 0 to 2π. Since this occurs as x varies from 0 to $\frac{2\pi}{|B|}$, the period of each of these functions is $\frac{2\pi}{|B|}$.

TRY IT

Sketch the graph of each function, and give its amplitude and period.

b. $y = 2 \cos \frac{1}{2}x$ **c.** $f(x) = -1.5 \sin \pi x$

Trigonometric functions of the form $f(x) = A \sin Bx$ or $g(x) = A \cos Bx$ are often useful models for describing waves and alternating quantities in real situations.

EXAMPLE

3. The typical voltage for electrical outlets in the United States is 110 volts. This is the *root-mean-squared* voltage. The actual voltage alternates *sinusoidally* between $\pm\sqrt{2} \cdot 110$ volts and a frequency (the reciprocal of the period) of 60 Hz. Write a function of the form $V(t) = A \sin Bt$ to model the outlet voltage as a function of time (t) in seconds.

$A = \sqrt{2} \cdot 110 \approx 155.6$

$p = \dfrac{1}{60} = \dfrac{2\pi}{B}$ Period $= \dfrac{1}{\text{frequency}}$

$B = 2\pi \cdot 60 = 120\pi$ Solve for B.

So $V(t) = 155.6 \sin 120\pi t$ models the outlet voltage.

d. A pendulum rocks from 4 inches left of its resting position to 4 inches right and back again in 2 seconds. Let D measure the position of the pendulum to the right of its resting position. Write a function of the form $D(t) = A \sin Bt$ to model the pendulum's position t seconds after it passes its resting position going to the right.

The sine and cosine functions are fundamental tools for modeling periodic, wavelike behavior. Such diverse phenomena as economic trends, sunspot frequency, and the propagation of light and sound can all be modeled using periodic functions.

REFLECT

1. How do you determine the amplitude and period of a periodic function from its graph?

2. How are the amplitude and period reflected in the equations of some periodic functions? Give examples to explain.

3. Describe a relationship in the real world that displays periodic behavior. Give a reasonable amplitude and period for the relationship.

Exercises

CORE

1. Getting Started Examine the graph of the periodic function.
  a. What is the range of the function?
  b. What evidence suggests that the function is periodic?
  c. Give the amplitude of the function.
  d. Give the period of the function.
  e. Give the average value of the function.

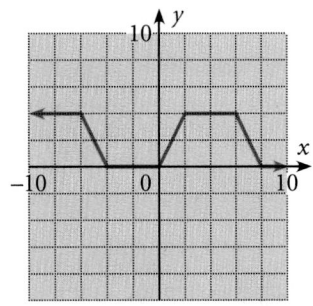

Write the word or phrase that correctly completes each statement.

2. The ____ of a periodic function is equal to half the difference between the maximum and minimum function values.

3. On the graph of a periodic function, the length of the basic pattern that repeats is the ____ of the function.

4. Sketch the graph of $y = \cos x$. Use the graph to find approximate values of four angle measures with cosines of -0.3.

5. Write the letter of the second pair that best matches the first pair.
  Trigonometric function: periodic function as
  (a) domain: period
  (b) sine function: cosine function
  (c) constant function: linear function
  (d) parabola: circle

Give the amplitude and period of each periodic function.

6.

Xmin = –6
Xmax = 6
Xscl = 1
Ymin = –4
Ymax = 4
Yscl = 1

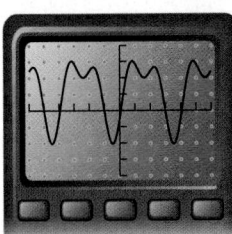

7.

Xmin = –4
Xmax = 4
Xscl = 1
Ymin = –6
Ymax = 6
Yscl = 1

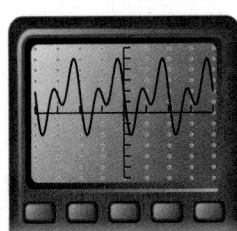

8. Jazzy Sounds This graph shows the change in air pressure from atmospheric pressure (1 atm) as a function of time, produced by a note played on a clarinet.

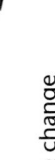
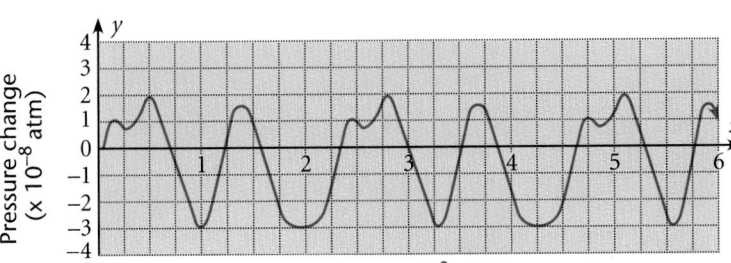

Pressure change (x 10⁻⁸ atm)

Time (x 10⁻³ sec)

a. Give the period and amplitude of the function.

b. The loudness of a note in decibels is given by the formula $D = 180 + 20 \log A$, where A is the pressure amplitude in atmospheres. How loud is the clarinet note?

c. The reciprocal of the period in seconds is the frequency of the note in Hertz (Hz). Give the frequency of the note being played on the clarinet. Refer to the table and decide which note is being played.

Note	C	C#	D	D#	E	F	F#	G	G#	A	A#	B
Frequency (Hz)	262	277	294	311	330	349	370	392	415	440	466	494

Sketch the graph of each function, and give its amplitude and period.

9. $y = \sin 2x$

10. $y = \cos \frac{1}{2}x$

11. $y = 2 \sin 3x$

12. $y = -5 \cos 2x$

13. $y = 13 \sin 5x$

14. $y = 0.5 \cos 0.25x$

15. $y = 2 \cos 2.5x$

16. $y = 3 \sin \frac{1}{2}x$

17. $y = -2 \sin 4x$

Give a sine function with each amplitude and period.

18. amplitude 4, period π

19. amplitude 1.5, period $\frac{\pi}{3}$

20. amplitude 9, period 10π

21. Surf's Up The peaks of an ocean wave are 8 feet higher than the troughs. The horizontal distance from one peak to the next is 20 feet. Write a function of the form $W(x) = A \cos Bx$ that models the wave height above the average sea level as a function of x, the horizontal distance measured from one peak in the direction of the wave. (Note: When the period is a distance, it is often referred to as the *wavelength*.)

22. Latitude Attitude When projected onto a 2-dimensional map, the orbit of the Space Shuttle traces an approximate sine curve on the earth's surface. The shuttle takes about 90 minutes to orbit the earth. Write a function that gives the shuttle's latitude t minutes after crossing the equator northward.

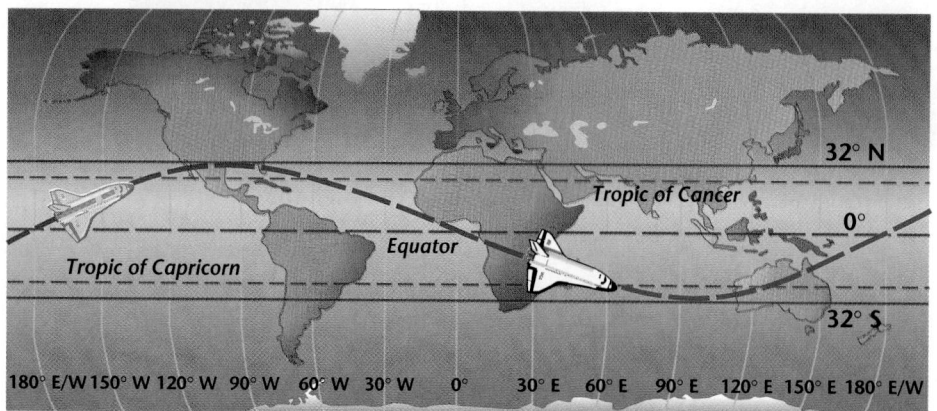

LOOK AHEAD

23. Sketch the graphs of $y = \sin x$ and $y = \sin\left(x - \frac{\pi}{2}\right)$. Describe how you can obtain the second graph through a translation of the first.

24. Sketch the graphs of $y = \cos x$ and $y = \cos(x + \pi)$. Describe how you can obtain the second graph through a translation of the first.

MORE PRACTICE

Give the amplitude and period of each periodic function.

25.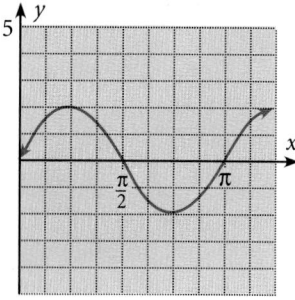

26.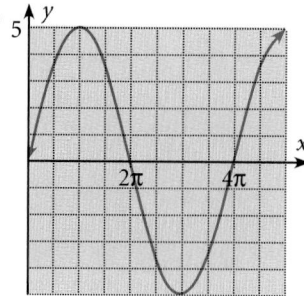

27.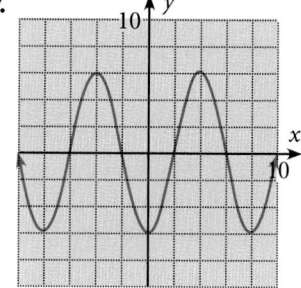

28. Sketch the graph of a periodic function with amplitude 6, period 4, and average value -2.

Give a sine function with the given amplitude and period.

29. amplitude 2, period 2π

30. amplitude 7, period $\frac{\pi}{3}$

31. amplitude 0.4, period 3

32. amplitude 6, period 4

33. amplitude 1.8, period 1.4

34. amplitude 3, period 5

Sketch the graph of each function, and give its amplitude and period.

35. $y = \cos 2x$

36. $y = \sin \frac{1}{4}x$

37. $y = 3 \cos x$

38. $y = 5 \sin 2x$

39. $y = -2.5 \sin 3x$

40. $y = -2 \cos 3\pi x$

41. $y = \frac{2}{3} \sin 0.5x$

42. $y = -4 \cos \frac{3}{2}x$

43. $y = 1.5 \sin 4x$

44. $y = 2 \cos 2.4x$

45. $y = 3 \sin \frac{\pi}{5}x$

46. $y = -0.8 \sin \frac{x}{2}$

47. $y = 5 \cos \frac{x}{2}$

48. $y = 0.5 \sin 3x$

49. $y = 2 \cos 4x$

50. It's Shocking In Europe, the typical outlet voltage is 220 volts. This is the root-mean-squared voltage. The actual voltage alternates sinusoidally with an amplitude of $\sqrt{2} \cdot 220$ volts and a frequency of 50 Hz. Give the period in seconds, the reciprocal of the frequency in Hertz. Write a function of the form $V(t) = A \cos Bt$ to model the outlet voltage as a function of time (t) in seconds.

51. Hop to It! As a boy bounces on his pogo stick, the height of his head varies between 1 foot above and 1 foot below a fence. Write a function that could model the height of the boy's head, over time, if he bounces once each second.

MORE MATH REASONING

52. Sketch the graph of the function $y = \tan x$ in the interval $-2\pi \le x \le 2\pi$. Give the period of the tangent function and explain why it has no amplitude.

53. Sketch the graph of the function $y = \cot x$ in the interval $-2\pi \le x \le 2\pi$. Discuss the features of the graph of this periodic function.

54. Swing Time April has a part in a show at an animal park. As the highlight of the show, she must cross a 28-foot wide lagoon filled with alligators. It takes April 6 seconds to swing from 18 feet right of the center of the lagoon to 18 feet left of center. As she is about to land, April sees a lion that has escaped from its enclosure! So, instead of letting go, she swings back and forth over the lagoon until the lion leaves.

a. Write and graph a function of the form $d(t) = A \cos Bt$ for April's distance to the right of the center of the lagoon t seconds after she starts swinging.

b. In what time interval of her first swing back and forth is April over the left bank?

c. The lion leaves 25 seconds after April starts swinging. Will April land on the left bank if she lets go at this time? If not, when is it next safe for her to let go?

← C O N N E C T → *You have graphed sine and cosine functions and used them to model periodic behavior. By translating sine and cosine graphs vertically and horizontally, you can create other useful periodic models.*

Recall that in Chapter 5 you graphed circles centered at the origin and considered other circles as *translations* of these. For instance, the graph of the equation $x^2 + y^2 = 4$ is a circle with radius 2 centered at the origin. The graph of $(x - 3)^2 + (y + 5)^2 = 4$ is a circle with the same radius but centered at $(3, -5)$. Replacing x by $x - 3$ and y by $y + 5$ effectively translates the circle 3 units right and 5 units down.

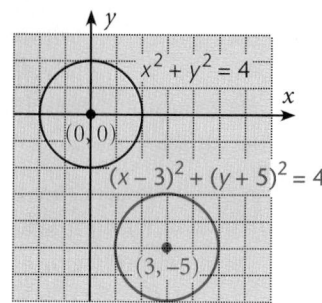

The same idea works for the graphs of periodic functions. A vertical translation of a periodic function changes its average value, while a horizontal translation shifts the maximums, minimums, and other features.

EXAMPLE

1. Sketch the graphs of $y = \sin 2x$, $y = 4 + \sin 2x$, and $y = 4 + \sin\left(2x - \frac{\pi}{2}\right)$ on the same coordinate plane and describe how their graphs are related.

    First graph: The graph of $y = \sin 2x$ is a sine curve with amplitude 1 and period π. The average y-value is 0.

    Second graph: Writing the second equation as $y - 4 = \sin 2x$ shows that its graph is a translation of the first graph 4 units up. (y has been replaced by $y - 4$.) This function has an average y-value of 4.

    Third graph: Since $2x - \frac{\pi}{2} = 2\left(x - \frac{\pi}{4}\right)$, the graph of $y = 4 + \sin\left(2x - \frac{\pi}{2}\right)$ is a translation of the second graph $\frac{\pi}{4}$ units to the right. It also has an average y-value of 4.

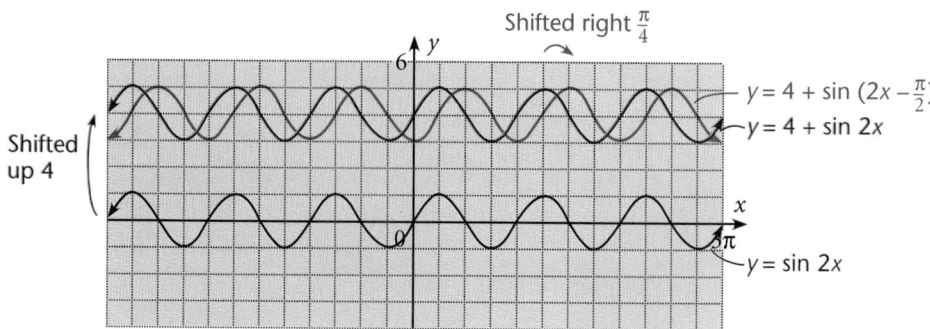

The vertical shift of a sine or cosine graph gives the average y-value. The horizontal shift of a sine or cosine graph is called the **phase shift.** With these, we can now summarize the features of sine and cosine functions.

Any periodic function of the form $y = k + A \sin B(x - h)$ or $y = k + A \cos B(x - h)$ has the following features.

$|A|$ = the amplitude $\qquad\qquad \dfrac{2\pi}{|B|}$ = the period

k = the average y-value $\qquad\qquad h$ = the phase shift

TRY IT

a. Sketch the graph of $y = -3 + 2 \cos \left(\frac{1}{3}x + \frac{\pi}{3}\right)$. Give the amplitude, period, average y-value, and phase shift of this periodic function.

In 10-3A, you examined the graph of the amount of daylight per day at latitude 50° N as a periodic function of time. In the following Explore, you will model this relationship and use your model to make predictions.

EXPLORE: THE LIGHT OF DAY

MATERIALS

Graphing utility

The amount of daylight per day at 50° N latitude varies between about 8 hours on December 21 and 16 hours on June 21. Let t be the number of days since the beginning of the year. For simplicity, assume there are exactly 365 days in a year. (So, $t = 1$ is January 1 of this year, $t = 366$ is January 1 of next year, and so on.)

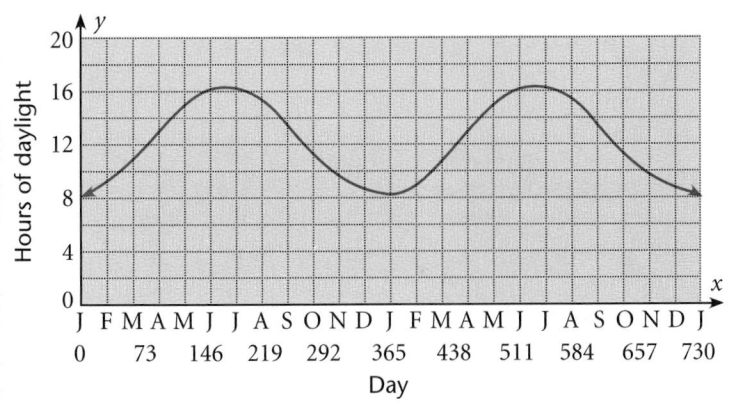

1. Decide if you want to model the number of daylight hours with a trigonometric function involving the sine or the cosine. Then give the amplitude, period, average value, and phase shift that you will use.
2. Write a periodic function $D(t)$ to model the number of daylight hours. Check that your model has the correct minimum and maximum values on the appropriate days.
3. At latitude 50° N, how many hours of daylight do you predict there will be on February 20 of each year? How many hours of daylight do you predict for today?
4. Could you use a different phase shift in your model without altering the predictions? Explain.

When a periodic graph has the simple wave shape of a sine curve, you can use either a sine function or cosine function as a model.

WHAT DO **YOU** THINK?

The graph shows the average human heart rate $H(t)$ at different hours of the day. Model the average heart rate t hours after midnight as a periodic function.

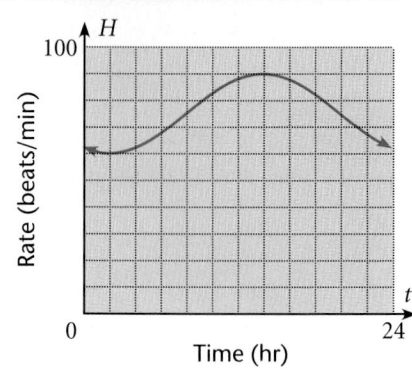

Brian thinks...

I'll write a function of the form $H(t) = k + A \sin B(t - h)$ to model the heart rate. The heart rate varies from 60 to 90, with an average of $k = 75$. The amplitude is $A = 15$, half of $(90 - 60)$. The period $\frac{2\pi}{B}$ is 24 hours, so $B = \frac{\pi}{12}$. The sine curve starts at $t = 8$, so the phase shift is $h = 8$.

My model is the function $H(t) = 75 + 15 \sin \frac{\pi}{12}(t - 8)$.

Andrea thinks...

I'll write a function of the form $H(t) = k + A \cos B(t - h)$. I also get $k = 75$, $A = 15$, and $B = \frac{\pi}{12}$. But the cosine curve starts at $t = 14$, so the phase shift is $h = 14$.

My model is the function $H(t) = 75 + 15 \cos \frac{\pi}{12}(t - 14)$.

CONSIDER

?

1. If a sine function models a situation well, then a cosine function will also model it well, and vice versa. Explain why sine functions and cosine functions work equally well as periodic models.

The concepts of average value, amplitude, period, and phase shift are widely used in physics and other sciences to study the wave nature of water, sound, light, and a wide variety of other relationships with periodic behavior.

REFLECT

1. How can you determine the average y-value and the phase shift from an equation of a sine or cosine function?

2. Describe the steps you take to find a sine or cosine model for a graph.

3. Describe a situation (not involving daylight or heart rates) in which a periodic function has an average value different from 0 or has a phase shift.

Exercises

CORE

1. Getting Started Examine the graph of this trigonometric function.

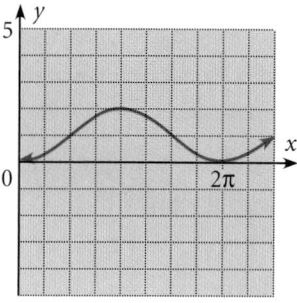

    a. Suppose that this is a graph of a sine function. What is the average y-value of the function, the amount the sine curve has been translated up?

    b. Find a starting point of the sine curve, a point where y equals the average value and the curve slopes upward.

    c. What is the phase shift, the amount the sine curve has been translated to the right?

2. Suppose that the graph in **1** is the graph of a cosine function. Give the average y-value and phase shift of the function.

3. Match each expression with the best phrase. Assume y is a sine function of x.

    a. average y-value   **i.** range of x-values in one cycle

    b. amplitude   **ii.** range of y-values in one cycle ÷ 2

    c. period   **iii.** horizontal translation

    d. phase shift   **iv.** vertical translation

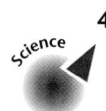

4. Body Heat The average human body temperature throughout the day can be modeled by a sine curve.

    a. Give the amplitude and period of the temperature.

    b. Give the average daily temperature and the phase shift.

5. Sketch the graph of a sine function with amplitude 1, period 4π, phase shift π, and average y-value 4.

6. Sketch the graph of a cosine function with amplitude 3, period 6, phase shift 4.5, and average y-value 3.

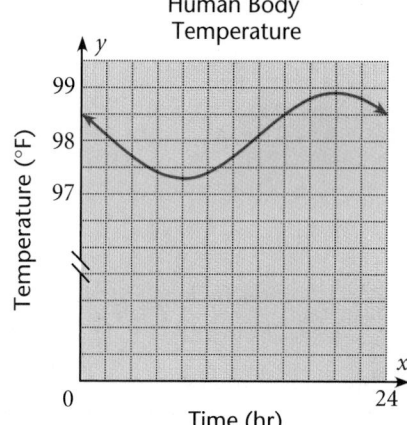

Human Body Temperature

Sketch the graph of each trigonometric function. Give the amplitude, period, average y-value, and phase shift of the function.

7. $y = \sin(x + \pi)$

8. $y = \cos\left(x - \frac{\pi}{6}\right) - 2$

9. $y = 3\cos\left(\frac{1}{2}x + \pi\right) - 1$

10. $y = 5 + 3\sin\left(2x - \frac{\pi}{5}\right)$

11. $y = 2.5 + 2\sin\left(3x - \frac{\pi}{4}\right)$

12. $y = \cos\left(6x + \frac{\pi}{2}\right) - 9$

13. $y = -2\sin\left(x - \frac{\pi}{4}\right) - 3$

14. $y = 1 - 3\cos\left(\frac{1}{2}x + \pi\right)$

Give a sine function with the given values.

15. amplitude 1, period 2π, phase shift π, and average value -3

16. amplitude 2, period π, phase shift $-\frac{\pi}{4}$, and average value 1.5

17. amplitude $\frac{1}{2}$, period 4, phase shift 1, and average value -8

18. If a sine function has a maximum at $(1, 2)$ and the next minimum is at $(7, 0)$, give an equation of the function.

19. The graphs of the functions $y = \sin(x + k)$, $y = \sin(2x + m)$, and $y = \sin(3x + n)$ are all shifted by a phase shift of $\frac{\pi}{2}$, that is, $\frac{\pi}{2}$ to the right. Give the values of k, m, and n.

20. Time and Tide Ocean tides rise and fall periodically. The scatter plot shows hourly tide heights from a permanent measuring stick at a point near Newport, Rhode Island. Copy the scatter plot and draw a sine curve that fits the data. Give an equation for the sine curve that you drew.

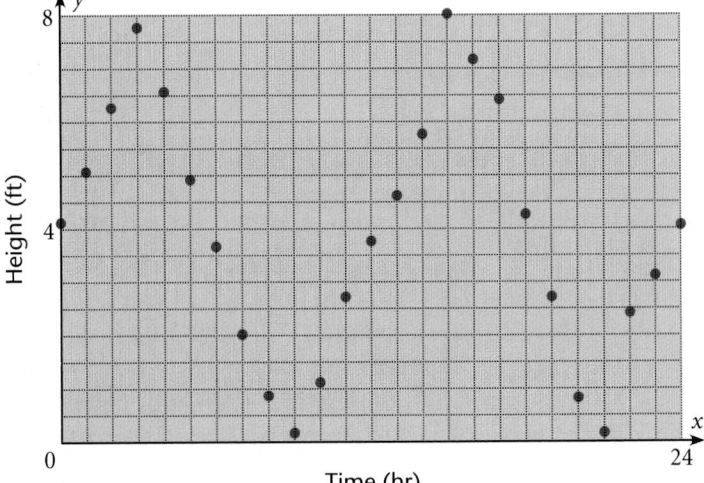

Time (hr)

 **LOOK BACK**

Solve each equation. [5-2, 9-2]

21. $6x^2 + 14x + 4 = 0$ **22.** $3^x = 8$

23. The point $(-3, 4)$ lies on the terminal side of an angle with measure θ. Give $\cos \theta$. [10-1]

MORE PRACTICE

24. Sketch the graph of a cosine function with amplitude 2, period π, phase shift $-\frac{\pi}{2}$, and average y-value 2.

25. Sketch the graph of a sine function with amplitude 4, period 10, phase shift 2, and average y-value -5.

26. Sketch the graph of a cosine function with amplitude 100, period 200, phase shift -50, and average y-value 1000.

Sketch the graph of each trigonometric function. Give the amplitude, period, average y-value, and phase shift of the function.

27. $y = \cos\left(x - \frac{\pi}{6}\right)$

28. $y = -3 \sin x - 6$

29. $y = 1 + 2 \cos\left(x + \frac{\pi}{2}\right)$

30. $y = 3 + 5 \sin(3x + \pi)$

31. $y = 5 + 4 \sin\left(\pi x - \frac{\pi}{3}\right)$

32. $y = 3 \cos(5x + 2)$

33. $y = 1.1 \sin\left(x + \frac{3\pi}{4}\right)$

34. $y - 2 = \cos(x - 12)$

35. $y + 4 = \sin(10x - \pi)$

36. $y = \frac{1}{3} \sin(2\pi x - \pi) + 4$

37. $y = 0.34 \cos(4\pi^2 x + \pi) - 2$

38. $y = \frac{2}{5}(\cos(x + 5)) - 3$

39. Ground Temperature The hourly underground temperature at a particular depth can be modeled by a sine function. The deeper you measure, the less the temperature varies throughout the day.

For the sine curve shown, give an equation that models the hourly temperature at a depth of 2 meters throughout the day.

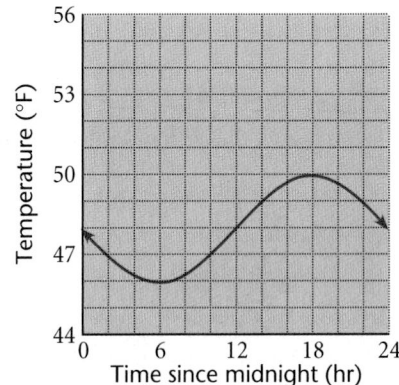

Give a sine function with the given values.

40. amplitude 1, period 7, phase shift -3.5, and average value -2

41. amplitude 2, period $\frac{1}{2}\pi$, phase shift π, and average value 3

42. amplitude 3, period π, phase shift $-\frac{\pi}{3}$, and average value 5

43. amplitude 4, period 9, phase shift 3, and average value -0.5

44. amplitude 5, period 6π, phase shift 6, and average value 0

45. If a sine function has a maximum at $(10, 1)$ and the next minimum is at $(11, 0)$, give an equation of the function.

MORE MATH REASONING

46. Use a Graphing Utility A sum or difference of two periodic functions is also a periodic function. Graph $y = \sqrt{2}(\sin x + \cos x)$. Find an equivalent sine function by determining the amplitude, period, average y-value, and phase shift of the graph.

47. Use a Graphing Utility How is the period of a sum or difference of two periodic functions related to the periods of the two functions?
a. Graph $y = \sin 3x + \cos 2x$. What is the period of this function?
b. Graph $y = 2 \cos 4x - \sin 6x$. What is the period of this function?
c. Make a conjecture about the period of a function of the form $y = \sin nx + \cos mx$, where n and m are positive integers. Justify your conjecture if possible.

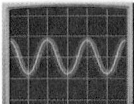
← C O N N E C T → *You have examined the graphs and features of sine functions and cosine functions. These functions are the basic tools for studying and modeling periodic behavior in a wide variety of situations.*

The Mayans, as well as many other civilizations, were keenly aware of the periodic nature of astronomical events and seasonal patterns. In the following Explore, you will model the periodic effect of the seasons on temperatures.

EXPLORE: RUNNING HOT AND COLD

MATERIALS

Graph paper

The table gives some mean daily temperatures during one year for the town of Roadrunner, New Mexico. The days are numbered beginning with day 1 on January 1.

Day	Mean Temperature (°F)	Day	Mean Temperature (°F)
1	27	200	83
12	28	213	81
21	28	224	81
38	31	239	73
51	35	248	74
66	39	257	68
83	47	272	62
95	55	287	57
104	57	301	46
120	62	314	45
138	75	329	38
155	78	340	32
171	85	351	29
188	82	365	28

1. Plot the data and connect the points to represent mean temperature as a function of the day of the year.

2. What is the mean annual temperature in the town of Roadrunner? What are the maximum and minimum mean daily temperatures? On what days do they occur?

3. Model the mean daily temperature in Roadrunner as a periodic function. Explain how you found each of the constants in your function and what they each mean in this situation.

4. Use your function to predict the mean temperature for day 291 and for today.

1. Explain what makes a function periodic.
2. Describe the general features of the graphs of sine and cosine functions.
3. What do the constants A, B, h, and k tell you about a periodic function given by an equation of the form $y = k + A \sin B(x - h)$?

Self-Assessment

1. The average value of the function $y = \sin x$ is
   (a) 1   (b) 0   (c) -1 (d) not here

2. The amplitude of the function $y = \sin x$ is
   (a) 1   (b) 2   (c) -1 (d) not here

3. Sketch a periodic function (not necessarily a sine or cosine function) with amplitude 4, period 6, and average value 3.

Sketch the graph of each trigonometric function. Give the amplitude, period, average y-value, and phase shift of the function.

4. $y = 4 + 2 \cos (3x + 9)$

5. $y = 0.5 \sin (12x - 30) - 5$

6. $y = -6 + 3 \cos (4\pi x - \pi)$

7. $y = 4 \sin \left(\frac{1}{2}x + \frac{\pi}{4}\right) + 3$

8. Give a sine function with amplitude 3, period 4, average y-value 2, and phase shift 1.

9. A *tsunami* is a gigantic wave caused by a bottom slide, earthquake, or volcanic eruption. In this nineteenth-century print by the Japanese printmaker Hokusai, a tsunami is shown breaking off Kanagawa, with Mt. Fuji in the background.

   When the island of Krakatoa exploded in 1883, the resulting tsunami was 100 feet to 130 feet high and traveled across the Pacific Ocean at 300 mi/hr. Tsunamis can span as much as 600 miles from crest to crest. Give a possible sine function that could model the height above mean sea level of a tsunami as a function of distance.

Give the value of each trigonometric ratio. [10-1]

10. $\sin 690°$

11. $\tan -135°$

12. $\cos \frac{19\pi}{4}$

Solve each equation. [5-2, 8-2, 9-2]

13. $2x^2 - 3x - 4 = 0$

14. $(x + 3)^2 = 3x + 7$

15. $x^3 - 3x^2 - 6x + 8 = 0$

16. $x^4 - 2x^3 + 3x^2 - 6x = 0$

17. $2^n = 24$

18. $\log 5x = -2$

19. Bear Weight Weight gain and loss is often a periodic function for wild animals. For example, from spring through early fall, a black bear gains weight, which will gradually be lost during hibernation. This graph records the weight of a black bear over one year. Model the bear's weight as a periodic function of time.

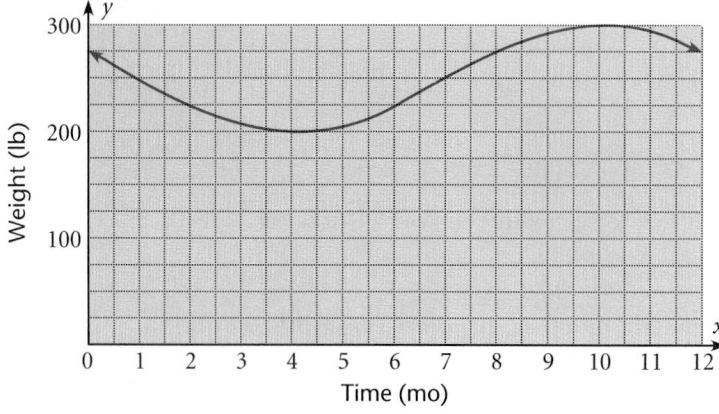

20. The *Mimosa pudica* is a common house plant known for the clocklike movement of its leaves. The mimosa leaves gradually spread apart for 12 hours and then close together for 12 hours. One leaf creates the periodic curve shown on the cylinder of a measuring device.

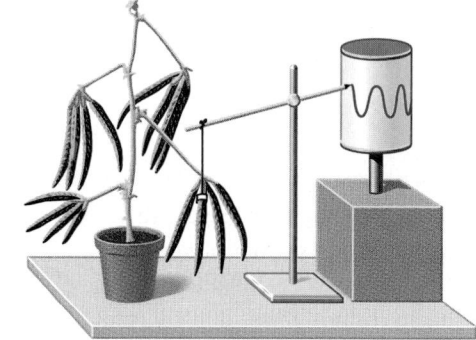

Choose a reasonable range of heights for one mimosa leaf and give a possible periodic function that could model the mimosa leaf's height as a function of time.

21. If a sine function has a maximum at $(4, 3)$ and the next minimum is at $(6, -1)$, give an equation of the function.

22. Earthquake! The shock waves from most earthquakes cause the ground to move up and down like waves on the surface of the ocean. Assume that 3 seconds after a quake hits, the ground beneath you reaches a maximum height of 7 inches higher than normal, and 9 seconds after the quake hits, the ground reaches a minimum height of 7 inches below normal. Write and sketch a possible function modeling the periodic motion of the ground during the quake.

Chapter 10 Review

In this chapter, you have extended your knowledge of functions by exploring the trigonometric functions and other periodic functions. You have discovered how trigonometry can be used to determine distances and angles, as well as model vectors, quantities, and periodic functions.

KEY TERMS

amplitude [10-3]

angle of depression [10-1]

angle of elevation [10-1]

angular speed [10-1]

arc length [10-1]

central angle [10-1]

cosecant (csc) [10-1]

cosine (cos) [10-1]

cotangent (cot) [10-1]

Heron's Formula [10-2]

initial side [10-1]

Law of Cosines [10-2]

Law of Sines [10-2]

linear speed [10-1]

period [10-3]

periodic function [10-3]

phase shift [10-3]

radian measure [10-1]

reference angle [10-1]

resultant vector [10-2]

secant (sec) [10-1]

sector [10-1]

sine (sin) [10-1]

tangent (tan) [10-1]

terminal side [10-1]

trigonometry [10-1]

trigonometric functions [10-3]

vector [10-2]

Write the word or phrase that correctly completes each statement.

1. Triangles that have the same shape, but are not necessarily the same size, are called ____ triangles.

2. In a right triangle, the ratio of lengths of the adjacent side of an acute angle to the hypotenuse is called the ____.

3. The ratio of the length of an arc of a circle to the radius is the ____ measure of the central angle of the arc.

4. The measure of the angle per unit time of a point moving along a circle is the ____ speed of the point.

5. The ____ of a periodic function is half the difference between the maximum and minimum y-values of the function.

6. A distance that the graph of a basic trigonometric function is translated to the right is the ____.

CONCEPTS AND APPLICATIONS

For each triangle, find each trigonometric ratio, length, or angle measure. [10-1]

7. a. sin A **b.** $m\angle A$ **c.** cos A
    d. tan B **e.** $m\angle B$ **f.** csc B
    g. cot B **h.** sec A **i.** csc A

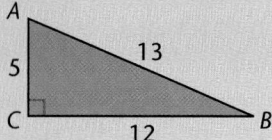

8. a. p **b.** q **c.** $m\angle Q$
    d. cos Q **e.** tan P **f.** sec Q
    g. sin P **h.** cot Q **i.** csc P

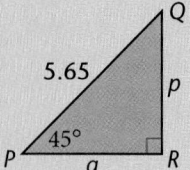

9. Convert each degree measure to radian measure. [10-1]
    a. 45°   **b.** 60°   **c.** 145°   **d.** 120°   **e.** 250°

10. Convert each radian measure to degree measure. [10-1]
    a. $\dfrac{\pi}{5}$ **b.** $\dfrac{3\pi}{2}$ **c.** $\dfrac{3\pi}{4}$ **d.** $\dfrac{5\pi}{3}$ **e.** $\dfrac{\pi}{9}$

Give each trigonometric ratio. [10-1]

11. sin $\dfrac{\pi}{2}$ **12.** cos $\dfrac{3\pi}{2}$ **13.** tan $\dfrac{5\pi}{4}$ **14.** sec $\dfrac{2\pi}{9}$

15. sin 175°   **16.** tan 270°   **17.** cos $\dfrac{7\pi}{2}$ **18.** sin $\dfrac{9\pi}{4}$

19. The radius of a circle and the measure of a central angle are given. Find the length of the arc and the area of the sector intercepted by the angle. [10-1]
    a. 5 cm, $\dfrac{\pi}{3}$ **b.** 11 m, $\dfrac{5\pi}{6}$ **c.** 4.5 in., 75°   **d.** 0.6 ft, 150°

20. A Ferris wheel in an amusement park has a radius of 20 ft. The wheel revolves once every 36 seconds. What are the angular and linear speeds of people riding on the outside edge of the Ferris wheel? [10-1]

21. A point on the terminal side of an angle with measure θ is given. Give sin θ, cos θ, and tan θ. [10-1]
    a. $(2, 5)$ **b.** $(-1, 6)$ **c.** $(-7, -3)$ **d.** $(4, -8)$ **e.** $(-3.5, 6)$

22. A 20-ft board is to be used to brace the side of a building at an angle of 80° with the ground. Will it touch the building below the window, which is 15 feet above ground? [10-2]

23. Use the Law of Cosines to find the indicated side or angle measure of $\triangle ABC$. [10-2]
    a. $a = 30$ cm, $b = 50$ cm, and $m\angle C = 30°$; find c.
    b. $a = 7$ ft, $b = 9$ ft, and $c = 10$ ft; find $m\angle C$.
    c. $a = 16$ m, $c = 10$ m, and $m\angle B = 45°$; find b.
    d. $b = 5.3$ yd, $c = 6.7$ yd, and $m\angle A = 88.5°$; find $m\angle B$.

24. Two sides of a sloped ceiling meet at an angle of 105.5°. If the length of the rafters on each side is 12 feet, how long is the cross-beam joining them? [10-2]

25. A plane is flying due north at a speed of 325 mi/hr. The wind is blowing east at a speed of 25 mi/hr. What are the resultant direction and speed of the airplane? [10-2]

26. Find the indicated side or angle of $\triangle ABC$. [10-2]
   a. $m\angle A = 14°$, $m\angle B = 68°$, and $a = 38$ cm; find b.
   b. $m\angle A = 53°$, $m\angle B = 40°$, and $c = 75.6$ ft; find a.
   c. $a = 20$ m, $c = 15$ m, and $m\angle B = 30°$; find b.
   d. $b = 2.2$ yd, $c = 4.1$ yd, and $m\angle A = 73.1°$; find $m\angle B$.

27. To measure the height of a tree, a landscape designer measures the angle of elevation to the tree top as 46°. She then moves 20 feet closer to the tree and remeasures the angle as 59°. How tall is the tree? [10-2]

Sketch each periodic function and give the amplitude, period, average y-value, and phase shift. [10-3]

28. $y = 2 \sin \frac{x}{3}$ **29.** $y = -2 \cos \pi x$ **30.** $y = 2 - \cos \frac{x}{2}$

31. $y = -2 \sin (3x + \pi) - 1$ **32.** $y = 2 \cos \left(x - \frac{\pi}{3}\right)$ **33.** $y = 2 - 1.5 \sin \left(x + \frac{\pi}{4}\right)$

34. Write an equation and sketch the graph of the function with each amplitude, period, average y-value, and phase shift. [10-3]
   a. a sine with amplitude of 2, period 3π, average y-value 2, and phase shift 4
   b. a cosine with amplitude $\frac{1}{2}$, period 4, average y-value 7, and phase shift -1

For each sine curve, give the amplitude, period, average y-value, and phase shift. [10-3]

35.
```
Xmin = -8
Xmax = 8
Xscl = 1
Ymin = -5
Ymax = 5
Yscl = 1
```
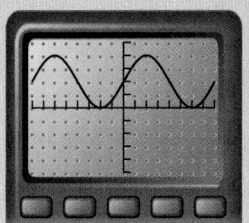

36.
```
Xmin = -8
Xmax = 8
Xscl = 1
Ymin = -5
Ymax = 5
Yscl = 1
```
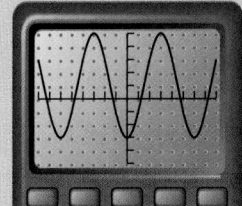

37. As you ride a 20-ft-radius Ferris wheel, your distance from the ground varies between 4 feet and 44 feet over time. When the Ferris wheel starts, your seat is at the position shown.

Suppose it takes you 12 seconds to reach the top and the wheel makes one complete revolution every 32 seconds. Write and graph a function that models your height as a function of time. [10-3]

CONCEPTS AND CONNECTIONS

38. Science A tsunami is a large, fast-moving ocean wave that causes the water to go below its normal level and then rise an equal distance above its normal level before returning to normal level. The period is usually about 15 minutes.

  a. Suppose a tsunami approaches a harbor with a normal depth of 90 meters, rises to a height of 40 meters above normal, and travels at a speed of 450 km/hr. Sketch the graph of a cosine function giving the water level at the mouth of the harbor as a function of the time since a crest passed. Use your graph to predict the height of the water after 2 minutes, 4 minutes, and 12 minutes.

  b. The wavelength of a wave is the distance that a crest of the wave travels in one period. It is also equal to the distance between two adjacent crests. What is the wavelength of the tsunami?

SELF-EVALUATION

Write a summary of what you learned in this chapter. Explain how the trigonometric functions may be important to you in a future career situation. How have concepts associated with trigonometry expanded your understanding of the mathematical processes you've observed in the past? Which techniques discussed in this chapter were confusing to you and why?

Chapter 10 Assessment

TEST

1. Use $\triangle XYZ$ to find each trigonometric ratio, length, or angle measure.

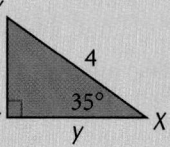

a. $\sin X$	**b.** x	**c.** $\cos X$
d. $\tan X$	**e.** $\cot X$	**f.** $\sec X$
g. $\csc X$	**h.** $m\angle Y$	**i.** $m\angle Z$

Convert each radian measure to degree measure.

2. $\dfrac{\pi}{3}$ **3.** $\dfrac{5\pi}{4}$ **4.** $\dfrac{3\pi}{2}$ **5.** $\dfrac{4\pi}{9}$

Convert each degree measure to radian measure.

6. $30°$ **7.** $90°$ **8.** $245°$ **9.** $320°$

Find the value of each trigonometric ratio.

10. $\cos \dfrac{\pi}{3}$ **11.** $\sin \dfrac{3\pi}{2}$ **12.** $\tan \dfrac{3\pi}{4}$ **13.** $\sin \dfrac{5\pi}{6}$

14. $\sin 135°$ **15.** $\cos 240°$ **16.** $\tan \dfrac{5\pi}{2}$ **17.** $\cos 5\pi$

18. What is the angular speed, in radians per second, of a large truck tire that rotates through an angle of $200°$ in 2 seconds?

19. The radius of a circle and the measure of a central angle are given. Find the length of the arc and area of the sector intercepted by the angle.

a. 8 cm, $\frac{\pi}{6}$ **b.** 12.4 in., $\frac{\pi}{2}$ **c.** 23 m, 42°   **d.** 6 ft, 125°

A point on the terminal side of an angle of rotation is given. Give the sin θ, cos θ, and tan θ.

20. $(5, 3)$ **21.** $(-6, -2)$ **22.** $(3, -3)$ **23.** $(-1, 7)$

24. Flying at an altitude of 1200 ft directly over a distressed fishing boat, a helicopter spots an ocean liner at a 15° angle of depression. How far from the boat is the ocean liner?

25. Find the indicated side length or angle measure.
   a. $a = 106$ cm, $b = 135$ cm, and $c = 165$ cm; find $m\angle C$.
   b. $\angle B = 36°$, $c = 16.4$ ft, and $b = 20.5$ ft; find a.
   c. $a = 27.2$ m, $b = 33.4$ m, and $c = 44.6$ m; find $m\angle B$.
   d. $\angle A = 43°$, $\angle B = 62°$, and $a = 6.5$ yd; find b.

26. The destination of a plane is due north. The plane is traveling 150 mi/hr, but there is a wind of 20 mi/hr from the west. What angle should the plane make with due north? What would the speed of the plane be in still air?

Sketch the graph of each function. Give the amplitude, period, average y-value, and phase shift.

27. $y = \frac{1}{2} \sin x$ **28.** $y = 2 \sin (x + \pi)$ **29.** $y = 3 - \cos \left(x - \frac{\pi}{2}\right)$ **30.** $y = 5 \sin \left(x + \frac{\pi}{3}\right) + 2$

Give a function with the given amplitude, period, average y-value, and phase shift.

31. a sine with amplitude $\frac{1}{2}$, period 4π, average y-value 2, and phase shift π

32. a cosine with amplitude 4, period 8, average y-value -5, and phase shift 2

33. A post sticks out of the sand at a beach. The top of the post is 76 cm above the beach. The depth of the water (in cm) at the beach varies with time due to the motion of the tides, according to the function $d = 40 + 60 \cos \left(\frac{\pi}{6}(t - 2)\right)$, where t is the time in hours since midnight.
   a. Sketch a graph of the function.
   b. What is the period between high tides?
   c. What is the earliest high tide of the day?

PERFORMANCE TASK

A weight attached to a spring or rubber band will bounce up and down in periodic motion that can be modeled by a sine function. Attach a spring or rubber band to your desk and attach a weight of some kind to the end. Use a watch with a second hand to time each bounce, measuring maximum and minimum heights of the weight. Write a function and draw a graph to model this motion. Discuss the trigonometric concepts involved and describe any possible inaccuracies in your data or in the model.

Chapter 11

FRIDAY — 30%

SATURDAY — 30%

SUNDAY — 30%

Project A
Rain, Rain, Go Away
What can you expect when the weather
report forecasts a 30 percent chance of
rain on three successive days?

Project B
That's Not Fair!
How do game designers decide
whether a game is fair?

Project C
**Figures Don't Lie,
But Liars Figure.**
Present some
misleading statistics.

752

I always enjoyed the challenge of math. But today, what I most appreciate about having taken math is that I developed thinking skills that help me create strategies to teach music!

I use math to calculate tempo, or speed relations in music. I also use math to determine the length of a piece, or to understand rhythmic relationships and meaning, as well as to recognize proportions in works of music.

Learning math enhances critical thinking, which is essential to our survival as human beings.

Thomas Wilkins
Resident Conductor
The Florida Orchestra
Tampa, Florida

11-1
Compound Events

In 11-1 you will calculate the probability of more than one event. You will use the following skills.

Find each probability. [Previous course]

1. P(selecting a vowel from the letters of the alphabet)

2. P(selecting a consonant from the letters of the alphabet)

3. P(person's birthday is December 17)

4. P(guessing wrong in a true-false test item)

5. P(guessing wrong in a multiple-choice test item, with answers A, B, C, D)

Evaluate to the nearest thousandth if feasible. [Previous course]

6. $(0.95)^4$

7. $1 - (0.98)^5$

8. $(365)^{40}$

9. $\dfrac{364}{365} \cdot \dfrac{363}{365} \cdot \dfrac{362}{365} \cdot \dfrac{361}{365}$

List the elements that are in set *A* and also in set *B*. [Previous course]

10. $A = \{0, 2, 4, 6, 8\}$; $B = \{0, 3, 6, 9, 12\}$

11. $A = \{vowels\}$; $B = \{consonants\}$

11-2
Sampling Methods

In 11-2 you will learn about issues involved in designing a survey. You will use the following skills.

For each of the following, how many outcomes are there and what is the probability of each one occurring? [Previous course]

12.

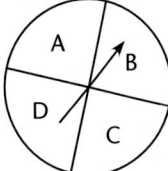

13.

Make a frequency table and a histogram using these numbers from a random number table. [Previous course]

1, 9, 2, 2, 3, 9, 5, 0, 3, 4, 0, 5, 7, 5, 6, 2, 8, 7, 1, 3,
9, 6, 4, 0, 9, 1, 2, 5, 3, 1, 4, 2, 5, 4, 4, 8, 2, 8, 5, 3

14. Make a frequency table.

15. Make a histogram.

IS IT COINCIDENCE?

Abraham Lincoln's inauguration in 1861 marked the first time in history when there were five living former presidents. At that time, James Buchanan, Franklin Pierce, Millard Fillmore, John Tyler, and Martin Van Buren were all alive.

On January 20, 1993, when Bill Clinton was inaugurated President, he became the forty-first person to hold that office. Clinton's inauguration also marked the second time in history when there were five living former presidents. When Richard Nixon resigned on August 9, 1974, he became the first former president of this time period. Following Nixon were Gerald Ford, Jimmy Carter, Ronald Reagan, and George Bush. Collectively, the five former presidents served in public office for nearly a century.

Would you have thought that two presidents had the same birthday? James Polk and Warren Harding were born on the same day, November 2, but in different years, 1795 and 1865, respectively.

Remarkably, *three* presidents have died on the same day, Independence Day. John Adams and Thomas Jefferson died on the exact same day, Tuesday, July 4, 1826. These two presidents signed the Declaration of Independence and died on the 50th anniversary of its signing. According to Jefferson's doctor, his last words were, "Is it the Fourth?" James Monroe also died on July 4 in 1831.

If presidents can have the same birthday, let's consider first ladies. There have been 42 of them, and both Ida McKinley and Barbara Bush were born on June 8.

?

1. How many living former presidents do you think it would be possible to have? Explain.
2. What is the probability that two presidents, chosen at random, have the same birthday?
3. Is it more likely to have five or more living former presidents in the future than it was in the past? Explain.

← C O N N E C T →   *You have used the Addition Counting Principle to find the number of ways two mutually exclusive events can occur. Now you will investigate the probability that at least one of two events will take place.*

Recall that the probability of an event is the fraction of time it is expected to occur. If an event E can occur m ways out of n possible equally likely ways, the probability of that event is $P(E) = \frac{m}{n}$. Probabilities range from 0 to 1.

We are often interested in the probability of a more complicated outcome, for instance, that event A occurs *or* event B occurs. In the Explore, you will investigate such probabilities.

EXPLORE: USE YOUR CENSUS

Some results of the 1990 U.S. census are shown below. (Numbers are rounded to the nearest thousand.)
- total population: 248,710,000
- number of males: 121,239,000
- number of females age 15−19: 8,708,000
- number of males age 15−19: 9,172,000

1. Find the probability that a randomly selected U.S. citizen is:
   a. male
   b. a female 15 to 19 years old
   c. a male 15 to 19 years old
2. Use your results from Step 1 to find the probability that a randomly selected U.S. citizen is female. How did you calculate this number?
3. What is the probability that a randomly selected U.S. citizen is 15 to 19 years old? Explain how you found this probability.
4. What is the probability that a randomly selected U.S. citizen is male *or* 15 to 19 years old, or both? How did you find this probability?
5. What is the difference between the situation in Step 3 and that in Step 4? How did this difference affect finding the requested probability?

Recall that two events that have no common outcomes are *mutually exclusive events.* If two mutually exclusive events are the only ones that can possibly occur, we say that the events are **complementary.** As you saw in Step 2 of the Explore, the probabilities of complementary events must add up to 1.

> The **complement** of event A is $\overline{A}$, where $\overline{A}$ denotes the event that A does not occur. If A and $\overline{A}$ are complementary events, $P(A) + P(\overline{A}) = 1$.

You've already worked with the game of Scrabble. Each game box is manufactured with 100 tiles, according to the following distribution.

Tile	Number	Points	Tile	Number	Points	Tile	Number	Points
A	9	1	J	1	8	S	4	1
B	2	3	K	1	5	T	6	1
C	2	3	L	4	1	U	4	1
D	4	2	M	2	3	V	2	4
E	12	1	N	6	1	W	2	4
F	2	4	O	8	1	X	1	8
G	3	2	P	2	3	Y	2	4
H	2	4	Q	1	10	Z	1	10
I	9	1	R	6	1	Blank	2	0

EXAMPLE

1. What is the probability that a randomly selected Scrabble tile is a vowel?

There are 100 tiles. Nine of them are A's, 12 are E's, 9 I's, 8 O's, and 4 U's. Since the total number of vowels is $9 + 12 + 9 + 8 + 4 = 42$, the probability of selecting a vowel is $\frac{42}{100} = 0.42$.

WHAT DO **YOU** THINK?

What is the probability that a randomly selected Scrabble tile is *not* a vowel?

Rita thinks...

I'll find the number of tiles that are not vowels and divide by 100.

There are $2 + 2 + 4 + 2 + 3 + 2 + 1 + 1 + 4 + 2 + 6 + 2 + 1 + 6 + 4 + 6 + 2 + 2 + 1 + 2 + 1 = 56$ consonant tiles and 2 blanks, for a total of 58 non-vowel tiles. Therefore, the probability that the tile is not a vowel is $\frac{58}{100} = 0.58$.

LeRon thinks...

The event that the tile is not a vowel is the complement of the event that it is a vowel. The two probabilities must add up to 1, so:

$P(\text{not a vowel}) = 1 - P(\text{vowel}) = 1 - 0.42 = 0.58$

a. What is the probability that a randomly selected Scrabble tile is worth more than 4 points?

b. What is the probability that it is worth 4 points or less?

The Venn diagram shows two events, *A* and *B*, in a sample space.

When looking for the probability *P(A or B)*, we cannot simply add the probability of *A* to the probability of *B* because this would "double count" the possibility of *A and B*. To remedy this, we subtract *P(A and B)* from the sum of the individual probabilities. The event *A or B* is a *compound event*, and its probability is a *compound probability*.

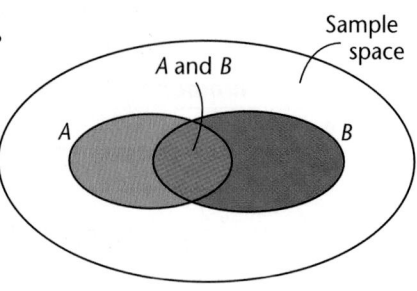

If *A* and *B* are events from the same sample space, then
P(A or B) = P(A) + P(B) − P(A and B).

EXAMPLES

2. If you roll a die, what is the probability that the number that comes up is less than 4 or is even?

P(less than 4 or even) = *P*(less than 4) + *P*(even) − *P*(less than 4 and even)

Three out of the six possible rolls on a die (1, 2, and 3) are less than 4, so *P*(less than 4) = $\frac{3}{6} = \frac{1}{2}$. There are three even rolls (2, 4, and 6), so the probability that the roll is even is also $\frac{1}{2}$. However, a roll of 2 is both less than 4 *and* even, and its probability, *P*(less than 4 and even) = $\frac{1}{6}$. Therefore:

P(less than 4 or even) = $\frac{1}{2} + \frac{1}{2} - \frac{1}{6} = \frac{5}{6} \approx 0.83$

3. In Scrabble, you are hoping that the first letter you draw is worth 5 or more points or is a vowel. What is the probability of this?

There are 100 tiles. Five of them (J, K, Q, X, and Z) are worth 5 or more points, and 42 are vowels. None of the vowels are worth 5 points or more.

P(≥ 5 or vowel) = *P*(≥ 5) + *P*(vowel) − *P*(≥ 5 and vowel)

$= \frac{5}{100} + \frac{42}{100} - \frac{0}{100} = \frac{47}{100} = 0.47$

CONSIDER

1. If *A* and *B* are mutually exclusive, what is *P(A and B)*? Write a formula for *P(A or B)* that is true only for mutually exclusive events.

c. In Scrabble, what is the probability that the first tile drawn is worth one point or is a consonant?

d. In a 500-member senior class, 180 students take Advanced Algebra, 80 take Spanish IV, and 40 take both. What is the probability that a student takes either Advanced Algebra or Spanish IV?

To find $P(A \text{ or } B)$, we add the probabilities of the two events, then subtract the probability of A and B both occurring. If A and B are mutually exclusive events, they cannot both occur at the same time, so $P(A \text{ and } B) = 0$.

REFLECT

1. In English, are the events that a letter is a vowel and that it is a consonant complementary? Is this true for Scrabble tiles? Explain.

2. Give examples of real-world events that are and are not mutually exclusive. Draw a Venn diagram to illustrate each pair of events.

3. When finding the probability of A or B, why is the probability of A and B subtracted from the sum of the individual probabilities?

Exercises

CORE

Getting Started Find each probability for a single roll of a six-sided die.

1. that you roll a 2

2. that you do not roll a 2

3. that you roll a 5 or a 6

4. that you roll an odd number or a 4

5. that you roll an odd number or a number greater than 4

Write the word or phrase that correctly completes each statement.

6. If the sum of the probabilities of two mutually exclusive events is 1, the events are ____.

7. Complementary events are an example of ____ events, because they cannot both occur at the same time.

8. In 1993, the probability that a randomly chosen U.S. citizen was in the armed services was about 0.0054. The probability that a randomly chosen U.S. citizen was female was about 0.5125. If the percentage of women in the armed services was 11.6%, what was the probability that a randomly selected U.S. citizen was female or in the armed services?

Refer to the table of Scrabble tiles on page 757 to help find each probability. Express answers as decimals.

9. that the first tile drawn is a blank

10. that the first tile drawn is worth 2 points

11. that the first tile drawn is worth 2 or 3 points

12. The table shows planets in the solar system. What is the probability that a randomly selected planet:
  a. has an equatorial diameter of less than 25,000 km?
  b. has an equatorial diameter of less than 25,000 km *and* has moons?
  c. has an equatorial diameter of at least 25,000 km *or* has no moons?
  d. What is the relationship between your answers from **b** and **c**? Explain why this is the case.

Planet	Equatorial Diameter (km)	Moons
Mercury	4,880	0
Venus	12,100	0
Earth	12,756	1
Mars	6,794	2
Jupiter	142,800	17(?)
Saturn	120,660	22(?)
Uranus	51,810	15
Neptune	49,528	8
Pluto	2,290(?)	1

13. At a school of 1000 students, 302 students drive their cars to school. There are 232 seniors, and the probability that a senior drives to school is approximately 0.56. What is the probability that a student is a senior or drives to school?

14. Senate Committees There are 100 U.S. senators, of which 29 are members of the Appropriations Committee and 21 are on the Committee on Banking, Housing, and Urban Affairs. If three senators are on both committees, what is the probability that a senator is on the Appropriations Committee or the Committee on Banking, Housing, and Urban Affairs?

Recall that the number of ways to choose r items out of a set of n items is $_nC_r = \dfrac{n!}{r!(n-r)!}$.

15. See You in Court Aline and Jerome are on the six-member student council. Four of the members are to be randomly chosen to be on the student court.
  a. How many different ways can four of the six student council members be selected?
  b. If Aline and Jerome are chosen, there are four other council members for the two remaining positions on the court. How many ways can two of the remaining four members be chosen?
  c. What is the probability that both Aline and Jerome are on the court?
  d. What is the probability that Aline and Jerome are *not* both on the court?

 ## *LOOK BACK*

Solve each equation. Where necessary, round answers to the nearest hundredth. [9-2]

16. $10^x = 25,000$

17. $0.01^n = 0.00001$

18. $0.02^n = 0.0003$

19. The lengths of two sides of a triangle are 6 and 7, and the measure of their included angle is 55°. Find the length of the third side and the area of the triangle. [10-2]

20. Graph $y = 2 \sin \frac{\pi}{4}(x - 2) + 1$. [10-3]

MORE PRACTICE

A set of dominoes usually consists of 28 tiles. Find each probability, expressing your answer as a decimal rounded to the nearest thousandth.

21. that a randomly chosen domino has at least one blank side

22. that a randomly chosen domino does *not* have a blank side

23. that a randomly chosen domino has *no* number greater than 3

24. that a randomly chosen domino has at least one number greater than 3

25. that a randomly chosen domino has the same number on both sides of the bar

26. that a randomly chosen domino has the same number (or a blank) on both sides of the bar or a 5

27. In a junior class of 180 students, 15 students were in the fall play and 22 were in the spring musical. If 8 students were in both events, what is the probability that a junior was in either the fall play or the spring musical?

28. Jacqui, Shelley, and Leilani are three of the twenty players on the softball team.
    a. In how many ways can the manager select nine of the twenty players to start the game?
    b. If Jacqui, Shelley, and Leilani are chosen to start the game, how many ways can the other six starters be chosen from the remaining seventeen players?
    c. What is the probability that Jacqui, Shelley, and Leilani all start the game?
    d. What assumption did you make when finding the probability in **c**? Do you think this is a valid assumption? Explain.

29. **It's a (Noble) Gas!** Of the 103 elements with official names, 6 are noble gases and 60 have atomic masses greater than 100 grams per mole. If two noble gases have atomic masses greater than 100 grams per mole, what is the probability that a randomly selected element is a noble gas or has an atomic mass greater than 100 grams per mole?

Science

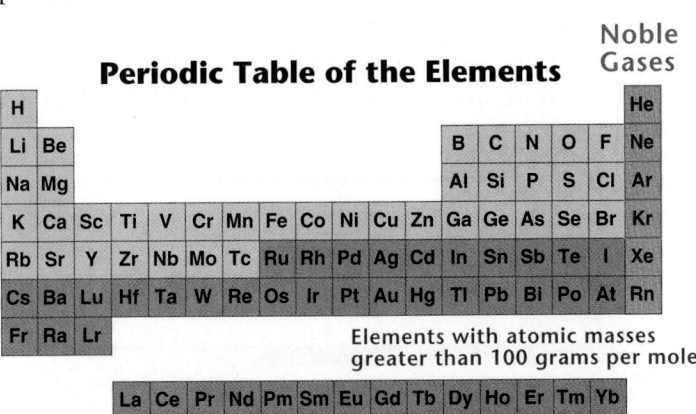

MORE MATH REASONING

30. Remember Your Principles! The Addition Counting Principle states that if A and B are mutually exclusive events, then $n(A \text{ or } B) = n(A) + n(B)$. Use this principle to show that, for mutually exclusive events, $P(A \text{ or } B) = P(A) + P(B)$.

31. For *three* events, A, B, and C:

$P(A \text{ or } B \text{ or } C) =$
$P(A) + P(B) + P(C) - P(A \text{ and } B) - P(B \text{ and } C) - P(A \text{ and } C) + P(A \text{ and } B \text{ and } C)$

a. Use a Venn diagram to show why this formula is valid.

b. Write a formula for $P(A \text{ or } B \text{ or } C \text{ or } D)$. Explain how you found this formula.

11-1
PART B Independent and Dependent Events

← CONNECT →   *You've computed the probability that one event **or** another occurs. Now you will explore the probability that two outcomes **both** occur. You will also see how to identify independent and dependent events.*

Sometimes the result of one event affects the probability of the second event. For instance, if you get an A on a final exam, the probability that you get an A for that course increases. However, the fact that you sat in the back seat on the way to school does not affect the probability of your earning an A.

When knowledge of whether an event occurs affects the probability of a second event, the events are **dependent.** If knowledge of the first event does not affect the probability of the second, the events are **independent.**

CONSIDER

?

Decide whether the two events are dependent or independent and explain why.

1. tossing a coin so that it lands heads and rolling a die so that an even number comes up
2. the temperature being over 90°F today and over 90°F tomorrow
3. the temperature being over 90°F today and seeing a green car tomorrow

The formal definition of independent events also provides a way to calculate the probability that two independent events both occur.

A and B are **independent events** if and only if $P(A \text{ and } B) = P(A) \cdot P(B)$.

1. Assume that membership in the National Geographic Society and being left-handed are independent events. If the probability that a U.S. citizen belongs to the National Geographic Society is $\frac{1}{24}$ and the probability that a U.S. citizen is left-handed is $\frac{1}{10}$, what is the probability that a U.S. citizen is a member of the National Geographic Society and left-handed?

Since the events are independent:

$P(\text{member and left-handed}) = P(\text{member}) \cdot P(\text{left-handed})$

$$= \frac{1}{24} \cdot \frac{1}{10} = \frac{1}{240} \approx 0.0042$$

Although the definition of independent events refers to only two events, the formula holds true for more than two events. If events A through N are independent, $P(A \text{ and } B \text{ and} \ldots \text{ and } N) = P(A) \cdot P(B) \cdot P(C) \cdot \cdots \cdot P(N)$.

2. At the local high school, 28% of the students are juniors, 18% take art, and 26% walk to school. Assuming these events are independent, what is the probability that a randomly selected student is a junior, takes art, and walks to school?

Since the events are independent:

$P(\text{junior, art, walks}) = P(\text{junior}) \cdot P(\text{art}) \cdot P(\text{walks})$

$$= 0.28 \cdot 0.18 \cdot 0.26 \approx 0.0131$$

The probability that a student is a junior who takes art and walks to school is about 0.0131, or 1.31%.

Assume all events are independent.

a. What is the probability that you roll a 6 on a die and a coin toss comes up tails?

b. In 1990, the probability that a U.S. worker lived in Los Angeles was about 1.4%. The probability that a person in Los Angeles drove to work was about 80.6%. What was the probability that a U.S. citizen lived in Los Angeles and drove to work?

c. You've saved your English paper on disk and are planning to print it. If the probability that the disk works is 98%, the probability that the computer works is 99.5%, and the probability that there is paper for the printer is 90%, what is the probability that you can print your English paper?

We all make decisions based on probability estimates. Sometimes, when the probability of an event is very small, we assume that it cannot happen. In the Explore, you will investigate the validity of this assumption.

The Chus have saved enough money to buy a house and have found the perfect home. The only drawback: the house lies in a floodplain, and there is a 2.5% chance that the area will be flooded in any given year. Should the Chus be concerned?

MATERIALS

Graphing utility

1. Suppose the Chus purchase the house. What is the probability that the house will not be flooded in the first year that they live there?
2. Assume that floods are independent events. Use your knowledge of these events to find the probability that the house will not be flooded in the first year *and* the second year. What is the probability that the house will be flooded in *at least* one of those years? Explain.
3. Write an equation for the probability that the house will not be flooded for the first *n* years. What type of equation is this? Graph the equation on a graphing utility.
4. What is the probability that the house will not be flooded for:
   a. 5 years?   **b.** 10 years?   **c.** 15 years?   **d.** 20 years?   **e.** 25 years?   **f.** 30 years?
5. How many years will it be before there is a 50% chance of the house being flooded at least once? a 70% chance?
6. Should the Chus be concerned about the possibility of a flood? Explain.
7. Identify other real-life situations like the one illustrated in the problem. If there is a low probability of an event occurring in any given year, should you conclude that the event will never happen? Explain.

We are often interested in finding the probability that something happens *at least* once. To do this, it is often easier to first find the probability of the complementary event—the probability that it *does not* happen at all.

EXAMPLE

3. Suppose that in a game of basketball, you have an 85% probability of making a free throw. Over the course of a game, you attempt five free throws. What is the probability that you miss at least one of them?

First, find the probability that you make all five. Assuming each free throw is an independent event:

$P(\text{make all } 5) = (0.85)^5 \approx 0.444$

This is the probability that you make all five free throws. Making all five is complementary to missing at least one, so:

$P(\text{miss at least one}) \approx 1 - 0.444 = 0.556$

The probability that you miss at least one of the free throws is about 55.6%.

4. A test that detects a particular disease is accurate 92% of the time. If test results are independent events, how many of these tests should be run on a patient to be 99.95% certain of detecting the disease?

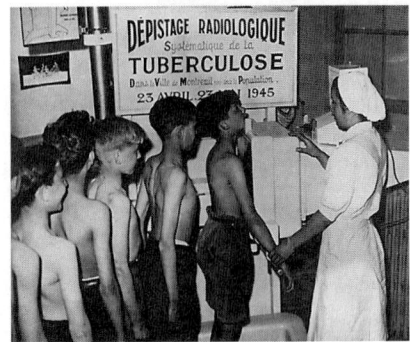

The probability that the test misses the disease is $1 - 0.92 = 0.08$, so the probability of n failures in a row is 0.08^n. We want this value to be less than or equal to 0.05%.

$$0.08^n \leq 0.0005$$

$\log 0.08^n \leq \log 0.0005$	Take logarithms of both sides.
$n \log 0.08 \leq \log 0.0005$	Use properties of logarithms.
$n(-1.10) \leq (-3.30)$	Use a calculator to approximate the logarithms.
$n \geq \dfrac{-3.30}{-1.10}$	Reverse the inequality when dividing by a negative number.
$n \geq 3$	

The test should be run 3 times to be 99.95% certain of detecting the disease.

d. Suppose that 10% of the students in each class at a particular college drop out each year. What is the probability that a new student will drop out before graduation in 4 years?

By working with probabilities of independent events, you can find the probability of success or failure for a series of such events. You can also use these probabilities to find how many safety devices or tests are needed to provide a desired success rate.

1. Give an example of two dependent events and an example of two independent events.

2. Explain how to find the probability that two independent events A and B both occur.

3. Suppose that the probability of an event happening in any given year is p. What is the probability that the event happens at least once in a span of n consecutive years? Explain how you found this probability.

4. Suppose that through probability experiments, you estimate $P(A)$ to be 0.5, $P(B)$ to be 0.6, and $P(A \text{ and } B)$ to be 0.4. Do you think that A and B are independent events? Explain why or why not.

Exercises

CORE

Getting Started Find each probability for tosses of a coin.

1. that two consecutive tosses land heads

2. that three consecutive tosses land tails

3. Are coin tosses dependent or independent events? Explain.

Decide whether the two events are dependent or independent, and explain why.

4. rolling a 6 on two consecutive turns in a game

5. having a part-time job and earning minimum wage

6. getting an A on a test and then getting another A on the next test

Let A, B, and C be independent events, and $P(A) = 0.35$, $P(B) = 0.14$, and $P(C) = 0.82$. Find each probability.

7. $P(A$ and $B)$ **8.** $P(B$ and $C)$ **9.** $P(A$ and $C)$ **10.** $P(A$ and B and $C)$

11. Rain or Shine The Lopez family reunion is to be held in the park on Saturday. Patty plans to attend the reunion if she does not have to work. There is a 50% chance she will have to work. The weather person estimates that there is a 40% chance of rain. What is the probability that Patty will attend the reunion in the rain?

12. Suppose you randomly choose a T-shirt and a pair of pants from your closet. If three of the twelve T-shirts are blue and four of the eight pairs of pants are jeans, what is the probability that you wear a blue shirt and jeans?

Health

13. Testing, Testing The definition of *independent events* can be used as a test to determine whether two events are independent. Suppose that medical researchers are testing a new drug to see whether it helps cure a disease. In the tests, 40% of the patients are given the drug, and 75% of all of the patients are cured. Specific results are shown in the table.

	Drug	**No Drug**	**Total %**
% Cured	30	45	75
% Not Cured	10	15	25
Total %	40	60	100

Are the events that a patient receives this drug and that the patient is cured of the disease independent or dependent? How can you tell? What does this tell you about the effectiveness of the drug?

14. I'm Due Suppose you toss a fair coin and it comes up heads 50 times in a row. What is the probability that it comes up tails on the next flip? Explain what this situation has to do with dependent and independent events.

15. It's a Yahtzee® The game of Yahtzee is played by rolling five dice. Players try to get different combinations of numbers by rolling the dice. The largest number of points that can be earned by a player in one turn is achieved by getting the same number on all five dice. This is called a Yahtzee.

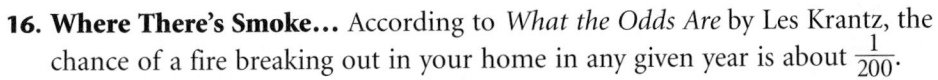

    a. What is the probability that a player will get a Yahtzee of threes when rolling all five dice?

    b. What is the probability that the player will get a Yahtzee of any kind when rolling all five dice?

    c. If a player rolls all five dice thirteen times during a game, what is the probability that the player will *not* get a Yahtzee on any of these rolls? What is the probability that a player will get *at least one* Yahtzee on one of these thirteen rolls?

16. Where There's Smoke... According to *What the Odds Are* by Les Krantz, the chance of a fire breaking out in your home in any given year is about $\frac{1}{200}$.

    a. Assuming that home fires are independent events, what is the probability, to the nearest tenth of a percent, that a fire does *not* occur in your home for:

        i. two consecutive years?   **ii.** three consecutive years?   **iii.** n consecutive years?

    b. The life expectancy of a U.S. citizen is nearly 76 years. What is the probability that a U.S. citizen will have at least one home fire over a 76-year life span?

    c. Do you think that home fires are truly independent events? Explain.

17. Redundant and Repetitive So that a single failure does not cause a disaster, high-risk machines are often designed with *redundancy*. Critical components have backup systems that take over if the original component fails. Suppose a guidance computer on a space shuttle has a 0.001 probability of failure.

    a. How many of these systems should be built into the shuttle so that the overall probability of failure is less than 0.0000001?

    b. What is the probability of failure if three of these systems are used?

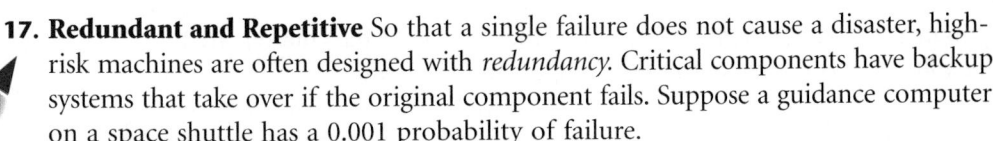

LOOK AHEAD

Write each product in simplest terms. Then rewrite each fraction as a decimal.

18. $\frac{7}{100} \times \frac{6}{99}$ **19.** $\frac{9}{10} \times \frac{9}{10}$ **20.** $\frac{5}{10} \times \frac{4}{9} \times \frac{3}{8}$ **21.** $\frac{364}{365} \times \frac{363}{365} \times \frac{362}{365}$

22. I'm a People Person Suppose that you apply for a summer job and 36% of the job applicants are called back for an interview. If you have an interview, the probability that you get the job is 25%.

    a. What is the probability that you will get the job?

    b. You are called for an interview. Given this knowledge, what is the probability that you will get the job?

MORE PRACTICE

Decide whether the two events are dependent or independent, and explain why.

23. missing the bus and then being late for school

24. your teacher choosing your name from a box to present a report, then after replacing your name, drawing your name later to answer a question

Let *A*, *B*, and *C* be independent events, and $P(A) = 0.42$, $P(B) = 0.25$, and $P(C) = 0.74$. Find each probability.

25. $P(A \text{ and } B)$ **26.** $P(B \text{ and } C)$ **27.** $P(A \text{ and } C)$ **28.** $P(A \text{ and } B \text{ and } C)$

29. Off Base A baseball team is about to bat in the bottom of the ninth inning. The opposing team's pitcher knows that he will be removed from the game if he allows a batter to reach base. The *on-base percentages* (probability that the batter will reach base) of the three batters due up next are 0.375, 0.348, and 0.279.

    a. Assuming that consecutive batters reaching base are independent events, what is the probability that the pitcher will not allow any of the three batters to reach base? Explain how you found this probability.

    b. Do you believe that these events are actually independent? In other words, would the event that one batter reached base (or did not reach base) have no effect on the next batter's chances of success? Justify your answer.

30. Balanced Babies A newly married couple is beginning a family, and the husband and wife want to have both a boy and a girl.

    a. Suppose the couple has two children. Find the probability that the second child is the same sex as the first. What is the probability that, after two children, the couple has a boy and a girl?

    b. For each number of children, find the probabilities that all of the children are the same sex and that the couple has at least one boy and one girl.

      i. three   **ii.** four   **iii.** five   **iv.** *n*

    c. How many children must the couple have for the probability to be greater than 90% that they will have a boy and a girl?

    d. How many children must the couple have in order to *guarantee* that they will have both a boy and a girl? Explain.

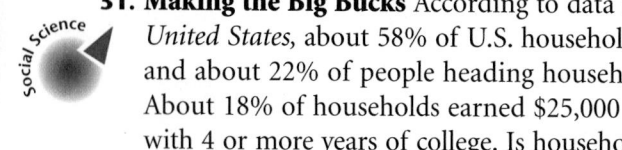

31. Making the Big Bucks According to data in the *1992 Statistical Abstract of the United States,* about 58% of U.S. households earned $25,000 or more in 1991, and about 22% of people heading households had 4 years or more of college. About 18% of households earned $25,000 or more and were headed by a person with 4 or more years of college. Is household income independent of educational attainment? Explain how you found your answer.

MORE MATH REASONING

32. Consider the probability of obtaining exactly one head in *n* tosses of a coin.

    a. Find the probability of this event for 2, 3, 4, and 5 tosses.

    b. Develop a general formula for *n* tosses, where *n* is a whole number.

    c. What happens to the probability in **b** as *n* increases? Why does this make sense?

33. Lightning Never Strikes Twice In John Irving's novel *The World According to Garp,* Garp buys a home that a plane had crashed into earlier. Garp feels certain that it cannot happen again since it is nearly impossible that such a crash could happen twice. Do you agree with Garp's reasoning? What does this have to do with independent and dependent events? Explain.

34. Guilt by Probability Imagine that you fit the description of a person accused of a crime: a male 15–19 years old, attending high school, height 6 feet or over. A prosecutor is trying to convince a judge that you should be tried for the crime.

"Although we have no actual evidence to link this person to the crime, the probability that he did it is overwhelming. The approximate probability that a randomly selected U.S. citizen is male is 0.49, that the person is between 15 and 19 years old is 0.07, that a person attends high school is 0.05, and that a person is 6 feet tall or more is 0.07. Therefore, the probability of a person having all of these characteristics is about 0.00012. He *must* be the one!"

a. Explain how the prosecutor came up with the probability of 0.00012 that a person would have all of these characteristics.

b. Assuming the individual probabilities are accurate, find one or more flaws in the prosecutor's argument that will convince the judge to let you go.

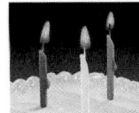

11-1 PART C Conditional Probability

← CONNECT →   *You know how to find the probability that two or more independent events occur. Now you will explore ways to find probabilities of dependent events.*

In many real-world situations, knowledge of one event affects our estimate of the probability of another. For instance, making the first cut when trying out for a team or being called back when auditioning for a play increases the probability that you will make the team or be in the play.

When the probability of event *B* depends on event *A*, this probability is called a **conditional probability.** The conditional probability that *B* occurs, given that *A* has occurred, is written $P(B|A)$.

In the figure, the probability of randomly choosing a point in square *A* is $\frac{1}{64}$. However, if you know that the point chosen is inside square *B*, then the probability that the point is in square *A* is $\frac{1}{4}$. So, $P(A|B) = \frac{1}{4}$.

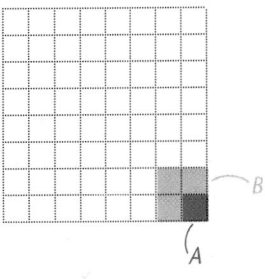

EXAMPLES

1. Suppose that you roll two dice, one green and one orange. What is the probability that you roll a sum of 8, given that the green die comes up 3?

We want to find $P(\text{sum is } 8 | \text{green is } 3)$. The only way for the sum of the two dice to be 8 is if the orange die comes up 5. Therefore:

$$P(\text{sum is } 8 | \text{green is } 3) = P(\text{orange is } 5) = \frac{1}{6}$$

2. In 1993, approximately 4.19 million U.S. workers were paid an hourly wage of $4.25 or less. About 2.24 million of these workers were 16 to 24 years old. What was the probability that a worker was age 16 to 24, given that the worker earned $4.25 or less?

$$P(\text{age } 16-24 | \text{earned } \$4.25 \text{ or less}) = \frac{2.24}{4.19} \approx 0.535$$

In 1993, the probability that a person earning $4.25 an hour or less was 16 to 24 years old was about 0.535, or 53.5%.

TRY IT

a. Suppose that you roll two dice. If the first die comes up 3, what is the probability that the sum of the dice is 6 or more?

EXPLORE: THE DRAWING ROOM

A store is holding a drawing to attract business. You are given one entry blank each time you shop at the store. The drawing is for the prizes shown.

When the drawing is held, there are 90 tickets in a large bin. Since you went to the store three times, three of these tickets have your name on them.

1. The drawing for third prize is held first. What is the probability that you win third prize?

2. The winning ticket is not replaced in the bin. What is the conditional probability that you win second prize given that you did *not* win third prize?

3. What is the probability that you win neither third nor second prize? Explain.

4. Suppose you do not win third prize or second prize. What is the probability that you win first prize now? that you win none of the prizes? Explain how you found these probabilities.

5. The winner of the $25 gift certificate claims that the drawing should have been done in the reverse order: first, second, and then third. Do you agree? Why or why not?

6. Repeat Steps 1–4, but assume that the winning tickets *are* replaced in the bin. Are the third-, second-, and first-place drawings dependent events when the winning tickets are replaced? when they are not replaced? Explain.

Drawing a series of tickets from a bin without putting the winning tickets back into the bin (as in Explore Steps 1–5) is called **sampling without replacement.** If the winning tickets are replaced, the method is called **sampling with replacement.**

EXAMPLES

In the game of Scrabble, tiles are usually drawn without replacement. Recall that there are 100 tiles, including 12 E's and 6 R's. Find each probability for the first two tiles drawn.

3. $P(E|R)$ (The probability that the second tile is an E if the first was an R.)

After the first tile is drawn, there are 99 left, and there are still 12 E's. So:

$P(E|R) = \frac{12}{99} = \frac{4}{33} \approx 0.121$

4. $P(E|E)$

The first tile is drawn and is an E. There are 99 tiles left, and 11 of the E's remain. Therefore:

$P(E|E) = \frac{11}{99} = \frac{1}{9} \approx 0.111$

TRY IT

There are twelve marbles in a bag. Five are yellow, four are red, and three are blue. Marbles are drawn from the bag without replacement. Find each probability for the first two marbles drawn.

b. $P(\text{yellow}|\text{blue})$ **c.** $P(\text{red}|\text{red})$ **d.** $P(\text{blue}|\text{blue})$

CONSIDER

?

1. If sampling is done with replacement, are the samples independent or dependent events? If sampling is done without replacement, are the samples independent or dependent events? Explain your answers.
2. If A and B are independent events, what is true about $P(A|B)$ and $P(A)$? Explain.

In 11-1B, you found a rule to calculate the probability of two independent events. We can now expand this rule so that it applies to *any* two events.

For events A and B, $P(A \text{ and } B) = P(A) \cdot P(B|A)$.

If A and B are independent, the probability of B is not affected by A, and $P(B|A) = P(B)$. So for independent events, the formula above is equivalent to $P(A \text{ and } B) = P(A) \cdot P(B)$.

5. In March 1993, the probability that a U.S. citizen, age 25 or older, was employed was about 61.8%. In this group of people, 27.8% had earned a bachelor's degree or more. What was the probability that a U.S. citizen, age 25 or older, was employed and had a bachelor's degree or more?

P(employed and $\geq$ bachelor's) = P(employed) $\cdot$ P($\geq$ bachelor's | employed)

$= 0.618 \cdot 0.278 \approx 0.172$

The probability that a U.S. citizen in this age group was employed and had a bachelor's degree or more was about 0.172 or 17.2%.

TRY IT

e. According to figures in *What the Odds Are* by Les Krantz, about 58.0% of used motor oil in the United States is reused in some way. Of this reused oil, 8.6% is refined and used as motor oil a second time. What is the probability that an ounce of old motor oil will be reused as motor oil?

When two events are dependent, conditional probability is used to show how the probability of one event is affected by the other. Conditional probability is used to analyze situations involving sampling without replacement.

REFLECT

1. If you wanted to win several prizes in a drawing, would you prefer that winning tickets be drawn with or without replacement? Explain.

2. Suppose that you know that the probability of events M and N both happening is 0.24, that the probability of M is 0.30, and that the probability of N is 0.75. Are M and N independent events? Explain.

3. Give an example of how you might use the idea of conditional probability in your daily life.

Exercises

CORE

Getting Started Decide whether the two events given (a) are dependent or independent, and (b) involve sampling with replacement, sampling without replacement, or neither.

1. rolling a 5 on a die, then choosing a red card from a deck

2. choosing a red card from a deck, then choosing a second red card without replacing the first card

3. choosing a red card from a deck, then picking a second red card after replacing the first

4. rolling a 2 on a die and then rolling a 2 again

Recall that there are 100 Scrabble tiles, including 4 D's, 3 G's, 1 J, and 8 O's. Find each probability for the first two tiles drawn without replacement.

5. $P(\text{D}|\text{G})$ **6.** $P(\text{D}|\text{D})$ **7.** $P(\text{J}|\text{J})$ **8.** $P(\text{O}|\text{O})$

Industry

9. It Pays to Advertise An advertising agency finds that 24% of the people who see an advertisement buy their product. They advertise on a television show seen by 17% of the viewing audience. Assuming that everyone watching the show sees the advertisement, what is the probability that a viewer sees the show and buys the product?

A game is played where a die is rolled by player 1 and then by player 2. Player 2 wins if the number she rolls is greater than or equal to the number rolled by player 1.

10. Does the game describe dependent or independent events? Explain.

11. Find the probability that player 2 will roll a number greater than or equal to 3.

12. Find the probability that player 2 will roll a number greater than or equal to 3, given that player 1 has already rolled a 3.

History

13. The peoples who immigrated to the United States from Europe and Asia from 1820 to 1992 are listed; **a–d** refer to this time period.
  a. 4,741,776 immigrants came from Ireland. What is the probability that an immigrant came from Ireland?
  b. Ireland is in Europe. What is the probability that an immigrant came from Ireland, given that the immigrant came from Europe?
  c. Given that 1,158,881 immigrants came from the Philippines, what is the probability that an immigrant came from the Philippines?
  d. The Philippines are in Asia. What is the probability that an immigrant came from the Philippines, given that the immigrant came from Asia?

Region	Number of Immigrants
Europe	37,400,991
Asia	6,706,139
All Countries	59,795,158

Health

14. According to figures from a National Health Interview survey, 83.1% of U.S. children were covered by health care insurance in 1988. 56.9% of children without health care insurance saw a doctor during that year. What is the probability that a child in the United States was not covered by health care insurance and the child did not see a doctor in 1988?

Health

15. Suppose the probability that a person has a particular disease is 0.005. If a person has the disease, a medical test gives a positive result 95% of the time. If the person does not have the disease, the test gives a false-positive result 1% of the time.
  a. Find the probability that a person has the disease and the test result is positive.
  b. Find the probability that a person does not have the disease and the test result is positive.
  c. What is the probability that a person whose test result is positive does *not* have the disease? Explain.

 ## *LOOK BACK*

Evaluate each expression. If necessary, round answers to the nearest hundredth. [9-2]

16. $\log_2 32$ **17.** $\log_3 \frac{1}{27}$ **18.** $\log 10^{15}$ **19.** $\ln 10$

20. In $\triangle RST$, $t = 6.5$, $r = 8.7$, and $s = 11.2$. Find $m\angle R$ and the area of $\triangle RST$. [10-2]

21. Graph $y = -\frac{1}{2} \cos 2\pi(x + 2) - 4$. [10-3]

MORE PRACTICE

Decide whether the two events given (a) are dependent or independent, and (b) involve sampling with replacement, sampling without replacement, or neither.

22. drawing a colored marble from a bag, putting it back, then drawing another

23. tossing a coin, then drawing a marble from the bag

24. drawing a marble, then drawing another without putting the first back in the bag

25. choosing two people for a team from a group of ten people

The game of Rummikub® is played with tiles. The black, red, orange, and blue tiles are numbered 1 to 13. For each color and number, there are two tiles. There are also two jokers for a total of 106 tiles. Find each probability for the first two tiles drawn without replacement.

26. $P(\text{red}|\text{red})$ **27.** $P(11|11)$

28. $P(\text{joker}|\text{joker})$ **29.** $P(11|5)$

30. $P(\text{red}|\text{joker})$ **31.** $P(\text{joker}|\text{red})$

32. Four More Years! From 1792 to 1992, incumbent presidents ran for reelection 24 times and were reelected 15 times. What is the probability that a candidate was reelected, given that he was the incumbent?

33. I Can Probably Tape That for You Approximately 98% of U.S. households have at least one television set. Of those households with a television, about 79% have a VCR. Find the probability that a U.S. household has a television set and a VCR.

34. But I Feel Fine! Suppose the probability that a person has a particular disease is 0.003. If a person has the disease, a medical test gives a positive result 98% of the time. If the person does not have the disease, the test gives a false-positive result 2% of the time. What is the probability that a person with a positive test result actually has the disease?

MORE MATH REASONING

35. The Johnstons have two children. Mr. Blair meets one of the children, a boy. To find the probability that both children are males, given that one is a male, Mr. Blair reasons that there are four possible ways a two-child family can occur.

Mr. Blair reasons that since the situation with two females cannot be true for the Johnston family, that possibility must be eliminated. He concludes that there is a 1 in 3 chance of two males. Do you agree with his reasoning? Explain.

First Child	Second Child
male	male
male	female
female	male
female	female

36. So You Hail From Lake County! According to 1990 census figures, of the 248,709,873 people living in the United States, 1,481,157 lived in a county named Lake County, 5,544,159 lived in Indiana, and 475,594 lived in Lake County, Indiana. What is the probability that a person lived in Indiana, given that he or she lived in Lake County? Explain your solution method.

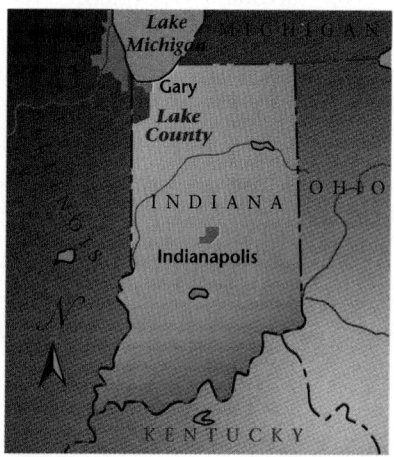

37. That Darn Machine! A company has two computer printers. People use printer A 65% of the time, since it only jams on 5% of the jobs it does, while printer B jams on 20% of its jobs.

a. If a printer jams, what is the probability that it is printer B?

b. In order for printer B to be responsible for 50% of the jams, what percentage of the time should it be used?

c. A repair person replaces a part on printer B, lowering its percentage of jams to 10%. What percentage of the time should printer B be used now in order for it to be responsible for 50% of the jams?

11-1
PART D   Making Connections

← **CONNECT** →   *You've seen how to find the probability that one event or another occurs, explored independent and dependent events, and found the probability that two or more events occur together.*

Now that you're familiar with ways to find probabilities of several events, you can find the probability that two people in a group—or two presidents in history—share a birthday.

Ignoring February 29, you must have 366 people in a room to be 100% certain that at least two of them have the same birthday. But how many people must be in a room to have a probability of 50% that at least two of them share a birthday?

1. Guess the number of people that must be in a room so that there is a 50% chance that at least two of them share a birthday.

2. If there are two people in a room, what is the probability that they have the same birthday? What is the probability that they do *not* have the same birthday?

3. A third person enters the room. What is the probability that the third person does not have the same birthday as either of the first two, given that the first two do not have the same birthday? What type of probability is this?

4. What is the probability that the second person does not have the same birthday as the first *and* that the third person does not have the same birthday as either the first or the second person? Explain how you found this probability.

5. Use your spreadsheet to make a table showing the number of people in a room, the probability that no two of them share a birthday, and the probability that at least two of them do share a birthday. What is the smallest number of people needed for there to be a 50% or greater chance that at least two of them share a birthday? Compare your result to your guess from Step 1.

6. If 50 people are in a room, what is the probability that at least two of them share a birthday? How many people would there need to be so that there is less than a 1% chance that no two share a birthday?

7. Counting President Clinton, 41 different people have been president of the United States. Is it surprising that two of them, James Polk and Warren Harding, had the same birthday? Explain.

REFLECT

1. Explain in your own words the difference between dependent and independent events.

2. When finding the probability of *A* or *B*, do you have to consider whether or not *A* and *B* are independent events? Why or why not?

3. You always seem to have your shoelaces untied. Your mother says, "On any given day, there is a probability of 0.01 that you will fall and hurt yourself if you do not tie your shoelaces!" Should you start tying your shoelaces? Justify your decision.

Self-Assessment

Decide whether the two events are dependent or independent, and explain why.

1. tossing heads on a coin and then tossing heads on another coin

2. spinning a 6 on a spinner and tossing heads on a coin

3. picking a vowel in Scrabble and then picking another without replacing the first

4. picking a vowel in Scrabble, replacing it, and then picking another

5. that you have a cold today and you have a cold tomorrow

6. that you get a telephone call from a friend and you lose a quarter in a vending machine

The table shows the distribution of the Scrabble tiles that are worth 1 point. Find each probability. Where necessary, round answers to the nearest hundredth.

7. that the first tile drawn is an A

8. that the first tile drawn is an A or an R

9. that the first tile drawn is a consonant and is worth one point. (Note: Two of the 100 tiles are blank.)

Tile	Number	Tile	Number	Tile	Number
A	9	L	4	S	4
E	12	N	6	T	6
I	9	O	8	U	4
		R	6		

10. that the first two tiles drawn are vowels if the first tile is replaced before drawing the second

11. that the first two tiles drawn are vowels if the first tile is not replaced before drawing the second

12. You toss a coin and then roll a die. Which of the following have probability $\frac{1}{6}$?
I. P(you roll a 6)   II. P(roll a 6 | heads)   III. P(heads, and roll is greater than 4)
(a) only I   (b) only II   (c) only III   (d) II and III   (e) I, II, and III

13. Explain why $P(A|B) = P(A)$ when A and B are independent events.

Evaluate each expression. If necessary, round answers to the nearest hundredth. [9-2]

14. $\log_4 32$ **15.** $\log_2 \frac{1}{64}$ **16.** $\ln e$ **17.** $\log 10^{-6}$

18. In $\triangle ABC$, $m\angle A = 42°$, $c = 11.8$, and $m\angle C = 107°$. Find b, a, $m\angle B$, and the area of $\triangle ABC$. [10-2]

19. As of 1994, there were 201 people in the Basketball Hall of Fame. Of these, 99 were players and 47 were coaches. One person, John Wooden, is in the Hall of Fame both as a player and as a coach. What is the probability that a Hall of Fame member is a player or a coach?

20. The table shows U.S. investment in foreign countries for 1993, in millions of dollars.

   a. What is the probability that a U.S. dollar invested abroad was invested in Asia and the Pacific?

   b. The 1993 investment in Japan was $31,393 million. What is the probability that a U.S. dollar invested abroad was invested in Japan, given that it was invested in Asia and the Pacific?

Region	Investment ($ millions)
South America	30,921
Asia and the Pacific	98,728
All Countries	548,644

   c. What is the probability that a U.S. dollar invested abroad in 1993 was invested in South America?

   d. The 1993 U.S. investment in Brazil was $16,908 million. What is the probability that a U.S. dollar invested abroad was invested in Brazil, given that it was invested in South America?

21. Does It Work? A medical research team is testing a new treatment for a disease. Of the patients in the study, 42% are given the treatment, and 90% of all patients are cured of the disease.

	Treatment	No Treatment	Total
% Cured	40	50	90
% Not Cured	2	8	10
% of Total	42	58	

Are the events that a patient received this treatment and that the patient is cured of the disease independent or dependent? How can you tell? What does this tell you about the effectiveness of the treatment?

22. That'll Never Happen A motorist always exceeds the speed limit on a particular stretch of highway when going to work to make sure she arrives on time. She estimates that one out of every 400 speeding cars gets a ticket.

   a. Assuming that tickets are independent events, what is the probability that she does not get a ticket for:

   i. one month (22 workdays)? **ii.** half a year (130 workdays)? **iii.** n consecutive workdays?

   b. What is the probability that this driver will get at least one speeding ticket within a year if she works 260 days that year?

23. In Security You are designing a computer security system for a company that requires a high degree of secrecy. The system requires users to enter a three-digit code number before they have access to the computer.

   a. What is the probability that a person who does not know the correct code will guess it correctly in one try?

   b. Suppose the person is allowed to try again. What is the probability that he or she will guess the correct code, given that he or she knows the first guess was wrong? Explain how you found this answer.

   c. The person who does know the password has a 5% probability of entering the code incorrectly. What is the probability that this person enters the code incorrectly twice in a row?

   d. You need to decide how many times a person should be allowed to try to enter the password correctly before the computer alerts the security guards that an unauthorized user is on the system. How many tries will you allow? Explain how you decided on this number.

11-2 Sampling Methods

In 1936, Literary Digest *magazine predicted that Kansas Republican Alfred (Alf) Landon would be elected president of the United States by a comfortable margin. This prediction was based on the largest response to any poll in history. Using telephone directories and club membership lists,* Literary Digest *sent questionnaires to over 10 million people, 2 million of whom returned their responses.*

Landon's opponent was Franklin Delano Roosevelt, who was completing his first term as president. The country was in the depths of the Great Depression, and it was Roosevelt who had instituted many expensive government programs to help the nation recover. But because of these progams, the U.S. budget deficit was growing rapidly. Landon was promising to reduce government spending.

Despite Roosevelt's popularity, the editor of Literary Digest *was confident of the prediction that Landon would win. The magazine had correctly predicted the winner of every presidential election since 1916.*

On election day, Roosevelt won with over 62% of the popular vote and an electoral vote count of 523, compared to 8 electoral votes for Landon—the most overwhelming victory ever. Roosevelt won every state except Maine and Vermont. Kansas newspaper editor Wilma Allen White noted, "Landon went down the creek in a torrent." Literary Digest *went bankrupt soon afterward.*

?

1. What are some things that should be considered when taking a poll?

2. In 1936, what problems might have been caused by using names from telephone books to choose poll subjects? Would these same concerns be valid today? Explain.

3. Many presidential polls today survey only a few thousand prospective voters, yet their results are far more accurate than the *Literary Digest* poll, which had more than 2 million respondents. Explain why this might be the case.

← CONNECT → *You've used equations to model trends in data. Now you will investigate issues involved in taking a data sample that is representative of an entire population.*

Suppose a politician hires you to predict whether she will win an election. Your job is to study a large group of people (citizens who are likely to vote in this election) and predict how this group will vote on election day. In statistics, this group is called the **population.**

Of course, it is too expensive and time-consuming to interview each likely voter. Instead, you question a subset of the voting population, called a **sample.** From the results of the sample, you make a prediction about the outcome of the actual election. The accuracy of your prediction depends partly on how well your sample represents the population at large. Your goal is to have a **representative sample.**

CONSIDER
?

1. In what ways might subscribers of a particular magazine fail to be representative of the nation as a whole?

When a sample is not representative of the population it is taken from, the sample is called **biased.**

TRY IT

State whether each sample is likely to be biased. Explain your reasoning.

a. A telephone survey about support for possible Social Security cuts is taken between the hours of 9 a.m. and 5 p.m. on weekdays.

b. A survey about whether or not student funds should be raised for the senior prom is taken in ninth grade English classes.

Random sampling techniques are often used to avoid sampling bias. A random sample is used so that every subject in the population has an equal probability of being chosen for the sample, and so that the selection of a particular subject has no effect on the chances of any other subject.

There are many methods that can be used to take random samples.

Describe how, in a neighborhood of 240 homes, a random sample of 30 households can be chosen for a survey.

Jacy thinks...

I'll print out a list of all 240 addresses, separate them, and put the slips of paper in a box. Then I'll mix the addresses thoroughly and draw 30 of them.

Rita thinks...

I'll assign one number from 1 to 240 to the address of each household. Then I'll generate 30 random numbers from 1 to 240 to identify the households to survey.

(Random numbers on a calculator range from 0 to 1. They can be converted to whole numbers from 1 to 240 by multiplying by 240, taking the integer part of the result, and adding 1, as shown.)

TRY IT

Imagine a bathtub full of M&M's®. You are to estimate what percentage of M&M's are of each color by selecting 100 M&M's at random.

c. What is the population for this problem?

d. State whether each approach will give you a random sample. Explain.

   i. You mix the M&M's well, then remove 100 with a scoop from the middle of the tub.

   ii. You ask each of 20 students to select 5 M&M's.

   iii. You ask each of 20 students to select 5 M&M's, but you blindfold the students before the selection.

The results of a sample can be displayed in a **histogram,** which is a bar graph that shows the frequency, percentage, or probability of outcomes. The outcomes must be divided into categories of equal size.

Suppose that the number of academic classes taken by 2124 students at a school is:

4 classes = 185 students
5 classes = 814 students
6 classes = 866 students
7 classes = 259 students

The histogram displays these results, showing the frequency of each outcome. Notice that the labels for the categories are shown on the horizontal axis, centered under the appropriate rectangles.

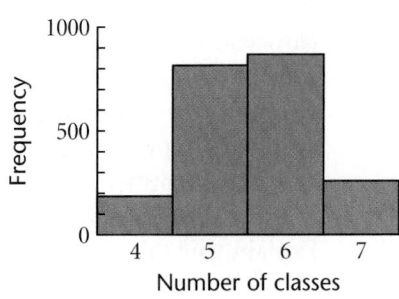

1. Suppose that a survey asks 500 people about the number of days each week that they eat dinner at restaurants. The survey has the following results. Make a histogram of the results.

0 dinners = 57 people = 11.4%   1 dinner = 179 people = 35.8%
2 dinners = 145 people = 29.0%   3 dinners = 42 people = 8.4%
4 dinners = 29 people = 5.8%   5 dinners = 25 people = 5.0%
6 dinners = 17 people = 3.4%   7 dinners = 6 people = 1.2%

The percentage of the population sampled is shown on the vertical axis. The categories for the histogram (number of dinners at a restaurant) are the whole numbers 0−7; these are shown on the horizontal axis. Rectangles of equal width are drawn to the appropriate height. The labels 0−7 are centered under the rectangles.

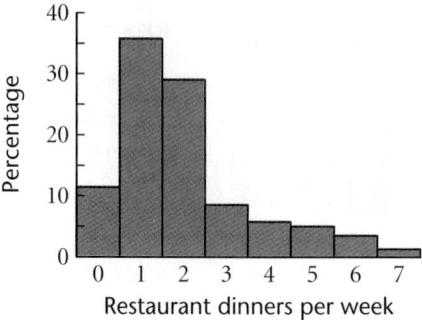

2. Assuming this sample is representative, find the probability that a randomly chosen person eats dinner at a restaurant twice a week or less.

We can find this probability by adding the percentages of people eating dinner in a restaurant 0, 1, and 2 times a week.

11.4% + 35.8% + 29.0% = 76.2%

We predict a probability of 0.762 that a person chosen at random eats dinner in a restaurant 2 times a week or less.

EXPLORE: RULER OF ALL I SURVEY

MATERIALS

Graph paper
Graphing utility (optional)

You are to survey twelve students in your class on a topic chosen by your class or teacher.

1. Decide how you will select a random sample of twelve students from your class population. Explain why your method gives each student an equal probability of being selected.
2. Use your method to identify twelve students. Then you or one of your classmates will be chosen to do the actual survey. Record the survey results and use a graphing utility to make a histogram showing the results of the survey. Make a copy of the histogram.
3. Now you will design a survey for your entire school. First, identify an issue that affects students in your school. If you were to survey students about this issue, would different groups tend to respond differently? For instance, would the grade level of a student tend to affect their opinion? Identify possible sources of bias in such a survey.
4. Propose a method that you could use to select a random sample of 50 students. Explain why this method selects a truly random sample.

The size of a sample is a critical issue in designing a survey. If a sample is too small, the results may not be representative. Suppose a pollster asked four people whether they were going to vote for Elena Munoz. If three said "Yes," it would not be reasonable to conclude that she is likely to win with 75% of the vote. However, if 3000 out of 4000 randomly selected voters supported her, you would have much more confidence in this estimate.

CONSIDER

2. What are the disadvantages of using too large a sample? Give some reasons that you might want to limit the size of a sample.

TRY IT

In each situation, would you study the entire population or a sample? Why?

e. You manufacture light bulbs and want to check that the bulbs last at least 500 hours.

f. You manufacture fuel tanks for the space shuttle and want to make sure that there are no leaks in the tanks.

An interesting example of statistical research, the **capture-recapture method,** is used to estimate wildlife populations.

Suppose you need to estimate the number of deer in a park. Under the capture-recapture method, a random sample of deer is captured, tagged, and released. Later, another random sample is chosen. The ratio of captured deer with tags to the total number captured allows you to estimate the total number of deer.

EXAMPLE

3. Suppose that a random sample of 50 deer in a state park is captured and tagged. Two weeks later, a random sample of 33 deer contains two with tags. Estimate the number of deer in the park.

The capture-recapture method assumes that the fraction of tagged deer in the second sample is equal to the fraction of tagged deer in the whole population.

$$\frac{\text{tagged deer in second sample}}{\text{deer in second sample}} = \frac{\text{tagged deer in population}}{\text{population } (P)}$$

$$\frac{2}{33} = \frac{50}{P}$$

$$2P = 1650$$

$$P = 825$$

Problem-Solving Tip

Use proportional thinking.

We estimate the deer population to be about 825.

By choosing an unbiased sample, you can make a prediction about the whole population. Surveys and polls determine the views of a subset of a population and use this information to estimate the views of the entire group.

1. What are the similarities and differences between the meaning of *bias* as it is used in everyday language and its meaning in statistics?

2. Explain why a sample of voters from a particular age group might be a biased sample of the voting population.

3. A random sample is more likely to be unbiased than one taken from a particular group. However, is it possible for a random sample to be biased? Explain your answer.

Exercises

CORE

Getting Started In each situation, state whether you think a sample or the entire population should be studied, and explain why.

1. A chef is making soup and wants to know if there is enough salt in it.

2. A political researcher wants to know how many people are going to vote in an upcoming election.

3. The president of a company wants to know how many people are going to come to the company picnic.

4. Explain the difference between a population and a sample.

Determine whether each statement is true or false. If the statement is false, change the underlined word or phrase to make it true.

5. When a sample of people is not representative of the whole population, that sample is called a <u>random</u> sample.

6. In random sampling, each member of the population has <u>an equal</u> chance to be selected for the sample.

Identify the population being studied in each situation. Would you study the entire population or a sample? Why?

7. A baking company wants to make sure that its bread does not contain more than the federally allowed amount of contaminants.

8. A medical research group wants to study the blood cholesterol level of children in the United States.

9. If you are doing a survey at your school, is the population for the study necessarily the entire school population? If so, explain why; if not, give an example of a school study where the population of the study would not be the school population.

10. Describe a method for randomly sampling 50 different restaurants about the average prices they charge for dinner.

11. Sketch a histogram for the data set 2, 5, 4, 6, 3, 4, 5, 3, 4, 4, 6, 2, 6, 1, 7, 3, 5, 4, 4, 3. Use percentages along the vertical axis. (Hint: Tally the data first.)

12. The table shows U.S. population age distribution figures, in millions, for the years 1980 and 1991.

Years	Total Aged 0–74	0–14 Years	15–29 Years	30–44 Years	45–59 Years	60–74 Years
1980	217.1	51.3	62.4	43.3	34.4	25.7
1991	239.2	55.1	57.4	61.6	36.2	28.9

a. Make a histogram of the data for each year showing percentages in each age group.

b. For each year, find the probability that a person is from 15 to 29 years old.

c. Describe the differences between the two histograms. What do these differences show about the U.S. population?

In each situation, explain why the sample obtained may be biased.

13. You are collecting information on the type of food people like to eat when they are shopping in a mall. You decide to ask every fifth person who walks by you, as long as they look like they wouldn't mind being interviewed.

14. You are interested in learning what percentage of women hold full-time jobs while raising a family. You decide to conduct random telephone interviews, using your local telephone directory each morning for one week.

15. The U.S. Census is intended to be a study of the entire population of the United States. What are some problems that might be encountered in doing this study?

16. Suppose that you can randomly select people for a survey by drawing names out of a hat or by making a list of names, assigning each a number, then using a computer to choose the numbers randomly. How would you decide which method to use?

17. A team of wildlife researchers captures and tags 40 caribou in a certain region. Two weeks later, they capture 30 caribou, 5 of which are tagged. What would be their estimate of the total number of caribou in the region?

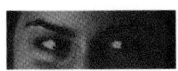 **LOOK AHEAD**

18. Suppose that the average height of a woman in the United States between the ages of 18 and 24 is $5'5\frac{1}{2}''$. Would you expect there to be more women in this age group between $5'5''$ and $5'6''$ or between $5'10''$ and $5'11''$? Explain.

19. Suppose your teacher gives two quizzes. The average score on both is 85. Scores on the first quiz range from 68 to 100, while scores on the second range from 77 to 93.

a. Sketch possible histograms of the scores on each of the two quizzes. Describe how these histograms differ.

b. On which quiz would you be more confident that your score was above 80? Why?

MORE PRACTICE

Identify the population being studied in each situation. Would you study the entire population or a sample? Why?

20. A boat manufacturer wants to make sure that the boats he sells do not leak.

21. A research team wants to see the effect of a new drug in treating a serious disease.

22. Sketch a histogram for the data set 5, 7, 5, 8, 6, 11, 5, 3, 7, 11, 9, 10, 7, 10, 8, 6, 9, 10, 2, 4, 9, 10, 2, 10, 2. Use percentages along the vertical axis.

23. The table shows how many U.S. households in 1991 had fewer than seven persons.

Social Science

Size	1 person	2 persons	3 persons	4 persons	5 persons	6 persons
Households (thousands)	23,590	30,181	16,082	14,556	6,206	2,237

    a. Make a histogram showing percentages for each household size.
    b. Find the probability that a household of 6 or less had more than 4 persons.

In each situation, explain why the sample obtained may be biased.

24. A researcher uses the Internet to conduct a survey about technology use.

25. You survey students in the school parking lot about whether or not they have jobs.

26. Describe a method for randomly sampling 30 different students about their participation in extracurricular activities.

Science

27. The Bear Facts In a national park, a random sample of 15 bears is captured and tagged. Later, a second sample of 12 bears is captured, 5 of which have tags. What is the estimated bear population of this national park?

MORE MATH REASONING

28. That's What I Expected In a case where different outcomes have different "payoffs," the *expected value* is found by multiplying the probability of each possible outcome by its payoff. Suppose that you are starting a new company. You feel that there is a 10% chance that you will earn $100,000 in the first year, a 30% chance that you will earn $50,000, a 40% chance that you will earn $25,000, and a 20% chance that you will *lose* $15,000. What is the expected value of the first year?

29. I'm Polling for Smythe You have been selected by candidate Joseph Smythe to conduct a survey of likely voters to project the winner of the state governor's race. In this survey, you can ask subjects their preference in one of three ways:
- by asking them if they plan to vote for Joseph Smythe
- by asking them whom they plan to support for governor
- by giving them a list of candidates and asking them to state their preference

Which method do you think would give the most unbiased results? Would any of them tend to overestimate the true percentage of voters for Smythe? Explain.

The Normal Distribution

← CONNECT → *You've explored ways to sample a population. When the results of a statistical sample show a particular pattern, the results can be modeled by the "normal" curve. Real-world data, including heights, shoe sizes, and test scores, are often approximately normally distributed.*

If you toss a coin 100 times, how many times do you think it will come up heads? Of course you predict 50, but you would not be surprised if it were 53, or 49, or 46. You would certainly be surprised, however, if heads came up 92 times or 13 times.

EXPLORE: PROBABLE COIN TOSSES

Suppose we simulate a poll by tossing a coin. Let heads represent a "yes" response and tails represent "no."

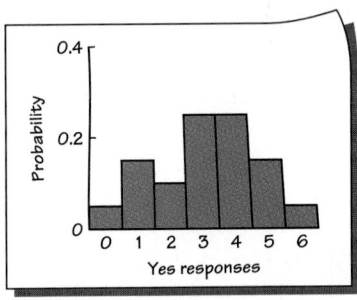

1. If you toss a coin six times, there are seven possible outcomes, from 0 heads (0 yes responses), to 6 heads (6 yes responses). Conduct four trials of this experiment and record your results. Find the probability of each outcome and construct a histogram of the results, plotting the number of yes responses on the *x*-axis and the experimental probability on the *y*-axis.

2. Conduct six more trials of this experiment. Combine these results with the results of the previous trials and construct a new histogram. Compare the histogram with all ten trials to the histogram with only four. What differences do you see?

3. Let the width of each rectangle in your histogram equal 1 and its height equal the probability of the outcome. Find the sum of the areas of all the rectangles in the histogram. Explain why your results make sense.

4. Combine the results of your ten trials with those of the other members of your class. Calculate the experimental probability of each outcome and construct a histogram showing the class results. How does this histogram compare to your ten-trial histogram?

5. Suppose your simulation had consisted of tossing a coin 100 times. Draw a sketch showing what you would expect the histogram of many such simulations to be. Explain why you think the histogram would look like this.

As you do more and more trials of an experiment, or take more and more samples from a population, the experimental probabilities of events tend to get closer and closer to the "true" probabilities.

One hundred simulations of 100 coin tosses gave the results shown in the histogram. In many situations, as you increase the number of trials, the distribution takes on the shape of the curve shown, the **normal distribution.**

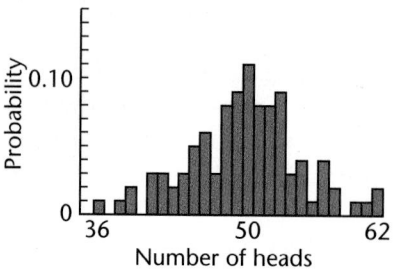
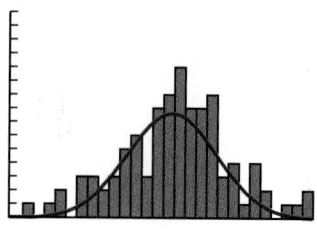

Notice that although results ranged from 36 to 62 heads, the numbers of heads were more frequently near 50, and values above 50 were about as likely as those below 50. When a data set is normally distributed, an item of data is more likely to be in a range near the mean of the data set than in a range of equal size far from the mean, and the data set is symmetric about the mean.

A normal curve can be tightly compressed around the mean, or it may be quite spread out. The **standard deviation** of a data set is a measurement of how far the data values deviate from the mean. About 68.2% of the data values in a normal distribution lie within one standard deviation of the mean.

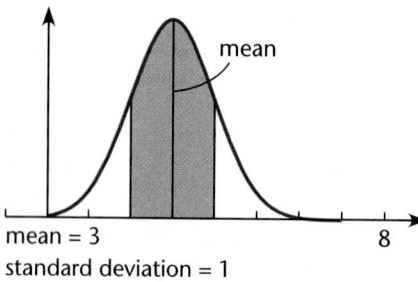
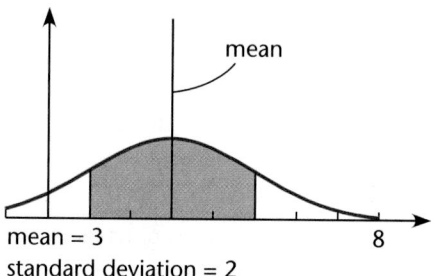

The probability that a randomly selected item of data lies between two other values is given by the percentage of area under the normal curve between those two values. Notice that the *tails* of the normal distribution contain very little area.

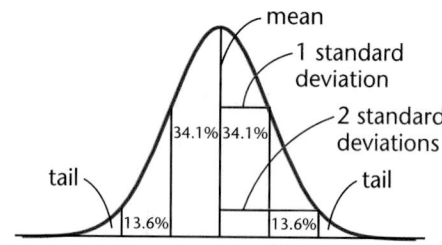

CONSIDER

1. To the nearest tenth, what percentage of normally distributed data values lie within 2 standard deviations of the mean?

2. To the nearest tenth of a percent, what percentage of the data values are more than two standard deviations above the mean? more than two standard deviations below the mean?

1. Suppose that a data set is normally distributed with a mean of 24 and a standard deviation of 7.

   a. What percentage of the data values lie between 17 and 31?

   Seventeen is one standard deviation (7) below the mean (24), and 31 is one standard deviation above the mean. Therefore, about 68.2% of the data values lie between these two values.

   b. What is the probability that a randomly selected value is above 38?

   Since 38 is two standard deviations above the mean, about 2.3% of the values lie above 38.

2. The heights of U.S. women, aged 18 to 24 years, are approximately normally distributed, with a mean of about 65.5 inches and a standard deviation of 2.5 inches.

   a. What is the probability that a randomly selected woman from this population has a height above 65.5 inches?

   The mean of the data set is 65.5 inches. Since half of the data values lie above the mean, the probability is $\frac{1}{2} = 0.5$ that a woman chosen at random is more than 65.5 inches tall.

   b. Find a range of heights that covers 95% of U.S. women, aged 18 to 24.

   Ninety-five percent of normally distributed data lie within two standard deviations of the mean. So heights two standard deviations above and below the mean will determine the range we need.

   $65.5 + 2(2.5) = 65.5 + 5 = 70.5$

   $65.5 - 2(2.5) = 65.5 - 5 = 60.5$

   About 95% of U.S. women in the given age range are between 60.5 and 70.5 inches tall.

Complete the statements for a normal distribution that has a mean of 10 and a standard deviation of 2.

a. Approximately 68% of the data will lie between ____ and ____.

b. Approximately 95% of the data will lie between ____ and ____.

c. Approximately 2.3% of the data will be greater than ____.

d. Find a range of heights that will include those of approximately 68% of U.S. women, aged 18 to 24.

e. The radius of a ball bearing is specified to be 0.5 mm ± 0.05 mm. If the machine manufacturing them produces ball bearings with a mean of 0.5 mm and a standard deviation of 0.025 mm, what percentage of the bearings will not meet the specifications?

The normal distribution is used to model many types of real-world data, from heights to the dimensions of mass-produced items. A data set that is normally distributed has an equal probability of being above or below the mean of the data, and is more likely to be in a range of values closer to the mean than farther away.

REFLECT

1. Give an example of a set of data that could be approximated by a normal distribution. Explain why the normal distribution would be a good model for this data.

2. Give an example of a set of data that the normal distribution would *not* model well. Explain how the distribution of this data is likely to be different from the normal distribution.

3. In your own words, explain how the standard deviation of a normal distribution affects the shape of its graph. If you score 20 points above average on a physical fitness test, is your achievement more remarkable if the standard deviation is 10 or if the standard deviation is 25?

Exercises

CORE

1. **Getting Started** Answer each question about normally distributed data.
   a. What is the probability that an item of data lies above the mean?
   b. What is the probability that an item of data lies within one standard deviation of the mean?
   c. What is the probability that an item of data lies within two standard deviations of the mean?

Determine whether each statement is true or false. If the statement is false, change the underlined word or phrase to make it true.

2. The higher the standard deviation of a normal distribution, the <u>less</u> the spread of its graph.

3. If a data set is normally distributed, the probability that an item of data lies below the mean is <u>less than</u> the probability that it lies above the mean.

4. A normal curve is symmetric with respect to a <u>vertical</u> line.

Suppose that a data set is normally distributed with a mean of 100 and a standard deviation of 1. Complete each statement.

5. Approximately 68% of the data values lie between ____ and ____.

6. Approximately 95% of the data values lie between ____ and ____.

7. Approximately 99.7% of the data values lie between ____ and ____.

8. Approximately 2.3% of the data values are greater than ____.

9. In the Clouds The heights of U.S. males from 18 to 24 years old are approximately normally distributed, with a mean of about 70 inches and a standard deviation of about 3 inches.

a. What is the approximate percentage of U.S. men, aged 18 to 24, that are:
    i. between 67 and 73 inches tall?   **ii.** between 64 and 76 inches tall?

b. What is the approximate probability that a randomly selected U.S. male in this age range is over 76 inches tall?

c. Suppose you see a group of five males in this age range who are *all* over 76 inches tall. What is the probability of this happening randomly? Would you be surprised to see such a group? Explain.

10. Enlightened Customer Service Lifetime Light Bulb Company guarantees that its bulbs will last for at least 1000 hours. If a bulb fails before 1000 hours of use, the customer can ask for a refund. Lifetime's research department has determined that the average life of the light bulbs is approximately normally distributed, with a mean of 1050 hours and a standard deviation of 25 hours.

a. Find the approximate percentage of light bulbs sold that will not last 1000 hours.

b. Do you think that the percentage of people who ask for a refund for a bulb that failed to last 1000 hours will be the same percentage you found in **a**? Explain.

State whether you believe that a normal distribution would be a good model for each data set. Explain your answers.

11. the weights of female babies born in the United States in a given year

12. the number of boats owned by U.S. families

Suppose that a data set is normally distributed with a mean of 2.0 and a standard deviation of 0.4. Complete each statement.

13. Approximately 68% of the data values lie between ____ and ____.

14. Approximately 95% of the data values lie between ____ and ____.

15. Approximately 99.7% of the data values lie between ____ and ____.

16. Approximately 2.3% of the data values are less than ____.

17. A machine produces nails whose diameters are to be 0.125 inches ± 0.005 inches. The nails produced typically have a mean diameter of 0.125 inches, with a standard deviation of about 0.0025 inches.

a. When the machine is operating normally, what percentage of the nails produced will not meet specifications? Explain.

b. If ten consecutive nails produced by the machine have a diameter of more than 0.130 inches, what would you do? Explain why you would take this action.

LOOK BACK

18. Find all of the roots of $2x^3 + 3x^2 - 23x - 12 = 0$. [8-2]

19. Solve $\frac{2}{x+1} = \frac{5}{x+3} - 1$. [8-3]

20. Find the length of $\widehat{WYX}$ and the area of sector $WVXY$. [10-1]

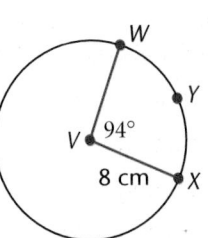

21. There are twenty marbles in a bag. Nine of them are yellow, seven are silver, and four are green. [11-1]

    a. If one marble is drawn from the bag, what is the probability that it is not green?

    b. If two marbles are drawn with replacement, what is the probability that both are silver?

    c. If two marbles are drawn without replacement, what is the probability that both are silver?

MORE PRACTICE

Suppose that a data set is normally distributed with a mean of 60 and a standard deviation of 10. Complete each statement.

22. Approximately 68% of the data values lie between ____ and ____.

23. Approximately 95% of the data values lie between ____ and ____.

24. Approximately 99.7% of the data values lie between ____ and ____.

25. Approximately 2.3% of the data values are greater than ____.

Suppose that a data set is normally distributed with a mean of 4.0 and a standard deviation of 0.5. Complete each statement.

26. Approximately 68% of the data values lie between ____ and ____.

27. Approximately 95% of the data values lie between ____ and ____.

28. Approximately 99.7% of the data values lie between ____ and ____.

29. Approximately 2.3% of the data values are less than ____.

30. A salad dressing manufacturer's label claims that a bottle contains 8 ounces of dressing. In fact, there is some variation involved in filling the bottles, so that the mean amount in a bottle is 8.05 ounces, with a standard deviation of 0.025 ounces. Assume a normal distribution for the following exercises.

    a. Estimate the probability that you will get less than 8 ounces when you purchase a bottle of salad dressing.

    b. Estimate the probability that you will get more than 8 ounces when you purchase a bottle of salad dressing.

    c. Estimate the probability that you will get more than 8.1 ounces when you purchase a bottle of salad dressing.

    d. Explain why the manufacturer might state that the bottle contains 8 ounces when the mean amount is actually 8.05 ounces.

31. Suppose that the mean blood cholesterol level of a group of patients in a study is 192 milligrams per 100 milliliters of blood and that the standard deviation is 24 milligrams per 100 milliliters of blood.

    a. About what percentage of the patients have cholesterol levels between 168 and 216?

    b. If a person's cholesterol level exceeds 240, the risk of coronary heart disease is approximately double that of the general population. About what percentage of these patients have cholesterol levels above 240?

MORE MATH REASONING

32. Use a Graphing Utility Investigate the graphs below.

  a. Set the window on your graphing utility so that x-values range from -5 to 5 and y-values range from 0 to 0.5. Then graph $y = \dfrac{1}{\sqrt{2\pi}}e^{-\frac{x^2}{2}}$. Describe the graph.

  b. Without clearing the graph of $y = \dfrac{1}{\sqrt{2\pi}}e^{-\frac{x^2}{2}}$, graph $y = \dfrac{1}{\sqrt{2\pi}}e^{-\frac{(x-2)^2}{2}}$. Compare the two graphs. Explain why the difference between them makes sense.

  c. Clear the graph of $y = \dfrac{1}{\sqrt{2\pi}}e^{-\frac{(x-2)^2}{2}}$. Now graph $y = \dfrac{1}{4\sqrt{2\pi}}e^{-\frac{x^2}{2(16)}}$. Compare this graph to the graph of $y = \dfrac{1}{\sqrt{2\pi}}e^{-\frac{x^2}{2}}$.

  d. $y = \dfrac{1}{\sqrt{2\pi}}e^{-\frac{x^2}{2}}$ is the graph of the *standard normal curve,* with mean 0 and standard deviation 1. Explain what you think the numbers μ (mu) and σ (sigma) mean in the equation $y = \dfrac{1}{\sigma\sqrt{2\pi}}e^{-\frac{(x-\mu)^2}{2\sigma^2}}$.

33. Over a long period of time, the annual percentage return on money invested in common stocks has been roughly normally distributed, with a mean of about 9% and a standard deviation of about 28%.

  a. Suppose a person invests $1000 in stocks and $1000 in a bank account paying 5% interest, compounded annually. Assuming the money invested in stocks grows at 9% per year, find the value of each investment after 3 years.

  b. What is the approximate probability that the average return on common stocks is -19% or worse? 37% or better?

  c. If you invest $1000 in the stock market, how much will you have after 3 years if you lose 19% each year? if you earn 37% each year? Explain why people might or might not choose to invest in stocks.

Brokers at the New York Curb Exchange, 1919

The standard deviation of a data set with n elements $x_1, x_2, x_3, x_4, \ldots x_n$, whose mean is $\overline{x}$, is given by:

$$\text{standard deviation} = \sqrt{\frac{\displaystyle\sum_{i=1}^{n}(\overline{x}-x_i)^2}{n}}$$

34. One day the advertised rents for one-bedroom apartments in a California city were, in dollars: 705, 700, 635, 660, 725, 650, 695, 600, 595, 590, 600, 550, 595, 660, 595, 650, 620, and 705.

  a. What is the mean of this data set?

  b. What is the standard deviation of this data set?

  c. Does this data set appear to be normally distributed? Explain why or why not.

← CONNECT → *You've seen the importance of unbiased sampling in collecting data and you've used a normal distribution as a model for real-world data.*

Statisticians sample data to estimate the probability distribution for an entire population. If the data sample shows certain characteristics, the normal distribution or another probability distribution can be used to model the distribution for the population as a whole.

EXPLORE: SAMPLE EXAMPLE

MATERIALS

Graphing utility (optional)

Your automobile company has just developed the technology to make a car that can convert into a pickup truck. You have been selected to design a phone survey to find the amount of money Americans would be willing to pay for this "trar."

1. What is your target population for this survey?

2. Describe how you could select a random sample from this population to survey. What problems with bias should concern you? Explain how you would attempt to ensure that your sample is not biased.

3. Suppose that your survey yields the following results, in dollars, for the first 25 respondents.

10,000	10,750	11,300	11,700	12,100
12,500	12,800	13,200	13,400	13,500
13,500	13,750	14,100	14,200	14,300
14,500	14,600	14,800	15,200	15,500
15,900	16,300	16,500	17,500	18,100

Make a histogram of this data, grouping data in $500 intervals. Do you think a normal distribution is a reasonable model for this data? Why or why not?

4. Estimate the percentage of potential customers that would be willing to pay $16,000 or more for the trar. Explain how you made your estimate. (If you believe that the distribution is normal, assume that the mean is $14,000 and the standard deviation is $2,000.)

1. Explain why it is important for statisticians and pollsters to choose an unbiased sample from the population they are studying.
2. What are some characteristics of a data set that would make the normal distribution a good approximation for the distribution of the data? What are some characteristics that would indicate that the normal distribution is not a good model?
3. Describe some circumstances where you might want to collect data from an entire population instead of from a sample.

Self-Assessment

1. Explain why statisticians take samples instead of studying entire populations.

2. Suppose you wanted to draw a random sample of 100 students within your school. Explain in detail how you would select the sample.

3. **Draft Lottery** In 1970 during the Vietnam conflict, the first draft lottery was held to select men to serve in the armed forces. Each of the 366 possible birth dates was placed in a drum. The first number drawn was September 14, so every person in the draft whose birthday was September 14 was assigned the number 1. The lower your number, the more likely it was that you would be drafted into the armed services.

The results by birth month were as shown. Do you think the lottery was biased or unbiased? Explain your reasoning.

Month	Average Number	Month	Average Number	Month	Average Number
January	201.2	May	208.0	September	157.3
February	203.0	June	195.7	October	182.5
March	225.8	July	181.5	November	148.7
April	203.7	August	173.5	December	121.5

Identify the population being studied in each situation. Would you study the entire population or a sample? Why?

4. A researcher wants to estimate the average number of patients an American dentist sees in one day.

5. A product designer wants to be sure that new improved Cheese Crispos are crunchier than the old Cheese Crispos.

6. Which of the following statements is *not* true of the normal distribution?
   (a) It is symmetric about its mean.
   (b) If data is normally distributed, approximately 68% of the data values lie within one standard deviation of the mean.
   (c) If data is normally distributed, about 10% of the data values lie more than two standard deviations from the mean.

7. The 1990 values of owner-occupied U.S. homes worth less than $500,000 are shown. Sketch a histogram for the data. Make the vertical axis the percentage of homes in the given category.

Value of homes (in $1,000s)	0−99	100−199	200−299	300−399	400−499
Total number of homes (in millions)	28.3	10.8	3.4	1.2	0.5

    a. Make a histogram of the data showing the percentage of homes in each range of values.

    b. Find the probability that the value of a home in this data set is less than $300,000.

8. Find the length of $\overset{\frown}{ADC}$ and the area of sector *ABCD*. [10-1]

9. Solve $\dfrac{4}{x-3} = \dfrac{4}{x+1} + 1$. [8-3]

10. Find all of the roots of $x^3 + 2x^2 - 5x - 6 = 0$. [8-2]

11. Suppose you have ten coins in your pocket. Three are quarters, five are dimes, and two are nickels. [11-1]

    a. If you take one coin from your pocket, what is the probability that it is a nickel?

    b. If you take one coin out of your pocket, replace it, and then take another coin out, what is the probability that both are quarters?

    c. If two coins are drawn without replacement, what is the probability that both are dimes?

12. A Fishy Game A game preserve warden is studying the population of fish in a pond. On Monday, he tags 200 fish and releases them back into the pond. At a later date, he collects 200 more fish and discovers that 12 of them are tagged.

    a. Analyzing only the mathematics of the problem, what would be the game warden's conclusion about the number of fish in the pond?

    b. Suppose the later date when the game warden caught fish was actually two years after the first date. How reliable is the estimate of the fish population? Explain.

13. Two normal distributions each have means of 100. Distribution A has a standard deviation of 10, while distribution B has a standard deviation of 25.

    a. Which distribution has a taller, narrower curve?

    b. In which distribution would you expect to find more data lying between 90 and 110?

    c. In which distribution would you expect to find more data lying between 80 and 100?

    d. In which distribution would you expect to find more data lying above 120?

14. Normal Bulbs A light bulb has an average life of 1000 hours with a standard deviation of 120 hours. Suppose the lifetimes of the bulbs are approximately normally distributed.

    a. Find the probability that a light bulb will last between 880 and 1120 hours.

    b. Find the probability that a light bulb will last less than 880 hours.

    c. Find the probability that a light bulb will last more than 1240 hours.

    d. If you were the manufacturer of this light bulb, what would you guarantee as its life? Explain your reasoning.

Chapter 11 Review

In this chapter you expanded your knowledge of probability and data analysis. You investigated probabilities of complex events and explored independent and dependent events. You worked with random sampling and histograms and used the normal curve as a model for some real-world data. Understanding probability and the use of statistics is important in many careers and is necessary for understanding daily news reports.

KEY TERMS

biased sample [11-2]

capture-recapture method [11-2]

complementary events [11-1]

conditional probability [11-1]

dependent events [11-1]

histogram [11-2]

independent events [11-1]

normal distribution [11-2]

population [11-2]

random sample [11-2]

representative sample [11-2]

sample [11-2]

sampling with replacement [11-1]

sampling without replacement [11-1]

standard deviation [11-2]

Write the word or phrase that correctly completes each statement.

1. Two events are said to be ____ if the occurrence of one influences the occurrence of the other.

2. A subset of a population is called a ____.

3. A ____ is a type of bar graph that shows the number, percentage, or probability of the outcomes in a data set.

4. Several names are written on slips of paper and placed in a bag. A series of names is drawn from the bag, and the drawn names are not put back in the bag. This is an example of sampling ____.

CONCEPTS AND APPLICATIONS

Decide whether the two events are dependent or independent, and explain why. [11-1]

5. rolling a 4 on a die and tossing heads on a coin

6. washing the car today and washing it tomorrow

7. a Democratic representative being elected from a district in 1996 and a Republican being elected from the same district in 1998

Suppose you have a set of 20 cards made up of 10 orange cards numbered 1 through 10 and 10 purple cards numbered 1 through 10. Find the probability of each event. [11-1]

8. that the first card drawn is a purple card or has an even number

9. that the first two cards drawn are orange cards if the first card is replaced before drawing the second

10. that the first two cards drawn are orange cards if the first card is not replaced before drawing the second

11. Bad Chip You work in the quality control department of a company that makes microchips. The probability that a chip is defective is 1%. If you test 200 chips, what is the probability that at least one is defective? [11-1]

Industry

In each situation, state whether you think a sample or the entire population should be studied and explain why. [11-2]

12. A school needs to know how many students will ride the bus this year.

13. A scientist wants to find the average weight of an adult grizzly bear.

14. A statistician conducting a capture-recapture study initially tags 20 elk. Two weeks later, she captures another 20, five of which are tagged. Her assistant thought that he was supposed to do the recapture work, caught 30 elk, and found that 8 were tagged. What would you do with the two results? [11-2]

Science

15. In 1994, the mean Mathematics SAT score for college-bound seniors was 479 and the standard deviation was 124. Assuming that the test scores are approximately normally distributed, find the approximate probability:
a. that a student scored between 355 and 603
b. that a student scored over 727

CONCEPTS AND CONNECTIONS

16. Social Science The table shows the number of U.S. families below the poverty level in 1991.

Social Science

Age of householder	15 to 24	25 to 34	35 to 44	45 to 54	55 to 64
Number (thousands)	955	2377	1648	806	627

Draw a histogram of this data. Describe any patterns you see and give reasons explaining why they might occur.

SELF-EVALUATION

Write a summary of what you learned in this chapter. Explain how you can apply the probability concepts in this chapter to an activity that you do often and how the data analysis techniques can help you interpret statistics quoted in news reports. Which techniques in this chapter were confusing for you, and which were easy to use?

TEST

Decide whether the two events are dependent or independent and explain why.

1. having cold weather one day and brushing your teeth the next morning

2. seeing the movie *Algebra Stories* and seeing *Algebra Stories II*

3. The probability that a car taken to a mechanic needs new brakes is 0.15; the probability that it needs a new muffler is 0.21; and the probability of both is 0.08. Find the probability that the car needs new brakes or a new muffler.

A bag of jelly beans contains 25 beans: 7 green, 3 red, 1 pink, 2 black, 8 yellow, and 4 orange. Find the probability of each event.

4. drawing a red bean, eating it, then drawing a yellow bean

5. drawing a green bean, replacing it, and then drawing an orange bean

6. not drawing a pink or black jelly bean in your first draw

7. In a capture-recapture study of fish in a lake, 25 redfish were tagged and released. Out of 124 redfish recaptured, 8 were tagged. Estimate the redfish population.

8. You want to conduct a survey of voters. If you go to a busy bookstore and survey every third person, will you get a random sample? If so, explain why; if not, explain how this sample might be different from the population you want to study.

9. Suppose twenty people were asked how many times a week they go to a shopping center. Their responses were: 4, 2, 1, 3, 2, 5, 1, 7, 6, 2, 4, 1, 4, 0, 2, 5, 3, 4, 3, 2. Make a histogram of this data. Then find the probability that a person polled went to a shopping center twice a week or less.

10. The average rainfall in an area is approximately normally distributed. Death Valley has a mean annual rainfall of 1.8 inches and its rainfall total has a standard deviation of 0.35 inches. Find the probability that Death Valley receives between 1.1 and 2.5 inches of rain in a given year.

PERFORMANCE TASK

You are the quality control expert for a machine shop that manufactures pistons for engines. The pistons must have a diameter of no less than 2.998 in. and no more than 3.002 in. The diameters of the pistons you manufacture are approximately normally distributed with a mean of 3 inches and a standard deviation of 0.001 inches. If a piston is too small, it must be discarded; if it is too large, it can be machined again.

You have been asked to estimate the percentage of pistons that meet the specifications the first time, the percentage that must be discarded, and the probability that at least one out of any set of 20 pistons will need to be machined again. Estimate these probabilities and explain how you made your estimates.

Chapter 12

Discrete Mathematics and Models

Project A
Are You Loyal?
How does a car company monitor customer loyalty?

Project B
From Here to There
How does a transportation manager determine the best routes for buses to follow?

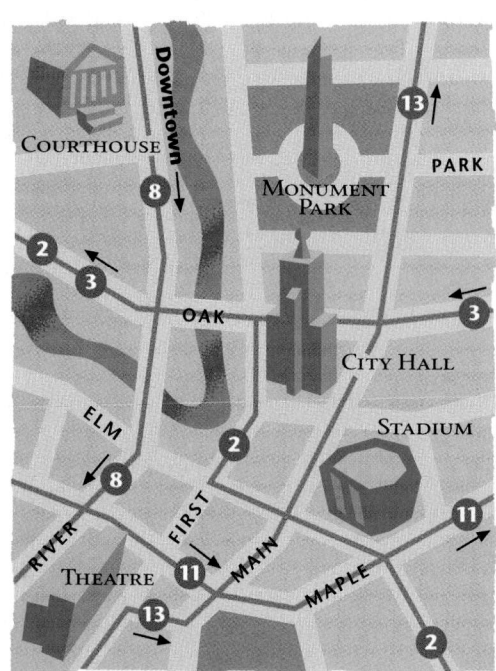

Project C
Color Me
How many colors do you need to use on a map to differentiate regions that are next to each other?

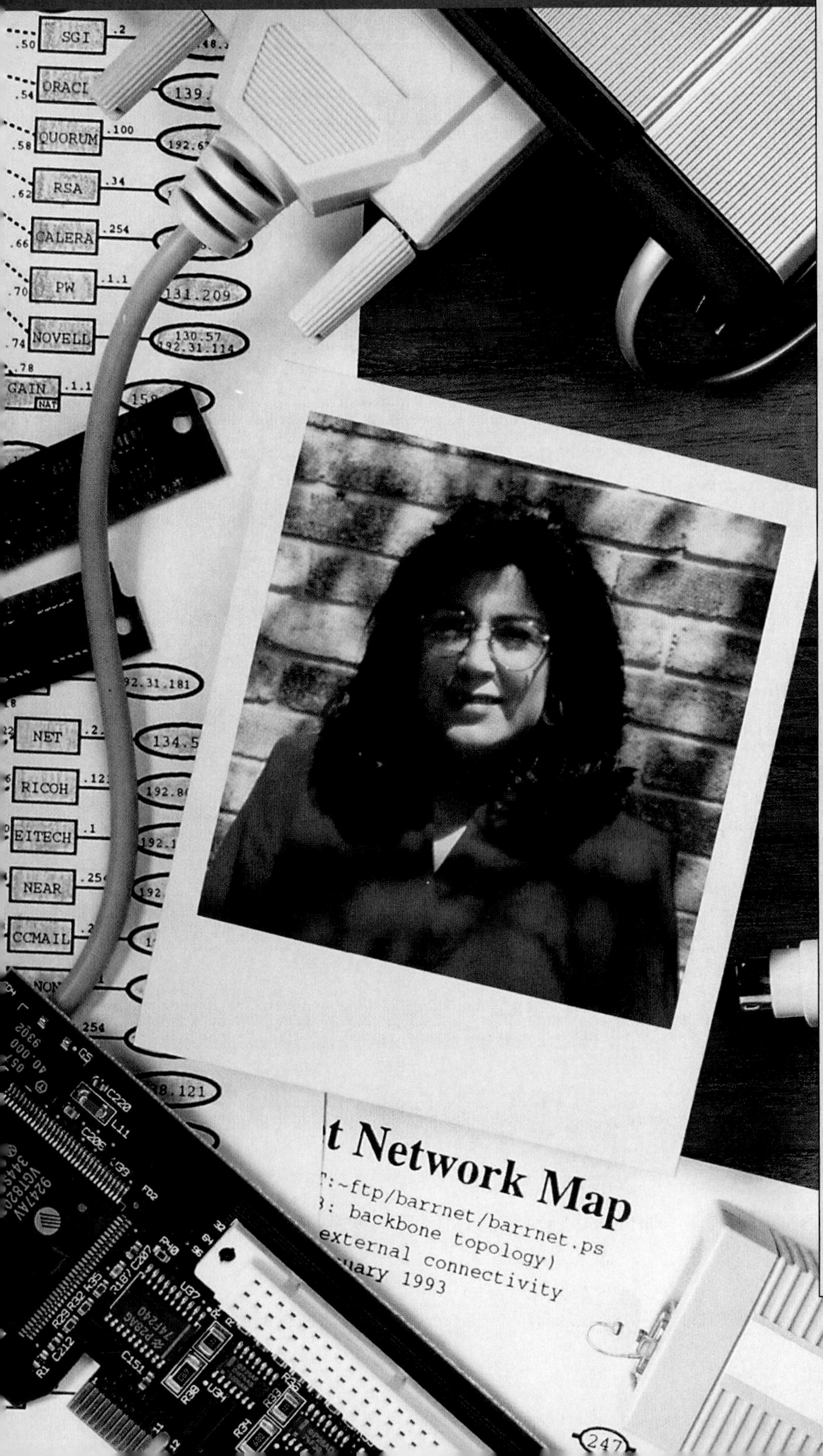

CINDA TAPIA RODRIGUEZ

Math was a challenge, so that made me concentrate and study even harder.

In my field, math plays a vital role in every aspect, from cost analysis to the configuration of a personal computer (PC). For example, we might measure the speed of the PC or the size of its storage, or determine the number of pixels on the screen, or use a complex algorithm for computations in a programming language.

I think students must study math. It is just as important as learning the English language to communicate.

Cinda Tapia Rodriguez
Computer Scientist
HQ Air Intelligence Agency
Kelly AFB, Texas

Chapter 12

Discrete Mathematics and Models

GETTING READY

12-1
Graph Theory

In 12-1 you will see how graph theory can model and optimize the performance of networks. You will use the following geometry skills.

For exercises 1–7, refer to the figure at the right. [Previous course]

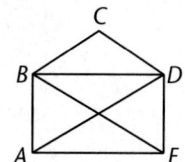

How many line segments have each of the following as an endpoint? [Previous course]

1. A **2.** C **3.** D

Without lifting your pencil or redrawing a line segment, draw each of the following. [Previous course]

4. triangle BDE **5.** quadrilateral $ABCD$

6. quadrilateral $ABDE$ and its diagonals   **7.** the entire figure

---

12-2
Recursion

In 12-2 you will investigate recursion in sequences and in probability matrices. You will use the following skills.

Write the first 5 terms of each sequence. [Previous course]

8. $a_1 = 15$ and $a_n = a_{(n-1)} + 3$

9. $a_1 = 6$ and $a_n = 6 \cdot a_{(n-1)}$

Solve each system. [Previous course]

10. $2 = x + 0.5y$ and $2.5 = x + 0.25y$

11. $10,000 = x + 0.2y$ and $4000 = x + 0.04y$

Let $A = \begin{bmatrix} 4 & 2 \\ -1 & 3 \end{bmatrix}$ and $B = \begin{bmatrix} 5 & -1 \\ 4 & 2 \end{bmatrix}$. Find each of the following. [Previous course]

12. $A + B$ **13.** AB **14.** A^2 **15.** AB^2

Give Me a Call

People in a large corporation can make millions of telephone calls per month from hundreds of locations to tens of thousands of destinations. There are thousands of large corporations, hundreds of thousands of smaller businesses, and millions of individuals making long-distance phone calls every hour. How do all of these calls make it through the jungle of wires, fiber-optic cables, and satellite links to reach their destinations?

Long-distance telephone companies grapple with this question every day as they try to maintain the efficiency of their networks. A network's performance is continuously monitored with data collected from around the country, which is displayed on a special wallboard. The wallboard shows whether a customer's call is delayed by a lack of capacity in the network. When this happens, the customer's call is routed through a third city that has the available capacity to complete the call. This happens so quickly that it is virtually undetectable by the caller.

Calls are rerouted through a switching system that takes only milliseconds to connect to another switch and set up your call. But none of this efficient, split-second switching would be possible without a mathematical plan for maintaining this complex network. The mathematics that enables this system to function has applications to airline scheduling, shipping, and many other network problems.

?

1. How do you think a country-wide telephone network is modeled before it is built? What types of mathematics are involved?
2. What might calling be like if all telephone switching were done by hand?
3. What timing and cost considerations do you think must be taken into account in running a large telephone network?

← CONNECT → *You have previously worked with polygons and polyhedrons. You will now study relationships that exist among the faces, edges, and vertices of polyhedrons. You will also examine the two-dimensional representations, called graphs, that arise from polyhedrons and in other contexts.*

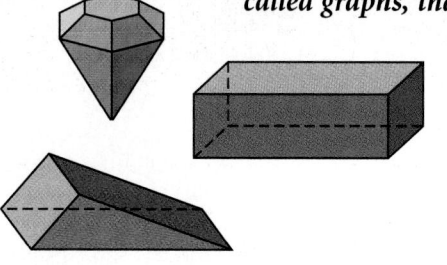

Recall that a **polyhedron** is a geometric solid with polygonal faces. Prisms, pyramids, boxes, and diamond shapes are all polyhedrons.

In the following Explore, you will look for a relationship among the numbers of faces, vertices, and edges of various polyhedrons.

EXPLORE: A SOLID RELATIONSHIP

The ancient Greeks showed that there are only five types of convex ("no dents") regular polyhedrons, that is, polyhedrons with congruent faces and an equal number of edges meeting at each vertex. These regular polyhedrons have 4, 6, 8, 12, or 20 faces and are called the Platonic solids after Plato.

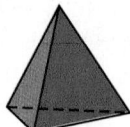
Tetrahedron

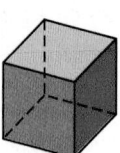
Cube

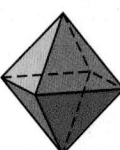
Octahedron

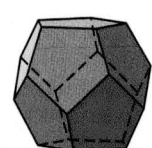
Dodecahedron

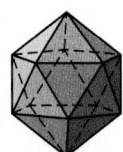
Icosahedron

1. Find and record the numbers of faces, vertices, and edges of each regular polyhedron.

> **Problem Solving Tip**
>
> Make an organized list or table.

2. Consider the numbers of faces, vertices, and edges you found for each polyhedron and the various sums of these numbers. Find a relationship among the numbers that holds for each regular polyhedron.

3. Test your relationship on these irregular polyhedrons.

a.

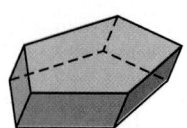

b.

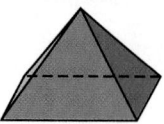

c.

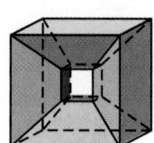

4. Does your relationship seem to hold for irregular polyhedrons that have no holes? with holes? Summarize your findings in a conjecture.

René Descartes (1596–1650) and Leonhard Euler (1707–1783) recognized that the relationship you discovered in the Explore holds for any convex polyhedron and, more generally, for any *simple* polyhedron, a polyhedron with no holes through it. The resulting formula was proved by Euler and is named for him.

> ### EULER'S FORMULA
>
> For any simple polyhedron with F faces, V vertices, and E edges,
> $F + V - E = 2$.

TRY IT

a. Suppose you are designing a polyhedral tent with ten faces (counting the floor) and eight vertices where edge rods connect. How many rods will the tent require?

Imagine shining a light through a wire model of a polyhedron onto a sheet of paper. The shadow forms a plane figure made up of vertices and edges. A plane figure consisting of vertices and edges that connect vertices, such as this, is called a **graph,** not to be confused with the graph of a function.

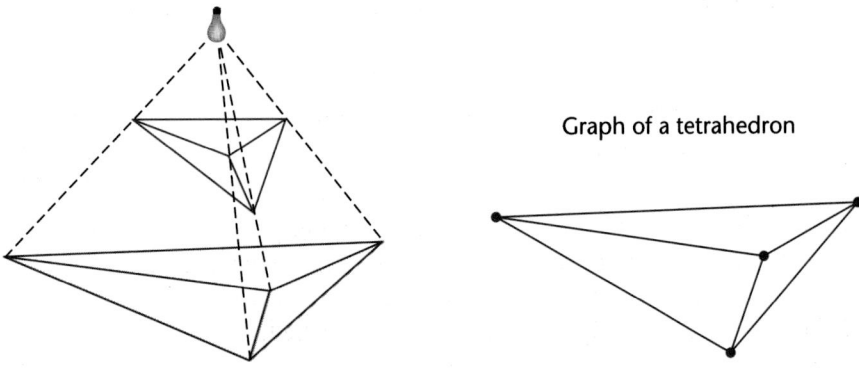

Graph of a tetrahedron

CONSIDER

?

1. Explain how Euler's Formula for a tetrahedron translates to a statement about the *graph* of a tetrahedron.

Graphs can be used to analyze polyhedrons and prove Euler's Formula, but they also have a wide variety of applications in other fields and situations. For instance, graphs can represent molecules, electrical circuits, irrigation systems, flowcharts, communication networks, and transportation routes.

EXAMPLE

An airline has flights connecting Chicago to New York, Dallas, Los Angeles, and San Francisco. In addition, the airline has flights connecting San Francisco directly with Los Angeles and Dallas. Draw a graph representing the airline connections available through this airline.

Represent each city by a vertex and each connection by an edge.

The arrangement of vertices in a graph is not critical. However, showing which pairs of vertices are connected by edges is critical. Notice that the edges of a graph can intersect without having a vertex at the intersection.

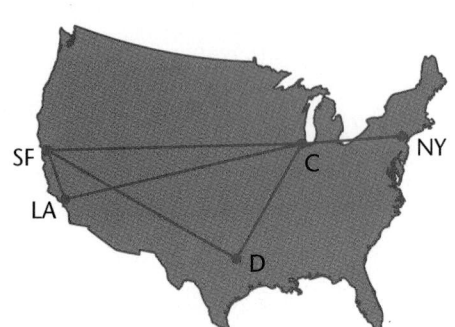

TRY IT

b. The high school soccer teams from Ames (A), Buchanan (B), Chavez (C), Delano (D), and Eton (E) have played the following games so far this year.

A has played B, C, and D.

B has played A and D.

C has played A and E.

D has played A, B, and E.

E has played C and D.

Draw a graph representing the soccer games played so far this year.

Graphs provide efficient visual models that can help you to analyze situations involving networks and their connections.

REFLECT

1. What kinds of figures form the faces of a regular polyhedron?
2. If one octahedron (8 faces) has 6 more vertices than another octahedron, what can you say about the number of edges of these polyhedrons?
3. Give an example of a graph consisting of vertices and edges that you've seen in a mathematical or real-life context.

Exercises

CORE

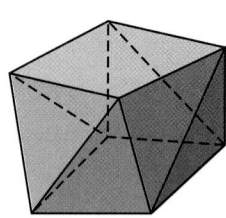

1. **Getting Started** Consider this polyhedron.
   a. How many faces does the polyhedron have?
   b. How many vertices does the polyhedron have?
   c. How many edges does the polyhedron have?
   d. Verify the relationship given by Euler's Formula for this polyhedron.

Write the word or phrase that correctly completes each statement.

2. A ____ is a plane figure consisting of vertices and edges that connect vertices.

3. A ____ is a solid figure with polygonal faces.

4. A single honeycomb in a beehive forms a polyhedron with a hexagonal cross section, as shown. Verify Euler's Formula for a honeycomb.

5. A simple polyhedron has 8 faces and 6 vertices. How many edges does it have?

6. A simple polyhedron has 18 edges and 8 faces. How many vertices does it have?

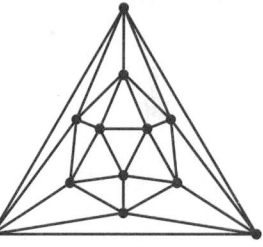

7. Analyze this graph representing an icosahedron.
   a. How many vertices and edges does the graph have? The graph divides the plane into how many regions?
   b. Restate Euler's Formula for graphs with edges that intersect only at vertices. (Hint: Use the number of regions into which a graph divides the plane in place of the number of faces of a polyhedron.)

8. **Party Line** The host (H) of a party chatted with each of his five guests. The architect (A) chatted with the teacher (T) and store manager (M), as well as with the host. The salesperson (S) chatted with everyone except the architect. The bank teller (B) was shy and chatted only with the salesperson and the host. Draw a graph showing who chatted with whom at the party.

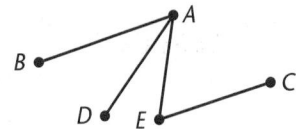

9. This graph shows five museums and several bus lines that can be taken to get from one museum to another. How many bus lines are there? How many bus lines would need to be added so that there would be a bus line between each pair of museums?

10. **Three Houses and Three Utilities** Suppose that three houses in a row are located directly across from three utility connections in a row (electricity, gas, and water). Is it possible to make separate connections from each house to each utility without any connections crossing? (Connections can be lines or curves in a plane.) Explain.

Problem-Solving Tip

Draw a graph of the situation.

11. If only one edge connects each pair of vertices, what is the greatest number of edges a graph can have if it has 3 vertices? 5 vertices? *n* vertices?

 **LOOK AHEAD**

12. Copy each graph. For each graph, choose a starting vertex and find a way to trace over each edge of the graph exactly once without lifting your pencil. Number the edges to show the order in which you traced the edges.

a.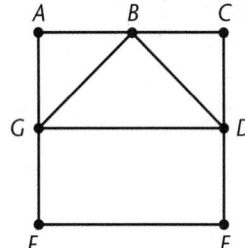

b.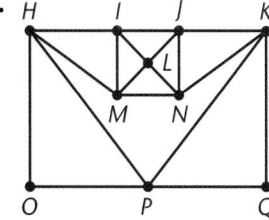

MORE PRACTICE

Verify Euler's Formula for each polyhedron.

13.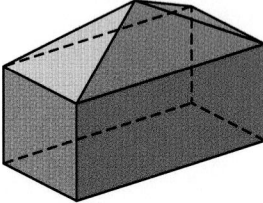

14.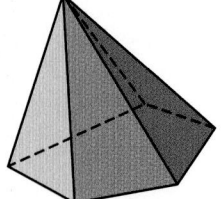

15. A cuboctahedron has 14 faces and 24 edges. How many vertices does it have?

16. A rhombicuboctahedron has 48 edges and 24 vertices. How many faces does it have?

17. **It's in the Mail** This graph shows how the mail travels between homes in Fernwood and homes in Greendale, 3000 miles away. Describe the steps involved in getting mail between these towns. If the mail takes an average of one day per edge on this graph, what is the typical time it takes for mail to be delivered from one town to the other?

Fernwood Post Office

Central Post Office

Greendale Post Office

Fernwood

Greendale

18. A snub cube has 60 edges and 38 faces. How many vertices does it have?

19. The following is a list of debates held so far this year between pairs of high school teams from Hamilton (H), Tyler (T), Wilson (W), Polk (P), and Lincoln (L).

H has debated T and L.

T has debated H, W, and L.

W has debated T and P.

P has debated W.

L has debated H and T.

Draw a graph representing the debates that have been held so far this year.

20. Cable TV Two competing cable television companies want to supply three neighborhoods with their services. Is it possible to connect each cable company with each of the three neighborhoods without crossing the underground cables? Explain.

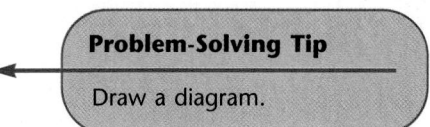

Problem-Solving Tip

Draw a diagram.

21. Describe a situation at school, work, or home that could be modeled by a graph. What do the vertices and edges of the graph represent in this situation? Sketch a possible graph for the situation.

MORE MATH REASONING

22. Holey Moley The polyhedrons shown are not simple since they have holes through them. A solid with one hole is called a *torus*, a solid with two holes is called a *double torus*, and so on.

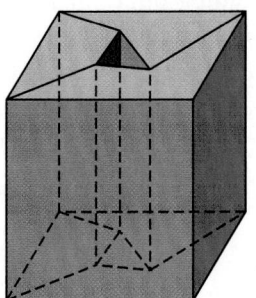　　　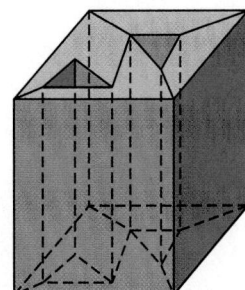

a. Show that Euler's Formula is not satisfied for the two polyhedrons shown.

b. The value of $F + V - E$ is the *Euler characteristic* of a polyhedron. Give the Euler characteristic of each polyhedron shown. Make a generalization of Euler's Formula that applies to polyhedrons with n holes, where n can be 0, 1, 2, and so on. Draw other models to help you see a pattern, if necessary.

23. Count Carefully Consider a regular convex polyhedron where p edges form the boundary of each face and q edges meet at every vertex. For any solid having F faces, E edges, and V vertices, show that each of the following identities is true.

a. $F = 2\dfrac{E}{p}$　　　　　**b.** $V = 2\dfrac{E}{q}$　　　　　**c.** $\dfrac{1}{p} + \dfrac{1}{q} = \dfrac{1}{E} + \dfrac{1}{2}$

Paths and Circuits

You've discovered how graphs can be used to represent polyhedrons, networks, and connections in a variety of situations. Now you will analyze and apply paths and circuits within graphs.

Suppose you are planning a hiking trip in the Great Smoky Mountains National Park in North Carolina. The map shows a system of trails that branch out from the Deep Creek campground. A graph is shown representing this network of trails.

The graph of this trail system is a **connected graph** because there is a **path,** a series of vertices and edges, connecting any two vertices in the graph. A path, such as *BCDB*, that ends at the same vertex as it begins without repeating edges is called a **circuit.**

A hiker might ask whether it is possible to start at Deep Creek campground and hike each trail without ever hiking the same trail twice; that is, can a path be found that traverses each edge exactly once? If such a path exists with different starting and ending points, then it is called an **Euler path.** If the path ends where it starts at Deep Creek campground, then it is called an **Euler circuit.**

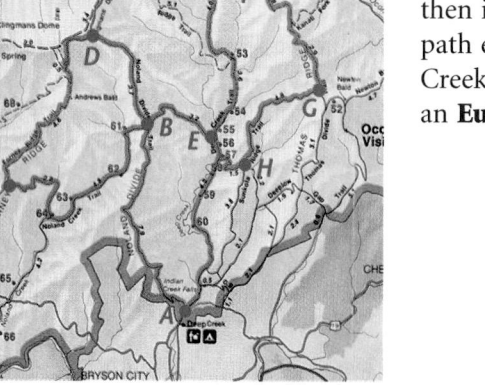

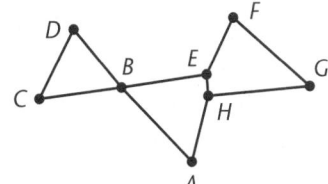

CONSIDER

1. There is no Euler path or Euler circuit starting at Deep Creek, but there is an Euler path starting at vertex *E* and ending at vertex *H*. Identify such a path.

In the following Explore, you will investigate Euler circuits, including the situation that originated the theory of graphs.

When Euler was a young man, the River Pregel ran through the Prussian city of Königsberg. The islands and banks of the city were joined by seven bridges, as shown.

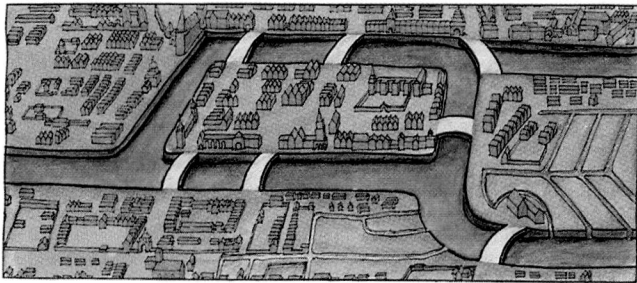

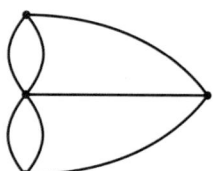

Graph of Königsberg (vertices) and its bridges (edges)

Was it possible to leave home, cross all seven bridges, and return home without crossing any bridge more than once? Euler was intrigued by this question and answered it in 1736, proving the first theorems in graph theory along the way.

1. First examine these graphs for Euler circuits using the following *trace test:* Copy each graph. For each graph, choose a starting point (vertex) and try to trace along each edge exactly once and return to the starting point without lifting your pencil or pen.

a. 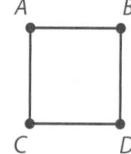 **b.** 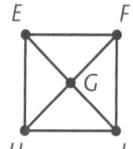 **c.**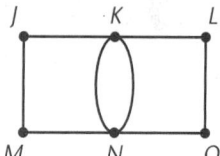

Which graphs have Euler circuits? Identify any Euler circuits you found.

2. Examine the vertices of each graph in Step 1. Decide if there are an odd or even number of edges meeting at each vertex, and label the vertex accordingly (O or E).

3. Look for a connection between the vertex labels in Step 2 and the graphs that have Euler circuits. Make a conjecture about a way to use vertices to decide whether a graph has an Euler circuit.

4. Use your conjecture to decide if it was possible to cross each bridge of Königsberg exactly once and return to the starting point. Verify your answer by using the trace test on the graph of Königsberg.

In the Explore, you counted the number of edges meeting at a vertex of a graph. This number is called the **degree of the vertex.** Euler proved that you can decide whether a graph has an Euler circuit or an Euler path simply by finding the degree of each of its vertices.

EULER'S TRAVERSABILITY THEOREM

- A connected graph has an Euler circuit if and only if it is connected and every vertex has even degree.

- A connected graph has an Euler path between two vertices *A* and *B* if and only if *A* and *B* have odd degree and all other vertices have even degree.

EXAMPLES

Decide whether each graph has an Euler circuit or path and identify one if so.

1.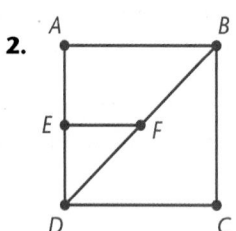

Vertices A, C, D, and F have even degree (2) and vertices B and E have odd degree (3). So there is an Euler path between B and E.

The path $BCDEFABE$ is an Euler path from B to E.

2.

Vertices B, D, E, and F all have odd degree (3), so there is no Euler circuit or path.

WHAT DO **YOU** THINK?

A driver for a bakery makes bread deliveries on each block of the region represented by the graph.

Plan an efficient delivery route for the driver to follow.

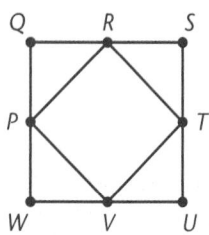

Darcy thinks...

I'll trace along the graph to find an efficient route. The driver can make two circuits, starting and ending at P, that hit every block exactly once. The path $PQRSTUVWPRTVP$ is an efficient delivery route.

Arturo thinks...

An Euler circuit would be an efficient route since it requires driving along each block only once. I'll check the vertices to see whether there is an Euler circuit. Vertices P, R, T, and V each have degree 4, and vertices Q, S, U, and W each have degree 2. Since all vertices have even degree, there is an Euler circuit. For example, the path $PWVUTSRQPRTVP$ is an Euler circuit.

CONSIDER

?

2. Are the Euler circuits found by Darcy and Arturo equally efficient? Explain your answer.

Determine whether each graph has an Euler circuit or path and identify one if so.

a.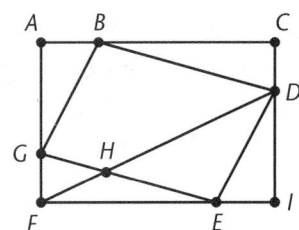

b.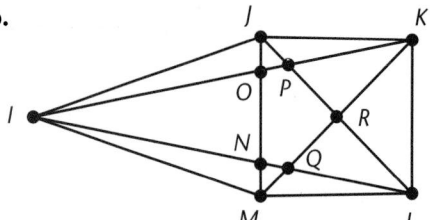

c. If someone walking in Königsberg didn't have to end up where he or she began, would it have been possible to walk and cross each bridge exactly once?

Euler's Traversability Theorem and the trace test are simple but effective tools for finding efficient routes and strategies in situations involving networks of connected objects.

REFLECT

1. What is a *path* on a graph? What is a *circuit*?
2. Explain what makes a path an Euler path. Why might the driver of a garbage or recycling truck want to find an Euler path?
3. How does knowing the degree of each vertex of a graph help you find an Euler path if one exists?

Exercises

CORE

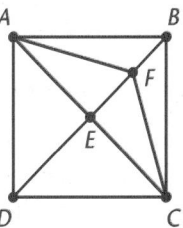

1. **Getting Started** Consider the connected graph shown.
   a. Give the degree of each vertex.
   b. Explain why there is no Euler circuit on this graph.
   c. Explain why there is an Euler path connecting *B* and *D*. Trace to find an Euler path between *B* and *D*.

Write the word or phrase that correctly completes each statement.

2. The ____ of a vertex of a graph is the number of edges in the graph that meet at that vertex.

3. A ____ is a series of vertices and edges that connects two vertices of a graph.

4. A graph is ____ if there is a path in the graph connecting any two vertices.

5. A path without repeating edges that begins and ends at the same vertex in a graph is a ____.

Decide whether each graph is connected.

6.

7.

8. Explain why each path is or is not an Euler path.

a.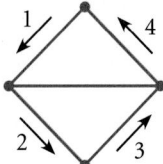

b.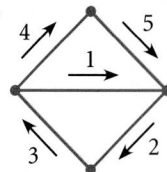

c.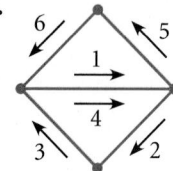

Give the degree of all vertices in each graph. Determine whether the graph has an Euler circuit or path, and identify one if so.

9.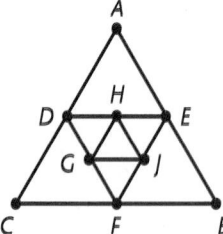

10.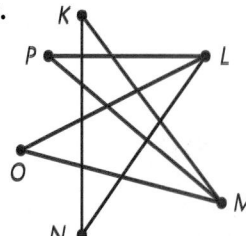

11.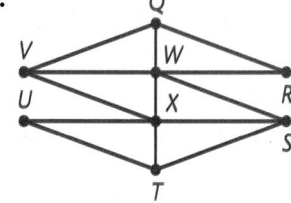

12. Fast Food To deliver meals to senior citizens unable to leave their homes, a volunteer for Meals-on-Wheels must drive along each of the streets represented by the graph. Plan an efficient route the driver can follow that begins and ends at the kitchen at *A*.

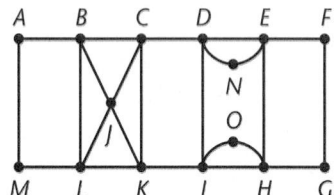

13. Paper Route Suppose you deliver newspapers to people living on each block of a 9-square-block subdivision, arranged in a square that is 3 blocks by 3 blocks. What would be an efficient route to deliver the newspapers?

> **Problem-Solving Tip**
>
> Draw a diagram and graph of the subdivision.

14. Sketch a system of streets, freeways, or highways near you and represent them as a graph. Is there an Euler circuit or path for this graph? Why might someone want to find such a path or circuit?

15. Do you think a graph that is not connected can have an Euler circuit? Explain.

16. By adding edges to a graph to eliminate vertices of odd degree, you can create a new graph that has an Euler circuit. Copy and label this graph. Add one or more edges so that the new graph has an Euler circuit. Identify the Euler circuit.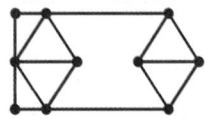

17. Back to Königsberg In the Explore, you considered the seven bridges of Königsberg. Suppose the people of Königsberg decided to build one more bridge. Could one more bridge be built so that a person could cross each bridge exactly once and return to the start? If so, draw a diagram to show where the new bridge should be built. If not, explain why.

18. Explain why an Euler path must start at a vertex of odd degree. (Hint: Think about the number of edges used each time a path passes through a vertex.)

19. If you remove one edge of an Euler circuit, what is true about the path that is left?

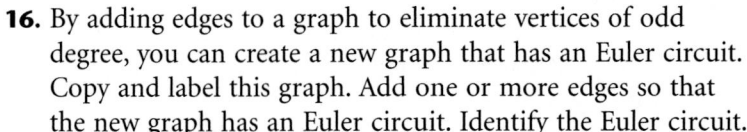 **LOOK BACK**

20. If $2500 is invested at 4% annual interest, compounded semiannually, what will the investment be worth in 10 years? [9-1]

21. a. How does the period of $y = 4 \sin 2x$ compare with that of $y = 6 \sin x$? [10-3]
  b. How does the amplitude of $y = 4 \sin 2x$ compare with that of $y = 6 \sin x$?

22. A pair of dice is rolled three times. Find the probability that exactly two of the rolls come up doubles (two ones, two twos, two threes, etc.). [11-1]

MORE PRACTICE

Decide whether each graph is connected.

23.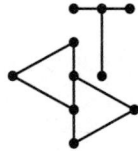

24.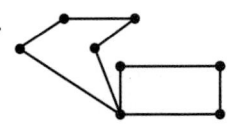

25.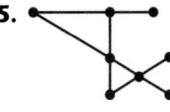

26. Explain why each path is or is not an Euler path.

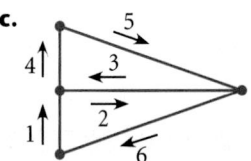

27. a. Summarize what must be true about the degrees of the vertices of a graph for the graph to have an Euler circuit. Sketch a graph to illustrate.
  b. Summarize what must be true about the degrees of the vertices of a graph for the graph to have an Euler path. Sketch a graph to illustrate.

Give the degree of all vertices in each graph. Determine whether the graph has an Euler circuit or path, and identify one if so.

28.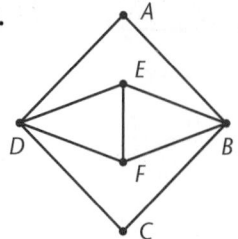

29.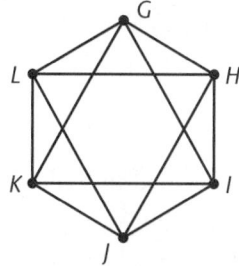

30.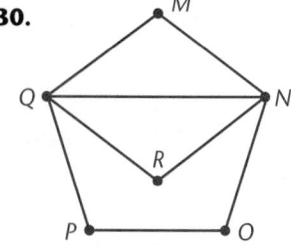

31. House Tracking Consider this floor plan of a house. Has the house been designed so that a person can walk through the house, passing through each doorway exactly once? If so, show how it can be done. If not, explain why it cannot be done.

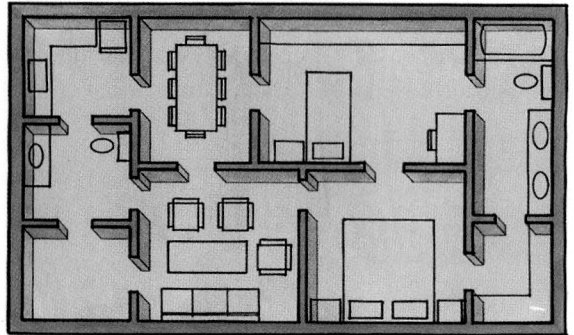

32. Copy and label this graph. Add one or more edges so that the new graph has an Euler circuit. Identify an Euler circuit.

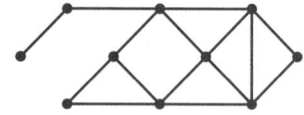

33. Every Home Should Have One! This graph represents the rooms (vertices) and hallways (edges) that are cleaned by a robot on one floor of a mansion. What is an efficient path to program the robot to take as it cleans rooms and hallways? (The robot need not finish where it started.)

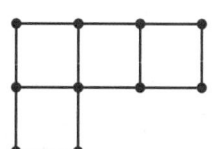

34. Parking Problems? This street map shows the locations of parking meters along several blocks. A parking-control officer wants to make two circuits of these blocks in order to check the meters on both sides of each street. Plan an efficient route for the officer to take.

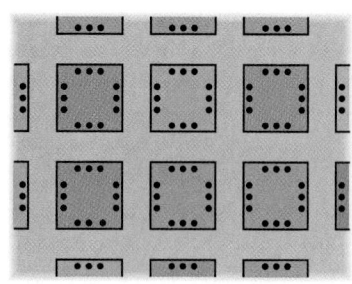

MORE MATH REASONING

35. Explain why a graph must have an even number of vertices of odd degree.

36. Scheduling Sundays At one time, the National Football League had two conferences with 13 teams each. The league officials decided that each team would play a total of 14 games. Eleven of the games would be with teams in their own conference and the remaining 3 games would be with teams in the other conference. Show that this is impossible.

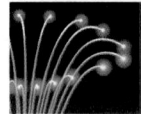
← CONNECT → *You have analyzed graphs, paths, and circuits. Now you will see how graphs and trees can help you optimize quantities such as distance and cost.*

Euler circuits and paths must contain each edge of a graph exactly once. Another interesting type of circuit or path is one that passes through each *vertex* of a connected graph exactly once. A path of this type is a **Hamiltonian path** and a circuit of this type is a **Hamiltonian circuit.** These are named after the Irish mathematician Sir William Rowan Hamilton (1805−1865), who invented and marketed an interesting puzzle based on this idea.

EXPLORE: THIS IS PUZZLING

Hamilton's puzzle consisted of a regular dodecahedron made of wood with a well-known city labeled at each vertex. The object was to use string to trace a connected route along the edges that passed through each city exactly once.

1. Solve Hamilton's puzzle using string and an actual dodecahedron, if available. Describe your solution and any strategies that helped you solve the puzzle.

2. Copy and label this graph representing a dodecahedron. Solve Hamilton's puzzle by tracing to find a circuit on the graph that passes through each vertex exactly once. Compare your solution with those of two classmates. Is there more than one solution?

3. If you solved the puzzle using an actual dodecahedron, imagine projecting your solution onto a flat piece of paper. Does the solution look like your graph in Step 2 or is it different? Does it depend on how you orient the dodecahedron?

MATERIALS

*Optional: String
Dodecahedron with a nail or pin
in each vertex*

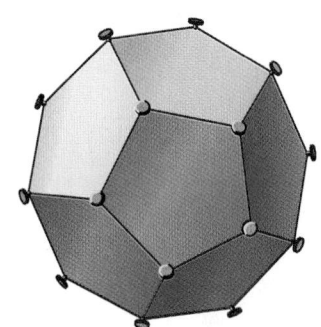

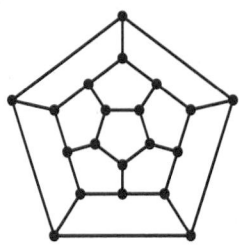

The degrees of vertices tell you whether a graph contains an Euler circuit, but there is no known general method for determining whether a graph contains a Hamiltonian circuit. As you saw in the Explore, each graph can be checked individually by tracing. Note that Hamiltonian circuits and paths need not include all edges, just all vertices.

There is often more than one Hamiltonian circuit for a graph. If the vertices of the graph represent cities, we might ask which Hamiltonian circuit minimizes distance or cost. This type of optimization problem is known as the *traveling salesperson problem*.

EXAMPLE

1. A salesperson starts in Dallas, Texas, and must visit Lubbock and Vernon, Texas, and Oklahoma City, Oklahoma, before returning to Dallas. The distances between these cities are shown on the graph. Find the shortest Hamiltonian circuit the salesperson can take.

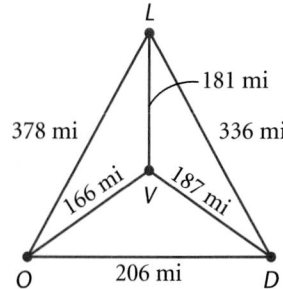

This tree diagram shows the total distances of several Hamiltonian circuits.

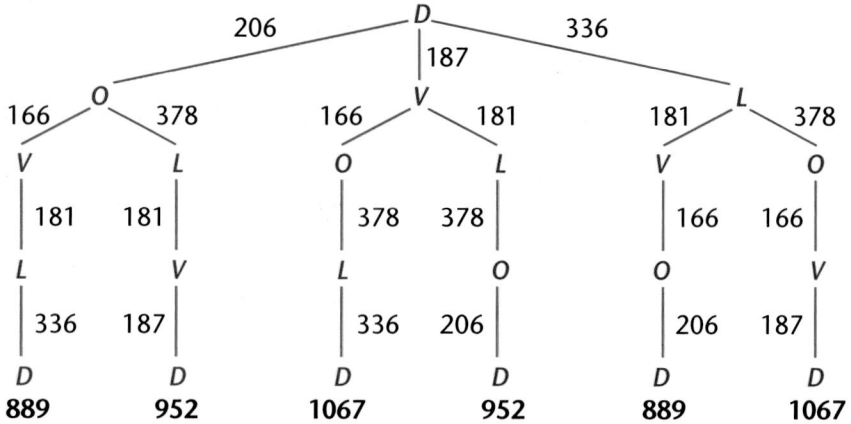

The shortest Hamiltonian circuit is *DOVLD* (or *DLVOD*, the same circuit listed in the opposite order), which is 889 miles long. The shortest route the salesperson can take is this circuit taken in either direction:

Dallas → Oklahoma City → Vernon → Lubbock → Dallas

or

Dallas → Lubbock → Vernon → Oklahoma City → Dallas

TRY IT

a. An inspector must plan his route beginning and ending at site *A* and visiting four factories, *B, C, D,* and *E*. The distances between the sites are shown on the graph. Find the shortest Hamiltonian circuit the inspector can take.

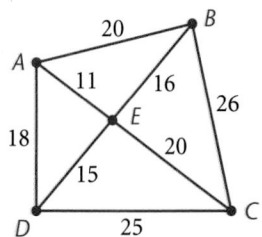

Tree diagrams are examples of another type of graph called a *tree*. In general, a **tree** is a connected graph that contains no circuits. A tree that contains every vertex of a graph and has no new edges is called a **spanning tree** of that graph. Here are three possible spanning trees for the graph in Example 1.

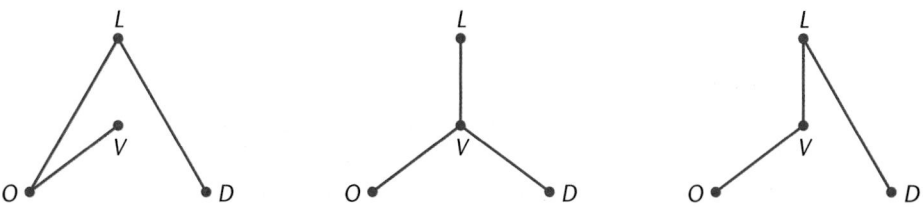

To solve a traveling salesperson problem, you may look for a Hamiltonian circuit with minimal length or cost. In other situations, such as laying phone or power lines, a solution must contain all vertices but need not contain any circuits. In these situations, we look for a **minimal spanning tree,** a spanning tree that minimizes the total length or cost of all edges.

There is a convenient method developed by J. B. Kruskal for finding minimal spanning trees. Suppose you are looking for a spanning tree *T* with the least total length in the connected graph *G*. Follow these steps to find a minimal spanning tree of *G*.

Step 1: Choose an edge of minimal length for the first edge of *T*.

Step 2: Consider each remaining edge with one vertex in *T* and one vertex not in *T*. Choose such an edge of minimal length and add it to *T*.

Step 3: Repeat Step 2 until the tree *T* contains all vertices of *G*. The resulting tree *T* is a minimal spanning tree of *G*.

EXAMPLE

2. This graph shows costs (in thousands of dollars) of laying a network of computer lines among 12 buildings of a college campus. Find a spanning tree that connects all of the buildings at a minimal cost.

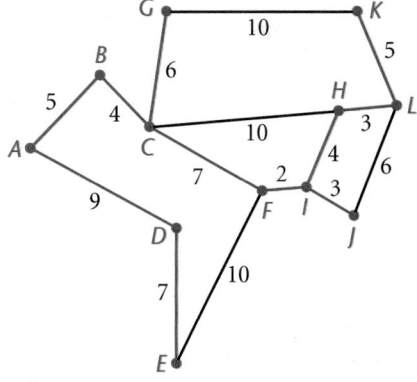

First choose *FI*, the edge with minimal cost (2). Edge *IJ* has the minimum cost (3) of the remaining edges with one vertex in *FI*. Of the remaining edges with one vertex in the tree *FIJ*, edge *IH* has the minimal cost (4).

Continuing in this manner until all vertices are included, we find the minimal spanning tree with edges *FI, IJ, IH, HL, LK, FC, CB, BA, CG, AD,* and *DE,* with a total cost of 55.

The resulting minimal spanning tree gives a total cost of $55,000 to lay a network of computer lines connecting the buildings.

b. Find a minimal spanning tree for this connected graph. What is the length of the minimal spanning tree?

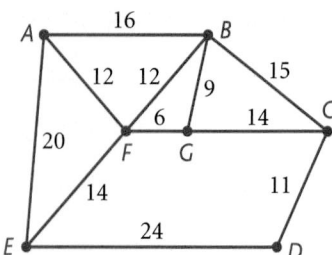

1. Why is there only one path connecting any two points in a tree?
2. Explain why a minimal spanning tree for a graph with *n* vertices must have *n* − 1 edges.

Analyzing graphs, finding Hamiltonian circuits, and designing spanning trees are useful skills for optimizing lengths, costs, and other quantities in many real-world situations. Much of the theory of graphs, such as the algorithm for finding minimal spanning trees, is easily implemented on computers, allowing companies to efficiently plan, operate, and monitor complex networks.

REFLECT

1. What makes a circuit in a graph a Hamiltonian circuit?
2. How is a tree different from other graphs?
3. Describe a traveling-salesperson-type problem. Also draw the graph, circuit, or tree that can help you solve the problem.

Exercises

CORE

1. Getting Started Decide if the path on each graph is a Hamiltonian circuit.

a.

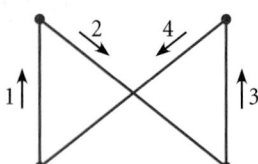

b.

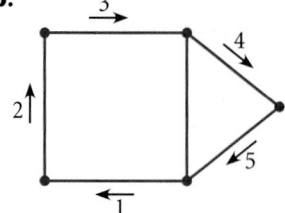

c.

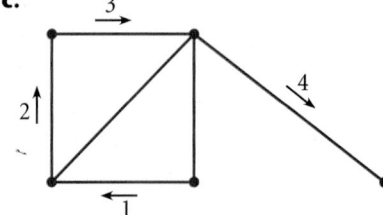

Determine whether each statement is true or false. If the statement is false, change the underlined word or phrase to make it true.

2. A Hamiltonian circuit is a circuit that passes through each <u>edge</u> of a graph once.

3. A tree is a connected graph that contains no <u>paths</u>.

4. A spanning tree is a tree that contains every <u>vertex</u> of a graph.

Give a Hamiltonian circuit for each graph.

5.

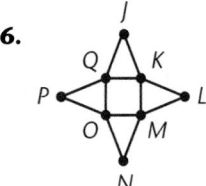

6.

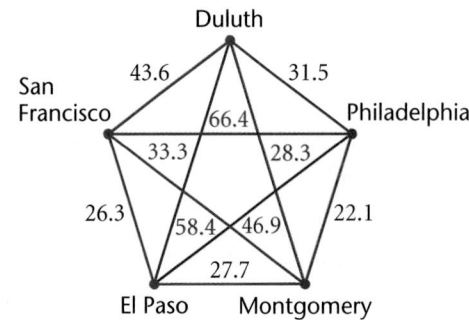

7. Draw a graph representing a cube, and give a Hamiltonian circuit for the graph.

8. Road Rally You've entered a cross-country road rally that starts in Duluth, with stops in San Francisco, El Paso, Montgomery, and Philadelphia, The graph shows the average driving times, in hours, between cities. The winner is the driver who stops at each city exactly once and returns to Duluth in the least amount of time. All speed limits must be obeyed. Which round-trip would you take to win the rally?

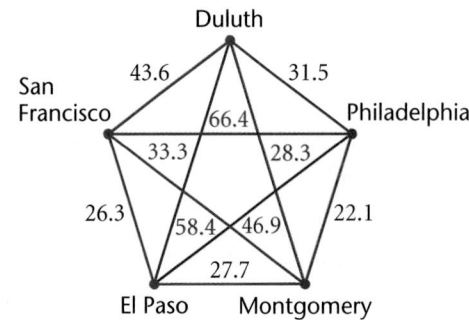

Decide whether each graph is a tree. Explain your reasoning.

9.

10.

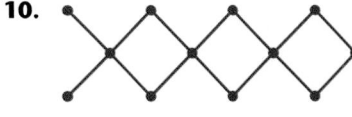

11. Jarring News Jar A contains one red ball and two blue balls. Jar B contains three red balls and two blue balls. A jar is chosen at random and then a ball is chosen at random from that jar. Use a tree to decide which color ball is most likely to be chosen. Give the probability of choosing that color ball.

12. In 1857, Arthur Cayley modeled molecules of chemicals called hydrocarbons using graphs in which vertices represent atoms of carbon or hydrogen and edges represent bonds between atoms. Using graphs, Cayley was able to predict the existence of new hydrocarbons.

A molecule of a saturated unbranched hydrocarbon consists of a column of carbon atoms surrounded by hydrogen atoms. The first two of these are methane and ethane, as shown. Draw graphs of the molecular structures of the next two saturated unbranched hydrocarbons, propane (C_3H_8) and butane (C_4H_{10}).

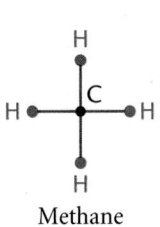

Methane
(CH_4)

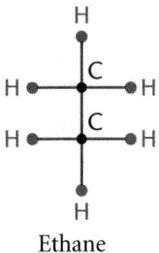

Ethane
(C_2H_6)

Draw a minimal spanning tree for each graph.

13.
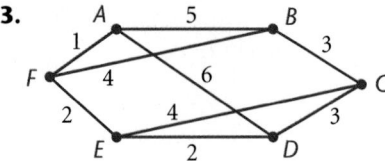

14.
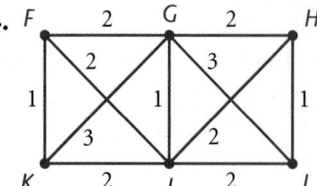

15. Suppose you need to connect these Maryland cities with the shortest possible length of telegraph lines. The distances, in miles, are shown on the graph. Find the minimum length of wire needed and show that there are two plans that give this length.

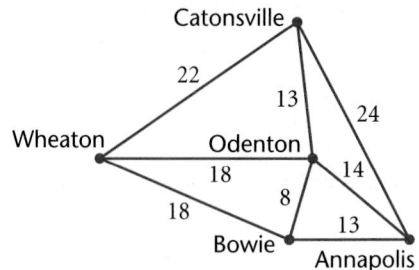

16. A group of marines is on a training exercise on an island in the Pacific Ocean. They plan to run communication wire between four key points on the island.

a. Measure and record the distance between each pair of sites.

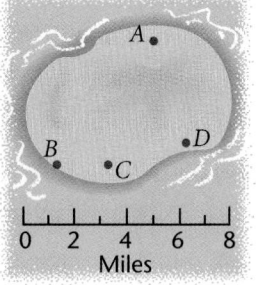

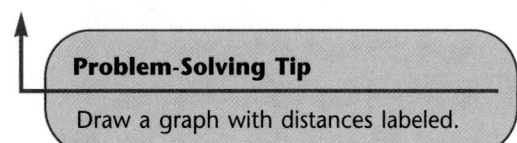
Problem-Solving Tip

Draw a graph with distances labeled.

b. Find and sketch a minimal spanning tree that shows how the sites can be connected using the least amount of wire. What is the minimum amount of wire needed?

 **LOOK AHEAD**

17. The first term of a sequence is 1 and each subsequent term is one more than twice the previous term. Write the first six terms of the sequence.

18. Multiply the matrix $A = \begin{bmatrix} 0.6 & 0.4 \\ 0.4 & 0.6 \end{bmatrix}$ by itself repeatedly to find A^2, A^3, and A^4.

MORE PRACTICE

Give a Hamiltonian circuit for each graph.

19.
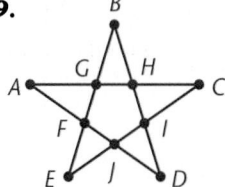

20.
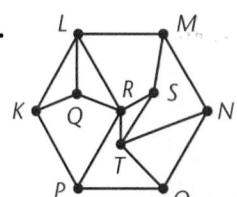

21.
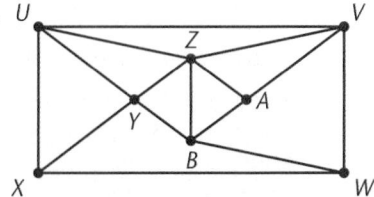

22. Draw a graph representing an octahedron, and give a Hamiltonian circuit for the graph.

23. Five towns are connected by commuter train service, as shown on the graph. The distances between towns are labeled on the graph. Determine a route that minimizes the round-trip distance required to visit each town exactly once and return to the starting point.

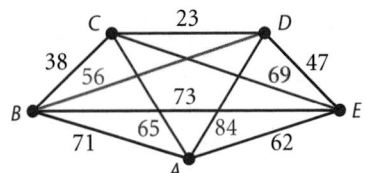

24. The graph shows the costs of driving between four cities. Give a round-trip route, starting and ending at *F*, that a driver could take to visit each city with the minimum transportation cost.

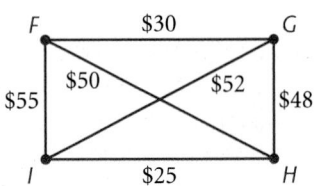

Decide whether each graph is a tree. Explain your reasoning.

25.

26.

27.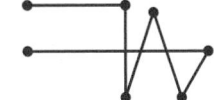

Draw a minimal spanning tree for each graph.

28.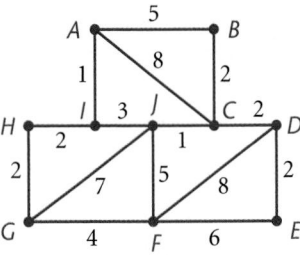

29.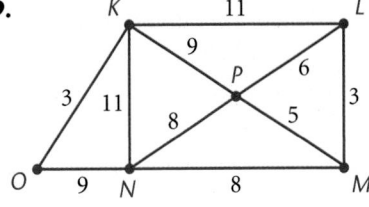

30.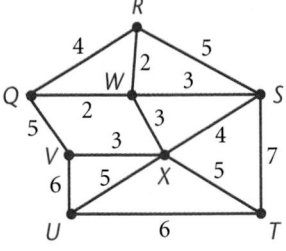

31.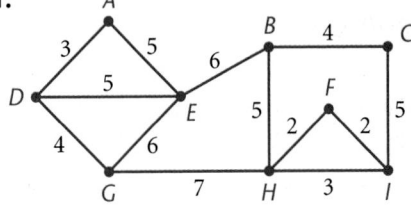

32. Oil Tree An oil company needs to build pipelines connecting five storage facilities, as shown on the map. Assume pipeline costs are $1000 per mile to construct and pipes can be run between any pair of facilities.

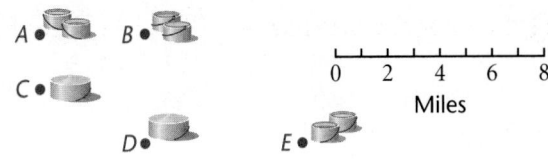

a. Measure and record the distance between each pair of storage facilities.

Problem-Solving Tip

Draw a graph with distances labeled.

b. Find and sketch a spanning tree that shows where to construct the pipelines to minimize the total cost of connecting the storage facilities. What is that minimum cost?

33. Spy Against Spy Agents *A, B, C, D, E, F, G,* and *H* are working undercover for the See-All Intelligence Agency. Each agent must be able to communicate directly or indirectly with every other agent. The table gives the *risk factors* associated with direct communication between agents. All other direct communications are too risky. What is the least possible total risk (the sum of the risk factors) in a connected communication system, where any two agents can pass information through some number of other agents?

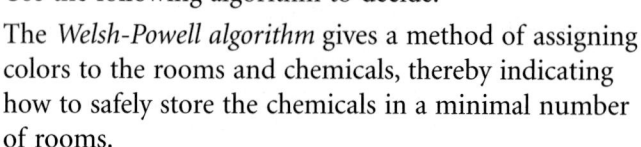

Agent Pairs	AB	AC	AE	AF	AG	BC	BF	CD	CF	CG	CH	DE	DH	EH
Risk Factor	9	3	8	3	4	10	6	6	4	5	7	6	3	5

MORE MATH REASONING

34. Welsh-Powell Algorithm Vertices in this graph denote chemicals. If two chemicals are connected by an edge, the chemicals should not be stored in the same room since accidental mixing could cause an explosion. How many rooms are needed to store the chemicals safely? Use the following algorithm to decide.

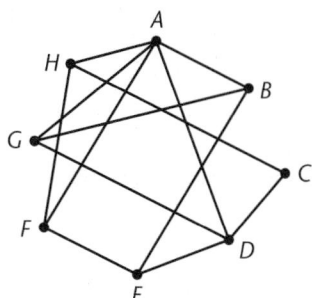

The *Welsh-Powell algorithm* gives a method of assigning colors to the rooms and chemicals, thereby indicating how to safely store the chemicals in a minimal number of rooms.

Step 1: Rename the vertices of the graph $V_1, V_2, V_3, \ldots, V_n$ according to their degrees: $\deg(V_1) \geq \deg(V_2) \geq \deg(V_3) \geq \ldots \geq \deg(V_n)$. (Break any ties arbitrarily.)

Step 2: Assign a color to the first uncolored vertex in the list of vertices ordered by degree. Then go through the vertices in numerical order, assigning this color to any vertex that doesn't share an edge with any other vertex of this color.

Step 3: If some vertices have not been assigned colors yet, return to Step 2.

Step 4: When all vertices are colored, these colors indicate the room assignments that will minimize risk.

12-1
PART D Making Connections

← **CONNECT** → *You have learned to analyze paths, circuits, and trees in graphs to find efficient and optimal solutions in situations that involve networks.*

Communications networks and transportation routes are some of the most complex networks in the world. Now you will see how graphs can help you analyze and efficiently use airline routes.

An accountant in the Boston branch of a company must arrange a trip to visit the company's branches in six other cities. Assume that there are direct flights between any two of the cities and that the cost of the flights is proportional to the total distance. How can the accountant plan the round-trip to minimize the distance and flight costs?

The table shows the distances between pairs of these cities and the graph shows one possible route (not with the minimum distance).

		BOS	GTF	MCI	LAX	MIA	MSP	YVR
Boston	BOS	—	1985	1255	2596	1258	1120	2513
Great Falls	GTF	1985	—	1036	1015	2267	700	540
Kansas City	MCI	1255	1036	—	1351	1245	401	1555
Los Angeles	LAX	2596	1015	1351	—	2330	1525	1079
Miami	MIA	1258	2267	1245	2330	—	1500	2800
Minneapolis	MSP	1120	700	401	1525	1500	—	1435
Vancouver	YVR	2513	540	1555	1079	2800	1435	—

The British mathematician Nicos Christofides found a strategy for solving traveling salesperson problems that is guaranteed to be no more than 50% greater in length than a minimal Hamiltonian circuit. Now you will use this method to find a route for the accountant's trip.

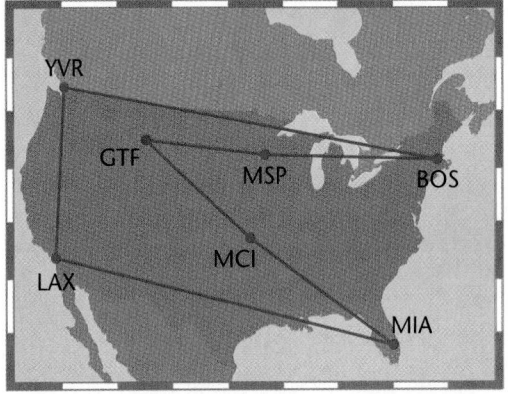

1. Find a minimum spanning tree for the graph with edges between each pair of cities.
2. Circle the cities connected to an odd number of other cities (vertices with odd degree). Add new edges between pairs of these cities until you create a circuit. (The circuit need not be Hamiltonian yet and may pass through cities more than once.)
3. Introduce shortcuts as needed to make the circuit Hamiltonian and to reduce the overall length of the circuit.
4. a. Give the total length of your circuit once you've made all the shortcuts you can.
   b. How much shorter is your route than the one shown by the map?
   c. Compare your results with those of another student and discuss the differences in your methods and final results.

While the process of pairing odd vertices and introducing shortcuts does not guarantee a minimal Hamiltonian circuit, it significantly eases the task of comparing all such circuits in order to find a minimum.

REFLECT

1. State Euler's Formula. Sketch a simple polyhedron and verify the formula.
2. What are some similarities and differences between Euler circuits and Hamiltonian circuits?
3. What makes a tree a spanning tree? What makes a tree a minimal spanning tree?
4. Describe a situation in which graphs could help you optimize a cost. What type of graph would help give the minimum cost?

Self-Assessment

1. Verify Euler's Formula for this polyhedron-shaped chisel.

2. The following pairs of people exchanged business cards at a convention:

   Alan and Bob, Chuck and Delia, Evan and Felicia, Alan and Evan, George and Delia, Hank and Iris, Evan and Iris, George and Iris, Hank and Bob

   Draw a graph representing the business connections made at the convention.

Decide whether each graph is connected.

3.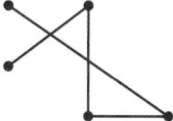

4.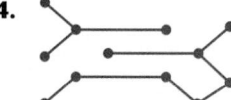

5. A polyhedron has 6 faces and 12 edges. How many vertices does it have?

Determine whether a mason installing the illustrated tile patterns could place the cement between the tiles following an Euler circuit. Explain your conclusions.

6.

7.

8. Bob has to check the traffic signals in town. The corners with signals are indicated on the map. Copy the graph and indicate a Hamiltonian circuit that Bob can follow to check the signals without passing the same corner twice.

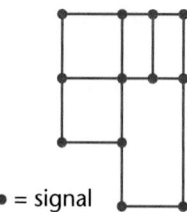

● = signal

9. More Bridges The river Seine cuts through Paris and the Ile de Cité in France as shown. Is it possible to walk around this area and cross every bridge exactly once, not necessarily ending where you began? If so, show an Euler path that accomplishes the trip. If not, show how a bridge could be added to make the trip possible.

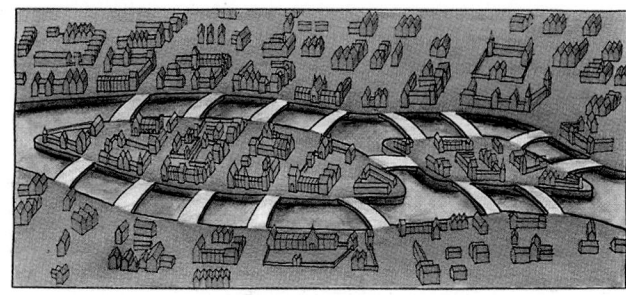

10. Can you trace along the edges of a pyramid, cross each vertex exactly once, and return to the vertex where you began? Explain.

Problem-Solving Tip

Draw a diagram or graph.

11. The graph shows the costs, in thousands of dollars, of installing a new high-speed communications network. Find a minimal spanning tree and give the minimum cost of installing the network.

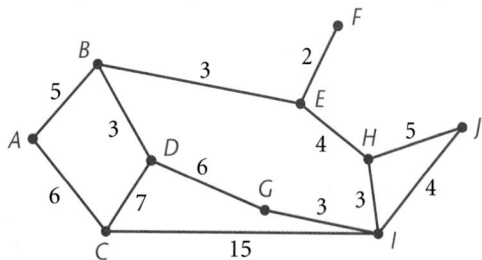

12. An aerospace company wants to establish a computer network connecting five of its factories, laboratories, and administrative buildings. The cost (in thousands of dollars) of linking any two sites is shown on the graph. If the company wants to build the network as cheaply as possible, how should it be built?

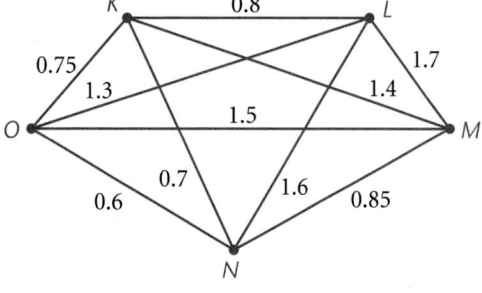

13. Bouncing Ball A ball is dropped from a height of 12 meters. It falls straight down and each rebound is $\frac{1}{3}$ of the distance it fell. How far will the ball travel before coming to rest? [4-2]

14. Suppose you start a retirement account by depositing $2000 at 9%, compounded continuously. With no further deposits, how much will your account be worth in 40 years when you retire? [9-1]

15. Wolf, Goat, and Cabbage Solve this problem, which appears in *Problems for the Quickening of the Mind,* thought to be compiled by Alcuin of York (ca. 775).

A man wishes to safely transport a wolf, a goat, and a head of cabbage from one side of the river to the other. The man can only take one thing across the river at a time, and he must not leave the wolf alone with the goat or the goat alone with the cabbage. How should he proceed in order to get all three safely across the river in the least number of trips?

16. Compare the amplitude and period of the functions $y = 3 \cos x + 2$ and $y = 5 \cos x - 2$. [10-3]

17. A three-person committee is to be chosen from a group of six women and four men. Give the probability that the chosen committee consists of two women and one man. [11-1]

18. Using Christofides's method in the Explore on page 825, find a round-trip that goes to each city shown in the graph.

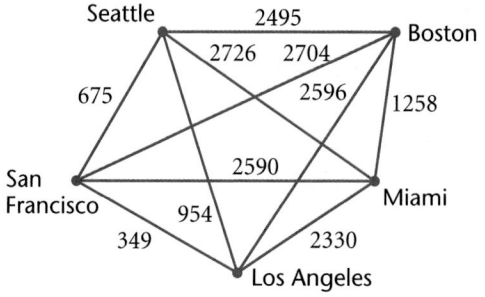

19. Soccer to Me Teams A and B have played several soccer games, with A winning two-thirds of the games. These teams are now in a play-off in which the first team to win two games becomes the champion. Assume the probability of A beating B in a game is two-thirds. Draw a tree diagram to determine the probability that A wins the play-off.

20. Trucking Lightly Suppose that seven dangerous chemicals are to be shipped from a factory to a remote processing site. The EPA forbids certain chemicals to be shipped on the same truck at the same time because of the danger of an explosion should the chemicals become accidentally mixed. A list of chemicals that cannot be shipped together is shown. Using the Welsh-Powell algorithm outlined in Exercise 34 on page 824, find a way to safely ship the chemicals simultaneously.

Chemical	Incompatible Chemicals
1	2, 3, 5
2	1, 5, 7
3	1, 4, 6, 7
4	3, 5, 7
5	1, 2, 4
6	3, 7
7	2, 3, 4, 6

Recursion and Creativity

In 1985, British zoologist Richard Dawkins wrote a computer program, called Biomorph Land, that surpassed all of his expectations. Biomorph Land defines a space of possible biological shapes constructed with short straight lines and branches. Dawkins created Biomorph Land to demonstrate visually that, although totally random selection could not produce a coherent design, selection by accumulated mutations could. The program draws a stick, adds branches to it, adds branches to the branches, and so on. The parameters allow forms to mutate at random. Being a zoologist, it was Dawkins's intention to try to generate known tree shapes. Here's what happened:

On the first day, the program generated trees, some of which did not exist in nature. So far, so good. As hours passed, the branching structures began to cross back upon themselves, forming little bodies instead of tree trunks. Then legs and wings appeared that were attached to the bodies. Dawkins had unintentionally created insects! As the program continued, scorpions, spiders, frogs, shrimp, Aztec temples, Gothic church windows, and kangaroos appeared. This reinforced Dawkins's notion that the process of development in living beings is recursive; that is, simple rules iterated over and over again produce the complexity of the final forms.

1. What do you think is meant by a recursive computer process?

2. In what sense is the development of life on Earth recursive?

Recursive Sequences

Earlier you explored arithmetic and geometric sequences. You saw how these sequences can be defined recursively in terms of common differences and common ratios. Now you will analyze and apply other sequences defined through recursion.

You may recall from Chapter 4 that a *recursive definition* of a sequence is a rule that tells how to find each term from previous terms. For example, the arithmetic sequence 1, 5, 9, 13, ... can be defined by the initial term $a_1 = 1$ and the **recursion formula** $a_n = a_{n-1} + 4$ for $n > 1$. Similarly, the geometric sequence 2, 6, 18, 54, ... can be defined by the initial term $b_1 = 2$ and the recursion formula $b_n = 3b_{n-1}$ for $n > 1$.

Recursion can be used to define a variety of sequences that may display arithmetic growth, geometric growth, periodicity, or even chaotic behavior.

EXPLORE: SUITABLE SUITS

MATERIALS

Graphing utility or spreadsheet software

When the need arises, environmental engineers wear protective suits that are designed to neutralize specific toxic chemicals. However, the ability of a suit to neutralize a chemical is usually reduced with prolonged exposure.

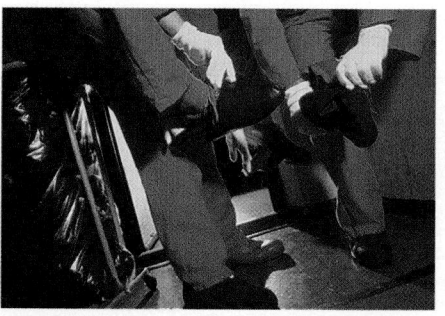

Suppose an engineer has put on a new protective suit and begins to clean up a chemical spill in a laboratory. During each hour of the cleanup, the suit neutralizes 30% of the toxic chemical on it and accumulates an additional 12 micrograms of the chemical.

1. Make a table or spreadsheet of the amounts of unneutralized chemical on the suit during each hour of the cleanup. Describe the growth of these values.
2. Do the values in Step 1 form an arithmetic sequence, a geometric sequence, or neither? Explain. Then give an initial term and a recursion formula for this sequence of values if possible.
3. The suit is safe to use until it has accumulated 35 micrograms or more of the toxic chemical. How long can the engineer safely continue to clean up the spill before the suit must be changed?
4. Reanalysis of the toxicity of the chemical indicates that the suit can be used safely with up to 40 micrograms of accumulated chemical. Does this make a significant difference in the amount of time the engineer can continue to work on the chemical spill? Explain.

Although the sequence in the Explore is neither arithmetic nor geometric, it shares features with both types of sequences. Its recursion formula can be written in the form $a_n = Aa_{n-1} + B$, where A and B are constants. Recursive sequences of this type have a variety of applications, including modeling medicine levels in the body.

EXAMPLE

1. Dr. Dossey has prescribed that a patient take 16 units of medicine orally every 4 hours. This medicine is quickly absorbed into the bloodstream. The medicine level in the bloodstream then falls to 75% of its previous level after 4 hours.

   The medicine level in the bloodstream should not exceed 65 units. Define a sequence giving the medicine level in the patient's bloodstream after each dose is taken and absorbed. Use your definition to decide how many doses the patient can safely take.

   There are 16 units of medicine in the patient's bloodstream after the first dose. The medicine level after each subsequent dose is absorbed is 75% of the previous level plus 16 units from the new dose.

   $$b_1 = 16 \qquad b_n = 0.75b_{n-1} + 16$$

   Some of the term values are shown in the spreadsheet and graph.

   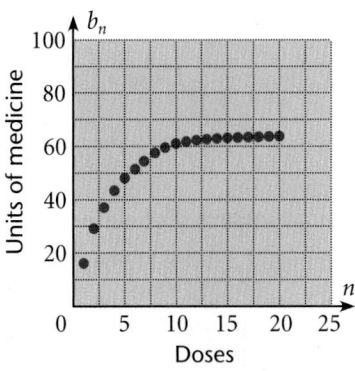

A	B
1	16
2	28
3	37
4	43.75
5	48.8125
6	52.609375
7	55.4570313
8	57.5927734
9	59.1945801
10	60.3959351
...	...
35	63.9972878
36	63.9979658
37	63.9984744
38	63.9988558
39	63.9991418
40	63.9993564
...	...

   The medicine level apparently approaches 64 units and never reaches 65 units. So the medicine level is safe for any number of 16-unit doses taken in 4-hour intervals. The doctor can continue the medication as long as needed to heal the patient.

The term values in Example 1 appear to approach 64. In fact, by using inductive reasoning, it is possible to find the following explicit formula for the nth term, which shows that the term values approach 64.

$$b_n = 64 - 64(0.75)^n$$

For example, $b_4 = 64 - 64(0.75)^4 = 64 - 20.25 = 43.75$.

CONSIDER

1. How can you tell that the term values of the sequence in Example 1 approach 64 from the explicit formula for the nth term?

Like the sequence in Example 1, every sequence with a recursive formula of the form $a_n = Aa_{n-1} + B$ has an explicit formula of the form $a_n = h + kA^n$, where h and k are constants.

EXAMPLE

2. Give an explicit formula for the sequence with the recursive definition $a_1 = 2$ and $a_n = 3a_{n-1} + 20$ for $n > 1$. Use your formula to find a_{10}.

Using the recursive definition, the sequence begins 2, 26, 98, 314, …. The explicit formula has the form $a_n = h + k3^n$. We can use this, along with the first two term values $a_1 = 2$ and $a_2 = 26$, to solve for h and k.

$n = 1$: $a_1 = 2$ and also $a_1 = h + k(3)$ $\rightarrow$ $h + 3k = 2$ ❶

$n = 2$: $a_2 = 26$ and also $a_2 = h + k(3^2)$ $\rightarrow$ $h + 9k = 26$ ❷

Solve this system of equations for h and k. Subtracting equation ❶ from equation ❷ eliminates h and gives $6k = 24$. Therefore, $k = 4$. Substituting this value into either equation and solving for h gives $h = -10$. Now we can write the explicit formula $a_n = h + k3^n$ using these constants.

$$a_n = -10 + 4 \cdot 3^n$$

Using this formula, $a_{10} = -10 + 4 \cdot 3^{10} = 236,186$.

Notice that the sequence does not converge since 3^n grows indefinitely.

TRY IT

a. Give an explicit formula for the sequence with the recursive definition $a_1 = 2$ and $a_n = 0.5a_{n-1} + 1.5$. Use your formula to find a_8. Does this sequence converge?

b. At the beginning of this year, Regina invested $1000 in a certificate of deposit that earns 6% simple annual interest. She expects to save $1000 per year, which she will add to the account at the beginning of each year. Assuming the interest rate stays at 6%, define a sequence that gives the amount in the account after each deposit. How much can Regina expect to have in her account after 10 deposits?

These are just some of the many applications of recursively defined sequences. Such sequences can also be used to model population growth, heating and cooling of objects, and even the complex behavior of chaotic systems.

1. Define *recursion* in your own words.

2. Explain the procedure you use to find an explicit formula for a sequence if it satisfies a recursion formula of the form $a_n = Aa_{n-1} + B$.

3. Why is an explicit formula for the nth term of a sequence sometimes more convenient than a recursion formula?

Exercises

CORE

1. Getting Started A sequence has first term $a_1 = 5$ and satisfies the recursive formula $a_n = 2a_{n-1} - 3$. Substitute $n = 2$ into the recursive formula to find a_2. Then substitute $n = 3$ into the formula to find a_3. Continue in this manner until you've listed the first ten terms of the sequence.

Determine whether each statement is true or false. If the statement is false, change the underlined word or phrase to make it true.

2. A <u>recursion formula</u> for a sequence is a formula for the nth term of the sequence in terms of previous terms.

3. An <u>explicit formula</u> for a sequence is a formula for the nth term of the sequence directly in terms of n.

Give the first eight terms of each sequence, and sketch a graph of the sequence.

4. $a_1 = 1$ and $a_n = 4a_{n-1} - 1$

5. $b_1 = -6$ and $b_n = -0.5b_{n-1} + 8$

6. Take That to the Bank Today Josephine deposited $400 to open a bank account that pays 4% simple annual interest. She plans to deposit $100 in the account one year from now, $100 two years from now, and so on. Define a recursive sequence that gives the amount in the account after each year. In how many years will Josephine have saved $1000?

7. Which of these is a recursion formula for a geometric sequence?

I. $a_n = 3(a_{n-1} + 3)$ II. $b_n = 4b_{n-1}$ III. $c_n = 2 + 2c_{n-1}$

(a) only I   (b) only II   (c) only III   (d) I and III   (e) I, II, and III

Give an explicit formula of the form $a_n = h + kA^n$ for each recursively defined sequence. Use your formula to find the tenth term and to determine whether the sequence converges.

8. $a_n = 2a_{n-1} - 3$; $a_1 = 3.5$

9. $a_n = 0.5a_{n-1} + 5$; $a_1 = 2$

10. $a_n = 1 - 3a_{n-1}$; $a_1 = -2$

11. $a_n = 1.5a - 16$; $a_1 = 32$

12. Ripcord A sky diver opens her parachute after reaching a free-fall speed of 90 feet per second. Suppose that her speed n seconds after opening the parachute is y_n, satisfying $y_{n+1} = 0.1y_n + 14.4$. Describe what occurs after the parachute opens.

13. Cool It! Janet took a casserole out of a 375°F oven to cool in her 75°F kitchen. A good model for how the casserole cools is given by Newton's Law of Cooling, which may be restated to say that the temperature change per minute is proportional to the temperature difference between the casserole and the room. In this case, the initial temperature is $T_0 = 375$ and $T_n - T_{n-1} = -0.15(T_{n-1} - 75)$ gives T_n, the temperature n minutes after Janet removes the casserole.
  a. Give the casserole temperature for several minutes after it is removed from the oven. When will the casserole first be under 175°F and ready to serve?
  b. Give an explicit formula for T_n. How warm will the casserole be if it sits for 30 minutes before being served?

14. Fibonacci's Rabbits The following situation was described and analyzed in the year 1202 by Italian mathematician Leonardo Fibonacci in his book *Liber Abaci*.

Suppose a rabbit colony begins with a pair of newborn rabbits, one male and one female. Assume that newborn rabbits mature in a month. Also assume that each mature rabbit pair mates once per month and has a litter of one male and one female rabbit a month later. This tree diagram shows the colony size for the first five months.

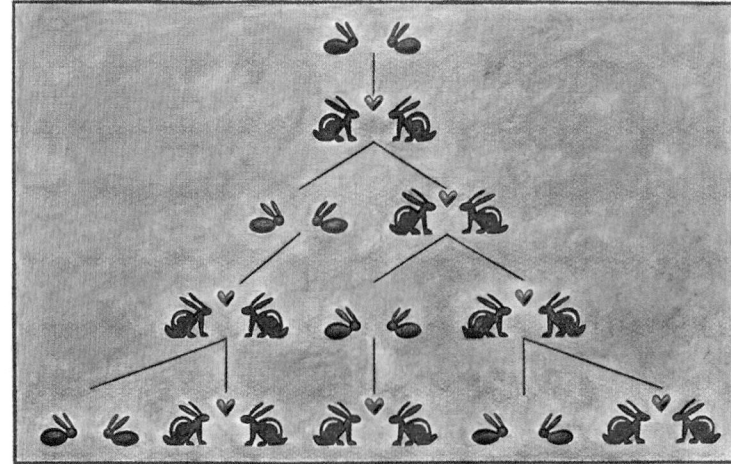

  a. Give the number of rabbit pairs for the sixth through the twelfth months.
  b. These monthly numbers of rabbit pairs form the *Fibonacci sequence*. In terms of the rabbit population, explain why the Fibonacci sequence satisfies the recursion formula $a_n = a_{n-1} + a_{n-2}$ for $n > 2$. This formula, along with the initial terms $a_1 = 1$ and $a_2 = 1$, gives the recursive definition of the Fibonacci sequence.

15. Recall that the golden ratio is the constant $g = \dfrac{1 + \sqrt{5}}{2} \approx 1.618034$.
  a. Compute ratios of consecutive terms of the Fibonacci sequence and show that the ratios get closer and closer to g.
  b. Show that the geometric sequence $1, g, g^2, g^3, \ldots$ satisfies the same recursion formula as the Fibonacci sequence.

Give the first six powers of each matrix.

16. $A = \begin{bmatrix} 0.6 & 0.25 \\ 0.4 & 0.75 \end{bmatrix}$

17. $B = \begin{bmatrix} 0.5 & 0.2 \\ 0.5 & 0.8 \end{bmatrix}$

MORE PRACTICE

Give the first eight terms of each sequence, and sketch a graph of the sequence.

18. $a_1 = 2$ and $a_n = 2a_{n-1} + 1$

19. $b_1 = -4$ and $b_n = -b_{n-1} - 2$

20. $c_1 = 3$ and $c_n = -2c_{n-1} + 4$

21. $d_1 = 6$ and $d_n = 0.6d_{n-1} + 0.4$

22. A deposit of $2000 is made in an account paying 5% interest, compounded annually. A withdrawal of $200 is made at the beginning of each subsequent year. Define a recursive sequence that gives the amount in the account after each withdrawal. In how many years will the account be empty?

Give an explicit formula of the form $a_n = h + kA^n$ for each recursively defined sequence. Use your formula to find the tenth term and to determine if the sequence converges.

23. $a_n = 2a_{n-1} - 7;\ a_1 = 4.5$

24. $a_n = -3a_{n-1};\ a_1 = 5$

25. $a_n = 0.5a_{n-1} + 4;\ a_1 = -3$

26. $a_n = -0.2a_{n-1} - 3;\ a_1 = 2$

27. $a_n = 5a_{n-1} + 12;\ a_1 = -3$

28. $a_n = -8a_{n-1} + 9;\ a_1 = 1$

29. Use a Graphing Utility Improvements in an experimental medicine lead to a mere 20% decrease in the medicine level in the bloodstream for each dose period. Assume the dosage is 20 mg and it is absorbed into the bloodstream immediately.
  a. Define a recursive sequence that gives the medicine level after n doses.
  b. Graph this sequence and use the graph to estimate the limit of the medicine level in the bloodstream.
  c. Give an explicit formula for the sequence. Use it to determine the exact limit of the medicine level in the bloodstream. Compare this with your estimate in **b.**

30. Moose on the Loose The population of moose in a region is currently 800, but it is declining 1% each year, due to natural causes. In addition, the region is losing 25 moose each year to poaching. How many moose will there be in the region in 10 years?

31. Golden Years You're saving your money and plan to invest some of it in a certificate of deposit earning 8% annual interest, compounded monthly. You'd like to invest enough so that you can withdraw $1600 at the end of each month for living expenses and never have the account run out of money. How large must the investment be so that the money will never run out?

MORE MATH REASONING

32. Calculate the first ten powers of the matrix $F = \begin{bmatrix} 1 & 1 \\ 1 & 0 \end{bmatrix}$ and describe how their entries are related to terms of the Fibonacci sequence.

33. In 1724, Bernoulli first derived this explicit formula for the nth term of the Fibonacci sequence. In the formula, g is the golden ratio equal to $\dfrac{1 + \sqrt{5}}{2}$.

$$a_n = \frac{1}{\sqrt{5}}(g^n - (-g)^{-n}) \text{ for } n = 1, 2, 3, \ldots$$

Verify that the formula gives the correct twelfth term. Then calculate the 50th term.

34. Limited Growth With unlimited resources, a population of 200 deer would grow by 60% per decade, giving the recursion formula $P_n = 1.6P_{n-1}$ for their population in n decades. However, limited resources restrict their population growth so that in reality it is modeled by the equation $P_n = 1.6P_{n-1} - 0.0024(P_{n-1})^2$.

a. Give the predicted deer population for the next several decades and graph this sequence. Describe the population growth and tell how the given resources limit the population.

b. Rewrite the equation, assuming a constant deer population of $P_n = p$ for all n. Solve your equation to find p, the constant deer population that can be supported by the given resources. How can this help to explain the population growth you noticed in **a**?

35. Consider the recursion formula $a_n = Aa_{n-1} + B$, where A and B are constants. Show that an explicit formula for the nth term is $a_n = \dfrac{B}{1 - A} + (a_0 - \dfrac{B}{1 - A})A^n$.

12-2
PART B Probability Matrices

• •

← CONNECT → *The idea of iteration and recursion can also be applied to matrices. Now you will investigate matrices with entries that represent probabilities. Analyzing these matrices will allow you to predict the long-term behavior patterns in situations undergoing transition.*

People are always changing their minds about one thing or another. They may switch product brands, change dry cleaners, or decide to support a different political candidate. The possible products, services, or candidates that can be chosen in a given situation are called **transition states.** The Russian mathematician A. A. Markov (1856–1922) showed that you can predict how many people will be in each transition state in the long run if you know the **transition probabilities** that people will switch from one state to another.

MATERIALS

Graphing calculator

A cable television network has done a study showing that, during a free preview, nonsubscribing households have a 3% probability of becoming subscribers, while current subscribers have an 85% probability of renewing their subscription. Out of 1,680,351 households, 10,116 households subscribe initially.

There are four possible transitions between the two states (subscribing and not subscribing).

We can enter the probabilities of these transitions in the **transition matrix** A, as shown.

Complete the following steps using this matrix to predict how many of these households will subscribe in the long run.

$$\begin{array}{c} \text{Before} \\ \text{After} \quad \begin{array}{cc} & \begin{array}{cc} \text{Yes} & \text{No} \end{array} \\ \begin{array}{c} \text{Yes} \\ \text{No} \end{array} & \begin{bmatrix} 0.85 & 0.03 \\ 0.15 & 0.97 \end{bmatrix} \end{array} \end{array}$$

Transition Matrix A

$$B = \begin{bmatrix} \text{Subscribers} \\ \text{Nonsubscribers} \end{bmatrix}$$

1. Enter the transition matrix A in your graphing calculator. Then enter the 2×1 matrix B with the numbers of current subscribers and nonsubscribers. Calculate the product matrix AB to predict the numbers of subscribers and nonsubscribers after the first free preview.
2. Repeatedly multiplying A by the subscriber-nonsubscriber column matrix produces the sequence of matrices AB, A^2B, A^3B, ..., giving the predicted numbers of subscribers and nonsubscribers after successive previews. Calculate A^2B, A^3B, and A^4B, and give the numbers of subscribers and nonsubscribers after the second, third, and fourth previews.
3. Notice that each column matrix in Step 2 is a power of A multiplied by B. Examine the successive powers of the transition matrix: A, A^2, A^3, ... Give several powers of A for exponents of 50 and more. Describe any patterns you notice.
4. Investigate A^nB for large exponents using some of the powers you found in Step 3. How many of the 1,680,351 households do you predict will subscribe in the long run?

In general, a transition matrix is a square matrix; the entries in each column are probabilities that add up to 1. In most cases, the powers of the transition matrix converge and its limit matrix can help you analyze long-term trends.

1. In a choice between Rocky Cola and Spike Cola, 80% of the people who prefer Rocky Cola will still prefer it over Spike Cola in a month. Only 60% of the people who prefer Spike Cola will still prefer it over Rocky Cola in a month.

Of 100 people who drink these colas, 45 prefer Rocky Cola and 55 prefer Spike Cola this month. How many of these people do you predict will prefer each brand of cola next month? in the long run?

Arrange the transition probabilities as shown. For example, the second entry in the top row is 0.4, which indicates that 40% of the people who prefer Spike one month will prefer Rocky the next month.

$$\text{After} \begin{array}{c} \text{Rocky} \\ \text{Spike} \end{array} \overset{\begin{array}{c}\text{Before} \\ \text{Rocky/Spike}\end{array}}{\begin{bmatrix} 0.8 & 0.4 \\ 0.2 & 0.6 \end{bmatrix}}$$

The transition matrix is $A = \begin{bmatrix} 0.8 & 0.4 \\ 0.2 & 0.6 \end{bmatrix}$. The matrix $B = \begin{bmatrix} 45 \\ 55 \end{bmatrix}$ represents the number of people that prefer each brand of cola this month. (Note that Rocky is listed above Spike, just as in the transition matrix.) The number of people that are expected to prefer each brand next month are given by AB.

$$AB = \begin{bmatrix} 0.8 & 0.4 \\ 0.2 & 0.6 \end{bmatrix}\begin{bmatrix} 45 \\ 55 \end{bmatrix} = \begin{bmatrix} 58 \\ 42 \end{bmatrix}$$

So 58 of the 100 people are expected to prefer Rocky Cola next month and 42 are expected to prefer Spike Cola.

To find the long-term trend, use a graphing calculator to find the limit of the powers of A.

The powers of A converge to the matrix

$$L = \begin{bmatrix} \frac{2}{3} & \frac{2}{3} \\ \frac{1}{3} & \frac{1}{3} \end{bmatrix}.$$

The top entries of L indicate that ultimately two-thirds of the people will prefer Rocky Cola, while the bottom entries indicate that ultimately one-third of the people will prefer Spike Cola. So out of the original 100, about 67 people will prefer Rocky Cola and about 33 will prefer Spike Cola.

Notice that you get the same result if you calculate LB, the limit of A^nB.

$$LB = \begin{bmatrix} \frac{2}{3} & \frac{2}{3} \\ \frac{1}{3} & \frac{1}{3} \end{bmatrix}\begin{bmatrix} 45 \\ 55 \end{bmatrix} = \begin{bmatrix} 66\frac{2}{3} \\ 33\frac{1}{3} \end{bmatrix}$$

CONSIDER

1. Explain why the matrix product *LB* would be the same no matter what the preferences of the original 100 people.

a. Find the limit of the powers A^n, where $A = \begin{bmatrix} 0.9 & 0.1 \\ 0.1 & 0.9 \end{bmatrix}$.

b. An optician has found that 85% of his customers who prefer glasses over contact lenses one month still prefer them the next month. Only 75% of his customers who prefer contact lenses over glasses one month still prefer them the next month. If half of the optician's customers prefer glasses and the other half prefer contact lenses this month, what percentage of customers will prefer each next month? in the long run?

Transition matrices apply in a wide variety of situations where probabilities determine change. Markov extended the idea of transitions governed by probabilities to a general class of processes, which are now known as Markov processes.

REFLECT

1. What is meant by transition states?
2. If the powers of a transition matrix converge, what do the entries of the limit matrix tell you?
3. Assume two candidates are running for office in an upcoming election. Explain how a transition matrix could help you analyze the prospects of each candidate at election time. What transition probabilities would you need to determine?

Exercises

CORE

1. Getting Started Let $A = \begin{bmatrix} 0.7 & 0.5 \\ 0.3 & 0.5 \end{bmatrix}$ and $B = \begin{bmatrix} 40 \\ 60 \end{bmatrix}$.

a. Multiply A by itself to find A^2, A^3, and A^4.
b. Multiply A and powers of A by B to find AB, A^2B, A^3B, and A^4B.

Write the word or phrase that correctly completes each statement.

2. If people are deciding between two candidates for an office, the likelihood that people supporting one candidate will support the other a week later is an example of a transition ____.

3. A ____ is a square matrix with entries in each column that are transition probabilities that add up to 1.

Decide whether each matrix is a transition matrix. Explain your reasoning.

4. $\begin{bmatrix} 0.6 & 0.2 \\ 0.4 & 0.8 \end{bmatrix}$

5. $\begin{bmatrix} 2 & 4 \\ 8 & 6 \end{bmatrix}$

6. $\begin{bmatrix} 0.2 & 0.3 & 0.5 \\ 0.8 & 0.7 & 0.5 \end{bmatrix}$

7. Calculate several powers of each transition matrix and give the limit matrix to which these powers converge.

a. $A = \begin{bmatrix} 0.3 & 0.6 \\ 0.7 & 0.4 \end{bmatrix}$ **b.** $B = \begin{bmatrix} 0.56 & 0.33 \\ 0.44 & 0.67 \end{bmatrix}$ **c.** $C = \begin{bmatrix} 0.8 & 0.25 \\ 0.2 & 0.75 \end{bmatrix}$

d. Make a conjecture about how various entries in a limit matrix for powers of a transition matrix are related.

8. Hold the Press! A newspaper has 2,000 subscribers in a town of 12,000 people. The editor-in-chief expects that, for the next subscription period, 92% of the current subscribers will resubscribe and 2% of the nonsubscribers will subscribe.

a. Write a transition matrix T with transition probabilities arranged as shown. (*Yes* means has subscribed and *no* means has not subscribed.) Then write a column matrix B with the current numbers of subscribers and nonsubscribers arranged as shown.

$$T = \begin{bmatrix} P(\text{yes} \to \text{yes}) & P(\text{no} \to \text{yes}) \\ P(\text{yes} \to \text{no}) & P(\text{no} \to \text{no}) \end{bmatrix} \begin{matrix} \text{After yes} \\ \text{After no} \end{matrix} \qquad B = \begin{bmatrix} \text{Subscribers} \\ \text{Nonsubscribers} \end{bmatrix}$$

Current yes   Current no

b. Calculate TB, T^2B, T^3B, and T^4B, and use these values to predict the numbers of subscribers and nonsubscribers in the next four subscription periods.

c. Find the limit L of powers of T. Then calculate LB and predict the numbers of subscribers and nonsubscribers the editor-in-chief can expect in the long run.

9. Months before an election, a survey indicates that 88% of the people favoring a ballot measure still favor it one week later, while the other 12% are against it. Of the people who are against the ballot measure, 95% are still against it one week later, while 5% are for it. This *transition diagram* shows the transition probabilities.

a. Write a transition matrix for this situation.

b. Find the limit of the powers of the transition matrix. If 10,000 people favor the measure right now and 10,000 people are against it, predict the support for the measure in one week, two weeks, three weeks, and in the long run.

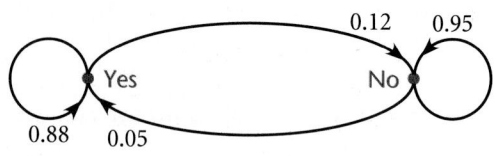

10. Burger Wars Brawny Burger has opened an outlet near Don's Grill, which gets 600 customers per week. Figures from other towns where these restaurants compete indicate that 18% of Don's customers will switch to Brawny in a week. On the other hand, only 8% of Brawny's customers will switch to Don's in a week.

a. Write the transition matrix for this situation and a column matrix representing the initial number of customers each restaurant gets per week.

b. How fast will Brawny Burger's business pick up in the first few weeks after opening? How many of the 600 customers that eat in the two establishments each week can Brawny expect to get in the long run?

11. Decide which exponential function is shown in the graph. [9-1]

    (a) $y = 2^x$ (b) $y = 3(2^x)$ (c) $y = 0.2(2^x)$

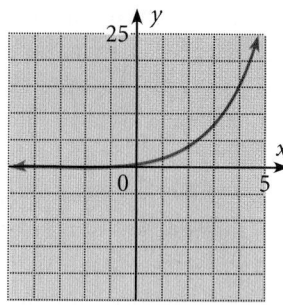

12. Solve and graph $2x + 3 < 7$. [2-3]

13. Solve $2x^3 - 9x^2 + 2x + 1 = 0$. [8-2]

14. How many radians does the second hand of a watch rotate through in 3 minutes? [10-1]

MORE PRACTICE

Decide whether each matrix is a transition matrix. Explain your reasoning.

15. $\begin{bmatrix} 0.1 & 0.4 \\ 0.9 & 0.4 \end{bmatrix}$ **16.** $\begin{bmatrix} 0.8 \\ 0.2 \end{bmatrix}$

17. $\begin{bmatrix} 0.7 & 0.44 \\ 0.3 & 0.56 \end{bmatrix}$ **18.** $\begin{bmatrix} -0.4 & 0.3 \\ -0.6 & 0.7 \end{bmatrix}$

Give the missing transition probabilities in each transition matrix.

19. $\begin{bmatrix} 0.43 & ? \\ ? & 0.04 \end{bmatrix}$ **20.** $\begin{bmatrix} 0.19 & 0.91 \\ ? & ? \end{bmatrix}$

Calculate several powers of each transition matrix and give the limit matrix to which these powers converge.

21. $A = \begin{bmatrix} 0.2 & 0.2 \\ 0.8 & 0.8 \end{bmatrix}$ **22.** $B = \begin{bmatrix} 0.06 & 0.83 \\ 0.94 & 0.17 \end{bmatrix}$

23. $C = \begin{bmatrix} 0.51 & 0.34 \\ 0.49 & 0.66 \end{bmatrix}$ **24.** $D = \begin{bmatrix} 0.7 & 0.54 \\ 0.3 & 0.46 \end{bmatrix}$

25. At a large party, 90% of the people having a good time will still be having a good time in an hour, while the rest will be bored. Of the bored people, 75% will still be bored in an hour, but the rest will start having a good time.
    a. If all 100 people at the party are happy when they arrive, how many bored people will there be after 1 hour? 2 hours? 3 hours?
    b. If the party went on forever, what is the limit of the number of bored people?
    c. Will the number of people who are bored be close to this limit by the end of the 6-hour party?

26. **Bart City** Between 6 a.m. and 9 a.m. on a typical weekday in Bart City, 9% of the people in the suburbs commute downtown each hour, and the rest stay in the suburbs. Meanwhile, 3% of the people downtown go to the suburbs, while the rest stay downtown. At 6 a.m., there are 20,000 people downtown and 60,000 in the suburbs. How many people will be downtown and how many will be in the suburbs at 7 a.m.? 8 a.m.? 9 a.m.?

27. Commuter Trend Thirty percent of the commuters in the Rome metropolitan area use a public transportation system; the remaining 70% commute via automobile. To attract more riders, the city recently added more security to its public transportation system. It is expected that one month from now 6% of those who are now commuting to work via automobile will switch to public transportation. At the same time, it is expected that 2% of those now using public transportation will switch to automobiles. If this trend continues, what percentage of commuters can be expected to use public transportation in the long run?

MORE MATH REASONING

28. An electronic security camera scans to three different positions: left, center, and right. To avoid predictability, the camera does not repeat the same scanning pattern, but instead scans according to the following probabilities.

Current position	Next position probability
Left	Left 0.1, center 0.9
Center	Left 0.45, center 0.1, right 0.45
Right	Center 0.9, right 0.1

Note: Movement from a position to itself means the camera stays in that position for one scanning cycle.

When the camera is turned on, it is in the center position.

a. Write the 3×3 transition matrix and initial column matrix.

b. Find the probabilities of the camera being in each of the three positions after the first cycle, second cycle, and third cycle.

c. In the long run, what are the probabilities that a scanning cycle will end in each of the three positions?

d. Repeat **c,** assuming the camera is initially in the left position. Describe how these results compare to those from **c.**

29. Victory Party? Weekly polls indicate a trend for the upcoming election. If a voter was in favor of Proposition Z one week, the probabilities of the same voter being in favor the next week is 0.8, of being against the proposition 0.15, and of being undecided 0.05. If the voter was against the proposition one week, the probabilities of being in favor the next week is 0.2, of being against 0.75, and of being undecided 0.05. Finally, if undecided one week, the probabilities of being in favor the next week is 0.3, of being against 0.4, and of being undecided 0.3.

The election is in twelve weeks, and the most recent poll indicates that 20% favor the proposition, 40% oppose it, and 40% are undecided.

a. If the trend continues, what percent of the voters will be in favor of Proposition Z at election time? opposed? undecided? Will the initiative pass?

b. Suppose that, at the voting booth, all undecided voters vote against the initiative? Will the initiative pass? Explain.

Making Connections

←C O N N E C T→ *You have explored recursion in sequences and in transition matrices. The idea of recursion is a powerful tool for analyzing mathematical models and writing efficient computer programs.*

The British mathematician John Conway invented a game called Life that allows geometric shapes to *evolve* generation by generation. The shapes evolve by iterating a few simple rules, yet this recursive process can create a surprising variety of behaviors in the evolving shapes.

EXPLORE: THAT'S LIFE

MATERIALS

Graph paper

You begin Conway's game of Life by choosing and shading a pattern of grid squares on graph paper. This pattern is the first generation. The object of the game is to find graphs for the following generations and observe how they evolve.

To find the squares in a new generation, first count the number of *neighbors* of each square near the pattern. The "neighbors" of a square are the shaded squares adjacent to that square. Each square can have up to eight neighbors. After counting neighbors, follow these rules to graph the next generation.

(A) Each shaded square with 2 or 3 neighbors remains *alive* and is shaded in the next generation; otherwise, the square is empty in the next generation.

(B) Each empty square with exactly 3 neighbors *comes to life* and is shaded in the next generation; otherwise, the square remains empty in the next generation.

1. Copy each pattern and graph the next four generations on empty sections of graph paper. Describe how each pattern evolves through the generations.

a. 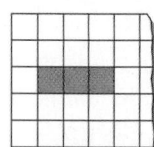 **b.** 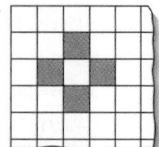 **c.**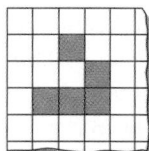

2. Graph a new pattern with three shaded squares in a horizontal row and a fourth shaded square just above the right-hand shaded square. Graph the original pattern and as many generations as needed to discover a pattern to the evolution. Describe how the pattern will keep evolving into future generations.

3. Design one or more patterns and explore their evolution. Describe the different types of behavior patterns possible in the evolution in the game of Life.

1. Discuss the concept of recursion and the types of mathematical models that can be generated through recursion.

2. How does a recursive definition of a sequence differ from an explicit definition?

3. Describe how recursion is involved in finding long-term behavior patterns in situations involving transition states and transition probabilities.

Self-Assessment

Give the first eight terms of each sequence, and sketch a graph of the sequence.

1. $a_1 = 3$ and $a_n = 0.2a_{n-1} + 10$

2. $b_1 = 1$ and $b_n = 2b_{n-1} + 5$

3. $c_1 = 0$ and $c_n = 2.4c_{n-1} + 1$

4. $d_1 = 2$ and $d_n = 0.5d_{n-1} - 3$

Give an explicit formula of the form $a_n = h + kA^n$ for each recursively defined sequence. Use your formula to find the tenth term and determine if the sequence converges.

5. $a_n = 2a_{n-1} - 7;\ a_1 = 3$

6. $a_n = 3a_{n-1};\ a_1 = 2$

7. I've Got a Headache Aspirin *washes out* of the bloodstream quite rapidly. The amount of effective aspirin left in the bloodstream is reduced by 50% approximately every half hour.

a. Suppose you take 650 mg of aspirin every four hours, as recommended. (Assume the aspirin is absorbed into the bloodstream immediately.) How long after the first dose will the aspirin level in your bloodstream be reduced to 10 mg? By what factor is the aspirin level reduced every four hours?

b. Define a sequence giving the aspirin level in your bloodstream after each dose. Give the limit of the term values, and tell what it represents in this situation.

8. A population of 40 sheep would grow by about 8% per year with unlimited resources. In reality, the recursive equation $P_n = 1.08P_{n-1} - 0.001P_{n-1}^2$ governs their population growth. Give enough terms of the sequence to determine the population growth and the population limit, given the available resources.

9. Which of these is a recursion formula for an arithmetic sequence?

I. $a_n = a_{n-1} - 3$ II. $b_n = 2b_{n-1} - 10$ III. $c_n = 2 + c_{n-1}$

(a) only I   (b) only II   (c) only III   (d) I and III   (e) I, II, and III

10. Factorial Recursion Give a recursion formula for the sequence of factorials with nth term $n! = n(n-1)(n-2) \cdot \cdots \cdot 3 \cdot 2 \cdot 1$.

11. In a town of 3000 people, there is only a 5% chance that a person who ate at Xin Wa's restaurant during one month won't return there next month. There is a 10% chance that a person who hasn't eaten at Xin Wa's in one month will dine there the next month.

    a. If 500 people dine at Xin Wa's during this month, how many do you predict will dine there sometime next month? the month after that?

    b. In the long run, how many of the 3000 people will eat at Xin Wa's at some point in a given month?

12. Clean as a Whistle A supermarket has found that 3% of their customers buying name-brand laundry detergent will switch to generic brand detergent in a month. Meanwhile, 11% of their customers buying generic brand detergent will switch to a name brand in a month. At present, twice as many customers buy name-brand detergent as those buying generic detergent. What percentage of these customers will buy generic detergent in the long run?

13. Examine the graph. Determine whether the graph has an Euler circuit, a Hamiltonian path, or both. Identify the circuit or path. [12-1]

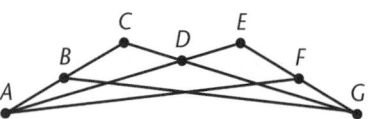

14. The probability that Karen gets a hit in each at-bat in a softball game is 0.455. What is the probability that she has a slump of eight at-bats without a hit? [11-1]

15. Sketch the graph of the periodic function $y = 6 + 2 \sin \pi x$. Identify the amplitude, period, and average value of the function. [10-3]

Decide which choice is correct.

(A) The quantity in Column A is greater.
(B) The quantity in Column B is greater.
(C) The two quantities are equal.
(D) The relationship cannot be determined.

Column A	Column B
16. a_{10}, if $a_1 = 1$ and $a_n = 2a_{n-1}$	b_{10}, if $b_1 = 1$ and $b_n = 3b_{n-1} - 2$
17. $1 + \frac{2}{3} + \frac{4}{9} + \frac{8}{27} + \cdots$	$2 + \frac{2}{3} + \frac{2}{9} + \frac{2}{27} + \cdots$

Calculate several powers of each transition matrix and give the limit matrix to which these powers converge.

18. $A = \begin{bmatrix} 0.4 & 0.6 \\ 0.6 & 0.4 \end{bmatrix}$

19. $B = \begin{bmatrix} 0.65 & 0.3 \\ 0.35 & 0.7 \end{bmatrix}$

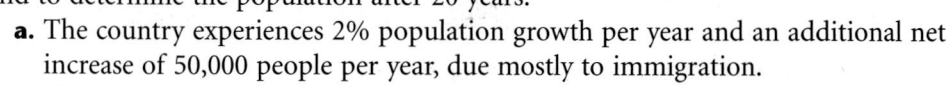

20. Population Modeling A country currently has a population of 10 million. Use the given rate of population growth in each case to model the population of the country and to determine the population after 20 years.

    a. The country experiences 2% population growth per year and an additional net increase of 50,000 people per year, due mostly to immigration.

    b. The country experiences 4% population growth per year and an additional net increase of 100,000 people per year.

    c. The country experiences 10% population growth per year and a decrease of 80,000 people per year, due mostly to emigration.

    d. The country experiences a 5% decline in population per year and emigration of 100,000 people per year.

Chapter 12 Review

In this chapter, you have studied two important modeling methods. The theory of graphs allows you to model connections between objects in a network. You can use graphs to find efficient and often optimal strategies for working with such networks. You've also seen how recursion, both in sequences and in transition matrices, allows you to make valuable predictions about growth and long-term behavior.

KEY TERMS

circuit [12-1]

connected graph [12-1]

degree of a vertex [12-1]

Euler circuit [12-1]

Euler path [12-1]

Euler's Formula [12-1]

Euler's Traversability Theorem [12-1]

graph [12-1]

Hamiltonian circuit [12-1]

Hamiltonian path [12-1]

minimal spanning tree [12-1]

path [12-1]

polyhedron [12-1]

recursion formula [12-2]

spanning tree [12-1]

transition matrix [12-2]

transition probability [12-2]

transition state [12-2]

tree [12-1]

Determine whether each statement is true or false. If the statement is false, change the underlined word or phrase to make it true.

1. A path in a graph that passes through each vertex exactly once and ends at the same vertex where it started is a <u>Hamiltonian circuit.</u>

2. An <u>Euler path</u> must cross each edge of a graph exactly once.

3. A spanning tree is a tree that contains each <u>edge</u> of a graph.

4. A formula for the nth term of a sequence in terms of previous term values is a(n) <u>explicit formula</u> for the sequence.

5. A <u>transition state</u> is a matrix containing transition probabilities.

CONCEPTS AND APPLICATIONS

6. What are the degrees of the vertices in this graph? [12-1]

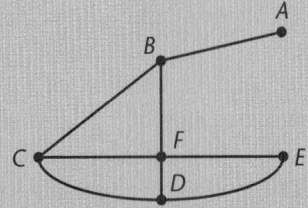

7. Determine whether the graph has an Euler circuit. If it does, identify the circuit. If not, explain why. [12-1]

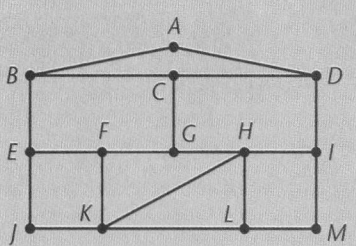

8. Explain how an Euler circuit is similar and different from a Hamiltonian circuit. [12-1]

9. A simple polyhedron has 11 faces and 27 edges. How many vertices does it have? [12-1]

10. Is there a way to walk through the rooms shown and pass through every doorway exactly once? Explain. [12-1]

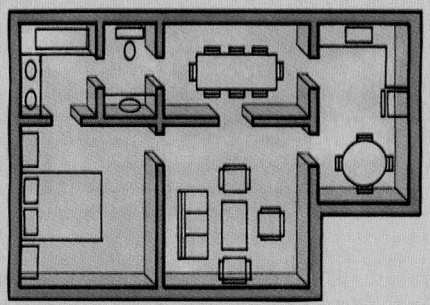

11. Consider the sequence with initial term $a_1 = 2$ and recursion formula $a_n = 0.8a_{n-1} + 2$. [12-1]
   a. Give the first six terms of the sequence.
   b. Graph the sequence.
   c. Give an explicit formula for the nth term of the sequence.

Decide which choice is correct.

(A) The quantity in Column A is greater.
(B) The quantity in Column B is greater.
(C) The two quantities are equal.
(D) The relationship cannot be determined.

Column A	Column B
12. a_6, if $a_1 = 2$ and $a_n = 1.5a_{n-1}$	b_6, if $b_1 = 1$ and $b_n = 2b_{n-1} - 1$
13. c_8, if $c_n = 5c_{n-1}$	d_8, if $d_n = 5d_{n-1} - 8$

Decide whether each matrix is a transition matrix. Explain your reasoning.

14. $\begin{bmatrix} 0.28 & 0.75 \\ 0.82 & 0.25 \end{bmatrix}$
   15. $\begin{bmatrix} 0.7 \\ 0.3 \end{bmatrix}$

16. How much money will you have after 20 years if you deposit $100 at 7%, compounded annually, and add $100 more at the beginning of each new year? [12-2]

17. A phone company wants to lay cable to connect five cities. The graph shows the cost of building each cable between cities. Find a minimal spanning tree that can help the company plan connections between the cities that will be as cost effective as possible. [12-1]

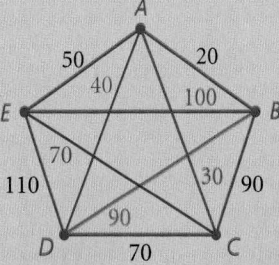

18. Find enough powers of the transition matrix $\begin{bmatrix} 0.5 & 0.4 \\ 0.5 & 0.6 \end{bmatrix}$ to determine the limit matrix to which these powers converge. [12-2]

19. Of 5000 voters in a town, 2000 initially support mayoral candidate Jones, while the rest support candidate Farley. The election is many months away. Each week, 15% of Jones' supporters switch their support to Farley, and 10% of Farley's supporters switch their support to Jones. How many supporters do you predict each candidate will have in a week? in two weeks? in the long run? [12-2]

CONCEPTS AND CONNECTIONS

20. City Planning As a city planner, you want to connect a monorail system to a shopping mall, the city airport, the civic center, a group of hotels, and the downtown business district. Devise a plan for constructing this network as cheaply as possible. Assign reasonable costs to each path of the network. Explain the methods you employed and the results obtained.

SELF-EVALUATION

Write a summary about what you have learned about discrete mathematical modeling. Compare and contrast discrete modeling with continuous modeling. Discuss the types of situations to which discrete modeling is applicable. Write a description of the areas where you had difficulty, and make a plan to review those areas. Be as specific as possible.

Chapter 12 Assessment

TEST

1. Abdul, Brenda, Carlos, Dede, and Ethan are neighbors in an apartment complex. Brenda knows Dede and Ethan. Carlos knows Abdul and Dede. Ethan knows Abdul and Brenda. Draw a graph that represents who knows whom.

2. Four cities and the distances between them are listed below. A salesperson must start in Atlanta and visit every city before returning to Atlanta. What Hamiltonian circuit will minimize the total round-trip distance?

   Atlanta to Washington, D.C.: 653 mi   Atlanta to Chicago: 791 mi

   Atlanta to Knoxville: 193 mi   Chicago to Washington, D.C.: 693 mi

   Chicago to Knoxville: 540 mi   Washington, D.C., to Knoxville: 488 mi

3. A simple polyhedron has 14 faces and 36 edges. How many vertices does it have?

4. Determine whether the graph has an Euler circuit or a Hamiltonian circuit. Show examples of such circuits or explain why none exist.

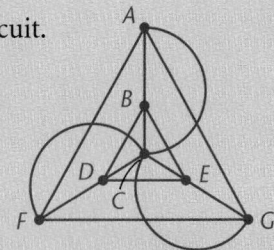

5. A sequence has initial term $a_1 = 6$ and recursion relation $a_n = 0.1a_{n-1} + 0.6$.

   a. Give the first 6 terms of the sequence.

   b. Graph the sequence.

   c. Give an explicit formula for the nth term of the sequence.

6. Find an efficient path that a street cleaner can take along the roads represented in this graph, so that she starts at O and never sweeps the same road twice.

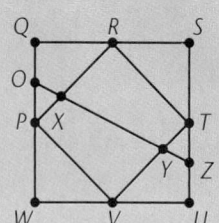

7. A magazine currently has 10,000 subscribers in a city of 100,000. The editors have found that 9% of their subscribers cancel their subscriptions each month, while 1% of the city residents that don't subscribe one month will open a subscription the next month. How many subscribers can the magazine expect next month? the month after that? in the long run?

8. Five cities are represented on this graph, along with the costs of connecting them with fiber-optic cable. Give a spanning tree that connects these cities as cheaply as possible.

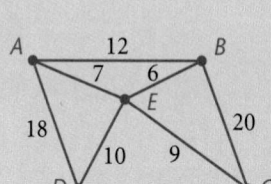

9. A deposit of $30,000 is made in a savings account paying 7% simple annual interest. If $1000 is withdrawn at the end of each year at the same time as the new interest is added, how long will it be before the account has grown in value to $35,000?

Decide which choice is correct.

(A) The quantity in Column A is greater.
(B) The quantity in Column B is greater.
(C) The two quantities are equal.
(D) The relationship cannot be determined.

Column A	Column B
10. c_8, if $c_1 = 4$	d_8, if $d_2 = 4$
11. a_5, if $a_1 = 1$ and $a_n = 2a_{n-1} + 2$	b_5, if $b_1 = 16$ and $b_n = 2.5b_{n-1}$

Decide whether each matrix is a transition matrix. Explain your reasoning.

12. $\begin{bmatrix} 0.01 & 0.98 \\ 0.99 & 0.02 \end{bmatrix}$

13. $\begin{bmatrix} 1.1 & 0.88 \\ 0.1 & 0.12 \end{bmatrix}$

Calculate several powers of each transition matrix and give the limit matrix to which these powers converge.

14. $A = \begin{bmatrix} 0.22 & 0.84 \\ 0.78 & 0.16 \end{bmatrix}$

15. $B = \begin{bmatrix} 0.69 & 0.19 \\ 0.31 & 0.81 \end{bmatrix}$

PERFORMANCE TASK

Choose five or more places you visit regularly. Estimate the travel distances between your home and each location. Determine the shortest, fastest, or cheapest route from your home to visit each of the five places and return home. Use a graph to illustrate and explain your methods.

◥ ENRICHMENT

CALCULATING INVERSE MATRICES

The method shown on page 185, Exercise 37, can be used to find the inverse of a 2×2 matrix. To find inverses of larger square matrices by hand, we use *row-equivalent operations* on a type of *augmented matrix*.

The row-equivalent operations for matrices are:

- interchanging any two rows of the matrix

- multiplying any row by a nonzero constant

- multiplying a row by a nonzero constant and adding the result to another row

An augmented matrix used to find the inverse of an $n \times n$ matrix consists of the original matrix and its identity matrix. For $A = \begin{bmatrix} -1 & 1 & 2 \\ 4 & 2 & -2 \\ -4 & -3 & 3 \end{bmatrix}$, this is:

$$\begin{array}{cc} A & I \\ \left[\begin{array}{ccc|ccc} -1 & 1 & 2 & 1 & 0 & 0 \\ 4 & 2 & -2 & 0 & 1 & 0 \\ -4 & -3 & 3 & 0 & 0 & 1 \end{array}\right] \end{array}$$

To find A^{-1}, use row operations to transform A (the left half of the augmented matrix) into I. The right half of the resulting matrix will be A^{-1}.

EXAMPLE

Find the inverse matrix for $A = \begin{bmatrix} -1 & 1 & 2 \\ 4 & 2 & -2 \\ -4 & -3 & 3 \end{bmatrix}$.

Start by forming the augmented matrix. As shown above, this is:

$$\left[\begin{array}{ccc|ccc} -1 & 1 & 2 & 1 & 0 & 0 \\ 4 & 2 & -2 & 0 & 1 & 0 \\ -4 & -3 & 3 & 0 & 0 & 1 \end{array}\right] \begin{array}{l} \text{Row (1)} \\ \text{Row (2)} \\ \text{Row (3)} \end{array}$$

Use row operations to transform the left half of the augmented matrix into I. First, obtain zeros in the first column except for its top entry.

$$\left[\begin{array}{ccc|ccc} -1 & 1 & 2 & 1 & 0 & 0 \\ 4 & 2 & -2 & 0 & 1 & 0 \\ -4 & -3 & 3 & 0 & 0 & 1 \end{array}\right] \begin{array}{c} 4❶ + ❷ = \\ -4❶ + ❸ \end{array} \left[\begin{array}{ccc|ccc} -1 & 1 & 2 & 1 & 0 & 0 \\ 0 & 6 & 6 & 4 & 1 & 0 \\ 0 & -7 & -5 & -4 & 0 & 1 \end{array}\right]$$

Now, obtain zeros in the top and bottom entries of the middle column.

$$
\begin{bmatrix}
-1 & 1 & 2 & | & 1 & 0 & 0 \\
0 & 6 & 6 & | & 4 & 1 & 0 \\
0 & -7 & -5 & | & -4 & 0 & 1
\end{bmatrix}
\begin{array}{c} -6\textbf{①} + \textbf{②} \\ \\ 7\textbf{②} + 6\textbf{③} \end{array}
=
\begin{bmatrix}
6 & 0 & -6 & | & -2 & 1 & 0 \\
0 & 6 & 6 & | & 4 & 1 & 0 \\
0 & 0 & 12 & | & 4 & 7 & 6
\end{bmatrix}
$$

Next, obtain zeros in the top two entries of the third column.

$$
\begin{bmatrix}
6 & 0 & -6 & | & -2 & 1 & 0 \\
0 & 6 & 6 & | & 4 & 1 & 0 \\
0 & 0 & 12 & | & 4 & 7 & 6
\end{bmatrix}
\begin{array}{c} 2\textbf{①} + \textbf{③} \\ -2\textbf{②} + \textbf{③} \\ \end{array}
=
\begin{bmatrix}
12 & 0 & 0 & | & 0 & 9 & 6 \\
0 & -12 & 0 & | & -4 & 5 & 6 \\
0 & 0 & 12 & | & 4 & 7 & 6
\end{bmatrix}
$$

Finally, multiply to obtain 1's in the left half of the matrix.

$$
\begin{bmatrix}
12 & 0 & 0 & | & 0 & 9 & 6 \\
0 & -12 & 0 & | & -4 & 5 & 6 \\
0 & 0 & 12 & | & 4 & 7 & 6
\end{bmatrix}
\begin{array}{c} \frac{1}{12}\textbf{①} \\ -\frac{1}{12}\textbf{②} \\ \frac{1}{12}\textbf{③} \end{array}
=
\begin{bmatrix}
1 & 0 & 0 & | & 0 & \frac{3}{4} & \frac{1}{2} \\
0 & 1 & 0 & | & \frac{1}{3} & -\frac{5}{12} & -\frac{1}{2} \\
0 & 0 & 1 & | & \frac{1}{3} & \frac{7}{12} & \frac{1}{2}
\end{bmatrix}
$$

The inverse matrix for $A = \begin{bmatrix} -1 & 1 & 2 \\ 4 & 2 & -2 \\ -4 & -3 & 3 \end{bmatrix}$ is $A^{-1} = \begin{bmatrix} 0 & \frac{3}{4} & \frac{1}{2} \\ \frac{1}{3} & -\frac{5}{12} & -\frac{1}{2} \\ \frac{1}{3} & \frac{7}{12} & \frac{1}{2} \end{bmatrix}$.

You can confirm this by checking that $A \times A^{-1} = A^{-1} \times A = I$.

As seen in 3-1C, matrix inverses can be used to solve matrix equations. For coefficient matrix A, constant matrix B, and variable matrix X, $X = A^{-1}B$.

TRY IT

Use augmented matrices to find the inverse of each matrix.

1. $\begin{bmatrix} 2 & 1 & -1 \\ 3 & 2 & 1 \\ -2 & 1 & -1 \end{bmatrix}$

2. $\begin{bmatrix} -2 & 1 & -2 \\ 2 & 1 & -1 \\ 2 & 4 & 2 \end{bmatrix}$

3. Use augmented matrices to find the inverse of the coefficient matrix. Then use the inverse matrix to solve:

$$2x + y - z = -5$$
$$x + 2y + z = -1$$
$$-x + y + 3z = 5$$

SOLVING SYSTEMS USING AUGMENTED MATRICES

On pages 850–851, you saw how to use row operations on one type of augmented matrix to find a matrix inverse. It is also possible to use row operations on another type of augmented matrix to solve a system of linear equations. The augmented matrix used consists of the matrix of coefficients and the matrix of the constants on the right-hand sides of the equations.

EXAMPLE

Solve: $3x - 2y = 5$
$-4x + 2y = -8$

Write the augmented matrix by combining the matrix of coefficients with the matrix of the constants: $\begin{bmatrix} 3 & -2 & | & 5 \\ -4 & 2 & | & -8 \end{bmatrix} \begin{matrix} \text{Row (1)} \\ \text{Row (2)} \end{matrix}$

Then, perform row operations until the coefficient matrix is transformed into the 2×2 identity matrix $\begin{bmatrix} 1 & 0 \\ 0 & 1 \end{bmatrix}$.

$$\begin{bmatrix} 3 & -2 & | & 5 \\ -4 & 2 & | & -8 \end{bmatrix} 4❶ + 3❷ = \begin{bmatrix} 3 & -2 & | & 5 \\ 0 & -2 & | & -4 \end{bmatrix}$$

$$\begin{bmatrix} 3 & -2 & | & 5 \\ 0 & -2 & | & -4 \end{bmatrix} ❶ + -❷ = \begin{bmatrix} 3 & 0 & | & 9 \\ 0 & -2 & | & -4 \end{bmatrix}$$

$$\begin{bmatrix} 3 & 0 & | & 9 \\ 0 & -2 & | & -4 \end{bmatrix} \begin{matrix} \frac{1}{3}❶ \\ \frac{1}{2}❷ \end{matrix} = \begin{bmatrix} 1 & 0 & | & 3 \\ 0 & 1 & | & 2 \end{bmatrix}$$

The solution to this system, as shown in the right-hand column of the final matrix, is $x = 3, y = 2$.

TRY IT

Solve each system of equations by using augmented matrices.

1. $5x + 2y = -6$
$-3x - 4y = 12$

2. $-x + 2y = 4$
$3x + y = -5$

3. $x + y = 1$
$2x + 3y = -1$

4. $x - 4y = 1$
$-3x + 2y = -8$

Synthetic division is an algorithm that simplifies the process of dividing a polynomial by a linear polynomial of the form $x - c$. Synthetic division shortens the division process by using only the coefficients of the dividend and divisor.

EXAMPLE

Divide $3x^4 - 2x^2 + 15x - 8$ by $x + 2$.

Notice that $x - c = x + 2$, so $c = -2$.

$$\begin{array}{r|rrrrr} -2 & 3 & 0 & -2 & 15 & -8 \\ \hline & 3 & & & & \end{array}$$
Write c and the coefficients of the polynomial.

Bring down the first coefficient.

$$\begin{array}{r|rrrrr} -2 & 3 & 0 & -2 & 15 & -8 \\ & & -6 & & & \\ \hline & 3 & -6 & & & \end{array}$$
Multiply -2 by 3 and write the result below 0.

Add 0 and -6.

$$\begin{array}{r|rrrrr} -2 & 3 & 0 & -2 & 15 & -8 \\ & & -6 & 12 & & \\ \hline & 3 & -6 & 10 & & \end{array}$$
Multiply -2 by -6 and write the result below -2.

Add -2 and 12.

$$\begin{array}{r|rrrrr} -2 & 3 & 0 & -2 & 15 & -8 \\ & & -6 & 12 & -20 & \\ \hline & 3 & -6 & 10 & -5 & \end{array}$$
Multiply -2 by 10 and write the result below 15.

Add 15 and -20.

$$\begin{array}{r|rrrrr} -2 & 3 & 0 & -2 & 15 & -8 \\ & & -6 & 12 & -20 & 10 \\ \hline & 3 & -6 & 10 & -5 & | \;\; 2 \end{array}$$
Multiply -2 by -5 and write the result below -8.

Add -8 and 10.

The last number in the bottom row represents the remainder; the other numbers are the coefficients of the quotient. Therefore, $3x^4 - 2x^2 + 15x - 8$ divided by $x + 2$ is $3x^3 - 6x^2 + 10x - 5$ with remainder 2.

TRY IT

Use synthetic division to find each quotient and remainder.

1. $\dfrac{x^4 - 3x^2 + 4x - 5}{x - 5}$

2. $\dfrac{x^4 + 1}{x + 1}$

3. $\dfrac{x^3 - x + 2}{x - 1}$

4. $\dfrac{6x^4 + 5x^2 + 31}{x + 2}$

COMPLEX RATIONAL EXPRESSIONS

A *complex rational expression* has a rational expression in its numerator and/or denominator. These are examples of complex rational expressions.

$$\frac{\dfrac{x^2+2}{x-1}}{\dfrac{x^3+5x-1}{3x^4+1}} \qquad \frac{\dfrac{a}{x^2}+\dfrac{b}{y}}{1+\dfrac{2}{x}} \qquad \frac{\dfrac{10}{x}+3x}{\dfrac{x^2+1}{x+1}-1}$$

EXAMPLE

Simplify $\dfrac{\dfrac{a}{x^2}+\dfrac{b}{y}}{1+\dfrac{2}{x}}$.

Method 1   The LCD of the denominators x^2, y, and x is x^2y. Multiply the numerator and denominator by x^2y.

$$\frac{\dfrac{a}{x^2}+\dfrac{b}{y}}{1+\dfrac{2}{x}} \times \frac{x^2y}{x^2y} = \frac{\left(\dfrac{a}{x^2}+\dfrac{b}{y}\right)(x^2y)}{\left(1+\dfrac{2}{x}\right)(x^2y)}$$

$$= \frac{ay+bx^2}{x^2y+2xy} \ \text{ or } \ \frac{ay+bx^2}{xy(x+2)}$$

Method 2   Simplify the numerator.

$$\frac{a}{x^2}+\frac{b}{y}=\frac{ay}{x^2y}+\frac{bx^2}{x^2y}$$

$$= \frac{ay+bx^2}{x^2y}$$

Simplify the denominator.

$$1+\frac{2}{x}=\frac{x}{x}+\frac{2}{x}=\frac{x+2}{x}$$

Proceed with the division problem.

$$\frac{\dfrac{ay+bx^2}{x^2y}}{\dfrac{x+2}{x}}=\frac{ay+bx^2}{x^2y}\cdot\frac{x}{x+2}$$

$$= \frac{ay+bx^2}{xy(x+2)}$$

TRY IT

Simplify each complex rational expression.

1. $\dfrac{\dfrac{x^2+3x}{x-1}}{\dfrac{x^2+10}{x^2-1}+1}$

2. $\dfrac{\dfrac{a}{x^2}+\dfrac{2}{xy}}{\dfrac{x+3}{y}}$

3. $\dfrac{x+\dfrac{y}{x+1}}{1+\dfrac{1}{x^2+1}}$

4. $\dfrac{\dfrac{m}{x}-\dfrac{n}{y}}{1+\dfrac{1}{x^2}}$

TRIGONOMETRIC INVERSE FUNCTIONS

The equation $y = \text{Sin}^{-1} x$ (or $y = \text{Arcsin } x$) represents the inverse function for $y = \sin x$. (The capital letter is used to specify the use of the inverse *function*, not a relation.) In $y = \text{Sin}^{-1} x$, y is an *angle measure* and x is a value of the sine function. Given a value for x, the inverse finds an angle measure whose sine is equal to that value.

Since the trigonometric functions are periodic, there may be an infinite number of angle measures that have a certain sine value. For instance, there are an infinite number of angles whose sine is 0.

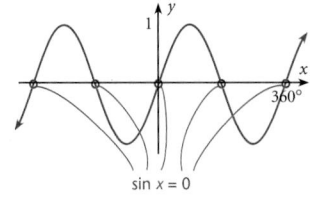

sin x = 0

So that $y = \text{Sin}^{-1} x$ is a function, its range is restricted to $-90° \leq y \leq 90°$. In this range, each sine value corresponds to exactly one angle measure. For instance, $\text{Sin}^{-1} 0 = 0°$.

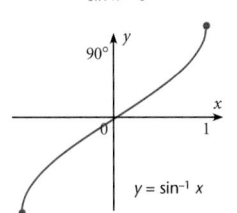

y = sin⁻¹ x

The restricted ranges for Sin^{-1}, Cos^{-1}, and Tan^{-1}, in degrees, are shown.

Function	$y = \text{Sin}^{-1} x$	$y = \text{Cos}^{-1} x$	$y = \text{Tan}^{-1} x$
Range	$-90° \leq y \leq 90°$	$0° \leq y \leq 180°$	$-90° < y < 90°$

EXAMPLES

Evaluate each expression. Express your answers to the nearest degree or hundredth of a radian.

1. $\text{Sin}^{-1} 0.5$
Using a calculator,
0.5 $\boxed{\text{INV}}$ $\boxed{\text{SIN}}$ $= 30°$
$\text{Sin}^{-1} 0.5 = 30°$.

2. $\text{Arccos } (-1)$
Using a calculator,
-1 $\boxed{\text{INV}}$ $\boxed{\text{COS}}$ $= 180°$
$\text{Cos}^{-1} (-1) = 180°$.

3. $\text{Tan}^{-1} (-0.327)$, in radians
Using a calculator,
-0.327 $\boxed{\text{INV}}$ $\boxed{\text{TAN}}$ ≈ -0.32
$\text{Tan}^{-1} (-0.327) \approx -0.32$.

4. $\text{Arcsin } (-0.51)$, in radians
Using a calculator
-0.51 $\boxed{\text{INV}}$ $\boxed{\text{SIN}}$ ≈ -0.54
$\text{Arcsin } (-0.51) \approx -0.54$.

TRY IT

Evaluate each expression. Express your answers to the nearest degree or hundredth of a radian.

1. $\text{Sin}^{-1} 1$, in degrees
2. $\text{Cos}^{-1} \frac{\sqrt{3}}{2}$, in degrees
3. $\text{Tan}^{-1} 1.445$, in radians
4. $\text{Arcsin } 0.3774$, in degrees
5. $\text{Arccos } (-3.56)$, in radians
6. $\text{Tan}^{-1} (-2)$, in radians

When a trigonometric inverse is shown with a lowercase letter, as in $y = \cos^{-1} x$ (or $y = \arccos x$), we find *all* relevant values of the angle measure. These are trigonometric inverse relations.

EXAMPLES

1. Solve $y = \cos^{-1}(-0.5)$. Find all possible solutions and give answers in degrees.

Find all angle measures whose cosine is equal to -0.5. Since $\cos x$ is a periodic function, there are an infinite number of such measures.

First, find the measure of the reference angle. To do this, find Cos^{-1} of the absolute value of -0.5. $\text{Cos}^{-1} 0.5 = 60°$.

Then, find all angle measures x, with $0° \leq x < 360°$, that satisfy the equation. Since the cosine is *negative*, apply the reference angle to quadrants II and III. A 60° reference-angle measure in these quadrants gives measures of 120° and 240°, respectively.

Finally, give all angle measures that satisfy the equation. The period of cosine is 360°, so the answers are:

$$120° + 360°n \text{ and } 240° + 360°n, \text{ where } n \text{ is an integer}$$

These answers include $-240°, -120°, 120°, 240°, 480°, 600°$, and an infinite number of other answers.

2. Solve $y = \sin^{-1} 0.7562$. Find all solutions from 0 to 2π. Round answers to the nearest hundredth.

Find the measure of the reference angle $\text{Sin}^{-1} 0.7562 \approx 0.86$.

Sine is positive in quadrants I and II. A reference angle measure of 0.86 radians corresponds to measures of 0.86 radians and $3.14 - 0.86 = 2.28$ radians in quadrants I and II, respectively. The domain is restricted to values from 0 to 2π, so $y = 0.86$ radians and $y = 2.28$ radians are the only solutions.

TRY IT

Find all solutions from 0° to 360°. Round answers to the nearest degree.

1. $y = \tan^{-1} \dfrac{\sqrt{3}}{3}$ **2.** $y = \arctan(-2.57)$ **3.** $y = \cos^{-1} 0.5714$

Find all solutions from 0 to 2π. Round answers to the nearest hundredth.

4. $y = \cos^{-1}\left(-\dfrac{\sqrt{2}}{2}\right)$ **5.** $y = \sin^{-1}(0.4772)$

We can use trigonometric inverse functions to help solve more complex trigonometric equations.

EXAMPLES

3. Solve $2 \cos x - \sqrt{3} = 0$. Find all solutions from 0° to 360°.

$2 \cos x = \sqrt{3}$

$\cos x = \dfrac{\sqrt{3}}{2}$ Solve for the trigonometric function.

$x = \cos^{-1} \dfrac{\sqrt{3}}{2}$ Take the inverse cosine of both sides.

The measure of the reference angle with a cosine value of $\dfrac{\sqrt{3}}{2}$ is 30°. Cosine is positive in quadrants I and IV. Applying a reference angle measure of 30° in these quadrants gives angle measures of 30° and 330°, respectively. These are the two solutions to the equation from 0° to 360°.

4. Solve $3 \sin (x - 0.32) + 7 = 6$. Find all solutions from 0 to 2π. Round answers to the nearest hundredth.

$3 \sin (x - 0.32) + 7 = 6$

$\sin (x - 0.32) = -\dfrac{1}{3}$ Solve for the trigonometric function.

$x - 0.32 = \sin^{-1} \left(-\dfrac{1}{3}\right)$ Take the inverse sine of both sides.

Find the possible values of $x - 0.32$. The measure of the reference angle with a sine value of $\dfrac{1}{3}$ is about 0.34 radians. Sine is negative in quadrants III and IV. Applying 0.34 in these quadrants gives angle measures of 3.48 and 5.94, respectively.

$x - 0.32 \approx 3.48$ or $x - 0.32 \approx 5.94$ Use both possibilities to solve for x.

         $x \approx 3.80$ or $x \approx 6.26$

TRY IT

Find all solutions from 0° to 360°. Round answers to the nearest degree.

6. $\cos x - 1 = 0$ **7.** $2 \sin x + 3 = 4$

8. $\sin x + 4 = 5$ **9.** $5 \tan (x + 5°) + 1 = 2.3$

Find all solutions from 0 to 2π. Round answers to the nearest hundredth.

10. $\tan x + 1 = 0$ **11.** $2 \cos x - 1 = 0$

12. $3 \tan x - \sqrt{3} = 0$ **13.** $2 \sin (x + 1.05) + 4.21 = 3.08$

TRIGONOMETRIC PROPERTIES AND IDENTITIES

There are several properties that show relationships among the trigonometric functions. Some of them are shown below.

Reciprocal Properties

$$\sec x = \frac{1}{\cos x} \qquad \csc x = \frac{1}{\sin x} \qquad \cot x = \frac{1}{\tan x}$$

Quotient Properties

$$\tan x = \frac{\sin x}{\cos x} \qquad \cot x = \frac{\cos x}{\sin x}$$

Pythagorean Properties

$$\sin^2 x + \cos^2 x = 1 \quad \tan^2 x + 1 = \sec^2 x \quad 1 + \cot^2 x = \csc^2 x$$

The Pythagorean properties are often seen in other forms. For instance, the expression $\sin^2 x + \cos^2 x = 1$ can be rewritten as:

$$1 - \sin^2 x = \cos^2 x \qquad \text{and as} \qquad 1 - \cos^2 x = \sin^2 x$$

Notice that the first two sets of properties make it possible to express any trigonometric expression in terms of sines and cosines alone.

A *trigonometric identity* is an equation that is always true. To prove a trigonometric identity, use trigonometric properties to transform *one* side of the original equation until it is identical to the other. (You may not work on both sides of the identity.) It is usually easiest to manipulate the more complicated side of the identity.

EXAMPLES

1. Prove that $\tan^2 x \cot x \csc x = \sec x$.

Work with the most complicated side first. It is often helpful to begin by writing all expressions on that side in terms of sines and cosines.

$$\tan^2 x \cot x \csc x = \sec x$$

$\dfrac{\sin^2 x}{\cos^2 x} \dfrac{\cos x}{\sin x} \dfrac{1}{\sin x} = \sec x$	Use reciprocal and quotient properties to express as sines and cosines.
$\dfrac{1}{\cos x} = \sec x$	Simplify.
$\sec x = \sec x$	Use a reciprocal property.

2. Prove that $\sin x = (1 - \cos^2 x) \csc x$.

$$\sin x = (1 - \cos^2 x) \csc x$$

$\sin x = (1 - \cos^2 x) \dfrac{1}{\sin x}$	Convert to sines and cosines.
$\sin x = \sin^2 x \dfrac{1}{\sin x}$	Use a Pythagorean property.
$\sin x = \sin x$	Simplify.

3. Prove that $\dfrac{1}{\sin x \cos x} - \tan x = \cot x$

$\dfrac{1}{\sin x \cos x} - \tan x = \cot x$

$\dfrac{1}{\sin x \cos x} - \dfrac{\sin x}{\cos x} = \cot x$

$\dfrac{1}{\sin x \cos x} - \dfrac{\sin^2 x}{\sin x \cos x} = \cot x$ Use the common denominator $\sin x \cos x$.

$\dfrac{1 - \sin^2 x}{\sin x \cos x} = \cot x$ Write as a single fraction.

$\dfrac{\cos^2 x}{\sin x \cos x} = \cot x$ Use a Pythagorean property.

$\dfrac{\cos x}{\sin x} = \cot x$ Simplify.

$\cot x = \cot x$ Use a quotient property.

4. Prove that $1 - \dfrac{1}{\tan^2 x + 1} = \dfrac{1}{\csc^2 x}$

$1 - \dfrac{1}{\tan^2 x + 1} = \dfrac{1}{\csc^2 x}$

$1 - \dfrac{1}{\sec^2 x} = \dfrac{1}{\csc^2 x}$ Use a Pythagorean property.

$1 - \cos^2 x = \dfrac{1}{\csc^2 x}$ Use a reciprocal property.

$\sin^2 x = \dfrac{1}{\csc^2 x}$ Use a Pythagorean property.

$\dfrac{1}{\csc^2 x} = \dfrac{1}{\csc^2 x}$ Use a reciprocal property.

TRY IT

Prove each identity.

1. $\tan x \cos x = \sin x$ **2.** $\cot^2 x \sec x \csc x \tan x = \csc^2 x$

3. $\sec x \cot x = \csc x$ **4.** $(\cos x + 1)(\cos x - 1) = -\sin^2 x$

5. $\dfrac{\sin x + 1}{\cos x} - \tan x = \sec x$ **6.** $(1 - \sin^2 x)\tan^2 x = 1 - \cos^2 x$

7. $\dfrac{\tan x}{\cos x} + \csc x = \sec^2 x \csc x$ **8.** $(\sin x + \cos x)^2 \sec x = 2\sin x + \sec x$

MEASURES OF CENTRAL TENDENCY

A *measure of central tendency* is a single central value that summarizes a set of numerical data. There are three common measures of central tendency.

The *mean* is the sum of all the data divided by the number of data points.

If the number of data is odd, the *median* is the middle value when the data are arranged in numerical order. If the number of data is even, the median is the average of the two middle values.

The *mode* is the value that occurs most frequently. If there is no value that occurs more than once, the data set has no mode. It is also possible for a data set to have more than one mode.

EXAMPLE

The unemployment rates in the civilian labor force for the months of 1993 are shown below. Find the mean, median, and mode of these values.

7.1, 7.0, 7.0, 6.9, 7.0, 6.9, 6.7, 6.8, 6.7, 6.5, 6.7, 6.4

Find the *mean:*

The number of data is 12, and the sum of the data is 81.7.

The mean is $\frac{81.7}{12} \approx 6.81$.

Find the *median:*

First, arrange the data from least to greatest.

6.4, 6.5, 6.7, 6.7, 6.7, 6.8, 6.9, 6.9, 7.0, 7.0, 7.0, 7.1

Since the number of data is even, take the average of the two middle values, 6.8 and 6.9.

The median is $\frac{6.8 + 6.9}{2} = 6.85$.

Find the *mode:*

The modes are 6.7 and 7.0, since these values occur most often.

TRY IT

Find the mean, median, and mode of each data set.

1. These data give minimum age requirements for obtaining a motorcycle license in Alabama, Arkansas, Florida, Georgia, Kentucky, Louisiana, Mississippi, Missouri, North Carolina, South Carolina, and Tennessee:
14, 16, 15, 16, 16, 15, 15, 15.5, 18, 16, 16

2. These data give record high temperatures (in °F) for Alaska, Arizona, California, Colorado, Hawaii, Idaho, Nevada, New Mexico, Oregon, Utah, and Washington:
100, 127, 134, 118, 100, 118, 122, 116, 119, 117, 118

STANDARD DEVIATION

As discussed on page 788, the standard deviation of a data set measures how far the data deviates from the mean. The standard deviation σ (Greek letter *sigma*) of a data set with n elements x_1, x_2, x_3, x_4, ..., x_n whose mean is $\bar{x}$ is given by:

$$\sigma = \sqrt{\frac{\sum_{i=1}^{n} (x - x_i)^2}{n}}$$

The expression $(\bar{x} - x_i)$ represents the deviation of an individual data value from the mean. $\sum_{i=1}^{n} (x - x_i)^2$ is the sum of the squares of these deviations.

EXAMPLE

The data in the table give the general sales-and-use tax percentages for ten states. Find the standard deviation of this data set.

AL	CO	HI	KY	MI	ND	RI	SC	VT	WY
4	3	4	6	6	5	7	5	5	4

First, find the mean of the data. $\bar{x} = \frac{4 + 3 + 4 + 6 + 6 + 5 + 7 + 5 + 5 + 4}{10} = 4.9$.

Then, find the sum of the squared deviations from the mean.

$0.9^2 + 1.9^2 + 0.9^2 + 1.1^2 + 1.1^2 + 0.1^2 + 2.1^2 + 0.1^2 + 0.1^2 + 0.9^2 = 12.9$

Finally, divide by the number of elements in the data set, in this case 10, and take the square root of the result. The standard deviation of this data set is

$\sigma = \sqrt{\frac{12.9}{10}} \approx 1.14$.

TRY IT

Find the standard deviation of each data set. Round answers to the nearest tenth.

1. 8, 4, 5, 5, 8

2. 10, 18, 12, 15, 16, 13

3. The average mortgage rate for home loans on houses purchased in the United States, 1985–1994

1985	1986	1987	1988	1989	1990	1991	1992	1993	1994
11.7	10.3	9.3	9.3	10.1	10.0	9.5	8.5	7.3	7.0

If a data set is normally distributed, about 68% of the data lies within 1 standard deviation of the mean and about 95% of the data lies within 2 standard deviations of the mean. To investigate intervals that are not a convenient multiple of the standard deviation, we use *z-scores*.

The z-score tells how many standard deviations a data value is above or below the mean. For instance, a z-score of -1.58 indicates that a data value is 1.58 standard deviations below the mean of the distribution.

For a value x in a normal distribution of data whose mean is $\bar{x}$ and standard deviation is σ, the z-score is $z = \frac{x - \bar{x}}{\sigma}$.

EXAMPLE

1. What is the z-score for 25 in a normal distribution whose mean is 20 and standard deviation is 3.6?

$$z = \frac{x - \bar{x}}{\sigma} = \frac{25 - 20}{3.6} = \frac{5}{3.6} \approx 1.39$$

Note that this means that 25 is about 1.39 standard deviations above the mean of this distribution.

The standard normal distribution table on page 875 shows the probability that a z-score of a data value is less than a particular z-value. Example 2 illustrates the use of this table.

EXAMPLE

2. In the United States, the heights of 18- to 24-year-old males are approximately normally distributed with a mean of about 70 inches and a standard deviation of about 3 inches. Find the probability that a randomly chosen male in this age group is under 6 feet tall.

The z-score corresponding to 6 feet (72 inches) is $z = \frac{x - \bar{x}}{\sigma} = \frac{72 - 70}{3} \approx 0.67$.

To use the table, we find the row corresponding to the first two digits of the z-score (0.6) and the column corresponding to the third digit (7).

z	0	1	2	3	4	5	6	7	8	9
0.6	.7257	.7291	.7324	.7357	.7389	.7422	.7454	.7486	.7517	.7549

The probability that a randomly chosen male in this age group is less than 6 feet tall is about 0.75.

Z-scores and the standard normal distribution table can be used to find the probability that the value of a selected item of data lies within a certain range.

EXAMPLE

3. Suppose that the mean blood cholesterol level of a group of patients in a study is 180 milligrams per 100 milliliters of blood and that the standard deviation is 20 milligrams per 100 milliliters of blood. What is the probability that a patient has a cholesterol level between 170 milligrams and 200 milligrams per 100 milliliters of blood?

To find this probability, find the probability that the patient's cholesterol is below 200 milligrams and subtract the probability that it is below 170 milligrams.

The z-score for 200 milligrams is $z = \frac{x - \bar{x}}{\sigma} = \frac{200 - 180}{20} = 1.00$. From the table, the probability that the cholesterol level is below 200 is 0.8413.

The z-score for 170 milligrams is $z = \frac{x - \bar{x}}{\sigma} = \frac{170 - 180}{20} = -0.50$. From the table, the probability that the cholesterol level is below 170 is 0.3085.

The probability that a patient's cholesterol level is between 200 and 170 milligrams is $0.8413 - 0.3085 = 0.5328$. About 53% of the patients have cholesterol levels in this range.

TRY IT

Find each z-score. Assume each data set is normally distributed.

1. for 12, in a distribution whose mean is 15 and standard deviation is 1.8

2. for 130, in a distribution whose mean is 100 and standard deviation is 15

3. for 24.1, in a distribution whose mean is 20.6 and standard deviation is 2.8

4. In the United States, the heights of 18- to 24-year-old females are approximately normally distributed with a mean of about 65.5 inches and a standard deviation of about 2.5 inches. Find the probability that a randomly chosen female in this age group is less than 5 feet 4 inches tall.

5. The net weights of packaged crackers are normally distributed with a mean of 12.12 ounces and a standard deviation of 0.05 ounces. The packages indicate that the net weight of the crackers is 12 ounces. What percentage of the packages have less than the advertised weight?

6. In 1994, the mean Mathematics SAT score for college-bound seniors was 479 and the standard deviation was 124. Assuming that the test scores are normally distributed, find the approximate probability that a student scored between 430 and 660. Round your answer to the nearest tenth.

HYPOTHESIS TESTING OF MEANS

If you sample the heights of 10 eleventh grade male students at your school, their average (mean) height will probably be somewhat different than the average height of all eleventh grade male students in the United States. This may be due to chance, or the students at your school could truly be different than the general population.

Hypothesis testing is used to investigate whether an *observed* difference in data is likely due to chance or whether it points to an *actual* difference between the group and the population. This "actual" difference is called a *statistically significant* difference.

The *significance level* of a test measures the probability that the observed difference in the means is due to chance alone. We will use a significance level of 0.05 (5%), a common choice for social science researchers.

There is a three-step process for comparing the mean of a population to the mean of a sample of a subset.

Step 1 Compute the *standard error* (S.E.) of the mean of the sample. The standard error of the mean is found by dividing the standard deviation (σ) by the square root of the number of data in the sample (n):
$$\text{S.E.} = \frac{\sigma}{\sqrt{n}}.$$

Step 2 Find the *z-value* for the mean of the sample. This is the difference between the sample mean ($\bar{x}$) and the population mean (μ) divided by the standard error: $z = \dfrac{\bar{x} - \mu}{\text{S.E.}}$.

Step 3 Compare the *z*-value to the values for the standard normal curve, using the significance level. For a 0.05 (5%) significance test, if $|z| \geq 1.96$, conclude that there is a statistically significant difference at the 0.05 significance level. This means that the probability that the difference is due to chance alone is less than or equal to 5%.

EXAMPLE

1. The birth weights of babies in the United States average about 115 ounces and have a standard deviation of about 30 ounces. Suppose the babies of 40 women who received monthly prenatal care averaged 125 ounces. Is there a statistically significant difference between the birth weights of these babies and those of babies in the general population at the 0.05 significance level?

   Step 1 The standard error for this data is S.E. $= \dfrac{\sigma}{\sqrt{n}} = \dfrac{30}{\sqrt{40}} \approx 4.74$.

   Step 2 The *z*-value is $z = \dfrac{\bar{x} - \mu}{\text{S.E.}} = \dfrac{125 - 115}{4.74} \approx 2.11$.

   Step 3 To conclude that there is a difference between these means at the 0.05 significance level, $|z|$ must exceed 1.96. Since $z \approx 2.11$, there is a significant difference between birth weights of babies whose mothers received care and those of babies in the general population.

EXAMPLE

2. Suppose that the scores on a standardized test have a mean of 500 points and a standard deviation of 100. Eighty students who take the test when it is snowing outside have a mean score of 487. Is there a significant difference between the scores of students who take the test when it is snowing and those of the general population? Use the 0.05 significance level.

Step 1 $S.E. = \frac{\sigma}{\sqrt{n}} = \frac{100}{\sqrt{80}} \approx 11.2.$

Step 2 $z = \frac{\bar{x} - \mu}{S.E.} = \frac{487 - 500}{11.2} \approx 1.16$

Step 3 To conclude that the means are different at the 0.05 level, $|z|$ must exceed 1.96. Since $z \approx 1.16$, we conclude that there is not a significant difference between the means.

News reports about statistical studies often state that the study found a "significant difference." In this context, *significance* has a precise mathematical meaning. If the sample size of the study is great enough, a very small numerical difference between two means may be statistically significant.

TRY IT

1. Suppose that the average height of a 17-year-old female is 5′5″ and the standard deviation of the height of 17-year-old females is 3 inches. Thirty 17-year-old females eat their vegetables every day. The average height of these 30 females is 5′6″. Can we conclude that there is a difference between the heights of females who eat their vegetables and the general population at the 0.05 significance level?

2. Now, suppose fifty 17-year-old females who eat their vegetables every day have an average height of 5′6″. Can we conclude that there is a difference between the heights of females who eat their vegetables and the general population at the 0.05 significance level now?

3. A company advertises that the average life of their lightbulbs is 1000 hours. The standard deviation of the lives of the bulbs is 50 hours. If a sample of 60 lightbulbs has an average life of 970 hours, can we conclude that the advertisement is likely to be untrue? Use the 0.05 significance level.

4. A blood pressure reading consists of two numbers. The diastolic pressure is the lesser of the two numbers. Suppose that the diastolic blood pressure of U.S. males in their thirties is normally distributed with a mean of 87 and a standard deviation of 15. In this age group, 150 men are placed on an exercise program, and the mean of their diastolic pressures drops to 84. Can we conclude that there is a significant difference between the diastolic blood pressures of men on this exercise program and those of the general population at the 0.05 significance level?

RESIDUALS AND LINEAR REGRESSION

One way to measure how well a line fits data is with **residuals.** For a given trend line or line of best fit, the residual for a data point is the difference between the y-value of the data point and the y-value predicted by the line.

EXAMPLE

1. Make a scatter plot of these data: $(2, 3.5), (4, 2), (-4, 0.5), (-2, -2), (0, 0.5)$. Draw a trend line and find the residual of each data point.

   The trend line shown is the line $y = 0.5x + 1$. Use this equation to find the predicted y-values and then the residuals.

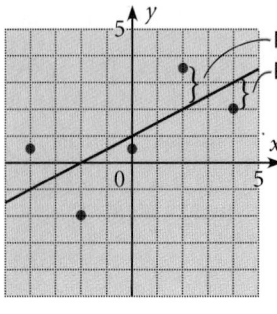

Residual = 3.5 − 2 = 1.5
Residual = 2 − 2 = −1

Data	$0.5x + 1$	Residual
$(2, 3.5)$	2	1.5
$(4, 2)$	3	−1
$(-4, 0.5)$	−1	1.5
$(-2, -2)$	0	−2
$(0, 0.5)$	1	−0.5

TRY IT

Make a scatter plot of each set of data. Draw a trend line and find the residual of each data point.

1. $(-3, -8), (-1, -5.5), (1, 0), (4, 6), (6, 7.5)$
2. $(-8, 8), (-6, 10), (-2, 8), (4, 6), (6, 1)$

Minimizing residuals is the basis for *linear regression,* the method most commonly used in science and statistics to find a line of best fit. Linear regression was developed in 1805 by the French mathematician Adrien Legendre. This method, also known as the *method of least squares,* finds the line that minimizes the sum of the squares of the residuals.

You can find the regression line $y = mx + b$ using technology or by calculating the means $\bar{x}, \bar{y}, \overline{x^2}$, and $\overline{xy}$, and then solving the following system of equations for m and b.

$$\bar{y} = m\bar{x} + b$$

$$\overline{xy} = m\overline{x^2} + b\bar{x}$$

EXAMPLE

2. These data are from a study by the Educational Testing Service and show the percentage of eighth-graders who watch 6 hours or more of television per day (x) and the average math score on the SAT exam (y) in ten states: (33, 231), (19, 246), (16, 256), (14, 263), (12, 259), (11, 267), (9, 276), (8, 274), (7, 276), (6, 281)

Make a scatter plot of the data. Find and graph the regression line and use it to predict the average math score on the SAT in a state where 25% of the eighth-graders watch 6 hours or more of television per day.

First calculate the values and means of x, y, x^2, and xy.

x	y	x^2	xy
33	231	1089	7623
19	246	361	4674
16	256	256	4096
14	263	196	3682
12	259	144	3108
11	267	121	2937
9	276	81	2484
8	274	64	2192
7	276	49	1932
6	281	36	1686

means 13.5   262.9   239.7   3441.4

Solve the system:
$$\bar{y} = m\bar{x} + b$$
$$\overline{xy} = m\overline{x^2} + b\bar{x}$$
$\rightarrow$
$$262.9 = 13.5m + b$$
$$3441.4 = 239.7m + 13.5b$$

Solving this system gives $m \approx -1.8755$ and $b \approx 288.2198$. The equation of the regression line is $y = -1.8755x + 288.22$.

When $x = 25$, $y \approx -1.8755(25) + 288.22 \approx 241.33$.

Therefore, in a state where 25% of the eighth-graders watch 6 hours or more of television, we expect an average SAT math score of about 241.

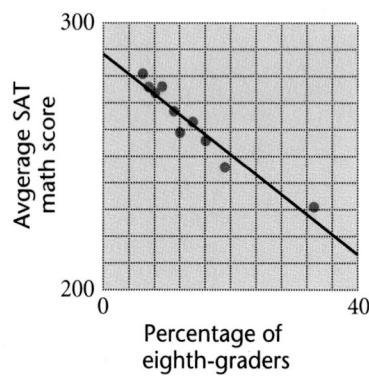

TRY IT

3. Make a scatter plot of the winning heights for the women's Olympic high jump for the given years. Find and graph the regression line and use it to predict the winning height in the 2020 Olympics.

Year	1956	1960	1964	1968	1972	1976	1980	1984	1988	1992
Height (in.)	69.25	72.75	74.75	71.5	76	75.75	77.5	79.5	80	79.5

CHOOSING A MATHEMATICAL MODEL

A common way to measure how well a set of data fits a particular model is with the **correlation coefficient,** usually denoted by r. The r-value for any model and set of data is a number between -1 and 1. An r-value close to 0 means that the model doesn't fit the data very well. An r-value close to -1 or 1 means that the model does fit the data well. The sign of r tells whether the data show a positive or negative association.

EXAMPLES

1. Plot the following data on a graphing utility and give the correlation coefficient for a linear model: $(-4, 3)$, $(-3, 2)$, $(-2, 2)$, $(-1, 1.5)$, $(0, 0.5)$, $(1, 1)$, $(1.5, 0)$, $(2, 0.5)$, $(3, -1)$, $(4, -0.5)$.

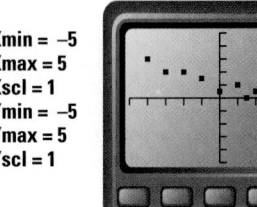

Xmin = –5
Xmax = 5
Xscl = 1
Ymin = –5
Ymax = 5
Yscl = 1

On most graphing utilities, the r-value is shown along with the equation of the regression line or curve for the given model.

EDIT **CALC**
1: 1-Var Stats
2: 2-Var Stats
3: SetUp
4: Med-Med
5: LinReg (ax+b)
6: QuadReg
7↓CubicReg

LinReg
y = ax+b
a = –.449012495
b = .9673518742
r = –.9484936177

The correlation coefficient for a linear model is $r \approx -0.95$. Since r is close to -1, a linear model fits the data well.

2. Plot the following data on a graphing utility and give the correlation coefficient for a power model: $(1, 0.5)$, $(2, 1.5)$, $(3, 3)$, $(4, 4)$, $(5, 5.5)$, $(6, 7.5)$, $(7, 9)$.

Xmin = 0
Xmax = 10
Xscl = 1
Ymin = 0
Ymax = 10
Yscl = 1

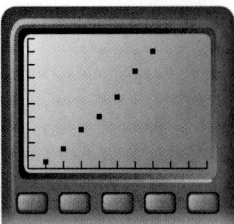

PwrReg
y = a*x^b
a = .5271878625
b = 1.477448691
r = .9984022746

Using power regression to model this set of data gives the equation $y = 0.52719x^{1.47745}$. The correlation coefficient is $r \approx 0.9984$, so the power model fits the data very well.

TRY IT

Plot each set of data on a graphing utility and give the correlation coefficient.

1. (5, 8), (6, 10), (7, 11.5), (8, 13), (9, 15), (10, 16.5): linear model

2. (2, 6), (3, 10), (4, 15), (5, 25), (6, 46), (7, 99): power model

3. (0, 13), (1, 25), (2, 53), (3, 100), (4, 190), (5, 385): exponential model

For a given set of data, compare the correlation coefficients for various models to help you decide which model to choose.

EXAMPLE

3. Choose a model that fits the following data. Plot the data and draw the regression line or curve. Then predict Nevada's population in the year 2000.

Years since 1900 (x)	Nevada Population (y)	Years since 1900 (x)	Nevada Population (y)
40	110,247	70	488,738
50	160,083	80	800,508
60	285,278	90	1,201,833

Compare the correlation coefficients for several reasonable models.

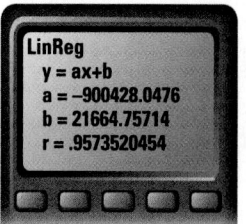  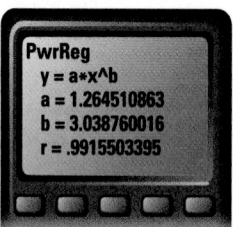

The exponential model fits the data best and gives the regression equation $y = 14659.87(1.0507)^x$. (Notice that the population of Nevada is growing at about 5% per year.)

When $x = 100$, the model predicts $y \approx 2,060,000$. So the population of Nevada is predicted to be about 2.06 million in the year 2000.

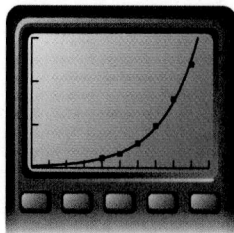

Xmin = 0
Xmax = 100
Xscl = 10
Ymin = 0
Ymax = 1500000
Yscl = 500000

TRY IT

4. The following data show wholesale prices of a dozen eggs. Choose a model that fits the data well. Plot the data and draw the regression line or curve. Use your model to predict the egg price in the year 2010.

Years since 1900 (x)	40	50	60	70	80	90
Egg Price (cents per dozen) (y)	18.0	36.3	36.1	39.1	56.3	70.9

INEQUALITIES FROM POLYNOMIAL, SQUARE ROOT, AND RATIONAL EQUATIONS

The equations you studied on pages 498, 566, and 603 have inequality counterparts.

Conditional Inequality

A conditional inequality is true for some but not all values of the variables involved. For example, $x - 5 > 4$ is only true for values of x greater than 9.

Sense

The inequalities $a > b$ and $c > d$ have the same sense, but $a > b$ and $e < f$ have the opposite sense. Sense is reversed if each side is multiplied by the same negative number.

EXAMPLES

1. **Polynomial inequality** To solve a quadratic inequality such as $y > 2x^2 + 1$, first plot the corresponding equation $y = 2x^2 + 1$ on a graph.

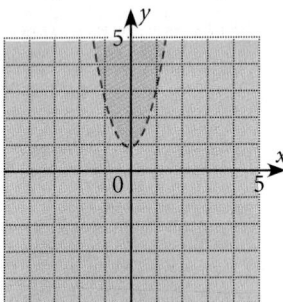

The shaded region includes all those points (values of x and y) for which the inequality holds true. Verify that this is correct for sample points in both the shaded and unshaded regions.

For $(x, y) = (1, 5)$, it is true that $5 > 2(1)^2 + 1$.

For $(x, y) = (5, 5)$, it is false that $5 > 2(5)^2 + 1$.

Points on the boundary do not satisfy the inequality because it is a strict inequality ($<$, not $\leq$).

2. **Square root inequality** The basic square root function is $y = \sqrt{x}$. What does the graph of $y \leq \sqrt{x}$ look like?

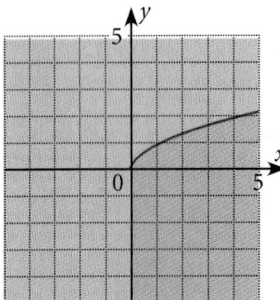

The shaded region includes all those points (values of x and y) for which the inequality holds true. Verify that this is correct for sample points in both the shaded and unshaded regions.

For $(x, y) = (1, 5)$, it is true that $1 \leq \sqrt{5}$.

For $(x, y) = (3, 5)$, it is false that $3 \leq \sqrt{5}$.

Points on the boundary satisfy the inequality because it is not a strict inequality.

3. **Rational Inequality** A spacecraft is traveling from Earth directly toward the moon, 240,000 miles away. If x is the distance to Earth in thousands of miles, then $240 - x$ is the distance to the moon. At these distances gravity accelerates the craft at $\frac{154}{x^2}$ m/sec^2 toward Earth and at $\frac{1.9}{(240 - x)^2}$ m/sec^2 toward the moon. At what distance from Earth will the net gravitational acceleration (caused by the Earth and by the moon acting upon the spacecraft) be toward the moon?

The net acceleration toward Earth, in m/sec^2, is given by the function

$$A(x) = \frac{154}{x^2} - \frac{1.9}{(240 - x)^2}, \text{ where } 0 < x < 240.$$

The solution of the rational inequality $\frac{154}{x^2} - \frac{1.9}{(240 - x)^2} < 0$, where $0 < x < 240$, gives the domain of values for x where the net gravitational acceleration is toward the moon. Graphing the function across the domain of x and tracing to find the x-intercept, on one side of which $A(x) < 0$, yields the solution $x > 216$ rounded to the nearest thousand miles. The net acceleration is toward the moon when the spacecraft is greater than about 216,000 miles from Earth, 90% of the way to the moon.

TRY IT

1. Graph the following inequalities. Identify two points that satisfy each inequality and two points that do not satisfy each inequality.
   a. $y \leq 3 + \sqrt{x + 2}$
   b. $x^2 + y < 3$
   c. $y \geq \frac{3 + x}{x^2}$

2. Hans designs and builds wood furniture. He is designing a new chest to have a volume between 48 cubic feet and 50 cubic feet. A chest too small would not hold enough supplies. A chest too big would not fit into the available space. All of the chests he builds are 2 feet wider than their height and 2 feet longer than their width. Hans can measure accurately to the nearest $\frac{1}{32}$ inch. What is the least value the height should be? What is the greatest?

INEQUALITIES FROM EXPONENTIAL
AND LOGARITHMIC EQUATIONS

The equations solved on pages 642 and 653 have inequality counterparts. An inequality is a statement that one real number is greater than or less than another. Inequality Signs and Absolute versus Conditional Inequality are discussed on page 870.

Conditional Inequality

A conditional inequality is true for some but not all values of the variables involved. For example, $x - 5 > 4$ is only true for values of x greater than 9.

Sense

The inequalities $a >$ and $c > d$ have the same sense, but $a > b$ and $e <$ have the opposite sense. Sense is reversed if each side is multiplied by the same negative number.

- If $a > b$ and $k < 0$, then $ka < kb$.
- If $a > b$ and if a, b, and n are positive, then $a^n > b^n$ and $a^{-n} < b^{-n}$.

EXAMPLE

1. The altitude of an aircraft is a function of outside air pressure. A minimum safe clearance above known obstacles is required. The higher the aircraft, the thinner the air around it, and the lower the pressure. Maintaining a maximum outside pressure generally correlates with maintaining a minimum required altitude. Assume a 2-mile minimum is required.

   When the outside pressure is less than P, the altitude (h), in miles, is given by $h > -\frac{100}{9} \log \frac{P}{B}$, where B is the atmospheric pressure at sea level. P and B must be measured in the same units.

   Find the altitude of an aircraft if the pressure at sea level is 30 inches of mercury and the outside air pressure is less than 18.2 inches of mercury.

   $h > \frac{-100}{9} \log \frac{P}{B}$

   $h > \frac{-100}{9} \log \frac{18.2}{30}$

   $h > \frac{-100}{9}(-0.217)$

   $h > 2.41$

   The aircraft is greater than 2.41 miles high, well above the 2-mile minimum safe altitude.

2. The value (A) of an original investment of P dollars with an interest rate $r\%$ compounded continuously for t years is $A = Pe^{rt}$ where the decimal expansion of the irrational number (e) begins $e = 2.718281828...$.

If a bank advertises that it will pay a minimum of 6% interest, starting upon deposit and compounded continuously for deposits of at least 3 years duration, what would be the value of a $2000 deposit after 3 years?

Where $r \geq .06$, and $t \geq 3$, $A = Pe^{rt} \geq 2000e^{(.06)(3)}$

$A \geq 2000e^{0.18}$
$A \geq (2000)(1.1972174)$
$A \geq 2394.4347$

The value of the deposit would be at least $2394.43.

TRY IT

1. The figure shows the graph of the exponential function $f(x) = y = e^x$.
  a. When $x = 0$, what is the value of $f(x)$?
  b. What is the domain of $f(x)$?
  c. Where in the domain is $f(x) < 0$?
  d. What is the range of $f(x)$?

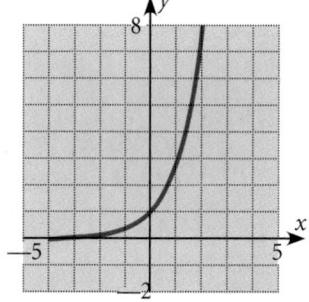

2. The figure shows the graph of the natural logarithmic function $f(x) = y = \ln(x)$.
  a. When $f(x) = 0$, what is the value of x?
  b. What is the domain of $f(x)$?
  c. What is the range of $f(x)$?

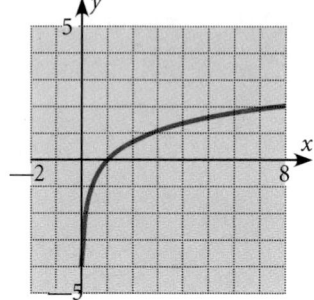

3. A bank will pay a minimum of 8% interest, starting upon deposit and compounded continuously for deposits of at least 10 years duration. What will be the value of a $5000 deposit after 10 years?

SPIRAL REVIEW

CHAPTER 1 MATHEMATICAL MODELS

1-1 GRAPHICAL MODELS

Use with or after Part 1-1A

Simplify. [Previous course]

1. $-2 + 14 - 25 - (-17) - 6$

2. $1 + 3 \cdot 5 - 4 + 1$

3. $2 \cdot 6 - 3 + 2 - 4 \cdot 6$

4. $2x^2(3x)^2$

5. $3a - 2b + 5(3b - 2a)$

6. $6(x + 2y)$

Evaluate. [Previous course]

7. $x^2 + 3x - 2$ for $x = -3$

8. $\dfrac{x^3}{x}$ for $x = -3$

9. $-2x^2$ for $x = -2$

10. $(x^4)^0$ for $x = -1$

Use with or after Part 1-1B

Simplify. [Previous course]

11. $-5 + (-4) - 3 + 7 + 6$

12. $15 + 32 + (-24) \div (-6)$

13. $-2.1 - 3.2 - (-13) + (-2.1)$

14. $14 + (-24) - 21 - (-32)$

15. $-2x^3 - 7x^3 + 4x$

16. $a + b - 4c - 3b + 6a$

Evaluate. [Previous course]

17. $-x^3 + 2x^2$ for $x = -5$

18. $(2x)^2 - 5x$ for $x = -1$

19. $4r^2 \cdot (-2r^3)$ for $r = 0.1$

20. $\dfrac{1}{x}$ for $x = 0.5$

21. $\left| 17 - x \right|$ for $x = -5$

22. $\left| 6 - x \right|$ for $x = 7$

Use with or after Part 1-1C

Evaluate. [Previous course]

23. $4y^2$ for $y = \dfrac{1}{4}$

24. $\dfrac{a + b}{ab}$ for $a = -2, b = -1$

25. $\dfrac{1}{2}bh$ for $b = 1.7, h = 2.4$

26. $\dfrac{1}{3}(a - b)$ for $a = -3, b = 9$

27. $\dfrac{2}{x}$ for $x = \dfrac{1}{8}$

28. $\dfrac{x + 3}{3}$ for $x = -2$

29. $3x(x - 4)$ for $x = -3$

30. $-(-2x)^3 \cdot (x)$ for $x = -1$

1-2 EXPERIMENTAL PROBABILITY AND SIMULATION

Use with or after Part 1-2A

Simplify. [Previous course]

1. $-(-2^2)^3$

2. $\dfrac{x^3 \cdot x^4 \cdot y^2}{y \cdot x^5}$

3. $\dfrac{-1}{\frac{1}{4x}}$

4. $\dfrac{x^{-2}}{x^{-5}}$

5. $\left(-\dfrac{1}{3}\right)^{-2}$

Evaluate for $x = -4$ and $y = -3$. [Previous course]

6. $6x$

7. 2^x

8. x^{-3}

9. $\left(\dfrac{1}{x}\right)^{-2}$

10. $-5xy$

11. $-2y^2$

12. y^3

13. $-ay^2$

Use with or after Part 1-2B

Simplify. [Previous course]

14. $6f - 4g + 3f - (-11f)$

15. $-4x^2 - x - 11 - 9x - 17 - 8x^2$

16. $-(3z - 2y + x) - (4z - 3y)$

17. $x - 1 - (x - 1) - (x - (x - 1))$

Solve. [Previous course]

18. $4y + y = 23$

19. $10p - 3 = 7p + 12$

20. $5a + 2a - 12 = 3a + 52$

21. $3c - 2 = 5c + 20$

Let $g(x) = x^2 - 5x + 3$. Find each of the following. [1-1C]

22. $g(-6)$ **23.** $g(5)$ **24.** $g(-3)$ **25.** $g(0.2)$

1-3 MATRICES

Use with or after Part 1-3A

Evaluate. [Previous course]

1. $\sqrt{3} \cdot \sqrt{3}$

2. $-\sqrt{\dfrac{36}{4}}$

3. $\sqrt{-9}$

4. $\pm\sqrt{1.96}$

5. $\sqrt{1.44} \cdot \sqrt{10{,}000}$

6. $\sqrt{18} \cdot \sqrt{50}$

7. $\left(\sqrt{13}\right)^2$

8. $\dfrac{\sqrt{27}}{\sqrt{3}}$

9. $\sqrt{2} + \sqrt{2}$

Identify the domain and range of each function. [1-1C]

10. $y = \dfrac{1}{2}x - 3$ **11.** $y = 3|x|$ **12.** $y = \sqrt{x - 1}$ **13.** $y = x^2 + 2$

14. $y = -4$ **15.** $y = \dfrac{1}{\sqrt{2x}}$ **16.** $\{(2, 5), (-3, 8), (7, 5), (2, 6), (3, 8)\}$

Use with or after Part 1-3B

Solve. [Previous course]

17. $\dfrac{18}{x} = \dfrac{6}{12}$ **18.** $\dfrac{3}{y} = \dfrac{17}{3}$ **19.** $\dfrac{x}{4} = \dfrac{10}{16}$ **20.** $\dfrac{12}{x} = \dfrac{x}{3}$

Simplify. [Previous course]

21. $-2 - 8 + 4(3 - 2^2)^3$ **22.** $-2^4 + 3(5 - 2 + 1)^2$ **23.** $\left(-\dfrac{1}{4}\right)^{-2} \cdot 2^{-3}$

24. $[(3x)^2 \cdot -2x^3]^2$ **25.** $\dfrac{(-3a^2b)^5}{(ab^{-1})^2}$ **26.** $\dfrac{x^{-3}y^2z^0}{x^{-4}y}$

Make a table of values for each equation. Include at least six entries. [1-1B]

27. $y = \dfrac{1}{x}$ **28.** $y = 3x^2 - 5$ **29.** $y = \dfrac{1 + x}{x}$ **30.** $y = 4 - x^2$

CHAPTER 2 LINEAR FUNCTIONS, EQUATIONS, AND INEQUALITIES

2-1 LINEAR FUNCTIONS AND EQUATIONS

Use with or after Part 2-1A

Evaluate the expressions for $x = 3$, $y = -2$, $z = -5$. [Previous course]

1. $7x^2$ **2.** $(-xy)^2$ **3.** $6xy$ **4.** $-2x \cdot 5y$

5. $3xz$ **6.** $2z - 4x$ **7.** $x(y - z)$ **8.** y^x

Use with or after Part 2-1B

Solve for x. [Previous course]

9. $3x + 1 = 7$ **10.** $4x - 3 = 10$ **11.** $2(x + 3) - 8 = 0$

12. $x^2 = 9$ **13.** $\frac{3}{2}x = 9$ **14.** $\frac{x}{2} + 1 = 7$

15. $(x + 3)(x - 3) = 0$ **16.** $x^2 + 6 = 42$

Find the domain and range of the following. [1-1C]

17. $\{(1, 3), (4, 9), (-2, 6)\}$ **18.** $f(x) = x^2 - 1$ **19.** $f(g) = \sqrt{2 + g}$

20. $\{(1, 3), (0, 9), (-2, 9)\}$ **21.** $f(x) = x^2 + 1$ **22.** $f(x) = -|x| - 3$

Use with or after Part 2-1C

Simplify. [Previous course]

23. $\dfrac{x^6}{x^2}$ **24.** $3(-2)^2 + 1$ **25.** $\dfrac{3x^2 + 9}{3}$ **26.** $\dfrac{2(x - 1)}{3(x - 1)}$

Let $f(x) = 2x^2 - 3x$. Find each of the following. [1-1C]

27. $f(0)$ **28.** $f(3)$ **29.** $f(-2)$

30. $f\left(\dfrac{1}{3}\right)$ **31.** $f(n)$ **32.** $f(0.7)$

Decide whether each equation represents a linear function. If so, give its slope and decide whether it represents direct variation. [2-1A]

33. $f(x) = \dfrac{2}{3}x$ **34.** $5 - 10x = 5y$ **35.** $yx = 1$ **36.** $y = 3|x| - 8$

2-2 FITTING LINEAR FUNCTIONS TO DATA

Use with or after Part 2-2A

Simplify. [Previous course]

1. $\dfrac{20m^3p}{4mn^2p}$ **2.** $(-1)^{10}$ **3.** $\dfrac{-5^3}{5^3}$ **4.** $x^4 + x^4$

5. $(x + 1)^2$ **6.** $(999)^0$ **7.** $(x + 3)(x - 2)$ **8.** $\dfrac{8x + 2y}{2}$

Factor completely. [Previous course]

9. $x^2 + 3x + 2$ **10.** $x^2 - 9$ **11.** $x^2 + x - 6$ **12.** $10x^2 + 6x - 2$

13. $x^2 + 7x + 6$ **14.** $x^2 - 8x + 12$ **15.** $x^2 - 3x - 10$ **16.** $3x^2 - 48$

Use with or after Part 2-2B

Evaluate each expression for $x = 4$, $y = -2$, $z = 7$. [Previous course]

17. $3x^2$ **18.** xyz **19.** $-7x^2$ **20.** $3x - 2y$

21. $\dfrac{x}{y}$ **22.** $x(y + z)$ **23.** $\dfrac{z^2}{xy}$ **24.** y^x

Solve and check each equation. [2-1B]

25. $x = 4(3 - 2) + 3$ **26.** $2x = 3(5 - 3)$ **27.** $2x = 5x - 7$

28. $3(2 - 3z) = 24$ **29.** $x = 9x - 72$ **30.** $0.8m = 0.2m + 24$

31. $6\dfrac{1}{2}z = 7 - \dfrac{1}{2}z$ **32.** $2y + 36 = -3y - 54$

Use with or after Part 2-2C

Give the slope for each linear equation. [2-1C]

33. $y = 3x + 5$ **34.** $y = 2 - 4x$ **35.** $y = \dfrac{2x}{3} + 1$ **36.** $y = \dfrac{x}{2} - 4$

37. $y = x$ **38.** $5 = 2x - y$ **39.** $y = 4(x - 1)$ **40.** $y = 3$

Give an equation for each line or function. [2-1C]
41. slope $= 4$, point $(3, 5)$ **42.** slope $= 2$, point $(1, 4)$
43. points $(2, 5)$ and $(4, 11)$ **44.** point $(-3, 5)$ and origin
45. slope $= 2$, y-intercept $= 7$ **46.** slope $= \dfrac{1}{2}$, y-intercept $= 6$

2-3 LINEAR INEQUALITIES

Use with or after Part 2-3A

Find the value of x that will result in a true proportion. [Previous course]

1. $\dfrac{1}{2} = \dfrac{x}{8}$ **2.** $\dfrac{3}{5} = \dfrac{18}{x}$ **3.** $\dfrac{5}{x} = \dfrac{25}{40}$ **4.** $\dfrac{x}{36} = \dfrac{5}{18}$

Simplify. [Previous course]

5. $\dfrac{2}{3} \div \dfrac{8}{9}$ **6.** 25% of 0.4   **7.** $\left| -7 - (-3) \right|$ **8.** $\sqrt{\dfrac{36}{49}}$

9. $(m^2)^3$ **10.** $-\sqrt{9}$ **11.** $x^3 + x^3$ **12.** -4^2

Use with or after Part 2-3B

Simplify. [Previous course]

13. $-4x(5x^2 - 3x)$ **14.** $\left| 5 - 8 \right|$ **15.** 7^{-1}

16. $\left(\sqrt{49} \right)^2$ **17.** $\dfrac{2a^2(a^2b)^3}{a^3b^2}$ **18.** $\dfrac{11 - (-19)}{6} - 4 \div 2$

19. $(2^5)\left(\dfrac{1}{2} \right)^3$ **20.** $\dfrac{c^8}{c^2}$

For each set of data: plot the points; find the centroid; find the slope of line AC; write the equation for the median-median line. [2-2B]
21. $\{A(0, 4), B(2, 3), C(4, 8)\}$ **22.** $\{A(2, 1), B(4, 5), C(6, 3)\}$
23. $\{A(-2, 5), B(1, 1), C(4, 3)\}$ **24.** $\{A(0, 0), B(25, 100), C(200, 50)\}$

Use with or after Part 2-3C

Simplify. [Previous course]

25. $\dfrac{-16 + 10}{-3}$ **26.** $5(x - 1) + 3(4 - x)$ **27.** $3x^3 + 2x(x^2 - 4)$

28. $\left| 4 - 11 \right|$ **29.** $3x^2 \cdot 4x^3$ **30.** $\dfrac{2.4 \times 10^3}{1.2 \times 10^{-8}}$

31. $-8(a^2)^3 a^{-5}$ **32.** $(f^3)^3$

Find the slope of the line represented by each equation. [2-1C]

33. $y = 3x + 2$ **34.** $y = -x + 1$ **35.** $f(x) = -4x - 1$

36. $y = \dfrac{2}{3}x - 3$ **37.** $y = \dfrac{x}{4} + 1$ **38.** $2x + 5y = 5$

39. $y = x + 2x$ **40.** $2y = 6x - 4$

CHAPTER 3 SOLVING SYSTEMS OF LINEAR EQUATIONS AND INEQUALITIES

3-1 SYSTEMS OF LINEAR EQUATIONS

Use with or after Part 3-1A

Use the matrices below to find each of the following, if possible. If not possible, explain why not. [1-3A]

$$A = \begin{bmatrix} 2 & 3 \\ -5 & -3 \end{bmatrix} \quad B = \begin{bmatrix} -1 & 1 & 4 \\ 0 & 2 & -1 \\ 2 & 3 & 1 \end{bmatrix} \quad C = \begin{bmatrix} -1 & -3 \\ 4 & 2 \end{bmatrix} \quad D = \begin{bmatrix} 4 & -8 & 4 \\ -6 & 2 & -6 \\ 2 & -4 & -6 \end{bmatrix}$$

1. $A + B$ **2.** $B + D$ **3.** $C - A$ **4.** $-3B$

5. $\frac{1}{2}D$ **6.** $3A - 2C$ **7.** $-C$ **8.** $D - A$

Use with or after Part 3-1B

Let $h(x) = |3x - 5|$. Find each of the following. [1-1D]

9. $h(1)$ **10.** $h(-1)$ **11.** $h(m)$ **12.** $h(0)$

13. $h(-3)$ **14.** $h(0.03)$ **15.** $h\left(\frac{5}{3}\right)$ **16.** $h\left(\frac{2}{3}\right)$

Solve and check each equation. [2-1B]

17. $3x - 4 = -1$ **18.** $6x + 15 = 3(5 + 3x)$ **19.** $5(m - 3) = 4m - 5$

20. $7 - 2(g - 4) = 5$ **21.** $2(x + 4) = -6$ **22.** $2(3x + 5) = 14$

Use with or after Part 3-1C

Give an equation for each line or function. [2-1C]

23. slope $= -2$, through $(7, 2)$ **24.** through $(5, 3)$ and $(2, 6)$

25. through $(9, 10)$, parallel to the graph of $f(x) = \frac{2}{3}x + 4$

26. through $(8, -8)$, perpendicular to the graph of $y = -0.8x + 2$

Solve and graph each inequality. [2-3A]

27. $4x \geq 8$ **28.** $2t - 1 < 9$ **29.** $\frac{2}{3}x \leq -6$

Solve and graph each equation. [2-3B]

30. $|x - 3| = 7$ **31.** $|2x - 7| = 11$ **32.** $|x| < 18$

33. $10 - |x + 3| \leq 15$ **34.** $|-6t + 3| = 9$ **35.** $|x| - 5 = 8$

Use with or after Part 3-1D

Solve each literal equation for x. [2-1B]

36. $x + b - 2(x - a) = 2a$ **37.** $2b - 5x - (2x - 3b) = 2$

38. $3a(5 + x) - 2a(x - 1) = 1$ **39.** $2(7b + 2x) + (3x - 2b) = b - x$

Solve each equation or inequality. [2-1B, 2-3A]

40. $5(x - 2) - 3(2x + 1) = 2 + 5x$ **41.** $4a - 12 < 2a + 2$

42. $\frac{2z - 3}{6} - \frac{z - 2}{3} = \frac{3z - 1}{12}$ **43.** $6(5 - 2x) \geq 5x - 2 - 5(x + 3)$

3-2 SYSTEMS OF LINEAR INEQUALITIES

Use with or after Part 3-2A

Simplify. [Previous course]

1. $\dfrac{x^{-2}y^3}{\frac{x}{y^2}}$

2. $\dfrac{-3^2 \cdot (-2)^2(-5)^2}{2^2(3)}$

3. $-\left| -2(4 - 3 + 2) \right|$

4. $\dfrac{3a^{-2}(4a)^3}{12a}$

Solve and graph each compound inequality. [2-3A]

5. $-4 \le 2x - 1 < 8$

6. $3x < -9$ or $4x > 32$

7. $-7 < 6 - 4x \le 18$

8. $-7 < 3x + 5 \le 17$

9. $4x - 1 < 11$ or $3x + 1 > 16$

10. $6 < 3(x - 4) \le 15$

Use with or after Part 3-2B

Let $h(x) = \dfrac{x^2 - 3x + 2}{x - 1}$ and $f(x) = \dfrac{|3x^2 - x|}{x - 3}$. **Find each of the following. [1-1C]**

11. $h(3)$

12. $h(-5)$

13. $h(0.2)$

14. $h(1.6)$

15. $f(-3)$

16. $f(0)$

17. $f(5)$

18. $f(0.1)$

Solve each equation. [2-1B]

19. $12 + 5x = 3x - 11$

20. $7x = 3 + 4x$

21. $8x - 4 = 6x + 10$

22. $4p - 9 = 5(2p + 3)$

23. $\dfrac{2}{3}x + 15 = \dfrac{1}{3}x - 12$

24. $67 = 4(3 - x)$

Use with or after Part 3-2C

Check whether each pair of matrices is a pair of inverse matrices. [1-3B]

$A = \begin{bmatrix} 1 & 2 \\ 1 & 1 \end{bmatrix}$ $B = \begin{bmatrix} 1 & 1 \\ 1 & 2 \end{bmatrix}$ $C = \begin{bmatrix} 2 & -1 \\ -1 & 1 \end{bmatrix}$

25. A and B

26. B and C

27. A and C

Find the equation of the median-median line for the set of data. [2-2B]

28. $(2, 3), (5, 5), (3, 1), (8, 6), (11, 2), (4, 1), (9, 5), (15, 3), (7, 4)$

CHAPTER 4 PATTERNS AND STRUCTURE IN ALGEBRA

4-1 ANALYZING ARITHMETIC GROWTH

Use with or after Part 4-1A

Calculate. [Previous course]

1. $3!$

2. $6!$

3. $6! - 3!$

4. $\dfrac{6!}{3!}$

5. $6!3!$

6. $10!$

Complete each table. [1-1B]

7.

x	1	2	3	4	5
y	13	20	27		

8.

x	1	2	3	4	5
y	$\frac{1}{2}$	1	$\frac{3}{2}$		

Use with or after Part 4-1B

Simplify. [Previous course]

9. $x^2 \cdot x^3$

10. $(x^3)^4$

11. $\dfrac{x^6}{x^2}$

12. $3x^2 + 2x^2$

13. $\dfrac{x^3 \cdot x^4}{x^2}$

14. $(3x^6)^{-1}$

15. $\dfrac{7x^2}{x^4}$

16. $\sqrt{x^6}$

For each table, write an equation relating x and y. [1-1B]

17.

x	3	4	5	6
y	6	8	10	12

18.

x	1	2	3	4
y	1	4	9	16

19.

x	1	2	3	4
y	5	6	7	8

20.

x	1	2	3	4
y	-2	-1	0	1

21.

x	1	2	3	4
y	-2	-4	-6	-8

22.

x	1	2	3	4
y	$\frac{1}{2}$	1	$\frac{3}{2}$	2

4-2 ANALYZING GEOMETRIC GROWTH

Use with or after Part 4-2A

Determine the number of solutions of the linear system in each graph.

Tell whether the system is consistent or inconsistent. Give the solution set. [3-1A]

1.

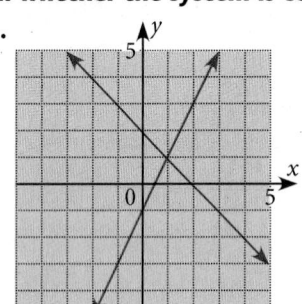

2.

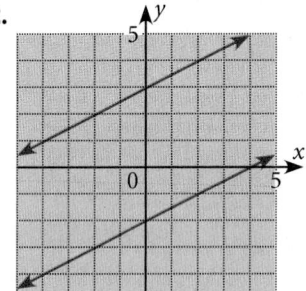

Use with or after Part 4-2B

Evaluate; given $x = -3$, $y = -2$, $z = 4$. [Previous course]

3. $4x^2$

4. xyz

5. $2z - 4x$

6. $\dfrac{y}{z}$

7. y^z

8. $2y - 3z$

9. $-3y + z$

10. z^{-1}

Let $f(x) = x^2 - 2x + 3$. Find each of the following. [1-1C]

11. $f(-3)$

12. $f(0)$

13. $f(5)$

14. $f(n)$

15. $f\left(\dfrac{1}{2}\right)$

16. $f(0.2)$

17. $f(-1)$

18. $f\left(\dfrac{1}{4}\right)$

Use with or after Part 4-2C

Simplify. [Previous course]

19. $(x + 3)(x - 2)$

20. $(x - 1)^2$

21. $(3x + 1)(2x + 5)$

22. $(x + 7y)(x - 2y)$

23. $(2x + 3)(3x - 2)$

24. $\left(\dfrac{1}{2}x + 1\right)(x + 4)$

Solve each literal equation for the indicated variable. [2-1A]

25. $A = \dfrac{1}{2}h(b_1 + b_2)$, for h

26. $V = \dfrac{1}{3}\pi r^2 h$, for h

4-3 ALGEBRAIC STRUCTURES AND FRACTAL GEOMETRY

Use with or after Part 4-3A

Write in factored form. [Previous course]

1. $2x + 2y$ **2.** $3x^2 - 9xy$ **3.** $5a^2b - ab^2$ **4.** $3y^2z - y^2$

Graph the following inequalities on a coordinate system. [3-2A]

5. $y < x + 2$ **6.** $x \geq -3$ **7.** $x + y > 4$ **8.** $2 < x < 4$
      $y < -x + 5$ $y < 2$ $y \leq 2x - 3$

Use with or after Part 4-3B

**Use the matrices below to find each product matrix, if possible.
If not possible, explain why not. [1-3B]**

$$W = \begin{bmatrix} -1 \\ -3 \end{bmatrix} \quad X = [-2 \quad 3] \quad Y = \begin{bmatrix} 4 & -2 \\ 1 & 2 \end{bmatrix} \quad Z = \begin{bmatrix} 2 & 3 & -1 \\ 3 & -5 & 2 \end{bmatrix}$$

9. WX **10.** WY **11.** W^2 **12.** YZ

13. XW **14.** XZ **15.** YW **16.** Y^2

Give a formula for the nth term of each arithmetic sequence. [4-1A]

17. $-6, 0, 6, 12, \ldots$ **18.** $\dfrac{-1}{2}, \dfrac{-3}{2}, \dfrac{-5}{2}, \dfrac{-7}{2}, \ldots$

19. $1.7, 2.6, 3.5, 4.4, \ldots$ **20.** $-11, -13, -15, -17, \ldots$

21. $18, 25, 32, 39, \ldots$ **22.** $50, 45, 40, 35, \ldots$

23. $8, 18, 28, 38, \ldots$ **24.** $6.3, 6.7, 7.1, 7.5, \ldots$

Use with or after Part 4-3C

Graph each inequality. [2-3C]

25. $y < -x + 3$ **26.** $y - 2x \leq 1$ **27.** $y + 3x > -2$ **28.** $y < x$
29. $y < |x|$ **30.** $y \leq |x - 2|$ **31.** $y \geq 2|x|$ **32.** $y \leq -|3x|$

**Write each system as a matrix equation $AX = B$. Solve using matrices, if possible.
If not possible, describe the system. [3-1C]**

33. $y - x = 2$ **34.** $3x = 4 + y$ **35.** $7x + 6y = 8$
      $x + y = 8$ $4.5x - 1.5y = -6$ $-2x - 3y = -1$

36. $2x + 4y = -21$ **37.** $3x - 2y = 4$ **38.** $y = x - 1$
      $y = -9 - 3x$ $x = 8 - 3y$ $y - 2 = -3x$

Use with or after Part 4-3D

Solve each system of equations. [3-1D]

39. $x = 2$ **40.** $x + y = 2$ **41.** $x + y + z = 4$
      $x + y = 5$ $x + y + 3z = 0$ $2x + y = 0$
      $x + y + z = 6$ $2x + y = 3$ $3x - 2y = 1$

42. $2x - 3y + z = 1$ **43.** $2x + 2y - z = 2$ **44.** $4x + y + 2z = 3$
      $x + 2y - z = 6$ $3x + y + 2z = 22$ $2x + 3y + z = 6$
      $-x + 4y + z = 20$ $x - y + 2z = 10$ $2x - 3z = -12$

CHAPTER 5 QUADRATIC FUNCTIONS AND RELATIONS

5-1 QUADRATIC FUNCTIONS

Use with or after Part 5-1A

Graph each system of inequalities on a coordinate plane. [3-2A]

1. $x > 2$
$y > -3$

2. $y \geq x$
$x \leq 3$

3. $x > 0$
$y < 0$

4. $x + y > 3$
$x - y < 6$

Solve. [4-3B]

5. $x^2 = 25$

6. $2x^2 = 18$

7. $\dfrac{x^2}{2} = 18$

8. $3x^2 + 5 = 17$

9. $x^2 = 6$

10. $25x^2 = 36$

11. $2x^2 - 6 = 4$

12. $\dfrac{3}{4}x^2 = \dfrac{1}{3}$

Use with or after Part 5-1B

Solve each system of equations. [3-1B]

13. $x + y = 10$
$x - y = 4$

14. $2x + y = 11$
$3x + y = 16$

15. $x + y = 0$
$x - y = 4$

16. $x + 2y = 8$
$x - 2y = 4$

For each arithmetic sequence, find the next term, common difference, and 101st term. [4-1B]

17. 4, 9, 14, 19, …

18. 3, 11, 19, 27, …

19. 0.8, 1.0, 1.2, 1.4, …

20. $-7, -9, -11, -13, \ldots$ **21.** 12, 7, 2, -3, …

22. $\dfrac{1}{3}, -\dfrac{2}{3}, -\dfrac{5}{3}, -\dfrac{8}{3}, \ldots$

Use with or after Part 5-1C

Factor. [Previous course]

23. $x^2 - 9$

24. $x^2 - 144$

25. $4x^2 - 9$

26. $16x^2 - 81$

27. $x^2 - y^2$

28. $36x^2 - y^2$

29. $49x^2 - 121y^2$

30. $25x^3 - 36x$

Give an equation for each line. [2-1C]

31. slope = 3, y-intercept = -2

32. slope = -2, contains (3, 4)

33. contains (0, 3) and (1, 6)

34. contains (2, 5) and (4, 11)

35. contains (4, 6), parallel to $y = 2x$

36. contains (2, 3), perpendicular to $y = \dfrac{1}{2}x + 1$

37. slope = -2, y-intercept = 0

38. slope = 0, contains (3, -2)

Use with or after Part 5-1D

Solve. [2-1B]

39. $7c = 10 + 2c$

40. $2h - 6 = h + 1$

41. $3(2x + 1) = 21$

42. $5a - 2(a + 1) = 10$

43. $0.5x - 30 = 1.1x$

44. $\dfrac{3}{4}x - 2 = \dfrac{3}{2}x$

45. $\dfrac{x}{3} + \dfrac{1}{4} = 6$

46. $9x - 6(x - 1) = 36$

Give the sum. [4-1B]

47. $\displaystyle\sum_{n=1}^{5} (3n)$

48. $\displaystyle\sum_{n=1}^{10} (n + 1)$

49. $\displaystyle\sum_{n=1}^{12} (2n - 1)$

50. $\displaystyle\sum_{n=1}^{20} (4n - 1)$

5-2 SOLVING QUADRATIC EQUATIONS

Use with or after Part 5-2A

Tell whether each sequence is geometric. If so, give the common ratio. [4-2A]

1. 10, 20, 40, 80, ...

2. 2, 4, 6, 8, ...

3. 500, 100, 20, 4, ...

4. $\frac{1}{2}, \frac{1}{4}, \frac{1}{8}, \frac{1}{16}, \ldots$

5. 1, −1, 1, −1, ...

6. $\frac{1}{3}, \frac{1}{6}, \frac{1}{9}, \frac{1}{12}, \ldots$

7. 4, 8, 12, 16, ...

8. $10^8, 10^7, 10^6, 10^5, \ldots$

Simplify. [4-3B, 4-3C]

9. $-\sqrt{-81}$

10. $\pm\sqrt{12}$

11. $\sqrt{-50}$

12. $2i\sqrt{-54}$

13. $3\sqrt{36}$

14. $-\sqrt{48}$

15. $\sqrt{16} + \sqrt{9}$

16. $\sqrt{16 + 9}$

Use with or after Part 5-2B

Find the degree of each polynomial expression. [Previous course]

17. $2x^3 + 5x$

18. $x^5 - 3x$

19. $x + 4$

20. $7 + 3x^2 - 6x^3$

21. $4(x)(x^2)$

22. $(x^2 - 2) + (x + 1)$

23. $3x^3 - (x + 3x^3)$

24. $(x^3)^2$

Find the centroid and median-median line of fit. [2-2B]

25. $A(0, 1)$, $B(6, 8)$, $C(12, 0)$

26. $X(1, 6)$, $Y(3, 10)$, $Z(8, 2)$

27. $T(9, 0)$, $U(10, 0)$, $V(20, -3)$

28. $D(-4, -2)$, $E(9, -6)$, $F(4, 5)$

29. $J(-1, 1)$, $K(0, 0)$, $L(1, 1)$

30. $P(50, 38)$, $Q(75, 42)$, $R(100, 50)$

Use with or after Part 5-2C

Find the slope. [2-1A]

31. $y = 2x + 3$

32. $y = -x + 1$

33. $y = 3$

34. $x = 2$

35. $3x + y = 2$

36. a line parallel to $y = 2x$

37. a line perpendicular to $y = 3x + 1$

Solve. [2-1B, 2-3C, 5-2B]

38. $x^2 = 9$

39. $x^2 - 4 = 0$

40. $3x(2x - 1) = 6x + 15$

41. $x^2 + 3x + 2 = 0$

42. $2x^2 + 3x - 2 = 0$

43. $|3x - 1| = 6$

Use with or after Part 5-2D

State whether the equation represents a *linear* function. If so, write the slope. [2-1A]

44. $y = 2x + 1$

45. $f(x) = x^2$

46. $f(x) = x - 7$

47. $f(x) = \frac{x}{2} + 3$

48. $3x + 2y = 6$

49. $y = 0.2x + 1$

50. $y = 3x(x)$

51. $x + \frac{y}{3} = 7$

Factor. [5-2D]

52. $x^2 - 3x + 2$

53. $2x^2 - x - 6$

54. $x^2 - 4$

55. $x^2 + 6x + 9$

56. $6x^2 + 11x + 4$

57. $10x^2 + 11x - 6$

58. $25x^2 - y^2$

59. $16x^2 - 81y^2$

60. $2x^2 + 7x + 3$

61. $6x^2 + x - 1$

62. $5x^2 - 8x - 4$

63. $12x^2 + 17x + 6$

5-3 CONIC SECTIONS

Use with or after Part 5-3A

Give the reciprocal of the given number. [Previous course]

1. 7   **2.** $-4\frac{1}{2}$ **3.** $\frac{2}{3}$ **4.** -1

5. x **6.** $\frac{1}{x}, (x \neq 0)$ **7.** $\frac{x}{2}$ **8.** $-x$

Solve for x. [2-1B, 2-3A, 2-3B, 4-3B]

9. $2\sqrt{x} = 20$ **10.** $\sqrt{5x} = 8$ **11.** $6x^2 = 72$

12. $9x^2 = 441$ **13.** $8 > -|x| + 6$ **14.** $|-4x + 1| = 12$

15. $|3 - x| < 1$ **16.** $3|x| = -15$

Use with or after Part 5-3B

Give a formula for the nth term of each geometric sequence. [4-2A]

17. 2, 6, 18, 48, ...   **18.** 0.1, 0.01, 0.001, 0.0001, ...

19. 4, −8, 16, −32, ...   **20.** 1, 2, 4, 8, ...

21. 100, 20, 4, 0.8, ...   **22.** 3, −3, 3, −3, ...

23. $\frac{8}{9}, \frac{2}{3}, \frac{1}{2}, \frac{3}{8}, ...$ **24.** 11, 5.5, 2.75, 1.375, ...

Use with or after Part 5-3C

Simplify. [4-3B, 4-3C]

25. $\sqrt{0.36}$ **26.** $\sqrt{121(x + y)^2}$ **27.** $\sqrt{\frac{36}{25}}$

28. $\sqrt{\frac{-12}{-3}}$ **29.** $-\sqrt{14}$ **30.** $i\sqrt{50} + \sqrt{-98}$

5-4 QUADRATIC SYSTEMS

Use with or after Part 5-4A

Solve. [2-1B, 2-3B]

1. $|x| = 3$ **2.** $2|x| = 10$ **3.** $|x| - 3 = 6$

4. $3|x + 2| = 8$ **5.** $|x - 3| = 5$ **6.** $|5 - x| = 11$

7. $2|x - 6| = 18$ **8.** $3|x - 2| + 6 = 24$ **9.** $8x = 23 + 3(2x - 5)$

Find the absolute value of each number. [2-3B, 4-3D]

10. $|-7|$ **11.** $|6i|$ **12.** $|5 - 2i|$ **13.** $|3 - 4i|$

14. $|5 + 12i|$ **15.** $|5 - 12|$ **16.** $|5 - 12i|$ **17.** $\left|-\left(-\frac{2}{3}\right)\right|$

Use with or after Part 5-4B

Find the greatest common factor of the pair of monomials. [Previous course]

18. $8x, 12x$ **19.** $7, 14y$ **20.** $10x^2, 15xy$

21. $4c^2, 6c^3$ **22.** $30x^2y, 90xy^2$ **23.** $5fg, 12gh$

24. $18x^2yz^3, 36xy^2z^2$ **25.** $7xy, 11yz$

Graph. [2-3C]

26. $y > |x - 2|$ **27.** $y \geq -x + 1$ **28.** $y < -|x|$ **29.** $y < -3$

30. $y + 3 \leq |-8|$ **31.** $y \geq |2x| + 1$ **32.** $y = |x + 1|$ **33.** $y < -3|x| + 2$

CHAPTER 6 COUNTING AND ARRANGING DISCRETE OBJECTS

6-1 COUNTING OBJECTS AND PERMUTATIONS

Use with or after Part 6-1A

Write each series in sigma notation and give its sum. [4-1B]

1. $6, 11, 16, 21, \ldots, 51$
2. $-4, -1, 2, 5, \ldots, 59$
3. $0.7, 0.65, 0.6, \ldots, 0$
4. $-14, -10, -6, \ldots, 38$
5. $11, 8, 5, 2, \ldots, -10$
6. $32, 28, 24, \ldots, 0$

Complete the square to find the vertex and line of symmetry of the graph of each function. [5-1C]

7. $y = x^2 + 8x$
8. $f(x) = x^2 - 20x - 60$
9. $g(x) = x^2 - 7x + 8$

Use with or after Part 6-1B

Simplify each expression. [4-3C]

10. $4i \cdot 4i$
11. $\sqrt{-7}\sqrt{-21}$
12. $i\sqrt{-9}$

13. $\sqrt{-8}\sqrt{6}$
14. $\sqrt{-\dfrac{49}{64}}$
15. $(2i)(3i)$

16. $(5 - i) - (i + 5)$
17. $(7 + 2i)(3 - 5i)$

Solve each equation using the Principle of Zero Products. If the equation cannot be solved by factoring, say so. [5-2B]

18. $x^2 - 4x + 4 = 0$
19. $x^2 + 7x + 12 = 0$
20. $x^2 + x - 30 = 0$
21. $3x^2 + 13x - 10 = 0$
22. $x^2 + 4x - 4 = 0$
23. $2x^2 + x - 4 = 0$

6-2 COMBINATIONS AND THE BINOMIAL THEOREM

Use with or after Part 6-2A

Write each geometric series in sigma notation and find its sum. [4-2B]

1. $1, -3, 9, -27, 81, -243$
2. $1, \dfrac{2}{3}, \dfrac{4}{9}, \dfrac{8}{27}, \dfrac{16}{81}$
3. $\dfrac{3}{4}, \dfrac{1}{2}, \dfrac{1}{3}, \dfrac{2}{9}, \dfrac{4}{27}$

Evaluate each expression. [6-1A]

4. $\dfrac{4!}{2!0!}$
5. $7! - 5!$
6. $\dfrac{7!}{5!}$
7. $\dfrac{6!}{(5 - 3)!}$

Use with or after Part 6-2B

Simplify each expression. [Previous course, 4-3B, 4-3C]

8. $\sqrt{(-6)^2}$
9. $-35 - (-18)$
10. $\dfrac{\sqrt{-20}}{\sqrt{-4}}$

11. $\sqrt{-49m^2}$
12. $-|-5|$
13. $42a^2b^3 \div (-7a^{-3}b^{-2})$

Find the distance between each pair of points. Express your answers as decimal approximations rounded to the nearest hundredth. [5-3A]

14. $(-4, 1), (0, 7)$
15. $(2.3, 3.7), (4.5, 2.1)$
16. $(-0.1, -0.25), (3.1, -1.4)$

CHAPTER 7 INVESTIGATING ROOTS AND POWERS

7-1 VARIATION AND INTEGRAL EXPONENT POWERS

Use with or after Part 7-1A

Give the common difference and next term of the arithmetic series. [4-1A]

1. $3, 6, 9, 12, \ldots$
2. $-5, -8, -11, -14, \ldots$
3. $\frac{1}{2}, 1, \frac{3}{2}, 2, \ldots$
4. $-7, -4, -1, 2, \ldots$
5. $24, 9, -6, -21, \ldots$
6. $2.3, 1.6, 0.9, 0.2, \ldots$

Find the number of *different* arrangements. [6-1B]

7. 3 letters followed by 3 digits
8. answers to 6 true-false questions

Use with or after Part 7-1B

For each quadratic function, find the vertex of its graph. [5-1C]

9. $f(x) = 2(x - 3)^2 + 2$
10. $g(x) = 5(x + 2)^2 + 9$
11. $h(x) = -3(x - 2)^2 - 5$
12. $h(x) = 3x^2 - 4$
13. $f(t) = -\frac{1}{3}(t - 3)^2 - 8$
14. $f(x) = \frac{2}{3}x^2 + 5$
15. $f(x) = m(x - n)^2 + p$
16. $k(t) = mt^2 - n$

Complete the square. [5-1D]

17. $x^2 + 4x +$ ___
18. $m^2 + 14m +$ ___
19. $y^2 - 6y +$ ___
20. $x^2 + 3x +$ ___
21. $c^2 + 8c +$ ___
22. $x^2 + 1x +$ ___
23. $y^2 - 5y +$ ___
24. $m^2 + 0.2m +$ ___

Use with or after Part 7-1C

Write an equation in the form $y = ax^2$ that contains each point. [5-1B]

25. $(2, 2)$
26. $(1, -3)$
27. $(-2, 16)$
28. $(5, -50)$
29. $(1, -5)$
30. $(2, 20)$
31. $(-2, -2)$
32. $(-4, 32)$

Evaluate each expression. [6-1B]

33. $_5P_3$
34. $_7P_6$
35. $_4P_2$
36. $_7P_2$
37. $_6P_6$
38. $_{10}P_2$
39. $_3P_3$
40. $_{15}P_4$

7-2 ROOTS, RADICALS, AND RATIONAL EXPONENTS

Use with or after Part 7-2A

Give a formula for the *n*th term of each geometric sequence. [4-2A]

1. $1, -1, 1, -1, \ldots$
2. $-7, 28, -112, 448, \ldots$
3. $10, 12, 14.4, 17.28, \ldots$

Rewrite each quadratic equation in standard form. [5-2A]

4. $x(x + 2) - 6 = 0$
5. $(3x - 1)(x + 5) = 7$
6. $7x(x + 2) = 5x^2 + 1$

Expand. [6-2B]

7. $(x + 3)^4$
8. $(x - 2)^3$
9. $(m + n)^5$
10. $(3x + 1)^4$
11. $(4 + x)^3$
12. $(3x - 5)^5$
13. $\left(x - \frac{1}{2}\right)^3$
14. $(x + 0.7)^4$

Use with or after Part 7-2B

Give each sum. [4-2B]

15. the first 10 terms of $4 + 8 + 16 + \cdots$

16. the first 6 terms of $3 + 9 + 27 + \cdots$

17. $1 + 4 + 16 + \cdots + 4096$ **18.** $1 + \dfrac{1}{2} + \dfrac{1}{4} + \dfrac{1}{8} + \dfrac{1}{16}$

Solve each equation by factoring. [5-2B]

19. $x^2 + 5x - 14 = 0$ **20.** $x^2 - 8x + 15 = 0$ **21.** $3x^2 - 10x - 8 = 0$

22. $6x^2 - 17x + 5 = 0$ **23.** $12x^2 + 25x = 7$ **24.** $x^2 = 4$

Use with or after Part 7-2C

Determine whether each geometric series converges. [4-2C]

25. $36 + 12 + 4 + \ldots$ **26.** $5 + 25 + 125 + \ldots$ **27.** $100 + 50 + 25 + \ldots$

Solve using the quadratic formula. Leave answers in exact form. [5-2C]

28. $2x^2 + 9x - 5 = 0$ **29.** $2x^2 - 3x - 4 = 0$ **30.** $x^2 - 5x - 2 = 0$

31. $x^2 + 12 = 7x$ **32.** $5x^2 - 3x = 2$ **33.** $3x^2 - x = 1$

Give the coordinates of the center of each circle. [5-3A]

34. $(x + 2)^2 + y^2 = 9$ **35.** $(x - 3)^2 + (y + 2)^2 = 36$

36. $(x - 3)^2 + (y - 2)^2 = 100$

Use with or after Part 7-2D

For each table, write an equation relating x and y. [1-1B]

37.

x	1	2	3	4
y	$\frac{1}{2}$	1	$\frac{3}{2}$	2

38.

x	0	1	2	3
y	1	3	5	7

39.

x	0	1	2	3	4
y	-1	1	3	5	7

40.

x	0	1	2	3	4
y	5	8	11	14	17

41.

x	0	1	2	3
y	-4	-2	0	2

42.

x	1	2	3	4
y	1	5	9	13

7-3 COMBINING FUNCTIONS

Use with or after Part 7-3A

Write an equation for each circle in standard form. [5-3A]

1. center $(3, -4)$, radius 3   **2.** center $(-4, -7)$, radius $\dfrac{1}{2}$

3. center $(-1, -3)$, radius $\sqrt{5}$ **4.** center $(0, 0)$, containing $(3, 4)$

5. center $(0, 0)$, containing $(5, 12)$ **6.** center $(2, -3)$, containing $(4, 6)$

Find the number of zeros of each function. [5-2A]

7. $x^2 - 3x + 4 = 0$ **8.** $3x^2 = 2$

9. $2x^2 = 12x - 18$ **10.** $(5n + 1)(2n + 1) = 2$

11. $5x^2 - 8x + 3 = 0$ **12.** $x^2 + 5x = 3$

13. $3x(4x - 2) + (3 - 2x^2) = 5$

Use with or after Part 7-3B

Solve and graph each equation or inequality. [2-3B]

14. $|x| = 4$ **15.** $|x - 2| = 3$ **16.** $|-3x| = 6$

17. $|6 - 2x| = 10$ **18.** $|x| > 3$ **19.** $|x - 6| \geq 1$

Give the coordinates of the foci of each ellipse. [5-3B]

20. $\dfrac{x^2}{16} + \dfrac{y^2}{9} = 1$ **21.** $\dfrac{x^2}{9} + \dfrac{y^2}{16} = 1$ **22.** $\dfrac{x^2}{16} + \dfrac{y^2}{36} = 1$ **23.** $\dfrac{x^2}{100} + \dfrac{y^2}{64} = 1$

Evaluate each expression. [6-1B]

24. $_5P_2$ **25.** $_{10}P_4$ **26.** $_5P_5$ **27.** $_8P_5$

Use with or after Part 7-3C

Complete each equation. [5-1D]

28. $x^2 + 12x + \underline{\quad} = (x + 6)^2$ **29.** $x^2 - 10x + \underline{\quad} = (x - 5)^2$

30. $x^2 + \underline{\quad} + 16 = (x + 4)^2$ **31.** $x^2 + \underline{\quad} + y^2 = (x + y)^2$

32. $x^2 - \underline{\quad} + 121 = (x - 11)^2$ **33.** $x^2 + x + \underline{\quad} = \left(x + \dfrac{1}{2}\right)^2$

34. $x^2 + \underline{\quad} + \dfrac{1}{25} = \left(x + \dfrac{1}{5}\right)^2$ **35.** $x^2 - \underline{\quad} + 4y^2 = (x - 2y)^2$

CHAPTER 8 POLYNOMIALS AND POLYNOMIAL FUNCTIONS

8-1 POLYNOMIAL FUNCTIONS AND THEIR GRAPHS

Use with or after Part 8-1A

Solve each linear system using either substitution or linear combination methods. [3-1B]

1. $18x + 12y = 96$ **2.** $x = 2y + 4$ **3.** $5x = 3y - 7$ **4.** $\dfrac{x}{2} - \dfrac{y}{5} = 1$

  $1.5x + y = 8$ $2x - 5y = 7$ $4x = -9y + 3$ $\dfrac{x}{6} - \dfrac{y}{7} = 1$

Find each constant of variation when y varies ... [7-1A]

5. directly with x, and $y = 18$ when $x = 3$.

6. inversely with x, and $y = 7$ when $x = 13$.

7. directly with x, and $y = 25$ when $x = 12$.

8. inversely with a, and $y = 12$ when $a = 60$.

Use with or after Part 8-1B

Solve each equation. Check your solution. [2-1B]

9. $8(4 + 3(x - 2)) = 2(8x + 3) - 25$ **10.** $12(3x - 5) = 8(5 - 2(x + 4))$

11. $5(t - 3) + 1 = 3t - 3(7 - t)$ **12.** $3(-8x - 5(3 - 4x) + 10) = 6x + 15$

Write each arithmetic series in sigma notation and find its sum. [4-1B]

13. $-1 + 5 + 11 + 17 + \cdots + 53$ **14.** $1 - 3 - 7 - 11 - \cdots - 39$

15. $-0.6 - 1.9 - 3.2 - \cdots - 13.6$ **16.** $2 + 5 + 8 + \cdots + 143$

Use with
or after
Part 8-1C

Write a quadratic function of the form $f(x) = a(x + h)^2 + k$
for each parabola. [5-1C]

17. vertex $(4, 3)$ and $a = -2$ **18.** vertex $(-1, 1)$ and $a = 0.5$

19. vertex $(2, -3)$ and $a = \dfrac{1}{2}$ **20.** vertex $(1, 2)$ and $a = 3$

Simplify. Write answers without negative exponents. [7-1C]

21. $(a^{-2}b)^2$ **22.** $\dfrac{x^4(xy^{-2}z^2)^{-2}}{x^{-3}y^2}$ **23.** $\dfrac{(3^2 \cdot 5^0 \cdot 2^{-3})^{-1}}{2^2 \cdot 3^{-3} \cdot 5^{-2}}$

24. $\dfrac{x^2y^3x}{y^3 \cdot y^{-3}}$ **25.** $\dfrac{x^3(y^2m)^{-2}}{(xy^2)^{-3}m^2}$ **26.** $\dfrac{(ab^5)^2c^{-3}}{(a^2b^3c)^{-1}}$

8-2 THE FUNDAMENTAL THEOREM OF ALGEBRA

Use with
or after
Part 8-2A

Give the complex conjugate of each number. [4-3D]

1. $2 + i$ **2.** $-3 + 2i$ **3.** 7 **4.** $6 - 3i$

For each pair of functions, find $f(g(x))$ and $g(f(x))$. [7-3B]

5. $f(x) = x + 3$ **6.** $f(x) = x^2$ **7.** $f(x) = 5x$ **8.** $f(x) = \dfrac{x + 3}{2}$

    $g(x) = -x$ $g(x) = x - 2$ $g(x) = 4x - 2$ $g(x) = 2x - 1$

Find the zeros of each function. Tell what method you used. [8-1C]

9. $f(x) = x^2 - x - 6$ **10.** $f(x) = x^4 - 10x^2 + 21$

11. $f(x) = 6x^3 - 12x^2 - 90x$

Use with
or after
Part 8-2B

Evaluate each expression. Where necessary, round answers to the
nearest hundredth. [7-2B]

12. $\left(\dfrac{3}{16}\right)^{\frac{1}{5}}$ **13.** $48^{\frac{2}{3}}$ **14.** $72.3^{1.03}$ **15.** $0^{5.623}$

16. $2.79^{3.25}$ **17.** $27^{\frac{4}{3}}$ **18.** $7.8^{0.7} \cdot 7.8^{1.3}$ **19.** $1^{7.3}$

Find the inverse of each function. [7-3C]

20. $f(x) = x - 2$ **21.** $f(x) = x^3 - 1$ **22.** $f(x) = 3x + 1$ **23.** $f(x) = 7 + x^5$

24. $f(x) = (x - 1)^3$ **25.** $f(x) = \dfrac{1}{x + 2}$ **26.** $f(x) = \sqrt{x - 1}$ **27.** $f(x) = \dfrac{-3}{x}$

Use with
or after
Part 8-2C

Use the discriminant to determine the number and nature of the roots
of each quadratic equation. [5-2D]

28. $2x^2 - 5x + 3 = 0$ **29.** $4x^2 + 23x - 6 = 0$ **30.** $1 + 2x + 3x^2 = 0$

31. $4x^2 - 12x + 9 = 0$ **32.** $x^2 - 2x + 15 = 0$ **33.** $35x^2 - 10x + 1 = 0$

Solve each equation. [7-2D]

34. $x + 3\sqrt{x - 2} = 0$ **35.** $\sqrt{3x - 2} = 5$

36. $\sqrt{3x + 7} - \sqrt{x - 2} = \sqrt{3x}$ **37.** $\sqrt{x + 2} - \sqrt{x} = 1$

38. $\sqrt{2x - 1} - \sqrt{x - 1} = 1$ **39.** $\sqrt{x} - \sqrt{x - 5} = 2$

8-3 RATIONAL EXPRESSIONS AND FUNCTIONS

Give each sum. [4-1B, 4-2B]

1. $\displaystyle\sum_{n=1}^{8} (7 - 5n)$

2. $\displaystyle\sum_{n=1}^{6} 3^n$

3. $\displaystyle\sum_{n=2}^{7} (4n + 3)$

4. $\displaystyle\sum_{n=1}^{4} 125(-0.125)^n$

Let $f(x) = 5x - 2$ and $g(x) = (x - 1)^2$. Find each value or expression. [7-3B]

5. $f(g(-2))$

6. $(g \circ f)(x)$

7. $f(f(3))$

8. $g(f(-7))$

9. $g(g(0))$

10. $(f \circ g)(a^2)$

11. $g(f(0.2))$

12. $f(g(\sqrt{x}))$

Simplify each expression. [4-3C]

13. $\sqrt{108}$

14. $-8\sqrt{-12}$

15. $-3\sqrt{6} \cdot 2\sqrt{54}$

16. $\sqrt{169 - 25}$

17. $|7 - 3i|$

18. $|-18i|$

19. $|-3 + 4i|$

20. $|-7|$

Solve each equation. Leave answers in exact form. [5-2C]

21. $x^2 + 8x - 4 = 0$

22. $3x^2 + 6x - 11 = 0$

23. $-2t^2 + 40t - 3 = 0$

24. $x^2 + 6x + 8 = 0$

25. $3x^2 - 4x - 2 = 0$

26. $x^2 + 2x + 3 = 0$

27. $3x^2 - 2x = 1$

28. $x^2 = x - 1$

Write an equation for each circle in standard form. Then state the center and radius of the circle. [5-3A]

29. $x^2 + y^2 + 8y = 0$

30. $4x^2 + 4y^2 - 80 = 0$

31. $2x^2 + 2y^2 - 50 = 0$

32. $x^2 - 6x + y^2 = 9$

33. $x^2 - 7x + y^2 + 11y = -26.5$

34. $x^2 + 10x + y^2 = 119$

Expand. [6-2B]

35. $(x - 2)^8$

36. $(x + y)^5$

37. $(5 + y)^4$

38. $(3x - 1)^7$

39. $(x + 2)^6$

40. $(3x - 2)^8$

41. $(x - y)^2$

42. $(x^2 - y^2)^3$

Use the matrices below to find each of the following, if possible. If not possible, explain why not. [1-3A, 1-3B]

$$A = \begin{bmatrix} 3 & 1 & 1 \\ 2 & 0 & -1 \\ 2 & 2 & 3 \end{bmatrix} \quad B = \begin{bmatrix} 0 & 1 & 0 \\ 1 & -1 & 1 \\ 1 & 2 & 2 \end{bmatrix} \quad C = \begin{bmatrix} -1 & 0 & 2 \\ 1 & 1 & 1 \end{bmatrix} \quad D = \begin{bmatrix} 1 & 1 \\ 0 & -1 \\ 2 & 1 \end{bmatrix}$$

43. $A + B$

44. $3C$

45. $C - D$

46. $2B - A$

47. BC

48. BD

49. CB

50. DC

Find the zeros of each function. [8-2A]

51. $f(x) = 2x^2 + 11x + 12$

52. $f(x) = x^4 - 10x^2 + 9$

53. $f(x) = x^4 - 8x^2 + 16$

CHAPTER 9 EXPONENTIAL AND LOGARITHMIC FUNCTIONS

9-1 EXPONENTIAL PATTERNS AND GROWTH

Use with or after Part 9-1A

Simplify. Write answers with positive exponents. [7-1C]

1. $3x^{-2}y^{-3}$
2. $(2x^{-2}y)^{-3}$
3. $(x^3y^{-2})^2$
4. $(-9x^2y^3)^{-1}$
5. $x^{25} \cdot x^{-10}$
6. $25x(-10x)$

Find the zeros of the function. [8-1C]

7. $f(x) = 6x^2 + 11x + 3$
8. $f(p) = 3p^2 + 2p - 1$
9. $f(x) = 3x^2 - 14x + 8$

Use with or after Part 9-1B

Simplify each expression. [4-3B]

10. $\sqrt{27m^3}$
11. $\sqrt{3}(\sqrt{6a} + \sqrt{15a})$
12. $\dfrac{36\sqrt{72}}{9\sqrt{12}}$
13. $\sqrt{32} - \sqrt{8} + \sqrt{18}$
14. $-\sqrt{6x^2}$
15. $2\sqrt{3} - 4\sqrt{5} + \sqrt{45} - \sqrt{75}$

Solve each equation. Indicate any necessary restrictions. [8-3D]

16. $1 = \dfrac{-1}{x - 4}$
17. $\dfrac{2}{4 - x} = \dfrac{3}{x^2 - 16}$
18. $\dfrac{x^2 + 3}{x + 1} + x + 1 = x + 3$

Use with or after Part 9-1C

Give an equation for each line or function. [2-1C]

19. slope is 1.5 and contains $(-6, 3)$
20. contains $(-1, -4)$ and $(-2, -1)$
21. has y-intercept -5 and slope -2
22. contains $(3, 4)$ and $(-2, 3)$

Solve each system of equations symbolically. [5-4A, 5-4B]

23. $x^2 + y^2 = 4$
$2x^2 + 2y^2 = 10$
24. $x^2 - y^2 = 1$
$x^2 + y^2 = 1$
25. $x^2 + y^2 = 25$
$y^2 = (x - 1)^2$
26. $y = x^2 - 3x$
$y = 2x$
27. $y - 4 = x^2$
$x^2 + y^2 = 16$
28. $2x + y = 3$
$4x^2 + y^2 = 5$
29. $y = x - 1$
$x^2 + y^2 = 9$
30. $y = 2x^2 + 1$
$y = -x^2 + 4$

Use with or after Part 9-1D

Find the distance between each pair of points. Round to the nearest hundredth. [5-3A]

31. $(3, 4)$ and $(12, 13)$
32. $(-2, 5.1)$ and $(1.2, -1)$
33. $(13, 14)$ and $(-7, 14)$
34. $(-2, -5)$ and $(6, 11)$
35. $(5, 11)$ and $(4, -7)$
36. $(3.1, 5.3)$ and $(-2.1, 1.4)$

Solve each equation. [7-2D]

37. $x - 8\sqrt{x} + 15 = 0$
38. $x - 5\sqrt{x} + 6 = 0$
39. $x - 2\sqrt{x} - 15 = 0$
40. $x + \sqrt{x} + 1 = 0$
41. $\sqrt[3]{x^2} - 2.2\sqrt[3]{x} - 4.2 = 0$
42. $x^8 - 77x^4 - 324 = 0$

9-2 LOGARITHMIC FUNCTIONS

Use with
or after
Part 9-2A

Solve each equation using the Principle of Zero Products.
If the equation cannot be solved by factoring, say so. [5-2B]

1. $2x^2 - 11x + 15 = 0$ **2.** $6x^2 + 5x - 4 = 0$
3. $7x^2 - 22x + 3 = 0$ **4.** $3x^2 + 13x - 30 = 0$

Let $h(x) = 3x + 2$ and $g(x) = 2x - 5$. Find each value or expression. [7-3A]

5. $(h + g)(-1)$ **6.** $(g - h)(0)$ **7.** $(g + h)(2)$ **8.** $h(-5)$
9. $(h \cdot g)(1)$ **10.** $h(-3) + g(-2)$ **11.** $(h - g)(2)$ **12.** $(g \cdot h)(-3)$

Use with
or after
Part 9-2B

Expand. [6-2B]

13. $(x + 3)^5$ **14.** $(2x - 1)^6$ **15.** $(3x - 2)^4$ **16.** $(x - 1)^7$
17. $(x - 6)^4$ **18.** $(x + y)^5$ **19.** $(5 - y)^5$ **20.** $(2 - x)^6$

Find the roots of each polynomial equation. [8-2C]

21. $x^3 - 5x^2 + 6x = 0$ **22.** $x^3 - 10x^2 + 31x - 30 = 0$
23. $2x^3 - 3x^2 - 39x + 20 = 0$ **24.** $4x^3 + 7x^2 - 21x - 18 = 0$
25. $6x^3 - 7x^2 - 14x + 15 = 0$ **26.** $2x^3 - 13x^2 + 10x + 25 = 0$

Use with
or after
Part 9-2C

Solve each equation. [4-3B]

27. $\sqrt{x} = 5$ **28.** $3x^2 = 75$ **29.** $\sqrt{2x} = 11$ **30.** $4x^2 = 324$
31. $2\sqrt{x} = 6$ **32.** $\sqrt{2x} = 6$ **33.** $\sqrt{-2x} = 6$ **34.** $2x^2 = 6$

Write an equation in the form $y = ax^2$ that contains each point. [5-1B]

35. $(1, 1)$ **36.** $(2, -28)$ **37.** $(-3, -9)$ **38.** $(2, 24)$
39. $(-2, 3)$ **40.** $(3, -2)$ **41.** $(-4, -1)$ **42.** $\left(5, \dfrac{1}{5}\right)$

CHAPTER 10 TRIGONOMETRY

10-1 TRIGONOMETRIC RATIOS

Use with
or after
Part 10-1A

Evaluate. [6-1A]

1. $11!$ **2.** $4 \cdot 5!$ **3.** $\dfrac{8!}{5}$ **4.** $\dfrac{10!}{8!}$

Find each constant of variation when y varies ... [7-1A]

5. directly with x, and $y = 16$ when $x = 2$.
6. inversely with x, and $y = 20$ when $x = 100$.
7. directly with x cubed, and $y = 128$ when $x = 4$.
8. inversely with x, and $y = 3$ when $x = 7$.

Evaluate each expression. [6-1B]

9. $_6P_3$ **10.** $_6P_6$ **11.** $_{20}P_4$ **12.** $_{10}P_9$

Use with or after Part 10-1B

Sketch a graph of each function. [7-1B]

13. $f(x) = -x^2 + 1$ **14.** $f(x) = x^3 + 1$ **15.** $f(x) = 3x^2 - 2$ **16.** $f(x) = -x^5$

Find the inverse of each function. [7-3D]

17. $f(x) = x + 3$ **18.** $f(x) = 8x$ **19.** $f(x) = \frac{2}{3}x$ **20.** $f(x) = 3x + 5$

21. $f(x) = \frac{x}{2}$ **22.** $f(x) = \frac{x + 7}{3}$ **23.** $f(x) = x^5$ **24.** $f(x) = \sqrt[5]{x} + 4$

Use with or after Part 10-1C

Give an equation for each line or function. [2-1C]

25. slope $= \frac{3}{2}$ and contains $(4, 2)$ **26.** $f(3) = 6$ and y-intercept -2

27. contains $(3.5, 1.2)$ and $(2, -4.0)$ **28.** $f(0) = 3$ and x-intercept 4

29. contains $(2, 3)$ and perpendicular to $y = 4x - 5$

30. contains $(5, -7)$ and parallel to $y = 2x - 7$

Find the zeros of each function. [8-1C]

31. $f(x) = 3x^2 - 2x - 5$ **32.** $f(x) = x^2 + 3x - 5$

33. $f(x) = x^4 - 13x^2 + 36$ **34.** $f(x) = x^5 - 26x^3 + 25x$

35. $f(x) = 6x^3 - x^2 - 15x$ **36.** $f(x) = x^3 - 8x^2 - 65x$

Use with or after Part 10-1D

Given each pair of reflection points on a parabola, find the equation of the line of symmetry. [5-1A]

37. $(-1, 1)$ and $(5, 1)$ **38.** $(3, 5)$ and $(-2, 5)$

39. $(-2, 6)$ and $(-8, 6)$ **40.** $(-5, -2)$ and $(1, -2)$

41. $(3, 2)$ and $(6, 2)$ **42.** $(1.2, -4)$ and $(3.6, -4)$

43. $\left(-\frac{3}{4}, \frac{1}{2}\right)$ and $\left(4\frac{1}{4}, \frac{1}{2}\right)$ **44.** $\left(5, -\frac{3}{2}\right)$ and $\left(-5, -\frac{3}{2}\right)$

Solve each equation. [9-1A]

45. $3^x = 81$ **46.** $4^{x-1} = 4096$ **47.** $16^x = 4$ **48.** $4^x = 8$

49. $125^x = 5$ **50.** $4^{-x} = 256$ **51.** $\left(\frac{1}{3}\right)^x = 243$ **52.** $\left(\frac{2}{5}\right)^x = \frac{25}{4}$

10-2 LAWS OF COSINES AND SINES

Use with or after Part 10-2A

Evaluate each expression. [7-2A]

1. $81^{\frac{1}{2}}$ **2.** $25^{-\frac{1}{2}}$ **3.** $36^{\frac{3}{2}}$ **4.** $81^{\frac{1}{4}} \cdot 81^{\frac{1}{4}}$

5. $(-27)^{\frac{2}{3}}$ **6.** $121^{\frac{3}{2}}$ **7.** $121^{-\frac{1}{2}}$ **8.** $\left(144^{\frac{3}{8}}\right)^{\frac{4}{3}}$

Evaluate each expression. Round to the nearest hundredth. [9-2A]

9. $\log_3 81$ **10.** $\log 45$ **11.** $\log_2 \frac{1}{32}$ **12.** $\ln 6$

13. $\ln e$ **14.** $\log_5 1$ **15.** $\log_{\frac{1}{2}} 81$ **16.** $3 \log_2 16$

Evaluate. If necessary, round to the nearest hundredth. [7-2B]

17. $6^{1.4}$ **18.** $81^{0.5}$ **19.** $3^{2.7}$

20. $1^{12.265}$ **21.** $4^{\frac{4}{5}}$ **22.** $2.6^{1.7}$

Use the given roots to write a simplified polynomial expression arranged with descending powers of x. [8-2B]

23. $x = 3, 1, 0$ **24.** $x = 4, -2, -1$ **25.** $x = \frac{1}{2}, -3, 4$ **26.** $x = 0, 3, -5, 6$

Solve each equation. Round to the nearest hundredth. [9-2B]

27. $10^x = 209$ **28.** $10^{6x} = 251$ **29.** $10^{6x} = 1000$ **30.** $e^x = 2.226$

10-3 TRIGONOMETRIC FUNCTIONS

Simplify each expression. [8-3A]

1. $\dfrac{m^3}{m^2 - 16} \div \dfrac{3m}{m - 4}$ **2.** $\dfrac{6x^3}{5y^2} \div \dfrac{2x^2}{5y^2}$

3. $\dfrac{y^2 - 16}{x - 2} \cdot \dfrac{x^2 - 4}{y + 4}$ **4.** $\dfrac{18x^2y^3}{2x^4y^5}$

In right $\triangle ABC$, the right angle is at C, $AC = 1.2$, and $AB = 1.3$. Find each ratio. [10-1A]

5. $\sin A$ **6.** $\cos B$ **7.** $\cot A$

8. $\sec A$ **9.** $\sin B$ **10.** $\tan A$

Find the composite functions. Use $f(x) = 2x$; $g(x) = x^2$; $h(x) = 2x - 1$; $j(x) = 3x + 2$. [7-3B]

11. $f(g(2))$ **12.** $g(f(2))$ **13.** $h(j(3))$ **14.** $j(h(3))$

The radius and measure of the central angle is given. Find the length of the arc intercepted by the angle. Round to the nearest hundredth. [10-1C]

15. 8 in., $\dfrac{\pi}{4}$ radians **16.** 20 in., $\dfrac{\pi}{2}$ radians **17.** 17.6 cm, 1.5 radians

CHAPTER 11 ADVANCED TECHNIQUES FOR CHANCE AND DATA

11-1 COMPOUND EVENTS

A sheet of paper about 10^{-7} km thick is repeatedly folded. Determine the total thickness of the paper after it is folded in half the indicated number of times. [9-1B]

1. 1 fold **2.** 2 folds **3.** 5 folds **4.** 8 folds

5. 11 folds **6.** 14 folds **7.** 16 folds **8.** 17 folds

Use with or after Part 11-1B

Find the value of an original investment of *P* dollars with an interest rate *r* compounded continuously for *t* = 10 years; use the formula *A* = *Pe*^*rt* for the following values. [9-1D]

9. $P = \$1000, r = 5.5\%$ **10.** $P = \$2000, r = 6.0\%$ **11.** $P = \$1000, r = 11\%$

12. $P = \$2000, r = 11\%$ **13.** $P = \$100, r = 5.5\%$ **14.** $P = \$2000, r = 5.5\%$

The radius of a circle and measure of a central angle are given. Give the length of the arc that is intercepted by the angle. [10-1C]

15. 6 in., $\dfrac{3\pi}{2}$ radians   **16.** 15 cm, 2.3 radians   **17.** 4.3 ft, 80°

18. 14 in., $\dfrac{5\pi}{8}$ radians   **19.** 112 mm, 1.1 radians   **20.** 3 km, 120°

Use with or after Part 11-1C

Give the sum of each arithmetic series. [4-1B]

21. $3 + 9 + 15 + \cdots + 201$

22. $75 + 73 + 71 + \cdots + 1$

23. $1 + 1.1 + 1.2 + \cdots + 10$

24. $1 + 3 + 5 + \cdots + 101$

25. $\dfrac{1}{2} + 1 + \dfrac{3}{2} + 2 + \cdots + 50$

26. $\dfrac{2}{3} + \dfrac{4}{3} + 2 + \dfrac{8}{3} + \dfrac{10}{3} + 4 + \cdots + 12$

Solve each equation. If necessary, round answers to the nearest hundredth. [9-2B]

27. $10^x = 2.5$ **28.** $10^{3x} = 0.125$ **29.** $e^x = 4.2$

30. $e^{3x} = 36$ **31.** $10^x = 0.00043$ **32.** $e^x = 1000$

33. $10^{3x-2} = 10,000$ **34.** $\log x = 2.31$

Find the missing side length(s) for $\triangle YWX$. If necessary, round answers to the nearest tenth. [10-2A, 10-2B]

35. $m\angle W = 76°, x = 12, y = 8$ **36.** $w = 6, m\angle X = 48°, y = 10$

37. $m\angle W = 112°, x = 9, y = 6$ **38.** $w = 7, x = 10, m\angle Y = 60°$

39. $m\angle X = 40°, m\angle Y = 50°, x = 5$ **40.** $m\angle W = 70°, m\angle X = 80°, x = 5$

11-2 SAMPLING METHODS

Use with or after Part 11-2A

Solve each equation. Give answers in exact form. [5-2C]

1. $2x^2 - 17x + 21 = 0$ **2.** $x^2 + 10x + 12 = 0$ **3.** $3x^2 - 13x + 4 = 0$

4. $2x^2 - 11x + 15 = 0$ **5.** $1.3x^2 + 2.1x + 0.7 = 0$ **6.** $3x^2 - 3x - 1 = 0$

Write using only positive exponents. [7-1C]

7. $\dfrac{a^5 y}{a^3 y^3}$ **8.** $\dfrac{15t^{-3}(xy)^{-1}}{x^2 y^{-1}}$ **9.** $\dfrac{a^{-3}b}{a^{-2}b^{-1}}$ **10.** $\dfrac{a^4 b^2 (a^2 b)^{-3}}{ab^2(a^{-3}b)^{-1}}$

Give the amplitude and period of each function. [10-3A]

11. $y = 2 \sin 2x$ **12.** $y = 3 \cos \dfrac{1}{2}x$ **13.** $y = 2 \cos 4x$ **14.** $y = 0.5 \sin \dfrac{1}{2}x$

15. $y = 4 \sin 4x$ **16.** $y = -\cos 5x$ **17.** $y = \dfrac{2}{3} \sin 3x$ **18.** $y = -4 \cos x$

Give each sum. [4-2B]

Use with or after Part 11-2B

19. the first 10 terms of $2 + 4 + 8 + \cdots$

20. the first 20 terms of $2 + 6 + 18 + \cdots$

21. S_6 for the series $1 + 1.1 + 1.21 + \cdots$

22. S_{20} for the series $-2 + 4 - 8 + \cdots$

23. $\displaystyle\sum_{n=1}^{6} 5^n$ **24.** $\displaystyle\sum_{n=1}^{8} \left(\frac{1}{2}\right)^n$

25. $\displaystyle\sum_{n=1}^{9} (-1)^n$ **26.** $\displaystyle\sum_{n=1}^{5} 3^n$

Solve the following equations. [8-2C]

27. $x^3 - 3x - 2 = 0$ **28.** $x^4 + 7x^3 + 9x^2 - 7x - 10 = 0$

29. $2x^3 + 3x^2 - 8x + 3 = 0$ **30.** $2x^4 - 13x^3 + 12x^2 + 17x - 10 = 0$

31. $x^4 - 4x^3 - x^2 + 36x - 72 = 0$ **32.** $2x^3 + 5x^2 - x - 1 = 0$

Solve each equation. If necessary, round answers to the nearest hundredth. [9-2C]

33. $\log x - \log 6 = \log 3$ **34.** $3 \log 2 + 2 \log 5 = \log x$

35. $3 \log x = \log 125$

CHAPTER 12 DISCRETE MATHEMATICS AND MODELS

12-1 GRAPH THEORY

Use with or after Part 12-1A

Let $f(x) = 4^{4-x}$. Evaluate $f(x)$ for each value for x. [9-1A]

1. $f(1)$ **2.** $f(0.2)$ **3.** $f(0)$ **4.** $f(4)$

5. $f(6)$ **6.** $f(1.3)$ **7.** $f(4.5)$ **8.** $f(2x + 3)$

For each angle measure, give an equivalent angle measure between 0° and 360°. [10-1E]

9. $445°$ **10.** $-40°$ **11.** $900°$ **12.** $-740°$

13. $\frac{\pi}{6}$ radians   **14.** $\frac{3\pi}{2}$ radians   **15.** $-\frac{7\pi}{6}$ radians   **16.** $-\frac{3\pi}{4}$ radians

Use with or after Part 12-1B

Find each value or expression. Let $f(x) = 4x - 2$ and $g(x) = x^2 + 3$. [7-3B]

17. $f(3)$ **18.** $f(g(2))$ **19.** $g(f(-2))$ **20.** $(f \circ g)(x)$

21. $(g \circ f)(2)$ **22.** $f(g(-5))$ **23.** $(f \circ g)(2)$ **24.** $f(g(m))$

Convert each angle to radians. [10-1B]

25. $45°$ **26.** $150°$ **27.** $315°$ **28.** $360°$

29. $225°$ **30.** $180°$ **31.** $75°$ **32.** $20°$

Use with
or after
Part 12-1C

Solve each equation. [7-2C]

33. $\sqrt{x} = 1.7$ **34.** $\sqrt{3x + 1} = 4$ **35.** $\sqrt{5x - 1} = 7$ **36.** $\sqrt[3]{x} = 7$

37. $\sqrt{x} = \dfrac{1}{4}$ **38.** $x^{\frac{1}{2}} = 12$ **39.** $x^{\frac{3}{4}} = 8$ **40.** $\sqrt[3]{x - 1} = 2$

Solve. [8-1C]

41. $x^3 + 4x^2 - 21x = 0$ **42.** $2x^2 + 5x = 3$

43. $x^3 + 6x^2 + 5x - 12 = 0$ **44.** $x^3 + 2x^2 - 49x - 98 = 0$

45. $x^4 - 10x^2 = -9$ **46.** $6x^3 + 20x^2 - 3x - 10 = 0$

47. $x^3 = 4x$ **48.** $15x^4 - 59x^3 + 64x^2 - 4x - 16 = 0$

Simplify each expression by rewriting as a single logarithm. [9-2C]

49. $\log 5 + \log 6$ **50.** $2 \log x$ **51.** $3 \log 7$

52. $\log 5^4 - \log 5^2$ **53.** $3 \log 2 + 4 \log 3$ **54.** $4 \log 7 + 2 \log 3$

55. $\log 8 - \log 3$ **56.** $\log m + \log n - \log p$

12-2 RECURSION

Use with
or after
Part 12-2A

Evaluate each expression. Round to the nearest hundredth. [9-2A]

1. $\log_3 243$ **2.** $\log_5 25$ **3.** $\log_2 \dfrac{1}{4}$ **4.** $\ln e$

5. $\log_7 1$ **6.** $\ln 2.5$ **7.** $\log_{\frac{1}{3}} 27$ **8.** $5 \ln 7$

Find the period (in degrees) of each function. [10-3A]

9. $y = \sin 3x$ **10.** $y = \cos \dfrac{1}{3}x$ **11.** $y = \sin 9x$ **12.** $y = \sin \dfrac{1}{2}x$

13. $y = \sin(-4x)$ **14.** $y = \cos\left(-\dfrac{5}{4}x\right)$ **15.** $y = \sin\left(-\dfrac{3}{2}x\right)$ **16.** $y = \sin \dfrac{11}{12}x$

Use with
or after
Part 12-2B

Find the remainder. [8-2B]

17. $(3x^3 - 5x + 2) \div (x - 2)$ **18.** $(2x^5 - 3x^3 + 4x - 5) \div (x + 1)$

19. $(x^4 + 2x^3 - 5) \div (x + 5)$ **20.** $(x^5 - 3) \div (x - 1)$

21. $(x^3 + 4x^2 + x - 6) \div (x + 2)$ **22.** $(2x^3 - 3x - 5) \div (x + 2)$

23. $(x^3 - 9x) \div (x + 3)$ **24.** $(x^4 + 5x^3 + 1) \div (x + 3)$

Solve each equation. [9-1B]

25. $5^x = 625$ **26.** $36^x = 6$ **27.** $2^{2x} = 256$ **28.** $4^{-x} = \dfrac{1}{64}$

29. $9^x = 27$ **30.** $\left(\dfrac{1}{7}\right)^x = 49$ **31.** $11^x = 1$ **32.** $2^{10x} = 32$

Find the amplitude of each function. [10-3A]

33. $y = 3 \sin 5x$ **34.** $y = -5 \cos 2x$ **35.** $y = \dfrac{1}{2} \sin 3x$ **36.** $y = -9 \sin 4x$

37. $y = 0.8 \sin 2x$ **38.** $y = \cos 3x$ **39.** $y = -2 \cos 3x$ **40.** $y = 1.5 \sin \dfrac{x}{2}$

MEASUREMENT CONVERSION FACTORS

Metric Measures Length

1000 meters (m) = 1 kilometer (km)
100 centimeter (cm) = 1 m
10 decimeter (dm) = 1 m
1000 millimeters (mm) = 1 m
10 cm = 1 decimeter (dm)
10 mm = 1 cm

Area

100 square millimeters = 1 square centimeter
(mm^2) (cm^2)
10,000 cm^2 = 1 square meter (m^2)
10,000 m^2 = 1 hectare (ha)

Volume

1000 cubic millimeters = 1 cubic centimeter
(mm^3) (cm^3)
1000 cm^3 = 1 cubic decimeter (dm^3)
1,000,000 cm^3 = 1 cubic meter (m^3)

Capacity

1000 milliliters (mL) = 1 liter (L)
1000 L = 1 kiloliter (kL)

Mass

1000 kilograms (kg) = 1 metric ton (t)
1000 grams (g) = 1 kg
1000 milligrams (mg) = 1 g

Temperature Degrees Celsius (°C)

0°C = freezing point of water
37°C = normal body temperature
100°C = boiling point of water

Time

60 seconds (sec) = 1 minute (min)
60 min = 1 hour (hr)
24 hr = 1 day

Customary Measures Length

12 inches (in.) = 1 foot (ft)
3 ft = 1 yard (yd)
36 in. = 1 yd
5280 ft = 1 mile (mi)
1760 yd = 1 mi
6076 feet = 1 nautical mile

Area

144 square inches = 1 square foot
($in.^2$) (ft^2)
9 ft^2 = 1 square yard (yd^2)
43,560 ft^2 = 1 acre (A)

Volume

1728 cubic inches = 1 cubic foot
($in.^3$) (ft^3)
27 ft^3 = 1 cubic yard (yd^3)

Capacity

8 fluid ounces (fl oz) = 1 cup (c)
2 c = 1 pint (pt)
2 p = 1 quart (qt)
4 qt = 1 gallon (gal)

Weight

16 ounces (oz) = 1 pound (lb)
2000 lb = 1 ton (T)

Temperature Degrees Fahrenheit (°F)

32°F = freezing point of water
98.6°F = normal body temperature
212°F = boiling point of water

SYMBOLS

$+$	plus or positive	$\log_a b$	the logarithm, base a, of b
$-$	minus or negative	a^n	the nth power of a
$\cdot$	times	$n!$	n factorial
$\times$	times	a_n	the nth term of a sequence
$\div$	divided by	$\displaystyle\sum_{k=1}^{n} a_k$	the summation $a_1 + a_2 + \cdots + a_n$
$\pm$	positive or negative; plus or minus	S_n	the nth partial sum of a series
$=$	is equal to	$|x|$	absolute value of x
$\neq$	is not equal to	$\sqrt{x}$	principal square root of x
$<$	is less than	$\bar{x}$	the mean of data values of x
$>$	is greater than	$x_1, x_2,$ etc.	specific values of the variable x
$\leq$	is less than or equal to	$y_1, y_2,$ etc.	specific values of the variable y
$\geq$	is greater than or equal to	$f(x)$	f of x, the value of the function f at x
$\approx$	is approximately equal to	$f \circ g(x)$	$f(g(x))$, the composition of functions f and g
$\%$	percent		
$\{\}$	set braces	$f^{-1}(x)$	the inverse function of $f(x)$
$a{:}b$	the ratio of a to b, or $\frac{a}{b}$	π	pi (approximately 3.1416)
$\cong$	is congruent to	e	the base of natural logarithms (approximately 2.71828)
$\perp$	is perpendicular to		
$\parallel$	is parallel to	(a, b)	ordered pair with x-coordinate a and y-coordinate b
$\sim$	is similar to		
$^\circ$	degree(s)	$\bar{A}$	the complement of event A
$\overleftrightarrow{AB}$	line containing points A and B	$_nC_r$	the number of combinations of r items out of n
$\overline{AB}$	line segment with endpoints A and B		
$\overrightarrow{AB}$	ray with endpoint A and containing B	$_nP_r$	the number of permutations of r items out of n
$\overrightarrow{AB}$	vector with origin A and endpoint B	$n(A)$	the number of ways an event A can occur
$\odot A$	circle with center A		
$\overparen{ABC}$	arc ABC	$P(A)$	the probability of event A
AB	length of $\overline{AB}$; distance between A and B	$P(B\,|\,A)$	the probability of event B, given that event A occurs
$\triangle ABC$	triangle with vertices A, B, and C	$\sin A$	sine of $\angle A$
$\angle ABC$	angle with sides $\overrightarrow{BA}$ and $\overrightarrow{BC}$	$\cos A$	cosine of $\angle A$
$\angle B$	angle with vertex B	$\tan A$	tangent of $\angle A$
$m\angle ABC$	measure of $\angle ABC$	$\csc A$	cosecant of $\angle A$
$\leftrightarrow$	corresponds to	$\sec A$	secant of $\angle A$
$p \rightarrow q$	p implies q	$\cot A$	cotangent of $\angle A$

RANDOM NUMBERS

RANDOM NUMBER TABLE

```
16247  67057  10251  98521  23049  90485  93472  54764  00881  21724
81610  35647  07547  50419  21362  85249  28479  33337  61331  58725
02190  78025  42193  97923  78377  86562  24007  91872  67410  46409
22649  91220  32179  21334  12788  40270  11138  82012  05998  10364
29001  56298  83778  69591  90123  04649  79227  25378  45715  52276

15234  02652  30047  49331  40652  73094  77908  06495  57351  84655
95577  61558  43018  33399  50975  19841  55339  80061  35990  70867
03283  51305  82814  21654  50927  38630  67102  80549  22337  07513
99335  43723  54336  85631  29536  09603  54311  96113  76841  44828
58948  06168  12821  68004  35025  10759  97747  32629  88242  00491

54133  08702  64190  41077  01227  97516  05049  56559  42675  47265
94799  15581  35844  12041  19406  87466  01987  47078  13721  48109
75132  50493  54738  45219  94101  96092  65224  75320  84902  26903
48977  35675  00748  76521  12774  65079  35629  65977  34438  77810
43718  63169  96092  60295  04520  84718  84185  83447  33832  56383

83235  42754  77728  24549  31299  33827  02580  08151  61013  64209
03943  82600  30461  68178  31421  45606  68730  67643  24547  02547
79539  24424  19473  67861  40210  93720  90758  15756  14016  87498
14345  28829  16266  16842  26986  54043  95243  46557  81167  23076
75046  17173  30543  53818  98718  05829  95943  80761  52074  82025

24104  86117  80507  08639  42463  75654  41821  60112  97561  19897
33613  79355  08460  86685  55409  23376  54838  88002  33788  44248
84566  42821  14117  23095  05460  41344  34675  45742  94992  30119
15381  02276  44307  16442  74366  89358  53839  02761  50312  57353
39197  98534  70506  15141  55602  88296  78648  94354  14021  26215
```

SIMULATION USING A RANDOM NUMBER GENERATOR

Many graphing utilities and computers have a random number generator (RAND), which returns a random number between 0 and 1. This feature, along with the greatest integer function (INT), allows you to simulate a variety of probability experiments.

INT(10 * RAND) — Press ENTER repeatedly to generate random digits from 0 to 9.

INT(6 * RAND) + 1 — Press ENTER repeatedly to generate random integers from 1 to 6. Use this to simulate rolls of a die.

INT(365 * RAND) + 1 — Press ENTER repeatedly to generate integers from 1 to 365. Use this to simulate days of the year, such as birthdates.

INT(n * RAND) + 1 — For any positive integer n, press ENTER repeatedly to generate integers from 1 to n.

(RAND < 0.5) — Press ENTER repeatedly to generate 0's and 1's with equal probability: for example, to simulate coin tosses (1 = heads, 0 = tails) or births (1 = girl, 0 = boy).

(RAND < p) — For any probability p, press ENTER repeatedly to generate 1's with probability p and 0's with probability $1 - p$. For example, 1 can simulate the failure of a machine part that has a probability p of breaking.

STANDARD NORMAL DISTRIBUTION

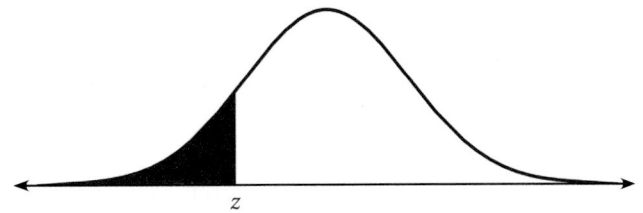

AREAS UNDER THE STANDARD NORMAL CURVE TO THE LEFT OF z

z	0	1	2	3	4	5	6	7	8	9
−2.5	.0062	.0060	.0059	.0057	.0055	.0054	.0052	.0051	.0049	.0048
−2.4	.0082	.0080	.0078	.0075	.0073	.0071	.0069	.0068	.0066	.0064
−2.3	.0107	.0104	.0102	.0099	.0096	.0094	.0091	.0089	.0087	.0084
−2.2	.0139	.0136	.0132	.0129	.0125	.0122	.0119	.0116	.0113	.0110
−2.1	.0179	.0174	.0170	.0166	.0162	.0158	.0154	.0150	.0146	.0143
−2.0	.0228	.0222	.0217	.0212	.0207	.0202	.0197	.0192	.0188	.0183
−1.9	.0287	.0281	.0274	.0268	.0262	.0256	.0250	.0244	.0239	.0233
−1.8	.0359	.0351	.0344	.0336	.0329	.0322	.0314	.0307	.0301	.0294
−1.7	.0446	.0436	.0427	.0418	.0409	.0401	.0392	.0384	.0375	.0367
−1.6	.0548	.0537	.0526	.0516	.0505	.0495	.0485	.0475	.0465	.0455
−1.5	.0668	.0655	.0643	.0630	.0618	.0606	.0594	.0582	.0571	.0559
−1.4	.0808	.0793	.0778	.0764	.0749	.0735	.0721	.0708	.0694	.0681
−1.3	.0968	.0951	.0934	.0918	.0901	.0885	.0869	.0853	.0838	.0823
−1.2	.1151	.1131	.1112	.1093	.1075	.1056	.1038	.1020	.1003	.0985
−1.1	.1357	.1335	.1314	.1292	.1271	.1251	.1230	.1210	.1190	.1170
−1.0	.1587	.1562	.1539	.1515	.1492	.1469	.1446	.1423	.1401	.1379
−0.9	.1841	.1814	.1788	.1762	.1736	.1711	.1685	.1660	.1635	.1611
−0.8	.2119	.2090	.2061	.2033	.2005	.1977	.1949	.1922	.1894	.1867
−0.7	.2420	.2389	.2358	.2327	.2296	.2266	.2236	.2206	.2177	.2148
−0.6	.2743	.2709	.2676	.2643	.2611	.2578	.2546	.2514	.2483	.2451
−0.5	.3085	.3050	.3015	.2981	.2946	.2912	.2877	.2843	.2810	.2776
−0.4	.3446	.3409	.3372	.3336	.3300	.3264	.3228	.3192	.3156	.3121
−0.3	.3821	.3783	.3745	.3707	.3669	.3632	.3594	.3557	.3520	.3483
−0.2	.4207	.4168	.4129	.4090	.4052	.4013	.3974	.3936	.3897	.3859
−0.1	.4602	.4562	.4522	.4483	.4443	.4404	.4364	.4325	.4286	.4247
−0.0	.5000	.4960	.4920	.4880	.4840	.4801	.4761	.4721	.4684	.4641
0.0	.5000	.5040	.5080	.5120	.5160	.5199	.5239	.5279	.5319	.5359
0.1	.5398	.5438	.5478	.5517	.5557	.5596	.5636	.5675	.5714	.5753
0.2	.5793	.5832	.5871	.5910	.5948	.5987	.6026	.6064	.6103	.6141
0.3	.6179	.6217	.6255	.6293	.6331	.6368	.6406	.6443	.6480	.6517
0.4	.6554	.6591	.6628	.6664	.6700	.6736	.6772	.6808	.6844	.6879
0.5	.6915	.6950	.6985	.7019	.7054	.7088	.7123	.7157	.7190	.7224
0.6	.7257	.7291	.7324	.7357	.7389	.7422	.7454	.7486	.7517	.7549
0.7	.7580	.7611	.7642	.7673	.7704	.7734	.7764	.7794	.7823	.7852
0.8	.7881	.7910	.7939	.7967	.7995	.8023	.8051	.8078	.8106	.8133
0.9	.8159	.8186	.8212	.8238	.8264	.8289	.8315	.8340	.8365	.8389
1.0	.8413	.8438	.8461	.8485	.8508	.8531	.8554	.8577	.8599	.8621
1.1	.8643	.8665	.8686	.8708	.8729	.8749	.8770	.8790	.8810	.8830
1.2	.8849	.8869	.8888	.8907	.8925	.8944	.8962	.8980	.8997	.9015
1.3	.9032	.9049	.9066	.9082	.9099	.9115	.9131	.9147	.9162	.9177
1.4	.9192	.9207	.9222	.9236	.9251	.9265	.9279	.9292	.9306	.9319
1.5	.9332	.9345	.9357	.9370	.9382	.9394	.9406	.9418	.9429	.9441
1.6	.9452	.9463	.9474	.9484	.9495	.9505	.9515	.9525	.9535	.9545
1.7	.9554	.9564	.9573	.9582	.9591	.9599	.9608	.9616	.9625	.9633
1.8	.9641	.9649	.9656	.9664	.9671	.9678	.9686	.9693	.9699	.9706
1.9	.9713	.9719	.9726	.9732	.9738	.9744	.9750	.9756	.9761	.9767
2.0	.9772	.9778	.9783	.9788	.9793	.9798	.9803	.9808	.9812	.9817
2.1	.9821	.9826	.9830	.9834	.9838	.9842	.9846	.9850	.9854	.9857
2.2	.9861	.9864	.9868	.9871	.9875	.9878	.9881	.9884	.9887	.9890
2.3	.9893	.9896	.9898	.9901	.9904	.9906	.9909	.9911	.9913	.9916
2.4	.9918	.9920	.9922	.9925	.9927	.9929	.9931	.9932	.9934	.9936
2.5	.9938	.9940	.9941	.9943	.9945	.9946	.9948	.9949	.9951	.9952

GEOMETRIC FORMULAS

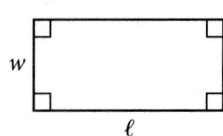

Rectangle

Area: $A = \ell w$

Perimeter: $p = 2\ell + 2w$

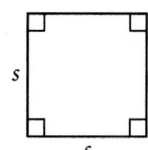

Square

Area: $A = s^2$

Perimeter: $p = 4s$

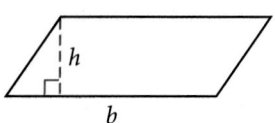

Parallelogram

Area: $A = bh$

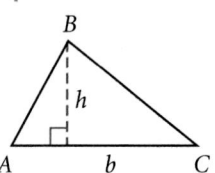

Triangle

Area: $A = \frac{1}{2} bh$

$m\angle A + m\angle B + m\angle C = 180°$

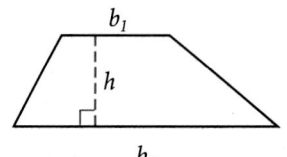

Trapezoid

Area: $A = \frac{1}{2} h(b_1 + b_2)$

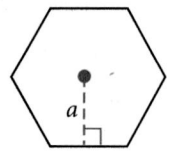

Regular Polygon

Area: $A = \frac{1}{2} ap$

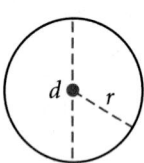

Circle

Area: $A = \pi r^2$

Circumference: $C = \pi d = 2\pi r$

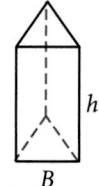

Right Prism

Volume: $V = Bh$

Lateral Area: $LA = ph$

Surface Area: $SA = ph + 2B$

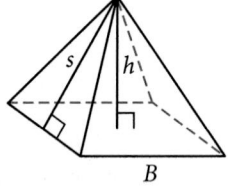

Regular Pyramid

Volume: $V = \frac{1}{3}Bh$

Lateral Area: $LA = \frac{1}{2}ps$

Surface Area: $SA = \frac{1}{2}ps + B$

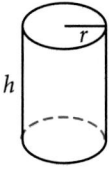

Right Cylinder

Volume: $V = \pi r^2 h$

Lateral Area: $LA = 2\pi rh$

Surface Area: $SA = 2\pi rh + 2\pi r^2$

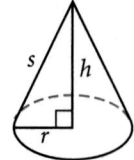

Right Cone

Volume: $V = \frac{1}{3} \pi r^2 h$

Lateral Area: $LA = \pi rs$

Surface Area: $SA = \pi rs + \pi r^2$

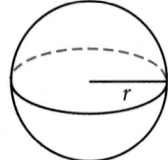

Sphere

Volume: $V = \frac{4}{3} \pi r^3$

Surface Area: $SA = 4\pi r^2$

ALGEBRAIC PROPERTIES

Properties of Equality

For any numbers a, b, and c:

Addition   If $a = b$, then $a + c = b + c$.

Multiplication   If $a = b$, then $ac = bc$.

Reflexive $a = a$

Symmetric   If $a = b$, then $b = a$.

Transitive   If $a = b$ and $b = c$, then $a = c$.

Properties of Inequality

For any real numbers a, b, and c:

Addition   If $a > b$, then $a + c > b + c$.

Multiplication   If $a > b$, then $ac > bc$ if $c > 0$ and $ac < bc$ if $c < 0$.

Transitive   If $a < b$ and $b < c$, then $a < c$.

Trichotomy   Either $a < b$, $a > b$, or $a = b$.

Triangle Inequality   If a, b, and c are side lengths of a triangle, then $a + b > c$, $a + c > b$, and $b + c > a$.

Field Properties

For any elements a, b, and c in a field with operations $+$ and $\cdot$:

Closure $a + b$ and $a \cdot b$ are in the field.

Commutative $a + b = b + a$ and $a \cdot b = b \cdot a$.

Associative $(a + b) + c = a + (b + c)$ and $(a \cdot b) \cdot c = a \cdot (b \cdot c)$.

Identities   There are elements 0 and 1 in the field so that $a + 0 = 0 + a = a$ and $a \cdot 1 = 1 \cdot a = a$ for any element a.

Inverses   There is an element $-a$ so that $a + -a = 0$ and, if $a \neq 0$, there is an element $\frac{1}{a}$ so that $a \cdot \frac{1}{a} = \frac{1}{a} \cdot a = 1$.

Distributive $a \cdot (b + c) = a \cdot b + a \cdot c$

Exponents and Radicals

For all real numbers a and b and integers m and n:

$$a^m \cdot a^n = a^{m+n}$$

$$(a^m)^n = a^{mn}$$

$$(ab)^m = a^m b^m$$

$$a^{-n} = \frac{1}{a^n}, \text{ and } \frac{1}{a^{-n}} = a^n$$

$$\frac{a^m}{a^n} = a^{m-n}, \text{ if } a \neq 0$$

$$\left(\frac{a}{b}\right)^m = \frac{a^m}{b^m}, \text{ if } b \neq 0$$

$$a^{\frac{m}{n}} = \sqrt[n]{a^m} = (\sqrt[n]{a})^m$$

Polynomials

Remainder Theorem   If a polynomial $P(x)$ is divided by $(x - a)$, where a is a constant, then the remainder is $P(a)$.

Factor Theorem   For any polynomial $P(x)$, if $P(a) = 0$ for a constant a, then $(x - a)$ is a factor of $P(x)$.

Rational Roots Theorem   Let $P(x) = a_n x^n + a_{n-1} x^{n-1} + \cdots + a_1 x + a_0$ be any polynomial with integer coefficients. If b and c are integers with no common factors and $\frac{b}{c}$ is a rational root of the equation $P(x) = 0$, then b is a divisor of a_0 and c is a divisor of a_n.

Logarithms

For any real number n and any positive numbers x, y, and $b \neq 1$:

$$y = \log_b x \text{ means } x = b^y$$

$$\log_b (xy) = \log_b x + \log_b y$$

$$\log_b \left(\frac{x}{y}\right) = \log_b x - \log_b y$$

$$\log_b (x^n) = n \log_b x$$

$$\log_b x = \frac{\log_a x}{\log_a b} \text{ for any } a > 0$$

ALGEBRAIC FORMULAS

Absolute Value
If a and b are any real numbers, then
$$|a| = a \text{ if } a \geq 0 \qquad\qquad |a| = -a \text{ if } a < 0 \qquad\qquad |a + bi| = \sqrt{a^2 + b^2}.$$

Matrix Inverses
If $ad - bc \neq 0$, then the inverse of $A = \begin{bmatrix} a & b \\ c & d \end{bmatrix}$ is $A^{-1} = \dfrac{1}{ad - bc} \begin{bmatrix} d & -b \\ -c & a \end{bmatrix}$.

Experimental Probability
$$P(E) = \frac{\text{number of successful trials for event } E}{\text{total number of trials}}$$

Theoretical Probability
If all outcomes are equally likely, $P(E) = \dfrac{\text{number of outcomes in the event } E}{\text{number of outcomes in the sample space}}$.

Geometric Probability
If A is a region contained in region B and point C is chosen at random from B, then
$$P(C \text{ is in region } A) = \frac{\text{area of region } A}{\text{area of region } B}.$$

Probability Formulas
$$P(\text{not } E) = P(\overline{E}) = 1 - P(E) \qquad\qquad P(A \text{ or } B) = P(A) + P(B) - P(A \text{ and } B)$$

$$P(A \text{ and } B) = P(A)P(B\,|\,A) \qquad\qquad P(A \text{ and } B) = P(A)P(B), \text{ if } A \text{ and } B \text{ are independent}$$

Arithmetic Sequence
An arithmetic sequence with first term a_1 and common difference d has nth term $a_n = a_1 + (n - 1)d$.

Geometric Sequence
A geometric sequence with first term a_1 and common ratio r has nth term $a_n = a_1 r^{n-1}$.

Arithmetic Series
An arithmetic series, $a_1 + a_2 + a_3 + \cdots$, has nth partial sum $S_n = \frac{n}{2}(a_1 + a_n)$.

Geometric Series
A geometric series, $a_1 + a_2 + a_3 + \cdots$, with first term a_1 and common ratio r, has nth partial sum $S_n = \dfrac{a_1(1 - r^n)}{1 - r}$. If $|r| < 1$, the series converges to $S = \dfrac{a_1}{1 - r}$.

Pythagorean Theorem
A right triangle with legs of lengths a and b and hypotenuse of length c satisfies $a^2 + b^2 = c^2$.

Distance Formula
The distance between (x_1, y_1) and (x_2, y_2) is $\sqrt{(x_1 - x_2)^2 + (y_1 - y_2)^2}$.

Midpoint Formula
The midpoint between (x_1, y_1) and (x_2, y_2) is $\left(\dfrac{x_1 + x_2}{2}, \dfrac{y_1 + y_2}{2} \right)$.

Quadratic Formula

The solutions of a quadratic equation in standard form $ax^2 + bx + c = 0$ are given by $x = \dfrac{-b \pm \sqrt{b^2 - 4ac}}{2a}$.

Multiplication Counting Principle

The number of ways a series of events, A_1 through A_k, can occur is $n(A_1) \cdot n(A_2) \cdot \cdots \cdot n(A_k)$.

Addition Counting Principle

If A and B are mutually exclusive events, then
$n(A \text{ or } B) = n(A) + n(B)$.

Permutations and Combinations

$$_nP_r = \frac{n!}{(n-r)!} \qquad _nC_r = \frac{n!}{r!(n-r)!}$$

If n items contain q copies of one item, r copies of another item, s copies of a third item, etc., then the number of distinguishable permutations of all n items is $P = \dfrac{n!}{q!r!s!\ldots}$.

Binomial Theorem

For any binomial $(a + b)$ and any positive integer n,
$$(a + b)^n = {_nC_0}a^n + {_nC_1}a^{n-1}b + {_nC_2}a^{n-2}b^2 + \cdots + {_nC_{n-1}}ab^{n-1} + {_nC_n}b^n.$$

Trigonometric Definitions

In $\triangle ABC$ with a right angle at C,

$$\sin A = \frac{a}{c} \qquad \cos A = \frac{b}{c} \qquad \tan A = \frac{a}{b}$$

$$\csc A = \frac{c}{a} \qquad \sec A = \frac{c}{b} \qquad \cot A = \frac{b}{a}$$

Arc Length and Sector Area

In a circle of radius r, the length of an arc intercepted by a central angle with radian measure θ is $s = r\theta$.

The area of a sector determined by a central angle with radian measure θ is $A = \frac{1}{2}r^2\theta$.

Law of Cosines

For any $\triangle ABC$, $c^2 = a^2 + b^2 - 2ab \cos C$.

Law of Sines

In any $\triangle ABC$, $\dfrac{a}{\sin A} = \dfrac{b}{\sin B} = \dfrac{c}{\sin C}$.

Area of a Triangle

The area of $\triangle XYZ$ is $\frac{1}{2}xy \sin Z$.

Heron's Formula

The area of $\triangle XYZ$ is $\sqrt{s(s-x)(s-y)(s-z)}$, where $s = \dfrac{x+y+z}{2}$.

Euler's Formula

For any simple polyhedron with F faces, V vertices, and E edges, $F + V - E = 2$.

GLOSSARY

absolute maximum

The largest y-value of a function $y = f(x)$. [p. 550]

absolute minimum

The smallest y-value of a function $y = f(x)$. [p. 550]

absolute value

The absolute value of any real number, a, written as $|a|$, is defined as: $|a| = a$ if $a \geq 0$ and $|a| = -a$ if $a < 0$. It is the number's distance from zero on the number line. [p. 135]

absolute value function

A function defined by an equation of the form $f(x) = a|x - b| + c$. [p. 144]

absolute value of a complex number

The absolute value of a complex number $a + bi$ is defined as: $|a + bi| = \sqrt{a^2 + b^2}$. It is the number's distance from the origin in the complex plane. [p. 293]

Addition Counting Principle

If A and B are mutually exclusive events, then $n(A \text{ or } B) = n(A) + n(B)$. [p. 424]

Addition Property of Equality

For any real numbers a, b, and c, if $a = b$, then $a + c = b + c$. [p. 87]

Addition Property of Inequalities

For any real numbers a, b, and c, if $a > b$, then $a + c > b + c$. [p. 128]

additive identity

The sum of a number and the additive identity is the original number. Zero is the additive identity for real numbers. [p. 272]

additive inverse

Two numbers are additive inverses if their sum is the additive identity. [p. 273]

algorithm

A procedure for solving a problem.

amplitude

The amplitude of a periodic function is half the difference between the maximum and minimum values of the function. [p. 730]

anagram

A word or phrase formed by rearranging letters in an existing word or phrase. [p. 428]

angle of depression or elevation

An angle of depression or angle of elevation to an object is formed by the line of sight and a horizontal line. The vertex of the angle is the eye of the person looking at the object. [p. 683]

angular speed

The rate of revolution of a rotating object, usually given in revolutions or radians per unit time. [p. 696]

arc

Two points on a circle and the continuous part of the circle between them.

arc length

The distance along the circumference of a circle between the two endpoints of an arc.

arc measure

The degree measure of an arc.

area

The number of square units contained in a plane region.

arithmetic means

Terms in an arithmetic sequence between two given terms. [p. 237]

arithmetic sequence

A sequence in which a constant (d) is added to a given term to get the next term. [p. 233]

arithmetic series

The sum of the terms in an arithmetic sequence. [p. 240]

association

When two quantities in paired values of data increase together, they have a positive association; when one increases as the other decreases, they have a negative association; and when they are unrelated, they have no association. [p. 7]

associative properties

For any numbers a, b, and c, $(a + b) + c = a + (b + c)$ and $(a \cdot b) \cdot c = a \cdot (b \cdot c)$. [p. 273]

asymptote

A line is an asymptote to a graph if the graph approaches the line more and more closely as x-values increase, decrease, or approach a constant. [p. 390]

base

The base of a power b^x is b. The base of a logarithm $\log_b x$ is b. [p. 474]

biased sample

When a sample is not representative of the population from which it is taken, the sample is biased. [p. 780]

binomial

A polynomial with two terms. [p. 443]

Binomial Theorem

For any binomial $(a + b)$ and any positive integer n, $(a + b)^n = {}_nC_0a^n + {}_nC_1a^{n-1}b + {}_nC_2a^{n-2}b^2 + \cdots + {}_nC_{n-1}ab^{n-1} + {}_nC_nb^n$. [p. 444]

bisect

Divide into two congruent halves.

boundary line

The edge of the graph of a linear inequality in a coordinate plane. [p. 142]

boundary point

An endpoint of the graph of an inequality on a number line. [p. 128]

branches of a hyperbola

The two parts of a hyperbola. The two branches approach the asymptotes of the hyperbola as the distance from the center increases. [p. 390]

center (of a circle, ellipse, hyperbola)

See *circle*, *ellipse*, and *hyperbola*.

central angle

An angle in the plane of a circle whose vertex is the center of the circle. [p. 688]

centroid

The balance point or center of gravity of a geometric object. In a triangle, the point where the medians intersect. [p. 110]

circle

The set of points in a plane equidistant from a given point. The distance is the radius of the circle and the given point is its center. [p. 373]

circuit

A path in a graph that ends at the same vertex as it begins without repeating edges. [p. 810]

circumference

The distance around a circle.

closure

A set of numbers is closed under an operation if, when the operation is performed on any two numbers in the set, the resulting number is also in the set. [p. 272]

coefficient

The numerical factor in a term containing variables.

combinations

Collections of items without regard to order. [p. 438]

combined variation

In a formula with several variables, if one variable varies directly with at least one other variable and inversely with at least one other variable, the variation is called combined variation. [p. 463]

common difference

The constant added to a term of an arithmetic sequence to get the next term. [p. 233]

common external tangent

A line tangent to two circles that does not intersect the line through their centers.

common logarithm

A logarithm with base 10. [p. 652]

common ratio

The constant that a term in a geometric sequence is multiplied by to get the next term. [p. 251]

commutative properties

For any numbers a and b, $a + b = b + a$ and $a \cdot b = b \cdot a$. [p. 273]

complementary angles

Two angles whose measures add to 90°.

complementary events

The complement of event A is $\overline{A}$, where $\overline{A}$ denotes the event that A does not occur. If A and $\overline{A}$ are complementary events, $P(A) + P(\overline{A}) = 1$. [p. 757]

completing the square

Adding a constant to a polynomial to make it a trinomial square. [p. 330]

complex conjugate

The complex conjugate of $a + bi$ is $a - bi$. [p. 292]

complex number

The complex numbers consist of all sums $a + bi$, where a and b are real numbers and $i = \sqrt{-1}$. [p. 287]

complex plane

A coordinate plane used for graphing complex numbers. The horizontal axis is the real axis and the vertical axis is the imaginary axis. [p. 291]

composite function

Let f and g be any two functions such that the range of g is in the domain of f. The composite (or composition) of f and g is the function $f(g(x))$ or $f \circ g(x)$. [p. 520]

compound inequality

A compound inequality is the result of combining two inequalities with *and* or with *or*. [p. 130]

conditional probability

When the probability of event B depends on event A, the probability is called a conditional probability, written as $P(B|A)$. [p. 769]

congruent

Having the same shape and size.

congruent angles

Angles with equal measures.

congruent segments

Segments with equal lengths.

conic sections

Figures determined by the intersection of a plane and a double-napped cone. Circles, ellipses, parabolas, and hyperbolas are conic sections. [p. 396]

connected graph

A graph that has a path connecting every pair of its vertices. [p. 810]

consistent system

A system of equations that has at least one solution. [p. 162]

constant

A quantity whose value does not change. [p. 13]

constant of variation

The proportionality constant in a variation equation. For instance, in $y = kx$, k is the constant of variation. [p. 460]

constant term

A term in a polynomial that is not multiplied by a variable. [p. 542]

constraints

See *linear programming*.

continuous

A function is continuous on an interval if its graph can be traced with a pencil without needing to lift the pencil. The graph has no "holes" or "jumps." [p. 548]

converge

If the terms of a sequence or the partial sums of a series approach a particular value, then the sequence or series converges. The value to which it converges is called the limit of the sequence or series. [p. 262]

cosecant (csc)

In a right triangle $\triangle ABC$ with right angle $\angle C$, the cosecant of $\angle A = \csc A = \dfrac{\text{length of hypotenuse}}{\text{length of opposite leg}} = \dfrac{c}{a}$. [p. 681]

cosine (cos)

In a right triangle $\triangle ABC$ with right angle $\angle C$, the cosine of $\angle A = \cos A = \dfrac{\text{length of adjacent leg}}{\text{length of hypotenuse}} = \dfrac{b}{c}$. [p. 681]

cotangent (cot)

In a right triangle $\triangle ABC$ with right angle $\angle C$, the cotangent of $\angle A = \cot A = \dfrac{\text{length of adjacent leg}}{\text{length of opposite leg}} = \dfrac{b}{a}$. [p. 681]

cross section

The figure formed by the intersection of a solid and a plane.

cubic

A cubic function is a polynomial function of degree three. [p. 543]

degree of a polynomial

The degree of a polynomial with one variable is the greatest exponent of the variable that appears in any term. [p. 542]

degree of a vertex

The number of edges meeting at a vertex of a graph. [p. 811]

dependent equations

If the graphs of two lines coincide, their equations are dependent equations. [p. 162]

dependent events

When knowledge that an event does (or does not) occur affects the probability of a second event, the events are dependent. [p. 762]

dependent variable

When the value of y depends on the value of x, y is called the dependent variable (and x is called the independent variable). [p. 16]

descending order

A polynomial is in descending order when the term with the greatest exponent is listed first, the term with the next greatest exponent second, etc., with the constant term last. [p. 544]

dilation

A transformation of the points in a plane. A dilation with scale factor k maps one point, the center of dilation, onto itself, and maps every other point P to a point P' on $\overrightarrow{CP}$ so that $CP' = kCP$.

dimension

The dimension of a matrix is given by the number of horizontal rows and the number of vertical columns. A matrix with m rows and n columns has dimension $m \times n$. [p. 50]

direct variation

y varies directly with x if $y = kx$ for some constant k. [p. 79]

discontinuity

A function has a discontinuity at a particular x-value if its graph has a jump, break, or hole. [p. 599]

discontinuous

A function is discontinuous if its graph has at least one discontinuity. [p. 599]

discriminant

The discriminant of a quadratic equation $ax^2 + bx + c$ is the quantity $b^2 - 4ac$. [p. 362]

distinguishable permutation

When some objects in a set are identical, some permutations do not give different arrangements. The distinguishable permutations are the different arrangements that can be formed. [p. 430]

distributive property of multiplication over addition

For any numbers, a, b, and c, $a \cdot (b + c) = a \cdot b + a \cdot c$. [p. 273]

domain

The domain of a function is the set of all possible values of the independent variable. [p. 22]

double root

If a quadratic equation has only one solution, this solution is called a double root. A quadratic equation has a double root if its discriminant equals zero. (See *multiple root*.) [p. 363]

e (number)

An irrational number, the base of natural logarithms; $e \approx 2.718281828....$ [p. 641]

edge of a graph

A connection between two vertices of a graph. [p. 805]

ellipse

An ellipse is the set of all points P in a plane where the sum of the distances from P to two fixed points is a constant. The two fixed points are the foci of the ellipse. The center of the ellipse is the midpoint of the segment joining the foci. The two points on the ellipse farthest from its center are the endpoints of the major axis. The minor axis joins the two points on the ellipse nearest its center. [p. 381]

entry

Each number in a matrix is an entry. [p. 50]

equal matrices

Matrices are equal if and only if they have the same dimension and all of their corresponding entries are equal. [p. 50]

equivalent equations

Equations with the same solutions. [p. 88]

Euler circuit

A circuit that contains all edges of a graph and can be drawn without tracing any edge more than once. [p. 810]

Euler path

A path that contains all edges of a graph and can be drawn without tracing any edge more than once. [p. 810]

Euler's Formula

For any simple polyhedron with F faces, V vertices, and E edges, $F + V - E = 2$. [p. 805]

Euler's Traversability Theorem

A connected graph has an Euler circuit if and only if every vertex has even degree. A connected graph has an Euler path between two vertices A and B if and only if A and B have odd degree and all other vertices have even degree. [p. 811]

event

Any specified set of outcomes in the sample space of a probability experiment. [p. 32]

experimental probability

A probability found by collecting data or performing an experiment. [p. 33]

exponent

The exponent of a power b^x is x. The exponent tells how many factors of the base are multiplied together. [p. 474]

exponential equation

An equation where the variable is an exponent. [p. 623]

exponential growth and decay

Exponential functions exhibit exponential growth or decay as x-values increase. If the base of the function is greater than 1, the function shows exponential growth; if it is a positive value less than 1, it shows exponential decay. [p. 627]

exponential function

A function of the form $f(x) = ab^x$, where a, b, and x are real numbers; $b > 0$; and $b \neq 1$. [p. 620]

exponential notation

The use of exponents to write a power; for instance, 2^3 is exponential form for $2 \cdot 2 \cdot 2$. [p. 474]

extraneous (extra) solution

An invalid solution sometimes produced when both sides of an equation are raised to a power. [p. 499]

Factor Theorem

For any polynomial $P(x)$, if $P(a) = 0$ for a constant a, then $(x - a)$ is a factor of $P(x)$. [p. 573]

factorial

For any integer $n > 1$, n factorial, written $n!$, is equal to $n \cdot (n - 1) \cdot (n - 2) \cdots 3 \cdot 2 \cdot 1$. For $n = 0$ or 1, $0! = 1! = 1$. [p. 424]

feasible region

The solution to the system of constraints for a linear programming problem. [p. 204]

field

A set with two operations, $+$ and $\cdot$, that satisfies the field axioms. [p. 273]

field axioms

The field axioms are: closure, the commutative properties, the associative properties, inverses, identities, and the distributive property of $\cdot$ over $+$. [p. 273]

foci (of an ellipse, of a hyperbola)

See *ellipse, hyperbola.*

fractal

A geometric pattern that shows self-similarity.

function

A relationship between two quantities in which the value of one quantity, the dependent variable, is uniquely determined by the value of the independent variable. [p. 22]

function notation

Function notation uses $f(x)$ (or $g(x)$, $h(x)$, etc.), instead of y, to represent the dependent variable. [p. 22]

Fundamental Theorem of Algebra

Every polynomial $P(x)$ of degree at least 1 and with complex coefficients has at least one complex zero. [p. 579]

general (*n*th) term

The general term or *n*th term in a sequence is denoted by a_n. [p. 233]

geometric means

Terms in a geometric sequence between two given terms. [p. 254]

geometric probability

A probability determined by comparing the areas (or perimeters, angle measures, etc.) of the "successful" regions to the total area of the sample space. [p. 33]

geometric sequence

A sequence in which a given term is multiplied by a constant (r) to get the next term. [p. 251]

geometric series

The sum of the terms of a geometric sequence. [p. 256]

golden ratio

The length-to-width ratio of a golden rectangle, $\frac{1 + \sqrt{5}}{2} \approx 1.618$.

golden rectangle

A rectangle whose length-to-width ratio is the golden ratio. A golden rectangle can be divided into a square and another golden rectangle.

graph (discrete math)

A plane figure consisting of vertices and edges connecting vertices. [p. 805]

great circle

A circle on a sphere whose center is the center of the sphere.

Hamiltonian circuit

A circuit that passes through each vertex of a connected graph exactly once. [p. 817]

Hamiltonian path

A path that passes through each vertex of a connected graph exactly once. [p. 817]

Heron's Formula

For any $\triangle XYZ$, the area $A = \sqrt{s(s - x)(s - y)(s - z)}$, where s equals half of the perimeter (the *semiperimeter*) of the triangle. [p. 720]

histogram

A bar graph that shows the frequency, percentage, or probability of outcomes. The outcomes must be divided into categories of equal size. [p. 781]

hyperbola

The set of all points P in a plane where the difference between the distances from P to two fixed points is a constant. The two fixed points are the foci of the hyperbola. The center of the hyperbola is the midpoint of the segment joining the foci. [p. 390]

identity matrix

See *multiplicative identity matrix*.

identity properties

Addition: There is a unique identity element, 0, so that for any a, $a + 0 = 0 + a = a$. Multiplication: There is an unique identity element, 1, so that for any a, $a \cdot 1 = a$. [p. 273]

image

The point or figure that results from a transformation, such as a reflection or rotation.

imaginary axis

The vertical axis in the complex plane. [p. 291]

imaginary number

A number of the form bi, where b is a real number. [p. 286]

imaginary part (of a complex number)

The imaginary part of a complex number $a + bi$ is bi. [p. 287]

imaginary unit

The imaginary unit is $i = \sqrt{-1}$. [p. 286]

inconsistent system

A system of equations with no solution. [p. 162]

independent events

When knowledge that an event does (or does not) occur does not affect the probability of a second event, the events are independent. A and B are independent events if and only if $P(A \text{ and } B) = P(A) \cdot P(B)$. [p. 762]

independent variable

When the value of y depends on the value of x, x is called the independent variable (and y is called the dependent variable). [p. 16]

index

In $\sqrt[12]{2}$, 12 is the index of the radical. [p. 486]

inductive reasoning

Making a conjecture by looking at examples and recognizing patterns. [p. 239]

inequality

Two expressions separated by an inequality symbol. [p. 128]

infinite sequence

A sequence that continues indefinitely. [p. 233]

infinite series

The sum of the terms of an infinite sequence. [p. 262]

initial side

In trigonometry, the initial side of an angle lies along the positive x-axis. [p. 700]

integers

The whole numbers and their opposites: …, $-3, -2, -1, 0, 1, 2, 3, \ldots$. [p. 278]

inverse function/relation

The inverse of a function or relation is obtained by interchanging the domain and range of the original relation. [p. 525]

inverse matrix

See *multiplicative inverse matrix*.

inverse variation

y varies inversely with x if $y = \dfrac{k}{x}$ for some constant k. [p. 461]

invertible matrix

If matrix A has an inverse, it is said to be invertible. [p. 181]

irrational numbers

The set of all real numbers that cannot be expressed as the ratio of two integers. [p. 278]

joint variation

If one variable varies directly with two or more other variables, but does not vary inversely with any other variable, the variation is called joint variation. [p. 463]

Law of Cosines

For any $\triangle ABC$, $c^2 = a^2 + b^2 - 2ab \cos C$. [p. 710]

Law of Sines

In any $\triangle ABC$, $\dfrac{a}{\sin A} = \dfrac{b}{\sin B} = \dfrac{c}{\sin C}$. [p. 718]

leading coefficient

The coefficient of the term of a polynomial with the greatest exponent. [p. 542]

least common denominator (LCD)

The least common denominator of two or more fractions is the least common multiple of their denominators. [p. 593]

limit

A fixed number approached by the terms of a sequence, the partial sums of a series, or the y-values of a function under certain conditions. [p. 262]

line of best fit

A trend line that is found mathematically, such as a median-median line or a regression line. [p. 109]

line symmetry

A figure has line symmetry if a line divides it into two mirror-image halves.

linear combination method

A method for solving a system of linear equations. The equations in the system, or multiples of these equations, are added to each other to eliminate all but one of the variables. [p. 169]

linear function

A function whose graph is a straight line. A linear function of x can be written in the form $y = mx + b$, where m and b are constants. [p. 79]

linear inequality

An inequality that has only first-degree variable terms and constants. [p. 142]

linear programming

A method of modeling and solving problems where limitations, or constraints, can be modeled by linear inequalities. [p. 204]

linear regression

A method for finding an equation for the line of best fit for a data set. The method is based on minimizing the sum of the squared vertical distances from the data points to the line of best fit. [p. 117]

linear speed

The distance an object travels per unit time. [p. 696]

literal equation

A formula involving several variables. [p. 88]

locus

The set of points that satisfies a particular condition or conditions.

logarithm

A value of a logarithmic function. [p. 651]

logarithmic function

The logarithmic function $y = \log_b x$ is the inverse of the exponential function $y = b^x$, where $b > 0$ and $b \neq 1$. [p. 651]

major arc

An arc of a circle that measures more than 180°.

major axis

See *ellipse*.

matrix

A rectangular array of numbers arranged between brackets. [p. 50]

matrix multiplication

The method for finding the product of matrices. When multiplying two matrices A and B, the entry in the ith row and jth column of the product matrix AB is the sum of the products of corresponding entries in row i of matrix A and column j of matrix B. [p. 59]

mean

The mean (or average) of a data set is the sum of the data divided by the number of items in the set.

median-median line

The line of best fit for a data set found by the median-median method. The method is based on dividing the data points into three groups, finding the median point for each group, and finding the line that is parallel to the line through the left- and right-hand median points and that contains the centroid of the triangle determined by the three median points. [p. 110]

median of a data set

The median of a data set is the value above which half the data lie and below which half the data lie. If the number of data is odd, the median is the middle value when the data are arranged in numerical order. If the number of data is even, the median is the average of the two middle values. [p. 110]

median of a triangle

A median of a triangle is a segment from a vertex to the midpoint of the opposite side. [p. 114]

minimal spanning tree

A spanning tree that minimizes the total length or cost of all edges. [p. 819]

minor arc

An arc of a circle that measures less than 180°.

minor axis

See *ellipse*.

monomial

A polynomial with one term. [p. 542]

multiple root

If a polynomial $P(x)$ has two or more equal factors of the form $(x - a)$, then a is called a multiple root of the polynomial equation $P(x) = 0$. [p. 579]

Multiplication Counting Principle

The number of ways a series of events, A_1 through A_k, can occur is $n(A_1) \cdot n(A_2) \cdot \cdots \cdot n(A_k)$. [p. 423]

Multiplication Property of Equality

For any real numbers a, b, and c, if $a = b$, then $ac = bc$. [p. 87]

Multiplication Property of Inequalities

For any real numbers *a*, *b*, and *c*, if $a > b$, then $ac > bc$ if $c > 0$, and $ac < bc$ if $c < 0$. [p. 128]

multiplicative identity

The product of a number and the multiplicative identity is the original number. 1 is the multiplicative identity for real numbers. [p. 273]

multiplicative identity matrix

A square matrix with a diagonal of 1's running from upper left to lower right and 0's for all other entries, sometimes denoted *I*. If *A* is an $n \times n$ matrix and *I* is the $n \times n$ identity matrix, then $AI = IA = A$. [p. 61]

multiplicative inverse (reciprocal)

Two numbers are multiplicative inverses if they multiply to 1. [p. 273]

multiplicative inverse matrix

A^{-1} is the multiplicative inverse matrix of matrix *A* if and only if their product (in either order) is the multiplicative identity matrix for *A*. [p. 61]

mutually exclusive events

Events that have no common outcomes. [p. 424]

natural log (ln)

A logarithm with base *e*. [p. 653]

normal distribution

A statistical distribution characterized by a bell-shaped curve. About 68% of data in a normal distribution lie within one standard deviation of the mean. [p. 788]

objective function

In linear programming, an equation that gives the value of a quantity to be optimized in terms of the variables in the problem. [p. 212]

optimal solution

In linear programming, the solution that gives the best possible value (maximum or minimum) of the objective function. [p. 212]

outcome

Any possible result of a probability experiment. [p. 32]

parabola

The graph of a quadratic function. [p. 308]

parallel lines

Coplanar lines that do not intersect. If two lines have the same slope, then they are parallel.

parameter

When the position of a point in an *x-y* plane is described in terms of a third variable, the third variable is a parameter. [p. 311]

parent function

The basic function for a family of functions. For instance, $y = x^2$ is the parent function of the family of quadratic functions. [p. 317]

partial sum

In a series, the sum of the terms up to and including a given term. [p. 240]

Pascal's Triangle

A triangular arrangement of numbers that gives the coefficients for a binomial expansion. The first and last numbers in each row are 1's, and each other number is the sum of the numbers above it to the left and right. [p. 445]

$$
\begin{array}{ccccccc}
 & & & 1 & & & \\
 & & 1 & & 1 & & \\
 & 1 & & 2 & & 1 & \\
1 & & 3 & & 3 & & 1 \\
\end{array}
$$
$$\cdots$$

path

A series of vertices, and edges connecting vertices, in a graph. [p. 810]

perimeter

The distance around the outside of a plane figure.

period

The length of the smallest repeating pattern in the graph of a periodic function. [p. 730]

periodic function

A function whose graph repeats itself in a consistent way. A function $f(x)$ is periodic if there is a constant $p > 0$, so that $f(x + p) = f(x)$ for all values of *x*. [p. 730]

permutation

An ordered arrangement of a set of items. [p. 429]

perpendicular lines

Two lines that intersect at right angles. If the product of the slopes of two lines is -1, then they are perpendicular.

phase shift

The horizontal shift of a sine or cosine graph. [p. 739]

point-slope form

The point-slope form of an equation of a line through a point (x_1, y_1) with slope m is $y - y_1 = m(x - x_1)$. [p. 93]

point symmetry

If a plane figure coincides with itself after a 180° rotation around a point, it has point symmetry with respect to the point. [p. 469]

polygon

A plane figure whose sides are three or more segments that intersect only at their endpoints. Consecutive sides cannot be collinear, and no more than two sides can meet at any one vertex.

polyhedron

A solid whose faces are polygons. [p. 804]

polynomial

Any expression of the form $a_n x^n + a_{n-1} x^{n-1} + \cdots + a_1 x + a_0$, where n is a nonnegative integer and $a_0, ..., a_n$ are constant coefficients. [p. 542]

polynomial equation

An equation of the form $P(x) = c$, where $P(x)$ is a polynomial and c is a constant. [p. 566]

polynomial function

A function where $f(x)$ is equal to a polynomial expression, such as $f(x) = -2x^4 + 7x^3 - x + 4$ or $y = -2x^4 + 7x^3 - x + 4$. [p. 542]

population

The entire group being investigated in a statistical study. [p. 780]

power

A base taken to an exponent. 3^5 is the fifth power of 3. [p. 474]

power regression

A power regression equation is an equation of the form $y = Ax^B$ used to model data. The curve of best fit is called a power regression curve. [p. 493]

pre-image

A point or figure to which a transformation is applied.

principal square root

The nonnegative square root of a nonnegative number. [p. 279]

Principle of Zero Products

If m and n are real numbers and $mn = 0$, then either $m = 0$ or $n = 0$. [p. 349]

probability

The probability of an event is the fraction of time it is expected to occur. (See *theoretical probability*.) [p. 32]

product matrix

The matrix that results from multiplying two or more matrices. (See *matrix multiplication*.) [p. 58]

quadratic equation

An equation that results when a quadratic function takes on a particular value. $y = 2x^2 + 3x - 7$ is a quadratic function; $12 = 2x^2 + 3x - 7$ is a quadratic equation. [p. 340]

quadratic form

An equation in quadratic form contains a trinomial with a variable raised to powers that are multiples of 2, 1, and 0. For example, $x^6 - 4x^3 - 5 = 0$ is in quadratic form. [p. 506]

quadratic formula

A general formula, $x = \dfrac{-b \pm \sqrt{b^2 - 4ac}}{2a}$, that can be used to solve any quadratic equation in the form $ax^2 + bx + c = 0$. [p. 354]

quadratic function

A function that can be expressed in the form $f(x) = ax^2 + bx + c$, where a, b, and c are real-number constants and $a \neq 0$. [p. 308]

quadratic-linear system

A system of equations with a linear equation and a quadratic relation. [p. 400]

quadratic-quadratic system

A system of quadratic relations. [p. 405]

quartic

A polynomial function of degree four. [p. 543]

radian measure

The radian measure of an arc (or the central angle that intercepts the arc) is the ratio of the arc's length to the radius of the circle. [p. 689]

radical equation

An equation that contains at least one radical expression. [p. 498]

radical symbol

The radical symbol is $\sqrt{}$. [p. 279]

radicand

The number inside a radical symbol. In $\sqrt[12]{2}$, 2 is the radicand. [p. 486]

radius

The distance from the center of a circle to a point on the circle. Also, a segment whose endpoints are the center of a circle and a point on the circle. [p. 373]

random sample

A random sample of a population is chosen so that every subject has an equal probability of being chosen for the sample, and the selection of a particular subject has no effect on the chances of any other subject being chosen. [p. 780]

range

The range of a function is the set of all possible values of the dependent variable. [p. 22]

rate of change

The amount that the value of one variable changes in response to a unit change in another. [p. 79]

rational equation

An equation involving rational expressions. [p. 603]

rational expression

A ratio of polynomials, such as $\frac{3x^2 + 2x - 5}{4x - 7}$ and $\frac{2x - 1}{x(x + 3)}$. [p. 587]

rational function

A function of the form $r(x) = \frac{p(x)}{q(x)}$, where $p(x)$ and $q(x)$ are polynomials. [p. 598]

rational numbers

Real numbers that can be expressed in the form $\frac{a}{b}$, where a and b are integers and $b \neq 0$. [p. 278]

Rational Roots Theorem

Let $P(x) = a_n x^n + a_{n-1} x^{n-1} + \cdots + a_1 x + a_0$ be any polynomial with integer coefficients. If b and c are integers with no common factors and $\frac{b}{c}$ is a rational root of the equation $P(x) = 0$, then b is a divisor of a_0 and c is a divisor of a_n. [p. 577]

real axis

The horizontal axis in the complex plane. [p. 291]

real numbers

All numbers on a number line. [p. 278]

real part (of a complex number)

The real part of a complex number $a + bi$ is a. [p. 287]

real roots

The zeros of an equation that occur at x-intercepts of the graph of the related function. [p. 556]

rectangular hyperbola

A hyperbola whose asymptotes are the coordinate axes. The graph of an inverse variation is a rectangular hyperbola. [p. 462]

recursion formula

A formula that tells how to find each term of a sequence from previous terms. [p. 830]

recursive definition

A definition of a sequence that includes the values of one or more initial terms and a recursion formula. [p. 233]

reference angle

The angle formed by the terminal side of an angle and the x-axis. [p. 702]

reflection

A transformation of the points in a plane that maps each point onto another point so that the line of reflection is the perpendicular bisector of the segment connecting corresponding points.

Reflexive Property of Equality

For any real number a, $a = a$.

regression line

A line of best fit found by linear regression. [p. 117]

relation

A set of ordered pairs. [p. 525]

relative maximum

The greatest y-value within a specified interval. [p. 550]

relative minimum

The least y-value within a specified interval. [p. 550]

Remainder Theorem

If a polynomial $P(x)$ is divided by $(x - a)$, where a is a constant, then the remainder is $P(a)$. [p. 572]

representative sample

In statistics, a sample that is representative of the population being studied. [p. 780]

resultant vector

The sum of two or more vectors acting on the same object. [p. 711]

rise

The vertical change between two points on a graph. [p. 80]

root(s) of an equation

The solution(s) of an equation in the form $f(x) = 0$. [p. 342]

rotation

A transformation of the points in a plane that turns each point around one point, the center of rotation. A rotation of $n°$ around center C maps every other point A onto A', so that $m\angle ACA' = n°$ and $AC = CA'$.

run

The horizontal change between two points on a graph. [p. 80]

sample

In statistics, a subset of the population being studied. [p. 780]

sample space

The set of all possible outcomes of a probability experiment. [p. 32]

sampling with replacement

Choosing a series of items from a set when you allow items that are chosen once to be chosen again. [p. 771]

sampling without replacement

Choosing a series of items from a set when you do not allow an item to be chosen more than once. [p. 771]

scalar multiplication

The process of multiplying a matrix by a number. The scalar product of a number r and a matrix A is the matrix rA. [p. 51]

scatter plot

A graph that shows a set of points, each based on paired data. [p. 6]

scientific notation

A number is in scientific notation if it is in the form $a \times 10^n$, where $1 \le a < 10$ and n is an integer. [p. 476]

secant (sec)

In a right triangle $\triangle ABC$ with right angle $\angle C$, the secant of $\angle A = \sec A = \dfrac{\text{length of hypotenuse}}{\text{length of adjacent leg}} = \dfrac{c}{b}$. [p. 681]

sector

A portion of a circle bounded by an arc and the radii drawn to its endpoints. [p. 694]

self-similarity

A figure has self-similarity if a part of the figure viewed at a particular scale resembles a corresponding part viewed at a different scale.

sequence

An ordered list of numbers. [p. 233]

series

The sum of the terms of a sequence. [p. 240]

sigma notation

Notation for a series that uses the Greek letter Σ (sigma). [p. 241]

simulation

An experiment designed to find an approximation for a theoretical probability. [p. 38]

sine (sin)

In a right triangle $\triangle ABC$ with right angle $\angle C$, the sine of $\angle A = \sin A = \dfrac{\text{length of opposite leg}}{\text{length of hypotenuse}} = \dfrac{a}{c}$. [p. 681]

slope

The steepness and direction of a line in a coordinate plane. The slope of a line is the ratio of the *change in y* (Δy) to the *change in x* (Δx) as you move from one point on the line to another. [p. 80]

slope-intercept form

The slope-intercept form of an equation of a line with slope m and y-intercept b is $y = mx + b$. [p. 92]

solution(s) of an equation

The values for the variables in an equation that make the equation true. [p. 86]

solution(s) of an inequality

The values for the variables in an inequality that make the inequality true. [p. 128]

spanning tree

A tree that contains every vertex of a graph. [p. 819]

square matrix

A matrix with the same number of columns and rows. [p. 61]

square root

A square root of a number a is a number c such that $c^2 = a$. [p. 279]

standard deviation

A measure of how far the data in a data set deviates from the mean. The standard deviation of a data set with n elements $x_1, x_2, x_3, x_4, \ldots, x_n$, whose mean is $\bar{x}$, is given by:

$$\text{standard deviation} = \sqrt{\frac{\sum_{i=1}^{n}(\bar{x} - x_i)^2}{n}}. \text{ [p. 788]}$$

standard form for a circle

The standard form of the equation of a circle with radius r and center (h, k) is $(x - h)^2 + (y - k)^2 = r^2$. [p. 374]

standard form for a hyperbola

The standard form of an equation of a hyperbola with center $(0, 0)$ and *vertices on the x-axis* is:
$$\frac{x^2}{a^2} - \frac{y^2}{b^2} = 1.$$

The standard form of an equation of a hyperbola with center $(0, 0)$ and *vertices on the y-axis* is:
$$\frac{y^2}{a^2} - \frac{x^2}{b^2} = 1. \text{ [p. 390]}$$

standard form for a quadratic equation

The standard form for a quadratic equation is $ax^2 + bx + c = 0$. [p. 342]

standard form for an ellipse

The standard form of the equation of an ellipse with center $(0, 0)$ and *major axis on the x-axis* is:
$$\frac{x^2}{a^2} + \frac{y^2}{b^2} = 1, \text{ where } a^2 > b^2.$$

The standard form of the equation of an ellipse with center $(0, 0)$ and *major axis on the y-axis* is:
$$\frac{x^2}{b^2} + \frac{y^2}{a^2} = 1, \text{ where } a^2 > b^2. \text{ [p. 381]}$$

substitution method

A method for solving a system of equations where you reduce the number of variables in one equation by substituting for the other variable(s). [p. 168]

supplementary angles

Two angles whose measures add to $180°$.

Symmetric Property of Equality

For any real numbers a and b, if $a = b$, then $b = a$.

symmetry

A figure has symmetry if it coincides with itself after some transformation.

system of linear equations

A set of two or more linear equations with the same variables. [p. 160]

system of linear inequalities

A set of two or more linear inequalities with the same variables. [p. 198]

tangent (tan)

In a right triangle $\triangle ABC$ with right angle $\angle C$, the tangent of $\angle A = \tan A = \frac{\text{length of opposite leg}}{\text{length of adjacent leg}} = \frac{a}{b}$. [p. 681]

term

A number in a sequence. [p. 233] Also, a monomial that is part of a polynomial.

terminal side

In trigonometry, the terminal side of an angle has its vertex at the origin and is located by a rotation from the positive x-axis. [p. 700]

theoretical probability

If an event E consists of m outcomes out of a sample space of n possible equally likely outcomes, the theoretical probability of that event is $P(E) = \frac{m}{n}$. [p. 33]

transition matrix

A matrix whose entries are transition probabilities. The probabilities in each column of a transition matrix add to 1. [p. 837]

transition probability

The probability of a change from one state to another. [p. 836]

transition state

The possible states that can be taken on in a situation involving change. [p. 836]

Transitive Property of Equality

For any three real numbers, a, b, and c, if $a = b$ and $b = c$, then $a = c$.

translation

A transformation that moves all points in a plane a fixed distance in a given direction.

tree

A connected graph that contains no circuits. [p. 819]

tree diagram

A diagram whose branches show the possible outcomes of a probability experiment. [p. 422]

trend line

A line drawn through scattered data so that about half the data lies above the line and half below it. The trend line helps show the association between the sets of data. [p. 6]

trigonometric function

A function that involves a trigonometric ratio.

trigonometry

The relationships among the angle measures and side lengths of triangles. [p. 680]

trinomial

A polynomial with three terms. [p. 542]

trinomial square

A trinomial that can be factored as the square of a binomial where the coefficients of the terms in the binomial are integers. [p. 331]

variable

A quantity whose value can change or vary. [p. 13]

vector

A quantity that is characterized both by a *magnitude* and a *direction*. [p. 711]

vertex (of a parabola)

The turning point of the parabola. [p. 309]

Vertex Theorem

If a linear programming problem has an optimal solution, then one of the vertices of the feasible region represents an optimal solution. [p. 216]

vertical asymptote

A vertical line that is an asymptote of the graph of a function. [p. 599]

vertices of a hyperbola

The two points on the hyperbola nearest its center. [p. 390]

vertices of an ellipse

The endpoints of the major and minor axes of the ellipse. [p. 381]

volume

The number of cubic units contained in a solid.

whole numbers

The nonnegative integers: 0, 1, 2, …. [p. 278]

***y*-intercept**

The y-value of a point where a graph crosses the y-axis. [p. 92]

zero(s) of a function

The value(s) of x for which the value of the function is zero. The real zeros of a function are the x-intercepts of its graph in the coordinate plane. [p. 342]

SELECTED ANSWERS

CHAPTER 1

1-1 Part A Try It

a. Negative association

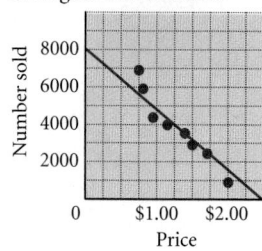

1-1 Part A Exercises

1. a–c.

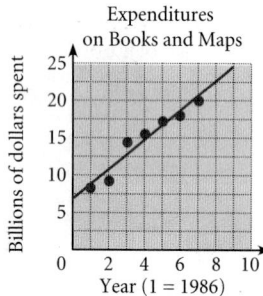

Expenditures on Books and Maps

c. Positive association
d. As the year number increases, the amount spent on books and maps increases.
3. Positive association
9. No association
10. a–b.

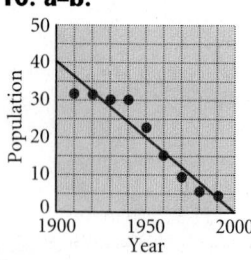

b. Negative association
c. Yes, around the year 2000
d. No **11.** Possible answer: Side length and area of a square **12.** Possible answer: Winning times and years in the Indianapolis 500
13. Possible answer: Speed of light (in a vacuum) and the height of the tide

14. a–b. Negative

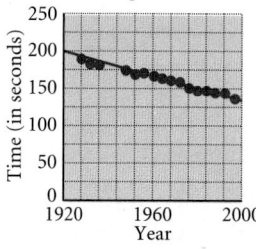

c. 145 sec **d.** 182 sec; 180 sec
15. Stays the same
17. Varies **19.** $y = x + 5$
27. a–b.

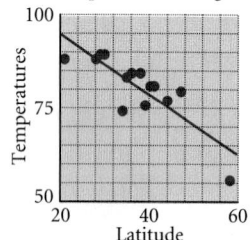

Latitude and Mean Temperatures in August

29. a–b.

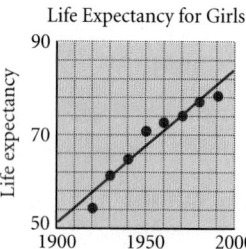

Life Expectancy for Girls

31. More data points usually increase confidence in predictions.

1-1 Part B Try It

a. $y = 5x$

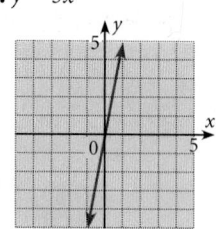

b. $y = 2x + 3$

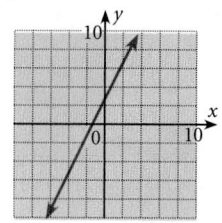

c. $t = 0.05d$ **d.** Dependent variable: t; Independent variable: d

1-1 Part B Exercises

1. a. Positive
b.

x	−2	−1	0	1	2	3	4	5
y	−6	−3	0	3	6	9	12	15

c. $y = 3x$ **d.** 75
e. $(-2, -6), (-1, -3),$ $(0, 0), (1, 3), (2, 6), (3, 9),$ $(4, 12), (5, 15)$
f.

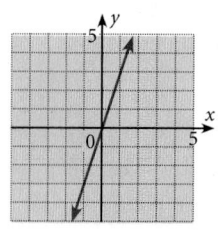

5.

x	0	1	2	3	4	5
y	6	7	8	9	10	11

$y = x + 6$

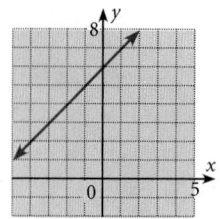

7.

x	0	1	2	3	4	5
y	1	4	7	10	13	16

$y = 3x + 1$

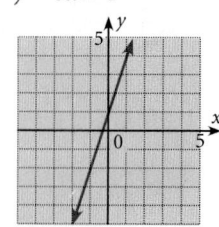

9.

x	1	2	3	4	5	6
y	3	6	11	18	27	38

$y = x^2 + 2$

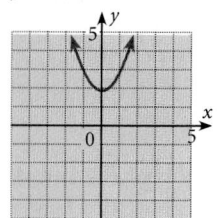

11. a. $s = 3n - 2$
b. $s = 133$ **c.** $n = 27$
15.

x	−2	−1	0	1	2	3
y	4	2	2	4	8	14

19. 225 cm² **21.** 540 mm²
23. 357.1 cm²
25.

x	0	1	2	3	4	5
y	0	6	12	18	24	30

$y = 6x$

27.

x	0	1	2	3	4	5
y	−1	1	3	5	7	9

$y = 2x - 1$

29.

x	0	1	2	3	4	5
y	−2	−1	2	7	14	23

$y = x^2 - 2$

31. a. $h = 70t$ **b.** 350
c. $h = 95t$ **d.** 125
e.

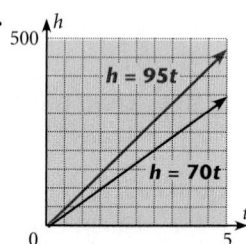

33.

x	0	1	2	3	4	5
y	5	5.5	6	6.5	7	7.5

35.

x	0	1	2	3	4	5
y	3	$3\frac{2}{3}$	$4\frac{1}{3}$	5	$5\frac{2}{3}$	$6\frac{1}{3}$

37.

x	−2	−1	0	1	2	3
y	−8	−1	0	1	8	27

39. a. 59°F **41. a.** About 30 mi/hr; 0 mi/hr **b.** D; H
c. A; C **d.** Moving at a constant speed (or stationary)
e. About 30 minutes after leaving Seattle **f.** D

1-1 Part C Try It

a. −21 **b.** Domain: all real numbers; Range: all real numbers greater than or equal to 3 **c.** No

1-1 Part C Exercises

1. a. $f(x) = 55x$ **b.** 220
c. There is only one value of $f(x)$ for each value of x.
d. Domain: nonnegative real numbers; Range: nonnegative real numbers
e.

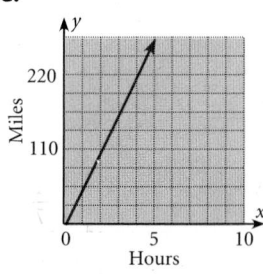

7. Not a function
9. Function; Domain: real numbers greater than or equal to one; Range: nonnegative real numbers
11. Not a function
15. a. $f(x) = 2x - 2$
b.

x	0	1	2	3	4	5
f(x)	−2	0	2	4	6	8

c.

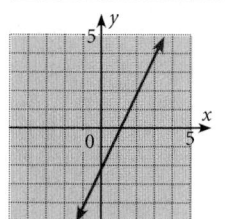

19. $\frac{1}{2}$ **21.** $\frac{1}{3}$ **23.** Function
25. Function **27.** Function
29. Function **31. a.** 0
b. −5 **c.** 0 **d.** −3 **e.** 4
f. $|n| - 5$ **33. a.** $A = 4\pi r^2$
b.

r	1	2	3	4	5
A	4π	16π	36π	64π	100π

c. i. $484\pi \approx 1{,}521$ cm²
ii. $146{,}410{,}000\pi \approx 45{,}996{,}000$ km²

1-1 Part D Self-Assessment

1. No association
2. Negative association
3. Positive association
4.

x	0	1	2	3	4	5
y	2	5	8	11	14	17

$y = 3x + 2$

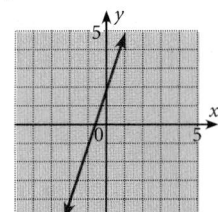

5. a–b.

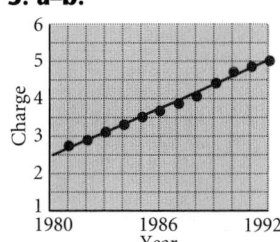

b. Positive association
c. About $2.50
6. a. No association
b.

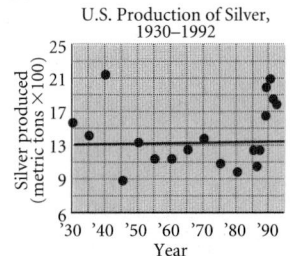

7.

x	0	1	2	3	4	5
y	0	6	12	18	24	30

$y = 6x$

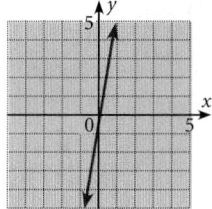

8.

x	0	1	2	3	4	5
y	3	2	−1	−6	−13	−22

$y = 3 - x^2$

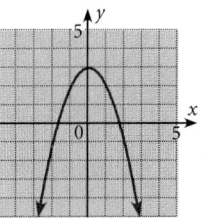

9. 37.5 in.² **10.** 80 cm²
11. a. 260 **b.** $c = 13r$
c. Independent: r; Dependent: c **d.** 31 minutes
12. Function **13.** Function
14. Function **15.** (d)
16. (c) **17. a.** −6 **b.** 0
c. 24 **d.** 0 **e.** $\frac{26}{25}$
f. $n^2 - 5n$
18. a. $y = 1.2x + 4$
b.

Distance	1	2	5	10
Fare	5.20	6.40	10	16

c. Domain: nonnegative reals; Range: all real numbers ≥ 4

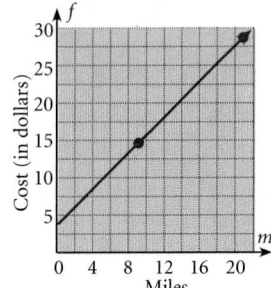

d. 14.80 **e.** Almost 21 miles

1-2 Part A Try It

a. $\frac{1}{3}$ **b.** $\frac{3}{8}$ **c.** $\frac{7}{10}$

1-2 Part A Exercises

1. a. {1, 2, 3, 4, 5, 6, 7, 8}
b. Spinning an even number
c. {2, 4, 6, 8} **d.** $\frac{1}{2}$
3. {green, yellow, blue}
5. {$\overline{AB}$, $\overline{AC}$, $\overline{AD}$, $\overline{BC}$, $\overline{BD}$, $\overline{CD}$}
7. 26 **9.** 8 **11.** 3 **15.** 0.23
19. a. 0.43 **b.** 0.32 **c.** 0.24
d. 0.25 **27.** Negative

29. 12 **31.** 6 **33.** 2 **35.** 3
37. a. 0.5 **b.** 0.3 **c.** 0.4
d. 0.5 **e.** 1 **f.** 0.4 **39.** 0.25
41. a. 0.02 ← U.S.
b. 0.70 ← Water
c. 0.03 ← South America
d. 0.30 ← Land

1-2 Part B Try It

a. Possible answer: Rolling a die **b.** Possible answer: Flipping a coin

1-2 Part B Exercises

1. a. 4; 6; 9; 1 **b.** 0.45
c. 0.20 **3.** Roll a die. Let "1" or "2" represent those eating in a restaurant. **5.** False
9. a. 0.75 **b.** No
10. a. Let 0, 1, 2, 3, 4, 5, and 6 represent success. One digit is needed per free throw. Two consecutive digits represent two free throws. **b. i.** 0.50
ii. 0.40 **iii.** 0.10
13.

Age	Male Drivers
Under 16	35,000
16	739,000
17	1,098,000
18	1,311,000
19	1,490,000

17. Table of random numbers; let four digits represent Anchorage residents.
19. Roll a die; let 1 or 2 represent small cars.
23. a. 0.41 **b.** Answers should be close to the theoretical probability, which is about 0.43.
25. About 7 trips

1-2 Part C Self-Assessment

1. 2 **2.** 3 **3.** 2 **4.** (c)
5. a. 0.50 **b.** 0.10 **c.** 0.20
d. 0.30 **e.** 0.05 **f.** 0
6. a. 0.33 **b.** 0.85 **c.** 0.48

7. Possible answer: Probability that a certain number of people will get sick from exposure to a virus. Numbers with many significant figures are cumbersome to use.
8. Negative association
9. a. 2 **b.** −22 **c.** −13 **d.** 44 **e.** $6n - 16$ **10.** Experimental
11. $\frac{1}{75} \approx 0.01$ **12.** 0.03
13. a. 0.50 **b.** 0.23
14. Possible answer: 0.25
15. Possible answer: 0.72
16. Possible answer: The northbound bus always arrives one minute after the southbound bus.

1-3 Part A Try It

a. 4 **b.** $\begin{bmatrix} 0 & 10 \\ 10 & 10 \end{bmatrix}$
c. Not possible
d. $\begin{bmatrix} 9 & 18 \\ 6 & -3 \end{bmatrix}$ **e.** $\begin{bmatrix} 9 & -2 \\ -14 & -23 \end{bmatrix}$
f.

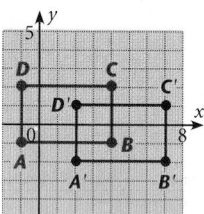

$$V + T = \begin{bmatrix} 2 & 7 & 7 & 2 \\ -2 & -2 & 1 & 1 \end{bmatrix}$$

g.

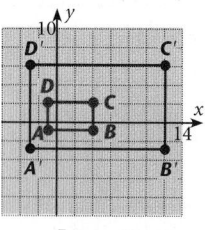

$$3V = \begin{bmatrix} -3 & 12 & 12 & -3 \\ & -3 & 6 & \end{bmatrix}$$

1-3 Part A Exercises

1. a. 3×4 **b.** −5 **c.** $i = 3$, $j = 2$
d. $\begin{bmatrix} 0 & 6 & -10 & 6 \\ 10 & -14 & 4 & -2 \\ 8 & 16 & 4 & 12 \end{bmatrix}$

3. $\begin{bmatrix} 12 & 0 \\ 7 & 0 \end{bmatrix}$ **5.** $\begin{bmatrix} 0 & 0 & 0 \\ 0 & 0 & 0 \\ 0 & 0 & 0 \end{bmatrix}$

7. $\begin{bmatrix} \frac{3}{2} & -\frac{7}{2} \\ 2 & 1 \end{bmatrix}$ **9.** $\begin{bmatrix} -3 & 7 \\ -4 & -2 \end{bmatrix}$

13. a. Use $A + B - C = \begin{bmatrix} 41 & 48 \\ 34 & 19 \end{bmatrix}$.
b. Male; Basic.
c. $1.05 \begin{bmatrix} 41 & 48 \\ 34 & 19 \end{bmatrix} \approx \begin{bmatrix} 43 & 50 \\ 36 & 20 \end{bmatrix}$
17. a. Total, 16 and older
$\begin{bmatrix} 117{,}914 & 116{,}877 \\ 6{,}874 & 8{,}426 \end{bmatrix}$

Men, 20 and older
$\begin{bmatrix} 61{,}198 & 60{,}174 \\ 3{,}170 & 4{,}109 \end{bmatrix}$

Women, 20 and older
$\begin{bmatrix} 50{,}455 & 50{,}535 \\ 2{,}555 & 3{,}028 \end{bmatrix}$

b. $\begin{bmatrix} 111{,}653 & 110{,}709 \\ 5{,}725 & 7{,}137 \end{bmatrix}$

c. $\begin{bmatrix} 6261 & 6168 \\ 1149 & 1289 \end{bmatrix}$

19. 0.36 **21.** $A = 3 \times 4$; $B = 3 \times 2$ **23.** $i = 1$, $j = 3$ in A
27. $\begin{bmatrix} -20 & 10 \\ -15 & -5 \end{bmatrix}$ **29.** $\begin{bmatrix} 15 & -3 \\ 21 & 18 \\ -6 & 0 \end{bmatrix}$
31. Not possible because the matrices do not have the same dimension.
33. $\begin{bmatrix} -5 & 6 \\ 3 & 1 \end{bmatrix}$ **35.** $\begin{bmatrix} 2.5 & -0.5 \\ 3.5 & 3 \\ -1 & 0 \end{bmatrix}$
37. $\begin{bmatrix} 24 & -2 \\ 20 & 10 \\ -10 & 8 \end{bmatrix}$
39.

	1970	1980	1990
Venezuela	3.71	2.17	2.14
Saudi Arabia	3.80	9.90	6.45
Nigeria	1.08	2.06	1.83
Indonesia	0.85	1.58	1.46

41. a^2: 1

1-3 Part B Try It

a. 3×5 **b.** $\begin{bmatrix} 0 \\ 20 \end{bmatrix}$
c. Not possible **d.** Not possible
e. $\begin{bmatrix} 3 & 4 \\ -9 & -12 \\ 15 & 20 \end{bmatrix}$

1-3 Part B Exercises

1. a. 2×2, 2×3 **b.** 5 **c.** 6
d. $1 \cdot 5 + 2(-3)$
e. $AB = \begin{bmatrix} 5 & 6 & -1 \\ 13 & 10 & 3 \end{bmatrix}$
Dimension 2×3
2.
$\begin{bmatrix} 1 \cdot 6 + 2 \cdot -1 & 1 \cdot 7 + 2 \cdot -2 \\ 4 \cdot 6 + 5 \cdot -1 & 4 \cdot 7 + 5 \cdot -2 \end{bmatrix}$
$= \begin{bmatrix} 4 & 3 \\ 19 & 18 \end{bmatrix}$
5. AB does not exist.
7. a. Yes **b.** Yes **c.** Total videos rented during 1992–1994 for each of the two stores. **9.** Not possible
21. $-4x$ **23.** $-6c - 11$
25. a. x-values increase by 1; corresponding y-values decrease by 3.
b–c.

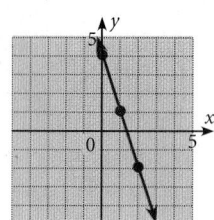

Straight line; $y = -3x + 4$
27. a. AB does not exist.
b. 4×1 **c.** AB does not exist.
29. $\begin{bmatrix} -22 \\ 4 \end{bmatrix}$ **33.** Not possible
37. $\begin{bmatrix} 36 & -12 & 33 \\ 68 & 0 & 29 \\ -13 & 23 & -98 \end{bmatrix}$
39. Yes
41. a. $\begin{bmatrix} 530 & 810 & 1060 & 620 \\ 710 & 910 & 1290 & 850 \end{bmatrix}$;
$\begin{bmatrix} .80 \\ .40 \\ .30 \\ .70 \end{bmatrix}$ **b.** $\begin{bmatrix} 1500 \\ 1914 \end{bmatrix}$
45. $AB = \begin{bmatrix} 9 & 8 & 4 \\ 9 & -47 & 59 \\ 18 & -28 & 52 \end{bmatrix}$
$AC = \begin{bmatrix} 9 & 8 & 4 \\ 9 & -47 & 59 \\ 18 & -28 & 52 \end{bmatrix}$
Thus $AB = AC$, but $B \neq C$.

1-3 Part C Self Assessment

1. (a) **2.** False **3.** False
4. a. 4×1 **b.** Does not exist **c.** 2×5
5. $\begin{bmatrix} 7 & -3 & 4 \\ -3 & 11 & 1 \\ 7 & 8 & 0 \end{bmatrix}$
6. $\begin{bmatrix} -44 & 20 & 24 \\ 8 & 0 & 36 \end{bmatrix}$
7. Not possible
8. $\begin{bmatrix} 7 & 12 & -9 \\ -9 & 26 & 10 \\ -14 & -4 & -14 \end{bmatrix}$
9. $\begin{bmatrix} 15 & -11 & 17 \\ 4 & 27 & -15 \\ -6 & -10 & -2 \end{bmatrix}$
10. $\begin{bmatrix} 95 & -28 \\ 13 & -5 \end{bmatrix}$
11. Not possible
12. $\begin{bmatrix} -69 & 79 & -7 \\ 30 & 36 & -7 \end{bmatrix}$
13. $\begin{bmatrix} 15 & -7 \\ 5 & -2 \end{bmatrix} \times \begin{bmatrix} 1 & 0 \\ 0 & 1 \end{bmatrix} = \begin{bmatrix} 15 & -7 \\ 5 & -2 \end{bmatrix}$
14. Yes **15.** 0.50 **16.** 0.30
17. a. 0.14 **b.** Yes
18. a. 15 **b.** $n = 3$
$\begin{bmatrix} 4 & 9 & 2 \\ 3 & 5 & 7 \\ 8 & 1 & 6 \end{bmatrix}$
19. a. 2×3
b. $1.1 \times \begin{bmatrix} 320 & 290 & 340 \\ 530 & 310 & 130 \end{bmatrix}$
$= \begin{bmatrix} 352 & 319 & 374 \\ 583 & 341 & 143 \end{bmatrix}$
20. a. Books Submitted (thousands)
$\begin{bmatrix} 376 & 438 & 156 & 94 \\ 372 & 470 & 148 & 104 \\ 360 & 474 & 151 & 110 \end{bmatrix}$;
$\begin{bmatrix} 0.015 \\ 0.011 \\ 0.025 \\ 0.021 \end{bmatrix}$ **b.** $\begin{bmatrix} 16{,}332 \\ 16{,}634 \\ 16{,}699 \end{bmatrix}$
c. Total books published in each year.

Chapter 1 Review

1. (d) **2.** (b) **3.** Yes; Domain {0, 1, 2, 3}; Range {1, 2, 3, 4} **4.** Not a function **5.** $y = 2x - 1$

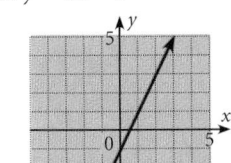

6. Independent variable = price per gallon; Dependent variable = average gallons purchased **7.** Negative association **8.** 10 gallons **9. a.** 1 **b.** 10 **c.** 5 **d.** $1\frac{1}{4}$ **e.** $n^2 + 1$ **10.** 0.14 **11.** 0.26 **12.** Experimental probability is based on observation of actual trials, and theoretical probability is calculated using logic. **13.** Let H = girl, T = boy; Probability: 0.44

14. $\begin{bmatrix} -4 & 8 \\ 8 & 0 \\ 2 & -3 \end{bmatrix}$ **15.** $\begin{bmatrix} 10 & -8 \\ -12 & -6 \\ 6 & 12 \end{bmatrix}$

16. [8 42]

17. $\begin{bmatrix} 63 & 19 & 42 \\ 58 & 37 & 61 \end{bmatrix} \times \begin{bmatrix} 65 \\ 79 \\ 102 \end{bmatrix} = \begin{bmatrix} 9,880 \\ 12,915 \end{bmatrix}$

18. a. i. $\begin{bmatrix} 1 & 1 & 1 & 1 \\ 0 & 0 & 0 & 0 \end{bmatrix}$

ii. $\begin{bmatrix} -9 & -9 & -9 & -9 \\ 1 & 1 & 1 & 1 \end{bmatrix}$

b. 0.01 **c.** Positive association

CHAPTER 2

2-1 Part A Try It

a. Linear; Not direct variation **b.** Not linear **c.** Linear; Direct variation **d.** Linear; Direct variation **e.** $\frac{1}{6}$ **f.** -4 **g.** 1.8

2-1 Part A Exercises

1. a. $20; $30 **b.** $y = 10x$ **c.** 10 **3.** $\frac{2}{3}$ **5.** $-\frac{4}{3}$ **9.** 1.28

11. Linear; Slope 6; Not direct variation **13.** Not linear **15.** Linear: Slope -2, Not direct variation **23.** $\frac{y-2}{x-1}$ **25.** Linear, slope 9; Not direct variation **27.** Linear, slope -2; Not direct variation **29.** Not linear **31.** Linear, slope $-\frac{6}{5}$; Not direct variation **33.** Not linear **35.** Linear, slope -1; Direct variation **37.** Linear, slope -1; Not direct variation **39.** $d = 2x$; Direct variation **41.** 8 **43.** $\frac{5}{2}$ **45.** 3 **47. a.** $C = \frac{21}{37} U$, where C is Confederate troop strength and U is Union troop strength.

2-1 Part B Try It

a. $x = 4$ **b.** $x = 6$ **c.** $z = 5$ **d.** $x = -4$ **e.** $t = \frac{d}{r}$; Light traffic $\frac{1}{2}$ hour; Heavy traffic $\frac{3}{4}$ hour

2-1 Part B Exercises

1. a. Original equation **b.** Subtract 8. **c.** Subtract $4x$. **d.** Divide by 2. **3. a.** $x = 4$ **b.** $x = -5$ **c.** $x = -2$ **5.** $y = 0.79x$ **9.** $x = 7$ **11.** $x = -2.4$ **13.** $x = 7$ **15.** No solution **19.** $x = 464$ **21.** $x = 2.25$ **23. a.** $t = 4.89m$ **25.** $\begin{bmatrix} 5 & -10 \\ 10 & -5 \end{bmatrix}$ **27.** (a), (c) **29. a.** $x \approx 1.4$ **b.** $x = 6$ **c.** $x \approx -3.1$ **31.** $c = -5$ **33.** $t = -3.2$ **35.** $b = 1$ **37.** $x = 70$ **39. a.** $1.5x + 1$ **b.** $10 = 1.5x + 1$; $x = 6$ **41.** $p = -12$ **43.** $x = 21$ **45.** No solution **47.** $z = -5$ **49.** $y = 5$ **51.** $T = 20$ **53.** $0 = 1200 - 1.5x$

2-1 Part C Try It

a. $y = 3x - \frac{4}{3}$; Slope 3; y-intercept $-\frac{4}{3}$ **b.** $y = \frac{3}{2}x - 3$ **c.** $y - 5 = -2(x + 3)$ **d.** $y - 2 = -1(x - 1)$ or $y - 7 = -1(x + 4)$ **e.** Parallel: (i) and (iv) Perpendicular: (iii) and (v)

2-1 Part C Exercises

1.

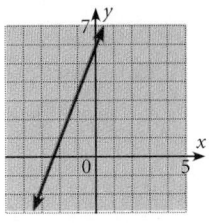

a. 2.5; The coefficient of x **b.** 6; The constant term **5.** $y = 2$ **7.** $y = \frac{1}{2}x - 1$ **11.** $y = -x + 2$ **13.** $(y - 0.12) = -0.015(x - 3)$ **15.** $y = -\frac{1}{3}x + 73\frac{1}{3}$ **21.** $y = -\frac{1}{2}x - 1$ **23.** $y = x + 1$ **25. a.** $y = -\frac{2}{3}x + \frac{13}{3}$ **b.** $y = \frac{3}{2}x - 8$

27. a.

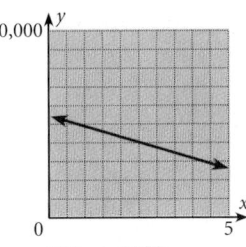

$y = -556x + 5380$

b. Slope is depreciation per year; y-intercept is value when new **c.** $3712 **29.** The right-hand graph **31.** $m = -3$; Possible answer: (10, 6) **33.** Perpendicular **35.** Parallel **37.** Perpendicular **39.** $y - 3 = 4(x - 1)$ **41.** $y - 5 = -\frac{3}{5}(x + 3)$ **43.** $y = -\frac{7}{5}x + 10$ **45.** $y = 0.06x + 6$ **47.** $y = 2x + 3$ **49.** $y + 5 = \frac{1}{2}(x - 4)$ **51.** $x = \frac{3}{7}$ **53. a.** $32.62 is total hourly cost per employee; $23.80 is fixed cost per week **b.** $C = 32.62x + 23.80$ **c.** $937.16 **d.** About 26.86 hours; $711.81

2-1 Part D Self-Assessment

1. Linear; Not direct variation; $\frac{3}{2}$ **2.** Not linear; Not direct variation **3.** Linear; Not direct variation; 0

4. Linear; Not direct variation; 1 **5.** Not linear; Not direct variation **6.** Linear; Direct variation; -7 **7.** 0.322; Joe's batting average in August **8.** $\frac{3}{2}$ **9.** $-\frac{11}{4}$ **10.** $\frac{7}{2}$ **11.** $m = -2$, $b = -1$ **12.** $m = 4$, $b = 3$ **13.** $m = -3$, $b = 12$ **14. a.** Auto mechanic, A; Management trainee, B **b.** A: $E = 7h$; B: $F = 5h + 20$ **c.** Auto mechanic **d.** A: 14.3 hours; B: 16 hours **15.** $x = -7$ **16.** $y = \frac{21}{2}$ **17.** $x = -162$ **18.** $w = 13$ **19.** $x = -4$ **20.** No solution **21.** In 1995 or 1996 **22.** $c = 8s + 45$; Fixed set up cost is $45; Charge per shirt is $8. **23.** $y = -x + 2$ **24.** $y = x + 3$ **25.** $y = -3x + 10$ **26.** $y = -\frac{1}{4}x - 4$ **27.** (b) **28.** (d) **29.** $110 **30.** 20 hours plus Saturday **31.** 8 weeks

2-2 Part A Try It

a. $y = \frac{5}{2}x + 35$ **b.** 60°F; 110°F; No, the thirtieth week will be the following autumn and the temperatures will be getting cooler at that time.

2-2 Part A Exercises

1. a. $-\frac{2}{3}$ **b.** 4 **c.** $y = -\frac{2}{3}x + 4$ **d.** 1 **5.** $y = \frac{1}{3}x + 25$; 35 **7.** $y = -x + 4$; 1.5 **9.** Possible answer: $y = 0.78x + 1.5$

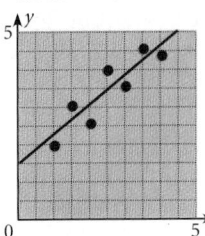

11. 9 **13.** (6, 8) **15.** (6.5, 2.5)

17. $y = -0.078x + 5.37$

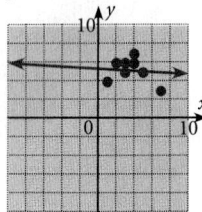

19. $y = -\frac{1}{4}x + 3; 2\frac{1}{4}$
21. $y = 2; 2$ **23.** Do not agree

2-2 Part B Try It

a. $\left(12\frac{1}{3}, 114\right)$ **b.** $(5, 6)$
c. $33, 34, 33$ **d.** $y = -\frac{2}{35}x + 14\frac{31}{35}$ **e.** 15.5 hours

2-2 Part B Exercises

1. $\left(5, \frac{22}{3}\right)$ **5. a.** $(1, 1),$
$(2, 7), (2, 18), (2, 23); (3, 35),$
$(4, 20), (4, 42), (5, 48);$
$(7, 65), (8, 63), (10, 101),$
$(11, 67)$ **b.** $(2, 12.5), (4, 38.5),$
$(9, 66)$ Centroid: $(5, 39)$
c. $\frac{107}{14}; y = \frac{107}{14}x + \frac{11}{14}$
d. Slope; about 7643 mi
9.

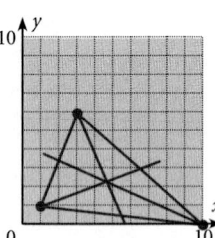

a. $\left(4\frac{2}{3}, 2\frac{1}{3}\right)$ **b.** $\left(4\frac{2}{3}, 2\frac{1}{3}\right)$
c. They are the same.
11. No association
13. Positive association
15. $-\frac{1}{3}$ **19.** About $(5, 15)$
21. a. First $(1, 20), (2, 12),$
$(2, 15);$ Second $(3, 10), (6, 7),$
$(9, 8);$ Third $(11, 3), (15, 6),$
$(13, 8)$ **b.** $(2, 15), (6, 8),$
$(13, 6);$ Centroid $\left(7, 9\frac{2}{3}\right)$
c. $-\frac{9}{11}; y = -\frac{9}{11}x + 15\frac{13}{33}$
23. a. $(1200, 120), (3200,$
$275), (5500, 340);$ Centroid
$(3300, 245)$ **b.** $y = \frac{11}{215}x + 76\frac{7}{43}$ **c.** About $230
d. The third, fifth, seventh, and eighth shows charge more than the median-median line would predict.

2-2 Part C Try It

a. $y = 2x$

2-2 Part C Exercises

1. (b)
3. a–b.

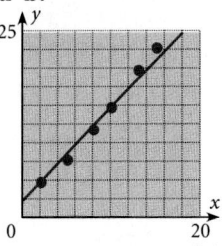

b. Possible answer: $y = \frac{5}{4}x + 2\frac{1}{2}$ **c.** $y = 1.41x + 1.36$

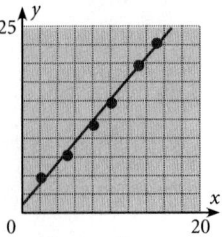

d. $y = \frac{30}{21}x + 1\frac{3}{14}$

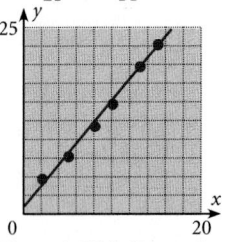

e. Yes; $y = 27.5;$ Regression: $y \approx 29.604;$ Median-median: $y \approx 29.786$ **9.** Possible answers: Total revenue for the year vs. week of the year, to predict revenue at year's end.
11. $y = -3$ **13.** $>$ **15.** $>$
17. a. Regression:
$y = -3.825x + 46.837$
Median-Median: $y = -5x + 50$
c. $y = 8.587, y = 0$
19. b. $y = 0.36x - 15.6$
c. Yes   **d.** $y = 0.33x - 14.1$

2-2 Part D Self-Assessment

1. Positive association
2. Possible answer: Positive association corresponds to positive slope and negative association corresponds to negative slope.   **3.** About 37

4. a.

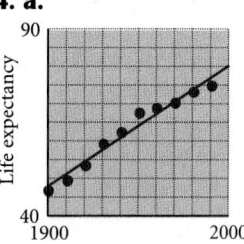

b. Possible answer: $y = 0.33x - 578.5$ **c.** About 91.4 years   **5.** Possible answer: Find the average of the x-coordinates and of the y-coordinates.   **6.** Possible answer: Organize data from low to high based on x-coordinates. Separate data into three (almost) equal-sized groups. For each group find the median of the x-values and of the y-values. Find the slope of the line through the first and third group medians. The median-median line has this slope and passes through the centroid of the triangle formed by the median points.   **7. a.** $m = 55;$ Speed in miles per hour
b. 23   **c.** No, if the trip started from home, the y-intercept would be zero.
8. $y = \frac{5}{3}x + 2$ **9. a.** Slope
b. At $y = 15.67928$
10. a. $y = 0.12x + 53.0$
b. About 149 gallons
11. a. Those less than or equal to $\frac{1}{12}$ **b.** At least 120 inches   **12.** Possible answer: Let x represent the child's age and let y represent the dosage in cc. Then $y = 0.45x + 0.5.$
13. a.

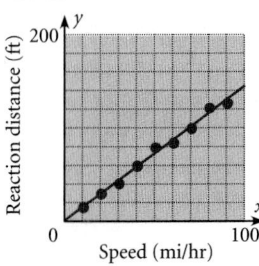

b. Possible answer: Reaction distance: $y = 1.44x + 3.1;$
Braking distance:
$y = 5.98x - 106.4;$ Linear regression   **c.** Possible answers: The reaction distance and braking distance at 100 mi/hr are expected to be about 147 ft and be 492 ft, respectively.   **14. a.** Male, 166.01 cm; Female, 156.73 cm
b. Possible answer: The slope is the ratio of the change in height to the change in humerus length.

2-3 Part A Try It

a. $x \geq 8$

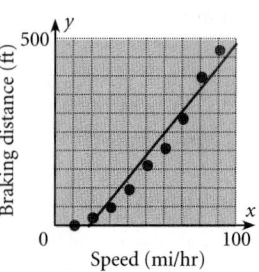

b. $s < -1.2$

c. $w < -2\frac{1}{2}$

d. $-1 \leq x < 5$

e. $x < -2$ or $x > 9$

2-3 Part A Exercises

1. a. iii   **b.** i   **c.** iv   **d.** ii
3. $x < 3$

5. $x < 0.6$

7. $v \leq -\frac{35}{9}$

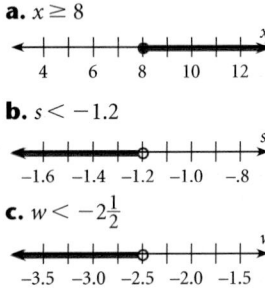

9. $647.06 or more
11. $-7 < x \le 4$

15. $x < -1.2$ or $x > 2.8$

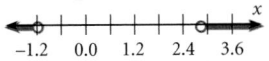

17. a. $1110 \le v \le 1850$
b. $v < 1110$ or $v > 1850$
23. Different directions;
Same distance. **25.** $x \ge 31$
27. $x \le -12$ **29.** $x > -9$
31. $x > 2$ **33.** At most
48.89 grams of fat per day.
35. $\frac{1}{4} < x \le 3$
37. All real numbers
39. $x < -5$ or $x \ge 15$

2-3 Part B Try It

a. $x \le -5$ or $x \ge 5$
b. $x < -5$ or $x > 5$

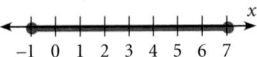

c. $x < -2$ or $x > 8$

d. $-1 \le x \le 7$

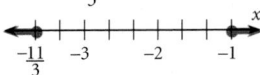

e. $-1 < x < 1$

f. $x \le -\frac{11}{3}$ or $x \ge -1$

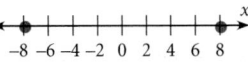

g. $x \le -11$ or $x \ge 3$

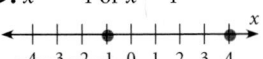

2-3 Part B Exercises

1. a. $|x| = 3$ **b.** $|x| \le 5$
c. $|x| > 8$
3. $x = -8$ or $x = 8$

7. $x = -4$ or $x = 4$

9. $x = -1$ or $x = 4$

11. $x = 7$ or $x = 9$

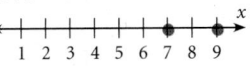

15. $-2 < x < 6$

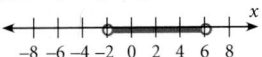

19. $-\frac{27}{5} \le x \le -1$

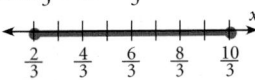

23. $\frac{2}{3} \le x \le \frac{10}{3}$

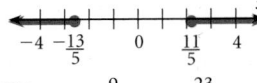

29. $x \le -\frac{13}{5}$ or $x \ge \frac{11}{5}$

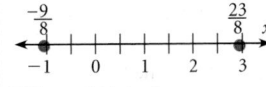

33. $x = -\frac{9}{8}$ or $x = \frac{23}{8}$

37. a. 6.01 inches;
5.99 inches **b.** $|d - 6| \le 0.01$
c. $d = \frac{5}{8} \pm \frac{1}{64}$ **43. a.** Let
x = gallons purchased.
$\left|x - \frac{12.36}{1.19}\right| \le 0.1$;
$10.287 \le x \le 10.487$
b. About 12 cents
45. a. Rational **b.** Irrational
c. Rational **d.** Rational
47. $x = 4$ or $x = 6$
49. $x = -2\frac{1}{2}$ or $x = 2\frac{1}{2}$
51. $x = -5$ or $x = 5$
53. $x = -8$ or $x = 3$
55. $|x| = 1.5$ **57.** $|x - 2| < 3$
59. $x < -3$ or $x > 5$
61. $x > -5$ or $x < -11$
63. $x < -5$ or $x > 5$
65. No solution
67. $t < -6$ or $t > 36$
69. $|x - 2.5| \le 0.02$
71. $x = -14$ or $x = -4$
73. $x = -7$ or $x = 11$
75. $-\frac{3}{2} < x < \frac{5}{2}$ **77.** $-\frac{7}{4} <$
$x < \frac{7}{4}$ **79.** $x \le -\frac{5}{2}$ or $x \ge 1$

2-3 Part C Try It

a.

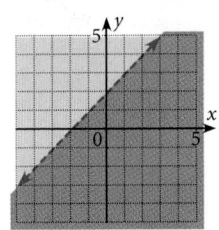

b.

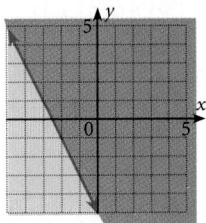

c.

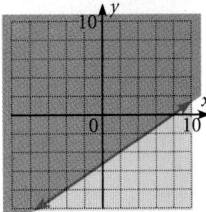

d.

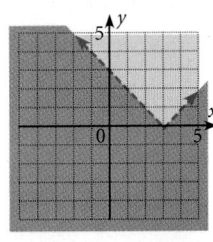

e.

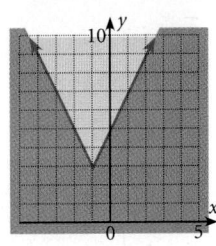

2-3 Part C Exercises

1. a. $y > -x + 2$ **b.** $x \ge 3$
c. $y \le -\frac{3}{2}x + 15$
3.

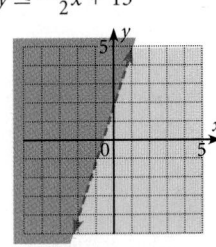

5.

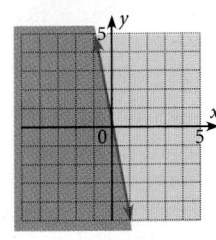

7.

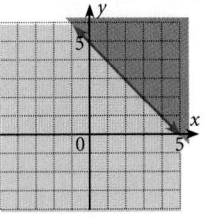

11. a. No **b.** Yes
15.

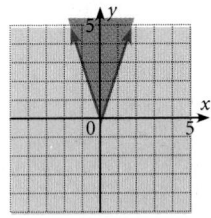

17.

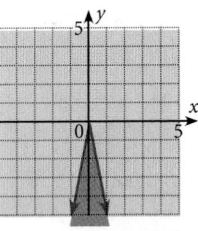

19.

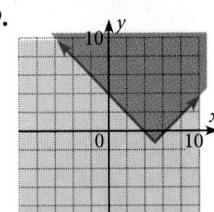

23. $x > 0$ and $y > 0$; Two
25. $y > x + 2$
27.

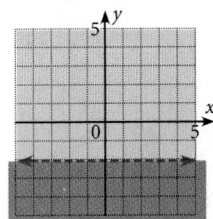

31.

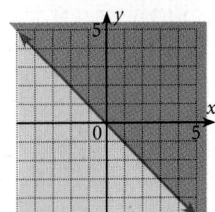

35.

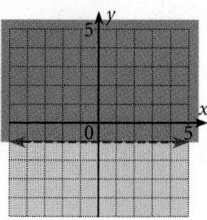

39. $100x + 75y \geq 450$ where $x =$ number of tablets of *High CEE* and $y =$ number of tablets of *Happy Balance*.

41.

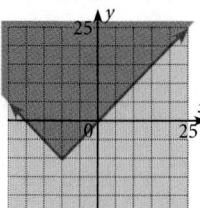

45.

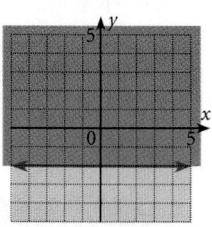

49. a. $g + r \leq 900$
b. $500 \leq g + r$
c. $15g + 25r \geq 500$
51. a.

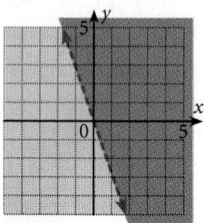

b. Yes **53.** $\frac{3}{100}$

2-3 Part D
Self-Assessment

1. $x > -11$ **2.** $t < -2$
3. $t \leq -3$ **4.** $x \geq -5$
5. $x \geq 6$ **6.** $x < -4$
7. $x < 1$ or $x > 4$
8. $-7 < x \leq 1$
9. $-2 < x < 3$
10. $x > 2$ **11.** $x > \frac{11}{2}$
12. $x > -1$ **13.** $2.5x \leq 40$
Take no more than 16 pills per day. **14.** 0.05
15. $x = -3$ or $x = 7$

---

16. $x = -\frac{4}{3}$ or $x = \frac{4}{3}$
17. $x = -9$ or $x = 7$
18. $x = -\frac{15}{2}$ or $x = -\frac{1}{2}$
19. $x = 2$ or $x = 6$
20. $x \leq -\frac{4}{3}$ or $x \geq 2$
21. $1 < x < 5$ **22.** All real numbers **23.** No solution
24. $x > 10$ or $x < 4$
25. $|x - 5.2| \leq 0.3$
26. $3 \times 108 < 360$
27. $y = 3x + 7$
28. $y = x + 5$
29. $\begin{bmatrix} 8 & -12 \\ 10 & 0 \\ -4 & 6 \end{bmatrix}$

30. $\begin{bmatrix} -4 & 2 & -6 \\ -4 & 6 & -2 \end{bmatrix}$

31. $\begin{bmatrix} 0 & 0 \\ 0 & 0 \\ 0 & 0 \end{bmatrix}$ **32.** (e)

33.

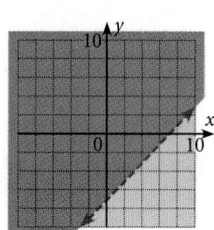

34.

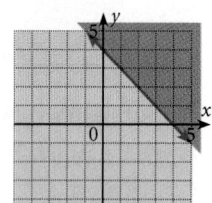

35.

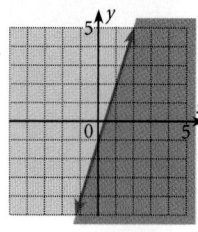

36.

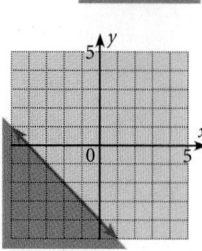

37.

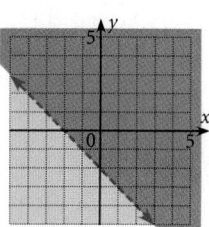

38.

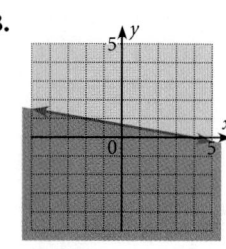

39. a. $0.05x + 0.06y \geq 500$
b.

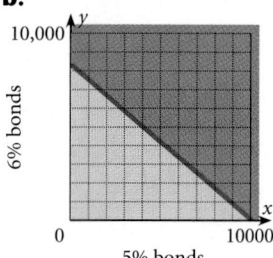

c. No, she will not earn $500 unless she invests at least $5000 in the riskier bond.
40. a. $15x + 7y \geq 2100$

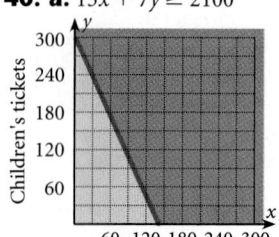

b. Intercepts represent the number of tickets that would need to be sold to adults only (or children only) if no tickets are sold to the other group.

Chapter 2 Review

1. False; Point-slope form
2. True **3.** True **4.** False; Median-median line **5.** True
6. a. 2 inches per year
b. No, an age of zero does not correspond to a height of zero. **c.** No
7. $m: \frac{3}{2}$; $n: \frac{5}{2}$; $p: -\frac{1}{3}$

---

8. $m: y = \frac{3}{2}x$
$n: y = \frac{5}{2}x - 5$
$p: y = -\frac{1}{3}x + 1$
9. $y = \frac{2}{3}x - 2$
10. $y = -x + 8$
11. $y = -\frac{1}{7}x + \frac{15}{7}$
12. $y = -\frac{1}{2}x + 9$
13. Negative slope: From left to right, it goes down. Positive slope: From left to right, it goes up. **14.** $x = \frac{1}{2}$
15. $x = -25$ **16.** $x = -65$
17. -9 **18. a.** -125 gallons per minute **b.** $y = -125x + 2850$ **c.** 2850 **d.** 22.8
19. a. Possible answer: $y = \frac{10}{3}x + 100$ **b.** About $267
20. $y - 10 = \frac{7}{6}(x - 5)$; 27.5

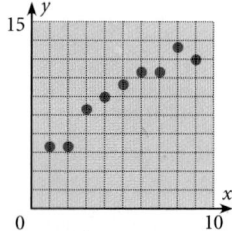

21. $y = 0.73x - 1408$; 1997
22. $x \leq 3$ **23.** $y \leq -9$
24. $-10 < x < -3$
25. $x < -9$ or $x > 2$
26. $x = -20$ or $x = -3$
27. $-4 < x < 3$
28. $y < -3x - 1$
29. $y \geq |2x + 14| - 1$
30. $y > 2x - 3$ **31.** $4x \leq 82$
32. $|x - 70| \leq 3$
33. $\frac{x}{600} + \frac{y}{1000} \leq 8$

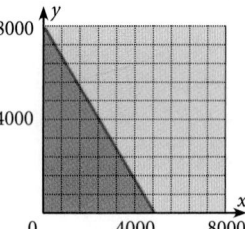

34. a. $40x + 25y \geq 450$

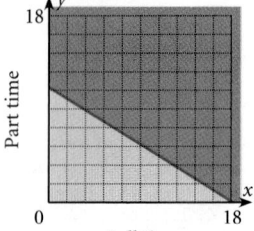

3-1 Part A Try It

a. (2, 3); One solution; Consistent

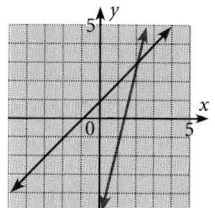

b. No solution; Inconsistent

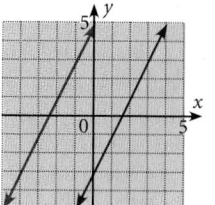

3-1 Part A Exercises

1. a. $y = -3x + 11$, $y = 2x - 3$

b.

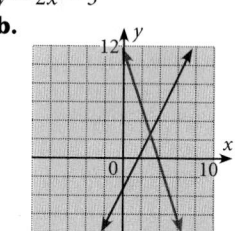

c. (2.8, 2.6); x-value: 2.8; y-value: 2.6 **5.** One solution; Consistent **7.** Infinitely many solutions; Consistent **9.** About $(0.7, -2.1)$, exact answer is $\left(\frac{5}{7}, -\frac{15}{7}\right)$. **13.** No solution **14.** About 31 minutes **17.** Infinitely many solutions; Consistent **19. a.** 31.5 miles

b. Carlottas: $d = 42t$; Friends: $d = 54\left(t - \frac{3}{4}\right)$

c. About (3.4, 142), exact answer is $\left(3\frac{3}{8}, 141\frac{3}{4}\right)$

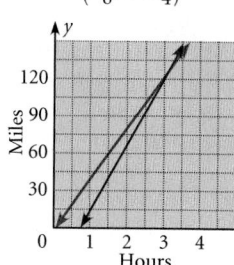

21. $-20x + 12y$ **23.** $x = \frac{9}{2}$
25. $y = \frac{12}{5}$ **27.** One solution; Consistent **29.** (2, 5)
31. (2.5, 1) **33.** (3, −4)
35. (8, 22) **37.** No solution
39. One solution; Consistent
41. One solution; Consistent
43. a. Possible answer: Whether they could make a greater profit **b.** $y = 0.42x$; $y = 0.77x - 240$ **c.** About 312 bags **d.** About 686 bags
45. 1.8 miles high
47. About 2003

3-1 Part B Try It

a. $\left(0, \frac{5}{2}\right)$; One solution; Consistent **b.** $\left(-\frac{11}{2}, -\frac{25}{2}\right)$; One solution; Consistent **c.** No solution; Inconsistent

3-1 Part B Exercises

1. a. $x = 3y + 3$
b. $2(3y + 3) + 4y = -14$; x
c. $10y + 6 = -14$; $y = -2$
d. $x = -3$ **e.** (−3, −2)
7. (2, 1) **9.** (4, 3)
11. 6 feet × 2 feet
13. (5, −2) **15.** (1, −1)
17. (2, −4); One solution; Consistent **19.** No solution; Inconsistent **21.** $\left(-\frac{23}{30}, \frac{7}{15}\right)$; One solution; Consistent
25. $y = -\frac{2}{3}x$ **27.** $\begin{bmatrix} 22 \\ 74 \end{bmatrix}$
29. 4000 T-shirts
31. (−20, −15); One solution; Consistent
33. (5, 1); One solution; Consistent **35.** No solution; Inconsistent **37.** Infinitely many solutions; Consistent
39. 600 gallons of regular, 400 gallons of premium
41. (3, 2), $\left(-\frac{39}{29}, \frac{40}{29}\right)$, $\left(1, \frac{10}{3}\right)$
43. 19 **45. a.** $x = \frac{ce - bf}{ae - bd}$, $y = \frac{af - cd}{ae - bd}$ **b.** Yes **c.** (2, −1)

3-1 Part C Try It

a. $\begin{bmatrix} 2 & 3 \\ -3 & 5 \end{bmatrix}\begin{bmatrix} x \\ y \end{bmatrix} = \begin{bmatrix} 8 \\ 7 \end{bmatrix}$

b. $\begin{bmatrix} 2.25 & -3.72 \\ 1 & 11.37 \end{bmatrix}\begin{bmatrix} x \\ y \end{bmatrix} =$ $\begin{bmatrix} 10.98 \\ 32.14 \end{bmatrix}$

c. (−2.04, −0.90)
d. (2.66, −0.17) **e.** Gold: $389.25; Silver: $4.87
f. No solution; Inconsistent
g. No solution; Inconsistent
h. No solution; Inconsistent

3-1 Part C Exercises

1. a. $\begin{bmatrix} 4 & 2 \\ 7 & 4 \end{bmatrix}; \begin{bmatrix} x \\ y \end{bmatrix}; \begin{bmatrix} 8 \\ 14 \end{bmatrix}$

b. $\begin{bmatrix} 4 & 2 \\ 7 & 4 \end{bmatrix}\begin{bmatrix} x \\ y \end{bmatrix} = \begin{bmatrix} 8 \\ 14 \end{bmatrix}$

c. $\begin{bmatrix} 2 & -1 \\ -\frac{7}{2} & 2 \end{bmatrix}\begin{bmatrix} 4 & 2 \\ 7 & 4 \end{bmatrix}\begin{bmatrix} x \\ y \end{bmatrix} =$ $\begin{bmatrix} 2 & -1 \\ -\frac{7}{2} & 2 \end{bmatrix}\begin{bmatrix} 8 \\ 14 \end{bmatrix}$

d. $\begin{bmatrix} 2 \\ 0 \end{bmatrix}$ **e.** (2, 0)

3. $\begin{bmatrix} 3 & -1 \\ 5 & -2 \end{bmatrix}\begin{bmatrix} x \\ y \end{bmatrix} = \begin{bmatrix} 6 \\ 2 \end{bmatrix}$

5. $\begin{bmatrix} 1 & -2 \\ 2 & 1 \end{bmatrix}\begin{bmatrix} x \\ y \end{bmatrix} = \begin{bmatrix} 3 \\ 1 \end{bmatrix}$

7. (10, 24) **9.** (1, −1)
13. $\begin{bmatrix} 1 & 1 \\ 425 & 550 \end{bmatrix}\begin{bmatrix} x \\ y \end{bmatrix} =$ $\begin{bmatrix} 50 \\ 25{,}000 \end{bmatrix}$

15. No **19.** $\begin{bmatrix} \frac{9}{16} & \frac{7}{16} \\ \frac{1}{16} & -\frac{1}{16} \end{bmatrix}$

21. No inverse exists.
23. No inverse exists.
25. $\begin{bmatrix} 1 & 0 \\ 0 & 1 \end{bmatrix}$

27. $\begin{bmatrix} 3 & 4 \\ -1 & 2 \end{bmatrix}\begin{bmatrix} x \\ y \end{bmatrix} = \begin{bmatrix} 10 \\ 0 \end{bmatrix}$; (2, 1)

29. $\begin{bmatrix} 22.3 & 14.3 \\ 7.5 & -15.2 \end{bmatrix}\begin{bmatrix} x \\ y \end{bmatrix} =$ $\begin{bmatrix} 15.4 \\ 3.3 \end{bmatrix}$; (0.63, 0.09)

31. Possible answer: $\begin{bmatrix} 13 & -1 \\ 1 & 1 \end{bmatrix}\begin{bmatrix} x \\ y \end{bmatrix} = \begin{bmatrix} 3 \\ 4 \end{bmatrix}$; (0.5, 3.5) **33.** 120 acres of tomatoes, 80 acres of peas
35. Large: 12 volts; Small: 9 volts

37. b. $\begin{bmatrix} -2 & 1 \\ -\frac{5}{2} & 1 \end{bmatrix}$

c. (−8, −14) **39.** 84,767

3-1 Part D Try It

a. $x = 2$, $y = 4$, $z = -1$
b. Mouse, $40; Track ball, $65; Joy stick, $75

3-1 Part D Exercises

1. a. 1; 2; y **b.** 4; 4; z
c. y; 1; 2; y; 2 **d.** (2, 2, 4)
3. (3, −1, 2) **5.** (4, 0, −3)
7. 4, 8, 12 **9.** 45°, 30°, 105°
13. $a = S(1 - r)$ **15.** $x < \frac{4}{3}$
17. $y > \frac{19}{2}$ **19.** (4, −1, −5)
21. $\left(-\frac{310}{21}, \frac{191}{21}, -\frac{188}{21}\right)$
23. $\left(\frac{1}{2}, 5, -2\right)$

25. $\begin{bmatrix} 2 & 5 & -3 \\ 3 & 3 & 7 \\ 5 & -4 & 6 \end{bmatrix}\begin{bmatrix} x \\ y \\ z \end{bmatrix} = \begin{bmatrix} 6 \\ 23 \\ 9 \end{bmatrix}$; (1, 2, 2)

27. $\begin{bmatrix} 3 & 2 & 1 \\ 2 & -1 & -1 \\ 5 & -4 & -2 \end{bmatrix}\begin{bmatrix} x \\ y \\ z \end{bmatrix} = \begin{bmatrix} 7.7 \\ 3.3 \\ 5.5 \end{bmatrix}$; (1.9, 1.5, −1)

29. $\begin{bmatrix} 1 & 1 & 1 \\ \frac{1}{4} & \frac{1}{2} & \frac{1}{3} \\ 0 & 2 & 3 \end{bmatrix}\begin{bmatrix} x \\ y \\ z \end{bmatrix} = \begin{bmatrix} 180 \\ 60 \\ 330 \end{bmatrix}$; (60, 30, 90) **31.** Granola $2.25/lb, dried fruit $1.80/lb, trail mix $2.70/lb **33.** Voe Callist was the winner with a score of 8.10.

3-1 Part E Self-Assessment

1. (c) **2.** (a) **3.** (d)
4. $\left(\frac{28}{11}, \frac{20}{11}\right)$; One solution; Consistent **5.** (1, 3); One solution; Consistent
6. (1, 5); One solution; Consistent **7.** $\left(\frac{3}{4}, -\frac{1}{4}\right)$; One solution; Consistent
8. No solution; Inconsistent
9. Infinitely many solutions; Consistent **10.** (3, 1); One solution; Consistent
11. (−1, −1); One solution; Consistent **12.** $\left(\frac{3}{4}, \frac{2}{3}\right)$; One solution; Consistent

13. 12 gallons of 35% linseed oil, 8 gallons of 25% linseed oil **14.** $w = \frac{V}{lh}$

15. $r = -\sqrt{\frac{A}{\pi}}$ or $r = \sqrt{\frac{A}{\pi}}$

16. $b_1 = \frac{2A}{h} - b_2$
17. $y = 8.71x - 1.51$; Linear regression; 20.3 million dollars **18.** During prime time: 10 spots; After prime time: 20 spots

19. $\begin{bmatrix} 3 & 7 \\ 2 & 5 \end{bmatrix}\begin{bmatrix} x \\ y \end{bmatrix} = \begin{bmatrix} -4 \\ 3 \end{bmatrix}$

20. $\begin{bmatrix} 3 & 4 \\ 1 & -3 \end{bmatrix}\begin{bmatrix} x \\ y \end{bmatrix} = \begin{bmatrix} 26 \\ 0 \end{bmatrix}$

21.
$\begin{bmatrix} 0.9 & -3.5 & 2.4 \\ 1.4 & 2.5 & 3.0 \\ -3.4 & -1.8 & -5.6 \end{bmatrix}\begin{bmatrix} x \\ y \\ z \end{bmatrix} =$

$\begin{bmatrix} -9.75 \\ 2.5 \\ 10.14 \end{bmatrix}$

22. In the year 2004
23. $(5, -3, 5)$
24. $\left(1, \frac{1}{2}, -3\right)$
25. *PC*-160: $1500, *PC*-250: $1800, *PC*-540: $2600

3-2 Part A Try It

a. $y \le -3x + 4$
$y < -\frac{2}{3}x - 2$

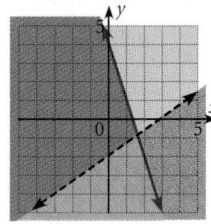

b. $y \ge -2$, $y \le 3x - 6$,
$y < -\frac{1}{2}x + \frac{7}{2}$

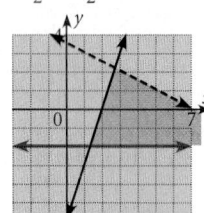

3-2 Part A Exercises

1.

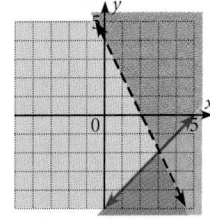

3.

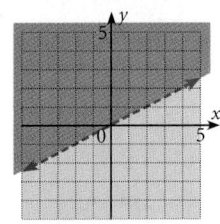

5.

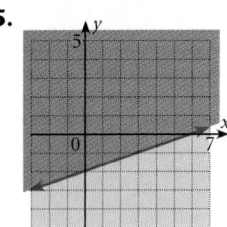

7. $0 \le x + y \le 12{,}000$
9. a. At least $32,500
b. Incomes less than $86,666.67 **c.** No
11.

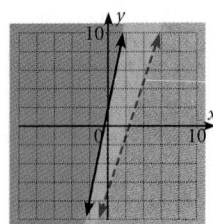

13. a. $\frac{x}{18}; \frac{y}{26}$
b. $\frac{x}{18} + \frac{y}{26} \le 16$
c.

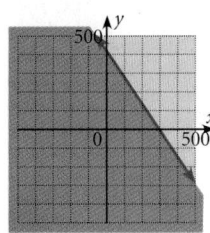

15.

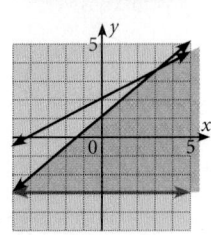

19. $x = 2$, $y = 4$; One solution; Consistent **21.** $s = 8$, $t = 6$; One solution; Consistent **23.** $x \ge 5$
25. $-1 < x < 9$
27.

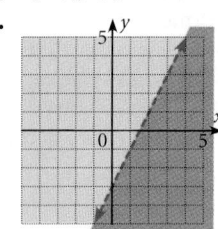

29.

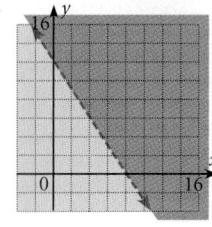

31. Possible answer: $F \ge 271$
33.

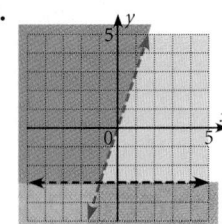

37.

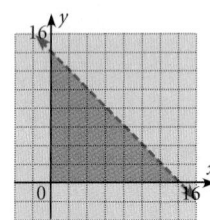

39. a. $r + x \le 1400$
b. $r \le 392$ **c.** Yes, $r \ge 0$ and $x \ge 0$
41.

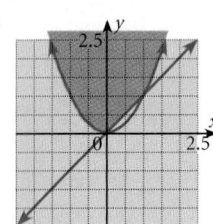

43. $\frac{\pi}{4}$

3-2 Part B Try It

a.

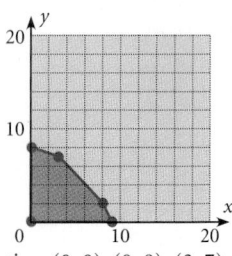

Vertices $(0, 0)$, $(0, 8)$, $(3, 7)$, $(8, 2)$, $(9, 0)$
b. Let $x =$ number of nonfiction books and let $y =$ number of fiction books.
$0 \le x \le 25{,}000$, $0 \le y \le 30{,}000$, $x + y \le 40{,}000$
c. Let $x =$ number of grams per serving of Blueberry Flakies and let $y =$ number of grams per serving of Corn Crunchies.
$x \ge 0$, $y \ge 0$, $x + y \le 50$, $3x + 6y \le 270$

3-2 Part B Exercises

1. a. $(0, 5)$ **b.** $(6, 2)$
c. $(8, 0)$ **d.** $(0, 0)$ **5.** $(0, 0)$, $(5, 0)$, $(2, 3)$, $(0, 5)$ **7.** Let $x =$ number of reserved seat tickets and let $y =$ number of general admission tickets that may be sold.
$x \ge 0$, $y \ge 0$, $x \le 500$, $x + y = 1500$; $(0, 0)$, $(0, 1500)$, $(500, 1000)$, $(500, 0)$

9. Let $x =$ number of inches of black beads and let $y =$ number of inches of orange beads.
$x \ge 0$, $y \ge 0$, $x + y \ge 12$, $x + y \le 24$, $x \ge 2y$, $x \ge 5$; $(12, 0)$, $(8, 4)$, $(16, 8)$, $(24, 0)$
11.

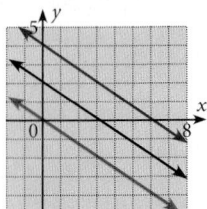

13. $(0, 0)$, $(5, 0)$, $(0, 3)$
15. $(0, 120)$, $(100, 120)$, $(200, 0)$, $(0, 0)$

17. Let x = number of ink drawings and let y = number of watercolors.
$x \geq 0$, $y \geq 0$, $0.3x + 0.5y \leq 120$, $0.2x + 0.2y \leq 60$; (0, 0), (0, 240), (150, 150), (300, 0)

19. Let x = number of public parking spaces and let y = number of employee parking spaces.
$x \geq 0$, $y \geq 0$, $x + y \leq 2500$, $x + y \geq 2000$, $x \geq 4y$, $y \geq 220$
a. (2000, 500), (1780, 220), (1600, 400), (2280, 220)

3-2 Part C Try It

a. 97; (3, 7) **b.** 60 pounds birdseed, 30 pounds mineral supplements

3-2 Part C Exercises

1. 26; (5, 7) **2.** −4; (2, 7)
3. $F = 15x + 25y$
5. $F = mM + nC$
7. $F = 600x + 300y$; Each performs 3 minutes; Cost is $2700. **11.** $x = -7$
13. $x = \frac{16}{9}$
15. $\begin{bmatrix} 10 & -22 & 4 \\ -2 & 0 & 18 \\ 6 & -12 & 4 \end{bmatrix}$

17. Not possible
19. $\begin{bmatrix} -2 & 1 \\ -\frac{5}{2} & \frac{7}{2} \end{bmatrix}$

21. $F = 2.59x + 3.57y$
23. $F = 50x + 150y$; 300 basic and 275 in-depth returns; $56,250
25. a. $F = 190x + 215y$; 1780 public spaces, 220 employee spaces; $385,500
b. $F = y$; 2000 public spaces and 500 employee spaces
c. $F = x$; 2280 public spaces and 220 employee spaces
27. No **29.** Let x = number of 10-point questions and y = number of 5-point questions.
$x \geq 0$, $y \geq 0$, $x + y \leq 6$, $7x + 3y \leq 25$
Vertices: (0, 6), $\left(1\frac{3}{4}, 4\frac{1}{4}\right)$, $\left(3\frac{4}{7}, 0\right)$, (0, 0)
Impossible: $\left(1\frac{3}{4}, 4\frac{1}{4}\right)$, $\left(3\frac{4}{7}, 0\right)$

b. (0, 0), (0, 1), (0, 2), (0, 3), (0, 4), (0, 5), (0, 6), (1, 0), (1, 1), (1, 2), (1, 3), (1, 4), (1, 5), (2, 0), (2, 1), (2, 2), (2, 3), (3, 0), (3, 1)
c. 10-point problem, 8 points; 5-point problem, 4.5 points; $F = 8x + 4.5y$
d. (1, 5); About $30\frac{1}{2}$ points
e. $\left(1\frac{3}{4}, 4\frac{1}{4}\right)$; Close to optimal solution

3-2 Part D Self-Assessment

1.
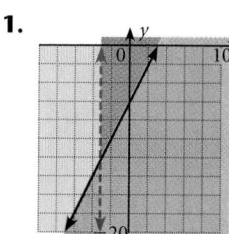

2.
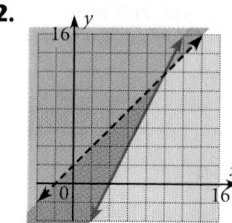

3.
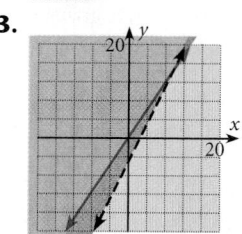

4.
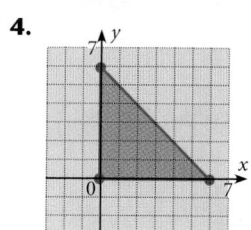

5.
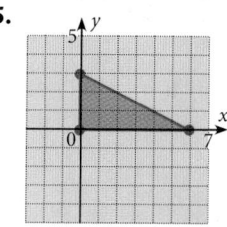

6.
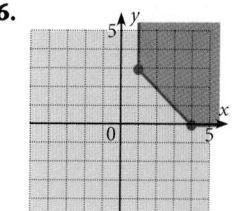

7. 520 (4, 8) **8.** 180; (1, 5)
9. $F = 70x + 10y$ **10.** $F = 0.2x + 0.1y$ **11.** $F = xR + yW$
12. $\begin{bmatrix} 3 & 3 & 13 \\ -3 & 12 & 9 \\ 6 & -8 & 9 \end{bmatrix}$
13. $\begin{bmatrix} 16 & 2 \\ -8 & -14 \end{bmatrix}$
14. $\begin{bmatrix} 34 & -11 & -36 \\ -9 & -14 & -18 \\ -7 & -14 & 17 \end{bmatrix}$
15. Not possible; Matrices do not all have the same dimension. **16.** (8, 2); One solution; Consistent
17. (−10, −26); One solution; Consistent
18. $m = -3$, $n = -2$; One solution; Consistent
19. Let x = number of ShuffleMan players and let y = number of WalkOn players. **a.** $P = 20x + 15y$; 1000 ShuffleMan and 500 WalkOn; $27,500
b. 1,000 ShuffleMan and 500 WalkOn; $23,500.
20. Let x = number of hardcover editions and let y = number of paperback editions. $x \geq 0$, $y \geq 0$, $x + y \geq 400$, $4x \geq y$
a. (80, 320), (400, 0)
b. $F = 19.50x + 6.95y$
c. 80 hardcover and 320 paperback **d.** $3784
21. Let x = number of basic stamps and let y = number of rare stamps. **a.** $x \geq 0$, $y \geq 0$, $y \leq 500$, $x \geq 3y$, $x \leq 2200$
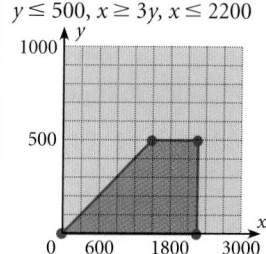

b. $F = 2x + 18y$ **c.** 2200 basic and 500 rare; $13,400 (if all stamps are sold)

Chapter 3 Review

1. Inconsistent **2.** Infinitely many **3.** Linear combination **4.** Inverse
5. Constraints
6. Linear programming
7. No solution; Inconsistent
8. $\left(\frac{14}{5}, \frac{3}{10}\right)$; One solution; Consistent **9.** (2, 1); One solution; Consistent
10. (3, 1); One solution; Consistent **11.** (0, 1); One solution; Consistent
12. $\left(\frac{48}{7}, -\frac{32}{7}\right)$; One solution; Consistent
13. $\begin{bmatrix} 3 & -7 \\ 2 & 1 \end{bmatrix}\begin{bmatrix} x \\ y \end{bmatrix} = \begin{bmatrix} 5 \\ 9 \end{bmatrix}$
14. $\begin{bmatrix} -1 & 1 \\ -2 & 3 \end{bmatrix}\begin{bmatrix} x \\ y \end{bmatrix} = \begin{bmatrix} 2 \\ 0 \end{bmatrix}$
15. $\begin{bmatrix} 3 & 6 \\ -1 & -2 \end{bmatrix}\begin{bmatrix} x \\ y \end{bmatrix} = \begin{bmatrix} 5 \\ -4 \end{bmatrix}$
16. (5, 1, 0)
17.
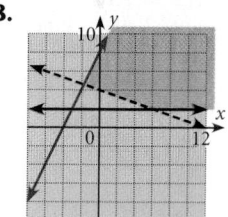

18.

19. (0, 2), (0, 5), (6, 2)
20. (0, 0), (0, 5), (2, 3), (3, 0)
21. (0, 0), (0, 300), (450, 0)
22. (0, 300); 1500 **23.** $51\frac{3}{7}$ grams of 10-karat gold and $68\frac{4}{7}$ grams of 24-karat gold
24. a. Let x = number of gold necklaces; let y = number of turquoise necklaces. $x \geq 0$, $y \geq 0$, $x + y \leq 50$, $x \leq 20$

b.

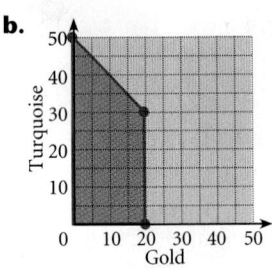

(0, 0), (0, 50), (20, 30), (20, 0)
c. $F = 80x + 50y$; Make 20 gold necklaces and 30 turquoise necklaces. Profit is $3100.

CHAPTER 4

4-1 Part A Try It

a. Yes; 6; 37 **b.** No **c.** Yes; -2; 27 **d.** -268
e. 15; $a_n = 15 + (n-1)6$

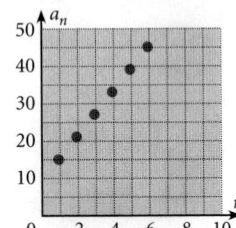

4-1 Part A Exercises

1. a. 3 **b.** 29, 32, 35, 38
c.

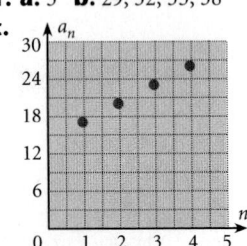

5. $5.74, $6.49, $7.24, $7.99; Yes

7.

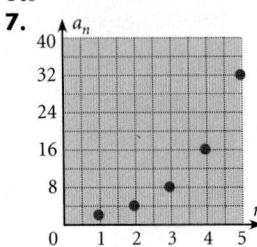

No **9.** Yes; $a_1 = -1$; $d = 2$
13. $a_n = 13 + (n-1)(-3)$
15. a. The prices have a common difference of 23¢.
b. $2.16 **c.** $(23n + 9)$¢

17. 851 **a.** $a_n = 851 + (n-1)(6)$ **b.** $a_1 = 851$; $a_{n+1} = a_n + 6$ **c.** $a_n = a_1 + (n-1)d$ **19. a.** 26, 33, 40
b. 22.6, 32.2, 41.8, 51.4
21. (2, 4) **23.** $\begin{bmatrix} 37 \\ -61 \end{bmatrix}$
25.

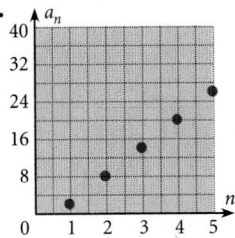

Yes; 6; 26 **27.** Yes; -4; -19
29. No **31.** $12.00, $10.51, $9.02, $7.53, $6.04, $4.55
33. $1.50 **35.** 23.6 and -4.4
37. Yes; -10; 2.5 **39.** No
41. $a_n = 7 + (n-1)(6)$
43. $a_n = 0.9 + (n-1)(-0.15)$ **45.** 39.5; $a_n = 39.5 + (n-1)(-1.5)$
47. a. $d = 10$; 20, 30, 40, 50, 60, 70 **b.** Change cell B2 to 100, and change each 10 to 25.

4-1 Part B Try It

a. 121 **b.** 87
c. $\sum_{n=1}^{21} (2n - 1) = 441$

4-1 Part B Exercises

1. a. $S_1 = 2$; $S_2 = 8$; $S_3 = 18$; $S_4 = 32$ **b.** 58 **c.** 30
d. $S_{15} = 450$ **5.** 3432
7. 1590 **9. a.** $(1 + 50) + (2 + 49) + (3 + 48) + \cdots + (25 + 26)$ **b.** 51; 25; 1275
c. 1275 **11.** -175
13. $1710 **15.** 189
17. $\sum_{n=1}^{7} (7n - 6) = 154$
23. 81, 243, 729 **25.** 2550
27. 500,500 **29.** 36,300
31. -41.8 **33.** 210
35. 7800 **37.** 1337.5
39. $\sum_{n=1}^{10} (7n - 5) = 335$
41. $\sum_{n=1}^{20} (-4n + 84) = 840$
43. a. $365 **b.** $66,795
45. a. $82 **b.** $460
47. a. 7 **b.** 6 **c.** 5, 4, 3, 2, 1, 0 **d.** 28

4-1 Part C Self-Assessment

1. No **2.** Yes; -10 **3.** Yes; 3.7 **4.** Yes; 0 **5.** Yes; -2
6. No **7.** An arithmetic sequence is an ordered list of numbers. An arithmetic series is the sum of the terms of an arithmetic sequence.
8. a. 15, 19, 23 **b.** 7, 18, 33, 52 **9.** 546 **10.** 540
11. 737.5 **12.** 7600
13. 315 **14.** -190
15. $\sum_{n=1}^{18} (5n + 1) = 873$
16. -8.5, 6, 20.5
17. $\begin{bmatrix} -42 \\ 63 \end{bmatrix}$
18. $(-3, 5)$ **19.** $y = \frac{1}{2}x - 4$
20. a. $45, $61, $77, $93, $109, $125, $141, $157
b. Yes, each term is $16 more than the previous term.
c. $124, the private contractor charges less once the service charge time reaches 90 minutes. **d.** Yes; Solve the system $y = 45 + 16(x - 1)$ and $y = 95 + 14.5(x - 4)$, and round the x-value up to the next integer, 6, giving the least number of 15-minute periods for which the private contractor charges less.
21. (b) **22.** Day 841
23. a. $14.50 **b.** $4.00
24. a. 1, 5, 14, 30, 55, 91, 140, 204 **b.** 1, 4, 9, 16, ..., or $a_n = n^2$
c. $\sum_{n=1}^{10} n^2 = 385$

4-2 Part A Try It

a. Yes; 1.5; 81 **b.** No
c. Yes; 0.75; 20.25 **d.** $a_n = 1280(0.5^{n-1})$ **e.** Answer will depend on current year. Value in 1996 ≈ $177.16

4-2 Part A Exercises

1. a. 2 **b.** 48, 96, 192, 384

c.

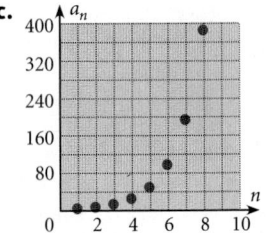

3. Yes; 4; 256 **7.** No
9. No **11.** 1250
15. a. 7800 mi/hr; 5150 mi/hr
b. Approximately 9:09 A.M.; No **17.** $a_n = -1(2^{n-1})$
19. $9259.26 **21. a.** 5
b. $a_n = 5(3^{n-1})$ **25.** 132
27. $(9, -5)$ **29.** No
31. Yes; $\frac{1}{4}$; $\frac{1}{256}$ **33.** No
35. Yes; -1.5; 20.25
37. Yes; -10; -10
41. $a_n = 256(1.75^{n-1})$
43. $a_n = 120(-0.5)^{n-1}$
45. $a_n = 2(1.9^{n-1})$
47. a. 50, 25, 12.5, 6.25, 3.125, 1.5625 **49.** $a_1 = 64$; $a_n = 64(4.5^{n-1})$

4-2 Part B Try It

a. 5461 **b.** 295.546875
c. $\sum_{n=1}^{6} 3(2^{n-1}) = 189$

4-2 Part B Exercises

1. a. 3 **b.** 54, 162 **c.** 2, 8, 26, 80 **5.** 124.9999872
7. -63.9375 **9.** -1
11. 7812 **15.** $\frac{728}{486} \approx 1.4979$
17. $\sum_{n=1}^{7} 4^{n-1} = 5461$
23. a. 200, 100, 50, 25, 12.5, 6.25, 3.125, 1.5625
b. 398.4375; About 0.39%
25. 5 **27. a.** Growing larger and larger **b.** The sums seem to approach 2.
29. 5115 **31.** 33.333333
33. 19,531 **35.** $\frac{3367}{2048} \approx 1.644$
37. 126 **39.** 3279
41. 104.16 **43.** 63 ft
45. $\sum_{n=1}^{7} 256(0.75)^{n-1} = 887.3125$
47. $\sum_{n=1}^{12} 3240\left(\frac{1}{6}\right)^{n-1} = \frac{2{,}176{,}782{,}335}{559{,}872} \approx 3888$
49. 0.8 **51.** About 13 hr since 9:00

4-2 Part C Try It

a. Yes **b.** No **c.** 270 in.

4-2 Part C Exercises

1. a. 0.25 **b.** 0.25; The absolute value of the common ratio is less than 1. **c.** $\frac{4}{3}$
5. Yes **7.** Yes **9.** $\frac{125}{6}$
13. 15 in.
17. $\sum\limits_{n=1}^{\infty} \left(\frac{1}{2}\right)^{n-1} = 2$
19. 8192 cm² **21. a.** $0.\overline{3} = 0.3 + 0.03 + 0.003 + 0.0003 + 0.00003 + \cdots$ **c.** $\frac{7}{9}$ **d.** $\frac{5}{33}$
e. $\frac{61}{99}$ **23.** $-3 < x \le -2$
25. Yes **27.** Yes **29.** No
31. $\frac{300}{11}$ **33.** $\frac{5}{3}$ **35.** 180
37. a. 600 ft, 510 ft, 433.5 ft, 368.475 ft **b.** About 1912 ft
39. $\sum\limits_{n=1}^{\infty} (0.1)^{n-1} = \frac{10}{9}$
41. $\sum\limits_{n=1}^{\infty} 16(-0.75)^{n-1} = \frac{64}{7}$
43. No, the ant will never reach the end. As the strip grows at least $1\frac{1}{4}$ in./sec, the ant walks 1 in./sec.

4-2 Part D Self-Assessment

1. Yes; 4; $a_n = 4^{n-1}$ **2.** No
3. Yes; -2; $a_n = -1(-2)^{n-1}$
4. No **5. a.** 12, 8, $5\frac{1}{3}$ **b.** 27, 45, 57, 65 **6.** 394.5703125
7. 1023 **8.** 24.9984 **9.** $\frac{63}{64}$
10. -547 **11.** 11,715
12. $3940\frac{20}{27}$ **13.** 64
14. -60.75 **15.** 18 **16.** 1
17. 0.42% **18.** $\sum\limits_{n=1}^{5} 7^{n-1}$
19. $\sum\limits_{n=1}^{\infty} 40(0.1)^{n-1}$
20. $0.45 + 0.0045 + 0.000045 + \cdots$; $\frac{5}{11}$ **21.** 108 in.
22. a. 3, 9, 15, 21, 27 **b.** 3, 9, 27, 81, 243 **23.** 19.5, 25, 30.5 **24. a.** 164,173, 153,096, 278,671, 299,285, 375,877, 275,371, 358,929, 665,005, 286,162; 317,397
b. $P_n = 4,877,185 + 317,397n$, where n is the number of decades since 1990. **c.** 5,829,376 **25.** (c)
26. (c) **27.** 3.125%
28. a. $S_n = 2^n - 1$

b. $S_n = \frac{1 - 2^n}{1 - 2} = 2^n - 1$
29. a. 0.004, 0.008, 0.016, 0.032, 0.064, 0.128, 0.256, 0.512 **b.** 2,147,484 in.; 33.89 mi **30.** 17.71°; 33

4-3 Part A Try It

a. No, 0 has no multiplicative inverse. **b.** No, 0 has no multiplicative inverse, and 0 is an integer. **c.** Yes, if a is a positive real number, then $\frac{1}{a}$ is a positive real number and $a \cdot \frac{1}{a} = 1$. **d.** Yes, the distributive property is true for any subset of the real numbers. **e.** No, most integers do not have a multiplicative inverse in the set of integers.

4-3 Part A Exercises

1. Possible answers:
a. $2 \cdot (3 \cdot 4) = (2 \cdot 3) \cdot 4$
b. $3 + (-3) = -3 + 3 = 0$
c. $4 + 0 = 0 + 4 = 4$
d. $2 \cdot (3 + 4) = 2 \cdot 3 + 2 \cdot 4$
e. $2 \cdot 4 = 8$, and 8 is a real number. **f.** $3 + 5 = 5 + 3$
3. -14.6 **5.** -2 **17. a.** Yes **b.** Yes, 0 for Ⓒ, 1 for ⓧ **c.** Yes **d.** Yes, all field axioms are satisfied. **19.** No, there is no additive identity element. **23.** Rational numbers are real numbers that can be written as a ratio of two integers **25.** No, $\pi + (-\pi) = 0$. **27.** 13.72 **29.** $\frac{5}{4}$
37. Closure property of multiplication **39.** Additive identity **41.** Multiplicative identity **43.** Commutative property of multiplication **45.** Method (a) is correct; Method (b) distributes 6 over both binomials.

4-3 Part B Try It

a. Rational; 15 **b.** Irrational **c.** Rational; $-\frac{4}{7}$ **d.** $\frac{3}{10}\sqrt{2}$
e. $-2|w|\sqrt{3}$ **f.** $4\sqrt{11} + 7\sqrt{5}$
g. $60|k|\sqrt{3}$

4-3 Part B Exercises

1. a. Real, rational, integer, whole number **b.** Real, rational, nonintegral rational number **c.** Real, rational, integer **d.** Real, rational, nonintegral rational number **e.** Real, irrational **f.** Real, rational, nonintegral rational number **g.** Not a real number **h.** Real, irrational **i.** Real, rational, nonintegral rational number
7. Irrational **9.** 3.9; Rational
11. $-4\sqrt{26} \approx -20.4$
13. $x = -2$ or $x = 2$
15. $x = 162$ **17.** $2|p|$
21. 147 **23.** $2\sqrt{2} + \sqrt{6} - 2\sqrt{3}$ **25.** $12x\sqrt{2}$
27. $-2\sqrt{5h}$ **29.** About 9.54 sec **33.** $(2, -3)$
35. Possible answer: Real numbers that can be expressed as ratio of integers; $\frac{7}{8}$ **37.** Decimal numbers or all numbers on a number line
39. About 208.7 ft × 208.7 ft
41. Rational; $\frac{5}{4}$ **43.** Rational; 0.1 **45.** Irrational
47. $3\sqrt{61}$; Irrational
49. $6\sqrt{10} \approx 18.97$
51. $-\frac{13}{5}\sqrt{6} \approx -6.37$
53. $x = -5$ or $x = 5$
55. $x = 243$ **57.** $x = 361$
59. $3|m|\sqrt{2}$ **61.** $5\sqrt{5} - 8\sqrt{7} - \sqrt{3}$ **63.** $19\sqrt{2}$
65. 3 **67.** $\sqrt{7}$ **69.** $8|m|$
71. About 0.007 sec **75.** No

4-3 Part C Try It

a. $5i\sqrt{2}$ **b.** $-4\sqrt{3}$ **c.** $-27i$
d. $-1 - 24i$ **e.** $11 - 71i$

4-3 Part C Exercises

1. a. -1 **b.** -1 **c.** $7i$
3. $10i$ **9.** -60 **13.** $-6i\sqrt{2}$
19. -1 **21.** $19 - 26i$
25. $-9 + 2i$ **29.** $(165 - 72i)$ volts **31.** $-22i$
33. $43\sqrt{5}$ ft; Irrational
35. $4i$ ohms **37.** $-\frac{1}{3}$; -2

39. 13

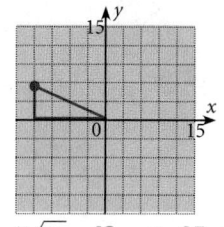

41. $i\sqrt{23}$ **43.** -9 **45.** $17i$
47. -4 **49.** $4i\sqrt{2}$ **51.** -5
53. $-9 - 15i$ **55.** $-25 + 13i$ **57.** $-9 - 20i$
59. $5i\sqrt{5}$ **61.** $116 - 8i$

4-3 Part D Try It

a–d.

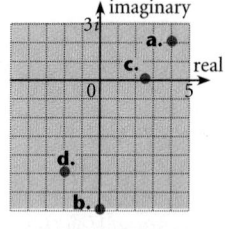

$1 + 2i$

e.

f.

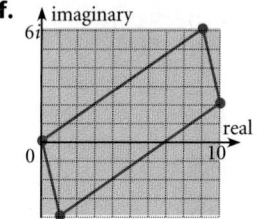

$10 + 2i$ **g.** 13 **h.** 6 **i.** $\sqrt{58}$

4-3 Part D Exercises

1. a. $4 + 2i$ **b.** $3i$
c. $-3 + 4i$ **d.** -4 **e.** $2 - 3i$
3., 5.

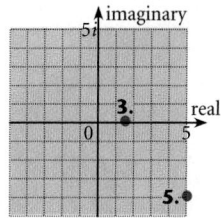

9. $14 + 7i$ **13.** 1 **15.** 19

19.

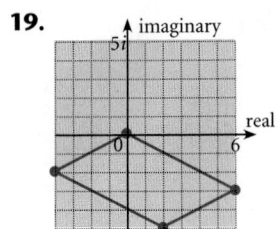

$2 - 5i$ **23.** $0 \le w \le 1100$, with w representing weight the school elevator can handle safely **33.** $\sqrt{274}$ **35.** $2\sqrt{3}$ **37.** 14 **39.** 29 **43.** $113 - 290i$ **45.** $\sqrt{3}$ **47.** $17 + 17i$ **49.** 49

51.

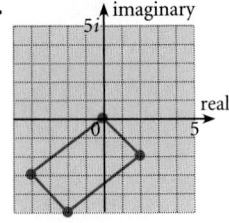

$-2 - 5i$ **53.** $2 + 3i$ **55.** $6 + 4i$

57.

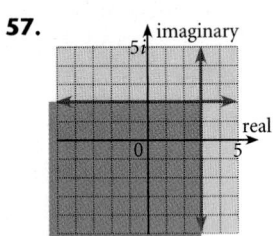

4-3 Part E Self-Assessment

1. Commutative property of multiplication **2.** Closure property of the real numbers under addition **3.** Multiplicative inverse **4.** Associative property of addition **5.** Additive identity **6.** Distributive property **7.** Yes **8.** No **9.** No **10.** No **11.** False **12.** False **13.** About 21.21 miles **14.** Complex **15.** Imaginary, complex **16.** Real, complex **17.** Imaginary, complex **18.** $90\sqrt{2}$ or about 127.28 ft **19. a.**

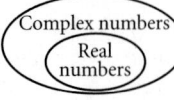

b.

c.

d.

20. -6 **21.** $6i$ **22.** $4\sqrt{2}$ **23.** $2i\sqrt{2}$ **24.** $3|n|$ **25.** $-\frac{2}{3}$ **26.** $2\sqrt{2}$ **27.** -42 **28.** -4 **29.** -1 **30.** $4i$ **31.** $-1 + 5i$ **32.** $-17 + 14i$ **33.** $-6 + 3i$ **34.** $26 - 7i$ **35.** $16 - 30i$ **36.**

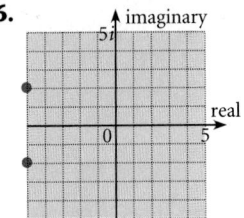

37.

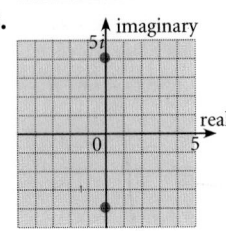

38.

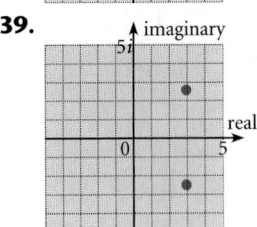

39.

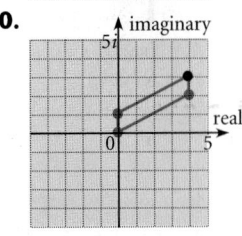

40.

$4 + 3i$

41.

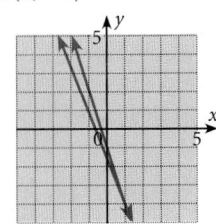

$-1 - 5i$ **42.** $4.3\sqrt{2}$ ft; Irrational **43.** 0.05 cm; Rational **44.** (c) **45.** (a)

46. $\begin{bmatrix} -8 & 11 \\ 3 & 0 \\ -4 & -7 \end{bmatrix}$

47. $(1, -4)$

48. 24 **49.** Possible answer: Matrix multiplication is not commutative.

$\begin{bmatrix} 1 & 1 \\ 0 & 1 \end{bmatrix} \times \begin{bmatrix} 1 & 0 \\ 1 & 1 \end{bmatrix} = \begin{bmatrix} 2 & 1 \\ 1 & 1 \end{bmatrix}$

$\begin{bmatrix} 1 & 0 \\ 1 & 1 \end{bmatrix} \times \begin{bmatrix} 1 & 1 \\ 0 & 1 \end{bmatrix} = \begin{bmatrix} 1 & 1 \\ 1 & 2 \end{bmatrix}$

Chapter 4 Review

1. (a) **2.** (c) **3.** (d) **4.** Possible answer: Arithmetic: 6, 12, 18, 24, ... Geometric: 2, 4, 8, 16, ... An arithmetic sequence has a common difference which is added to each term to get the next term. A geometric sequence has a common ratio which is multiplied by each term to get the next term. **5.** Geometric; -2; $-12(-2)^{n-1}$ **6.** Arithmetic; 20; $5 + 20(n - 1)$ **7. a.** 10, 14, 18; 2, 8, 18, 32 **b.** 18, 54, 162; 2, 8, 26, 80 **8.** 276 **9.** 980 **10.** 1533 **11.** $\frac{127}{128}$ **12.** 120 **13.** 27,993 **14.** $\sum_{n=1}^{21} (3n + 1) = 714$ **15.** $\sum_{n=1}^{5} 8^{n-1} = 4681$

16. 330 bricks **17.** 3.125 mg; 0.0488281 mg **18.** Associative property of multiplication **19.** Closure property of the real numbers under multiplication **20.** Additive inverse **21.** Multiplicative identity **22.** Possible answer: $2 \cdot 4 = 4 \cdot 2$ **23.** Possible answer: $1 + 1 = 2$, and 2 is not in the set. **24.** Possible answer: $(8 - 3) - 4 \ne 8 - (3 - 4)$ **25.** Possible answer: $(3 \cdot 2) \cdot 4 = 3 \cdot (2 \cdot 4)$ **26.** Possible answer: $3 \cdot \frac{1}{3} = \frac{1}{3} \cdot 3 = 1$ **27.** Possible answer: $2 \cdot (3 + 4) = (2 \cdot 3) + (2 \cdot 4)$ **28.** $-\frac{1}{6}$ **29.** -0.46 **30.** 4.2; 4.2i **31.** 26; $24 + 10i$ **32.** 15; 15 **33.** -10; Rational, complex **34.** $7i$; Complex **35.** $6\sqrt{2}$; Irrational, complex **36.** $\frac{2}{5}i$; Complex **37.** -6; Rational, complex **38.** $7\sqrt{3}$; Irrational, complex **39.** $1 - 2i$; Complex **40.** i; Complex **41.** $21 + i$; Complex **42–44.**

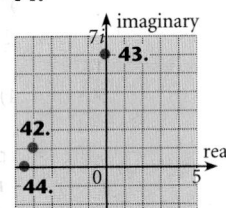

45.

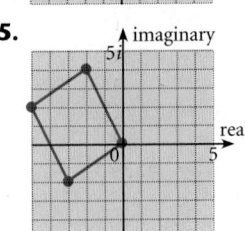

$-5 + 2i$ **46.** $(104 - 48i)$ volts **47.** About 3.25 cm

CHAPTER 5

5-1 Part A Try It

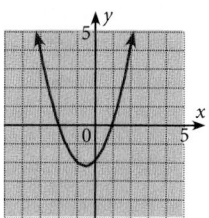

a. $\left(-\frac{1}{2}, -\frac{9}{4}\right)$ **b.** $x = -\frac{1}{2}$
c. Minimum $y = -\frac{9}{4}$

5-1 Part A Exercises

1. a. $(1, -2)$; $x = 1$ **b.** -2;
1 **c.** $(2, -1)$ **d.** $(-1, 2)$
3. $\left(1\frac{1}{4}, 6\frac{1}{8}\right)$; $x = 1\frac{1}{4}$;
Maximum $= 6\frac{1}{8}$ **7.** $x = 2$
9. $x = -2.3$ **15.** Quadratic;
$y = x^2$ **21.** Yes;
$y = x^2 + 0x - 6$ **23.** 81 in.^{2};
9 in. $\times$ 9 in. **25.** 2.5 sec
after the initial kick **27.** $\frac{5}{4} \le$
$t \le \frac{7}{4}$ **29.** 18 **31.** 36
33. Yes; $y = 4x^2 + 5x + 0$
35. Not quadratic
37. $x = 1$ **39.** $x = -8.05$
41. $x = -0.4$ **43.** $(-3, -9)$;
$x = -3$; Minimum $= -9$
45. $(0.35, 0.1125)$; $x = 0.35$;
Maximum $= 0.1125$
47. b. $h(0) = 500$ m, $h(4) =$
413.6 m, $h(6) = 311.6$ m,
$h(8) = 170.4$ m, $p(0) = 0$ m,
$p(4) = 300$ m, $p(6) = 450$ m,
$p(8) = 600$ m **c.** $t \approx 8.83$ sec;
Horizontal distance $\approx$
662.50 m **d.** At about $t =$
9.90 sec; Horizontal distance $\approx$
742.46 m **49.** Quadratic;
$y = 4x^2 + 1$ **53. a.** $A =$
$w^2 + 10w$ **c.** 35 ft $\times$ 45 ft;
The graph includes $(35, 1575)$,
so the width is 35 ft and the
length is $35 + 10 = 45$ ft.
55. a. $y \approx -0.0434x^2 +$
$8.703x - 420.396$
b. The vertex would
represent the price and profit
where the profit is maximum.

5-1 Part B Try It

a. $y = \frac{5}{2}x^2$ **b.** $y = -\frac{5}{2}x^2$;
$(2, -10)$

c.

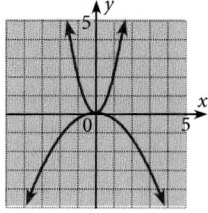

5-1 Part B Exercises

1. a. Upward: $f(x)$ and $j(x)$;
Downward: $g(x)$ and $h(x)$
b. $f(x), g(x), h(x), j(x)$
c. Maximum at vertex: $g(x)$
and $h(x)$. Minimum at vertex:
$f(x)$ and $j(x)$. They are all
$(0, 0)$.
3. a. $(0, 0)$ **b.** The axis of
symmetry is the y-axis or
$y = 0$ for all 3 graphs.
c. $y = 0.5x^2$ and $y = 2x^2$
open upward, $y = -3x^2$
opens downward. Widest to
narrowest:
$y = 0.5x^2, y = 2x^2, y = -3x^2$
5.

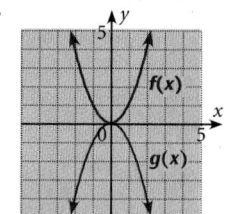

13. 9 times as high; 8.1 ft
14. 32.4 m below
21. $y = \frac{3}{2}x^2$; $y = -\frac{3}{2}x^2$
27. $x^2 + 4x + 4$
29. $4x^2 - 4x + 1$
31. $(x + 3)^2$ **33.** $(x + 2.5)^2$
37.

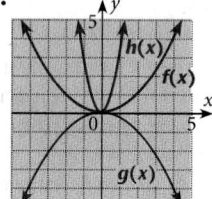

39. $y = 0.1x^2$; $y = -0.1x^2$
41. $y = 101x^2$; $y = -101x^2$
43. $y = 0.0064x^2$
45. a. 36 ft **b.** 72 ft/sec
c. 65.6 ft/sec **d.** 64.16 ft/sec;
64.016 ft/sec; 64.0016 ft/sec

5-1 Part C Try It

a.

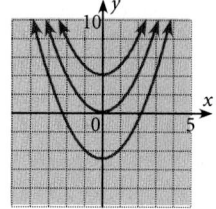

For $y = x^2$, $V = (0, 0)$;
For $y = x^2 + 4$, $V = (0, 4)$;
For $y = x^2 - 5$, $V = (0, -5)$
b.

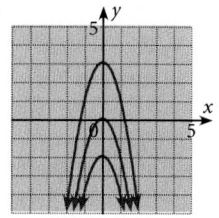

For $y = -2x^2$, $V = (0, 0)$;
For $y = -2x^2 + 3$, $V =$
$(0, 3)$; For $y = -2x^2 - 2$,
$V = (0, -2)$ **c.** $(0, 6)$;
Minimum; $x = 0$
d. $(3, -12)$; Minimum; $x = 3$
e. $(-\pi, 1066)$; Maximum;
$x = -\pi$

5-1 Part C Exercises

1. a. a **b.** k **c.** h **d.** a
e. k **f.** h
3.

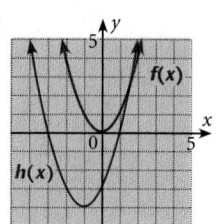

5.

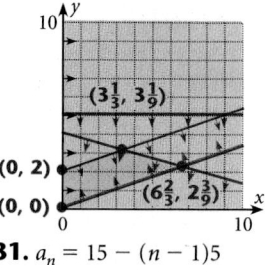

7. $(5, 7)$; Minimum
9. $(3, -3)$; Maximum
11. a. It takes 1.2 sec; 24 ft up
b. $h(t) = 0$ at about 2.42 sec
13. $f(x) = -3(x + 5)^2$
17. Reflect over the x-axis,
then translate 7 units to the
right and 3 units downward.
20. \$7.50 **27.** $y = 0.5x - 1$

29.

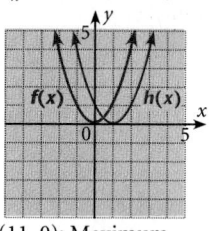

$(3\frac{1}{3}, 3\frac{1}{9})$
$(0, 2)$
$(0, 0)$
$(6\frac{2}{3}, 2\frac{3}{9})$

31. $a_n = 15 - (n - 1)5$
33.

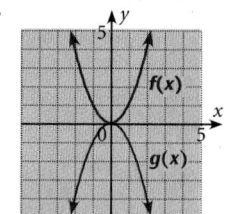

37. $(11, 0)$; Maximum
39. $(-4, 3)$; Maximum
41. $f(x) = -3x^2$
43. $f(x) = (x - m)^2 + 2m$
45. $f(x) = -16(x - 1.87)^2 +$
56.2 **47.** Translate 3 units
upward and 5 units to the
right. **49.** Reflect over the
x-axis, then translate 2 units
to the right and 4 units
upward.
51. $f(x) = \left(x + \frac{1}{2}\right)^2 - 6\frac{1}{4}$
53. $f(x) = -\left(x - \frac{1}{2}\right)^2 + 3\frac{1}{4}$
55. a. 19%; 64%
b. 1%; 16%
c. $1 - r^2 = -1(r + 0)^2 + 1$;
Vertex: $(0, 1)$; Maximum;
$(1 - r)^2 = 1(r - 1)^2 + 0$;
Vertex: $(1, 0)$; Minimum;

5-1 Part D Try It

a. $y = (x + 3)^2 - 9$;
$(-3, -9)$; $x = -3$
b. $f(x) = (x - 5)^2 - 115$;
$(5, -115)$; $x = 5$ **c.** $g(x) =$
$\left(x - \frac{5}{2}\right)^2 - \frac{5}{4}$; $\left(\frac{5}{2}, -\frac{5}{4}\right)$; $x = \frac{5}{2}$
d. $y = \left(x + \frac{7}{2}\right)^2 - \frac{61}{4}$;
$\left(-\frac{7}{2}, -\frac{61}{4}\right)$; $x = -\frac{7}{2}$
e. $y = -3(x + 1)^2 + 4$;
$(-1, 4)$; $x = -1$ **f.** $f(x) =$
$2(x - 1)^2 - 9$; $(1, -9)$; $x = 1$

5-1 Part D Exercises

1. a. -1 **b.** 9; 9 **c.** 8, 3
d. 3; 8 **3.** $y^2 + \underline{-14y} + 49 =$
$(y - 7)^2$ **7.** $n^2 + 0.5n +$
$\underline{0.0625} = (n + 0.25)^2$

11. $y = (x - 4)^2 - 21$; $(4, -21)$; $x = 4$; Minimum $= -21$

13. $y = \left(x + \frac{3}{8}\right)^2 + 3\frac{55}{64}$; $\left(-\frac{3}{8}, 3\frac{55}{64}\right)$; $x = -\frac{3}{8}$; Minimum $= 3\frac{55}{64}$

15. $f(x) = -5(x - 1)^2 + 5$; $(1, 5)$; $x = 1$; Maximum $= 5$

17. $m = -3\left(k - \frac{3}{2}\right)^2 - \frac{13}{4}$; $\left(\frac{3}{2}, -\frac{13}{4}\right)$; $k = \frac{3}{2}$; Maximum $= -\frac{13}{4}$

19. a. $H(t) = -16t^2 + 7500t + 448,800$ ft; $H(t) = -16(t - 234.375)^2 + 1,327,706.25$ ft
b. About $1,327,706$ ft (or 251.5 mi); About 234 sec (or 3.9 min) after it is released.
23. $(-2, -6)$; Minimum; 2
25. $(-3, -4)$; Minimum; 2
27. $(x - 13)(x + 3)$
29. $(x + 9)(x - 1)$ **31.** $y^2 + -12y + 36 = (y - 6)^2$
33. $d^2 + 7d + \frac{49}{4} = \left(d + \frac{7}{2}\right)^2$
35. $r^2 + 2r + 1 = (r + 1)^2$
37. $p^2 + \frac{3}{2}p + \frac{9}{16} = \left(p + \frac{3}{4}\right)^2$
39. $y = (x + 2)^2 - 4$; $(-2, -4)$; $x = -2$; Minimum $= -4$ **41.** $v = (d + 4)^2 - 23$; $(-4, -23)$; $d = -4$; Minimum $= -23$
43. $y = \left(x + \frac{5}{2}\right)^2 - \frac{9}{4}$; $\left(-\frac{5}{2}, -\frac{9}{4}\right)$; $x = -\frac{5}{2}$; Minimum $= -\frac{9}{4}$ **45.** $g(x) = (x + 0.3)^2 - 11.09$; $(-0.3, -11.09)$; $x = -0.3$; Minimum $= -11.09$
47. $f(x) = -\left(x + \frac{3}{2}\right)^2 + 2$; $\left(-\frac{3}{2}, 2\right)$; $x = -\frac{3}{2}$; Maximum $= 2$ **49.** $y = -2(x - 5)^2 + 47$; $(5, 47)$; $x = 5$; Maximum $= 47$
51. a. $\left(7 - \frac{1}{2}m\right)$; $(640 + 80m)$ **b.** $R = -40m^2 + 240m + 4480$ **c.** $5.50

5-1 Part E Self-Assessment

1. a. Upward: $f(x)$ and $h(x)$; Downward: $g(x)$ and $j(x)$
b. $j(x)$, $f(x)$, $g(x)$, $h(x)$
c. Maximum: $g(x)$ and $j(x)$
Minimum: $f(x)$ and $h(x)$

---

2. Possible answer: $(-1, 4)$
3. Possible answer: $(11.2, 11)$
4. Possible answer: $(-10, -5)$
5. a. $y = 5x^2$; $y = -5x^2$
b. $y = -\frac{3}{4}x^2$; $y = \frac{3}{4}x^2$
c. $y = \frac{1}{5}x^2$; $y = -\frac{1}{5}x^2$
6. (d) **7. a.** Moon: $h(t) = -0.8(t - 18.75)^2 + 281.25$; Earth: $h(t) = -4.9(t - 3.061)^2 + 45.918$ **b.** About 281.25 m; About 45.918 m
8. a. 1 **b.** 3 **c.** 2
9. $(4, 16)$; $x = 4$; Maximum
10. $(-1, 0)$; $x = -1$; Minimum **11.** $(0, 0)$; $x = 0$; Minimum
12.

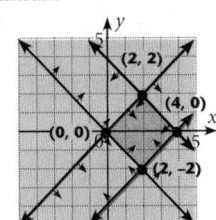

13. 10 **14.** 84 **15.** 52
16. -22 **17. a.** Reflection over x-axis; $y = -2x^2$
b. Translation 5 units to the right; $y = -2(x + 5)^2$
c. Translation 5 units upward; $y = -2(x + 5)^2 + 6$
18. a. $\ell = 600 - 2w$; $A(w) = w(600 - 2w)$
b. The equation can be written $A(w) = -2w^2 + 600w$.
c. $45,000$ ft^2; 150 ft $\times 300$ ft
19.

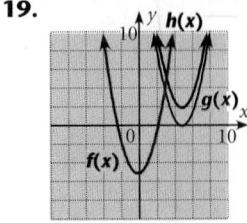

20.

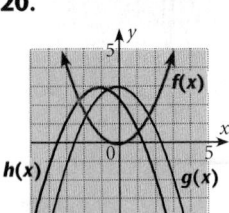

21. $f(x) = (x + 5)^2 - 25$; $(-5, -25)$; $x = -5$; Minimum $= -25$

---

22. $y = (x - 3)^2 - 6$; $(3, -6)$; $x = 3$; Minimum $= -6$
23. $g(x) = 2(x + 2)^2 + 2$; $(-2, 2)$; $x = -2$; Minimum $= 2$ **24. a.** $y = 0.009(x - 50)^2 + 4.5$ **b.** 50 yrs. old; 4.5 accidents per million driving miles
25. a. At the focus
b. At the focus

5-2 Part A Try It

a. $x = -2$ or $x = 0$
b. $x = 1$ **c.** $x \approx -1.2$ or $x \approx 2.2$ **d.** $x = -4$ or $x = -2$

5-2 Part A Exercises

1. a.

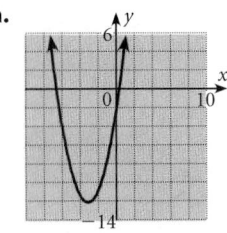

b. $x = -7$ or $x = 1$
c. $x \approx -6.5$ or $x \approx 0.5$
d. -6.5 and 0.5 **e.** -7 and 1
f. -6.5 and 0.5 **3.** Two
7. a. $x = -3$ or $x = 3$
b. $x = 0$ **c.** No real solution
9. $x \approx \pm 2.8$ **11.** No real solution **15.** $0 = x^2 + 8x + 16$ **17.** About 4.47 m/sec; About 4.61 m/sec
21. $x \approx -7.5$ or $x \approx -0.5$
23. $x = -\frac{1}{2}, \frac{1}{2}$ **25.** $x = 2, 3$
27. $(4, 16)$; $x = 4$; Minimum
29. $(0, 0)$; $x = 0$; Minimum
31. $16 - 6i$ **33.** $-i$
35. $x \approx \pm 2.1$ **37.** $x \approx \pm 4.0$ **39.** $x = -1.5$
41. $x \approx -11.0$ or $x \approx 3.2$
43. $0 = 2x^2 - x - 6$
45. $0 = x^2 + 2x - 5$
47. $x \approx 7.2$ or $x \approx 0.1$
49. $x = 0$ or $x = \frac{1}{2}$
51. $x \approx 12.87$ or $x \approx -6.34$
53. $x \approx -0.65$ or $x \approx 4.65$
55. a. $A = 500(1 + r)^2$
b. About 4.88% **57. a.** $v = 10\left(1 - \frac{r^2}{0.25}\right)$ **b.** About 0.35 cm from the center **c.** 0.5 cm

---

5-2 Part B Try It

a. $x = 3$ or $x = -2$ **b.** $x = 0$ or $x = 7$ **c.** $x = -2$ or $x = -4$ **d.** $x = \frac{1}{2}$ or $x = -4$
e. $x = -1$ or $x = -\frac{6}{5}$
f. $x = \frac{1}{2}$ or $x = \frac{2}{3}$

5-2 Part B Exercises

1. a. $x^2 + 8x + 15$
b.

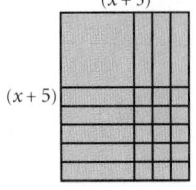

c. $(x + 5)$ and $(x + 3)$
d. $(x + 5)(x + 3)$ **3.** C
9. $x = 4$ or $x = -2$
11. Cannot be solved by factoring **13.** $x = 0$ or $x = -2$
15. $x = -6$ or $x = 2$
17. $x = -1$ or $x = \frac{7}{3}$
19. $b = 3$ or $b = -16$
21. a. $16t^2 - 400 = 0$; 5 sec
b. $16t^2 - 600 = 0$; No
23. $x \approx \pm 2.4$ **28.** 11 in. by 7 in. **29.** $(-5, -25)$; $x = -5$; Minimum $= -25$
31. $(-1.25, 2.875)$; $x = -1.25$; Minimum $= -2.875$
33. $x = 1$ **35.** $x = 8$ or $x = 3$ **37.** $x = 2$ or $x = -14$
39. $x = 2$ or $x = -5$
41. $x = \pm 4$ **43.** $x = -3$ or $x = -1$ **45.** $x = \frac{5}{2}$ or $x = 1$
47. $x = \frac{2}{5}$ **49.** $x \approx \pm 3.3$
51. 5 in. **53.** 6 ft

5-2 Part C Try It

a. $x = 7.5$ or $x = -1$
b. $x = -0.42$ or $x = -1.58$
c. After about 4.24 sec
d. $(2, 2)$ **e.** $(-1.75, -7.125)$

5-2 Part C Exercises

1. a. $a = 2$, $b = 7$, $c = 3$
b. $x = \dfrac{-7 \pm \sqrt{(7)^2 - 4(2)(3)}}{2(2)}$
c. $x = \dfrac{-7 \pm \sqrt{49 - 24}}{4}$
d. $x = \dfrac{-7 \pm 5}{4}$
e. $x = \dfrac{-7 - 5}{4} = -\dfrac{2}{4} = -\dfrac{1}{2}$; $x = \dfrac{-7 + 5}{4} = -\dfrac{12}{4} = -3$

5. $x = -3$ or $x = -4$
7. $x = -4 \pm 2\sqrt{3}$
9. $x = \frac{5 \pm \sqrt{57}}{4}$
11. About 2.41 m
15. $k = 7.47$ or $k = -1.47$
19. $t \approx \pm 1.97$ or $t \approx \pm 0.95i$
21. a.

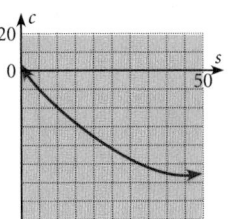

b. 5.6 mi/hr; 10.2 mi/hr; 15.7 mi/hr **25.** $h = 3.46$ cm; $b = 8.56$ cm **27.** $(0, -6)$, $(0, 2)$ **29.** $(-6, -40)$
33.

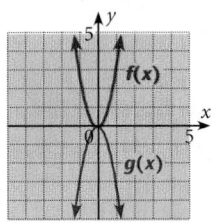

37. $x = \frac{-9 \pm \sqrt{41}}{2}$
39. $x = -\frac{1}{2}$
41. $x = 1 \pm i\sqrt{3}$
43. $x = 5$ or $x = -1$
45. $x = -0.5$ or $x \approx -1.67$
47. $x \approx 5.06$ or $x \approx 0.12$
49. $t = -6.58$ or $t = 15.60$
51. 11.33, 7.79
53. a. Yes **b.** $d = v_h t$

5-2 Part D Try It

a. Two real roots **b.** One real root **c.** Possible answer: $x^2 + 4x + 8 = 0$

5-2 Part D Exercises

1. a. $2; > 0$ **b.** $0; < 0$
c. $1; = 0$ **5.** Two complex conjugate roots. **9.** Two complex conjugate roots.
11. Possible answer: $x^2 + 4x + 8 = 0$ **13.** $x = 0.50$ and $x = \frac{2}{3}$; $y < 0$ for $x < \frac{1}{2}$ or $x > \frac{2}{3}$; $y > 0$ for $\frac{1}{2} < x < \frac{2}{3}$
15. Two **19.** None
25. 2,500 items or 10,000 items **29.** $y = \pm\sqrt{4 - x^2}$
31. Two complex conjugate roots **33.** Two real roots

---

35. Two complex conjugate roots **37.** None **39.** None
41. Two **45.** Never
47. a. $-\frac{b}{a}, \frac{c}{a}$ **b.** $-\frac{3}{2}, \frac{1}{6}$
c. Possible answer: $x^2 - 9x + 20 = 0$

5-2 Part E Self-Assessment

1. (c) **2.** The quadratic formula gives exact values of the zeros. **3.** $x = -1$ or $x = 3$
4. $x \approx \pm 2.6$ **5.** $x \approx -1.1$ or $x \approx 4.6$
6.

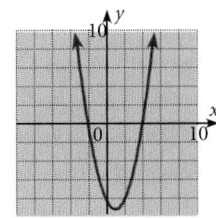

$f(x) = -\frac{20}{9}(x - 4)(x + 2)$
7. $11 - 15i$ **8.** $-1 + i$
9. -1 **10.** $30 + 5i$
11.

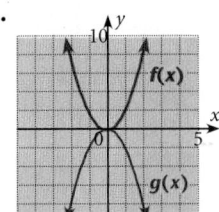

12.

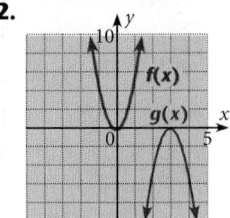

13.

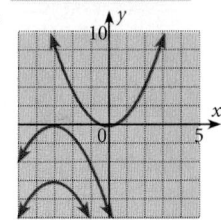

14. a. Graphing
b. Quadratic formula
c. Discriminant **15.** $x = -2$, $x = -4$ **16.** $x \approx \pm 1.4$
17. $b = \frac{1}{2}$, $b = -3$ **18.** $t \approx 15.3$, $t \approx 2.6$ **19.** $x = 0$, $x \approx 3.1$ **20.** $x = -1$
21. 26 and 28, or -26 and -28 **22.** $y = -\frac{5}{2}$, $y = 1$

---

23. $x = -2 \pm \sqrt{15}$
24. $x = \frac{9 \pm \sqrt{201}}{4}$
25. $t = 1$ or $t = 4$
26. $k \leq -4\sqrt{5}$ or $k \geq 4\sqrt{5}$
27. The 75-ft-high ball
28. Two real roots **29.** Two complex conjugate roots
30. Two real roots **31.** Two real roots **32. a. i.** About 4.17 sec **ii.** About 5.39 sec **iii.** About 6.13 sec
b. $h_0 = 1043.9$ ft
33. a. $x + \frac{1}{2}p$; $x^2 + p + \frac{1}{4}p^2$
c. $\left(x + \frac{1}{2}p\right)^2 = q + 4\left(\frac{1}{4}p\right)^2$;
$x = -\frac{1}{2}p + \sqrt{q + \frac{p^2}{4}}$;
d. $-4 + 3\sqrt{3}$

5-3 Part A Try It

a. 5 **b.** $2\sqrt{10} \approx 6.32$
c. $3\sqrt{13} \approx 10.82$ **d.** $x^2 + y^2 = 4$ **e.** $x^2 + y^2 = 5$
f. $(x - 3)^2 + (y - 4)^2 = 49$
g. $(x + 2)^2 + (y + 1)^2 = 3$
h.

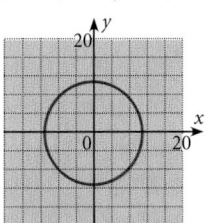

i.

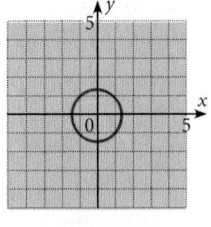

j.

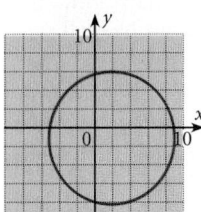

k.

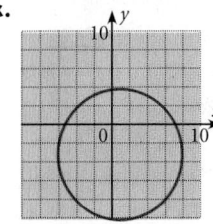

5-3 Part A Exercises

1. a. $(0, 0)$; 13 **b.** $(9, 3)$; 7
c. $(0, 0)$; $\frac{1}{2}$ **d.** $(1, -5)$; 5
3. $x^2 + y^2 = 256$
5.

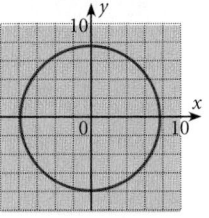

9.

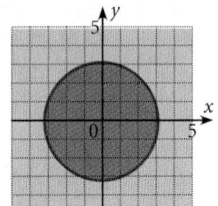

11. $x^2 + y^2 = 4$ **17.** 9.43
19. $x^2 + y^2 = 34$
21. a. $x^2 + y^2 = 23.04$;
$x^2 + y^2 = 92.16$;
$x^2 + y^2 = 207.36$;
$x^2 + y^2 = 368.64$;
$x^2 + y^2 = 576$
b. i. 4% **ii.** 36%
23. $(x + 3)^2 + (y - 3)^2 = 16$
29. $(x + 4)^2 + (y + 1)^2 = 21$; Center $(-4, -1)$; Radius $= \sqrt{21} \approx 4.58$
31.

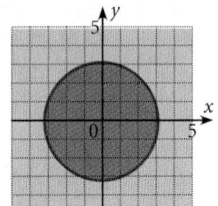

35. $a_n = 1 + 3(n - 1)$
37. $a_n = 81\left(\frac{1}{3}\right)^{n-1}$
39. $k = 5 \pm 2.2i$
41. $n = 4.3$ or $n = -0.3$
43. $x^2 + y^2 = 36$
45. 11 **47.** 8.77
49. $y = \pm\sqrt{16 - x^2}$
51. $y = \pm\sqrt{225 - x^2}$
53. $y = \pm\sqrt{17 - x^2}$
55. $x^2 + (y + 5)^2 = 25$; Center $(0, -5)$; Radius $= 5$
57. $(x + 3)^2 + (y - 1)^2 = 24$; Center $(-3, 1)$; Radius $= 2\sqrt{6} \approx 4.90$ **59.** $\left(x - \frac{7}{2}\right)^2 + \left(y + \frac{11}{2}\right)^2 = \frac{125}{2}$
Center $(3.5, -5.5)$; Radius $= \frac{5}{2}\sqrt{10} \approx 7.91$

61. a. $x^2 + y^2 = 0.25^2$

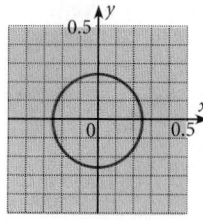

b. ± 0.15, Using the *Trace* command, locate $y = 0.2$ and check the corresponding x-value. Note that $y = 0.2$ occurs twice, once on either side of the x-axis. **63.** It is a sphere with center $(10, -3, 8)$ and radius 5.

5-3 Part B Try It

a.

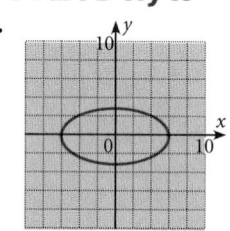

$(-3\sqrt{3}, 0), (3\sqrt{3}, 0)$
b. $\frac{x^2}{64} + \frac{y^2}{36} = 1$

5-3 Part B Exercises

1. a. 4 **b.** $(-4, 0), (4, 0)$
c. 2 **d.** $(0, -2), (0, 2)$
e.

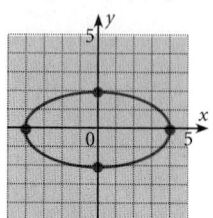

3.

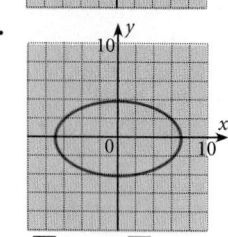

$(-\sqrt{33}, 0), (\sqrt{33}, 0)$
5.

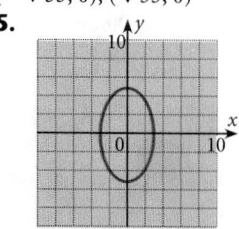

$(0, -4), (0, 4)$

936

---

9. $\frac{x^2}{9} + \frac{y^2}{4} = 1$ **15.** 4
17. About 95.78 feet
19. Eccentricity = 0.66
25. Center $(2, -1)$; Foci $(2 - 4\sqrt{3}, -1)$, $(2 + 4\sqrt{3}, -1)$; Lines of symmetry $x = 2, y = -1$
27.

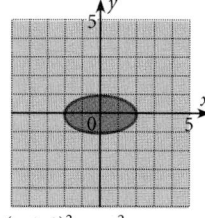

29. $\frac{(x+1)^2}{5} + \frac{y^2}{10} = 1$; Center $(-1, 0)$ **33.** $\left(\frac{14}{9}, -\frac{22}{9}\right)$
35. No solution **37.** $(2 + i, 6 + 3i), (2 - i, 6 - 3i)$
39. Foci $(-3, 0), (3, 0)$
41. Foci $(0, -\sqrt{7}), (0, \sqrt{7})$
43. Eccentricity = 0.75
45. Eccentricity = 0.47
47. $y = \pm\sqrt{1 - \frac{x^2}{9}}$
49. $y = \pm\sqrt{4 - \frac{4x^2}{25}}$
51. $\frac{(x+4)^2}{18} + \frac{y^2}{36} = 1; (-4, 0)$
53. $\frac{(x-3)^2}{32} + \frac{(y-5)^2}{64} = 1$; $(3, 5)$
55. $\frac{x^2}{33,062,500} + \frac{y^2}{32,500,000} = 1$
57. a. i. $\frac{(x+1)^2}{9} + \frac{(y+2)^2}{9} = 1$
ii. $\frac{(x+3)^2}{12.5} + \frac{(y+2)^2}{25} = 1$
iii. $\frac{(x+1)^2}{9} + \frac{(y-2)^2}{6} = 1$
iv. $\frac{(x+3)^2}{36} + \frac{(y-5)^2}{36} = 1$

5-3 Part C Try It

a.

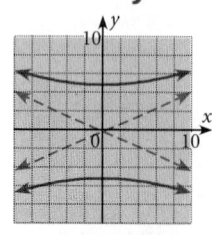

Foci $(0, -13), (0, 13)$
b.

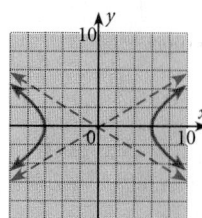

Foci $(-4\sqrt{3}, 0), (4\sqrt{3}, 0)$
c. $\frac{y^2}{4} - x^2 = 1$

5-3 Part C Exercises

1. a. 4 **b.** $(-4, 0), (4, 0)$
c. 2 **d.** $y = \frac{1}{2}x, y = -\frac{1}{2}x$
e.

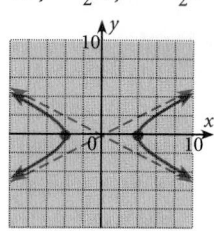

3.

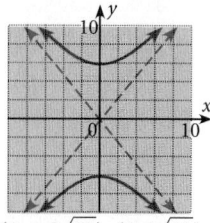

Foci $(0, -\sqrt{61}), (0, \sqrt{61})$;
Asymptotes $y = \pm\frac{6}{5}x$
5.

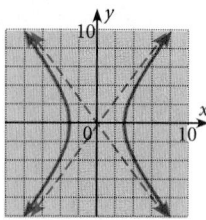

Foci $(-5, 0), (5, 0)$;
Asymptotes $y = \pm\frac{4}{3}x$
7. $\frac{x^2}{9} - y^2 = 1$ **11.** 10
15.

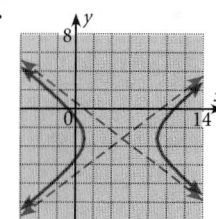

Center = $(5, -3)$; Foci $(0, -3), (10, -3)$; Lines of symmetry: $x = 5$ and $y = -3$
19. $\frac{(x+1)^2}{16} - \frac{y^2}{16} = 1$; $(-1, 0)$
20. $\frac{(y-2)^2}{9} - \frac{x^2}{9} = 1; (0, 2)$
21. $\frac{(y+4)^2}{\frac{49}{2}} - \frac{(x+2)^2}{\frac{49}{3}} = 1$; $(-2, -4)$
22. $\frac{(x-300)^2}{10,000} - \frac{y^2}{80,000} = 1$
23. a. 32% **b.** 28% **c.** 0%
d. 68% **25.** $3\sqrt{2}$
27. $12\sqrt{5}$ **29.** Two real roots **31.** Two real roots
33. Center = $(0, 0)$; Foci $(0, -5\sqrt{5}), (0, 5\sqrt{5})$; Asymptotes $y = \pm\frac{1}{2}x$

---

35. Center = $(0, 0)$; Foci $(0, -2\sqrt{5}), (0, 2\sqrt{5})$; Asymptotes $y = \pm 2x$
37. Center = $(0, 0)$; Foci $(0, -\sqrt{33}), (0, \sqrt{33})$; Asymptotes $y = \pm 4\sqrt{2}x$
39. Center = $(-6, 1)$; Foci $(-6, 1 - 2\sqrt{19})$, $(-6, 1 + 2\sqrt{19})$
43. $\frac{(x-3)^2}{9} - \frac{y^2}{9} = 1; (3, 0)$
45. $\frac{(x+2)^2}{5.25} - \frac{(y+1)^2}{10.5} = 1$; $(-2, -1)$
47. $y = \pm\sqrt{4 + \frac{x^2}{9}}$
49. $y = \pm\sqrt{1 + \frac{x^2}{4}}$
51. $y = \pm 2\sqrt{x^2 - 9}$
53. a. $\frac{x^2}{9} - \frac{y^2}{16} = 1; (-5, 0)$
b. At about $(3.5, 2.4)$

5-3 Part D Self-Assessment

1. $(x - 2)^2 + (y + 4)^2 = 81$
2. $\frac{x^2}{36} + \frac{y^2}{11} = 1$
3. $\frac{x^2}{4} - \frac{y^2}{4} = 1$
4. Circle; Center $(0, 0)$; Radius 5 **5.** Hyperbola; Center $(0, 0)$; Vertices $(-5, 0), (5, 0)$ **6.** Ellipse; Center $(0, 0)$; Foci $(0, -\sqrt{7})$, $(0, \sqrt{7})$ **7.** Parabola; Vertex $(-4, -2)$ **8.** Circle; Center $(1, -3)$; Radius 2
9. Hyperbola; Center $(-4, 1)$; Vertices $(-4, -5), (-4, 7)$
10. Ellipse; Center $(-3, 2)$; Foci $(-3 - 2\sqrt{3}, 2)$, $(-3 + 2\sqrt{3}, 2)$
11. Hyperbola; Center $(-8, 10)$; Vertices $(-8 - \sqrt{5}, 10)$, $(-8 + \sqrt{5}, 10)$ **12.** Ellipse; Center $(-2, 0)$; Foci $(-2, -2\sqrt{2}), (-2, -2\sqrt{2})$
13. A circular tub would have the shock waves focus on the wave propagation machine. A hyperbolic tub would not reflect the waves in a useful way. **14.** An orbit is a closed path. A parabolic or hyperbolic path can only be traveled once, as it continues infinitely. **15.** $(x + 2)^2 + (y - 4)^2 = 22$; Circle; $(-2, 4)$

16. $\frac{(x+2)^2}{14} + \frac{(y-2)^2}{7} = 1$; Ellipse; $(-2, 2)$

17. $(y+2)^2 - \frac{(x+2)^2}{2} = 1$; Hyperbola; $(-2, -2)$

18. First solve for y. Set $y_1 = $ positive half of the conic; Set $y_2 = $ negative half of the conic. Then graph both.

19. About 43.5 million miles, $a = \frac{c}{\text{eccentricity}} = \frac{7.4}{0.205} \approx 36.1$ and $36.1 + 7.4 = 43.5$.

20. The ball would go into the pocket, anything originating from one focus of an ellipse and bouncing off the edge heads for the other focus.   **21.** $a_n = 2^{n+1}$

22. $a_n = 1 - 3n$

23. $a_n = -16\left(-\frac{1}{4}\right)^{n-1}$

24. Two complex conjugate roots   **25.** One real root

26. Two complex conjugate roots   **27.** Two complex conjugate roots   **28.** In hyperbolic geometry, the sum of the angles measures less than 180°. In spherical geometry, the sum measures greater than 180°.

29.

$(0, 4)$; $y = -4$

5-4 Part A Try It

a.

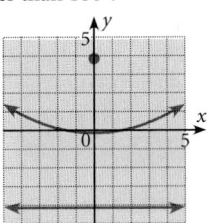

$(1.30, -1.09)$, $(-2.30, -11.91)$

b.

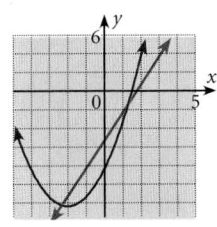

$(0, 6)$, $(8, 0)$

---

c. $\left(\frac{8 - \sqrt{13}}{3}, \frac{4 - 2\sqrt{13}}{3}\right) \approx$ $(1.46, -1.07)$

d. $(3, 4)$, $(-2, -1)$

5-4 Part A Exercises

1. About $(0.3, 0.3)$, $(2.8, -3)$

3.

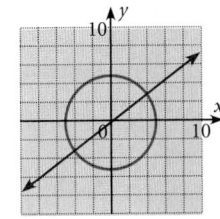

$(4, 3)$, $(-4, -3)$ **5.** $(0, 0)$, $(4, 4)$ **7.** $(0, -1)$, $\left(\frac{4}{3}, \frac{5}{3}\right)$

9. 3 cm × 4 cm

11.

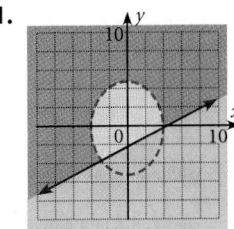

13. $\begin{bmatrix} 6 & 2 \\ 2 & 7 \end{bmatrix}$

15. Yes   **17.** $(2\sqrt{5}, 0)$, $(-2\sqrt{5}, 0)$ **19.** $(3, 10)$, $(-3, 10)$ **21.** $(4.5, 2.5)$

23. 3 m × 7 m   **25.** $(3, 4)$, $(4, 3)$ **27.** $(3, 1)$, $(-3, 2.5)$

29. $(0, -3)$, $(4, 5)$

31. $(4, 3)$, $\left(-\frac{56}{13}, -\frac{33}{13}\right)$

5-4 Part B Try It

a.

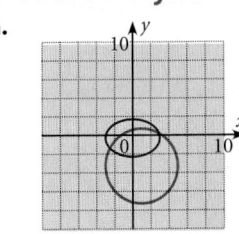

$(-2.5, -1.1)$, $(2.9, 0.5)$

b. $\left(\pm \frac{\sqrt{-2 + 2\sqrt{321}}}{4}, \frac{-1 + \sqrt{321}}{4}\right) \approx (\pm 1.45, 4.23)$

5-4 Part B Exercises

1. $(3, 4)$, $(-3, 4)$

3.

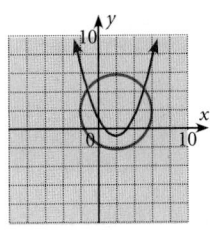

$(5.1, 4.5)$, $(-1.2, 4.5)$

5. $(-6, 8)$ **7.** Two points: $\left(\frac{4}{5}, \pm\frac{\sqrt{10}}{5}\right) \approx \left(\frac{4}{5}, \pm0.6\right)$

9. Two points: $\left(\pm\frac{4\sqrt{7}}{7}, \frac{32}{7}\right) \approx (\pm1.5, 4.6)$

11.

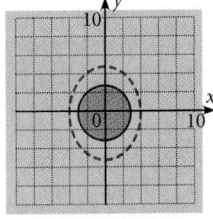

13.

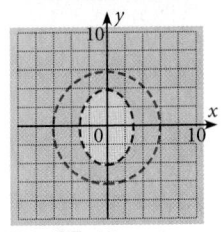

15. 720   **17.** 22

19. No solution

21. $(1.87, 2.78)$, $(1.87, -2.78)$

23. No real solutions

25. Infinitely many solutions

27. Four points: $(\pm\sqrt{17}, \pm2\sqrt{2}) \approx (\pm4.12, \pm2.83)$

29. 1994: 781 units @ $34; 1995: 976 units @ $29

31. $4 + 2i$, $-4 - 2i$

5-4 Part C Self-Assessment

1.

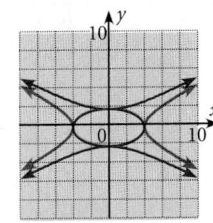

Hyperbola with vertices on the x-axis, hyperbola with vertices on the y-axis, and ellipse; the first hyperbola intersects the ellipse at $(-4, 0)$ and $(4, 0)$, the second intersects the ellipse at

---

$(0, -2)$ and $(0, 2)$. The two hyperbolas do not intersect one another.   **2.** $(4.6, 3.8)$, $(4.6, -3.8)$, $(-4.6, 3.8)$, $(-4.6, -3.8)$ **3.** $(2.3, 0.3)$, $(-2.3, 0.3)$ **4.** $(-2, 7)$, $(1, -2)$ **5.** 3 cm × 19 cm

6. Possible answer: Ellipse $\frac{x^2}{16} + \frac{y^2}{9} = 1$ Parabola $y = -x^2 - 3$

7. $(\pm\sqrt{-2 + 2\sqrt{101}}, -1 + \sqrt{101}) \approx (\pm4.25, 9.05)$

8. $(4, 3)$, $(3, 4)$ **9.** Four points: $(\pm\sqrt{10}, \pm\sqrt{6}) \approx (\pm3.16, \pm2.45)$

10. $(2.99, -0.28)$, $(2.01, -2.22)$ **11.** No

12. Yes   **13.** $(-4, 0)$, $(4, 0)$

14. $(-2 - 3\sqrt{11}, 3)$, $(-2 + 3\sqrt{11}, 3)$

15.

$\qquad$

16.

$\qquad$

17. 4 Ultra glorks, 16 glorks

Chapter 5 Review

1. False; Hyperbola   **2.** False; Quadratic formula   **3.** True

4. False; Hyperbolas (instead of functions)   **5.** False; Zeros

6. False; Major axis   **7.** False; Vertex   **8.** $(0, -2)$, 0.75, no, none, down 2   **9.** $f(x) = 0.4(x - 1.6)^2 - 7$, $(1.6, -7)$

10. $(-5, 0)$, -8, yes, left 5, none   **11.** $f(x) = -3(x - 2)^2 + 5$, yes, right 2, up 5

12.

13.

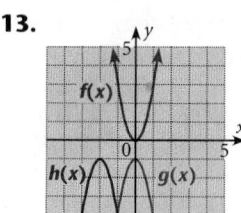

14. $f(x) = (x + 3)^2 - 9$;
$(-3, -9)$; $x = -3$;
Minimum $f(x) = -9$
15. $y = (x - 4)^2 - 11$;
$(4, -11)$; $x = 4$ minimum;
$y = -11$
16. $g(x) = 3\left(x + \frac{3}{2}\right)^2 - 7\frac{3}{4}$;
$V = \left(-\frac{3}{2}, -7\frac{3}{4}\right)$; $x = -\frac{3}{2}$;
Minimum $g(x) = -7\frac{3}{4}$
17. 15 products leads to 229 successful contacts, the monthly minimum. Complete the square to obtain $y = -(x - 15)^2 + 229$. **18.** $x = 7$; Possible answer: Use the Principle of Zero Products because the equation in standard form factors easily. **19.** $x = 0.4$ or $x = -2$; Possible answer: Use the Principle of Zero Products because the equation factors. **20.** $x = -9$ or $x = 7$; Possible answer: Use the Principle of Zero Products because the equation factors. **21.** $x = 2 \pm \frac{\sqrt{66}}{3}$; $x \approx -0.7$ or $x \approx 4.7$; Possible answer: Use the quadratic formula because the equation cannot be factored. **22. a.** $h(t) = -4.9t^2 + 10t + 0$ **b.** No; His maximum will be about 5.1 meters. **23.** Two real roots **24.** Two real roots **25.** Circle; Center = $(0, 0)$, radius = 9 **26.** Hyperbola; Center = $(0, 0)$; Vertices $(6, 0)$, $(-6, 0)$ **27.** Ellipse; Center = $(1, -2)$; Foci $(1 + \sqrt{5}, -2)$, $(1 - \sqrt{5}, -2)$ **28.** 28,620,000 mi, $c = 0.205a = 0.205(36,000,000) = 7,380,000$, and $36,000,000 - 7,380,000 = 28,620,000$.

29. $(2.8, 6.6)$, $(-2.4, -3.8)$
30. $(-2.4, 1.6)$, $(-1.5, -1.8)$, $(1.5, -1.8)$, $(2.4, 1.6)$
31. $(5, 10)$, $(-5, -10)$
32. $(\pm\sqrt{3}, 2) \approx (\pm1.73, 2)$
33. About 4 times/day or 56 items/day, set cost = revenue and solve. **34.** The parabolic mirror reflects the parallel light rays toward the common focus. The hyperbolic mirror then reflects the light toward its focus, which is where the eye is located.

CHAPTER 6

6-1 Part A Try It

a. 35 **b.** 6 **c.** 720 **d.** 6

6-1 Part A Exercises

1. a.

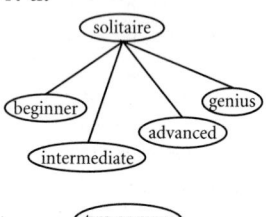

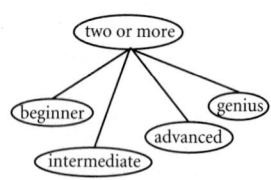

b. 8 **3. a.** 4 **b.** 3 **c.** 7
5. 16 **7.** 3,628,800 **9.** 714
11. 48 **13. a.** 1,352; 35,152; 36,504 **b.** 1,200; 27,600; 28,800 **15.** 60 **17.** 60
19. 362,880 **21.** 40,200
23. 720 **25.** 27 different ways **27.** 6000 **29.** 45
31. 12 **33.** True; $n! = n(n - 1)(n - 2) \times \cdots \times 1$ and $n(n - 1)! = n(n - 1)(n - 2) \times \cdots \times 1$

6-1 Part B Try It

a. 55,440 **b.** 60,480 **c.** 120
d. 34,650

6-1 Part B Exercises

1. a. 6; 5; 4; 3 **b.** 360

c. 720 **5.** STU, SUT, TSU, TUS, UST, UTS
7. a. 3,628,800 **b.** 24
9. 3,628,800 **11.** 40,320
13. 32,760 **17.** 4,989,600
19. 360 **21.** $(3, -2)$
23. 7th term **25.** $(5, 0)$, $(-5, 0)$ **27.** 120; 60 **29.** 30
31. 13,800 **33.** 9 **35.** 12
37. 10,897,286,400
39. 10,080 **41.** 1,663,200
43. 420 **45.** 60
47. 181,440 **49.** 5040
51. b. 39,916,800

6-1 Part C Self-Assessment

1. 64 **2. a.** There are 16 types of parakeet available. **b.** The number of types available would be reduced to 12. **3.** 24 **4.** 6840
5. a. 720 **b.** 24 **c.** 360
6. 165,765,599
7. 479,001,600 **8.** 60
9. About $(-4.61, 3.84)$, About $(0.99, 5.92)$
10. $\left(\frac{1}{3}, \frac{13}{9}\right)$, $(2, 2)$
11. $-38 + 42i$ **12.** 64
13. 6,375,600; $\frac{1}{6,375,600}$
14. a. 72 **b.** 432 **c.** 120
15. 336 **16.** 1,814,400
18. 20 **19.** 20 different varieties

6-2 Part A Try It

a. 56 **b.** 21 **c.** 210
d. $\frac{2}{17} \approx 0.118$

6-2 Part A Exercises

1. a. Yes, it involves combinations. **b.** No, it does not.
3. 44,352,165 **5.** 1 **11.** 66
13. 65,536 **15. a.** 15 **b.** 20
17. a. $\frac{5}{28} \approx 0.18$
b. $\frac{15}{28} \approx 0.54$ **c.** $\frac{5}{7} \approx 0.71$
19. $x^2 + 10x + 25$ **21.** $x^4 - 8x^3 + 24x^2 - 32x + 16$
23. 3876 **25.** 1 **27.** 1
29. 1 **31. a.** 56 **b.** 93
33. About 0.399
35. a. 201,376 **b.** 4,368
c. $\frac{39}{1798} \approx 0.0217$
39. 34,650

6-2 Part B Try It

a. $x^5 + 10x^4 + 40x^3 + 80x^2 + 80x + 32$ **b.** $27c^3 - 108c^2 + 144c - 64$
c. $729x^6 + 1458x^5 + 1215x^4 + 540x^3 + 135x^2 + 18x + 1$ **d.** $-32y^5 + 800y^4 - 8000y^3 + 40,000y^2 - 100,000y + 100,000$

6-2 Part B Exercises

1. a. 6 **b.** $_5C_0, 3_5C_1, 9_5C_2, 27_5C_3, 81_5C_4, 243_5C_5$
c. $x^5 + 15x^4 + 90x^3 + 270x^2 + 405x + 243$
5. $193,536p^2$ **7.** $1,306,368x^2, -2,239,488x, 1,679,616$
9. $x^7 - 7x^6y + 21x^5y^2 - 35x^4y^3 + 35x^3y^4 - 21x^2y^5 + 7xy^6 - y^7$ **11.** $8x^3 + 6x^2 + 1.5x + 0.125$
13. $x^5 + 10x^4 + 40x^3 + 80x^2 + 80x + 32$ **15. a.** 32
b. 10 **c.** 26 **d.** $\frac{13}{16} \approx 0.813$
17. a. 0.25 **b.** 0.375
21. $x = 3, 4$ **23.** 7 **25.** 3
27. $6048c^5$ **29.** (A)
31. $x^7 - 14x^6 + 84x^5 - 280x^4 + 560x^3 - 672x^2 + 448x - 128$ **33.** $32x^5 - 240x^4 + 720x^3 - 1080x^2 + 810x - 243$ **35.** $x^4 + 0.4x^3 + 0.06x^2 + 0.004x + 0.0001$ **37.** $x^3 + 0.9x^2 + 0.27x + 0.027$
39. $-0.01024 + 0.128x - 0.64x^2 + 1.6x^3 - 2x^4 + x^5$
41. $x^3 + 3x + \frac{3}{x} + \frac{1}{x^3}$
43. $-117 - 44i$
45. Located on a diagonal starting with a 1 in the 4th row; $t_n = {}_{n+2}C_3 = \frac{n(n + 1)(n + 2)}{6}$
47. $(0.65x + 0.35y)^3 = 0.274625x^3 + 0.443625x^2y + 0.238875xy^2 + 0.042875y^3$

6-2 Part C Self-Assessment

1. 15 **2.** 35 **3.** 7 **4.** 70
5. 210 **6.** 11 **7.** (b)
8. $x^4 + 48x^3 + 864x^2 + 6912x + 20736$ **9.** $16a^4 - 32a^3b + 24a^2b^2 - 8ab^3 + b^4$
10. $-27 + 54y - 36y^2 + 8y^3$

11. 6th, 7th, 8th, 14th, 21st, and 28th days; The number of rejection reactions are extremely high on those days compared to the others.
12. Add each pair of two adjacent numbers in row n to get the number between them in row $(n + 1)$ and insert 1s at both ends of the row.
13. $\frac{3}{54,145} \approx 0.000055$
14. 30; No **15.** About 0.035
16. -115 **17.** $x = 10, -2$
18. $x = -10, 7$ **19.** 24
20. There are 792 choices of 5 students, and with 8 teachers there is a total of 6336 possible classes. **22.** 8120
23. 210 **24.** $\frac{26,670}{100,947} \approx$ 0.264

Chapter 6 Review

1. $n!$ **2.** Multiplication
3. Permutation
4. Combination
5.

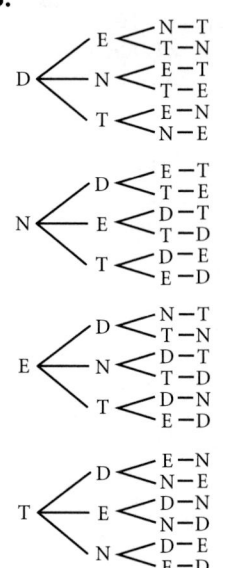

6. 20 **7.** 1296 **8.** 40,320
9. 96 **10.** 30240 **11.** 5
12. $\frac{1}{13} \approx 0.077$ **13.** 7
14. 120 **15.** 6,720 **16.** 1
17. 39,916,800 **18. a.** 11
b. 358,800 **c.** 13,800
19. 120 **20.** 1,663,200
21. 45,360 **22.** 2520
23. 35 **24. a.** 210 **b.** 112
25. 35 **26.** 84 **27.** 45

28. 1 **29. a.** 23,535,820
b. 5,852,925
30. a. 25,827,165
b. $\frac{1}{25,827,165} \approx 3.87 \cdot 10^{-8}$
31. $\frac{6}{1105} \approx 0.00543$
32. $243x^5 + 810x^4 + 1080x^3 + 720x^2 + 240x + 32$
33. $16x^4 - 64x^3 + 96x^2 - 64x + 16$ **34.** $216 + 432y + 288y^2 + 64y^3$ **35.** $\frac{15}{128}$
36. About 1.3×10^{130}
37. 2.09×10^{13}

CHAPTER 7

7-1 Part A Try It

a. 75 cd **b.** 6 hr **c.** 72
d. $\frac{1}{2}$ amp **e.** 4.32 units

7-1 Part A Exercises

1. a. $y = kx$ **b.** $k = 3$; $y = 3x$ **c.** $y = 96$ **d.** $x = 16.5$
e. Possible answer: (12, 36), (32, 96), (16.5, 49.5)

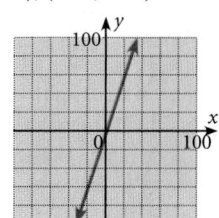

f. x increases; y increases
5. 6 **7.** $\frac{50}{3}$
9. a.

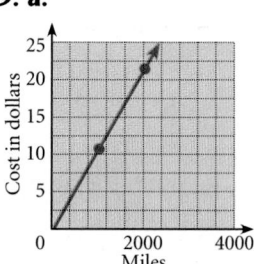

b. \$0.99 **11.** $F = \frac{kmM}{r^2}$
13. y is halved. **15.** y is decreased by a factor of $\frac{1}{4}$.
21. $x \approx -1.1$ or $x \approx 6.1$
23. $x \approx -0.8 + 1.4i$ or $x \approx -0.8 - 1.4i$ **25.** $\frac{1}{4}$
27. 15 **29.** 64
31. 600 hours **33.** Width varies directly with volume and inversely with height.

35. Area varies directly with the square of the radius.
37. About 194,000 watts
39. \$125

7-1 Part B Try It

a.

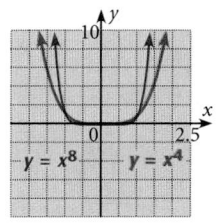

b.

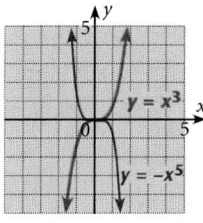

7-1 Part B Exercises

1. a. Quadratic **b.** Possible answer: $(-1, 1)$, $(0, 0)$, $(1, 1)$
c. Line symmetry **d.** The positive and negative x-values result in larger positive y-values the farther they get from 0. **e.** More steeply
f. Less steeply over most of the interval, but more steeply when x is very close to 1.
3. B **7.** Graph 1 is $y = x^9$ and graph 2 is $y = x^{13}$.
9.

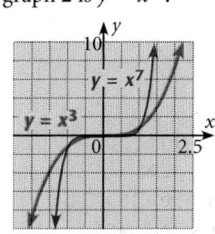

11.

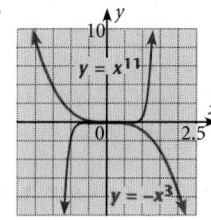

13. b. i. 21.5 hp **ii.** 38.5 hp
iii. 3.5 in. **15.** $y = x^2$ and $y = x^4$ are even functions, and $y = x^3$ and $y = x^5$ are odd functions.

17. $\frac{x \cdot x \cdot x \cdot x}{x \cdot x}$
19. $(-3k)(-3k)(-3k)$
21. $v \cdot v \cdot v \cdot v \cdot v \cdot v \cdot v \cdot v$
23. 0.00736 **25. a.** Cubic
b. Possible answer: $(-1, -1)$, $(0, 0)$, $(1, 1)$
c. Point symmetry **d.** As the x-values get farther from 0, the y-values get farther from 0. For positive x-values, the y-values are positive, and for negative x-values, the y-values are negative.
e. More steeply **f.** Less steeply over most of the interval, but more steeply when x is very close to 1. **27.** C
31. Graph 1 is $y = x^{11}$ and graph 2 is $y = x^{15}$.
33.

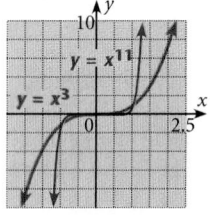

37.

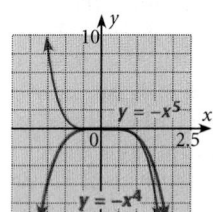

39. a. $y = p^4$; $0 \le p \le 1$
b. i. 0.01 **ii.** 0.06 **iii.** 0.24
iv. 0.66 **41.** About 107%

7-1 Part C Try It

a. $81k^4$ **b.** $-16a^4$ **c.** $16a^4$
d. n^{12} **e.** 10^4 or 10,000
f. $\frac{1}{c^9}$ **g.** m^{80} **h.** $\frac{2x^{16}y^9}{5}$
i. 1.503×10^{-10} Joules

7-1 Part C Exercises

1. False **4.** False **8.** False
13. $4m^3$ **17.** $\frac{-4}{m^3}$ **21.** $-10x$
27. $\frac{9x}{2}$ **31.** 596,000 mi^2
33. 3×10^{-4} m
35. 6.25×10^3
37. a. About 9.46×10^{12} km
b. About 1.23×10^{23} km

43.

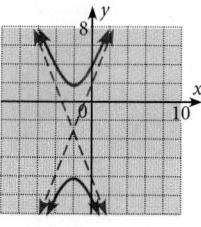

45. $-8h^3$ **47.** $108p^5$
49. x^3 **51.** 20^6 **53.** $-\frac{1}{243}$
55. 14^{15} **57.** $-12m^4$ **59.** $\frac{1}{2}$
61. $2c^{16}$ **63.** $128k^{28}$ **65.** c^3
67. $\frac{3y^{18}}{8x^{16}}$ **71.** 6,592,800 mi^2
73. 1.08×10^{25} atoms
75. 1.008×10^5 **77.** 2.31×10^{-5} mi/sec **79.** $x = \frac{1}{2}$
81. $x = \frac{13}{3}$ **83. a.** No
b. Evaluate a^b first, then take the result to the c power.

7-1 Part D Self-Assessment

1. a. $0 \le x \le 1, 0 \le y \le 1$, All of the curves intersect at $(0, 0)$ and $(1, 1)$. **b.** 1: $y = x$; 2: $y = x^2$; 3: $y = x^3$; 4: $y = x^4$
2. Exponent **3.** Direct; Inverse **4.** 5 **5.** 27 **6.** 50
7. $20\frac{5}{6}$ **8.** 968 **9.** $x \approx -0.56$ or $x \approx 3.56$ **10.** $x = 4$ or $x = -5$ **11.** $x \approx -0.14 - 1.25i$ or $x \approx -0.14 + 1.25i$
12. 4.5 newtons **13.** 56
14. 1 hour **15. a.** $g = kd$; $k \approx 0.035$ **b.** 456 mi
16.

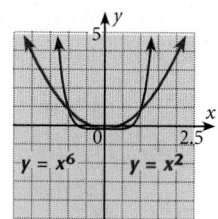

17.

18. $(0, 0)$, $(1, 1)$ **19.** Less steeply **20.** More steeply over most of the interval, but less steeply when x is very close to 1 **21.** (d) **22.** (D)

---

23. (C) **24.** $\frac{1}{47}$ **25.** 1
26. $-\frac{5y^9}{x^6}$ **27.** $-16p^{18}$
28. $\frac{2d^5}{243}$ **29.** $\frac{1.5}{10^{11}}$
30. 5.67×10^{13}
31. 1.043×10^{-10}
32. 0.000000008035
33. 600,000,000 **34.** 3 units
35. a. 1.17×10^{15} ft^3
b. 7.81×10^{23} grains of sand

7-2 Part A Try It

a. 64 **b.** $\frac{1}{5}$ **c.** 3 **d.** 8
e. $\sqrt[5]{c^{12}}$ **f.** $h \approx 241M^{-\frac{1}{4}}$
g. $(m^2n)^{\frac{5}{6}}$ **h.** 6 **i.** $\sqrt{m}\sqrt[4]{n}$

7-2 Part A Exercises

1. a. $a^{\frac{3}{4}} = \sqrt[4]{a^3} = \left(\sqrt[4]{a}\right)^3$
b. $\sqrt[5]{a^2} = \left(\sqrt[5]{a}\right)^2 = a^{\frac{2}{5}}$
3. $\sqrt[3]{7}$ **5.** $19^{\frac{1}{4}}$
7. $\sqrt[7]{(a+3b)^5}$ **9.** $\sqrt[3]{n^{10}}$
11. $(2x-y)^{\frac{5}{6}}$ **13.** $\sqrt[7]{a^6b^8}$ or $|b|\sqrt[7]{a^6|b|}$ **15.** Negative
17. Does not exist
19. $A = \frac{A_L}{\sqrt[5]{2.7^3}}$ **21.** 10
23. $\frac{1}{7}$ **25.** 243 **27.** 6
29. $5^{\frac{1}{6}} = \sqrt[6]{5}$ **33.** $\frac{\sqrt{6}}{3}$
36. a. $T = 2\pi\left(\frac{\ell}{g}\right)^{\frac{1}{2}}$
b. About 2.2 sec **37.** 0.75
39. 1.8 **41.** $\frac{3}{5}$ **43.** $\frac{23}{8}$
45. $\sqrt[4]{6}$ **47.** $15^{\frac{1}{3}}$ **49.** $b^{\frac{3}{2}}$
51. $\sqrt[5]{(x-y)^2}$
53. $(m+2n)^{\frac{3}{4}}$
55. $\frac{1}{\sqrt[5]{y+3z^2}}$
57. $x^{-\frac{2}{5}}y^{-\frac{1}{5}}$ or $\frac{1}{x^{\frac{2}{5}}y^{\frac{1}{5}}}$
59. $5^{\frac{5}{9}}h^{\frac{10}{9}}k^{\frac{5}{3}}$ **63.** 3 **65.** $\frac{1}{10}$
67. 729 **69.** $\frac{1}{9}$ **71.** 29
73. 2 **75.** $\sqrt{x}$ **77.** 25
79. a. About 0.14 L/hr
b. About 9.3 L/hr
c. About 44.4 L/hr
81. a. $W = w(b-35)^{-\frac{1}{3}}$
b. Alex

7-2 Part B Try It

a. 3125 **b.** 12.64 **c.** $x^{2.94}$

7-2 Part B Exercises

1. Linear regression
3. Linear regression **5.** 343
7. 9 **9.** 2187 **13.** 2.10
15. 3.9 **17.** $a^{6.06}$
21. a. About 37,131 in.^{2}
b. About 3107 in.^{2}
23. $(x-3)^2 + (y+2)^2 = 36$
25. 24 **27.** 2520 **29.** 8
31. 121 **33.** 243 **35.** 1
37. 33.84 **39.** 0.21
41. 2.92 **43.** 1.23
45. 104.23 **47.** $e^{2.34}$
49. $a^{-6.766}b^{10.455} = \frac{b^{10.455}}{a^{6.766}}$
51. $x^{2.61}$
53. a. $y = 28.24x^{0.219}$
b. About 77.4 years
57. a. Inversely **b.** About 106 strides per minute
c. 1.69 kg

7-2 Part C Try It

a. $x = 256$ **b.** $x = 62$
c. $x = 0$ or $x = 1$ **d.** $x = 7$

7-2 Part C Exercises

1. a. $\sqrt{x} = 5$ **b.** $x = 25$
c. $3 + \sqrt{25} = 8$, checks
5. $x = 2$ **7.** No solution
9. $x = -1$ **13.** $x = 30$
15. $x = 64$ or $x = -64$
17. $x = 32$ or $x = -32$
21. $d = \pm\sqrt{\frac{kMm}{F}}$
23. $m = \frac{F}{4\ell^2f^2}$
25. a. $r = \sqrt{\frac{A}{\pi}}$
b. 8.29 in. **27.** $16 - t^2$
29. $x^2 - 14x + 49$ **31.** $x - 6\sqrt{x} + 9$ **33.** $x = 144$
35. $x = \frac{76}{3}$ **37.** No solution
39. $x = 11$ **41.** $x = -128$
43. $x = -1$ **45.** $x = 9$
47. $x = 125$ **49.** $x \approx 20.72$ or $x \approx -20.72$ **51.** $s = \frac{gt^2}{2}$
53. $d = (5 \times 10^9 t)^{\frac{2}{3}} \approx 2.92 \times 10^6 t^{\frac{2}{3}}$
55. a. $r = \frac{1}{2}\sqrt{\frac{S}{\pi}}$
b. About 1820 km
57. a. $p = 1 - \sqrt[30]{1 - P_{30}}$
b. About 0.04 **c.** About 0.91

7-2 Part D Try It

a.

$x = 4$ **b.** $x = 5$ **c.** $x = 1$
d. No real solutions

7-2 Part D Exercises

1. a. $\sqrt{x} + 1$
b. $x + 2\sqrt{x} + 1$ **c.** 2 **d.** 1
e. 1 **f.** 1, 1 **g.** Checks
3.

$x = 11$ **5.** $x = 9$ **7.** $x = \frac{25}{36}$
9. $y = -\frac{7}{6}x + \frac{67}{12}$ **17.** No real solution **19.** No real solution **21.** About 6420 ft
23. 10 **25.** 55 **27.** $x = 8$
29. $x = 6$ **31.** $x = 16$
33. $x = -2$ **35.** $x = -3$
45. $x = 1$ **47.** $x = 4$
49. $x = 25$ or $x = 49$
51. About 2.9 m **53.** $x = \frac{5}{4}$

7-2 Part E Self-Assessment

1. $x = 1$ is extraneous.
2. (b) **3.** (d)
4. a. 1: $y = x^2$; 2: $y = \sqrt{x}$; 3: $y = \sqrt[4]{x}$; **b.** $(0, 0)$, $(1, 1)$
5. a. 792 **b.** 120
6. $(x+1)^2 + (y-4)^2 = 4$
7. (C) **8.** (D) **9.** 3
10. $k^{\frac{5}{6}} = \sqrt[6]{k^5}$
11. $x^{\frac{1}{4}} = \sqrt[4]{x}$
12. $x^{0.8}y^{-8.2} = \frac{x^{0.8}}{y^{8.2}}$
13. $|c|^{\frac{5}{6}} = \sqrt[6]{|c^5|}$
14. $m^{1.82}n^{4.68}$ **15.** -1
16. 8 **17.** 125 **18.** 1.95
19. 0.17 **20.** 10
21. $(x + y^2)^{\frac{3}{2}}$ **22.** $\sqrt[4]{xy^3}$
23. a. $v \approx 3.86\sqrt{d}$ **b.** $d \approx \frac{v^2}{14.9}$ **c.** About 518 mi/hr

24. $x = 38.44$ **25.** $x = 10$
26. $x = 8$ **27.** $x = -20$
28. $x = 4$ **29.** $x = 3$
30. $x = 49$ or $x = 9$
31. $x \approx 7.30$ **32.** $x \approx 2.03$
33. $x = 5$ **34.** $x = 9$ or
$x = 1$ **35.** $r = \sqrt[3]{\dfrac{3V}{4\pi}}$
36. 5% **37. a.** $k \approx 21.5$
b. About 232,362 ft^2
c. About 82.8 pounds

7-3 Part A Try It

a. $-x + 1$; $-5x - 5$; $-6x^2 - 13x - 6$ **b.** $-2x^3 + 3x^2 + 5x - 5$; $-2x^3 - 3x^2 + 5x + 3$; $-6x^5 + 23x^3 - 3x^2 - 20x + 4$ **c.** -56

7-3 Part A Exercises

1. a. 3 **b.** 4 **c.** 7 **d.** -1
e. 12 **f.** $3x + 1$ **g.** $-x + 1$
h. $2x^2 + 2x$ **3.** 17 **5.** 210
7. $-3k^2 + 2k + 1$
9. $2x - 3$; $-4x + 7$; $-3x^2 + 11x - 10$ **11.** $x^3 + 3x^2 + 2x - 2$; $x^3 - 3x^2 - 2x - 2$; $3x^5 + 2x^4 - 6x^2 - 4x$
13. $3x^4 + x^3 - x^2 + 5x + 7$; $3x^4 - x^3 - x^2 - 5x - 1$; $3x^7 + 14x^5 + 12x^4 - 2x^3 - 4x^2 + 15x + 12$
15. a. 2 **b.** 18 **c.** -42
16. a. $r(x) = 480$
$v(x) = 18(x - 40)$
b. $p(x) = 480 + 18(x - 40) = 18x - 240$ **c.** $624
19. $(f + g)(x) = x^2 - 5$
21. $x^3 + 3x^2 + 3x + 1$
23. $27c^3 + 54c^2 + 36c + 8$
25. No solution **27.** 6
29. -20 **31.** $2n + 5$
33. $-2x$; $4x$; $-3x^2$
35. $7x - 1$; $x + 3$; $12x^2 - 5x - 2$ **37.** $x^2 + 2x + 2$; $-x^2 + 2x - 6$; $2x^3 - 2x^2 + 8x - 8$ **39.** $3x^2 - 3x + 1$; $-x^2 - x + 5$; $2x^4 - 5x^3 + 6x^2 + x - 6$
41. $(f + g)(x) = 2x$
43. $(f + g)(x) = -2x$
45. a. $y = 0.66x - 1196.32$, where x is the year; $y = 0.55x - 1087.1$
b. $y = 1.21x - 2283.42$
c. 1988

7-3 Part B Try It

a. 3; -1 **b.** x^2; $x^2 - 2x + 2$
c. $c = 0.04m$

7-3 Part B Exercises

1. a. $f(g(x)) = f(x + 4)$
b. $3(x + 4) - 1$ **c.** $3x - 11$
3. 7 **5.** 19 **7.** $3x^3 - 5$
9. a. $f(x) = 0.8x$ **b.** $g(x) = 0.75x$ **c.** $(f \circ g)x = 0.6x$
d. Ira pays $36. **11.** 5; 9
15. $4x^2 - 4x + 1$; $2x^2 - 1$
17. $2x^2 + 5x + 2$; $2x^2 - 3x + 2$ **19.** $27x^3 - 3x$; $3x^3 - 3x$ **21.** $4x$ **23.** $2x^2$
27. $f(g(x)) = x$; $g(f(x)) = x$
29. -11; 5 **31.** -13; 13
33. 19; 25 **35. a.** $c(d) = d - 5$ **b.** $s(d) = 0.8d$
c. $s(c(d)) = 0.8d - 4$; $c(s(d)) = 0.8d - 5$ **d.** After, to save an extra dollar.
37. 9; 9 **39.** x^2; $x^2 - 2x + 2$
41. $x^2 + 2$; $x^2 + 4x + 4$
43. $x^2 + 2x - 3$; $x^2 + 4x - 1$
47. Average temperature: (Let February = 2, March = 3, etc.) $v = 2.786m + 53.07$; Apparent temperature in terms of average temperature: $p = 0.96v - 1.74$; Apparent temperature in terms of month: $p = 2.67m + 49.21$

7-3 Part C Try It

a. Relation is a function; Inverse relation is also a function. **b.** Relation is a function; Inverse relation is not a function.
c.

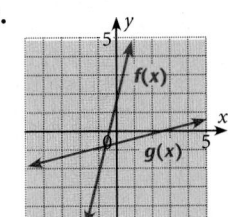

$f(g(x)) = 4\left(\dfrac{x-2}{4}\right) + 2 = x$;
$g(f(x)) = \dfrac{(4x + 2) - 2}{4} = x$
d. $f^{-1}(x) = \dfrac{x + 1}{4}$
e. $h^{-1}(x) = \sqrt[5]{7x}$

7-3 Part C Exercises

1. a. Yes, for each x there is exactly one y. **b.** $f^{-1} = \{(-2, -4), (1, -1), (-2, 0)\}$; No, the number -2 in the domain is matched with two members of the range.
c.

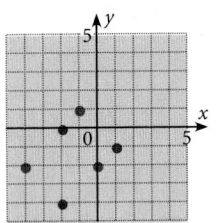

The graph of f^{-1} is the reflection of the graph of f over the line $y = x$. **5.** Relation is not a function; Inverse relation is not a function.
7.

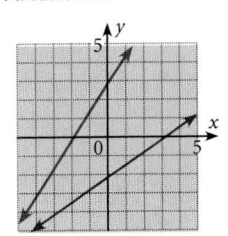

9.

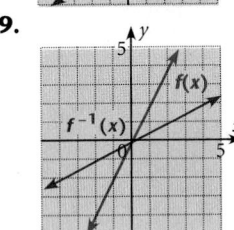

13. $f(g(x)) = 4\left(\dfrac{1}{4}x\right) = x$; $g(f(x)) = \dfrac{1}{4}(4x) = x$
15. $f(g(x)) = -2\left(-\dfrac{1}{2}x + 2\right) + 4 = x$; $g(f(x)) = -\dfrac{1}{2}(-2x + 4) + 2 = x$
19. $f^{-1}(x) = \dfrac{x - 8}{3}$
21. $f^{-1}(x) = \dfrac{3x - 7}{4}$
23. $f^{-1}(x) = \sqrt[3]{x + 5}$
25. a. $f(x) = 2\pi x$
b. $f^{-1}(x) = \dfrac{x}{2\pi}$; The radius corresponding to a circumference of x. **c.** $f(f^{-1}(x)) = 2\pi\left(\dfrac{x}{2\pi}\right) = x$ **27.** $\dfrac{1}{2}$
29. $f(g(x)) = (x - 3) + 3 = x$; $g(f(x)) = (x + 3) - 3 = x$
31. $f(g(x)) = 0.1(10x) = x$; $g(f(x)) = 10(0.1x) = x$

33. $f(g(x)) = 3\left(\dfrac{x - 1}{3}\right) + 1 = x$; $g(f(x)) = \dfrac{(3x + 1) - 1}{3} = x$
35.

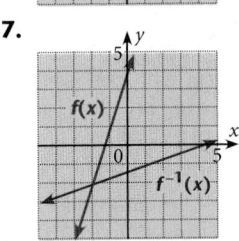

37.

39. $f^{-1}(x) = x + 2$
41. $f^{-1}(x) = \dfrac{x - 7}{3}$
43. $f^{-1}(x) = \dfrac{2}{x}$
45. a. $r = \sqrt[3]{\dfrac{3m}{19.3 \times 4\pi}} \approx 0.2313\sqrt[3]{m}$
b. About 0.63 cm **47.** They are reciprocals.

7-3 Part D Self-Assessment

1. $7x$ **2.** -21 **3.** $-3x + 6$
4. $10x^2 + 9x - 9$ **5.** -8
6. $10x - 3$ **7.** $10x + 12$
8. -11 **9.** $3x - 4$; $x - 6$; $2x^2 - 3x - 5$ **10.** $2x^2 + 3x - 7$; $-2x^2 + 3x + 7$; $6x^3 - 21x$ **11.** $3x^2 - 7x + 7$; $-x^2 - 7x - 5$; $2x^4 - 14x^3 + 8x^2 - 42x + 6$
12. $x^3 + 2x^2 + 7x + 2$; $x^3 - 2x^2 - 3x + 10$; $2x^5 + 5x^4 + 22x^2 + 22x - 24$
13. a. Consumption, the coefficient of t is larger.
b. $I(t) = 0.37t + 2.3$, by computing $C(t) - P(t)$
c. i. 2.3 quadrillion Btu
ii. 6 quadrillion Btu
iii. 9.7 quadrillion Btu
iv. 13.4 quadrillion Btu
14. 0.375 **15.** $x = 53$
16. No real solutions
17. $x = 4$ **18.** 25; 29
19. 6; 12 **20.** 101; -101
21. -122; -735
22. $f(g(x)) = 3$; $g(f(x)) = 11$

23. $f(g(x)) = 2x - 2$; $g(f(x)) = 2x - \frac{2}{3}$

24. $f(g(x)) = x^2 - 3$; $g(f(x)) = x^2 - 6x + 9$

25. $f(g(x)) = \frac{x+5}{2}$; $g(f(x)) = \frac{x+1}{2}$

26. a. $S = 4\pi r^2$ **b.** $r = \frac{d}{2}$ **c.** $S = \pi d^2$ **27.** Yes; No

28. $f(g(x)) = (x+5) - 5 = x$; $g(f(x)) = (x-5) + 5 = x$

29. $f(g(x)) = 2\left(\frac{1}{2}x - 2\right) + 4 = x$; $g(f(x)) = \frac{1}{2}(2x+4) - 2 = x$ **30.** $f^{-1}(x) = 4x$

31. $f^{-1}(x) = -\frac{1}{3}x + 4$

32. $f^{-1}(x) = \frac{\sqrt[3]{x}}{2}$

33. $f^{-1}(x) = \frac{5x+3}{2}$ **34.** (e)

35. a. $f(x) = 4x + 5$

b. $f^{-1}(x) = \frac{x-5}{4}$; Number of family members as a function of total cost. **c.** Possible answer: A family paid \$25 for tickets to the concert. How many family members attended? (Answer is 5.)

Chapter 7 Review

1. Directly **2.** Extraneous solution **3. a.** Direct **b.** Joint **c.** Joint **d.** Inverse

4. a.

b. $y = x^7$ has a much steeper (narrower) climb than $y = x^3$, but they both have the same general shape. Common points: $(0, 0)$, $(1, 1)$, and $(-1, -1)$.

5. $\frac{1}{x^3}$ **6.** $\frac{5}{w^{10}}$ **7.** $2a^2|b|^3\sqrt{2}$

8. $-\frac{2b}{a^3}$ **9. a.** 1.1×10^4 ft

b. 8.93×10^5 times as fast

10. 16 **11.** 0.02 **12.** 2048

13. 12,063,414.74

14. $x^2 \cdot \sqrt{x} \cdot \sqrt[4]{x}$

15. $4^{\frac{4}{3}} \cdot 2^{\frac{5}{6}}$ **16.** $6^5 x^{\frac{16}{5}} y^{\frac{24}{5}}$

17. $\frac{(729)^{\frac{1}{3}}}{(64)^{\frac{1}{3}}} = \left(\frac{729}{64}\right)^{\frac{1}{3}} = \frac{9}{4}$

---

18. $x = \frac{18}{5}$ **19.** $x = 8$

20. $x = 1$ **21.** $x = 4$

22. -8 **23.** $-15x^2 + 8x + 12$ **24.** 11 **25.** $-15x + 20$

26. $-15x - 4$ **27.** $\frac{x-2}{3}$

28. $-\frac{x-6}{5}$ **29.** x

30. a. $P_R(x) = 1.5x$

b. $P_S(x) = 0.7P_R(x)$

c. $P_S(x) = 1.05x$

31. a. $W = \frac{kV^2}{R}$; $k = \frac{4}{3}$

b. $W = \frac{4V^2}{3R}$ **c.** Lower, because W varies inversely with R. **d.** $W = 80$ watts

CHAPTER 8

8-1 Part A Try It

a. Cubic function

b. Quartic function **c.** Fifth-degree polynomial function

8-1 Part A Exercises

1. a. -7 **b.** 5 **c.** 6 **d.** 5

9. $0 \le x < 9.2$ **11.** $2x^5 + x^4 - 9x^3 - 3x^2 + 5x - 26$; $x^4 + 9x^3 - 7x^2 - 3x - 16$

15. $x^3 - 4x^2 - 9x + 36$; 1; 3

17. $-4x^4 + 100$; -4; 4

19. (a) -1.2 (b) -2

21. (a) -2.2 (b) 3.2

23. D **27.** C **29.** $-x^6 + x^4 - 37x^3 + 2x^2 + 12x + 5$; $x^6 + x^4 - 7x^3 + 8x^2 + 20x - 19$ **31.** $3x^5 + 4x^4 + 5x^3 - 7x^2 + 2x + 4$; $2x^6 + 3x^5 - 4x^4 - 5x^3 - 5x^2 - 12$

37. $V(x) = 4x^3$; $A(x) = 18x^2$; $V(1.5) = 13.5$ cm³; $A(1.5) = 40.5$ cm²

8-1 Part B Try It

a. No; No **b.** Given intervals are possible answers. Maximums: $y \approx 9.9$ at B between $x = -3$ and $x = -2$, $y \approx 50.8$ at D between $x = -1$ and $x = 2$ Minimums: $y \approx -5.9$ at C between $x = -2$ and $x = -1$, $y \approx -22.3$ at E between $x = 2$ and $x = 3$ **c.** About 24.9 **d.** About -81.4

8-1 Part B Exercises

1. a. No **b.** No **c.** E **d.** B

---

9. a. Absolute minimum: $y \approx -34$ at C **b.** A: $y \approx -30$, relative minimum for $-3 \le x \le -1$; B: $y \approx 0$, relative maximum for $-1 \le x \le 1$ **11. a.** Absolute maximum: $y \approx 46$ at A **b.** Given intervals are possible answers. A: $y \approx 45$, relative (and absolute) maximum for $-3 \le x \le 1$; B: $y \approx 7$, relative maximum for $1 \le x \le 3$

13. $f \circ g$ does not exist $g \circ f = \{(-2, -5), (4, 7)\}$ **15.** Yes; $r = 0.4$ **17.** $y \approx -45.33$

19. D; The only quadratic shown **23.** No maximum; Absolute minimum at $y \approx -0.04$ **25.** No maximum or minimum

27. Absolute maximum $y = 3$

29. A: $y \approx -16$, relative (and absolute) minimum; B: $y \approx 0$, relative minimum **31.** A: $y \approx -2$, relative minimum; B: $y \approx 2$, relative maximum

8-1 Part C Try It

a. 0.3, 6.2 **b.** $x = 0, 3, -2$

c. $x = 1, -1, 5, -5$

8-1 Part C Exercises

1. a. $x = -4, 1, 4$ **b.** $x = -4, 1, 4$ **c.** 0 **7.** $x \approx -1.73, 3.61$ **9.** $x \approx \pm 3.72, \pm 1.08$; Possible answer: By quadratic formula **11. a.** 14 yards at 20 yards towards the goal line **b.** 2 yards **c.** About 41.6 yards from the start or 1.6 yards beyond the goal line

14.

x	0	1	2	3	4	5	6
3^x	1	3	9	27	81	243	729

18.

x	0	1	2	3	4	5	6
3^{-x}	1	$\frac{1}{3}$	$\frac{1}{9}$	$\frac{1}{27}$	$\frac{1}{81}$	$\frac{1}{243}$	$\frac{1}{729}$

21. Possible answer: Note where the graphs cross the x-axis. **23.** $x = -2, 0, 3$

25. $x = -2, 1, 2$ **27.** Three zeros at $x = -2, 0, 2$

29. Two zeros at $x \approx -1.87$, 0.87 **31.** Increasing, except in the interval from 1 to 1.02.

8-1 Part D Self-Assessment

1. $-0.4, 4$ **2.** $-3, 2$ **3.** $-1, 3$ **4.** $-0.05, 1$ **5.** 1, 7

6. $-1, 5$ **7.** T **8.** F **9.** T

10. T **11.** 24 **12.** (A)

13. (D) **14.** (A) **15.** (A)

16. Let $x =$ length of one side of cut in inches

a. $0 < x < 9$ **b.** $V(x) = (18 - 2x)x(18 - 1.5x)$ or $V(x) = 3x^3 - 63x^2 + 324x$

c. Graph $V(x)$. Find a relative maximum in the appropriate domain. **d.** About 3.4 in. × 12.9 in. × 11.2 in.; 491 in.³

17. Does not form a geometric sequence **18.** 250 yd × 500 yd **19.** $x \approx 3.1$

20. $x \approx -2, -1.3, 2, 2.3$

21. $x \approx -2, 1, 2$ **22.** $x \approx -0.9, 0.6, 1.7$ **23. a.** $y \approx 1.8$

b. $y \approx -12.6$ **c.** Any two of $x \approx -2, -1.3, 2, 2.3$

24. $x = 0, 3, 4$; Possible answer: By factoring

8-2 Part A Try It

a.

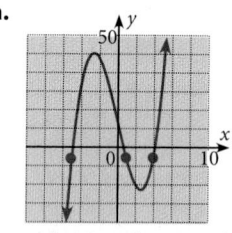

$x = -5$ or $x = 1$ or $x = 4$

b.

$x = -1$ or $x = 0$ or $x = 3$

c.

3; The graph of $y = 2x^3 + 5x^2 - 2x$ has 3 points where $y = 5$.

8-2 Part A Exercises

1. a. $-2, 1, 4$ **b.** $x = -2, 1, 4$ **c.** $x = 0$ (or -1.5 or 4.5); Yes **3.** $x = -0.25$ or $x = 1$
5. $x \approx 0.25$ or $x \approx 0.84$
7. $x = -3$ or $x = 0$ or $x = 1$
9. $x \approx -3.5$ or $x \approx -2.3$ or $x \approx -0.4$ or $x \approx 1.2$
11. $151{,}200$ **15.** $x = 1, -6$
17. $x = 0$ or $x = 1$ or $x = 3.5$
19. $x \approx 3.9$ **21.** $x \approx -0.7$ or $x \approx 3.2$ **23.** $x \approx 1.6$ or $x \approx 3.0$ **27.** $x \approx 3.1$ or $x = 4$
29. $x \approx 1.1$ **31. a.** $V(r) = \frac{2}{3}\pi r^3 + 4\pi r^2$, Cubic
b. About 3.54 cm **33.** No

8-2 Part B Try It

a. $x = -10$ or $x = 0$ or $x = 2$
b. $x = -3$ or $x = 0$ or $x = 3$
c. $x = \pm\frac{\sqrt{6}}{2}$ or $x = \pm i\sqrt{2}$
d. $x^2 + 4x + 5$ remainder 14
e. $x^2 - x + 2$ remainder 3
f. $P(5) = 5^4 - 4 \cdot (5)^3 - 6 \cdot (5)^2 + 3 \cdot 5 + 10 = 625 - 500 - 150 + 15 + 10 = 0$

8-2 Part B Exercises

1. a. $16x$ **b.** $x^2 - 6x - 16$
c. 8, 2 **d.** 8, −2 **3.** $x = -1$ or $x = 0$ or $x = 5$ **5.** $x = -\frac{3}{2}$ or $x = 0$ or $x = 2$ **7.** 3; 3; 9; 5; Quotient $x + 3$; With remainder 5 **9.** $3x - 5$ remainder 2 **11.** $x + 8$ remainder 32 **13. a.** $-\frac{1}{2}$
b. Yes **c.** Yes **15.** 49
17. 10 **23.** $6x^2 - 5x - 21$
25. $x - 5$ is a factor of $Q(x)$.
27. $P(x) = x^3 + 2x^2 - x - 2$
29. a. $M(t) = -0.001t^2(t - 100)$; $m(t)$ has zeros at 0 and 100 **31.** Undefined; 6; Undefined **33.** $x = \pm 3$, or $x = \pm i\sqrt{2}$ **35.** $x = -3$ or $x = 0$ or $x = \frac{1}{2}$ **37.** $x = -1$ or $x = 0$ **39.** $x = \pm\sqrt{2}$
41. $4x - 3$ remainder 15
43. $x^3 + x^2 + x + 1$ remainder 0 **45.** $x - 1$ remainder -2 **47.** $2x^3 + 3$ remainder -12 **49.** $x^7 + x^6 + x^5 + x^4 + x^3 + x^2 + x + 1$ remainder 0 **51.** About 0.60 ft or 7.2 in. **53.** $x - 4$ is a factor of $P(x)$. **55.** 5

57. -31 **59.** 62 **61.** 300
63. $P(x) = x^3 - 3x^2 - 18x + 40$ **65.** $P(x) = x^4 - 15x^3 + 58x^2 - 86x + 60$
67. $b = 2$ **69.** Quotient: $x + 1$; Remainder: $-2x + 2$

8-2 Part C Try It

a. $x = -5$ or $x = 1$ or $x = 2$
b. $x = -1$ or $x = -\frac{1}{2}$ or $x = 2$

8-2 Part C Exercises

1. a. No; Yes
b. $(x - 1)(2x^2 + 7x - 4)$
c. $-4, \frac{1}{2}$ **d.** $1, -4, \frac{1}{2}$
e. $(x - 1)(x + 4)(2x - 1)$
7. $x = -\frac{1}{3}$ or $x = 1$ or $x = \frac{5}{2}$
13. $x = -4$ or $x = 2$ or $x = 3$
15. One; $x = -5$ or $x = i$ or $x = -i$ **17.** Yes; -1 and 1; 6
21. $\begin{bmatrix} -4 \\ 19 \\ 1 \end{bmatrix}$ **23.** $x = -3$ or $x = 2$ or $x = 4$ **25.** $x = -2$ or $x = 2 \pm 3i$ **27.** $x = -\frac{7}{2}$ or $x = \frac{1}{3}$ or $x = 1$ or $x = 3$
29. $x = -3$ or $x = 1$ or $x = \frac{7}{2}$ **31.** $x = -2$ or $x = 1$ or $x = \frac{1 \pm \sqrt{7}}{3}$ **33.** $x = \pm 1$ or $x = 2$ **35.** Roots are 1 and -4; 1 is a multiple root of $x^3 + 2x^2 - 7x = -4$
37. No; 3 **39.** No; 3
41. Yes; $x = \pm\sqrt{3}$; 4

8-2 Part D Self-Assessment

1. $(x^3 - 3x^2 + 3x - 1) = (x - 1)^3$ so root is 1; No
2. 1, 2, or 3 **3.** Possible answer: $P(x) = (x - 5)(x + 6)(x - 7)$; $Q(x) = (x - 5)^2(x + 6)(x - 7)$
4. a. Graph looks like a parabola but does not intersect the x-axis; $g(x) = 0$ has no real roots **b.** Graph has two x-intercepts; $h(x) = 0$ has two real roots **5.** $x = 5$ or $x = -2$ **6.** $x = 4$ or $x = \pm\sqrt{3}$ **7.** $x = -4$ or $x = 2 \pm 2i\sqrt{3}$ **8.** $273; $57,152
9. $\frac{x^2}{100} + \frac{y^2}{36} = 1$ **10.** 25! or 1.55×10^{25} **11.** $x = 2$
12. $x = 0$ or $x = 16$

13. $x^3 - 2x^2 + 10x - 36$ remainder 177 **14.** $3x^2 - 9x + 25$ remainder -58
15. a.

d vs h graph

Cubic shape
b. About 83.2 m

8-3 Part A Try It

a. 2 ohms **b.** $2.1 + 2.7i$ ohms **c.** $1.2 + 0.9i$ ohms
d. $\frac{(x + 2)(x^2 + 4)}{3x - 2}$ **e.** $-\frac{ab^2}{6}$
f. $\frac{6x^2}{2x - 3}$ **g.** $\frac{(z + 5)(2z - 3)}{3z + 4}$

8-3 Part A Exercises

1. a. Yes **b.** No **c.** Yes
d. Yes **3.** $\frac{1}{9}$ **5.** $\frac{1}{8}$ **7.** $-4 - 6i$ **9.** $\frac{a(1 - r^{10})}{1 - r}$; 204.6
11. $\frac{1}{a - 2}$ **15.** $\frac{1}{x}$ **17.** $\frac{1}{2y - 1}$
19. $\frac{(b + 5)(b + 9)}{6(b - 6)}$
21. a. $\frac{2800}{400 + w}$ hr; $\frac{2800}{400 - w}$ hr
b. About 6 hr 50 min; About 7 hr 11 min **23.** $\frac{4}{15}$ **25.** $\frac{4}{21}$
27. $\frac{2}{3}$ **29.** -1 **31.** $-16 + 12i$ **33.** $0.5 - 0.9i$
35. $-\frac{5y^2}{8x^2}$ **37.** $\frac{y - 1}{2y + 1}$
39. $\frac{3y + 2}{5y + 2}$
41. $\frac{t(t^2 + 4)(t - 2)^2}{2(t^2 - 2t + 4)}$
43. $\frac{1}{2x^3}$ **45.** $\frac{4}{3y(y - 3)}$
47. $\frac{c(2c + 1)}{c + 2}$ **49.** $\frac{b - 1}{b + 2}$
51. For $x = -3, x = -2$, and $x = 1$ **53.** $\frac{8}{x}$

8-3 Part B Try It

a. $\frac{2}{(x + 1)(x - 1)}$ **b.** $\frac{s^2 + 2}{s(s^2 - 4)}$

8-3 Part B Exercises

1. a. $\frac{a + 3}{4a}$ **b.** $\frac{6}{c + 1}$ **c.** 1
3. $2(b + 3)(b - 3)$
5. $(x + 3)^2(x - 3)$
7. $\frac{15m + 2}{20m^2}$ **9.** $\frac{5p^2 + 7}{p(p + 1)}$
11. $\frac{2(7x + 4)}{(x - 3)(2x + 1)}$

13. $\frac{r(r - 4)}{2(r - 2)}$ **15.** $\frac{12(\ell + 1)}{\ell(2\ell + 1)}$, where ℓ is the length of the shorter rectangle; $1\frac{2}{3}$ in.
17. $3\sqrt{5}$ **19.** 13
23. $5a(2a + 1)(2a - 1)$
25. $12(a - 2)$
27. $(b + 2)^2(b - 3)$
29. $\frac{a^2 + 4a - 4}{2a(a + 1)(a - 1)}$
31. $\frac{x^2 + 7}{(x + 5)(x - 3)}$
33. $\frac{a - 14}{(a + 2)(a - 2)}$
35. $\frac{3n^2 - n + 4}{(3n - 4)(n - 2)(3n + 1)}$
37. $-\frac{11m + 7}{(m + 5)(m - 3)}$
39. a. Total number of tickets were sold
b. $\frac{S(3.3p^2 + 1.1px - 2x^2)}{p(p - x)(p + 2x)}$; About 4650 tickets were sold.
41. a. $\frac{120(x - 5)}{x(x - 10)}$
b. 5 bracelets per hr

8-3 Part C Try It

a.
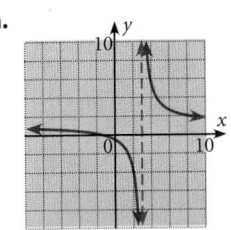
b.
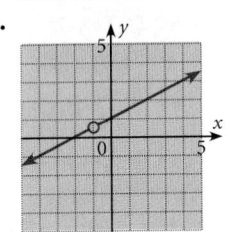
c.
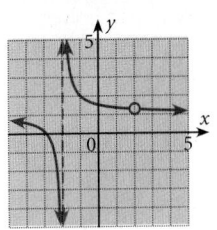

8-3 Part C Exercises

1. a. Zero at $x = 0$; Undefined at $x = -1$ because division by 0 is undefined
b. $x = \frac{5}{3}$; Undefined at $x = 0$ because division by 0 is undefined

c. Zero at $x = 0$ and 3; Undefined at $x = -\frac{5}{2}$ because division by 0 is undefined **5.** At $x = 1$ **7.** At $x = 5$ and $x = 2$ **9. a. ii,** $f(0) = 0$; Asymptote at $x = -2$, hole at $x = 3$ **b. iii,** $f(-5) = 0$; "Hole" at $x = -2$ **c. i,** Function is never negative; Asymptote at $x = -1$

11.

x	-3	-2	-1	1	2
$g(x)$	$\frac{1}{9}$	$\frac{1}{4}$	1	1	$\frac{1}{4}$

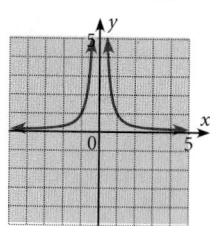

Asymptote at $x = 0$ **17.** $p = \frac{1}{3}$ or $p = -1\frac{1}{4}$ **19.** $y = -7$ or $y = 2$ **21.** None **23.** At $x = -1\frac{1}{2}$ and $x = 5$ **25.** At $x \approx -0.23$ and $x \approx -1.43$ **27. a.** $m \geq 0$ **b.** No **c.** No **35.** $f(x) = \frac{(x-2)(x-5)}{x+4}$ **37.** Vertical asymptote at $x = -c$; Horizontal asymptote at $y = a$

8-3 Part D Try It

a. $x = \pm 1\frac{1}{2}$ **b.** $p = 0$ or 7 **c.** $y = -\frac{8}{13}$

8-3 Part D Exercises

1. a. $3a + 21 = 8a - 4$; $a = 5$ **b.** $6x + 3 = 50$; $x = \frac{47}{6}$ **c.** $y^2 = 4y - 4$; $y = 2$ **5.** $y = \frac{12}{11}$ **7.** $x = 4$ **9.** No solution **11.** $y = 1$ **13.** $p = 50$ cm, $q = 12.5$ cm **15.** $h = \frac{4r}{3}$ **17.** $-\frac{8}{3} \leq x \leq 2$ **19.** No solution; $x \neq 0$ **21.** $a = \frac{7}{2}$; $a \neq \frac{5}{2}$ **23.** $b = 1\frac{1}{4}$ or $b = -1$; $b \neq -4$ and $b \neq -\frac{2}{3}$ **25.** $p = -\frac{11}{3}$ or $p = -1$; $p \neq \pm 11$ **27.** $b = \frac{3}{4}$; $b \neq 1$ **29.** No solution; $x \neq -4$ and $x \neq -1$ **31.** Jogger: 6 mi/hr; Hiker: 4 mi/hr **33.** No solution **35.** 1 min 20 sec

944

8-3 Part E Self-Assessment

1. $\frac{11}{7}$ **2.** $-\frac{7}{8}$ **3.** $\frac{x^2 + 7}{(x+5)(x-3)}$ **4.** $\frac{-3(2p-1)}{(p+3)(p-3)(p+2)}$ **5.** $\frac{a(2a+1)}{(a-1)(a-5)}$ **6.** $-\frac{y(3y+2)}{(y+1)(y-1)}$ **7. a.** Set the numerator equal to zero and solve for x. **b.** Look for zeros in the denominator. **c.** It has the factor $(x-3)$ in both the numerator and the denominator. **8.** At $x = -2$ and $x = -4$ **9.** At $x = -4$ and $x = -1\frac{1}{2}$

11.

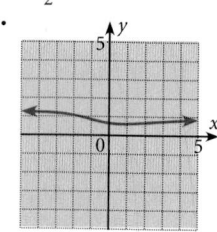

No discontinuities

13.

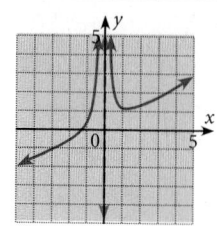

Asymptote at $x = -5$

15.

x	-3	-2	-1	1	2
$k(x)$	$-\frac{13}{9}$	$-\frac{7}{8}$	0	1	$\frac{9}{8}$

Asymptote at $x = 0$

16. $30 + x$; $14.70 + 0.79x$; $\frac{14.70 + 0.79x}{30 + x}$; 15 lb **17.** $a = 0$ **18.** $n = -11$ **19.** $x = -\frac{1}{2}$ **20.** $x = 1$ **21.** $S_n = \frac{n(n+1)(2n+1)}{6}$ **22.** 4.083% **23.** 0.0113

24. About 12.005 ft **25.** $5(x+4)$ **26.** $(w+6)^2(w-6)$ **27.** $p^3(p^4-1)$ **28.** $(t-2)(t-3)(t+4)$ **29.** 7 mi/hr **30.** 1.6 watts per m^2 **31.** $4\pi r^3$; $6\pi r^3$; $\frac{2}{3}$

Chapter 8 Review

1. Degree **2.** $x - r$ **3.** R **4.** Denominator **5.** Asymptote **6.** $f(x) = 72x^4 - 2$; 72; 4 **7.** $g(x) = 8x^3 + 8x^2 + 11x$; 8; 3 **8.** $h(x) = -2.8x^{10} + 4.5x^8 + 5.6x^6$; -2.8; 10 **9.** c, line of positive slope **10.** b, parabola opening down **11.** a, cubic function **12.** d, no quartic graph is shown **13. a.** Quartic **b.** No; There is no upper limit on y-values. **c.** Yes; At $x \approx \pm 1.2$, the y-coordinate reaches its lowest value. **d.** Given intervals are possible answers. Relative maximum $y = 3$ for $-1 < x < 1$; Relative minimums $y \approx 0.8$ for $-2 < x < 1$ and $1 < x < 2$. **14. a.** $1.42 **b.** $6.00 **c.** $10.58 **15. a.** 3 **b.** Zeros at $x = 1$, $x \approx -1.8$ and $x \approx 1.6$ **c.** $f(1) = 0$, $f(-1.8) \approx 0.60$, $f(1.6) = 0.2$ **d.** Possible answer: Examine the graph closely using the zoom in feature, or solve by other means. **16.** $x = 0, 4,$ and -3 **17.** $x = \pm 2i$ or $x = \pm 4i$ **18.** $f(3) = 53$; No **19.** $f(3) = 0$; Yes **20.** Not a factor **21.** Yes; $x^4 - x^3 + 5x^2 - 5x$ **22.** $h(3) = 2$ **23.** $x = \pm 7$ **24.** $x = -\frac{3}{2}$ or $x = 1$ or $x = \frac{3}{2}$ or $x = 2$ **25.** $15x^2 - 2x - 8 = 0$ **26.** $(x-3)(x+2)(x+3)$ **27.** $\frac{6x^3 + 20x^2 - 40x + 25}{(3x+2)(4x-5)}$; $3\frac{1}{24}$ **28.** $2x^3(x-2)$; 0 **29.** $\frac{2(4x^4 - 54x^3 - x + 1)}{25x^3(x-1)}$; -3.69 **30.** Zeros at $x = 3$; Discontinuities at $x = -1$ and $x = -2$ **31.** Asymptote at $x = -3$ **32.** Asymptote at $x = -2$, "hole" at $x = 3$

33. $x = \pm 2$ **34.** $x = 0$ **35.** Possible answer: $\frac{600(2x^2 + 10x + 25)}{x^2(x+5)^2}$ where x is the distance to the closer street light.

CHAPTER 9

9-1 Part A Try It

a. About 115,417,000 **b.** $x = 3$ **c.** $x = 3\frac{1}{2}$

9-1 Part A Exercises

1. a. Yes **b.** No **c.** No **d.** No **e.** Yes **5.** 1 **7.** 243 **9.** 3 **11.** 3^{h+5} **17.** $1,402.54 **21.** $x = 1\frac{2}{3}$ **25.** $x = -3$ **31.** $x = 4$ **33.** $x = \frac{1}{7}$ **35.** $x = 5$ **37.** $x = 1$ **39.** $x = -2$ **41.** $x = -3$ **43.** 8 **45.** $\frac{1}{2}$ **47.** $8\sqrt{2} \approx 11.31$ **49.** $\frac{1}{16}$ **53.** $x = -1$ **55.** $x = -4$ **57.** $x = \frac{3}{4}$

9-1 Part B Try It

a. $3\frac{1}{8}g$ **b.** 40,000 years **c.** About 4.381×10^9 kg

9-1 Part B Exercises

1. a. $18,696 = $9,494(b)^{10}$ **b.** $b^{10} \approx 1.96924$ **c.** $(1.96924)^{\frac{1}{10}} \approx (b^{10})^{\frac{1}{10}}$ **d.** $1.0701 \approx b$ **e.** 0.0701; 7.01% **3.** About 18,568,760 metric tons **5.** About 22,414,280 metric tons **7. a.** 8 mg **b.** 4 mg **c.** 1 mg **9.** About $4,132.85 **13.** 65,536 **17.** $x = -\frac{256}{17} \approx -15.06$ **19.** $x^2 + 9x + 15$ remainder 38 **21.** $2x^2 + 8x + 26$ remainder 107 **23.** About 82,080,000 **25.** About 172,597,000 **27.** Harborview; Harborview **29.** About 3.23%; About 105.1×10^9 ft^3 **31. a.** In Europe between 1900 and 1950 **c.** About 700 billion; About 11.3 billion **d.** About 1.76%; Increasing

9-1 Part C Try It

a.

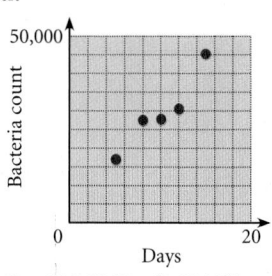

$C \approx 11{,}263.58 \cdot (1.0941)^x$;
$C(18) \approx 56{,}800$

9-1 Part C Exercises

1. Linear **2.** Exponential
5. 24 **7.** 2.31 **9. a.** 7.2%
b. i. About $25,690
ii. About $51,489
iii. About $103,195
iv. About $1,176,190
13. Union: $P = \$7(1.5)^t$;
Confederacy: $P = \$7(2)^t$
($t = 0$ in 1861) **a.** $15.75;
$28.00 **b.** $23.63; $56.00
c. $35.44; $112.00
15. $g^{-1}(x) = \dfrac{\sqrt[3]{x}}{2}$
17. They are reflections of
each other over the line $y = x$. **19.** $y \approx 0.187(1.1726)^x$
21. a. $P(d) \approx$
$4942.34(0.8244)^x$
b. i. About 716
ii. About 273
iii. About 4942

9-1 Part D Try It

a. $372.96 **b.** About 14 yr
c. Answer will depend on
current year. Possible
answers:
1996: $996,739,490.10;
1998: $1,146,523,319.75;
2000: $1,318,815,734.48;
2002: $1,516,999,184.90;
2004: $1,744,964,415.27

9-1 Part D Exercises

1. About 14 yr **5.** $f(0) =$
2500; $f(1) \approx 2{,}366.21$; $f(2) \approx$
2239.59; $f(6) \approx 1797.31$;
$f(10) \approx 1442.37$
9. $3,729.56 **12. a.** 0.487;
0.736; 0.903 **b.** 0.330; 0.551;
0.753

---

13. a. $y = \$2500e^{0.055t}$

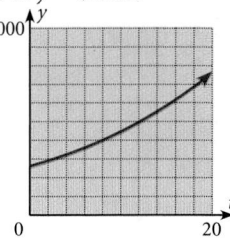

b. Yearly: $5,581.19,
Quarterly: $5,672.73,
Monthly: $5,693.96,
Continuously: $5,704.70
c. 5.5%; $2641.35; 7%:
$2681.27; 10%: 2762.93
15. The partial sums
approach e; Yes; 2.718 or e
17. $x = 0$ or $x = 1$ or $x = 3$
19. $x = \frac{3}{2}$ or $x = \pm i$
21. About 5.83 yr
23. About 40 yr **25.** $f(0) =$
785; $f(1) = 939.82$; $f(3) =$
1,347.07; $f(6) = 2{,}311.57$;
$f(10) = 4{,}748.97$
27. a. $634.43 **b.** $656.21
c. $661.38 **d.** $664.02
29. $362,544.48
31. a. $96.62
b. $107,432.02, by calculating
$\dfrac{600{,}000}{1.035^{50}}$ **c.** $3,350,956

9-1 Part E Self-Assessment

1. $f(0) = 3$; $f(1) = 6$; $f(2) =$
12; $f(6) = 192$; $f(10) = 3072$
2. $f(0) = 1200$; $f(1) = 1320$;
$f(2) = 1452$; $f(6) \approx 2125.87$;
$f(10) \approx 3112.49$
3. $f(0) = 150$; $f(1) \approx 82.32$;
$f(2) \approx 45.18$; $f(6) \approx 4.099$;
$f(10) \approx 0.372$
5.

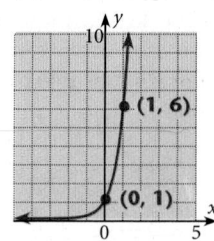

7. $x = 4$ **8.** $x = 1.5$
9. $x = -2.5$ **10.** $1.35 \times$
10^{10} yr **11.** 33.22 days; Yes
12. 25,937; 174,494
13. $x = -2$ or $x = 0$ or
$x = 7$ **14.** $x = -1$ or $x = 2$
or $x = 5$

---

15. $x = 12$ **16.** (c)
17. a. $121.90 **b.** $122.14
18. (D) **19.** (C)
20. a. 16.2% **b.** 31.9%
21. a. $y = 165(1.05946)^n$
b. E: 165; F: 174.81; F#:
185.21; G: 196.22; G#: 207.88;
A: 220.25; A#: 233.34;
B: 247.22; C: 261.92;
C#: 277.49; D: 293.99;
D#: 311.47; E: 329.99

9-2 Part A Try It

a. -2 **b.** -3 **c.** $x = 81$
d. $x = \frac{1}{16}$ **e.** $x = 3$
f. $x = 128$

9-2 Part A Exercises

1. a.

x	-2	-1	0	1	2
y	$\frac{1}{9}$	$\frac{1}{3}$	1	3	9

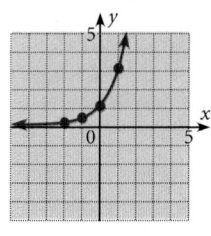

b.

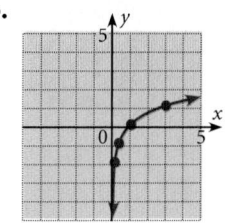

5.

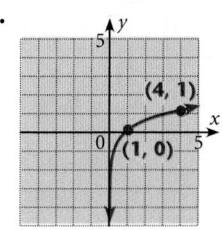

9. $2^2 = 4$ **11.** $\log_{\frac{1}{4}} 64 = -3$
13. $\log_8 4 = \frac{2}{3}$
15. $\log_2 \frac{1}{64} = -6$ **17.** The
ground motion of the earth-
quake that measures 6.5 is
one hundred times greater
than the one that measures
4.5, $10^{6.5\,-\,4.5} = 100$
19. -2 **21.** 1.36 **23.** 0

---

25. -4 **29.** $x = 0.125$
31. $x = \pm 4$ **33.** $x = 2$
35. $x = \pm 2$ **39.** $z^{-4} = \dfrac{1}{z^4}$
41. 400,000 or 4×10^5
45. $\log_3 729 = 6$
47. $\log_5 \frac{1}{25} = -2$ **49.** $7^2 =$
49 **51.** $\left(\frac{1}{3}\right)^2 = \frac{1}{9}$ **53.** 3
55. 6.35 **57.** -3 **59.** -3
61. $x = 10^{100}$ **63.** $x = 1\frac{1}{3}$
65. $x = 64$ **67.** $x = \frac{1}{9}$
69. $(1, 0)$ and $(b, 1)$

9-2 Part B Try It

a. $x \approx 2.40$ **b.** $x \approx -1.60$
c. $x \approx 0.83$ **d.** $t \approx 13.86$

9-2 Part B Exercises

3. $x \approx -0.77$ **5.** $m \approx 1.14$
7. $n \approx 0.80$ **9.** $x \approx 1.46$ or
$x \approx -5.46$ **11.** $x \approx 125.00$
13. ≈ 849.12 **15. a.** About
17.33 yr **b.** About 31.32 yr
c. About 57.56 yr **d.** About
287.82 yr **17.** About 1.98
months **21.** $x = \frac{3}{4}$
23. $x = 2$ **25.** $-i$ **27.** $\frac{2i}{3}$
29. $x \approx 1.18$ **31.** $x \approx 1.87$
33. $r \approx -3.70$ **35.** $x \approx 1.52$
37. $t \approx -0.02$ **39.** $x \approx$
26.00 **41. a.** About 8.66 yr
b. About 15.66 yr **c.** About
28.78 yr **d.** About 143.91 yr
45. b. $y \approx 48.398 +$
$5.499(\ln x)$ **d.** About 62.9
in.; About 64.0 in.

9-2 Part C Try It

a. $\log\left(\dfrac{x}{y^3}\right)$ **b.** $\log\left(\dfrac{k^2 m^3}{n + 10}\right)$
c. $\log x + \log x + \log x +$
$\log y + \log y$ **d.** $x = 3$

9-2 Part C Exercises

1. a. D **b.** C **c.** A **d.** B
5. $\log (xy)$ **7.** $\log \dfrac{a^3}{b^5}$
9. $\log (x^3 y^4)$ **11.** $\log t +$
$\log u + \log s$ **13.** $3 \log g +$
$3 \log h$ **15.** $x = 6$
17. $t \approx 4.57$ **19.** $x = 3$
21. a. About 3,597 parsecs
b. About 6.91×10^{16} mi
25. 55° **27.** $(90 - x)°$
29. $x \approx 13.15$
31. $h \approx 67.55$ **33.** $\log \dfrac{M}{N}$
35. $\log (a^8 b^2)$ **37.** $\ln(bc^6)$

39. $5 \log x + \log y$
41. $4 \log c + 4 \log d$
43. $\frac{1}{2} \log m + \frac{1}{2} \log n$
45. a. After 15.03 yr, in 2005
b. After 32.30 yr, in 2022
c. After 334.56 yr, in 2325
47. $x \approx 1.77$ **49.** $x \approx 15.19$
51. $x = 3.25$
53. a. $h = \left(-\frac{100}{9}\right) \log \frac{x}{30}$

9-2 Part D Self-Assessment

1. They are reflections of each other over the line $y = x$. **2.** (15,625, 6)
3.

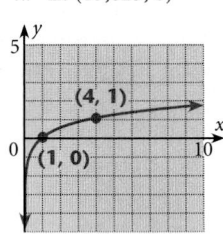

(4, 1)
(1, 0)

5.

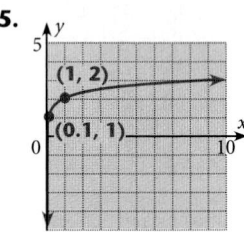

(1, 2)
(0.1, 1)

6. $10^4 = 10,000$
7. $\log_2 8 = 3$ **8.** $4^{-2} = \frac{1}{16}$
9. $\log 0.001 = -3$
10. $6^0 = 1$ **11.** $\log_{81} 27 = \frac{3}{4}$
12. 2 **13.** -3 **14.** 0.95
15. 5.33 **16.** About 15.53 hr
17. (D) **18.** (D) **19.** $-2i$
20. $\frac{3+i}{2}$ **21.** $\frac{6-17i}{25}$ **22.** i
23. $\log(xy^2)$ **24.** $\log\left(\frac{a^3}{b^2}\right)$
25. $\ln\left(\frac{m^8}{n^3}\right)$ **26.** $2 \log x +$ $3 \log y$ **27.** $\log c - \log d$
28. $\frac{1}{2} \log m + \log k$
29. About 6.53 **30.** $x = 32$
31. $x = \frac{1}{3}$ **32.** $x = 5$
33. $x = \frac{1}{81}$ **34.** $x \approx 2.58$
35. $x \approx 0.15$ **36.** $x \approx 10.73$
37. $x \approx 316,227.77$
38. $x = 6$ **39.** $x \approx 2.88$
40. $x = 3$ **41. a.** After 26.78 yr, in 2018
b. After 124.46 yr, in 2115
c. After 230.62 yr, in 2222
42. About 5.61%

Chapter 9 Review

1. (c) **2.** Inverse
3.

(1, 4)
(4, 1)
(0, 1)
(1, 0)

4. $x = \frac{1}{3}$ **5.** $x = 2$ **6.** $x = \frac{3}{2}$
7. a. \$21,589.25
b. \$22,080.40 **c.** \$22,255.41
8. 20 sec **9.** $\log_4 1024 = 5$
10. $10^4 = 10,000$
11. $\log_6 \frac{1}{36} = -2$ **12.** $4^{-1} =$ 0.25 **13.** $(0.5)^2 = \frac{1}{4}$
14. $\log_{36} 6 = \frac{1}{2}$
15. a. About 1.24%
b. About 81.3 million
c. 224.24 yrs after 1990, in 2214 **16.** 5 **17.** 5 **18.** -4
19. -3 **20.** $x = 4$
21. $x \approx -1.67$ **22.** $x \approx 1.35$
23. $x = 0.5$ **24.** About 6.56% **25.** $S \approx 85.05$ dB

CHAPTER 10

10-1 Part A Try It

a. $\sin A = \frac{4}{5}$, $\cos A = \frac{3}{5}$; $\tan A = \frac{4}{3}$, $\csc A = \frac{5}{4}$; $\sec A = \frac{5}{3}$, $\cot A = \frac{3}{4}$; **b.** 53.1°
c. About 8.06 m

10-1 Part A Exercises

1. a. 5; 12 **b.** 12; 5
c. $\sin K = \frac{12}{13}$; $\sin L = \frac{5}{13}$; $\cos K = \frac{5}{13}$; $\tan K = \frac{12}{5}$; $\sec L = \frac{13}{12}$ **5.** $\frac{5}{13}$ **9.** $\frac{5}{12}$
11. $\sin 37° \approx 0.6018$; $\cos 37° \approx 0.7986$; $\tan 37° \approx$ 0.7536; $\csc 37° \approx 1.6616$, $\sec 37° \approx 1.2521$; $\cot 37° \approx$ 1.3270 **15. a.** About 16 ft
b. About 11 ft **19.** $m\angle B \approx$ $25.84°$ **21.** $x \approx 10.83$
25. $m\angle D \approx 69.78°$
27. About 1203 ft **31.** $x^7 +$ $21x^6 + 189x^5 + 945x^4 +$ $2835x^3 + 5103x^2 + 5103x +$ 2187 **35.** $\frac{15}{17}$ **37.** $\frac{8}{15}$
39. $\frac{17}{8}$ **41.** $\frac{15}{8}$ **43.** $\frac{15}{17}$

45. $\sin 1° \approx 0.0175$; $\cos 1° \approx$ 0.9998; $\tan 1° \approx 0.0175$; $\csc$ $1° \approx 57.2986$; $\sec 1° \approx$ 1.0002; $\cot 1° \approx 57.2900$
47. $\sin 77° \approx 0.9744$; $\cos 77° \approx 0.2250$; $\tan 77° \approx$ 4.3315; $\csc 77° \approx 1.0263$; $\sec 77° \approx 4.4454$; $\cot 77° \approx$ 0.2309 **49.** About 43.27
51. $m\angle K \approx 31.97°$ **53.** $r \approx$ 7.98 **54.** $m\angle R = 28°$
56. About 4.53° **57.** No
59. a. $\sqrt{3}$ **b.** About 35°

10-1 Part B Try It

a. $\frac{\pi}{6}$ **b.** 210° **c.** ≈ 0.1951
d. ≈ 5.908 **e.** ≈ 0.3249
f. ≈ 1.4142 **g.** 2 **h.** $\sqrt{2}$
i. $\sqrt{3}$

10-1 Part B Exercises

1. a. $\frac{1}{6}$; $\frac{\pi}{6}$ **b.** (ii) **c.** $\frac{1}{4}$; 45°
d. (i) **5.** $\frac{5\pi}{9}$ **7.** $\frac{6\pi}{5}$ **9.** 156°
11. 80° **13.** $90\pi \approx 282.74$; $\frac{3\pi}{2} \approx 4.71$ **15.** 0.5 **19.** 1
21. a. About 6851 mi
b. About 0.62 radians; About 35.46° **23. a.** 100π in.^{2}; 12.5π in.^{2} **b.** 2 slices, 25π in.^{2}; 3 slices, 37.5π in.^{2}
c. Yes **25.** $\frac{5\pi}{4}$ **27.** $\frac{4\pi}{3}$
29. $\frac{7\pi}{4}$ **31.** $\frac{4\pi}{5}$ **33.** 225°
35. 100° **37.** 276° **39.** 171°
41. About 1.31 radians
43. 0.5 **45.** 0 **47.** ≈ 0.9902
49. ≈ 0.6667 **51.** $\sqrt{2}$
53. 120°, $\frac{2\pi}{3}$ **55. a.** About 16.76 cm^2 **b.** For $\theta = 2\pi$, $A = 2(2\pi)r^2 = 4\pi r^2$.

10-1 Part C Try It

a. 8π cm **b.** About 940 mi
c. About 10,472 m^2
d. About 3142 cm/min or 1.88 km/hr

10-1 Part C Exercises

1. a. 6 cm
b.

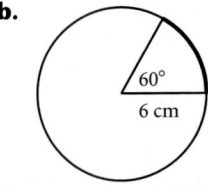

$\frac{\pi}{3}$ **c.** 2π cm

5. $6.5\pi \approx 20.42$ cm
7. $\frac{7\pi}{2} \approx 11.00$ cm **9.** About 684 mi **11.** About 77.05%
15. About 2094 mi **16.** $40\frac{1}{3}$ radians/sec **19.** $6x + 9$
21. $4\pi \approx 12.57$ in.
23. $\frac{55\pi}{6} \approx 28.80$ in.
25. $12\pi \approx 36.70$ cm
27. About 11.24 mi
29. 50π in.$^2 \approx 157.08$ in.^{2}
31. 18π in.$^2 \approx 56.55$ in.^{2}
33. About 2460.44 cm^2
35. About 10,838 mi^2
37. 168π cm/sec ≈ 527.79 cm/sec ≈ 19.00 km/hr
39. About 28.92 mi/hr

10-1 Part D Try It

a. 142°; II **b.** 240°, III
c. 285°; IV **d.** 31°; I
e. $\sin 330° = -\frac{1}{2}$; $\cot 330° =$ $-\sqrt{3}$; $\sec 330° = \frac{2\sqrt{3}}{3}$
f. 0; Undefined; 1 **g.** $-\frac{\sqrt{3}}{2}$; $-\frac{1}{2}$; $\sqrt{3}$

10-1 Part D Exercises

1. a. $\overrightarrow{CA}$ **b.** $\overrightarrow{CB}$ **c.** $\angle ACB$
d. Hypotenuse: $\sqrt{10}$, opposite: 1, adjacent: 3
e. i. $-\frac{\sqrt{10}}{10}$ **ii.** $\frac{3\sqrt{10}}{10}$
iii. $-\frac{1}{3}$ **iv.** $-\sqrt{10}$
v. $\frac{\sqrt{10}}{3}$ **vi.** -3 **5.** 61°; I
9. $\sin = \frac{5}{13}$; $\cos = \frac{12}{13}$; $\tan =$ $\frac{5}{12}$ **11.** $\frac{\sqrt{2}}{2}$ **13.** $-\sqrt{3}$
15. 2 **19.** $\theta_e(t) = 15t$; $\theta_s(t) = 72t$; After about 6.32 hr **23.** 270°; Between III and IV **25.** 216°; III
27. $\sin = -\frac{3}{5}$; $\cos = -\frac{4}{5}$; $\tan = \frac{3}{4}$ **29.** $\sin = \frac{15}{17}$; $\cos = \frac{8}{17}$; $\tan = \frac{15}{8}$ **31.** $\frac{\sqrt{3}}{2}$
33. $\frac{\sqrt{2}}{2}$ **35.** $\frac{\sqrt{3}}{3}$ **37.** $-\sqrt{3}$
39. $-\frac{2\sqrt{3}}{3}$ **41.** $x = \frac{\pi}{3}$ or $x = \frac{5\pi}{3}$ **43.** $x = \frac{5\pi}{6}$ or $x = \frac{7\pi}{6}$

10-1 Part E Self-Assessment

1. (b) **2.** (a) **3.** (a)
4. About 241.5 ft **5.** About 57.74 m **6.** 48π

7. 8.1π cm$^2 \approx 25.45$ cm^2
8. b. $\frac{r}{3960} = \cos\theta$; $r = 3960\cos\theta$ **c.** About 3046.8 mi **d.** About 999.7 mi **e.** About 997.9 mi; About 0.2% difference **9.** About 19.2° **10.** About 11.20 rev/sec
11. a. 16π radians/sec **b.** About 1.106 m/sec **12.** 1
13. $\frac{1}{2}$ **14.** $\frac{\sqrt{3}}{2}$ **15.** -1
16. x **17.** About 5.22 ohms
18. $x = \pm 6$ **19. a.** 225°
b. About 12,316,300 mi^2
20. a. About 21.27 cm
b. About 17.20 cm
21. $\sin 87.77° = \frac{r}{r+3}$; About 3958.34 mi **22.** One mile north of any circle of latitude near the South Pole whose circumference is $\frac{1}{n}$ miles where n is a counting number.

10-2 Part A Try It
a. $f \approx 17.0$ **b.** $\angle F = 130.5°$

10-2 Part A Exercises
1. a. $a^2 = b^2 + c^2 - 2bc \cos A$ **b.** $a^2 = 24^2 + 15^2 - 2(24)(15)(\cos 65°)$; $\cos 65° \approx 0.423$ **c.** $a \approx 22.29$
7. 4.6 **9.** 12.2
11. a. About 45.4 m/min
b. About 48.5 m/min; Somewhat faster than in part a
13. 37.5° **15.** 90°
17. About 77.2°, 43.5° and 59.3° **19. a.** $(-16, -9)$
b. $x = -16$, $y = -9$
21. $x = 81$ **23.** $x = \frac{1}{16}$
25. 7.4 **27.** 74.5 **29.** 12.4
31. 1730 mi **33.** 60°
35. 90° **37.** 103.8°
39. 349.3 mi/hr on a heading of 7.4° north of due west.

10-2 Part B Try It
a. 20.1 **b.** 9.7 **c.** $m\angle F = 74°$; $d \approx 5.9$; $e \approx 15.7$
d. $m\angle K = 39°$; $g \approx 25.1$; $k \approx 25.6$ **e.** 26.9 **f.** 194.1

10-2 Part B Exercises
1. $\frac{f}{\sin F} = \frac{g}{\sin G} = \frac{h}{\sin H}$
3. 17.8 **5.** 166.0 **7.** About 3534 m **9.** 51.6 **11.** 2065.6

13. About 181.07 cm^2
15. $m\angle B = 27°$; $a \approx 12.4$; $c \approx 11.9$; Area ≈ 33.5
17. $m\angle A \approx 24.1°$; $m\angle B \approx 38.0°$; $m\angle C \approx 117.9°$; Area ≈ 73.3
23.

25. 42.1 **27.** 37.9
29. 3782.9 **31.** 18.8
33. Boat A: About 414.6 m; Boat B: About 218.3 m
35. $m\angle A = 134°$; $a \approx 11.9$; $b \approx 4.8$; Area ≈ 13.9
37. $m\angle A \approx 34.7°$; $m\angle B \approx 12.3°$; $c \approx 80.6$; Area ≈ 538.8
39. $m\angle A \approx 34.0°$; $m\angle B \approx 22.5°$; $m\angle C \approx 123.5°$; Area ≈ 9.3 **41.** About 133 ft
43. a. $m\angle R \approx 148.5°$; $m\angle T \approx 7.5°$; $t \approx 4.5$ or $m\angle R \approx 31.5°$; $m\angle T \approx 124.5°$; $t \approx 28.4$ **b.** $m\angle R \approx 18.4°$; $m\angle T \approx 137.6°$; $t \approx 29.9$
c. No such triangle exists

10-2 Part C Self-Assessment
1. 21.4 **2.** 116.1 **3.** 21.2
4. 5.5 **5.** 237.1 **6.** $x\sqrt{3}$ or $1.7x$ **7.** About 47.0 m
8. a. About $(10.7, -1.3)$
b. $\left(\frac{32}{3}, -\frac{4}{3}\right)$ **9. a.** About 95.82 lbs **10.** $x = 64$
11. $x = \frac{3}{2}$ **12.** $x = 100{,}000$
13. $x = 5$ **14.** (e)
15. About 2.22×10^{-8} cm
16. 38.0° **17.** 140.4°
18. 39.3° **19.** 90°
20. 25.8° **21.** No
22. a. About 96.1° **b.** About 17,570 m^2 **23.** About 65.3
24. a. About 66.8 ft
b. About 63.7 ft **25.** (B)
26. (A) **27.** $m\angle B = 44°$; $a \approx 13.0$; $c \approx 13.6$; Area ≈ 61.7 **28.** $m\angle A \approx 16.8°$; $m\angle B \approx 23.2°$; $c \approx 25.4$; Area ≈ 57.2 **29.** $m\angle B = 82.5°$; $m\angle C = 82.5°$; $a \approx 2.3$; Area ≈ 10.5

30. $m\angle C = 20°$; $a \approx 57.7$; $c \approx 20.0$; Area ≈ 499.9
31. $m\angle A \approx 43.2°$; $m\angle C \approx 104.8°$; $b \approx 1.3$; Area ≈ 1.1
32. $m\angle A \approx 46.6°$; $m\angle B \approx 104.5°$; $m\angle C \approx 28.9°$; Area ≈ 46.5 **33.** About 69.6 newtons **34.** Not possible
35. a. $\frac{2ab}{(c^2 - (a - b)^2)} = \frac{1}{1 - \cos C}$; $2ab - 2ab \cos C = c^2 - a^2 + 2ab - b^2$; $a^2 + b^2 - 2ab \cos C = c^2$, which is the Law of Cosines. **b.** For a right triangle, $\cos C = \cos 90° = 1$ and $1 - \cos C = 0$, so Snell's formula has a zero denominator.
c. $\frac{1}{\sin A} = \frac{bc}{2\triangle}$ where $\triangle$ represents the area of the triangle. $2\triangle = bc \sin A$ and $\triangle = \frac{1}{2}bc \sin A$, or Area $= \frac{1}{2}bc \sin A$.
36. a. The angle is obtuse.
b. There is no triangle that satisfies the given information.

10-3 Part A Try It
a. 2; 4
b.

Amplitude = 2; Period = 4π
c.

Amplitude = 1.5; Period = 2 **d.** $D(t) = 4 \sin \pi t$

10-3 Part A Exercises
1. a. $0 \le y \le 4$ **b.** The section from $x = -10$ to $x = -2$ is identical to the section from $x = 2$ to $x = 10$.
c. 2 **d.** 12 **e.** 2
7. Amplitude = $\frac{7}{2}$; Period = 2
9. Amplitude = 1; Period = π

10. Amplitude = 1; Period = 4π **11.** Amplitude = 2; Period = $\frac{2\pi}{3}$
15. Amplitude = 2; Period = $\frac{4\pi}{5}$
17.

Amplitude = 2; Period = $\frac{\pi}{2}$
19. $y = 1.5 \sin 6x$
21. $W(x) = 4 \cos \frac{\pi}{10}x$
23. Translate the first graph $\frac{\pi}{2}$ units to the right. **25.** 2; π **27.** 6; 8 **29.** $y = 2 \sin x$
31. $y = 0.4 \sin \frac{2\pi}{3}x$
33. $y = 1.8 \sin \frac{10\pi}{7}x$
35. Amplitude = 1; Period = π **37.** Amplitude = 3; Period = 2π
39. Amplitude = 2.5; Period = $\frac{2\pi}{3}$
41. Amplitude = $\frac{2}{3}$; Period = 4π
43. Amplitude = 1.5; Period = $\frac{\pi}{2}$
45. Amplitude = 3; Period = 10 **47.** Amplitude = 5; Period = 4π
49. Amplitude = 2; Period = $\frac{\pi}{2}$ **51.** $H(t) = \sin 2\pi t$
53. Period = π; No amplitude, and vertical asymptotes at $x = k\pi$.

10-3 Part B Try It
a.

Amplitude = 2; Period = 6π; Average y-value = -3; Phase shift = $-\pi$

10-3 Part B Exercises
1. a. 1 **b.** $\left(\frac{\pi}{2}, 1\right)$ **c.** $\frac{\pi}{2}$

5.
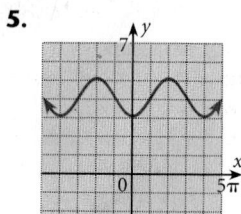

7. Amplitude = 1; Period = 2π; Average y-value = 0; Phase shift = $-\pi$

9. Amplitude = 3; Period = 4π; Average y-value = -1; Phase shift = -2π

13. Amplitude = 2; Period = 2π; Average y-value = -3; Phase shift = $\frac{\pi}{4}$ **15.** $y = \sin(x - \pi) - 3$ **17.** $y = \frac{1}{2}\sin\frac{\pi}{2}(x - 1) - 8$ **19.** $k = -\frac{\pi}{2}$, $m = -\pi$, $n = \frac{3\pi}{2}$

21. $x = -2, -\frac{1}{3}$ **23.** $\frac{4}{5}$

25.
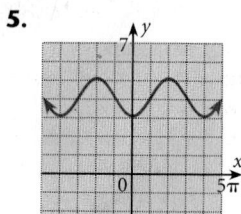

27. Amplitude = 1; Period = 2π; Average y-value = 0; Phase shift = $\frac{\pi}{6}$

29. Amplitude = 2; Period = 2π; Average y-value = 1; Phase shift = $-\frac{\pi}{2}$

31. Amplitude = 4; Period = 2; Average y-value = 5; Phase shift = $\frac{1}{3}$

33. Amplitude = 1.1; Period = 2π; Average y-value = 0; Phase shift = $-\frac{3\pi}{4}$

35. Amplitude = 1; Period = $\frac{\pi}{5}$; Average y-value = -4; Phase shift = $\frac{\pi}{10}$

37. Amplitude = 0.34; Period = $\frac{1}{2\pi}$; Average y-value = -2; Phase shift = $-\frac{1}{4\pi}$ **39.** $T(t) = 2\sin\frac{\pi}{12}(t + 12) + 48$

41. $y = 2\sin 4(x - \pi) + 3$

43. $y = 4\sin\frac{2\pi}{9}(x - 3) - \frac{1}{2}$

45. $y = \frac{1}{2}\sin\pi(x + \frac{1}{2}) + \frac{1}{2}$

47. a. 2π **b.** π

10-3 Part C
Self-Assessment

1. (b) **2.** (a)

---

3. Possible sketch:
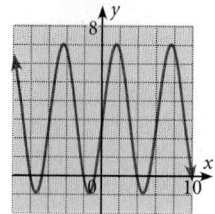

4. Amplitude = 2; Period = $\frac{2\pi}{3}$; Average y-value = 4; Phase shift = -3

5. Amplitude = 0.5; Period = $\frac{\pi}{6}$; Average y-value = -5; Phase shift = 2.5

6. Amplitude = 3; Period = $\frac{1}{2}$; Average y-value = -6; Phase shift = $\frac{1}{4}$

7. Amplitude = 4; Period = 4π; Average y-value = 3; Phase shift = $-\frac{\pi}{2}$

8. $y = 3\sin\frac{\pi}{2}(x - 1) + 2$

9. Possible answer: $130\sin\frac{\pi}{300}x$, where x is the number of miles and y is in feet. **10.** $x = \frac{3 \pm \sqrt{41}}{4}$, or $x \approx -0.85$ or $x \approx 2.35$ **11.** $x = -1$ or $x = -2$ **12.** $x = -2$ or $x = 1$ or $x = 4$ **13.** $x = 0$ or $x = 2$ or $x = \pm i\sqrt{3}$

14. $n \approx 4.58$ **15.** $x = \frac{1}{500}$

16. $-\frac{1}{2}$ **17.** 1 **18.** $-\frac{\sqrt{2}}{2}$

19. Possible answer: $y = 50\sin\frac{\pi}{6}(x - 7) + 250$

20. Possible answer: $y = 2\sin\left(\frac{\pi x}{12}\right) + 16$, assuming a 4-inch difference between highest and lowest leaf positions

21. $y = 2\sin\frac{\pi}{2}(x - 3) + 1$

22. Possible answer: $H(t) = 7\cos\frac{\pi}{6}(t - 3)$

Chapter 10 Review

1. Similar **2.** Cosine
3. Radian **4.** Angular
5. Amplitude **6.** Phase shift
7. a. $\frac{12}{13}$ **b.** About 67.38°
c. $\frac{5}{13}$ **d.** $\frac{5}{12}$ **e.** About 22.62°
f. $\frac{13}{5}$ **g.** $\frac{12}{5}$ **h.** $\frac{13}{5}$ **i.** $\frac{13}{12}$
8. a. About 4 **b.** About 4
c. 45° **d.** $\frac{\sqrt{2}}{2}$ **e.** 1 **f.** $\sqrt{2}$
g. $\frac{\sqrt{2}}{2}$ **h.** 1 **i.** $\sqrt{2}$ **9. a.** $\frac{\pi}{4}$
b. $\frac{\pi}{3}$ **c.** $\frac{29\pi}{36}$ **d.** $\frac{2\pi}{3}$ **e.** $\frac{25\pi}{18}$
10. a. 36° **b.** 270° **c.** 135°
d. 300° **e.** 20° **11.** 1

---

12. 0 **13.** 1 **14.** About 1.305 **15.** About 0.0872
16. Undefined **17.** 0
18. $\frac{\sqrt{2}}{2} \approx 0.707$
19. a. $\ell = \frac{5\pi}{3} \approx 5.24$ cm; $A = \frac{25\pi}{6} \approx 13.09$ cm²
b. $\ell = \frac{55\pi}{6} \approx 28.8$ m; $A = \frac{605\pi}{12} \approx 158.4$ cm²
c. $\ell = 1.875\pi \approx 5.9$ in.; $A \approx 4.219\pi \approx 13.3$ in.²
d. $\ell = \frac{\pi}{2} \approx 1.6$ ft; $A = \frac{3\pi}{20} \approx 0.47$ ft²
20. $\frac{1}{36}$ revolution/sec or $\frac{\pi}{18}$ radians/sec; $\frac{10\pi}{9}$ or about 3.49 ft/sec
21. a. $\sin\theta = \frac{5\sqrt{29}}{29}$; $\cos\theta = \frac{2\sqrt{29}}{29}$; $\tan\theta = \frac{5}{2}$

CHAPTER 11

11-1 Part A Try It

a. 0.05 **b.** 0.95 **c.** 0.98
d. 0.44

11-1 Part A Exercises

1. $\frac{1}{6} = 0.1\overline{6}$ **3.** $\frac{1}{3} = 0.\overline{3}$
5. $\frac{2}{3} = 0.\overline{6}$ **9.** 0.02 **11.** 0.15
13. 0.404 **15. a.** 15 **b.** 6
c. $\frac{2}{5} = 0.4$ **d.** $\frac{3}{5} = 0.6$
17. $n = 2.5$ **19.** About 6.07; About 17.2 **21.** 0.250
23. 0.357 **25.** 0.25
27. $\frac{29}{180} \approx 0.161$
29. $\frac{64}{103} \approx 0.621$

11-1 Part B Try It

a. $\frac{1}{12} \approx 0.08$ **b.** About 1.13% **c.** About 87.76%
d. About 34.39%

11-1 Part B Exercises

1. $\frac{1}{4}$ **3.** Independent
7. 0.049 **9.** 0.287 **11.** 20%
13. Independent
15. a. $\frac{1}{1776} \approx 1.29 \times 10^{-4}$
b. $\frac{1}{1296} \approx 7.72 \times 10^{-4}$
c. About 99%; About 1%
17. a. 3 **b.** 0.000000001
19. $\frac{81}{100} = 0.81$
21. $\frac{47,831,784}{48,627,125} \approx 0.984$

---

23. Dependent **25.** 0.105
27. 0.3108 **29. a.** About 0.294 **b.** No **31.** Not independent

11-1 Part C Try It

a. $\frac{2}{3} = 0.\overline{6}$ **b.** $\frac{5}{11} = 0.\overline{45}$
c. $\frac{3}{11} = 0.\overline{27}$ **d.** $\frac{2}{11} = 0.\overline{18}$
e. 0.04988

11-1 Part C Exercises

1. (a) Independent
(b) Neither
3. (a) Independent
(b) Sampling with replacement. **5.** $\frac{4}{99} \approx 0.040$
7. 0 **9.** 0.0408 **11.** $\frac{2}{3}$
15. a. 0.00475 **b.** 0.00995
c. About 0.677 **17.** -3
19. 2.30

21.
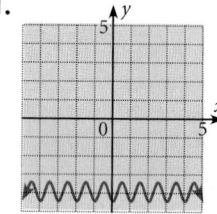

23. (a) Independent **(b)** Neither **25. (a)** Dependent **(b)** Sampling without replacement **27.** $\frac{1}{15} \approx 0.07$
29. $\frac{8}{105} \approx 0.08$ **31.** $\frac{2}{105} \approx 0.02$ **33.** About 0.77
35. No **37. a.** About 0.683
b. 20% **c.** 33.3%

11-1 Part D
Self-Assessment

1. Independent
2. Independent
3. Dependent
4. Independent
5. Dependent
6. Independent **7.** 0.09
8. 0.15 **9.** 0.26 **10.** 0.18
11. About 0.17 **12.** (e)
13. For any two events A and B, $P(B \text{ and } A) = P(B) \cdot P(A|B)$. If the events are independent, then $P(B \text{ and } A) = P(B) \cdot P(A)$, so $P(B) \cdot P(A|B) = P(B) \cdot P(A)$. If $P(B) \neq 0$, this gives $P(A|B) = P(A)$. If $P(B) = 0$, then $P(A|B)$ is undefined.

14. 2.5 **15.** −6 **16.** 1
17. −6 **18.** $b \approx 6.36$, $a \approx$ 8.26; $m\angle B = 31°$, Area ≈ 25.09 **19.** $\frac{145}{201} \approx 0.72$
20. a. About 0.180
b. About 0.318 **c.** About 0.0564 **d.** About 0.547
21. Dependent
22. a. i. About 0.95
ii. About 0.72 **iii.** $\left(\frac{399}{400}\right)^n$
b. About 0.48 **23. a.** $\frac{1}{1000}$
b. $\frac{1}{999}$ **c.** 0.0025

11-2 Part A Try It

a. Biased; Possible answer: Many people at home during these hours are retired, and would be more likely to react negatively to such cutbacks than is typical. **b.** Biased; Possible answer: Many freshmen would not be interested in the Senior Prom and so would be less likely to support raising funds than students in general. **c.** All the M & M's in the bathtub **d. i.** Assuming the mixture is truly well-mixed, this is adequate. **ii.** Not random because students may have preferences for certain colors. **iii.** Random, if the M&M's are mixed well. **e.** Sample; Possible answer: To test the entire population would leave no bulbs for actual use. **f.** Population; Each fuel tank is too important to risk error.

11-2 Part A Exercises

1. Sample **3.** Population
5. False; Biased **7.** All bread produced by the company; Sample **9.** No
11.

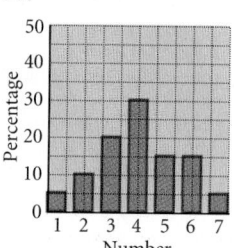

15. Getting everyone to respond, giving everyone a questionnaire, and reaching the homeless and people who are moving is difficult.
17. About 240 **19. a.** The second quiz results are clustered together. **b.** The second, because all scores were 77 or above.
21. Population: Everyone with the disease; Sample
23. b. About 0.091
27. About 36 bears

11-2 Part B Try It

a. 8; 12 **b.** 6; 14 **c.** 14
d. 63 in. to 68 in. **e.** About 5%

11-2 Part B Exercises

1. a. 0.50 **b.** About 0.68
c. About 0.95 **5.** 99; 101
7. 97; 103 **9. a. i.** About 68% **ii.** About 95%
b. About 2.3% **c.** About 6.44×10^{-9} **11.** Yes
13. 1.6; 2.4 **15.** 0.8; 3.2
17. a. About 5% **b.** Stop the use of the machine
19. $x = -\frac{1}{2} \pm \frac{\sqrt{15}}{2}i$
21. a. $\frac{4}{5} = 0.8$ **b.** $\frac{49}{400} \approx$ 0.12 **c.** $\frac{21}{190} \approx 0.11$ **23.** 40;
80 **25.** 80 **27.** 3; 5 **29.** 3
31. a. About 68%
b. About 2.3%
33. a. Stocks: $1,295.03; Bank: $1,157.63 **b.** About 16%; About 16% **c.** $531.44; $2,571.35

11-2 Part C Self-Assessment

1. Possible answer: It is often not practical or possible to survey an entire population.
2. Possible answer: Get a student list, number each student, and have a computer generate 100 random numbers to select students.
3. Biased **4.** Population: American dentists; Sample
5. New improved Cheese Crispos; Sample **6.** (c)

7. a.

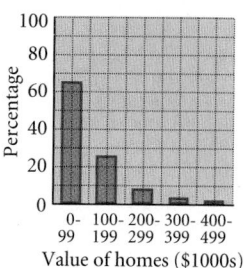

b. About 0.96
8. $\ell = \frac{632\pi}{225} \approx 8.82$ in.; $A = \frac{5056\pi}{1125} \approx 14.12$ in.^{2}
9. $x \approx -3.47$ or $x \approx 5.47$
10. $x = -3$ or $x = -1$ or $x = 2$ **11. a.** $\frac{1}{5} = 0.2$
b. $\frac{9}{100} = 0.02$ **c.** $\frac{2}{9} = 0.\overline{2}$
12. a. About 3333 **b.** Poor
13. a. A **b.** A **c.** A **d.** B
14. a. About 68%
b. About 16%
c. About 2.3%

Chapter 11 Review

1. Dependent **2.** Sample
3. Histogram **4.** Without replacement **5.** Independent
6. Dependent **7.** Dependent
8. $\frac{3}{4} = 0.75$ **9.** $\frac{1}{4} = 0.25$
10. $\frac{9}{38} \approx 0.24$ **11.** About 0.87 or 87% **12.** Possible answer: Population, an exact number is needed and the population is limited and easy to survey. **13.** Sample
14. Possible answer: Use $\frac{13}{50}$ as the tagged/total ratio.
15. a. About 68%
b. About 2.3%

CHAPTER 12

12-1 Part A Try It

a. 16
b. Possible answer:

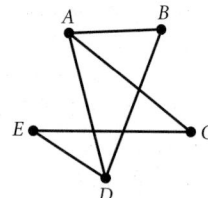

1. a. 10 **b.** 8 **c.** 16
d. 10 (faces) + 8 (vertices) − 16 (edges) = 2 **5.** 12
7. a. $V = 12$, $E = 30$; 20 regions **b.** $R + V - E = 2$
9. 4; 6 **11.** 3; 10; $_nC_2$ or $\frac{n(n-1)}{2}$, assuming that no edge connects a vertex to itself and no pair of vertices is connected by more than one edge. **13.** 9 (faces) + 9 (vertices) − 16 (edges) = 2
15. 12 **17.** About 4 days

12-1 Part B Try It

a. Euler path; Possible answer: *DIEDHEFHGBDCBAGF*
b. Euler circuit; Possible answer: *IMNQMLQRLKRP-KJPOJIONI* **c.** No

12-1 Part B Exercises

1. a. *A:* 4, *B:* 3, *C:* 4, *D:* 3, *E:* 4, *F:* 4 **b.** Not all vertices are even (*B* and *D* are odd).
c. *B* and *D* have odd degree, but all the other vertices have even degree. Possible answer: *DAEDCEFCBFAB*
7. Connected **9.** *A:* 2, *B:* 2, *C:* 2, *D:* 4, *E:* 4, *F:* 4, *G:* 4, *H:* 4, *J:* 4; Euler circuit
11. *Q:* 3, *R:* 2, *S:* 3, *T:* 3, *U:* 2, *V:* 3, *W:* 5, *X:* 5; No Euler circuit or path **15.** Yes, *ABCDA* is an Euler circuit for the graph shown.

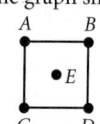

19. It is an Euler path for the graph that remains after the edge is deleted. **21. a.** It is half as large. **b.** It is $\frac{2}{3}$ as large. **23.** Not connected
25. Connected **27. a.** Each vertex must be of an even degree. **b.** Two vertices must have odd degree; the rest must be even.

29. $G, H, I, J, K,$ and L all have degree 4; Euler circuit **31.** No; There are more than two rooms (which represent vertices) with an odd number (3) of doors (which represent edges). **35.** Each edge connects two vertices, so the sum of the degrees of the vertices is an even number (twice the number of edges).

12-1 Part C Try It

a. Either $ADCBEA$ or $AEBCDA$ (both are 96 units long)

b.
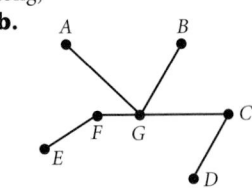

66

12-1 Part C Exercises

1. a. Yes **b.** Yes **c.** No
5. Possible answer:
$ABCDEFGA$
7. Possible answer:
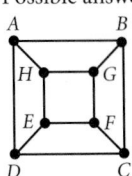
Possible answer:
$ABCDEFGHA$ **9.** Not a tree, contains a circuit
11. Blue; $\frac{8}{15}$
13.
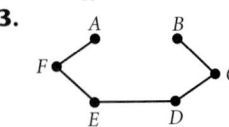

15. 52 mi **17.** 1, 3, 7, 15, 31, 63 **19.** Possible answer: $AGBHCIDJEFA$
21. Possible answer: $UXWBYZAVU$
23. $ABCDEA$ **25.** Yes, the graph contains no circuits and is connected. **27.** Yes, the graph has no circuits and is connected.

---

29. Possible answer:
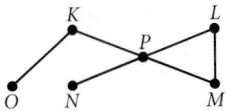

33. 30

12-1 Part D
Self-Assessment

1. $F = 6, V = 8, E = 12,$
$F + V - E = 6 + 8 - 12 = 2$
2. Possible answer:
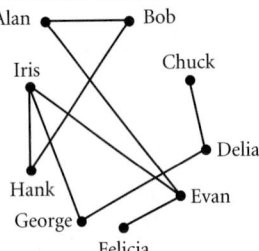

3. Connected **4.** Not connected **5.** 8 **6.** No, there exist vertices of odd degree. **7.** Yes, all vertices are of even degree.
8.
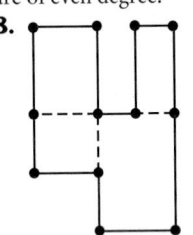

9. Yes **10.** Yes
11.
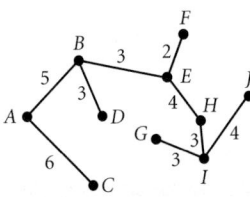

Minimum cost: $33,000
12. Possible answer: Link K to L, K to N, M to N and N to O. **13.** 24 m
14. $73,196.47 **15.** Bring the goat across, go back and bring the cabbage (or the wolf) across, bring the goat back, bring the wolf (or the cabbage) across, and go back and bring the goat across.

---

16. The amplitudes are 3 and 5, so the second function is greater by 2. The periods are 2π for each, so they are equal. **17.** $\frac{1}{2}$ **18.** Start in any city and travel the path formed by Seattle to Boston to Miami to Los Angeles to San Francisco to Seattle. **19.** $P(A \text{ winning}) \approx \frac{20}{27}$ **20.** 3 trucks minimum

12-2 Part A Try It

a. $a_n = 3 - 2\left(\frac{1}{2}\right)^n$;
$a_8 = 2.9921875$; Yes, it converges to 3.
b. $a_n = 1.06a_{n-1} + 1000$ and $a_1 = 1000$; $13,971.64

12-2 Part A Exercises

1. $a_2 = 7$; First ten terms: 5, 7, 11, 19, 35, 67, 131, 259, 515, 1027
9. $a_n = 10 - 16\left(\frac{1}{2}\right)^n$;
$a_{10} \approx 9.98$; Converges
11. $a_n = 32$; $a_{10} = 32$;
Converges **13. a.** In about 7 minutes
b. $T_n = 75 + 300(0.85)^n$;
$T_{30} \approx 77.29°F$
17. $B^1 = \begin{bmatrix} 0.5 & 0.2 \\ 0.5 & 0.8 \end{bmatrix}$,
$B^2 = \begin{bmatrix} 0.35 & 0.26 \\ 0.65 & 0.74 \end{bmatrix}$,
$B^3 = \begin{bmatrix} 0.305 & 0.278 \\ 0.695 & 0.722 \end{bmatrix}$,
$B^4 = \begin{bmatrix} 0.2915 & 0.2834 \\ 0.7085 & 0.7166 \end{bmatrix}$,
$B^5 \approx \begin{bmatrix} 0.2875 & 0.2850 \\ 0.7126 & 0.7150 \end{bmatrix}$,
$B^6 \approx \begin{bmatrix} 0.2862 & 0.2855 \\ 0.7138 & 0.7145 \end{bmatrix}$
19. $-4, 2, -4, 2, -4, 2, -4, 2$ **21.** 6, 4, 2.8, 2.08, 1.648, 1.3888, 1.23328, 1.139968
23. $a_n = 7 - \frac{5}{4}(2)^n$; $a_{10} = -1273$; Does not converge
25. $a_n = 8 - 22\left(\frac{1}{2}\right)^n$;
$a_{10} \approx 7.979$; Converges
27. $a_n = -3$; $a_{10} = -3$;
Converges **29. a.** $a_n = 0.8a_{n-1} + 20$ and $a_1 = 20$
b. About 100 mg

---

c. $d_n = 100 - 100(0.8)^n$; 100
31. At least $240,000
33. $a_n = \frac{1}{\sqrt{5}}[g^n - (-g)^{-n}]$;
$a_{12} = 144 = \left[\left(\frac{1+\sqrt{5}}{2}\right)^{12} - \left(-\frac{1+\sqrt{5}}{2}\right)^{-12}\right] \cdot \frac{1}{\sqrt{5}}$
$a_{50} = 12,586,269,025$

12-2 Part B Try It

a. $\begin{bmatrix} 0.5 & 0.5 \\ 0.5 & 0.5 \end{bmatrix}$

b. Next month, 55% prefer glasses, 45% prefer contacts; In the long run, 62.5% prefer glasses, 37.5% prefer contacts.

12-2 Part B Exercises

1. a. $A^2 = \begin{bmatrix} 0.64 & 0.6 \\ 0.36 & 0.4 \end{bmatrix}$;
$A^3 = \begin{bmatrix} 0.628 & 0.62 \\ 0.372 & 0.38 \end{bmatrix}$;
$A^4 = \begin{bmatrix} 0.6256 & 0.624 \\ 0.3744 & 0.376 \end{bmatrix}$
b. $AB = \begin{bmatrix} 58 \\ 42 \end{bmatrix}$,
$A^2B = \begin{bmatrix} 61.6 \\ 38.4 \end{bmatrix}$,
$A^3B = \begin{bmatrix} 62.32 \\ 37.68 \end{bmatrix}$,
$A^4B = \begin{bmatrix} 62.464 \\ 37.536 \end{bmatrix}$
5. No, entries are not probabilities.
7. a. $L = \begin{bmatrix} \frac{6}{13} & \frac{6}{13} \\ \frac{7}{13} & \frac{7}{13} \end{bmatrix}$
$\approx \begin{bmatrix} 0.4615 & 0.4615 \\ 0.5385 & 0.5385 \end{bmatrix}$
b. Limit = $\begin{bmatrix} \frac{3}{7} & \frac{3}{7} \\ \frac{4}{7} & \frac{4}{7} \end{bmatrix}$
$\approx \begin{bmatrix} 0.4286 & 0.4286 \\ 0.5714 & 0.5714 \end{bmatrix}$
c. Limit = $\begin{bmatrix} \frac{5}{9} & \frac{5}{9} \\ \frac{4}{9} & \frac{4}{9} \end{bmatrix}$
$\approx \begin{bmatrix} 0.5556 & 0.5556 \\ 0.4444 & 0.4444 \end{bmatrix}$

9. a. $T = \begin{bmatrix} 0.88 & 0.05 \\ 0.12 & 0.95 \end{bmatrix}$

b. Limit $= \begin{bmatrix} \frac{5}{17} & \frac{5}{17} \\ \frac{12}{17} & \frac{12}{17} \end{bmatrix}$

$\approx \begin{bmatrix} 0.2941 & 0.2941 \\ 0.7059 & 0.7059 \end{bmatrix}$

1 wk: $\begin{array}{l} \text{for} \\ \text{against} \end{array} \begin{bmatrix} 9,300 \\ 10,700 \end{bmatrix}$

2 wks: $\begin{array}{l} \text{for} \\ \text{against} \end{array} \begin{bmatrix} 8,719 \\ 11,281 \end{bmatrix}$

3 wks: $\begin{array}{l} \text{for} \\ \text{against} \end{array} \begin{bmatrix} \approx 8,237 \\ \approx 11,763 \end{bmatrix}$

long run:

$\begin{array}{l} \text{for} \\ \text{against} \end{array} \begin{bmatrix} \approx 5,882 \\ \approx 14,118 \end{bmatrix}$

11. (a) **13.** $x = \frac{1}{2}$ or $x = 2 \pm \sqrt{5}$ **15.** No, not all columns add to 1. **17.** Yes, all the entries are probabilities, the columns add up to 1, and the matrix is square.

19. $\begin{bmatrix} 0.43 & 0.96 \\ 0.57 & 0.04 \end{bmatrix}$

21. $A^2 = A^3 = A^4 = \begin{bmatrix} 0.2 & 0.2 \\ 0.8 & 0.8 \end{bmatrix}$;

Limit $= \begin{bmatrix} 0.2 & 0.2 \\ 0.8 & 0.8 \end{bmatrix}$

23. Limit $= \begin{bmatrix} \frac{34}{83} & \frac{34}{83} \\ \frac{49}{83} & \frac{49}{83} \end{bmatrix}$

$\approx \begin{bmatrix} 0.4096 & 0.4096 \\ 0.5904 & 0.5904 \end{bmatrix}$

25. a. 10; About 17; About 21 **b.** About 29 **c.** Yes, about 26 will be bored.
27. 75% **29. a.** In favor: 51.6%; Opposed: 41.7%; Undecided: 6.7%; Yes, it will pass. **b.** Yes, the initiative will pass, because 51.6% in favor represents a majority.

12-2 Part C Self-Assessment

1. 3, 10.6, 12.12, 12.424, 12.4848, 12.49696, 12.499392, 12.4998784 **2.** 1, 7, 19, 43, 91, 187, 379, 763

3. 0, 1, 3.4, 9.16, 22.984, 56.1616, 135.788, 327.890816
4. 2, −2, −4, −5, −5.5, −5.75, −5.875, −5.9375
5. $a_n = 7 - 2(2)^n$; $a_{10} = -2041$; Does not converge
6. $a_n = \frac{2}{3}(3)^n$; $a_{10} = 39,366$; Does not converge
7. a. About 3 hr; $\frac{1}{256} \approx 0.0039$
b. $a_n = \frac{1}{256}a_{n-1} + 650$ and $a_1 = 650$; About 652.549 mg
8. Approximate growth: 40, 42, 43, 45, 46, 48, ...; Limit: 80 sheep **9.** (d)
10. $a_n = n \cdot a_{n-1}$
11. a. 725; About 916
b. 2000 **12.** About 21.4%
13. Hamiltonian path; Possible answer: *ABCDEFG*.
14. About 0.0078
15. Amplitude = 2; Period = 2; Average y-value = 6 **16.** (A)
17. (C)

18. Limit $= \begin{bmatrix} 0.5 & 0.5 \\ 0.5 & 0.5 \end{bmatrix}$

19. $L = \begin{bmatrix} \frac{6}{13} & \frac{6}{13} \\ \frac{7}{13} & \frac{7}{13} \end{bmatrix}$

$\approx \begin{bmatrix} 0.4615 & 0.4615 \\ 0.5385 & 0.5385 \end{bmatrix}$

20. a. $a_n = 1.02a_{n-1} + 50,000$ and $a_1 = 10^7$; About 16,074,000
b. $a_n = 1.04a_{n-1} + 100,000$ and $a_1 = 10^7$; About 24,889,000
c. $a_n = 1.1a_{n-1} - 80,000$ and $a_1 = 10^7$; About 62,693,000
d. $a_n = 0.95a_{n-1} - 100,000$ and $a_1 = 10^7$; About 2,302,000

Chapter 12 Review

1. True **2.** True **3.** False; Vertex **4.** False; Recursive formula **5.** False; Transition matrix **6.** *A:* 1, *B:* 3, *C:* 3, *D:* 3, *E:* 2, *F:* 4 **7.** No Euler circuits, some vertices have odd degree.

8. Possible answer: Both types of circuits begin and end at the same vertex; An Euler circuit must cross each *edge* exactly once, while a Hamiltonian circuit must pass through each *vertex* exactly once. **9.** 18
10. Yes; Start in one of the rooms with three doors and end in the other room with three doors. **11. a.** 2, 3.6, 4.88, 5.904, 6.7232, 7.37856
b.

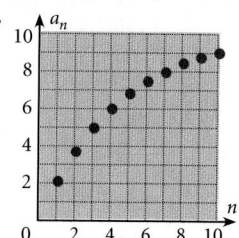

c. $a_n = 10 - 10(0.8)^n$
12. (A) **13.** (D) **14.** No, the entries in the first column do not add up to 1. **15.** No, the matrix is not square.
16. $4486.52
17.

A
50   20
E   40   30   B
D   C

18. Limit $= \begin{bmatrix} \frac{4}{9} & \frac{4}{9} \\ \frac{5}{9} & \frac{5}{9} \end{bmatrix}$

$\approx \begin{bmatrix} 0.4444 & 0.4444 \\ 0.5556 & 0.5556 \end{bmatrix}$

19. After one week: Jones 2000, Farley 3000; After two weeks: Jones 2000, Farley 3000; In long run: Jones 2000, Farley 3000.

CREDITS

PHOTOGRAPHS

Front Cover   **Left** Cheryl Fenton*   **Right** Antonio M. Rosario/ The Image Bank

Spine   **Left** Cheryl Fenton*   **Right** Antonio M. Rosario/The Image Bank

Back Cover   **TL** Thomas Kitchin/Tom Stack & Associates **TCL** Giraudon/Art Resource, NY   **TCR** Jerry Jacka Photography **TR** Jon Feingersh/Tom Stack & Associates   **BL** Art Resource **BCL** Jerry Jacka Photography/Courtesy: Museum of Northern Arizona, Flagstaff   **BCR** Cheryl Fenton*   **BR** Antonio M. Rosario/The Image Bank

Front Matter   **vBR** Gregory Sams/SPL/Photo Researchers **viiB** David L. Brown/Tom Stack & Associates   **viii** Nathan Bilow/ Allsport   **ixT** Masahiro Sano/The Stock Market   **ixC** John Bavosi/ SPL/Photo Researchers   **ixB** Thomas Mangalsen/Images of Nature **xT** Tim Davis/Photo Researchers   **xC** John Madere/The Stock Market **xB** Bob Daemmrich/Stock, Boston   **xiiB** K. Scholz/ Superstock, Inc. **xiv** J. Wes Bobbitt/Black Star   **xvii** Gary Larson/Farworks, Inc./Universal Press Syndicate

Chapter 1   **5(inset)** David Young/Tom Stack & Associates **5(background)** David Muench/Tony Stone Images   **6** Kunio Owaki/The Stock Market   **7R** W. Strode/Superstock, Inc.   **7L** Lester Lefkowitz/Tony Stone Images   **8** UPI/Bettmann Archive   **10** J. Irwin/ Superstock, Inc.   **14** Fridmar Damm/Leo de Wys Inc.   **19** David Madison   **21** Gregory Sams/SPL/Photo Researchers   **23** Richard Nowitz/Photo Researchers   **27** The Fine Arts Museums of San Francisco, gift of Mr. & Mrs. John D. Rockefeller III   **32** P. R. Production/Superstock, Inc.   **36** Adam Hart-Davis/SPL/Photo Researchers   **38T** Patricia J. Bruno/Positive Images   **43** JoeSam., San Francisco   **45T** Rijksmuseum, Kröller-Müller   **45C** A . Michael Noll **45B** Charles Falco/Science Source/Photo Researchers   **46** CDC/Science Source/Photo Researchers   **50** Cathlyn Melloan/Tony Stone Images **55T** M. Granitsas/The Image Works   **55B** B. Daemmrich/The Image Works   **66** B. Daemmrich/Tony Stone Images

Chapter 2   **74** Timothy Shonnard/Tony Stone Images **77(border)** Frank P. Rossotto/The Stock Market   **77** Library of Congress   **82** Carolyn Brown/Photo Researchers   **84** Marc Muench/Tony Stone Images   **85** Bob Firth   **88** Louis Bencze/Tony Stone Images   **89** Charles Krebs/Tony Stone Images   **92L** Kevin Horan   **92R** Harry Benson   **94** Brian Parker/Tom Stack & Associates **95** Giraudon/Art Resource, NY   **105** Johnny Johnson/DRK Photo **109** Greg Vaughn/Tom Stack & Associates   **110** Tim Davis* **112L** Anne Dowie*   **112R** Gary Withey   **114** Donald C. Johnson/The Stock Market   **116T** Connie Coleman/Tony Stone Images   **119** David Madison/Bruce Coleman Inc.   **121** Globus Brothers Studios/The Stock Market   **125T** Jonathan Wright/Bruce Coleman Inc.   **125B** Tim Davis*   **126** Des & Jen Bartlett/Bruce Coleman Inc.   **127T** Culver Pictures   **132** Brenda Lewison/The Stock Market   **137L** Chuck Savage/The Stock Market   **137R** © IFA/Bruce Coleman Inc.   **146** Tom McHugh/Photo Researchers   **148** Kevin Morris/Tony Stone Images **149** David M. Dennis/Tom Stack & Associates   **151** Esbin Anderson/Photo 20-20

Chapter 3   **159(background)** Leo de Wys Inc./De Wys/Sipa/Baudet   **160** Gary Larson/Farworks, Inc./Universal Press Syndicate. Geoffrey Nilsen Photography*   **164** Ed Bock/The Stock Market   **167L** Darrell Gulin/Tony Stone Images   **167R** Stephen Simpson/FPG International   **170** Vandystadt/Allsport   **174** UPI/ Bettmann Archive   **180** R. A. Lee/Superstock, Inc.   **183** Archive Photos   **185** Marty Cordano/DRK Photo   **189T** Al Michaud/FPG International   **189B** J. Barry O'Rourke/The Stock Market   **191** Lucy Stone/Tony Stone Images   **194** Federal Communications Commission **196** Mike & Elvan Habich/Animals, Animals   **197T** Jon Feingersh/ The Stock Market   **197B** AT & T Archives   **202T** Cindy Lewis **202B** Michael W. Davidson/Photo Researchers   **203** Francis Lepine/ Earth Scenes   **204** Mauritius/Superstock, Inc.   **205** Dr. Fred Espenak/ SPL/Photo Researchers   **207** M. Taylor/ Superstock, Inc.

209 M. Grecco/Stock, Boston   **212** Brian Parker/ Tom Stack & Associates   **214** John Mason/The Stock Market   **217** Edward H. Mitchell   **219** Rosenfeld Images/The Stock Market   **220T** Breck P. Kent/Earth Scenes   **220B** A. Walter/Superstock, Inc.

Chapter 4   **231** John Elk III/Bruce Coleman Inc.   **234** Lick Observatory   **241** David L. Brown/Tom Stack & Associates   **245** Rod Planck/Tom Stack & Associates   **248** The Mansell Collection **252L** CNRI/SPL/Photo Researchers   **257** Henry Groskinsky/Peter Arnold, Inc.   **259** Eastcott-Momatiuk/Woodfin Camp & Associates **260** J. C. Carton/Bruce Coleman Inc.   **261** Geoff Tompkinson/SPL/ Photo Researchers   **263** Robert Mathena/Fundamental Photographs **268** Mark Burnett/Stock, Boston   **274** Brock May/ Photo Researchers **282** Lew Long/The Stock Market   **283** Seiko Corporation   **284** C. G. & M. Kohler/FPG International   **295B** William Strode/Notre Dame University   **298** David Madison/Bruce Coleman Inc.

Chapter 5   **304L** John Shaw/Tom Stack & Associates **307(inset)** Ray Nelson/Phototake   **307(background)** Telegraph Colour Library/FPG International   **310** Arthur M. Siegelman/FPG International   **311** Vince Streano/The Stock Market   **314** Eduardo Garcia/FPG International   **317** David Muench/Tony Stone Images **321** Ric Ergenbright/Tony Stone Images   **322** Jean Miele/The Stock Market   **328** James Blank/The Stock Market   **330** Guy Marche/FPG International   **335** Telegraph Colour Library/FPG International **340** A. Mercieca/Superstock, Inc.   **341** D. Middleton/Superstock, Inc. **343** David Madison   **347** George A. Plimpton Collection/Columbia University, Rare Book and Manuscript Library   **351** Wedding, 1991, Polaroid Polacolor ER photograph, © William Wegman/Pace MacGill Gallery/Geoffrey Nilsen Photography*   **352** Will & Deni McIntyre/ Tony Stone Images   **358** "Vince and Larry ®" ©1985 US DOT, photo byCesar Rubio*   **367** Henneghien/Bruce Coleman Inc.   **368T** Bob Daemmrich/Stock, Boston   **371** Ulrike Welsch/Photo Researchers **373** Scott Camazine/Photo Researchers   **377** Dave Lawlor/FPG International   **378** M. C. Escher/Cordon Art-Baarn-Holland **379** Shattil-Rozinski/Tom Stack & Associates   **382** John Maher/Stock, Boston   **383** K. Scholz/Superstock, Inc.   **388** NASA/Superstock, Inc. **389T** P. I. Production/Superstock, Inc.   **389C** Vince Streano/Tony Stone Images   **389B** John Livzey/Tony Stone Images   **393** Cern, P. Loiez/SPL/Photo Researchers   **394** Dr. Vic Bradbury/SPL/Photo Researchers   **397** Chuck Pefley/Tony Stone Images   **399** David C. Tomlinson/Tony Stone Images   **401** Richard H. Smith/FPG International   **403** W. Kaufmann/JPL/SS/Photo Researchers   **409** Finley Holiday Film   **410** Courtesy of Raytheon Marine Co.   **411** Bridgeman/Art Resource, NY   **412** Kunio Owaki/The Stock Market

Chapter 6   **418B** E. R. Degginger/Bruce Coleman Inc. **428** Nathan Bilow/Allsport   **431** Lee Boltin Photography   **433** Archive Photos   **435** Charles Gupton/Stock, Boston   **436** David Muench* **441** Masahiro Sano/The Stock Market   **442** Giraudon/Art Resource, NY   **443** Steve Solum/Bruce Coleman Inc.   **446** John Kelly/Tony Stone Images   **448** Archive Photos   **449** Earl Fansler Photographers Inc.   **450** Greg Vaughn/Tom Stack & Associates   **451** Gary Wagner/ Stock, Boston

Chapter 7   **456T** Brady/The Bettmann Archive   **457(background)** Sam Minkler*   **459** Dorothea Lange/Library of Congress **460** A. Devaney/Superstock, Inc.   **465** Goodyear Tire and Rubber **466** Manfred Gottschalk/Tom Stack & Associates   **471** Buick Motor Division   **473** John Bavosi/SPL/Photo Researchers   **478** Brian Parker/ Tom Stack & Associates   **480T** Art Wolfe/Tony Stone Images **480B** Michael Stuckey/Comstock, Inc.   **481** Bill & Sally Fletcher/Tom Stack & Associates   **483** Richard Megna/Fundamental Photographs **485** Paul Merideth/Tony Stone Images   **486** Damian Strohmeyer/ Allsport USA   **488** Thomas Mangalsen/Images of Nature   **489** Brent P. Kent/ Earth Scenes   **490** Richard Megna/Fundamental Photographs **492T** Dominique Braud/Tom Stack & Associates   **492B** Jan Yellin/ Shooting Star   **493** UPI/Bettmann   **494** Stan Osolinski/FPG International   **495** Muybridge/Photo Researchers   **496** R. King/Superstock, Inc.   **497** M. Taylor/Superstock, Inc.   **498** D. Ellersen/Superstock, Inc.

501 Dennis Hallinan/FPG International   502 NASA/ Peter Arnold, Inc.   504 Scala/Art Resource, NY   509T Archive Photos 509B Richard Megna/Fundamental Photographs   510 Michael Stuckey/Comstock, Inc.   512 Mark Newman/Tom Stack & Associates 513(background) Marc Webber   513 Mauritius/ Superstock, Inc. 520 Eugen Gebhardt/FPG International   523 ATC Productions 1993/ The Stock Market   524 M. Roessler/Superstock, Inc.   532 Michele Burgess/The Stock Market   533 E. Nagele/FPG International

Chapter 8   538R Renee Lynn*   538BL Henri Matisse, French, 1869–1954, Apples, oil on canvas, 1916, 116.8 cm x 89.4 cm, gift of Florene May Schoenborn and Samuel A. Marx, 1948.563/The Art Institute of Chicago   539(background) Norman Owen Tomalin/ Bruce Coleman Inc.   542 Patricia Lanza/Bruce Coleman Inc. 544 Tom Tracy/The Stock Market   551 John Madere/The Stock Market   553 J. R. Eyerman/Life Magazine ©1952 Time Inc.   560 Joe Bator/The Stock Market   565TR Inga Spence/Tom Stack & Associates 565C Tim Davis/Photo Researchers   565BR Kevin Horan/Stock, Boston   565BL Peter Menzel/Stock, Boston   565(background) Gary Braasch/Woodfin Camp & Associates   576 Will & Deni McIntyre/ Photo Researchers   583 John Shaw/Bruce Coleman Inc.   584 Larry Ulrich/DRK Photo   585 Fred Ward   594 David Ulmer/Stock, Boston 598 Mark C. Burnett/Photo Researchers   601 Jon Riley/Tony Stone Images   602 Diane Schiumo/Fundamental Photographs 603 Photoworld/FPG International   605T Emory Kristof/National Geographic Society   605C Pierre Mion/National Geographic Society 605B Emory Kristof/National Geographic Society   607 David Madison   610 Mark Burnett/Photo Researchers

Chapter 9   616L UPI/Bettmann   616R E. Nagele/FPG International   619 Kim Westerskov/Tony Stone Images   623B Lionello Fabri/Photo Researchers   628 Sylvain Coffie/Tony Stone Images 629 Peoria Area Convention and Visitors Bureau   631 Telegraph Colour Library/FPG International   632 Chuck Savage/The Stock Market   633 American Gas Association   634 Pekka Parviainen/SPL/ Photo Researchers   635 Michael J. Howell/ Stock, Boston   639 Steve Leonard/Tony Stone Images   644 Bob Daemmrich/Stock, Boston 647 Francois Gohier/Photo Researchers   649 Ron Kuntz/UPI/ Bettmann Newsphotos   653 Ron Dahlquist/ Superstock, Inc. 655 Bob Daemmrich/The Image Works   656 Bob Daemmrich/Stock, Boston   659 Sunil Malhotra/Reuters/Bettmann   662 Bob Daemmrich/Stock, Boston   663 Robert Cundy/FPG International 666 Mark D. Phillips/Photo Researchers   667 Mike O'Brine/Tom Stack & Associates   670 Andrew Rafkind/Tony Stone Images 671 Kimimasa Mayama/Reuters/Bettmann

Chapter 10   676L David Muench   676R Monte Costa 677(background) Peter Bradshaw, Imperial College of London, courtesy of Parabolic Press   687 Dan McCoy/Rainbow   692 David Madison/Bruce Coleman Inc.   696 Richard During/Tony Stone Images   698 Stephen Frisch*   699 Washnik Studio/The Stock Market 709 Virginia Historical Society, Richmond, VA   717 Tom Bean/Tony Stone Images   722T Greg Vaughn/Tom Stack & Associates 722B Kenneth Noland   724 Robert Weinreb/Bruce Coleman Inc. 725 Mark C. Burnett/Photo Researchers   726 David Muench 729 David L. Brown/Tom Stack & Associates   731 Express Newspapers/ Archive Photos   732 Naval Research Laboratory, Stennis Space Center   735 American Stock/Archive Photos   739 David Muench   742 Kip Peticolas/Fundamental Photographs   745 The Fine Arts Museums of San Francisco, Achenbach Foundation for Graphic Arts, 1969.32.6   746 Underwood Photo Archives, SF

Chapter 11   759 U.S. Coast Guard   763 National Geographic Society Image Collection   764 Michael O' Leary/Tony Stone Images 765 Photo from European Picture Service/FPG International 766 Robert E. Daemmrich/Tony Stone Images   769 Harold M. Lambert/Archive Photos   772 Chuck Savage/Stock Market 774B Bob Daemmrich/The Image Works   780 Robert E. Daemmrich/ Tony Stone Images   785 Joe McDonald/Animals, Animals 789 David Madison   795 Arnold Sachs/Archive Photos

Chapter 12   803(background) Jim Foster/The Stock Market 805 John Hart, courtesy Electronic Visualization Laboratory at University of Illinois at Chicago   806 Mark Burnett/Photo Researchers 807 Scott Camazine/Photo Researchers   810 Larry Ulrich/DRK Photo

814 Anne Dowie*   825 Frank Rossotto/The Stock Market 830 P. Ginter/The Stock Market   835 Kennan Ward/The Stock Market   836 Darrell Jones/The Stock Market   840 Enell/Archive Photos   842 Jean Pragen/Tony Stone Images   844 Michele Burgess/The Stock Market

The Bettmann Archive: xii, 49, 78, 104, 127B, 140, 175, 242, 557, 590, 638, 773, 779L, 793. **Cheryl Fenton:*** 3(background), 75(background), 116B, 157(background), 229(background), 252R, 271(background), 305(background), 368B, 418T, 419(background), 421, 424, 437, 538TL, 548, 559, 562, 568, 597, 609, 617(background), 691, 697, 753(background), 758, 800, 801(background). **Ken Karp:*** xiii, 60, 129T, 129B, 187, 240, 325, 439C, 439B, 444, 476, 589, 599, 622, 623T, 665, 740, 757, 781T, 781C, 812. **Lifesmith Classic Fractals:*** xiiT, 271(insets), 287, 291, 295T, 296, 297, 354, 829, 832. **Liza Loeffler:*** 86, 91, 102, 265, 275, 292, 439T, 566, 570, 571, 587, 596, 715, 838. NASA: vi, 122, 123, 266, 405, 514, 586. **Geoffrey Nilsen Photography:*** vT, vBL, viiT, 2, 34, 64, 156T, 156B, 159(inset), 161, 184, 199, 206T, 213, 304TR, 304BR, 313, 336, 462–463, 627, 630, 661, 767. **Bill Reitzel:*** 12, 38B, 156C, 172, 176, 193, 200, 206B, 477, 518, 522, 636, 756, 781B. **Cesar Rubio:*** xiiC, 380, 456B, 625, 771, 774T, 779R, 779(background). Look Forward/Look Back icons photographed by Ken Karp*.
*Photographed expressly for Addison-Wesley Publishing Co., Inc.

TEXT AND ART

CHAPTER 1   p. 45: A. Michael Noll, *Computer Composition with Lines*, 1964, copyright ©1965 A. Michael Noll   p. 69: *Lo-Shu* (Magic Squares) from Theoni Pappas, *The Joy of Mathematics*, San Carlos, CA: Wide World Publishing/Tetra, 1989, p. 82; copyright ©1986, 1987, 1989 Theoni Pappas.

CHAPTER 4   p. 231: text excerpt from Kendrick Frazier, "Solstice Watchers of Chaco," *Science News* 114(9), 26 August 1978, pp. 148–151.

CHAPTER 5   p. 398: pseudosphere and sphere from *For All Practical Purposes: Introduction to Contemporary Mathematics*, 2nd Edition, NY: W. H. Freeman and Company; copyright ©1988, 1991 by COMAP, Inc.

CHAPTER 10   p. 746: sensitive plant art from Edward S. Ayensu & Philip Whitfield, eds., *The Rhythms of Life*, NY: Crown Publishers, 1982, p. 54. Copyright ©1981 Marshall Editions Limited.

ILLUSTRATIONS

Sam Assefa: 811a, 816d, 827b, 847b **Molly Babich:** 250a, 267a, 339a, 578 **Christine Benjamin:** 94b, 98a, 130a, 134c, 149a, 210a, 228b, 237a, 239a, 254b, 264, 304a, 426a, 432a, 549a, 552f, 610a, 826d, 826e, 834a **Bruce Bowles:** 58a, 221a, 308a, 338c, 361a, 415a, 776a **Cindy Brodie:** 28a, 69b **Warren Budd & Assoc.:** 18a, 20b, 461a, 531a **Gary Carlson:** 371a, b, d **Steve Dinnino:** 315a, 345a, 404b **Don Dudley:** 24a, 66b, 245a, 327b, 672a, 698a, 828a **Joe Heiner:** 74a; Large Icons: 4, 76, 158, 230, 231, 306, 420, 458, 540, 618, 678, 754, 802; Small Icons: 77, 103, 127, 159, 197, 249, 271, 307, 339, 371, 399, 459, 485, 513, 565, 585, 619, 679, 709, 729, 755, 779, 803, 829 **John Hersey:** 52a, 74b, 83a, 107e, 124b, 150a, 256a, 281a, 434a, 438a, 680b **Laszlo Kubinyi:** 85b **Nina Lisowski:** 399c, 829b, c, d **Karen Minot:** 563b, 567a, 590b, 683a, 685d, 714c, 724a, 725b **Helene Moore:** 167c **Tony Morse:** 127a, 211a, 228a, 686a, 688a, 699b, 755a **Deborah Morse:** 103a, 167c, 372a, 398b, 585a **Andrew Muonio:** 100a, 141a, 487a, 526a, 543a **Laurie O'Keefe:** 126a **Bill Pasini:** 270a, 484a, 619b, 626a, 679a, 685a, 706b, 736a, 775a **William Rieser:** 33b, 34b, 36a, 41a, 165a, 166a, 175b, 208a, 310a, 324a, 332a, 338b, 348a, 360c, 363a, 393b, 508a, 509a, 770a, 792a, 794a **Rob Schuster:** 57a, 635a, 640a **Elwood Smith:** 31a, b, 616c, 800a **Susan Todd:** 183b, 215d, 272a, 285a, 316a, 370a, 378b, 392d, 436a, 445a, 464a, 515a, 527a, 584a, 595a, 610c, 682b, 727c, 729b, c, d, 733b, 749c **Joe Van Der Bos:** 2a, c, 97d, 101a, 113b, 123b, 133a, 133b, 134d, 142a, 243a, 254a, 258a, 262a, 273a, 422a, 423a, 469a, 561a, 576b, 619a, 683b, 683d, 693a, 721b, 722b, 726b, 728a, 737a, 752b, 800b, 822d, 837a **Cameron Wasson:** 467b **John Weber:** 127c **Sarah Woodward:** 380a, 385d, 490a, 676c, 752a

INDEX

graphing polynomial functions, 543, 547, 548, 549, 554, 567, 582–583

graphing precipitation and temperature, 532

graphing a probability equation, 764

graphing quadratic functions, 324–326, 329

graphing radical equations, 491, 504

graphing rational equations, 592

graphing a recursive sequence, 835

graphing the standard normal curve, 793

graphing trigonometric functions, 732

histogram, 794

histogram of a sample, 782

inverse matrix, 181

inverse variation, 461

line of best fit, 170

linear equations, 14, 19, 104

linear regression, 153

linear systems on, 161–162, 167

matrices to find probability, 184

matrix equations on, 179, 180

matrix multiplication, 65, 66

matrix operations, 60

matrix to solve quadratic equations, 353

maximum volume, 563

median–median line, 118

modeling decompression, 608

power regression, 493, 497, 510

prediction with graphs, 268

prediction with linear graphs, 100

predictions with lines of fit, 123

quadratic function for three data points, 335

quadratic functions, 309, 314, 315

random events, 44

regression functions, 524

regression line, 117–120, 125

roots of a polynomial equation, 571

scatter plot, 7, 12–13, 28, 104

sequences, 255

Sierpinski gasket, 21

solving linear equations, 86, 91

solving linear systems, 194

solving linear systems using matrices, 184

solving quadratic equations, 340–343, 346, 347

solving quadratic systems, 411

solving quadratic-linear systems, 401, 404

solving quadratic-quadratic systems, 405–407, 409, 410

solving three-variable systems using matrices, 189, 193

TRACE feature, 86

transition matrix, 837

volume of a cone, 570

volume and surface area of a cylinder, 561

Graph(s)

connected, 810–813

discontinuous, 599

exponential, 619–648

of functions, 308–326, 542–551

histogram, 781–782

of polyhedrons, 804–806

of quadratic–linear systems, 400–402

of rational functions, 598–600, 603–605

scatter plot, 6–9, 12–13, 28, 104

theory of, 800–828

tree, 818–820

Graph theory, 800–828

Great circle, 679

Growth

decay and, 627–630

exponential, 627–630

exponential functions and, 621–624

recursion and, 830–834

H

Hamilton, Sir William Rowan, 817

Hamiltonian circuit, 817

Hamiltonian path, 817

Hardy, G.H., 5

Health, 19, 30, 43, 46, 54, 125, 133, 147, 149, 150, 164, 199, 202, 371, 383, 450, 473, 479, 559, 568, 635, 648, 662, 672, 675, 740, 741, 765, 766, 773, 774, 778, 786, 792, 831, 835, 839, 844

Heron's Formula, 720

Hexagonal numbers, 232, 241

Histogram, 781–782, 794

History, 11, 14, 27, 29, 32, 36, 49, 66, 69, 77, 78, 82, 85, 100, 102, 104, 124, 126, 127, 159, 170, 174, 192, 197, 231, 232, 242, 248, 254, 271, 274, 285, 286, 291, 295, 315, 330, 347, 367, 370, 378, 380, 398, 399, 404, 416, 421, 426, 431, 435, 436, 437, 443, 445, 447, 450, 459, 482, 490, 493, 513, 533, 565, 582, 590, 598, 619, 625, 628, 634, 638, 669, 686, 699, 706, 708, 709, 724, 728, 729, 755, 756, 759, 770, 773, 774, 776, 779, 795, 804, 805, 811, 817, 821, 828, 829, 834, 836

Horizontal asymptote, 603

Horizontal shift, of a sine or cosine graph, 738–740

Hubble, Edwin, 482

Hyperbola(s), 388–392

asymptotes of, 390

branches of, 390

center of, 390

definition, 390

focus of, 390

as graphs of inverse relationships, 462

rectangular, 395, 462

standard form of the equation of, 390, 393

vertices of, 390

Hyperbolic geometry, 398

I

Identity

additive, 272, 273

multiplicative, 62, 273

Imaginary axis, 291

Imaginary number, 286–288

Imaginary plane, 367

Imaginary unit, 286

Inconsistent system of linear equations, 162

Independent events, 762–765

Independent variable, 16

Index, roots and, 486

Inductive reasoning, 239–241

Industry, 9, 12, 29, 45, 48, 54, 57, 64, 99, 100, 108, 109, 125, 139, 140, 141, 159, 167, 189, 191, 194, 197, 207, 209, 211, 217, 220, 223, 225, 227, 248, 254, 315, 327, 329, 334, 335, 338, 346, 359, 360, 365, 379, 410, 412, 414, 415, 416, 417, 437, 448–449, 496, 502, 537, 541, 551, 553, 554, 556, 560, 563, 565, 566, 568, 570, 576, 585, 591, 597, 601, 607, 612, 629, 631, 633, 645, 655, 673, 675, 767, 773, 775, 778, 784, 786, 789, 791, 792, 793, 794, 796, 798, 803, 818, 822, 823, 825, 827, 828, 837, 838, 840, 847, 849

Inequality (inequalities)

absolute value and, 135–138, 149

addition property of, 128

boundary line, 142–143

boundary point, 128

compound, 130–131, 136

definition of, 128

exponential, 872

graphing quadratic systems of, 403, 408, 409, 412

graphs of circles and, 377

as limitations, 149

logarithmic, 872

multiplication property of, 128

one-variable, 128–131

quadratic, 870

rational, 870

square root, 870

symbols, 128

systems of, 198–227

tolerance and, 149

two-variable, 142–145

Infinite sequence, 233

Infinite series

geometric, 262–265

limit of, 262–265

sum of, 262

Initial side, of an angle on the coordinate plane, 700

Integer programming, 220

Integer(s), 278

as exponents, 467–470, 475, 476

Interest

compound, 502, 640, 641, 658–659

simple, 88

Inverse
additive, 273
multiplicative, 273
operations, 177
Inverse function(s), 525–528
exponential, 650–653
Inverse matrices, 61, 177–183
Inverse relationships, 461–462,
525–528
graph of, 462
Inverse variation, 461–463
Invertible matrix, 181
Irrational numbers, 278–281
square roots, 279–281
Iteration, 271
Julia sets and, 295
matrices and, 836–839
recursion and, 830–834
shape evolution and, 843–844

J

Joint variation, 463
Julia, Gaston, 295
Julia sets, 295, 296, 297

K

Karmarkar, Narenda, 197
Kepler, Johannes, 380, 490
Kerrich, John, 32
Khachian, L.G., 197
Kinetic energy, 345
Koch, Helge von, 264
Koch snowflake, 264
Krantz, Les, 42, 48
Kruskal, J. B., 819

L

Lange, Dorothea, 459
Latitude, 679
Law of Cosines, 710–713
Law of Sines, 717–721
**Leading coefficient, of a
polynomial,** 542
Least common denominator, 593
Leibniz, Gottfried von, 264
Limit, 262–265
Line(s)
parallel, 95
perpendicular, 95
vertical, 96
Line of best fit, 109, 170
median-median line, 109–112
regression line, 117–120
Line symmetry, 471
**Linear combination, method for
solving systems of equations,**
169, 187
Linear equation(s)
consistent system of, 162
dependent, 162

finding equations for lines, 92–95
graphing, 14–16
graphing to solve, 86–89
inconsistent system of, 162
point–slope form of, 93
quadratic relations and, 400–402
slope and, 81
slope–intercept form of, 92
solving by linear combination, 169, 187
solving by substitution, 168–169, 187–188
solving systems graphically, 160–163
solving systems symbolically, 168–173
solving systems using matrices, 177–182
solving systems with three variables, 186–190
systems of, 158–196
trend lines and, 104–106
Linear function(s), 453
compared to quadratic functions, 308
definition, 79
direct variation and, 78–81
graphing, 78–81, 86–89
and quadratic relations, 400–402
slope of graph of, 80
Linear inequalities
constraints and, 204–208
objective function for, 212–216
optimal solution of, 212–216
systems of, 198–227
Linear programming, 197
feasible region in, 204–208
for making business decisions, 204–223
modeling constraints with linear inequalities, 204–208
optimal problem solutions, 212–216
Vertex Theorem, 216
Linear regression, 117–120, 153
Linear speed, 696–697
Literal equation, 88
Literature, 330, 370, 378, 392, 421, 433, 436, 553, 562, 590, 625, 769, 779, 834
Logarithm(s)
common, 652
definition of, 651
exponents and, 663–666
natural, 653
properties of, 663–666
for solving exponential equations, 657–659
Logarithmic equation(s), solving, 663–666
Logarithmic form, 651
Logarithmic function(s), 650–675
definition of, 651
Logarithmic regression, 662
Logic, 21
arrangements, 428–430
circuits and paths, 810–813

combinations, 438–440, 443–445
compound inequalities, 130–131
counterexample, 272
encoding and decoding, 66–67
graph theory, 800–828
mutually exclusive events, 424, 756
networks, 804–806, 810–813, 824–826
optimization, 817–820
patterns, 4–30
sequences, 232–238
series, 239–245
simulation and, 39–42
tree diagrams, 422–423, 818–820
Logistics function, 670
Longitude, 679

M

Magnitude, of a vector, 711–713
Major axis, of an ellipse, 381
Mandelbrot, Benoit, 271, 297
Mandelbrot set, 291
Mapping
matrices and, 52, 72
tree diagrams and, 422–423
Marsalis, Wynton, 485
Mathematical structure. *See also*
Numbers; Properties; Theorems
arithmetic sequences, 232–238
arithmetic series, 239–245
geometric sequences, 250–256
geometric series, 256–258
inequalities, 128–131, 142–145
types of numbers, 278–281
Mathematics, definition of, 5
Matrix (matrices)
adjoint of, 185
data handling and, 50–53
definition, 50
determinant of, 176, 185
dimension, 50
encoding and decoding with, 66–67
entry, 50
equal, 50
inverse, 61, 177–183
invertible, 181
multiplication, 58–62, 65, 66
multiplicative identity, 61
operations on, 50–53
probability, 836–839
product, 58
scalar multiplication, 51
solving systems of equations with, 177–182
square, 61
transformation, 52
transition, 837
**Maximum(s), of polynomial
functions,** 548–551, 561, 582–583
Maximum point
of a parabola, 309, 324–326
of a quadratic function, 323

Polynomial equation(s)
  factors of, 570–574
  graphing to solve, 566–567
  multiple roots of, 579
  roots of, 556, 570–574, 577–580
Polynomial function(s), 542–544
  See also Quadratic function(s)
  maximums and minimums of,
    548–551, 561, 582–583
  zeros of, 555–558, 574
Population, in statistics, 780
Power regression curve, 493
Power series, 258
Power(s). *See* Exponent(s); Root(s)
Prediction
  using arithmetic series, 246
  using exponential regression,
    635–637
  using geometric series, 268–269
  using graphs of functions, 86–89
  using inverse variation, 461
  using a median–median line, 109–112
  using power regression, 493, 510
  using probability matrices, 836–839
  using recursive sequences, 830–834
  using samples, 779–799
  using scatter plots, 6–9
  using trend lines, 104–106, 122–123
Principal square root, 279
Principle of Zero Products, 349,
  557–558
Prisoner values, 297
Probability
  certain event, 32, 34
  combinations and, 440
  complementary events, 756–759
  compound, 758
  compound events, 755–778
  conditional, 769–772
  counting methods, 422–425, 762
  definition of, 31
  dependent events, 762–765
  event, 32
  experimental, 32–34
  factorial, 424–425
  geometric, 33–34
  impossible event, 32, 34
  independent events, 762–765
  matrices, 836–839
  mutually exclusive events, 424, 756
  outcome, 32
  sample space, 32
  sampling, 771
  sampling methods, 779–799
  simulation and, 38–42, 46–47
  theoretical, 32–34
  transition, 836
Problem Solving
  Problem solving is fundamental to
    the presentation of mathematics
    in this book and is found
    throughout.

Problem-Solving Strategies
  Analyze the Information Given, 719
  Check Answers Graphically, 648
  Check Answers for Sense, 180, 342,
    515
  Draw a Diagram, 256, 259, 570, 596,
    687, 694, 809, 814, 827
  Draw a Graph, 546, 808, 814, 822,
    823, 827
  Draw a Picture, 36
  Look for a Pattern, 14, 78, 232, 244,
    280, 322, 438
  Make a Chart, 434
  Make an Organized List, 119, 428,
    434, 580, 732, 804
  Make a Plan, 257
  Make a Sketch, 412
  Make a Table, 260, 732, 804
  Solve an Equation, 171, 194
  Use Proportional Thinking, 783
  Write an Inequality, 202
  Write a Proportion, 586
Problem-Solving Tip, 14, 36, 78, 119,
  171, 180, 194, 202, 232, 244, 256, 257,
  259, 260, 280, 322, 342, 412, 428, 434,
  438, 480, 515, 546, 570, 580, 586, 596,
  648, 687, 694, 719, 732, 783, 804, 808,
  809, 814, 822, 823, 827
Product matrix, 58
Properties
  absolute value and square root, 280
  addition, 53
  addition property of equality, 87
  addition property of inequalities, 128
  associative, 53
  change of base property for loga-
    rithms, 668
  commutative, 53
  of inverse functions, 527
  of logarithms, 663–666
  multiplication property of equality, 87
  multiplication property of inequali-
    ties, 128
  of square roots, 280
Proportional thinking. *See* Direct
  variation; Similar figures
Pyramidal numbers, 248
Pythagoras, 232
Pythagorean Theorem, 282, 284
  for real numbers, 293
  spherical right triangle and, 706
  trigonometric ratios and, 682, 703

Q

Quadratic equation(s)
  discriminant of, 361–364
  factoring, 348–350
  projectile motion and, 368
  solving graphically, 340–343
  standard form of, 342, 349

**Quadratic form, of radical equa-
  tions,** 506–507
Quadratic formula, 354–356
  derivation of, 354
Quadratic function(s), 308–312, 543
  completing the square, 330–332
  fitting data to, 335
  of the form $f(x) = ax^2$, 316–318
  of the form $f(x) = a(x-h)^2 + k$,
    323–326
  graphs of, 316–318, 336
  maximum and minimum values of,
    549
  translations of, 323–326
  zeros of, 342, 577–580
Quadratic programming, 412
Quadratic systems, 399–415
Quadratic-linear systems, 400–402
  solving graphically, 400–402
  solving symbolically, 401–402
Quadratic-quadratic systems,
  405–408
  solving graphically, 405–406
  solving symbolically, 406–408
Quartic function(s), 543
  maximum value of, 550
  minimum value of, 550

R

Radian measure, 688–690
Radical equation(s), 498–500,
  503–507
  extraneous solution, 499
  quadratic form, 506–507
Radical symbol, 279
Radicand, 486
Radius, of a circle, 373
**Random numbers, simulations
  with,** 39–41
Random sampling, 780–784
Range
  definition, 22
  identifying, 22–24
Rate of change, 79
  arithmetic sequence, 233
  geometric sequence, 251
Ratio(s)
  golden, 416, 834
  trigonometric, 680–684, 700–703
Rational equation(s), 603–605
Rational exponent, 486–489
Rational expression(s), 586–589
  adding and subtracting, 592–595
Rational function(s), 598–600,
  603–605, 608
Rational numbers, 278–281
Rational Roots Theorem, 577–578
Real axis, 291
Real numbers, 272–275, 278–281
  properties of, 53, 272
Rectangular hyperbola, 395

X

x-intercept
> of a polynomial function, 555–558
> of a quadratic function, 342

Y

y-intercept, definition, 92
y-values
> of a quadratic function, 323–326
> for sine and cosine functions,
> 738–740

Z

Zeno's paradoxes, 262, 264
Zero, as an exponent, 475
Zero Products, Principle of, 349,
> 557–558
Zeros
> complex, 577–580
> Descartes' Rule of Signs for the
> number of, 582
> of a polynomial function, 555–558,
> 574
> of a quadratic function, 342
> of a sine function, 732